HANDBOOK OF MARRIAGE AND THE FAMILY

CONTRIBUTORS

John Sirjamaki, *State University of New York at Buffalo* • Jesse R. Pitts, *Oakland University* • Sheldon Stryker, *Indiana University* • Reuben Hill, *University of Minnesota* • Roy H. Rodgers, *University of Oregon* • Charles E. Bowerman, *University of North Carolina* • F. Ivan Nye, *Washington State University* • Marvin B. Sussman, *Western Reserve University* • Paul C. Glick, *United States Bureau of the Census* • Murray A. Straus, *University of Minnesota* • Panos D. Bardis, *University of Toledo* • Morris Zelditch, Jr., *Stanford University* • John Mogey, *Boston University* • Ruth Shonle Cavan, *Rockford College* • Winston Ehrmann, *American Association of University Professors* • Lee G. Burchinal, *United States Department of Health, Education and Welfare* • Jessie Bernard, *Pennsylvania State University* • Edward Z. Dager, *Purdue University* • Donald A. Hansen, *Purdue University* • Muriel W. Brown • Richard K. Kerckhoff, *Washington School of Psychiatry* • Gerald R. Leslie, *Oklahoma State University* • William M. Kephart, *University of Pennsylvania*

HANDBOOK
OF MARRIAGE
AND THE FAMILY

Edited by HAROLD T. CHRISTENSEN

PURDUE UNIVERSITY

RAND McNALLY & COMPANY
CHICAGO

RAND McNALLY SOCIOLOGY SERIES

Edgar F. Borgatta, Advisory Editor

ALFORD, *Party and Society*

BAKAN, *The Duality of Human Existence*

BORGATTA AND CROWTHER, *A Workbook for the Study of Social Interaction Processes*

CHRISTENSEN, ED., *Handbook of Marriage and the Family*

DEMERATH, *Social Class in American Protestantism*

DENTLER, *Major American Social Problems*

FARIS, ED., *Handbook of Modern Sociology*

GLOCK AND STARK, *Religion and Society in Tension*

HADDEN AND BORGATTA, *American Cities: Their Social Characteristics*

KAPLAN, ED., *Science and Society*

MARCH, ED., *Handbook of Organizations*

NYE AND HOFFMAN, *The Employed Mother in America*

SCOTT, *Values and Organizations*

WARREN, *The Community in America*

WARREN, ED., *Perspectives on the American Community*

WEBB, CAMPBELL, SCHWARTZ, AND SECHREST, *Unobtrusive Measures*

Preface

By *handbook* is meant a manual or reference work giving comprehensive coverage of a field. The field of concern here, known as marriage and the family, has had perhaps more than its share of both popular interest and loose writing. This handbook will not have a popular appeal: it is not a how-to-do-it manual for the layman explaining the way to success in ten easy lessons, or anything like that. Rather, it is a serious, systematic analysis of the subject under treatment, aimed at the professional worker in the field. The sledding is tough in places, but that is because some of the problems are difficult and as yet unresolved. It is in the nature of science that phenomena be examined objectively and realistically, regardless of their complexity, the urgency of the occasion, or the vested interests of the investigators.

Although family phenomena have been exposed to serious study for approximately a century, it is only in recent years that the rigors of the scientific method have come to be applied to them, and it is only now that scholars are starting to concern themselves with the integration of disjointed materials and with systematic theory building. It is toward this latter goal that the present handbook is aimed. What the editor and the contributors have attempted is to take stock of past accomplishments, present resources, and future potentials. We have wanted to know where we have been, where we are, where we are going, and how to get there—as a profession. Hopefully, we have laid bare major discontinuities in knowledge and have added to the incipient theory from which researchable hypotheses designed to eliminate the gaps and overlaps must come. Honest self-examination, such as this, is a prerequisite to any coming of age of the field.

Although written especially for the professional, this handbook is set up to serve a diversified and large audience. In the first place, marriage and the family is a field that draws from many of the intellectual disciplines; in the second place, there is the professional-in-training as well as the professional-on-the-job; and in the third place, there are three separate levels of activity relative to the field: research, teaching, and application, or what has been called "social engineering." Thus, this treatise should prove useful to advanced students of family phenomena, whether upper classmen or at the graduate level, in pursuit of their careers; to college professors from various departments, whether engaged in teaching or research or both; and to a variety of other specialists such as social workers, marriage and family counselors, lawyers, legislators, governmental functionaries, personnel workers in business and industry, independent researchers, and authors. On the college campus, it should find a place in courses in anthropology, sociology, psychology, home economics, education, and medicine, to name only those most clearly applicable.

There have been earlier attempts to synthesize marriage and family materials (see Ch. 1 below). These—all valuable—run all the way from simple reference lists; to bibliographies made more functional by annotations and cross-references; to inventories and abstracting services; to critiques and criteria-building endeavors; to symposia of one kind or another, where selected readings are placed in juxtaposition within the covers of a single book; and finally to the integrating efforts of single authors, focused either upon selected phenomena or, in rare instances, upon the field as a whole. But, so far as we know, this present attempt is the first *team* approach to theory building for the *over-all* family field.

Several well-defined steps have been followed in the process: (a) First of all, a prospectus was prepared, giving the purpose, tentative outline, and nature of the proposed approach. (b) This was then circulated to a few leaders in the field for reactions and criticisms, and was revised on the basis of suggestions received. (c) Prospective authors for the various chapters were invited to participate and placed under contract; selection was on the bases of demonstrated scholarship, competence in their respective subfields, and promise of producing creative leads for use by future scholars. (d) The authors were then further instructed on

the nature of the proposed handbook and of their particular jobs, and were requested to submit chapter outlines. (e) These detailed outlines, when received, were reconciled with each other, and the revised over-all outline was then sent to all authors so that each could see what others would be doing as well as himself. (f) The authors then prepared their manuscripts, and these, after being turned in, were edited to eliminate undesirable gaps and overlaps and to coordinate for style. (g) Finally, there were in many instances exchanges between editor and author to iron out differences and to insure a minimum uniformity and a systematic coverage.

Our conception of the Handbook may be seen from the following excerpts from instructions given to the chapter authors:

Emphasis is to be upon systematic treatment, with an eye toward research sophistication and theory building.

We are aiming at a definitive job that will be useful to scholars for years to come. Each of us will want to make a serious effort to review the relevant literature dealing with his subject and to structure that literature and existing knowledge in a useful theoretical form.

Each chapter should describe the relevant empirical studies and decide what can be generalized from them; the aim, in other words, is for empirically based theory building. We want more than a rehash of what is found in textbooks, though an analytical review of core materials is a necessary *part* of the job. We will want to indicate the status of present knowledge in the field and also to suggest what the "next steps" in development might be. As authors select their materials and decide upon their emphases they should keep in mind such questions as: Where has the best work been done? Where is the most novel and promising work now being done? What needs to be undertaken in order to fill in the gaps and round out the theory?

Thus, every chapter has been originally and separately produced for this volume, and every author has been encouraged to be creative. What does such diversity do to our need for unity and for systematic treatment? A small price has been paid, of course, but at this stage of the field's development, complete consensus is too much to ask. There is value in throwing the products of creative minds into juxtaposition, especially when ideas are made to take each other into consideration in striving toward the goal of synthesis, as is attempted here. By the initial outlining of the field into logical categories, the setting up of uniform goals to guide all contributors, and the careful editing along the way to coordinate the materials, the editor has hoped to achieve the necessary harmony that a book like this requires. Nevertheless, the editing has not been so extensive as to deny an author his own personal style, or his particular point of view on controversial issues, or the privilege of developing his major arguments, even though this occasionally may mean some repetition of materials from other chapters. The editor believes that no duplication, in the sense of identical treatment, remains; there are a few instances of the same topic being treated in two or more chapters, but always in differing contexts. Yet it seems to him that some of this is both inevitable and desirable—inevitable in that phenomena *are* amenable to more than one orientation, and desirable in that multiple treatment from varying points of view *is* sometimes needed in order to see a phenomenon in balanced perspective.

The reader should find the table of contents and especially the index to be valuable in running down the various complementary but interrelated treatments of a topic. There is some cross-referencing of interlocking subjects within the text itself, but full exploration often will require more. In addition to the index, there are up-to-date, comprehensive reference lists at the end of each chapter which can direct the interested reader to supplementary materials.

The book is organized with the family as the center of attention. It has been designed to be comprehensive but not encyclopedic. Peripheral specialities—such as child development, youth culture, gerontology, women's roles, health practices, sexual behavior, household economics, and demographic analysis—have been either ignored or relegated to subsidiary positions and treated only when they bear upon the *family* as such. Contributions from a number of the intellectual disciplines—sociology, anthropology, psychology, physiology, home economics, medicine and psychiatry, and so on—have been drawn upon, but only when their data are descriptive of *family* phenomena. Core problems have been selected and treated, with a view toward a unified theory, empirically supported; but always with the *family* at the focus.

Specific organization divides the book into five parts: I is essentially theoretical; II is basically methodological; III and IV report substantive findings, first concerning the family as an institution in society, and second concerning the internal workings of the family viewed as a small-group association; and V deals with applications, along with related normative considerations. But the distinctions are ones of relative emphasis more than of mutually exclusive categories: a methodological chapter might illustrate with substantive materials, for example, just as a substantive chapter may describe its material within the framework of methodological and theoretical problems. Although the over-all concern has been with theory building, it is recognized that sound theory is based upon solid research, concerning relevant substantive phenomena, resulting in generalizations capable of application.

Not only is this volume the product of 24 separate authors, but from the time of its inception to the end it has had the benefit of valuable suggestions from numerous others. Without in any way wishing to sidestep his own responsibility for over-all planning, follow-through, and final decisions, the Editor would like to gratefully acknowledge help from the following: Edgar F. Borgatta for the original idea and its early clarification; Robert O. Blood, Edward Z. Dager, Evelyn M. Duvall, Reuben Hill, Walter Hirsch, Gerald R. Leslie, Eleanore Luckey, and F. Ivan Nye for their critiques of the prospectus; Carolyn Cummings, Edward Z. Dager, David Ellison, Donald Hansen, Reuben Hill, John Mogey, F. Ivan Nye, Robert Perrucci, Murray Straus, and Marvin Sussman for serving as critics on first drafts of Chapters 1 and/or 24; Judy Broadwell, Dorothy Butcher, Alice S. Christensen, Nelle D. Foster, and Donna Sieredzki for many hours of typing and assistance in mailing the manuscripts; and from John Applegath and Lucia Boyden of Rand McNally for their cooperative approach and detailed assistance in seeing the work through to publication.

Harold T. Christensen

West Lafayette, Indiana
March 10, 1964

Contents

PART **I** Theoretical
Orientations

CHAPTER I

Development of the Family Field of Study

HAROLD T. CHRISTENSEN
Purdue University

Love, sex, marriage, and parenthood are subjects of intrinsic interest to nearly everyone. Perhaps this is so because they represent experiences common to all mankind, and also because the motives which impel them and the consequences which spring from them are rather deep-seated in human personality and far-reaching in terms of human satisfactions. Family phenomena constitute important factors back of both personal happiness and social stability (Christensen, 1958, pp. 29–32).

There has developed a vast literature on the family, running all the way from superstition-based folklore, to imaginative fiction, to poetic outpourings, to philosophical speculations, to popularized magazine articles and advice columns, and finally to reports of scientific investigations. Much of this has been piecemeal, impressionistic, and contradictory. It is only in recent years that the family institution has been viewed under the searchlight of science, and, although the activity has been considerable and the results promising, there remains the task of pulling the various elements together into a unified and valid theory. Such a theory would organize the eclectic findings now available, giving them deeper meaning, and would lay out a framework for future research and theory building in the family field. This book is intended as a serious step toward such a goal.

DEFINITIONS[1] AND DELIMITATIONS

The terms marriage and family are so interrelated that the tendency is to speak of them in the same breath. They nevertheless are not synonomous. *Marriage* is an institutionalized mating arrangement between human males and females, whereas *family* refers to marriage plus progeny; family, in other words, signifies a set of statuses and roles acquired through marriage and procreation. Thus, it is customary to view marriage as a precondition of family organization, and to consider the family as a product of marital interaction.

[1] Although the field has been moving toward a standard usage of terms, this goal has not been entirely achieved. For an expanded treatment of many of these and some other definitions, see Zelditch's discussion below, pp. 465–469.

Neither are marriage and *mating* the same thing. The former is a sociological concept, the latter a biological one. The mating phenomenon is shared with other animals, whereas marriage is strictly human. Mating, even on the human level, may be quite impersonal, random, and temporary. Marriage, on the other hand, is a social institution, and it assumes some permanence and conformity to societal norms. Marriage is society's way of controlling sex and fixing responsibility for adult sexual matings. In this connection it is worth noting that all societies, both past and present, prescribe marriage for the majority of their members. Marriage, in other words, is a universal social institution, and, although extramarital sexual contacts frequently are permitted, it is the marriage arrangement that is most strongly sanctioned for most men and women during most of their life spans.

The least common denominator of family organization is the so-called *nuclear family* (sometimes referred to as the "conjugal family," since in it the marriage bond is of primary importance). It consists of husband, wife, and their immediate children. The marriage of one man to one woman is known as *monogamy,* and it is such a marriage plus the resulting offspring that make up a nuclear family. Sometimes nuclear families are joined or extended into larger family units. If the joining is at the point of the marriage relationship, so that one person has two or more spouses and hence simultaneous membership in two or more nuclear families, the phenomenon is that of *polygamy*. Polygamous marriages technically are referred to as *polygyny* if the arrangement is one man with multiple wives; as *polyandry* if it is one wife with multiple husbands; and as *bigamy* if the number of mates, whether polygynous or polyandrous, is limited to two. In extremely rare instances marriage has involved multiple mates on both sides, that is, several males married to several females, a phenomenon known as *group marriage*. If the joining of nuclear families is on the basis of

blood relationship, so that several generations of offspring are included within one family unit, we have what is known as the *consanguine family*. For example, the typical Chinese family of a generation and more ago was made up of the oldest living male together with his spouse, the spouses of his married male descendants, and all of his unmarried descendants for as many generations as they extended. Upon marriage, daughters moved out of the family and into another, and sons recruited new members as wives. Usually these large, multi-generational families lived under one roof, or in a close cluster of houses, and functioned together as a unit.

The consanguine family sometimes has been referred to as the *joint family,* a term not used as frequently today as in times past. More recently it has been labeled an *extended family* (Murdock, 1949). We prefer, however, to keep the more descriptive term, "consanguine," for this special type of family organization; and to use the term "extended family" in a more generic sense to include *all* nuclear family groupings, whether the extension is along the line of husband-wife relationships (polygamy), parent-child relationships (consanguine), or even is accomplished by adoption (a not uncommon practice in both preliterate and modern societies). Nevertheless, this distinction is not generally adhered to; in the chapters to follow "extended family" is frequently used in the Murdock sense.

It is possible, of course, to classify marriage and family phenomena in an almost infinite number of ways, depending upon one's point of reference. From the referent of personal affiliation, there are the *family of orientation* into which one is born and from which he gets his first and most basic socialization, and the *family of procreation,* which is established later on through marriage and reproduction. From the referent of lineage tracing come *patrilineal* if it is through the male line, *matrilineal* if through the female line, and *bilineal* (or *bilateral*) if somewhat equally through both family lines. From the referent of residence practices, one describes the custom of a newly married couple moving in with the husband's clan or village as *patrilocal,* with the wife's clan or village as *matrilocal,* and where a new or independent residence is established as *neolocal.* From the referent of authority patterns, it is customary to refer to the father-dominated family as *patriarchal,* the mother-dominated family as *matriarchal,* the child-dominated family as *filiarchal,* and where relationships are democratically structured as the *equalitarian family.* And then there is *term marriage,* a relatively rare practice in which the wedding contract is for a specified period of time, say two years, after which husband and wife are free to go their own ways. There is *quasi-marriage,* which regularizes sexual unions and sets up at least a semblance of family life on a lesser approval or status level than regular marriage, such as concubinage, the keeping of mistresses, and consensual or common-law marriages. Finally, there is what—perhaps only half-seriously—has been labeled *sequential polygamy,* where a person has more than one mate, not at the same time, but in succession over a lifetime, a practice becoming increasingly common in modern nations having high rates of divorce.

In United States census usage, a *household* includes all persons who occupy a given house, apartment, or other residential unit; and a *family* "consists of two or more persons living in the same household who are related to each other by blood, marriage, or adoption." Thus, not all households contain families, for a household may have one person living alone, or more than one person none of whom is related to any other. Furthermore, some households may contain more than one family. A *married couple* is defined as a husband and wife who are members of the same household, and a *husband and wife family* is defined as a family in which husband and wife are enumerated as members of the same family. The great majority of families are "heads of households with relatives in the household,"

and are labeled *primary families.* A few, however, are designated as either secondary families or subfamilies. A *secondary family* is a husband-wife family without its own household, that is, living with another and unrelated family in a subordinate position. A *subfamily* is a husband-wife family living with relatives; it is not enumerated separately in the census count of families, since by definition it is considered a part of the family to which it is related, which heads up the household of which it is a part.

Although some of these distinctions may seem arbitrary, they demonstrate the need for precision in the classification and analysis of quantitative data (compare especially Ch. 9 below). For present purposes, it is sufficient to emphasize that a household is a residential group, while the family is a group bound together by the relatedness of its members, whether this relatedness be by blood, by marriage, or by adoption.

It must be recognized that classification, at best, is somewhat arbitrary. Furthermore, the arbitrariness of definitions may be excused so long as these definitions fit the purposes at hand and are at the same time made explicit for all to understand. For some purposes, census data would be even more useful if the Bureau would rule out of its family category all groupings except parent-child combinations, that is, rule out childless married couples and blood-related combinations of the same generation, and rule in nuclear families that happen to be separated in residence and hence are not of the same household (cf. pp. 304–305).

STAGES IN DEVELOPMENT

Attention now is to be focused, not upon the development of the family itself, but upon a brief history of family studies. (For a history of the family as such, see Ch. 11.) The development of investigations concerning marriage and the family may be seen as falling into four periods or stages, which can be labeled according to their dominant orientations: Preresearch, Social Darwinism,

Emerging Science, and Systematic Theory Building. The first of these stages extended up to about the middle of the nineteenth century; the second for a fifty-year period to the beginning of the twentieth century; the third for another fifty-year period up to the middle of the twentieth century. The fourth, which we are still in, started about 1950 and offers promise of continuing in its present line of development for an indefinite time into the future.

But the arbitrariness of this scheme must be recognized. Shifts in orientation have been more or less gradual, so that an entirely accurate picture might be that of a gradual time continuum rather than a series of separate stages. Furthermore, on both logical and empirical grounds either fewer or more stages than these four could be specified, and the breaking points could be otherwise located. Hence, the divisions between stages must not be regarded as being sharp or the stages themselves as being entirely discrete. Nevertheless, there are real advantages, by way of expositional convenience and heuristic utility, in seeing the development of family study in terms of a limited number of sequential steps with breaking points located at the easily remembered midcentury and turn-of-the-century marks.

In a previous attempt at stage construction, Komarovsky and Waller (1945) described the period 1896–1914 as characterized by concerns over the family's origin and evolution, as well as with the alleviation of certain social evils; the period 1915–1926 as involving a shift to greater interest in the contemporary family, studied empirically and statistically for the first time; and the period 1927–1944 as marked by the emergence of the social-psychological approach, including the new use of case studies to complement a continuing emphasis on quantitative methods. Since they were writing as part of a symposium commemorating the fiftieth anniversary of the founding of the *American Journal of Sociology,* it is understandable that this event would dictate both the starting and closing points of the

fifty-year period they covered. Their analysis is to be incorporated into what follows, except that this chapter starts earlier and continues later, and attaches the essential features of their first period to the second half of the nineteenth century, in which it starts, and their second and third periods to the first half of the twentieth century, of which they clearly are a part.

Preresearch (Prior to about 1850)

It probably can be said that systematic study of the family did not begin until a little over a century ago. Before then, thinking on this subject tended to be largely emotional and either superstitious or highly speculative. Each society had its family folklore, to be sure, but these guidelines by and large were in the form of traditional beliefs, religious pronouncements, moralistic exhortations, poetic fantasies, and philosophical speculations. People listened to old wives' tales such as "love is blind," "two can live as cheaply as one," "out of sight, out of mind," and "absence makes the heart grow fonder" (Christensen, 1958, pp. 11–12), which were untested and often contradictory, as illustrated by the opposing generalizations contained in the last two listed. This is not to say that the modern world is entirely rid of mythology and untested assumptions regarding marriage and the family. Not by a long way! Neither is it to suggest that everything that is not modern is in error. But the shift toward systematic investigation and, in recent decades, toward the rigorous application of scientific methods nevertheless has been dramatic.

To review the mainstreams of prescientific thought on family themes, it certainly would be necessary to include such notables as William Shakespeare, Robert and Elizabeth Browning, and Walt Whitman in the literary realm; Confucius, Christ, and Saint Augustine in the religious realm; and Plato, Aristotle, and John Locke in the philosophical realm. But to examine the works of such as these would be merely touching the surface of a vast and varied literature that has accumulated since the beginning of written language. Furthermore, and what is most important, it would be missing the mark, for the present treatise confines itself essentially to the *empirical study* of family phenomena, meaning *scientific research*.

Social Darwinism (Second Half of the Nineteenth Century)

Beginning about midway through the nineteenth century and lasting for approximately fifty years, there developed a body of scholarly literature which dealt with the family in broad institutional and historical perspective. The cue was taken from Charles Darwin's *Origin of Species,* published in 1859, and *The Descent of Man,* published in 1871. Darwin, a biologist, had great influence over his contemporaries in the humanities and emerging social sciences. He for the first time traced the evolution of biological organisms from lower life forms through successive stages to the more complex levels, including man. His rather convincing evidence for biological evolution suggested to social thinkers that perhaps social forms and institutions develop in much the same way. Thus, arguing by analogy, they began to look for evidence to support the assumption of social evolution. This consuming interest which dominated the social science scholars of the period became known as "Social Darwinism." It was used to explain the evolution of marriage and the family, as well as of other social institutions.

Exemplars of this line of reasoning are Herbert Spencer, who published *Synthetic Philosophy* in 1860; J. J. Bachofen, who published *Das Mutterrecht* in 1861; Henry Sumner Maine, with *Ancient Law* in 1861; Lewis Morgan, with *Ancient Society* in 1877; Edward Westermarck, with *History of Human Marriage* in 1891; E. B. Tyler, with *The Matriarchal Family System in the Nineteenth Century* in 1896; Friedrich Engels, with *The Origin of the Family, Private Property and the State* in 1902; August Bebel, with *Women in the Past, Present and Future* in 1902; G. E. Howard, with *A History of Matrimonial Institutions* in 1904; and—outliving the period—Robert Briffault, with *The Mothers* in 1927 (Zimmerman, 1947).

But this is to name only some of the most outstanding social evolutionists of the period; there are others. Although they differed among themselves concerning the specific lines of development that the family was presumed to have followed (see Ch. 11 for these descriptions), they all saw it as evolving universally through certain natural stages. The general approach was to search the literature rather than resort to original field studies, and to look for proof perhaps more than for truth. Nevertheless, the investigations were empirical in nature, were focused, and were somewhat systematic. They were large-scale, mostly anthropological, with chief attention to "primitive" peoples, and their main concerns were with the origin and evolution of the family institution, colored by the optimistic belief that there had been "progress" (Komarovsky & Waller, 1945). Hill tells us that

These early reports were macroscopic in scope, covering great sweeps of social space and social time, comparing marriage, kinship, and socialization patterns in several societies with a view to establishing phases of evolutionary development of family forms. The methods of data collection were poor, resting upon historical and anecdotal records of doubtful validity built up from reports of travellers and missionaries with minimal training in ethnography. Methods of analysis were descriptive and impressionistic, producing few firm propositions that could be left unchallenged (1962, p. 425).

But Hill recognized Frederic Le Play as being an exception, and cited an article by John Mogey (1955) in which the contributions of Le Play which were ahead of his time are pointed up. Le Play, who published *Les Ouvriers Européens* in 1855 and *L'Or-*

ganization de la famille in 1875, emphasized the need for empirical facts and created his own instruments of data collection, thus anticipating the social survey, the research interview, the family budget questionnaire, and the method of participant observation— methods not generally adopted by researchers until later in the twentieth century.

Paralleling Social Darwinism during the latter part of the nineteenth century and the very first part of the twentieth century was an urgent concern over social problems and social reform. The Industrial Revolution had brought on or intensified such conditions as poverty, child labor, woman's restlessness accompanying emancipation, prostitution, illegitimacy, and divorce. The relationship of these to the family was quickly seen, and the result was a small amount of research, but considerably more agitation, directed toward social reform. There were moralistic attacks on social evils and cries for legislation to help correct them. Even Le Play's more solid research on budgets and consumption patterns were action-oriented and directed toward the establishment of national policies on the family (Bell & Vogel, 1960b; Komarovsky & Waller, 1945; Mogey, 1955).

Emerging Science (First Half of the Twentieth Century)

Social Darwinism, with its emphasis on large-scale comparative studies emphasizing evolution and progress, and its accompanying moralizing and attacking of social evils, carried over into the early part of the twentieth century. Its strength quickly lessened, however, and in time almost completely faded out as the new science, with its value-free position and its more rigorous methodology, took over. The pioneering efforts of Le Play finally bore fruit; his empirically oriented point of view and sound research methods were rediscovered by twentieth-century investigators and then added to, to make this next fifty years an age of emerging science. The development

of social survey techniques in England at about the turn of the century, by Booth, Rowntree, and others, came about quite independently of Le Play and was concerned more with poverty than with the family; yet it was applicable to family research and in time the two streams merged. The transition, though gradual, was far-reaching indeed; family study was not very scientific in 1900, considerably so in 1950.

Komarovsky and Waller, it will be recalled, saw the decade 1915–1926 as one in which family study concerns shifted from the past to the present and from loose, large-scale investigations to more scientific methods applied to more narrowly defined problems. They wrote:

During this period the study of the social problems of the family continued to occupy a central place, and the basic conceptual framework remained much the same. Methods and materials, however, were changing, as richer and more accurate sources were supplied through official channels and the records of private agencies; and methods were improved by the growing separation of science and morality; the emphasis on empirical, rather than merely logical, verification; and the increasing prestige of quantitative methods. Such studies as Colcord's *Broken Homes* (1920), Hall and Brooke's *American Marriage Laws* (1920), Patterson's *Intermarriages* (1924), and Richmond and Hall's *Child Marriages* (1925) exemplified this more elaborate and accurate investigation of contemporary life (Komarovsky & Waller, 1945, pp. 445–446).[2]

These authors also pointed out that, during this decade, women's problems continued to receive considerable attention; sex study, together with certain radical proposals, came into prominence; and the study of the social psychology of the family had its beginning. Regarding this latter, they pointed to the works of Cooley, Thomas, Park, and Burgess among the sociologists, and to Freud, Adler, and Jung among the psychoanalysts.

[2] By permission of The University of Chicago Press.

Flugel, a follower of the early psycho-analysts, published his *Psychoanalytic Study of the Family* in 1921. Mental hygiene books were numerous about this time; and social work, with its emphasis upon individual adjustment, was achieving professional status.

But, although the above description was for the decade 1915–1926, Komarovsky and Waller recognized that these new developments had their roots in the years immediately preceding. This was especially true for the use of statistics, which began soon after the turn of the century. They also recognized that these trends continued in their development for the next two decades approximately, which is as far as their study was carried.

Substantively considered, the most pronounced characteristic of twentieth-century family study is its emphasis upon the internal relationships of family members. Cooley, Park, Mead, Thomas, and others contributed to this emphasis, but it is Ernest W. Burgess who has done most to both conceptualize it and assist in its development. In a 1926 article he spoke of "the family as a unity of interacting personalities"; to which later was added, "each with a history in a given cultural milieu" (Nimkoff, 1948, p. 478). Interest in studying the family broadly, as a social institution, has materially shifted to an interest in studying it more narrowly and internally, as an association. This is the social-psychological approach. It began early in the century, although in a diffuse fashion at first, received its conceptualization with Burgess' now-famous statement, and then underwent intensive development during the several decades following. It has been expressed through expanding research, teaching, and counseling on such phenomena as dating, mate selection, marriage adjustment, parent-child relationships, and personality formation within the family context.

Methodologically considered, the dominant orientation of family study within the present century is to the scientific method.

Here, too, the emphasis began early and developed rapidly, especially over the most recent decades. Lewis M. Terman's *Psychological Factors in Marital Happiness,* published in 1938, and Ernest W. Burgess and Leonard S. Cottrell's *Predicting Success or Failure in Marriage,* published in 1939, were landmarks in this development. They introduced statistical prediction into the field and were instrumental in stimulating a surge of research activity along similar lines over the quarter century that has followed (see Ch. 6 of this Handbook). Workers in the family field became research-minded, and the problems to which they applied themselves became many and varied—although, as has been said, the greatest increase in activity was in studying the family as a small-group association. The social survey, which was introduced by Le Play but which did not really catch on until several decades later, was further explored and refined, and many new research techniques were also developed. Certainly by 1950, and probably much before, it was proper to speak of the *scientific study* of marriage and the family.

Of course, the use of the historical method in family study in the late nineteenth century did not entirely die out. Notable examples of its more recent continuation are Goodsell's *A History of the Family as a Social and Educational Institution,* published in 1915, Calhoun's *A Social History of the American Family from Colonial Times to the Present,* published in 1917, Frazier's *The Negro Family in the United States,* published in 1939, Zimmerman's *Family and Civilization,* which appeared in 1947, and Sirjamaki's *The American Family in the Twentieth Century,* published in 1953. But these, in contrast to their predecessors, did not ride the evolutionary theme, were less evaluative, and were far better documented.

Systematic Theory Building
(1950 to the Present)

In the second half of the twentieth century, there emerged a new and strong interest in theory building. Quantitative research has continued apace, but the researches undertaken are less eclectic and more systematic from the vantage point of theory. Furthermore, there are serious attempts to pull together and assess the various researches of the past, and to first delineate and then synthesize the several schools of thought or theoretical frames of reference which have been used in family study (see below).

Since the trends to be described in the next section all reach their zenith in the present stage of family study, there is no point in doing more here than briefly characterize the period.

There is, however, one recurrence in substantive interest which requires mention. Hill (1962) presented evidence to show that the attention of some family researchers is turning again to cross-cultural and comparative studies and asked the question, "Has scholarly writing on marriage and the family now come full circle?" His 58-item bibliography cited numerous contemporary studies of this nature, most of which have taken place since 1950. It is to be noted, nevertheless, that these recent comparative family studies are so different as to be almost of another variety from the earlier ones. They are narrower in scope, are in the main nonjudgmental and value-free, are generally based upon original field data, systematically gathered, with the use of carefully constructed schedules to test specified hypotheses, and they ordinarily involve the use of one or more sophisticated statistical techniques in the analysis. Their major concerns are with discovering, first, relationships which are generalizable across cultures and, second, the effects of cultural variables upon family phenomena. They are, in other words, more scientific and more suitable to sound theory building than were their earlier counterparts.

In summary, the family field of study may be viewed as having followed the three stages of growth of an intellectual discipline as outlined over a century ago by Auguste Comte. The first stage was the *theological,* which lasted up to the middle of the nineteenth century and which we have called preresearch, since its primary character was superstition and "revelation." The second was the *metaphysical* or philosophical, which was characterized by speculative and value-oriented investigations and which took up the last half of the nineteenth century. The third was the *positivistic* or scientific, which stresses the necessity of empirical, value-free investigation, and which has characterized the twentieth century.

Still another way of viewing the development of family study is to consider it in terms of the Hegelian dialectic. The sweeping but loose Social Darwinism of the latter half of the nineteenth century might be thought of as the *thesis.* Its exponents were library-based scholars, relying upon common sense, logic, and erudition, and concerning themselves with mankind as a whole. Then came the reaction or *antithesis* during the first half of the twentieth century, in which family scholars became determined to eliminate value judgments and to make their researches specific, objective, and scientific. And finally, during the past decade or so, family scholars are commencing to react against the previous reaction and to seek a *synthesis* of the best of the movements represented by the earlier thesis and the antithesis. There are reactions against the triviality of some problems that are researched, against their lack of theoretical orientation, against the absence of integration with other research, in short, against *rank empiricism,* as some choose to call it.

This effort toward synthesis which characterizes the present day is no simple return to the speculative theorizing of an earlier period. Rather it is an attempt to incorporate research into theory, and theory into research.

TRENDS IN FAMILY STUDY

Whereas the previous section attempted to see time sequences or stages according to the dominant orientations of family study activity, this one focuses upon the activities themselves, with the time dimension in the background. The two approaches, one organized around time and the other around function, are to be regarded as complementary. The seven specific trends which are designated are particularly characteristic of the approximately 15-year period from 1950 on, and it may be presumed that they will continue into the future perhaps even at an accelerated pace, if past trends are any indication. As a matter of fact, they all had their beginnings in earlier times but have been gaining in momentum at what appears to be an exponential rate.

Several recent writers have made serious attempts to see and list dominant trends (Burgess, 1946; Burgess, 1947; Cottrell, 1948; Cottrell, 1953; Dager, 1959; Ehrmann, 1955; Ehrmann, 1956; Ehrmann, 1957; Ehrmann, 1958; Ellis & Doorbar, 1952; Goode, 1959; Hill, 1951a; Hill, 1951b; Hill, 1955; Hill, 1958; Hill, 1962; Hoffman & Lippitt, 1960; Kelley & Nesbitt, 1946; Kephart, 1957; Komarovsky & Waller, 1945; Mogey, 1962; Mowrer & Mowrer, 1951; Nimkoff, 1948; Nye & Bayer, 1963; Rockwood, 1942; Walters, 1962; Winch, 1957). The writer's own listing, though built with an eye upon primary sources, has been influenced profoundly by these previous analyses of studies in the marriage and family field.

Acceptance of the Scientific Point of View

It has been only in recent years that family study has been characterized by the scientific frame of reference. As noted earlier, writings concerning the family were largely superstitious or speculative prior to about 1850. Then there was a half-century of methodologically loose, large-scale, comparative analyses, followed by another half-century in which the focus was narrowing to a consideration of the family as a small-group system to be studied internally, and the methodology was tightening in line

with the rigors of scientific standards. But it was not until about the middle of the 1920's that the family came to be viewed from a social-psychological standpoint, and not until the late 1930's and early 1940's that the development of this newer emphasis took form in terms of concrete research (Hill, 1955; Hill & Simpson, 1956).

Science seeks to investigate systematically a phenomenon for the purpose of revealing its true nature. It is interested in both the properties of the phenomenon and the relations existing among these properties which explain the action or behavior taking place. Primary attention is given to relations among properties, since it is from these that the scientist is able to achieve his ultimate goal: prediction. He must rely upon information received through one or more of the five senses; his data, in other words, must always be empirical data, not mere hunches. Furthermore, the phenomenon must be studied objectively, not subjectively, so that his generalizations spring from the data alone and not from personal bias. If these two conditions hold—reliance upon empirical data and objectivity of the study methods —the generalizations can always be retested for the sake of verification. Thus, in time there can be built up a body of trusted knowledge and theory, so that, knowing the conditions of a phenomenon, it becomes possible to predict the probable outcome. Essentially, therefore, the attitude of science is that of value-free truth-seeking; the method is that of the objective analysis of empirical data; and the aim is that of predictive theory.

But it has taken a long time for students of the family to come around to this point of view, longer, perhaps, than in some other social science specialities, and social science as a whole has been slower to develop than either the biological or the physical sciences. The essential reason is that social science deals with people, who have feelings and vested interests. Since the social scientist is closer to his data, it is more difficult for him to remain objective. And the family scholar has been heavily subjected to pressures and taboos which have retarded the development of his discipline (Christensen, 1958; Hill, 1958; Komarovsky & Waller, 1945).

Although there have been obstacles, and although the development of a scientific point of view has been slow, the trend has been consistent and far-reaching, even if not complete. Komarovsky and Waller (1945) emphasized this shift from a speculative and reform-oriented approach, which relied upon moral justification and logical verification, to an approach that is value-free and empirically based. But they also pointed out that

Taboos concerning the study of family relation are still strong; and the teacher in the field, what with the transferences of his students and the projections and displacements of his colleagues, is in a peculiarly exposed position. Since the research worker is also usually a college teacher, academic imperatives and restrictions put their stamp upon his writing. Such things help to account for the conservative tone, and the frequent lack of incisiveness, in the sociological writings concerning the family (p. 450).

But, although this statement, written nearly two decades ago, still has some validity, there is reason to suppose that it is less true now, that the scientific point of view in family study is more prevalent.

Increasing Respectability of the Field

Komarovsky and Waller (1945) also listed as a difficulty in family research the desire for privacy on the part of normal married couples. They pointed out that it is easier to study badly adjusted couples, which explains why a disproportionate amount of the research has centered on them, but that it somehow has seemed unethical and in poor taste to violate the sanctity of the normal marriage by researching it. Here, too, while conceding the point, the writer would presume that there has been a change over the past two decades in the direction of a greater

willingness of families to be studied. Recent sex and fertility research, to mention only the most striking examples, bears this out; respondents have not been found to be reluctant.

Hill and Simpson (1956) pointed out that progress in family research has had to wait, not only for the emancipation of scientists from the moral impediments of the culture, and for the development of adequate methods, but for the willingness of families to be studied. Yet they feel that significant changes have come about on all three counts. Hill (1958) tells us that

So long as family scholars were content to describe and analyze ancient and exotic families, the issue of the propriety of family study was not raised. . . .

The first studies of contemporary families were repugnant to the prevailing moral sentiments as a violation of the sanctity of the home. Bereavement studies, courtship studies, and studies of family in crisis were vulnerable to censorship and negative sanctions. Literally within the past decade have these areas become safe for protracted study in the United States (p. 5).

Hill goes on to show, however, that in a number of the European countries there is still considerable resistance to being studied on the part of families, and that such resistance is reinforced by religious and political pressures. But progress is being made.

This earlier resistance to and later partial acceptance of the right of the family researcher to have access to intimate data represents a type of transition which certain other sciences also have gone through. Take medicine, for example. There were public outcries with accompanying opposition when the male physician started replacing the midwife at childbirth, and when medical research and instruction first turned to the use of human cadavers. The use of live animals for research and instruction meets with opposition in some quarters even now. Yet it was only by overcoming such obstacles that medical science has been able to advance.

Advances in the scientific study of the family have been paralleled by comparable advances in the applications of research findings (see Part V of this Handbook). Family life education has become almost academically respectable, for example, and marriage counseling is rapidly becoming a recognized and accepted profession. No doubt these two phenomena reinforce each other, that is, lifting the quality of the research is bringing about greater public acceptance, which means both greater willingness to be researched and greater demand for the products of research, which in turn gives additional stimulus to the research efforts. Although there still is some distance to be traveled, it can be noted that family research is accepted, if not demanded, by the public, and that even conservative foundations and government agencies are increasingly giving it financial support (Hill, 1958).

More Attention to Personal Adjustment Within the Family Context

If family study had remained at the level of large-scale institutional analysis, it would have seemed somewhat remote to the individual, and we would not have expected him either to resist or to become very interested. But, with the shift of attention to the internal workings of the immediate family in one's own society, the individual quite naturally became very much concerned. He both resisted, because he feared the intrusion, and he in time accepted, because he saw the applicability of findings to his own situation. Science began probing within the family system much as it had earlier into the workings of the human body, and in both instances there developed new data for personal adjustment.

Hill (1958, and elsewhere) described this movement as a shift from macroscopic to microscopic studies and spoke of recent attempts at "Cracking the Family Nucleus Through Interaction Process Analysis." It began sometime after the start of the twentieth century, received its first clear conceptualization in the mid 1920's when Burgess described the family as "a unity of interacting personalities," and has continued with increasingly sophisticated research, at an accelerating pace. The Terman and the Burgess and Cottrell prediction studies of the late 1930's put the focus upon marital adjustment, where it has remained to a considerable extent ever since. But there have been elaborations of these early prediction devices, and among recent research concerns are empathy, interpersonal competence, intrafamily communication, interaction process analysis, and role perception in family decision-making (Hill, 1958, p. 29).

As part of this trend, there has come to be considerable interest in youth problems as these relate to the family—in juvenile delinquency, to be sure, but also in the more normal premarriage processes of dating, courtship, and mate selection. And interest likewise has expanded at the other end of the spectrum to problems of the middle and older years.

Not only has the trend been toward more studies of the family as a small-group association, but this emphasis characterizes scholarly activity within the United States much more than in the rest of the world (Hill, 1958).

In response to this shift toward personal and applied interests in family research, and possibly also as a stimulus to it, has come a similar development on the educational scene. In most colleges and universities, academically oriented courses which treat the family as a social institution have yielded ground to functionally oriented courses on marriage and family relationships which are intended to aid in personal adjustment (see Ch. 21 of this Handbook).

Proliferation of Substantive Reports

The relaxation of taboos concerning family research, together with the emerging sophistication and greater personal applicability of this research, have resulted in a rousing crescendo of publications on the subject. Hill (1958) has surveyed all serious family literature from some 30 countries for the period 1945–1956. He concluded that the majority of the careful descriptive writing on the family has been done since about 1925, and that most systematic analyses of empirical data have been concentrated in even more recent years, starting about 1945. Furthermore, he reported a steady increase in volume over the period studied, and showed for the United States that marriage and the family has for several years ranked with the first four of 24 fields of study tabulated in the American Sociological Association's annual census of research. Nye and Bayer (1963) more recently have followed this comparison for another five years, showing again that marriage and the family ranks high in number of projects and that this number continues to increase, although by 1961 the field had slipped to sixth place among the 24. A subsequent count for the year 1963 showed that the field was back up to second place. Whatever these variations, possibly due to inaccuracies in reporting and classifying, it can be said that marriage and the family continues to rank high among the fields of sociological research.

The United States claimed over half of the family publications coming from the 30 countries studied by Hill (1958). The other industrialized nations, where social science is also firmly established, came next in rank. Another difference noted was the greater tendency for scholars in this country to publish in professional journals, whereas larger proportions elsewhere published in books.

For some years now the *Journal of Marriage and the Family* (formerly *Marriage and Family Living*) has carried the largest number of research articles on the family of any single journal (Dager, 1959; Ehrmann, 1958; Walters, 1962). Although the other articles are scattered throughout perhaps a hundred additional journals, they tend to be concentrated in about a dozen, chief of which are the following: *American Journal of Sociology, American Sociological Re-*

view, American Anthropologist, Child Development, Journal of Consulting Psychology, Sociology and Social Research, and *Social Forces.* To illustrate the international flavor recently developing, it can be mentioned that the September, 1962, issue of the *International Journal of Comparative Sociology* (published in India) was built around the theme "The Family in Its Social Setting," and Volume 14, Number 3, 1962, of the *International Social Science Journal* (published in France by UNESCO) was a special issue devoted to "Changes in the Family."

A number of bibliographies of literature in the marriage and family field have appeared, mostly since 1950. Ludlow's (1951) was among the first and was the most comprehensive for its day. Foote and Cottrell (1955) produced an extensive though selective list for the period 1945–1954. Hill's (1958) trend report for 1945–1956 carried a 908-item list which was both classified and annotated. The *Journal of Marriage and the Family* has been publishing yearly reviews of family research, starting with 1954 (Dager, 1959; Ehrmann, 1955; Ehrmann, 1956; Ehrmann, 1957; Ehrmann, 1958; Walters, 1962); these have featured bibliographies plus descriptive summaries of trends and accomplishments. And there have been others (Ellis, 1954a; Ellis, 1954b; Ellis & Doorbar, 1953; Kelley & Nesbitt, 1946; Komarovsky, 1940; Rockwood, 1942; Winch, 1957).

Bibliographies can help the student keep abreast of the vast family literature which is accumulating. But bare lists are of limited value. They become increasingly useful if they are classified into subject-matter categories, or are annotated, or are accompanied by analysis. Hill's bibliography cited above is the only one that meets all three of these standards.

Abstracting is another practice designed to assist scholars in keeping up in their fields. Three abstracting services have become available in recent years: the *Journal of Marriage and the Family* has a regular section devoted to abstracts of current family literature;

Psychological Abstracts and *Sociological Abstracts*, though encompassing wider fields, also include marriage and the family in their coverage.

Not only have professional reports of family study been very much on the increase, but accompanying this is an expanding body of popular literature, which capitalizes upon current interest and need, and which in quality ranges all the way from the accurate reporting of research findings, geared to popular consumption, to the sensationalized distortions of cheap journalism (for expanded treatment see Ch. 24).

Elaboration of Organizational Programs

Programs which both stimulate and support family study are an important part of the development of recent years. In some ways these newer programs are a result of today's widespread interest in family phenomena, but also they have been among the forces which have helped to *produce* this interest and activity.

A little over a quarter of a century ago, Ernest R. Groves called together a small group from the social science disciplines and helping professions for the purpose of discussing ways of preserving family values in our society. Those attending were so enthusiastic that the experiment was repeated, and it is now an annual affair involving some two or three hundred invited participants. It has become known as the Groves Conference on Marriage and the Family. Its multidisciplinary approach and strong research and counseling emphases make it one of the most significant programs in the family field today.

An even more significant development was the organization of the National Council on Family Relations in 1938. This group brings together outstanding workers in research, teaching, and professional service. It holds annual conferences and publishes what has become the leading professional journal in the field, the *Journal of Marriage and the Family*, which, by providing an out-

let, encourages the development of both research and theory. The Research Section of the organization has done much over the years to stimulate research and set standards for its development. In 1950, NCFR voted to develop a special fund for the encouragement of family research, to be administered by its Research Section. This was named the Ernest W. Burgess Fund, in honor of one of the field's most eminent pioneers (Hill, 1951a, pp. 27–28). Earnings from the fund are periodically used as prizes to outstanding family researchers. These, known as Ernest W. Burgess Awards, are considerably valued and hence serve as incentives toward quality research. Recipients are carefully selected on the basis of best design, or best publication, or the person's over-all contribution to family research (the bases of selection have occasionally shifted), and the awards are prominently announced.

Over the years, the National Council on Family Relations has either sponsored or cosponsored at least three special gatherings of family researchers for the purpose of exchanging views on methodology and theory. The first was a two-day conference in August, 1945, at the University of Chicago, to discuss research then shaping up in the area of war and the family. The second was a three-week interdisciplinary workshop in August, 1950, also at the University of Chicago, where experienced scholars worked with outstanding graduate students to inventory and evaluate the research methods and orientations then in use. Hill (1951a) gave a very comprehensive report of this fruitful experience. The third was a one-week workshop, assisted by the Elizabeth McCormick Memorial Fund, and held in the Fund's offices in Chicago during late October and early November, 1956. Participants were from the related disciplines of sociology, psychology, psychiatry, child development, and parent education; attention was focused upon stock-taking in terms of knowns and unknowns in family research; and the papers, which had been prepared and circulated ahead of time, were subsequently published in a special issue of *Marriage and Family Living* (National Council on Family Relations, 1957).

As recently as 1964 there was organized a Section on the Family of the American Sociological Association. Its purpose is to foster quality research and the development of family theory through organized meetings, publications, and other means that may be deemed appropriate. Membership is open to ASA members with an interest in and a major commitment to these goals.

Of a quasi-professional nature are the various White House Conferences, which have enjoyed the highest governmental sponsorship and cooperation from numerous national agencies. The first White House Conference on Children and Youth met in 1910 and has convened at 10-year intervals ever since, celebrating its Golden Anniversary in 1960. In that year also was held the first White House Conference on Aging. Of special interest to students of the family was the White House Conference on Family Life (also called the National Conference on Family Life) held in 1948—the first of its kind, but many hope not the last (see pp. 175–176).

A promising development has been the recent establishment at certain universities of Family Study Centers. The first of these was organized at the University of Chicago during the early 1950's; of late its program has been broadened somewhat and its name changed to Community and Family Study Center. In 1957 the Minnesota Family Study Center was organized at the University of Minnesota. It is an interdivisional agency set up to facilitate graduate training and research in the family field. Some additional universities are now giving consideration to adopting this type of organization, for it has the obvious advantages of aiding interdisciplinary coordination and easing the securing of financial sponsorship for research.

On the international scene, note must be taken of the work of the International Seminar on Family Research, and of the recently organized standing Committee on Family Research of the International Sociological Association. The International Seminar on Family Research holds yearly, week-long workshops, involving about 15 to 20 invited participants from a variety of countries, and focusing upon the examination and cross-fertilization of research methods, concepts, and findings. It held its first session in Cologne, Germany, in 1954, and most of the subsequent meetings have been held in various other countries. During the first few years it was sponsored by the UNESCO Institute for Social Sciences, but more recently it has been taken over by, and is now a function of, ISA's Committee on Family Research. In addition to handling this operation, the Committee on Family Research also carries on continuing activity designed to stimulate worldwide family research, particularly in those countries where research activity has been low, and with special regard to cross-cultural teams cooperating on cross-cultural projects.

Refinements in Research Methodology

With the early twentieth-century shift to a scientific point of view and to an emphasis upon quantification, methodology tended at first to remain piecemeal and underdeveloped. Researchers followed a line of least resistance by staying with the most accessible data, gathered in the easiest manner, and frequently without the use of hypotheses, or concern over the relevance of findings to theory (Ellis & Doorbar, 1952; Hill, 1958).

But the trend, particularly strong in recent years, has been away from what Mowrer and Mowrer (1951) called the "seine or basket method" of collecting data, accompanied by simple analysis, and has been toward the systematic use of hypotheses, tied in with previous work on the problem, involving the employment of increasingly elaborate techniques for both gathering and analyzing the data, and resulting in accretive theory. In short, there has been a marked movement in the direction of greater scientific sophistication. (Compare Ch. 7 of this Handbook.)

A part of this movement is the growing tendency for greater coordination of research effort. This takes two forms: first, there is the emerging practice of researchers banding together into interdisciplinary and/or cross-cultural teams; and, second, there is the increasing practice of researchers staying with the same theme and following through with a series of consecutive studies so that their results become cumulative over time. Hill (1958) gave recent examples of both types of development and underlined the significance of this shift away from one-shot, isolated research, where the researchers do not have the benefit of cross-stimulation and where their findings fail to add up. He presented evidence of increasingly greater documentation in research reports, of progress toward a gradual accumulation of family theory.

From his trend data for the period 1945–1956, Hill listed additional evidence of an increasing attention to the scientific method in family study. Specifically, he showed that there have been shifts toward: (a) The use of more representative samples, although most studies in this country are still based upon nonrepresentative samples, such as college students; (b) a greater reliance upon direct observation in data gathering, although interviews, questionnaires, and tests are still by all odds most frequently used; (c) a greater reliance upon probability statistics in data analysis; (d) a more frequent testing of theoretically derived hypotheses; and (e) a more frequent assumption of a statistically oriented analytical stance. Interestingly, the United States ranked below countries from Europe and Asia in the use of representative samples and direct observation, but considerably above the other countries in the use of probability analysis, hypothesis testing, and analytical stance.

Nye and Bayer (1963), covering the period 1947–1961, found substantiation for some of the trends mentioned above. They reported increases in (a) the practice of documenting from previous research, (b) the use of formally stated hypotheses, and (c) the employment of tests of significance. Ranking data-gathering techniques, however, they reported that the questionnaire and the interview remained highest and increased at the expense of census and other secondary data, which as a source slipped to third place, and that direct observation remained low and decreased in the period from 1952–1956 to 1957–1961. They also reported a trend toward smaller samples, probably due to the proportional decline in the use of census data and also possibly to an increase in small-group research and in the use of more expensive techniques in data gathering. Finally, they reported that the major dependent variables dealt with were, in descending order, dating–courtship–mate selection, marital satisfaction, marriage roles, parent-child relationships, and sexual behavior; and that the major independent variables to which these were related were sex of the subject, social class, age, religion, education, and place of residence. No analysis of trends over time in the use of these variables was made.

Starting about 1950, there have come into use a whole series of new or newly adapted research techniques. Chief among these are direct observation of family behavior, tape recording of interactional or interview materials, role-playing interviews, projective techniques, sociometric devices, record linkage, and experimental controls (Hill, 1958; Hill & Simpson, 1956). Most of these, and others, are discussed in Part II of this Handbook.

Methodological improvement is taking place, in large part, because of the willingness of family researchers to look critically at what they are doing. An important aspect of the self-examination now taking place in the field is an effort to establish criteria for evaluating research. Hill (1951a) made a start in this direction, and Foote (1957) carried the attempt still further. Foote polled a group of active family researchers and found the following nine criteria recognized, listed in descending order of frequency mentioned: technical competence, contribution to theory, continuity with other research, centrality to family understanding, newness of findings, practical value of results, nontriviality of problem, development of research tools, and clarity of presentation. He nevertheless acknowledged the tentativeness of this approach and urged that the audience—or consumers of family research and not just fellow professionals—also be taken into account in appraising the worth of studies.

The problem is complex, and it is probably fair to say that no acceptable or generally recognized standard for judging family research exists at the present time. But it is needed, both as a bench mark to help researchers gauge their work and as a set of rules to guide editors in selecting articles and committees in selecting award winners.

New Concern Over Theory Building

As has been seen, systematic theory building became a major concern in family study starting about 1950; it is perhaps the dominant orientation at the present stage of development of the discipline. In its formative stages, any intellectual discipline is apt to show an absence of theoretical sophistication and hence lack of comparability among its investigations. But if empirical research, regardless of the technical perfection of its methodology, is to be anything more than random observation, it must be seen within a theoretical context. Hill and Simpson pointed to an upswing in both methodological and theoretical concerns starting about midcentury, but concluded that "most current research is sophisticated in method but needs to grow in theoretical relevance" (1956, p. 96).

Already noted in this recent concern for, and trend toward, theory building, are the appearance of more and better bibliographies, especially valuable when classified and annotated; the introduction of abstracting

services, which facilitate the task of keeping up in the field; and the exploring of possible criteria for assessing the excellence of research. Each of these developments contributes to theory in that it encourages comparison and integration.

There are at least four additional developments in theory building presently taking place within the family field: critical self-examinations by family scholars, inventorying for research propositions, attempting integrated analyses of research findings, and identifying theoretical frames of reference. The first three are given brief treatment here, and the fourth is examined in the following section.

Thirty or more separate critiques of family research have appeared over the past 15 or 20 years (Burgess, 1946; Burgess, 1947; Cottrell, 1948; Cottrell, 1953; Dager, 1959; Ehrmann, 1955; Ehrmann, 1956; Ehrmann, 1957; Ehrmann, 1958; Ellis & Doorbar, 1952; Foote, 1954; Foote, 1957; Foote & Cottrell, 1955; Goode, 1959; Hill, 1951a; Hill, 1951b; Hill, 1955; Hill, 1958; Hill & Simpson, 1956; Hoffman & Lippitt, 1960; Kelley & Nesbitt, 1946; Kolb, 1948; Kolb, 1950; Komarovsky & Waller, 1945; Mogey, 1962; Mowrer & Mowrer, 1951; National Council on Family Relations, 1957; Nimkoff, 1948; Nye & Bayer, 1963; Rockwood, 1942; Rockwood, 1952; Walters, 1962; Winch, 1957). This is at the rate of better than one per year. Most of these critiques have been accompanied by bibliographical lists and trend analyses and have attempted to describe gaps and shortcomings as well as to suggest needed lines of development.

Hill and associates (Hill, Katz, & Simpson, 1957) are undertaking the job of inventorying the entire field of marriage and family research from 1900 on. Their concern is over the need for an orderly summarization, integration, and systematization of the materials of the field. Attention is being paid to methodological procedures, substantive findings, and theoretical developments; and the end product, hopefully, is to be a handbook encompassing interrelated hypotheses and propositions of wide scope. The project is described as a "propositional inventory."

William J. Goode, working independently of the Hill team, is engaged in a similar project. He is aiming "to publish an essentially skeletonic arrangement of related propositions, which will contain most of the published sociological findings and hypotheses relating to the family." [3]

The completion of these two propositional inventories will most certainly represent a major advancement for family theory.

Hill (1958) spoke of an emerging concern over the importance of checking on the generalizability of findings. It is expressing itself in attempts to test the reliability of generalizations over time and across groups and cultures. Murdock's (1949) use of the Cross-Cultural Survey files on 250 societies to arrive at generalizations on family structure is a good example. Another example is Cavan's (1963) summary of family materials for the United States by region, social class, and ethnic composition. An important, but not entirely resolved, problem in this approach is the determination of which elements of a phenomenon are universal and which are relative to the particular period or particular culture being studied; in other words, how much of family phenomena can be generalized, and to what extent and in what ways do time and space operate as intervening variables?

In recent years there have appeared a number of publications which seek to pull together scattered findings and to synthesize them into theory. Among those which have focused upon a single area of family study are Winch's (1950) treatment of personality formation within the family setting, Barron's (1951) analysis of intermarriage, Katz and Hill's (1958) use of their propositional inventory to summarize studies of residential propinquity as a factor in mate selection, Hoffman and Lippitt's (1960) review of the child's behavior and development within the

[3] From a personal communication to the author received July, 1963.

family, Jacobsohn and Matheny's (1962) analysis of studies in mate selection, and Smith's (1962) formulations concerning American youth culture. Several books of readings have entered the market over the past decade. These cover marriage and family more broadly, and, by careful selection plus editorial comments, try to bring order out of partial chaos. Among these are Sussman's *Sourcebook in Marriage and the Family* (1963); Winch, McGinnis, and Barringer's *Selected Studies in Marriage and the Family* (1962); and Bell and Vogel's *A Modern Introduction to the Family* (1960a). Finally, there are comprehensive treatments of the field by single authors, such as Kirkpatrick's research- and theory-oriented *The Family: as Process and Institution* (1963).

TOWARD A SOCIOLOGY OF THE FAMILY

The maturity of any scientific discipline depends upon both the adequacy of its research and the level at which its empirical findings are organized into meaningful theory. How is it with marriage and the family?

Emerging Frames of Reference

The relatively recent concern over theory building, described above, has resulted in the delineation of several distinct theoretical approaches in the family field of study. Hill and his collaborators have been most responsible for isolating, labeling, and describing these various schools (Hill, 1951a; Hill, 1951b; Hill, 1955; Hill, 1958; Hill & Hansen, 1960; Hill, Katz, & Simpson, 1957). Five of the approaches have been sufficiently developed, and are sufficiently promising as frameworks for future research, to justify careful and expanded treatment in this volume. They therefore have been made to provide the contents of Chapters 2, 3, 4, and 5. The plan for the present section is to mention several peripheral or abortive approaches, and then to follow with brief characterizations of the five which are most central to our present concern.

Peripheral approaches. Certain approaches must be regarded as peripheral because of their particularistic nature or their failure to keep the family in focus. Although undoubtedly important in their own right, they hardly can be described as approaches to *family* study as such. Three illustrations will be used.

1. There is what Hill (1951b, and elsewhere) has termed the household economics–home management approach. It is the one traditionally used by home economists employing the technology of management and dealing essentially with the resources of time, money, and energy. Hill feels that home economists, until recently at least, "have skirted family values and family relationships in their research." He explained:

In examining over a hundred experiment station bulletins by home economists and rural sociologists supposedly studying family living since they were so titled, I found almost no mention of children, husband-wife concerns, or family activities as a family. The studies were heavily on expenditures and levels of living, facilities, standards of performance, use of time, nutritional standards, housing, health, and so on. The conceptual framework of the research home economists is more closely allied to farm management than family operation. It is really household management; consequently, it is hard to integrate their findings with other theories about the American family (Hill, 1955, p. 275).

Feeling that this approach has failed to generate a full-fledged conceptual framework for family study, and that it either remains at the level of description or in some instances merely ties in with frameworks or theories developed elsewhere, Hill and Hansen (1960, p. 299, note 2) decided to drop it from their later classification. Whether a distinct theoretical framework for this approach will eventually emerge is yet to be seen.

2. Another approach, at first delineated by Hill (1951b, and elsewhere) but later dropped by Hill and Hansen (1960, p. 300, note 2) is what has been called the learning theory–maturational approach. It has been used almost entirely by psychologists and child development specialists, who, by definition, are concerned chiefly with the individual. Its emphasis therefore, has been upon the personality of the growing child, with biological maturation and the mother-child relationship as the principal processes receiving attention. Although the learning and development of the child are seen against the background of the family, it is the child and not the family which is at the focus of study; the child's maturation and socialization are traced within the family context, to be sure, but other family characteristics and processes are largely ignored. For family study proper

. . . it is necessary to consider only approaches which can deal with the family as a whole and/or with the full array of its internal relationships. The promise that learning theory showed a decade ago of developing such a framework has not been realized, and today it still focuses exclusively on the individual (Hill & Hansen, 1960, p. 300).

3. Finally, there is the psychoanalytic approach, which remains peripheral to family study for the same reason as does learning theory, that is, it focuses upon the individual rather than upon the family per se. Freud first introduced the idea of universal unconscious drives, to which his followers have added the contributions of social and cultural influences. Present-day family literature is full of such psychoanalytic concepts as identification, fixation, transference, narcissism, latency period, oedipus complex, ambivalence, sublimation, and superego, to give but a few examples.

There is no denying that psychoanalytic thought has had a powerful influence on family study (Flugel, 1921; Mowrer & Mowrer, 1951). In recent years, even psychoanalytically oriented clinicians have been recognizing the importance of family inter-action to personal pathology and treatment. They have been attempting to integrate psychoanalytic and sociological concepts, to correlate individual behavior with social be-havior within the family context, and to get at individual treatment through family treatment (Ackerman, 1957; Ackerman, 1958; Alexander, 1963; Barrabee, 1957; Chance, 1959; Kronhausen & Kronhausen, 1959; Pollak, 1956; Simpson, 1957; Spiegel, 1954). Nevertheless, the approach remains essentially focused on personality, and the concepts developed are less applicable to the family *as such* than to members of the fam-ily considered separately. Although there are occasional references to dyads, as with the oedipus and electra complexes, no attention is paid to the larger pluralities. Further-more, when stages of development are traced, the reference is to personal develop-ment, not family changes over time, and when transference is dealt with, it is from person to person, not transactions between the family and other social systems.

Home economists, psychologists, psycho-analysts, and others have made very signifi-cant contributions to family study and will continue to do so. It is only that they have come at the family indirectly, and so have not arrived at theoretical frameworks par-ticularly suited to *family* analysis.

One of the most promising attempts at bringing together psychological, sociological, and psychoanalytic theory pertaining to fam-ily phenomena is that made by Parsons and Bales (1955; see also Chs 3 and 18 of this Handbook).

Sociological approaches. Since sociology, first and foremost, is concerned with group phenomena, and since the family most cer-tainly is a group, it follows that the major theoretical frameworks for family analysis will be sociological. Recognition of this fact in no way implies that sociology is above or better than its sister disciplines, but only that the family falls more clearly at the focus of its interest.

Employing Hill's conceptualization (Hill & Hansen, 1960), this Handbook recognizes five separate theoretical frameworks for family study, each with a sociological orien-tation. The first of these focuses upon the family as an institution; the second upon the family as a social system; the third upon interaction among family members; the fourth upon situational settings which affect family member behavior; and the fifth upon life cycle stages in family development. Only the last named, which also is the most recent, has been consciously formulated with the conceptual demands of family research in mind. The previous four grew up like Topsy, with the conceptual formulations developing after sufficient studies had accu-mulated and a certain amount of internal consistency among them had been discov-ered.

1. The institutional approach (see Ch. 2 below) was perhaps the first to develop, and in the beginning was rather broad-scaled, descriptive, and moralistic. It was also his-torical. Both anthropologists and sociologists took it up. Concern was with the origin and evolution of the family institution and with comparisons over space as well as time. No-tions of improvement and progress were strong. In more recent years scholars using this approach have tended to become value-free and to replace pure description with a greater amount of empirical testing and analysis, but the emphasis remains on historical and cross-cultural design.

2. The structural-functional approach (see Ch. 3 below) also has developed from the positions of both anthropology and sociol-ogy. It views the family as a social system, with constituent parts bound together by interaction and interdependence. It is con-cerned with whether any given element is either functional or disfunctional to the total system, determined by the extent to which it either adds or subtracts from the system's operation. Attention focuses upon both the internal workings of the family system and upon relationships between the family and other social systems. It concentrates on such

questions as how systems are organized and how they operate. Bell and Vogel (1960a) used this frame of reference for building their recent book of readings on the family.

3. The interactional approach (see Ch. 4 below) has developed from the fields of sociology and social psychology. It began about the middle of the 1920's when Ernest W. Burgess, a follower of George Herbert Mead and a symbolic interactionist, first described "the family as a unity of interacting personalities"; and for the past few decades it has received the major attention of family scholars. It strives to interpret family phenomena in terms of internal processes: role playing, status relations, communication problems, decision making, stress reactions, and the like. Within this approach, little attempt is made to view the over-all institutional or cross-cultural or transactional relationships of the family considered as a unit in society—the meat of the two approaches previously mentioned.

4. The situational approach (see latter part of Ch. 4 below) is in some ways similar to the interactional just discussed, in that it, too, views the family as a unity of interacting personalities. However, where the interactionist focuses upon interaction as such, the situationalist views the family as a social situation affecting behavior, that is, as a unified set of stimuli external to family members and acting upon them. Bossard and Boll (1943) have been its chief users in the United States, and they and others have dealt with such phenomena as family table talk, family rituals, space utilization policies, and the like. Although most work to date has centered upon individual behavior as influenced by family situations, the framework lends itself to consideration of stimuli from outside the family as well. Hill and Hansen (1960) recognized the parallel development of a similar approach in psychology, called the psychological-habitat approach, but they rejected this as being too individualistic and hence lacking in family orientation.

5. The developmental approach (see Ch.

5 below) is the most recent to come into use and is the only one to have been consciously formulated in advance of the research it seeks to organize. It, too, in common with the interactional and situational approaches, views the family as a unity of interacting personalities. But its point of departure is not interaction per se, nor situationally influenced behavior, but rather the family life cycle or stages of development through which the family and its members travel. Earlier approaches tended to neglect the time dimension, and hence failed to deal adequately with family change. The developmental approach, while borrowing certain concepts from other fields, is seeking to correct this deficiency by organizing the borrowed tools and adding others to deal specifically with the unifying theme of family change.

For additional detail on these five sociologically oriented frames of reference the reader is referred to Hill and Hansen's (1960) rather comprehensive and sophisticated formulations already cited, and then especially to the remaining chapters in Part I of this Handbook.

Requisites to Family Theory

The existence of competing frames of reference serves to underline the state of flux which characterizes the field today. But it also gives evidence of growth, for until very recently family study has been quite eclectic, sporadic, and without standardizing guides of any significance. Now, at least we have some of the issues clearly drawn, some of the ideas firmly conceptualized, and many—perhaps most—of the theoretical frames of reference isolated and fairly well formulated.

Interdisciplinary concerns with a sociological focus. Delimitation of the field is a primary requisite to any theory. In seeking to accomplish this, it usually has been found that phenomena tend to cluster around recognizable foci, but with their peripheries being much less distinct and frequently overlapping with each other. For this reason, scientists generally have been content with clearly defining the foci of their disciplines without bothering to draw exact dividing lines between them, and then referring to the interstitial areas by the use of joint terms such as astrophysics, biochemistry, and social psychology.

Since family phenomena are ubiquitous in society, it follows that they are of legitimate interest in small or large part to every one of the human and social sciences. But if the scientific disciplines are adequately differentiated, it also follows that each will approach the field from a different perspective. Thus, the anthropologist might be expected to focus upon preliterate and folk societies and to be primarily concerned with cultural patterns; the biologist is apt to concentrate upon problems of reproduction, growth, heredity, and health; the psychologist upon the functioning of the individual, whether as an organism in nature or as a person in society; the economist upon the earning, allocating, managing, and consumption of family income; the political scientist upon the family as an element in the power structure and governing processes of the society; and so on. It will be noted that none of these holds the family *as such* within clear focus; rather, each rightly chooses to concentrate upon the central concern of its discipline—culture, health, personality, income, power structure, and so on—though frequently studied within the family context, to be sure, and though contributing to family understanding in the long run.

The important point here is that only sociology is in a position to study the family per se, that is, to analyze its structure and processes, to see what it is like as a human social grouping. Sociology, by definition, focuses upon social interaction, upon *group* phenomena. Group interaction is the very essence of family life, which argues for a *sociological orientation* in family study. It is the *sociology of the family,* therefore, that must be regarded as making primary contributions to family theory at this writing.

Nevertheless, it again must be emphasized that we are regarding sociology merely as the integrating framework for family study, not as its pre-emptor. Certainly the other disciplines have legitimate interest in family phenomena (just, for example, as sociology has a legitimate interest in economic phenomena, though this would not be its focus, nor would the sociologist make any claim to proficiency in economics). But theory demands clarity and a division of labor consistently followed. More efficacious than interdisciplinary competition for an area of study such as the family is multidisciplinary cooperation.

Sociological focus allows for the family to be viewed first as an association and second as an institution. Putting this another way, concern is over both internal processes where family members are seen as constituting an interacting group, and patterned regularities where the family is considered as a unit in the social structure.

Furthermore, sociological treatment of the family permits it to be viewed as either an independent or dependent variable—or both, within a framework of interdependence. Regarded as an association, it would be an independent variable when seen as acting upon or affecting its members, and as a dependent variable when seen as being changed, such as either strengthened or weakened, by actions of its members. Regarded as an institution, the family may be seen as an independent variable when it changes or influences other institutions, such as religion, the economy, or the state, and as a dependent variable when it is affected by these institutions. Thus, the family may be studied as both actor and acted upon, and each type of analysis may be turned either inward toward the members of a family or outward toward society at large.

Special theories versus general theory. Hill's (Hill & Hansen, 1960, and elsewhere) delineation of family study into five conceptual frameworks is a major accomplishment. Yet graduate students tend to be trained in only one line of attack, the one represented by their own major professor, and as long as this remains true, there is certain to be confusion in either understanding or appreciating the literature from the other schools of thought. Furthermore, no family theorist so far has arisen to transcend the boundaries of the separate schools or to integrate them into a general theory, and until this occurs no consistent body of cumulative theory can be expected (Hill, 1955; Hill, 1958). Martindale made a similar point with reference to the development of theoretical approaches in sociology: "That the schools are true alternative formations of theory has been established beyond all doubt. They form independent systems of concepts that cannot be arbitrarily intermixed. This fact appears over and over again whenever one type of theory attempts to account for evidence of another branch" (1960, p. 538).

Perhaps a general theory of marriage and the family is too much to expect. Certainly we do not have it now. If agreement upon a broad disciplinary frame of reference, say the sociological, can be reached, a step in the direction of general theory will have been taken. Yet even within the one discipline there is room for difference, as demonstrated by the existence of five competing conceptual frameworks, all sociological in that they focus upon the family as a group, but differing from each other in basic assumptions, conceptualizations, and methods of analysis.

Unless, or until, a general theory is developed, the next best thing is to become familiar with the alternative theories now in existence. This will be of help both in interpreting the research of others and in designing the research that is to be one's own. Mogey has pointed out that "certain enquiries call for one theory while others are insoluble by that approach" (1962, p. 421), and agreed with Hill and Hansen (1960) that choice of theory may be just as important as choice of problem or choice of technique.

Theory building in the family field is an unfinished job and perhaps will remain so. Yet there has been progress and there will be more. It is too early to tell whether a general or over-all theory will eventually emerge. But even with a recognition that differing interests legitimately exist, it is possible and desirable to work for further clarification of ideas and greater complementation of effort.

The joining of research and theory. It should be evident by now that by theory we do not mean mere speculation. Neither is the collecting and classifying of facts sufficient, although this does lay down the necessary base for theory building. Winch and his collaborators distinguish between *properties,* which are simply descriptions in answer to the "how" questions, and *relations,* which involve analysis and which get at the "why" questions of science. In general, they contend, property studies are theory-free, while relation studies are theory-bound. They then say:

A scientific theory is a statement of the way in which abstract variables are related and from which verifiable hypotheses are deducible. The key word here is "verifiable." Although a theory may be suggested by an insight, an intuition, a dream, or any other bit of experience, to satisfy the requisites of science it cannot end there. A theory must culminate in a statement from which testable hypotheses are deduced, tested, and verified or rejected before we can accept or reject the theory (Winch, McGinnis, & Barringer, 1962, pp. 4–5).

Goode (1959) distinguished among three types of family theory—(a) where the theory available to the over-all discipline, say sociology, is applied to the family subfield; (b) where theory development works from the specific findings of the family subfield to the building of general theory in the discipline; and (c) where a unit of the family subfield is treated as a closed system and the interrelationships of important variables within that system are studied. He then said:

With respect to all three types of theory development, of course, "theory" means the systematic interrelations among empirical propositions, not speculation or philosophy. Since it is empirically based, it does not endeavor to prove value judgments, however important these are in our private lives (Goode, 1959, p. 186).

Merton (1957) pointed to a battle among sociologists between large-scale theorists who make sweeping generalizations without waiting for detailed observation or testing, and radical empiricists who test and verify but often on trivial problems and without seeing their meaning or significance. He claimed, however, that there is no logical reason for these two camps to be pitted against each other, and argued for a marriage between them. Empirical studies need to be theory-oriented, and theory needs to be empirically confirmed. Theory—which is the accumulation of interrelated propositions derived from research, and hence is more than methodology, or than general sociological orientations, or than the basic concepts of the discipline, or even than the empirical findings standing by themselves—can be used to help structure the research design and to avoid such errors as *post factum* interpretation. Research, on the other hand, serves to initiate, clarify, verify, and reshape theory. Theory and research ideally play reciprocal roles; sometimes one comes first and sometimes the other, but they fit together in a continuous, mutually reinforcing cycle.

Hill (1955) named three functions served by family research, two of which relate to theory: verifying or refuting assertions and theories, filling in existing theoretical gaps, and exploring questions raised by the consuming public. Hill, Katz, and Simpson (1957) have described their ongoing "propositional inventory" which seeks to codify or organize a half-century of marriage and family research materials into a set of interrelated hypotheses and propositions.

In sum, what the field requires is **theo-**retically oriented research and empirically

oriented theory. This means the avoidance of both radical empiricism and armchair theorizing. It will result in a stable and expanding body of interrelated knowledge, known as *theory*. The theory will be founded upon certain basic assumptions or *postulates,* upon a set of clearly defined *concepts,* and upon empirical findings or *generalizations*. But it will not be true theory until the generalizations are interrelated into *propositions* of a higher order.

Some Needs and Next Steps

Although progress toward a scientific discipline with an adequate theory has been considerable, as has been noted, there still are a number of deterrents and unresolved problems in family study which should be pointed out.

Deterrents to development. Komarovsky and Waller, writing about two decades ago, had this to say: "The worker in this field is shackled by taboos and ancestral superstitions, which he has the more trouble in combating because they are in his mind as well as in his environment. We are able to observe only what the mores permit us to see. At any given period sociological writing on the family reflects the moral problems of the time, and that is as true today as it ever was . . . " (1945, p. 443). They went on, however, to show progress in the direction of a value-free science. They also pointed to methodological deterrents, but recognized progress there as well. It seems likely that the last two decades have seen continual improvements, both attitudinal and methodological.

Kirkpatrick (1963, pp. 8–10) took a similar view. He saw the difficulties facing family study in terms of (a) emotional obstacles and (b) intellectual obstacles. The first include such things as biases, fears, and wishful preconceptions; a conservative attitude; the romantic complex; surviving sex taboos; and the tendency to view family phenomena as being comic. The second refer to the complexity of the phenomena, including the existence of confused terminology, and to ignorance and dogmatism external to the researcher, such as strongly believed folklore.[4]

Hill (1955, pp. 273–275) summarized obstacles to family research under five headings: (a) the resistance of families to be studied, (b) the lack of adequate research tools, (c) the existence of competing conceptual approaches, (d) the twin evils of "prima donnism" and "discipleship," and (e) the paucity of research workers and/or the time and facilities at their disposal. But he did recognize promising developments with respect to most of these, and in describing the increase in family research characteristic of recent years, he reminded that it had to await: (a) the willingness of families to be studied, (b) the emancipation of scientists from blinders imposed by the mores, and (c) the formulation of better methods and theory (Hill & Simpson, 1956).

Administrative considerations. With the shift in research interest away from institutional analysis and toward more or less personal phenomena having immediate applicability has come an increased respectability of the field, a whetted public interest manifested through an elaborate scientific and popular literature, and an expanded programming for the field, including such developments as the founding of national organizations, the establishment of family study centers, the setting up of national and international workshops, and the defining of criteria and the offering of awards for excellence in family research. These trends

---

[4] F. Ivan Nye, in reading a preliminary draft of these paragraphs, commented as follows: "I feel there is an additional problem in that some of our radical wing try to justify their own deviant behavior or wishes by attacking mores which are serving the society very well. They are not mature enough, or objective enough to take responsibility for their departure from the mores but defend such departures by attacking the structure of the society. I'm suggesting that those who attack the present family norms are about as likely to be lacking in objectivity as those who uncritically support the status quo."

already have been noted, and continuing developments must be expected. Here four additional, though closely related, trends are pointed up, which although also under way, are in great need of further development.

1. First and foremost is self-examination, or what might be labeled "disciplinary introspection." The recent growth of classified bibliographies, abstracting services, propositional inventories, evaluational standards, and critiques coming from within the field has been noted. Hill (1958) spoke of such developments as "perspective taking," and indicated that he regarded them as hallmarks of emerging maturity for the field. Workers in marriage and the family need to be professionally introspective in their teaching, counseling, and other applied activities, as well as in research (cf. Burgess, 1946; Burgess, 1947). In other words, the field is ripe for evaluational research—research turned inward, research about research, and research about the applications of research. In this manner the field can become self-correcting.

2. Closely related to the above is the need for an adequate dissemination of current knowledge in the field (Burgess, 1946), including factual data, methodological procedures, and theoretical formulations. This means an accurate dissemination to the consuming public and to fellow scholars, both within the country and abroad. Hill (1962) and Mogey (1962) have pointed especially to the need for international teamwork in research to the end of cross-fertilization, the lifting of methodologically underdeveloped areas, and the building of cross-cultural theory. The recently organized Committee on Family Research of the International Sociological Association is now working toward these goals. Bibliographies, abstracts, and the other introspective devices mentioned in the paragraph above can assist in dissemination. In addition, there may be need for more and better publications. Nye and Bayer (1963), for example, argued for the addition of both a new journal to stimulate methodological research, and a new

book on family theory (perhaps unknowingly anticipating this present Handbook).

3. The trend toward more coordination of research efforts (Hill, 1958) needs to be continued and expanded. This can take several forms: individual workers or teams staying with one research problem long enough to produce cumulative results, researchers familiarizing themselves with the literature of others in their own and related fields, and the setting up of collaborative teams across disciplines. There needs to be not only a better dissemination of information, but also better communication and cooperation among workers of varying orientations (Burgess, 1946; Mowrer & Mowrer, 1951). Nye and Bayer (1963) also argued for cooperation from nonfamily-trained sociologists, that is, for cross-fertilization *within* the field.

4. Greater efforts should be made to interest more well-qualified workers in family research, to free them from other responsibilities, to provide them with adequate facilities, and to assist them by means of conferences, workshops, family study centers, and the like. In other words, there needs to be more attention given to providing research supports. As it is, hardly anyone is giving full time to family research (Hill, 1955; Nimkoff, 1948), facilities are inadequate, and funds are woefully meager. There recently have been breakthroughs in securing grants from foundations and governmental agencies, but these sources need to be further developed and utilized. Better financing could mean improved training programs and more productive research across the board. The setting up of a National Family Research Center has been suggested (Nimkoff, 1948).

Utilitarian considerations. To "pure" scientists, questions of utility are hardly relevant. The task of science, they say, is the discovery of truth, regardless of values and applications; these latter are best left to the theologian, the philosopher, and the social engineer. Nevertheless, many if not most family researchers take the implicit

position that, although values should not influence the generalizations of their science, they can and must help decide the kinds of problems to be studied. Foote (1954) made this view explicit by claiming that the only real justification for research is the contribution it can make to common welfare. Part V of this Handbook gives special attention to applied interests, and the final chapter especially focuses upon the value issue. Here, however, it may be well to list several of the outstanding problems for solution.

1. There is the problem of eliminating bias and vested interest from the research process, of creating a value-free science. Although the trend over a half-century or more has been in this direction, there is still some distance to go. The requirement is not that scientists as persons divest themselves of self interests and value judgments, but only that they keep these out of the scientific process, making sure that their research generalizations spring only from the empirical facts investigated.

2. Even if it be accepted that values have no place in the formulation of generalizations, there is still the question of how the researcher relates to the people he is studying. Should he be always objective and detached, or should he be interested in his subjects and committed to their betterment? Foote and Cottrell (1955) have argued for the latter, decrying the tendency of researchers to assume a disinterested spectator role, and outlining their preferred procedure called "participant experimentation." Kolb (1948; 1950), on the other hand, claimed that the field has been limited by its own value position; he criticized family researchers and educators for promoting the values of adjustment and stability, which, he said, are anti-individualistic and deterring factors in personality growth. Whether, or to what extent, research can be combined with educational and therapeutic interests is still open to question.

3. Another but closely related problem has to do with public relations. Assuming

that applied interests have their place, how best can family researchers keep in touch with the consumer market? One aspect of the problem requires a bridging of communication gaps between the researcher and the helping professions and the general public. This presents conceptual and terminological difficulties, as well as tendencies toward distortion in popularized reporting. An additional aspect of the problem requires tact in dealing with certain sensitive areas until resistance can be overcome. Although progress has been made, family researchers are still handicapped by such things as the lack of religious data on most vital statistics records and by the lack of complete acceptance of sex teaching and research in many sectors of society.

4. There is the question, also closely related, of what effects the work may have upon the consuming public. Can one be realistic without appearing pessimistic, for example? College students sometimes complain of the approach being too negative, too problem centered, simply because it is analytical. Perhaps the research *has* disproportionately emphasized family problems, with the result that the normal family has been neglected (Komarovsky & Waller, 1945). If so, this needs to be corrected. But if the problems are there they must be looked at; realism is the only road to rectification, and hence ultimately to optimism. It may be, however, that the analytical approach in family life education and research is discouraging some and oversensitizing others, causing relatively normal persons to be anxious or to exaggerate the problems before them. The question is one of delicate balance: how to be positive without being pollyannaish; how to be analytical without squeezing out love or making people overly problem-conscious.

Method-theory considerations. Because of the close interrelationship existing between method and theory, it might be well here to view them together. The central need, of course, is for many of the trends already pointed out to continue, such as quantifica-

tion coupled with case study analysis; the use of meaningful research designs, including formally stated hypotheses; the improvement of data-gathering processes; the willingness to make value-free generalizations; the replication, integration, and codification of research findings; and the delineation of theoretical frames of reference. There are other noteworthy developments also, some of which have been mentioned earlier in this chapter and many of which are treated at appropriate points in the chapters to follow. For present purposes, it seems appropriate to give special though brief reminders of four of the most pressing needs.

1. There is a strong need to improve the validity and reliability of the data used. Too much of family literature, even today, is based upon nonrepresentative samples and data which have been loosely gathered, to say nothing for the moment about poor conceptualization, design, and analysis. The frequent result is distorted generalization. Nevertheless, it would be a mistake to assume that representative samples are the only ones allowable. Hoffman and Lippitt (1960) correctly pointed out that the testing of relationships among variables often requires the use of homogeneous and nonrepresentative samples. They distinguished between "statistical generalization" and "theoretical generalization," and in regard to the latter they said that "the greater accessibility of nonrepresentative samples may at times be an acceptable reason for using them" (p. 1004; cf. Winch, McGinnis, & Barringer, 1962, p. 9). These authors, in the treatise cited, also gave an excellent critical summary of major methodological problems in such issues as obtaining access to the data, overcoming distortion in verbal reports, and making promising approaches in observation. Although their focus was upon child development, their rather comprehensive treatment of various research techniques and problems can be recommended for family sociologists as well (pp. 985–1005). Nye and Bayer (1963) likewise dealt with some of

these issues, stressing such needs as a greater and more sophisticated use of scale construction, replacing isolated items dealt with separately, and a further exploration and utilization of so-called lie tests (not the same lie-detector tests used in crime detection) to insure accuracy in reporting.

2. There is an equally strong need to become concerned over and, insofar as possible, to measure *causation* among the variables being studied. The movement from a mere description of properties to the testing of relationships among properties has been a notable one. Relationships may be spurious, however; the establishment of statistical association is not the proving of *cause and effect* relationships. This latter, a central concern of science, is difficult to accomplish, and especially so in the social sciences, because of the complexity and frequent inaccessibility of the data and because of practical difficulties in carrying out controlled experiments on people. But it is far from impossible, and increases in its use have already been noted. Winch, McGinnis, and Barringer (1962, Ch. 1) have explained the scientific method as applied to family study and, as part of their helpful discussion, outlined the classical design of an experiment, together with approximations to it, useful to social scientists. In the classical experiment, both experimental and control groups are observed both before and after the introduction of a factor into the experimental group. This is the surest way to test causation, for it controls all relevant variables except the one being tested, and it observes the operation of the latter over time. Three less useful, but more easily administered, variations of this are: (a) eliminating the control group but retaining the time dimension; (b) eliminating the time element but retaining the control group; and (c) eliminating both or, in other words, studying just one group or individual case at one given time, the weakest of all. More attention must be given to longitudinal design with appropriate controls.

3. Closely related to the above—or even a part of it—is the need for better control over intervening variables. Typically, this has been accomplished, or partly so, by restricting the analysis to a relatively homogeneous group or stratum of society. Nye and Bayer (1963, p. 299) reminded, however, that no group is entirely homogeneous, therefore the "control" is only partial. Furthermore, when research is so restricted, its generalizations are likewise restricted and do not have anything approaching universality. As possible alternatives to the homogeneous sample, they suggested frequency-distribution control and ecological matching, and they cited research where the so-called third variable is handled, not just passively by being neutralized, but actively as one of the conditions affecting the relationship. This approach would seem to offer promise for modern cross-cultural researchers, for their task is one of both determining the effects of culture upon the phenomenon studied and determining the "universals" in family phenomena, that is, the elements which are unaffected by cultural variation (Christensen, 1960). Regarding the latter, Mogey (1962, p. 423) called upon students of the family to develop generalizations which are "culture-free and of world relevance," which of course will be impossible without determining if and to what extent culture intervenes. Hoffman and Lippitt (1960) referred to the size of the "causal jump" in the sequential framework of research as one of its most frequent problems, and emphasized the need for operationalizing the intervening steps or variables involved in order to tell what causes what.

4. As has been said several times, there is urgent need for better theory. Critics of family research have described it as being amateurish, trivial, scattered, often sterile, and sometimes moralistic. These are harsh words, and they are at best only partially true. Furthermore, they are less true today than yesterday. But there is still need for correcting what Goode (1959, p. 186) spoke of as a "hornet's nest of conceptual and terminological problems." There is still need

to isolate and then integrate, insofar as seems feasible, the theoretical frameworks which can guide the discipline. And there is still need to find and then specify the relationships among empirical generalizations in order to constitute true theory.

For some time at least, family theory is likely to remain middle-ranged and multi-focused, although an eventual general theory for the field is a possibility that must not be ruled out. But, in any case, it is to theory that we must look for both the interpretation of empirical data and the generation of researchable hypotheses.

REFERENCES

Ackerman, N. W. An orientation to psychiatric research on the family. *Marr. & fam. Living,* 1957, 19, 68–74.

Ackerman, N. W. *The psychodynamics of family life.* New York: Basic Books, 1958.

Alexander, I. E. Family therapy. *Marr. & fam. Living,* 1963, 25, 146–154.

Barrabee, P. The family as a unit of treatment in mental health therapy. *Marr. & fam. Living,* 1957, 19, 182–186.

Barron, M. L. Research on intermarriage: a survey of accomplishments and prospects. *Amer. J. Sociol.,* 1951, 57, 249–255.

Bell, N. W., & Vogel, E. F. (Eds.) *A modern introduction to the family.* Glencoe, Ill.: Free Press, 1960. (a)

Bell, N. W., & Vogel, E. F. Toward a framework for functional analysis of family behavior. In N. W. Bell & E. F. Vogel (Eds.), *A modern introduction to the family.* Glencoe, Ill.: Free Press, 1960. Pp. 1–33. (b)

Bossard, J. H. S., & Boll, Eleanor S. *Family situations.* Philadelphia: Univer. of Pennsylvania Press, 1943.

Burgess, E. W. New foundations for marriage and the family: research. *Marr. & fam. Living,* 1946, 8, 64–65.

Burgess, E. W. The family and sociological research. *Soc. Forces,* 1947, 26, 1–6.

Cavan, Ruth S. *The American family.* (3rd ed.) New York: Crowell, 1963.

Chance, E. *Families in treatment: from the viewpoint of the patient, the clinician, and the researcher.* New York: Basic Books, 1959.

Christensen, H. T. *Marriage analysis: foundations for successful family life.* (2nd ed.) New York: Ronald Press, 1958.

Christensen, H. T. Cultural relativism and premarital sex norms. *Amer. sociol. Rev.,* 1960, 25, 31–39.

Cottrell, L. S. The present status and future orientation of research on the family. *Amer. sociol. Rev.,* 1948, 13, 123–129. Discussed by E. W. Burgess, Ruth S. Cavan, & Mirra Komarovsky, *loc. cit.,* pp. 129–136.

Cottrell, L. S. New directions for research on the American family. *Soc. Casewk,* 1953, 34, 54–60.

Dager, E. Z. A review of family research in 1958. *Marr. & fam. Living,* 1959, 21, 287–299.

Ehrmann, W. A review of family research in 1954. *Marr. & fam. Living,* 1955, 17, 169–176.

Ehrmann, W. A review of family research in 1955. *Marr. & fam. Living,* 1956, 18, 168–176.

Ehrmann, W. A review of family research in 1956. *Marr. & fam. Living,* 1957, 19, 279–294.

Ehrmann, W. A review of family research in 1957. *Marr. & fam. Living,* 1958, 20, 384–396.

Ellis, A. 1953 classified bibliography on human sex relations. *Int. J. Sexol.,* 1954, 7, 1–12. (a)

Ellis, A. 1953 classified bibliography on marriage and family relations. *Marr. & fam. Living,* 1954, 16, 145–161, 254–263. (b)

Ellis, A., & Doorbar, Ruth R. Recent trends in sex, marriage and family research. *Marr. & fam. Living,* 1952, 14, 338–340.

Ellis, A., & Doorbar, Ruth R. Classified bibliography of articles, books, and pamphlets on sex, love, marriage, and family relations published during 1952. *Marr. & fam. Living,* 1953, 15, 156–175.

Flugel, J. C. *The psycho-analytic study of the family.* London: Hogarth Press, 1921.

Foote, N. N. Research: a new strength for family life. *Marr. & fam. Living,* 1954, 16, 13–20.

Foote, N. N. The appraisal of family research. *Marr. & fam. Living,* 1957, 19, 92–99.

Foote, N. N., & Cottrell, L. S. *Identity and interpersonal competence.* Chicago: Univer. of Chicago Press, 1955.

Goode, W. J. Horizons in family theory. In

R. K. Merton, L. Broom, & L. S. Cottrell (Eds.), *Sociology today.* New York: Basic Books, 1959. Pp. 178–196.

Hill, R. Interdisciplinary workshop on marriage and family research. *Marr. & fam. Living,* 1951, 13, 13–28. (a)

Hill, R. Review of current research on marriage and the family. *Amer. sociol. Rev.,* 1951, 16, 694–701. (b)

Hill, R. A critique of contemporary marriage and family research. *Soc. Forces,* 1955, 33, 268–277.

Hill, R. Sociology of marriage and family behavior, 1945–56: a trend report and bibliography. *Current Sociol.,* 1958, 7, 1–98.

Hill, R. Cross-national family research: attempts and prospects. *Int. soc. sci. J.,* 1962, 14, 425–451.

Hill, R., & Hansen, D. A. The identification of conceptual frameworks utilized in family study. *Marr. & fam. Living,* 1960, 22, 299–311.

Hill, R., Katz, A. M., & Simpson, R. L. An inventory of research in marriage and family behavior: a statement of objectives and progress. *Marr. & fam. Living,* 1957, 19, 89–92.

Hill, R., & Simpson, R. L. Marriage and family sociology, 1945–55. In H. L. Zetterberg (Ed.), *Sociology in the United States.* Paris: UNESCO, 1956. Pp. 93–100.

Hoffman, Lois W., & Lippitt, R. The measurement of family life bariables. In P. H. Mussen (Ed.), *Handbook of research methods in child development.* New York: Wiley, 1960. Pp. 945–1013.

Jacobsohn, P., & Matheny, A. P., Jr. Mate selection in open marriage systems. *Int. J. comp. Sociol.,* 1962, 3, 98–123.

Katz, A. M., & Hill, R. Residential propinquity and marital selection: a review of theory, method, and fact. *Marr. & fam. Living,* 1958, 20, 27–35.

Kelley, I. B., & Nesbitt, Margaret. The family, education, and child adjustment. *Rev. educ. Res.,* 1946, 16, 71–80.

Kephart, W. M. Some knowns and unknowns in family research: a sociological critique. *Marr. & fam. Living,* 1957, 19, 7–15.

Kirkpatrick, C. *The family: as process and institution.* (2nd ed.) New York: Ronald Press, 1963.

Kolb, W. L. Sociologically established family norms and democratic values. *Soc. Forces,* 1948, 26, 451–456.

Kolb, W. L. Family, sociology, marriage education, and the romantic complex. *Soc. Forces,* 1950, 29, 65–72.

Komarovsky, Mirra. Selected bibliography on the family. *Amer. sociol. Rev.,* 1940, 5, 558–565.

Komarovsky, Mirra, & Waller, W. Studies of the family. *Amer. J. Sociol.,* 1945, 50, 443–451.

Kronhausen, E., & Kronhausen, Phyllis C. The therapeutic family—the family's role in emotional disturbance and rehabilitation. *Marr. & fam. Living,* 1959, 21, 29–35.

Ludlow, W. L. *A syllabus and bibliography of marriage and the family.* New Concord, O.: Radcliffe Press, 1951.

Martindale, D. *The nature and types of sociological theory.* Boston: Houghton Mifflin, 1960.

Merton, R. K. The bearing of sociological theory on empirical research. In *Social theory and sociological structure.* (2nd ed.) Glencoe, Ill.: Free Press, 1957. Pp. 85–101.

Mogey, J. M. The contributions of Frederic LePlay to family research. *Marr. & fam. Living,* 1955, 17, 310–315.

Mogey, J. M. Changes in the family: introduction. *Int. soc. sci. J.,* 1962, 14, 411–424.

Mowrer, E. R., & Mowrer, Harriet. The social psychology of marriage. *Amer. sociol. Rev.,* 1951, 16, 27–36.

Murdock, G. P. *Social structure.* New York: Macmillan, 1949.

National Council on Family Relations. Proceedings of the Family Research Conference. Special issue of *Marr. & fam. Living,* 1957, 19, 1–128.

Nimkoff, M. F. Trends in family research. *Amer. J. Sociol.,* 1948, 53, 477–482.

Nye, F. I., & Bayer, A. E. Some recent trends in family research. *Soc. Forces,* 1963, 41, 290–301.

Parsons, T., & Bales, R. F., with Olds, J., Zelditch, M., Jr., & Slater, A. *Family, socialization and interaction process.* Glencoe, Ill.: Free Press, 1955.

Pollak, O. *Integrating sociological and psychoanalytic concepts.* New York: Russell Sage Foundation, 1956.

Rockwood, L. D. Trends in family life research. *J. home Econ.,* 1942, 34, 647–654.

Rockwood, Leino D. A proposal for the direction of family research in the next decade. *J. home Econ.*, 1952, 44, 23–27.

Simpson, G. Empiricism and psychoanalysis in the sociology of the family. *Marr. & fam. Living*, 1957, 19, 382–384.

Smith, E. A. *American youth culture.* New York: Free Press, 1962.

Spiegel, J. P. New perspectives in the study of the family. *Marr. & fam. Living*, 1954, 16, 4–12.

Sussman, M. B. (Ed.) *Sourcebook in marriage and the family.* (2nd ed.) Boston: Houghton Mifflin, 1963.

Walters, J. A review of family research in 1959, 1960, and 1961. *Marr. & fam. Living*, 1962, 24, 158–178.

Winch, R. F. The study of personality in the family setting. *Soc. Forces*, 1950, 28, 310–316.

Winch, R. F. Marriage and the family. In J. B. Gittler (Ed.), *Review of sociology, 1945–55.* New York: Wiley, 1957. Pp. 346–390.

Winch, R. F., McGinnis, R., & Barringer, H. R. (Eds.) *Selected studies in marriage and the family.* (Rev. ed.) New York: Holt, Rinehart, & Winston, 1962.

Zimmerman, C. C. *The family and civilization.* New York: Harper, 1947.

CHAPTER 2 The Institutional Approach

JOHN SIRJAMAKI
State University of New York at Buffalo

The systematic study of families began with the rise of anthropology in the eighteenth century and of sociology in the nineteenth. As one subject of their inquiry, social scientists at this time investigated the family customs of various peoples, and sought to explain uniformities and diversities in them. These queries led them to make more comprehensive studies of family systems in societies, and to speculate about the historical development of the family.

In these larger surveys, anthropologists and sociologists dealt with families as institutions. They meant by family institutions the established practices by which societies control the association of the sexes in marriage and family and sanction the reproduction and socialization of human generations. In Spencer's analogy, they likened institutions to social organs of societies which, in turn, they conceived of as living organisms (Spencer, 1880–1897). Through comparative studies of family institutions in societies, they assembled empirical data and formulated theories about families. In the course of these studies, they developed their method of investigation into what has been labeled "the institutional approach to the study of the family."

Today, these early studies are seldom read, and their institutional approach is depreciated and has become difficult to understand. The reasons for this lie in the continuing intellectual progress of the social sciences. In sociology, the school of positive organicism, within which the institutional approach was nurtured, has fallen into disfavor, and its particular conception of institutions has been discarded. The other modern schools of thought—the conflict, social behavorial, and functional schools—define and use institutions differently in their investigations; the formal school scarcely uses the term at all (Martindale, 1960b). In anthropology, too, the concept has become obscure. As these sciences, moreover, develop experimental and statistical methods of investigation, social scientists resort to other than institutional explanations of the phenomena they study. They employ other concepts, too, which displace institutional terms and develop newer theories which arise from their current researches.

THE COMPARATIVE METHOD

But the eclipse of the institutional approach is more apparent than real. As its founders developed this approach, they dealt with the cultures of societies and the historical growth of institutions, and made it a method of cultural and historical analysis. Clearly, social scientists cannot afford to neglect the cultures and histories of the societies which they study. They actually retain the institutional approach, therefore, but under another name and with some changes.

At present, the mode of investigation which they use to study societies culturally and historically is the comparative method. The institutional approach has developed into the comparative method; they now are one and the same thing. As the comparative method, the institutional approach constitutes the principal method of investigation in anthropology; it is one of several major methods in sociology.

The comparative method derives its name from its method of analysis. It involves the systematic collection of cultural practices or historical cases from societies in different places and times, and a comparison and evaluation of them to discover their constant and essential traits and to separate their variable or unessential traits. It follows an inductive process of reasoning known in logic as the method of concomitant variation.

Used in family studies, the comparative method makes possible a cultural and historical analysis of family organization and institutions in societies. It permits cross-cultural generalizations about families which reveal their universal character in world societies and their particular character in individual societies in the same or different regions or periods. It provides a means to interpret historical changes in families, and to relate these to other social and cultural changes in societies. These functions of comparative analysis are of enormous importance; they make the comparative method indispensable to the scientific understanding of the family.

To continue to speak of the institutional approach, despite its submergence in the comparative method, is still desirable in family studies. This usage retains a central emphasis on the concept of institution and stresses the institutional features of marriage and family. The concept of institution, moreover, aids in analysis of family organization and of family patterns and norms which are incorporated in it. Its use also makes clear the assumptions of the comparative method, which distinguish it from other methods of investigation.

Meaning of "Institutions"

Paradoxically, the meaning of "institutions" is ambiguous in the social sciences now. However, according to *The Oxford Universal Dictionary,* the word has existed in the English language since 1450 and has several meanings, of which social scientists principally use two. One is the definition of institutions as established practices in the social and political life of a people (1551); the other is the orderly arrangement and regulation of human activities (1821).

These meanings of "institutions" are restated in scientific terminology in a number of ways. Sumner (1906) defined "institutions" as consisting of a concept (idea, notion, doctrine, interest) and a structure (framework, apparatus, functionaries). Chapin (1935) defined them as behavior patterns and differentiated diffuse or cultural institutions, such as language, and nucleated institutions, such as schools and government. The latter, he held, are marked by distinctive attitudes, symbolic and utilitarian culture traits, and values. For Martindale (1962), institutions are standardized solutions to the problems of collective life in societies.

At present, many sociologists define "institutions" to denote the systems of norms which organize human behavior and bring it under the control of rules. They also use the concept in its infinitive form: to institutionalize, to indicate the process by which behavior comes under the regulation of norms. Anthropologists similarly employ "institutions" to signify a system of norms which underlie culture patterns.

Whatever definitions they use, however, social scientists agree in postulating the fundamental importance of institutions in organizing human behavior into stable patterns of activity, which makes possible the biological, social, and cultural continuity of societies. This postulate rests on a number of assumptions about the nature of societies, of which several have especial pertinence to families.

Assumptions Concerning Man and Society

The first assumption is that men, born creatures of genus Homo, with their bisexuality, biological reproduction, generalized primate characteristics, and intelligence achieved through natural evolution, are made into human beings by their experiences in societies. They are born to parents and families which have custody over them, and who rear them to the social life and culture of their societies. Each generation of the young enjoys a prolonged childhood in which to grow, and its members possess the intellect and acquire the language to learn their cultures. Thus, they take on human nature and mind and develop into mature persons who carry their societies and civilizations onward in time. The family is the core institution in the reproduction and socialization of human beings.

A second assumption is that societies have institutions which differ in number and kind in relation to their cultures and their time and place in history, and therefore prescribe normative behavior differently. Each society possesses institutions which bind its members absolutely, and define standards of morality for them. But societies support few if any institutions universally; the determination of right conduct depends on the cultures of individual societies. Through family institutions, it follows, societies provide certain sexual arrangements for their members, but there is variation

between societies in what these are and in the sanctions for them. This is, of course, the theory of cultural relativity.

The third assumption is that societies alter their institutions when they face changed conditions and require fresh solutions to new problems of existence. All societies experience social and cultural changes brought on by a host of social, economic, political, and other causes. To adjust to altered circumstances, they modify old institutions, devise new ones, and realign the number and order of institutions in their social organization. They modify family institutions, accordingly, to ensure the stability of the family in periods of social change.

COMPARATIVE FAMILY STUDIES

Comparative—or institutional—family studies are either historical or cross-cultural in their methods of investigation. Historical studies deal with family organization in societies and analyze social changes over periods of time by use of historical and cultural data. Cross-cultural studies deal with family organization in existing societies at a given point in time, and utilize comparative methods of analysis to understand them. [Cf. Part III of this Handbook.]

In both kinds of studies social scientists are concerned with the social behavior of persons, who interact in groups to create the social order and culture of societies. Therefore, they pursue comparative studies in a social-behavioral rather than an organismic frame of analysis, with sociologists employing the concepts and theories of symbolic interaction, pluralistic behavior, or social action, and anthropologists those of their science. Most family studies mentioned in this Handbook are behaviorial in orientation. But some comparative family studies nevertheless appear in the organismic tradition (Sumner & Keller, 1927; Zimmerman, 1947). Others follow a functional method of analysis (Goode, 1963; Levy, 1949).

Stated in behavioral terms, comparative studies are concerned with family organization in societies, and with family institutions in the social organization of societies. Whether historical or cross-cultural, their focus is on societies, and on how societies control the sexes in marriage and family to accomplish the functions of reproduction and socialization. Societies denote both peoples and the total systems of interaction which these people compose. Social organization signifies the organization of societies, which occurs through an integration of family, economic, political, and other institutions in their social orders; the number, hierarchy, and sets of institutions vary with societies. Family organization denotes the family systems which societies have, and are based on their marriage and family institutions.

Areas of Investigation

In analysis of family organization, comparative studies concentrate on five areas of investigation. [More extensive treatments of social structure and family organization are to be found in Chs 3, 12, and 13 of this Handbook.] A first one concerns the family and kin groups which exist in societies, and the nature of their social structure and culture patterns. Such family groups are nuclear and extended families, with various recognition in modern societies of kindreds and lineages; in primitive societies sibs, clans, and other kin groups occur in addition. These family and kin groups differ in size and composition of members, marital, parental, sibling, and kindred relations, systems of authority, functions, and residential groups and households. They vary also in consanguineal and affinal ties which unite family members and nurture sentiments of kinship among them.

A second area of investigation deals with the marriage and family institutions of societies. Comparative studies analyze types of marriage, kinship structure, methods of courtship and mate selection, rules concerning residence after marriage, descent, succession to office, inheritance of property, family authority, separation and divorce of spouses, remarriage, child-rearing practices, and other family customs. Anthropologists summarize their data by family culture constructs which are invaluable for comparative analysis. Sociologists consider family institutions within the larger organization of societies.

Still another area is that of the social and cultural roles of family and kin groups. In primitive societies, families are paramount groups which carry on nearly all enterprises; their roles therefore are indispensable to existence. Family groups are always important but are only one of many kinds of groups in modern societies, and perform fewer, more specialized roles. Moreover, family members, as individuals and as families, belong to many other groups and organizations, such as business firms, schools, churches, and political parties. They are employed by these organizations and active in their affairs, and follow separate institutionalized practices in performance of roles in them. As a result, they establish a relationship of families to economic, political, religious, and other organizations, and determine a division of labor between family and them. They relate families also to social classes, subcommunities, labor forces, and other aggregations in their societies.

This study of the social participation of family and kin groups necessitates analysis more directly of the social organization of societies. This is a fourth area of inquiry. Societies have different types of social organization based on different sets and rank order of institutions, and accordingly make different use of family institutions. Primitive societies utilize family institutions continuously in their social organization; modern societies, including ours, employ them much less so. Certain societies, such as theocratic or military ones, make still other use of family institutions in their social orders. So do religious, racial, and ethnic subcommunities, which often give family institutions more importance than do the societies in which they exist.

Finally, an investigation of families requires that they be studied over historical time and under diverse conditions to discover the social changes which occur. As a universal association of the sexes, the family is enormously durable, and its great adaptability is one reason for this. Family and kin groups meet altered conditions of existence with institutionalization of new behavior and innovations in family organization. A study of family development and change is a fifth area of investigation, and constitutes a major interest of comparative studies.

Use of Ideal Types

As their method of investigation, historical and cross-cultural studies rely on comparisons of family organization and institutions in and between societies at same or different times and places. To ensure valid comparisons of them, however, some classification of societies or families into types within which they are actually comparable is necessary. Purely random comparisons, made between societies highly diverse in cultures or belonging to widely different periods, lead to capricious and erroneous conclusions. Therefore, comparative studies establish typologies of societies or families, and pursue their investigations by reference to this structuring.

In their use of typologies, comparative studies do not differ significantly from other scientific investigations. A classification of persons or things into categories is often necessary for analysis. But comparative studies nevertheless differ from most other studies in that they utilize ideal types, while the latter usually employ empirical types or theoretical models. Ideal types are hypothetical constructs based on idealized or "pure" characteristics; empirical types are classes based on important traits or common properties defined operationally to aid in scientific investigation.

Social scientists resort to ideal types in comparative studies because their knowledge of societies or institutions is insufficient, and they are unsure of the essential properties of the persons or things which they investigate. This is nearly always the case when they deal with ancient or primitive societies which are removed in time and place and whose cultures are hard to determine. It is true also of modern societies which have undergone rapid social change, or whose cultures have not been subject to extensive analysis. But societies, at all times, are highly complex and diverse, and complete understanding of them, and therefore classification of their institutions, is never easy.

For these reasons, social scientists construct ideal types of societies or institutions based on pure or exaggerated traits, which they conceive of as hypothetically concrete entities useful in comparative studies. They adhere to two criteria in developing ideal types. One is that they select traits which are empirically possible and conform with scientific knowledge of them. The other is that they select traits which are causally relevant to the societies or institutions whose social and cultural activities they analyze (Martindale in Gross, 1959; Weber, 1949).

Thus constructed, ideal types serve three principal functions in scientific investigation. Their use, first, enables social scientists to make valid and precise comparisons between societies separated in time and place. Second, social scientists employ them as devices for historical analysis. They derive the types from the basic forms in which institutions have appeared in world societies and which also represent historical phases in their development. In comparisons of institutions, social scientists employ relevant historical and cultural data of the societies they deal with, as well as follow social changes in institutions through time. Third, they use ideal types to develop hypotheses about institutions—the ideal types are not hypotheses in themselves—which they put to test by the methods of science.

When their knowledge of institutions is sufficient, social scientists will employ empirical types or theoretical models in preference to ideal types. At this stage, they no longer need ideal types to classify institutions which are obscure to them and are able to carry on their studies with other methods of research. Therefore, they properly discard further use of ideal types, and, indeed, the scientific mission of ideal types is completed.

In historical and cross-cultural studies, however, social scientists have not, and probably never will, attain this level of knowledge, and so continue to find ideal types necessary to their investigations. Therefore, ideal types abound in comparative studies. Familiar examples are the concepts of church and sect, the historical forms of capitalism, the races of man, urban and rural ways of living, the pattern variables, and mass society. In family sociology, institutional and companionship families, typologies of kinship systems, and forms of marriage are other examples. So also are Riesman's inner- and other-directed personality types, and Parsons' typology of the American kinship system. Parsons' analysis, it should be noticed, has aroused considerable contention among social scientists, some of which stems from misconceptions which they have of ideal types.

METHODS OF HISTORICAL FAMILY STUDIES

Social scientists face special difficulties when they attempt to explain historical changes in family institutions. One reason is because families do not have a historical time of origin in human societies, but rather seem to have undergone an evolutionary development which relates them to families which exist subculturally among animals and birds. Another is that families do not lend themselves readily to historical analysis because historical evidence of families as families is nearly impossible to get. Human life is brief, and family groups are transitory; families commonly vanish without leaving historical traces of themselves. Family institutions similarly disappear and are difficult to reconstruct thereafter, espe-

cially when written records are absent or inadequate. A third reason is that family groups seldom are powerful enough to make history and are not remembered, therefore, in historical annals. Some family dynasties appear, to be sure, but ordinarily they are short-lived; and they are preferably analyzed, in any case, as status groups or other entities rather than as family groups, or by other assessments of their achievements.

To deal with historical changes in families, social scientists employ several methods of analysis which permit them to use historical evidence without writing histories. Some follow a practical expedient of selecting societies from several periods for comparison, and use historical and cultural data from these societies to analyze their family organization (Goodsell, 1915; Queen & Adams, 1952). But others prefer to utilize systems of theory which enable them to investigate and interpret social and cultural changes, and hence family changes, too, in societies over time.

Evolutionary Hypotheses

One method of historical analysis, which social scientists of the nineteenth century employed, was to account for the development of the family in terms of evolutionary progress. By application of Darwinian concepts to the social evolution of societies, some of them contended that the human family had originated in prehistoric times in inchoate form. Thereafter, it acquired a polygynous and then monogamous character, as societies advanced through stages of barbarism and savagery to the civilization of western Europe. Having this conception of lineal evolution, these scientists argued about the priority of the mother-children family, to which the father was attached at a later time, or the father-family dominated by patriarchs who controlled its women and children. The names of Spencer (1880–1897), Tyler (1874), Bachofen (1861), and L. Morgan (1877) are familiar as advocates of evolutionary hypotheses about the development of the family. [See also Ch. 11, pp. 403–411 of this Handbook.]

Few social scientists now subscribe to theories of lineal evolution, but some hold nevertheless to conceptions of a more complex social and cultural evolution. In general, they consider evolution to consist of orderly, adaptive changes societies make to changing conditions of existence, which may be identified by stages, sequences, or patterns of development for purposes of analysis (Sumner & Keller, 1927; White, 1949). They intend by these stages to designate broad cultural-historical periods of social evolution, and do not impute teleological purpose to social changes which occur in them. Thus, archeologists employ cultural stages of development when they deal with prehistoric peoples and their cultures, as do anthropologists in their historical reconstructions of past societies (Strong, 1953). On occasion, they include some consideration of family evolution in their studies and devise cultural stages to deal with families in prehistoric periods.

To some extent, the present disinterest of social scientists in social evolution stems from attacks made on it by the functionalist school of anthropologists in the 1920's. This group succeeded in replacing evolutionary with functional explanations of culture within their own science; some members opposed evolutionism so violently that they also became antihistorical in their anaylses of social and cultural change (Malinowski, 1945). For this reason, it is interesting to notice that certain other functionalists, this time sociologists, are attempting to reinstate evolutionary hypotheses to explain social change (Parsons et al., 1961).

The *Gemeinschaft-Gesellschaft* Typology

A second method of analysis, highly favored by social scientists, explains historical change in societies by their transition from primitive or agricultural to industrial nations. Such European scholars as Toennies (1940), Maine (1861), and Durkheim (1947), also in the nineteenth century, developed this mode of explanation to account for the social and cultural changes which engulfed the European countries of their time. They distinguished agricultural from industrial societies by their different ideal types of social organization. Of the many pairs of terms which they and their followers proposed, *Gemeinschaft* and *Gesellschaft* are the most familiar and widely used today. To establish these types, they identified the basic social groups, institutions, and social relations which characterize each of them. As societies advance culturally, they move from the more simple (*Gemeinschaft*) toward the more complex (*Gesellschaft*) social order, which brings social and cultural changes to them and alters the number and importance of their groups and institutions (Toennies, 1940).

Utilization of these typologies aids historical analyses of families because family institutions are included in the social organization of societies, and are involved in the realignment of institutions which occurs when societies change in their social orders. Societies with a *Gemeinschaft* social order make important and continuous use of family institutions in their social life and activities. But societies with a *Gesellschaft* social order make much less and more specialized use of them, and separate family groups from other organized groups. The transition of societies from one to the other, therefore, produces major changes in families, whose scale and direction social scientists investigate by historical and cultural data.

To enlarge on these contentions, societies with a *Gemeinschaft* social order consider family and kin groups as basic social groups, and family institutions are paramount in their social orders. Such family groups in primitive and agricultural societies are numerous and variable: they comprise, in one or another of them, nuclear and extended families, such consanguineal groups as lineages, sibs, phratries, moieties, sections, kindreds, and demes, and clans, which are both kin and residential groups. These groups also vary in their functions, with clans often settled in villages, commonly carrying on economic, recreational, political, and military activities, and sibs constituting family groups which act together in life crises and ceremonial activities; sibs and moieties also regulate marriage (Murdock, 1949). Said in another way, through family and kin groups, primitive peoples win economic subsistence, rear their young, maintain social and political control, pursue religious activities, and ensure individual and group maintenance. Of necessity, their family institutions support and perpetuate the particular family groups which occur in them, and interrelate with other institutions as well. Under these circumstances, family and kin groups ascribe most statuses and allocate most roles for members, and create close, personal, and lasting relations among them. Persons are, in truth, born, reared, work, and die within family and kin groups in these societies.

In modern nations, which have *Gesellschaft* social orders, family groups and institutions, in contrast, no longer provide this continuous organization of the lives and activities of people. Rather, such societies have many organized groups in addition to family groups which carry on specialized activities in a complex division of labor by means of separate and specialized institutions. The family groups in them are predominantly nuclear, but include variable groupings of kindred also; they perform functions of marriage, reproduction, socialization, and affection and pursue some social activities as families. Their members join other organizations, adhere to other institutions in them, compartmentalize roles, and enter status relations with many, but primary relations with few, persons. They win their more important statuses through achievement in organizations, although families ascribe some statuses for them.

Social scientists have found these ideal types of social order highly useful as analytic devices. They make possible a holistic conception of societies and facilitate cross-cultural comparisons among them. Moreover, they serve to locate the factors which instigate social change in societies and to put the investigation of institutions into historical perspective. Then, also, they generate hypotheses about societies which can be made subject to cultural and historical analysis and can be tested empirically.

But ideal types such as these also have limitations which weaken their validity for purposes of research. Principally, they oversimplify the cultural variations which occur in societies and prevent adequate consideration of them. Primitive and especially modern societies are never so uniform that they divide conveniently into dichotomies of social organization. Moreover, modern societies utilize, in various combinations, both types of social order in their subcommunities. For these reasons, social scientists sometimes have increased the number of types to three—folk, rural, and urban—or provided the types with subclasses, or aligned the types and subclasses along a continuum (Becker & Boskoff, 1957; Loomis & Beegle, 1950; Redfield, 1930).

In comparative family studies, the utility of the types is weakened further by frequent failure to construct them properly and by inept historical analysis. A case of this occurs in historical explanations of family changes in the United States which some sociologists make in terms of loss or specialization of family functions (Ogburn, 1933). In their functional analyses they compare the American family in early (colonial, frontier, rural) and modern (urban, industrial) society, evaluating changes in family functions which have occurred, but without analysis of the social organization of the United States then and now except by general historical information. As a substitute for historical analysis, they establish family changes by comparative census or other data, and ascribe the changes to urbanization and industrialization of the country. Consequently, they tend to reduce historical and cultural to technological explanations of social change, and to imply a technological determinism to account for changes in family functions (Ogburn, 1955).

Community Types as a Basis for Analysis

A third method of historical analysis, suggested by Weber (1958) and made explicit by Martindale (Martindale, 1960; Weber, 1958, preface), explains social and cultural change by the transition of societies from one form of community to another, with accompanying changes in their social life and order. Essentially, this method expands the dichotomies of social order and increases their utility and versatility as means of interpretation. Communities, to these writers, denote populations which have a social organization, a culture, and exist as social groups, and hence provide their members with a total human experience. This definition lays stress on communities as social groups which have solved, through their social order and institutions, the problems of collective life for members; and it rejects the notion of communities defined as territorially unified groups, which has been their traditional meaning in the social sciences. In this sense, communities constitute the basic forms of human association and aggregation in societies; they are variously band, tribal, village, urban, and national communities. Societies have a predominant form of community organization, but retain also other lesser forms of community. Moreover, societies have subcommunities: these are ethnic, racial, cultural, and religious groups which have a distinctive social life and order, but are never entirely enclosed in membership. A comparative analysis of community organization of societies affords a means to follow social and cultural change in them. [Cf. Mogey's conceptualization of community found in Ch. 13, pp. 511–514, below.]

The kinds of communities which societies possess vary with their cultures, government, economic development, settlement, and time and place in history. In the Paleolithic period, ancient men lived in small bands of related families which collected their food in certain areas and lacked fixed abodes. About 6000 B.C., tribes in the Near East learned to domesticate plants and animals and became village dwellers who developed Neolithic cultures. Their villages thereafter diffused the world over and have been the most durable form of community ever to exist; the bulk of the world's population even today lives in them. Cities emerged as stable urban communities in the Near East after 3100 B.C., and city-states were the dominant form of society throughout antiquity. In medieval Europe, agricultural villages were the major communities in the feudal order of society; the renaissance of cities in the eleventh and twelfth centuries reintroduced urban communities. After 1500, with the advent of early modern times, the nation-states of Europe appeared. Today, national communities are paramount in most countries of the world, and have even become partially obsolescent now. For this reason, some forms of international state exist, although international communities are still inchoate. At present, countries of Asia and Africa are advancing from village communities to nation-states in large cultural and political strides, omitting the city-state stage of development through which Western nations passed (Sirjamaki, 1964).

As they are defined, village, tribal, urban, and national communities are ideal types of community. Each has its own distinctive social organization in which some set of institutions is paramount, and within which the institutions are accommodated to each other in rank order of importance. Family and kin groups, again, are powerful in village communities, and family institutions predominate in their social order. Family groups and institutions similarly prevail in tribal communities, but in various combinations with political and religious groups and institutions. Political, religious, economic, and family institutions, in various number and hierarchy, are dominant in the social order of urban communities; their precise number and rank of significance have varied historically with the cities of the world. Political and economic institutions are paramount in national communities, with family, religious, educational, and other institutions reduced in importance but never neglected in their social organization. Subcommunities exist in tribal, urban, and national communities. They also have a social organization in which one or several institutions prevail over other institutions.

The utilization of this typology of communities for historical analysis of family organization is clear, perhaps, from this discussion. A comparative study analyzes family institutions within the context of the social organization of societies; the forms of community make explicit the nature of the social organization which particular societies have, and aid in analysis of it. Their use also facilitates analysis of family organization and of the relation of families to other groups and institutions in societies. Moreover, they aid in investigation of family changes in societies. As societies advance to higher forms of community, they align the institutions in different number and rank order in their social organization, and experience social changes in family organization in this process.

METHODS OF CROSS-CULTURAL FAMILY STUDIES

In cross-cultural studies, social scientists increasingly deal with contemporary societies, both modern and primitive. They have the advantages in research which the study of living peoples affords: the possibility of visiting them, access to viable cultures, direct observation of behavior. Moreover, they have historical knowledge of existing societies, with further sources of information about them available in universities, libraries, and government offices. In addition, they are able to undertake research projects as groups of scholars, often to cooperate with foreign scholars as well, and to secure funds for researches from universities, foundations, or governments. For these reasons,

they may employ more rigorous methods of investigation than have been possible in past historical comparisons.

Among anthropologists, the cross-cultural method reigns supreme and has been developed to a high level of competence. Since they study nonliterate peoples mostly, anthropologists have to visit them in their native lands. Therefore, they lay great stress on field studies and on interviews and participant observation of primitive peoples as methods of data collection. In field work, they embellish these procedures with other techniques if possible or deemed necessary, such as use of sampling or projective tests. They enter field studies with some ethnographic, archeological, and historical knowledge of the peoples they investigate and check the validity of their findings with this fund of scientific information.

To ensure comparability of cases, anthropologists select samples of societies according to criteria of size, distribution, and representativeness in areas or continents. Thereafter, they pursue cultural comparisons in and between societies, and utilize both ideal and empirical types to classify societies or institutions. They refine their methods of analysis further as particular problems of investigation require.

Recently, anthropologists and especially sociologists have pursued cross-cultural family studies in modern societies, comparing two or three of them, perhaps, with respect to some family institution. These social scientists have, for the most part, carried on family researches in their own countries, and then attempted to extend or replicate them in other countries in order to check generalizations cross-culturally. But they represent also an increasing number of social scientists who cooperate with foreign scholars in comparative researches and thus compose an international community of scholars in their sciences. In some cases, they form teams of scholars which undertake large-scale investigations and are able to utilize sophisticated methods of study which trained personnel and ample funds make possible (Hill, 1962).

Since these social scientists carry on comparative studies under many circumstances, they follow various methods of research. If, however, the larger projects are considered as models, they use procedures which include, in one study or another, careful research designs, systematic testing of hypotheses, field surveys, interviews, questionnaires and other methods of data collection, selection of samples, and various scales and measures. In addition, they solve, as much as they can, the problems of communication in two or more languages and the special training required of field investigators. They devote their studies to a variety of research problems: family migration, family planning, marriage and divorce, courtship practices, urbanization of families, fertility control, patterns of child-rearing, and others. The list of these subjects indicates that cross-cultural studies are not restricted to historical analyses of families and permit the use of any reliable methods of research which are feasible.

FAMILY LITERATURE

Further exposition of the comparative method is possible through consideration of published historical and cross-cultural family studies. Because the bibliography on institutional family analysis is enormous, only a survey of it, with comment reserved for a few books, is feasible. But this review of family literature, organized under headings which designate basic forms of community, will indicate the volume and scope of such studies, as well as the kinds of societies to which they have been devoted. It will reveal also the body of theory to which social scientists have been partial, and how they have put it to account in family studies.

Village and Tribal Communities

The investigations of primitive societies by anthropologists provide the most complete institutional studies of families which are available. This is perhaps to be expected, because family and kin groups are paramount among primitives, and studies of these societies could not proceed far without analysis of their family institutions. Primitive societies have, of course, a social organization of the *Gemeinschaft* type; and indeed they have supplied the cultural norms by which this type has been constructed.

Murdock (1949) has classified the social organization of primitive societies into 11 types based on their distinctive family and kinship structure and patterns. His types are, in effect, subclasses of *Gemeinschaft* social order and enhance its utility in explanation of family organization. He designates his types as the Eskimo, Hawaiian, Yuman, Fox, Guinea, Dakota, Sudanese, Omaha, Nankanse, Iroquois, and Crow. After developing these types, he proceeded to discuss transitions between them and attempted to reconstruct the historical processes by which they emerged.

While virtually all anthropologists, at one time or another, investigate family organization, few, if any, devote their entire attention to it and so are not, in this sense, family specialists. An exception appears to be Lewis (1959; 1961), who has steadfastly made the family the center of his interest, and has published notable studies of families in contemporary Mexico. But most anthropologists are concerned with the general culture of primitive societies, and they study family organization only as an essential step toward larger cultural analysis. Therefore, they deal with family organization only as completely as they desire, and proceed thereupon to relate it to social and cultural organization. From anthropologists have come a great number of skillful and enlightening analyses of primitive family organization: the range and quality of their output is revealed below in Chapters 3, 12, and 13.

Urban Communities

A comparable knowledge of family organization in the city-states of antiquity is lacking. Much information on families in the classical societies nevertheless is available: historians and archeologists have recovered evidence of family customs from the remains of dead cities and from the written records left behind by their ancient inhabitants. From these data, historians have reconstructed family organization in urban communities to some extent and added their own informed, intuitive interpretations. But their knowledge is fragmentary and discontinuous, and most of it necessarily is descriptive. Few social scientists have ventured to study family institutions in the ancient societies (Goodsell, 1915; Zimmerman, 1947). To do this requires interdisciplinary skills which few of them have and an interest in the institutional analysis of families. Historians, conversely, ordinarily lack training in the social sciences and do not undertake family studies on their own.

But analysis of family organization in the ancient cities, were it pursued sufficiently, would be enormously valuable for historical understanding of families. These cities had a community organization radically different from that of Neolithic villages, with sets of institutions dominant commonly religious, political, economic, and family. Accordingly, priest-kings, priestly strata, government officials, and military leaders ruled the cities; they exercised powers of state, waged wars with professional armies, and subjugated other cities and peoples. Urban dwellers were citizens of their cities and owed loyalty to their rulers and not only to family and kin groups.

Two classic studies of early antiquity, Fustel de Coulanges' *The Ancient City* (1889) and Glotz's *The Greek City and Its Institutions* (1930), although concerned with the growth of cities, reveal some of the social changes which families underwent in urban communities. Family and kin groups, even tribes, persisted in the cities of antiquity, to an extent not always clear now, and performed traditional family functions. But family members were urban citizens and had to surrender family autonomy to city-states. With the growth of government, temple worship, schools, and other institutions, families lost or shared functions with

them. But they tended to retain control of their own family and marriage practices, and to maintain the autonomy of the home. When the city-states intervened in family organization, their concern principally was to regulate the sale, inheritance, or bequest of private property which involved families, and to establish the conditions and wages of individual and family labor. As early as Hammurabi's code, this interest in private property in land and manufactured goods was manifest.

The transition of families to urban communities occurred also in medieval Europe, with states and the Catholic Church exerting strong influences on them. Historians know the medieval period much more fully than they do the period of antiquity, and their knowledge of families is greater also. But it tends, again, to be descriptive, and to be greater in areas in which there has been much research. These include studies of royal, noble, and merchant families, family legislation, church control of matrimonial institutions, and marriage customs.

Nevertheless, good studies of selected family patterns exist, and larger analyses of family organization in feudal society, medieval cities, and agricultural villages are possible, as certain volumes which deal only incidentally with families indicate (Bloch, 1961; Homans, 1941; Mundy, 1954). [See also Ch. 11 of this Handbook.]

National Communities

After 1500, the countries of Europe developed as nation-states and experienced the social and cultural advances which brought them into their modern historical period. Both historical and cultural knowledge of modern nations is vast, and understanding of family organization in them is large, too. But historical analyses of families have continued to be largely descriptive, although with greater awareness of the cultural events which influence them. These include, as examples, the rise of capitalism, the industrial revolution, democratic governments, New

World settlement, and large-scale urbanization. A discussion of several books which treat the history of families will illustrate contemporary efforts to analyze these developments.

In *Family and Civilization,* Zimmerman (1947) considered the same problems of institutional family analysis discussed in this chapter, but reached different conclusions concerning them. He opposed an interpretation of family history in terms of evolutionary theory and of the typologies of social order. More than this, he dismissed analysis of primitive family organization as irrelevant to that of civilized families. Instead, he proposed a theory of a cyclical movement of families through a sequence of ideal types in historical societies: trustee, domestic, and atomistic family systems. The cycle of development is reversible, at least from atomistic to domestic families, and the three systems of families may coexist as, indeed, they do in modern societies. This is an organismic cycle theory of family history, sensed intuitively for the most part, but argued with use of historical data.

Zimmerman contended that family, state, and church are principal institutions which contest for power in historical societies. When families dominate in control of power, the trustee family system prevails: family and kin groups are trustees rather than outright owners of the wealth, property, and rights which belong to them. When family groups share power with state or church, the domestic family system exists. It is a middle type of family system often restored from the atomistic family system by action of government or church. When persons and families have much freedom from family, state, and church controls, and pursue private and public goals of individualism, the atomistic family system results. This is the modern family in most Western countries, and it is a family in trouble in Zimmerman's belief.

Zimmerman discouraged adequate consideration of his theory of cyclical family change by his strident tone of controversy and unconvincing use of historical evidence. Nonetheless, he dealt with important issues in family sociology which deserve a wider hearing. In terms of the types of community used in this chapter, his trustee family system appears to be that of primitive peoples, whose family and kin groups hold power in their communities. Zimmerman obscured their identity when he called them the family system of barbarian peoples who founded the classical societies. His domestic family system resembles family and kin groups of urban dwellers in the ancient city-states: in them, both family and state sanctions supported stable families. But his atomistic family, although some characteristics he attributed to it derive from families in national communities today, has its origin in organismic thinking, and his criticism reflects his own judgment of it.

In *A Social History of the American Family,* Calhoun (1917–1919) treated the family as a social institution which maintained social control over marriage and family life and composed with other institutions the social order of the United States. In the main, he subscribed to an evolutionary point of view, but one which emphasized the constant adaptation of institutions to the changing conditions of life in societies. However, he made explicit use of neither evolutionary theory nor the dichotomies of social order to explain changes in the family. He relied rather on what he called "social forces," by which he meant the social and cultural advances in American society exemplified by modern capitalism, slavery, immigration, urban growth, and similar factors. His volumes are the best history of the American family available at this time.

A conception of family history in terms of evolutionary adjustment pervaded *The American Family in the Twentieth Century,* by Sirjamaki (1953), although its analysis was sociological rather than historical. Sirjamaki considered family institutions as cultural norms and dealt with them in the social order of the United States from the colonial period to the present. For purposes of analysis, he employed Malinowski's conception of institutions as organized social groups and attempted to apply it to American families. In addition, he used the concepts of majority and minorities families to deal with family institutions of status subcommunities, and analyzed the cultural configurations of the majority family. But he had no clearly stated institutional theory to explain social change in American families. Rather, his orientation was eclectic, utilizing, among other things, some functional analysis and family life cycle theory.

In *The Changing American Parent,* Miller and Swanson (1958) employed their own version of the dichotomies of social order to explain changes in child-rearing practices in the United States. They used the ideal types, entrepreneurial and bureaucratic families, which they derived from Burgess' institutional and companionship families but revised on the basis of what they conceived were important changes in the national economy over the last two centuries. Furthermore, they substituted the "colleague family" for the "companionship family" to indicate the emerging middle-class family in which spouses are relatively equal in status and perform professionalized family roles. In advancing this economic typology of families, the authors demonstrate limited knowledge of the history of the theory they used and of the historical development of families.

Specialized Studies

At present, no other more comprehensive historical studies of American family organization exist, and none which deals with it in the national community of the United States. To some extent, family textbooks provide an interpretation of present family institutions, but few espouse comparative methods of analysis or have much historical perspective. However, the materials for large-scale historical analysis are available in the increasing number of monographs which have dealt extensively with selected aspects of American family behavior, and which provide both historical and cultural data. These specialized studies are well known, and are concerned with matters such as sexual behavior (Kinsey et al., 1948; Kinsey et al., 1953), premarital sexual behavior (Ehrmann, 1952), divorce (Goode, 1956), engagement and courtship (Burgess & Wallin, 1953; Terman et al., 1938), and employed mothers (Nye & Hoffman, 1963). In addition, studies of cultural subcommunities have appeared: on Negro families (Frazier, 1948), on the Puritan family (E. S. Morgan, 1944), and on the polygamous family of early Mormondom (Young, 1954).

A number of institutional studies of family organization in other countries have been published, and more are promised. Among recent publications are studies of the Russian family (Mace & Mace, 1963); Israeli families (Spiro, 1956; Spiro, 1958); and English families (Young & Wilmott, 1957). Other family studies deal with Asian and other countries which have experienced important changes in family organizations. These include analyses of Indian families (Kapadia, 1958; Ross, 1961); Chinese families (Lang, 1946; Levy, 1949; Yang, 1959); and Japanese families (Dore, 1958; Vogel, 1963).

Contemporary Cross-Cultural Studies

Of contemporary cross-cultural family studies, Goode's *World Revolution and Family Patterns* (1963) constitutes, to rephrase its title, a revolution in comparative family analysis. It represents a vast, successful effort to describe and interpret family changes which have occurred in countries of Asia and Africa as their peoples have modernized. The family revolution which Goode discusses is the emergence of the conjugal family system among them, thus repeating or paralleling its appearance in Western countries, and making it a universal form in the present world. By conjugal family he means the small family, based on husband-wife and parent-children ties, neolocal, multilineal, mate selection based on free choice, and having more kinship ties and control by kinship than the purely nuclear family does. [Contrast Mogey's conceptualization of family types below, pp. 526–527.]

To support his thesis, Goode established the basic patterns of the conjugal family system by examination of cultural and historical data in the United States and Europe. Thereupon he investigated family organization and family changes in Arabic Islam, sub-Saharan Africa, India, China, and Japan. He paid particular attention to such family patterns as mate selection, forms of marriage, age at marriage, fertility, infanticide, family groups, divorce and remarriage, and the position of women. As sources of data, he utilized ethnographies, histories, monographs, articles, census data, and social surveys. He compiled from them a vast amount of information and employed it with impressive scholarship to support his hypotheses.

While Goode's conclusions are probably right in general—as societies become national communities, they tend to develop similar family organization—he is less convincing, it is fair to say, in his historical than in his cross-cultural analyses. One reason for this, perhaps, is his predilection for functional analysis, which caused him to discuss the "fit" of the conjugal family system with modern economic organization. To explain family changes, he relied on urbanization and industrialization as dominant social forces, although he is careful to recognize that they are not monolithic factors. He added ideologies (without much analysis of them, however) as a third factor in causing family changes, for which he provided ample evidence through the mass of data he had assembled.

Other cross-cultural family studies in modern countries are, as Hill's (1962) survey shows, still largely in progress. But those of West Indian nations, principally Puerto Rico and Jamaica, are the more numerous and complete to date. The governments of these countries, concerned with rapid population growth and large-scale migration, have encouraged social scientists to study their family organization and especially fertility control. As a result, several excellent volumes on families which include extensive analysis of domestic issues have been published (Blake, 1961; Hill, Back, & Stycos, 1959). Other studies, variously comparing American, European, and Asiatic families in some family institution, have resulted in articles in scientific journals (e.g., Christensen, 1960; Christensen & Carpenter, 1962). Some of these are of a high quality and promise volumes of similar calibre which summarize all of their findings. Textbooks which view the family in cross-cultural perspective include those by Blitsten (1963), Queen and Adams (1952), and Stephens (1963).

CONCLUSIONS

These last remarks foretell a much increased use of the comparative method in family studies. As more social scientists produce more institutional family analyses, they accumulate cultural and historical data on families and enlarge scientific knowledge of family organization in world societies. With this greater abundance of data, they are able to employ the comparative method more extensively and to extend it to more areas of investigation. Until now, they have been restricted in their use of comparative studies by the relative paucity or unreliable character of family data, in modern as much as in primitive societies. They still have far to go to assemble sufficient family data, but they are at least started in cross-cultural studies which promise to increase their information on families.

As they persevere in comparative studies, social scientists also lift the incubus of evolutionism which has haunted the comparative method, especially in the area of institutional family analysis. They now tend to investigate historical changes in families, employ the methods of science to do so, and no longer resort to evolutionary explanations of social change. More social scientists, it may be, are more adept in cross-cultural than historical comparisons, but they utilize both historical and cultural evidence in their investigations and are inclined to appraise human institutions in historical perspective. Clearly, they do not pursue their studies in ignorance of the time factor, or believe that historical knowledge of institutions is unimportant to scientific knowledge of them.

Social scientists employ the comparative method to realize its advantages in investigation. They consider it principally as a method of historical and cultural analysis. More specifically, they utilize it when they deal with family organization and family institutions in the over-all social organization of societies. They employ it also to test scientific generalizations cross-culturally in order to determine their universal character or only limited application. Without constant comparisons, they cannot build a scientific knowledge of families or rise above common-sense understanding of them. They use it also to follow family changes and to relate family changes to social changes in societies.

In brief, they employ the comparative (institutional) method to invest their family studies with cultural content and historical meaning.

REFERENCES

Bachofen, J. J. *Das Mutterrecht.* Stuttgart, 1861.

Becker, H., & Boskoff, A. (Eds.) *Modern sociological theory in continuity and change.* New York: Dryden, 1957.

Blake, Judith. *Family structure in Jamaica.* New York: Free Press, 1961.

Blitsten, Dorothy R. *The world of the family.* New York: Random House, 1963.

Bloch, M. *Feudal society.* Trans. L. A. Manyon. Chicago: Univer. of Chicago Press, 1961.

Burgess, E. W., & Wallin, P. *Engagement and marriage.* Philadelphia: Lippincott, 1953.

Calhoun, A. W. *A social history of the American family from colonial times to the present.* Cleveland: Clark, 1917–1919. 3 vols.

Chapin, F. S. *Contemporary American institutions.* New York: Harper, 1935.

Christensen, H. T. Cultural relativism and premarital sex norms. *Amer. sociol. Rev.,* 1960, 25, 31–39.

Christensen, H. T., & Carpenter, G. R. Value-behavior discrepancies regarding premarital coitus in three western cultures. *Amer. sociol. Rev.,* 1962, 27, 66–74.

Dore, R. P. *City life in Japan.* Berkeley: Univer. of California Press, 1958.

Durkheim, E. *The division of labor in society.* Trans. G. Simpson. Glencoe, Ill.: Free Press, 1947.

Ehrmann, W. W. *Premarital dating behavior.* New York: Dryden, 1952.

Frazier, E. F. *The Negro family in the United States.* New York: Citadel, 1948.

Fustel de Coulanges, N. D. *The ancient city.* Boston: Lee & Shepard, 1889.

Glotz, G. *The Greek city and its institutions.* New York: Knopf, 1930.

Goode, W. J. *After divorce.* New York: Free Press, 1956.

Goode, W. J. *World revolution and family patterns.* New York: Free Press, 1963.

Goodsell, W. *A history of the family as a social and educational institution.* New York: Macmillan, 1915.

Gross, L. (Ed.) *Symposium on sociological theory.* New York: Harper & Row, 1959.

Hill, R. Cross-national family research: attempts and prospects. *Int. soc. sci. J.,* 1962, 14, 425–451.

Hill, R., Back, K. W. & Stycos, J. M. *The family and population control.* Chapel Hill: Univer. of North Carolina Press, 1959.

Homans, G. C. *English villages of the thirteenth century.* Cambridge: Harvard Univer. Press, 1941.

Kapadia, K. M. *Marriage and family in India.* (2nd ed.) Bombay: Oxford Univer. Press, 1958.

Kinsey, A. C., Pomeroy, W. B., & Martin, C. E. *Sexual behavior in the human male.* Philadelphia: Saunders, 1948.

Kinsey, A. C., Pomeroy, W. B., Martin, C. E., & Gebhard, P. H. *Sexual Behavior in the human female.* Philadelphia: Saunders, 1953.

Lang, Olga. *Chinese family and society.* New Haven: Yale Univer. Press, 1946.

Levy, M. J., Jr. *The family revolution in modern China.* Cambridge: Harvard Univer. Press, 1949.

Lewis, O. *Five families.* New York: Basic Books, 1959.

Lewis, O. *The children of Sanchez.* New York: Random House, 1961.

Loomis, C. P., & Beegle, J. A. *Rural social systems.* New York: Prentice-Hall, 1950.

Mace, D., & Mace, Vera. *The Soviet family.* New York: Doubleday, 1963.

Maine, H. S. *Ancient law.* London: Murray, 1861.

Malinowski, B. *The dynamics of culture change.* New Haven: Yale Univer. Press, 1945.

Martindale, D. *American social structure.* New York: Appleton-Century-Crofts, 1960. (a)

Martindale, D. *The nature and types of sociological theory.* Boston: Houghton Mifflin, 1960. (b)

Martindale, D. *Social life and cultural change.* Princeton: Van Nostrand, 1962.

Miller, D. R., & Swanson, G. E. *The changing American parent.* New York: Wiley, 1958.

Morgan, E. S. *The Puritan family.* Boston: Trustees of the Public Library, 1944.

Morgan, L. *Ancient society.* Chicago: Kerr, 1877.

Mundy, J. H. *Liberty and political power in Toulouse.* New York: Columbia Univer. Press, 1954.

Murdock, G. P. *Social structure.* New York: Macmillan, 1949.

Nye, F. I., & Hoffman, Lois W. *The employed mother in America.* Chicago: Rand McNally, 1963.

Ogburn, W. F. Changing family functions. In *Recent Social Trends.* New York: Wiley, 1933. Pp. 661–708.

Ogburn, W. F. *Technology and the changing family.* Boston: Houghton Mifflin, 1955.

Parsons, T., et al. *Theories of society.* New York: Free Press, 1961.

Queen, S. A., & Adams, J. B. *The family in various cultures.* Philadelphia: Lippincott, 1952.

Redfield, R. *Tepoztlan: a Mexican village.* Chicago: Univer. of Chicago Press, 1930.

Ross, Aileen D. *The Hindu family in its urban setting.* Toronto: Univer. of Toronto Press, 1961.

Sirjamaki, J. *The American family in the twentieth century.* Cambridge: Harvard Univer. Press, 1953.

Sirjamaki, J. *The sociology of cities.* New York: Random House, 1964.

Spencer, H. *The principles of sociology.* New York: Appleton, 1880–1897. 3 vols.

Spiro, M. E. *Children of the Kibbutz.* Cambridge: Harvard Univer. Press, 1958.

Spiro, M. E. *Kibbutz: venture in utopia.* Cambridge: Harvard Univer. Press, 1956.

Stephens, W. N. *The family in cross-cultural perspective.* New York: Holt, Rinehart & Winston, 1963.

Strong, W. D. Historical approach in anthropology. In A. L. Kroeber (Ed.), *Anthropology today.* Chicago: Univer. of Chicago Press, 1953. Pp. 386–397.

Sumner, W. G. *Folkways.* Boston: Ginn, 1906.

Sumner, W. G., & Keller, A. G. *Science of society.* New Haven: Yale Univer. Press, 1927. 4 vols.

Terman, L. M., with Buttenwieser, P., Ferguson, L. W., Johnson, W. B., & Wilson, D. P. *Psychological factors in marital happiness.* New York: McGraw-Hill, 1938.

Toennies, F. *Gemeinschaft und Gesellschaft.* Trans. C. P. Loomis & publ. as *Fundamental concepts of law.* New York: American Book, 1940.

Tyler, E. B. *Primitive culture.* Boston: Estes & Lauriat, 1874.

Vogel, E. *Japan's new middle class.* Berkeley: Univer. of California Press, 1963.

Weber, M. *The methodology of the social sciences.* Trans. E. Shils & H. A. Finch. Glencoe, Ill.: Free Press, 1949.

Weber, M. *The city.* Trans. & ed. D. Martindale & Gertrud Neuwirth. Glencoe, Ill.: Free Press, 1958.

White, L. A. *The science of culture.* New York: Farrar, Straus, 1949.

Yang, C. K. *The Chinese family in the communist revolution*. Cambridge: MIT Technology Press & Harvard Univer. Press, 1959.

Young, K. *Isn't one wife enough?* New York: Holt, 1954.

Young, M. & Willmott, P. *Family and kinship in East London*. Glencoe, Ill.: Free Press, 1957.

Zimmerman, C. C. *Family and civilization*. New York: Harper, 1947.

CHAPTER **3**   # The Structural-
Functional
Approach

JESSE R. PITTS
Wayne State University

This chapter does not aim to be an exhaustive review of the structural-functional literature on the family, partly because extensive bibliographies already exist (Hill, 1958; International Committee, 1951–   ), and partly because a definition of what a structural-functional article is would be difficult to make. Most researchers do not announce their colors when writing an article, nor do they limit themselves to one approach. Furthermore, there are few articles that could not be seen, if one wished, as containing features of the structural-functional approach.

Certain controversies, such as the universality of the nuclear family and those involving cross-cousin marriage (Homans & Schneider, 1955; Mandelbaum, 1963; Needham, 1962), are dealt with in other chapters. For the same reason, this chapter does not deal at any length with the relations between social structure and personality structure.

This chapter, then, discusses some of the main features of what is commonly described as the structural-functional approach. It applies this approach to the analysis of the structure of the nuclear family and its rela-tions with the institutions of solidarity, the economy, the polity, and the other organizations that specialize in socialization and tension reduction.

BASIC FEATURES OF THE STRUCTURAL-FUNCTIONAL METHOD

The structural-functional method of approaching social facts refers essentially to a type of analysis that stresses the integration of parts within a whole, the social system to which the parts belong. The method originated in the biological sciences because of the obvious insufficiencies of the Aristotelian concept of causality for explaining the relation between the parts of a living organism. A concept of causality which uses the model of a tool-using man (*homo faber*), who causes something to happen which remains separate and independent from him once he has "caused" it to be, and in which the direction between cause and effect is always from the former to the latter (except, perhaps, in the case of Pygmalion), is insufficient in a situation where the effect cannot be separated from its cause without the "cause" being affected. Such is the case in living organisms. Here, the causal chain is not one way—the action is reciprocal. Cause and effect are interdependent, and they have jointly, in their interdependence, a "causal" relationship to a third effect which is the preservation of the body (a biological system) as a living organism similar to itself through time and space.

This similitude through time and space is described by *equilibrium* and *homeostasis* (Cannon, 1939), words which imply at once the irritability of living matter, the comparative stability of its inner structure, and the powerful forces which operate to keep this stability within a narrow range of possible fluctuations.

The initial concept of cause and effect has now become two factors of the equilibrium, and these two factors—or any number that are separated by analysis—are *functions* of one another, that is, they have a *reciprocal action* which can be partially described by a ratio (of movement, of size, or of numbers). Sometimes these factors have negative feedback actions on one another, which means that they tend to dampen each other's departure from the equilibrium state. Such is the relation between the production of cortisone and the production of ACTH. Usually, however, the equilibrating mechanisms utilize other relationships than those between the two factors under consideration. Hence, *interdependence within a system stable over time,* described by a *ratio or a coefficient,* and occasional *negative feedback* represent a *functional relationship* between variables of an organic system.

If physiology knew all of the dimensions of the relationship, it would utilize the language of law rather than the language of function. But it does not. Medicine utilizes the language of function because, among all of the relationships of an organ with the rest of the body, it may want to specify the one most strategic to the maintenance of the system. The heart, for instance, needs oxygen and nourishment from the blood; it accounts for a certain percentage of the circulatory system; it sends out a shock wave which is transmitted to the circulatory system; its weight influences the center of gravity of the body: all of these are relations which could be described in functional terms. But the one that is actually called a function is that of the heart in pumping the blood through the heart. The blood as such does not have a reciprocal action upon the pumping action (except Newtonian reaction). To secure reciprocal action we have to specify the boundaries of the system that contains both blood and heart. The action of the blood upon the heart is a part of the broader function, which is to provide nourishment and oxygen ot all parts of the body.

Structural-Functionalism in Family Sociology

Often enough, this is the only effective meaning of function in sociology: a relationship has been identified between two variables, and this relationship is deemed necessary for the continued existence of each of the variables and/or of the system that contains them. Perhaps even the word "necessary" is excessive, since "very important" or even "preferable" might be quite satisfactory to describe the relationship. For instance, the statement, "the isolated conjugal (nuclear) family is functional to an industrial society," does not mean that it is *necessary* and/or *sufficient.* Sociology does not have the data to permit such claims. Isolated conjugal families exist in preindustrial societies, hence they are not a sufficient condition of industrialization.[1]

A good example of the reciprocal action

[1] In all large preindustrial societies the statistically dominant form of family is the conjugal (nuclear)— or rather a "shriveled patrilinear family"—reduced to the conjugal type, with, perhaps, for a limited time, one ascendent and/or one unmarried sibling. Death and poverty prevent anything larger (Collver, 1963; Gamble, 1954). Hence, where the isolated conjugal family might make an important difference is in the group where the patrilineage is effectively prevalent, that is, the middle and upper classes, and also to displace the patrilineage as the goal of the poor man's ambition.

that is implied in functional statements would be the proposition that industrialization is functional to the isolation of the conjugal family. If the statement had been made to the effect that the isolation of the conjugal family (in middle and upper classes) is *necessary* to industrialization, a statement that industrialization was taking place in a given society would imply that isolation of the conjugal family was also taking place. *Necessary* and *necessary and sufficient* statements about two variables in a closed system are automatically reciprocal. However, in a closed system made of many factors *all* factors are necessary to explain any state of any *one* of the factors, and *none* is by itself *sufficient*. At best one may distinguish a *strategically* important relationship and describe it in terms of mechanical and/or logical integration. If there is such integration between the isolation of the nuclear family and industrialization *within a given society,* the two factors should be "functions" of one another. By limiting the relevance of the analysis to a given society, the other factors have been implicitly held constant as far as their bearing upon the strategic relationship is concerned, an assumption that can be made only within narrow limits.

Another example of reciprocal action would be, for instance, the statement that easily penetrable but solidary neighborhoods are functional to the integration of the isolated nuclear family in a mobile industrial society. Is the other side of the reciprocal relation the statement that the isolation of the nuclear family is functional to the development of easily penetrable but solidary neighborhoods as mechanisms for integrating a mobile industrial society? If the alternative to the neighborhood is the extended family, then the proposition becomes tautological. However, the alternative could be greater reliance on formal organization (police, medical professions, municipal civil service) and more tightly knit class groups than are found in America, at least within the middle class.

The negative feedback mechanisms could affect several of the possible relationships between the two variables, "mobile and isolated nuclear family" and "solidary but easily penetrable neighborhoods." The solidary dimension restricts the *penetrable* dimension to the level compatible with a homogeneity and closure in turn compatible with the maintenance of solidarity. On the other hand, the mobility restricts the solidarity to a level compatible with the ease of penetration and ease of departure. However, these are not truly negative feedback mechanisms. They are reciprocal relationships within the family-neighborhood system. A true negative feedback would be: if mobility exceeds a certain limit, the neighborhood denies its services until it has made sure of the residential commitment of the new family. It thus creates a force for lower turnover, a force, however, that may not be very effective, because mobility is overwhelmingly determined by the occupational system. Or, if mobility decreases below a certain point, the solidarity becomes too great (people become "too nosy"), and families move away to reduce their level of interaction. The second of these negative-feedback mechanisms is essentially a form of social control, and this is often what is implicit in the descriptions of sociological negative-feedback mechanisms: *norms keep deviance within limits.* Purely structural feedback mechanisms require a type of knowledge that we do not have, unless it is a purely thermostatic effect: socialization ends when it is accomplished; reproduction ends when the family deems it has reproduced enough.

A true system-oriented structural-functional analysis should always be capable of showing at least some reciprocal action. Often enough, the reciprocal action is omitted, perhaps because the author is not sure of the boundaries of his final system of reference. As Gouldner noted, Mertonian functionalism does not stress the concept of system as does Parsonian functionalism (1959, p. 243). Rather it stresses the fact that integration is not perfect, that factors can have more disutility (*dysfunction*) for the social system than utility, and that one should not automatically associate certain functions with certain structures. Alternative structures and *functional equivalents* (see Merton, 1957) at once open the road to many insights but decrease the possibility of extrapolating functional relationships from one social system to another. What functional analysis gains in flexibility it loses in capacity for generalization, unless one secures a much more systematic knowledge of the *functional prerequisites* of social systems than exists now.

Parsons (1949; 1951; 1959; 1961) on the contrary, has stressed the importance of the system concept in structural-functional analyses. An inductive approach to this problem would be, for instance, to try and relate the level of *labor mobility* which must exist in order to maximize production in an industrial economy with the *stability of income and social environment* which must exist in order to maximize the capacity of the family to fulfill its functions as a tension reducer, educator, and creator of solidarity. One current analysis has it that the isolated conjugal family has lower requirements of ecological and social stability than the extended family and, as a result, is more compatible with ("functional to") the mobility requirements of an industrial society.

Unhappily enough, this type of analysis, which starts from a knowledge of the structure and the functional requirements of the systems involved, is rather rare. Much structural-functional analysis begins with the statement of a correlation: a relationship between a pattern of family behavior and a pattern of economic, political, or class behavior is perceived by the observer, who then reinforces his belief in the reality of the relationship—often certified by statistical measurement—by showing how the relationship benefits one or even both of the social systems involved. The problem resides in the fact that there has been little effective analysis of the nature and strength of the equilibrium of the over-all system or of the interacting subsystems. This is partly because much structural-functional analysis is circular. Too often, it is a discovered relationship which defines this equilibrium. Since there is not enough background knowledge of the relationships between the family and other social systems to build a network that in turn would define the equilibrium, the latter, as it exists now, offers little resistance to *ad hoc* construction and speculative conjecture—which, of course, tend to sweep the reader by their logical coherence.

Although Parsons is a master of the insightful (rather than statistical) inductive approach, his labor of love has been to create a theory of social systems which might permit a classification of concrete social systems and an identification of the functional prerequisites for each classification. He starts with an abstract (analytical) model of the total society and differentiates it into four basic subsystems which specialize in coping with the four functional problems of the total society: *adaptive* (economic), *goal attainment* (political), *integrative* (institutional), and *pattern maintenance* (motivational). Bell and Vogel (1960) give a summary description of the schema, which has the great advantage of trying to do for sociology what Goode (1959) thought was very likely indispensable: to develop social systems which are not contiguous with "concrete" social systems and, it may be added, to make the reasoning of the sociologist less easily contaminated by the role he plays in these concrete structures. By emphasizing the use of these subsystems as points of reference and differentiating them in turn into four sub-subsystems (like so many Ukrainian dolls), and by defining functional relations as being essentially relations of *input and output* between subsystems or between sub-subsystems, Parsons may well have increased the generalizability of structural-functional analyses.

Parsons has also attempted a typology of the kinds of exchange that takes place between the major subsystems, and within each of these major subsystems between their own four sub-subsystems. However, the characteristic of subsystems and the typology of exchanges that takes place between them are of such a broad logical extension (in formal logic terms) that they lose much in comprehension. What Parsons gains in stressing exchanges, he loses in the ambiguity of their meaning.

To take one of the more precise exchange typologies, Bell and Vogel (1960) described the interchange between the nuclear family qua motivational system with the economy as: (1) labor-wages; (2) family assets–consumer goods. On the surface, this is not a particularly striking statement, but it could lead to some insights, in particular that it is *the family that produces labor* rather than the individual. The exchanges take place in two markets which are dominated, one (labor) by the economy and the other (retail) by the family. Unbalances in the exchanges lead to the triggering of homeostatic mechanisms involving other subsystems.

In this context, Parsons has raised acutely the problem of levels of analysis, that is, the problem of delineating the boundaries of the system which contains the effective exchange. This is a problem which has plagued sociological analysis in a way dissimilar to physiology, where system boundaries are clearer. The determination of structural negative-feedback mechanisms (as opposed to normative ones) is likely to require more accurate system references than are now available.

As a sort of abstract frame to be superimposed on the relationships between roles, role expectations, institutions, and collectivities, the schema has yet to be used by many sociologists. Most let their IBM cards and/or their intuition guide them. Functional analysis becomes the identification of the strategic variable in a multivariable system, a statement of logico-meaningful integration of structural parts (small organizations move more easily than large organizations), or a statement of what structures have what functions for larger systems. Sometimes the boundaries of the system are stated; more often they are not. Questions of origin (what came first) and the motivation of the actors are often ignored.

No doubt Parsons (1951) hopes that eventually a construct of exchanges held together by a comprehensive body of theory will replace the present disparate structural-functional statements. As Davis (1959) has pointed out, structural-functional analysis developed in a climate of struggle where sociology was trying to establish itself either against other disciplines, or against approaches that seem to condemn sociology to remain some sort of historical philosophy. Durkheim opposed it to the reductionism of the utilitarians and of the psychologists: functionalism required the assumption of a social system with its own laws of integration and where the notion of individual purpose was irrelevant. Malinowski (1939) and Radcliffe-Brown (1935) adopted structural-functional analysis as an alternative to cataloguing, trait-distributionism, and metaphysical evolutionism.

No science of man is likely to be built in a vacuum: it is unlikely that the sociologist would be content to note correlations that had no more meaning to him than chemical relationships have to a layman. All sciences require a broad framework which gives significance to the direction of research and offers hope of unifying the findings. If a broader theory such as the Pythagorean concept of the world which inspired Copernicus and Kepler, the prescience of atomic theory which sustained chemistry, the theory of evolution which from the end of the eighteenth century inspired botanists, zoologists, paleontologists, is not available to social science, a "functional equivalent" will be necessary to sustain the scientist in his efforts. What have been these equivalents for the users of the structural-functional method? A sympathy for the logic of primitive societies as against Christian nationalism and colonial omnipotence; a belief in the general wisdom of the social body, or at least in the complexity of the relationships between factors, so that social change has always unintended consequences. To the rashness of the revolutionary, social science opposes the humanitarian scepticism of the new patriot. Indeed, in the 1930's only the monistic approach of Marxism could compete with the multifactorial approach of structural-functional analysis. The latter permitted some contact with the broad picture without falling immediately into ideology. Hence, the preference of structural-functional analysis for macro-sociology, which keeps in focus the equilibrium of the total society.

In fact, much of the analysis of the relationships of the family to economic and political structure comes from a confrontation between present-day America and societies seen on different steps along the road which America has traveled earlier. By using a modification of the Spencerian model of differentiation, Parsons has developed (or perhaps merely systematized) a model for role specialization as a means for maximizing efficiency and reducing conflict. If one accepts a neo-Darwinian formula, where specialization implies better performance, but where values give the long-range directionality of performance (rather than mere adaptation), one has the essence of the use of the structural-functional method as a tool for the analysis of change in social systems.

Analysis, helped finally by comparative studies of some scope, searches for the emergence of American or Western forms in various societies, and the discrepancies become "residues" which lead to more refined theoretical formulations of the functional relationships between industrialization and rules of descent, isolation of the nuclear family, or the relationship between political authority and the nuclear family.

The alternative to the sweep (sometimes stimulating, sometimes misleading) of structural-functionalism is a dehydrated statistical correlationism, which is unlikely to result in any cumulative building of science because of the lack of agreement in the definition of concepts and the resulting lack in the homogeneity of the data collected. In the present state of social science, the looseness of structural-functional analysis is functional to its growth. It ties it to the preoccupations that make men move. When computers have been harnessed to data collected by teams of "foreigners," new developments will be possible, and perhaps sociological analysis will be able to look at earth from the vantage point of the planet built by its own theory, and keep the same enthusiasm in its researchers, henceforth strangers in a world they never made.

Components and Functions of the Family

By *family* is usually meant the *nuclear family* made up of husband-wife and children. This is to be differentiated from the *extended family* which "includes two or more nuclear families united by consanguineal kinship bonds such as those between parent and child and between two siblings" (Murdock, 1949, p. 23).

The *nuclear family* may be defined as the *socially sanctioned cohabitation of a man and woman who have preferential or even exclusive enjoyment of economic and sexual rights over one another and are committed to raise the children brought to life by the woman.* Thus, the nuclear family is formed by the institution of *marriage,* which establishes under what conditions a man and a woman can cohabit with the approval of the community, practice sexual intercourse, and support each other economically. Murdock defined marriage as existing "only when the economic and the sexual are united into one relationship, and this combination occurs only in marriage" (1949, p. 8).

Parenthood is the institution which regulates the rights and duties of the married couple toward the children borne by the wife and the conditions under which children can be adopted. The purpose of the relationship is to assure the society of biological and cultural continuity. It is the reproductive and the educative function of the family.

Both of these components (marriage and parenthood) of the nuclear family represent long-term commitments of all parties to one another and are marked by some form of ceremony by which the community acknowledges the solidary collectivity made by the family, gives its approval, promises support against trespassers, and recognizes the seriousness of the commitment made by the bride and groom to one another and, as parents, to their future children.

Thus, the basic functions of the nuclear family for the community are to maintain its members in physical and mental health by economic cooperation and tension reduction, to reproduce the species, and to train the children to make them available for community roles. These functions can be described more generally as the providing of the society with socialized motivation, not only from the children but also from their parents, as is discussed below.

There are all sorts of anthropological oddities which can make a shambles of any attempt at generalization, even of the type contained in definitions. In some African tribes (Herskovits, 1937) a rich and barren woman can "marry" another woman, i.e., commit herself to be responsible for the social placement and economic support of the latter's children, who will now continue her lineage. In most nonliterate societies the husband-wife role system—core of the marriage institution in the West—is relatively brittle and undeveloped as compared with the institution of parenthood, and specifically with the mother-child role system.

Nevertheless it would seem that a nuclear family pattern characterized by equally well developed institutions of marriage and parenthood is the most effective organization for combining the satisfaction of the organic and psychological needs of its members with the necessity for continuing the society and its culture. Whether or not the nuclear family, combining marriage and parenthood, is

a cultural universal will be discussed in Chapter 12. A structural-functional approach tinged with evolutionism is satisfied with the statement that the trend in humanity is toward its strengthening and in particular toward the strengthening of the institution of marriage.

A study of the facilities and conditions of action with which the nuclear family is designed to cope should support this contention.

THE FAMILY IN EQUILIBRIUM WITH THE ORGANIC, PERSONALITY, AND SOCIAL SYSTEMS

The structural-functional approach does not involve merely the relation of the nuclear family to the over-all social system: it involves also the relationship of the family to the personality system and the organic system, that is, to the psychological and biological characteristics of the human species.

This section analyzes how the human family copes with certain situational givens which are the result of universal characteristics of the human body, the human personality, and the most general features of social systems as reflected in the structure of any human society. A traditional approach would speak of the organic, psychological, and structural *conditions* of the human family. A true functional approach must assert the reciprocal flow of causality and raise the issue of the impact of family structure upon organic structure, for instance. It speaks of *facilities* as well as of *conditions*.

Biological Conditions and Facilities

In Chapter 15, the biological substratum of sexual behavior is presented in detail, hence, there is no need to dwell on this aspect of the organic system except to summarize briefly some of the crucial findings.

1. Hormonal changes do not have in the human species the overwhelming motivational

force that they have in other animals. The inhibitory power of the cortex (Pavlov, 1927) facilitates a more complex *scheduling* of biological satisfactions, which, in turn, permits the allocation of these satisfactions to social roles marked by reciprocity and exchange. This inhibitory power of the cortex is very likely the reason why it takes longer for man to reach ejaculation—a median of two minutes according to Kinsey (Kinsey et al., 1948)—than for the males of practically all mammals, including the elephant, the whale, and the primates. This, in turn, permits the human female, who seems to be slower in becoming sexually aroused, to reach an *orgasm,* which is not necessarily correlated with impregnation. Other female animals, when in oestrus, seem to need copulation as one might need breathing when one is short of air, but do not seem to experience orgasm. The human species is thus unique in having sexual pleasure without the penalty of overpowering biological impulse. This is more true for women than for men, since the latter experience a measure of internal sexual stimulation in the accumulation of the secretions of the prostate gland. Orgasm in women is, even more than in men, available as a reinforcer for role relationships unrelated to biological needs. On the other hand, if women had the same capacity for aggressive sexual arousal as men, the incest taboo between mother and son could never have been institutionalized. Furthermore, the capacity of women to do without sexual intercourse for much longer periods than men gives the former a crucial bargaining advantage in their relationships to men.

2. The relation between hormones and maternal behavior is perhaps less overshadowed by the inhibitory effect of the cortex than is the relationship between hormones and female sexuality. No doubt the evidence as to the impact of hormones such as progesterone is hard to factor out from psychological influences, but its relation to behavior seems well established by the studies of D. Levy (1942) and Benedek (1952). What is most interesting is that there is a strong possibility of a reciprocal action between maternal behavior and the capacity to have children. A certain percentage of sterile women who adopt children conceive after adoption, which leads to the hypothesis that maternal behavior may induce physiological changes favorable to impregnation in women previously sterile. From a structural-functional standpoint, such results would be expected, and psychiatrists have expressed a belief in this dual relationship between role and organism (see H. Deutsch, 1944–1945). On the other hand, the weight of medical evidence accumulated so far does not support this conclusion—granted that a proper research design on the problem is very difficult to implement (see Hanson & Rock, 1950; Tyler, Bonapart, & Grant, 1960).

3. The genetic constitution of the human species seems to make the problem of genetic compatibility between man and woman one of the bars to fecundity. Newly married couples not practicing birth control take a median time of three months with a mean of approximately 11 months before launching a successful pregnancy (Westoff et al., 1961, p. 55). Given a sex ratio of approximately one to one, this means that, once random promiscuity is ruled out by cultural factors, the most effective way of impregnating a woman is by insuring cohabitation with a man for long periods of time.

On the other hand, it is likely that incest rules and rules of exogamy make less likely the matching of genetic recessives in the fertilized egg, so that, in the final analysis, rules of exogamy probably increase the likelihood of female fecundity.

4. The human child is not physically (nor emotionally) ready to discharge the most complex social roles until he or she is about 16 or 17. The formative years of the human species are about one-third of his life expectancy, and the human child is relatively helpless for an inordinate number of years compared to all other mammals. As a result, in situations where life is "brutish and short," it meant that there was a strong likelihood that a child would be deprived of one or both biological parents before his growth was terminated. The *isolated* conjugal family is not really possible under these circumstances, since there will be need of substitute parents to complete the socialization process.

5. The fact that children take so long to grow means that every nuclear family will have children of various stages of growth at any one time, capable of different tasks and requiring more or less supervision. The coordination of this heterogeneous group requires organization and leadership. The family being the source of the early and major rewards is also the most likely source of control.

6. Perhaps as important as the sexual characteristics of the human organism are the differences in muscular strength between the sexes. These differences are more crucial in the case of an economy based upon hunting and plow agriculture than in one based upon gathering and horticulture (or modern industry). Even when the strength differential is not strategic, the disabilities placed upon women by childbirth and child care limit her capacity to produce food. *The use of fire* permits the integration of these differences into a division of labor, the immediate result of which is a sharp increase in the available food supply, combined with effective surveillance and training of infants, who are highly vulnerable for at least six years after birth. Women specialize in preparing and cooking meals, thus increasing considerably the range of foods which can be chewed by the human jaw and digested by the human stomach. Although industrialization has reduced the meaning of the strength differential, immobilization imposed by child-rearing is still a basic limit on the occupational activity and career potential of the married woman.

On the other hand, the specialization of women in the lighter tasks of home management may well have resulted in developing body types, genetically stabilized through marital selection, of which the muscular strength differential has been exaggerated. Peasant women show less difference than city women, especially city women of the upper classes for whom physical weakness was, until two generations ago, a valued status symbol. Conspicuous fragility is still a mark of femininity.

7. Finally, there seems to be a human tendency, in common with many animals and with most primates, for strong males to establish dominance over many females and to beat off attempts of younger males to have sexual intercourse with the females they control. The classical description of this was made by Zuckerman (1932). There may well be a biological push toward polygyny, just as male sexual aggressiveness seems to be a biological given. The normal distribution of biological traits warns that, whatever the traits are, they are unequal in their strength among human beings. The relative uniformity of social behavior is insured in man through *cultural and social constraints,* rather than through the uniformity of biological traits. In fact, it is because the biological is rarely determinant that social conformity can be secured, at greater costs, of course, to those human animals on both extremes of the biological range.

Psychological Factors and Processes

Very little is known of the personality system of infrahuman animals, and it is very possible that some of the behavior ascribed to semireflexive drives of an organic character may actually be due to some basic aspects of the animal personality structure. For instance, the tendency toward polygyny may well be due to a desire to monopolize the mother, present in the animal when suckling at his mother's nipples, which becomes generalized to all females when sexual drives push the male to want females once more. Among children, the desire to possess the mother exclusively, as well as a strong reluctance to part with or share any object from which gratification has been secured or from which gratification is anticipated, seem to be common proclivities. The tendency toward jealousy is not something which the society has to foster. Rather, society must attempt to guide and limit its expression (Davis, 1936).

What are some of the other psychological factors most strategic to an understanding of family structure, that is, which will act both as facilities and limitations upon family structure? In the past, this question has often been asked under the form, What are the universal features of human nature? It is not an easy question to answer, because human nature is never observed outside the context of role behavior, and it is difficult to distinguish regularities due to social structure and regularities due to inherent properties of the human personality system. As it is, the present chapter describes properties which are not completely dependent upon the enforcement of the incest taboos and which seem most immediately relevant to the family structure.

1. It seems likely that the human psychological system is characterized by the importance of nonmetabolic pleasure. Pleasure in humans is easily triggered by stimulation

which has little to do with the satisfaction of bodily needs such as eating or elimination. Not only the sex organs, but the mouth, the anus, the whole skin area, probably even the whole musculature of the child, are "eroticized." This may well be true for other animals, but probably not to the same extent as in the human species. This is organ pleasure. It has a diffuse quality; its feeling tone spreads over stimuli that are spatially or temporally connected with the immediate pleasure-giving stimuli, so that the former can evoke the pleasureable feeling tone. This diffuseness probably is back of the human personality's capacity for *stimulus generalization*. It provides a capacity for the personality to resonate to a whole range of stimuli that are metabolically indifferent.

2. Because of this capacity for stimulus generalization, objects as stimuli can become easily *conditioned*, even if their connection to the initial response is at third, fourth, or fifth remove. This is the basis of symbolization, as a result of which, the symbolic meanings of objects can be much more important than their intrinsic significance as goal satisfiers. Pleasure from organ stimulation can be displaced to nonorganic experience, that is, to experience where there is no direct contact with the stimulus.

3. The prolonged helplessness of the human child requires the agency of a powerful person in order to secure metabolic needs and pleasureable stimulation. It is through role behavior, that is, by reaching complementarity of behavior with a powerful person (the parent), that pleasant experience is gained. Thus, the mother-child relationship (a social role) becomes the source and the promise of greater pleasure than could be provided by discrete organ stimulations. In fact, the human body very quickly becomes relatively desensualized except for the sexual parts. From organ pleasure one moves to role pleasure and to its counterpart, role anxiety, aroused by threats to the mother-child relationship. The sensualization of the mother-child relationship parallels the relative desensualization of the body, and anxiety acts as another source of stimulus generalization.

The discussion of the importance of nonmetabolic pleasure and role anxiety as forces behind stimulus generalization points to the importance of the early experiences of the child for the development of the capacity to generalize, which is itself a basic component of I.Q. It would seem that the development of a strong mother-child or mother-surrogate relationship through a certain rhythm of stimulation, gratification, and deprivation is functional to the capacity to differentiate the environment, to relative desensualization of the body, to the use of the body as a tool, and to the manipulation of symbols in order to secure ends valued by the mother-child relationship. By the time he is four years of age, the child's basic cognitive structures have become differentiated; these are, of course, affected by hereditary factors, but they are likely to have been decisively influenced by the early interaction of parent and child. Once differentiated, they may be much more insulated from role experience —"broken home," unhappily married parents, and the like—than they were before.

The experience and speculations of Hebb (1949; 1955) on the crucial importance of early "cell assemblies," the studies of Spitz on hospitalism (Spitz, 1945; Spitz, 1949; Spitz & Wolfe, 1946), as well as those of Goldfarb (1945), and the studies of Bowlby (1953) on early love deprivation, tend to support this hypothesis. However, the critique of Spitz's findings by Pinneau (1955a; 1955b; Pinneau & Jones, 1955) and the nondefinitive but somewhat contradictory data on a Lebanese foundling home reported by Dennis and Najarian (1957), leave one with a feeling of "no verdict." Even the data on extremely isolated children discussed by Davis (1940; 1947) or those reported by Singh and Zingg (1942) in their book on so-called wolf children are inconclusive. Although Anna made slow progress, Isabelle, to quote Davis (1947), "achieved a normal mentality within two years" after she was found.

Identity, ambivalence, and regression. A functional approach does not have to concern itself with the problem of whether or not identity is a property of the personality system which antecedes social structure. The relationship between identity and family structure is a reciprocal one. The nuclear family stimulates the development of identity through the unique placement of the child, first within the family in terms of his age, sex, birth order, the use of a name, second through differentiating him from others of identical sex and age through his family origin.

One of the major consequences of the existence of identity as a property of the personality system is the necessity for neutralizing the aggression toward parental figures which would threaten both the identifications at the core of the identity and the pattern of role relationships which defines the family.

The process of growth and learning forces the parent to withdraw gratification and even to punish behavior which was tolerated at earlier age levels, in order to force personality differentiation upon the child. Certainly, the parent is aided by maturational factors such as muscle coordination and growing strength which provide some autonomous reinforcement for "spontaneous growth," but the parent cannot avoid *threatening* the first developments of identity made by the child *in order to promote a more complex identity.* Thus, anxiety and aggression toward the parent are bound to be generated. Even though the child wants to be like the parent, he discovers too late that for this he must give up his *previous* identity. Hence, feelings toward parents are bound to have an *ambivalent* character, although in most cases the positive feelings are stronger and more prominent in consciousness. If the child were less dependent, negative feelings would lead to his moving out of the field and to decreasing the interaction rate with his parents.

The fact that family roles are by necessity and social pressure difficult to shed can lead to such a level of ambivalence or even such dominant hostility that psychological equilibrium and basic family functions are threatened. There are few loves like family loves, but there are also few hatreds like family hatreds, and a good proportion of the crimes of violence center on the family. It is a source of a reverse Homans effect: in a minority of cases, the more interaction there is between some family members, the greater the dislike they have for one another.

Things would be simpler for the human personality if it could ignore or completely extinguish memories and feelings which are not functional to present role demands and the present identity. As it is, the personality has to push into the unconscious, by various mechanisms of defense, those elements which are dysfunctional; however, they remain there and are capable of influencing role behavior under certain circumstances.

Chapters 4 and 18 cover the problems attendant on socialization and analyze the processes of identification and internalization as they relate to the child. This chapter concerns itself more with the properties of the personality as they affect the behavior of parents within the family system. Here the phenomenon of *regression* is crucial.

In regression, the personality, facing difficult problems of socialization or performance, falls back on more primitive levels of organization where these demands did not bear upon the identity. Since these earlier levels do not correspond to present age, sex, and social status, regression leads to behavior incompatible with complex role requirements. The personality reactivates primitive internalizations which gave it unconditional support and protection. The process decreases anxiety and permits some tension reduction through narcissistic behavior.

Regression can be "acted out" in the realm of disguised phantasies (dreams). It thus serves the ego by reinforcing the internal equilibrium and permits a new mobilization of energy for performance at the higher level of organization which is demanded by the personality's value commitments. Regression requires a social setting where the behavior of the personality (verbalization, phantasy, "acting out") can be insulated from the society where its inappropriateness would cause conflict. *Sleep* is one of the ways in which regression occurs, permitting tension reduction through dreams. The human personality, in order to maintain a high level of role behavior, requires long and regular periods of sleep in secure quarters.

The nuclear family is the social setting where much (though not all) regression takes place. For this purpose, it must be able to isolate its members from the rest of the social structure, and its members have to be able to tolerate a good deal of unproductive behavior—in terms of social values—from one another. Sexual intercourse and parenthood are examples of complex behavior which have very powerful regressive components.

Parental identification with the child. Indeed, the reactivation of obsolete role patterns is the raw material of parental identification with the child. Parenthood activates the more primitive parental images which were cathected and internalized by the parents when they were the age of their own child. Much regressive income is derived from parental roles, which leads one to believe that fatherhood is nearly as much a need of the masculine personality as motherhood is a need of the feminine personality.

From these regressive components comes much of the spontaneity and nurturant characteristics of the parental role and of the marital roles as well. These characteristics, in turn, are responsible for the creation of the secure islands so indispensable to the spouses and particularly to the child. They suspend the operation of objective evaluative criteria. On the other hand, they render parental roles less amenable to rationalizations in terms of therapeutic manipulation, all the more so when the parent is under stress and has greater needs for tension reduction. Hence it is difficult, on the whole, for a parent to improve much upon the performance of his own parent whose image is the raw material of his own parental role. The problem is compounded by the fact that the child is often unable to communicate his anxiety or his anger because of lack of communication tools and/or his fear of reprisals. Parenthood is often acted out in the dark —in the dark of the unconscious and in the dark as to what impact it has on the child.

On the other hand, the regressive components in parental identification permit the vicarious experiencing of the child's need satisfactions as if they were one's own. This has a sedative effect upon the pains of low status and upon the fear of death which is a realistic and conscious fear of man, increasing with exposure and age. And, in turn, this vicarious experiencing of the parent may lead him to try to force his ambitions upon the child and thus violate the latter's identity.

Sex role and identity. Another aspect of the personality structure important for the understanding of the nuclear family is that the resolution of the oedipal conflict is less thorough in women than in men, which led Freud to mention that the superego of woman is less developed than that of man. This is because the repression of nurturant needs is never as complete in the girl in the latency stage as it is in the boy, given the greater sexualization of the relationship to the father. The boy experiences his father more as a threat than does the girl. The latter gives up the mother (a certain type of relationship to the mother) only to secure a nurturant relationship to the father which is muted but not abolished by the incest taboo. As a result, the personality of woman is more interested in the security of relationships than it is in conformity to impersonal rules. This is "functional" to the role that woman plays in the family, especially in the conjugal system, where she is more supportive than judgmental. On the other hand, it implies a lesser capacity than man's for assuming roles where affective neutrality and conformity with impersonal standards and competitive achievement (that is, role tenure is not secure) are the norm. This disability should limit the capacity of most women to reach the higher rungs of the occupational ladder, regardless of their level of formal education, except in careers where high expressive and nurturant potentials are required.

Social Structure and Processes

Some of the aspects of the organic and personality systems most immediately relevant to the family system have been examined briefly. What are some of the basic features of the social structure which the family has to meet?

1. The society must reproduce itself, and, conversely, keep its numbers within certain limits so as to be able to maintain possession of its territory and live on its resources. These are demographic and political imperatives.
2. The society must receive from the family: a supply of individuals motivated to fulfill the roles of its structure, which entails the capacity to internalize the values and norms from which these roles evolve; a commitment to the collectivity as a source of new roles and new role definitions, regardless of personal deprivation; a capacity to cooperate with other individuals toward whom identification is weak, even if this cooperation is immediately depriving; and, finally, a capacity to furnish work and increase the stores of wealth available to the total society.

Thus, reproduction, conformity, loyalty to the over-all collectivity, group participation, and labor are the essential requirements the society makes upon the nuclear family. Reproduction, of course, underlies all of the last four categories. The reason for mentioning it separately is that it permits taking into account some of the biological and ecological aspects of the milieu in which the family must operate.

Development of leadership roles. Another structural requirement which the family has to meet is that of developing leadership. Like any enduring small group, it has a necessity to differentiate roles on the *power* axis. Furthermore, this leadership is of two types, normally not combined in the same individual: *instrumental* leadership and *expressive* leadership (see Bales & Slater, 1955). *Instrumental leadership* deals with what Homans (1950) has called the external system, that is, the solution of system problems relating to the external environment such as work and political tasks. *Expressive leadership* deals largely with Homans' internal system, the harmonization of roles, the reduction of tensions, the increase in individual commitment to the system. As Parsons (1955) has said, the effectiveness of leadership depends on a strong coalition between the instrumental and expressive leaders.

Parsons (1955), in fact, has shown how the structure of the child's personality reflects the social structure of the nuclear family. Personality differentiation and increased role participation go hand in hand. The two axes of differentiation give, when applied to the family, a high power-instrumental leader (father), a high power-expressive leader (mother), a low power-instrumental follower (son), a low power-expressive follower (daughter). The great advantage of the family is that these four roles are filled, on the average, by people whose ages and sexes fit especially well the functional requirements of a small group. Hence, the family is a stronger, longer-lasting, and more efficient small group than any other.

There is a certain amount of circularity about this argument, since the role skills that are brought to group formation beyond the family were learned in the family. It would not be surprising, therefore, if small groups which are goal-oriented imitated the nuclear family structure—and hence the nuclear family would be bound to come out as an ideal small group.

Another strand to this line of reasoning is that the family has certain sociological slots inherent to its structure that are ready to mold the character of the participants, due account being taken of their sex-role ascription. A tantalizing hypothesis would be to project that in a family of boys only, one boy is bound to assume many of the responsibilities of the low power-expressive role, that is, of the "daughter role," while in a family of girls only, one girl will take up the low power-instrumental role, the "son role." The isolation of this "sociological-slot" factor would be particularly difficult, given the fact that birth order would also be a factor—eldest siblings being more instrumental—and sibling rivalry would lead brothers or sisters to specialize in different fields so as not to compete too openly and painfully. The sister of the glamor girl would strive for school achievement, the brother of the honor student would go in for athletics and aggressive dating.

It must be acknowledged, however, that Brim's (1958) article gives results among five- and six-year-olds that seem to contradict the above analysis.

The incest taboo and the oedipus complex. Chapter 12 contains a discussion of the classical explanations of the incest taboo, which follow the classical structural-functional approach, most of which have been summarized by Murdock (1949).

The problem in many structural-functional analyses is that one can rationalize what is, on the assumption that if the system exists it must be viable and that all items of the structure must contribute to viability, or, at least, to use Merton's language, that the function of a structural item must outweigh its dysfunctions. Since there is no reference to the goals of the individuals involved in the system, one may describe patterns that are rational but which are not "real," and in fact are quite arbitrary and incapable of ever being tested.

A step forward would be to bridge some of the gaps between the motivation of the individual who follows the structural pattern and the functions of the pattern for the social system. Unless institutionalized patterns can be hooked to role expectations, the chances of structural-functional analysis being an arbitrary construction are too real to ignore. Is this possible for the incest taboo?

In order for the incest taboo to exist, there must be a long-lasting association between a man and a mother of children. Once fire,

cooking, clothing, and shelter become basic aspects of human biological needs, the benefits of economic cooperation between mobile man and a woman rendered partly immobile by pregnancy and baby care become obvious, simply on a least-effort basis. Barring gross inequalities of skill among men, the most efficient combination is one man associated with one woman. Sexual intercourse is a reinforcement of the man-woman tie, but what must be explained is how sexual intercourse becomes the monopoly of the parents.

S. Freud (1920; 1924; 1927) has given the most systematic explanation in terms of the resolution of the competition between the child and father for possession of the mother. Around four to six years of age, organ pleasure in the child is much more concentrated upon the penis, and his hostility toward the father results in fears of reprisal, that is, castration anxiety. Yet the feeling toward the father is not altogether negative, since he is also protective and helpful, and is respected by the mother. The feelings toward the father are ambivalent. The ambivalence is resolved by a primary type of identification with the father, where the instinctual part of the personality (the id) develops an anti-instinctual force (the superego). Castration anxiety is detached from the body and becomes moral guilt. Anna Freud (1945) described this process as "identification with the aggressor," which explains why the son becomes like the person who frustrates him rather than like the one who gratifies him. The fact that superego formation is essentially derived from the id explains why the superego is not reality-oriented. Its action is essentially nonrational, immune from the pressures of expediency.

S. Freud and Anna Freud's description of the internalization of the father figure lacks clarity, but the linking of the development of sexual identity with the internalization of the incest taboo seems a profound insight. Three aspects of this internalization seem undeniable: (a) the training of the child into the observance of the incest taboo is done at an early age, anywhere between four to seven; (b) there is a powerful need for the child to learn whatever there is to be learned in this regard; (c) finally, although the training is rarely overt and clearcut, it is, nevertheless, efficacious, since the focusing of sexual drives after puberty does not overthrow the avoidance structures built in early childhood. Let us describe a mode of the learning of the incest taboo inspired by Parsons' (1955) revision of the Freudian model, where sociological variables are made explicit.

1. The child becomes aware of the sexual differences between boys and girls and between father and mother. He discovers two categories of which he is a member: *sex*, which includes one of the parents, and *age*, which excludes both parents. Sex is a category that permits identification in the sense of *wanting to be like* his parent of the same sex and *wanting to be with* the parent of the opposite sex. Age, on the other hand, separates clearly what is expected from the grownups from what is expected of the children. The children must abandon some initiative in favor of being held to lower expectations. There are things which grownups can do that children cannot.

2. The awareness of sexual differences means at the same time the discovery of the special relation between mother and father. Since mother respects and "backs up" father, to have mother or to maximize one's relationship with her, son must become like father. But in the age category falls the prohibition of sexual behavior with mother; at the time the son discovers what he has in common with father, he also learns he cannot use it sexually. C. Kluckhohn used to remark that an anthropological universal is the fact that sexual matters are everywhere "sensitive" areas for discussion. In no case do husband and wife have sexual intercourse in full view of their children. The latent cue is: This is not for you. The conditioning used by the parents conveys to the child that the grownup father has a relationship with the mother that is free of the anxiety which he (the child) feels about losing her, and that it is a relationship which is unique, not shared with children. The relationship is denied to him because he

belongs to the category, children. However, there are two things the child can do in order to become more like his father: to deny himself organ pleasure (and bear with pain—big boys don't cry) and to work.

3. Work means behavior that is no more conditioned by body pleasure and is much less directly tied to relationship pleasure than was anal sphincter control. Work, however, is evaluated directly by the same-sex parent and is rewarded, while the commitment to work is rewarded expressively by the cross-sex parent. The mother rewards imitation of the father in terms of work. The father supports and guides the work activity, which is still not free from all erotic aspects, since much of it is play or is full of phantasy elements. It demonstrates a commitment to be like the father which the latter rewards, largely regardless of success, even though he guides and corrects it. Hence, the father figure is not as negative as some of the classical Freudians have described him. The father gives the child guidance; the son gives the father admiration and omnipotence. For the father, the relationship with the son has many regressive features. It reactivates childish structures in the father, structures closer to organ pleasure, although he cannot let these dominate the relationship. The father identifies with the son as a prolongation of his life span, as a claim to eternity and omnipotence.

4. The incest taboo, then, implies the abandonment of adult-like claims, of jealousy toward the father, and implies rewards for becoming like the father by working and giving up organ pleasure. It often involves also some hostility toward the mother for not preferring him to the father. Up to a point ambivalence in learning situations (see Amsel, 1962) seems to result in stronger drives toward the more powerfully rewarded goal, hence the massive repression of hostility, of dependency, and of organ-directed pleasure which conflicts with that goal. Some of the libido invested in the mother and the father is diverted to same-sex peers, and this may help in reducing the intensity of the conflict. The Garden of Eden of the father's relation to the mother is repressed, only to reappear in a new form after puberty when the demands for organ pleasure are reactivated by hormonal changes in the body.

Thus, the incest taboo is taught by a process of latent conditioning which becomes part of the child's basic identity. As a result, the symbolic meanings of the mother and father are never displaced by changes brought about by aging. The mother can never become another female; the father can never become a decrepit rival to be vanquished and turned out. The relationship to the parents can be reversed when the grown child, to a certain extent, plays the "parent" to his impotent father or mother, but the attitudes of love and respect are fixated forever.

5. So far, it is the mother-son incest that has been studied. The low sexual excitability of women is probably a factor in permitting the taboo to be elaborated, in view of the fact that the mother's power over her son is very great. If she were more sexually excitable, it is likely that she would find it much more difficult to enforce the taboo. The same is true for the daughter in relation to the father. The diffuseness of sexual feelings prevents the girl child from direct sexual provocation of the father who, in turn, is deterred by the added definition of sexual possession as a symbol of masculine power and prowess. Possessing one's daughter is not prowess.

6. There is another corollary to this analysis of the incest taboo within the context of the oedipus complex, that of the frequency of some form of romantic love. Man's desire for a woman, which appears after puberty, is a return of that he repressed; the desire for a woman all one's own and the relationship with her is overvalued, just as the vision of the mother-father couple was overvalued before massive repression set in. This does not mean that every society accommodates romantic love or encourages it as our society does (see Goode, 1959), but it does mean that man never, as a modal phenomenon, regards his wife as chattel. Even if he did not choose her, she has a unique meaning for him in terms of his usually exclusive sexual rights over her.

7. Another corollary of the incest taboo is the homosexual taboo. It is obvious that the push toward the repression of organ pleasure and toward the positioning of the same-sex parent as instrumental leader would be threatened if the male child were, for instance, rebutted in his sexual approaches to the mother but found a willing homosexual partner in his father or brother. The securing of work would be jeopardized if the child could secure rewards by presenting himself sexually to his father

and to the other males of the society. This is a typical functional argument. A psychological argument is that the very perception of the mother as the legitimate sexual object of the grownup father builds in the male identity of the child the choice of a female as a sex object. Homosexuality threatens the sexual identity of the child (see Parsons, 1954; Parsons & Bales, 1955).

Thus the structure of the family, the integration and conflicts of the parent-child and husband-wife roles, are crucial for the very structuring of the human personality, its capacity to develop a value-oriented identity capable of extensive role playing within a presumption of supportive reciprocity, an identity capable of work as well as of play.

STRUCTURE AND FUNCTION OF THE NUCLEAR FAMILY

The following sections analyze the basic institutions of the nuclear family, their range of variability, and the differential importance of the functions they discharge for the individual and for the society.

The Institution of Marriage

Sexual control and the commitment to parenthood. The incest and homosexual taboos make it imperative that sexual partners be chosen from outside the nuclear family. Sexual needs in men can be demanding, and in other mammals lead to fighting among males. Marriage, by reserving exclusive or preferential rights of specified adult males over certain women, *reduces the incidence of sexual competition among men and is thus a force for social order.* Western societies try to proscribe sexual intercourse except in marriage, while Murdock (1949, p. 263) stated that premarital license prevailed in 70 per cent of the cases for which he had data. However, this license affects mainly the immature young, girls whose fecundity is low and who are under the control of their parents, and boys who are not yet members of adult society. When sexual intercourse involves grown adults, there are strong taboos which, first of all, respect the sexual rights of the husband. Taboos on adultery are absent in only five societies out of the 148 for which data are available. However, most nonliterate societies allow, *under certain conditions,* relatives or even age-mates (Masai) to have access to one's wife. These *privileged* relationships "serve to counteract the sexual deprivations that men would otherwise suffer in those societies which impose prolonged continence during pregnancy and nursing" (p. 269).

Indeed, in most societies, if marriage takes place, it is not so much to provide a legitimate sexual outlet as to tie two families together by obligations of solidarity (Lévi-Strauss, 1949, Chs 1 & 2) and, as Malinowski emphasized, it is to establish legitimate parenthood, which means that "no child should be brought into the world without a man—and one man at that—assuming the role of sociological father, that is, guardian and protector, the male link between the child and the rest of the community" (1930, p. 137). When, then, can marriage take place?

The procreative problem of the society is to maintain its members at a level compatible with safety and comfort. The model of a stationary population can be used as a starting point. In such a case, *the first functional requirement is that the supplementary mouth to be fed should be admitted to the human community only when there is sufficient surplus generated to take care of him.* Given the difficulty of impregnating the human female, prolonged cohabitation between men and women and consequent maternity is allowed only between a man and a woman who are physically developed to a point where their economic cooperation can generate the surplus necessary for the care of the infant. This capacity is determined by adult society. Marriage is the ceremony whereby this maturity is certified and whereby a man commits himself to economic and sexual cooperation with a given woman. Family and property, as Malthus pointed out, are institutions which, by making married partners responsible for

the care of their children with the means they own, put powerful pressure against excess fertility. The demographic imperative has been extremely well analyzed by Davis and Blake (1956), who pointed out the relationship between premarital sexual taboos, age of marriage, restrictions upon marital sexuality, birth-control devices, infanticide, and the population balance of a given society. Their conclusion was that primitive societies use more abortion and infanticide, while industrial societies utilize the postponement of marriage and even the denial of marriage for some males and females (plus birth control).

The marriage custom does operate both as a pressure to get married and as a proscription to those who are not socially ready for the commitment. One psychological force intervenes as a factor which must be controlled if it is not to jeopardize social structure, and this is *romantic love.* Goode (1959) has listed the ways romantic love is controlled so as to prevent it from destroying the functions of marriage as a creator of solidarity ties between families of equal rank in promoting the power and prestige of dynasties, or, more simply, to prevent it from joining a couple both parties of which are not ready to assume the economic or educative burdens of parenthood. The institutions of the bride price and the dowry make quite clear the importance of the economic qualification for marriage.

Murdock (1949, p. 21) emphasized the meaning of the *bride price* as a compensation for the loss of work represented by the loss of a daughter, and he noted that the bride price is much more frequent when the rules of residence for the new couple are patrilocal, especially when the bride is removed from her local community. Beyond its economic value, the bride price serves as a symbol of the commitments of the families to one another, and it gives them a vested interest in the stability of the new nuclear family, since the bride's family is more likely to adjust to the loss of the girl if it is accompanied by a gain in wealth and less likely to look forward to a cancellation of the bargain. *Dowries* are much less frequent than bride prices, but this does not mean that the man's family contributes nothing. Usually the dowry, when given, is proportional to the contribution of the man's family to the new couple. It is substantial where the economic contribution of the bride through labor is largely negative (Chinese gentry, upper-class Europe).

Dowry and bride price are means whereby the heads of families are able to control the marriage of their offspring, for it is very rare that the amount can be secured and set aside by either the future bride or groom without the cooperation of their families. Marriages based on mutual choice have been accompanied by a considerable shrinking of the importance of the dowry or bride price, although there are some functional equivalents in the hope chest, the trousseau, and the gifts made by kin and friends at the time of the wedding. In contemporary Western societies, the costs of the wedding are a substantial burden borne by the bride's family in return for social prestige.

Marriage as creator of solidarity. For the families of the bride and groom, marriage represents an occasion to extend the network of solidarity. Lévi-Strauss cited the answer of an Arapesh who was asked why he did not marry his own sister: "Don't you want to have a brother-in-law" (1949, p. 601). Hence, marriage for the two families of orientation is an alliance, an opportunity, at least for one of the two lineages involved, of continuing itself through legitimate grandchildren, and a public testimony of its standing in the community. The marriage then appears as an exchange of equal values.

When the extended family is the most important source of support and solidarity in a society, after the immediate parents, a marriageable offspring represents an investment for the parents, work capital, an element of political support, a proof of successful discharge of the socialization function, and last but not least, an object of affection and vicarious identification. Marriage represents, between the two contracting parties, an exchange of values. To have an exchange, one must have a community which defines the noncontractual rules of contract and what is of sound value. Granted that every exchange contains idiosyncratic components (one has to value more what one gets than what one gives away), the rough equivalence of the values exchanged must be accepted by the community if the latter is to underwrite the exchange. When marriage is a major means of extending the solidary network of families, the number, strength, and reputation of the extended family are an important aspect of the values exchanged. All family members are interdependent in regard to their marriage chances, and this fact acts as a source of social control over these members: marriage becomes a problem of corporate action, which in turn requires centralized decision powers for the corporate group.

Mutual interdependence for marriage chances is a factor for the "politicization" of the extended family. A marriage becomes the public assessment of the extended family's past performance. This is true also for the isolated nuclear family, even when a change in solidary patterns from extended kin to neighborhood and occupational groups has made the marriage of a grown child a matter of importance only for the bride and groom and their nuclear families of orientation.

From the analysis of marriage as exchange, one can deduce the expectation that equivalence of social rank is the rule between the contracting families.

Another corollary is that when the extended family position is relevant to the marriage-market position of any one nuclear family, the political authority of the extended family is the final authority on the desirability of a given match.

When evaluation of the marriage requires political understanding of the complex issues involved, the bride and the groom, unless the latter is well advanced into mature adulthood, have little "originating power" over whom they marry, although they may be allowed preferential choices among a field selected by family authorities.

Since families are more effectively extended the higher the social class, the role of romantic love in originating marriage declines in the upper classes.

When class groups are composed of extended families related to one another by marriage or as branches of the same lineage, marriage is the crucial determinant of social mobility. The differential marginal utilities of money, present power, and ancientness of lineage for various extended families can permit a family of lower rank to contract a prestigeful alliance through the gift of a huge dowry to an upper-class family. A certain amount of *commercium* follows *connubium*, although in a strictly patrilineal, patrilocal system the increased commercium may not be terribly high. Often what the "brilliant marriage" of a daughter eventually permits is a better marriage for her brother.

A corollary of this type of marriage in a society where there is some mobility is that a man with ambitions has an interest in delaying his marriage until he has secured a high position in which his marriage-market value is maximum. In turn, this is possible only if a man in his late twenties or thirties has access to desirable girls, a more common situation when the families control the social exposure of young, unmarried girls than when the peer group does.

Finally, postponement of marriage is difficult unless some form of prostitution or common-law arrangement with lower-class girls is possible. The only major exception to this rule seems to have been the Ireland described by Arensburg and Kimball (1940), where postponement of marriage of the heir until the parents retired seems to have taken place without recourse to such sexual outlets.

It was seen that the dowry and the bride price were means for the heads of the family to control the marriage of the young. Furthermore, bride prices are often not the type of property that can be secured easily outside of the social system. In nonliterate societies, it is often made up of ceremonial money and requires the family, whether nuclear or extended, to enter the market specific to the social system in order to secure this special type of money (Gray, 1960). Hence, the preparation of marriage stimulates a greater commitment of the family to the community values and a greater amount of interaction with other families. Following the lead of Slater (1963), one might say that the creation of a strong dyad requires the compensatory reassertion of the duties of the dyad to the broader society, and that the preparation for marriage and the marriage ceremony itself have, besides the exchange and alliance components discussed above, a certain primal functionalism in preventing dyad isolation and dissolution.

Monogamy, polygyny, polyandry. In the Murdock sample of societies (1949), 193 were characterized by marriage patterns permitting polygyny, 43 allowing monogamy alone, and two allowing polyandry. Of the 193 societies which permitted polygyny, 61 showed an incidence of polygynous marriage of 20 per cent or less of the total number of marriages. In general, since the sex ratio is close to 1:1 (except in warlike tribes), and because most men find the breadwinning for one woman and her children to be quite enough to occupy their time, monogamy will be the dominant form of marriage, even in societies which make of polygyny the preferred form.

The motivational forces behind marriage are not identical in man and in woman. If we accept a biological or, more likely, a psychological force pushing toward the monopolization of women by the sexually active male, there will be an inherent tendency toward polygyny among men, which will be checked by the institutional requirements of responsibility for the burdens of parenthood. In motivational terms, women are sexual prizes to men and also items of conspicuous consumption; this is less true for women in regard to men. When the economic institutions permit the realization of high economic rewards for executive capacity, that is, if agriculture or husbandry is extensive and private property well institutionalized, polygyny will be possible for the rich and the powerful, especially when family ties are the only effective way to mobilize effective political support.

Thus, if we have an assymetry of motivation between man and woman as regards the desire for several mates, we have also an assymetry of motivation as regards children. The desire for children and the interest in children has biological and psychological roots which are much more extensive in women than in men. The primary motivational focus for women in marriage is the parent-child relationship. The primary motivational focus for men is the possession of the woman. As a result, women will accommodate to marriage forms as long as the mother-child relationship is safeguarded. Nevertheless, insofar as the relationship of the wife to her husband reawakens the regressive components of the father-daughter relationship, she will also wish for exclusive possession of her husband in the same way as she enjoys exclusive possession of he children. But just as many if not most societies do not allow romantic love to guide marriage choice, this desire of women will not be allowed institutional expression except in the more advanced Christian societies. In fact in many polygynous societies where the marital tie is not a great source of psychic income, where domestic help is scarce, and where the wife does share in the prestige brought to her husband by his possession of several wives, she may push her husband to marry again: she thus gains a helper and a release from sexual duties which are perhaps of low reward value for her.

The structural-functional analysis being made here accepts the fact that conformity to institutional patterns is one of the primary needs of the personality, but it also states that the institutional patterns can frustrate or poorly satisfy some nonextinguishable needs, so that it is possible to speak of the motivational costs of an institutional pattern. The above analysis of the motivational assymetries between the marriage partners leads to this conclusion: in the absence of value pressures, and economic conditions being favorable, some form of polygyny will be the likely pattern for the males of higher rank. In Western societies and in particular in Latin countries, the mistress is the functional equivalent of the plural wives. As the bargaining position of women increases in society, there will be pressures toward monogamy.

This is not to say that psychological pressures toward monogamy are nonexistent in men. However, they will be of a more differentiated nature, that is, less regressive. For instance, monogamy through personal choice is likely to permit a higher level of intimacy than polygyny would permit: the more isolated the nuclear family, the more dependent the husband will be upon this intimacy. Reciprocally, the isolation of the nuclear family is probably conditional upon the reinforcement of the marital tie and its capacity to provide stimulation and tension reduction on the peer level rather than merely on the more regressive levels of husband's omnipotence and mother-child symbiosis.

The socialization of children in polygynous marriages can be accomplished apparently as well as in monogamous marriages, especially when the power and prestige of the father are mediated to the child not only by the mother but by members of the community at large. Polygyny is likely to create a large supply of men committed to the community roles requiring high skill and responsibility, such as priesthood, war leadership, estate management, and headship of lineages. In fact, if the death rate is not high enough, there is a possibility of strong competition between the sons of the polygynous father (since there is likely to be less mutual identification between sons of different mothers than between sons of a monogamous couple), which can degenerate into fratricidal warfare. When political power is less efficacious in securing economic power, polygyny will make more difficult the consolidation of huge family estates because of the fragmentation caused by the large numbers of heirs.

Polygyny will be functional when, because of the exposure of men to war, hunting, deep-sea fishing, there are more marriageable women than men. The demographic imperative will favor a form of polygyny. To an unknown extent, it may have a eugenic effect by limiting the reproductive potential of the weaker men and increasing the reproductive potential of the more successful. On the other hand, when the sex ratio is close to 1:1, monogamy is the marriage form which will guarantee the greatest fecundity, since it increases the frequency of sexual contacts per nubile woman.

Polygyny has certain built-in problems, partly due to the fact that, even if the institutions of marriage do not recognize the wishes of the wife for exclusive possession of her husband, they cannot eliminate jealousy among plural wives. Even if the direct expression of sexual jealousy is tabooed, there will be jealousy relating to the allocation of work tasks and the claims of the children to the favors and estate of their father. Authority of the first wife over all others, a separate household for each wife and her children, regular visits by the husband to all wives, and perhaps, above all, sororal polygyny, where the co-wives have learned to get along as sisters, are ways of coping with these strains.

Polyandry is the rarest form of marriage, as could be expected from the fact that it denies man exclusive control over the sexual favors of his wife. Murdock (1949) claimed that when women make "an insignificant contribution to the economic life, as among the Todas, polyandry becomes a satisfactory adjustment" (p. 36). A polyandrous system can secure maximum fecundity from a small number of women. In the case of both the Todas and of the Marquesans there is evidence of female infanticide. The Todas practice mostly fraternal polyandry, which must reduce some of the strains of sexual jealousy. Paternity of the children is ascribed in a ritual manner unrelated to sexual intercourse.

Linton (1949) has explained polyandry as the response of society to great poverty when a single male cannot support a wife and children with any degree of reliability. Hence, it is not so much the insignificant contribution of the wife to economic life that one must incriminate, but the aleatory contribution of the husband. Similar patterns are found in certain tribes of sub-Saharan Africa, where women have a sort of legitimated concubinage relationship with one or two other men who commit themselves to economic services to herself and her children in return for sexual favors which increase their prestige in the community. M. G. Smith has called this pattern "secondary marriage" (1953).

These are social patterns the psychological cost of which must be such that when there is an opportunity to escape from them, they must fall into desuetude. In Western societies they are sometimes found in the more disorganized lower classes.

Marriage as a source of tension reduction. Regardless of how little tender interaction may take place between husband and wife, they are likely to have a regressive meaning for one another, in terms of the oedipus complex and also because of the duration and intensity of the interaction which takes place within the marriage. As long as the lineage is a main center for protection and subsistence, as long as the same-sex peer groups and the relationships to parents are still the main source of comfort, the meaning of marriage will reside in the commitment to parenthood. In modern societies marriage has come into its own as the main source of tension reduction.

Marriage is a role system in which there is bound to be relatively high interaction and complementarity of function without bargaining. Each spouse acts by doing a specialty as a reward for the other rather than as an exchange of equal values. Thus, breadwinning on the one hand, home management on the other, lovemaking for both have a "closed market" in the home. This does not mean that either spouse tolerates gross failures, but that within broad limits each is assured of a noncompetitive appreciation of his or her actions by the other. This is a major source of support for the personalities involved in the marriage.

On the other hand, the division of labor creates a problem of communication between the spouses because they lack knowledge of the difficulties involved in each others' labor. Children, extended family politics, and village gossip are the more common objects of noninstrumental communication, while same-sex peers are the main tension reducers in the area of work.

The Institution of Parenthood

As Malinowski (1930) pointed out, the core of marriage in primitive societies has been commitment to parenthood. Most primitive and preindustrial societies have difficulties in maintaining their population equilibrium, and the valuation of fecundity is high even while the understanding of the causes of sterility is low. Hence, practically all societies allow a husband to repudiate a barren wife, who is looked upon as a failure, or at least to take another wife or a concubine (China) to give him legitimate heirs. In Roman Catholic societies, which prohibit divorce, the extended family is or was until recently an important political and economic unit: a barren couple can contribute to the support and care of the children of another nuclear family which belongs to the extended family. In societies where the nuclear family has reached a high degree of isolation, as in the United States, and where fecundity considerations are not legitimate grounds for divorce, the nuclear family is able to adopt children so as to perform its parenthood function. Catholic societies tend to discourage adoption unless it represents merely a change of legal and inheritance

status for children born within the extended family.

The assumption of parenthood is usually marked by ceremonies which symbolize the public relevance of its responsibilities. In Western societies, registration and baptism mark the introduction of the child into the broader communities of church and state. The structure of parenthood sets the distribution and duration of parental authority, responsibility of parents for the actions of their children, and certain patterns of distance.

For Goode (1960b), the essence of parenthood lies in the social placement of the child. Through his legitimate birth, the child acquires a set of rights and obligations toward which the whole community can orient itself. Parenthood gives the child a sociological identity.

How much marital stability and interaction are necessary for the effective discharge of parental roles is unknown. Legitimation per se may require little interaction beyond the marriage ceremony (Nayar). The Freudian model of superego formation, so crucial to the socialization process, would require rivalry between the child and a husband figure for possession of the mother. Although the presence of the husband-father seems modal and preferable, children can use other male relatives as role models.

Structural strains in parenthood. The major structural problem of parenthood is that the maintenance of a reciprocal pattern in the parent-child relationship is difficult, due to the shifting pattern of personality needs and changing components of the role set experienced by the child.

Both personality needs and the requirement of order require a stabilization of the interaction pattern. The parent in particular finds the stabilization process most appealing, not only because of the regressive valence of the parental role for his personality, but also because parenthood is more of a part-time role for him (less so for her), while sonhood or daughterhood is a much more fulltime role. No doubt it is part of the parental role to promote growth. The tendency is to promote growth when the parent believes the child is ready for it, which usually means that the parent believes himself (herself) ready to cope with it. Yet the pattern of growth of the child is largely beyond the parent's control. Hence, the meshing of expectations cannot be taken for granted. The role demands of the school are part of the public record. The role demands of the peer group upon the child are largely unknown, especially when peer-group membership is determined by the choice of the child.

The result is that the pattern of parenthood tends to have two disjunctions. The first comes when the parent, who is burdened by the dependency of the child, pushes him to grow, a push that is largely functional to the learning of the incest taboo but which can result in premature school placement. The second comes when the child, in response to physical and social growth, makes claims for independence which the parent is reluctant to grant because to do so increases his problem of control and decreases the regressive valence of the relationship (loss of power, loss of dependency, realization of parental aging, and growing alienation from the world of the young). These are some of the sociological factors behind the minor revolutions that affect the parent-child relationship, particularly in the child's adolescence. The problem is compounded by the fact that the child's adolescence means a rupture in identity, so that there is no stable pattern of growth but rather moments of growth where demands for autonomy are warranted and moments of regression when the granting of autonomy would be frightening to the claimant.

The sibling group. The existence of siblings is functional to the growth of the parent, because roles with younger children can take up the deficit in regressive income created by the growth of the oldest child. The latter, when not given the benefits of primogeniture, is likely to experience more discontinuity in his parent-child roles than do his younger siblings.

Within the structure of parenthood must be described the *sibling group,* which is created on the basis of (a) the solidarity fostered by the parents and the community as a moral imperative which transforms much of the initial sibling rivalry into the desire to nurture; and (b) the solidarity and positive feelings that come from continued interaction (Homans, 1950) and coping with similar problems of conforming to parental authority and of mitigating some of it through evasion patterns. One may speculate that when both parents tend to be relatively gratifying, as in the American middle-class family, this is one of the reinforcements of which the sibling group is bereft.

When the sibling group is an effective work or political organization, the requirements of coordination and control are likely to make functional a hierarchy between siblings. Primogeniture is a solution where older age is likely to be correlated with greater experience and strength. Furthermore, the ascriptive quality of primogeniture reduces competitive strains within the sibling group. A high death rate gives cadets a reasonable chance to replace their older brothers, so that the frustrations of the system are not as great as its benefits.

Elder-brother prerogatives which are not backed by primogeniture are difficult to maintain in adulthood, when the age differential loses much of its meaning. Joint family enterprises are difficult to maintain if the existence of money wages in the community permits comparability of work contributions and militates against the assumption that work contributions are equal as well as the division of proceeds (see Rosenfeld, 1958).

The rituals of death. The rituals of death would seem not to belong to the structure of the nuclear family, but the hypothesis here is that they are as intrinsic to this structure as is the incest taboo. Indeed the rituals of death, involving feelings of parents toward their children and children toward their parents, express clearly the facts that within the nuclear family the bodies of the participants are all symbolic cues and that the relationships are never determined by the cathectic meaning of the body, except perhaps for the suckling baby. Although the corpse soon becomes repugnant and arouses anxiety as a symbol of death, the corpse of the parent usually inspires in the adult son or daughter a feeling of grief and requires certain duties of careful laying out and burial. Distaste is repressed, just as sexual trends to the parents were repressed at ages five and six. Yet the fear of the corpse is not due only to these intrinsic valences of the stimulus. The fundamental ambivalence of family relations creates a problem of guilt for the survivors, not only because in most societies the death of the parent often means an increase in power and wealth for his heirs, but also because death represents an unwelcomed realization of the aggressive wishes that have been harbored more or less unconsciously toward the departed. Malinowski (1925) and Warner (1937) have focused upon the relationship of the community to the bereaved family. Opler (1936) has demonstrated how the ambivalent feelings result in care of the sick and fear of the dying. Goody (1962) has shown how the magnitude of death ceremonies seems directly related to the importance of the property complex within the society, which would tend to support the theory of ambivalence.

One might hazard that the relative simplification of death duties in our American society is due in no small part to the decline of ambivalence in relation to the old parents, given the fact that the property of the latter plays a smaller and smaller role in the determination of life chances for the heirs.

Basic Institutional Features of the Nuclear Family

The division of labor. Zelditch (1955) has shown conclusively that in all but a very few societies, instrumental roles, which include political and economic leadership, are played by the husband-father, while expressive roles are played by the wife-mother.

Parsons (1955) has made a cogent case for the importance of this type of division of labor for the socialization of the child in any society. Slater (1961) argued against the universality of this pattern and stated that it describes a situation of an earlier era in which mothers were subordinate. Today, he has claimed, at least in the mobile loose-network family described by Bott (1957), the integrated family with low role differentiation is probably more functional to socialization than the differentiated role pattern the prototype of which would be the classical German family. This is because the "de-differentiated" pattern may permit better internalization of the parental image, more specifically of the father role, since learning theory shows that only a previously rewarding figure can become an effective punisher and trainer. Bergen's (1961) rejoinder makes a valid theoretical distinction, pointing out that Parsons was addressing himself to a different system level than Slater: Parsons was talking about the nuclear family in relation to the wider social system. The father deals with external-system problems, the wife with internal-system problems. How these system problems become allocated in roles is another question. Indeed, there is a confusion in the use of the term *role*. According to Bergen, Parsons should have used the terms instrumental *position* and expressive *position* rather than *role*.

This has left Slater dissatisfied, as it might well do. How does one bridge the gap between position and role and verify the roundness of the theoretical construct? Although Kotlar (1962) has collected data which support Parsons' analysis, a refinement of the analysis would first require the statement that the roles of the father and mother are not uniformly instrumental, on the one hand, or expressive, on the other. Within the household, the mother is the instrumental leader so far as the homemaker role is concerned. She directs servants, plans meals, furnishings, and decorations, organizes parties. The total output to her family is tension reduction and pattern maintenance (upper-middle-class pattern, for instance). Within the role system, she may enlist her daughter as trainee. She is the instrumental leader here, and she is the instrumental leader for developing in her daughter the skills necessary, not only to homemaking, but also to her more general status as a young female, such as grooming, neatness, poise.

In relation to the boy, the mother is not an expert in masculine behavior: instead, she is a "consumer" of masculine qualities. She may demand certain performances, but they are specifically in terms of human relations. She may teach manners and tidiness and demand performance of homework and music assignments. Since she is not a man, she is demanding performance in tasks that she knows men must do. The boy, however, usually checks with his father, often unconsciously, to see whether her demands are legitimate. While he is obeying one parent on the premises, he is identifying with another one, often away from the premises. It is precisely because of the content dissonance between the feminine anchorage of the mother's role and her role in "reinforcing" masculinity that the child needs the reassurance that the father is backing her up, and he tests this repeatedly. Furthermore, there is a feeling tone dissonance in the mother's role. On the one hand, she operates as an instrumental proxy in the training of the boy; on the other, she has an expressive role in rewarding the boy's masculinity, just as the father has an expressive role toward his daughter in rewarding her femininity. These rewarding role systems are as important in reinforcing the internalization of proper role models as are the instrumental-expert-training roles.

It is possible that the dissonances between the expressive and the instrumental roles toward the son make for a greater "conditionality of love" than is the case when the mother has a small effective instrumental role in bringing up the prepubertal and postpubertal boy. On the other hand, the father must provide a corrective to the mother's training, which is excessively rigid and contaminated by feminine values. By being a "friendly companion," he offers expertise and at the same time expressive rewards for the son's "catching on." Thus, while in Europe the unrealistic unconditional support given by the mother becomes part of the typical female amorality, in the American family the father-son coalition is against the unrealistic virtue of women.

The American pattern of relative de-differentiation may make more necessary the establishment of a marital consensus that is no more guaranteed either by the father's unquestioned power or by a sharp tion between father and daughter.

Slater mentioned, quite correctly it would seem, the isolation of the American boy from other male role models besides his father. The typical boy of the American nuclear family is given no young uncle, no more or less "black-sheep" uncle, no senior older brother as alternative role models. If the "good men" of television fiction as well as the mothers and teachers reinforce super-ego structures, the reinforcement of the ego must be done by the peer group and the father. The peer group is closer to the id; the father is closer to the superego. It is because of his contact with the real world that the father can be such an effective socializer. By specifying and "humanizing" the values of mothers and teachers, the father prevents disanchantment, cynicism, or the typical European transfer of superego object from the aloof father to the aloof state.

Hence the product of the equalitarian de-differentiated family should be a more inner-oriented person, capable of give and take, of assimilating the high rate of structural change characterized by "institutionalized individualism" (Parsons, 1962a) which requires an individual responsiveness to cues but is undeterred by them from the main purpose—to be an honest success in building up the progress of society.

Male superiority. A generalized male superiority is a basic theme of the structure of the nuclear family in all known societies. This does not mean that the father-husband (or the mother's brother in matrilinear societies) dominates all interaction sequences, but that the community roles in which he participates—wars, markets, ceremonials—have a priority over most family roles—at least that the family roles "stretch" as far as is compatible with these fulfillments in order to maximize the capacity of the husband to participate in the community roles. This male superiority also functions to further the incest-taboo training of the boy: it points clearly to the superiority of masculine identification over the preservation of the nurturant relationship with the mother, and for the girl it shows that the winning of a man is also more important than the preservation of nurturant relationships with the mother. In fact, male superiority is all the more necessary where kinship relationships are more central to the community and there are few achievement patterns differentiated from the family context.

A functional analysis of male superiority in terms of its mediating the requirement of the community to the family requires a mechanism for mediating the requirements of the family to the society. The high valuation of female fecundity and the patterns protecting her during pregnancy are one factor. Another which enters more immediately into the patterns of decision-making for the husband-father is his affection for his wife and especially for his children. Through this affection is mediated to the community the needs of the family as a parental system and as a conjugal system. It is interesting to note that as men have become potentially more independent of women, in terms of home management and cooking (after all, there are restaurants and laundries), the affectional ties have become more prominent as a factor of decision.

The higher the skill and responsibility of the man in extra-familial roles, the greater is the effective superiority of the husband in family decision-making. Fougeyrollas (1951) has validated this statement for French families ranging from the working class to the fringes of the upper-middle class. At the highest class levels, several elements diminish the power differential between husband and wife. In the status groups where graceful living is more the claim to supremacy than is male achievement, the wife, who directs many of the representative functions of the family, develops a level of skill and responsibility that gives her a strategic position. Protection of her sizeable property rights through legal measures (dowry, alimony), capacity to mobilize her kin network for assistance, a decline in the pressures against adultery make the wife under 45 a potential prize in the seduction game, and thus decrease her dependency upon her husband for status.

On the other hand, the power functional for the mediation of social needs may not be functional to the tension-reduction system. An upper-class husband avoids the blunt use of his power, as does, and for the same reasons, the lower-class wife.

Illegitimacy and Divorce

Very illuminating discussions of divorce and illegitimacy from a structural-functional point of view are to be found in Davis (1939a; 1939b) and in Goode (1956; 1960; 1961a; 1961b; 1963). Only a few remarks are necessary to summarize the propositions and perhaps add certain details to their presentation.

If the first function of marriage, especially in primitive and preindustrial societies, is to insure legitimate parenthood, one would expect that the pressures against illegitimacy would be much greater than those against premarital sexuality, as well as against divorce. In any society, the cohabitation of two people who depend upon one another and yet dislike one another is one of the most unpleasant experiences of life. Its impact upon growing children is noxious and can seriously endanger the socialization function of the family. Hence, every society has structural means for ending a marriage which cannot fulfill its function of procreation, economic collaboration, sexual control, socialization, and tension reduction.

In Arab countries, illegitimacy is low

while divorce is relatively frequent; recorded instances of the latter have approached or even exceeded the more reliably computed United States rates (Goode, 1961a; Goode, 1963). Murdock (1950) mentioned that more than half of the primitive societies for which he had data seemed to surpass the United States in divorce rates.

Lineage tensions versus conjugal tensions. There are probably two types of divorce, one generated by lineage tensions, and the other by conjugal tensions. Sterility and failure to integrate with the patrilinear or matrilinear line are probably more important when the conjugal pair is integrated with the lineage. Sterility is an important cause when, as among the pastoral tribes of subSaharan Africa, fecundity is highly valued in women. Since sterility can be the result of genetic incompatibility, divorce and remarriage can make fecund women who might otherwise have remained sterile. Failure to get along with in-laws can threaten the economic efficiency of the extended family and of the nuclear family. Lack of virginity is frequently, and adultery is usually, a reason for repudiation of the bride, if not, in the latter case, for her actual execution, thus putting on women the responsibility for maintaining the functions of marriage in relation to sexual control. No doubt wives who are not supported properly or whose husbands behave in dishonorable fashion might be permitted to return to their parents; these problems are likely to be more acute in isolated nuclear families or in "shriveled patrilineages of few numbers" than in cases where the couple is integrated to a strong patrilineage and failure of the husband can be more easily compensated by the exertions of relatives.

In the isolated conjugal system of industrial societies, failures of tension reduction are a major cause of divorce. This is also a problem in preindustrial societies, but, often enough, the conjugal family in these societies is not necessarily an important source of tension reduction. Same-sex peer groups, mother-daughter relationships, and mother-son relationships, as in India (Gore, 1962),

can be the effective centers of tension reduction. Thus, marital maladjustment does not always have the catastrophic repercussions it can have in the American nuclear family, for instance.

Tension-reduction deficit is likely to be a man's complaint, since the wife has in her children a source of socialized regression not available to her husband to the same extent. The conclusion is that the wife is less likely, even in the United States, to initiate divorce action for this reason than is the husband.

Finally, when a major function of marriage is alliance between two lineages, the husband thinks twice before divorcing his wife, for then instead of an alliance he may have created bitter enmity with her lineage.

When families are weak and poor, this problem is relatively minimal and the bride price of small value. Hence, under these conditions, structural hindrances to divorce are fewer than those which bear upon high-ranking lineages. This is valid in Western societies as well.

Even when lineage considerations are minor, as in the American middle and upper classes, divorce is much rarer as one goes up the social scale, until he reaches the café-society fringe (Goode, 1956). Certainly, the higher the class, the more the nuclear family is willing to subordinate tension reduction to representation and socialization functions and to the duties to uphold the dominant mores concerning the "sanctity" of marriage. But the higher the social class, the greater the social and psychological resources to maintain role complementarity and emotional compatibility or to minimize marital contact when contact is frustrating (Purdah in India, travel in Europe and in classical China, mistresses in Europe, concubines in China and South America).

If the Parsonian analysis of a trend toward a more effective specialization of the nuclear family into early socialization and tension reduction is correct (Parsons, 1953; Parsons, 1961b; Parsons & Bales, 1955), the Western family and in particular the American family should be more effective in these functions than classical Western families and the families found in pre-industrial and/or nonliterate societies. Indices to test this proposition are not easy to elaborate. One may be that "there is to-day a larger percentage of the total (American) population of marriageable age married and living with their spouses than at any time in the history of reliable census data; this is true in spite of divorces (since most divorced persons remarry) and separations" (1961b, p. 275). Indeed more than half the divorces take place between childless couples, and a large majority of divorcees remarry successfully (Jacobson, 1959). Given the fact that the divorce rate is probably more reliable as an index of broken homes in the United States than in any major country except the Scandinavian ones (fewer unregistered common-law marriages and desertions), and also given the fact that there are fewer social pressures to maintain "empty shell families" (Goode, 1961) which certainly do not fulfill functions of tension reduction, it might seem that the 75 per cent or so of American families that endure are probably fulfilling better their function of tension reduction and are probably exacting a lower price for the other functions than the 98 or 99 per cent of Indian families that endure only to be broken up by a high death rate. Another argument could be made in terms of the fact that, when there is a choice between marriage patterns, the modern Western type seems to be the preferred one. On Darwinian terms this should be because it represents a better solution to the problems of social living. The major contribution of the Soviet revolutions to the welfare of its citizens may well have been the promotion of an equalitarian, specialized nuclear family.

Courtship patterns and divorce. It is interesting to note that pre-Meiji rural Japan had a high rate of divorce and yet allowed relatively free marital choice to the young peasants. This was apparently in sharp contrast with the Chinese rural pattern, in which marriage was decided and arranged by family elders. In view of the fact that

the integration of the Japanese wife with her husband's family was delayed by groom service or the wife's continuing service to her parents (Goode, 1963), it is possible that the high rate of divorce was due to lineage causes—failure of integration—as much if not more than to conjugal incompatibility. Hence, there was a lack of integration between a courtship pattern functional to the "shriveled patrilinear family" of poor rural folk (which was very comparable to the isolated conjugal-family system of the West) and the authority of the parents, which remained supreme during their life span.

Fortes (1949, p. 93 & passim) described a similar high divorce rate among the Tallensi, where unsupervised courtship by males resulted in frequent elopements followed by haggling over bride price and great pressures on the part of the wife's patrilineage for her return. Such conflicting pressures would seem a better explanation for the high rate of "trial marriages" than mere psychological incompatibility. Here, the pressures would seem to come more from the bride's family than from the husband's family, as they did in Japan.

The Meiji restoration, by diffusing Samurai patterns through the lower classes in Japan, made the parents take a much more active part in the selection of the bride, and hence there was a decrease in the type of divorce due to in-law incompatibility. On the other hand, since World War II and the diffusion of Western patterns, there has been an increase in the type of divorce which is due to failure of the marriage to provide mutual support and tension management for the husband and wife.

The consideration of the elopement pattern of the Tallensi leads to a consideration of the element of rebellion in certain types of marriages. Since the choice of spouse finds much of its motivational fuel in early internalization of parental roles, and since, on the other hand, falling in love and the commitment to marriage is a declaration of independence from one's family of orientation, one may expect that courtship will often involve components of rebellion which push one toward a marital choice not most in line with one's basic internalizations. Hence, relatively unsupervised courtship involves a pattern of trial and error which may result in some form of "trial marriage" until the components of rebellion are exhausted, as it were, and there is effective motivational compatibility. When marriage further implies patrilocal residence and integration of a relative stranger, the problem is all the greater, at least until the stranger has borne a son for the lineage.

Looking at the divorce rate of the United States, where there is a high freedom of courtship and a high degree of isolation of the nuclear family, one also finds that the bulk of divorces involve the trial and rebellion type of marriage. Glick (1957) showed that girls married for the first time at ages 14 to 17 have a remarriage rate more than twice as high as the rate for women married for the first time at ages 20 to 21. Women married for the first time at 18 and 19 have a rate between the two. Of women married for the first time at 14 to 17 during the period 1940 to 1949, only two-thirds were still living with their first husbands in 1954.

All of this suggests functional relationships which can be stated as follows:

In societies and social classes where the nuclear family is tightly integrated into the extended family, whether patrilinear or matrilinear, lineage malintegration is a frequent source of marital instability, unless the lineage authorities completely determine the marriage.

The more important the tension management functions of the marriage, the more likely marriage will be determined by autonomous courtship marked by trial and error.

The earlier the age of marriage when male courtship is the determinant of choice, the more likely the failure of conjugal integration at first marriage.

In the United States, courtship has two components: the pattern of dalliance described by Waller (1938) and the component of mutual choice characterized by the going-steady, engagement, and marriage sequence. The dalliance pattern is largely exploitative, and the effective reference groups are the same-sex peer groups. Particularly in the female group, sexual activity in the dating pattern is a form of juvenile delinquency in relation to the parental norms of sexual chastity, and for the boys, it is an affirmation of masculine identity in terms of autonomy and sexual aggressiveness. On the other hand, the values which associate sex with marriage are strong enough to force young couples who have had premarital sexual intercourse, usually under male initiative, into marriages which neither partner truly wants or is emotionally qualified and ready for—either in order to secure escape from emotional dissonance (sex without marriage) or because pregnancy has occurred, especially when the exploitative aspect of the dalliance pattern does not permit effective contraceptive planning.

Christensen and Meissner (1953), using data from Tippecanoe County, Indiana, compared "178 cases of marriage where conception was rather definitely premarital and 989 where it was definitely postmarital. Divorce percentages within these two groups were found to be 18.54 and 6.27 respectively." The fact of social class intervenes here, of course, since early female marriage and premarital conception are both functions of interrupted schooling and low sophistication concerning birth control.

The present pattern of early steady dating represents a decline in the dalliance pattern, dalliance being reduced to the ages of about 14 to 16. As parental opposition to sexual intercourse declines, and with the generalization of birth-control knowledge, there should be a further decline in dalliance, as a late-adolescent pattern.

More and more, going steady represents the functional equivalent of a trial marriage connected with sexual intercourse, but, reciprocally, sexual intercourse is more and more reserved for the trial marriage represented by the steady relationship. Thus, there is still the Christian connection between love and sexuality, although not necessarily between sexuality and marriage. The one change in norms still required is the abandonment by the male of the preference for the virgin wife, which seems to insure him a "closed market" for sexual performance and satisfies the regressive psychological components of the identification of the bride with the oedipal mother. Denmark (see Christensen & Carpenter, 1962) seems to have gone further in this direction than has the United States. The decline in the incidence and risks of dalliance, the decline in the double standard, and the final institutionalization of steady dating in the United States might actually increase the average age at marriage. It is likely to decrease the range of marriage age, especially reducing teenage marriages, thus resulting in a decline of the type of divorce which results from premature commitment.

The Honeymoon

An element of the institution of marriage that is relatively specific to the Western world is the honeymoon.

The honeymoon permitted the isolation of the couple from other social ties, the suspension of work obligations on the part of both bride and groom, so that a sort of Edenic state of affairs was created where bride and groom would satiate their desire for complete possession of one another. In the upper classes, the honeymoon might last several months, financed by a gift from the groom's family. It was not a pattern that the lower classes could easily afford, except for a few days at most.

To understand the long honeymoon pattern, one must describe the pattern of courtship which used to be characteristic of bourgeois Europe. If the "pretender" was acceptable to the family, he was allowed to court his bride-to-be under chaperoned conditions. This courting retained much of the flavor of the *roman courtois* tradition, in which the knight worshipped his lady and made her the queen of his thoughts and the spectator of high deeds accomplished in order to deserve her. This was perhaps more pronounced in Italy and Spain, but it was also the pattern in France.

The virginity of the future wife is a crucial value in this context. In terms of the personality system, the future wife partakes of many features of the pre-oedipal mother, she who has not been possessed by anyone, who is going to be the sole property of the suitor; yet the overt gradient of subordination is more from the girl to the man, who acts as if his fiancée were of a superior essence to him.

The future wife, on the other hand, has led a very sheltered life in which there has often been a semihysterical repression of the elementary facts of sexuality. She has had very little role autonomy, except in the secrecy of her peer-group relationships, and no contact with men except those of her own family. The period of engagement is a period of heightened sexual tension, yet with very few occasions to relieve this tension. She is treated with utmost respect by her fiancé, but her role as wife is likely to be much more sharply subordinated to her husband's life than her role as courted girl would lead her to imagine. This is a clear instance of role discontinuity.

The honeymoon has a function as an item of conspicuous leisure and expenditure, but much more important is the opportunity provided by the isolation of the new dyad from both families of orientation to learn the new roles of husband and wife toward each other and toward the world. The honeymoon status in fact permits other members of the society to cooperate in the learning process through indulgence over errors, and it eliminates for the bride the ambiguities of role transfer, for in a foreign setting she is known only as the wife of a traveler. All the reinforcement she receives is for her new role as wife. Furthermore, the sexual reward for developing role adjustment is a powerful one, and the honeymoon permits a peak level of sexual activity on the part of the new couple.

In the classical bourgeois pattern, the husband was the initiator, not only sexually but socially. The status of married women was immeasurably superior to that of unmarried girls. Under these conditions, there was great likelihood that the wife would develop a strong transference upon her husband-educator, so that even if the marriage had been completely arranged by her parents and she had had little opportunity to know her husband beforehand, she was likely to grow in love with him. Her role in the marriage would change from that of a virgin-mother prototype to that of an obedient-daughter prototype, where the gradient of authority was very clearly on the side of her husband. The shift was aided by the fact that in the bourgeois marriage the median age differential was about 10 years in favor of the husband.

In a situation where the component of sexual initiation of the bride was very obvious, the honeymoon removed this action from the context of the family of orientation, where the resonances with the incest tensions might be too great—more in connection with the father-daughter role perhaps, but also with the mother-son role and to some extent also with the in-laws of opposite sex—for the main protagonists of the sexual drama.

The honeymoon fits well into the context of the Christian tradition in which marriage makes man and woman of one flesh. It emphasized the marriage ties in a situation where lineage pressures were very strong. As a result, it worked as a pressure toward neolocalism, and certainly emphasized the fact that henceforth the overriding loyalty of the spouses had to be to one another. The Garden of Eden was something which each one owed to the other. It was the fulfillment of the infantile fantasy which had been denied by the incest taboo. Even if the new couple had to return to live within the orbit of the husband's family, the marriage tie had received a reinforcement which was bound to weaken the lineage ties and strengthen the trend toward bilateralism.

Finally, the honeymoon acts as a tension reducer for the remainder of the marriage, because it makes clear that marital bliss depends upon an isolation which cannot last. As a memory, it permits the spouses to bear the monotony and the discomforts that married life is sure to bring. The wife, in particular, finds the honeymoon a fantasy to which she can repair.

In modern United States, many of these functions have been detached from the honeymoon. Marriage is likely to be the result of a better acquaintance than used to be the case in bourgeois Europe. There are more peer relationships in the courtship, and as a result the role reversals in courtship and marriage do not exist to the same extent. Hence, the function of the honeymoon as a bridge over role discontinuity is not as crucial.

For Protestants and assimilated Jews, the pattern of premarital intercourse during engagement has probably become the majority pattern. Burgess and Wallin (1953) said that 45 per cent of the couples they studied reported premarital intercourse with spouse. Kanin and Howard (1958) reported 43.5 per cent of their 190 couples acknowledging premarital intercourse. Very likely, the loss of virginity is no more a major feature of the honeymoon.

Hollingshead (1952) reported the average honeymoon in his New Haven sample to be nine days, which means that one or two weeks is usually the time couples spend. The median cost was $287 at 1950 prices. The honeymoon has become more expensive in terms of the salaries earned by the young husbands, and as a result, is shorter even among the rich. The increased pressure of hard work, even among the upper-middle class, makes it difficult to justify long idleness, and, above all, the parties are less ignorant about their social roles. Going steady has trained the pair into marital patterns. Kanin and Howard (1958) reported that only 47 per cent of the 77 couples who had had premarital intercourse had a wedding trip, in contrast to 87 per cent of the 100 pairs not reporting premarital intercourse, and the pattern held regardless of social class.

The Balance Between Marriage Ties and Lineage Ties

It was stated above that the honeymoon was bound to strengthen the marriage system against the lineage. What are some of the structural mechanisms by which the lineage is protected against the development of the nuclear family as an independent center?

When marriage is patrilinear and patrilocal, the integration of the inmarrying wife with the husband's family is more complete and more exclusive of her own ties to her family of orientation, the younger she is when she marries. The most extreme case is found in India, but good examples are found in the Arab world and in black Africa.

In China also, the trend was toward early marriage made by the parents before the adolescent could develop any personal choices. In the poorer groups, it would often entail taking the future bride into one's household as a baby or as soon as she could be of some help. This was the institution of the *t'ung yang hsi*. Similarly, a boy might join the household of a family without male heir as *chui-fu* many years before formal marriage with the daughter of his adoptive family. Here, the age differential of the bride and groom was of secondary importance. It happened, in fact, that the wife could be several years older than her husband without threatening the patrilinear pattern of descent. Goode (1963, pp. 285–291) reported conflicting evidence, but it is clear that the pattern of child marriage did not dominate China as it dominated India.

Within the Chinese upper classes as well as within the European aristocracy, early marriage is an item of conspicuous consumption. The wealth necessary for the support of the new nuclear family and its future children does not depend upon work but upon the property of the families of orientation. In China and in the European aristocratic families, where continuity of the line is important, there is a premium on early marriage of the eldest son in order to secure succession—especially when, as in Europe, he follows a military career.

As soon as the age of marriage for girls exceeds the teens, it is likely that her integration into the patrilineage will not be as complete as it is when marriage takes place at 15 or 16. The older she is at marriage and the stronger her ties to her own family, the more the "bilateralization" of the descent system.

Another factor preventing the development of a strong conjugal system is a low level of interaction and intimacy between husband and wife. Structural factors which make intimacy more difficult are: (a) the "paternalization" of the husband-wife relationship through a higher age differential at marriage. This is reinforced when values tend to separate sexuality from maternity in the whore-madonna complex. In such a system, the man is relatively inhibited in his sexual relationships with his "virgin" wife, who is the mother of his children, and expects more satisfactory relationships with women who do not have this exalted position. The availability of concubines, geishas, and mistresses permits sexual satisfaction and somewhat more informal relations with women who have no claims upon the husband. This is all the more reinforced by belief patterns that devalue womanhood as against manhood, stressing woman's insatiable sexuality, fickleness, and lack of moral commitment, so that a man must guard himself from being too influenced by women if he does not want to ruin his family. A major theme of fiction is the Circe theme (*Nana, The Blue Angel,* and others). (b) A great differential in formal education between husband and wife. This affects mainly middle- or upper-class wives, for their husbands are the only ones likely to have received formal education. (c) Isolation of the wife from the community, extreme examples of which are the Indian purdah, the Arab's women's quarters and veils, and to a lesser extent the classical Spanish ideal which restricts severely the exposure of women to public gaze. Isolation of the wife reduces the value of her conversation.

THE NUCLEAR FAMILY AND THE INTEGRATIVE SYSTEM

Having outlined some of the basic structural features of the nuclear family, this chapter now analyzes the functional relationship between it and the integrative system of the society, that is, those aspects of the society that specialize in maintenance of order, development of solidarity, and social control. First, the relationship of the nuclear family to the adolescent peer group from which the spouses graduate into marriage is described, and how the loyalties of the new family to the families of origin are allocated through rules of residence and rules of descent is discussed. Then, the discussion turns briefly to the process which has promoted the isolation of the nuclear family toward a pattern already well known in the United States, that is, essentially the process of the decline of the patrilinear descent system in preindustrial societies.

The Family and the Peer Group

The starting point in this section is the nuclear family at the time of its founding through marriage. Marriage creates new solidary obligations for bride and groom to each other, to their future children, to their respective families of origin—or of *orientation* as Warner has named them—and to their spouse's family of orientation.

There are two functional problems involved here: one is a problem of securing new loyalties and the other the problem of ranking them. The obligations to the families of orientation are inherent in the structure of parenthood. The nuclear family is a powerful source of solidarity and order because the gap for the individual between compliance and palpable increments in security and value is small. The habits of past cooperation are well developed. The problem, in marriage, is in fact to operate a change in loyalties so that bride and groom, instead of giving priority to his or her family of orientation, give priority to the new family of procreation.

A likely solution is to weaken the ties to the families of orientation during adolescence, while not endangering the socialization process. The structure that fulfills this function is the development of same-sex peer groups which become progressively strong and stable, especially after puberty. The same-sex peer group permits consolidation of the sexual identity and becomes a focus of dependent feelings (see Parsons, 1942; Parsons & White, 1961). It shares with the paternal figure the physical power born of the strength of the many, as against the weakness of one member. It shares with the maternal figure the capacity to support the member even though he fails to perform in conformity with paternal or school norms. It thus receives much of the dependent feelings that were directed toward the parents, and it places the youth in a mild climate of competition among peers who judge one another on the basis of standards of their own choosing.

The contribution of the peer group to socialization has been discussed elsewhere (see Pitts, 1960; Pitts, 1961; Pitts, 1963). A crucial factor to remember is that the norms of the peer group, although essentially derived from the dominant values (Elkin & Westley, 1957), contain a delinquent valence which is essential to the maintenance of peer-group boundaries. This delinquent valence is inherent in *every* peer group; it defines its identity and permits it to develop indigenous leadership and communication patterns. This is because the peer group aims to facilitate value achievement among its members, due account being taken of their other role claims; and one of the easiest ways to do this is to reduce the achievement pressures bearing upon the members by a conspiracy which leaves authority unaware of what could actually be done, if the peer group were not engaged in the stretchout or the slowdown or even organized cheating. Davis, who wrote so perceptively of the "sociology of parent-youth conflict" (1940), was mistaken in thinking that this conflict is essentially characteristic of modern industrial society.

The adolescent peer group is bound to be more delinquent than other peer groups because it is not harnessed to the more socially meaningful roles of work, religion, or warfare. It is oriented to play, sexual experimentation in the form of play, and to the expression of ambivalent feelings toward parental authority (Parsons, 1942; Parsons, 1943; Parsons, 1947; Parsons, 1949). Here the peer group permits the adolescent to move out of the field. It transforms into a generalized "age struggle" the more personalized and dangerous "parent-youth conflict" (see Bloch & Niederhoffer, 1958). The family and the community at large keep pressure upon the adolescent peer group because of its delinquent valence and also to create a "relative appreciation" for graduation from the peer group, the activities of which are defined as "kid's stuff" or "teenage stuff." The peer group has to bear a certain stigma for its delinquency, which can be tolerated only insofar as it does not affect crucial role contexts and does not exceed certain limits.

Certain functional statements are possible. For example, insofar as there is a strong wish to control the marriage of the daughter, her peer-group activities are restricted. This restriction in turn reinforces the reluctance to have adolescent girls attend universities, where peer-group life is extensive. The evidence available here is the behavior of the bourgeoisie and aristocracy of classical Europe which, until recently, did not allow their daughters the benefit of university education.

Furthermore, the more intense the commitment of the adolescent to the peer group, the greater his or her independence from the family of orientation. Insofar as bilinear descent seems to be more often connected with neolocal residence, the conclusion would be that the family system with that type of descent and residence pattern would have more intense adolescent peer-group life than societies following a patrilineal, patrilocal descent system.

The evidence here is somewhat contradictory. If one considers the classical European upper class which practiced a form of patrilineal descent and patrilocal residence, he finds that the youth of these social classes enjoyed a long period of irresponsibility, often centered in the universities and the army, and with relatively strong peer-group attachments—except that intimate friendships and lover-mistress relationships were notably stronger than the peer group as such. The basic reference group remained the status group with its intensive *salon* activity, oriented to gratuitous and expressive behavior; and the status groups were dominated by well-established families, usually in the main urban centers. The upper-status and mature group conception of the good life is not too far distant from adolescent play. Hence, there was no real youth culture, nor was there a true youth society. There was enough dyadic and peer-group life to decrease considerably the strength of the emotional dependence upon the family of orientation, but no development of new norms. When the father was ready to retire or not too far from his death, the "youth," by now in his late twenties or early thirties, would settle down and get married, return to the ancestral home or to the paternal factory, and continue the life of his father. If his elder brother died, he would take his place. Otherwise, he would remain in the army or the civil service. Hence, the maximum of emotional independence from parents—best exemplified by the British boarding-school system—was combined with the maximum of cultural conformity.

In England, peer-group and intense intimate relationships between men kept the emotional involvement in the marriage comparatively low. In France, it could be the intimate friendships and the lover-mistress relationships that would reduce the commitment to the marriage system. It was "middle class" to love one's wife.

In the United States, peer-group life becomes very intense in the early teens at all levels. Moreover, in a highly achievement-oriented society such as the United States, there has been less and less upper-class legitimation for an irresponsible youth culture (which tends to flower only in the rebellious lower class). The trend could be described as going from Joe College to the Freedom Rider (see Parsons, 1962b, p. 117). The peer group has to exchange participation in more meaningful "adult" role contexts— gainful employment, extracurricular but school-integrated activities, the semisacred sports—against a smaller delinquent valence. Furthermore, the peer group is a major, if not the major, agency of social control in the courtship process. It pushes its members toward strong heterosexual commitments (even though these commitments weaken it ultimately) and mediates class values with enough regard to personal charisma to insure class endogamy without rebellion. It carries the adolescent's main emotional investments from family of orientation to peer group to potential marriage partner.

In Europe, as in the United States, the girl does not develop as strong a peer-group life as does the boy. Heterosexual involvement in both Scandinavia and the United States (and to a growing extent in western Europe) reduces her commitment to the peer group at an earlier age. Mother-daughter relationships preserve an importance that is far out of proportion to the importance of the mother-son tie. However, the marriage system is equipped to handle the mother-in-law problem on the wife's side. There is an avoidance pattern between son-in-law and mother-in-law supported by jokes and the expectation of some hostility. The mother-in-law, however, is likely to have a cooperative relationship with her married daughter. She helps at childbirth, she helps at her daughter's illnesses. She does not intrude as a judge of her daughter's performance.

Such is not the case with the husband's mother. She is more likely to see herself as a rival, and to judge her daughter-in-law's performance. On the other hand, the taboos against her intrusion in the new family are much greater. The tie between herself and her married son is much more distended than that between the married daughter and her mother. Hence, there is less expectation of the continuation of a relationship of high intensity between the groom's mother and his new household, and the likelihood of petty friction is less. In a neolocal residential pattern there is no reason for her presence in the son's household.

Komarovsky (1950; 1956) is right in pointing out that involvement of the husband's mother with her son's household is predictive of much greater pathology than involvement of the wife's mother with her daughter's household. The existence of a "silver cord" between grown man and mother is more abnormal and much rarer than the existence of strong attachment between grown daughter and her mother. As a result, the structural protections against mother-in-law trouble from the groom's side are not as strong as they are in dealing with the wife's mother. Mother-in-law trouble from the husband's side is more destructive—though rarer.

This discussion has led to the problem of ordering the ties which are on the one hand created by the marriage—ties to the spouse, ties to the in-laws—and those which, on the other hand, existed prior to the marriage. Precisely whose line do the children continue, what social responsibilities left by dead or sick adults will they assume, who will they feed and defend if the need arises? From which group of relatives will children receive the property which they can use as facilities of production?

Rules of descent essentially decide these issues and rank these obligations, by giving absolute priority to either the family of the father (*patrilineal descent*) or to the family of the mother (*matrilineal descent*). More specifically, in the case of patrilineal descent, this is done by emphasizing obligations through the male line (property descends from the father) and in the case of matrilineal descent, by emphasizing obligations to the female line (property descends from the mother's brother). *Bilinear descent* divides obligations more nearly equally between the two families of orientation. (The anthropologists also describe a fourth rule called *double descent,* which selects various relatives within both the father's and the mother's families.)

Rules of Residence and Descent

In Chapter 12 and to some extent in Chapter 13 are thorough discussions of the rules of descent and of the integrative, economic, and political factors with which they are in equilibrium. Only a few comments are necessary to illustrate the use of the structural-functional method in relation to this problem.

A typical structural-functional approach would be to determine what conditions are associated with what kinds of rules of descent. The major hypothesis, stated by Linton (1936), sees the rules of residence as having a decisive influence upon the rules of descent that are institutionalized. This is a straight causal relation made functional by the reciprocity of the causal relationship, although the main causal flow is depicted as going from rules of residence to rules of descent.

From a structural point of view, the first problem that occurs in either patrilocal or matrilocal residence is the integration of the stranger. This is the functional problem of minimizing friction and maximizing reciprocity, given the fact that a new person must be assimilated into the solidary systems of the family and of its immediate network of relatives and neighbors. The marriage ceremony contributes to the solution of this problem by warning the community of the change of status and locale of the bride and groom. And here an axiom can be stated: *harmonization of masculine roles is more problematical than the harmonization of female roles.*

Masculine roles are instrumentally oriented. Their coefficient of uncertainty and their competitive component, which contains more or less sublimated aggression, make harmonization at once more difficult and more essential, since masculine roles are above all concerned with the provision of sustenance and security. Hence, a consequence is that the "capital" that already exists in role harmonization and knowledge of the instrumental theater (hunting or fishing grounds) is not easily given up. Barring neutralizing factors, marriage establishes the new couple with or near the husband's group. Out of 250 societies tabulated by the Cross-Cultural Survey, 146 are patrilocal and 22 are patri-matrilocal (Murdock, 1949). Furthermore, even when residence is matrilocal or neolocal, it rarely compels the man to leave the community, while more than half of the patrilocal societies for which information is available require the wife to leave the community, and thus bear the burden of being the stranger. Being a stranger forces her to concentrate her efforts on maximizing her relationship to her husband and to her children. She is less crippled in her role efficiency by being a stranger, however, than her husband would be.

Aberle (1961) stated, after Lippert (1931, p. 237), that matrilocal residence tends to be related to a situation where women make a strategic contribution to the problem of existence, such as primitive agriculture where women do much of the productive labor. Lowie (1920) and Murdock (1949) have outlined the conditions which tend to promote various shifts in the rules of residence. Neolocal residence is "favored by any influence which tends to isolate or emphasize the individual or the nuclear family." Among such influences are: monogamy, "since the nuclear family is somewhat submerged under polygyny;" . . . "any influence which tends to undermine or inhibit large local aggregations of kinsmen" such as the growth of territorial states; the development of private property; "individual enterprise in the economic sphere," personal freedom in the choice of marital partners; individual migration (Murdock, 1949, p. 203).

Patrilocal residence is promoted by any change in culture or the conditions of life which significantly enhances the status, importance, and influence of man in relation to the opposite sex. Among such factors are the development of a pastoral economy, polygyny, the development of movable property which can be accumulated in quantity, herds, slaves, money.

The relation between rules of residence and rules of descent is demonstrated by the fact that in less than 10 per cent of societies having patrilocal and matri-patrilocal rules of residence is there matrilineal descent, while in cases of matrilocal or avunculocal residence (residence with the mother's brother), there are 71 per cent of cases of matrilineal descent and 29 per cent of cases of bilinear descent (Murdock, 1949, p. 39). The fit is far from perfect, of course, but territorial propinquity implies the necessity of higher levels of interaction which, as Homans (1950) reminded, fosters positive sentiments and higher levels of integration. (Rules of residence involve many rights, and some of them may not follow the dominant rules of descent.)

In some ways, bilinear descent seems to fulfill more of the needs of the personality system, in view of the fact that the mother's family, for instance, is not likely to relinquish all interest in the married daughter, niece, or cousin. Furthermore, resemblance in physical features is bilateral in impact, so that identification with the children of a daughter is hard to avoid. In fact, no unilinear system does away *completely* with

obligations to the matrilineal line, or to the patrilineal line in the case of matrilineal societies. Descent is a question of ranking obligations rather than of denying them. In view of the addictive aspect of nuclear family internalizations, especially to parental figures, so closely involved in the formation of the incest taboo, it is very likely that *in the absence of other factors, the trend of descent systems is bilinear*. As a matter of fact, the World Ethnographic Sample (Aberle, 1961) shows that out of 564 societies, the bilateral-bilinear system accounts for 204 societies. Double descent accounts for another 28. Patrilineal descent still is most frequent (248), and matrilineal descent is least frequent (84).

Another functional requirement of the organization of loyalties and obligations known as the descent system is the need to preserve the existence of a community distinct from the family. Hence, the number of relatives with whom a child can be affiliated must be limited, given the fact that theoretically he could have double the number that each of his parents have. As a result, rules of descent limit the relevance of whole sections of relatives. Patrilinear descent reduces the relevance of the maternal relatives, matrilinear descent reduces the relevance of the paternal relatives, and bilinear descent cuts off the furthest relatives of both mother and father. Bilinear descent has the advantage that the gradient of loyalty and obligation is likely to be more coincidental with the gradient of gratification and interaction, especially when marriage does not involve a change in community for either spouse.

The interesting problem, then, is to determine what structural advantages of unilinear descent systems are sufficient to neutralize the preferences of the personality system for the bilinear system.

The great advantage of the unilinear descent system over the bilateral *kindred* is that the lineage can easily develop into a corporate group with leadership and capacity to act as a unified body. Radcliffe-

Brown (1935a) and Linton (1936) insisted upon the ease of specification and simplification of jural rights and the greater predictability of succession found in unilinear descent groups, as compared with bilateral descent groups, as factors explaining the predominance of unilinear descent groups. As compared with the bilateral kindred, unilinear descent groups can have the same effective relatives. In the bilateral kindred, only siblings have the same relatives, hence they can never be true groups except from the vantage point of the individual member. As Murdock observed, "kindreds interlace and overlap, they do not and cannot form discrete and separate segments of the entire society. The kindred cannot act as a collectivity, nor hold land or property since it has no continuity over time" (1949, p. 60).

Hence, the importance of property ownership gives the second advantage of the unilinear descent system. As long as the society does not have a complex, well-institutionalized property system, the continued presence of the lineage is indispensable to maintain the *seisin,* that is, physical control over the property. This is all the more true as the property, instead of being easily abstracted into *capital,* remains involved with particular meanings or with magic. When knacks and special skills seem necessary in order to utilize the property effectively, it is transmitted through the lineage, usually through the patrilineage. This was the case with the ancient crafts and with the agriculture in which magic played an important role. As property becomes more movable, more easily transformed into money terms, as the seisin of the individual is more protected by law and the state, instead of by the relatives, the disadvantage of the nuclear family as against the lineage tends to disappear. The problem of the harmonization of roles does not require some form of patrilocalism. This has been the case in the industrial West.

Further analysis of the functional relationship between rules of descent and political organization and of the factors behind

the decline of the patrilinear descent system can be found in Chapters 12 and 13 and in Goode (1963). The analysis of the decline of the patrilinear descent system in preindustrial societies is, in fact, a good example of the use of the structural-functional method to study social change. It has followed essentially the lines of argument laid down by Parsons (1942; 1943; 1961a; 1962b; Parsons & Bales, 1955) and M. Levy (1949) which relate the growing isolation of the nuclear family from lineage and extended kin network to the functional requirements of industrialization, nationalism, and the contagion of value systems oriented to individualism and achievement. Parsons sees in this a process of differentiation by which the nuclear family becomes increasingly specialized and effective in promoting socialization and tension reduction, while it becomes detached from an extended kin network which has lost to bureaucratized structures the functions of economic production, political and economic security, and education, and where tribe and caste have been replaced as sources of solidarity by the nation and achievement-based primary-type groups.

The Isolation of the Nuclear Family

A crucial aspect of the Parsonian functional analysis is the diagnosis of the American family as having reached the maximum level of isolation, just as American society has reached the maximum level of industrialization and general role differentiation. The analysis, when applied to preindustrial societies, traces their steps down the road traced by Puritan America.

For Parsons, the isolation of the nuclear family was functional to the requirements of all economic systems centered on industry, which require a high level of mobility within the labor force and a *system of valuations and rewards emphasizing occupational achievement* rather than familistic achievement (filial piety, good family management, continuation of family traditions, and the like). The assumption is that extended family systems, usually of the patrilineal variety, restrict the mobility of the males. This restriction is a result of several factors. One is that diffuse family obligations are exchange systems equilibrated over time, like hospitality obligations. A diffuse system of obligations requires long-range availability, and the "goods" to be returned must be of the same diffuse nature as the goods received. If one removes himself from the field, he precludes his capacity to repay benefits secured previously. Extended family obligations thus interfere with geographic mobility. They also interfere with occupational mobility by fostering a "copybook" identification with the father, which guarantees the latter his authority. Thus, sons follow their father's occupation and, as long as applied science is not an important part of the occupational techniques, the experience of the father gives him an automatic executive position which parallels the authority due to status.

What perhaps needs emphasis in the analysis is the specification that the isolation of the nuclear family is functional to the middle-class and managerial groups rather than to the lower classes—which have usually known the pattern out of necessity—or to the upper classes where it weakens their dynastic proclivities (cf. Pitts, 1958).

The Parsonian analysis has been challenged by various authors, particularly Sussman and Litwak. Sussman (1959), basing his argument on his own data and data collected by Dodson (1951) and Sharp and Axelrod (1956), has pointed to the network of visiting and aid that exists between both working-class and middle-class families and concluded that the nuclear family is not isolated, or that social mobility does not require in present-day United States the isolation of the nuclear family (Litwak, 1959–1960; Litwak, 1960a; Litwak, 1960b).

These discussions are actually based upon a misunderstanding of what constitutes isolation. First, isolation does not require no contact with relatives. If anything, better and cheaper means of communication (tele-

phone, automobile) have permitted nuclear families to maintain contact with their families of orientation, with collaterals and affinals, better than was the case in the past. Furthermore, patterns of aid do exist, but they are clearly subordinated to the need of maintaining the autonomy and self-respect of the recipient families. Help is more easily accepted when it is made of imponderables and when it occurs in situations of catastrophe which do not challenge the recipients' capacity, in normal circumstances, to take care of their own affairs. Help during illness is the one category of aid which has the highest incidence, but even it affects less than half of Sussman's sample (50 families). The help pattern seems especially to affect the respondents as recipients of financial aid from *their parents. Among siblings, financial aid, advice, and valuable gifts are rare.* It is probable that the most intimate friends would have scored as high or higher. In the Hough study (Sussman & White, 1959), it was found that, in the working class, banks came ahead of relatives as sources of financial aid, in the same way that clergymen were ahead of relatives when assistance in terms of personal trouble was required.

The meaning of the kinship network in the bilinear descent system which is present in contemporary United States—due account being taken of certain class differences to be analyzed presently—must be found in the rather thorough differentiation of economic and political factors from the sentimental factors imbedded in kinship. In fact, the modern family has partly solved certain problems that have plagued the patrilinear and the bilateral extended family systems: the conflict between nuclear family interest versus the affectionate ties between its members and their respective families of orientation which are expected by custom; the affection for siblings versus the rivalry which exists among the siblings for recognition by the parents; the affection and solidarity among siblings versus their commitment to the interests of their own families of procreation.

One of the factors which has helped to

solve these problems is indeed the decline in the power of property, as compared with the purchasing power gained by work, so that the expectation of inheritance has ceased to be an important factor in the relationships between married children, their siblings, and their parents, except in the upper-class group. Consumer credit, the easy mortgage, social security, the family doctor, have enabled many working-class families and most middle-class families to utilize kinship as a potential source of friendship and no more as the source of (more or less mandatory) advice and ascriptive solidary obligations. For the first time, the nuclear family can have gratuitous relationships with its network of kin and, as a result, the relationships are likely to be less charged with ambivalence. With the help of modern communications, it is very likely that these gratuitous relationships have never been so frequent and so strong as they are today (Cumming & Schneider, 1961, p. 501).

Whenever a successful relative attempts, in the manner described by Litwak (1959–1960), to secure recognition from the extended kin for his occupational prowess (a force for continued contact with collaterals, according to him), this may also create severe strain, and the relative has to allow himself to be exploited in return for the admiration. Otherwise, his court does not last very long, and the young, in particular, are not always likely to participate in a hero worship which by comparison downgrades their own parents' achievement level.

In the middle class, a cousin calls from his hotel room to announce that he is in town. The ambiguity about hospitality duties within the middle class that used to give rise to many cartoons prior to World War II has been resolved in favor of decreased duties—unless the cousin is also a friend. In the relationships between members of the bilateral kindred, the burden of proof is upon him who would ask for help. There is, as in the American neighborhood, an expectation that people in situations of serious emergency will ask for help (in fact,

not asking for help comes close to being an insult, if the emergency is a result of an "Act of God"), but the good standing of a nuclear family depends on its capacity to cope with its own normal problems. Assistance flows more easily from ascriptive authority to ascriptive subordination, from parent to adult child, from aunt or uncle to nephew or niece, and perhaps even more easily from grandparent to grandchild. In this latter instance, the parent must allow the child his autonomy, and to that extent the child is allowed his own dependent relationships with grandparents without impugning directly the capacity of the nuclear family to take care of its own. Contributions to the expense of college education would be a good example of such aid.

The conclusion, then, is that extended family relationships have been largely preempted of their political and career meanings. The relationships that are probably as strong as before, and certainly more frequent, are the protracted ones with parents after one's own marriage (Sussman & Burchinal, 1962) and the long grandparent-grandchild relationships which may be expected for the coming generations, which will combine long life with early marriage. Thus, the average American girl is more likely to attend her granddaughter's wedding and, in fact, is likely to have for her great-granddaughter the position in relative age and closeness to death that her mother had with her own grandmother. Young grandmothers and numerous great-grandmothers are two results of the present trend. Apple (1956) has made a classical analysis of the grandparental roles.

Close to a majority of men today will live to see their grandsons on their way to success or to failure. Thus, a man will be dealt by fate several new chances for vicarious identification, a boon to the man who starts from a low status, a warning to exercise tolerance and humility for the man who starts at a high status and for whom the problem is to maintain rather than to achieve.

Value Factors in the Decline
of Patrilinear Descent Systems

A major component of Parsonian functionalism is the stress upon values. In discussing Parsons' analysis of the relationship between industrialization and isolation of the nuclear family, most writers have focused only on the component of role integration and neglected completely the value element. No doubt Parsons has stressed that values are probably the one factor most resistant to change in any one society, but where they do change, their impact upon the society is much more pervasive than are changes in economic, political, or integrative structures.

At the present time, two major "religious movements" are sweeping the world and result in pervasive changes in the norms that motivate individuals within their societies. One is *Marxism-Leninism,* which represents the result of a fusion of the scientific spirit with Eastern Catholicism, and the other is *liberal individualism,* which represents the fusion of the scientific spirit with the Protestant tradition and, to a lesser extent, with the more collectivistic Catholic tradition. These two religious movements express themselves through various ideologies which are more or less congruent with the existing cultural traditions and the core institutions of the societies exposed to their impact. Although they are opposed in many aspects, they agree on the premises of the complete equality of women, the belief in economic and social progress, and the importance of occupational achievement rather than extended family membership as the basis for status.

The elites of underdeveloped countries have three reference groups: one is made of their traditional collectivities (tribe, caste); another is their emerging nation; and the third consists of the elites of major Western countries where the traditional family patterns such as the low status of women are regarded as signs of cultural inferiority. The desire to be modern, to be Western, has often led to the passing of legislation which testified to the conscious commitment of the elites of India, Japan, Egypt, and elsewhere to Western patterns. However, this does not mean that these Western patterns are readily institutionalized among the masses, nor often enough among the upper classes. Changes in family structure must contend with the fact that family roles have high regressive components, and to that extent a certain "repetition compulsion" does exist—even though consciously held ideas may be completely at variance with the structure of these regressive components. Also, a problem resides in the fact that, although the upper classes may be committed to Western patterns of women's rights, abolition of primogeniture, neolocal residence, and freedom of occupational choice for the sons, their class position reinforces the secondary gains of the patrilineal extended family patterns. Those who take to the new patterns most willingly are, of course, the middle classes, such as the Japanese Sarari men described by Vogel (1963).

As was previously mentioned, one of the beliefs that bolster patrilinear descent patterns, at least the stem family if not the patrilinear extended family, is the belief that women, although good as mothers, are dangerous as peers, either because of their excessive sexuality or because of their inherent perversity. It is interesting to parallel this belief in the wickedness of women with the Tallensi belief that witchcraft is hereditarily transmitted by women to women (Fortes, 1949). Fortes advanced the idea that this belief is functional to preserving trust within the male line: most bad things come from women. The two Western religious movements mentioned earlier condemn this systematic imputation of ethical inferiority to women.

In Arab countries and in various sub-Saharan tribes (for example, the Masai), clitorectomy is practiced as a means, supposedly, to reduce the strength of women's sexuality (Berque in Goode, 1963, p. 147). Nasser made this operation illegal in Egypt in 1958. In most Arab countries, women now have the suffrage. In Algeria, their participation in the resistance movement has gained them a new ethical stature in the eyes of the urban masses. Furthermore, they are gaining access to schooling of the Western type, which increases their communication capacity in the marriage.

In India, the belief in the desirability of the nuclear family as the preferred pattern does not seem to be very extensive, and the most progress in this direction appears to have been made upon those who have been in contact with Western ideas. However, the most important change in India resides in abandoning the exclusive emphasis upon the patriline. The joint family ideal persists, with less opportunity in the cities for actual joint living, but with a stronger mutual-aid pattern than is common in the Western world. A transition to the classical French pattern of shifting coalitions (Pitts, 1963) within the kindred can be expected to replace the patrilinear joint family characterized by very early marriage and the complete assimilation of the wife to her husband's lineage.

An interesting case in the relation of societal values to the trend away from the patrilinear family is that of Japan. Bellah (1957) insisted that in the particular form Buddhism took in Japan, as compared to China, there was implicit more activism: a duty to transform the present world according to the divine law (p. 78) and a stress upon political loyalty that overshadowed family loyalty (pp. 81–82, 164). Virtues more congenial to the stability of the patrilinear extended family are those of harmony, balance, the cult of the esthetic, and a respect for the world as it is. Any value system which emphasizes political loyalty with an ascetic and activist content, instead of loyalty for its own sake, will come into conflict with the extended patrilineage. The value elements for the development of a centralized state are present.

The stress upon achievement for the sake of the group in Japan has two consequences.

One is the adoption pattern, by which it is possible for the head of the family to adopt a capable stranger and give him the care of the lineage, if he sees no one among his own sons capable of doing this in acceptable fashion. The second is to play down individual mobility, contrary to the Chinese system, in which history is a graveyard of gentry families. It is service to the group that counts rather than personal success. There is less particularistic pressure against recognition of the capable than in China or India. As a result, the striving for recognition is less disruptive than in China and even less than in the United States, for instance.

The present transition in Japan has been that the focus of loyalty, instead of being on the land-based *Ie* (patrilineage) and the emperor, has been shifting to the nuclear family and to the urban-based industrial and commercial firm (Vogel, 1963). Because of the universalistic components of the value system, the land-based Ie with its primogeniture pattern (though the main heir was not always the oldest son) "spun off" many new families which went to seek their fortunes in the cities and took up a feudal type of vassalage in industrial firms. The loyalty to the Ie became ceremonial, or merely a reserve for catastrophes. There was no development of clans or sibs which might have stood between the state or the firm and the cadet's nuclear family.

An interesting problem is that the emphasis upon vertical superordination-subordination relationships (what F. Kluckhohn, 1958, would call "lineal emphasis") does render more difficult the development of equalitarian relationships between husband and wife. In the nuclear family of Japan the parental system remains stronger than the conjugal system. This is correlated with a lower level of female employment than in China, and especially a low level of employment for married women. Japanese culture has been able to integrate many aspects of Western civilization without as much strain upon its basic values and family systems.

Christianity is a force which has made for

the development of the bilateral kindred to the detriment of the patrilineal lineage, basically because it reinforced the marital tie in such a way that concubinage was not a legitimate outlet for sexual needs, and repudiation for barrenness was no longer the husband's prerogative. By reinforcing the marital tie, it automatically weakens the lineage ties of the husband. The Catholic Church also helped develop strong national states, which in turn weakened the patri-lineage. However, in the nineteenth and early twentieth century, the Catholic Church became afraid of the diffusion of atheism among the working class and lower-middle class and saw in the multiplication of republican governments a major threat to itself. It allied itself with the aristocratic and bourgeois lineages against centralized republican regimes (France, Italy, Spain). The stem family was seen as the ideal—along with emphasizing patriarchal authority of divine right, downgrading individual aspirations for success, and Church guidance rather than a state-controlled school system diffusing the heresies of the Enlightenment.

The stem family and Church organizations were functional to one another. Large families used the convents as schools and as outlets for surplus girls and Church careers for surplus boys. The Church was thus insured a strong recruitment among the wealthier and more powerful classes, which offered it some protection against the state. This variant of Catholicism was given its most systematic description by Le Play (1864; 1871).

Greenfield (1961) has correctly emphasized the importance of Puritanism in promoting the isolation of the nuclear family, which in America antedated and facilitated extensive industrialization. Puritanism extended the Christian trends toward the liberation of women, even though it began by making sexuality a greater focus of sin than it had been in Catholic practice. In particular, it made fornication a great sin for man; the result was an increased pressure for early marriage, since the outlet of prostitution was frowned upon. Puritanism made of marriage an individual affair, that is, marriage was above all a means to one's salvation and required the consent of one's will. As a result, romantic love received a level of legitimation as a source of marriage that had been lacking in Catholic countries.

Furthermore, Puritanism did not extol obedience to one's parents to the extent that was preached by Catholicism. The early departure of half-grown boys from their families was seen as an act of courage rather than defiance, for children had to find their own salvation in the world. Thus, it has been difficult, in the face of such a value system, for the American upper classes to stabilize themselves as dynasties. The prestige of personal achievement as a mark of salvation is much greater than mere descent from illustrious ancestors. Furthermore, the equalitarian bias in American values has made it difficult for upper-class families to claim a superiority of breed that would give them a recognized quasi-monopoly on high levels of achievement, something that the English gentry has maintained.

The importance of the values of self-reliance and personal autonomy and the belief in the superiority of the future in contrast to the past, are largely incompatible with the type of patriarchal domination characteristic of patrilineal extended families found in an upper-class status. As a sort of "American ideology," now relayed in Catholic countries by a new emphasis upon personalism, it has given a high prestige to the middle-class pattern in all Westernized countries outside the Soviet orbit.

The analysis of the isolation of the nuclear family through the use of motivational factors departs from the classical equilibrium theme of the structural-functional approach. Direction in the analysis is resumed by showing institutional patterns to be specifications of value patterns. The reversibility of structural-functional items, well exemplified by Durkheim's analysis of ritual and the strength of collective representations, does not obtain here. The nuclear family does not "cause" the development of individualistic Puritan values. It may make members of isolated conjugal families vulnerable to such a value pattern, but since the conjugal family is the family system most commonly experienced anywhere in the world, a positivistic approach—which would explain the development of norms from the extrapolation of what is—would not be valuable here.

Hence, in explaining the prevalence of the isolated conjugal family in the United States and the renouncement of "aristocratization" among many upper-middle-class families in contemporary Europe, priority must be given to the value system. The structural-functional approach can encompass the value analysis by referring to the equilibrium between motivational systems and role systems. It does this by bringing into play, in order to explain social facts (a family pattern), two nonsocial systems; the cultural system and the personality system.

Social Class and Neighborhoods

Between the world of strangers and the protective intimacy of the nuclear family, the first intermediary layer was the extended kin network. In the Western world, this has been replaced, for most purposes, by a more flexible grouping known as social class. The geographically centered community is replaced by the abstract solidarity of the nation and the more limited solidarity of the one-class neighborhood.

Some functional needs. The functional needs behind these statements are as follows:

1. The nuclear family needs to create around itself, as much as possible, an area where social interaction is dominated by expectations of mutual support as compared to the immediate reciprocities of market exchange.
2. The expectation of mutual support is especially important in relation to the problems of maintaining a certain level of achievement in the face of the uncertain worth of offspring and of competitive pressures from above and below. This statement assumes that the process of identification with children has, for con-

sequences, a desire to give them as many advantages as possible so as to facilitate their retention, or even betterment, of the status inherited from their parents.
3. In the absence of strong lineages, and when the problems of achieving stable expectations and reciprocity are difficult, the multirank local community is an important center of solidarity. It is hard for newcomers to gain admission.
4. Conversely, when the nation-state is able to guarantee many rights and obligations for all its citizens, regardless of local origin, and when there is a permanent need for additional contributions on the part of local structures (or simply on the part of their members), the effective stranger is usually welcomed. The community is not an important center of solidarity, since it can be entered and left at will. The nuclear family sees the community as a facility rather than as a binding order.

The combination of (1) and (2) gives the caste, estate, and social class as the structural solutions to the needs for solidarity in the fact of differential achievement. The units of caste and estate are extended families, while the units of social class are nuclear families.

Social class considered generally. The class peer groups are made of intimate friends and of the informal networks that coagulate around the work place, the church, and the club. They provide the nuclear family, most often through the intermediary and origination of the husband (Babchuk & Bates, 1963), with entertainment and information for job and investment opportunities, and make it easier in general for the breadwinner to maintain his occupational standing in the face of competition from below or even from above.

The class peer groups have a great advantage over the extended family in that, wherever the pursuit of occupation takes one, it is easy to claim entrance to the class peer group equivalent to the one left behind through recommendations or through entry into civic clubs or church membership. The capacity to contribute effectively to the power and prestige of the peer group is a sufficient passport for admittance and for receiving services which make adjustment to the whole community easier (Litwak, 1961).

Class peer groups are often very effective in preventing gross downward mobility which might be due to the illness or death of the husband-father, and have permitted widows and their small children to retain the style of life and protective network characteristic of their class level.

Peer groups are usually more effective the higher one moves up in the middle class. In contemporary American society, class membership is more effective than extended family membership in solving the problem of competition and solidarity, because there is little pressure for a nuclear family to limit its achievement capacity in order to remain integrated in the class. If one's level exceeds the group, he moves up to the higher level, with the limitations to be discussed presently.

If one looks at the relationship between social class and the nuclear family from the standpoint of the Parsonian type of exchange functionalism, one could outline the following interchanges: the social class gives the nuclear family support and protection. The support is often given tangibly through income opportunities, but also through the rewards implicit in membership, since class membership is a public testimony to a certain level of achievement. Support is also given through the tension reduction induced by mutual entertainment. Protection is given essentially by discrimination against outsiders and usually includes immunities to prosecution of minor crimes by police. In return for support and protection, the nuclear family commits itself to a given standard of value achievement, which is constantly tested by its capacity to *express* its conformity through style of life. Only when capacity is not seen as a failure of motivation or skill can failure to conform not lead to expulsion from the class (the family is no longer invited).

The nuclear family also commits itself to exercise leadership in favor of the class by discriminating against outsiders and by passing on information which can be of use to the members of one's status group (the class in its interactional expression).

The social class furthermore protects the socialization and tension-management function of the nuclear family by isolating it from achievement levels it could not hope to realize, and the constant vision of which could only lead to frustration and a breakup of the husband and wife's closed markets in the conjugal system. It maintains the gap between present status and hoped-for achievement at a bearable level. In return, the nuclear family commits itself to the socialization of the children into patterns which insure their *commitment* to the class level of value achievement. This is why, in the higher class levels, full membership is contingent upon the demonstration that the socialization function of the family is being pursued effectively and that social climbing has not absorbed so much of the family's energy that it is crippled in its socialization function. If the latter is the case, the family is likely to need much more support than it can give the class group to which it claims admittance. Hence, it is unlikely to be admitted except to a marginal status, where it will have to demonstrate undeviating conformity to class patterns in all its behavior. Thus, the family is led to fulfill the Davis-Moore function of the social class in relation to the social system—by insuring a sufficient supply of motivations and becoming trained and eager for roles requiring high skills and responsibilities.

It is likely that the insulation from higher standards which is accomplished by the social class helps the family in its socialization function. In particular, it prevents the children from being prematurely exposed to higher standards than their families are capable of, thus losing their respect for their parents with deleterious effects upon superego formation.

One of the problems of the lower class. and particularly the Negro lower class, in an achievement-oriented society like the United States, is that the lowest position gives very little protection of this sort. This frequently means that extra-familial role participations by the children are likely to lead to premature disenchantment with their parents. [Compare the above paragraphs with Cavan's discussions of social class, pp. 541–544.]

Neighborhoods and the family. A major structural complement of the isolated nuclear family has been the residential neighborhood of suburbia and subsuburbia, where the levels of solidarity reached can compare quite favorably with those to be expected from the more remote elements of the extended family. Based upon relatively homogeneous levels of income and style of life, they increase in strength in the lower-middle and middle-middle classes, where the incidence of the working wife is comparatively low. They are characterized by the Republic of Children, where there is much communal sharing of play facilities and refrigerator raiding, by coffee-klatching networks, all reinforced by such formal organizations as the PTA, the Cub Scouts, and, in certain cases, the church. Although *turnover of membership is relatively high,* they preserve the capacity to assimilate the newcomer into a network of jovial conviviality which has definite tension-reduction values. Its usefulness as an informal police force, baby-sitting cooperative, consumers' union, and source of entertainment cannot be gainsaid. It is a unique institution in the Western world, and it is interesting to note that English working-class families, removed from their slums and placed into suburban housing, did not seem to re-create there a neighborhood group of similar strength (Young & Willmott, 1957; compare Mogey, 1955). Fellin and Litwak (1963, p. 375) have shown the relative incompatibility between extensive family connections and integration of the nuclear family into the neighborhood.

It is true that the nature of the exchanges within the neighborhood are of goods and services of comparatively low value, although there is a latent commitment to help in emergencies which may even go so far as the collection of money. The terms of solidarity are influenced by the likelihood of long-range reciprocity and the need to remain on equal footing with your neighbors. Here, the comparative uncertainty as to who is or will remain an effective member of the neighborhood acts as a limiting factor. [Compare Mogey's discussion of neighborhoods, pp. 519–522.]

Interactional networks. The functional principle that emerges in connection with the analysis of relationships between the nuclear family and the other solidary systems is that the solidarity is more easily maintained and the commitment greater when the boundaries of the group are sharper; and the boundaries are all the more sharp when the world beyond them is defined as dangerous. Kinship has a great advantage, since the obligations are related to kinship terminology, and the distinction between who is kin and who is not is clear. The boundaries of the kindred are not as clear as those of the lineage, but they are clearer so far as ego is concerned than are the boundaries of occupational peer groups or even of neighborhood peer groups.

But in the United States lower-middle and middle-middle classes, the activation of the collateral and affinal network is rarer than the activation of the occupational peer group and neighborhood. What the kindred gains in sharpness of definition in relation to these groups, it loses in scarcity of activation. In fact, the group which has the greatest level of activation is the class peer group and its core of intimate friends. On the other hand, the boundaries of these groups are more fuzzy, so it might still be easier to call upon a brother for emergency help than to call upon a class peer group, especially when needing help might threaten the definition of the right to belong to the group.

The problem for all solidary groups rooted in various amounts of particularism is that the total society has provided on a universalistic basis for practically all emergencies through health insurance, tuition loans, credit unions. Activation is more and more limited to emotional support.

The boundary for the couple within our nuclear society is very sharp and is maintained through the exclusiveness of sexual love. In fact, the isolation of the conjugal family is reinforced by the assumption that the married couple shares something that cannot be shared by anyone else. How the marital couple is reinforced by various structural features is discussed below.

The main reinforcement is to restrict the social life of the married couple either to same-sex affairs, occupational peer-group activities, "lunch with the girls," or couple-to-couple relationships which split off into same-sex interaction: the wives talk to the wives; the husbands talk to the husbands (Parsons, 1942). In the lower-middle and middle-middle classes, there generally is no flirtation. In the upper-middle class, there may be flirtation and extramarital necking at large parties which are part of its style of life, but there is not likely to be any lasting relationship between a wife and someone else's husband without the serious step of divorce being brought up by the woman of the pair.

Furthermore, romantic love, however legitimate for adolescents and young adults, is seen as being somewhat abnormal for grown men. Once it has welded the marital bond, it is not supposed to burn again in the heart of the man: his occupation should be his passion. Hence, not only structurally but also motivationally the marriage tie is protected against disruption.

If the marriage is to be efficacious as a source of solidarity and nurturance, the woman has to have assets which decrease the maturity and education differential that existed between herself and her husband in the classical bourgeois marriage. Low age differential, low or no educational differential, and increase in the wife's earning potential are some of the characteristics of the modern middle-class marriage.

As the marriage becomes more efficacious as a tension reducer and a focus of solidarity

(the classical marriage gave the husband the support of passive compliance and the illusion of omnipotence, but denied him the more valuable type of peer-group support which can be given by a woman who knows the man's world), there is less demand for such experiences in extra-familial role participations. As a result, the primary character of kin networks (in particular collaterals) and of other peer groups declines. They become more relations of entertainment and less relations of mutual support. They can be left more easily and entered into more easily.

Bott (1957) has demonstrated correlations between the tightly integrated conjugal system and the loose network affiliations of the couple, on the one hand, and the more loosely integrated conjugal system of couples with tight and usually separate network affiliations, on the other hand. Upper-middle and upper-class English families are characteristic of the latter; American upper-middle-class families are more characteristic of the former.

The lower social class. By lower class is meant that segment of society which has an unstable connection to the labor force, partly because the trained capacity that it offers is of low quality and low reliability, partly because the demand for its skills is very fluctuating. It corresponds to Warner's lower-lower class rather than to all of Hollingshead's class V. The capacity of the husband to discharge his breadwinner's role is impaired. In fact, the economic penalties of the lower-class position bear more heavily upon the men than upon the women, for the latter in hard times are still in demand for domestic services and receive easier treatment from welfare agencies and from men of higher classes. Adolescent children, also, are likely to earn sums that are not much inferior to those earned by mature men. Little in the breadwinning role reinforces the prestige and authority of the lower-class male. In a situation of failure in relation to middle-class achievement values, treated as a subordinate in many extra-occupational contexts, deprived of much peer support, the lower-class male is likely to bring to the conjugal and parental systems a burden of tension that these systems cannot cope with. Blood and Wolfe (1960) showed that lower-class women are consistently the least satisfied of all women with their marriages (pp. 226, 228–229).

Lower classes in both France and the United States have been characterized by comparatively high rates of family instability. Around Paris, in the working-class suburbs of the early 1950's, it was estimated that one-third of the marriages were of the common-law variety. A man may or may not register his household formation as a legal marriage, then desert, and following this episode, set up a common-law establishment with another woman without any statistics registering the "divorce."

In the poorer section of the American Negro working class and in the lower-lower white class, this pattern is common, so that the effective unit of the family is the mother-daughter system, with a powerful "matrifocal" if not matrilinear tendency. It is only in the mother-daughter relationship that stability is found, for reasons to be seen presently.

The lower-class male finds himself in a difficult predicament. The age and sex roles which he has learned from the environment are difficult for him to realize in the occupational world: he is dependent, he obeys, he has to take a passive role in production which conflicts with the definition of the male role. The pains of low status are diminished by adolescent peer-group membership, which extols masculine values more easily accessible—such as sexual prowess and physical aggression—than occupational achievements. Yet the nurturant needs of the lower-class adolescent or young adult are, if anything, greater than in higher social classes. He is often pushed into early marriage, where the conflicts between breadwinning responsibilities and low opportunity create tensions. Being threatened in masculine role identification, he compen-

sates by domineering and sexually exploitative relationships with his wife, who responds by passivity or more or less covert aggression. He remains heavily committed to the masculine peer group and soon anticipates extra-marital affairs as a mark of superior masculinity (Green, 1941; Rainwater & Weinstein, 1960).

His commitment to the marriage is low, and "taking off" has the advantage of reopening the elusive future. Refusing to settle down returns to one's social-status problem an aspect of adolescent play. It is not final: one is "available" for the breaks which might come his way. If the man deserts his wife, she is entitled to state aid, which might well exceed what the man has given her from his wages.

Now that society's standard of living is higher, a divorce often can be secured for two- or three-weeks' wages, while in the past it might have cost four- to six-weeks' wages. A certain amount of the secular trend in the American divorce rate is to be accounted for by the increased registration of working-class marriage and separation.

The problem in Western society is that the psychological pressures toward irresponsible sexual exploitation of women by men are a constant force: the man-child gets a woman to take care of him simply because he is a man, he has a penis. The regressive resonance of this pimp role, with many oedipal overtones, feeds the fantasies of people in all classes and finds an outlet in literature and movies. Other themes are: the man-child takes women away from other men; women will do anything for their man regardless of his failings. There are four undercurrents in these themes which are positive in relation to the over-all societal value system: the valuation of masculinity, the valuation of competition, the valuation of the unconditional commitment of women to men, the valuation of masculine independence in relation to women's nurturance, which permits in fiction the "private eye," or the cowboy, to tear himself from the embrace of the love-hungry woman. A lower-class man who is blocked from achievement in the more differentiated role patterns can reject them and find a second order of legitimacy in the primitive masculine values, which the over-all society can never reject completely because of their fantasy value and their kernel of conformity.

Thus, these regressive mythologies have an important function in mitigating the pains of lower-class status. The peer group, in a manner outlined by Cohen (1955), develops a variant normative pattern which is overdetermined—compulsive, Parsons would say—and which sustains irresponsible mating behavior in the lower class, especially in societies where the achievement values are strong and where the class system is fairly open, as is the case in the whole Western world.

Here, the pains of low status are likely to be very high, and the psychological usefulness of regressive antioccupational and antimarital achievement fantasies have to be greatest. Furthermore, as Goode (1963) has pointed out, the bargaining power of the lower-class girl is low. Although a lower-class male can reach ideals of primitive masculinity, lower-class girls are much less likely to reach ideals of primitive femininity, and if their family does not back them up, they are relatively defenseless against sexual exploitation. Very often, premarital conception is the only way that the lower-class woman can force the marriage, because it is a point where social controls bear strongest, and fatherhood does have some prestige value for the lower-class male.

As the income and occupational stability of the lower-class man increase, one of his immediate goals is to enforce the classical pattern where only the husband works for gain. There is a rigid division of labor within the family, which leaves child-rearing and home management to the wife, while the husband works outside and makes the crucial decisions unilaterally. Often, he turns over the bulk of his pay check to his wife, reserving for himself some pocket money to spend in peer-group entertainment. Marital stability, the chastity of the daughters, and being a good provider become values held in opposition to the marital instability, promiscuity of daughters, and working-wife patterns of the "trash."

The case of the Caribbean. In this connection, there still remains to be analyzed an interesting paradox of marriage patterns in the Caribbean Islands, where a large part of the urban and rural proletariat live in conditions similar to those of the lower class in the United States, and where *consensual unions* are common. This seems to have challenged the requirement of marriage as a condition to parenthood so well expressed by Malinowski. Henriques (1953), Braithwaite (1957), and R. T. Smith (1956) have claimed that there is little or no ethical pressure against illegitimacy in the Caribbean, and that there is a lower-class norm born of circumstances which legitimizes consensual unions and accepts children born under any circumstances. Smith rendered the high incidence of male unemployment responsible for this situation.

Blake (1955; 1961) and Goode (1960) have pointed out that, although the punishments for illegitimacy in the lower classes are small, nevertheless there can be no question as to what the ideal norm is, and that eventually the majority of men and women do get married, usually when the man is able to fulfill the breadwinning role with more stability.

Henriques, Braithwaite, and R. T. Smith spoke in terms of a lower-class subculture, while Blake and Goode had a social disorganization model in mind. From the point of view of producing children for whom there is little or no surplus of resources available, there is indeed "disorganization." On the other hand, the pattern provides a sexual outlet for lower-class males while cutting down on the fertility of women as compared to what it might have been had the women been legally married (Blake, 1955). Furthermore, "social placement" is not as crucial a problem in the urban and rural lower class where there is little or no property to be transmitted and where most of the extra-familial roles available to the growing adolescent—especially occupational roles—are "residual" ones.

Finally, it may be suggested that, in relation to the societal norms, illegitimacy brands children born under its stigma and constituting a substantial percentage of the lower class, with a disability that legitimizes their low class position *in their own eyes*. The pattern acts in the Caribbean and in many South American and even European settings (rural or urban) in the way the "drop-out" stigma acts in America. "Disorganization" is thus functional to the social class system. (This may come under the heading of "cynical functionalism.")

True enough, some neutralization of the pains of stigma and low status is necessary. This is how the variant subculture develops, and it promotes a second order of legitimacy out of values bearing on the definitions of masculinity, fertility, and male independence. In fact, this subculture represents a major contribution of social class to the family: it protects it from constant exposure to achievement levels (whether they bear on occupation, patterns of consumption, or standards of family behavior) which would degrade the present performance of the family unbearably.

However, the ideologies which exist—and these are ideologies rather than values, that is, responses to strain, neutralization of contradictions and of the pains of low achievement levels—cannot hide completely the fact that these lower-class patterns are deviant ones. Following them is still one of the penalties of a lower-class status. Within a total societal reference, increased prestige is accorded the man, woman, or couple that marries officially and then follows the regular patterns of legitimacy. If there were a true alternative value pattern there would be no pressure, as soon as means became available, to change behavior and demonstrate conformity with the dominant value pattern.

Social class and fertility. Davis and Blake (1956) have analyzed very well the factors which must be controlled in order to achieve a level of reproduction commensurate with the society's welfare. Most societies, until relatively recently, had institutions which resulted either in slow growth or in stationary populations: age of marriage; incidence of celibacy; type of marriage, whether monogamous or polygamous; taboos on intercourse within certain periods; infanticide; use of birth control or abortion. These institutions had functional consequences which usually kept the population within the limits of subsistence. Economic, political, class factors, and even the demographic subculture of families (Berent, 1953) influence the number of children which families have. The class factor is of concern here.

The usual correlation between fertility and class has been an inverse one: the farmer and the unskilled laborer have large families, and the middle class has small families. Statistics do not usually give rates for the upper-middle class or the upper class, since they are too small in numbers and are lost in the middle-class indices.

The possibility of a complete reversal of fertility rates seems a challenge to the structural-functional analytical scheme: Why should those groups least able to rear children have more than those most able to afford them?

First, the farmer's family can utilize the labor of his children, so a high fertility as a means of providing a family with its labor force makes relatively good sense. Given the fact that a good percentage of industrial workers come from farms, one must expect a true "cultural lag" due to motivational factors, as mentioned above.

Second, in the classical working-class family, where children went to work from the age of 12 onward, they were an effective source of income; the greatest periods of a family's prosperity were encountered when it had several children contributing to the family funds. Furthermore, children were one's old-age security. Here again, a large family, given the fact of a higher death rate, makes good sense. And one would again expect some cultural lag before working-class families realized the fact that children are no more of much use as contributors to the family treasury in times when compulsory schooling extends to 16 and when great pressures are upon working-class children to stay in school until 18.

The relatively high fertility of working-class families (see Blood & Wolfe, 1960, p. 130), and especially of the nonmiddle-class-oriented lower-lower class, is also explained by the general lack of planning capacity—the refusal of the man to use contraceptives which supposedly would decrease his pleasure and the reluctance of poorly educated wives to use "unnatural" methods like pills, diaphragms, and so on (see Rainwater & Weinstein, 1960). Often, in fact, in the lower-class family the mother-baby relationship is the most satisfying one, and the wife can at best be ambivalent toward family planning which deprives her of the occasions for a regressive, symbiotic relationship in which she is most needed and most powerful.

One can expect that the ambitious middle class restricts fertility in order to permit concentration of socialization efforts upon fewer children and greater success, in addition to the greater representative claims on the wife's time. However, as one reaches the upper-middle class and the upper class, resources are sufficient for the hiring of mother surrogates. Further, in the stable upper class and in the stable upper-middle class, increasing pride in lineage puts a premium upon a large kin network requiring, to start with, a large number of children. Hence, particularly in Catholic countries where the dynastic ambitions are more in tune with the societal value system, one would expect to find higher fertility rates in the upper-middle and upper classes than in the middle-middle and lower-middle classes. This is what the writer's own data show for France (Pitts, 1958).

Even in the United States, the incidence of four-child families among the upper-middle class, following the ideology of the professionalization of motherhood, may well have reversed the usual demographic differential. To a certain extent, the fourth child has become an item of conspicuous consumption, although perhaps this is only a marginal component of the motivation to have him. Certainly, as compared to the 1920's and 1930's, the upper-middle class woman of the 1940's and 1950's could not confess preferring external activities to motherhood. There are impressionistic indications that in the 1960's the pendulum is swinging back in the other direction, to three- and two-child families, so that there may be a disappearance of the birth-rate differential, except for the lower-lower class.

THE NUCLEAR FAMILY AND THE ECONOMIC SYSTEM

Technology and the Family

Relations between the types of food-gathering economies have already been touched on in the discussions of rules of residence and rules of descent in this chapter, and they are also discussed in Chapters 12 and 13. Nimkoff & Middleton (1960), following in the technologically oriented path of Ogburn (1938), used the World Ethnographic Sample compiled by Murdock (1957) to relate types of family to types of economies and compared the modern industrial society "with its small independent family" to the "simpler hunting and gathering society." The resemblance of their family types was due to their limited need for family labor and to a common physical mobility; "The hunter . . . pursues the game; the industrial worker, the job" (p. 225).

In discussing Japan and India, Nimkoff (1960) left open the possibility that the joint family may not be as dysfunctional (because of nepotism, low mobility, low economic priorities, passivity) to industrialization in India as a formal analysis would lead one to believe. The problem here, of course, is that the structures that may have been highly functional to the discovery of a social system (the factory system in a free market dominated by competitive corporations) may not necessarily be the ones required for its adoption as a proven device. With the reference of a market economy for costs indications and the unproblematical nature of consumer desires, a semiplanned economy may require less mobility, especially when urbanization creates a concentrated job market. On the other hand, the joint family may be much more dysfunctional for the middle and upper classes, where entrepreneurial decisions are made.

Occupation and the Family

The classical relations between the family and the economy have considered the impact of unemployment (Bakke, 1940; Cavan & Ranck, 1938; Komarovsky, 1950) and shown the working of the homeostatic mechanisms in re-establishing role equilibrium under stress. A crucial element, when unemployment occurs, seems to be the "definition of the situation," that is, whether the wife and children define the unemployment of the father as an external catastrophe often affecting friends and neighbors or due to a personal failing of the breadwinner. In fact, this is a principle that applies generally to all "economic" factors. It is rare that they have an intrinsic meaning, and furthermore it is often difficult to decide whether a factor is merely "economic," that is, centering on the techniques of work and the production of labor or the decisions to consume, or whether it belongs to the social class system. A typical instance is the problem of occupation.

The relations between occupations and family structure have been studied relatively little. Aberle and Naegele's article (1952) deals with social class rather than with occupational structure per se. What is needed is better conceptualization than has usually been forthcoming. The folklore used to pity the doctor's wife, although now that medical practice has become more office-centered, the commiseration has declined. On an impressionistic basis, the divorce rate among airline pilots and SAC crews seems high, but this may be due to the type of personalities the job selects rather than to the type of occupational pressures that bear upon the family. The same may be said of the entertainment profession. The night shift is probably not favorable to family stability, nor is the occupational life of the waitress, of the furniture mover, and of the trucker. The folklore has described the troubles of the "PK's" (preachers' kids), and in particular of the minister's daughter. The civil servant and the traveling salesman would be interesting types to compare in terms of the impact of their occupation—security, risks, hours, remuneration—upon their family structure.

Research so far has mostly centered upon the functional relationship between the type of organizational culture shared by a family and the patterns of child-rearing practiced by this family (Miller & Swanson, 1958), or on the power structure and the pattern of task allocation (Gold & Slater, 1958).

Structural Impacts of the Wife's Gainful Employment

One of the most interesting problems concerning the relationship between the nuclear family and the economic system has been that of the allocation of family power as related to the occupational roles of husband and wife. A common assumption made by most structural-functional studies (in particular, Goode, 1963), which hold the value factor constant, is that the possibility of independent employment decreases the dependence of the wife upon her husband and his family and increases her bargaining power within the conjugal society. As a result, she gains greater legitimacy for the continuation of her ties to her own family of orientation. This, in turn, reinforces the trend toward bilateralism. Furthermore, she is less likely to accept with good grace that her hard-earned income should go to sub-sidize her husband's family. Hence, salaried employment by the wife is likely to be a force for the isolation of the nuclear family from the patrilineage. The stress is on *salaried* employment. In Arab countries, women often do the bulk of the routine tasks—gathering wood, hoeing, tending the sheep, bringing in the water—so that they actually do more productive work than their husbands. Nevertheless, there is no wage in-volved, and her hard work is simply part of the low status of women in general. Her economic contribution does not mean in-creased bargaining power, because the wife does not control the produce of her labor. The same was true of the Japanese girl in-dentured to a textile factory, prior to World War II. No doubt the particularly hard-working and able Arab women would not be easy to replace, and hence could gain more bargaining power in the marriage, but where the valuation of labor is low, the possibilities of using work prowess as a bar-gaining point are restricted.

Woman's work and status. In the United States, the problem of woman's work and her status within the family and the com-munity has been the focus of much, but somewhat inconclusive, research. What are the components of the problem?

Industrialization removes many of the differential strength handicaps which affect women. There are few roles that bar them on this basis, and Soviet Russia has given proof of this—if proof were needed. Psy-chologically, there can be some debate as to whether women's personality systems permit as thorough a socialization into professional patterns. The greater interest of women is in expressive relationships, which are dys-functional to complex organizations, espe-cially in the higher executive range. The experience of Soviet Russia does not con-tradict this statement, for even there the higher executive jobs seem to be over-whelmingly the prerogatives of men; this is true in managerial occupations and in medicine, where specialists are usually men,

while general practitioners (who are per-haps closer in training to our Masters of Nursing Science) are usually women.

The increase in female employment in the United States and western Europe tends to take place in the white-collar expressive, teaching, or nurturant occupations. Effective time-motion studies of many secretarial, re-ceptionist, or data-processing jobs would probably show that half of their function is a tension-reduction and expressive one, the usefulness of which is to dilute the com-petitive strain bearing upon the men and to give the latter noncontingent feminine re-wards. As the competitive pressures become greater in the world of affairs, the need to "have women around" increases. It de-creases the tension-reduction burden of the nuclear family.

Effects upon the power structure. In a small group such as the nuclear family, final authority belongs to those who carry the roles which embody the highest prestige and are the most strategic to the welfare of the family taken as a whole. Another functional requirement is that final authority should be assigned without ambiguity.

The problem of ambiguity raises an in-teresting question, for, more than *absolute* prestige or strategic character, it is the *dif-ferential* aspect of these values as between husband and wife that is important in de-termining the final authority within the family.

In relation to prestige, the first observa-tion is that housekeeping is universally an activity of low status. In upper-class strata it is delegated to servants. It is repetitious, monotonous, and although capital goods have increased the efficiency of housework (vacuum cleaners, gas or electric stoves with automatic timers, washing and drying ma-chines, refrigerators), it remains essentially a low-skill activity which requires for suc-cessful discharge a high sense of responsi-bility rather than complex training. The same is true of parenthood, especially care of the infant and prepubertal child.

In upper-class strata, the representative

functions assume greater strategic importance for the status of the nuclear family,
and they require greater skill than housekeeping on the part of the wife. This increases the relative value of her contribution
to the nuclear family and gives her some
leverage. On the other hand, the occupational or citizen roles of her husband are
likely to have very high prestige, which
re-establishes the differential.

From these considerations, one could arrive at the following propositions:

1. Insofar as personality factors do not inter-
vene decisively in reversing the allocation of
authority within the family, the authority of
the husband is all the greater as the skill and
responsibility of his extra-familial roles are
greater.
2. Where the differential prestige is comparatively low, the authority of the male is reinforced by a sharp division of labor barring
women from any deliberative part in instrumental decisions which do not concern the
training of daughters or the management of
the home.
3. Where women in lower-class groups also
participate in gainful employment, the basis
of male authority reverts to superiority in
strength.

Most research on authority patterns has
been done in connection with the gainful
employment of the wife, the common hypothesis being that contribution of the wife
to family income increases her relative
power in the household: she participates in
a more valued activity than housework, and
she has some control over the disposal of
her earnings. Early research such as that by
Blood and Hamblin (1958) did not show
any "reliable" increase in power of the
working wife. Heer's article (1958) shows
that, in a sample of Irish Catholics where
general personality dominance has been
held constant, "for both working class and
middle-class, the differences in family decision making dependent on the work status
of the wife still . . . remain" (p. 39). On
the other hand, the test of dominance was

the response of husband and wife together
to the question, "Now I would like to know
something about decisions in your family.
When there is a really important decision on
which you two are likely to disagree, who
usually wins out?" The index is based upon
subjective evaluation and may not be too
valid.

In Hoffman's (1960) study, there was an
attempt to hold constant the factor of commitment to a traditional ideology of male
dominance versus commitment to a more
equalitarian attitude. She used information
gathered from grammar-school children
about the decision behavior of their parents,
plus a mailed questionnaire, to ascertain the
parents' ideological commitment. As did
the authors of the previous two articles, she
matched couples having working wives
with couples of which the wife was not
working. There was no significant difference in the power scores of the matched
pairs.

As did the previous authors, she reported
data describing changes in role allocation
within the household: husbands taking
more part in the household activities and
making more routine decisions, wives taking less part and making fewer routine decisions.

Middleton and Putney (1960) found that
families with working wives were "significantly more patriarchal in decisions than
those in which the wife does not work, in
direct contradiction to findings of previous
studies" (p. 608). Middleton and Putney's
sample was small (40) and used a Strodtbeck discussion technique.

Blood, working over some of the data collected by the Detroit Area Study (1963),
found that the power of the wife concerning
the purchase of car, house, insurance does
increase with the wife's employment. Her
economic power increases, although not
necessarily her power in noneconomic areas.

The contradictions of these studies are
due in part to their reliance upon data of
uncertain validity. The data, further, are
often of low comparability, and the sample

sizes have been too small to permit the types of refined breakdown on class and ideological commitment that one might desire. Heer (1963) shows some of the conceptual refinements which are necessary in order to make the studies more meaningful.

Effects upon socialization. Before leaving the problem of the wife's employment, it is necessary to mention the impact of the working mother upon the socialization function of the nuclear family. A full discussion of the evidence is found in Chapter 18.

Nearly all of these studies bearing upon this problem begin with the question, more or less openly stated, of whether employment of the mother is "bad" for the children. Employment is seen as a factor which theoretically could disrupt the equilibrium of the parental system. The findings tend to show that what seems to matter most is the "contract" that husband and wife have with one another and with their children. This is a socio-cultural system which is behind the marriage and the assumption of parenthood. The wife-mother's employment secures its meaning from this contract, and from the conformity with the milieu in which the couple and its children have to live. The motivation of the wife, the more or less covert impact that the wife's employment has upon the masculine image of the father, the interpretation by the children of their mother's motivation for working, all have a far greater impact upon the socialization of the child and the authority distribution in the family than does the sheer absence or presence of the mother from home.

Employment can be a source not only of money but also of social contacts, which can be used for tension management, and of successes, which can be strengthening to the ego. As a result, certain marriages can be re-equilibrated by the wife's employment, especially when the interaction rate with the husband has declined for some reason (greater job commitment of the husband, increasing divergence of interests, departure of children). The wife's employment can be

part of a plan for social climbing, or it can be a recognition that the conjugal ties are not as successful a source of tension management as the wife anticipated. Employment then means achievement, contacts with other people, and lesser demands for stimulation upon the marriage. Often enough, a decline in demands decreases marital frustration and makes for a better equilibrium. On the other hand, the assumption of outside employment may signal the wife's abandonment of her marriage as a source of financial security and emotional support and the beginning of the road to divorce.

Must sociology abandon the struggle for generalities in the face of the many varieties of meaning that the wife's employment may have? Probably not, but the variables which must be isolated require a much finer breakdown into status groups and attitudes toward social mobility, the character dispositions of parents (see Heer, 1958), the neighborhood and the high-school subcultures, the incidence of peer grouping and steady dating (see Douvan, 1963), the age and sex of the children, and so forth. Hence, to isolate the significant variables, much larger samples are necessary than have been heretofore available, and this, in turn, may require a more integrated research approach than the dispersed and uncoordinated efforts of individual researchers and their small teams that have prevailed up to now.

The results secured so far have the merit of having lifted the problem out of the scope of social ethics. Research can now leave behind its preoccupation with the beneficial or harmful character of gainful employment by wife and mother.

Consumption Patterns

An interesting aspect of the relationship between the nuclear family and the economy is the one between consumption and authority structure. In the classical working-class family, the surplus of income over routine consumption was very small. The worker who conformed to the values of the "poor but honest" group would turn over practically all of his pay to his wife, retaining only some pocket money for a few rounds at the saloon, the pub, or the bistro. All purchases were made by the wife, who usually also made all the clothing for the family. Given the fact that the margin for error was small, precise management of income was indispensable. Within the home, the wife was the main authority, and, in fact, she exercised more executive functions in her role than the man ever had occasion to exercise in his roles, given his subordination in the occupational world. As mentioned previously, the masculine identification can be asserted only on an expressive level: femaleness and the home are somewhat devalued against maleness and the working man's club (saloon, pub, bistro). Tough talk, revolutionary ideology, militant trade-unionism, drinking bouts, occasional collective expeditions to the local house of prostitution, an occasional swat to the children and to the wife were the means whereby the men often recaptured some status superiority. Another way was to limit what the wife had to use as expense money and to increase the share given to the man's amusement, letting the wife scrounge as she might, including entering the labor market.

With the increase in take-home pay, there is an increase in standard of living, which in turn increases the entertainment valence of the home. The radio, the television, the larger spaces, all give the working man's home (apartment in Europe, detached house in the United States) a more middle-class appearance. The purchase of a house or a car, the purchase of household appliances, the increasing expenditure of money on consumer durables and insurance leads to an increasing participation of the husband in family budgeting. The sharp division between the man's world and the woman's world tends to break down, with the working man actually increasing his participation in home management. One might predict,

on a simple equilibrium model, that there is a decline in the pressure for the manifestation of masculinity on the expressive level, and a more equalitarian atmosphere in the home (see Moscovici, 1961).

The old pattern made the home a market-place where values from the feminine world were exchanged for values of the masculine world. The husbands lived in their peer group, which, in the working class, replaced the patrilineage. The women lived in the world of women, constituted by their neighbors, female relatives, but foremost by their own mothers (see Young & Willmott, 1957, pp. 9, 11, 28–56). Today, there is more cooperation within the marriage system. The children are no more sent to work at a tender age, either in factories or in home industries, and the relation of power which was functional to the taskmaster role is no longer necessary.

Labor power. According to the Parsonian model of functionalism, the nuclear family can be analyzed into four functional subsystems: economic, political, integrative, and pattern maintenance. For our purposes, it is primarily a motivational system specializing in socialization, tension management, and pattern maintenance. Its relationships with the economy can be described as an interchange which goes as follows: labor against purchasing power, and consumer spending against consumer goods. This involved the family in two major markets: the labor market and the retail market.

Following the input-output model of the relation between family and economy, one is led to one novel and fruitful conception: that it is not so much the individual that produces labor power as it is the nuclear family, and this becomes relevant the more disciplined and "alienated" (in the sense of complete separation of the work task from the family context, whether ecologically or in the irrelevance of the product of labor to the utility of the family) the labor becomes. The amount of labor a family can produce depends upon what energy it needs for the fulfillment of other role systems. The more effective it is as a center of tension management, the more it can produce alienated labor.

One of the major trends in factory work has been the growing alienation of labor and also the upgrading of the skill and responsibility required for the performance of factory work as compared with farm labor or the household industries not covered by traditional crafts, such as weaving or spinning. Hence, it would seem that the improvement of the nuclear family's capacity for producing tension reduction would be functional to the growing demand of industry for work units of reliable quality and quantity. If the isolated nuclear family is proven to be the social unit most capable of producing effective tension management, then one might say that industrialization reinforces the trend toward this form of family, especially among those groups which furnish labor of high skill and responsibility; conversely, the nuclear family is the only unit capable of furnishing the type of work needed by modern industry. The production of consumption goods which increase the capacity of the nuclear family to provide tension management, such as movies, radio, television, and leisure time, is also functional.

In turn, the isolation of the nuclear family and the improvement of its tension-management capacity, especially among lower-class families, permits a reinforcement of the economizing function in the retail market, due to the fact that the entertainment function of purchasing is less necessary as a factor of tension management for the wife (or for the Arab husband). Standardized service and single pricing are some of the economic gains that are immediately possible.

The labor market. Turning to the labor market, one finds that the requirements of the family for consumer goods are steady, honorable employment, which defines the instrumental function of the father-husband, and a stable flow of purchasing power. The

first was given by the various forms of farming, but not the second, in view of the vagaries of the weather, disease, and the uncertain levels of feudal exactions from the landlord.

The requirements of capitalistic industry are for a labor force which can at all times be kept at the level required by the marginal utility of labor, which itself is determined by the price the entrepreneur can secure in the market. For the rural instabilities of the weather and blight, capitalistic industries substitute the instability of the market: hence, it cannot guarantee honorable employment or a steady flow of purchasing power, although it can usually provide a higher return for hours of labor than farming could.

One institution which stabilizes employment to a certain extent is the city, which permits the working-class family to change employers without having to change home, school, and neighborhood. Other institutions which stabilized income were friendly societies, savings banks, and insurance schemes, sometimes sponsored by the state, by the city, or by the friendly societies themselves. The extension of consumer credit by retail stores was another; and, perhaps above all, so was the development *of the family firm* which committed itself to the maintenance of its workers on a relatively noncontingent basis. In return, the employees gave a broad work commitment and renounced discussion of wage rates and hours and comparisons between conditions made by the firm and its competitors. With the help of vegetable gardens attached to company housing and the short-week pattern in times of slack demand, the family firm was able to reduce considerably the uncertainty in the flow of purchasing power attendant on the fluctuations of the market economy. Since the Great Depression, the generalization of unemployment insurance and the stabilization of the business cycle through state intervention has made unnecessary the services provided by the family firm and the corner grocery store. (For the family firm in Japan, see Abegglen, 1958, Ch. 2.)

Family Farms and Firms

Another problem in the relations of the family with the economy is the fusion of the economic and family roles that one finds in the family farm and in the family firm at the executive levels. Although the farm or the firm as economic systems require role differentiation on the basis of economic rationality with affective neutrality, and allocation of roles on the basis of proven capacity only, the family has an ascriptive system of role allocations and operates on the basis of family rationality (that is, values which stress solidarity and respect and affection regardless of performance) in a climate of affectivity.

The fusion of these two role systems tends to result in a combination of both systems in their concrete expressions. The father, being an executive, keeps his relation to his children, and particularly to the sons who work with him, on a business level, somewhat cold and aloof, which permits him to supervise them and reward them according to their performance. On the other hand, the sons learn economic procedures, not as procedures which can be changed at will if they do not prove profitable, but as sacred instructions from their father. As such, challenging their efficacy is equivalent to challenging the legitimacy of their father's position as chief of the enterprise. Since his position is ascribed, his teachings are not challengeable, even if he should die. Furthermore, the family executive positions are not alterable by reasons of performance.

The fusion of firm and family, on the other hand, results in the harnessing of a powerful motivational system to the performance of economic action: work is not alienated, and large quantities of it are produced. Moreover, the techniques are traditional. Capital is economized with great celerity, since savings increase assets of the family in a tangible way. Whenever technology is stagnant, the economies of size limited, raw material expensive (as in the luxury trades), and hard work crucial, the family firm is a rather effective economic form. Otherwise, if the family firm has to compete with corporations, the distortion of role allocation and role differentiation by family rationality decreases the effectiveness and efficiency of the production unit and results in capital losses. (Weber pointed out the necessity of separating the household from the production unit if "the maximum rationality of capital accounting" were to be secured [1947, p. 277]).

It is interesting to note that, at the beginning of the extension of the factory system to the textile industry, the weavers and the spinners who had been working at home with their whole family, just as they would have worked a farm, merely moved the family to the factory and supervised the work of the wife and children there. Smelser (1959) showed how technological change led to a breakup of the family as a production unit and advanced the idea that this was at the root of the many worker disturbances that took place in the 1820's after the worst economic deprivation was past. Legal pressures for the departure of the children from the factory, followed by the married women, forced the development of the modern working-class family where the husband works far from his family during the day and has no more supervisory functions in the factory other than those assigned to him on the basis of skill. The shortening of the hours of work freed the adult employees for family activities, although at first these were more often peer-group than home activities for the husband.

THE NUCLEAR FAMILY AND THE POLITY

By polity is meant here those organizations that specialize in the production of political power, that mobilize motivational and nonmotivational resources for the attainment of societal ends, and that can use force to increase the required level of compliance by individuals or groups of individuals. In modern society, the polity is usually equivalent with the organisms of government. There has been comparatively little study of the relationship between the polity and the family, whether nuclear or extended.

Development of Central Authority

In patrilinear or matrilinear societies, the lineage acts as a political unit responsible for the compliance of its members with the decisions of the community executive. In the nuclear family, the father is responsible for the compliance of his wife and children; in Western societies, his legal responsibility is limited to financial obligations. In the United States, the father is held accountable only partially for damages his minor children may commit.

The feudal system was a political system which organized compliance by extending family types of loyalties into personal allegiance to a chief, who in turn had personal loyalties to a higher chief, until the highest authority, the king, received the personal commitment of the highest vassals. A main problem in this type of political organization is that a vassal can easily lead his own vassals into rebellion against the central authority, for the lower vassals know only their own lord as authority and focus of loyalty.

The development of central authority resulted from the generalization to the king of people's attachment to the church, which backed the king by giving him the endorsement of divine right, and also from the development of the urban centers, which tended to favor bilateral descent, guild loyalty, and the development of the town as a corporate entity. (Weber [1958] held that this did not occur in classical China, where the clans retained primary loyalty and where the geographical propinquity of urbanism did not result in the development of loyalties

capable of overriding lineage claims.) In feudal Europe, the town often developed against the lord's authority and implied rejection of all liege obligations except the more remote ducal or kingly authority: "town air made free."

In underdeveloped countries today, the striking aspect of the polity is that, just as in feudal Europe, the central authority is weak. Village elders reach an adjustment among themselves, or with their landlords, and the central government has hardly any impact upon local affairs (see Bailey, 1960). Conscription, which might rid the community of excess youth, may be better tolerated than orders which change the local economic and leadership patterns. (One of the major advantages that the Communist movement has in underdeveloped countries is that it is often the only effective form of long-range centralized political control in the area.) Taxation is not even very effective, unless it is indirect taxation, by which the contribution of the state in creating markets and a rational monetary system is in direct exchange for the sales tax or customs duties that are imposed.

The development of state authority over the nuclear family requires the setting up of a solidary collectivity at the level of the nation. The development of a common language, of money, of a legal system which can effectively protect the family against the oppression of local leadership and guarantee the right to move away from the local community, security against external enemies, the provision of employment—these are some of the contributions that the state must be able to make if it is to secure compliance with its orders from the nuclear families. State authority is more easily enforced if the nuclear family is not embedded in a lineage capable of providing aid and protection and able to muster much support for active resistance to this authority. In Western society, the upper classes are much more in this position than the middle and lower classes, but in mountain areas there are sections of modern society where the authority of the state over rural families is rather limited.

Revolutionary Governments and the Nuclear Family

The traditional form of the isolated nuclear family is not the most efficient organization conceivable for the production of economic wealth, since it prevents the specialization and full-scale utilization of female labor in factory employment. Hence, governments which wanted to create capital fast have tried to reduce the nuclear family to the minimum by restricting opportunities for marital interaction and cohabitation. They have transformed child care and food-processing into specialties devolving on a small number of women, while other women assume economic tasks traditionally reserved for men.

To a certain extent, this has been the policy of all Western societies at war and most systematically of the Hebrew kibbutz and the Chinese commune.

The ideology behind the Hebrew kibbutz seems to have been one of equalitarianism, not only on the economic and political levels but also on the sexual level. It aimed to free the Jewish woman from the bonds and restraints placed upon her by the classical Jewish tradition. As the charismatic appeal of the movement has declined, due partly to an increase in military security, the number of recruits lacking semireligious faith in the movement has increased. The complexity in the division of labor has increased, with greater pressures upon equalitarianism in the reward system and significant impact upon the self image of children. The claims of the nuclear family have grown, manifested by the increase in its role in residential upkeep and feeding (Vallier, 1961; Talmon-Garber, 1962).

An important aspect of the decline in psychic income accruing from the surrender of much family privacy in favor of the building of the kibbutz in Israel has been the decline of the prestige of the kibbutz.

Today, members are less often thought of as heroes and more often as country hicks (Talmon-Garber, personal communication, 1963). Talmon-Garber (1959) has described the kibbutz as originally formed to be a sort of primary group including both men and women, where the nuclear families eventually coagulated and became very powerful sources of loyalty, especially when the parent-child relationship, far from being weakened, became stronger. It might be added that the kibbutz at one time was the incarnation of the national state. Since the independence of Israel, this is less and less true. So, in between the national state and the nuclear family, the kibbutz becomes more like a community and less like a brotherhood.

In China the same movement was undertaken in order to break up the *Tsu* (the patrilinear clan loyalty), which would be superseded by loyalty to a community reorganized by the Communist party and to an exalted concept of the state. The commune has superseded the *Tsu* and taken over many of its covert functions such as helping the family in its wedding or funeral arrangements, coping with financial emergencies, schooling, and the like; and through community dining halls it takes care of the basic food needs of the family. Thus, a considerable amount of woman power is freed for the mechanized labor which in our society is being displaced by automation. The woman is freed from subjection and from the necessity of combining work in the fields or factory and work at home. In this system she would seem to be, as in Soviet Russia, at a definite advantage. As a matter of fact, both in the Soviet Union and in China, what seems to have been a condition for economic revolution and for the massive development of the factory system is a change in the family system which freed the woman from much home drudgery (the Russian scarcity of living space and furniture) and from the care of small children through the organization of state nurseries (cf. Yang, 1959).

In nineteenth-century Europe, this freedom was often secured by the nuclear family boarding its children from a very tender age in farming homes, which made such care a sort of home industry. The preservation of the classical family model as the ideal, however, probably reduced the amount of woman power available to industry and decreased the rate of capitalization by compelling the firm to pay wages to the husband which could keep alive not only himself but also his non-productive wife and children.

Under conditions of revolutionary fervor and of charismatic group formation, the nuclear family can be considerably distended. Psychic income is derived from the *bund* and from identification with the omnipotent state. This is especially true for the young adults. The movement prolongs adolescence and gives women a taste of freedom. As the charismatic appeal wanes, as the state wishes to increase the birth rate (somewhat jeopardized by the distention of the nuclear family), it has to strike a new bargain with the family. If the previous analysis of the organic, psychological, and structural roots of women's needs is correct, the new power and prestige of women should be used to promote the interest of the nuclear family and insist on a greater amount of privatization.

In periods of high-speed social change, the state undermines all agencies of social control which can compete with it as centers of loyalty, including the nuclear family: it accepts disorder through promiscuous sexuality and private aggression in order to maximize control of the production of work and of the weapons of mass warfare.

This, in fact, was the position of the Soviet Union in the period of war communism from 1919 to 1922 and to a lesser degree up to 1934. The state had encouraged easy divorce and common-law marriage. This was in line with the ideological reaction against the bourgeois family and had great appeal to the lower class in view of the fact that it legitimated the pattern which many lower-class individuals practiced as it were out of necessity.

Timasheff (1946) has outlined well the dysfunctional results of such a policy especially as far as the birth rate is concerned. When the state is not able to replace the socialization function of the nuclear family, and it is unlikely to be able to do so on any large scale, the weakening of the nuclear family results in the multiplication of psychopathic types of children who grow up to become threats to society. There are strong signs that the nuclear family, both in the marriage and parenthood systems, is increasing its strength as a center of loyalty, socialization, and tension management. Indices of this trend would be a more insistent demand for housing and consumer durables, and the development of romantic love as a theme in literature (cf. Dunham, 1960). Russian life is becoming more "privatized."

Youth Movements as Socialization Agencies

Another attack upon the family as a center of loyalty is made through the development of youth movements which utilize the adolescent rebellion inherent in the socialization process. They legitimate and thereby increase rebellion, only to drain it by utilizing youth organizations as shock troops in the promotion of new social patterns.

The youth organizations do help the family in its socialization functions, by promoting independence from parental ties and by providing entertainment and tension release. They also deflect adolescent rebellion aimed at the parents.

On the other hand, the organizations force the parents, insofar as they do not want the deflected aggression to fall back with renewed vigor upon them, to increase their conformity to the state. In order to maintain the nuclear family as a center of tension reduction, the parents find themselves pressured to follow the political en-

thusiasm of their children, or at least not
to oppose it.

In families deeply embedded in the network of extended kin, such as are common
in the upper class, resistance to the state's
pressure through children is high, partly
because the child knows that his standing
in life is more likely to depend upon his
family's standing and particularistic network than upon his performance in youth
organizations. In the isolated nuclear families of urban centers, the state's pressure is
maximal—partly, as Geiger (1956) pointed
out, because success in Soviet Russia
depends upon economic opportunities controlled by the state, which uses these opportunities, as much as possible, to reward
conformity with its ideology. The decline of
political pressure might give the Soviet
Golden Youth some opportunity to escape,
all the more if their parents have built good
networks of *blat* (pull).

In societies where the government is essentially conservative in terms of social
structure, youth movements tend to be radical either in the left-wing or right-wing direction. University and even high-school
adolescents who are reasonably well adjusted in their families follow the opinions
of their parents just as in the United States
(see Maccoby et al., 1954), but give them a
radical twist. Those who are poorly adjusted embrace radical versions of opinions
opposite to their parents'. Where the society is not highly politicized, as in the
United States, adolescent rebellion finds
other channels, except in those comparatively few families where politics is an important focus of interest.

Privacy Needs of the Family

The crucial need of the nuclear family, if
the latter is to perform its tension-reduction
function adequately, is privacy. This provides a guarantee that whatever behavior
takes place within the home is, within broad
limits, immune from public sanctions imposed by the state. As long as no member

of the family brings the complaint to the
state, the state does not endeavor to prosecute. Given the weakness and ignorance of
children, mistreatment of the latter by parents goes unpunished unless neighbors or
school authorities complain to the state
authorities. In these situations, the state
finds itself caught in a dilemma: on the one
hand, each family has its punishment subculture, so that physical punishment which
might upset New England Protestants
seems quite effective and legitimate to a
family of Sicilian immigrants; on the other
hand, if the state interferes in the administration of parental punishment, it runs the
risk of destroying a parental authority it is
not capable of replacing, with consequences
that may be worse than those of "excessive
punishment."

The same analysis applies to the level of
care that is given by parents to children.
The state prefers to help out indirectly by
school lunch programs. Social-work agencies
substitute to some extent for an absent
father and guide a mother in the promotion
of proper care standards. Often the presence
of the husband creates severe problems between social agencies and the family, because of the implicit attack on the family's
privacy and the father's competence. In the
same way, the state prohibits intrusion by
third parties into the home through wire-
tapping and the utilization of private knowledge for purposes of blackmail. In defending the privacy of the home, the state
imposes upon itself restraints similar to
those which guarantee the medical, legal,
religious, and even social-work professions
the right of privileged communication—and
for essentially the same reasons.

Many of the laws regulating private behavior are symbolic of value commitment,
and their efficacy is mainly that of inducing
guilt in the personalities of participants. As
long as public peace is maintained, the state
cannot prosecute without creating more disorder than order. The state uses its prestige
to bind marriages; it serves, with the
church, as a witness of the commitment

that spouses make to one another. Through its divorce laws, it permits, under certain conditions, and at the cost at times of harrowing and humiliating procedures, the undoing of the marriage. There are limits to the extent laws can interfere with the private customs of families. Le Play (1864) ascribed to the equalitarian inheritance laws of the French Revolution the breakup of the *famille souche,* but modern evidence (Roussiers, 1934) showed that the practice of primogeniture had largely disappeared even in noble families at the time of the French Revolution. Laws which violate common mores can make it easier for the alienated and/or "progressive" to call upon the state to enforce rights that the mores refuse them. In the midst of the subcultures and ideologies serving to neutralize the pains of low achievement, laws must clarify what the dominant norms are so as to increase their pressure upon superego constituents in the personality and give weapons to those who desire to maintain higher levels of conformity or promote state policy.

The state contributes to the definition of the masculine and feminine roles by encouraging the involvement of men and women in political activities which are in resonance with their activities in the nuclear family. Men concern themselves with labor issues, national and international affairs; women concern themselves with schools and community affairs which relate to the immediate socialization problems met by the nuclear family. In European countries, this division of political labor is more difficult, simply because the state controls education, and community administration is more directly controlled by the high-prestige national civil service.

There seems to be a relationship between the extension of suffrage to women and the development of the equalitarian family; its titular head is no longer able to mediate to the state the interest of women *qua* women. Feminine suffrage recognizes the separate identity of women outside of marriage ties. By guaranteeing this identity, it makes the marriage a more effective free contract, especially when the matrix of past custom is to subordinate the woman to her parents or to her in-laws.

In return for this suffrage, the wife-mother has to accept willingly the discomfort that citizen duties may entail. In return for a more positive valuation of femininity as against masculinity, she is duty-bound to show more spartan fervor. The woman who votes must not detain the warrior or complain if the state manufactures guns rather than washing machines.

An interesting question is raised by the problem of the teenage vote. By restricting voting to those 21 or older, the state underwrites the dependency of the adolescent upon his family and, more crucial, implies that there are no *legitimate* adolescent interests which cannot be satisfactorily mediated to the polity by his parents. In the matter of schools or constructive leisure opportunities for the adolescent who is neither a "jock" nor an intellectual athlete, this may be debatable. Some lower-class "juvenile delinquency," which in middle-class youth may be called "high spirits," may be a response to this breakdown in communication between the adolescent and the adult world.

THE FAMILY
AND THE MOTIVATIONAL SYSTEM

Previous sections of this chapter have concentrated upon the relations of the nuclear family with the integrative, economic, and political systems of the total society. The following pages analyze the relations of the nuclear family to some organizations having motivational primacy, that is, which concentrate on socialization and/or tension management, such as the school, the church, the doctor-patient relationship, and the practice of prostitution.

The Nuclear Family and the School

The school is the first organization in which the child has to work in order to receive praise. In order for him to be able to work, the family must have developed in the child certain psychological structures which permit him to manipulate his body as a tool rather than as a source of pleasure, and to manipulate symbols—letters and numbers—in an effectively neutral way. How much reading and number readiness is a result of identification processes and how much is a result of the unfolding of conflict-free aspects of the ego (genetic intelligence) is not known. What is likely, however, is that the family structure, the presence of a positive father figure, the level of anxiety, uncertainty, role reliability, and verbalization that the child encounters in the first four or five years of his life have great importance for his performance in the first grades of school (cf. M. P. Deutsch, 1960). The social-class differential in learning performance is not likely to be explained by genetic selection.

Another important relationship between the family and the school is the need for cultural congruence. Families who do not back up the school are less likely to facilitate the performance of their children; and they are less likely to back it up if the inner culture of the family and the culture of the school are too divergent. The Great Cities Project of the Ford Foundation is predicated on this assumption, and it attempts to increase parental support of the school and the cultural levels of lower-class children and simultaneously of their families.

Another interesting aspect of the relationship between school and family is the level of achievement pressure that the school places upon the child.

The American school system is, much more than the European school system, a "total institution," that is, it involves a greater commitment of the child. Partly because of its mixture of permissiveness and pressure for achievement (which parallels the mother's role) and partly because of its legitimation of the peer group and of the peer group's integration to the school (school senate, hall guards, clubs, competitive sports), the level of achievement pressure is extremely high—though it may not be the type of academic achievement French students are accustomed to strive for. On the other hand, the American high school provides more types of student careers than the purely academic one, and the peer group, instead of being purely tension-reducing, as in France, is much more involved in achievement and in training the student in its particular type of "competitive solidarity." This eventually expresses itself in rigidly segregated sororities or fraternities or their informal equivalent. The emotional "rinsing out" which the American child can experience in his school is quite different from the limited commitment and the highly delinquent peer group (in verbal fantasy) that the French child experiences in his.

Hence, the American family must be much more tension-reducing than the equivalent French family. The American family does this by increasing its primary-group component to the detriment of its "bureaucratic dimension." The type of socialization pressure meted out by the American father and mother is, in total, less demanding, much more tolerant, and much more supportive than in the French, Italian, German, or Dutch family—which is not to say that it requires less "work" on the part of the American parents.

Finally, all school systems exchange, in return for the parents' endorsement of their cultural mission, a generalized support for the legitimacy of parental authority. Through all sorts of cues, the school reminds the child of his parents' supreme responsibility for him, and of his own responsibility to them. The child works at school for his family of orientation, just as in the future he will work for his family of procreation.

The Family and the Church

Just as the sociology of folklore is rather good at describing some of the functions of prostitution or of the "office wife," it is also sensitive to the functions of the church as providing the crucial rites of passage for the family (baptism, confirmation or first communion, wedding, funeral) and in helping the socialization of the children and the emotional equilibrium of the wife.

It might simply be added that the significance of ritual here resides in its irrational character. Through ritual, the church gives an ascriptive quality to the new roles that are being entered into. Its contact with the highest values legitimizes changes in status, makes the continuance of each status largely independent of actual performance, and makes it clear that regression to old patterns is blocked forever. In the same way that the state as representative of social order takes official cognizance of the marriage vows, of the birth of children, and of the departure of a citizen from this world, the church, as representative of moral commitment, also registers, witnesses, and pledges itself to assist its parishioners in carrying out their family duties.

In Catholic countries, the church played an important role in extolling the importance of chastity and of obedience to parents, and these were useful in permitting the control of girls for the marriage policy of the family. In most Catholic churches except those of Germany and the United States, church attendance is mainly that of women, girls, prepubertal boys, and the elderly (upper-middle-class and upper-class males have a higher rate of attendance than males of other classes, either out of conviction or out of civic duty). Even in Protestant churches, while the male-female differential is lower than in Catholic countries, it is substantial.

In either Protestant or Catholic countries, prior to the acceptance of female employment by the middle class, the unmarried women or the widows stayed close to the church's shadow so as to certify to their continued chastity. Christianity has given a peculiar merit to chastity; and to the extent that it reinforced successfully the pa-

rental teachings, it actually permitted women more mobility and social participation, since the internalization of the norms rendered chaperonage less necessary. This was all the more possible when Protestantism demanded high chastity for men and reduced the pressures upon the unaccompanied girl. European travelers at the time of the American Revolution marveled at the freedom that could be allowed young Yankee girls without any fear of untoward consequences.

It is interesting to note that Sunday school is accepted by most middle-class-oriented families as an obligation, even when they have few or any conscious religious convictions. There is, of course, the conspicuous-consumption component, but this is not sufficient to explain the continued interest in Sunday school. Even in countries where a high percentage of the working-class and lower white-collar group vote Communist and affect atheistic views, many allow their children to receive instructions in catechism. What, then, is the contribution of the church to the socialization of children? This question does not imply that any of these contributions (functions) is a "reason" for letting the children attend.

The contribution of the church is to reinforce parental dominance over the children. First, like the regular school system, it endorses parental authority. Second, by displacing the pre-oedipal image of the parents onto God (God and the Virgin in Catholic countries), it provides a source of unconditional support for the child in the latency stage, at a time when he discovers the conditionality of his parents' love and is under severe school pressure.

Furthermore, the concept of God decreases the demands of the child for perfection and omnipotence in his parents. It is easier to forgive them their weaknesses and their injustices, since only God is perfect, so that the authority of the parents withers slowly rather than crumbling prematurely with the discovery that the parental idols have feet of clay. By making children and parents equal in front of God and established values, it tends to prevent a premature disenchantment which might alienate the child from these values.

In the Soviet Union, now that the regime is consolidated, the youth organizations, which among other functions are equivalent to Sunday school, teach the children obedience to their parents for the greater glory of the Communist society.

The church also contributes to the family by taking the sting out of failure in this world. By so doing, it reinforces the structure of the "closed markets" and helps each mate to accept the other's deficiencies in living up to the latent marriage contract. By stressing and rewarding motivational conformity ("giving oneself to God") rather than actual wordly success in implementing values, the church reduces the sting of failure and prevents the latter from threatening the commitment of the faithful to values. In learning-theory terms, the church tries to prevent the lack of "reinforcement" from extinguishing conformity.

Furthermore, Christianity enables those who have to do the most adjustment in the family, the women, to gain a special ethical dignity because of their forbearance. The feminine values of meekness, charity, and pity were given much higher standing in the Christian ethos than previously. Religious women accept more easily frustrations in their marital life that would lead others to overt counteraggression. By raising the ethical dignity of women, Christianity promotes the trend toward equality. American Protestantism has gone further in this direction and in fact has succeeded in convincing American men that women, independently of their role as mothers, are more moral than men.

The Doctor-Patient Relationship

Parsons and Fox (1952) have described the relationship between the American pattern of hospitalization and the nuclear family. The hospital isolates the medical deviant from his family, prevents secondary gain, and reduces the emotional burden on the nuclear family.

At the present time, the doctor-patient relationship seems to be an important structural complement to the isolated nuclear family. It relieves this isolation in a way which preserves more of the autonomy of the family than would be the case if the trust and confiding that are usual features of the doctor-patient relationship were transferred to the extended family network. For many working and middle-class families, the doctor, basing himself on the "magic" of science, has taken on much of the role of the minister. For a certain percentage of middle-class families (probably overisolated), the psychiatric social worker, the clinical psychologist, the psychiatrist, the psychoanalyst have become the omniscient "dutch uncles" that help them to confront their experiences of reality and reduce tensions that are beyond the capacity of the nuclear family. The overisolation may have been caused by characteristics of the component personalities but also by mobility away from the parental ethnic culture and/or social class.

It is interesting in this context to note the recent complaints about the growing office-centeredness and impersonality of medical practice. The patients seem to be referring to a relative deprivation from a transference situation which had given to the American doctor a prestige probably unequaled in the Western world.

The Nuclear Family and Prostitution

As Davis (1937; 1961) has so well shown, there is a functional relationship between the existence of the nuclear family in stratified society and the existence of prostitution. It was seen at the beginning of this chapter that the easily triggered sexuality of man and the all-season availability of woman was a powerful force in making for stable male and female relationships in human societies. Marriage eliminates women from being an object of contention between men and makes sexual release for the male conditional on his accepting responsibility for the husband and father roles. As Davis pointed out, it is the fact that sex is the reinforcer of nonsexual ends that makes the disappearance of prostitution very unlikely in any complex society; what *would* do away with prostitution (sex for money) is a conception of sex as needing no more justification than temporary pleasure, but this also would do away with marriage (sex for maintenance, protection, and collaboration in parenthood). A desacralization of sex would also make more problematical the maintenance of the incest taboo.

Besides these general factors, Davis mentioned as basic "causes" of prostitution "the unequal scale of attractiveness"—the unattractive male has to offer special inducements in order to secure sexual satisfaction —and "social inequality between classes and between male and female." Thus, women use sex—the desire of men for coitus—as a means of securing the rewards that men have to give; in other words, there is a little bit of the prostitute in every woman.

The functional advantage of prostitution as an institution is that it permits a relatively small number of women to take upon themselves the opprobrium and to serve the sexual and other psychological needs of those many men who cannot be satisfied by regular institutionalized means. In the Western world, these needs have been highest when men have postponed marriage until their late twenties in order to better their position in the marriage market; when there is a substantial number of men who must forgo marriage so as to permit a brother a better marriage; when the working man cannot attain access to some of the feminine esthetic values through an overburdened, tired, and poverty-ridden wife, and finds that the house of prostitution is the only place where a brief contact with softness and charm is possible; when sexual access to unmarried women is severely restricted; when sexual prowess is highly valued as a sign of masculinity; and when sexual unresponsiveness on the part of wives is seen as a sign of their special virtue. These conditions were classically those of the nineteenth century in the urban Western world.

A certain amount of the demand for prostitutes' services has declined with the decline of the Victorian respect for frigidity in wives, the decline in the age of marriage, the disappearance of the chronic bachelor population, the inclusion of the beauty parlor in the working-class wife's budget, and the greater sexual accessibility of unmarried women. Last but not least, there has been a decline in certain countries of the Western world of the valuation of sexual prowess as the major badge of masculinity, often under the impact of a renewed Catholicism in the upper and middle classes. In Protestant countries, there was usually less stress upon sexual prowess as a particular source of prestige, especially among the middle classes.

An interesting aspect of prostitution is that of the *geisha type,* where much of the commodity transacted is not sexual release but a high grade of entertainment and tension reduction. The geisha of Japan, or the party girl in America, or the demi-mondaine of France (the role "Gigi" was being groomed for), specializes in a combination of sex and companionship aimed at uppermiddle and upper-class consumption. In fact, the prestige of the prostitute increases as she increases the amount of nonsexual interaction that accompanies the purely sexual acts; that is, as she increases the primary character of the relationship.

Davis has mentioned the functional relationship between the need for a peer type of interaction with women and the development of a class of sophisticated prostitutes of the geisha variety, when the wives are made incapable of such interaction by the limitation of their experience and their formal education. In the Western world, this limitation of the wife's experience is largely a thing of the past, especially in the middle class and in the middle-class-oriented working class. However, there are certain drawbacks to communication in the marital relationship which tend to create a tension-management deficit in the *higher reaches of the occupational world*. These are due to the complex nature of decision-making and the difficulty of communicating problems to a person who, however well educated, does not know the basic elements of the problems. Also, the inability or unwillingness of the husband to communicate may be due to his fear of destroying the omnipotent image he has come to depend upon in his relations with his wife. He is afraid to weaken the structure of this closed market by inviting comparisons with others, perhaps more successful or less prone to error.

Under these circumstances, the husband may be in the market for a type of relationship which starts at a lower level of value commitment. The secretary, for instance, is in a sense a greater connoisseur of business values than is the housewife, just as the nurse is a greater connoisseur of medical values. Support from such connoisseurs in these areas has more tension-reduction value than the automatic support of the wife. Furthermore, through his position of authority, the man insures the likelihood of a favorable judgment, not so much through a form of bootlicking, but through the normal identification that women employees tend to develop toward their employers. By initiating an illicit sexual relationship with the secretary, for instance, the employer disvalues her, and for this reason can afford to reveal himself more intimately and secure support regardless of his business or sexual sins. He also makes more certain that the support he receives does not go as much to his status as to his personality. Employer and secretary become "partners in sin."

The interesting aspect of these relationships is that they may not go as far as adultery. But the wife knows very well that the relationship of the secretary with her husband, all the more if she is young and pretty, can seldom be "innocent." The term "office wife" covers most of the meanings described here.

American society, in order to protect the isolated conjugal family, makes it very difficult for a man to have meaningful social contacts with women after he is married. The world of work is the only place where these contacts are legitimate, and this is very likely the locus of American adultery, whether effective or subliminal.

To a certain extent, the world of work provides some isolation to the adulterous pattern and prevents it from having too much impact on the world of home. On the other hand, there is very likely an equilibrium between the level of tension reduction the husband secures at home and the level he secures at the office. The reader can draw the functional consequences for himself.

What of the wives, left at home or "taken for granted"? Some, of course, participate in the world of work and share in the more or less subliminal adultery pattern. If Freudian psychology has described the characteristics of the female personality adequately, one must draw the conclusion that the attachment to the father is never as completely resolved in the woman's personality as is the attachment to the mother in the man's. Hence, omnipotent authority has a tension-reducing meaning for wives that it cannot normally have for husbands, because of the castrating threat implied to men by such power. This kind of omnipotent authority figure has all the more tension-reduction valence if the incest taboo is respected: the priest, the doctor, and even the employer can be the ideal incarnations of the father figure. They reduce certain tensions that a more equalitarian marriage pattern cannot cope with.

The modern American family has to cope with a longer post-parental period than has been the case in the past, at a time when the middle-class husband is likely to be most intently committed to his occupation. The problem for the wife is to maintain emotional equilibrium and communication with her husband when the children are no more a common "work" problem. Certainly, the development of occupations which utilize the nurturant and expressive capacities of women are one answer, and the world of work is seeing a growing number of middle-aged women returning to or entering the labor force. The university is also likely to see a growing number of these returnees, especially in the United States, where the university seems to be emerging as the Cathedral of modern times.

REFERENCES

Abegglen, J. G. *The Japanese factory.* Glencoe, Ill.: Free Press, 1958. Pp. 11–25.

Aberle, D. Matrilinear descent in cross-cultural perspective. In D. M. Schneider & E. K. Gough (Eds.), *Matrilineal kinship.* Berkeley: Univer. of California Press, 1961.

Aberle, D., & Naegele, K. Middle-class fathers' occupational roles and attitudes toward children. *Amer. J. Orthopsychiat.,* 1952, 22, 366–378.

Amsel, A. Frustrative nonreward in partial reinforcement and discrimination learning: some recent history and a theoretical extension. *Psychol. Rev.,* 1962, 69, 306–328.

Apple, D. The social structure of grandparenthood. *Amer. Anthropologist,* 1956, 58, 656–663.

Arensburg, C. M., & Kimball, S. T. *Family and community in Ireland.* Cambridge: Harvard Univer. Press, 1940.

Babchuk, N., & Bates, A. P. The primary relations of middle-class couples: a study in role dominance. *Amer. sociol. Rev.,* 1963, 28, 377–384.

Bailey, F. W. *Tribe, caste and nation.* Manchester: Manchester Univer. Press, 1960.

Bakke, E. W. *The unemployed worker.* New Haven: Yale Univer. Press, 1940.

Bales, R. F., & Slater, P. E. Role Differentiation in small decision-making groups. In T. Parsons & R. F. Bales, with M. Zelditch, Jr., J. Olds, & P. Slater, *Family, socialization and interaction process.* Glencoe, Ill.: Free Press, 1955. Pp. 259–306.

Bell, N., & Vogel, E. *A modern introduction to the family.* Glencoe, Ill.: Free Press, 1960.

Bellah, R. N. *Tokugawa religion.* Glencoe, Ill.: Free Press, 1957.

Benedek, T. *Psychosexual functions in women.* New York: Ronald Press, 1952.

Berent, J. The relationship between family sizes of two successive generations, *Milbank mem. fund Quart.,* 1953, 31, 39–50.

Bergen, B. J. Comment. *Amer. J. Sociol.,* 1961, 67, 308–311.

Blake, Judith. Family instability and reproductive behavior in Jamaica. In Milbank Memorial Fund, *Current research in human fertility.* New York: Author, 1955. Pp. 24–41.

Blake, Judith. *Family structure in Jamaica.* New York: Free Press, 1961.

Bloch, H., & Niederhoffer, A. *The gang.* New York: Philosophical Library, 1958.

Blond, G. *The great story of whales.* Trans. J. Cleugh. Garden City, N.Y.: Hanover, 1955.

Blood, R. O. The husband-wife relationship. In F. I. Nye & Lois W. Hoffman, *The employed mother in America.* Chicago: Rand McNally, 1963. Pp. 282–305.

Blood, R. O., & Hamblin, R. L. The effect of the wife's employment on the family power structure. *Soc. Forces,* 1958, 36, 347–352.

Blood, R. O., & Wolfe, D. M. *Husbands and wives: the dynamics of married living.* Glencoe, Ill.: Free Press, 1960.

Bossard, J. *The sociology of child development.* New York: Harper, 1954.

Bossard, J., & Boll, Eleanor. *Ritual in family living.* Philadelphia: Univer. of Pennsylvania Press, 1950.

Bott, Elizabeth. *Family and social network.* London: Tavistock, 1957.

Bowlby, J. *Child care and the growth of love.* Ed. Marjory Fry. London: Penguin, 1953.

Braithwaite, L. Social stratification in Trinidad. *Soc. & econ. Stud.,* 1953, 2, 5–175.

Braithwaite, L. Sociology and demographic research in the British Caribbean. *Soc. & econ. Stud.,* 1957, 6, 523–571.

Brim, O. G. Family structure and sex role learning by children: a further analysis of Helen Koch's data. *Sociometry,* 1958, 21, 1–16.

Burgess, E. W., & Wallin, P. *Engagement and marriage.* Philadelphia: Lippincott, 1953.

Cannon, W. B. *The wisdom of the body*. New York: Norton, 1939.

Cavan, Ruth S., & Ranck, Katherine H. *The family and the depression*. Chicago: Univer. of Chicago Press, 1938.

Christensen, H., & Carpenter, G. R. Value behavior discrepancies in premarital coitus. *Amer. sociol. Rev.*, 1962, 27, 66–74.

Christensen, H., & Meissner, Hanna H. Studies in child spacing: III, premarital pregnancy as a factor in divorce. *Amer. sociol. Rev.*, 1953, 18, 641–644.

Cohen, A. K. *Delinquent boys*. Glencoe, Ill.: Free Press, 1955.

Collver, A. The family cycle in India and the United States. *Amer. sociol. Rev.*, 1963, 28, 86–96.

Cumming, Elaine, & Schneider, D. M. Sibling solidarity: a property of American kinship. *Amer. Anthropologist*, 1961, 63, 498–507.

Davis, K. Jealousy and sexual property. *Soc. Forces*, 1936, 19, 395–405.

Davis, K. The sociology of prostitution. *Amer. sociol. Rev.*, 1937, 2, 744–755.

Davis, K. Illegitimacy and the social structure. *Amer. J. Sociol.*, 1939, 45, 215–233. (a)

Davis, K. The forms of illegitimacy. *Soc. Forces*, 1939, 18, 77–89. (b)

Davis, K. Extreme isolation of a child. *Amer. J. Sociol.*, 1940, 45, 564–574. (a)

Davis, K. The sociology of parent-youth conflict. *Amer. sociol. Rev.*, 1940, 5, 523–535. (b)

Davis, K. Final note on a case of extreme isolation. *Amer. J. Sociol.*, 1947, 50, 432–437.

Davis, K. *Human society*. New York: Macmillan, 1949.

Davis, K. The myth of functional analysis. *Amer. sociol. Rev.*, 1959, 24, 757–772.

Davis, K. Prostitution. In R. K. Merton & R. A. Nisbet (Eds.), *Contemporary social problems*. New York: Harcourt, Brace, & World, 1961. Pp. 262–288.

Davis, K., & Blake, Judith. Social structure and fertility: an analytical framework. *Econ. Develpm. & cult. Change*, 1956, 16, 211–235.

Dennis, W., & Najarian, P. Infant development under environmental handicaps. *Psychol. Monogr.*, 1957, 71, No. 7 (Whole No. 436).

Deutsch, Helene. *The psychology of women*. New York: Grune & Stratton, 1944–1945.

Deutsch, M. P. Minority groups and class status as related to social and personality factors in scholastic achievement. *Monogr. No. 2*. Ithaca, N.Y.: Society for Applied Anthropology, 1960.

Dodson, F. Patterns of voluntary association among urban working class families. *Amer. sociol. Rev.*, 1951, 16, 681–693.

Dore, R. P. Function and cause. *Amer. sociol. Rev.*, 1961, 26, 843–853.

Douvan, Elizabeth. Employment and the adolescent. In F. I. Nye & Lois W. Hoffman, *The employed mother in America*. Chicago: Rand McNally, 1963. Pp. 142–164.

Dunham, V. Eros in contemporary Russian poetry. *Soc. Probl.*, 1960, 7, 339–351.

Durkheim, E. *The rules of sociological method*. (8th ed.) Trans. Sarah A. Solovay & J. H. Mueller. Chicago: Univer. of Chicago Press, 1938.

Elkin, F., & Westley, W. A. The myth of adolescent culture. *Amer. sociol. Rev.*, 1957, 20, 680–684.

Erikson, E. H. *Childhood and society*. New York: Norton, 1950.

Fellin, P., & Litwak, E. Neighborhood cohesion and mobility. *Amer. sociol. Rev.*, 1963, 28, 364–367.

Fortes, M. *The web of kinship in the Tallensi*. London: Paul, 1949.

Fougeyrollas, P. Prédominance du mari ou de la femme dans le ménage. *Population*, 1951, 6, 83–102.

Freud, Anna. *The ego and the mechanisms of defense*. London: Hogarth, 1945.

Freud, S. *A general introduction to psychoanalysis*. New York: Liveright, 1920.

Freud, S. The passing of the oedipus complex. In *Collected papers*. Vol. 2. London: Hogarth, 1924.

Freud, S. *The ego and the id*. London: Hogarth, 1927.

Gamble, S. D. *Ting Hsien, a north China rural community*. New York: Institute of Pacific Relations, 1954.

Geiger, K. Changing political attitudes in totalitarian society: a case study of the role of the family. *World Pol.*, 1956, 8, 187–205.

Glick, P. *American families*. New York: Wiley, 1957.

Gold, M., & Slater, C. Office, factory, store— and family: a study of integration setting. *Amer. sociol. Rev.*, 1958, 23, 64–74.

Goldfarb, W. Effects of psychological deprivation in infancy and subsequent stimulation. *Amer. J. Psychol.*, 1945, 102, 18–33.

Goode, W. J. *After divorce.* Glencoe, Ill.: Free Press, 1956.

Goode, W. J. The theoretical importance of love. *Amer. sociol. Rev.*, 1959, 24, 38–47.

Goode, W. J. Illegitimacy in the Caribbean social structure. *Amer. sociol. Rev.*, 1960, 25, 21–30. (a)

Goode, W. J. *Die Strucktur der Familie.* Cologne: Westdeutscher Verlag, 1960. (b)

Goode, W. J. Family disorganization. In R. K. Merton & R. A. Nisbet (Eds.), *Contemporary social problems.* New York: Harcourt, Brace, & World, 1961. Pp. 390–458. (a)

Goode, W. J. Illegitimacy, anomie, and cultural penetration. *Amer. sociol. Rev.*, 1961, 26, 910–925. (b)

Goode, W. J. *World revolution and family patterns.* New York: Macmillan, 1963.

Goody, J. *Death, property, and the ancestors.* Stanford, Calif.: Stanford Univer. Press, 1962.

Gore, M. S. The husband-wife and mother-son relationships. *Sociol. Bull.*, 1962, 1–2, 91–102.

Gough, E. Kathleen. The Nayars and the definition of marriage. *J. royal anthropol. Inst.*, 1959, 89, 23–34.

Gouldner, A. W. Reciprocity and autonomy in functional theory. In L. Gross (Ed.), *Symposium on Sociological Theory.* Evanston, Ill.: Row, Peterson, 1959. Pp. 241–270.

Gray, R. F. Singo bride price and the question of the African wife purchase. *Amer. Anthropologist*, 1960, 62, 54–57.

Gray, R. N., & Smith, T. C. Effect of employment on sex differences in attitude toward the parental family. *Marr. & fam. Living*, 1960, 22, 36–38.

Green, A. The "cult of personality" and sexual relations. *Psychiatry*, 1941, 4, 344–348.

Greenfield, S. Industrialization and the family in sociological theory. *Amer. J. Sociol.*, 1961, 67, 312–322.

Hanson, F. M., & Rock, J. Effect of adoption on fertility and other reproductive organs. *Amer. J. Obst. & Gyn.*, 1950, 59, 311–320.

Hebb, D. O. *The organization of behavior: a neuropsychological theory.* New York: Wiley, 1949.

Hebb, D. O. Drives and the C.N.S. *Psychol. Rev.*, 1955, 67, 243–254.

Heer, D. M. Dominance and the working wife. *Soc. Forces*, 1958, 36, 341–347.

Heer, D. M. The measurement and basis of family power. *Marr & fam. Living*, 1963, 25, 133–139.

Heinicke, C. M. Some effects of separating two-year-old children from their parents: a comparative study. *Hum. Relat.*, 1956, 9, 105–176.

Henriques, F. *Family and colour in Jamaica.* London: Eyre & Spottiswoode, 1953.

Herskovits, M. J. A note on "woman marriage" in Dahomey. *Africa*, 1937, 10, 335–341.

Hill, R. Sociology of marriage and family behavior, 1945–56. *Current Sociol.*, 1958, 7, 1–41.

Hill, R., & Hansen, D. The identification of conceptual frameworks utilized in family study. *Marr. & fam. Living*, 1960, 22, 299–311.

Hoffman, Lois W. Mother's employment and effects on the child. *Child Develpm.*, 1961, 32, 187–197.

Hoffman, Lois W. Parental power relations and the division of household tasks. *Marr. & fam. Living*, 1960, 22, 27–35.

Hollingshead, A. B. Marital status and wedding behavior. *Marr. & fam. Living*, 1952, 14, 308–311.

Homans, G. C. *The human group.* New York: Harcourt, Brace, 1950.

Homans, G. C., & Schneider, D. M. *Marriage, authority and final causes.* Glencoe, Ill.: Free Press, 1955.

Huang, L. J. A re-evaluation of the primary role of the Communist Chinese woman: the homemaker or the worker. *Marr. & fam. Living*, 1963, 25, 162–166.

International Committee for Social Sciences Documentation. *International bibliography of the social sciences.* Paris: UNESCO, 1951–   . 12 vols to date.

Int. soc. sci. J. 1962, 14, 411–549.

Jacobson, P. H. *American marriage and divorce.* New York: Rinehart, 1959.

Kanin, E. J., & Howard, D. H. Post-marital consequences of pre-marital sex adjustments. *Amer. sociol. Rev.*, 1958, 23, 556–562.

Kinsey, A. C., Pomeroy, W. B., & Martin,

C. E. *Sexual behavior in the human male.* Philadelphia: Saunders, 1948.

Kluckhohn, F. Family diagnosis: variations in the basic values of family systems. *Soc. Casewk,* 1958, 29, 63–72.

Komarovsky, Mirra. *The unemployed man and his family.* New York: Dryden Press, 1940.

Komarovsky, Mirra. Functional analysis of sex roles. *Amer. sociol. Rev.,* 1950, 15, 508–516.

Komarovsky, Mirra. Continuities in family research: a case study. *Amer. J. Sociol.,* 1956, 62, 42–47.

Kotlar, Sally L. Instrumental and expressive marital roles. *Sociol. & soc. Res.,* 1962, 46, 186–194.

Le Play, F. *Les ouvriers Européens.* Paris: Imprimerie Royale, 1855.

Le Play, F. *La réforme sociale en France.* Tours: Mame, 1864.

Lévi-Strauss, C. *Les structures élémentaires de la parenté.* Paris: Presses Universitaires, 1949.

Levy, D. M. Psychosomatic studies of some aspects of maternal behavior. *Psychosomatic Behav.,* 1942, 4, 223–227.

Levy, M. *The family revolution in China.* Cambridge: Harvard Univer. Press, 1949.

Linton, R. *The study of man.* New York: Appleton-Century, 1936.

Linton, R. The natural history of the family. In Ruth N. Anshen (Ed.), *The family: its function and destiny.* New York: Harper, 1949. Pp. 30–64.

Lippert, J. *The evolution of culture.* New York: Macmillan, 1931.

Litwak, E. The use of extended family groups in the achievement of social goals. *Soc. Probl.,* 1959–1960, 7, 177–187.

Litwak, E. Geographical mobility and extended family cohesion. *Amer. sociol. Rev.,* 1960, 25, 385–394. (a)

Litwak, E. Occupational mobility and extended family cohesion. *Amer. sociol. Rev.,* 1960, 25, 9–21. (b)

Litwak, E. Voluntary associations and neighborhood cohesion. *Amer. sociol. Rev.,* 1961, 26, 258–271.

Lowie, R. H. *Primitive society.* New York: Boni & Liveright, 1920.

Maccoby, Eleanor E. Review article. In National Manpower Council, *Work in the lives of married women.* New York: Columbia Univer. Press, 1958. Pp. 150–172.

Maccoby, Eleanor E., Matthews, R., & Merton, H. The family and the political behavior of youth. *Publ. opin. Quart.,* 1954, 18, 23–34.

Malinowski, B. Parenthood—the basis of social structure. In V. F. Calverton & S. D. Schmalhausen (Eds.), *The new generation.* New York: McCauley, 1930.

Malinowski, B. The group and the individual in functional analysis. *Amer. J. Sociol.,* 1939, 44, 938–964.

Malinowski, B. *Magic, science and religion.* Glencoe, Ill.: Free Press, 1948. (First published in 1925.)

Mandelbaum, M. A note on Homans' functionalism. *Brit. J. Sociol.,* 1963, 14, 113–117.

Merton, R. K. *Social structure and social theory.* Glencoe, Ill.: Free Press, 1957.

Middleton, R., & Putney, S. Dominance in decisions in the family: race and class differences. *Amer. J. Sociol.,* 1960, 65, 605–609.

Miller, D. R., & Swanson, G. E. *The changing American parent.* New York: Wiley, 1958.

Mogey, J. M. Changes in family life experienced by English workers moving from slums to housing estates. *Marr. & fam. Living,* 1955, 17, 123–128.

Moscovici, S. *Reconversion industrielle et changements sociaux.* Paris: Colin, 1961.

Murdock, G. P. *Social structure.* New York: Macmillan, 1949.

Murdock, G. P. Family stability in non-European cultures. *Ann. Amer. Acad. pol. & soc. Sci.,* 1950, 272, 195–201.

Murdock, G. P. World Ethnographic Sample. *Amer. Anthropologist,* 1957, 20, 664–687.

Needham, R. *Structure and sentiment, a test case in social anthropology.* Chicago: Univer. of Chicago Press, 1962.

Nimkoff, M. F. Is the joint family an obstacle to industrialization? *Int. J. comp. Sociol.,* 1960, 1, 109–118.

Nimkoff, M. F., & Middleton, R. Types of family and types of economy. *Amer. J. Sociol.,* 1960, 67, 215–225.

Nye, F. I. Maternal employment and the adjustment of adolescent children. *Marr. & fam. Living,* 1959, 21, 240–244.

Nye, F. I., & Hoffman, Lois W. *The employed mother in America.* Chicago: Rand McNally, 1963.

Nye, F. I., Perry, J. B., & Ogles, R. H. Anxiety and anti-social behavior in preschool children. In F. I. Nye & Lois W. Hoffman,

The employed mother in America. Chicago: Rand McNally, 1963. Pp. 82–94.

Ogburn, W. F. The changing family. *Family,* 1938, 19, 139–143.

Opler, M. An interpretation of ambivalence in two American Indian tribes. *J. soc. Psychol.,* 1936, 7, 82–116.

Orenstein, H. The recent history of the extended family in India. *Soc. Probl.,* 1961, 8, 341–350.

Parsons, T. Age and sex in the social structure of the United States. *Amer. sociol. Rev.,* 1942, 7, 604–616.

Parsons, T. The kinship system of the contemporary United States. *Amer. Anthropologist,* 1943, 45, 22–38.

Parsons, T. *The social system.* Glencoe, Ill.: Free Press, 1951.

Parsons, T. The incest taboo in relation to social structure and the socialization of the child. *Brit. J. Sociol.,* 1954, 5, 101–117.

Parsons, T. The social structure of the family. In Ruth N. Anshen (Ed.), *The family: its function and destiny.* New York: Harper, 1959. Pp. 241–274.

Parsons, T. Toward a healthy maturity. *J. Hlth & hum. Behav.,* 1960, 1, 163–173.

Parsons, T. An outline of the social system. In T. Parsons et al. (Eds.), *Theories of society.* Vol. 1. New York: Free Press, 1961. Pp 30–79. (a)

Parsons, T. A sociologist's view. In E. Ginzberg (Ed.), *Values and ideals of American youth.* New York: Columbia Univer. Press, 1961. (b)

Parsons, T. Individual autonomy and social pressure: an answer to Dennis H. Wrong. *Psychoanal. & psychoanal. Rev.,* 1962, 49, 70–79. (a)

Parsons, T. Youth in the context of American society. *Daedalus,* 1962, 91, 97–123. (b)

Parsons, T., & Bales, R. F., with Olds, J., Zelditch, M., Jr., & Slater, P. *Family, socialization and interaction process.* Glencoe, Ill.: Free Press, 1955.

Parsons, T., & Fox, Renee. Illness, therapy and the modern urban American family. *J. soc. Issues,* 1952, 8, 31–44.

Parsons, T., & Smelser, N. *Economy and society.* Glencoe, Ill.: Free Press, 1956.

Parsons, T., & White, W. The mass media and the structure of American society. *J. soc. Issues,* 1960, 16, 67–77.

Parsons, T., & White, W. The link between character and society. In S. M. Lipset & L. Lowenthal (Eds.), *Culture and social character.* New York: Free Press, 1961. Pp. 89–135.

Pavlov, I. P. *Conditioned reflexes.* Trans. G.V. Anrep. London: Oxford Univer. Press, 1927.

Pinneau, S. R. Reply to Dr. Spitz. *Psychol. Bull.,* 1955, 52, 459–462. (a)

Pinneau, S. R. The infantile disorders of hospitalism and anaclitic depression. *Psychol. Bull.,* 1955, 52, 429–452. (b)

Pinneau, S. R., & Jones, H. E. Mental development in infancy and childhood and mental abilities in adult life. (Rev. ed.) *Research,* 1955, 25, 415–437.

Pitts, J. R. The bourgeois family and French economic retardation. Unpublished doctoral dissertation, Harvard Univer., 1958.

Pitts, J. R. The family and the peer group. In N. Bell & E. Vogel (Eds.), *A modern introduction to the family.* Glencoe, Ill.: Free Press, 1960. Pp. 266–286.

Pitts, J. R. Introduction to Volume II. In T. Parsons et al. (Eds.), *Theories of society.* New York: Free Press, 1961. Pp. 685–716.

Pitts, J. R. Continuities and change in bourgeois France. In S. Hoffman et al. (Eds.), *In search of France.* Cambridge: Harvard Univer. Press, 1963. Pp. 235–304.

Radcliffe-Brown, A. R. On the concept of function in social science. *Amer. Anthropologist,* 1935. Reprinted in *Structure and function in primitive society.* Glencoe, Ill.: Free Press, 1952. Pp. 178–187. (a)

Radcliffe-Brown, A. R. Patrilineal and matrilineal succession. *Iowa law Rev.,* 1935, 20, 286–303. (b)

Rainwater, L., & Weinstein, Karol K. *And the poor get children.* Chicago: Quadrangle Books, 1960.

Rosenfeld, H. L. Process of structural change within the Arab village extended family. *Amer. Anthropologist,* 1958, 60, 1127–1139.

Roussiers, P. de. *Une famille de hoberaux pendant six siècles.* Paris: Didot, 1934.

Schlesinger, B. The changing patterns in the Hindu joint family system of India. *Marr. & fam. Living,* 1961, 23, 170–175.

Seligman, B. Incest and descent. *J. royal anthropol. Inst.,* 1929, 59, 243–245.

Sharp, H., & Axelrod, M. Mutual aid among relatives in urban populations. In R. Freedman et al., *Principles of sociology.* New York: Holt, 1956. Pp. 433–439.

Siegel, Alberta E., Stolz, Lois M., Hitchcock, Ethel A., & Adamson, Jean. Dependence and independence in children of working mothers. *Child Developm.,* 1959, 30, 533–546.

Singh, T. A. L., & Zingg, R. M. *Wolf children and feral man.* New York: Harper, 1942.

Slater, P. E. Parental role differentiation. *Amer. J. Sociol.,* 1961, 67, 296–308.

Slater, P. E. On social regression. *Amer. sociol. Rev.,* 1963, 28, 339–364.

Smelser, N. *Social change in the industrial revolution.* Chicago: Univer. of Chicago Press, 1959.

Smith, M. G. Secondary marriage in Northern Nigeria. *Africa,* 1953, 23, 298–323.

Smith, M. G. *Kinship and community in Carriacou.* New Haven: Yale Univer. Press, 1962. (a)

Smith, M. G. *West Indian family structure.* Seattle: Univer. of Washington Press, 1962. (b)

Smith, R. T. *The Negro family in British Guiana.* London: Routledge & Paul, 1956.

Spitz, R. A. Hospitalism: An inquiry into the genesis of psychiatric conditions in early childhood. Part I. *The psychoanalytic study of the child.* Vol. 1. New York: International Univer. Press, 1945. Pp. 53–74.

Spitz, R. A. Motherless infants. *Child Developm.,* 1949, 20, 145–155.

Spitz, R. A., & Wolfe, K. M. Anaclitic depression: an inquiry into the genesis of psychiatric conditions in early childhood. Part II. *The psychoanalytic study of the child.* Vol. 2. New York: International Univer. Press, 1946. Pp. 313–342.

Sussman, M. B. The isolated nuclear family: fact or fiction? *Soc. Probl.,* 1959, 6, 333–340.

Sussman, M. B., & Burchinal, H. Parental aid to married children: implications for family functioning. *Marr. & fam. Living,* 1962, 24, 320–332.

Sussman, M. B., & White, R. C. *Hough: a study of social life and change.* Cleveland: Western Reserve Univer. Press, 1959.

Talmon-Garber, Yonina. Social structure and family size. *Hum. Relat.,* 1959, 12, 121–146.

Talmon-Garber, Yonina. Social change and family structure. *Int. soc. sci. J.,* 1962, 14, 468–487.

Timasheff, N. S. *The great retreat.* New York: Dutton, 1946.

Tyler, E. T., Bonapart, J., & Grant, J. Occurrence of pregnancy following adoption. *Fertility & Sterility,* 1960, 11, 581–589.

Vallier, I. Structural differentiation, production imperatives and communal norms: the kibbutz in crisis. *Soc. Forces,* 1962, 40, 233–242.

Vogel, E. *Japan's new middle-class: the salaried man and his family in a Tokyo suburb.* Berkeley: Univer. of California Press, 1963.

Waller, W. *The family: a dynamic interpretation.* New York: Dryden, 1938.

Warner, L. *A black civilization.* New York: Harper, 1937.

Weber, M. *The theory of social and economic organization.* Trans. A. M. Henderson & T. Parsons. London: Oxford Univer. Press, 1947.

Weber, M. *The city.* Trans. & ed. D. Martindale & Gertrud Neuwirth. Glencoe, Ill.: Free Press, 1958.

World Health Organization. Deprivation and maternal care: a reassessment of its effects. *Publ. Hlth Papers,* No. 14. Geneva: Author, 1962.

Yang, C. K. *The Chinese family in the Communist revolution.* Cambridge: Harvard Univer. Press, 1959.

Young, M., & Willmott, P. *Family and kinship in East London.* Glencoe, Ill.: Free Press, 1957.

Zelditch, M., Jr. Role differentiation in the nuclear family: a comparative study. In T. Parsons, & R. F. Bales, with M. Zelditch, Jr., J. Olds, & P. Slater, *Family, socialization and interaction process.* Glencoe, Ill.: Free Press, 1955. Pp. 307–351.

Zuckerman, S. *The social life of apes and monkeys.* London: Paul, 1932.

CHAPTER **4**   # The Interactional and Situational Approaches[1]

SHELDON STRYKER
Indiana University

Sociology by definition, as the word seems to be commonly understood by its practitioners today, is the study of human interaction and its products. Given this state of affairs, if the present chapter is to be anything less comprehensive than a full review of sociological theories having relevance for the family, its focus obviously must be delimited. Fortunately, when the phrase "interactional approach" is used by sociologists in a more restrictive sense than that noted above, its meaning is indicated by what some have called "role theory," or by what the writer would prefer to call "symbolic interaction theory."[2]

[1] Thanks are due my colleague John H. Gagnon for his critical reading of sections of this chapter. I may not have done justice to his perceptive remarks.

[2] The latter usage seems to me to be preferable. For some, the two rubrics cover identical, or almost identical, ground. For others, "role theory" has, at best, only a tangential relationship to "symbolic interaction theory." Thus, for example, on the one hand, a comprehensive statement of role theory by Sarbin (1954) makes no distinction between the two. On the other hand, Biddle's (1961) assessment of role theory explicitly excludes materials stemming from symbolic interactionism.

SOME PRELIMINARY DISTINCTIONS

This chapter intends to examine closely symbolic interactionism, particularly in those respects in which its ideas have pertinence for a sociology of the family.

In order to do so, it will be necessary first of all to distinguish between symbolic interactionism as *theory,* and symbolic interactionism as *conceptual framework*. While both will be treated, this distinction must be kept in mind in order to avoid wholesale confusion. As theory, symbolic interactionism presents a set of propositions seeking to explain the social psychological processes of socialization and personality development. As conceptual framework, symbolic interactionism presents a set of concepts from which sociologists have approached important variables in social life in general, family life in particular. Those who view the family from the framework of symbolic interaction presumably aspire to the development of theory which fits the data of the family as social unit; by and large, as will be suggested, this task remains to be done. In drawing the distinction between theory and conceptual framework, the intention is not to compare invidiously what has been done with respect to socialization, and with respect to family life more generally, but only to provide a clearer indication of the challenge which faces those who find the ideas of symbolic interactionism worth working with.

This presentation has a second—and secondary—interest in what has been called the "situational approach." Although situationism has been seen as a distinctive theoretical framework (Hill & Hansen, 1960), it shares with symbolic interactionism essential assumptions, conceptions, and methodological predispositions; and it shares as well common historical roots, particularly in the writings of W. I. Thomas. It thus seems appropriate to treat the situational approach in the context of interactionism.

After reviewing the history of the ideas encompassed by symbolic interactionism, attention will be turned to explicating the position in its contemporary form insofar as it forms a coherent theory. Then, the way in which the ideas have been utilized in work on the family will be examined, after which an attempt will be made to evaluate the position from the standpoint of its application to the family. Attention will be drawn to what seem to be major gaps and limitations of the position, and some attempt will be made to provide a set of suggestions as to the potentialities of the position for work yet to be done. Insofar as it is possible, the presentation of the situational approach will parallel (in much briefer form) this treatment of symbolic interactionism.

Before proceeding with these primary tasks, a few preliminaries may aid the reader in assessing this chapter as a whole.

As has been repeatedly noted, usually in recriminatory tones, much of the work of sociologists who have concerned themselves with the family has been done without self-conscious reference to generalized theoretical schemes or even systematic conceptual frameworks (although family sociologists are by no means peculiar in this respect). There are undoubtedly a good number of

reasons for this, not the least of which is the irrelevance of much of what goes on under the label "theory" or "theorizing" to the real world in which sociologists are presumably interested.

A generous appraisal of this a-theoretical stance of family sociology would see in it the recognition, not necessarily or even typically conscious, of the futility of theorizing in the absence of a reasonably clear picture of the "facts": the data to be explained. While, ideally, theory-building and fact-gathering go hand in hand, fact-gathering in the absence of theory is both reasonable and more rewarding to a developing science than is theorizing in the absence of data. Sociologists have elevated to the status of an unassailable dogma the "no theory without research, no research without theory" dictum. There can be no argument with the first half of this phrase, nor with the second half *when relevant theory exists*. But when, as is frequently the case at this stage of our knowledge, such relevant theory does not exist, a precondition for its development is some awareness of the facts which it is the business of the theory to explain. Facts, certainly, must be gathered from some "point of view." But, a point of view and a theory are not the same thing.[3]

Given the current eminence of the term, there is a most curious ambiguity surrounding the word *theory*. At the risk of caricature, it is possible to note these variations in usage: (a) theory refers to any general idea associated with the history of a discipline; (b) theory refers to any guess about how some part of the world works; (c) theory refers to the superstructure of concepts, on a most general level, deemed to be appropriate for the description and analysis of the world or some part thereof. A more inclusive and yet more specific usage sees (d) theory as

---

[3] These assertions presume a particular view of theory, one increasingly but by no means universally held by sociologists, and of the criteria in terms of which theory is to be judged. What this view is will be made clear in the body of the chapter.

. . . a set of assumptions or postulates with which one approaches some part of the empirical world, a set of concepts in terms of which this part of the world is described, and a set of propositions emerging from the assumptions and relating the concepts about the way this part of the world "works" which are checked against observations of that world (Stryker, 1959, p. 111).

It is this last conception of theory which is presumed in this chapter. Theory, so conceived, is stillborn insofar as it does not emerge from data and lead to empirical work which, in some sense, tests that theory. Such a test, ideally, is direct; most testing is likely to be indirect. Yet testing there must be, and the theory must call for and stimulate such testing. The alternative is, at best, sterile word-mongering; at worst, it is stultifying dogma.

Patently, a conceptual framework or approach—a set of concepts in terms of which the world is described—is, in these terms, not a theory even though it is an essential part of a theory. It provides the terms which can be connected in propositional form within the theory. A theory is testable. A conceptual framework cannot be tested; it can only be judged in terms of its scope, its logical characteristics, and its fertility—the degree to which work, organized around its concepts, is stimulated.

This view of theory, and of a conceptual framework, has specific consequences for what follows in this chapter. For most sociologists, perhaps, the label "symbolic interaction" connotes an orientation to problems on the level of social psychology. Yet it is true, as is made eminently clear in a recent volume which attempts to demonstrate the viability of the position (Rose, 1962), that representatives of the position also see it as applicable to more distinctively sociological problems. It is at this point that the distinction posited between theory and conceptual framework is pertinent. While the writer agrees that the set of ideas of symbolic interactionism can indeed inform the student of social organization and social process, it is

his estimate that only with respect to particular social psychological problems can it be said to constitute a theory. With respect to a more general sociology of the family, this set of ideas forms a conceptual framework. It may be well to add that, in the writer's view, this in itself is no mean accomplishment.

As is implicit in what has already been said, this exposition will presume that insofar as symbolic interactionism is a theory, it is a relatively specialized one. That is, as theory it is designed to deal with a limited range of human behavior; it is not an all-encompassing theory of human behavior and ought not be so regarded. This presumption is by no means shared by all who call themselves symbolic interactionists. Nor, for that matter, would all who assume that mantle agree with all that has gone before or all that will come after in the present chapter. There is no orthodox symbolic interaction position, a fact which says much for the intellectual "life" of the position.

SYMBOLIC INTERACTION THEORY

Historical Development

The single most important source of symbolic interaction theory is George Herbert Mead, the philosopher-psychologist who helped shape the "Chicago School" of American sociology during the first third of this century, and whose ideas will be examined later in this section. But Mead was not alone in structuring this position; Charles Horton Cooley and William Isaac Thomas, along with Mead, are the immediate intellectual predecessors of the sociologists who today identify themselves with symbolic interactionism.

In part as a matter of convenience, and in part simply to keep this attempt to provide historical perspective within reasonable bounds, the starting point in the discussion will be William James. There are alternatives: one might reasonably begin with Hegel and the conception of the dialectic process; or one might start with the Scottish Moral Philosophers, especially Adam Smith and Adam Ferguson, and their stress on the significance of sympathy in social life.

James, Baldwin, and Dewey. In James's work, there are a number of elements of consequence for symbolic interactionism, which is squarely in the tradition of pragmatic philosophy. For one thing, his philosophy was " . . . a device that would permit him to accept mind as an independent reality . . . for reconciling idealism with science" (Martindale, 1960, p. 301); for another, James's writings can be read as an attack on the strict determinism of the science of his day. These elements, it will become clear, form part of the philosophic undergirding of symbolic interactionism.

But, closer to the level of substantive theory, the particular significance of James, from the perspective of an emerging symbolic interaction framework, lies in his psychology. His treatment of "habit" was, in effect, an attack on the then current instinct theories (although he still made considerable use of instinct doctrines). In his examination of "consciousness," and in his discussion of the types of self that grew out of this examination, he prepared the way for new insights into the relations of man and society.

One of the four types of self, suggested James, is the social self, a derivative of the recognition a man receives from others.

> Properly speaking, *a man has as many selves as there are individuals who recognize him....* But as the individuals . . . fall naturally into classes, we may practically say that he has as many different social selves as there are distinct *groups* of persons about whose opinion he cares (James, 1892, p. 179).

Thus, a significant segment of one's personality is seen as being rooted in his interaction with others, that is, in his social relationships.

Influenced by James, James Mark Baldwin carried this theme further, and so contrib-

uted to the stream of ideas in symbolic interaction theory. One of the first to look at the process of personality development in terms of learning, Baldwin saw the child as moving through three stages. In the first, the *projective stage,* the child discovers that persons are distinct from objects. Next, in the *subjective stage,* as he imitates the behavior of others, he learns that there are feeling states associated with this behavior. Finally, in the *ejective stage,* the child associates these feeling states with his conceptions of persons and thus becomes aware that others have feelings as he himself does (Baldwin, 1906, p. 17). For Baldwin, then, personality development was also in good part a product of self-other relationships.

The importance of John Dewey in the present context follows from his insistence upon the intimate interrelationship of personality and society. For Dewey, personality organization was primarily a function of habit, social organization primarily a function of custom. But custom *is* collective habit (1930, p. 58). Thus there can be no fundamental opposition between person and social order; that is, the individual cannot be set in contrast to society. Personality develops within a social context. Further, "To talk about the priority of 'society' to the individual is to indulge in nonsensical metaphysics. But to say that some pre-exisiting association of human beings is prior to every particular human being who is born into the world is to mention a commonplace" (p. 59).

Charles Horton Cooley. The ideas just traced were brought into sociology largely through Charles Horton Cooley; it is noteworthy that James, Baldwin, and Dewey are among the few non-literary sources specifically cited by Cooley.

That which is distinctively social, and so the special concern of the sociologist, is, according to Cooley, mental and subjective: to deny this is to be guilty of "dodging life itself" (1926). The "real person" consists in a personal idea; society is a relationship among personal ideas.

So far as the study of immediate social relations is concerned the personal idea is the real person. That is to say, it is in this alone that one man exists for another, and acts directly upon his mind. My association with you evidently consists in the relation between my idea of you and the rest of my mind. If there is something in you that is wholly beyond this and makes no impression on me it has no social reality in this relation. . . . Society, then, in its immediate aspect, *is a relation among personal ideas.* . . . Society exists in my mind as the contact and reciprocal influence of certain ideas named 'I', Thomas, Henry, Susan, Bridget, and so on. It exists in your mind as a similar group. . . (Cooley, 1902, p. 84).

It follows from such considerations that, in Cooley's (1902, p. 87) words, "the imaginations which people have of one another are the solid facts of society," and that the task of sociology is to observe and interpret these mental activities. Systematic autobiography is clearly indicated as the prime "method" of the discipline.

Beginning as he did with an organic view of social life, Cooley was led to the view that individual and society—both consisting in personal ideas—are two sides of the same coin. No society exists independent of individuals; and no individual has existence apart from society: the two are but the collective and distributive aspects of the same thing, which is, Cooley noted, "Human Life" (1902, p. 1). It follows that "there is no view of the self, that will bear examination, which makes it altogether distinct, in our minds from other persons" (pp. 91–92).

The self, then, is defined and developed in social interaction; it is a social product. Specifically, it is a product of the process summed up in the phrase "looking-glass self." The social reference for the self " . . . takes the form of a somewhat definite imagination of how one's self—that is, any idea he appropriates—appears in a particular mind, and the kind of self-feeling one has is determined by the attitude toward this attributed to the other mind. A social self of this sort might be called the reflected or

looking-glass self." There are three principal elements in the self-idea making up the social self: the imagination of our appearance to the other person; the imagination of his judgment of that appearance; and some sort of self-feeling, such as pride or mortification. "We always imagine, and in imagining, share, the judgments of the other mind" (Cooley, 1902, pp. 151–153).

This conceptualization has a number of important consequences: there can be no individuality outside the social order; individual personality is a "natural" development from the existing social unit and the state of communication within that unit; and an important element in this development consists in the expectations of others.

It is in primary groups that the self evolves; these are the "springs of life" for both the individual and larger units of social organization. Characterized by intimacy, face-to-face association, and cooperation, these groups are primary in that "they are fundamental in forming the social nature and ideals of the individual," in that "they give the individual his earliest and completest experience of social unity," and in that they are the continual source of more elaborate relationships. The family, the play group, and the neighborhood group are the most important of primary groups, since these "are ascendent in the open and plastic time of childhood" (Cooley, 1909, pp. 23–27).

William Isaac Thomas. As Martindale noted, with regard to the work of William Isaac Thomas, "At every critical point Thomas' affinities are with the pragmatists and symbolic interactionists" (1960, p. 349). For present purposes, it is Thomas' emphasis on the substantive and methodological significance of "situations," on the correlative of these, namely, definitions of the situation, and on the strategic significance of life histories or personal documents for the developing science of sociology which require consideration. While other aspects of Thomas' views are at least tangentially relevant—for example, his development of a character typology out of the culture-personality relationship, and his emphatic denial of the abnormality of social disorganization—it is the former which are most closely related to the major themes of symbolic interactionism.

Basic to Thomas' position is the assumption that any account of human behavior is incomplete insofar as it refuses to cope with the subjective, as well as the objective, facts of experience. The task of sociology is to analyze "behavior," defined as forms taken by the processes of adjustment undergone by both individuals and groups as they relate to other individuals and groups. Adjustment processes occur only in situations, i.e., are responses to objective conditions in which individuals and groups are embedded. But, to phrase the point in contemporary language, acting as intervening variables in this relationship between objective conditions—the situation—and adjustive processes are subjective components of experience—definitions of the situation. Nowhere in the literature is there a more straightforward and succinct statement of the significance of the subjective in human life than Thomas' assertion that "if men define situations as real, they are real in their consequences" (Thomas & Thomas, 1928, p. 572).

Both situation and definition of the situation must of necessity be incorporated into any account of human behavior.

The total situation will always contain more and less subjective factors, and the behavior reaction can be studied only in connection with the whole context, i.e., the situation as it exists in verifiable, objective terms, and as it has seemed to exist in terms of the interested persons (p. 572).

An adjustive effort of any kind is preceded by a decision to act or not act along a given line, and the decision is itself preceded by a *definition of the situation,* that is to say, an *interpretation,* or *point of view,* and eventually a policy and a behavior pattern (Thomas, 1937, p. 8).

As Thomas repeatedly stressed, it is the fact that the "same" objective situation does not lead to identical behavior that necessitates the introduction of this subjective variable.

The meaning of this key term, situation, shifted through the course of Thomas' career, and, indeed, as Volkart (1951, p. 29) suggested, at no point can it be said to have been defined with sufficient precision to make it really useful either descriptively or analytically. In *The Polish Peasant* (Thomas & Znaniecki, 1918–1920), the situation is defined in terms of the primary concepts of that work, value and attitude.

The situation is the set of values and attitudes with which the individual or the group has to deal in a process of activity and with regard to which this activity is planned and its results appreciated. Every concrete activity is the solution of a situation. This situation involves three kinds of data: (1) The objective conditions under which the individual or society has to act, that is, the totality of values—economic, social, religious, intellectual, etc.—which at the given moment affect directly or indirectly the conscious status of the individual or the group. (2) The pre-existing attitudes of the individual or the group which at the given moment have an actual influence upon his behavior. (3) The definition of the situation, that is, the more or less clear conception of the conditions and consciousness of the attitudes (Vol. 1, p. 68).

Later (1931, p. 176), he noted that the term refers to the "situation of social relationships," involving "all the institutions and mores," as well as values and attitudes. Least precise, but perhaps more indicative of what the term was intended to convey is his reference to the situation as representing "the configuration of the factors conditioning the behavior reaction" (1927, p. 1).

It was Thomas' view that an approach to human behavior through the comparative study of situations represents the best approximation to the controlled experiment available to the sociologist.

A study of the concrete situations which the individual encounters, into which he is forced, or which he creates will disclose the character of his adaptive strivings and the process of adjustment. The study of the situation, the behavior in the situation, the changes brought about in the situation, and the resulting change in behavior represent the nearest approach the social scientist is able to make to the use of experiment in research (1931, p. 177).

Since situations of necessity include a subjective component—definitions of the situation—students of behavior must find appropriate techniques to capture this part of reality. Thomas found these techniques in what he, generically, called personal documents: case studies, life histories, diaries, letters, autobiographical statements—in short, anything which would serve to reveal the situation from the point of view of the actor(s) within it.

Critical of purely observational or statistical studies because of their failure to capture such "meaning," Thomas nevertheless recognized the deficiencies of personal documents and the utility of more objective procedures. The principal function of personal documents is to bring to light the important variables affecting behavior, to suggest hypotheses with respect to the way these work, and to provide the basis for the interpretation of mass data; they cannot, in themselves, test and verify hypotheses. This last is the principal function of statistical studies which can serve to provide "inferences . . . as to the relative effect of situations on the behavior" (Thomas & Thomas, 1928, pp. 565–567).

What is needed is a continuous and detailed preparation and study of life histories along with the available statistical studies, to be used as a basis for the inferences drawn. And these inferences in turn must be continuously subjected to further statistical analysis as it becomes possible to transmute more factors into quantitative form. The case study method and the "natural history" method must not only precede the more scientifically acceptable method in order to produce realistic hypotheses and indicate what units should be defined and isolated; they must also be used as a general background of reference to the more limited statistical findings . . . (Thomas, 1931, p. 190).

The fundamental significance of definitions of the situation is clear: all "self-determined acts" are preceded by and dependent upon them, and "a whole life policy and the personality of the individual himself" issue from them. A child is always born into an ongoing group which has developed definitions of the general kinds of situations which it faces and rules of conduct based on these definitions: moral codes are the product of "successive definitions of the situation." In general, the child cannot create his own definitions and follow their implications without societal interference. But since individuals tend to a "hedonistic selection of activity" and society to a "utilitarian selection," there will always be rivalry between individual spontaneous definitions and societal definitions. The problem of socialization, thus, becomes the problem of bringing the individual to internalize societal definitions. And the family is the primary defining agency (1925, pp. 42–43). Finally, where there are—for whatever reason—rival social definitions of the situation, none of them fully constrains the individual; under these circumstances, we can expect both social and personal disorganization (1927, p. 13).

Parenthetically, it should be noted that Thomas did not see the relation of society to individual as a one-way street, as the emphasis in the foregoing might imply. This is made abundantly clear in Volkart's (1951) excellent statement.

George Herbert Mead. The ideas, both explicit and implicit, in the foregoing received somewhat more systematic treatment at the hands of George Herbert Mead. Mead, however, did not simply take over this thinking, for in point of fact he found it necessary to criticize severely those whose positions seem closest to his own (1930; 1934, p. 224).

Much of Mead's thought is presented in the context of the next section of this chapter. To avoid redundancy, the present review is more brief and terse than Mead's importance warrants. In Mead's view, termed social behaviorism,[4] the problems of man's behavior were to be approached from the standpoint of society. In line with fundamental developments occurring within psychology, Mead insisted on giving these problems a behavioristic bent, but without sacrificing mental activities in doing so. "Social psychology is behavioristic in the sense of starting off with an observable activity—the dynamic, on-going social process, and the social acts which are its component elements—to be studied and analyzed scientifically" (Mead, 1934, p. 7). From the social process, both mind and society derive.

The basic dictum of Mead's theory, then, is that social psychology starts its studies with ongoing social acts. The social behavior of the individual, and his personality, are developments from these. In what many consider his greatest contribution, Mead pointed to language as the nexus between the social process and emergent personality.

Communication through language depends, for Mead, on "significant symbols," gestures (any part of a social act which stands for, or is a sign of, those parts of the social act yet to occur) which come to have the same meaning for participants in the social act. Meaning, here, refers to activity which is aroused in response to a gesture: the meaning of a gesture lies in future phrases of social activity. "The meaning of what we are saying is the tendency to respond to it. You ask somebody to bring a visitor a chair. You arouse the tendency to get the chair in the other, but if he is slow to act, you get the chair yourself" (p. 67).

Language is a system of significant symbols; it is, in the sense noted above, shared behavior. Human social life is premised on the existence of such a system. Through language, precisely articulated social organization is possible; and through language, intelligent adaptation becomes possible as well. Through language, society and individual "interpenetrate," to use Martindale's phrase (1960, p. 356).

Mead dealt with the problem of personality largely in terms of the concept of "self." For Mead, the self develops insofar as the human organism becomes able to view its own activity objectively—that is, from the standpoint of others with whom that organism is implicated in the social process. This development is made possible, again, through language behavior. Making use of significant symbols implies that one takes the role of the other with whom one is communicating. In effect, one learns what he is, that is, what body of activities is associated with the symbol which is his name, by taking the role or the attitudes (Mead did not distinguish between these) of others toward himself through the use of significant symbols. "The self as that which can be an object to itself, is essentially a social structure, and it arises in social experience" (Mead, 1934, p. 140).

The self is structured into two phases, the "I" and the "me." "Taken together they constitute a personality as it appears in social experience" (p. 178). The "me" is the equivalent of social roles, the organized attitudes of others which one incorporates into his self. The "I," which Mead used in accounting for spontaneity, creativity, and change in social experience, represents the response of the organism to these organized attitudes of others.

In general terms, the personality develops in two stages, the earlier being "play," and the latter, "the game." A child's play frequently takes the form of "being" someone else—an imaginary companion, mother, teacher, the little boy across the street. Such play involves, then, taking the role of various and discrete particular others. Organized social life, however, implies a more complex situation; it is for this that Mead suggested the counterpart of the game. Involved in a game, a player must respond to an intricately related pattern of others; if he is to play his role, he must incorporate the roles of all the other participants. He must, to use

[4] This term is apparently C. W. Morris', rather than Mead's, and was used in the subtitle of the posthumously published volume, *Mind, Self and Society* (1934), edited by Morris.

Mead's phrase, take the role of the generalized other; in so doing, he becomes a part of the game—that is, he is able to play his own role in the ongoing social process.

A Contemporary Formulation

The broad ideas which are the heritage of contemporary symbolic interactionists having been sketched, attention will be turned now to the way these—with appropriate emendations—have been molded into a coherent theory.[5] [Cf. a briefer but somewhat parallel formulation in Ch. 18, pp. 744–746]

The reader must be reminded of three points made earlier. First, there can be no pretense that all who take these ideas seriously would agree with this formulation of the position; while there is certainly a hard core of agreement, there are also important differences among representatives of the position. Secondly, this immediate presentation focuses on symbolic interactionism as a social psychological theory, and will largely ignore its more general sociological implications, on the grounds that it is with reference to particular social psychological problems that it forms a coherent theory.

Thirdly, the assumption is being made that symbolic interactionism is indeed a theory in the sense alluded to in the introduction to this chapter. Not all symbolic interactionists seem to believe that this is the case. Some, apparently, see it as no more than a set of sensitizing concepts, that is, as a packaging of ideas which alert the investigator to (probably) important variables in the world with which he is dealing. This, for example, appears to be the view held by Strauss (1956). While not as rigorously formulated as theory ideally should be, and while the deductive potential of these ideas —in the strict sense of deduction—has never been fully demonstrated, symbolic inter-

action as social psychological theory seems to have the properties which qualify it as a theory.

The problems to which the theory is addressed. As a social psychological theory, symbolic interactionism addresses itself to facets of the general problem of the relationship between person and society, conceived, in Cooley's happy phrase, as two sides of the same coin. It seeks the answers to a set of interrelated questions about two "middle range" problems: the problem of socialization and the problem of personality organization.

Socialization, broadly, refers to the process by which the human organism acquires the characteristic ways of behaving, the values, norms, and attitudes of the social units of which he is a part. The focus here is on development—that which happens over time to the neophyte. Where early symbolic interactionists tended to restrict their interest to the socialization of the infant or the child, current researchers have broadened the inquiry to the entire range of neophyte-organized social unit relationships: the recruit entering the army, the student entering the university, the bride entering a new set of family relationships, and the like. And while earlier writers tended to conceive of the organized social units holistically, on the level of the total society, current workers concern themselves with the impact on the person of a variety of smaller units which, taken together, constitute a society in a larger sense.

The problem of personality organization —the twin of the problem of socialization— refers to the development of persistent behavior patterns. The task of a social psychology is to account for such organization as exists insofar as it depends upon social relationships: organization cannot be assumed, but must be demonstrated and explained. Symbolic interaction theory largely limits its considerations to the normal, that is, to the person without gross physical, physiological, or psychological defect. This does not imply that the theory concerns

---

[5] The statement to follow borrows freely from my earlier formulation of symbolic interaction theory (Stryker, 1959). It makes primary use, as well, of more recent presentations of the position by Rose (1962) and Martindale (1960).

itself only with personal organization. In point of fact, one of the strengths of the theory is that it can explore personal disorganization as well—this was a principal focus in Thomas' work, as it is in the work of such latter-day investigators as Alfred Lindesmith and Howard Becker—and that it can do so in the same terms in which it explores personal organization. Thus, it can treat these as two aspects of the same problem, rather than as different problems, and can provide answers to both without invoking principles lying outside the theoretical scheme proper.

The major problems which symbolic interaction theory attempts to explicate have purposely been stated in highly general form, for a more specific statement depends on the assumptions and concepts with which the theory approaches these parts of the world.

Assumptions. The initial assumption of the position is that insofar as interests are social psychological, man must be studied on his own level. Symbolic interactionism is anti-reductionist; it assumes that there are valid principles of human behavior as the product of social interaction which cannot be derived from, or inferred from, the study of non-human forms. This assertion rests on the principle of emergence. Emergence suggests the existence of qualitative differences as well as quantitative continuities among the precipitates of the evolutionary process. These qualitative differences are presumed to be man's capacity for complex symbolic productions, and his capacity for the storage over long periods of time of a virtual infinity of these productions. If man is qualitatively different from other animal forms, it follows that theory developed from the study of other forms cannot completely account for his behavior. While interest in the continuities in the animal world is certainly legitimate, and thus the approach to man's behavior from the background of animal research of value, the task of at least some social psychologists is to focus on that which is different in man;

this is what the symbolic interactionists propose to do.

A second assumption is that the most fruitful approach to man's social behavior is through an analysis of society. This assumption involves no assertion of some metaphysical priority of society over the individual; rather, it rests merely on the common-sense observation that any given individual is born into a complex structure of interacting persons—that is, a society— which comes "complete" with a culture, a set of values, meanings, and expectations. This last, however, does not mean that symbolic interactionism is committed to a cultural determinism. Rose has suggested eight reasons why this is so:

(a) Some of the interaction between individuals is on a non-cultural or natural sign level, so that some learned behavior is universally human and independent of specific cultures. (b) Most cultural expectations are for ranges of behavior rather than for specific behaviors. . . . (c) Most cultural expectations are for certain roles, rather than for all individuals, and for certain situations, rather than all situations, and the individual has some "freedom of choice" among the roles and situations he will enter. . . . (d) Some cultural expectations are for variation rather than conformity. . . . (e) The cultural *meanings* indicate possibilities for behavior, not requirements or "pressures" for a certain kind of behavior (as the cultural *values* do). The fact that a chair is an object to be sat on, for example, does not mean that the chair is only to be used for sitting or that one must always sit when a chair is available. (f) The culture, especially our culture, is often internally inconsistent, and one may move from one culture or subculture to another, so that there are conflicting cultural expectations for an individual. This does not mean solely that the individual has a choice between the two conflicting patterns of behavior he is exposed to, or can make a synthesis of them, but also that he can—within the limits permitted by the culture—define for himself somewhat new patterns suggested by the variation among the old ones. (g) . . . [W]henever the individual is "blocked" in carrying on behavior expected within the society, he has some possibility of innovating—within the limits of cultural tolerance—to devise new behavior patterns that will take him around the block. The self—Mead's "I"—is a creative self. . . . (h) Finally, the symbolic interactionist does not exclude the influence of biogenic and psychogenic factors in behavior, even though he does not incorporate them into his theory (1962, pp. 14–15).

The relative "reality-status" of society and individual is a philosophic issue which has long plagued students of human behavior. Social psychologists of one persuasion have contended that society is *the* ultimate reality, while social psychologists of another variety have given ontological precedence to the individual, some denying the reality of society. Symbolic interactionism bypasses rather than resolves the argument, doing so by beginning its analysis with the social act, and from interaction deriving both society and the individual. This formulation permits an articulation between sociology and social psychology which alternative frameworks can forge, if at all, only with great difficulty. Sociology and social psychology begin with the same "building bricks": social actions. The former builds in one direction to the behavior of collectivities; the latter builds in another direction to the behavior of individuals. Those whose problems bridge the two disciplines, as is true of perhaps most students of the family, are provided with a framework facilitating movement from one level to the other, permitting systematic transactions between the two levels. Martindale (1960) has made these connectives explicit by using the term *social behaviorism* as a generic rubric including within it pluralistic behaviorism, symbolic interactionism, and social-action theory, thus making the point that sociologists and social psychologists such as Tarde, Giddings, Chapin, Cooley, Mead, Thomas, and Weber share certain key ideas.

A third assumption is that the human being is actor as well as reactor. The human being does not simply respond to stimuli from the external environment; in fact, the external environment of the human

organism is a selected segment of the "real" world, the selection occurring in the interests of behavior which the human being himself initiates. Thus, what is environment and what serves as a stimulus depend on the activity in which the human organism is engaged: objects become stimuli when they serve to link impulses with satisfactions. Humans do not respond to the environment as physically given, but to an environment as it is mediated through symbolic processes—to a *symbolic environment*. Since this is true, and since men can produce their own symbols, men can be self-stimulating; they can respond to their own internal symbolic productions.

It is this assumption which leads to the fundamental methodological principle of the theory, namely, that the investigator must see the world from the point of view of the subject of his investigation. If men select and interpret the environment to which they respond, an explication of social behavior must incorporate these subjective elements. As Rose (1962, p. x) noted, this assumption and its methodological consequences distinguish symbolic interactionists from those who work in the "positivist" or "behaviorist" traditions in sociology and psychology.

A fourth assumption, which differentiates current symbolic interaction theory from its forerunners and, in another way, from the variants of Freudian theory, concerns the equipment with which the newborn is presumed to enter life. The infant is presumed to be neither social nor anti-social, but a-social. The infant is not born "human"; it has the potentiality for human development. It is an active organism; it has "impulses," but these impulses do not have particular content, nor are they channeled or directed by nature toward any specific ends.

On a somewhat different plane, and perhaps better cited as a predilection with important methodological consequences than as an assumption of the theory, is the tendency on the part of adherents of this theory to remain close to the world of everyday experience. "That is, empirical research tends to use observations from a selected portion of 'everyday' life; abstraction is left for conceptualization, analysis, and generalization" (Rose, 1962, p. ix). The theory develops out of such experience, and it is basically with such experiences that it seeks to deal.

Major concepts. If the capacity for symbolic behavior qualitatively differentiates man from the rest of the animal kingdom, and since man's primary mode of symbolization is language, a principal concern must be with language and its correlatives. This is not, of course, to identify symbolization with language, nor to deny the relevance of other modes of symbolization to social relationships. Greatest attention has, however, been paid to language, although in recent years there has been some analysis of other forms of symbolic interaction (e.g., Goffman, 1959; Stone, 1959).

The starting point is with the *act:* behavior by an organism stemming from an impulse and requiring for its completion some adjustment to appropriate objects in the external world. Sociologists are concerned with *social acts,* that is, acts in which the appropriate objects are other individuals.[6] But other individuals are not only social objects—they do not simply "stand still"—rather, they too act with reference to the initial actors. Thus every social act implicates at least two individuals, each of whom takes the other into account in the processes of satisfying impulses.

Thus far, there is no requirement that the "individuals" referred to above be human; but given man's complex nervous system there ensue possibilities apparently peculiar to man.

Social acts occur over time; they have a

history. This makes possible the appearance of *gestures,* defined as any part of the act which comes to be an indication of those parts of the act yet to occur. In responding to one another, individuals may be involved in what Mead called a "conversation of gestures": they may come to use early stages of another's acts as indicators of later stages. Such gestures have meaning. Vocal sounds, other physical movements, attire—all can serve as gestures, and all may have meaning. The meaning of a gesture (an early stage of an act) is the behavior which comes after it (the later stages of an act): meaning is, by definition, behavior, rather than being purely ideational or rather than residing "in" the sound, movement, or attire.

Some gestures come to have an additional property: they may mean the same thing—that is, they may imply the same set of subsequent behaviors—to both the organism which produces the gesture and the organism which perceives it. When this occurs, the gesture becomes a *significant symbol.*

Language, to the degree that it is social and not purely private, is a system of significant symbols. This asserts that language is a system of shared meanings and implies that language is a system of shared behavior. It is obvious that not all words are "understood" by parties to a "conversation," and it is obvious that not all words carry precisely the same shade of meaning, in the behavioral sense of meaning, to all. Yet meaning must be sufficiently shared for communication between human beings to take place. Social interaction presupposes these characteristics of linguistic and other symbols.

Symbols arise in the context of social acts, and they function in completing these acts. In this sense, they reflect the interests from which acts stem. We respond to symbols as predictors of later behavior, both on our own part and on the part of others. Since these symbols serve to anticipate further behavior, they provide a basis for adjusting—or, in Mead's usage, adapting—our activity

[6] Miyamoto (1959) calls this usage "loose," and refers to another usage found in Mead: ". . . an organized action of two or more individuals that is directed toward some common goal." Given Miyamoto's concerns, which are in the direction of problems of social organization and disorganization, this comment may be justified. Given the concerns of this chapter, the usage provided has it advantages.

before that behavior has occurred. Consequently, symbols function in the context of a social act in place of that which they symbolize, and organize behavior with reference to that which is symbolized. It is in this sense that Rose (1962) referred to a symbol as an incipient or telescoped act. To phrase the point in another manner, it can be said that symbols entail a plan of action.

Some symbols represent relatively discrete phenomena, but some represent generalizations of behavior toward objects; these are *categories*. To categorize is to apply a class term to a set of objects, and thus to signify that a number of different things are, for certain purposes, to be treated as the same kind of thing. Categorization or classification is essential to activity, for life would be impossible if one were forced to respond to every object in the world as unique. Categories, or class terms, are of course symbols, and as such they share the characteristics of symbols. They have meaning, they serve as cues to behavior, and they organize behavior.

Humans respond to a classified world, one whose salient features are named and placed into categories indicating their significance for behavior. In short, as previously noted, humans respond to a symbolic environment. Persons frequently enter situations in which their behavior is problematic, that is, in which action is not so routinized that we may legitimately speak of habit operating. Before they can act in other than a random manner, they must somehow represent the situation to themselves in symbolic terms: they must define the situation. The products of this defining behavior are termed *definitions of the situation*.

Such definitions do not necessarily exist in fully articulated form when one enters a novel situation, although it sometimes is the case that they do: persons sometimes self-consciously prepare to meet situations by constructing elaborate definitions. More typically, however, definitions are the product of a probing process in which tentatively held definitions are repeatedly tested against the reality of the situation and reformulated on the basis of this experience. There is, in other words, a continual dialectic of action on the basis of putative definitions, reactions from others which serve partially to validate or invalidate these definitions, and revision of the definitions as the basis for further action.

A particularly important kind of category is that called *position*. Others have used the term *status* here. Position seems preferable in order to avoid the hierarchical implications of status. Positions may certainly be hierarchized, but they need not be, and thus it is important to maintain this conceptual distinction. Positions are socially recognized categories of actors, any general category serving to classify persons. By this usage, father, sergeant, and teacher are positions, as are black sheep, divorcee, and intellectual. The significance of such categories is that they serve as cues to the future behavior of the persons so categorized, and they organize behavior toward these persons. In attaching a position designation to a person, we are led to expect certain behaviors from him and we behave toward him on the basis of these expectations. To the expectations with regard to behavior attached to a position the term *role* is given. These expectations are social in the same sense that symbolic behavior is always social: the ultimate meaning of the positions to which these expectations apply is shared behavior. They are social in another and frequently neglected sense, namely, that it is impossible to talk about *a* position without explicit reference to some context of *other* positions. One cannot talk meaningfully about the behavior of father except with reference to the behavior of mother, child, and so on. Every position assumes some counter-position, and every role presumes some counter-role. To use these terms is necessarily to refer to interpersonal relations.

The foregoing discussion has been, of necessity, oversimplified. Persons are frequently, if not typically, categorized in many ways, including some which provide contradictory cues to their behavior and so allow no clear means of organizing responses to them. Patently, many problems of interaction stem from this fact (Turner, 1962).

To this point, the discussion of categories has been couched in terms of an actor responding to objects in the external world, including people, in functionally relevant ways: position, for example, refers to an actor's definition *of others,* and is, in this sense, external to the actor. Typically, although not necessarily, a person also applies such categories to himself: he responds to himself, as he responds to other persons, by naming, defining, classifying himself. To engage in this kind of behavior is to have a *self.* Self can be defined in various ways, each calling attention to slightly different aspects of the same activity. Mead defined the self as that which is an object to itself, an elliptical way of saying that an organism has a self to the degree that he views his own activities objectively, i.e., from the standpoint of others. Others have defined the self as a set of responses of an organism which serve to organize the responses of the same organism. Whatever the nuances of definition, self refers to an activity, to reflexive activity, and not to an object, thing, or essence. From the standpoint of symbolic interaction theory, it is an indispensable concept, but it contains many dangers. In particular, it is difficult to avoid the tendency to reify the concept.

The individual defines himself in terms of socially recognized categories and their corresponding roles. Since these roles necessarily imply relationships to others, the self necessarily implies such relationships. One's self is the way one describes to himself his relationships to others in a social process.

The discussion thus far has presumed but not made explicit the process of *role-taking,* or, alternatively, *taking the role of the other.* Role-taking refers to the anticipation of the responses of others implicated with one in some social act. There is no necessary element of "feeling with," that is, of sympathy, in this conception of role-taking: one can anticipate the behavior of another without becoming emotionally identified with that other. It is on this basis that the concepts of role-taking and empathy may be differentiated; this distinction is, however, not consistently made in the literature.

The role-taking concept can perhaps best be elucidated through an illustration. Consider the classroom instructor who is in the process of presenting to his students an especially difficult idea. Perhaps he observes in his students, as he speaks, the blank and somewhat uneasy looks that suggest to him that the words he ordinarily uses to cover the topic do not allow the discussion to proceed beyond the immediate issue.[7] He then casts about for words which will allow him to clarify the idea, and so allow him to move beyond it to further materials. Presumably, he selects words in terms of what he knows or guesses about the backgrounds and experiences of the students before him. He will, in other words, attempt to put himself in the place of his students, anticipating their response to the words he will use. He takes the role of the other.

Role-taking may involve the anticipation of the responses of some particular other. More frequently, perhaps, since one's interaction is likely to be with multiple others either physically or symbolically present, it involves the anticipation of responses of what Mead called the *generalized other.* To revert to the classroom illustration: the instructor must deal with the class not as discrete individuals but as an organized unit, the members of which can be expected to behave in differentiated yet related ways. To take the role of the generalized other is to see one's behavior as taking place in the context of a defined system of related roles.

[7] Any instructor of my generation who has attempted to use his experiences in, say, World War II as the basis of illustration in a recent freshmen class will recognize the problem.

What is being emphasized here is the role-taking *process* as it plays its part in what Turner (1962) called role-making. There is, in the literature, wholesale confusion which results from the failure to recognize that what is called role theory refers sometimes to the tradition deriving from Mead, sometimes to the tradition deriving from Ralph Linton (1936), and sometimes to an agglomeration of both traditions; and from the failure to recognize that these are very different lines of thought and analysis. The distinction between the two is well made in the following passage:

An initial distinction must be made between taking the existence of distinct and identifiable roles as the starting point in role theory, and postulating a tendency to create and modify conceptions of self- and other-roles as the orienting process in interactive behavior. The latter approach has less interest in a group and the specific content of each role than in observing the basic tendency for actors to behave *as if* there were roles. . . . Roles "exist" in varying degrees of concreteness and consistency, while the individual frames his behavior as if they had unequivocal existence and clarity. The result is that in attempting from time to time to make aspects of the roles explicit he is creating and modifying roles as well as merely bringing them to light; the process is not only role-taking but *role-making*. . . . *The idea of role-taking shifts emphasis from the simple process of enacting a prescribed role to devising a performance on the basis of an imputed other-role* . . . [T]esting inferences about the role of alter is a continuing element in interaction. Hence the tentative character of the individual's own role definition and performance is never wholly suspended (Turner, 1962, pp. 21–23).

The concept of *significant other* represents the recognition that, in a fragmented and differentiated world, not all the persons with whom one interacts have identical or even compatible perspectives; and that, consequently, in order for action to proceed, the individual must give greater weight or priority to the perspectives of certain others.

To speak, then, of significant others is to say that given others occupy high rank on an "importance" continuum.

The concept of *reference group* currently much in vogue does not seem to add anything novel to the generalized-other concept—although it may be a preferable term in that it seems to offend less the sensitivities of the self-consciously scientific—at least insofar as it is used to refer to those systems from which one derives expectations for his own behavior. Borgatta (1960), in what is perhaps the most penetrating critique of role and reference-group theory extant, found it possible to discuss the ideas covered by these rubrics without making use of the term *reference group*, although it should be added that he also found it questionable that the concept of role advances the discussion to any great extent.

One last set of concepts needs to be mentioned; extended treatment of these does not seem to be necessary. As is evident, symbolic interaction theory makes unashamed use of a full range of so-called mentalistic concepts. In fact, the case may be put more strongly: its judgment is that any proposed theory seeking to deal with socialization and with personality which rules out such concepts distorts the facts of human experience.

Thus such concepts as *thinking, volition,* and *self-consciousness* find a place within this theory. Usage of these terms is, however, not traditional: where frequently they are defined in such a way as to place them outside the bounds of scientific discourse, symbolic interaction gives them behavioral referents and so permits their treatment within the conventions of scientific procedure. Thinking is defined as the internal, subvocal manipulation of language symbols. Volition becomes the process of selecting from the alternatives that are symbolically present in the experience of the individual. And self-consciousness is the activity of viewing oneself from the standpoint of others.

Major propositions. The propositions to be reviewed have been selected on the basis of their relevance for family sociology. Given present space limitations, it is impossible to do full justice either to the complexities of the questions raised or the propositions forwarded as tentative answers to these questions.

The problems of socialization and personality raise a number of interrelated questions, among them how meanings are developed in the human neophyte; how the self develops and is structured; how thinking and objectivity arise in the course of experience; how personal organization comes into being and is maintained; and how personal disorganization arises.

The human infant, active but unorganized, is born into an ongoing set of social relationships which are premised upon a system of shared meanings. The infant acts, but randomly: he thrashes his arms, he exercises his vocal cords, he contorts his face. The adult responds selectively to these actions, ignoring some, focusing on others. In response to, say, the crying of the infant, the adult feeds it, or changes it, or turns it over on its stomach. Eventually, the adult will find that response which completes the act in the desired way, that is, which stops the crying. There is, in this situation, an impulsive act which is, incipiently, a gesture, and there is incipient meaning as well. The incipient meaning is that part of the act supplied by the response of the adult. Over time, the cry of the infant becomes specialized, and the response of the adult narrows. The significant point here is that it is the adult who completes the act and who, therefore, supplies the meaning of the gesture.

The adult's response is, of course, limited by the repertory of meanings available in the social unit of which he is a part. Further, the adult will have defined the situation, including his positional relationship to the infant—for example, that of father to son—and this definition will invoke the set of expected behaviors we call the role of the father. This set of expected behaviors will not precisely delimit the adult's response—only rarely are expectations so narrowly restrictive as to permit no alternatives—but, rather, will call up a range of possibilities. If the father is a middle-class American, and if he takes the cry of the infant to indicate the possibility that the infant is thirsty, he will give the infant milk or water, but not wine or whiskey. The meanings attached to the gestures of the infant are social meanings, and they are supplied through his relationships with already socialized participants in an ongoing society.

The early activity of the child will include random vocalization. Eventually, as he gains control of his vocal apparatus, he will imitate sounds that others make. Others respond to the initially random vocalization by selecting out particular sounds and reacting to these. They respond as well to the imitated sounds by doing things which contain the adult meanings of these sounds. For the child, the correspondence between sound and meaning will be vague in the first stages, but in the process of interaction over time the correspondence will become more pronounced. So, for example, the child may use the sound "ba" to refer to any approximately round object—ball, orange, egg —which he rolls on the floor. The response of the parent to the rolling of an egg will soon make clear that an egg is not a "ba" and is not to be rolled. In the course of time, child and parent will come to agree on what is and what is not a ball, and a significant symbol will have come into existence. A sound, at first meaningless to, although produced by the child, comes to mean for the child what it already means to the adult and to the society of which the adult is a part.

The self comes into existence in this same way. Others supply us with a name, and they provide the meaning attached to that symbol. They categorize us in particular ways, and on the basis of such categorization they expect some set of behaviors from us. On the basis of these expectations, they act with reference to us. The ways in which they act toward us define our self. We come to categorize ourselves as they categorize us, and we come to act in ways implied in these categories and, so, appropriate to their expectations.

But we are not simply controlled by others' definitions and expectations. The evolution of the self is, of course, gradual. This development is one of increasing complexity, for as the child moves into the social world he comes into contact with a variety of persons in a variety of self-relevant situations. At any particular point in time, beyond the earliest, he has a conception of self, derived from past experience, which interacts with present expectations. Further, he comes, or may come, into contact with differing expectations as to how he is to behave, and differing identifications on which these expectations are based. He has available, consequently, through the role-taking process a variety of perspectives from which to view and to evaluate his own behavior, and he can act with reference to self as well as with reference to others. In short, the socialization process as it has been described makes possible the appearance of objectivity in the behavior of the individual. And, since these processes may be internalized through the mechanism of symbolization, there is also present the possibility of self-control.

These processes have been discussed as though they were peculiar to infancy and to childhood. It should be evident that they are equally applicable to later stages of the life cycle. Socialization is a lifetime process, the self is never "finally" formed, and self-other interaction ceases only with death. Infancy and childhood provide the prototypes of these processes, but the processes do not terminate then. The peculiar significance of infancy and childhood is a function of the simple fact that they are first, that the self is unstructured and so the person is more malleable and change a greater possibility. There is no need, from this point of view, to "explain away" radical changes in behavior patterns at later stages by arguing that only the particular manifestations of behavior have altered while the underlying pattern remains intact.

The individual, through time as well as at the same time, occupies a variety of positions in networks of social relationships. If he responded in each of these in terms of unique sets of role expectations and self definitions, his behavior would be discontinuous and disorganized. Usually, however, there is continuity and organization in the behaviors of a given individual. The question is: how can such personal organization be accounted for?

The basic answer suggested by symbolic interaction theory makes use of the concepts of self, role, and definition of the situation. On entering an ongoing social situation, one prepares to respond to that situation by defining it. This definition includes the assignment of positions to others, and thus the setting up of a range of expectations concerning their behavior. It also includes an assessment of self; that is, one also assigns positional identities to oneself. Others in the situation are, of course, engaged in the same kind of activity. The interplay of behaviors that ensues is a function of such defining activity. A crucial question thus becomes that of the congruence of definitions —situation, role, and self—of the interacting persons.

Congruence permits efficient, organized behavior. Expanding this, and again noting that the individual moves through a variety of interpersonal situations, the congruence of definitions, and so of the behavioral expectations these imply, is fundamental to the continuity and organization of behavior. Personal organization is thus a function, not simply of that which the individual carries around with him, but of the relationship between that which he carries with him—in the form of self-concepts—and the situations in which he interacts with others as these are mediated symbolically.

When one asks what kinds of social conditions foster or permit such congruence, the generalized answer is that when meanings are widely shared in a society, or among those persons within a society with whom one actually interacts, congruence is likely. Note that there is no assumption that meanings are necessarily shared widely, although the fact that we can speak of a society at all is prima facie evidence that this condition exists to at least a minimum degree.

What happens when meanings are diverse? Reversing the point recounted above, but maintaining the same explanatory principle, it may be said that incongruities in definition and so incongruities in expectations will result, and that personal disorganization is the outcome. There are a number of possible types of incongruity, and it can be suggested that not all will have the same disorganizing impact on the individual: conflicts or lack of coordination between self concepts and the expectations of others; conflicts among aspects of self called into play in the same situation; conflicts in expectations deriving from significant others within the same organized group; conflicts in expectations deriving from significant others who themselves are in our ambience but do not relate to one another; and the temporal succession of expectations which do not articulate.

Finally, changes in identities occur when others fail to validate self-concepts by behaving in appropriate ways. Generally, the behavior of others provides cues on the basis of which further performance in terms of an identity is possible. If these cues are not provided, then such performance is no longer possible, and the identity will fade. [The reader will be impressed with similarities between role theory, as discussed above, and game theory, as explained on pp. 695–711 of this Handbook.]

Methodological predilections. Rose has suggested three methodological characteristics of symbolic interaction: (a) the tendency to focus on the level of common experience; (b) the assumption that human behavior and social life are in constant flux:

"Social life is assumed to be 'in process' never 'in equilibrium'"; (c) "the assumption that all social objects of study . . . are 'interpreted' by the individual and have social meaning" (1962, pp. ix–x). As already suggested, the last leads to the demand that the investigator see the world from the standpoint of his subjects; this demand has been called the fundamental methodological principle of the theory.

Given this demand, the problem of procedure is set: how can we capture the point of view of the person(s) whose relationships are being studied? Cooley suggested a process he called "sympathetic introspection," by which he essentially meant that the investigator is to obtain the experience of his subjects and then plumb his own consciousness in the effort to understand this experience. But, from the standpoint of anything approaching the canons of a would-be science of social psychology, this is obviously hopelessly inadequate.

With Thomas, the life history and case document became the tools with which to meet the methodological imperatives of the theory, and in Thomas and Znaniecki (1918 –1920) there is a concrete demonstration of what these tools can accomplish in sophisticated hands.

At the time Thomas and Znaniecki achieved their major synthesis of symbolic interactionism, it was quite clear to both of them that their definition of sociological materials was such as to require special methods of study. How does one quantify definitions of the situation? What measurements apply to life organization. . . ? Thomas and Znaniecki advocated the life history, the detailed personal narrative, and the exhaustive study of the individual case as the methods appropriate to their materials. . . . Inevitably, with the development of methodological sophistication it became clear that the case or life history is only a technique and not a self-sufficient method, but this does not obscure the importance of its development or its consistency as a technique with the particular definition of sociological subject matter of symbolic interactionism (Martindale, 1960, p. 353).

This methodological sophistication is a recent development, although the implication should not be read into this statement that lack of methodological sophistication was, or is, characteristic solely of those who advocated the use of case materials as the answer to sociology's prayers for techniques suitable to its domain of inquiry. Through the 1930's, the sociological literature reflected the polemics of those who argued for case methods as opposed to statistical methods and the equally polemic arguments of those who plumped for statistical methods as opposed to case methods; and, to a lesser extent, this pseudo-argument appears today. It is undoubtedly true that many of those whose theoretical leanings are to symbolic interactionism find case material congenial, and they seek to exploit such materials in their research. It is also true that many of these same persons are either overtly or covertly "anti-statistical"; indeed, it seems fair to say that for some the major grounds for attraction to symbolic interaction theory is the support it appears to give for rejecting the use of statistical techniques.

But there seems to be no necessary logical basis for this antagonism; the commitment to the methodological rule of studying the world through the eyes of the subject does not preclude one from making use of statistics either in the descriptive or the analytic sense. Nor does this commitment necessarily wed the investigator to the life history or the case material. Other demands preclude a full defense of this assertion; but the researches of many social psychologists whose work stems from one or another phase of symbolic interaction theory (Rose, 1951; Stone, 1959; Stryker, 1956; Wallin, 1950) strongly argue its validity.

In part, the tendency to focus on everyday experience also reflects the methodological importance attached to definitions of the situation. Rose (1962) suggested that this tendency results in an emphasis on observation as opposed, for example, to experimentation under "artificial," controlled conditions. It is certainly the case that experimentation

has not been frequently used in the interests of testing the implications of symbolic interaction theory. Again, however, there seems to be no necessary reason for its exclusion, provided that one's attitude toward experimentation is that what "works" in the world outside should also "work" in the laboratory, rather than the reverse; and provided that one finds it legitimate to study the connections between abstract variables rather than situations in their "full" complexity.

There need be no apology for this concern with common experience. Only the naive will assume that it follows from this concern that analyses must lack subtlety; for those who are unconvinced, a reading of— among many others—Goffman (1959) should provide proof enough. This concern requires defense only if symbolic interaction theory is regarded as a complete theory of social behavior, which view this chapter has rejected.

The social process bias, the third of the methodological characteristics listed by Rose, has been in evidence throughout this presentation of the theory. An assessment of this feature of symbolic interaction theory will be reserved for the section of the chapter in which the theory is evaluated. At this point, it is sufficient to note that this emphasis is also, in part, responsible for the predilection toward the life document. Cooley once suggested, in all seriousness, that the ideal sociological "method" was the motion picture, for then life in process could truly be captured. The spirit of this remark is preserved in those who find case materials the ideal "method."

SYMBOLIC INTERACTIONISM IN FAMILY SOCIOLOGY

Development of the Ideas

Given the fact that the center of development of these ideas was the University of Chicago, it is not surprising that symbolic interaction theory found its way into family sociology through Ernest W. Burgess. Nor is it surprising that these ideas found a ready audience among sociologists and others with an interest in the family.

Burgess. It is noteworthy that Burgess, writing in 1926, could say that when he gave for the first time a course on the family nine years earlier,

But among all the volumes upon the family, ethnological, historical, psychological, ethical, social, economic, statistical, radically realist, or radically idealist, there was to be found not a single work that even pretended to study the modern family as behavior or as a social phenomenon. . . . So far as I know, the description by Professor Thomas of the large family group among the Polish peasants was the first study of the family as a living rather than as a dead form (1926, p. 3).

This was a point in time when sociologists generally were groping toward interaction as the distinctive subject matter of their discipline; and it was a point in time when family sociology as a distinctive speciality began to emerge. Given the emphasis on socialization, on the significance of primary relationships, and on studying behavior in its natural habitats, it seems inevitable that those with a concern for studying the family as a "living form" would find the ideas of Mead, Cooley, and Thomas congenial.

These ideas find clear expresion in Burgess' proposal that the family be studied as a "unity of interacting personalities." Searching for a way to organize materials for his course, Burgess began by developing typologies of families. He found particularly useful a classification of families in terms of the patterns of personal relationships tying husband and wife, parent and child together.

This study of the patterns of personal relationships in family life led directly to the conception of the family as a unity of interacting persons.

By a unity of interacting personalities is meant a living, changing, growing thing. I was about to call it a superpersonality. At any rate the actual unity of family life has its existence not in any legal conception, nor in any formal contract, but in the interaction of its members. For the family does not depend for its survival on the harmonious relations of its members, nor does it necessarily disintegrate as a result of conflicts between its members. The family lives as long as interaction is taking place and only dies when it ceases (1926, p. 5).

In the interaction of personalities, the family develops a conception of itself. It becomes a unit, with ties as a unit to the community and the larger society. Interaction as a principle of social life applies not only to internal family relationships, but to the relations of the family and its environment.

The conception of the family as a unity of interacting personalities is elucidated through the distinction between individual and person suggested by Park:

The person is an individual who has status. We come into the world as individuals. We acquire status, and become persons. Status means position in society. The individual inevitably has some status in every social group of which he is a member. In a given group the status of every member is determined by his relation to every other member of that group. The individual's self-consciousness—his conception of his role in society, his "self," is based on his status in the social group or groups of which he is a member (Park & Burgess, 1921, p. 55).

Pointing out that every person has a more or less aware conception of his own role in a family, and a sense of the roles of others in the family as well, Burgess referred in quite contemporary terms to the consequences for conceptions of roles of stable and rapidly changing societies, to conflicts in conceptions of family life, and to conflicting roles.

Burgess took issue with those (specifically, in this context, with Trigant Burrow) who regarded conceptions of self and other as illusions lacking reality, and in so doing emphasized the premises of symbolic interaction theory.

These social images, these conceptions of ourselves and others . . . seem to many of us the very substance of human nature and personality. . . . What is human nature but the capacity to have social images, to put oneself in the other person's place and look at oneself, so far as one is able, in the mirror of the attitudes of other persons? . . . For the study of human nature, personality, and groups like the family, the basic reality is just this social image, and this conception of one's role in the family, in the congenital group and in the community. Intimate studies of family life reveal that the actual problems of human beings center, in general, around the struggle to realize our conceptions of our roles. . . . For it is in his social images, his memories, his wishes, his dreams, his illusions, his faiths that a human being really lives. . . . (1926, p. 9).

Roles are, then, the social reality of the personality; but they are not absolutes. They are, rather, relative to social situations. They may become obsolete in relation to changes in life conditions. They may become formal and mechanical, losing the spontaneity and "human quality" which initially characterized them (1926, p. 9).

Waller. The first full-scale treatment of the family from the point of view of symbolic interactionism appeared in Willard Waller's *The Family: A Dynamic Interpretation* (1938). Presented as a text dealing with middle-class family life, this work has few of the marks of that genre. Rather, it is suffused with Waller's creative speculation, deriving largely from insights gained from case materials collected in the course of his own researches.

Waller's starting point was precisely with the ideas already reviewed. He proposed to study the family as a unity of interacting personalities, supplementing that formula with John Dollard's addendum, "each with a history" (1938, p. 15). Interaction, a set of processes by virtue of which society exists, takes place in the mind: "all our commerce with our fellows is mental and imaginative." Such interaction has certain special characteristics: (a) great changes take place in interacting elements in the process of interaction, particularly as a function of the experience of crisis; (b) the cause of much of the behavior of a human being is within the human being himself; (c) society, in any ultimate sense, exists in the mind and in imagination; and (d) elements which interact interpenetrate, becoming part of one another (pp. 19–20).

In elaborating the framework to be used, Waller exhibited characteristic sensitivity and balance. The sociological view of personality is valuable, but we need not and must not on that account fall into the fallacy of a cultural determinism. Accepting the Burgess dictum that the role is the ultimate social reality, he noted that there are other important realities as well. The family may usefully be seen, as Burgess suggested, as a superpersonality, but it would be dangerous to push the analogy too far; it is better simply to note that the family tends to be a more or less closed system of social interaction, and that, while family events often must be explained through extra-family variables, they can frequently be explained by reference to other family events. "The family is thus a partially closed causal system" (p. 25).

Waller did not intend these considerations to be restrictive, nor a barrier to the sociologist's traditional interest in institutional interrelationships and total societies. Rather:

The conception of the family as a unity of personalities acting upon one another furnishes the correct approach to the study of the relation of the family and society. . . . In order to understand the relation of the family to society, we must describe concrete processes of interaction within the family group and relate them to larger social processes which are taking place in the greater society. This discussion has suffered in the past from a too static view and from a tendency to relate the abstract conception of the family to an abstractly conceived society. . . . These are valuable interpretations, but their value would be greatly enhanced if it were possible to trace concretely the interaction processes involved (1938, pp. 25–26).

Noting that "the natural history of the family furnishes the best possible orientation for the study of processes of interaction in the family," Waller outlined five stages of family experience: life in the parental family, courtship, the first year of marriage, parenthood, and the stage of the empty nest.

Life in the parental family was, for Waller, the story of the formation of personality. The central concept of his treatment is habit. Relying primarily on Cooley and Mead, he traced the emergence of the self through the processes of symbolic interaction. Although not unaware of the dangers involved, in something of a tour de force he then attempted to integrate ideas relevant to personality development with the concept of habit, the formulation of which he took largely from Dewey. He proposed to treat attitudes as the equivalent of habit, as tendencies to act. He regarded "definition of the situation" as an account of the way in which habits of the new members of a group are influenced by established habits of group members. The individual's life organization is the objective aspect of habits, his life viewed as arrangements organized to satisfy habits. One's philosophy of life is the consequence of habits. Character is the product of interacting habits corresponding to the mores. Emotion, phantasy, imagination, memory, and intelligence are the consequences of interruptions of habits. Adjustment involves the modification of habits in response to changed situations. Roles, which are social realities, are habits, sometimes having great propulsive power; and these rest upon other habits. And, finally, the Freudian mechanisms, and mental conflict, may be interpreted in terms of the interaction of habits.

Making use of novels, case materials, and —almost incidentally—such research as existed at that time, Waller used the framework sketched as the underpinning of a series of novel formulations and tentative explanations of family-related behavior. Given present space limitations, this treatment will restrict attention primarily to one such formulation—that having to do with divorce as a social process, for one can see clearly here the use to which the ideas of symbolic interactionism are put. But no presentation of Waller's work could be satisfactory without at least mention of his account of certain courtship processes.

Waller stressed the degree to which courtship is a bargaining process—indeed, he saw marriage itself in the same light—and, in so doing, introduced the possibility of "definite exploitative attitudes" in the paired relationships involved. These exploitative attitudes may be seen in dating, which Waller regarded as aim-inhibited association deprived of its goal of permanent mating, intervening between puberty and mating. It is in this connection that he presented his conception of the rating-dating complex. This complex is a function of a competitive setting, and refers to the manner in which one achieves and retains prestige through the dating of prestigeful others. Since this assumes a competitive order, the outcome of this process, he suggested, is generally for assortative dating on the basis of comparable prestige. It also is likely to generate antagonism between the sexes, creating a favorable environment for exploitation. Even further, those who lose out in this competitive process are likely to develop protective accommodations and definitions of the situation.

Exploitation frequently characterizes the courtship process per se, since courtship is also a competitive bargaining relationship, albeit of a different order than dating. Emotional involvement in courtship often, perhaps usually, develops unevenly. If the difference in levels of involvement is great, the probability of exploitation is high. The exploiter is likely to be that person who is least concerned with continuing the relationship. "Control in these extra-marital relationships follows a principle which we may accurately, if somewhat ungrammatically, designate as the principle of least interest. That person is able to dictate the conditions of association whose interest in the continuation of the affair is least" (Waller, 1938, p. 275). This principle has a number of interesting consequences. It creates the great possibility that a relationship will stabilize on the level of exploitation with unpleasant results for one of the pair. Once a relationship becomes exploitative, it is not likely to develop further. The realization of the traumas connected with unequal involvement leads people to resist the development of love attitudes. Marriages which do occur out of such courtships are likely to be unsatisfactory. And those who are exploited in one affair may turn exploiter in the next.

Waller's aim, in his treatment of divorce as a social process, was to answer the question: why, given marriages which are just as "bad," do some terminate in divorce and others not?[8] Traditional sociological analyses, at the level of societal processes as in Ogburn's work, can explicate the "whys" of increasing divorce rates, but must be supplemented if this question is to be treated. For this, Waller proposed to focus on the individuals playing roles within the social process, and on the structure of personality which both determines and is determined by this interaction. It is worth noting, and it is in line with Waller's methodological premises, that he insisted this mode of analysis can stand alone at the same time that he suggested that a more complete account of divorce would include analyses of societal processes and depth analyses in the psychoanalytic vein.

Divorce cases differ from near-divorce cases in that in the former one or both parties have a sufficiently strong desire to escape to make them willing to pay the penalties of divorce.

It illuminates the problem somewhat to reflect that in many cases one develops this desire

[8] This account of the divorce process, as Waller saw it, has been drawn from his "text," rather than from his pioneering study of divorce, *The Old Love and the New* (1930). While the latter provides a better picture of the use of the case "method," being based principally on the intensive analysis of 33 case documents, the former provides a better view of Waller's attempt at systematically theorizing with respect to divorce.

to escape because the process of adjustment to life without the other person has already begun; love has been withdrawn and centered upon the self, habits have been formed on a separate basis, and so on. In so far as this process tends toward completion, the other person operates as a thwarting agent; the whole marriage is a frustration. One therefore develops the appropriate affects to carry him through the situation, an example of functionally determined emotion. This is a reason for the bitterness which enters into the divorce process and so often disappears just afterwards. Such situations also account for many of the cases in which married persons fall violently in love with outsiders (1938, p. 538).

Marriage in American society is becoming defined as an exclusively erotic relationship, and consequently is inherently unstable. In a period of transition in norms, the old norms operate with differential effectiveness on individuals and segments of society. The non-divorce of unhappy marriages thus represents a type of culture lag. The "startling" conclusion is that high divorce rates are not transitory, and we can take no solace from the "comfortable doctrine" that this is the case.

Divorce in particular cases is the end product of a process of alienation. This process develops out of crises which occasion successive redefinitions of the marital relationship in terms of greater alienation and greater instability.

Alienation is a summatory social process; like mating, it is a process in which each response leads to the next in line and the motive for each new step is furnished by the experiences of the process up to that point; it is characteristic of such processes that they cannot easily be arrested (p. 540).

Alienation, then, rests on a series of crises. Typically, there occurs early in the process a disturbance of erotic relationships arising out of lack of rapport. Then, what may have been privately considered becomes a matter of public definition through the overt mention of the possibility of divorce. At some point, the fiction of marital solidarity is broken, and others become aware of the situation. There is likely to be real shock involved for the married pair—they lose face, and each blames the other—but after this the marriage is on a quite different plane. "One may regard the destruction of the fiction of solidarity, if it is at all complete, as a master of [sic] symptom of alienation; once this has been destroyed, it is ordinarily rebuilt with difficulty, and the process enters a new phase" (p. 541).

The decision to break the relationship is followed by a crisis of separation, often traumatic, and eventually, by divorce itself. While the act of divorce is a crisis for which the parties typically have had time to prepare themselves, it is nevertheless significant in that it marks the point at which "the actual work of reconstructing one's life can begin."

Typically, crises furthering alienation are followed by crises of reconciliation, for marriage exerts strong pulls; the gap between the couple only gradually widens. As this process takes place, the couple begins making necessary adjustments: attitudes change in anticipation of situations, and in reaction to actual changes in the situations. These adjustments are not simple, for the attitudes of marriage are habits with considerable propulsive force. As alienation continues, these habits—sex, response, ego, food, and so on—are frustrated, and the response to frustration is akin to the mourning behavior in reaction to bereavement. When habitual behavior is forestalled, it at first tends to persist along the same channels, and there ensues a reactivation of memory and an activation of phantasy life. The rearrangements which follow blocked habit, akin to the mourning process, result in changes in personality which reinforce alienation. "New habits and new purposes are formed, and the tissue of rationalization and fictions by which one has been enabled to support a marriage or to tolerate one's role in marriage is destroyed" (p. 544).

But the account of the divorce process remains incomplete, suggested Waller, until the ways in which the divorcing couple remain interdependent are noted. The couple "need" one another, in part because of the joy of conflict and the "strange" joy derived from examining sore spots in their relationship. While this tendency appears as a kind of partial suicide, it is rather an assertion of self at the expense of that which the self holds most dear. In part, too, this "need" for one another reflects the interdependence of the alienation process: "each one needs for his role the continued support of the other. Each is able to achieve his own forward movement only by the continued participation of the other in the process" (pp. 547–548).

Waller was one of the most articulate defenders of the use of personal documents in the period in which this was seen as a distinctive method in opposition to a statistical method. There are, he wrote, two kinds of social scientists, "those who want what they say to be true and as demonstrable as possible, whether it is significant or not, and those who do not so much care whether what they say is exactly true as whether it is significant if it is true, or if it has some truth in it" (1930, p. 315).[9] Waller identified himself as one of the latter. While he noted that statistics may be used imaginatively, and case studies unimaginatively, he clearly conceived the reverse to be the more likely. And he unequivocally rejected the argument that case studies provide an inadequate base for generalization as compared with statistical analyses of mass data: "Now no generalization can be so clearly buttressed by facts as one which is definitely supported by one or two well understood cases; generalization from statistics is ever more tenuous and inconclusive than generalization from persons" (pp. 316–317).

Hill. In a variety of contexts, but perhaps particularly in his revision of Waller's *The Family* (1951), Reuben Hill has added substantially to the analysis of the family from the standpoint of symbolic interactionism.

[9] From *The Old Love and the New* by Willard Waller, by permission of Liveright, Publishers, N.Y. Copyright © R, 1958, by Willard Waller.

He has done so, in part, by toning down many of Waller's characteristic extravagances; by making it clear that whatever the intuitive appeal of the insights provided by Waller and others in their application of symbolic interaction ideas to familial relationships, the ultimate utility of these insights depends on systematically gathered evidence; and by showing, through example, that responsible scholarship in this area requires the confrontation of assertion by evidence and the willingness to alter assertion in the face of recalcitrant fact.

But Hill's contribution is more creative than the foregoing may imply. In particular, in a foreshadowing of what he now sees as a distinctive theoretical orientation to family research—the developmental approach (Hill & Hansen, 1960)—Hill has enlarged on Waller's tentative use of the stages of the "natural history" of the family by pointing up the significance of the fact that the various members of a family reach critical points of their life cycles in an unsynchronized fashion. In so doing, he has added a dynamic dimension to a mode of analysis which, for all of its emphasis on process, is frequently—perhaps even typically—limited to a consideration of statics.

The family as a group of interacting personalities differs from most primary groups in its age and sex composition. Its members, being of different ages, differ in their desires and needs, grow at different rates of speed, and differ in their levels of comprehension of how to handle the problems of living together in a family. At any moment, children are striving to meet their growth needs, parents to reconcile their own inner desires with their parental urges to serve their young. At rare times during the family life cycle, the family members are sufficiently reciprocal in their need to love and be loved, for example, to mutually support and sustain one another. Quite as naturally, upon occasion, goals, needs and strivings of family members are in conflict. Thus, each family may be seen as an arena of interacting personalities, each striving to obtain the satisfaction of his own basic desires. Limited and supported by the pattern of family life which has evolved in interaction with the larger so-ciety of which it is a part, each family achieves its own tempos and rhythms of living. Parents, who themselves have urgent needs, make most of the adjustments in building complementary roles between themselves and their children. They are often patient and understanding with the infant, but once he graduates from infancy to childhood he is recognized as expressing a will, and parents insist that he too must make his quota of adjustments.

If we hold the entire family in focus, we see that many of the clashes between members during the family's life cycle are due to the imcompatibility of the diverse developmental strivings of family members at critical points of growth. By the same token, much of the unity and cohesion between family members is a product of the mutual meeting of needs within the family sphere (Waller & Hill, 1951, p. 27).

The manner in which Hill brings the apparatus of symbolic interaction conceptions, enriched by the life cycle conceptions noted above, to the analysis of family patterns may be seen in his treatment of parent-adolescent and parent–post-adolescent child relations in the later stages of the family cycle (Waller & Hill, pp. 425-431). The starting point is with the concept of habit. Parents have difficulties in adjusting to their maturing children in part because of the rewards parents receive for habits of protection, guidance, and direction of their children through preschool and school ages, in part because playing parental roles represents fulfillment of years of anticipatory socialization, and in part because the roles of their children through this period reinforce the habitual patterns of the parent.

But parents are trained in roles which are pertinent only through this period; they are not trained for roles which permit decreasing intensity of relationships with children. More, both parents have difficult problems of role transition at a point when children are experiencing such problems as well. The teen-ager seeks independence, i.e., to leave his dependent childhood role. The mother has built a role which assumes a dependent other, and is likely to find it painful to release her child to the world precisely because of this. Her problem is accentuated under contemporary circumstances—coming earlier and in more vigorous condition to this launching stage, and a more abrupt transition given fewer children relatively close in age. The father's reaction is affected to some extent by the mother's, reflecting the intimate connection of their roles. Further, he must face the evidence of unrealized and unrealizable ambitions, and of lessened virility, both of which represent threats to the male role in a society such as our own. In this situation, then, parents need to be needed, at a point in time when their offspring are least likely to appear to need them. Thus the consequence of the differential phasing of life-cycle requirements is the incompatibility of family members.

A persistent interest of family sociologists has been in the conditions and consequences of family crises, and much of the work dealing with such crises has been done from the standpoint of symbolic interaction. Hill has contributed perhaps the most systematic research to date in this area (1949); and, on the basis of his own study together with that of others as well, has developed the underpinnings of a general theory of family crises (Waller & Hill, 1951, Ch. 21; see also Ch. 19 of this Handbook).

Family disorganization includes all situations in which the family loses a member; viewing the family as an interacting unity of personalities, it also includes the more subtle breaks in the configuration of the family which are seen in the alienation of one family member from another. Any rupture of family relationships which forces reorganization of family patterns constitutes a crisis. More fully,

a crisis is an event which strains the resources which families possess, cannot be resolved by the repertory of ready-made answers provided by the mores or built up out of the family's previous experience with trouble, and requires the family to find new (and usually expedient) ways of carrying on family operations. Viewed from the perspective of habit, a crisis is that which interrupts the run of habit (Waller & Hill, 1951, p. 456).

Whatever the source of crisis, once one set of habits is disrupted, other sets are disrupted as well and complete family paralysis becomes an objective possibility. Most crises involve a loss of morale, for role patterns within the family are sharply disturbed. Thus, for example, the loss of a family member requires the reallocation of his roles, and creates confusion and delay in the process.

A given event may or may not produce a family crisis. Whether it does will depend on at least three variables: the hardships involved in the situation or event itself; the resources of the family, i.e., its role structure, flexibility, and previous experience with crisis; the definition the family attaches to the event, whether the family regards the event as if it is or is not a threat to status, goals, and objectives. In line with fundamental assumptions of symbolic interaction theory, Hill has emphasized the significance of these definitions of the situation. Noting that there are three possible definitions of a crisis-precipitating event, the objective definition formulated by an impartial observer, the cultural definition formulated by the community, and the subjective definition formulated by the family, he argued that the third is the most important for the student of crisis proneness in families.

The researcher and the community stand outside the situation looking in, but the family members are on the inside, and family attitudes toward the event tend to be determined by the family's particular patterns of interaction, its resources, its values, and its previous experience with similar hardships. Not infrequently families with resources adequate to meet the hardships of sickness or job loss crack under stress because they define such hardship situations as insurmountable. Accident proneness is disproportionately high among individuals who lack self-confidence and are characterized by anxiety. Crisis proneness in families may also prove related to outlook—to whether or not the event is defined as challenging or crisis-provoking (Waller & Hill, 1951, p. 462).

In these terms, an event produces a crisis only as it interacts with the crisis-meeting resources of a family *and* with the family's definition of the situation.

Adjustment to family crises takes place at three levels of increasing complexity: the level of the individual facing the situation, the level of dyadic interaction (e.g., the married pair), and the level of the family as a unit. As a family,

Adjustment to crisis which threatens the family depends upon the adequacy of role performance of family members. The family consists of a number of members interacting with one another, and each member is ascribed roles to play in the family's life. The individual functions as a member of the family largely in terms of the expectations which other members place upon him; the family succeeds as a family largely in terms of the adequacy of role performance of its members. One major effect of crisis is to cause changes in these role patterns. Expectations shift, and the family finds it necessary to work out different patterns. In the process the family is slowed up in its affectional and emotion-satisfying performances until the new patterns are worked out and avenues for expressing affection are open once more (Waller & Hill, 1951, p. 464).

Cottrell and others. The prominence accorded to Burgess, to Waller, and to Hill here should not be taken to imply that only these men have made significant contributions to the effort systematically to conceptualize and analyze family behavior in terms of the framework of symbolic interaction. Many others, writing both before and after Waller, share in this development.

So, for example, Leonard S. Cottrell has consistently championed the utilization of the ideas of symbolic interactionism in studying the family. In an early paper, Cottrell (1933) proposed that marriage be viewed as a problem in the adjustment of roles, conceived as an organization of habits

and attitudes appropriate to a given position in a system of social relationships. He argued cogently the need to recognize the importance, particularly in the marriage relationship, of reciprocal expectations of behavior, noting that such expectations are an integral part of the concept of role. Recognizing that analysis based on these premises is only partial, neglecting larger cultural and economic factors, for example, he proposed that unique role patterns are chief determinants of the success or failure in marriages of persons from similar cultural backgrounds; and he offered a set of propositions for the study of marriage adjustment:

First, marriage adjustment may be regarded as a process in which marriage partners attempt to re-enact certain relational systems or situations which obtained in their own earlier family groups. Or, in other words, marriage partners tend to play the habitual roles they evolved in their childhood and adolescence.

Second, the kinds of roles that marriage partners bring to the marriage will determine the nature of their marriage relationship and the degree of adjustment that they will achieve.

Third, that maladjusted marriages may be regarded as results of the failure of marriage situation [sic] to provide the system of relationships called for by the roles which the marriage partners bring to the marriage (1933, p. 109).

In another essentially programmatic paper, Cottrell (1937) has suggested that the social psychological aspects of fertility might well be explicated through research based on the symbolic interaction framework. And he has repeatedly stressed the significance for students of family relationships (and of social psychology, more generally) of research into the empathic—or role-taking—responses (e.g., 1948; 1950). Much of the current work in this area derives from the impetus provided by Cottrell; and the direction this work has taken reflects Cottrell's insistence on the necessity of finding adequate means of operationalizing the role-taking concept.

While it is not possible to review these in any detail, mention should be made of the variety of textbooks which, to a greater or lesser extent, develop around and extend themes of symbolic interactionism. Such, for example, are works by Kirkpatrick (1955), and by Cavan (1953). It is an interesting fact about family sociology that a principal medium for conceptual and theoretical writing is the textbook. It is also the case that the texts tend to be theoretically eclectic, as perhaps they must be, given the starting point of interest in the substantive area of the family rather than in problems of abstract theory as such. Starting with a substantive interest, it seems almost inevitable that texts will treat a variety of types of data on a variety of levels, from genetics to sociology. Nevertheless, insofar as they focus on interaction patterns within the family unit, such works as cited find their basic outlook in symbolic interactionism and contribute to the development of this framework in family sociology.

[In addition to the examples discussed above, the reader should be aware of two important applications of symbolic interactionism to family phenomena found in this Handbook. See Bernard's use of game theory to explain marital behavior, Ch. 17; and Dager's treatment of socialization and personality development, Ch. 18.]

An Assessment

The presentation, to this point, has focused on symbolic interactionism as a set of ideas—its historical development has been reviewed, a contemporary formulation as a theory of socialization and personality development has been sketched, and the ways in which its ideas appear in the writings of sociologists of the family have been considered. As yet, however, there has been little attempt made to assess these ideas in the context of family sociology. This is the concern of the present section.

Criteria to be considered. One vital element in the assessment of a set of ideas which claims scientific status is its relationship to research. But to frame a response to

the question of the relationship of ideas to research in a useful way requires that the question itself be given greater specification. A number of rather crucial issues must be faced, and working rules laid out.

The introduction to this chapter, it may be recalled, drew a distinction between theory and conceptual framework, and suggested that symbolic interactionism constitutes a theory when addressed to problems of socialization and personality development but a conceptual framework insofar as the more general problems of a sociology of the family are concerned. With respect to a theory, it is appropriate to ask whether it has stimulated research, whether such research as it has stimulated serves to test it, and whether this research indicates its validity. With respect to a conceptual framework, however, it is again appropriate to ask whether it has stimulated research, but it becomes inappropriate to ask more than that. A conceptual framework—since it includes no explicit propositions about empirical relationships which are presumed to obtain in the world outlined by the framework—cannot be tested in the same sense that a theory can. One can legitimately ask only whether a conceptual framework has been fruitful.

Whatever one's questions about the relationship of ideas to research—that is, whether these include more than the question of fertility—there remain a number of other problems. What, for example, constitutes "research"? Does this term cover the many instances found in the literature in which someone reflects, however wisely, on a case or two drawn from their experience? Does research imply at least an approach to rigor, with attention paid to such matters as an adequate sampling routine, the utilization of controls, systematic observation, and precise analysis? Must a research flow explicitly from a given theory or conceptual framework, in the sense that the researcher recognizes the antecedents of his own efforts, before it is "counted" to the credit of the theory or framework? Alternatively, should a research be used to indicate the fertility of a framework if there seems to be little connection between the antecedents "recognized" by the researcher and what he actually does? And, finally but not exhaustively, suppose that a research has stemmed explicitly from a theory other than that which is being assessed, yet may be read to support the implications of that under consideration, is it legitimate to use it in the assessment of the latter theory?

It is a great temptation, particularly for one who believes that symbolic interactionism, both as a theory and as a conceptual frame, holds considerable promise to (a) use the term research loosely, (b) require only that there be a connection, whether recognized by the researcher or not, between the ideas and the research, (c) count all work done in the name of the ideas, regardless of the ties of the work to the ideas, and (d) bring to bear all research that can be interpreted to fit the theory, whether in fact oriented to it or not. But precisely because the set of ideas is held in esteem, it becomes important that none of these be done. It becomes much more important that the assessment be critical in order that the present gaps be better indicated and the opportunities for important work revealed. While wise reflections, "unrecognized" contributions, and evidence from work done from the standpoint of other theories and frames are important to the development of theory, they ought not be used in the assessment of that theory. Indeed, they cannot be so used if the evaluation of a set of ideas in terms of its validity and fertility is to be more than an empty gesture. It is for this reason that the works of such men as Strodtbeck (1951; 1954) and Bales (1950; 1955), which at certain points relate closely to symbolic interactionism, have not been incorporated into this chapter.

Level of accomplishment. Given, then, rather strict criteria as the basis for judgment, it must be said that symbolic interaction theory—as a theory of socialization and personality development—has not as yet received adequate test. Nor has it stimulated the amount of research which might be expected simply in terms of its longevity and its prominence in the literature. Comparatively recently, Sarbin (1954) could write: "A few years ago, only impressionistic and anecdotal materials were available to document the self-role-interaction scheme of human conduct" (p. 225)[10]; and could quote Kluckhohn and Murray approvingly to the effect that, despite the obvious importance of role-training and role-playing for personality formation, these had hardly been approached on an empirical level.

Yet the judgment expressed above, based as it is on an over-all impression of a roughly 40-year time span, must be tempered. "The number of empirical investigations cited in this chapter indicate that the subject has 'opened up,' that since 1948 social psychologists in increasing numbers have employed self, role, and interaction as key conceptions" (Sarbin, 1954, p. 225). Much of the work on which Sarbin based his assertion derives from theoretical standpoints other than symbolic interactionism. The assertion is nevertheless reasonable, for there is a small but growing literature of sophisticated researches which directly test symbolic interaction theory.

At this point, it is symbolic interactionism as a theory of socialization and personality development which is of concern; the question is, how does this theory stand up against such evidence as has been gathered specifically to test it? Because this chapter is addressed to symbolic interactionism in the particular context of the family, only a selected portion of this research will be reviewed. Many of the studies have nothing to do, directly, with the family as a substantive field; and only sufficient of them will be reviewed to indicate that the theory as it has been presented, with its obvious implications for important aspects—but not the whole—of the family sociologist's field, is beginning to be tested.

Before turning to this research, however,

[10] From G. Lindzey (ed.), *Handbook of Social Psychology.* 1954. Addison-Wesley, Reading, Mass.

it will serve the assessment purpose of this section to ask: why is it that this research is all of relatively recent origin?

One major part of the answer to this question has frequently been overlooked, despite its simplicity: sociology, as a discipline, has not been oriented to the strict testing of theory. It is certainly safe to say that few of the theories—even narrowly defined—with which the sociological literature abounds have been subjected to adequate testing. A review of the research literature seeking to test almost any of these, if criteria of selection like those suggested above were utilized, would produce meager results. In this connection, it must be remembered that symbolic interactionism finds its "natural" home among social psychologists whose background is sociology rather than psychology. While there are some psychologists whose work is in this tradition, they are comparatively few; and the experimental mentality they represent has only recently been directed toward the "self-role-interaction scheme of human conduct."

But to note that the discipline as a whole has lacked a strict-test-of-theory orientation does not in itself answer the question. Another part of the answer lies in the fact that the theory itself is rarely stated in testable terms. As has frequently been pointed out, the concepts embodied in its propositions are often imprecise in meaning, and thus the propositions themselves are open to various interpretations. This, in turn, reflects the complexity of the phenomena to which the concepts refer. In particular, it reflects the difficulty of pinning down for research purposes concepts which refer to social processes. When, for example, the attempt is made to give empirical specification to the role-taking concept in the context of a particular study, the requirements of clear observation conflict with the processual requirements of the concept itself; to "see" it precisely requires treating structurally and cross-sectionally that which is in process and is dynamic.

Further, the concepts which the theory employs as well as the problems it seeks to explicate are social in their very nature. Thus, they necessitate for their effective use observations of interpersonal relationships. Unfortunately, the techniques which have been best developed and are most frequently used are individual in their orientation and derivation: attitude scales, questionnaires, case histories. As a consequence, in general, characterizations of relational phenomena have been inadequate. By way of illustration, marital success—clearly a product of a relationship—has been indexed by responses of married pairs taken individually even by researchers who are most sensitive to the requirements of symbolic interaction theory. Burgess and Cottrell's (1939) pioneer work in this area is a case in point.

And, finally, a tendency remarked earlier seems partly responsible for the paucity of explicit tests of symbolic interaction theory. As noted, there seems to be an affinity between the theory and the use of case methods, and, at least frequently, an affinity between preference for case materials and an anti-quantitative bias. While there is no necessary connection between quantitative methods and a methodology oriented toward strict testing of theory, nor between non-quantitative methods and an aversion to such testing, empirically these pairings appear to exist.

Cottrell (1950), in his discussion (written from the point of view of symbolic interactionism) of neglected problems in social psychology, called for work on the self, empathic responses, the situation, and motivation. It is with respect to the first two that the most thorough testing of theory has been accomplished.

Illustrative research. A central proposition of the theory is that self is a product of the responses of others. Miyamoto and Dornbusch (1956), studying 195 volunteer subjects from two fraternities and two sororities and using a procedure developed by Dymond (1949), found that the presumed relationship between others' responses and self-conceptions held, that subjects' perceptions of others' responses bore an even closer relationship to self-conceptions, and that subjects' self-conceptions related more closely to estimates of generalized attitudes toward them than to the perceived attitudes of members of a particular group.

Couch (1958), using the Twenty Statements Test devised by Kuhn (Kuhn & McPartland, 1954) as a basis for inferences concerning self-conceptions, found that certain expected relationships between these conceptions and estimates of others' evaluations did appear. That is, Couch hypothesized that his subjects' estimates of their own performances would reflect the estimates of their co-workers less when these subjects had strong affiliations with groups and institutions other than those invoked in the experimental situation. In general, his results supported this expectation. Couch also predicted, on the grounds that our culture teaches females more than males to be dependent upon immediate others, that females' self-evaluations would reflect more closely the evaluations of their co-workers; this prediction was borne out.

Reeder, Donahue, and Biblarz (1960) asked enlisted military personnel to rank themselves and others as leaders and workers, and asked as well that their subjects estimate how most others in their groups would rank them. The responses provided indices of self-conceptions, actual responses of others, and perceived generalized other. Relationships among all three were found: on the average, high self-rankers were given higher rankings by others, and perceived themselves as being ranked high by the others (perceived generalized other). When the distribution of persons in high, middle, and low self-ranked categories was compared with objective group ratings, it was found that only in the low self-rating category did objective ratings correspond; here, all of the low self-rankers were given low ratings by others. The authors formulated the hypothesis that persons whose self-rating disagreed with the actual ratings of them by others were operating with reference groups other than the one in which the study took place. Their data support this hypothesis, and this finding fits well with that reported previously from Couch's study.

More closely related to the family is a research reported by Sarbin (1954, pp. 243–244) from an unpublished study by Sarbin and Van Spanckeren. If, these researchers suggested, the development of the self is a function of the "looking-glass" principle, then we may expect that persons whose early socialization is a product of role-taking relationships with many significant others will have different self-concepts than persons whose early socialization is mediated by few parent figures. They also suggested that it follows from the theory being considered that the former set of persons will be more socially adjusted than the latter and will share many common characteristics. Findings supported these hypotheses: persons with more significant others in childhood tended to have similar self-concepts, and these self-concepts were more "social" and extended, and more homogeneous, than the self-concepts of persons exposed to few significant others in childhood.

From the theory, one expects that persons with self-concepts which are congruent with the perceptions of others will be more "adjusted" than will those persons for whom an incongruity exists. This hypothesis is supported by the work of Goslin (1962), who found that adolescents who perceive themselves differently from the way they are perceived by others are likely to receive a low degree of acceptance from these others. Low acceptance also relates to inability to take the role of the others, as we would expect, given the presumptive relationship between role-taking and self-conceptions. Finally, Goslin found that low acceptance is associated with self-conflict.

In a series of studies, Luckey (1960; 1961) established a relationship between satisfaction and congruency of subjects' self-conceptions and conceptions held of them by their spouses.

The research cited above helps to establish

the validity of the view which sees self-concepts as tied to others' responses. It is, however, insufficient in that the theory specifies a causal relationship: others' responses produce self. Support for the causal inference may be found in Videbeck (1960), who experimentally manipulated others' reactions and traced their impact on self-ratings. Videbeck's work, in its essential aspects, has been replicated (Maehr, Mensing, & Nafzger, 1962) and in general supported.

An attempt to test systematically implications of symbolic interaction theory with respect to the conditions of accuracy in role-taking may be found in Stryker (1956). Four propositions were drawn from Mead: (a) social activities are imbedded in a structure of roles, i.e., are self-other patterns; (b) to engage in social activity, one must take the role of other(s) implicated in that activity; (c) a significant segment of the role one must take consists of attitudes; and (d) ability to take the role of the other is predicated upon a common universe of discourse, a system of common or social meanings. From these propositions, 15 hypotheses concerning accuracy in role-taking in adult offspring-parent relationships were derived. These hypotheses were tested using an index of role-taking accuracy based on correct predictions of others' responses to a family ideology scale. Of 147 individual tests, 57 (39 per cent) produced results clearly supporting the theory. Only one test produced results contradicting the theory. Of the remaining tests, almost all produced results in the direction of those hypothesized, but not at statistically significant levels. Concluding that the theory exhibits, in terms of these findings and considerations of alternative explanations of them, a basic soundness, it was also suggested that the theory required qualification in order to account better for the findings of the research. Specifically, it was suggested that it is necessary to take into account differentials in the degree to which rationality, utilitarianism, and organization exist in various sets

of social relationships, that structural variables such as these be explicitly incorporated into the theory, rather than treated implicitly as constants.

A somewhat fortuitous finding, legitimately introduced here because of the concern of the researchers with the implications of the theory being considered, relates again to the conditions of accurate role-taking. Sarbin and Faberow (1952) asked subjects to regress, under hypnosis, to various childhood periods. Some could do so easily and accurately; others could not. The differences between the two categories of persons seemed to be a function of their security in adult roles, a difference which is explicable in terms of the theory.

From propositions describing role learning in terms of interaction, including the process of role-taking, Brim (1958) was led to hypothesize that cross-sex siblings will have more of the traits of the opposite sex than will same-sex siblings, and that the younger rather than the older siblings will show this effect more markedly. While the complexities of Brim's analysis cannot be presented here, the data he reviewed support these hypotheses.

Turning to the consequences of role-taking, the findings of various researchers are apparently contradictory. Buerkle and Badgley (1959) faced their subjects, 36 couples whose marriages were "in trouble" and 186 couples whose marriages were "not in trouble," with a series of hypothetical family situations in which a husband and wife must deal with conflicting roles. These subjects could resolve the dilemmas by choosing solutions which either involve taking the role of the other or not. The findings of this study indicate that the couples "in trouble" chose the role-taking solution less frequently, and were characterized by less sympathy and agreement on a course of action to take. Sarbin and Jones (1955) found a positive relationship between role-taking skill and a measure of social adjustment. On the other hand, Locke, Sabagh, and Thomes (1956) found no significant relationship between empathy—defined in their study as "taking the role of another person with sufficient accuracy so that one can predict his responses"—and marital adjustment. Stryker (1957) found a positive, statistically non-significant relationship between the role-taking accuracy of adult offspring vis-à-vis their parents and adjustment to these parents. More important, however, is his finding that there is a statistically significant *inverse* relationship between role-taking accuracy and adjustment for parents vis-à-vis their offspring. Data presented in this research tie this finding to tradition-oriented, dependent parents whose attitudes conflict with those of their offspring. Thus it is suggested that, for parents with these characteristics, accurate role-taking can lead to maladjustment.

Meanings in terms of theory. The meaning of these findings for symbolic interaction theory is not easy to assess. These researches, in general, use adjustment in the sense of happiness or satisfaction with a relationship. Whether the theory postulates adjustment in this sense as a consequence of role-taking accuracy is not at all certain or clear. Mead, for example, used the term adjustment as a synonym for the process of effective adaptation rather than in the manner of the research cited. The theory requires that a husband be able to take the role of his wife in order to adapt his responses effectively to her, whatever his goals, and does not require that he be happy or satisfied with his relationship to his wife.

Further, these researches—in their operational procedures if not in their modes of conceptualizing variables—frequently treat role-taking as an attribute of the person rather than a characteristic of the relationship. In short, adequate measurement of role-taking would seem to require a close specification of the interactive context in which the process occurs, and the treatment of role-taking as a reciprocal rather than a one-way process. To complicate matters even more, it appears clear that various types and levels of role-taking must be dis-

tinguished if this kind of research is to make headway (Farber, 1962).

One more general problem of the research reviewed deserves comment. Many of the studies cited dealing with either self-concepts or role-taking used techniques which depend on the ascription of others' responses. That is, the measurement techniques required that person A respond to a scale or a set of statements for himself and to predict how other(s) would respond to these. Such techniques have been criticized (Cronbach, 1955; Gage & Cronbach, 1955) on the grounds that the "scores" derived in this way contain a variety of components, or independent sources, some of which are simple artifacts of response sets of predictors and the others. These scores, then, are "impure," in that they do not adequately index knowledge of others, role-taking accuracy, or related concepts. It is not as yet known whether this fact requires substantial revision of conclusions reached on the basis of the research, or whether the implications of the research for symbolic interaction theory need to be re-examined. Stryker (1957), for example, has argued that insofar as the theory postulates that one's social behavior is predicated on the symbolic anticipation of others' responses, the diverse sources of role-taking accuracy are irrelevant: one must act on the basis of these anticipations, regardless of how they are derived. Whether this is indeed the case or not remains to be investigated. It should be noted, however, that the finding of one study (Scodel & Mussen, 1953) does not stand up when "pure" accuracy scores are used rather than "impure" scores. These researchers found a negative correlation between role-taking accuracy and authoritarianism (a characteristic of a person rather than of a relationship). Ewer (1962), replicating their procedure, obtained a similar result when "impure" scores were used, but found that this correlation disappeared—or possibly reversed direction—when a "pure" score was used.

Symbolic interactionism as conceptual frame. Thus far, the discussion has been of symbolic interactionism qua theory. It turns now to symbolic interactionism qua conceptual framework. Here, attention will be strictly limited to work done in the context of the family. The criteria for inclusion have been relaxed somewhat however: the presentation which follows includes researches which may not, taken by themselves, be explicit about their connection with symbolic interactionism, but which are the product of investigators who have made apparent in other contexts their orientation to this conceptual frame.

There will be no attempt to mention all of the research which may be said to be motivated by symbolic interactionism, in part because much of it is presented in other chapters of this volume, in part because—since research in the family, as previously noted, tends to be eclectic with respect to its theoretical sources and allegiances—other frameworks have equal claim to much of the work. Hill and Hansen (1960) referred to "the hundreds of studies" stimulated by the symbolic interaction framework. While this may be an overgenerous estimate, given such criteria as have been imposed for the present discussion, it suggests the impossibility of complete coverage.

Nor will there be any real attempt to review the specific findings of such studies as are mentioned; this task is best left to those chapters of this Handbook in which the more substantive questions of a sociology of the family are pursued. Thus, what follows will be severely restricted, both in content and in scope. It is simply an attempt to document major foci.

The principal focus of efforts deriving from the conceptual framework of symbolic interactionism, it will come as no surprise, is with interpersonal relations within the family, treated as a more or less closed system.

One subset of these efforts concerns the parent-child relationship, at various stages of the life cycle. Mowrer (1954) has sought to study the way in which generalized attitudes of family members operate to struc-ture the roles of children by investigating the affectional adjustment of twins, seeing the use of twins as a methodological device which controls differentials in responses to children due to differences in time of entry into the family system. Carter (1954) raised the question of whether experiences shared with parents (such as mobility, parent employment, marital status of parents, and size of family) or relationships with parents (such as parental expectations, strictness, favoritism, and identification with parents) relate more closely to feelings about self, and found that self-feelings are more closely related to the latter. Wallin (1954a) found that the marital happiness of parents has an impact on their children's attitudes toward marriage, for both males and females, but with some interesting differences between the sexes in this regard: females are generally more favorable to marriage than are males for all categories of parental happiness; and females of divorced parents are relatively optimistic with regard to their own possibilities for marital happiness.

A series of studies inquires into the attachment of adult offspring to their parents, both in the sense of affectional ties and dependence. Wallin (1954b) examined and found wanting an hypothesis suggested by Komarovsky (1950) concerning sex differences in attitudes toward in-laws: namely, greater female attachment to and dependence upon family of orientation. This hypothesis was also examined by Stryker (1955) in a study of the adjustment of married offspring to their parents. These researches have been tied together by Komarovsky (1956) into a case history of the interplay between theory and research, highlighting the progressive refinement of theory in the face of evidence. Albrecht (1954) reported on the relationship of parents over age 65 with their children, finding a general high degree of independence together with close affectional ties. The same researcher (Albrecht, 1953) dealt with the existent or remembered relationships of these older persons with their own parents. Lu (1953) examined parent-child authority patterns as these relate to conflict and affection, finding a positive relationship between degree of authority and conflict, a negative relationship between degree of authority and affection. Wallin and Vollmer (1953) inquired into the relationship of college students' ratings of their parents' marital happiness and their attachment to their parents, finding a positive relationship between happiness ratings and degree of attachment, a negative relationship between these ratings and conflict with parents.

Perhaps the largest number of studies issuing from the symbolic interaction framework is concerned with the husband-wife relationship. The first major study of marital adjustment from the standpoint of the interaction of roles in the family setting was Burgess and Cottrell's (1939) effort to predict success or failure in marriage. A significant segment of the family literature published each year follows out leads provided in this work, although the bulk of these are oriented to specific findings rather than to the underlying conceptual scheme which provided the framework for the original study. Seminal as well is the Burgess and Wallin (1953) study of the variables predictive of success in engagement and marriage, a work which in many ways represents an attempt to deal with problems arising in the Burgess and Cottrell research. [See Ch. 6 of this Handbook.]

A study which actually succeeds in treating the family as an interacting unit in its methodology is Lu's (1952b) research into the impact of home discipline and reaction to authority on marital roles: he found that dominant roles in marriage were more frequently assumed by persons who reacted negatively to discipline imposed by their parents, especially their mothers, and that equalitarian roles were more frequently taken by persons who had close affectional attachments to their mothers. Lu (1952a) also found that equalitarian spouse relations were associated with good marital adjustment, and that dominance of either husband

or wife in the marriage relationship was associated with poor marital adjustment.

Representing a somewhat different order of inquiry into the marital relationship are a series of more recent studies. Buerkle, Anderson, and Badgley (1961) rejected, on the basis of their data, the hypothesis that altruism relates to marital adjustment, but found that adjusted more than maladjusted couples used these techniques of resolving conflict: accurate role-taking vis-à-vis partners' plans, being or appearing to be sympathetic with partners' plans, remaining ignorant of partners' plans. Buerkle (1960) related self-attitudes to marital adjustment, finding that the salience of family-related responses on the Kuhn Twenty Statements Test was higher for adjusted wives than for maladjusted, and also finding that the use of consensual (references to groups) rather than subconsensual (evaluative and qualifying references to self) responses to this test differentiated adjusted from maladjusted couples. Komarovsky is currently conducting research systematically inquiring into marriage communication, dealing with such questions as privacy and self-disclosure both as ideal norms and as actual behavior, the existence of significant others apart from spouse who may act as confidant for the person, and the impact of these on marital stability.

Deriving from symbolic interactionism, as well, has been an interest in the empathic or role-taking process as it takes place in paired relationships ranging from dates to marriages. Vernon and Stewart (1957) found an association between role-taking accuracy with respect to satisfaction in dating behavior and degree of dating involvement. Kirkpatrick and Hobart (1954) related dyadic empathic responses to the various stages of pair intimacy from favorite date to marriage, finding no consistent trend in degree of empathy by stage, but finding that members of married pairs were more empathic with respect to one another than were favorite dates. A replication of this study by Hobart (1956) produced similar results. An as yet unpublished study by Foote and associates reports an attempt to follow through on the theoretical suggestions made by Foote and Cottrell (1955) with respect to the development of interpersonal competence by increasing the empathic ability of young couples through role-playing practice.

Dating and courtship relationships have received attention in terms of other aspects of symbolic interactionism as well. Much of this attention has derived from Waller's discussion of the competitive and exploitative elements in the rating-dating complex. Smith (1955) found that competition was a major theme of dating behavior in the college students he studied. Blood (1955), on the other hand, questioned at every point the Waller picture of the norms which presumably govern casual dating relationships. Much of the data of the Burgess and Wallin (1953) study of engaged couples is also oriented to Waller's theorizing with respect to dating and the process of falling in love; these authors, too, found that theorizing unwarranted. A still different interest in courtship is exemplified by Brim and Wood (1956) who investigated the congruence of responses of couples who were new dates, were frequently dating, were going steady, were engaged, or were married to the Twenty Statements Test, finding, in general, congruence in responses which was not allied with stage in the courtship process. Kirkpatrick and Hobart (1954) and Hobart (1956) also pursued this kind of interest.

Closely allied to, but not adequately contained in, the categories of research already reviewed are studies of family-related roles and role expectations. Komarovsky (1946) investigated the contradictions in parental expectations with respect to the role of college women and their impact on the role of these women. Wallin (1950) pursued the same line of inquiry, but shifted the focus to contradictions between parental expectations and the college woman's conception of her own role. Both studies found considerable contradiction, although Wallin was less inclined to see these as seriously affecting his subjects than Komarovsky. Motz (1950) traced variations in conceptions of marital roles by status groups, and later (1952) developed a role conception inventory as a tool for studying expectations with respect to the role of women. Rose (1951) documented the inconsistency, confusion, and lack of realism among college women in their expectations with respect to adult roles. Neiman (1954) reported on the attitudes of persons at three age levels (11–14, 15–18, and 20–24) toward the feminine role, and noted the progressively important impact of peer groups on these attitudes. Hobart (1958) examined the effects of romanticism during courtship on marriage role conceptions.

Reflecting in various ways the influence of symbolic interactionism are a number of studies which focus on the reactions of families to stress. Although these have been concerned with interpersonal relations within the family, they differ to some extent from most of the work cited above in that interpersonal relations tend to be treated as intervening variables, with some characteristic of the family as a total unit the dependent variable (the crisis itself is the independent variable). Thus Angell (1936) sought to investigate the integration—bonds of unity of which he conceived common interests, affection, and a sense of economic interdependence to be most pertinent—and the adaptability, or capacity to meet difficulties by shifting activity, of families faced with economic crises. Cavan and Ranck (1938) used essentially similar concepts in their study of family reactions to depression-induced crises. Koos (1946; 1950) concerned himself with family adequacy, a concept closely related to those used in the earlier studies, in his researches into the reactions of lower-class and middle-class families to a number of different "troubles." The most satisfactory research into the impact of crises on families yet published, in terms of sampling procedures and size of sample, and in terms of adequacy of instruments and analytic techniques, is Hill's (1949) study of the adjustment of families to war-derived separation and return. The Hill research is perhaps especially notable for the way in which it effectively used and interwove statistical and case-study techniques.

While these have been the major foci of research from the standpoint of symbolic interactionism, other interests have been manifested as well. So, for example, Phillips (1957) followed out suggestions made by Cottrell (1942) in developing and examining empirically a "role-theory" approach to adjustment in old age. Deutscher (1958; 1962) investigated the socialization processes by which parents become prepared for postparental life. Hill, Stycos, and Back (1959) made use of the framework in structuring and analyzing the results of an effort at fertility control.

Gaps and potentialities. These assertions, then, summarize the appraisal of symbolic interactionism to this point. (a) Symbolic interaction theory has not stimulated a great deal of research, but in recent years there have been a number of studies oriented to its test in a meaningful way. (b) Such research as does exist indicates the basic validity of the theory. (c) The theory, however, requires some modification—largely in the form of the introduction of social structural variables—if it is to deal adequately with its problems. (d) Symbolic interactionism as a conceptual framework has motivated a good deal of research, more than could be referred to in the present context, even when this term is used in a relatively restricted manner.

But such considerations of research support and fertility do not exhaust the grounds on which an appraisal must be made. Other criteria apply as well, whether the concern is with symbolic interactionism qua theory or qua conceptual framework. In particular, these have to do with gaps and limitations, intrinsic or more or less fortuitous, and with potentialities not yet realized.

One can hardly have an ordinary conversation without making frequent use of the word situation. Such popularity must be deserved, and I have little doubt that its function in communication is important, though I sometimes suspect its utility is quite as great in preserving an illusion of understanding as it is in conveying genuine comprehension.

When we move over into more technical conversations, we also find the term widely used by students of social behavior. Indeed, sociology can be thought of as a discipline devoted to the analysis of social situations. Here again, however, it must be said that in the ready use of this term we do not always find the ends of precise communication well served.

A social psychologist of my orientation would, of course, be quite lost if you deprived him of the word situation or situational field. But, in spite of the embarrassment it would cause me I must confess that the use of the word in social psychology is almost as vague as it is in general conversation. This is as true among those who aspire to a rigorous experimentation as it is among those who operate with less refined research procedures (Cottrell, 1950, p. 711).

Cottrell's words ring as true today as they did over a decade ago; a major problem of the social psychologist is to conceptualize "situations" in a way which serves the purpose of analysis, and which does not reduce to the science-defeating banality of saying that every situation is particular and so different. Nor will it do to dissolve the real world, including social structure external to the person, in an all-embracing "definition of the situation." It is a perversion of Thomas to use, as many do, his dictum that "if men define situations as real, they are real in their consequences" to deny the significance for social behavior of the external realities to which the definitions refer.

Nor is it satisfactory to deal with a second major problem facing symbolic interactionism as theory and as framework, that of motivation, by defining the problem out of existence through the idea of a vocabulary of motives, again as some have done. Foote (1951) has sought to develop a theory of motivation in terms consistent with symbolic interactionism, but, especially on an empirical level, work on this crucial issue has barely begun.

It is intriguing that a framework which emphasizes process to the degree that symbolic interactionism does, abstracting its basic concepts from the flow of social behavior, has paid so little systematic attention to the time dimension of social relationships. Life may be a never-ending stream, but that figure does not serve analytic purposes well. The problem of time exists for the framework on many levels. The most microscopic involves the bounds of a unit of interaction; the development of adequate research procedures to deal with process awaits a viable answer to this question. On a more macroscopic level, the problem of time becomes one of delineating stages in sequences of development. Here, although symbolic interactionists have not made much use of it, the life cycle conception is neither foreign to the framework (as can be seen, for example, in Waller's work) nor does it create any particular strains for the framework. Here, too, the concept of "career" has been developed by persons identified with this point of view, for example, Becker and Strauss (1956).

Stone (1959) has pointed out what he called the "discursive bias" in the framework as it has developed from Mead. That is, he suggested, symbolic interactionists have largely restricted themselves to an emphasis on verbal communication as the currency of social interaction. He especially called attention to the significance of appearance through his own work. Goffman (1959), another who has gone beyond traditional formulations, called attention to impressions unwittingly given off by participants in the social process. Suggestions such as these open the way to expanding the scope and power of symbolic interactionism.

This expansion, however (whether in these directions or along more conventional lines), requires greater attention to the related tasks of conceptual clarification and devising appropriate empirical procedures. Symbolic interactionists have not been noteworthy for their insistence on precise definition, although they are no different in this respect from adherents of other frameworks in sociology. Yet unless concepts are rigorously defined, there can be little hope for advances in observational or measurement procedures. Of particular importance for the further development of symbolic interactionism are more adequate means of capturing the subjective components of behavior.

Most of the research cited above deals with internal family relationships; it regards, as stated, the family as a more or less closed system. While this is a methodologically necessary device, for certain purposes, the tendency to accept it as a description of reality has meant that comparatively little attention has been given to the interplay between family roles and extra-family roles, or to the impact of what in the language of another framework is called the external system on the family as a functioning unit. Neither of these deficiencies seems to be a necessary consequence of symbolic interactionism; indeed, the conceptions of self and role as these are developed in the theory would seem to provide admirable vantage points for viewing these processes.

Another gap in the work issuing from symbolic interactionism is in terms of institutional or cultural patterns. Specifically in the context of family research, these interests, as Hill and Hansen (1960) noted, have been quite foreign to this framework. Whether this is a necessary gap, in the sense that the framework cannot deal with these, is moot. A conception of culture as widely shared and stabilized definitions of situations, for example, might well serve to illuminate at least some problems on this level.

The possibilities of exploiting this point of view in family-related research seem almost limitless. Only a few can be suggested here. There is much to be done in studies of early socialization; we know little about the earliest emergence of the self in children, for example, or about the subtleties of communication in early parent-child relations which may structure the self that emerges. Nor do we really know about the impact of children on the self-conceptions or role relationships of parents; there has been a tendency, in spite of the emphasis on reciprocity in theoretical formulations, to treat the parent-child relation as a one-way street. On such questions, symbolic interactionists have been to this point largely satisfied with inferences based on the work of others and with the demonstration that the language of the theory can be used to describe this work.

The question of self-conception or identity in relation to the family remains virtually virgin in many respects. What accounts for the differentials which obviously exist in the salience of family identities? What are the consequences of these differentials in degree of commitment to a family identity for parent-child relations, for husband-wife relations, for the family as a functioning unit? What kinds of extra-familial identities are compatible with family identities? What kinds are not? What determines whether or not a family-related identity is invoked in given situations?

Finally, the question of differential consequences of role-taking needs to be explored. Much prescriptive social science assumes the adjustive consequences of accurate role-taking; the evidence is that it may or may not be. But what are the conditions under which role-taking is adjustive or not? Perhaps this ties to the stages of the life cycle. Perhaps it is a matter of differences in role-relationships as couples move through the sequence of dating, courtship, early marital relationships, and later marital relationships.

THE SITUATIONAL APPROACH

As mentioned, this chapter has a secondary interest in what has been called the situational approach to the study of the family. This approach tends to be seen as the equivalent of "the sociological approach" by James H. S. Bossard, with whom it is almost completely identified among sociological students of the family; and it is seen as a distinctive theoretical orientation by Hill and Hansen (1960) in their review of alternative frameworks available for sociological research into the family.

Similarity to Interactionism

Treatment of the situational approach in the present context obviously assumes that it bears some strong relationship to symbolic interactionism as this latter orientation has been presented here. While it is not the intention of this statement to argue that situationalism and symbolic interactionism are identical, or that the situational approach is without certain differentiating characteristics, the decision to incorporate the materials which follow implicitly argues that that which unites the two views is more important than that which makes them different, and that the measure of similarity is greater than the measure of distinctiveness. Whether or not this is indeed the case can perhaps be better judged after the position itself has been reviewed. The possibility should not be overlooked, however, that the assumption of greater similarity will have biased this review.

In presenting the situational approach, attention will focus on the writings of Bossard, notwithstanding the fact that others—e.g., Lowell J. Carr—have made contributions as well. It was Bossard who offered the most systematic attempt to delineate this position; and, as noted above, it is Bossard with whom the position is associated within family sociology.

Bossard's own review of the development of the situational approach emphasizes the movement in a variety of disciplines toward the scientific study of behavior—the entire response or adjustment pattern of the individual—from the standpoint of environment. This kind of study was named the "situational approach," and conceived in this context, "situation" was synonymous with the stimuli arising from conditions exterior to the organism which play upon that organism[11] (Bossard & Boll, 1943, p. 10).

[11] It is, it seems to me, significant that the word used is "organism," rather than individual or than person, for this permits such phenomena as self and role, for example, to be considered as part of the environment in that these are not functions of the organism, per se, but rather of the interplay between organism and others in a social setting.

Within sociology itself, suggested Bossard, the situational approach rests upon Cooley's work—the ideas of the self as a social product, society and individual as two sides of the same coin, the looking-glass self; upon the work of Thomas and Znaniecki with its "fundamental theme of the relationship between personality and the environing culture"; upon the idea of definition of the situation as elaborated by Thomas, as well as upon other themes appearing in Thomas' writing which have already been examined. Thomas, he suggested, defined the sociological approach by distinguishing between constitutional and situational studies of personality development. Situational studies concern stimuli to which individuals react. Their principal objective is to uncover the determinants of the individual's behavior in his relationships with other individuals and with society (p. 14).

In facing the problem of defining the concept of situation, Bossard turned to the literature and sought to draw from it the general ideas contained in the contemporary situational approach. These he saw as (a) the idea that the stimuli to be included are all external to the organism (and, thus, situation is not coterminous with environment, for the latter includes all things to which a responder responds); (b) the idea that the stimuli which comprise situations are organized with reference to one another—they do not operate independently of their particular relationships to one another; (c) the idea that a situation is organized around some focal point or person, and becomes an emergent force acting on the person. In these terms, then, a situation is defined as "a number of stimuli, external to the organism but acting upon it, organized as a unit and with a special relatedness to each other as stimuli of the specific organism involved" (p. 25).

Situations, so defined, may be approached in a variety of ways: from the standpoint of structure, which Bossard took to mean a cross-sectional, "still-life" analysis of elements within a situation, and their position and relationship to one another; from the standpoint of process, a "motion picture" analysis of the interaction of elements as they undergo mutually induced modifications; from the standpoint of content, or the analysis of the ideas, attitudes, words—in short, "culture"—for which structure and process act as vehicles.

Bossard saw a number of implications as flowing from the situational approach as he conceived it. Most significant for present purposes is his insistence that the situational approach is distinctive, commensurate with the study of the personality reacting to situations; and his correlative insistence that the situation is a distinctive field for investigation, to be studied in its own right without reference to the ways in which individuals react to them (pp. 33-34).

Social situations differ, suggested Bossard, from those studied by the physiologist and the psychologist in that they are not created by the investigator but rather accepted and studied by the student as they are found. This compels the student to identify situations with existing organizations of stimuli, typically in a form which is restricted to a specific group of which the person is a member. The family is one such group, and a most significant one, both because it is of primary importance for behavior and because it is a methodologically strategic place to begin the total task of situational analysis.

It is apparent that if the situational approach is to have substance and utility in the study of the family, a workable classification of family situations must be developed. After reviewing a variety of classificatory schemes, Bossard offered one which reflects a survey of the literature, an analysis of case records, and the interpolation of situations which seemed to him logically required for relative completeness. While full presentation of this classification seems pointless, it is worth noting that the major axes of the scheme are intra-family relationships, further divided into affectional and subjectual relationships, family patterns, and external factors. The subtypes of affectional relationships range from excess of affection at one extreme to frank rejection at the other. Each subtype may cover a variety of more specific situations, e.g., the possessive home, the oversolicitous home, and the overindulgent home represent three variants of the excess of affection situation. The family pattern axis refers to family situations defined in terms of size (e.g., the large family), organization (e.g., the cooperative family), activity (e.g., the community-benefactor family), and values and goals (e.g., the social-climber family). The external factors axis includes socio-economic status (e.g., the disgraced home), neighborhood (e.g., the misfit-in-the-neighborhood family), and health (e.g., the home of the defective).

Methodologically, Bossard was committed to the life history or case study procedure for carrying out the program implicit in his classification of family situations. Correlatively, he doubted the adequacy of more formal procedures (Bossard, 1956, Ch. 2; Bossard & Boll, 1950, Ch. 10).

The operation of ritual . . . like the processes of family table talk, family entertainment, and word usages, which were subjects of our earlier studies, elude for the most part the straitjacket of the questionnaire method, the naivete of a statistical table, or the balance sheet of a social accounting system (1950, p. 208).

Bossard (1954, Ch. 4) accepted the view of the family as a unity of interacting persons; he saw situational analysis within sociology as resting on the seminal ideas of Cooley and Thomas; he saw behavior as adaptation; he insisted sociologists must study situations as they "really are" in the everyday world; and his predilection was for the use of personal documents as a method of research. In these respects, the situational approach as formulated by Bossard is close kin to symbolic interactionism.

Distinguishing Characteristics

What may be considered different in the situational approach when compared with symbolic interactionism seems to be a function of three emphases appearing in Bossard's writings: (a) his assertion that situations can and ought to be studied independently of the way in which individuals define them; (b) the correlative intent to focus, in his own work, on that which subjects define rather than on their definitions; (c) his introduction into conceptual discussion of such considerations as the various ways in which situations can be approached—as structure, as process, and as content.

In one sense, the first two of these can be regarded as correctives to the particular directions taken in work done from the standpoint of symbolic interactionism over the years rather than as departures from that framework itself. As formulated by Thomas, symbolic interactionism calls for "equal time" to be given to situations and to definitions. Clearly, as indicated previously, the latter has been the principle concern, to the neglect of the former. Bossard's work sought to balance the books in some degree.

The strongest case for the distinctiveness of the two frameworks can be made on the grounds of Bossard's insistence on the independence of situation and definitions of situation, the interdependence of the two being a cardinal tenet of symbolic interactionism. But the force of this argument seems to be weakened by the demonstration in Bossard's own work of the failure of this methodological principle in a program of research. At so fundamental a point as the classification of family situations, it is quite apparent that definitional elements enter. Further, the dependence of this work on personal documents almost necessarily interweaves definitions of the situations with the situations themselves. Throughout Bossard's writings, materials referring to definitions enter; as has been true of others, Bossard was too good a sociologist to permit his methodological rules to stand in the way of his analyses.

The introduction of conceptual considerations such as those noted above does not seem to distinguish the situational approach from symbolic interactionism, or from any other approach which is sociological in its derivation and its concerns. These and other conceptual emphases appearing in Bossard's work, rather, represent the stock in trade (whether expressed in Bossard's language or not) of sociology itself. In a broad sense, the situational approach *is* the sociological approach.

As this suggests, every sociologist who has studied the behavior of members of a family from the standpoint of his discipline has practiced the situational approach which Bossard advocated. Under these circumstances, it does not make sense to raise the question of its fertility. Apart from Bossard and his associates, only a few sociologists—for example, Blood (1953)—appear to relate their work explicitly to a distinctive situational approach.

Bossard himself, writing alone or with associates at the William T. Carter Foundation, was prolific, dealing with a wide range of topics including family table talk and modes of expression, the role of the guest in the home, bilingualism and its impact on the child, ritual in family life, and the impact of large families. Virtually all of his work was based on case documents he and his associates gathered, and his work reflects impressively both the strengths and the weaknesses of this procedure.

CONCLUDING REMARKS

The intent of this chapter has been to present symbolic interactionism and to appraise it critically both as a theory of socialization and personality development and as a conceptual framework for the study of the family. The spirit in which the chapter has been written is that of a partisan of symbolic interactionism. Partisanship, however, does not require apologetics; nor does it require an uncritical attitude. Hopefully, both have been avoided in the presentation.

In fact, the kind of partisanship symbolic interactionism "deserves" is that which maximizes sharp critical reactions. If the position is strong, then such reactions can only increase its strength in the long run. The presumption in this chapter has been that the position does not need the kind of defense which reduces its function to that of increasing the sensitivity of the observer to important variables in social life. Given this latter view, there need be no attempt to achieve precision in definitions, no attempt to formulate theory in the sense that this term has been used here, and there is no reason for holding the ideas of the position responsible for dealing with empirical data. To permit symbolic interactionism to be reduced to a set of sensitizing concepts only shortchanges the position.

But it is far from a completely satisfactory theory, particularly in its application to the wide range of data in which the sociologist of the family is interested. Obviously, what has been said above implies the belief that it can become more satisfactory. If this is to occur, its deficiences must be clearly seen.

It would have been possible to write a far more flattering statement of the role symbolic interactionism has played for students of family behavior—by de-emphasizing the distinction between theory and conceptual framework, by relaxing the criteria of research used in the appraisal section, and so on. One inadvertent consequence of not doing so, and one that is certainly not intended, is that the student reading this chapter may be discouraged from pursuing the further theoretical development of symbolic interactionism and the attempt to develop its implications in the special context of the family. There are certainly gaps and limitations. These are also opportunities.

REFERENCES

Albrecht, Ruth. Relationships of older people with their own parents. *Marr. & fam. Living,* 1953, 15, 296–298.
Albrecht, Ruth. Relationships of older parents with their children. *Marr. & fam. Living,* 1954, 16, 32–35.
Angell, R. C. *The family encounters the depression.* New York: Scribner, 1936.

Baldwin, J. M. *Mental development in the child and the race.* New York: Macmillan, 1906.

Bales, R. F. *Interaction process analysis.* Cambridge, Mass.: Addison-Wesley, 1950.

Bales, R. F., & Slater, P. Role differentiation. In T. Parsons & R. F. Bales, with J. Olds, M. Zelditch, Jr., & P. Slater, *Family, socialization and interaction process.* Glencoe, Ill.: Free Press, 1955. Pp. 259–306.

Becker, H. S., & Strauss, A. Careers, personality and adult socialization. *Amer. J. Sociol.,* 1956, 62, 253–263.

Biddle, B. J. *The present status of role theory.* Columbia: Univer. of Missouri, Social Psychology Laboratory, 1961.

Blood, R. O., Jr. A situational approach to the study of permissiveness in child rearing. *Amer. sociol. Rev.,* 1953, 18, 84–87.

Blood, R. O., Jr. A retest of Waller's rating complex. *Marr. & fam. Living,* 1955, 17, 41–47.

Borgatta, E. F. Role and reference group theory. In L. S. Kogan (Ed.), *Social science theory and social work research.* New York: National Association of Social Workers, 1960. Pp. 16–27.

Bossard, J. H. S. *The sociology of child development.* (2nd ed.) New York: Harper, 1954.

Bossard, J. H. S. *The large family system.* Philadelphia: Univer. of Pennsylvania Press, 1956.

Bossard, J. H. S., & Boll, Eleanor S. *Family situations.* Philadelphia: Univer. of Pennsylvania Press, 1943.

Bossard, J. H. S., & Boll, Eleanor S. *Ritual in family living.* Philadelphia: Univer. of Pennsylvania Press, 1950.

Brim, O. G., Jr. Family structure and sex role learning by children: a further analysis of Helen Koch's data. *Sociometry,* 1958, 21, 1–16.

Brim, O. G., Jr., & Wood, Nancy. Self and other conceptions in courtship and marriage pairs. *Marr. & fam. Living,* 1956, 18, 243–248.

Buerkle, J. V. Self-attitudes and marital adjustment. *Merrill-Palmer Quart.,* 1960, 6, 114–124.

Buerkle, J. V., Anderson, T. R., & Badgley, R. F. Altruism, role conflict and marital adjustment. *Marr. & fam. Living,* 1961, 23, 20–26.

Buerkle, J. V., & Badgley, R. F. Couple role-taking: the Yale interaction battery. *Marr. & fam. Living,* 1959, 21, 53–58.

Burgess, E. W. The family as a unity of interacting personalities. *Family,* 1926, 7, 3–9.

Burgess, E. W., & Cottrell, L. S., Jr. *Predicting success or failure in marriage.* New York: Prentice-Hall, 1939.

Burgess, E. W., & Wallin, P. *Engagement and marriage.* Philadelphia: Lippincott, 1953.

Carter, D. C. The influence of family relations and family experiences on personality. *Marr. & fam. Living,* 1954, 16, 212–215.

Cavan, Ruth S. *The American family.* New York: Crowell, 1953.

Cavan, Ruth S., & Ranck, Katherine H. *The family and the depression.* Chicago: Univer. of Chicago Press, 1938.

Cooley, C. H. *Human nature and the social order.* New York: Scribner, 1902.

Cooley, C. H. *Social organization.* New York: Scribner, 1909.

Cooley, C. H. The roots of social knowledge. *Amer. J. Sociol.,* 1926, 32, 59–79.

Cottrell, L. S., Jr. Roles and marital adjustment. *Publ. Amer. sociol. Soc.,* 1933, 27, 107–115.

Cottrell, L. S., Jr. Research in causes of variations in fertility—social psychological aspects. *Amer. sociol. Rev.,* 1937, 2, 678–685.

Cottrell, L. S., Jr. The adjustment of the individual to his age and sex roles. *Amer. sociol. Rev.,* 1942, 7, 617–620.

Cottrell, L. S., Jr. The present status and future orientation of research on the family. *Amer. sociol. Rev.,* 1948, 13, 370–382.

Cottrell, L. S., Jr. Some neglected problems in social psychology. *Amer. sociol. Rev.,* 1950, 15, 705–712.

Couch, C. J. Self-attitudes and degree of agreement with immediate others. *Amer. J. Sociol.,* 1958, 63, 491–496.

Cronbach, L. J. Processes affecting scores on "understanding of others" and "assumed similarity." *Psychol. Bull.,* 1955, 52, 177–193.

Deutscher, I. Married life in the middle years: a study of the middle class urban postparental couple. Unpublished doctoral dissertation, Univer. of Missouri, 1958.

Deutscher, I. Socialization for postparental life. In A. M. Rose (Ed.), *Human behavior and social processes.* Boston: Houghton Mifflin, 1962. Pp. 506–525.

Dewey, J. *Human nature and conduct.* New York: Modern Library, 1930.

Dymond, Rosalind F. Empathic ability: an exploratory study. Unpublished doctoral dissertation, Cornell Univer., 1949.

Ewer, Phyllis A. The source of empathy scores in relation to an independent variable: a methodological study. Unpublished master's thesis, Indiana Univer., 1962.

Farber, B. Elements of competence in interpersonal relations: a factor analysis. *Sociometry,* 1962, 25, 30–47.

Foote, N. N. Identification as the basis for a theory of motivation. *Amer. sociol. Rev.,* 1951, 16, 14–21.

Foote, N. N., & Cottrell, L. S., Jr. *Identity and personal competence: a new direction in family research.* Chicago: Univer. of Chicago Press, 1955.

Gage, N. L., & Cronbach, L. J. Conceptual and methodological problems in interpersonal perception. *Psychol. Rev.,* 1955, 62, 411–422.

Goffman, E. *The presentation of self in everyday life.* Garden City, N.Y.: Doubleday, 1959.

Goslin, D. A. Accuracy of self perception and social acceptance. *Sociometry,* 1962, 25, 283–296.

Gross, N., Mason, W. S., & McEachern, A. W. *Explorations in role analysis.* New York: Wiley, 1958.

Hill, R. *Families under stress.* New York: Harper, 1949.

Hill, R., & Hansen, D. A. The identification of conceptual frameworks utilized in family study. *Marr. & fam. Living,* 1960, 22, 299–311.

Hill, R., Stycos, J. M., & Back, K. W. *The family and population control: a Puerto Rican experiment in social change.* Chapel Hill: Univer. of North Carolina Press, 1959.

Hobart, C. W. Disagreement and non-empathy during courtship: a restudy. *Marr. & fam. Living,* 1956, 18, 317–322.

Hobart, C. W. Some effects of romanticism during courtship on marriage role opinions. *Sociol. & soc. Res.,* 1958, 42, 336–343.

James, W. *Psychology.* New York: Holt, 1892.

Kirkpatrick, C. *The family: as process and institution.* New York: Ronald Press, 1955.

Kirkpatrick, C., & Hobart, C. Disagreement, disagreement estimate and non-empathic imputations for intimacy groups varying from favorite date to married. *Amer. sociol. Rev.,* 1954, 19, 10–19.

Komarovsky, Mirra. Cultural contradictions and sex roles. *Amer. J. Sociol.,* 1946, 52, 184–189.

Komarovsky, Mirra. Functional analysis of sex roles. *Amer. sociol. Rev.,* 1950, 15, 508–516.

Komarovsky, Mirra. Continuities in family research: a case study. *Amer. J. Sociol.,* 1956, 62, 42–47.

Koos, E. L. *Families in trouble.* New York: King's Crown Press, 1946.

Koos, E. L. *The middle-class family and its problems.* New York: Columbia Univer. Press, 1950.

Kuhn, M., & McPartland, T. An empirical investigation of self attitudes. *Amer. sociol. Rev.,* 1954, 19, 68–75.

Linton, R. *The study of man.* New York: Appleton-Century-Crofts, 1936.

Locke, H. J., Sabagh, G., & Thomes, Mary M. Correlates of primary communication and empathy. *Res. Stud. State Coll. Washington,* 1956, 24, 116–124.

Lu, Y. Marital roles and marriage adjustment. *Sociol. & soc. Res.,* 1952, 36, 364–368. (a)

Lu, Y. Parental role and parent child relationship. *Marr. & fam. Living,* 1952, 14, 294–297. (b)

Lu, Y. Home discipline and reaction to authority in relation to marital roles. *Marr. & fam. Living,* 1953, 15, 223–225.

Luckey, Eleanore B. Marital satisfaction and congruent self-spouse concepts. *Soc. Forces,* 1960, 39, 153–157.

Luckey, Eleanore B. Perceptual congruence of self and family concepts as related to marital interaction. *Sociometry,* 1961, 24, 234–250.

Maehr, M. L., Mensing, J., & Nafzger, S. Concept of self and the reaction of others. *Sociometry,* 1962, 25, 353–357.

Martindale, D. *The nature and types of sociological theory.* Boston: Houghton Mifflin, 1960.

Mead, G. H. Cooley's contribution to American social thought. *Amer. J. Sociol.,* 1930, 35, 693–706.

Mead, G. H. *Mind, self and society.* Chicago: Univer. of Chicago Press, 1934.

Miyamoto, S. F. The social act: reexamination of a concept. *Pac. sociol. Rev.,* 1959, 2, 51–55.

Miyamoto, S. F., & Dornbusch, S. A test of interactionist hypotheses of self-conceptions. *Amer. J. Sociol.,* 1956, 51, 399–403.

Motz, Annabelle B. Conceptions of marital roles by status groups. *Marr. & fam. Living,* 1950, 12, 136, 162.

Motz, Annabelle B. The role conception inventory: a tool for research in social psychology. *Amer. sociol. Rev.,* 1952, 17, 465–471.

Mowrer, E. R. Some factors in the affectional adjustment of twins. *Amer. sociol. Rev.,* 1954, 19, 468–471.

Neiman, L. J. The influence of peer groups upon attitudes toward the feminine role. *Soc. Probl.,* 1954, 2, 104–111.

Park, R. E., & Burgess, E. W. *Introduction to the science of sociology.* Chicago: Univer. of Chicago Press, 1921.

Phillips, B. A role theory approach to adjustment in old age. *Amer. sociol. Rev.,* 1957, 22, 212–217.

Reeder, L. G., Donahue, G. A., & Biblarz, A. Conceptions of self and others. *Amer. J. Sociol.,* 1960, 66, 153–159.

Rose, A. M. The adequacy of women's expectations for adult roles. *Soc. Forces,* 1951, 30, 69–77.

Rose, A. M. (Ed.) *Human behavior and social processes.* Boston: Houghton Mifflin, 1962.

Sarbin, T. R. Role theory. In G. Lindzey (Ed.), *Handbook of social psychology.* Vol. 1. Cambridge, Mass.: Addison-Wesley, 1954. Pp. 223–258.

Sarbin, T. R., & Faberow, N. L. Contributions to role-taking theory, II. a clinical study of self and role. *J. abnorm. soc. psychol.,* 1952, 47, 117–125.

Sarbin, T. R., & Jones, D. S. An experimental analysis of role behavior. *J. abnorm. soc. Psychol.,* 1955, 51, 236–241.

Scodel, A., & Mussen, P. Social perceptions of authoritarians and non-authoritarians. *J. abnorm. soc. Psychol.,* 1953, 48, 181–184.

Smith, E. A. Dating and courtship at Pioneer College. *Sociol. & soc. Res.,* 1955, 40, 92–98.

Stone, G. P. Clothing and social relations: a study of appearance in the context of community life. Unpublished doctoral dissertation, Univer. of Chicago, 1959.

Strauss, A. (Ed.) *The social psychology of George Herbert Mead.* Chicago: Univer. of Chicago Press, 1956.

Strodtbeck, F. L. Husband-wife interaction over revealed differences. *Amer. sociol. Rev.,* 1951, 16, 468–473.

Strodtbeck, F. L. The family as a three-person group. *Amer. sociol. Rev.,* 1954, 19, 23–29.

Stryker, S. The adjustment of married offspring to their parents. *Amer. sociol. Rev.,* 1955, 20, 149–154.

Stryker, S. Relationships of married offspring and parent: a test of Mead's theory. *Amer. J. Sociol.,* 1956, 62, 308–319.

Stryker, S. Role-taking accuracy and adjustment. *Sociometry,* 1957, 20, 286–296.

Stryker, S. Symbolic interaction as an approach to family research. *Marr. & fam. Living,* 1959, 21, 111–119.

Thomas, W. I. *The unadjusted girl.* Boston: Little, Brown, 1925.

Thomas, W. I. The behavior pattern and the situation. *Publ. Amer. sociol. Soc.,* 1927, 22, 1–13.

Thomas, W. I. The relation of research to the social process. In W. F. G. Swann et al., *Essays on research in the social sciences.* Washington: Brookings, 1931. Pp. 179–194.

Thomas, W. I. *Primitive behavior: an introduction to the social sciences.* New York: McGraw-Hill, 1937.

Thomas, W. I., & Thomas, Dorothy S. *The child in America.* New York: Knopf, 1928.

Thomas, W. I., & Znaniecki, F. *The Polish peasant in Europe and America.* Boston: Badger, 1918–1920. 5 vols.

Turner, R. H. Role-taking: process versus conformity. In A. M. Rose (Ed.), *Human behavior and social processes.* Boston: Houghton Mifflin, 1962. Pp. 20–40.

Vernon, G. M., & Stewart, R. L. Empathy as a process in the dating situation. *Amer. sociol. Rev.,* 1957, 22, 48–52.

Videbeck, R. Self-conception and the reaction of others. *Sociometry,* 1960, 23, 351–359.

Volkart, E. H. (Ed.) *Social behavior and personality: contributions of W. I. Thomas to theory and social research.* New York: Social Science Research Council, 1951.

Waller, W. *The old love and the new.* New York: Liveright, 1930.

Waller, W. *The family: a dynamic interpretation.* New York: Dryden, 1938.

Waller, W., & Hill, R. *The family: a dynamic interpretation.* New York: Dryden, 1951.

Wallin, P. Cultural contradictions and sex

roles: a repeat study. *Amer. sociol. Rev.,* 1950, 15, 288–293.

Wallin, P. Marital happiness of parents and their children's attitude to marriage. *Amer. sociol. Rev.,* 1954, 19, 20–23. (a)

Wallin, P. Sex differences in attitudes to "in-laws": a test of a theory. *Amer. J. Sociol.,* 1954, 59, 466–469. (b)

Wallin, P., & Vollmer, H. M. Marital happiness of parents and their children's attitudes to them. *Amer. sociol. Rev.,* 1953, 18, 424–431.

CHAPTER 5

The Developmental Approach

REUBEN HILL
University of Minnesota

ROY H. RODGERS
University of Oregon

In contrast to the long crescive histories of its predecessors, the developmental approach to family study has had a short history, beginning only in the 1930's, with the major portion of its development occurring in the last 10–15 years. As a consequence of its relative youth, it has had the benefit of the accumulation of empirical findings and generalizations stimulated by the other approaches discussed in previous chapters of this Handbook. The developmental approach has borrowed a great many of its concepts from these other approaches. The result has been a theoretical eclecticism and a tendency to internal inconsistency which may only be an indication of its conceptual adolescence. Before tracing in detail the emergence of what is unique about family developmental "theory," a statement of the properties of the approach as it appears in contemporary literature should be of help.

Hill and Hansen (1960), in discussing the characteristics of the developmental conceptual framework, have pointed to the fact that it is not presently a unique approach, but rather a joining together of various parts of some of the previous theoretical efforts.

Thus, it brings together from rural sociologists the idea of stages of the life cycle, from child psychologists and human development researchers concepts of developmental needs and tasks, from the sociology of the professions the idea of the family as a set of mutually contingent careers, and from the structure-function and interactional theorists such concepts as age and sex roles, plurality patterns, functional prerequisites, and other concepts which view the family as a system of interacting actors. By so doing, it combines into one approach an attempt to account for the societal-institutional, interactional-associational, and individual-personality variables of family phenomena. Furthermore, it directs its attention to the longitudinal career of the family system, rather than focussing statically on the family at one point in time. Herein lies its peculiar character. Most previous work in family theory which has attempted to account for change in the family over time has also tended to be macroanalytic in character, thus losing sight of the dynamics of interaction in the family system and accounting primarily for broad institutional pattern changes. When there has been microanalytic study of the family in which the interactions among actors have been studied, little accounting for change over time has been attempted. The developmental approach, in contrast, attempts both to be microanalytic and to account for changes in patterns of interaction over the family's life span.

The assumptions which appear to underlie the work carried out within this framework have been listed by Hill and Hansen as follows:

1. Human conduct is best seen as a function of the preceding as well as the current social milieu and individual conditions.
2. Human conduct cannot be adequately understood apart from human development.
3. The human is an actor as well as a reactor.
4. Individual and group development is best seen as dependent upon stimulation by a social milieu as well as on inherent (developed) capacities.
5. The individual in a social setting is the basic autonomous unit (1960, p. 309).

The two conditions of relative youth and theoretical eclecticism account for the most exciting aspects of the developmental approach. The theorist who attempts to work in this area cannot help being aware that he is operating in an expanding intellectual endeavor. The developmental approach is by no means a closed theoretical system with a large body of empirical data supporting it. Indeed, Hill and Hansen observed, "It is too soon to say whether the developmental approach will turn out to be a variant or an extension of interactional analysis rather than a unique approach in its own right" (1960, p. 308).

It will become increasingly apparent as the history of the growth of this approach is reviewed that there has been considerable effort expended in attempting to bring the concepts borrowed from the various approaches to human behavior into a unified framework. If, as Martindale (1960, p. 538) contended, a bona fide theoretical system cannot be arbitrarily mixed with other systems, then it will be necessary to continue

to evaluate the theoretical integrity of the developmental approach. But, as Rodgers (1962, p. 10) has observed, there is some basis for believing that the joining of concepts from such a wide diversity of sources may not be as incongruous as at first appears. Referring to the fact that the interactional approach probably falls within the framework of what Martindale (1960, pp. 294–303) called the "social behavioristic school" of sociology, he pointed out that many of the child psychology and human development theorists, e.g., Wundt, James, Dewey, and Watson, have much the same behavioristic philosophical tradition. It may well be that this common tradition will form the foundation for the eventual construction of an independent theory of family behavior.

The other essential condition of a fully developed theory, verification through empirical testing, is also yet to be accomplished. Although numerous research studies have included attention to the developmental characteristics of the data, none has been designed for the exclusive purpose of testing the developmental theoretical framework. As Merton (1957) has pointed out forcefully theory and research are interdependent activities in which each contributes significantly to the growth and development of the other. The developmental approach to family study is an excellent contemporary example of this essential relationship in the scientific study of human behavior. Attention may now be turned to a detailed description of the emergence, development, refinement, and present status of the developmental approach.

HISTORY THROUGH 1948

In the early history of the developmental approach, three essentially independent streams of thought are discernible. Each will be examined for its peculiar contribution to the approach. A discussion will follow of the concerted effort which attempted to merge them in the first integrated statement of the developmental viewpoint. This effort occurred in 1948 and, therefore, provides a convenient bench mark signifying the close of the primitive period of developmental theory and the beginning of a theoretically more sophisticated approach.

The Family Life Cycle as a Demographic Independent Variable

In the earliest conceptualizations, the family life cycle was seen essentially as a control factor or as an independent variable which might explain certain kinds of family phenomena. Thus, the literature reflected attempts to explain expenditure patterns, levels of living, and consumption patterns by the stage of the life cycle in which the family was located, in much the same way that other properties of the family such as income, occupation, or social class might be used.

The earliest adaptation of the life cycle to family data is found in the analyses of levels of living of families. B. Seebohm Rowntree, in his classic survey of primary and secondary poverty in York, England, at the turn of the century, advanced a theory of the life cycle of families: a period of poverty when the children are young, followed by one of relative prosperity when the children grow up and become earners, and finally a second period of poverty in old age, when the grown children leave home to establish families of their own (Rowntree, 1906, pp. 136–138).

Sorokin, Zimmerman, and Galpin (1931) utilized the life-cycle concept in their analysis of the economic life history of the rural peasant family which focussed on the changing family-member constellation. This publication, according to Nelson (1955), stimulated interest in family life-cycle analysis in rural sociology and precipitated a number of similar studies. Several of these (Blackwell, 1942; Duncan, 1941; Kirkpatrick, Cowles, & Tough, 1934; Lively, 1932; Loomis, 1934) employed a four-stage family cycle defined in terms of expanding and contracting family size or based on the ages of children.

Turning from the rural sociologists, the same use of the family life-cycle stages is seen in the work of the United States consumption economist Bigelow (1948), who developed a more elaborate set of stages of the family cycle, noting periods of deficit financing and recovery associated with the balance between income and expenditures at various points in the family's existence. While these were certainly pioneering efforts and set the patterns for much of the later work in family development, the divisions of the family life cycle were rather crude and paid little or no attention to the interactive process characteristic of the family system at different stages of development.

The Family Life Cycle as Process

In preceding chapters it has been amply evident that attention has been given to the analysis of processes of family interaction, particularly in the work undertaken within the conceptual framework of symbolic interaction. It has remained to make these analyses specific for stages of family development. As family life-cycle categories became more explicit, it seemed likely that specification of family interactive processes for each of these categories would follow.[1] The work of Glick provides the transition from the treatment of life-cycle stages as a demographic category to its utilization as a sensitizing concept for descriptive writing about the content of family living over the family life span.

---

[1] At least two family sociologists had organized courses on the family designed around the stages of the family life cycle before 1948. Lemo Dennis Rockwood of Cornell University drew from writings of novelists to explicate the processes of family interaction by stages of the life span. Robert G. Foster, at the Merrill-Palmer School of Detroit, drew from the studies of rural sociologists on family expenditure patterns and from personality research on child development to give content to the stages of family development. Both courses carried the title "Family Development." Unfortunately for the development of the approach in the country at large, their conceptual achievements were never published and therefore did not influence the direction taken in this early period.

The first hints are to be found in a series of analyses based on United States census materials published by Glick in 1947. At first glance, this work might appear to be only a further elaboration of the demographic categories. On closer examination, however, it is clear that Glick was interested in far more than shaping up the family life-cycle stages as an independent variable. In this work, and to a greater extent in the article and the census monograph which followed (Glick, 1955; Glick, 1957), Glick attempted to bring about an understanding of the implications for families of life in the various periods of the life span.

First of all, Glick's approach demonstrated the changes that had occurred historically in the life-cycle patterns of American families. He did this by comparing the family life-cycle stages of the family in 1890 with those in 1940 (Glick, 1947) and, later, in 1950 (Glick, 1955; Glick, 1957). By computing the median ages of husband and wife at first marriage, birth of last child, marriage of last child, death of one spouse, and death of remaining spouse, he highlighted a number of interesting trends which had real significance for the family as an association of actors. The most outstanding findings were that both men and women were marrying earlier in 1940 and 1950 than they did in 1890, that the childbearing period was much shorter than in 1890, that the launching of the last child from the family occurred considerably sooner, that a greater share of the marriage experience involved only the husband and wife without children present in the home, and that, due to the longer life expectancy and short child-rearing periods, an essentially "new stage" appeared in the 1940 and 1950 families after children had left and before one of the spouses was claimed by death. He then proceeded to show some of the effects of these changes on the family, including the greater possibility for the wife to be engaged in gainful employment, differences in the family situation as a result of fewer children being born, and differences resulting from the

earlier marriage and longer life span of the spouses. Thus, Glick's work constitutes a bridge between the interest in the stages of the family life cycle as demographic categories to the specification of content within those stages. [Cf. Ch. 9, p. 324].

A second publication might be cited as anticipating the family life cycle as process. Entering the arena of family life from another angle, housing, a conference on housing for family living, chaired by Lawrence K. Frank and financed by the Woman's Foundation, observed the pressures placed upon the family by the changing needs for living space over the life span. Utilizing a four-stage cycle similar to that of the rural sociologists, which stressed the changes occurring with expanding, stable, and contracting family size, a conference committee chaired by Evelyn M. Duvall identified four stages, which they labelled "the early years, the crowded years, the peak years, and the later years." The content of family interaction for each of these stages has been sensitively described in the conference publication edited by Frederic Gutheim (1948), by relating numbers and ages of the children and ages of the parents to the demands for space and equipment within the home. Needs of children and parents are shown colliding with the inflexibilities of housing designs to produce a highly suggestive report for architects as well as for students of family living.

Contributions of Human Growth and Development Research

Research in the growth and development of the human individual has been done on the scientific level since before the turn of the century. With the establishment of the Children's Bureau within the federal government and the founding of a number of centers for child development research under grants from the Laura Spelman Rockefeller Foundation in the 1920's, considerable impetus was given to this movement (Frank, 1962). This chapter will not review the large body of research findings produced by these centers, since this has been done most effectively elsewhere (Carmichael, 1954; Mussen, 1960) and would carry us far afield. The significance of this work to this Handbook lies in the careful and extensive documentation of the orderly maturational changes in the physical, intellectual, emotional, and social characteristics of the individual. The cumulative results of the research demonstrated that these changes were not independent of one another, but were interdependent aspects of growth of the individual as a total person. Although the great bulk of the research was carried out in laboratory, educational, and clinical settings, it became increasingly clear that the family situation was a significant variable in the manner in which these changes took place. It is not suprising, then, that the human growth and development effort is the source of the developmental rationale which is so central to the approach under consideration. It was this rationale which allowed those working with the family development approach to shift from a study of the family at one point in time, or from the comparison of two points in time, to a longitudinal study of the family at a microanalytical level.

Much of the developmental rationale is embodied in the concept of "developmental task," the history of which has been discussed by Duvall (1957, pp. 517–522). According to Duvall, the idea was probably first used by Williams (1930) and later by L. K. Frank in working with the staff of the Progressive Education Association's Adolescent Study at the University of Chicago. It appeared then in other published works (Blos, 1941; Havighurst, Prescott, & Redl, 1942) in an increasingly specific form. The definition of the concept has not changed since it was stated by Havighurst as follows: "A developmental task is a task which arises at or about a certain period in the life of an individual, successful achievement of which leads to his happiness and to success with later tasks, while failure

leads to unhappiness in the individual, disapproval by the society, and difficulty with later tasks."[2] This idea has remained a central concern of the developmental approach.

This, then, was the state of the family development approach prior to 1948. As has been said, there was no conscious awareness of a common theoretical point of view, but three essentially independent streams of thought which were yet to be incorporated into a single approach. It remains to trace the manner in which these streams were joined. As may be imagined, this did not happen all at one time. However, there was one significant event which may be viewed as the first major attempt at synthesis, in that there was a conscious awareness of each of the streams and a concerted effort to form one compatible approach to the study of the family.

The Joining of the Streams

The first attempt at systematizing a framework to cope with problems of family change over time was undertaken in 1948 on the occasion of the preparation for the National Conference on Family Life convened at the White House by President Truman. A committee on the Dynamics of Family Interaction, chaired by Evelyn M. Duvall and Reuben Hill, was charged with bringing together an intelligible framework which would facilitate both the summarizing of research to date on problems peculiar to the family at different stages of its development and descriptions of the natural history of families as small groups from their formation in engagement and marriage to their dissolution in divorce and death. Duvall and Hill prepared a two-dimensional outline for plotting the developmental tasks of children and of parents for each stage of the family life cycle, with implications for services arising out of the

[2] From R. J. Havighurst, *Human Development and Education*, p. 2. New York: Longmans, Green, 1953. Courtesy of David McKay Company, Inc.

problems involved in the achievement of each developmental task in American society (Duvall, 1957, p. 519). Thus, the demographic categories of the life cycle of the rural sociologists and the concepts of "developmental tasks" of the child development specialists were joined.

Eight subcommittees of specialists[3] on the various developmental levels were appointed by the cochairmen to prepare reports on the various life-cycle stages to give content to the outline prepared by Duvall and Hill, eventuating in a report, *The Dynamics of Family Interaction*. The national conference used both this report and its rudimentary framework in organizing its discussion groups and work sessions, thus giving a major impetus to what was to become the developmental approach to family study. Published in mimeographed form for the national conference (Duvall & Hill, 1948), the committee's background papers were widely read and discussed among family-oriented scholars. The report itself foreshadows the later shape of the developmental conceptual framework, since many of the elaborations and amplifications which occurred in the latter's evolution date from contact with the committee's background papers.

If the developmental approach during this period appears vague and ill-defined, it must be remembered that at this point in its history there was no explicit set of underlying assumptions, no clearly defined cluster of interrelated concepts, and, most certainly, no set of postulates which might be considered essential to a concretely stated theory. Much work remained before the approach could even be considered "conceptual framework."

THE EMERGING DEVELOPMENTAL CONCEPTUAL FRAMEWORK

Hill and Hansen defined a conceptual framework as "clusters of interrelated but not necessarily interdefined concepts generally applicable to the arena of marriage

[3] Including the pioneers Rockwood and Foster, mentioned in note 1.

and the family" (1960, p. 300). In the years since 1948, there has emerged such a body of concepts, although it is not yet fully developed and, as already noted, still not clearly distinct from other approaches. Nevertheless, there continue to be a considerable number of family theorists who are devoting their efforts to work in what they consciously term the "developmental approach." In order to trace this process of elaboration, it is necessary to continue to draw from a variety of sources for material. Much of the work is unpublished, with conferences, graduate seminars, master's theses, and doctoral dissertations providing significant contributions.

Definition of the Family

In Chapter 1, it was seen that a variety of definitions of the family are being utilized, depending upon the conceptual approach being followed. The family may be broadly defined as an institution or as an association, according to the emphasis taken by the theorist. To this point, there has been no discussion of the definition of the family utilized in the developmental approach. Indeed, historically, there was none until after the 1948 conference. Implicit in the work of that conference and in some of the later work, however, is a definition of the family which has become increasingly explicit. It is clear in looking back that this view of the family arose out of the symbolic interactionist view of society. E. W. Burgess, whose contributions were discussed in detail in the preceding chapter, very early defined the family as "a unity of interacting personalities" (1926). The emphasis on developmental tasks, arising as it did out of the human growth and development stream, laid great stress on the personality results of the total developmental process. In Chapter 4, it was also shown that such men as James and Dewey, who were closely associated with human growth theory, were also important predecessors to the work of the symbolic interactionist theorists. It was to this common stream of intellectual endeavor that Rodgers (1962, p. 10) was pointing in trying to account for the apparent theoretical eclecticism of the developmental approach. It was also these same factors which led Hill and Hansen (1960, p. 308) to be somewhat cautious in claiming independent conceptual framework status for the approach. Be that as it may, the emphasis on personality in the symbolic interactionists blended well with the developmental approach.

This basic approach to the family as a unity of interacting personalities was carried further in Hill's revision of Waller's classic text (Waller & Hill, 1951). Hill introduced the idea of the family as a closed system when he stated: "Any family group tends to be more or less a closed system of social interaction. . . . In order to explain events within the family of interaction, we must often have recourse to events outside the system, but we may also very frequently explain family events by means of other family events" (Waller & Hill, 1951, p. 25). The implicit view of the family as a closed system of interacting personalities paved the way for yet two other streams of thought to join the three that were already a part of the developmental approach. It was not long until specific concepts from the interactional and social-system schools of sociological theory were brought to bear on the problems studied by those involved in the family development enterprise.

The University of Chicago Workshop on Family Research

In the summer of 1950, an interdisciplinary workshop in marriage and family research was called by Evelyn Duvall, who was then Executive Secretary of the National Council on Family Relations. In one of the groups of this workshop were a number of participants of the 1948 conference. This group made further significant efforts in producing a conceptual framework for developmental study of the family.

One of the participants, Eleanor Godfrey, had recently completed a doctoral study of Illinois farm families under Talcott Parsons (Godfrey, 1951). She had developed several family types, using the structural-functional approach and the functional prerequisites earlier developed by Parsons (1949, pp. 6–7). She had demonstrated that her types of families were distinctly different in the manner in which they went about meeting the functional prerequisites. The presentation of this material at the 1950 workshop had two effects on the family development approach.

The first effect was to indicate that structural-functional theory could contribute much to the developmental study of the family. As has already been indicated, the view of the family as a system was already implicit in what had been produced previously. Godfrey showed that this view was quite compatible with structural-functional theory. Secondly, the groups went on to apply the idea of developmental tasks not only to individuals within the family, but to the family as a system as well. Godfrey had shown that the family system is organized to meet the basic functional prerequisites necessary for survival as a system. The workshop participants formulated a set of family developmental tasks for the establishment stage of the family life cycle based upon these functional prerequisites. They pointed to the fact that these family developmental tasks must satisfy biological requirements, cultural imperatives, and personal aspirations and values (Hill, 1951, pp. 21–22).

The workshop of 1950, therefore, provided a second and essential synthesis for the family development approach. At this point, the view could probably have been stated as follows: the family, as a closed system of interacting personalities, is organized in such a way as to meet certain functional prerequisites through the accomplishment of certain individual and developmental tasks. However, the quality of interaction in the family system is distinctly different at varying developmental levels, or stages of the life cycle. This statement could not be termed a conceptual framework, although the sources of the concepts to be used in such framework had now become clear.

The remainder of the history of the emergence of the conceptual framework involves a number of concurrent efforts which took place in the decade of the 1950's and which are still going on in 1964.

Graduate Seminars in Family Development Theory

Since the 1948 National Conference on Family Life, a number of graduate seminars in family development theory have been held at the University of North Carolina and at the University of Minnesota under the direction of Reuben Hill. The major burden of these seminars has been to push further the developmental conceptual framework by systematizing, specifying, and interdefining its concepts. Starting with little more than the working papers produced by the 1948 conference, each group attempted to bring to bear whatever material had become available as well as relevant conceptualizations from other disciplines. With Hill providing the continuity, each seminar was able to build on what the previous seminar had accomplished. A number of those now working with this approach had their first contact with it in one of these seminars. Several master's theses and doctoral dissertations have been stimulated by participation in the seminars (Blalock, 1954; Blood, 1952; Rodgers, 1962). It would be impossible at this point to document the contributions of a specific seminar group, but it is possible to indicate the accumulated contribution which the seminars as a whole have made.

The first seminars began with the acceptance of the definition of the family as a closed system of interacting personalities. As there was increasing sensitivity to the fact that the family was engaged not only in interactive behavior internally within the system, but also in transactive behavior with other systems of the society, the view of the family has changed to that of a *semi-closed* system. The stages of the family life cycle have been viewed as being a function of the quality of interaction which arises out of the developmental level of the members of the family group. Family life-cycle stages have tended to be defined in terms of the dominant developmental tasks being faced by individual members in the family and by the family as a system. One of the continuing points of issue has been the manner in which a particular set of stages might be defined, since a major problem arises out of the question of which member or members are to be focussed on in the determination of stages. The tendency has been to define stages in terms of the status of husband and wife when children are not a part of the family, and to focus on one or more of the children, most frequently the oldest child, when children are present. This in essence follows the lead of Glick (1947; 1955; 1957) and of the Committee on the Dynamics of Family Interaction (Duvall & Hill, 1948).

The developmental task concept has been a central focus of the seminar work. In order to deal with the individual, the family as a system, and the social setting of the family, the seminars have followed the 1950 workshop (Hill, 1951, pp. 21–22) in viewing the developmental tasks as being a result of the combination of individual maturational levels, family pressures, and social age and sex norms.

The seminars placed much emphasis on perfecting a set of concepts which could be used to analyze this family system and the patterns of interaction which occurred over its life cycle. A publication by Bates (1956) provided a set of core concepts for accomplishing this task. In attempting to reformulate the major sociological concepts of position, role, and norm, Bates presented three basic definitions which were easily adapted to the developmental view (Bates, 1956, p. 314):

1. Position: A location in a social structure which is associated with a set of social norms.
2. Role: A part of a social position consisting of a more or less integrated or related subset of social norms which is distinguishable from other sets of norms forming the same position.

3. Norm: A patterned or commonly held behavior expectation. A learned response, held in common by members of a group.

In his discussion, Bates further pointed out certain postulates which were of considerable assistance. He said that in any given culture there is a limited number of roles making up a limited number of positions, that each position contains dominant and recessive roles, that a role is always paired with a reciprocal role of another position, and that in a pair of related positions there is always at least one pair of reciprocal roles composed of reciprocal norms requiring certain kinds of expected behavior (Bates, 1956, pp. 315–317). The seminar groups took these definitions and defined the family as a system of positions composed of reciprocal roles defined in terms of both familial and societal norms. A family has only a limited number of positions, and each is rather clearly defined in terms of the roles which make it up. Furthermore, roles of specific positions have differing sets of norms applied to them at different developmental levels, so that change in the system can be accounted for by the changing developmental levels of the occupants of the positions specified by the age norms.

Later, the work of Gross, Mason, and McEachern (1958) provided some additional concepts. In addition to defining the concepts of position and role in much the same way Bates had done, this work gave evidence that the occupant of a position does not always meet the expectations or norms applied to that position. The concept of *role behavior* was used to define the actual behavior of the occupant of a position with reference to a particular role (Gross, Mason, & McEachern 1958, p. 64). A special kind of role behavior which had reward or punishment implications with respect to the performance of the occupant of a reciprocal role was called a *sanction* (p. 65). These two concepts provided a method of analyzing that aspect of the developmental task concept of which it was stated that "successful achievement . . . leads to his happiness

and to success with later tasks, while failure leads to unhappiness in the individual, disapproval by the society, and difficulty with later tasks" (Havighurst, 1953, p. 2).

Constantly aware that the developmental approach is concerned primarily with the longitudinal rather than the cross-sectional analysis of the family system, the seminar groups felt keenly the need for concepts which could handle the aspect of change in the family system through time. At about the same time that the Bates article appeared, some working papers of Irwin Deutscher's analysis of the postparental couple became available. These papers, which were later published, provided the necessary help. In dealing with changes which occurred in roles over time, Deutscher used the term *role sequence* to describe the series of roles which an occupant of a position is called upon to play as he moves through the life cycle (Deutscher, 1959, p. 18). In addition, he devised the term *role cluster* to define the set of roles being played by the incumbent of a position at any one point in time (p. 24), and the term *role complex* to define two or more sets of role clusters being played concurrently by two or more incumbents in an interlocking system (p. 26).

There remained one other dimension of the family life cycle for which concepts were considered necessary. This was the total life span of the individual within the family and the life span of the family system. Bernard Farber, in the study of the effects of a severely retarded child on family integration, had conceptualized the family as a set of mutually contingent careers (Farber, 1956). His model for the study of families as mutually contingent careers, interestingly enough, followed very closely the conceptualization of the family as a system of roles which had been emerging in the family development approach. Thus, the concept of *positional career* and of *family career* met the needs of the framework in this area.

Although the manner in which the development of the conceptual framework has been described gives the impression of a smooth progression of steps, it must be emphasized that these events took place over several years, with bits and pieces being added as additional insights were gained through the struggles of a particular seminar group. Many blind alleys were encountered, but there were also a number of those exciting breakthroughs which are such a satisfying part of the intellectual enterprise. It was only recently that the cumulative work of these seminars was brought together in published form along with certain additions (Rodgers, 1962). This work will be considered in greater detail below. What has been discussed represents the major contributions of the various seminar groups over slightly more than a decade of time. During this same decade, there appeared another major contribution to the developmental approach which provided considerable stimulus to the seminars and to other workers in the area.

The Initial Major Publication

The name of Evelyn Duvall has appeared frequently in the discussion of the developmental approach and rightfully so, for she has been a continuing major stimulator and contributor. It was she who published the first book-length treatment of the approach (Duvall, 1957). This publication, since revised (Duvall, 1962), has remained the only text in family development available to students. Duvall's objectives in the two editions of her publication appear to be twofold. In the first instance, she stated explicitly that she wanted to make more widely available the materials of the 1948 conference and the 1950 workshop, which had long since gone out of print, so that others might be prompted to do further work in the family development area (Duvall, 1957, p. 522). Secondly, she has expanded in a major way the implications of the family life-cycle stages for family interaction. In a series of chapters which comprise the major portion of the book, she developed in considerable detail the individual and family developmental task concepts as they apply to a specific stage of the life cycle by drawing heavily on research in sociology and human growth and development. Duvall was not so concerned with attempting to develop new theoretical formulations in the approach as she was with exploiting and expanding what had already been accomplished. While recognizing the unfinished nature of the conceptual approach, she was concerned that the insights which the approach provides for an understanding of the dynamics of family behavior be made available. Her emphasis, therefore, was on the functional aspects of the family development approach:

Each chapter is designed to put into the hands of the readers effective tools for a professional attitude toward families. Consequently, throughout the book, there are outlines and detailed analyses for meeting the problems that arise in the family life cycle such as: child-proofing the home for the rearing of children; checking the child's readiness for school; gathering information on how to prepare a child for a new baby brother or sister; building in safety features in the home during the middle and later years; learning to live with in-laws; adjustment to bereavement.
Readings are more extensive than is usual in a book of this kind so that they may (1) stimulate the study of the family and (2) functionally serve the professional worker who is currently concerned with the problems of families and family members (Duvall, 1957, pp. v–vi).

Both of Duvall's major goals have been adequately accomplished. For those who were primarily concerned with the extension of the conceptual issues, the book stimulated as much by what it did not say as by what it said. For the far greater audience who were not disturbed by the as yet poorly developed conceptual framework, there was much profit in reading the text. Since Duvall had been so intimately involved in both the theoretical and functional aspects of the family development approach, there was no one better qualified to meet the needs of both groups.

The publication of the book still left a

gap in the family development approach. Although there had been work of various sorts in progress for over a decade, there was yet no published statement of the conceptual framework as it was developing. Hill and various collaborators had discussed it briefly on at least three occasions (Hill, 1958; Hill & Hansen, 1960; Hill, Katz, & Simpson, 1957) with some indications of the characteristics of the framework. Recently, however, there has appeared an attempt to synthesize the accumulation of work done into one unified work.

A Further Attempt at Synthesis

In 1962 Rodgers published his doctoral study, which had two stated objectives: "The first is to make a further attempt to bring together into a more consistent body a set of concepts which may be utilized to analyze the family developmentally. Having done this, an attempt will be made to develop a set of categories of the family life cycle which may be used to test the conceptual framework developed" (Rodgers, 1962, p. 10). Having been a participant in the family development seminars both at the University of North Carolina and the University of Minnesota, he had been closely involved with the developmental conceptual framework as it was emerging. Citing the fact that considerable use had been made of the stages of the family life cycle in research, yet they have infrequently been devised out of any explicit conceptual scheme, Rodgers contended that these stages might have more explanatory power if they were so developed.

Using the work of Duvall (1957) as his primary reference, he identified some of the weaknesses that existed in the set of stages traditionally used in research. Chief among these was the fact that, although the approach had always been concerned with the total family system, most stage schemes have tended to be devised in terms of the husband, wife, and one of the children—most often the oldest child (Duvall, 1957, p. 8). Duvall justified the use of the oldest child

as the basic determinant of stage divisions on the grounds that "a family grows through a given stage with its oldest child, and in a sense 'repeats' as subsequent children come along" (Duvall, 1957, p. 9), although she recognized that this was not an entirely satisfactory solution to the conceptual problem of accounting for various plurality patterns in families.

Rodgers rejected this idea on the basis that it does not account adequately for the differences in role patterns which the addition of children to the family group initiates, and that it gives a false impression of a smooth progression from one life-cycle stage to the next. In his data he found considerable heterogeneity of role patterns, both in terms of numbers of children and spacing of children. He suggested that devising a more rigorous conceptual framework would force the researcher to adopt a different approach to the construction of family life-cycle categories. (He used the term *category* in preference to *stage* on the grounds that the categories are analytical devices constructed by the researcher, rather than any "real" condition of families [Rodgers, 1962, pp. 23–24].)

A second major criticism of previous sets of life-cycle stages is their inability to handle "abnormal" families. Rodgers pointed out that there was no way to account for families in which the death of a spouse or child occurred prior to the launching of all children, nor to handle families in which divorce, disability, or other events might interrupt the smooth progress from one stage to the next. He attributed this weakness, too, to the lack of a rigorous conceptual framework (pp. 69–72).

In attacking the problem of the conceptual framework, Rodgers drew heavily on the work of the seminars in which he had participated. Bringing together the concepts discussed above, he showed how they may be placed in an interlocking framework for analysis of family life-cycle data. Adapting a technique used by Bates (1956, p. 314), he presented three figures which depict graphically the longitudinal aspects of the family system (Rodgers, 1962, pp. 45–47). Rodgers showed the *position* as made up of a set of *roles*, which in turn are composed of *norms*. It was pointed out that the dynamic aspect of roles is accounted for by the concept of *role behavior*. In addition, a special form of role behavior of a reward-punishment quality is known as a *sanction*. Two of Rodgers' figures are reproduced here. Figure 1 depicts the longitudinal aspect of a single position. Both the longitudinal character of a single role, the *role sequence,* and the longitudinal feature of a role cluster, the *positional career,* are illustrated. Figure 2 brings two positions together in a *role complex* at one point in time, and more positions are added over time, resulting in the longitudinal expression of a role complex in the *family career.* For clarity, the figures do not show the reciprocal relationships which exist between roles within the various complexes.

After discussing the relevance of the functional prerequisites to the framework and the manner in which the normative pressures arise in the system, thus bringing about change, Rodgers turned to a discussion of the developmental task concept. He noted that such terms as *happiness, un-*

happiness, success, and *failure* are not concepts which can be readily tested. However, he pointed out that the developmental task idea may be restated in the vocabulary of position, role, and norms. This redefinition is stated as follows:

A developmental task is a set of norms (role expectations) arising at a particular point in the career of a position in a social system, which, if incorporated by the occupant of the position as a role or part of a role cluster, brings about integration and temporary equilibrium in the system with regard to a role complex or set of role complexes; failure to incorporate the norms leads to lack of integration, application of additional normative pressures in the form of sanctions, and difficulty in incorporating later norms into the role cluster of the position (Rodgers, 1962, pp. 54–55).

He pointed out that, while a developmental task may be viewed longitudinally as a particular kind of role sequence, not all role expectations are related to the developmental nature of a position and, thus, not all role sequences are developmental tasks. However, since the approach is concerned primarily with the developmental quality of

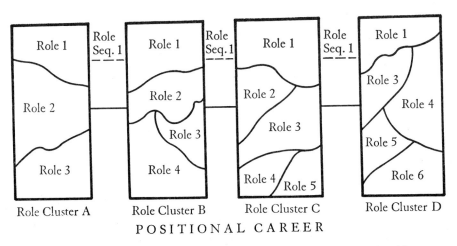

POSITIONAL CAREER

Fig. 1. Role Sequence, Role Cluster, and Positional Career (Reproduced with Permission from R. H. Rodgers, *Improvements in the Construction and Analysis of Family Life Cycle Categories.* Kalamazoo: Western Michigan Univer., 1962, p. 46).

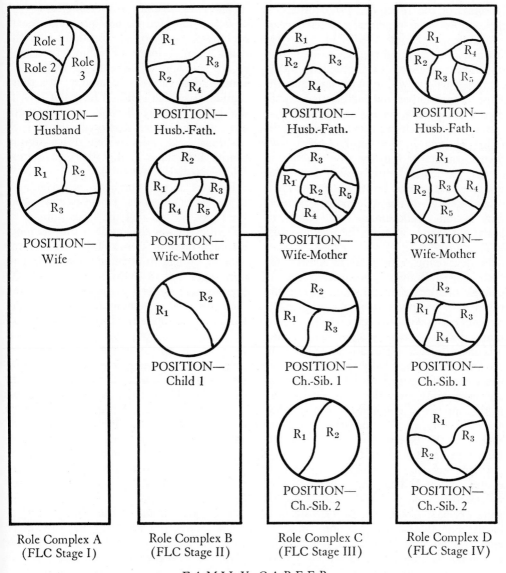

Role Complex A (FLC Stage I)

Role Complex B (FLC Stage II)

Role Complex C (FLC Stage III)

Role Complex D (FLC Stage IV)

FAMILY CAREER

Fig. 2. The Family Career (Reproduced with Permission from R. H. Rodgers, *Improvements in the Construction and Analysis of Family Life Cycle Categories.* Kalamazoo: Western Michigan Univer., 1962, p. 47).

family dynamics, it is to be expected that considerable emphasis will be placed on such developmental role sequences (pp. 55–56).

This framework also accounts for those family systems which are "abnormal" in the sense that premature death, divorce, disability, and other events may be handled. All that the analyst needs to ascertain is the positions which are occupied and the roles which are a part of these positions (p. 70).

In terms of the functional prerequisites, if the position which normally meets a particular demand is not filled, some other position will be required to take on that function. This is the sort of thing which is being expressed by the widow who says that she must be both father and mother to her children. Conceptually, she is simply stating that certain roles which are usually a part of the father position in the family system have been incorporated into the mother position in that particular family system. Thus, for example, the role of breadwinner, which is often recessive in the wife-mother position, may become a dominant role when the husband-father position in the family system is unoccupied.

In developing a new set of family life-cycle stages, Rodgers encountered the inevitable problem of making certain compromises with his conceptual scheme in order to render it operational. His framework demanded a set of stages which identified and accounted for change in all of the positions occupied in the family system over the entire career of the system. Clearly, this was an impossibility, since there is great variance in the number of children born to families, and, therefore, in the number of positions that have the potential of being occupied. However, he pointed out that there are four positions which, if occupied, are always easily identified. These are husband-father, wife-mother, oldest child, and youngest child (p. 62). A set of life-cycle categories based upon these four positions would account for more of the possible role patterns in the family system than a set based upon the spouses and only one child. Particularly, such a set of stages would identify the extreme differences in role patterns which might exist in families which have children of the developmental level of teenagers at the same time that there are infants present, as opposed to a family in which there were only teenagers or only infants (p. 68). These differences are not discernible in a set of stages in which only one child position is identified.

The set of stages devised for his research includes 24 distinct role complexes (pp. 64–65), as opposed to the eight-stage system of Duvall (1957, p. 8). In addition to the developmental levels of infant, preschool, school-age, and adolescent, he included a young adult category to account for those families in which children have not yet left the home but are beyond the adolescent level. He contended that occupants of such positions have roles which differ significantly from those in the adolescent period (Rodgers, 1962, pp. 65–66).

Rodgers noted a number of disadvantages in the set of categories which he developed. He cited the fact that the large number of categories makes the research process more complex both in terms of having a large enough sample to account for all role pattern types and in terms of the complexity of statistical analysis involved. In addition, they still do not account for all of the potential role complexes which varying plurality patterns may provide. A further limitation, which no set of stages has handled, involves the varying role patterns arising out of the sex composition of the children in families. He stressed, however, that these are not theoretical but technical limitations arising out of the inability to operationalize all of the elements demanded by the conceptual framework. For a specific research problem, a set of categories to account for these factors could be a part of the research design (pp. 72–75).

The contribution to the family development approach of this work has two facets. First, Rodgers has brought together in one place the theoretical work of over a decade and attempted to place it in a meaningful conceptual framework. Second, by having available such a framework, it is now possible to carry out tests of the developmental approach. These tests may be made both in terms of the logical and conceptual consistency of the framework itself and through empirical research. To this point, most of those who have used the developmental approach have assumed that it was a valid theoretical system. As will be seen in the following section, little research has been carried out which actually tests the conceptual framework in any rigorous manner. Rodgers' own test of the framework was far from adequate, although he attributed this more to methodological problems than to theoretical weakness (pp. 185–187). Both the theoretical and methodological problems in the family development approach will be discussed in the final section of this chapter. It must be noted at this point, however, that only as rigorous tests of a theoretical system are carried out can there ever be developed a true sociological theory.

A Contemporary Statement of the Developmental Approach

In making a statement concerning the present status of the developmental framework, the writers recognize its unfinished nature. No attempt is made here to extend its horizons further, but it is hoped that the tradition of critical analysis and additional refinement of the framework may be continued, since there remains much to be done.

The most frequently used concepts in the framework cluster around four distinct issues of conceptualization:

1. Concepts about the family as a totality dealing with its basic nature and having to do with the definition of the family caught by the framework, such as those which describe the family as a small-group association, a nuclear family group, or a relatively closed boundary-maintaining system, and differentiates it from other expressions of the family rendered residual by the framework, such as the family as a domestic institution, the extended family, the kindred, and the household.

2. Concepts of structure, such as position, role, norms, role clusters, and role complexes, which tell what recurring and reciprocal features may be seen internally, using this framework.

3. Concepts of direction, goal, purpose, and the phenomena of equilibrium-seeking which illuminate the functioning features of the family.

4. Concepts dealing with the sequential regularities observable in the family over its life history, such as role sequences, careers of family positions, intercontingencies of careers, and stages of development.

In espousing the view of the family as a social system, the developmental approach emphasizes the interrelatedness of parts which exists in the family association. The concept of system carries with it the idea that change in one part of the system brings about changes in other parts of the system, a state of interdependency which in the family involves positions and roles. The units of the system are positions occupied by actors, of whom there are a limited number in the family. Family development concerns itself primarily with two types of positions: (a) age positions modified by gender, which in the family may in turn be modified by the norms of ordinal position, (b) relatedness positions which are interrelated in normatively specified ways as paired positions: husband-wife, brother-sister, father-daughter, father-son, mother-daughter, and mother-son.

The family as a boundary-setting and boundary-maintaining system appears to operate with a limited number of relatedness positions in our society. If fewer than this number appear in the table of organization, there is a *deficit* in structure; if more, an *excess* of structure. A childless pair, a one-child family, a one-parent family, families with only boys or only girls, are all pure examples of families with a *deficit in structure,* full organization requiring two parents and at least two children of each sex to fill all the positions in the family structure. A three-generation family, a family with stepchildren, or a family with children born out of wedlock to siblings, would suggest *excess of structure* when viewed against the full table of organization, and would present problems in boundary setting and boundary maintenance.

Viewing the family as a boundary-maintaining system suggests that it is partially closed, semiautonomous, and when coping with internal issues may seem to exclude the world from its affairs. Nevertheless, the family provides for liaison with other associations, building liaison roles into family positions and rules for transacting business with the church, the school, and the marketplace. Thus, for example, the occupational role of the adult-male husband-father is a role which involves norms of the "provider" within the family but also "employee" norms relevant to the economic system of the society. Change in the normative content of this role brings about change in the behavior of occupants of positions both in the family system and in the economic system of which it is a part. It may be that, at times, the normative content of such a role places the incumbent in such a stressful situation that his role behavior is unsatisfactory in one or both systems. That is, the liaison role may begin so to threaten the boundary maintenance of the family system as to bring about heavy sanctions from incumbents of other positions in the family. Thus, the executive who becomes so involved in business matters that he has little time or energy for interaction with his family may begin to hear demands for spending more time with the family. These illustrations point up the tenuous balance between liaison contacts and boundary maintenance in the contemporary vision of the family as a semiclosed system.

Unique to the family development approach is its capacity to put its concepts to work over the natural history of family formation, expansion, contraction, and dissolution. We use this property in undertaking the exposition of the approach, weaving in the appropriate concepts as we put the family framework into motion over the life span.

Changing role content of positions. To account for change in the family system, the developmental approach focusses primarily on the changing role content of the positions, due chiefly to changes in age norms for these positions. Expectations for behavior are not the same for infants as for preschool toddlers, or for school-age as opposed to adolescent children. Since the family is a system, change in the role content of a specific position brings about change in all positions containing roles reciprocal to the changing position. Secondary sources of change in role expectations might be changing historical conditions or changing family situations. However, the developmental approach has not dealt extensively with these factors other than to note their effects upon the ability of the family to handle the developmental changes which are occurring. Thus, for example, an economic recession is of interest primarily because of its implications for the family system in handling the changes in role complexes of a developmental type. The same would be true of a family crisis arising out of some extrafamily or intrafamily stressor event (Duvall, 1962, pp. 477-515).

Age-role expectations have been extended as developmental tasks for every age level by human development specialists, including not only the familiar expectations for infants and children, but also for young, middle, and late adulthood. The bridging between position-role theory and developmental task theory has been attempted by Rodgers (1962) in invoking the concept of positional developmental tasks. The device of constructing developmental tasks ceases to be individual and becomes positional developmental as the age, sex, ordinal, and relatedness properties of the position in which the ego is located are taken into account. For example, in working up the positional developmental tasks of any member of a family, the analyst would start with the relatedness position and the age position occupied by the member, and would note from the relatedness position the sex, and, if a child, the ordinal position. Thus, there could be an adolescent, oldest daughter, eldest sister in a family of three girls and two boys, all siblings younger, father middle-aged, mother middle-aged. The ages of the other children become important and their ordinal positions need to be noted before the construction of the various positional developmental tasks for the adolescent member can be seriously completed.

The web of intercontingent tasks for such an age composition is fascinating to weave, and the strains and stresses expected in such a network soon become evident. Some age compositions bring more dovetailing and meshing of developmental tasks of children and parents, of husband and wife, and of siblings with siblings than others, leading analysts to identify compatible and incompatible stages of family development. Havighurst, in commenting on the work in family development from the viewpoint of human development, recognized the interdependence phenomenon the family development approach renders salient:

This committee made a step forward in the use of the concept by showing how each member of the younger, middle, and older generations in the family has his own developmental tasks, and how the successful achievement of one person's tasks is dependent on and contributory to the successful achievement by others in the family of their appropriate tasks (Havighurst, 1953, p. 331).

Family developmental tasks. Matching the positional developmental task concept, which can be linked so well into the changing internal system of the family over its natural history, is the concept of *family developmental task,* which bridges the gap between the family and the society of which it is a part. Recognizing the heavy responsibilities laid upon families by every society in the world and more specifically in our own, the students of family development deduced that there would be basic tasks for families just as there have been for other associations in the society, and just as the students of personality have identified them for individuals. Ready-made for their use were the so-called family functions, identified by sociologists and anthropologists as services provided by families for their members and for the larger society. If all families recognized these as task assignments, we would in effect have the core tasks which all families could be expected to undertake: (a) reproduction, (b) physical maintenance, (c) protection, (d) education and socialization, (e) recreation, (f) status-conferring, and (g) affection-giving. These can be seen to divide between services imperative for social survival and stability and services to individual members of the family.

When these basic tasks for families are particularized by the sequences in which they must be performed and the hierarchy of importance which they have at different points in time, they become family *developmental* tasks. Thus, the family development task concept permits the analyst to highlight for each stage of development the tasks that have primacy, those which are secondary, and those which are still to be activated. The Duvall text (1962) is organized around these several family developmental tasks for eight stages of development.

The payoff for a dynamic framework is to put it into action, and this can be done at two levels of generality: at the individual family level as an outline for collecting detailed case histories, and at the modal family level, which requires the identification of stages of development. At the individual family level, each family has its own pattern of growth, and the concepts can be put to work plotting the sequences of change in individual positions and in the family as a whole from its formation at wedding day to its dissolution. The framework makes an excellent tool to make up descriptive case histories that are rich in inter- and intrapersonal data in a family and cultural context which can be used for counseling or educational purposes.

At the level of modalities, it is thought that all families in a society have enough in common to make it possible to chart their development in stages of the family life span. The family development framework does not permit working with short time periods of seconds, minutes, days, or months; nor do the categories permit specificity in handling short episodes of inter-

	Stage 1 (Phase A) Establishment	Stage 1 (Phase B) Expectant	Stage 2 Childbearing	Stage 3 Preschool Family	Stage 4 School-Age	Stage 5 Adult Trainees	Stage 6 Young Adult Launching	Stage 7 Middle Years	Stage 8 Aging Years
Age Composition	H 22 W 20	H 23 W 21	F 24–26 M 22–24 S_1 30–2	F 26–30 M 24–28 S_1 2–6 S_2 0–4 S_3 0–2	F 30–37 M 28–35 S_1 6–13 S_2 4–11 S_3 2–9 S_4 0–7	F 37–44 M 35–42 S_1 13–20 S_2 11–18 S_3 9–16 S_4 7–14	F 44–52 M 42–50 (S_1 20–28,f) (S_2 18–26,m) (S_3 16–24,f) (S_4 14–22,m)	H 52–65 W 50–64	H 66–72 W 64–77
Size	2	2	3	3–5	5–6	6	6–2	2	2–1
Interpersonal Relations Maintained	1	1	3	3–10	10–15	15	15–1	1	1–0
Years in Stage	1	1	2	4	7	7	8	14	7–13
Years Married	0	1	3	7	14	21	29	43	43–50
Positions in Family	Husband Wife	H W	H-Father W-Mother Child	H-F W-M Son-Brother Daughter-Sister	H-F W-M S-B D-S	H-F W-M S-B D-S	H-F-GF W-M-GM S-B-Uncle D-S-Aunt	H-GF W-GM	H-GF W-GM
Positional Developmental Tasks (Age and Relatedness Positions)	Young Adult DT	Young Adult DT	Parent DT Infant DT	Parent DT Infant DT Child DT	Parent DT Infant DT Child DT Preadoles. DT	Parent DT Child DT Preadoles. DT Teenage DT	Grandparent DT Parent DT Teenage DT Young Adult DT	Postparental Adult DT Grandparent DT	Grandparent DT Aging DT
Major Family Goal	Adjusting to living as married pair	Adjusting to pregnancy	Reorganization around needs of infants and pre-school children	Reorganization of unit around needs of infants and pre-school children	Reorganization of family to fit into expanding world of school-agers	Loosening of family ties to permit greater freedom and heavier responsibility to members	Reorganization of family into equalitarian unit and releasing of members	Reorganization of family around marriage pair. Strategy of disengagement	Disengagement

Fig. 3. Schema Depicting Stages of Family Development and Accompanying Changes in Family Structure and Functioning

action such as the interact or the inter-activity. The student must be content with the uneven time spans covered by stages of family development. These stages are a con-venience to permit stopping the process of development and concentrating on the prop-erties of the family at this and that point in its development. In actuality, the stages merge into one another imperceptibly, so one gets the impression rather of continuity than of stages with sharp breaks, yet there are analytical advantages in making such breaks.

From the family development framework, three criteria are suggested for demarcating the stages of development for which demo-graphic data are readily available: changes in observable number of positions in the family (family size), changes in age compo-sition, and changes in occupational status of the breadwinner(s).

A simple but powerful criterion for di-viding up the life span is change in family size, which permits inferring stages of ex-pansion, of stability, and of contraction: (a) childless young marrieds, (b) expanding stage (addition of first child to closing of family), (c) stable stage (period of child rearing until first child leaves home), (d) contracting stage (period of launching of children until last child has left), (e) post-parental childless stage.

A second criterion involves the age com-position of the family, which reflects indi-rectly the *family's complex of age-role ex-pectations in reciprocity* at any one time in the history of the family. To play fair with the conceptual framework, a stage would be changed each time the role complex changed in any degree. If one were engaged in undertaking case studies of individual families, this procedure would be most in-teresting to follow, but in seeking to differ-entiate stages of development for large numbers of families, it would be highly im-practical to designate a new stage each time the complex of age-role expectations changed, since there would be almost as many different combinations of stages (fam-

ily careers) as there are families in the study. Two solutions have been attempted which constitute compromises, the Duvall (1957) system which produces eight stages, and the Rodgers (1962) system of 24 stages. Duvall suggested that it is sufficient to change stages of development each time the oldest child shifts from one significant age category to another, since his experiences present new and different problems which the family has not yet encountered and bring about the most modification of role content in all other positions in the family. Rodgers sought to improve on the Duvall scheme by shifting stages not only when the oldest child graduates from one significant age category to the next, but also when the youngest child makes these changes. Both see the significant age categories in which changes would be expected to occur in our society as being: infant, preschool child, school child, adolescent, and young adult. Using the age composition of the family, it is possible, within the expanding, stable, and contracting stages demarcated by the criterion by changing plurality patterns, to differentiate a number of new stages, desig-nated by the age position of the combina-tions of oldest and youngest child.

The third criterion involves the change in the age-role content in the husband-father position which occurs with his retirement from active employment. For the mother who has not been gainfully employed, re-tirement from active mothering occurs with the launching of her last child into mar-riage and is captured in the shift in the family's role complex from the launching center to the postparental stage. The post-parental childless stage identified by the first criterion now is differentiatable into two stages: postparental middle years and retirement aging years.

Figure 3 constitutes an expository schema for illustrating in summary form the use of the major concepts of the family devel-opment framework over the family life span. The stages of family development pre-sented in the chart utilize all three criteria described above and show both the changes in ages of the incumbents and the changes in family size, as well as the changes in family structure and functioning that might be expected to be characteristic of the modal families in the United States over the life span. It is assumed that the modal couple married at the median age (U.S. Census, 1960) and had two boys and two girls every two years. The modal family does not have that many children, but this assumption is made for expository reasons. Daughters were launched at 20, sons at 22, and the father retired at 65.

The changing age composition provides the basis for identifying age positions suggesting specific positional developmental tasks for each stage. Size over time also flows from age composition, as does the number of interpersonal relations which must be maintained. Positions in the family giving the relatedness structure flow from the sex and ordinal composition of the family. The Major Family Goals follow from the stages but are the bare organizing base for the family developmental tasks, which are too numerous to be listed in a chart (for a listing of these for the establishment stage, see Duvall, 1962, p. 128). Figure 3 provides a basis for studying the relative vulnerability of families to crisis by stages, making possible the gathering of data about economic, medical, and interpersonal stresses upon the family by stage of the family life cycle.

The reader should remember that the framework of this contemporary statement of the family development approach has yet to be tested empirically in a comprehensive manner. Nevertheless, considerable research has appeared since 1950 which has utilized aspects of the approach in one way or another. An appraisal of this research is the burden of the section which follows.

RESEARCH REFLECTING THE DEVELOPMENTAL APPROACH

In looking at the research undertaken since 1950, it is possible to distinguish the same two emphases underlined in the evolution of the conceptual framework itself. That is, the research published is divided between studies emphasizing life-cycle stages as an explanatory variable and those which seek to particularize the family interaction processes over time through the device of the life-cycle stage. The review of these two emphases is selective, sampling rather than exhausting the research that might be cited, and pointing up in the process the approach's potential for further research.

Life-Cycle Stages as Explanatory Variables

It was pointed out that most of the work with family life-cycle stages which involved the use of the stages as explanatory variables had to do primarily with levels of living of families. It is interesting, therefore, to discover that the recent research has continued the same general focus, though possibly with a slightly different emphasis. The studies cited here are concerned with the family's transactive behavior with the economic system, as a basic consuming unit of the society. The life-cycle stages, then, have been utilized as independent variables to explain variable consumption behavior.

In 1955, Consumer Behavior, Incorporated, published an entire volume devoted to papers on the topic, *The Life Cycle and Consumer Behavior* (Clark, 1955). An interpretive essay by Riesman and Roseborough opens the volume by discussing the significance of "Careers and Consumer Behavior" (pp. 1–18). A second paper, by Janet A. Fisher, reviews the place of "Family Life Cycle Analysis in Research on Consumer Behavior" (pp. 28–35), not only in the United States but also in several western European countries. A presentation, by Lansing and Morgan, sets forth an analysis of "Consumer Finances Over the Life Cycle" (pp. 36–51), utilizing data gathered in the annual Survey of Consumer Finances conducted by the Survey Research Center of the University of Michigan. This discussion devotes considerable attention to the development of a set of family life-cycle stages for analysis of such behavior which were used in some later work by Lansing and Kish (1957), to be discussed below. The stages were: young single; young married, no children; young married, youngest child under six; young married, youngest child six or over; older married, with children; older married, no children under 18; older, single; and other (Clark, 1955, p. 37).

In commenting on this paper and the one by Fisher, Blood made a plea for not "freezing" the stages to be used prematurely and stated further, "Using economic data as a criteria, it would be useful to test the effectiveness of the alternative ways of categorizing families with children" (Clark, 1955, p. 52). While Lansing and Morgan used the age of the youngest child to determine stage divisions, Blood noted three other methods which he suggested deserve exploration: (a) age of oldest child, (b) average age of children, and (c) number of children (p. 52). In discussing this same set of stages, Rodgers (1962, pp. 179–181) noted several limitations: (a) The categories "young, single" and "older, single" are not really stages of the family life cycle at all, in the sense that behavior of such individuals does not occur in family role-complex situations and could not be attributed in any way to interaction in the family. (b) In using the designation "young married" and "older married," age of household head is confounded with life-cycle stage, which Rodgers sees as a distinct variable. (c) The "other" category includes a variety of role-pattern situations which would make it difficult to attribute the behavior analyzed to a specific kind of family role complex. These comments notwithstanding, the work of Lansing and Morgan and, later, Lansing and Kish has made a significant contribution to this area of consumer research.

Further analysis of the data from the Survey of Consumer Finances attempted to compare the "explanatory power" of family life-cycle stages with that of categories of age of head of household (Lansing & Kish, 1957). The dependent variables upon which the tests were carried out included home ownership, indebtedness, gainful employment of the wife, income in excess of $4,000, purchase of a new automobile, and purchase of a television set. Since none of the traditionally employed statistical techniques was applicable to the data, the analysts devised three measurements of varying statistical sophistication (pp. 516–517). In each instance, family life-cycle categories were found to be of superior explanatory power. Lansing and Kish concluded: "Advantages of the family life cycle over age probably can be shown for many economic, social, political, and psychological variables as well as for the few shown here. Of course, contrariwise, there are characteristics for which age is a better explanatory variable; mortality and morbidity come to mind immediately. . . . But we believe that the life cycle should be adopted more widely as an independent variable to be used in place of or parallel to age" (p. 518). Unfortunately, there have been no further publications of this type with attempts to improve upon the statistical methods used.

In an effort at partial replication of the Lansing and Kish analysis, Rodgers (1962, pp. 168–187) compared the explanatory power of age of head of household with his schema of life-cycle stages (24 stages) and the Duvall schema (8 stages), employing the same statistical techniques used by Lansing and Kish. The dependent variables tested included home ownership, automobile purchases, employment of wife, and income in excess of $4,000. Rodgers confirmed that both schemata of life-cycle stages were superior to age of household head alone in predicting economic behavior of the family, but found that the simpler Duvall schema of eight stages did better than his more elaborate system of 24 categories.

There were real differences between the Rodgers study and the Lansing-Kish initial test, so that the fact of confirmation is the more remarkable. (a) The Lansing and

Kish sample was drawn by a complex sampling design representative of the United States population, while the Rodgers study drew from a limited metropolitan area. (b) The Lansing and Kish data were cross-sectional, while the Rodgers data were longitudinal, representing the entire life span of each family studied. (c) The Lansing and Kish categories differed in several respects from the Rodgers categories, both with regard to family life stage and age of household head. Rodgers, therefore, suggested caution in claiming superiority for any set of life-cycle stages until statistical techniques appropriate to life-cycle data analysis have been developed, and until more is known about the properties of the life-cycle stage variable itself.

The family life-cycle concept has been extensively used in a recent publication on housing (Foote, Abu-Lughod, Foley, & Winnick, 1960). In studying the expenditures for housing in the data of the Survey of Consumer Expenditures for 1950, Winnick discovered interesting differences by family life-cycle stage within income groupings. He found the highest percentage of home ownership, when income is controlled, to be in those families with maturing children, i.e., oldest child 16 years of age or older. The findings with regard to average housing expenditure produced similar results (Foote et al., 1960, p. 50).

In analyzing varying types of housing demands, Abu-Lughod and Foley compared the stages of the family life cycle with a "housing cycle" made up of dwelling-unit size, tenure status, mobility, and locational preference (Foote et al., 1960, pp. 97–118). Their findings are summarized in Table 1.

The authors pointed out, "This brings into focus the major problem of most housing consumers today: *during the period when space is most necessary, it is often unobtainable; once it has been achieved, it is soon unnecessary*" (pp. 112–113).

In yet another volume of the *Consumer Behavior* series, the stage of the life cycle as an explanatory variable in consumer choice appears in the research design for a study, entitled "Patterns of Decision-Making and the Accumulation of Family Assets," under the joint direction of Reuben Hill and Nelson Foote (Hill, 1961, pp. 57–80). Although the final report of the research is yet to be published, some preliminary findings indicate that the developmental conceptual framework was of considerable utility in meeting the research goals outlined by Hill. By breaking his sample into generational

TABLE I

THE MEDIAN FAMILY AND HOUSING CYCLE[a]

Stage of Family Cycle	Age of Husband	Family Size	Income	Dwelling Unit Size	Median Tenure	Mobility	Locational Preference
I: Pre-child (constant size)	23–24	2	$3,000	1–3	Rental	1 move to own home	Center city
II: Child-bearing (expanding size)	25–34	3–4	4,000	3–4	Rental	High; 2–3 moves (one may be intercity)	Middle and outer rings of center city
III: Child-rearing (constant size)	35–44	4	4,300	6	Owned	1 move to owned home	Periphery of city or suburbs
IV: Child-launching (declining size)	45–51	4–3	4,500	6	Owned	1 move to second home	Suburbs
V: Postchild (constant size)	52–64	2.5–2	3,800	6	Owned	Unlikely to move	
VI: Widowed	Age of wife 61–72	1	—		Widow	relinquishes owned home and takes up residence as "subfamily" in home of a grown child.	

[a] Reproduced with permission from Table 19, p. 99, Foote, Abu-Lughod, Foley, & Winnick, *Housing Choices and Housing Constraints* (New York: McGraw-Hill, 1960). Calculations are based on median values for the United States for 1950 from various sources.

subsamples, significant differences in decision-making behavior were revealed.

The studies which have been discussed represent the manner in which the family life cycle has been used in recent research as an independent variable. In much of this research, there is a definite awareness that the explanatory power of the life-cycle stage is based upon the unique qualities of family interaction which exist in the various stages. In order to highlight further these varying qualities, however, it will be necessary to review research which has had this as its central concern.

The Family Life Cycle as Process

The research reflecting life-cycle stage processes may be divided into two kinds. There is research which has focussed on a particular stage of the life cycle and has attempted to analyze specific characteristics of the stage. Thus, for example, there are studies of husband-wife interaction in the establishment stage, of new parenthood, and of interaction in the postparental stage. On the other hand, there have been research studies which have attempted to analyze the characteristics of the entire career of the family. As might be expected, there are considerably more examples of the former than of the latter. As yet, there has been no single study designed specifically to test in full the developmental conceptual framework as it has been set forth in this chapter. The work cited here, however, is suggestive of what is being done to determine how role complexes of the family system change over time. Those studies which concentrate on one specific stage of the life cycle will be discussed first, following the chronological order of stages from establishment to dissolution of the family.

Newly married couples. There is a basic research problem which centers at what Duvall (1957) has termed the establishment stage of the marriage, as the couple shift from the engaged status to that of a married couple. Divorce and separation statistics (Monahan, 1962) demonstrate quite clearly that the most vulnerable years of marriage are the early years, and that the most vulnerable of these is the first year of marriage. Monahan has suggested that the first year might therefore be viewed as the stormiest, most conflictual, and most in need of marital guidance. Yet, when students of marital adjustment and marital happiness look at married couples by number of years married, they discover that the first year has the highest scores for marital happiness, and that satisfaction with marriage appears to decrease through the first decade and a half, rising and levelling off with the launching of children into jobs and marriage (Blood & Wolfe, 1960; Bowerman, 1957; Terman, 1938). The inferences from Monahan's divorce and separation statistics run in the opposite direction from those drawn from cross-sectional studies of married couples by duration of marriage. Monahan's data tell something about those who are most critically dissatisfied with marriage, but give no information about those who remain married, many of whom may also be quite unhappy. The cross-sectional sample studies of married couples, on the other hand, may also be giving spurious results, since each of the investigators was comparing couples of different durations of marriage, yet was charting the results as if they were drawn from a cohort of married couples that had been followed over their entire family life span. Their research may be contrasted with that of Burgess and Wallin (1953), involving a truly longitudinal study of great cost which followed 1,000 engaged couples with measures of their adjustment to each other in engagement, after three years of marriage, and again after 15–20 years of marriage. With three measures at different periods of the marriage for every couple, considerably firmer generalizations have been made. Burgess and Pineo have found that, for most couples, disillusionment between engagement and the third year of marriage is not characteristic, but Pineo did report subsequent disenchantment with the marriage during the child-bearing and child-rearing years (Pineo, 1961).

Probably the most outstanding example of the developmental approach to the pre-parental stage of the family life cycle, which also extends into early parenthood, is still in the data-gathering stage. The Child Research Branch of the National Institute of Mental Health is engaged in a longitudinal study, covering a period of five years, on the development patterns in the infant and in the young family, under the direction of Wells Goodrich, to whom we are grateful for access to several working papers and unpublished reports. The rationale for the project is stated as follows:

Human development is influenced by a progressively changing interaction of biological and social forces, developmental change being most clearly manifested in a series of transition situations through which nearly all individuals pass. Certain phenomena reflecting this biosocial interaction in early stages of growth are considered to have high predictive power for understanding personality at later phases. The broad objective of this research program is to bring those biosocial interaction situations under direct observation, preferably as they occur in the natural course of events (Goodrich, 1961, p. 12).

The plan of the project, which began in July, 1959, involves gathering data at five points in the early period of the family life cycle: (a) the relationship in the fourth month of marriage; (b) the relationship in the seventh month of the first pregnancy; (c) developmental characteristics of the newborn infant; (d) mother-father-infant characteristics in the first three months of life; (e) developmental characteristics of the child in the third year. With regard to the first phase, data have been gathered on modes of conflict resolution, cohesion-disruption of the marital relationship in seven areas of interaction (food, housekeeping, relatives, friends, occupation, affection, and parenthood), marital role perceptions of husband and wife, role participation of

either a shared or segregated kind, level of conflict, level of marital satisfaction, and level of affective involvement (Goodrich, 1961, pp. 7–9). There has also been developed a "theoretical model of successive developmental transactions," which was designed to capture the possible relationships between variables and the state of adaptedness at one point in time, as well as possible changes through time (p. 15).

The transition to parenthood. As has been seen, the orderly changes which occur in the family system over time are of central concern to the developmental point of view. One of the most significant kinds of change is brought about by the addition of new positions to the system. This, of course, means that as these new positions are occupied, the network of role relationships and reciprocities must be rearranged. It is of considerable interest, therefore, to find that relatively few empirical data are available on the characteristics of the family system during the expanding phase of the family life cycle. Although there are innumerable books with advice to new parents, most of the research findings for this period deal with the infant and young child as an *individual* and not with the family system. That is, while there is a wealth of data gathered in the human growth and development research enterprises, there is a dearth of data gathered in the family context.

An exception is LeMasters' study of "Parenthood as Crisis" (1957; cf. Dyer, 1963). Although limited in its generalizability due to a small and specialized sample (46 cases) of urban middle-class parents, it does attempt to determine the effect of the entry of the first-born child upon the family. Conceptualizing the family as a small social system, and recognizing the reorganization demanded by the addition of a new member, LeMasters hypothesized that the birth of the first child would be a crisis event. His data fully support his hypothesis. "Extensive" or "severe" crisis in adjusting to the first child was reported by 83 per cent of the couples studied. Of the 38 pregnancies in which severe crisis was reported, 35 were reported as planned by the couple, thus negating the possibility that the crisis was due to lack of desire for children. In addition, 34 of those who reported the birth to be a crisis rated their marriages as "good" or better. LeMasters reported that his impressionistic evaluation of the couples indicated that they were personally adjusted and that the crisis could not be attributed to neurotic conditions. In attempting to account for his findings, he suggested that the crisis couples appeared to have over-romanticized parenthood and were unprepared for the realities of living with a baby. In addition, all of the mothers who had had professional training or extensive professional work experience ($n=8$) prior to parenthood had experienced severe crisis symptoms. The birth of the child brought about an extreme disruption in the content of their concurrent role clusters with marked role discontinuity from the childless to the parental status. LeMasters concluded that, in contrast to the usually accepted view, parenthood, not marriage, is probably the real "romantic complex" in contemporary American culture.

Families with school-age children. It is with entry into the educational system of the American society that occupants of child positions become deeply involved in transactional relationships outside the family system. This, of course, involves role changes within the system. A study suggestive of the changes which occur in these role relationships was carried out by Bowerman and Kinch (1959). Although focussing on the changes in orientation toward family and peers of the individual child, the findings reflect clearly the developmental framework's concern with the individual as a part of an interrelated system. The authors found that, with increased peer orientation between the fourth and tenth grades, orientation toward the family decreased primarily in those situations where there was poor adjustment in family role relationships with respect to the child. That is, the transactive

role behavior patterns set up by the child were clearly a function of the family role relationships during the period of increasing peer orientation (Bowerman & Kinch, 1959, p. 211). This research suggests that considerable insight into family dynamics may be gained by a more intensive study of families during this period of initial extensive contact outside the home on the part of children.

Families of adolescents. The fact that there is considerable research on adolescence is probably due to the problem orientation which American culture has taken to this period of life. Yet, if the developmental approach is to be taken seriously, adolescence cannot be understood apart from antecedent parent-child relations in the family system. Unfortunately, research which compares family characteristics in the pre-adolescent period with those of the adolescent period is notably absent. The work of Bowerman and Kinch (1959) is a step in this direction, although it stops at the threshold of adolescence. Lacking any comparative studies which focus on family role dynamics, the next best alternative would be studies of role patterns within the adolescent stage per se.

A series of publications which focus on both role conceptions and role behavior during the adolescent period and which follow from a developmental approach have been produced by Johannis and his associates (Johannis, 1957a; Johannis, 1957b; Johannis, 1958a; Johannis, 1958b; Johannis & Cunningham, 1959; Johannis & Rollins, 1959a; Johannis & Rollins, 1959b; Johannis & Rollins, 1960). With one exception (Johannis & Cunningham, 1959), these publications were based upon a study of a large sample of high school sophomores. Data were gathered on participation of family members in child care and control, family economic activity, household tasks, and social activity. In addition, perceptions of the teenager with respect to decision-making in these areas and attitudes of teenagers toward family relationships were analyzed.

In the area of *child care,* Johannis found that only 7 of 16 activities were shared by 50 per cent of the families and that, generally, more mothers than fathers, more fathers than teenage daughters, and more teenage daughters than teenage sons participated in this area (1957a). *Economic activities* were shared by half the families in only 3 of 9 areas, with mothers being primarily the household purchasing agents, while fathers were chiefly concerned with providing spending money, paying bills, making major expenditures such as the purchase of the family car, and wage earning. Children had their highest participation in areas having to do with *individual use,* such as clothing (1957b). Fifty per cent of the families shared only two of the 18 *household tasks* investigated. As might be expected, mothers carried the major responsibility, with teenage daughters being second most frequently involved. Fathers primarily carried responsibility for locking up at night and making household repairs. In two male areas, taking care of garbage and trash and yard care, teenage sons had the highest participation (1958a). These findings indicate a clear division of responsibility in household tasks. Finally, the highest joint participation of all was found in *social activities,* with all 10 of the activities in this area of family life reported as shared by over 50 per cent of the respondents. Nevertheless, there was some differentiation in this area. There was low participation on the part of both fathers and mothers in visiting children's friends and in club membership. Teenage sons entertained guests in the home the least frequently of any family members, while teenage daughters used the family car least. In general, it was found that teenagers seek their social activity outside the family to a greater extent than parents, sons more so than daughters (1958b).

These findings may be conceptualized as reports of role behavior in families with teenaged children. Data which approximated role definitions were also gathered with respect to the same four areas of family activity (Johannis & Rollins, 1959b; Johannis & Rollins, 1960). As the developmental approach would indicate, these two areas are not independent of one another, since conception of the role governs to a great extent the role behavior. It might be expected that responses to a question concerning who decides who will participate in a particular area would be somewhat influenced by who actually participated in the area. Without discussing the findings in detail, they may be summarized as follows: one-half or more of the families were reported by the teenage respondents to share decision-making in 15 of 53 activity areas. Fathers were seen as the chief decision-makers in 13 of the areas, with mothers superior in all other areas. At no time did the teenager of either sex perceive his own decision-making participation as superior to the mother. Decision-making participation was seen as superior to the father on the part of teenage sons in three areas: seeing that children wear the right clothes, seeing that children get dressed, and visiting children's friends. The teenage daughter was seen as participating more often than fathers in decision-making in 11 activities, all relating to household tasks, in addition to the three in which teenage sons participated more often.

As the authors concluded, it is obvious that joint decision-making has not become a common pattern in American homes, if these data are to be viewed as valid. Although it appears from the data that mothers are more often the decision-making leaders, Johannis and Rollins reported that there was "a high level of sharing for fathers and mothers on the general question concerned with decision making in the family" (1959b, p. 74). They also stated that, "These data also tend to support the Parsons-Bales-Zelditch hypothesis that the female adult will be the expressive leader and play the integrative supportive role in the family . . . ," though they raise some doubts as to the universality of the hypothesis on the basis of their data (Johannis & Rollins, 1960, p. 60).

Probably the most significant aspect of this work is the clear evidence it gives for sharp role differentiation by age and sex in the adolescent stage of the family life cycle. The data would take on increased importance if they could be compared with similar data from the preadolescent stage to discover the changes in role complexes which may occur in these two phases of the family career.

Launching families. Although no research has been cited which compares the preadolescent and adolescent family situations, there is available a study which compares some aspects of the adolescent family in which no children have yet left the home with families in which some children have been launched. Connor, Johannis, and Walters (1954) compared conflict areas in the family between parents and adolescent children as reported by launched female adolescents who were college students. These respondents were asked to report conflicts which had occurred with parents during high school, and also conflicts with parents at the time of the study. Both the percentage of students reporting conflicts and the number of conflicts reported declined between high school and college. The investigators observed that this may be a function of the absence of the adolescent from the home as well as of the maturation process.

The largest group of conflicts during both periods centered on dating and mate selection, but conflicts concerning other activities outside the home declined 50 per cent after departing from the home. Conflicts with regard to parental behavior, especially nagging, increased during college. It is of interest that no significant relationships were found between conflicts and background characteristics of respondents such as age, education, ordinal position, family size, place of residence, or parental occupation (Connor, Johannis, & Walters, 1954, p. 186). Although a great deal more information than is provided by this report would be desirable, it serves to show that there are significant events other than marriage of children which might be seen as having launching implications of concern to the family development theorist.

Postparental families. With increased life expectancy and smaller family size, there has arisen a new sensitivity to the importance of the postparental period of the family life cycle. The study of aging behavior takes on increased significance when placed in the context of the family's development. Evidence for this position may be found in research efforts of the kind which are now to be considered.

In a study of adjustment in the postparental period, Axelson (1960) compared a "quasi-postparental" (one or more children under 18 years of age remaining in the home) with a "true post-parental" group of individuals. No statistically significant differences were found between the two types of postparental couples in their responses to seven areas of adjustment. However, significant differences within the groups did appear. Women of both groups reported significant decreases in concern for children's welfare and financial worries, and significant increases in activities with husbands and satisfaction with marital adjustment. At the same time, significant decreases in participation in community activities were reported. A concomitant finding which was statistically significant for the true postparental female was an increase in loneliness. Both types of postparental males reported significant increases in activities with wife and satisfaction with marital adjustment. To be sure, postparental husbands also reported significant decreases in concern for the welfare of children and financial concerns, along with decreases in community activities. Quasi-postparental males reported a significant increase in interest in daily work. Loneliness among these males did not appear to be as important as among females (Axelson, 1960, pp. 67–68).

One investigator (Sussman, 1953; Sussman, 1955) has examined the idea that urbanization and mobility in modern American society may serve to cut off contacts between parents and their launched children and reduce the traditional visiting and helping that previously occurred in rural situations. His findings in regard to help patterns between generations of middle-class urban families did not support such an assumption. He found evidence of considerable help in the form of nursing care, house repair, gifts, provision for vacations, financial assistance, and child care exchanged between generations, primarily from parents to married children (Sussman, 1953). In fact, he concluded that such exchanges actually aid both parents and children in their adjustments to the new situation.

If a pattern of moderate help is established after marriage, parents and children's families are more likely to develop a clear understanding of one another's newly created roles, to learn behavior in relation to these, and to establish more easily common frames of reference which assist in the solution of problems of mutual concern to them. Also, parents find in their new activities adequate substitutes for former child rearing roles now decreased in importance (Sussman, 1953, p. 27).

In examining another dimension of this stage of family development, Sussman asserted that parents feel the need of increased social contacts and new activities to replace the void created in their lives by the departure of children (1955, p. 338). He found that postparental couples increased the number of activities together both within and outside the home, such as playing games, conversation, entertaining, dining out, watching television, and attending movies and concerts. Women more than men needed to be active. Major ventures were undertaken, such as home redecorating, repairing, and travel. If, however, the married children remained residentially close by, less need for such activities was expressed.

Deutscher's work (1959) has already been mentioned in connection with his creation of concepts needed to study the transitions between one role complex and another over the family's natural history. This conceptual development was undertaken to cope with the special problems of the transitions from parental to postparental phases of the family cycle. His general hypothesis was that the "transition to the postparental phase of the family cycle presents the urban middle class spouse with a crisis situation in terms of his role definitions and role behavior" (p. 31). The data obtained in this study of 31 middle-class couples in Kansas City lend little support for this general statement. It would appear to the contrary, that the continuity provided in roles in other areas of life facilitates the transition in such a way that it is seldom defined as a crisis by middle-aged parents. Only three of the 49 individuals personally interviewed defined the postparental situation as "worse" than the preceding phases of the family cycle. Twenty-two of the 49 actually defined postparental life as "better," and 15 considered it to be just as good. Although this is a transitional period in the lives of middle-aged parents, it is not a transition which most of them have difficulty making.

In accounting for those who favorably defined the postparental situation, as opposed to those who defined it less favorably, Deutscher found that those who made the transition most comfortably were more likely to be deeply involved in concurrent roles in other realms such as occupations, social organizations, and so on. He found no relationship between the number of roles which were continuous or the amount of mutual activity shared by husband and wife and the tendency to define the postparental situation favorably. Deutscher brought to his problem greater conceptual sophistication than any of his predecessors and coined concepts of role sequences, concurrent role clusters, and complementarity of roles between positions, which he put to work in designing his study, with the consequence that his findings may be placed into a small growing body of theory about transitions and family change.

Families in retirement. In an entire volume of the *Journal of Social Issues* devoted to adjustment in retirement, Streib and Thompson utilized a control-group design to investigate further some of the patterns of the postparental family in the retirement phase as compared with those who remained gainfully employed (1958). Streib reported that older persons accepted the achievement orientation of their children, although they showed some concern for the manner in which social mobility could affect the family relationships adversely. Retirees were found to stress status striving less than the closely matched control groups who were still gainfully employed. It is interesting that the data indicated that family solidarity was not adversely affected by social mobility. Streib found a high degree of similarity between parental expectations for their children and the behavior of the married children, which he took to be an indication of family solidarity. Finally, he stated, "In the minds of older parents, affectional ties are more important than financial assistance, although as one might expect in view of their greater economic deprivation, retirees tend to stress the importance of financial assistance more than older parents who are still working" (Streib, 1958, pp. 59–60).

Although these studies of retirement and the preceding studies of the postparental years indicate problem areas in the postparental period, the general picture is one of ability to handle this area of life, especially when married children are still present in the vicinity. However, one study provides another interpretation of the psychological and social processes of the period. In an attempt to develop a theory of aging, investigators in the Kansas City Study of Adult Life (Cumming, Dean, Newell, & McCaffrey, 1960) reported a general constriction in life space among aging couples, which they termed a kind of "social disengagement." Of particular interest to the developmental approach are findings about the time of the perception of constriction in life space. The data indicate that perception of constriction comes some time before actual constriction occurs (Cumming et al., 1960, p. 30). In the 50–59 age category, 41 per cent of the men and 51 per cent of the women perceived such constriction, although, presumably, this was somewhat prior to the onset of actual reduction in their life space. In addition, the perception of constriction in the nonworking female increased sharply between the age categories 50–54 and 55–59, while the working female's perception of constriction increased only modestly. In subsequent age categories, the nonworking female continued to show a higher perception of constriction than her working counterpart. From the developmental point of view, this may be an indication of the effect of the departure of children, although the authors did not believe the evidence was strong enough to claim that such a statement was supported.

Corollary to the finding among the females were the data which showed a precipitous increase in perception of restriction among the working males in the 65–69 age category. While again the data are not adequate enough to confirm definitely, there is an indication of the anticipation of retirement.

In contrast to the ever expanding, growing characteristics of the other periods of the life cycle, the work of Cumming and her associates would indicate that the developmental tasks of aging may be directed toward coping with a shrinking world, and a sort of anticipatory socialization process occurs. Not only are there decreasing social and group normative pressures which define the roles of the aging and level fewer sanctions for conforming or nonconforming role behavior, but there are also indications that the aged individual himself disengages from the society. The implications of this work certainly demand continuing investigation.

Multiple-stage analyses. Most of the studies of the family life cycle as process reviewed to this point have focussed on the content of interaction within a specific stage or on the transitions from one stage to another. Several studies which have attempted analyses of several stages or of the family career as a whole now come under our purview.

Since the work of Glick (1947; 1955; 1957) has already been reviewed in considerable detail, it suffices here to say that it gives perspective on the total life span of the family and makes an unrivaled contribution in providing national data on changes in the length of life-cycle stages for different historical periods.

As will be indicated later in discussing the methodological difficulties of implementing the developmental approach, the great shortcoming of multiple-stage analyses to date is that they are for the most part "synthetic longitudinal" studies, rather than bona fide cohort analyses based on sequential measures of the same families over a life span. Generalizations based on cross-sectional data arranged to give the impression of change over the family life span should be accepted with great caution.

Among the best of these cross-sectional analyses is the study of urban family structure and functioning by Blood and Wolfe (1960), carried out in Detroit with an area-probability sample of over 700 families. Measures of a number of structural variables (power, division of roles, and kinship relations), of marital success variables (marital satisfaction, love relationships, companionship in marriage), and of variables of effectiveness of family functioning (family size control, emotional support and morale, and economic achievements) were worked out for families at different stages of family development. Blood and Wolfe held out childless couples married five years or more in order to compare their problems and achievements on these same variables by duration of marriage with the couples in each of the stages of family development through which couples with children pass.

Their findings defy brief summary, but it may be said that there are less dramatic variations among families with children by stage of development than there are among childless couples of comparable durations of marriage, especially with respect to husband's power, marital satisfaction, and satisfaction with love. Childless marriages maintain a more even tenor over the life span with respect to wife's employment status, wife's satisfaction with companionship, and wife's satisfaction with the standard of living.

Comparing couples with children after different stages of family development, Blood and Wolfe reported an increase in husband power from the honeymoon stage (childless couples married less than four years) to the childbearing period (oldest child under six years), but thereafter a decline in authority in every stage until retirement. In general, the presence of growing children has a deteriorating effect on the marital relationship, indicated by a decline in satisfaction with companionship, with understanding, with love, and general marital satisfaction. These declined regressively in each of the child-rearing stages until the postparental stage, when the children have all been launched, at which time most of these conditions improve.

Remembering that these are not the same couples being followed over time, but couples of different durations of marriage and different stages of family development interviewed at one point in time, the Blood and Wolfe tables suggest that there are certain stages of the family life cycle that are more likely to be beset with crises and conflicts and with indifference and disenchantment than others, and that these are found in the middle and later periods of child rearing. Longitudinal studies of the content of interaction in these problematic stages should be undertaken forward in time, as these families launch their children into jobs and marriage, to throw light on the reasons for the upswing in marital relations from the nadir point of the family with adolescents to an improved position in the postparental period. The research on this question by Deutscher and by Sussman has been retrospective; what is needed is a longitudinal design which follows the same families forward in time to differentiate between families which improve with the departure of children, families in which relations deteriorate with their departure, and families which maintain good relations both before and after launching.

A remarkable research program involving several projects in sequence is under way at Cornell University's Department of Child Development and Family Relationships, under Professor Harold Feldman. Feldman and his associates have begun with a cross-sectional sample of 852 couples drawn from an upper middle-class urban setting in Syracuse, New York, with the objective of mapping the transitions couples move through from early marriage to old age. They note the points at which the husband-wife relationship experiences the greatest changes, in order to analyze these points of change intensively to discover the mechanisms involved. Following this "mapping" study, the investigators have undertaken a longitudinal study sampling several social classes and all possible duration-of-marriage cohorts, with the objective of following them over time as they shift from one stage of family development to the next, beginning with the transition which occurs as newly married dyads reconstitute their relationships into a family triad with the coming of the first child. Thereafter, the research program is to be terminated with a cross-cultural verification study extending the same basic research design to two cross-cultural settings, one a society characterized by traditionalism and the extended family system (Philippine Islands) and the other a society in which experimentation is under way with methods which would replace the traditional forms of family organization (an Israeli kibbutz).

In the initial cross-sectional study, Feldman and Meyerowitz (1962 undertaken) developed an 11-stage family life cycle to sort out the effects of duration of marriage, parenthood status, the first infant, and subsequent infants on the husband-wife relationship. Aspects of the husband-wife relationship in which measures were undertaken included the distribution of power, response to modes of handling marital conflict, initiative in verbal communication, communication time, and satisfaction with the present state of marriage. Comparing childless couples married 2–5 years and still without children with "honeymooners" married less than two years and childless, in order to capture the effects of length of marriage, the investigators found relatively little change on any of these variables. For the group married longer, conversations centered more on objective than on affective topics, the effect of being married longer resulting in somewhat more detachment for these couples.

In comparing the effect of becoming parents while isolating the duration-of-marriage influences, the investigators compared those married 2–5 years who had and who did not have children. Those with children spent less time daily in conversation with their spouse, but the consequence of conversation was more integrative. Couples with children reported fewer expressive experiences (argue or have gay times), but the proportion of these experiences which were disintegrative was lower than for the childless group. In sum, couples with children found they had less time for spousal interaction and reported a lower sensitivity in emotional experiences.

Focussing upon the effects of the first infant as against subsequent infants upon the husband-wife relationship, Feldman and Meyerowitz were limited to comparing responses of those with one child only against the childless, and a comparison of the "one child only" with multiparous couples, allowing length of marriage to remain uncontrolled. They found that the first infant was more disruptive of the husband-wife relationship than subsequent children. Seasoned couples reporting on second and later births in the family provided evidence of significantly fewer disintegrative experiences, less repressive modes of solving conflict, more gay times together, and more satisfaction with marriage at this time.

The genius of the Feldman program lies in the progressive control which his long-term design permits, beginning with a macroscopic exploratory cross-sectional study, following up with a segmented longitudinal study focussing microscopically and almost experimentally on the most significant points of transition in family development, and concluding with cross-national verification of the relationships uncovered.

The Feldman research is significant also for its demonstration of the range of statistical techniques that may be applied to family-development data. A major problem in coping with life-cycle data has been to discover methods of statistical analysis appropriate for summarizing and expressing associations sequentially for the same individuals. The Feldman project has employed highly sophisticated statistical techniques and has shortened the time required for computations through the employment of high-speed computers, suggesting the applicability of these techniques for life-cycle analysis.

The several researches cited are suggestive of the potential which the developmental conceptual approach has for an understanding of family dynamics over the life span. Yet, clearly, these efforts have only approximated an empirical test of the framework as it has been outlined in this chapter. There remain a number of unresolved issues of both a theoretical and methodological nature. The task of the final portion of this chapter is to point up these issues.

UNSOLVED PROBLEMS IN THEORY AND METHOD

Let us begin with an evaluation of the present status of the conceptual framework. Is it justifiable to treat the developmental approach as a distinct theoretical framework in its own right? Is what has been described here only a potpourri of concepts from a variety of approaches to the study of human behavior with little internal consistency and interrelatedness? Or, as Hill and Hansen (1960) have suggested, is it possibly not more than an extension of the interactional framework with a few new concepts added? Is it justifiable, on the other hand, to term it a general theory of human family behavior under which other approaches may be subsumed? To attempt an answer to these questions, it is best to return to the issue raised at the outset of this chapter: What is a conceptual framework?

If it is accepted that a conceptual framework is a set of "interrelated but not necessarily interdefined concepts," while a theory is a "set of interrelated concepts, a set of underlying and unifying assumptions, and a set of postulates," the developmental approach may be evaluated accordingly. First, it is clear that the approach is not only a set of interrelated concepts, but to an increasing degree these concepts are being interdefined. To this extent, the approach qualifies as a conceptual framework. Moreover, these concepts encompass far more than can be accounted for in the interactional framework, since there have been built into the approach concepts which cope with the institutional settings, individual behavioral, intersystem transactional, and longitudinal aspects of family dynamics. The approach transcends the interactional framework, since these latter concepts are not quasi-related annexations, but integral parts of the conceptual system.

On the other hand, it is certain that full theory status may not be claimed for the approach. The assumptions of the framework are not at present completely formulated so as to provide the kind of unity usually found in a well-stated theory. No explicit set of postulates has yet been set forth, although a number of propositions which are logical extensions of the framework may well serve as the rudiments for such a set of postulates. It is weakest of all in its lack of buttressing empirical verification and in its provincial character, since most of its generalizations are probably culture-bound. Verification through concrete studies runs into a number of methodological booby traps which deserve attention.

Operationalizing Concepts

In any research effort, there exists the essential bridging step of translating the theoretical statement into operational terms. This process always involves the levels of abstraction of concepts which require attention before operational indices may be constructed. Some concepts refer to directly observable behavior, still others may be one, two, or more steps removed from such behavior. The further removed the level of abstraction from the directly observed actions, of course, the more difficult is the operationalizing task. In examining the concepts in most frequent use in the developmental framework, it may be seen that many are at a sufficiently high level of abstraction to create problems of operationalizing. The concept of "norm," for example, may not be directly observed, but must be inferred from interactions of two or more actors. Thus, there is at least one level of abstraction involved in the empirical study of age norms. Since a role has been defined as a set of related norms, two levels of abstraction are involved. Role performance and sanctions may also be said to be at this second level of abstraction. On the third level of abstraction may be found the concepts of position, role cluster, role complex, and role sequence, all of which involve the determination of some type of relationship between a set of roles, either intrapositional or interpositional. The concept of positional career may be located at the fourth level of abstraction, since the dynamic of orderly change over time is added into the structural concept of position. Finally, family career probably lies at the fifth level of abstraction, since it combines the intercontingency of several positional careers over time. The problem of the investigator is to gather data, either by direct observation from which he infers his higher-level concepts, by selecting proxy variables to stand for these higher-level concepts, or by training his informants to respond to him at the appropriate level of abstraction set by his concepts. These problems have not as yet been satisfactorily solved for the developmental areas of family research.

Problems of Data Collection

To take full advantage of the conceptual framework of family development practically dictates a system of longitudinal data collection and analysis. But following couples from engagement period or wedding through their family span to the dissolution of the family is fraught with many practical difficulties, not the least of which includes the possibility that the researcher will not live to see his project completed. There are the difficulties of sampling, of securing the couples' cooperation and commitment over such a long period, of maintaining contact with the families for a long time, of committing oneself to a study of the necessary duration, and the many other organizational and personnel changes that lessen the chances of research continuity (Hill, 1962). There are very real problems of morale maintenance, as families tire of being studied, and, more seriously, the possible effects on the families of being trained to make more plans or be more permissive with children, as a consequence of the questions asked, until they no longer represent the population from which they were originally drawn.

Alternatives to the longitudinal study in dealing with the time dimension are compromises of variable validity. Five are sufficiently differentiated to justify attention here: (a) the synthetic pattern of development constructed from cross-sectional data; (b) retrospective history-taking; (c) segmented longitudinal study; (d) segmented longitudinal panels with controls; and (e) the intergenerational panel combining retrospective histories (backward-oriented) and panel interviews (forward in time). Each of these alternatives justifies individual attention, since each seeks to minimize one or more of the enormous costs incurred if a truly longitudinal study were to be carried out.

Synthetic patterns of development from cross-sectional data. This method is both the most frequent and the least defensible of the compromises in current use. A cross-section of the population is taken by sampling categories of "years married," and the data obtained on a given variable are treated as if they were longitudinal. Cross-sectional studies are suggestive of hypotheses about what is happening over time as couples age, but may provide erroneous generalizations, since they do not control for generational differences in value orientations and styles of life which have been influenced by historical circumstances. Take, for example, the impressions one would get from cross-sectional data of gainful employment of wife over the life cycle, compared with longitudinal data on this question, for a three-generation sample in Minneapolis–St. Paul. The rapidity of social change has so affected behavior that findings obtained by aggregating the three generations together cross-sectionally mask the tremendous changes that have occurred when each generation is studied longitudinally. Viewed cross-sectionally, wives begin the marriage with a majority in the labor force, and the proportion employed declines to about one-third during the childbearing years, turning up only slightly with the entering of the youngest children in school, to drop off sharply in the later years to less than 20 per cent gainfully employed.

Separating the three generations from each other and following each cohort longitudinally, quite different generalizations emerge. Only 5 per cent of the wives in the grandparent generation began marriage in the labor force, and the number increased slowly from the second year of marriage to the twentieth year, when it was still less than 10 per cent, rising sharply during the third decade to 20 per cent employed, where it remained for the balance of the life span. The parent generation began marriage with 20 per cent of wives employed and dropped

progressively to less than 10 per cent in the fifth year of marriage, when the proportion employed climbed steadily and sharply to 60 per cent employed in the third decade of marriage and dropped to 40 per cent in the fourth decade. The married-child generation began marriage with 62 per cent of wives employed, dropping to 28 per cent in the fifth year and returning to 40 per cent in the 6–10 year period.

From the longitudinal data, it is possible to see that in each successive generation more of the wives have worked during the first several years of marriage, and more have returned to work as their children grew up. Similar accelerations appearing in the acquisition of homes and durable goods are completely masked in synthesizing the life cycle through cross-sectional samples of years-married categories.

To be sure, the cross-sectional study avoids many of the costs of the truly longitudinal study in the ease of sampling, of securing cooperation for only one interview, and of manageability in analysis. Attrition and nonresponse problems are minimized. A poorly designed cross-sectional study can be interrupted and redesigned, but the longitudinal study, once under way, becomes difficult to change if the data are to be comparable from one wave of measurements to the next. Nevertheless, the synthetic pattern of development built from cross-sectional data can rarely be more than suggestive of developmental patterns; it is a poor substitute for the more costly longitudinal study.

Retrospective history-taking. This is a method for manipulating the time machine backward through the device of recall by the respondent. If the study is to cover the entire span of development, the informants will be in their sixties and seventies and not the most trustworthy of collaborators. Certain behaviors simply may not be successfully elicited back in time from such respondents: marital happiness, marital communication, value consensus, authority patterns and allocation of roles, parent-child and sibling-sibling relationships. On the other hand, from their Minnesota study Hill and Foote found residential histories, job histories, automobile and durable-goods purchases, and family composition histories not too difficult to obtain from the most aged respondents (Hill, 1961). When checked with the testimony of generations of the same line, the histories by the grandparents appeared substantially accurate.

An advantage of the method of retrospective history-taking over some of the other compromises is that the data are not wedded to the stages of development established a priori by the researcher and so may be altered on the basis of analysis of the historical data obtained to discover new points of significant change in family development. It is also a relatively inexpensive way of operating the time machine, since years and decades may be covered in a two-hour interview, but it does require as respondents families that are far enough along in the life span to have a life history to record. Moreover, the method is limited to issues that can be studied in the past tense. Some of the most interesting variables involve data which should be carried forward in time, e.g., the spacing and controlling of births, or the creation of patterns for coping with children's needs in the absence of the mother in the labor force. The one variable has long-run implications, the second may be studied in the short run, but both would be better suited to cohorts of young families moving forward in time than to aged families reminiscing about the past. [Cf. "record linkage," p. 309.]

Segmented longitudinal studies. In this category of solutions are placed the many studies which deal with a segment of the family life span to test hypotheses about family change at selected points in developmental time. A number of the studies already cited in the section on research relevant to the developmental framework have been of this type: Deutscher (1959), Goodrich (1961), LeMasters (1957), and Streib (1958). They have employed the principles of the longitudinal method over

short periods moving forward in time, as in the panel study, or backward in time by retrospective interviews. The losses due to attrition are less in these segmented longitudinal studies than in the long-term type, as are the training effects from being studied over long periods of time. The returns contribute piecemeal to theories of the middle range about family development; indeed, this may be the way most of the hypotheses in family development will be tested in the near future, but many questions of theory cannot be answered in this fashion. Do good parent-child relations in the adolescent years make for good relationships between middle-aged parents and their married offspring as asserted by Dinkel (1943) and questioned by the findings from the Stryker study (1955)? Do families become more competent in dealing with critical situations over time? The questions of continuity and discontinuity of change in family development are also less likely to be adequately answered by these short-run longitudinal studies.

Segmented longitudinal panels with controls. Ingenious and more promising than any of the other compromises listed so far is a design developed by Feldman (1962). When carried to its full term, this approach could involve careful sampling of categories of the population according to the stage of family development in which they are located. The orderliness of developmental change would be caught by undertaking interviews in two or more waves to capture the patterns characteristic of the stage of development in which they are presently located (in the first wave) and then undertaking interviews in a second wave late enough so that many families would have changed stages. Those who have not changed would be treated as controls to be compared with the first set of families who have changed.

This design would be particularly useful for capturing changes in quality of interaction from the childless companionate to the role complex of new parents (Feldman's current emphasis), from preschool to school age, from young adult to launching center, from launching center to postparental stage, and from postparental stage to aging family (after retirement of father). These are all stages in which developmental theory suggests high likelihood of discontinuity in roles and, possibly, sharper breaks in the role content of the positions in the family. By sampling families on the upper edge of each stage, it should be possible to see enough of them make the shift during the study period to have enough changers to match the non-changers and thus obtain excellent contrast data.

The design copes with the large issue of costs, of attrition, of tiring, of the so-called training effects of having been studied, better than the other compromises listed, but it depends heavily on the adequacy of the stage categories developed to date.

The intergenerational panel combining retrospective histories and panel interviews forward in time. This compromise on the longitudinal study was developed by Hill and Foote in 1958 for a study of changing patterns of family planning and decision-making, where the focus was to be on long-term financial planning and consumption (Hill, 1961, pp. 57–80). It was reasoned that attention to the careers of families up to the present (through retrospective interviews) and systematic recording of the planning and fulfillment of plans over a year's period (through waves of panel-type interviews forward in time) would provide evidence of competence in planning and judgment in decision-making (family consumership) of rare quality for family development.

An intergenerational sample of intact three-generation families representative of Minneapolis–St. Paul was selected, despite the possibility of undue residential stability. The advantages it offered for the family development framework were substantial. The population of families would be regionally homogeneous, largely urban, and intergenerationally linked, thus holding constant the variables of region, urbanity, and varia-

tions in private family culture. Moreover, it would offer depth historically and permit intergenerational comparisons in which continuity in the transmission of family culture could be noted. Such data permitted the researchers to take into account changes due to historical circumstances such as wars, depressions, and periods of inflation. Patterns of family spending and consumption change over time, partly because family members grow older and their needs and interests change, and partly because historical settings shift. From intergenerational data it is possible to distinguish the continuities and changes that can be generalized as part of life-cycle development from those that are adventitious or due to historical circumstances.

A sequential system of interviews in four waves, once every three months, enabled the interviewers to encompass a complete annual cycle, thus accounting for seasonal variations in routine. The repeated interviewing enabled the study to conform to the principles of a longitudinal study for the year of data-gathering. To supplement this year's data with retrospective history-taking, the study relied upon the respondents' memories and powers of verbalization, as assisted and checked by the testimony of prior and succeeding generations.

Interview content for successive waves of interviews divided in such a way that part was repeated at each wave and part was different. The former dealt primarily with recent and immediately prospective purchase plans, or other changes in family status, and their fulfillment or modification, whereas the latter dealt with the intergenerational history of the family and its long-range financial goals and commitments. Thus, in four waves a life-cycle pattern for each family on residential mobility, family composition, occupational careers, and financial growth was obtained.

At each wave, expectations of purchases and any other changes in family status during the next three months were elicited and the extent of commitment to the proposed change probed. On the second and subsequent waves, changes in the family inventory and other areas being studied were noted and discrepancies between expectations and outcomes discussed. An account of the reasons for postponement, the change in importance now ascribed to the expected but postponed purchase or action, and the interplay of family members about the purchase (action) or failure to buy (act) was obtained. This concentration on *what happens between waves* distinguishes this longitudinal study of decision-making from most panel studies, which merely observe changes in opinion on issues at different points in time or collect evidence of fulfillment or nonfulfillment of purchase plans at specified points in time. The advantages of taking soundings at different points in time is lost unless linkages of a process nature are made in between to account for change or nonchange, wherever this is discrepant with expectations.

This intergenerational panel combining retrospective histories and panel interviews forward in time has many advantages over the truly longitudinal study, with only a few of its disadvantages. It is, however, more costly than the other compromises listed. It elicits data which can test the categories of family development, since it is not dependent a priori on the adequacy of the stages already identified; indeed, Rodgers' work (1962) on developing new life-cycle categories was drawn from the Minnesota data. It avoids the organization problems of the lifetime longitudinal study and successfully deals with the issues of attrition and possible training effects. By joining the theoretical interest of sociology in family development with its methodological interest in intergenerational comparisons, this design provides a device for obtaining the benefits of longitudinal study without having to follow families for 30 or 40 years. By comparing generations of the same lineal families over their histories from marriage to the present, and by observing their behavior over a 12-month period, an effective compromise of the several considerations in longitudinal study has been at least partially achieved.

Problems of Data Analysis

The issues in data analysis center in two areas, the complexity of the data and the applicability of the statistical techniques. The problem of the complexity of the data becomes particularly acute when longitudinal or modified longitudinal designs are involved. Rodgers (1962), for example, developed a 24-category family life cycle and analyzed a sample of families, some of whom had been married for over 60 years, with the median years married being 38. If data on changes in the family were gathered only once each year, this would mean a basic table with over 1,400 cells. If attempts are made to analyze more than one variable at a time, the complexity of analysis increases rapidly. These facts make it quite clear that electronic data-processing is the only practical method of analysis for family life-cycle data. In this regard, the work of Orcutt, Greenberger, Korbel, and Rivlin (1961) in simulating with electronic computers microanalyses of socioeconomic systems is of some interest. This publication would indicate that, given the basic knowledge necessary for developing the computer analysis program, some highly complex kinds of manipulations may be carried out. It must be kept in mind, of course, that this work did not deal with actual data, but only simulated data variations based upon probabilities programmed into the computer.

The second problem, statistical methods, appears to be a more difficult one. The statistical methods commonly used in social research have been developed primarily for analysis of cross-sectional data. In addition, they carry with them certain basic assumptions concerning the data. Although it is true that these assumptions are often not met by those who use the statistics, it would appear that this problem becomes increasingly important in longitudinal analysis.

One of the basic assumptions of many statistical operations, for example, is independence of variables and between samples. If comparisons are attempted between various life-cycle stages, it is doubtful that independence of these stages can be assumed, since what occurs in an earlier stage of the life cycle is certainly related to what occurs in later stages. Feldman and his associates have used such highly sophisticated statistics as analysis of variance, factor analysis, and multiple regression (1961, pp. 9–10). It would be of interest to know to what extent the assumptions of these techniques have been met by the data being analyzed. It may be that a number of new statistical techniques more applicable to life-cycle data will have to be developed.

NEW DIRECTIONS FOR RESEARCH IN FAMILY DEVELOPMENT

Four areas for further research are suggested by this examination of the problems facing the advocates of the developmental approach to family study: (a) analysis of the impact of varying plurality patterns and variable spacing patterns on family careers; (b) analysis of the transitions in internal role patterns of families, discontinuities and continuities, as families shift from one stage to another in the family career; (c) classification and description of "deviant families" of various sorts which leave the cohort of so-called normal families and do not finish a family career, such as the childless, the divorced, the widowed, families with stepparents or stepchildren, three-generation households and so on; (d) cross-cultural studies of family careers to validate the limits of the categories of family development. Work in these four areas should go far toward advancing family development to where it may become a theory of family behavior. Let us examine these areas briefly.

The conceptual framework of the developmental approach deals quite directly with changing role patterns in the family over its life cycle. This means that the plurality patterns at any point in the life cycle are of direct relevance. There is little research at this juncture which would serve to indicate how varying plurality patterns affect these role patterns. Most family life-cycle stages have been based on the husband and wife and only one child, usually the oldest. This leaves the issue of additional family members as relevant to changing role patterns almost unexplored. In addition, the manner in which these additional members are added, i.e., the spacing patterns, would also appear to be relevant. These two factors, as has been seen, were what led Rodgers to his more complex set of life-cycle stages (1962, pp. 61–62). His work, however, has done little more than scratch the surface of this highly complex problem.

The second area, learning more about the internal role patterns of families at various stages of the life cycle, has been treated above in the discussions of research on the life cycle as process and on the methodological problem of gaining entry to the semiclosed family system. It is sufficient to note that there is much to be discovered here.

The problem of "deviant" families has not been raised before in this chapter. It becomes apparent in reviewing the family-development literature that little attention has been paid to families that do not follow the "normal" progression of stages from establishment to dissolution in the death of the partners. The conceptual framework which has been presented, however, is certainly capable of analyzing families in which occur such events as premature deaths of either children or parents, disabilities of a physical or mental variety, divorce, separation, and others. These situations occur with such frequency as to be better viewed as contingent rather than "abnormal" experiences of family life. Knowledge of the manner in which they affect the role patterns of families would be of considerable value.

The proposal of Feldman and his associates to carry their investigations to the Philippine family and Israeli kibbutz settings is an important beginning in meeting the need for more data of a cross-cultural nature. If the developmental approach is to become a general theory, it most certainly should be able to account for family behavior in other than American settings. When we have accumulated enough such studies, we will be in a position to determine whether the developmental approach is indeed a valid theory of family behavior or whether it should be abandoned in favor of more fruitful approaches.

CONCLUSIONS

In quick review, this chapter has identified the origins and properties of the family development framework and summarized the major researches which have been related to it. The framework has been seen as normative, culture-bound to the United States, possibly to urban middle-class American families, and not yet empirically tested for variations by subcultures within the United States. Its major concepts are difficult to operationalize, and it has the misfortune of requiring in some measure the longitudinal method of data collection which brings with it high costs and serious problems of attrition and contamination. Yet the approach permits families to be viewed as growing, changing organizations and provides categories for studying them over time. It permits families to be compared fruitfully with nonfamily groups in composition and history. It permits placing families in the context of other organizations specifying functions and interdependencies. It provides a set of lenses to focus on interpersonal relations within the family and on the family as a collectivity with its own properties. Finally, it provides a beginning tool for the helping professional who works with families, urging him to visit families in their home settings, to interview when members are together, and to expect strain and stress in all living families at some points in the life span, thus providing a set of predictive norms which can be revised by further experience against which adequacy of family functioning may some day be viewed.

REFERENCES

Axelson, L. J. Personal adjustment in the post-parental period. *Marr. & fam. Living,* 1960, 22, 66–68.

Bates, F. L. Position, role and status: a reformulation of concepts. *Soc. Forces,* 1956, 34, 313–321.

Bigelow, H. F. Financing the marriage. In H. Becker & R. Hill (Eds.), *Family, marriage and parenthood.* Boston: Heath, 1948. Pp. 393–421.

Blackwell, G. W. Correlates of the state of family development among farm families on relief. *Rural Sociol.,* 1942, 17, 161–174.

Blalock, Ann. A conceptual scheme for analyzing families as small groups. Unpublished master's thesis, Univer. of North Carolina, 1954.

Blood, R. O. Developmental and traditional child rearing philosophies and their family situational consequences. Unpublished doctoral dissertation, Univer. of North Carolina, 1952.

Blood, R. O., & Wolfe, D. M. *Husbands and wives: the dynamics of married living.* Glencoe, Ill.: Free Press, 1960.

Blos, P. *The adolescent personality.* New York: Appleton-Century, 1941.

Bowerman, C. Adjustment in marriage: overall and in specific areas. *Sociol. & soc. Res.,* 1957, 41, 257–263.

Bowerman, C. E., & Kinch, J. W. Changes in family and peer orientation of children between the fourth and tenth grades. *Soc. Forces,* 1959, 37, 206–211.

Burgess, E. W. The family as a unity of interacting personalities. *The Family,* 1926, 7, 3–9.

Burgess, E. W., & Wallin, P. *Engagement and marriage.* Philadelphia: Lippincott, 1953.

Carmichael, L. (Ed). *Manual of child psychology.* (2nd ed.) New York: Wiley, 1954.

Clark, L. H. (Ed.) *Consumer behavior.* Vol. 2. *The life cycle and consumer behavior.* New York: New York Univer. Press, 1955.

Connor, Ruth, Johannis, T. B., & Walters, J. Parent-adolescent conflicts: current and in retrospect. *J. Home Econ.*, 1954, 46, 183–186.

Cumming, Elaine, Dean, Lois R., Newell, D. S., & McCaffrey, Isabel. Disengagement—a tentative theory of aging. *Sociometry*, 1960, 23, 23–35.

Deutscher, I. *Married life in the middle years.* Kansas City, Mo.: Community Studies, 1959.

Dinkel, R. M. Parent-child conflict in Minnesota families. *Amer. sociol. Rev.*, 1943, 8, 412–419.

Duncan, O. D. Analysis of farm family organization in Oklahoma. Unpublished doctoral dissertation, Louisiana State Univer., 1941.

Duvall, Evelyn M. *Family development.* Philadelphia: Lippincott, 1957. (Rev. ed., 1962).

Duvall, Evelyn M., & Hill, R. L. (Cochairmen.) *Report of the committee on dynamics of family interaction.* Washington, D.C.: National Conference on Family Life, 1948. (Mimeographed.)

Dyer, E. D. Parenthood as crisis: a re-study. *Marr. & fam Living*, 1963, 25, 196–201.

Farber, B. A model for the study of the family as mutually contingent careers. Urbana: Univer. of Illinois, 1956. (Mimeographed.)

Feldman, H. The development of husband-wife relationships. Ithaca, N.Y.: Cornell Univer., 1961. (Mimeographed.)

Feldman, H., & Meyerowitz, J. H. Renewal proposal: development of husband-wife relationships. Ithaca, N.Y.: Cornell Univer., n.d. (Mimeographed.)

Feldman, H., & Meyerowitz, J. H. The personal relations of primaparous couples. Paper read at Seventh Int. Sem. on Fam. Res., Int. Sociol. Ass., Washington, D.C., Sept., 1962.

Foote, N. N., Abu-Lughod, Janet, Foley, Mary M., & Winnick, L. *Housing choices and housing constraints.* New York: McGraw-Hill, 1960.

Frank, L. K. The beginnings of child development and family life education in the twentieth century. *Merrill-Palmer Quart.*, 1962, 8, 207–227.

Glick, P. C. The family cycle. *Amer. sociol. Rev.*, 1947, 14, 164–174.

Glick, P. C. The life cycle of the family. *Marr. & fam. Living*, 1955, 17, 3–9.

Glick, P. C. *American families.* New York: Wiley, 1957.

Godfrey, Eleanor. A construction of family typologies and their initial verification. Unpublished doctoral dissertation, Radcliffe Coll., 1951.

Goodrich, D. W. Developmental patterns in the infant and in the young family. Bethesda, Md.: National Institute of Mental Health, 1961. (Mimeographed.)

Gross, N., Mason, W. S., & McEachern, A. W. *Explorations in role analysis.* New York: Wiley, 1958.

Gutheim, F. (Ed.) *Houses for family living.* New York: Woman's Foundation, 1948.

Havighurst, R. J. *Human development and education.* New York: Longmans, Green, 1953.

Havighurst, R. J., Prescott, D. A., & Redl, F. Scientific study of developing boys and girls has set up guideposts. In B. L. Johnson (Ed.), *General education in the American high school.* Chicago: Scott, Foresman, 1942. Ch. 4.

Hill, R. L. Interdisciplinary workshop on marriage and family research. *Marr. & fam. Living*, 1951, 13, 21–22.

Hill, R. L. Sociology of marriage and family behavior, 1945–56: a trend report and annotated bibliography. *Current Sociol.*, 1958, 7, No. 1.

Hill, R. L. Patterns of decision-making and the accumulation of family assets. In N. Foote (Ed.), *Consumer behavior.* Vol. 5. *Models of household decision-making.* New York: New York Univer. Press, 1961.

Hill, R. L. Methodological problems with the developmental approach to family study. Paper read at Seventh Int. Sem. on Fam. Res., Int. Sociol. Ass., Washington, D.C., Sept. 1962.

Hill, R. L., & Hansen, D. A. The identification of conceptual frameworks utilized in family study. *Marr. & fam. Living*, 1960, 22, 299–311.

Hill, R. L., Katz, A. M., & Simpson, R. L. An inventory of research in marriage and family behavior: a statement of objectives and progress. *Marr. & fam. Living*, 1957, 19, 89–92.

Johannis, T. B. Participation by fathers, mothers and teenage sons and daughters in se-selected child care and control activity. *Coordinator*, 1957, 6, 31–32. (a)

Johannis, T. B. Participation by fathers, mothers and teenage sons and daughters in selected family economic activity. *Coordinator,* 1957, 6, 15–16. (b)

Johannis, T. B. Participation by fathers, mothers and teenage sons and daughters in selected household tasks. *Coordinator,* 1958, 6, 61–62. (a)

Johannis, T. B. Participation by fathers, mothers and teenage sons and daughters in selected social activity. *Coordinator,* 1958, 7, 24–25. (b)

Johannis, T. B., & Cunningham, K. R. Conceptions of use of non-work time: individual, husband-wife, parent-child and family—a methodological note. *Coordinator,* 1959, 8, 34–36.

Johannis, T. B., & Rollins, J. M. Attitudes of teenagers toward family relationships and homogamy of social characteristics of their parents. *Sociol. & soc. Res.,* 1959, 43, 415–420. (a)

Johannis, T. B., & Rollins, J. M. Teenager perception of family decision making. *Coordinator,* 1959, 7, 70–74. (b)

Johannis, T. B., & Rollins, J. M. Teenager perception of family decision making about social activity. *Coordinator,* 1960, 8, 50–60.

Kirkpatrick, E. L., Cowles, Mary, & Tough, Roselyn. The life cycle of the farm family. *Res. Bull.* No. 121. Madison: Univer. of Wisconsin, Agricultural Experiment Station, 1934.

Lansing, J. B., & Kish, L. Family life cycle as an independent variable. *Amer. sociol. Rev.,* 1957, 22, 512–519.

LeMasters, E. E. Parenthood as crisis. *Marr. & fam. Living,* 1957, 19, 352–355.

Lively, C. E. The growth cycle of the farm family. *Bull.* No. 51. Wooster: Ohio Agricultural Experiment Station, 1932.

Loomis, C. P. *The growth of the farm family in relation to its activities.* Raleigh: North Carolina State Coll., Agricultural Experiment Station, 1934.

Martindale, D. *The nature and types of sociological theory.* Boston: Houghton Mifflin, 1960.

Merton, R. K. *Social theory and social structure.* Glencoe, Ill.: Free Press, 1957.

Monahan, T. C. When married couples part: statistical trends and relationships in divorce. *Amer. sociol. Rev.,* 1962, 27, 625–633.

Mussen, P. H. (Ed.) *Handbook of research methods in child development.* New York: Wiley, 1960.

Nelson, L. *Rural sociology.* (2nd ed.) New York: American Book, 1955.

Orcutt, G., Greenberger, M., Korbel, J., & Rivlin, Alice. *Microanalysis of socioeconomic systems: a simulation study.* New York: Harper, 1961.

Parsons, T. *Essays in sociological theory, pure and applied.* Glencoe, Ill.: Free Press, 1949.

Pineo, P. C. Disenchantment in the late years of marriage. *Marr. & fam. Living,* 1961, 23, 3–11.

Rodgers, R. H. *Improvements in the construction and analysis of family life cycle categories.* Kalamazoo: Western Michigan Univer., 1962.

Rowntree, B. S. *Poverty: a study of town life.* London: Macmillan, 1906.

Sorokin, P. A., Zimmerman, C. C., & Galpin, C. J. *A systematic sourcebook in rural sociology.* Vol. 2. Minneapolis: Univer. of Minnesota Press, 1931.

Streib, G. F. Family patterns in retirement. *J. soc. Issues,* 1958, 14, 46–60.

Stryker, S. The adjustment of married offspring to their parents. *Amer. sociol. Rev.,* 1955, 20, 149–154.

Sussman, M. B. The help pattern in the middle class family. *Amer. sociol. Rev.,* 1953, 22–28.

Sussman, M. B. Activity patterns of postparental couples and their relationship to family continuity. *Marr. & fam. Living,* 1955, 17, 338–341.

Terman, L. M., with Buttenwieser, P., Ferguson, L. W., Johnson, W. B., & Wilson, D. P. *Psychological factors in marital happiness.* New York: McGraw-Hill, 1938.

Waller, W., & Hill, R. L. *The family: a dynamic interpretation.* (Rev. ed.) New York: Dryden, 1951.

Williams, F. *Adolescence—studies in mental hygiene.* New York: Rinehart, 1930.

PART II Methodological Developments

CHAPTER **6**   **Prediction Studies**[1]

CHARLES E. BOWERMAN
University of North Carolina

Why do some marriages work out to the satisfaction of everyone concerned, while others fail? Is it possible to make an intelligent guess concerning the outcome of a given marriage? These are crucial questions for an individual facing marriage because the penalty of failure is great, and any assistance he could obtain to help him make a decision might lessen the probability of failure. These questions also present a challenge to the social scientist whose aim is the explanation and prediction of human behavior. As knowledge of marital interaction and the factors affecting it develops, prediction is seen as an opportunity to put the knowledge to practical use, as well as being a means for developing and testing theory.

This chapter will summarize some of the ways in which social scientists have gone about the task of trying to predict marital success, and will discuss the methodological problems involved in this kind of research. First, the main steps in the prediction process will be reviewed to obtain an over-

view of the kinds of problems to be discussed.

NATURE OF THE PREDICTION PROCEDURE

The initial step in any prediction study is to define and measure the variable which it is desired to predict, called the dependent, or criterion, variable. A number of studies have used divorce or separation as the basis for defining a marriage as unsuccessful, sometimes because data on divorced people were readily available, and sometimes because they thought of these cases as the extreme of unsuccess. Other investigators developed measures of the subjective reactions of individuals to the marriage, in terms of their happiness, satisfaction, or judgment of success of the marriage. Whatever concept of success the investigator selects as most relevant for the purposes of his study, he needs to define it with as much precision as he can and develop a measure of it which is as valid and reliable as possible.

The next step in the process is the identification of variables that can be used for pre-

[1] The author wishes to express appreciation for the contributions made by Bert Adams, James McCorkel, Daniel McMurray, and George Noel in seminar discussion of many aspects of this paper.

diction, called the independent variables. In premarital prediction, these variables are ones that are observable before the marriage. Examples of some of the premarital variables that have been used in prediction studies are: social class background, religious participation, amount of conflict with parents, marital adjustment of parents, age at time of marriage, and indications of the adjustment of the couple prior to marriage. It is assumed that if relationships can be found between such variables and later success in marriage, the variables can be used to predict success. Ideally, the investigator would like to find predictive variables that helped him explain *why* some marriages turned out more successfully than others. It has been much easier, however, to find relationships than to be able to explain why they occur.

Prediction does not necessarily have to be from the premarriage to the postmarriage period. Partly for this reason, and partly to try to account more accurately for differences in marital adjustment, many of the prediction studies have included questions about the period since marriage. Certain of these are continuations of the same variables existing prior to marriage, like some of the personality measures, while others are situations or conditions that occur only after marriage, such as the number of children or whether the wife is working. The search, then, is for predictive variables that will help explain the processes and differences in marriage, that will provide a basis for accuracy in prediction, and that can be measured with a high degree of accuracy.

The next step is to collect data from a sample of couples on both the predictor and criterion variables. A number of ways have been used to select samples and collect data. Suffice it to say here that the objective is to draw a sample of sufficient size and representativeness to permit detailed analysis of the data and to arrive at generalizations with some degree of confidence. The relationships between predictive items and the criterion variable are tested for the sample, and those items that are found to be useful for prediction are combined in some way to form a prediction score. Several different methods have been used for obtaining prediction scores, as will be described in the next section. As well as providing a means for prediction, this process should also provide some empirically tested generalizations about the kinds of characteristics and processes that affect the interaction of marriage, and for which kinds of people, and under what conditions.

If the data on the predictor variables were collected at one period of time and the measures on the criterion variable were obtained at a later time, and if the scorings of the two sets of variables were independent of each other, then the model used for relating the two provides a basis for predicting for individuals, and the amount of error in prediction is indicated by the degree of correlation. The correlation also indicates the success of the theory. In most studies, however, all of the data have been collected at one period of time, so that couples had to be asked about things in the past that were to be used for prediction. In this case, the relationships that are found need to be tried out on a new sample to see how they do, in fact, predict.

As can be seen from the above, the emphasis in this chapter is to be upon *quantitative* methods of prediction, characterized by explicit specification of variables, measurement, and the search for quantitatively expressed propositions. It should be pointed out that the writer feels that quantitative prediction of this sort, toward which research is aimed, differs only in degree from more informal kinds. Even common-sense folk predictions of how marriages will turn out have some conception of the nature of the success they are anticipating, and apply generalizations of a sort that have resulted from the accumulation of the wisdom of the ages and of the predictors' own experiences. The predictions of the expert counselor may approximate the methods used in quantitative research in that he will use generalizations based on his experience and on relevant research findings and theory. His methods of measurement are different, but may in some cases be better for his purpose. If he had the results of more formal prediction research available, his own case predictions could be based on these, but with modifications he might wish to make for a particular case if he thought it would vary from the generalized prediction due to individual factors not taken into account for the general case.

From this point of view, there is no contradiction between quantitative, or statistical, prediction and clinical, or case, prediction, since quantitative methods can in the long run provide the clinician with a more accurate basis for the generalizations he would otherwise have to make for himself, and since it will be a long time, if ever, before statistical prediction will be able to take into account a sufficiently large complex of factors with enough precision to rule out the need for supplementing statistical prediction with the insights gained from intimate knowledge of a particular case.

There are at least two criteria for judging the worth of marital prediction studies: accuracy and usefulness. Accuracy is a matter of the amount of error, or number of mistakes, made in prediction. The size of a correlation coefficient between predicted values of an adjustment score and the values achieved after marriage would be one measure of accuracy. If divorce or separation were the criterion being predicted, the proportion of predictions which were incorrect would indicate the inaccuracy. Experts differ on the amount of accuracy in prediction of marital success they believe will eventually be possible, but they agree generally that considerably more accuracy than we now have can be achieved. Judgment of accuracy is not as simple as it might appear from the examples given. Also to be taken into account are such things as the improvement in prediction over other methods, such as pure chance, the consequences of making a particular kind of error or an error of a certain magnitude, and the effect that would be found in practical application of prediction on the error measurement if some people did not marry because of an unfavorable prediction.

Usefulness is another basis for judging success of prediction. Practical usefulness is affected by the degree of accuracy which can be depended on in making a prediction. Practical usefulness would be increased if the methods of prediction could also tell a couple what *kinds* of difficulties they could expect to meet and under what *conditions*. This kind of prediction would provide assistance for control, rather than merely predicting a final outcome of the marriage. Prediction can also be evaluated in terms of theoretical usefulness. In this sense, prediction leads to generalizations which provide explanation and understanding of marriage processes and interaction, and serves as a means for testing theory. It is the contention of this chapter that as prediction of marital success is increasingly based on a growing body of theory, the accuracy of prediction will also increase, and it will become more useful for diagnosis and control, either individual or social.

SUMMARY OF MAJOR PREDICTION STUDIES

The methods used in major prediction studies will be reviewed in this section because of the important contribution they have made in the development of prediction methods, and as a basis for later discussion of general methodological problems in prediction. The studies selected for inclusion are those which used fairly complicated methods of measuring marital success, collected data from a moderately large sample, and included a wide range of questions about the premarital period in the effort to do as good a job of total prediction as possible. These studies differ from a large number of smaller studies which have investigated the relationship between marital adjustment and one or a few variables, but did not attempt total prediction in the same way. These large-scale prediction studies are the ones which concern us most.

The earliest of these studies were truly pioneering efforts. The investigators had relatively little previous research on which to pattern their work. Several small relationship studies had been published, and the earlier work of Davis (1929), Hamilton (1929), and Bernard (1933) was particularly helpful in providing a few guides. But there was virtually no body of theory on which to base the selection of variables. The study by E. W. Burgess and L. S. Cottrell (1939) was among the first large quantitative investigations in the entire field of sociology, so there were few methodological guidelines. L. M. Terman's study, made at about the same time (1938), reflected current interest in trait psychology, and used a slightly more sophisticated methodology following from a longer quantitative tradition in psychology. Later prediction studies were able to benefit from the insights of these first two, and so made certain improvements in method.

Burgess-Cottrell

Ernest W. Burgess and Leonard S. Cottrell published the preliminary results of their study in 1936 and their monograph in 1939. Data from this study were obtained from married couples by questionnaire. Approximately 7,000 questionnaires were distributed to married couples by students or other persons interested in helping with the study. An additional mailing list of persons listed in newspapers as having been divorced was used, and 250 forms were left in mailboxes of apartment houses. These methods yielded 526 questionnaires completed by couples who had been married between one and six years and were residents of Illinois. The sample obtained in this manner was predominantly middle class, 82 per cent lived in Chicago or its suburbs, over half had been to college, 56 per cent had no children and only 10 per

cent had two or more, the median age of husbands was 26.1 and of wives 23.4, and 71 per cent had been married between two and four years.

The questionnaire contained items about the premarital background of the husband and the wife as well as postmarital items on attitudes and experiences in the marriage. Most of the questionnaires were filled out by either the husband or the wife, but there was no control over possible collaboration. With this method of data collection, it was not possible to judge the accuracy of premarital items concerning the spouse, the degree to which the answers on marital satisfaction were biased by the possibility that the spouse would see what was put down, or the extent to which the ratings represented the point of view of only one person.

The criterion of success used in this study was the Index of Marital Adjustment. The investigators defined a well-adjusted marriage as "one in which the patterns of behavior of the two persons are mutually satisfying."[2] This was viewed as an abstraction and therefore not directly measurable. However, according to the values in our society, they assumed that this concept of adjustment would be related to the degree of agreement about crucial matters in the marriage, the number of common interests and activities, demonstration of affection and confidence, the number of complaints, and expression of personal well-being. The questionnaire contained 26 items that had been constructed to measure these five types of indicators. In order to combine responses of all 26 items into a single score for the person, every possible response to an item had to be given a score, or weight, such as 5 for most favorable, 4 for less favorable, and 0 for least favorable. The adjustment score would be obtained by adding the weights of the responses to all items that a person checked.

In deriving the weights to be used, a con-

[2] From E. W. Burgess & L. S. Cottrell, *Predicting Success or Failure in Marriage.* © 1939. By permission of Prentice-Hall, Inc.

tingency table was constructed to show the relationship of each item to a question which asked for an appraisal of the marriage as very happy, happy, average, unhappy, or very unhappy. The authors pointed out some of the objections to using the happiness question by itself as a criterion, such as its subjective nature, that it might be defined in various ways by different people, that husband and wife might rate the marriage differently, and that there might be a halo effect in the rating. However, it was believed to be the most valid *single* indication of the happiness of marriage for their purposes. Their analysis indicated that responses to the question had considerable reliability. For example, 72 per cent of 251 couples agreed exactly with each other on the rating they gave their marriage (although independence of responses could not be assured), there was approximately 70 per cent agreement on the ratings made of happiness of each set of their parents, and independent ratings of the marriage by an outsider agreed with that of the couple in 90 per cent of the cases within one category. These findings were taken as sufficient evidence of reliability to permit use of the happiness question to validate the items in the adjustment index and to serve as a basis for weighting items.

The maximum weight assigned to an item was roughly proportionate to the size of the tetrachoric correlation coefficient between the item and the happiness question. Other responses were given weights according to the relationships found in the contingency table. If there were a big difference in distribution of happiness responses between two categories of an item, the weights would differ more than if the happiness distributions were more similar. For example, weights of 10, 2, 0 would be assigned if the persons giving the first two responses differed greatly in their answers to the happiness question, but persons with the last two responses indicated similar degrees of happiness. (The happiness question, incidentally, was not included among the items in the index.) This weighting system gave a possible score range from 0 to 192 on the Index of Marital Adjustment.

The mean adjustment score of the 526 couples used in the study was 140.8, and the standard deviation was 38.8. There was a tendency for scores to pile up toward the "favorable" end of the distribution, with 43 per cent scoring 160 and over, and only 18.8 per cent under 100. The tetrachoric correlation between the adjustment scores and the happiness ratings was .92 for the entire sample. When tested in a new sample of 68 cases, this correlation was .95. As an indication of validity of the index (whether it really measured what it was intended to measure), the mean adjustment score for the 61 marriages in the sample which had resulted in divorce and the 65 where there was separation but not divorce was found to be approximately 91, compared with a mean of 116 for the 60 marriages where divorce or separation had only been contemplated, and 151 for those reporting that neither divorce nor separation had been contemplated.

The items concerning the premarital background of husband and wife were used in two ways. First, the association of each item with the marital adjustment score was used as a basis for discussing the effect of individual basic factors on marital success and, second, those items which had a relationship with marital success were weighted and combined into a prediction score for correlation of the entire set of items with marital adjustment. The background items were grouped under five basic factors for purposes of seeking an explanation of the effect of background on marital adjustment, and the items were discussed in terms of their implications for basic, underlying factors. The five factors they attempt to account for, with the items used in each, are as follows:

(1) *Impress of cultural background.* An index was constructed for the husband and another for the wife from 9 items about their family

background: occupations of fathers, education of parents, religious preference and participation, economic and social status, number of siblings and birth order, and happiness of parents' marriage. Similarity of background and rural vs. urban residence in childhood were also included in this factor. The data were interpreted as providing evidence for the hypothesis that marital adjustment is affected by differences in values and attitudes associated with different kinds of family background, and that similarity of cultural background of husband and wife contributes to successful adjustment.

(2) *Psychogenic characteristics.* These were thought of as ways in which individuals tend to react to others, as determined by relationships with family members during childhood. Items of this kind included degree of attachment and amount of conflict with parents, happiness of parents' marriage, marital status of parents, size of family, birth order, and attachment to siblings.

(3) *The social type,* as determined by the social roles of the persons, included questions on age and state of health at time of marriage, amount of formal education, religious affiliation and participation, number of organizational memberships, number of same-sex friends, and previous marital status. The results supported the expectation that mature, stable, conventional, and conforming individuals make the best adjustment to marriage.

(4) *The economic role.* This included the questions about occupation of the husband and wife at time of marriage, occupational mobility, monthly income, and savings.

(5) *Response patterns* were indicated by age differences at time of marriage, length of acquaintance and duration of courtship, and the approval of the marriage by the parents of the couple.

The marital prediction score was derived from the items mentioned under these five basic factors. The weights assigned to the different response categories of an item were based on inspection of contingency tables relating the item with the marital adjustment score. The maximum weight was determined by the degree of relationship, and weights for other categories were roughly proportionate to the difference in adjustment of respondents in each category (Bur-

gess & Cottrell, 1939, pp. 275–283). This procedure was followed even when it produced weights that were not consistent with expectation. For example, the question about the number of organizations that the wife had belonged to was given weights as follows: none, 5; one, 0; two, 10; three or more, 20; and no response, 0. The reversal between none and one is probably the result of sampling variation; thus, even though the weights assigned in this manner will produce larger correlations with the adjustment scores from which they were derived, they may not be the best weights in a new sample.

The marital prediction score for an individual was obtained by adding the weights of his response categories. These prediction scores were then correlated with the marital adjustment scores, to obtain a product-moment correlation of .51. The relationship was also shown in a contingency table (Table 1).

TABLE 1

RELATION BETWEEN THE PREDICTION SCORES
AND MARRIAGE-ADJUSTMENT SCORES[a]
(Percentage Distribution)

Premarital Prediction Score	Marital-Adjustment Score				Number of Cases
	Very Low	Low	High	Very High	
700–799	0.0	10.0	10.0	80.0	10
620–699	1.5	12.1	25.8	60.6	66
540–619	5.8	21.9	29.2	43.1	137
460–539	27.6	29.4	25.9	17.1	170
380–459	39.8	31.1	15.1	14.0	93
300–379	57.2	25.7	11.4	5.7	35
220–299	75.0	25.0	0.0	0.0	8
TOTAL					519

[a] From Burgess & Cottrell (1939), p. 284.

Since the background items about both husband and wife were in the majority of cases answered by only one of the couple, the reliability of the prediction score was checked by having another 70 couples fill out pairs of questionnaires independently, each one answering questions about backgrounds of both. The correlation between husband and wife prediction scores was .88 for the sample of 70 couples. Another 38 persons filled out the prediction schedule a second time after a period of eight months to two years, and the prediction score correlated .88 with that of the earlier period.

As an additional attempt to interpret the effect of background factors on the adjustment, the weights of the items in each of the five basic factors described above were added separately, providing a prediction score for each factor. The multiple correlation between these five prediction scores and marital adjustment was .56, not much better than the original zero order correlation of .51. The authors used the partial regression coefficients as a basis for suggesting some conclusions about the relative importance of these factors, such as the finding that the economic-role items added little to the others and had little relation to adjustment when other factors were held constant. The weakness of their factor interpretation was pointed out by the authors in stating their belief that the items used were not very accurate indicators of the basic factors they believed to be important, and that some basic factors were probably not included at all (pp. 328–329).

Terman

The study by Louis M. Terman and his associates (Terman, 1938) borrowed extensively from the Burgess-Cottrell schedule for items to be used in the Index of Marital Happiness and for many of the background items. Its primary substantive difference was its search for personality correlates of marital happiness that could be used for prediction. An earlier exploratory study (Terman & Buttenwieser, 1935) had found a number of items from the Bernreuter Personality Inventory and the Strong Interest Test that were related to marital happiness. These and other items from the exploratory study were included in the larger investigation.

The data for this study were collected from 792 married couples by self-administered questionnaire. In contrast to the Burgess-Cottrell study, which obtained one questionnaire for the marriage, Terman had questionnaires filled out by both the husband and the wife. Data were collected in a group situation with up to 50 couples in the group, under the supervision of a project member. Care was taken to explain the nature of the project and to assure anonymity; couples were spaced so there could be no collaboration. Subjects were obtained from the Institute of Family Relations in Los Angeles, the Family Relations Center in San Francisco, church and Sunday school groups, PTA's, social clubs, study clubs, and women's clubs. This method of sample selection was believed to obtain a "reasonable representation of the middle and upper-middle classes of urban and semi-urban Californians" (Terman, 1938, p. 13). Although about 10 per cent of the sample were clients of a family relations counseling center, there was also a large proportion of subjects with welfare or self-betterment interests. Whereas members of the Burgess-Cottrell sample had been married a relatively short time, the median length of marriage for the Terman sample was 11.4 years, with 11 per cent married over 20 years.

The Index of Marital Happiness was constructed from replies to nine items (Terman, 1938, pp. 51–54): common interests, average extent of agreement or disagreement about 10 areas of marital interaction (e.g., handling finances, recreation, religion, demonstration of affection), manner of handling disagreements, frequency of regret of marriage, guess as to whether one would marry the same person again, contemplation of divorce or separation, subjective rating of degree of marital happiness, length of unhappiness, and a complaint score derived from checking a list of 57 possible complaints for the men and 53 for the women. These items were considered possible indices of a central happiness factor, reflecting the general factor from several angles. The test of their belonging in the index was the degree of intercorrelation of each item with each other item for both husbands and wives. The average of the 72 intercorrelations for the above nine items used in the index was .57, and the range was .22 to .84. Four items with lower intercorrelations had been eliminated from this set. The weight for each item was assigned in accordance with the average size of intercorrelation of that item with the other eight and the amount of husband-wife correlation for the item. It was assumed that the items which were most highly correlated with others had the greatest saturation of the general factor, and the husband-wife correlation was considered an indication of reliability. Since the effective weight of any item in its influence on the total score distribution depends on the standard deviation of values received by the respondents on that item, category weights were assigned for each item to produce standard deviations proportionate to the total weight desired for the item (Terman, 1938, p. 58). The sums of these weights were used as scores on the Index of Marital Happiness. Scores ranged from 2 to the maximum of 87, with a mean of 68.40 for the 792 husbands and 69.25 for the wives. The standard deviations were 17.35 and 18.75 for husbands and wives, respectively, and the distributions were highly skewed negatively, as was the distribution of scores in the Burgess-Cottrell study. The correlation between happiness scores of husband and wife was .59. This was about as high a correlation as Terman had expected, since the reactions of husband and wife to the marriage are not necessarily similar, yet there should be a moderate correlation if the measure is reliable.

The majority of items in Terman's Index of Marital Happiness are the same as items used in the Burgess-Cottrell Index of Marital Adjustment. Terman did not use the Burgess-Cottrell items on type of leisure-time preference, frequency of kissing spouse,

degree of confiding, or the seven questions about feelings of unhappiness or loneliness, but included in his index a subjective rating of the happiness of marriage, admission of present unhappiness, and contemplation of separation or divorce. Terman used a long checklist of specific complaints rather than the open-end questions asking for a listing of complaints against spouse and marriage. Although the techniques for deriving weights were substantially different for the two studies, Burgess and Cottrell found a correlation of .90 between their scores and the score for their items when given Terman's weights. (In an index of this kind, including a number of items with only moderate intercorrelations, rather crude methods of weighting can be expected to give a fairly good approximation to the "best" weights that would maximize the relation between the set of items and an external variable.)

In his search for personality correlates of marital happiness that could be used for prediction, Terman drew 71 items from the Bernreuter Personality Inventory and 128 items from the Strong Interest Test that had been related with marital happiness in his exploratory study. He also added 34 items of opinion about the ideal marriage, giving a total of 233 personality items. He believed that items of this kind would obtain the habitual response patterns of the subjects and disclose interests, attitudes, and preferences that predispose a person to happiness or unhappiness in a marriage.

His analysis of the personality correlates revealed by his data was based on comparison of 300 of the happiest and 150 of the unhappiest couples, matched on age, years married, schooling, and occupation of the husband. The percentages of happy and unhappy husbands and wives giving each response were compared and the critical ratio of the difference computed. The tetrachoric correlation was also computed between the responses of happy husbands and wives and between unhappy husbands and wives to see if similarity of response by the couple was related to happiness or unhappiness. Of the original 233 items, 101 from the husband's schedule and 97 from the wife's schedule showed high enough significance of differences on at least one of these two tests to be retained for the prediction scale. Weights of up to two points for an item were assigned on the basis of the happy-unhappy comparisons, and up to two points for differences in husband-wife correlation between happy and unhappy groups, giving a maximum weight of four (Terman, 1938, pp. 122–141). A prediction score for personality items was obtained by adding the weights of these items. In his discussion of the relationship of various personality items to marital happiness, Terman clustered them according to traits such as escape, benevolent, defensive, domineering, and self-confident.

In addition to the personality items, 26 background items were found to have high enough relationship with marital happiness to be included in the prediction scale. Critical ratios were computed for the difference in mean happiness scores of persons in each response category. The entire sample of 792 couples was used for most of this analysis, and prediction weights were given proportionate to the size of the critical ratios (pp. 260–264).

A subsample of 200 couples was chosen to correlate the happiness scores with the scores on the personality and the background items. Not only did this permit inclusion of some subjects not used in deriving the item weights, but it included subjects having a less skewed distribution of happiness scores than did the total sample, it excluded couples married less than two years and those with less than two years of high school education, and no one over 60 years of age was included. The correlation between the scores on personality items and marital happiness was .47 for the 200 husbands and .46 for the wives. The prediction score from the background items correlated with the happiness score .35 for husbands and .29 for wives—a considerably lower relationship than that found by Bur-

gess and Cottrell. The multiple correlation of personality and background scores with marital happiness was .54 and .47 for husbands and wives, respectively.

Terman also constructed a scale of sexual adjustment in marriage, which had a correlation of .49 with marital happiness for both men and women, and when added to the prediction items in a multiple correlation raised the correlation by .05 for men and .10 for women. His analysis of the sex-adjustment items adds considerably to understanding the relationship of sexual adjustment to marital adjustment, but these items, at least in the form he used them, do not contribute to premarital prediction.

Thus, both of these early studies, from different sections of the United States, with different methods of sampling and data collection, one placing sole reliance on background items and the other placing less emphasis on background but heavy emphasis on personality items, obtained almost identical correlations between their prediction scores and scores on criterion variables that were fairly similar in content.

Terman and Oden

Terman's longitudinal study of gifted children provided an opportunity to test further the predictability of marital adjustment using another sample, and by following up the sample to see if later divorce was predictable from previous happiness and aptitude scores (Terman & Oden, 1947). In 1940, 317 of the gifted men and their wives and 250 gifted women and their husbands filled out the marriage blank, including aptitude and happiness items. The marital happiness index was based on Terman's earlier index, with the addition of three items about preference for spending leisure time with spouse and three items about satisfaction with spouse. The weighting of items was similar to that in his earlier study, except that more differentiation of weights was given at the favorable end of each item, producing total scores with a distribution more closely approximating a normal curve.

The marital aptitude test included personality and background items from the earlier study that had been related to marital happiness, plus some additional items thought to be promising. The weighting of prediction, or aptitude, items was done in the same manner as in the previous study. The resulting correlations between marital happiness and the aptitude scores for the 1940 gifted sample was very similar to that found for the couples in the earlier study; for husbands the correlation was .52 with personality scores, .35 with childhood and family background, and the multiple correlation with both was .53. For the wives, correlations were .45 with personality, .32 with background, and .48 for the multiple correlation.

A follow-up study in 1946 found 41 men and 45 women who had taken the aptitude and happiness tests in 1940 and were either separated or divorced at the time of the second study. When the mean scores in the 1940 tests for these broken marriages were compared with those for the unbroken marriages, husbands and wives whose marriages were intact had significantly higher scores on both marital happiness and marital aptitude than did the persons whose marriages had been broken. The critical ratios between the two groups were 4.10 for husbands and 5.39 for wives on marital happiness, and 3.04 and 5.03, respectively, on the marital aptitude test.

In support of his contention that the marital aptitude test reveals a general tendency existing before and after marriage and that it affects the probability of adaptation to the necessities of marriage, Terman gave evidence of the relationship between 1940 scores on aptitude and earlier data collected on the gifted persons. Women rated in 1928 as having "some" or "marked" nervous symptoms had a significantly lower aptitude score 12 years later. Social-adjustment ratings as early as 1922 showed a significant relationship with marital aptitude in 1940,

and social-adjustment ratings in 1928 had even higher relationships. Further analysis of these longitudinal data would add to our knowledge of such relationships over extended periods of time.

Locke

The study by H. J. Locke (1951) differed from previous ones in at least two significant respects. It was based on a comparison of a divorced group and a group identified as happily married, and an attempt was made to obtain a sample that was representative of these two groups for an entire county. Names of divorced couples were drawn from the county courthouse records, and there was success in locating and securing cooperation from 201 couples and 123 additional divorced individuals. A third of the happily married sample was suggested by divorced persons, and the rest were couples who had been identified by a random group of married persons in the county as happy couples. As in previous studies, only white persons were included. Data for the divorced group were gathered between 1939 and 1944 and for the married group during the last three years of that period. Contact was made by Locke or trained assistants who enlisted cooperation and had the persons fill out a questionnaire. Anonymity was promised, and the interviewer remained to assure independence of response when both of the couple were present, and to answer questions when needed.

This method of selection produced a sample that was fairly representative of the population from which it was drawn, with respect to educational level, nationality (mostly native born), date of birth, religious preference (almost exclusively Protestant), and economic level. A high degree of persistence and ingenuity produced the low refusal rate of only 15 per cent for the divorced and 5 per cent for the married.

Although the main analysis in this study consists of a comparison of responses of divorced and happily married persons on predictive items, these two groups are thought of as representing two extremes of marital adjustment. A marital adjustment test was constructed, with adjustment defined as "the process of adaptation of the husband and the wife in such a way as to avoid or resolve conflicts sufficiently so that the mates feel satisfied with the marriage and with each other, develop common interest and activities, and feel that the marriage is fulfilling their expectations" (Locke, 1951, p. 45). His marital adjustment test included 19 of the Burgess-Cottrell items, 2 from Terman, and 8 new items (pp. 48–52). Weights for each item were based on the percentage difference in response of the divorced and happily married, and men and women were scored separately. The resulting adjustment scores differentiated sharply between divorced and married persons, with a critical ratio of 24.0 for men and 28.4 for women. Locke had also included all items from the Burgess-Cottrell Index of Marital Adjustment, and these 26 items with the original weights produced scores for his sample that correlated between .83 and .88 with Locke's adjustment scores for the four groups of married and divorced men and women.

There was little overlapping in scores of the divorced and happily married, as would be expected, because adjustment weights had been derived so as to differentiate between the two groups, and also because the married group was selected as being happily married rather than randomly selected with respect to happiness. It is also likely that the divorced responded with a negative halo, particularly since 40 per cent of the men and 30 per cent of the women had remarried. In looking at the records of the divorced who had high adjustment scores overlapping the married group, Locke found that adultery or attention paid by the mate to a person of the opposite sex was given as a major reason for the divorce in over 80 per cent of the cases. This caused him to question the accuracy of marital adjustment tests, for even if most reactions

to the marriage are favorable, one or two problems may lead to divorce.

The correlation between adjustment scores of husband and wife was considerably lower than that found in previous studies—.36 for the married and .04 for the divorced. For the married group, the lower correlation may have resulted partly from abbreviating, or truncating, the distribution of happiness scores by selection of the happier couples. The divorced also represent a truncated distribution, which would lower the correlation, and responses about the earlier marriage could not be expected to be completely reliable, particularly for those who had remarried.

Locke's questionnaire included prediction items that had shown a relationship with adjustment in previous studies, plus a number of new items which he believed would add to the prediction. As the basis for discussion of the relationship of each item with adjustment, the percentage distributions for divorced and married men and women were compared, and evidences from other studies for the relationship were presented. His premarital background-type items included several on courtship and engagement, parental influences, sexual behavior, and occupational status. Several items concerning sexual behavior and adjustment in marriage, present educational and occupational level, and number of children were also among the prediction items.

Although grouped for purposes of discussion, the background items were considered one at a time, rather than being regarded as indicators of more general underlying variables. In dealing with his personality variables, however, he did try to use them to describe four personality traits and two more general personality patterns. Each subject checked the extent to which he thought he and his spouse had each of 16 personality traits. In addition to comparing responses of the divorced and married, couples with the highest and lowest adjustment scores in each of these groups were also compared.

Six items were considered as indicators of a trait called *directorial ability*—"assumes responsibility readily," "engages in disciplining the children," "is a leader," "able to make decisions readily," "has determination," and "not easily influenced by others." A second general trait was called *adaptability,* using the items "giving in in arguments," "not being dominating," "slowness in getting angry," and "quickness in getting over anger." *Affectionateness* included the items "affectionate" and "demonstrates affection." The other four items, "makes friends easily," "likes belonging to organizations," "cares what people think," "has sense of humor," were discussed under *sociability.* The two general personality patterns which Locke discussed are *sociability* and *conventionality,* each supported by three items (1951, pp. 319–337). Although these personality items were grouped for discussion and interpretive comments about the effect of the general trait, their internal consistency was not reported, nor were they combined into separate scales to look at their interrelationships or their combined relationship with adjustment. A number of these personality items apply best to the period after marriage, so they would have to be modified if used for premarital prediction.

A final group of items dealt with marital interaction expected in the companionship type of family—intimacy of communication, equality between husband and wife, shared versus individual enjoyment of activities, and equality in taking the lead in various activities. These are *contingency* items, included to show the effect of postmarital interaction, but might be modified for purposes of premarital prediction.

All of the above were included in Locke's list of predictive items, regardless of whether they referred to the period before or after marriage. Prediction weights for each item were derived in the same way as those used in the adjustment items, described above. These items could possibly be used for prediction from one period of marriage to another, but considerable selection and modification would be needed for their use in premarital prediction. Unfortunately, after all Locke's discussion of prediction, no prediction scores were worked out to show the relationship between the entire set of items and his adjustment scores, or the difference in prediction scores between divorced and happily married couples.

Karlsson

A companion study to Locke's, conducted by Georg Karlsson in Sweden, provided a direct comparison of results in two countries (Karlsson, 1951; Locke & Karlsson, 1952). Karlsson selected a random sample of 100 married couples from the civil register and obtained from them the names of couples believed to be happily married, 90 of whom he then interviewed. The same source provided names of 39 unhappy couples, and 51 of the couples in the random sample were interviewed. Twenty-five legally separated couples also were included, making a total of 205 couples and 13 additional individuals in the sample studied. Data were collected by personal interview, with husbands and wives in different rooms and the interviewer and the subject going through the questionnaire together. The sample compared rather closely with the census distribution of the total population of Sweden on several demographic characteristics, and so was considered to be fairly representative in those respects.

The items which Karlsson used in his Index of Marital Satisfaction were almost identical with those used by Locke. Weights of the items were determined in the same manner, also, by comparing the distribution of responses by the couples selected as happily married with answers given by separated couples (Karlsson, 1951, pp. 95–99). The total scores obtained from summing these item weights differentiated well enough between the two groups used in the weighting so that a 2×2 table relating scores for the two groups had less than 5 per cent of the cases in the nonmodal cells.

As further validation of the satisfaction scores, means were computed for the four groups in the sample, and a significant difference was found between means of the happily married, random couples, unhappily married, and separated men and women. The correlation ratio of satisfaction scores for the four groups was .70 for husbands and .73 for wives. The correlation between scores of husband and wife was .72. This is somewhat higher than the husband-wife correlation in Terman's sample, possibly because of the wider range of scores forced by Karlsson's method of sample selection, and cannot be compared with the low correlations reported by Locke, since Locke's correlations were worked out separately for the two extreme groups.

Karlsson included prediction items in his questionnaire that had been related to marital satisfaction in other studies, and also added a number of new items designed to measure characteristics which he believed would correlate with satisfaction. As Locke had done, he included both premarital and postmarital questions, thinking of prediction in terms of relationship with satisfaction rather than using it in the sense of predicting from one period of time to another. To find the relationship of each prediction item to adjustment, he compared responses given on the item by 153 husbands and 140 wives having the highest adjustment scores with responses given by 57 husbands and 73 wives who had the lowest adjustment scores. Of the 77 items which had been found to be predictive for either husband or wife in Locke's study, Karlsson found 50 to be significant for the husbands in his sample, and 47 for the wives (Locke & Karlsson, 1952, p. 13).

For further analysis of the relationship of prediction items to adjustment, he grouped the former under the following headings: (a) General Background, a conglomerate grouping of about 60 items, many of which were background, personality, and interactional items drawn from other studies

for comparison, and including questions about the marriage period as well as premarital questions; (b) Adaptability I, consisting of items dealing with adjustment in other situations plus some of the Minnesota Multiphasic Personality Inventory items; (c) Adaptability II, which included self and mate ratings on personality traits judged to indicate adaptability; (d) Personality, or the ratings on a number of additional personality traits; (e) Communication I, including several general questions about the amount of husband-wife communication; and (f) Communication II, an index of how much was known about the spouse's wishes based on the number of correct guesses to 25 questions. The weights of each of these six groups of items were added separately to form six different prediction scores. The correlation coefficients in Table 2 were found when Karlsson related these scores with each other and with the index of marital satisfaction (Karlsson, 1951, p. 150). The multiple correlation of all six prediction scores with the marital satisfaction scale was .84 for husbands and .91 for wives.

It will be noted that these correlations are considerably higher than those found in any other study. Karlsson suggested that this might be partly attributable to the fact that his study included a number of items dealing with the marital process, and that some of these items may actually be another way of measuring satisfaction. This is a plausible explanation, since the background score which accounts for most of the relationship includes a number of questions which ask for an evaluation of certain aspects of the marriage. It should also be pointed out that the method of weighting predictive items was such as to produce the highest possible discrimination of scores between well-satisfied and poorly satisfied couples. Since the sample was selected in a way that would tend toward a bimodal distribution of satisfaction scores, a high correlation was almost inevitable and cannot be considered indicative of results that

TABLE 2

INTERCORRELATIONS[a]

HUSBANDS

	Gen. Back.	Adapt. I	Adapt. II	Pers.	Comm. I	Comm. II
Marital Satisfaction	.76	.38	.64	.43	.64	.48
General Background		.47	.53	.31	.61	.42
Adaptability I			.31	.22	.36	.22
Adaptability II				.28	.64	.49
Personality Traits					.24	.22
Communication I						.43

WIVES

	Gen. Back.	Adapt. I	Adapt. II	Pers.	Comm. I	Comm. II
Marital Satisfaction	.84	.53	.75	.59	.71	.56
General Background		.61	.67	.56	.55	.56
Adaptability I			.47	.38	.45	.37
Adaptability II				.57	.65	.60
Personality Traits					.53	.37
Communication I						.41

[a] From Karlsson (1951), p. 150.

would be obtained with a random sample. The inclusion of questions about the post-marital period, the method of weighting, and the use of a sample representing extremes can account for correlations higher than those found in the Burgess-Cottrell and Terman studies. However, Locke might have found a higher correlation also, for the same reasons.

The contribution of this study lies not only in the testing of results of American studies in another culture, but in the steps taken toward the development of measures of basic variables such as adaptability and communication, as they apply to prediction. Although Karlsson's measures apply to the marriage period, they could be modified for use with premarital prediction.

Burgess and Wallin

The most ambitious study of this kind reported to date is that of E. W. Burgess and Paul Wallin (1953), starting with data from a sample of 1,000 engaged couples and following up with them after three or more years of marriage. The original sample of engaged couples consisted of persons contacted by students in colleges and universities in the Chicago metropolitan area and who were formally or informally engaged to be married. The sample was restricted to couples living in metropolitan Chicago, at least one of whom had been to college for a year or more. Approximately 6,000 sets of questionnaires were given to contact persons for distribution to engaged couples. The first 1,000 complete pairs of questionnaires constituted the sample for the study. The man and the woman each filled out a questionnaire and were instructed to do so independently, although no check was made on their compliance with this request. A short schedule about the couple was filled out by the contact person for three-fourths of the couples, and a personal interview with almost one-fourth provided additional data.

About two-thirds of the engaged couples gave their names and addresses, although they were told that they could remain anonymous if they wished. The contacting person also gave his own name and address and some identifying sign, such as initials, to match the couple with a code number for each case. This information was used in the follow-up of the couples between 1940 and 1943. On the basis of 131 known broken engagements, it was estimated that 150 of the original 1,000 couples broke their engagement. Those, along with 33 couples who were already divorced or separated and 10 couples whose marriage was broken by death, were dropped from further study. Only 42 couples refused to cooperate in the follow-up study, but others were lost because they could not be located. Marriage questionnaires were obtained from the remaining 666 couples. A separate questionnaire was filled out by husband and wife under supervision of an interviewer, assuring independence of response.

About three-fourths of these couples had been married from 3 to 5 years, 9 per cent 2 to 3 years, and 18 per cent between 5 and 9 years. Like the Burgess-Cottrell sample, these couples were predominantly middle class, with higher than average education, income, and occupational status.

Burgess and Wallin used several criteria of marital success instead of a single composite index. In analyzing the indices used by Burgess and Cottrell, Terman, Locke, and Karlsson, they classified the items in each index under eight components: adaptability, common interests, consensus, demonstration of affection, happiness, permanence, satisfaction, and sex satisfaction. The relative importance given these components, by adding their item weights, varied considerably in these four studies, without any rationale given for this variation. Since the intercorrelations of items were only moderate, Burgess and Wallin felt that the composite score derived from such heterogeneous items had an ambiguous meaning. Consequently, they developed multiple criteria of marital success, with a separate index for nine different components which they thought would be somewhat different and more meaningful for evaluating types of success in the marriage (Burgess & Wallin, 1953, Ch. 15).

Three of these indices were of a general nature: permanence (attitudes toward separation or divorce), happiness of the marriage, and general satisfaction with the marriage. The six specific indices were: specific satisfactions and dissatisfactions with a number of aspects of marriage and spouse; consensus, or degree of agreement about family matters; love for mate and perception of reciprocation; sexual satisfaction; companionship; and compatibility of personality and temperament, based on self and other ratings on 15 traits. Each of these indices was constructed from appropriate items from previous studies, plus new items thought to be useful in measuring the component. Although a scoring key was provided for each index, the method of determining weights was not described, nor was any test of internal consistency reported for the items in each index.

Since the use of multiple criteria assumed that more accurate measures could be obtained for components than for an index made up of heterogeneous elements, an important contribution could have been made by demonstrating that (a) there was a high degree of internal consistency among the items in each index, suggesting a unidimensional scale, and (b) that each index was measuring a different dimension, as indicated by moderate or low intercorrelations among index scores. A correlation of .82 for husbands and also for wives was reported between the marital happiness and the general satisfaction index, so these may have been measuring essentially the same thing. Correlations between the happiness and satisfaction indices and the remaining indices ranged, for husbands, between .44 and .65. The correlation between general and specific satisfaction was .60, but other intercorrelations among the component indices are not reported.

In their treatment of the predictive items Burgess and Wallin distinguished between premarital and postmarital items, the latter considered as contingencies. The prediction items from the engagement schedule were grouped under five headings. (a) Background items included those dealing with the parent-child relationship, social participation, economic background, and sex attitudes and behavior. (b) Ten prediction items were included under "engagement history," and asked about rating of physical appearance, attitudes of friends and parents toward the marriage, marriage plans, and length of association. (c) The personality items consisted of 42 questions from the Thurstone Personality Inventory that had discriminated between neurotic and non-neurotic persons in other studies. The weighting of these items for prediction was based on the critical ratios between mean engagement success scores of couples with the four combinations of neurotic versus non-neurotic responses of the man and woman. (d) Burgess and Cottrell had found a correlation between marital adjustment and the score on a number of postmarital contingency items of .51, and when this score had been included with the five background scores, the multiple correlation with marital adjustment was raised from .56 to .61. Burgess and Wallin followed this lead and constructed 14 items which could be answered during the engagement period anticipating various contingency conditions, such as whether the wife expected to work after marriage, the number of children expected, and where they expected to live. (e) An Index of Engagement Success was constructed from items modified from those used in the Burgess-Cottrell marital adjustment index. In the follow-up study, Burgess and Wallin found that men and women who had broken their engagements had lower average scores on this engagement success index than those who married, although the differences were not large. For example, 52.9 per cent of the men and 46.3 per cent of the women whose engagements were later broken had scores of 150 or over, compared with 60.7 per cent of the men and 61.4 per cent of the women who married. The test-retest reliability of the engagement success index was .75 and .71 for 81 men and women, respectively, who answered the same questions after a six-months' interval.

Prediction scores for each of the above five sets of items answered during engagement were correlated with "marital success" scores from the marriage questionnaire. Except for the personality items, the method of weighting prediction items was not reported, nor was it clear which measure of marital success had been used. These correlations ranged from .21 and .19 for anticipated contingency to .39 and .36 for engagement success scores, for men and women respectively. These correlations are considerably lower than those found in the studies obtaining their prediction data at the same time as the marriage data, and support the contention that biased responses are obtained when questions about the premarital period are answered after marriage. On the other hand, Burgess and Wallin did not report the prediction results for the couples whose marriages were broken. If these had been included in the correlation, it probably would have been somewhat higher. There probably is also a lowering of the correlation, especially between the personality items and the engagement success index, because collaboration was not controlled in collecting the engagement data, and one would expect less reporting of unfavorable characteristics and reactions.

The multiple correlation between the five groups of prediction scores and the multiple criteria of success (sum of individual scores?) was reported as .50 for 600 men. The correlation for women was not given. The authors stated that another expectancy table was worked out, based on a different classification of prediction items and with weights based on mean engagement adjustment scores of response combinations of the man and woman, but the results of this work were not reported (Burgess & Wallin, 1953, pp. 551–554).

An interesting experiment in forecasting was reported, in which judges gave predictive ratings from case materials collected during engagement on 14 factors in the relationship, and these scores for 229 couples correlated with the marital adjustment score at .42 for men and .39 for women (Burgess & Wallin, 1953, Ch. 17). A new rating scale based on a factor analysis of the 14 factors was used by three judges with even better results for prediction.

The data for this study were the most comprehensive of any in this field done up to date, and were used as the basis for a very insightful discussion of the engagement and marriage period. The use of case materials for illustration and suggested explanation is excellent, and the study provides numerous hypotheses for further investigation. Taken as a whole, Burgess and Wallin's report represents a significant contribution to the development of research and theory in this area. Nevertheless, limitations of data analysis and reporting, some of which are indicated above, are regrettable, particularly with respect to some of the crucial aspects of measurement and prediction.

METHODOLOGICAL PROBLEMS IN PREDICTION

Although the studies just reviewed have made important substantive and methodological contributions, progress toward the goal of achieving prediction of marital success has been rather limited.

Some Replication Studies

There have been several other studies which have partially replicated previous work. In one of these, Kelley (1939) gave 300 couples, before marriage, the Terman questions on background and personality,

and two years after marriage obtained data on marital happiness, using Terman's index. The correlation between prediction and happiness scores, corrected for attenuation, was .50 for husbands and .56 for wives. In another study, King (1952) gave the Burgess-Cottrell prediction and adjustment items to a sample of southern Negroes and obtained results comparable to those of the original study. Stroup (1953) also used the Burgess-Cottrell schedule with a sample of married couples randomly picked from the telephone listings in Akron, Ohio. He obtained a correlation of .36 between prediction and adjustment scores, using the original Burgess-Cottrell weights, and when he worked out new weights based on his sample, the correlation increased to .58. He found no significant differences between correlations of couples married one to six years and those married longer.

The picture is a little more favorable when efforts to find predictive variables are looked at. Numerous individual items have been discovered which correlate with a measure of marital adjustment in at least one study. However, Hill was able to find only 12 items whose relationship with adjustment had been confirmed in at least three studies (Waller & Hill, 1951, p. 358). In interpreting results of studies, many of these items are considered only as indicators of more basic variables, and it cannot yet be claimed that many explanatory variables have been established that fit into a theory of marital interaction and adjustment.

The upper limit has probably been reached, or nearly so, in the accuracy of prediction that can be expected from use of the methods of the early prediction studies. During the last two decades, there have been a number of smaller relationship studies contributing directly or indirectly to the problem of prediction. Many of these are characterized by efforts to improve the techniques of data collection, to develop better measures of the variables, to use concepts with broader theoretical relevance, and to use more elaborate methods for analyzing the data. These trends, which are apparent in some of the contemporary studies, grow out of criticisms which have been made of earlier prediction attempts and reflect increased concern over improved research methodology as well as the need for development of theory as the basis for explanation and for the selection of variables for prediction.

A Critique of Criticisms

Many of the questions and criticisms raised about the early marital prediction studies were raised about all quantitative research in sociology, particularly when subjective aspects of behavior were being studied. "Can such a subjective thing as happiness really be measured?" "Will people give honest answers to such personal questions?" "How can you deal quantitatively with a characteristic that means different things to different people and that changes over a period of time?" "How can such a complex phenomenon be handled with enough accuracy to predict?" "What is the value for individual prediction of data based on the study of groups of classes of individuals?" Those kinds of questions dealing essentially with the validity of quantitative research have been fairly well settled to the satisfaction of most and will not be dealt with here. The question is no longer one of whether this kind of behavior can be studied quantitatively, but rather what aspects of it can best be studied quantitatively and with what degree of accuracy. Error-free data may not be attainable by any method, yet much of the error is due to things we are gradually learning to control and account for with constantly improved methods of research design, data collection, and analysis.

The substantive results of the prediction and correlational studies of marital success, as they have contributed to generalizations about the nature and basis of marital adjustment, will be discussed in other chapters of this volume and are summarized in the available literature. Some of the main methodological features of these studies have been reviewed here because an awareness of methods is necessary for a correct assessment and interpretation of their results and because subsequent studies are built on the shoulders of their predecessors. For the same reasons, this section will attempt to summarize, in a constructive way, some of the principal criticisms that can be made of these studies.

Representativeness of sample. One of the most frequent criticisms of research in this area deals with the selection of samples for study. It is a time-consuming and expensive process to get a large, representative sample, and most of the studies have had insufficient resources for obtaining the sort of sample they would have preferred. There are also problems in getting cooperation of couples who have been randomly selected, so researchers have used "captive" groups or gained cooperation through students or other easily available informants. The studies by Locke, Karlsson, and Stroup made particular efforts to obtain representative samples, but in general it can be said that the data of the prediction studies represent a middle-class, fairly well-educated population, with a possible bias toward higher adjustment. As a result, little is known about marriages other than those of white, middle-class couples, and the basis for generalization even about those is not very secure, although the similarities of findings among studies often lends support.

Size of sample. The small size of samples has been a limiting factor in the sort of analysis of the data that could be made. A narrow emphasis on prediction leads to an item-by-item look at relationships, with resulting weights that are added together in a prediction score. Analysis would often have been more meaningful and possibly would have led to improved prediction if there had been more cross-classification of predictive variables to see their joint relationships with adjustment, and if control variables had been used to test for spuriousness or to see how relationships differed for subgroups in the sample. Hill's (1949) study of the effects of the crises of separation and reunion of the family in wartime is an excellent example of the use of more elaborate methods of data analysis, even with very limited sample size. Burgess and Wallin (1953) made some very useful analyses of their engagement data, and many of the smaller studies have elaborated their analyses to try to find an explanation of how and why their variables were related.

Some of the limitations of the prediction studies due to unrepresentative sampling could have been partially overcome by more attention to subgroup analysis. For example, comparison of relationships for lower-status couples having low education with findings for couples having higher status and education would have given a rough indication of the effects of sampling bias on these variables. Although these studies can be criticized for their relatively simple level of data analysis, elaboration with several variables at a time requires larger samples than any of the studies have had. Modern data processing equipment now makes it possible to handle a large number of cases and a number of variables at a time, so that future studies should not be so handicapped by this kind of limitation.

Reliability of response. Reliability of response is affected by the conditions under which the data are obtained. The Burgess-Cottrell schedule and the engagement schedule for the Burgess-Wallin study were given to the subject by an intermediary, and were filled out under unknown conditions. Many of the questions will be answered differently if the spouse is present to see the answer given. The later studies have recognized this problem and have had the data collected in the presence of the investigator or his representative. Certain sources of unreliability can be minimized if subjects are made aware of the purposes and nature of the research, have confidence in the integrity of the investigator, are assured of anonymity or confidentiality, and are convinced that

their answers will not be seen by their spouse or other persons who know them.

There is considerable evidence that under proper conditions people will give frank and honest answers even to questions that reflect unfavorably on themselves. The highly skewed distribution of marital success scores has been noted as evidence that subjects will not give honest answers to this type of question. There has, of course, been some unreliability of this sort, but score distributions are also affected by the questions asked and the weighting system used for scoring. Furthermore, we would *expect* the majority of marriages to be on the favorable end of the continuum, since people enter marriage with expectations of a pleasant relationship, attempt to make the relationship pleasant because of social expectations and personal convenience, and leave it if it is not tolerable.

Retrospective versus longitudinal design. Since prediction requires the use of evidence from one period of time to anticipate occurrences at a later time, a longitudinal research design in which data are collected before marriage as well as at several stages during marriage would be the ideal. With the exception of the studies by Burgess and Wallin, Terman and Oden, and Kelley, the prediction studies have collected all of their data from couples after marriage, or if divorced couples were included, after the divorce had taken place. The unreliability of retrospective data has been recognized by those doing the studies, and they point to the necessity of confirming findings in longitudinal follow-ups. At the early stages of research in a new area, the use of retrospective data is probably the most efficient, until concepts and measurements are well developed, major dimensions of the problem are mapped out, and there are some hypotheses available for more exact testing. Nevertheless, the unreliability of response inherent in retrospective data must be taken into account in interpreting the results of the research.

There are three sources of unreliability

inherent in the use of retrospective data: faulty memory, change in perception, and change in the variable being measured. These three sources of unreliability are related to three different kinds of data which may be collected after marriage for purposes of establishing predictive factors. First, there are certain objective facts, such as age at marriage, church membership and attendance, place of residence, and length of engagement. Memory of such facts should be fairly accurate. Second, there are questions about subjective reactions or evaluations of situations, people, and relationships at an earlier period of time, such as happiness during childhood, conflict or closeness to parents as a child, happiness of parents' marriage, or attachment to friends and siblings. The recall of such subjective reactions will be less reliable than that of objective occurrences, since the perception of the situation is affected to some degree by subsequent events and relationships. For example, a person with a happy marriage might perceive his earlier relationships with parents differently than he would if his marriage had been unhappy. Finally, there are data about personal characteristics, values, role relations, individual and common interests, and the like. These variables do not pertain to any period of time, but are continuously relevant, not only in the effect they may have, but as they may change through time as part of an ongoing process.

There are at least two kinds of problems in dealing with variables of this latter type. One is that of ascertaining the stability of the characteristic so that relationships with these variables during marriage can be anticipated from a stable variable at an earlier period. Otherwise, hypotheses derived from empirical findings of relationships at the time of marriage would have little value for prediction in a longitudinal study. The other problem is that of studying the processes involved in a dynamic relationship in which personal traits, interests, and roles both affect the marriage interaction and are affected by it.

As a hypothetical illustration, suppose a high negative correlation had been found between marital success and an index of neuroticism of married couples. The neurotic index would be useful for prediction if it could be shown that the index was stable for an individual throughout the period of time studied; that neurotic persons before marriage remained that way and became unhappy, and the non-neurotic persons stayed that way and became happy. It is more probable, however, that the correlation between neuroticism before marriage and adjustment after marriage would be much lower than that found for the married period, since some premarital neurotics would become unhappy, but others would change in reaction to a happy marriage, while some non-neurotics would become happy but others would react neurotically to an unhappily developing marriage. In this latter case, it would be concluded that the neurotic index by itself was too unreliable a measure to use for prediction. However, if other variables could be introduced in the analysis to find the conditions under which neurotic scores changed, there would be an understanding of the processes taking place as well as a further basis for prediction.

The statement of this difficulty has been somewhat lengthy in order to indicate the kind of dilemma which any prediction study must face—the choice between a longitudinal design which requires a long period of time and great expense for data collection, and a cross-sectional design depending on retrospective data with its greater unreliability [cf. pp. 203–207 of this Handbook].

Sources of bias. Since the degree of relationship between premarital prediction and marital adjustment scores is often cited in the literature as evidence of success or lack of success in prediction, there are several sources of bias affecting a correlation coefficient or other measure of relationship which should be recognized as due to methods of sampling or data analysis. Since any measure of relationship can be considered as a "correct" description of the degree of relationship for a particular set of data, bias is thought of as any source of systematic distortion of the relationship as it would be applied to a generalization for a larger population. The following paragraphs deal with sources of bias other than those resulting from nonrandom sampling, which was discussed above.

Several procedures have led to an artificially high estimate of the "true" relationship. (a) When prediction scores are derived from item weights assigned according to their discrimination on the dependent variable, the measures are not independent of each other and normally produce larger correlations than would be found in another sample using the same weights. This has usually been pointed out by the authors in their insistence that results must be tested in a new sample. The study by Stroup, it will be recalled, demonstrated that the correlation could be raised considerably when new weights were derived for his own sample. (b) Although generally the effect of random unreliability of measurement is to reduce the correlation between variables, the type of systematic unreliability suspected of retrospective data about the premarital period, or of data about a marriage which has resulted in divorce, would tend to raise the correlation. (c) As Karlsson suggested, correlations may be raised by inclusion in the prediction score of postmarital items which are also indices of adjustment. Such items should be kept separate from the temporally distinct prediction items and used for another level of analysis. (d) A correlation can be raised by removing the cases in the middle of the distribution. In the studies which have attempted to obtain couples at both extremes, the happily married at one end and the unhappy or divorced and separated at the other, items discriminating between these two extremes have been found, but the resulting correlations were higher than would be expected in a representative sample.

On the other hand, certain biasing effects in the opposite direction can be seen. (a) If a sample is taken from one extreme of the values of one variable, then the correlation will be lower than for a sample taken from the entire range of values. If some of the studies have obtained subjects in a way that tended to draw disproportionately from the "happy" end of the adjustment continuum, as has been claimed, then their correlations under-represent the relation for the entire population, assuming that the same tendencies hold for the under-represented segments. A correction for continuity can be applied to correct for this situation only if the form of the total population distribution is known. (b) The type of composite index of adjustment used in the prediction studies includes several dimensions. To the extent that certain prediction items are more closely predictive of one component of the index than of others, the additive model for combining diverse components into one index reduces the degree of relationship. (c) The same point can be made with reference to the additive combination of predictive items. A fictitious example will illustrate this point. Suppose one has two predictive variables, each with two values, and the mean adjustment score for each of the four combinations is as follows, with an equal number of cases in each cell.

	Item 1		
	−	+	Total
Item 2 + 80	100	90	
− 20	50	35	
Total 50	75	62.5	

If one predicts only from item 1, he predicts a mean score of either 50 or 75. If he predicts from item 2 alone, values of 35 or 90 would be predicted. If he predicts from knowledge of both items, using the information about the relationship between the two predictive items in the four cells, he gets the most accurate mean predictions of 20, 50, 80, and 100. But if he uses the items only in an additive manner, the average of the marginal means for the four response combinations are used, giving predictions of

42.5, 55, 70, and 82.5, as an approximation to the first set—which produces less information and predictive efficiency. An extension of this principle would lead to the multiple classification of all predictive items, which is a staggering thought, and impossible without an extremely large sample.

The solution to this difficulty would seem to lie in the development of a relatively small number of basic, unidimensional predictor variables, and the use of a model for prediction that would take their interrelationships into account to maximize the relationship between the set and the criterion variable. Burgess and Cottrell, Terman, and Karlsson were attempting to approximate such a solution when they divided prediction items into several types, added weights of these groups of items to get separate prediction scores, and combined them for correlation with the multiple regression model. A special instance of the point just made is the failure to take into account the joint responses of husband and wife in analysis of the data and in the development of prediction scores.

Theory Development

A number of methodological problems have been discussed which have been encountered in prediction studies and which need to be taken into account in future studies. Although there are a few special problems of application, the research methods used in this field do not differ in any essential way from those of social science research in general, and the growing body of research techniques now provides guides for the design and conduct of research far beyond the level of available technology of just a few years ago.

There is probably fairly general agreement that improvement in marital prediction lies not only in the application of better research techniques, but depends even more on the development of a body of theory on which prediction research can be more effectively based. The major prediction studies were initiated during a period when there were only the crude beginnings of any theory about marriage and family interaction, and the theory in related areas was of little help. Consequently, the items used for predictor variables were selected on an *ad hoc* basis and were often treated in the interpretation as indicators of more basic causal variables. For example, Sunday school attendance during adolescence was correlated with later marital adjustment, but was considered to be primarily an indicator of conventionality. Such attempts to interpret findings contributed in a significant way in the initial stages of theory development, but the research can be said to have been guided by theory only in a very limited sense.

A special theory, such as that concerning marriage interaction and adjustment, can be thought of as the network of propositions relating the particular variables to be taken into account in describing, understanding, and explaining those aspects of marital behavior in which the investigator is interested. Such special theories may develop with relative independence from the more general body of sociological theory, but in the long run must become a part of the general theory and will contribute to its development. Conversely, as theory in related areas develops, portions will be incorporated into the special theory. For example, developments in social psychology have contributed significantly to the specific theory about marriage and the family, and vice versa.

One goal of a theory is to provide a network of independent variables that can be brought to bear on the understanding and explanation of any particular dependent variable on which one wishes to focus. Marital prediction theory can be thought of as that segment of the total body of theory that selects as the dependent variable a certain aspect of the marital situation which is felt to be important for the welfare of individuals or society, and includes independent variables which precede the dependent variable in time so that a portion of its variability can be "accounted for" and anticipated. Prediction research should therefore be viewed as contributing to the development of the total body of marriage and family theory by examination and elaboration of concepts dealing with marriage interaction and adjustment, so they can be more effectively measured, by pointing to the need for development of those elements of theory concerned with sequences and processes of marital behavior, and by providing a test for certain theoretical propositions.

At the same time, theory and research focused on other problems provide elements that may be used for marital prediction. For example, the work in socialization, dating and mate selection, personality theory, and marriage interaction contributes to the development of concepts and propositions of use in prediction.

These points have been stressed because there seems to have been some tendency to think of marital prediction research in terms of developing formulas for use in practical prediction problems and as independent of other types of research and theory about marriage and the family. Current recognition of the need to base further prediction efforts on a more comprehensive theory has probably been a major reason why there have been no large prediction studies initiated recently. Instead, there have been a number of smaller studies attempting to test hypotheses concerning some of the elements that would fit into such a theory.

The following section discusses some of the other measures of marital success that have been proposed, and outlines one type of conceptual scheme for the definition and measurement of marital adjustment that would seem to have some promise for research and theory development.

DEFINITION AND MEASUREMENT OF MARITAL ADJUSTMENT

In reviewing over 60 studies published since 1940 which employed a measure of marital success, the writer found 23 that used a measure based on the Burgess-Cottrell, Terman, or Locke indices or some combination or modification of these. By comparison, only 10 of the studies used a single-item rating, and 12 studies, using records or demographic data, had divorce or separation as the criterion. The remaining 15 studies used some other measure of adjustment, such as role tension, empathy, similarity of interests, or number of problems in the marriage.

Some Attempts to Improve Measurement

Locke and Wallace (1959), noting the tendency of marital adjustment and prediction tests to use an increasing number of items, explored the possibility of obtaining measures of similar accuracy with shorter tests. They constructed a test of marital adjustment containing only 15 items and a prediction test with 35 items, selecting items from previous studies which had the highest discrimination, which seemed to cover the main areas included in other tests, and which did not seem to overlap other questions in content. They obtained correlations between these short-form tests of .47 for a sample of 118 couples. Since this is approximately the size of correlation found in other studies for this type of sample, they concluded that the short forms were approximately as reliable as longer forms.

There have been several attempts to design indirect measures of adjustment which would avoid the use of the direct, obvious questions believed to reduce the reliability of the traditional index. Kirkpatrick (1937) developed an Index of Community of Interests for which subjects were given a checklist of 60 items and asked to check those which they enjoyed doing, and those they enjoyed with their spouses. The individual Family Interest Score was the percentage of individual interests which were enjoyed with spouse. Scores were found to discriminate between couples identified by students as well or as poorly adjusted.

In a study comparing the Kirkpatrick Family Interest Scale with the Terman Marital Happiness Scale, Taves (1948) compared scores on both scales of a control group of 93 individuals with an experimental group of 89 persons. The experimental group had been motivated by a 15-minute talk to make their marital adjustment seem favorable compared with that of other people. He found that the differences in mean scores in the Terman scale were significantly higher for the experimental group, whereas the means for the Family Interest Scale were almost identical for the two groups. He concluded that situational factors that might affect motivation were much more likely to influence responses on the direct scale than on an indirect type of scale. The two scales had a correlation of .71. However, another study by Frumpkin (1953), using 107 married college students, obtained a correlation with self-ratings of marital happiness of only .31 for men and .24 for women with the Kirkpatrick scale, compared with .83 and .87 between self-ratings and scores on the Burgess-Cottrell scale. These studies do not settle the issue of relative reliability of the two kinds of scales. Since they would seem to be measuring two different aspects of adjustment, possibly each is valid and useful.

A different approach to the measurement of marital success was suggested by Farber (1957). His objective in developing the Index of Marital Integration was to obtain a measure which focuses on consensus and interpersonal relations, is simple to administer and score, is not an overt evaluation of marriage, and is based on the assumption that marital integration is a combination of integration of ends and of means. The instrument combines a consensus index, based on a ranking of 10 domestic values by husband and wife, and a role-tension index, derived from self and other ratings on 10 personality traits. Each of the two indices is given weights of 0 to 3 for each score quartile, and the Index of Marital Integration is the total of these two index scores. Significant relationships were found when he used this measure to test four hypotheses drawn from the literature.

Another measure of interaction in marriage was reported by Buerkle and Badgley (1959). Noting the criticism that marital adjustment and aptitude tests measure the reaction of only one person, rather than the couple, they constructed an index of the couple interaction. The Yale Marital Interaction Battery included 40 items in which husband and wife were presented with hypothetical conflict situations in the marriage and asked to indicate which of four reactions they would have if this were to happen to them. The four reactions were arranged to represent different degrees of role-taking. A couple received a high score on an item when both gave the high role-taking response, or when the pattern of response showed high agreement on the basis for action. They found 14 of these items which met the criteria of a Guttman scale. These scale scores, divided into high-, medium-, and low-score groups, differentiated significantly between a sample of 36 couples who were receiving marital counseling and 186 couples who were attending a club for religious couples. In summarizing the results of their study, Buerkle and Badgley pointed out that little is now known about the patterns of marital interaction that lead to stability, and they questioned the assumption that empathy is necessary in all types of marriages; since the implications of various interactive models have not been investigated, the democratic-equalitarian model may not be the only one which can explain marital stability at the present time.

In constructing measures of marital success, some researchers have thought of success in terms of an over-all evaluation, using happiness with the marriage or other generalizing questions. Others have claimed that the criterion of success should take into account the level of husband-wife interaction in various marital situations. The major prediction studies have combined several types of questions in their measures, some dealing with evaluation of the marriage, some with more specific matters of agreement and disagreement, and some involving still other dimensions.

It is clear that no single measure of success will be satisfactory for all purposes, and the writer believes it is necessary to aim toward the development of a set of measures that are interrelated in a meaningful way and that may be used for a variety of research purposes. Such measures should emerge from a conceptualization of the process of marital interaction that will be useful for diagnosis and analysis as well as for prediction.

The writer would like to outline a conceptual scheme that might provide a useful framework for measurement. The first and most specific level deals with adjustments made by the couple in a number of basic areas of marital interaction, called adjustment areas. The second level attempts to get at the effects of this interaction as it results in several types of orientation toward the spouse and toward the perceived effects of the marriage on various individual and group goals of each person in the marriage. The third level consists of the general evaluation of the marriage made by the individual as he takes into account, in some value-weighted manner, the previous interactions and orientations.

Adjustment Areas

Take as the basic unit of the adjustment process an interaction sequence arising when some act is initiated or there is need for a decision to be made so that one or both partners may act. Each sequence involves the accommodation of each person to the other, whether it be as simple a matter as moving out of the way so the other may pass, giving up an evening at home so that both may go to a movie, staying at home while the other goes out, accepting a statement that one is loved, or watching while the other punishes the children. The amount of accommodation required can be viewed as a function of the amount of difference between the two in attitude or desired direction of behavior, and of the intensity of the feeling about what should be done. For example, a decision about religious upbringing of the children would require more accommodation if the wife were a very devout Catholic and the husband an equally devout Baptist than if they were both Protestants with low religiosity. The accommodation that an individual makes in such an interaction sequence can be thought of as his adjustment. In other words, marital adjustment is that behavior which serves to reduce differences between marital partners with respect to a particular marital situation, or interaction sequence. [Cf. Bernard's discussion below, pp. 730–733.]

Marital interaction takes place in an infinite number of such sequences, and each is unique in some respects. However, there may be clusters of situations toward which individuals tend to develop characteristic types of adjustment. If such clusters can be isolated, then, by knowing the kind of adjustment an individual made to a sample of situations from this cluster one could predict what his adjustment would be to other situations in the cluster, or in a generalized way to the cluster as a whole. Such hypothetical clusters will be referred to as adjustment areas. An adjustment area, then, includes those interaction sequences toward which the adjustments of the individual are essentially similar, and which differ from adjustments made in other areas. This does not say that the adjustments made within an area are the same in all respects, but only that they are sufficiently similar in nature so that it is useful to consider them together. One might then say, for example, that a particular person made a very good adjustment with his spouse about economic and financial matters in the marriage, about methods of rearing the children, and about religion, but made a somewhat poorer adjustment about recreational matters and in-laws, and a very poor adjustment about sex relations.

There are at least two approaches to the measurement of adjustment areas. One would be to select samples of behaviors thought to represent several areas, and find out if the intercorrelations between the adjustment indicators clustered in the manner hypothesized—high intercorrelations between items within an area, and relatively low correlation between areas. The other approach would be to assume a generalizability of the adjustment if persons are able to think of adjustment for the area as a whole. In his study of the length of time required to achieve adjustment in marriage, Landis (1946) asked couples to indicate how long adjustment had taken in six areas: sex relations, spending family income, social activities, in-law relationships, religious activities, and mutual friends. Also, several of the marital prediction studies asked couples to indicate the amount of agreement or disagreement about such areas of the relationship. The fact that couples are able to respond to such questions and that the studies have been able to use the answers to obtain meaningful results is evidence that people are able to think of their marital interaction in such a generalized way.

A study by Bowerman (1957) attempted to develop Guttman scales to measure adjustment with the spouse in nine areas of the relationship: family expenditures, recreation, relationships with in-laws, relationships with friends, religious beliefs and practices, sex relations, homemaking duties and responsibilities, philosophy of life, and bringing up children. It was assumed that the degree of adjustment of each individual about any aspect of the relationship is a function of: (a) the amount of similarity or difference in attitude about that type of situation which is perceived to exist; (b) the extent to which a given difference in attitude or behavior is disturbing to the individual; (c) the amount of overt disagreement reported; (d) the manner and intensity of expressing disagreement; (e) expressions of satisfaction or dissatisfaction with the way they get along about this kind of thing; and (f) expressed satisfaction with the pattern of dominance in making decisions about such matters. One question was constructed

as an indicator of each of these six elements of adjustment, and identical questions were used for all adjustment areas with the insertion of a phrase which designated the area.

The resulting questionnaire was given to a sample of 102 couples, mostly from adult education classes and PTA groups, by student assistants who were present to prevent collaboration of husband and wife. The six items in each of the nine adjustment area scales had coefficients of reproducibility between .80 and .86, with simple scoring and a minimum number of category combinations. Intercorrelations between scores of husband and wife ranged from .44 to .68. Correlations among area adjustment scores for this sample are given in Table 3.

A rough cluster analysis led to the grouping of the adjustment areas into three types of adjustment situations. The first group deals with adjustments about *family-centered matters,* including the areas of family expenditures, household duties and responsibilities, bringing up children, and philosophy of life. The second can be thought of as concerning adjustments about more *person-centered matters,* and included the areas of sex adjustment and recreation. The last group included adjustments about friends, in-laws, and religious practices which can be viewed as centered in *activities taking place primarily outside of the home* and not involving the internal operation of the family.

The same adjustment-scale items were also used in a study by Glen T. Nygreen (1954) of 461 married college student couples. He obtained coefficients of reproducibility of .86 or over on each scale, using simple scoring and dichotomized responses. Furthermore, eight of these scales, omitting the one on adjustment about philosophy of life, were used in a study by David A. Gover (1962, pp. 43–45) in which he obtained reproducibility coefficients from .82 to .87 with simple scoring for a sample of 361 married women randomly selected from Greensboro, North Carolina.

Much more work is obviously needed in

TABLE 3

CORRELATIONS BETWEEN AREA ADJUSTMENT SCORES[a]

Adjustment with Respect to:	Husbands								
	I	2	3	4	5	6	7	8	9
1. Family Expenditures	—	.48	.48	.50	.21	.46	.44	.51	.49
2. Recreation		—	.28	.42	.14	.40	.33	.35	.31
3. Relationships with In-Laws			—	.22	.16	.37	.40	.31	.35
4. Relations with Friends				—	.27	.28	.48	.53	.49
5. Religious Matters					—	.18	.20	.26	.44
6. Sex Relations						—	.44	.40	.50
7. Homemaking Duties							—	.53	.60
8. Philosophy of Life								—	.65
9. Bringing up Children									—

Adjustment with Respect to:	Wives								
	I	2	3	4	5	6	7	8	9
1. Family Expenditures	—	.28	.39	.42	.28	.21	.49	.46	.49
2. Recreation		—	.24	.54	.12	.39	.48	.36	.41
3. Relationships with In-Laws			—	.38	.06	.29	.36	.48	.23
4. Relations with Friends				—	.17	.35	.49	.63	.43
5. Religious Matters					—	.06	.15	.32	.40
6. Sex Relations						—	.30	.34	.27
7. Homemaking Duties							—	.53	.48
8. Philosophy of Life								—	.52
9. Bringing up Children									—

[a] Based on data reported in Bowerman (1957).

developing measures of marital adjustment areas. The author holds no brief for the particular areas that have been selected in these studies. It may be useful to define adjustment areas more limited in scope than these, and other areas of importance might be added to the list. However, the work cited here illustrates the possibility that adjustment areas, as defined here, could be isolated and that unidimensional measures of a generalized kind might be developed.

Orientation Toward Spouse and Marriage

In the previous section the process of adjusting in marriage was seen as taking place through the accommodations made in innumerable interaction sequences, and it was suggested that these sequences could be clustered into adjustment areas for measurement and analysis. A second level of conceptualization, which can be thought of as adjustment in an evaluative sense, would be concerned with the kind of orientation that develops during the adjustment process to the spouse and to the perceived effects of the marriage on individual life goals.

It might be helpful to distinguish three types of orientation toward the spouse, corresponding to three aspects of the relationship which are significant in the original mate-selection process and in determining later satisfaction: (a) affectional orientation—feelings of love, affection, closeness; (b) associational orientation—enjoyment of being with, feeling of interests in common, companionship; and (c) norm and value orientation—agreement on major values and ways of acting, respect for beliefs and opinions of the other, respect for the other as a person. These three types of orientation are seen as related to each other, although different in content.

As the relationship of marriage develops through time, the original orientations toward the spouse are modified; they may become more, or less, favorable, and the basis on which the orientation is held becomes much broader and presumably more stable. These orientations develop in part as a crystallization of attitudes toward the other emerging from interaction in various adjustment areas, and in turn become factors affecting subsequent interaction sequences. For example, a person takes a more adaptable approach in interaction with someone whose values and opinions he respects highly, but over a period of time too large a difference of opinion will lead to a modification of his attitude toward the values of the other person.

The author is using eight-item Guttman scales in a current study to measure each of these three types of orientation of adolescents toward their parents. These could be modified, by changing the referent, and might provide measures of a useful dimension of marital interaction.

In addition to orientations toward the spouse, which sum up some of the significant aspects of the relationship, individuals also develop attitudes toward the way in which the marriage itself has affected important segments of their life. For example, a person may feel that marriage has restricted his personal freedom and mobility, has been of great importance in raising his social status and enhancing his occupational opportunities, has provided a haven of peace and comfort in the home, has retarded and restricted his personality development, or has improved his range of social activities. Perceptions of this sort might be divided into those related to family-maintenance goals (home, children, existence of primary group, and the like), person-centered goals (freedom, physical well-being, personality development and expression, having a confidant, and the like), and external goals (job

satisfaction and advancement, obtaining and keeping friends, social status). These orientations toward the marriage emerge as the original expectations of marriage are modified through experience, and are balanced against the satisfactions achieved in interaction. They are also significant elements in affecting various interaction sequences and orientations toward spouse.

General Evaluation of Marriage

This concept refers to the summary evaluation which individuals make of their marriage in its entirety, as would be suggested by statements that the marriage was fairly satisfactory, or was extremely happy, or that they had not made a very good adjustment in their marriage, and so on.

Experience with the use of the single question about the degree of marital happiness indicates that individuals are able to make such an evaluation with some reliability and validity. This kind of evaluation of marriage can be thought of as a function of adjustments made to the variety of marital situations and of the orientations to spouse and marriage, where these are weighted according to the values and expectations of the individual. For example, adjustments about religious matters would have relatively more effect on the general evaluation of persons who had strong religious beliefs, and one might expect to find social class differences in the effect of various orientations to spouse on marital satisfaction. Measurement at this level is important, therefore, not only as a criterion for prediction of "how the marriage will turn out" but also to enable study of the effects of other levels of adjustment on general marital satisfaction.

The indices of marital adjustment which have been used in the prediction studies might serve very adequately for measurement of this dimension. However, there would seem to be an advantage in a unidimensional scale based on several general evaluation items. In an attempt to develop such a scale, Bowerman's (1957) study, mentioned earlier, included 13 questions which asked for an evaluation of the marriage in general terms, such as the degree of happiness, success in achieving desired goals in the marriage, amount of quarreling, how many disappointments and disagreements there had been in marriage, and so on. These items formed a Guttman scale with a reproducibility of 90 per cent for the sample of 102 couples. The Burgess-Cottrell adjustment items were also included in the questionnaire, and, in testing for validity, the product-moment correlation between the two sets of scores was found to be .82 for husbands and .86 for wives.

This 13-item scale was also used in Nygreen's (1954) study of married college students. Reproducibility for his sample was only .82, with simple scoring, probably because of the highly skewed distribution of satisfaction as suggested by all indicators. He obtained a husband-wife correlation of .56, fairly close to that found by Terman in his study (1938). The scale has also been used in a study by Straus of married college couples (1960), and a seven-item version of the scale has been used in two community studies in Greensboro, North Carolina (Gover, 1962; Gulick & Bowerman, 1961). Gover correlated the scores of 64 women with scores obtained from the same items answered one to three months earlier for the other study and obtained a product-moment correlation of .72, suggesting a moderately high reliability for the short form of the scale. Both reliability and validity could undoubtedly be improved by further work on the scale, but it has seemed to operate fairly well for several diverse population groups in distinguishing 10 or more degrees of marital satisfaction.

Advantages of Multiple Criteria

The need for a battery of measures of different levels of adjustment and evaluation of marriage has been suggested. At one level would be several measures of the adjustment made by an individual to important areas of interaction in the marriage; at another level would be measures of the affectional, associational, and value orientations toward spouse and the effects marriage is thought to have on important life goals of the individual; and finally there would be a scale of general evaluation of the marriage. Although the utility of some such system of multiple criteria will be apparent to the reader, a few of the advantages will be discussed as the writer sees them.

This approach would provide an integrated set of measures that would focus on a number of important facets of the marriage interaction, yet which could be interrelated as elements in a theory of marriage for descriptive, explanatory, and predictive purposes. Descriptively, very little is known about the kinds of adjustment problems couples have in marriage, how adjustments about various family problems affect feelings toward the spouse, and how these contribute to the evaluation of the marriage as successful or unsuccessful.

As an illustration of one kind of analysis that can be made of these components, Bowerman's study of adjustment areas (1957) obtained a multiple correlation of .78 for men and .83 for women between the scale of general evaluation of marriage and scores on the nine adjustment areas. The sums of the Beta weights in the regression equation for the three groups of areas described earlier were .51 for men and .74 for women for the four family-centered areas, .49 and .46, respectively, for the two personal-centered areas, and —.04 and —.05, respectively, for the three external-centered areas. These findings would tentatively support the conclusion that general satisfaction with marriage is more affected by adjustments about internal family matters for women than it is for men, and that satisfaction for wives is more dependent upon family-centered adjustments than on adjustments about person-centered matters, whereas these are equally important for men. For this sample, adjustment about matters outside the family had little effect on general marital satisfaction when other adjustments were held constant. With improved measures and a larger sample, this kind of analysis could be elaborated to provide a useful description of the kinds of adjustments made by various categories of individuals and how the various levels of adjustment and interaction were interrelated.

Explanatory studies of marital adjustment would benefit from the use of a set of multiple criteria by being able to look more specifically at the way in which various causal and conditional variables affected different aspects of the marital relationship. For example, Which kinds of adjustments are most affected by early marriage? Does the relative importance of various orientations toward spouse and the marriage in affecting marital satisfaction differ by social class, or by authoritarian versus equalitarian structure of the husband-wife relationship? Do individuals who have a high dependence on the continuance of the marriage for personal or social reasons tend to make more adaptive adjustments than persons with similar levels of general satisfaction who do not have a strong dependence? Under what conditions of area adjustment and orientation to the marriage does low general evaluation lead to a decision to seek a divorce?

Measurement of a set of criteria such as these should lead to improvement in the accuracy and usefulness of prediction. It has been pointed out that the indices of success that have been used in prediction studies include several different dimensions. Predictive variables may be related to some of these but not to others, and the components of the index may have more relevance for satisfaction for some individuals than for others. Accuracy of prediction should be improved by making a prediction for each separate adjustment area, using variables which are specifically related to those areas, then combining the predicted area adjustments and orientations in equations to estimate the general evaluation expected for that combination of adjustments.

This procedure would have the added advantage of being able to take into account subgroup differences in relative importance of various areas and orientations in the overall evaluation of marriage. For example, if a multiple regression model turned out to be most accurate for this purpose, the dependent variable would be general evaluation, and the independent variables would be area adjustments and orientations, with the value of each of these independent variables determined by separate prediction models. The regression coefficients would represent the relative importance of each independent variable for evaluation, holding constant all other variables. These constants could be determined either on an individual basis, making up a personal equation for each individual, or on a group basis, having a separate prediction equation for each major value subgroup, thus avoiding the criticism that both measurement and prediction are biased toward middle-class values and do not take into account individual variations in types of adjustment.

In addition to increasing accuracy of prediction, the kind of prediction model made possible by a set of multiple criteria would increase the usefulness of prediction. Predictions could be made more specific by indicating not only the total evaluation of marriage that could be anticipated, but in what respects the marriage might be considered satisfactory or not, and in which areas difficulties are most likely. An individual making a decision about marriage, or a counselor, would thus have a more detailed type of prediction on which to help base a decision and to plan the future. Such predictions would still be actuarial, or statistical, in nature, and modifications for the individual case would still be useful; however, it is important to work toward as accurate and useful a model as possible to provide a broad empirical base around which case analysis and prediction can be made.

In summary, this section has tried to emphasize the need for a set of interdependent measures of several levels of marital adjustment, interaction, and evaluation which would be helpful for a number of research purposes and which would fit into a developing theory of marital adjustment, and the factors related to it, in a unified way. The outline of one possible conceptual system has been discussed. Any particular research problem would utilize only a portion of this system; but if there were a standardized set of theoretically interrelated measures of the sort suggested, segmented research could contribute more systematically to the development of theory.

CONCLUSION

This chapter has not attempted to summarize the substantive results of the marital prediction studies. These are included in other chapters of this volume, and excellent summaries can be found in Kirkpatrick (1947; 1963, pp. 385–394) and in Locke (1951, pp. 342–357), as well as in the numerous marriage and family texts.

The prediction studies have made an important contribution to the development of theory, both in the descriptive results they have provided and in their interpretive formulations. They pioneered in conceptualizing the nature of the prediction problem, led in the development of measures of marital adjustment, and explored a number of possible predictive variables. At a time when many social scientists were in doubt about the quantifiability of concepts such as marital adjustment, or satisfaction, they demonstrated that at least some level of accuracy in measurement is possible. The findings and tentative generalizations derived from these studies have found their way into the marriage and family texts and the popular literature. It seems probable that the kind of thinking involved in the prediction studies has added in some measure to the rationality of popular thinking about problems of mate selection and adjustment in marriage.

Not least among the contributions of the prediction studies is the stimulation they have given for other studies, which are providing additional findings and developing basic variables that will contribute to an eventual explanatory theory of premarriage behavior and marital interaction, out of which can be drawn the variables for more accurate and useful prediction in the future.

REFERENCES

Bernard, Jessie. An instrument for the measurement of success in marriage. *Publ. Amer. sociol. Soc.*, 1933, 27, 307–324.

Bowerman, C. E. Adjustment in marriage: over-all and in specific areas. *Sociol. & soc. Res.*, 1957, 41, 257–263.

Buerkle, J. V., & Badgley, R. F. Couple role-taking: the Yale marital interaction battery. *Marr. & fam. Living*, 1959, 21, 53–58.

Burgess, E. W., & Cottrell, L. S. The prediction of adjustment in marriage. *Amer. sociol. Rev.*, 1936, 1, 737–751.

Burgess, E. W., & Cottrell, L. S. *Predicting success or failure in marriage.* New York: Prentice-Hall, 1939.

Burgess, E. W., & Wallin, P. *Engagement and marriage.* Philadelphia: Lippincott, 1953.

Davis, Katherine B. *Factors in the sex life of twenty-two hundred women.* New York: Harper, 1929.

Farber, B. An index of marital integration. *Sociometry*, 1957, 20, 117–134.

Frumpkin, R. M. The Kirkpatrick scale of family interests as an instrument for the indirect assessment of marital adjustment. *Marr. & fam. Living*, 1953, 15, 35–57.

Gover, D. A. Employment as a factor in the marital adjustment of middle- and working-class wives. Unpublished doctoral dissertation, Univer. of North Carolina, 1962.

Gulick, J., & Bowerman, C. E. *Adaptation of newcomers in the Piedmont industrial crescent.* Chapel Hill: Univer. of North Carolina, Institute for Research in Social Science, 1961.

Hamilton, G. V. *A research in marriage.* New York: Boni, 1929.

Hill, R. *Families under stress: adjustment to the crises of war separation and reunion.* New York: Harper, 1949.

Karlsson, G. *Adaptability and communication in marriage: a Swedish predictive study of marital satisfaction.* Uppsala, Sweden: Almqvist & Wiksells, 1951.

Kelley, E. L. Concerning the validity of Terman's weights for predicting marital happiness. *Psychol. Bull.,* 1939, 36, 202–203.

King, C. E. The Burgess-Cottrell method of measuring marital adjustment applied to a non-white Southern urban population. *Marr. & fam. Living,* 1952, 14, 280–285.

Kirkpatrick, C. Community of interest and the measurement of marriage adjustment. *Family,* 1937, 18, 133–137.

Kirkpatrick, C. *What science says about happiness in marriage.* Minneapolis: Burgess, 1947.

Kirkpatrick, C. *The family: as process and institution.* (2nd ed.) New York: Ronald Press, 1963.

Landis, J. T. Length of time required to achieve adjustment in marriage. *Amer. sociol. Rev.,* 1946, 11, 666–677.

Locke, H. J. *Predicting adjustment in marriage: a comparison of a divorced and a happily married group.* New York: Holt, 1951.

Locke, H. J. & Karlsson, G. Marital adjustment and prediction in Sweden. *Amer. sociol. Rev.,* 1952, 17, 10–17.

Locke, H. J., & Wallace, K. M. Short marital adjustment and prediction tests: their reli-ability and validity. *Marr. & fam. Living,* 1959, 21, 251–255.

Nygreen, G. T. Marital adjustment in the University of Washington married student community. Unpublished doctoral dissertation, Univer. of Washington, 1954.

Straus, M. A. Leisure and marital satisfaction of college married couples. *Marr. & fam. Living,* 1960, 22, 360–361.

Stroup, A. L. Predicting marital success or failure in an urban population. *Amer. sociol. Rev.,* 1953, 18, 558–562.

Taves, M. J. A direct vs. an indirect approach in measuring marital adjustment. *Amer. sociol. Rev.,* 1948, 13, 538–541.

Terman, L. M., & Buttenwieser, P. Personality factors in marital compatibility. *J. soc. Psychol.,* 1935, 6, 143–171, 267–289.

Terman, L. M., with Buttenwieser, P., Ferguson, L. W., Johnson, W. B., & Wilson, D. P. *Psychological factors in marital happiness.* New York: McGraw-Hill, 1938.

Terman, L. M., & Oden, Melita H. *The gifted child grows up: twenty-five years' follow-up of a superior group.* Stanford, Calif.: Stanford Univer. Press, 1947.

Waller, W., & Hill, R. L. *The family: a dynamic interpretation.* (Rev. ed.) New York: Dryden, 1951.

CHAPTER **7**   **Field Research**

F. IVAN NYE
Washington State University

The term *field research* may have several different referents. It may involve a place away from the center of research operations, off campus, out of town, or in another society. It may refer to a method of selecting samples and handling extraneous or interfering variables, that is, employing "control" and "experimental" groups that have selected themselves with respect to the independent variable rather than having been selected by the investigator. It sometimes has referred to a type of research that is descriptive (public opinion polling, for example) rather than analytical. It has sometimes had reference to particular techniques of obtaining data, that is, questionnaires and structured interviews as opposed to depth interviews. Even size of sample has sometimes been included, with field studies considered to involve large numbers of individuals compared to the smaller numbers involved in laboratory studies.

Of these, the most basic to the writer is the second, the selection of control and experimental groups. This approach affords a reasonably adequate distinction between field study problems and procedures and those of the classical experiment carried out under laboratory conditions (see Ch. 8). In field study, individuals have either selected themselves or "been selected" by someone other than the investigator, in that the independent event has occurred prior to the study. For example, if the investigator is studying the relationship of the size of the family of orientation to premarital pregnancy, it is obvious that the individuals have been "placed" in families of different sizes by processes other than those controlled by the investigator.

If the method of selection of control and experimental groups is taken as the primary characteristic of field study, as it is proposed to do here, it follows that the other characteristics will vary. The place, however, is likely to be outside the laboratory, since behavior is to be studied under natural rather than artificial conditions. Descriptive studies will usually be done by field study methods, but so will most analytical research on the family. Field study can employ large numbers of subjects much more easily than laboratory research, but field study can also involve very small samples. A variety of data-gathering techniques can be employed, including questionnaires, interviews (both structured and depth), observation (systematic or random), and the use of recorded data gathered for other purposes. Some of these also can be employed in laboratory research.

Even when the single criterion of selection of experimental and control groups is employed, there may be a question concerning the classification of one type of research, experimental design studies carried out in the community. One design involves the selection of two similar communities, one of which is exposed to an educational or action program, while the other is not. Another involves the random selection of patients, clients, or prisoners, for example, one category of whom subsequently is exposed to a set of conditions while the other is not. Although spatially this type of research occurs outside the laboratory, and the problems of control of extraneous variables are difficult, it nonetheless falls within the experimental design of random selection of respondents followed by exposure and non-exposure to the independent variable, with subsequent measurement of the dependent variable. It might, therefore, more properly be viewed as laboratory than as field research, and consideration of it is reserved for Chapter 8. As it happens, family researchers have devoted little attention to this design, although it could be employed profitably in studying such phenomena as induced changes in family attitudes, knowledge of facts concerning the family, and perhaps others.

This chapter, therefore, regards field study as including that research in which individuals in experimental and control groups have been self-selected prior to the design of the research. Incidentally, it includes descriptive research also, since in it no prior attempt at defining independent and dependent variables is made and the family phenomena occur in their natural setting rather than being induced in the laboratory.

There is some overlapping of subject matter with the previous chapter, inasmuch as most predictive studies have been field studies, and the same is true with respect to demographic research (Ch. 9). To avoid needless duplication, methodologies and findings of these two areas are avoided here, to the extent this is possible, and attention centered on the more general problems of field research on the family.

THE RATIONALE OF FIELD STUDY

The values of most societies (and of most researchers) do not permit the manipulation of human beings with respect to the more important and permanent types of social relationships. It would be, for example, ridiculous to propose that couples marrying be instructed for research purposes about the number of children they are to bear and rear. This is true of most aspects of family behavior. Relatively limited, simple aspects of family interaction can be manipulated. For example, Walters, Connor, and Zunich in an unpublished study were able to manipulate within the laboratory situation the amount and type of maternal control exercized over small children and to show differences in control by social class. However, to test satisfactorily in the laboratory situation the effects of such basic independent variables as maternal overprotection, partiality in treatment of children, or authoritarian control over children seems to penetrate so far into the realm of the improbable that few family researchers appear to have seriously contemplated such projects. [For positive arguments, see Ch. 8.]

An alternative to experimental work with human families is the observation and manipulation of animal families. The above limitations on the control and manipulation of people appear to have been the principal reason for use of laboratory animals in psychological research. Family researchers and particularly family sociologists, however, are unconvinced that the family life of rats has much relationship to human family life. The problem is twofold. (a) Most of the significant family variables—values, affection, ideologies, etc.—cannot be transmitted to lower animals and manipulated at will. (b) The other problem is the one of generalizing from animal relationships to human relationships.

Although the independent family variables that can be transmitted and manipulated among animal groups are limited, some things can be done. For example, Calhoun showed that crowding rats into a limited space changes their courtship and parental behavior. "When a population of laboratory rats is allowed to increase in a confined space, the rats develop acutely abnormal patterns of behavior that can even lead to the extinction of the species" (1962, p. 139). However, before this finding would have much significance for humans, it would be necessary to show that crowding has similar effects among other higher animals and, finally, that the same phenomena can be shown to occur among humans. Such long, difficult, and expensive research processes have not been carried through, and this approach to family research, although it may have some potential, has not yet made an appreciable contribution. The difficulty or impossibility of employing social variables in animal research suggests that, at most, this approach will be limited to a few essentially physical or physiological variables.

Besides the limitations on the type of independent variables that can be used in animal family research, the problem of generalization from animal relationships to human relationships has appeared impossible to the sociologist. Aware of great intrasociety differences among social classes, major religious groups, farm and urban residential categories, et cetera, in addition to the infinitely greater differences in family behavior among societies, the sociologist generally has been unwilling to assume that any cause-effect relationship in group relations of animals can be assumed to be valid for humans.

Given the limitations on the kinds of family research problems appropriate to experimental research with humans (see Ch. 8) and the problems and limitations in employing animals for family research, it has been necessary for the researcher to observe, describe, and manipulate (statistically) family behavior in its natural setting. Researchers have not been particularly happy with this situation, but the choices have been limited insofar as most of the more important family behavior is concerned: either observe, describe, and manipulate the data (not the behavior), or give up the idea of researching family behavior.

Field study then, as defined here, is not experimental in the classical sense that similar experimental and control groups are selected by the researcher prior to the event, and then the experimental group only is subjected to the influence of the independent variable. Rather, individuals who already have experienced the independent variable are labeled the "experimental" and those who have not, the "control" group. To the extent that the two groups are similar in other respects, and only to that extent, can field studies approximate experimental conditions. Family researchers are presently committed to the assumption that such matching is possible, and feasible, and most believe that this approach is the best choice for advancing the understanding and description of the human family group.

SOME RECENT TRENDS

To obtain more than an impressionistic idea of techniques currently and recently employed in family research, a review was made of publications from 1947 through 1961 (Nye & Bayer, 1963). Family research articles were analyzed from four professional journals: *American Sociological Review, American Journal of Sociology, Social Forces,* and *Marriage and Family Living.* These journals were selected because each has published a substantial amount of family research over at least a 15-year period. The family research articles were analyzed with respect to technique employed for gathering data, statistical tests employed (if any), sample size, independent and dependent variables, number of previous studies cited, and hypotheses (if any) tested.[1]

Data-Gathering Techniques

The review of 456 studies published between 1947 and 1961 indicates that questionnaire and interview techniques of data-gathering have dominated family research in recent years (Table 1). This was less true in the period 1947–1951, when one-third used secondary sources as the only or one of the sources of data. However, this fraction had declined to little more than one-eighth in the more recent period, while questionnaires or interviews separately and combined were employed in four-fifths of the studies in the more recent period. The dominance of these latter techniques suggests that more and more studies are starting with a problem and then collecting the data to illuminate it, rather than starting

[1] This discussion has drawn heavily on Nye and Bayer (1963).

with the data available and then devising the problem. Of course, this generalization is a little too sweeping, since the researcher with a problem may find that some secondary materials fortuitously provide very appropriate and adequate data.

The review shows the continued dominance of the questionnaire, alone or combined with interviews. Interviews appear to have leveled off at about 20 per cent of the total studies; secondary sources appear to be declining; and observation shows little sign of becoming a major technique. This leaves the questionnaire as the instrument in over half of all the published studies, with no other technique close to it.

Sample Size

The trend in sample size appears to be downward during this 15-year period (Table 2). All categories under 1,000 showed proportional increases, with decreases in samples over that size and in the use of census or other secondary materials (which ordinarily would involve large numbers). The increase in studies with samples of 100

TABLE 1

TECHNIQUE REPORTED IN GATHERING RESEARCH DATA
BY FIVE-YEAR PERIODS, 1947–1961[a]

Technique for Gathering Data	1947–1951 N=71		1952–1956 N=194		1957–1961 N=191	
	Number	Per Cent	Number	Per Cent	Number	Per Cent
A. Interview	8	11.3	42	21.6	39	20.4
B. Questionnaire & standardized tests	29	40.9	68	35.1	96	50.4
C. Census, records, & articles	22	31.0	59	30.5	25	13.1
D. A & B above	5	7.0	10	5.2	16	8.4
E. A & C above	2	2.8	3	1.5	2	1.0
F. B & C above	1	1.4	3	1.5	1	0.5
G. A, B, & C above	2	2.8	0	0.0	3	1.5
H. Observation	0	0.0	5	2.6	1	0.5
I. B & H above	0	0.0	2	1.0	0	0.0
J. Discussion groups	2	2.8	0	0.0	0	0.0
K. Not reported	0	0.0	2	1.0	8	4.2
Total	71	100.0	194	100.0	191	100.0

[a] From Nye & Bayer (1963).

TABLE 2

SAMPLE SIZE OF RESEARCH REPORTED, BY FIVE-YEAR PERIODS, 1947–1961[a]

Sample Size	1947–1951 N=71		1952–1956 N=194		1957–1961 N=191	
	Number	Per Cent	Number	Per Cent	Number	Per Cent
0–29	1	1.4	9	4.6	10	5.2
30–99	7	9.8	26	13.4	30	15.7
100–499	17	24.0	63	32.6	78	40.9
500–999	9	12.7	21	10.8	33	17.3
1000–1999	12	16.9	14	7.2	11	5.8
2000 +	9	12.7	22	11.3	14	7.3
Census & Records in Which Size is Not Reported	14	19.7	30	15.5	9	4.7
Not Reported	2	2.8	9	4.6	6	3.1
Total	71	100.0	194	100.0	191	100.0

[a] From Nye & Bayer (1963).

or less coincides very closely with the proportion of studies employing interviews as the technique for gathering data. For example, in the 1957–1961 period, 20.4 per cent employed the interview, and 20.9 per cent used samples of less than 100 cases. It may be that the cost of interviewing has been instrumental in reducing sample size in family research. It is not clear, however, why samples of 100 to 1,000 have been increasing and of over 1,000 decreasing.

Statistical Tests

It may be surprising to note that in the 1947–1951 period, only about one-third of the research projects employed *any* type of test of significance; in the remainder there

TABLE 3

STATISTICAL TESTS REPORTED IN RESEARCH ARTICLES
BY FIVE-YEAR PERIODS, 1947–1961[a]

Statistical tests employed	1947–1951		1952–1956		1957–1961	
	Number	Per Cent	Number	Per Cent	Number	Per Cent
None	50	70.4	118	60.8	89	46.6
Chi square	13	18.3	43	22.2	66	34.6
T-test	1	1.4	13	6.7	21	11.0
Critical ratios	6	8.4	14	7.2	5	2.6
Mann-Whitney U-test	1	1.4	0	0.0	2	1.0
F-ratio	1	1.5	6	3.1	3	1.6
Other	4	5.6	8	4.1	17	8.9
Level of significance cited, test used not reported	0	0.0	2	1.0	12	6.3
Total	76	106.9[b]	204	105.1[b]	215	112.6[b]

[a] From Nye & Bayer (1963).
[b] Percentages add to more than 100, and total number of tests is more than number of articles, because some articles involved more than one test of significance.

was nothing more than an intuitive estimate of whether more than sample error was involved in sample differences (Table 3). The proportion lacking tests for significance had declined but was still large in 1957–1961, including over 46 per cent of the published studies. Chi square has been the "work horse" throughout the period. In the most recent years, however, a substantial scattering of techniques has occurred ("other," 8.9 per cent; "test not reported," 6.3 per cent).

This may reflect the increased use of a variety of new nonparametric techniques.

Variables Employed

The task of finding and showing which independent variables have been related to which dependent ones is formidable, and the present effort to carry it through is not entirely satisfactory (Table 4). The principal problem is one of classification, since

TABLE 4
INDEPENDENT AND DEPENDENT VARIABLES EMPLOYED IN
MARRIAGE AND FAMILY RESEARCH, 1947–1961[a]

		1	2	3	4	5	6	7	8	9	10	11	12	13	14	15	16	Total
		Dependent Variables																
Independent Variables	1	3	16	5	4	1	3	7	7	4	5	0	11	12	0	3	23	104
	2	0	1	1	3	0	0	0	0	0	0	0	3	3	0	0	2	13
	3	0	3	0	0	0	0	1	0	0	0	1	1	3	0	0	4	13
	4	2	14	3	7	3	0	12	4	5	4	3	9	8	2	2	16	94
	5	0	0	2	0	1	1	5	1	9	4	0	5	0	3	0	6	37
	6	0	3	0	5	6	3	6	0	9	3	1	6	2	2	5	11	62
	7	0	2	0	0	3	1	4	0	3	2	1	3	0	3	7	9	38
	8	0	0	0	1	1	1	1	1	1	0	0	4	0	0	0	1	11
	9	0	0	0	0	2	0	3	0	1	0	0	5	1	1	2	4	19
	10	1	7	0	5	2	0	7	2	3	2	0	10	2	3	2	18	64
	11	0	5	0	0	1	0	0	0	2	1	0	10	0	1	1	6	27
	12	0	10	2	6	5	1	2	7	9	5	3	10	8	3	1	9	81
	13	0	0	0	0	0	0	1	0	0	0	0	4	1	0	0	2	8
	14	4	4	3	1	1	2	3	4	3	2	0	8	3	2	3	7	50
	15	1	9	5	10	3	2	8	1	3	2	6	20	8	2	2	16	98
	16	6	37	6	8	5	5	23	12	14	6	4	32	8	5	3	36	210
	17	3	13	7	6	7	2	17	4	12	10	1	17	10	5	9	30	153
	18	0	0	0	0	1	0	0	0	0	0	0	4	3	0	0	0	8
	19	3	18	7	7	10	1	16	9	10	8	3	31	10	4	8	53	198
Total		23	142	41	63	52	22	116	52	88	54	23	193	82	36	48	253	1,288[b]

Independent variables

1. Age
2. Age at marriage
3. Dating patterns
4. Education
5. Employment of wife-mother
6. Family composition
7. Family relationships
8. Length of marriage
9. Marital adjustment
10. Marital status
11. Personality characteristics
12. Place of residence
13. Premarital sexual experience
14. Race & ethnic origin
15. Religion
16. Sex
17. Social class
18. Type of marriage ceremony
19. Miscellaneous

Dependent variables

1. Age at marriage
2. Dating, courtship, & mate selection
3. Family composition
4. Family planning, birth control, & sterility
5. Family solidarity
6. Inlaw relationships
7. Marital roles
8. Marital status
9. Parent-child relationships
10. Parental roles
11. Religious behavior
12. Marital success, failure, & satisfaction
13. Sexual behavior & attitudes
14. Social & personality problems of children
15. Socialization of children
16. Miscellaneous

[a] From Nye & Bayer (1963).
[b] The total number of articles involved is 456. The number of analyses is substantially larger (1,288) because there are several analyses reported in most articles.

the contents of these variables do not fall neatly into a manageable number of categories. Therefore, Table 4 represents only a rough approximation.

Three subjects, (a) dating, courtship, and mate selection, (b) marital success or failure, and (c) marital roles, are dependent variables to which independent variables had been related more than 100 times. Independent variables had been related to two other dependent variables—parent-child relationships and sexual behavior—more than 80 times. These five categories of dependent variables accounted for almost half of the analyses covered in this review.

A comparable concentration was found among independent variables. Sex had been employed in over 200 analyses, and social class in more than 150. Age, education, place of residence, and religious affiliation also were very frequently employed as independent variables.

Finally, some idea may be obtained about the frequency with which an independent variable has been related to a given dependent variable. Four combinations were made 20 or more times: (a) sex of respondent related to dating, courtship, and mate-selection behavior; (b) sex with marital roles; (c) sex with marital success or failure; and (d) religion with marital success or failure. Three other analyses had been made 15 or more times: (e) age with dating, courtship, and mate selection; (f) social class with marital roles; and (g) social class with marital success or failure.

It may be noted that the two most frequent classes of dependent variables—dating, courtship, and mate selection and marital success or failure—are rather closely related. Combined, they represent over one-quarter of the analyses reported here. This suggests something of a preoccupation in the past decade and a half with these areas of family behavior.

Numerical Trends

Family research projects have grown consistently in numbers, at least since the end of World War II. Precise growth rates are difficult to determine, because of inadequate compilations of projects and differences in criteria for listing. Nevertheless, approximate measures are possible.

According to listings in the annual surveys of research in progress made by the American Sociological Association, the family was second in number of listings in 1952. In 1955 and 1956 it was third; second in 1957; fifth from 1958 through 1960; sixth in 1961; but back to second in 1962. Prior to 1962, the trend seemed to be for family research to increase at a slower rate than some of the other sociological research areas. Whether the 1962 figures indicate a new concentration on family research will have to await the 1963 and 1964 figures.

THE FORMULATION OF PROBLEMS

The Place of Theory in Generating Problems

In one of the recent reviews of the field, Goode (Merton, Broom, & Cottrell, 1959, p. 179) opened his discussion of family theory by saying, "In the field of the family, theory has generally been neglected." He followed the general statement with a brief discussion of the works of Zimmerman, Durkheim, Malinowski, Parsons, Davis, and Homans—not an inconsiderable array of theorists, it would seem to the writer. However, to the researcher, family theory does appear lacking in continuity and integration, and at least the broader theories, such as Parsons and Bales's (1955) and Zimmerman's (1947), offer few testable hypotheses. Whether the family has less theory than other areas of sociology, or whether this condition is merely one that is generally true of all young and undeveloped disciplines, goes beyond the scope of the present analysis. (The writer has heard almost identical pessimistic statements made with respect to the two other substantive areas of sociology with which he has had substantial contact, rural and criminology.)

Regardless of evaluative statements about

the state of family theory, its impact on family research, especially as a source of fruitful hypotheses, has been limited.

There is one exception to this generalization, Freudian theory. This body of assumptions and postulates based on the rather slender foundation of clinical experience and insight has been so extensively elaborated by followers and practitioners that almost any family behavior can be "explained" by it. These elaborations provide a basis for testing implications and applications of the theory, if not of its central structure. A notable example of such testing was provided by Sewell and associates in their research on the relationship of childhood training practices to personality development in children (Sewell, Mussen, & Harris, 1955). They successfully tested the idea that specific practices affected personality characteristics and that there was a broad parental attitudinal base underlying the training practices. No support was found for either assumed relationship.

This finding, although attacked on methodological grounds by clinicians and other exponents of Freudian theory, appears to have had a marked deterring effect on the application of Freudian theory to these aspects of child care. Thus, a general theory in this instance provided a basis for testable hypotheses, although the researcher found it necessary to restate the relevant part of the theory before such tests could be made (Sewell, 1956). In this instance, the research failed to support the theory and cast doubt on its usefulness with respect to childhood training practices. It nevertheless illustrates one function of research, to demonstrate the falsity or inadequacy of theory.

Presumably, the broader the family theory and the smaller its foundation in facts, the more often such tests of theories are likely to produce negative findings. It has been suggested that hypotheses based on deductions from general theory are less likely to be supported than those developed from the observation of uniformities in behavior. It

appears, however, that some of the inferences from Freudian theory to family behavior may provide a fruitful basis for continued theory testing. It may also be that some broader family theories, such as that of Zimmerman's *Family and Civilization* (1947) and even older theoretical treatises, might be at least partially tested. The lack of such tests may have been partly a function of the lack of development of empirical methodology and limitation of funds for family research at the time the theories were propounded.

One further question should be considered, however. If it is true that hypotheses deduced from broad theories are less likely to be substantiated than those stemming from observation, is it worth while, given the present development of the field, to use broad theories as a source of hypotheses? The disadvantage of employing them is that they have so few connections with the family phenomena they are intended to organize and explain that their immediate potential for such explanation is not great and may not warrant the investment of research resources. However, broad theories may "locate" specific research in the development of the substantive area, and thus reduce fragmentation and discontinuity in research. The large-scale theoretical treatises often perform an unintended service to the researcher. Although he may not find profitable hypotheses as logical deductions from general theory, he may find concepts which can lead to better organization of family behavior, or he may find some incidental observation of the theorist which stimulates new directions for research. For example, the writer has found the concepts of *instrumental* and *expressive* parental functions developed by Parsons and Bales (1955) helpful in better organizing the tremendous number and variety of parental behaviors, although the originators' use of the concepts in relating the behavior to sex and age appears to add little substantial new understanding of family behavior.

The use of "miniature" family theories is another matter.[2] These are specific, limited, close to the behavior they are intended to explain, and may be inspired by direct observation. Some examples of such small-scale theories are Waller's "rating and dating" hypotheses [see pp. 643–645], Winch's theory of "complementary needs" [see pp. 665–670], the idea of "maternal deprivation" [see pp. 768–771], and Goode's (1959) recently propounded ideas of the relationships of social class, social control, and love. Whether these are considered theories or hypotheses (like, for example, the aggression-frustration hypotheses) is debatable. Whatever their label, they spell out relatively limited, specific research problems and are capable of being supported or refuted by research.

Family researchers have shown a disposition to use these small theories. For example, the Winch theory has been the subject of numerous and continuing research. (For a recent view of this, see Schellenberg & Bee, 1960.) Such miniature theories seem appropriate to the present level of development in the family area. To date, better use might have been made of these small theories in two ways: (a) "Tests" of them have not always been appropriate; for example, one researcher in testing Waller's "rating and dating" hypothesis included engaged couples in the sample. (b) The other shortcoming has been that researchers have not been aware of the existence of the theory, or it has not occurred to them that it was appropriate. Although the researcher has a convenient reference point for selecting a sampling technique, or test of significance, no

such convenient and adequate source is available in theory.

Besides miniature theories dealing directly with family behavior, a potentially useful development may come through the use of theories of limited range in other areas of behavioral research. For example, Merton's rather widely employed theory of "social structure and anomie" (1957) might well be applied to predict a differential distribution of deviant sexual behavior.

Other Sources of Research Problems

Other common sources of family research problems include subjects of public or agency concern (such as young marriages and unwed or employed mothers), personal experiences and problems of researchers, gaps in knowledge disclosed by teaching, counseling, or action programs, and problems suggested by previous research. The source of the problem makes it neither a good nor a poor one from a scientific point of view. However, family problems suggested by public interest or personal experiences may lack a theoretical background which is automatically available for those suggested by theory or previous research. In this case, the tasks of providing adequate intellectual tools and, subsequently, of integrating findings into the common body of knowledge are greater, also, because the origin of the problem is independent of the accumulated knowledge of the field.

The problem of covering previous research is common to all research enterprise. In the recent review of family research, cited earlier, the writer and an associate checked published articles to determine the amount of attention given to this matter (Nye & Bayer, 1963). As a rough approximation, they counted previous studies on the subject that were cited by each author (Table 5). An appreciable number mentioned no previous studies, although the proportion in this category had declined considerably. In the last five-year period, about a third cited 10

---

[2] The concept "minature theory" was expounded by Hans Zetterberg in the first edition of his book *On Theory and Verification* (1954). In the second edition (1963), he proposes that we stop thinking of sociological theory and consider as an alternative concern "theoretical sociology." In developing the latter proposal, he would emphasize theoretical propositions and hypotheses as the level of generalization appropriate to the present development of sociology.

TABLE 5

NUMBER OF REFERENCES TO PREVIOUS STUDIES CITED IN RESEARCH
ARTICLES BY FIVE-YEAR PERIODS, 1947–1961[a]

Number Studies referred to	1947–1951 N=71		1952–1956 N=194		1957–1961 N=191	
	Number	Per Cent	Number	Per Cent	Number	Per Cent
None	11	15.5	24	12.4	16	8.4
1–2	13	18.3	36	18.6	23	12.0
3–5	22	31.1	49	25.2	35	18.3
6–10	13	18.3	54	27.9	54	28.3
11–15	7	9.8	14	7.2	37	19.4
16–20	3	4.2	10	5.1	12	6.3
21 +	2	2.8	7	3.6	14	7.3
Total	71	100.0	194	100.0	191	100.0

[a] From Nye & Bayer (1963).

or more previous studies. Of course, because of the accumulation of research, there were more studies available to cite in the latter period. It nevertheless appears that researchers are devoting increased time to covering previous research, although an appreciable number still publish as if they had been working in a vacuum.

Statement of the Problem

Statements of problems in family research have varied from none (with at least the possibility that the researcher even lacked a problem in mind) to very elaborate formulations. Some research appears to be done starting with a dependent family variable and relating to it "the usual social variables" of age, sex, religious affiliation, social class, etc. Not much, of course, can be expected to emerge from this level of formulation. More frequent is a statement of the type of specific relationships to be studied. Occasionally found is a statement of not only the specific relationships desired but also any general assumptions or theoretical positions which might be illuminated by the findings. For example, in a recent doctoral dissertation, the specific problem concerned changes in personality attributable to a functional marriage course. The research

seemed to hold promise also for testing the more general problem of whether adult personality can be changed appreciably (Wetzel, 1962).

Ordinarily, opportunities to question general assumptions are greater than anticipated and, as Merton has said, one of the important research processes is the interaction between the data and the researcher's frame of reference, in which new insights are opened up as the analysis proceeds (1957, pp. 103–108).

Hypotheses

In textbook models, hypotheses are deduced from theory and supported or rejected on the basis of the outcome of the research. However, as noted above, a minority of current family (or other sociological) research follows this model. Of course, hypotheses are also based on relevant previous research, clinical experience, or observation. In Nye and Bayer's (1963) survey of research, the frequency with which hypotheses were stated formally or clearly implied was checked (Table 6). The review revealed a rapid trend toward formalization of this aspect of research, with over half of the family projects currently employing stated hypotheses and only one-fifth employing

TABLE 6

Type of Hypotheses Reported in Research Articles
By Five-Year Periods, 1947–1961[a]

Hypotheses	1947–1951 N=71		1952–1956 N=194		1957–1961 N=191	
	Number	Per Cent	Number	Per Cent	Number	Per Cent
Formal	11	15.15	88	45.3	103	53.9
Implied	21	29.6	50	25.8	47	24.6
None	39	54.9	56	28.9	41	21.5
Total	71	100.0	194	100.0	191	100.0

[a] From Nye & Bayer (1963).

neither formal nor implied ones. Nevertheless, a number of exploratory projects are still being developed in which researchers apparently feel that hypotheses are unnecessary or premature.

One matter of procedure with respect to hypotheses is receiving variable treatment: the form, either null or directional. There seems to be general agreement that only the former is appropriate when the investigator questions an existing theory or when insufficient or contradictory evidence is present. However, sometimes a null hypothesis is employed in family research when the investigator expects to find a statistical relationship between variables. This procedure is somewhat confusing and, in a general sense, illogical. It is rationalized on the grounds that statistical procedures are available only for testing the hypotheses that two population parameters are not identical. However, rationale and procedures have been given by Wallis and Roberts (1956) for initial statement of the direction of the alternative hypotheses, which not only allows the hypotheses to reflect the general theoretical position but also reduces by half the probability of accepting a hypothesis of no difference when a difference exists. The use of the alternative directional hypothesis, whenever appropriate, would reduce the number of inconclusive analyses of family behavior.

Conceptualization of Family Attributes and Behavior

Current family research typically devotes little attention to precise statements of concepts. This is time saving (and space saving) but does not contribute to rigorous thinking by the investigator or to good communication between investigators. For example, the idea of "role" becomes a concept with multiple meanings: status role (Parsons, 1951); a part of the structure of a position (Bates, 1956); and behavior related to a given position (Gross, Mason, & McEachern, 1958). Besides these different conceptualizations, inconsistency sometimes can be found in the use of concepts even within a given paper.

Since the exhaustive examination and exposition of a concept is a major operation, it is obvious that something less will usually be undertaken. However, as a minimum, such attention could be devoted to the dependent variable, at least.

There is one conceptual operation that is rarely specified in current family research: the working, or operational, definition of the concept. It is implied, of course, in the nature of the item, index, or scale employed, but it could be spelled out explicitly as well. For example, occupation of the male head is used most frequently as the criterion of social class. There is rarely any thought that it is a sufficient measure. It *may* be the most reliable one and, for some purposes, may be very useful. But, from a conceptual point of view, what is missing is a specification of which aspects of social class are measured and which are not.

TECHNIQUES OF DATA COLLECTION

Questionnaires

Questionnaires should be considered to include at least two techniques: personal administration and mailing. The troublesome problem of nonresponse applies mainly to the mailed questionnaire. There is some justification also for differential consideration of the questionnaire technique employed within a given community as compared with studies that are nationwide or regional in scope.

The questionnaire administered to a group of respondents by the researcher personally is a particularly versatile technique but limited in use to only a few populations, most of them composed of school children. Usable responses of 99 per cent are not uncommon, provided good motivation is provided and anonymity guaranteed (Nye, 1958). In addition to direct, structured instruments, the technique is appropriate to the use of a number of projective and disguised devices including the Group Rorschach, the Thematic Apperception Test, error choice, and disguised intelligence tests. Anonymity can be assured, which is impossible in an interview situation. Questions can be answered when they arise and additional instructions issued. It cannot, however, provide the "depth" rapport that is sometimes obtained in interviews.

It might be argued, of course, that such excellent rapport which permits obtaining guarded personal material sometimes cannot be achieved by the questionnaire and that its use, therefore, should be limited to the development of hypotheses and insights. A more serious limitation than that of the types of questions which can be asked has to do with the restricted number of populations which can be reached. This has led to disproportionate concentration on students in schools and universities. It must be limited to those who can read and, among these, adapted to their level of comprehension.

The mailed questionnaire, in principle, can sample wherever the mails go. In practice, however, it is limited to a given society and, within it, to groups whose members are labeled so that samples can be drawn. Thus, nationwide studies usually employ area samples and interviews in order to locate a random sample of individuals. Nationwide samples from more limited groups, such as the American Sociological Association, can be made. But such lists are obviously restricted by their special characteristics, and even with respect to a profession such as sociologist, only a part of the category (and a nonrepresentative part) will belong to the association. Even with these limitations, questionnaire studies of such groups may be useful. For example, data for professional directories are usually collected in this way.

Thus, the mailed questionnaire can tap wider groups—groups that could not be assembled for a personally administered questionnaire. But it has several disadvantages: an appreciable nonresponse category, lack of opportunity to explain questions, and loss of control over the conditions under which the form is completed. For these reasons, it probably never would be chosen if the researcher possessed the option of having his respondents assembled so that he could administer the instrument personally; but, as already noted, this condition is limited essentially to students.

Of the problems of mailed questionnaires, that of nonrespondents is the subject of most concern. The comment of Selltiz, Jahoda, Deutsch, and Cook (1959) that a return of only 10 to 50 per cent must be expected probably represents the opinion of a substantial number of researchers. This picture is, however, unrealistic. Slocum, Empey, and Swanson (1956) have shown that responses of over 90 per cent can be obtained, with some consistency. They have obtained more than 94 per cent return in a study of student attitudes toward their university.

Some of these studies were conducted under unusually favorable conditions. Nearer to average conditions for a questionnaire project within a given study was one dealing with the employment of mothers conducted by Nye (in Nye & Hoffman, 1963) in which a 78 per cent return was obtained. In this project, the researcher was familiar with the community, having conducted a previous study there. The project received the endorsement of a local citizens' committee and active support from some of the members of the committee. All mothers of children in the first and tenth grades in the public and parochial schools were included. The name and address of each parent was made available by the schools. Each was sent an eight-page questionnaire with a covering letter and a return-addressed envelope. No identification was placed on the questionnaire, but the respondent was given a post card with his name on it to be returned separately, indicating that she had returned the questionnaire. This permitted anonymity, yet made a follow-up possible. Respondents were promised a brief report on the project if a majority wished it. The first returns were about 40 per cent, which falls within the limits suggested by Selltiz and his associates for questionnaire response (1959). However, the final return was almost double the initial one. The additional returns were obtained by two follow-up letters; by an appeal to the officers of all church, civic, and recreational groups in the community; by a television appeal by the researcher and four community leaders; and by a final special-delivery letter. *The size of the response in a mailed questionnaire is largely a function of the ingenuity and persistence of the researchers.*

With nonresponse, the question arises as to differences between those who do and do not respond. Researchers have frequently reported under-response among those of low educational attainment and those who have no strong feeling on an issue. In the above study, it was possible to check the social characteristics of the respondents against data for the total population of parents of tenth-grade students obtained from the students in the classroom. This check failed to show heavier nonresponse in the low education group. Whether or not this bias develops may depend to an extent on the part of the country in which the study is conducted and on the length and wording of the questionnaire. Since much explanatory research does not involve controversial issues, the intensity of feeling about issues will be a problem in a minority of questionnaire studies, primarily in those dealing with public opinion.

How important is the nonresponse category? The type of study is crucial in answering this question. If the purpose is descriptive—for example, how the public intends to vote—it is hardly tolerable, since the objective is for the sample to represent the whole. This is true of an entire range of studies—for example, how frequently middle-class Americans visit with kin outside the nuclear family. It is much less crucial for explanatory studies in which a relationship between variables is sought.

Drawing an analogy from medical research, it is hardly necessary to take a nationwide probability sample of children in order to test the polio vaccine. Yet Chein strongly opposes this position (Selltiz et al., 1959, pp. 541–543). What Chein seems to overlook is that those who respond to a questionnaire are themselves *a probability sample of people who will return questionnaires* on this topic. This population has a sampling distribution of its own. The confusion occurs in equating this population with a larger population of which it is a part.

Even so, there is a possibility of the nonresponse producing a spurious relationship, if characteristics of the nonrespondents are related to both the independent and dependent variables. For example, in studying the relationship of employment of mothers to the attitudes of mothers toward children, if only employed mothers who enjoy their relationship to children respond, whereas among nonemployed mothers both those who enjoy and who reject their children respond, a spurious relationship would be introduced. Analyses of the nonrespondents in the Nye study referred to above have not disclosed a selective response of this type, but it could occur.

An additional problem with mailed questionnaires is the loss of control over the completion of the instrument. The researcher cannot prevent the respondent from discussing the questions with his spouse or others, or even from having someone else complete it. These problems, however, are not as great as they might at first appear. The respondent is under little if any compulsion to return the questionnaire, so if his interest is not secured, he is more likely to ignore it than to go to the trouble of having someone else do it. The likelihood of the latter happening is probably greatest in studies in which a number of similar people are readily available. For example, in studies of college students, respondents have reported that they gave their questionnaire to their roommates.[3] It is less likely that a questionnaire eliciting information from the female head of a family would be filled out by her husband or by the female head of another household.

These problems may be serious in special instances, however, as when the design of the project calls for the husband and wife

to report their attitudes and behavior without knowledge of the response of the spouse. Such designs would be better accomplished by a structured interview.

One further distinction should be made between personally administered and mailed questionnaires, namely, content. Normally, it is possible to secure somewhat deeper rapport when the researcher is present and can make an oral presentation and answer questions. Researchers have under these conditions been able to obtain information concerning some types of delinquent behavior and some aspects of sexual behavior. Mailed questionnaires have usually not attempted to secure such information, although Axelson (1963) has obtained data concerning attitudes toward sex by mailed questionnaire. Nye (in Nye & Hoffman, 1963), in attempting as part of a larger study to get at drinking behavior, felt that the data obtained were inadequate and that the inclusion of questions on drinking behavior in a mailed questionnaire probably contributed to nonresponse on the whole instrument.

To sum up briefly, the researcher who chooses the questionnaire technique is likely to have reasonably adequate numbers of cases, so that even relatively low associations between variables can be reliably established. It is likely that the relationship can be studied employing a number of contingent conditions and that generalizations may be established for a number of strata in the population. With the personally administered questionnaire, he should have minimum nonresponse problems. With the mailed questionnaire, even if ingenuity and perseverance are displayed, he must anticipate a relatively large proportion of nonrespondents. For descriptive purposes, this is a major limitation, but for explanation it is less serious.

Interviews

It has already been noted that interviews were employed as the data-gathering tech-

[3] It is felt that special attention needs to be devoted to such matters involving high school and college students, of whom an appreciable minority feel rebellious against the adult world, its rules and objectives. To outwit and confuse the representatives of the adult world provides personal satisfaction and status in their reference groups. Such interest can be overcome in most adolescents by especially effective appeals to their interest in the subject of the research and sense of responsibility in contributing to the advancement of knowledge in an important area. This will not be effective with every respondent, however, and for those who deliberately submit invalid responses, a lie scale is suggested.

nique in about one-fifth of the research reports recently published in four major sociological journals (Table 1). This shows it second in frequency of use only to the questionnaire. Since it is more expensive and time consuming than the questionnaire and requires the consent of the subjects (which observation and the use of secondary documents do not), its use is best rationalized in terms of limitations of those techniques. Hyman has noted that advantages over the questionaire include the facts that interviews can be obtained from illiterates, that questions coming later in the interview cannot influence answers given earlier (as could be the case with the questionnaire), and that the interviewer can clarify, obtain additional information, and record his own observations. Advantages over participant observation and recorded documents include the fact that the specific behavior sought may not spontaneously happen and that secondary documents may not include the needed information (1954, pp. 16–17).

In addition, it has generally been assumed that interviews solve or largely solve the problem of nonresponse. The assumption is that the respondent who would ignore a questionnaire will agree to a personal request for an interview. The facts appear to provide only limited support for this. Some questionnaires have obtained a higher proportion of returns than some interview studies. The writer has obtained questionnaire returns as high as 92 per cent, and others have obtained 94 (Slocum et al., 1956) and 95 per cent (Caudle, 1962). However, most interview studies have a smaller proportion of nonrespondents than most questionnaire studies.

It is not correct, however, to assume that selecting the interview technique solves the response problem. Goode has quoted a number of studies to show that refusals of interviews have varied from as little as 1.3 per cent to as much as 45 per cent (1956). In his study of postdivorce adjustment, he stated that 19 per cent of those contacted for interviews refused. However, an additional 17 per cent could not be located; therefore, of the 665 cases, data were obtained from only 433, or two-thirds of those drawn in the sample. Goode concluded that refusal rates of 15 to 20 per cent must be considered normal, "though any researcher is troubled by losses beyond 8–10 per cent" (1956, pp. 351–352).

Thus, it appears that the selection of the interview technique usually provides a better opportunity for reduction of nonresponse but does not automatically (or generally) solve the problem. That it can be solved, however, seems to be demonstrated by Stycos' research in Puerto Rico. He foresaw resistance to questions on sexual behavior and birth control techniques as one of the principal methodological problems and, by taking careful and elaborate precautions, obtained 144 interviews with only a single refusal (1955, pp. 266–283). This degree of success is unusual, however, and Hill's (1949) rate of 15 per cent refusals seems more reasonable for studies dealing with personal aspects of family behavior. Thus, the interview stands between the large nonresponse typical of mailed questionnaires and the almost complete response that can be expected in personally administered anonymous questionnaires.

Structured interviews. The structured interview is useful for testing previously formulated hypotheses with, at most, limited usefulness either in further delineating the problem or in formulating hypotheses. It presupposes that the items adequately tap the phenomena and that the response categories provide responses that classify the behavior or feelings of the respondent with little distortion. Since such assumptions cannot always be justified, the research sacrifices something in versatility for speed, ease in processing, and comparability of data from schedule to schedule and from interviewer to interviewer. It possesses most of both the virtues and vices of a questionnaire. In fact, many structured interview schedules could be as well completed by educated respondents if used as personally administered questionnaires.

One of the larger recent research projects employing highly structured interview schedules is reported in *Family Growth in Metropolitan Areas* (Westoff et al., 1961), in which 1,165 couples, randomly selected from seven metropolitan areas, were interviewed. The schedule included items on social background and contraceptive practices. It also employed open-ended questions and, interestingly enough, was accompanied by personality instruments obtained by the mailed questionnaire. Refusal rates were relatively low, with 6 per cent refusals on the interview and 19 per cent nonreturn on the mailed questionnaire. It may be that the high return of the personality instruments was partially a product of the previous interview. This combination of interview and questionnaire may possess considerable potential. It reduces the length of each and allows the researcher to obtain the part of his data with each technique that is most appropriate to it.

Semistructured interviews. The interview that allows or requires the probing of "why" or "how" questions elicits information unavailable from the structured interview or from most questionnaires. Goode considered this important in obtaining information that respondents were inclined to falsify (1956). It is at least equally useful for preliminary studies concerned with developing hypotheses or possible additional hypotheses (Hill, Stycos, & Back, 1959, pp. 31–35). Such probes might well provide material for the concluding section of a report, frequently entitled "Suggestions for Further Research." The semistructured (or even unstructured) interview is peculiarly appropriate to new research areas in which the researcher has little idea of the important independent variables. To neglect its potential in such areas is to invite a sterile project. Conversely, to employ extensive probes in a project designed to test well-formulated hypotheses may waste a great deal of the respondent's and the inter-

viewer's time, piling up material not appropriate for statistical treatment. Such material is not particularly useful in "explaining" relationships, since it is intuitive on the part of the respondent insofar as relationships are concerned. It can, of course, be employed descriptively as "reasons given by respondent for the action."

Basically, the semistructured interview performs two major functions: (a) searching for hypotheses for the current or future research projects and (b) obtaining specific, uniform responses for tests of hypotheses. It may, on occasion, also be employed to check the veracity of the respondent. It is a versatile instrument, particularly in a continuing project in which the completion of one set of analyses is the basis for the start of additional research. However, it is frequently wastefully used, in that the probe data may not be utilized and might have been dispensed with in the planning of the project.

Focused interviews. This is a special type that is not readily placed on a structured-unstructured continuum. It focuses on a particular event or experience (which provides the structure) but emphasizes the informants' frame of reference beyond that point (Merton, Fisk, & Kendall, 1952). Its obvious uses are in the experimental situation in which the respondent can be subjected to a particular experience and then interviewed concerning his feelings and reactions.

The focus of this technique on a single event limits its usefulness in family research, in which most studies involve a wider range of phenomena. However, it might be employed to study selected significant events which the researcher knows has recently occurred, such as a divorce, birth of a first child, retirement from employment, or loss of employment. It can obtain feelings and behavior which are more idiosyncratic than is true of most structured instruments. It centers on such psychological variables as the feelings that the interviewee had about the event and the intensity of his feelings. The development of these potentials by family researchers might add a useful psychological dimension to the familiar sociological variables.

Unstructured interviews. The completely unstructured interview is, presumably, a therapeutic rather than a research technique. Since the area of research interest is such a small part of total social behavior, economy of time and funds requires that the most casual conversation be directed to the area of research concern, which means that the interview has some structure.

To immerse oneself in the phenomenon to be studied, through observation and relatively unstructured interviews, is equally effective as a source of hypotheses and ineffective as a means of testing them. The decision to employ it as a source of hypotheses will depend on the amount of theory and previous research in the area and the interviewer's felt degree of familiarity with the problem. The need for such experience seems obvious in the study of family life in other societies. It is less obvious in the study of the family in a social class other than that of the investigator, but the need may be present.

For example, some of the earlier studies of family life among the lower social classes produced eulogistic pictures based on lack of excessive supervision or demands for conformity to middle-class standards. Later studies correctly identified the lack of supervision as neglect and indifference rather than permissiveness. Since most family researchers have reared or are rearing children by middle-class standards and are observing their neighbors doing the same, the mere intensity and duration of these experiences may make it particularly difficult to comprehend patterns of behavior which are not only different in specific aspects but which also occur in a social milieu which is different in many ways from their own. On a descriptive or narrowly analytical basis, the researcher may need to know little of this milieu, but for explanation and interpretation it is likely to be crucial. It is

insufficient to assume that the milieu of another social class differs from that of the investigator and then to attempt to deduce the differences on an intuitive basis.

Extended participant observation by the investigator provides an orientation to a subcultural world different from his own. It should be said, however, that such orientation is still subjective and is not a substitute for thorough objective data concerning the social systems of the subculture, only one or two of which are to be the primary concern of the investigator.

Other Sources of Survey Data

Census data are regarded by the writer as survey data; however, this is one of the subjects of Chapter 9 and need not be treated in detail here. It is sufficient to observe that these data are generally reliable and from adequate samples (or a total population), but the fact that they are gathered for limited, descriptive purposes severely restricts their contribution to family research.

Case studies, and clinical data in general, are more useful as sources of hypotheses than for testing them. In principle, case study data may be employed to test hypotheses in the same manner as census data. However, census data are usually descriptive, factual data which have been gathered with the expectation that they will be used by others, and considerable care has been exercised in their collection and description. Much case study material, in contrast, is subjective in nature and gathered with the object of aiding the intuitive judgment of the person who gathered it or a fellow therapist. Its usual purpose is treatment, not analysis and description. Ordinarily, there is no thought of sampling in the selection of cases. To complicate the matter further, case material is usually confidential, and permission to use it for research purposes often is difficult to obtain. Under these circumstances, it is questionable whether utilizing already collected case material for testing hypotheses is a wise use of research resources.

By contrast, case material, because it provides intimate and detailed contact with the phenomena, holds high potential for the generation of hypotheses—particularly for the discovery of fruitful independent variables. However, it is a moot question whether many family scientists have the training and experience to employ the technique fruitfully. It may be that the most productive arrangement for the use of the technique is a collaboration of the researcher with the therapist or administrator who has the training and experience to employ the technique adequately. The researcher needs the insight of the practitioner as much as the practitioner needs research.

Summary

The questionnaire is still the dominant technique for data-gathering in family research, accounting for as many published studies in major sociological journals as all other types combined, with interviews employed as the data-gathering technique in about one-fifth. Administered questionnaires and mailed questionnaires are sometimes thought of as synonymous, but, in fact, they have quite different advantages and limitations. Both critics and some researchers who employ mailed questionnaires err in the assumption that low returns must be expected. Good techniques and favorable conditions have produced returns of 75 to 95 per cent. Likewise, the profession errs in discounting nonresponse in interview studies. Present information suggests that 10 to 15 per cent must be expected. Some structured interview data could be obtained by the questionnaire, while some questionnaire studies would benefit by a preliminary investigation employing unstructured or semistructured interviews. Recent studies show that both techniques can sometimes be used with profit on the same project.

ANALYSIS OF DATA

Control of Extraneous Variables

Family sociologists have shown an awareness of the general problem of the intrusion of extraneous variables into data analyses. There are, however, two specific problems that warrant attention. First, the control over extraneous variables has been relative rather than absolute. For example, limiting an analysis to the middle class by employing selected occupations does not fully control social class, because this "homogeneous" category covers a considerable range of income, prestige, and power dimensions. To say that social class is completely controlled by this or any other technique in common practice is something of an exaggeration and leaves the impression that variables are eliminated when their effects are only reduced. Whether it is practicable at present to go further in such control may be debatable. Of course, it can be accomplished by severely limiting the analysis to a very homogeneous population, such as female classroom teachers in rural areas between certain ages with given levels of experience and training. The gain in such additional homogeneity may not be worth the extra time and expense, however. In any event, the degree to which homogeneity is accomplished might be more specifically stated in research reports than it is currently.

The second problem requiring attention is the matter of alternatives to homogeneity. Some writers in employing "homogeneous" samples leave the impression that if this is not the only device for achieving control, it is, in any event, obviously the best. However, homogeneity is obtained only by limiting the analysis to a small segment of the society. For example, in Sewell's classic study of parental child-rearing practices and personality development of children, he employed children from rural, middle-class, native-born parents (1952). He carefully limited his generalizations to this relatively small stratum. As a result, we know almost

TABLE 7

SOCIAL CHARACTERISTICS OF MOTHERS EMPLOYED FULL-TIME AND NOT
EMPLOYED, AND OF MATCHED SAMPLES OF THE SAME EMPLOYMENT CATEGORIES[a]

| Social Characteristics[b] | Original Sample | | Matched Sample | |
	Employed Full-Time %	Not Employed %	Employed Full-Time %	Not Employed %
Preschool children	23.3	64.8	29.1	30.3
Large families	27.3	45.8	27.6	27.7
Upper status	18.0	27.8	22.1	22.5
Low education	8.9	17.1	10.0	10.0
Remarriage	13.0	11.9	15.1	15.5

[a] From Nye & Hoffman (1963), p. 267.
[b] Social Characteristics:
  Preschool children—one or more present in home
  Large family—four or more children
  Upper status—professional, semi-professional, and business other than family operated
  Low education—grade or junior high school only
  Remarriage—widowed or divorced and remarried.

nothing about this important relationship in the balance of society.

It seems well to call attention to several alternative methods which have some advantages. The term *frequency distribution control* has been used to describe the practice of sampling a general population, then controlling social class, family size, and other extraneous variables by subsampling the experimental and control groups to equalize the distribution of each of the extraneous variables (Selltiz et al., 1959). An example is shown in Table 7, in which family size, presence of preschool children, economic status, education of mother, and proportion of broken homes are roughly equalized. In this instance, about 60 per cent of the sample is lost, which necessitates a large original sample. This technique provides, in effect, a stratified sample in which the stratification is accomplished after the data are collected.

The homogeneous strata technique involves a test of relationships in a narrow segment of the population. Frequency distribution control involves large losses of numbers. In projects in which it is desired to sample the general population, but where it is not feasible to obtain a large sample, stratification by ecological area may provide the best technique. A variation of this was employed by the writer: he selected a random sample of city blocks, interviewed all subjects who met his criteria for the experimental group, then interviewed the family geographically nearest to each of these for his control group. This procedure has been termed "ecological matching." It was found that this effectively matched the groups by income of the father, education of both the father and mother, and occupation of the father (in Nye & Hoffman, 1963). This results in a cluster sample with two individuals to a cluster. It is likely that it would prove equally effective for matching religious affiliation, race, and family size.

Partial correlation can be employed if the data meet the assumptions of parametric statistics. Random selection would be even more effective—in principle—if control and experimental groups could be randomly selected and the experimental group then subjected to the independent variable. This can be done with experiments in teaching, counseling, with certain simulated problems, and perhaps with some social work services. It could hardly be argued, how-ever, that the researcher can control by random selection such variables as family size, age at marriage, or patterns of rela-tionships within the family. The outlook is not optimisitic for manipulation or simula-tion of the more significant variables in family behavior. Therefore, it is felt that random selection of experimental and con-trol groups, with the introduction of the independent variable after the selection of the groups, is one of the least promising devices for controlling extraneous variables in family research. [For a more optimistic appraisal, see Ch. 8.]

Elaboration in Field Research

Although family research has reflected an awareness of possible spurious relationships, it is less clear that family researchers have as fully appreciated the potential of de-liberately introducing extra variables into any analysis in order to clarify and more precisely specify the relationship between variables. This process owes much to the work of Kendall and Lazarsfeld (Merton & Lazarsfeld, 1950, pp. 133–196), although it is not clear that all of the concepts they proposed are necessary or useful.[4]

It may be, however, that a more general concept, that of "contingent condition," will prove adequate for most purposes (Selltiz et al., 1959). Nye found this useful in a recent analysis of employment status and maternal dissatisfaction. A low general as-sociation was found between the two, with more dissatisfaction among mothers not employed. When family size was intro-duced as a contingent condition, it was found that the relationship held only in families of three or fewer children, but in

[4] Kendall and Lazarsfeld also strongly stressed time sequence. Many family variables, however, cannot realis-tically be assigned to a given instant. For example, when does "size of family" occur? Presumably, at the time of birth of a given child, but it remains a signi-ficant "active" variable until the child moves out of the parental home. For most family analyses, it would be artificial to designate it as either antecedent or in-tervening.

these families the relationship was higher than for the general sample. It could there-fore be said that the association between maternal employment and a relatively high degree of satisfaction with children *is con-tingent upon* a small number of children. Actually, for families of four or more chil-dren, the direction of the relationship was reversed (Nye & Hoffman, 1963).

The Kendall-Lazarsfeld and other con-ceptualizations add little to the technical manipulation of the data, but conceptualiza-tion assists in communication and in the meaningful integration of findings into the accumulated body of knowledge.

THE USE OF SERENDIPITOUS FINDINGS

It is agreed that serendipitous (unsought, unforeseen) findings are among the most important products of research. For exam-ple, it was the appearance of unaccountable empirical findings that led to the develop-ment of reference group theory (Merton & Lazarsfeld, 1950, pp. 40–105). It is not clear, however, that family sociologists are fully utilizing such findings to test presently ac-cepted assumptions or to reconstruct general propositions on the basis of the findings. For example, since neglect, rejection, and cruelty to children have been shown to be closely related to pathological personality and behavioral problems, it has been rather uncritically assumed that the most favor-able climate for the maturation of children is the complete opposite of these conditions: preoccupation with children, absolute af-fection, and total absence of punishment. Some of Nye's (1958) data question this, insofar as affection and disciplinary tech-niques are concerned. Children of rejecting or indifferent parents showed the most de-linquent behavior, but those with com-pletely accepting parents, who were "never" unfair, etc., showed about the same level of delinquency as those with "intermediate" parents. In recent research at Cornell Uni-versity, Devereux (1962) has reported more socially desirable behavior in children whose parents employed intermediate levels of control and punishment. Such findings can be employed to revise current theories of personality formation.

Feldman (1962) recently reported decline in marital satisfaction with the birth of a child. This finding, along with research by Christensen and Philbrick (1952) and Farber and Blackman (1956), may challenge the general assumption that children inevitably make marriages happier. In the present period of development of the field, in which there are few formally stated theories, the testing of such implicit assumptions, preferably by design, but if not, by skillful use of serendipitous findings, may be an important function of research.

THE CHALLENGE OF LONGITUDINAL RESEARCH

If it were intended to describe here only the survey research which has employed longitudinal design, such summary could be accomplished in little more than a paragraph. It is felt, however, that such design provides an uncommonly promising opportunity to move beyond the present accomplishments of family research.

The best-known longitudinal project in family research is the Burgess and Wallin (1953) study of 1,000 couples, who were restudied after five- and 15-year periods. This has permitted a panel study of marriage relationships with true predictions and before-and-after studies of the same individuals. It has resulted in numerous publications. [Cf. pp. 228–231.]

A group of studies, perhaps larger in aggregate, and extending over a 35-year period, were undertaken in the related area of child development by Harold Jones and associates at the University of California. This group of projects is said to have resulted in 227 studies (Jones, 1960). Other, more limited, longitudinal projects include Sewell's (1952) study of child-rearing practices, Terman's (1950) work on geniuses, which includes a study of their marriages, Moss and Gingles' (1959) study of early

marriage, and Havighurst and others' study of adolescence (Havighurst et al., 1962). To these might be added Buck and Bible's (1961) study of educational achievement because of certain interesting aspects of the methodology. Also, it should be noted that longitudinal family research from recorded data becomes possible through a method which is known as "record linkage" [see p. 309].

It is felt that longitudinal research has three major advantages:

1. It permits behavior to be recorded at or near the time it occurs, minimizing errors of recall.
2. It allows experimental and control groups to be matched on the basis of measurements conducted before the independent event occurred.
3. It provides conditions under which the time sequence of independent and dependent variables can be established with some certainty.
4. It provides opportunity to observe change in the same individual.

Of these four, the principal advantages are the more adequate control of extraneous variables and the establishment of the time sequence between variables. To the extent that both are accomplished, research moves closer to legitimate causal inference.

Objections to longitudinal design are that it requires stable research personnel with a long-term commitment to the project, and that data collection is difficult and expensive. However, the most frequent objection (and probably the most serious one) is the loss of subjects over an extended period. In the Burgess and Wallin project, 1,000 couples were selected initially. Of these, 150 broke their engagements and were eliminated for that reason. Several died and, for purposes of the study, those divorced before the restudy were eliminated. This left approximately 800 in the project. Of these, 666 were interviewed after five years. In the 15-year restudy, about 400 were interviewed. In one of the University of California studies, the Berkeley Growth Study, 49 of 61 were still in the project after 30 years.

The loss in the related studies appears to be more. In the Havighurst study, no direct statement of loss of students is found, but it appears to be less than 20 per cent for a 10-year period. In the Buck study of educational achievement, 80 per cent were still included after 10 years.

Thus, it appears that, although appreciable losses occur, contact can be maintained with most subjects. The loss of respondents is here regarded as a variable which is explainable in terms of the time and money invested in the follow-up, the ingenuity of the researchers, and the rapport established and maintained with the respondents. Thus, loss of respondents is not a unique problem of longitudinal analysis. It is similar to refusals of interviews, failure to locate the person to be interviewed, and nonresponse to mailed questionnaires.

In summary, it can be stated that longitudinal analysis has been almost entirely neglected in family survey research and argued that, in this neglect, a most promising technique for improved family research has been overlooked. [Cf. Ch. 8.]

PUBLIC RELATIONS AND RAPPORT

Public relations and rapport are general problems of survey research in that the research takes the time of the respondent and may at some point often involve information which he hesitates to communicate (or at least he may think that such communication might be involved). Such problems are in no sense peculiar to family research, but there is some reason to believe that the study of family relationships, attitudes, and personality encounters public relations and rapport problems more frequently and with greater intensity than is true of social science research in general.

Rapport Problems

Although rapport and public relations deal with related phenomena—the acceptance of and cooperation with the research project—it is useful to distinguish between the two. Rapport involves the relationship of the researcher or one of his staff to an individual respondent, first to secure his participation and then to obtain data in sufficient detail and without distortion. The principles and techniques for obtaining rapport are discussed in most general methodology texts and in all books devoted to interviewing (see, e.g., Hyman, 1954; Kahn & Carnell, 1957). Since these are discussed in great detail in general sources, it will suffice here to list only a few of the issues involved, with special attention to survey research. The researcher or his staff member must deal with questions such as the following, many of which will occur to his respondents:

1. Can this research be taken at face value? Is it research, or is a salesman concealed behind the clipboard? Am I being investigated personally by the government, a prospective employer, or someone else? Is the research really trying to get some other type of information about me than that which the question seems to ask?

2. Is the research important enough to enough people so that I should invest my time in it? Will it be published and available to the public?

3. Can the problem be researched, or are social phenomena so complex that nothing valid can be produced? Is the researcher competent to deal with the problem?

4. Will personal replies be kept confidential, or will they be published or some nonresearch use be made of them that would be inconvenient or embarrassing? If I am not asked to sign the questionnaire, is there some secret identification?

5. Can the interview or questionnaire be completed in a reasonable length of time? Will there be follow-up interviews or questionnaires which will take more time?

6. Is the subject one of personal interest, or will it be boring, complicated, or obscure so that the process itself will be uninteresting or frustrating?

Such questions underlying rapport confront the researcher at the individual level.

In instances in which the approach is from researchers to individual adults, these and related problems of rapport may be the only ones involved in securing adequate cooperation.[5]

Public Relations Problems

But in studies involving groups of children or others in institutional settings, some person or group of persons must give permission for the research to be conducted. The interaction here is better considered as public relations, since such institutions are finally responsible to and are the concern of the public. The responsible official must not only consider whether he views the research as worth while, but whether his superiors or ultimately the public would believe it to be good use of institutional time and facilities. He may also feel it necessary to evaluate the effect of a possible negative public reaction on his own professional prospects.

In the present discussion, it is assumed that the research project is intrinsically worth while. (It is the writer's feeling that research which is not justified in terms of its anticipated contribution should not be inflicted on the general public.) If the project is both important and well conceived, this can usually be communicated to the responsible official; therefore, it is his anticipation of objections from parents or other categories of the public which is usually the main source of objection to the project, rather than his own personal negative feelings.

The nature of objections of parents and others to survey research has been reported fragmentally as interesting or distressing side comments in the methodology section of research reports. It seems worth while here to propose some reasons for such objections.

Sexual behavior and attitudes. Although questions concerning sexual behavior have been employed successfully, it appears that this phenomenon provokes the most frequent and strongest negative emotions of any subject. [Cf. pp. 616–618.] For example, in Nye's research on delinquency in 1955, two questions concerning sexual behavior provoked considerable discussion, whereas none of those involving stealing or drinking aroused any comment. The matter is complicated by the news potential of the subject. In the above instance, the local newspaper headlined the study as "Little Kinsey Study in ———," although only two items of some 200 dealt with sex.

Enough similar experiences have been reported so that the researcher may expect that sex questions put to high school or younger students will result in the refusal of school authorities to cooperate, or if not that, then protests from parents and possibly others. The most frequent objections have been that such items are construed by adolescents as an endorsement of irregular sexual behavior, may intimate that such behavior is widespread, or the subject may be considered unfamiliar to the respondent. Exposure to questions concerning sex is assumed to encourage sexual misbehavior. Another objection, less likely to be stated, is that if the child had participated in irregular sexual behavior, such behavior might become known in the school and community to the disadvantage of the child or parents.

Therefore, the reasons for employing sex questions with high school populations must be compelling and the defense of such items ready.

Other objectionable items. Income and parent-child questions have frequently provided a basis for objections. The grounds seem to be that they reveal adult behavior which the adults might prefer to have remain secret. Also, parents have sometimes stated that they don't want adolescents to think of their own parents' personal or parental behavior in evaluative terms.

It seems that almost any question can

[5] Public relations occasionally become a source of problems when several individuals in the same social system are interviewed. Since they are in interaction, comments made by one may influence the willingness of others to cooperate. The writer is indebted to Walter Slocum for this observation.

provide the basis for an objection. In one recent survey (Urdal et al., 1963) parents objected to questions concerning occupational aspirations of students.

Motivations for opposing surveys. Opposition may be genuinely based on some of the above objections that the survey is detrimental to the child or the parent. There is no evidence that surveys encourage antisocial behavior, but neither is there evidence that they do not, and, in the absence of evidence, the argument cannot be countered with complete effectiveness. The objection that such parental behavior or information regarding parental behavior might become community knowledge can be countered by elementary precautions concerning the processing of the data.

An emerging problem in schools, as pressures to teach more subjects mount, is the time required for students to complete the questionnaires. The problem is most serious in schools near major universities, but it exists elsewhere, too. A related problem is the interruption of plans of the individual teachers. As more responsibilities are placed on the public schools, school officials can be expected to ask more searching questions about the importance of the research.

More diffuse and difficult problems are posed by a generalized dislike of questionnaires and interviews or, on the more general level, of social science research. The dislike of questionnaires and interviews, per se, is generally a problem only in research directed toward adults themselves. They infrequently have serious objection to the inconvenience that it might cause their children or school officials. This, therefore, is primarily a rapport problem rather than one in public relations.

A generalized hostile attitude toward social science research may be based on the feeling that it is a waste of time, an invasion of privacy (without specifying how it violates privacy), that social scientists are radicals trying to change the *status quo,* on a guilty conscience, or on generalized "free-floating" feelings of frustration and hostility which seek expression in any safe place.

Whatever the reason, this attitude can lead an official to oppose any family research, whatever its nature. In the general public, it represents an attitude which is ready to seize on any item in a study as being harmful, however little objective foundation there may be for such disapproval.

Such generalized negative attitudes, if held by a key official, may block a research project in a given area indefinitely. In a parent or other member of the public, they can lead to noisy objections, to questioning the integrity of the researchers, and may provide material which is picked up and publicized by the local press. Such negative attitudes in the general public need not block a project, but they can be assumed to exist in some proportion of the population, and some plan for dealing with them might be devised as part of the over-all research strategy.

Suggested strategies. In the past, public relations problems have been considered to be primarily to gain acceptance of the project by officials, that is, to convince them personally of the worth of the project. It is believed that this period is coming to an end. Officials are aware of human relations problems and know that the social scientist has research tools with which to attack them. However, as social science becomes more widespread and more important in institutional and political decision-making, it seems to be arousing or creating greater opposition in the general population. Survey researchers must be prepared to cope with this more diffuse type of opposition.

The writer does not pretend to have all of the answers to dealing with such opposition. The following proposals are made to open up the subject and to provoke discussion. It is assumed that generalized negative attitudes toward social science research cannot be changed by changing items on the instrument or by any other limited action. It must be expected that they will exist to some extent in any given community, and so the research must be planned to operate within such a social milieu.

Assuming the presence of some individuals within a community who have negative attitudes toward family research, it is a matter of first priority to have active support within the community. A very effective type of support might come from a lay group with official sanction within the community. For example, a lay group on problems of youth appointed by the local judge can speak with authority for a research project in juvenile delinquency. Such local leadership with a liaison with the local newspaper provides more local power than is likely to be generated by individuals hostile to social science research. In effect, such local leadership speaks positively for the research project, counterbalancing possible negative arguments and influence. Obviously, a situation such as this does not exist everywhere, but there may be an appropriate local group which would be glad to sponsor a project appropriate to their function. It is doubtful that an effective group of this type could be created for the sole purpose of providing support. Genuine local concern and interest appear to be the essential ingredients in effective community support.

Where organized support does not exist, an alternative is complete official support, that is, not only the approval of the immediate official but also of the group who employ him and who are ultimately responsible to the people. For a school official, it is the school board. This is not an easy route, since such officials frequently try to think of all possible objections that might be made by everyone in the county or other unit involved. It may be necessary with such policy boards to stress the positive contributions of the research as justifying positive action. If one attempted to remove everything from the project to which anyone might object, there would be nothing left. Such policy-making boards are not readily accessible to the researcher, and since they are considered to be conservative in outlook, this approach to community support is less attractive than the first.

Some researchers have taken the position that the consent of the official is all that is necessary, since this provides access to the respondents, and if the official is censored locally, that is his hard luck. Such an approach seems unrealistic for several reasons. It is unethical, in that the official who has no personal interest is left to defend the project and take local censure. Beyond that, he is unlikely to cooperate again with that researcher or others in the same general area. Furthermore, he will communicate any negative feelings concerning the project to others who have institutional responsibilities. The researcher (and others identified with him) may find other doors closed as a result of such irresponsible attitudes toward public relation problems.

Certain procedures for maximizing positive local support for research projects have been suggested. It is appropriate to consider, also, measures to minimize negative reactions to family research. Reduction of opposition, however, cannot be equated with its complete elimination. Reduction of negative forces lessens the amount of positive support necessary, but it does not eliminate negative attitudes or the need for positive support for family research.

A first step is the re-examination of the content and organization of the schedule or questionnaire. Items dealing with sexual behavior or attitudes can be expected to provoke opposition. Since numerous descriptive studies of sexual behavior have been made, it may be questioned whether such items for descriptive purposes are useful. Unless sexual items are necessary in the test of hypotheses, they might be eliminated. Overly long and complicated questionnaires and interviews create frustration and hostility.[6] Finally, identifying the respondent may be a sore point. If it can be dispensed with, opposition is likely to be less intense; if not, an adequate coding

[6] A former colleague, Prodipto Roy, described a technique for shortening data-collecting instruments, namely, to ask whether each item (a) was important for describing the phenomenon, (b) was needed as a control variable, or (c) was necessary for testing one of the stated hypotheses. If the answer to all of these was "no," the item was dropped (personal communication).

system which permits removal of the signature from the questionnaire would reduce opposition on this score.

A second strategy for minimizing negative reactions is the elimination of compulsory participation. In early studies employing students as respondents, children were given no choice but to complete the questionnaires (or, at least, pretend to do so). Students occasionally turned in blank questionnaires or completely invalid ones, but, in principle, all participated. This compulsory participation has provoked opposition from parents, and, presumably as a consequence, from teachers. Some parents have also taken the position that they should be permitted to forbid the participation of their children.

Such voluntary participation will have to be accepted by family researchers and to do so gracefully (and "voluntarily") may be expected to disarm some opposition to the project. At the same time, the elimination of some of the respondents poses problems in data interpretation. Efforts will have to be made to persuade all of those in the sample to cooperate voluntarily in order to keep nonresponse at a minimum. When parents are given an opportunity to hold their children out of the projects, the burden of the negative decision can be placed on them. Under such circumstances, the child of the indifferent parent will be in rather than outside the project.

To sum up, the position has been taken that rapport and public relations are crucial aspects of family survey research. Rapport is involved in the direct relations between researcher and interviewer. Ordinarily, interviews and mailed questionnaires have rapport problems, but not public relations problems. Good public relations are crucial in projects involving an intermediary official between researcher and subjects, an official who must agree and perhaps facilitate the project and who is susceptible to pressure from the public.

It is suggested that all communities in which there is some acquaintance with social research have some latent opposition to it. Such opposition must be overcome by drawing on positive attitudes toward social science research and by disarming opposition to the extent that it is centered on the project. Some opposition is believed to be grounded in political, economic, or religious conservatism or in "free-floating" hostility which seeks some object for expression. It cannot be disarmed but must be neutralized by equal or more influential positive forces.

To date, public relations strategy has received little attention in methodological literature. If techniques employed and results obtained were reported regularly and fully, this aspect of research operations would be advanced greatly, especially if failures were reported as well as successes.

TIME PERSPECTIVE

It is the writer's feeling that family (and other) sociologists are spending too little time on a given project. There is a tendency to count publications as though all were of equal value—at least those published in a given journal. This has led to giving minimum attention to a project or to any part of it. Some of the more prolific writers publish 10 or more articles in a year. These are of acceptable quality by present standards, or they would not be published. The question is whether these researchers might not contribute more to the discipline by devoting the same amount of time to half or a third that number of papers.

Individually, and as a discipline, we seem to be running to catch up with someone, or to reach some self-imposed goal. This frequently leads to poorly conceived problems, oversight of previous research and theory, questionable measurement, inadequate analysis, and complete neglect of the use of the findings to revise existing theoretical assumptions or to suggest new directions for its development. Lack of time, and to some extent lack of other resources, appears to be the explanation for the neglect of longitudinal studies of family life, a method which would seem to offer opportunity for the most complete utilization of technique and theory presently available to researchers.

Hopefully, the next decade may bring to family sociologists what they most need: time to read, to look, to talk, and to ponder.

REFERENCES

Axelson, L. J. A study of the marital adjustment and role definitions of husbands of working and non-working wives. Unpublished doctoral dissertation, Washington State Univer., 1963.

Bates, J. Position, role, and status: a reformulation of concepts. *Soc. Forces,* 1956, 34, 313–321.

Buck, R. C., & Bible, B. L. Educational attainment among Pennsylvania rural youth. *Bull.* No. 686. University Park: Pennsylvania State Univer., 1961.

Burgess, E. W., & Wallin, P. *Engagement and marriage.* Philadelphia: Lippincott, 1953.

Calhoun, J. B. Population density and social pathology. *Sci. Amer.,* 1962, 206 (2), 139–148.

Caudle, Ann H. Financial management practice of employed and non-employed wives. Unpublished doctoral dissertation, Florida State Univer., 1962.

Christensen, H. T., & Philbrick, R. E. Family size as a factor in the marital adjustments of college couples. *Amer. sociol. Rev.,* 1952, 17, 306–312.

Devereux, E. C., Jr. Evaluation of theory pertaining to family research. Paper read at Nat. Counc. on Fam. Relat., Storrs, Conn., 1962.

Farber, B., & Blackman, L. S. Marital role tensions and number and sex of children. *Amer. sociol. Rev.,* 1956, 21, 596–601.

Feldman, H., & Meyerowitz, J. H. The personal relations of primiparous couples. Paper read at Nat. Counc. on Fam. Relat., Storrs, Conn., 1962.

Goode, W. J. *After divorce.* Glencoe, Ill.: Free Press, 1956.

Goode, W. J. The theoretical importance of love. *Amer. sociol. Rev.,* 1959, 24, 38–47.

Gross, N., Mason, W. S., & McEachern, A. W. *Exploration in role analysis: studies in the school superintendency role.* New York: Wiley, 1958.

Havighurst, R. J., Bowman, P. H., Liddle, G. P., Mathews, C. V., & Pierce, J. V. *Growing up in River City.* New York: Wiley, 1962.

Hill, R. *Families under stress.* New York: Harper, 1949.

Hill, R., Stycos, J. M., & Back, K. *The family and population control.* Chapel Hill: Univer. of North Carolina Press, 1959.

Hyman, H. Interviewing in social research. Glencoe, Ill.: Free Press, 1954.

Jones, H. E. Personality development in children. In I. Iscoe & H. W. Stevenson (Eds.), *Personality development in children: papers by Harold E. Jones (and others).* Austin: Univer. of Texas Press, 1960.

Kahn, R. L., & Carnell, C. F. *The dynamics of interviewing: theory, techniques, and cases.* New York: Wiley, 1957.

Merton, R. K. *Social theory and social structure.* Glencoe, Ill.: Free Press, 1957.

Merton, R. K., Broom, L., & Cottrell, L. S., Jr. *Sociology today.* New York: Basic Books, 1959.

Merton, R. K., Fisk, Marjorie, & Kendall, Patricia. *The focused interview.* New York: Columbia Univer., Bureau of Applied Social Research, 1952.

Merton, R. K., & Lazarsfeld, P. *Continuities in social research: studies in the scope and method of "the American soldier."* Glencoe, Ill.: Free Press, 1950.

Moss, J. J., & Gingles, Ruby. The relationship of personality to the incidence of early marriage. *Marr. & fam. Living,* 1959, 21, 373–377.

Nye, F. I. *Family relationships and delinquent behavior.* New York: Wiley, 1958.

Nye, F. I., & Bayer, A. E. Some recent trends in family research. *Soc. Forces,* 1963, 41, 290–301.

Nye, F. I., & Hoffman, Lois W. *The employed mother in America.* Chicago: Rand McNally, 1963.

Parsons, T. *The social system.* Glencoe, Ill.: Free Press, 1951.

Parsons, T., & Bales, R. F., with Olds, J., Zelditch, M., Jr., & Slater, P. *Family, socialization and interaction process.* Glencoe, Ill.: Free Press, 1955.

Schellenberg, J. A., & Bee, L. S. A re-examination of the theory of complementary needs in mate selection. *Marr. & fam. Living*, 1960, 22, 227–232.

Selltiz, C., Jahoda, Marie, Deutsch, M., & Cook, S. W. *Research methods in social relations*. New York: Holt, 1959.

Sewell, W. H. Infant training and the personality of the child. *Amer. J. Sociol.*, 1952, 58, 150–159.

Sewell, W. H. Some observations on theory testing. *Rural Sociol.*, 1956, 21, 1–12.

Sewell, W. H., Mussen, P. H., & Harris, C. W. Relationships among child training practices. *Amer. sociol. Rev.*, 1955, 20, 137–148.

Slocum, W., Empey, L. T., & Swanson, H. S. Increasing response to questionnaires and structured interviews. *Amer. sociol. Rev.*, 1956, 21, 221–225.

Stycos, J. M. *Family and fertility in Puerto Rico*. New York: Columbia Univer. Press, 1955.

Terman, L. M. Predicting marriage failure from test scores. *Marr. & fam. Living*, 1950, 12, 51–54.

Urdal, L., et al. *Dropouts: an analysis of personal variables within the school situation*. Olympia, Wash.: Superintendent of Public Instruction, 1963.

Waller, W. & Hill, R. *The family: a dynamic interpretation*. New York: Dryden Press, 1951.

Wallis, W. A., & Roberts, H. V. *Statistics, a new approach*. Glencoe, Ill.: Free Press, 1956.

Westoff, C. F., et al. *Family growth in metropolitan America*. Princeton: Princeton Univer. Press, 1961.

Wetzel, Rita J. An investigation of students' personality characteristics and their modification following a marriage course. Unpublished doctoral dissertation, Florida State Univer., 1962.

Winch, R. *Mate selection*. New York: Harper, 1958.

Zetterberg, H. L. *On theory and verification in sociology*. (2nd ed.) Totawa, N.J.: Bedminster Press, 1963.

Zimmerman, C. C. *Family and civilization*. New York: Harper, 1947.

CHAPTER **8**   Experimental
Research[1]

MARVIN B. SUSSMAN
Western Reserve University

Recently, 10 people were asked (this was a convenient, not a random, sample) to state what came to their minds when they heard the words "laboratory or experimental research." All described with slight variations a picture of men and women working on "guinea pigs" in a clean and sterile laboratory with equipment and materials that suggested precision, accuracy, measurement, and other controls usually associated with experimentation in the physical sciences. This imagery is probably almost universal.

When probed further concerning research in the behavioral sciences and specifically in the area of marriage and the family, the individuals' responses became diffuse and reflected the conclusion one reaches after reviewing the literature: that there is an insufficient use of experimental techniques and procedures in studies of marriage and the family. From a review of the basic books on research methods in the social sciences, one finds that very little

space is devoted to "laboratory or experimental research."

TERMS

The reader by this time may be confused by the introduction of such terms as *laboratory, experiment,* and *research*. It becomes important, therefore, at the beginning of this inquiry to define terms and to relate these definitions to the topic under discussion in this chapter.

Research is systematic investigation into a subject in order to discover new knowledge, principles, and facts. Research implies formulation of significant questions and/or appropriate hypotheses to be tested in order to derive facts and principles and new knowledge.

Design is the arrangement of all conditions necessary to undertake research successfully. These arrangements include techniques, procedures, and methods for collecting and analyzing data most efficiently. The term *research design* is commonly used to differentiate between the more usual definition of design as a preliminary sketch or fashion artistically or skill-

[1] Acknowledgement is made to Lawrence E. Riley, former research assistant in the Department of Sociology at Western Reserve University, for his assistance in the development of this chapter.

275

fully conceived and the notion of design as a plan for the successful achievement of a research aim.

Methodology is a system of logical principles upon which a science is based and from which are derived the procedures and techniques utilized in research. McKinney (1957) has defined methodology as "the principles of organized investigation—the 'norms' by which procedures and techniques are selected and articulated" (p. 186). *Procedure* includes specific techniques. It is "a general form or system of operating investigation." *Technique* is "a specific fact-finding or manipulating operation adapted from the basic procedure" (p. 187).

The difference between procedure and technique may be illustrated by the following example. It is decided to use a procedure essentially statistical for a study of the relationship between early age at marriage and dependency. Terms and concepts are defined, the problem is well formulated and articulated, and specific hypotheses are postulated. The techniques for utilizing the statistical procedure are dependent upon the nature and scope of the problem. In this instance, a large number of cases is required. Records on age at marriage, place of residence at marriage, unemployment status of spouse, etc., are studied for a specific population over a given time period. The technique of record linkage developed by Christensen (1958) may be used. Another technique would be to interview a sample from a universe of sufficient size to permit adequate utilization of the statistical procedure. Several techniques may be employed to satisfy the statistical procedure used for the study of the relationship between early age at marriage and dependency.

Experiment is manipulation of conditions by the researcher in order to ascertain the causal relationships of *X* and *Y* variables.

Laboratory, according to Bijou and Baer (1960), has no essential place in research. It is an area of physical space where causal factors are controlled by manipulation and

conditions for studying causality are established more easily than elsewhere. Outside of these characteristics, the laboratory has no special features.

"LABORATORY RESEARCH"

The methodology of science encompasses at least five general procedures: (a) the statistical, (b) the experimental, (c) the typological, (d) the historical, and (e) the case study (McKinney, 1957). This scheme is broad and yet inclusive enough to contain the basic procedures of any methodology.

In most instances, laboratory research is identified as an advanced technique of the experimental procedure in which there is control and manipulation of relevant variables. The laboratory situation is a contrived one, where the conditions of the research are regulated so that an independent variable can be manipulated and so that the effects of this manipulation upon a dependent variable can then be observed. Generally, two groups are used, with manipulation occurring in one group and not in the other. Leaving one group unmanipulated constitutes control. Measures are made on both groups at designated times in relation to manipulation. A change in a dependent variable resulting from manipulation should be readily observable (Bijou & Baer, 1960).

A common form of manipulation in the laboratory setting is the introduction of a stimulus which changes a condition or state of being or situation for one group, while a second group remains unchanged because the stimulus is withheld from it. In this instance, the laboratory conditions for both groups are identical, and both groups are similar in characteristics. The difference between them is that one receives a stimulus and the other remains unstimulated. Campbell (1957) has stressed that manipulation and control are two basic characteristics of a true experimental design.

The introduction of the term *laboratory* and the phrase *laboratory research* has added very little to the development of experimental research in the social sciences. *Laboratory* conveys the image expressed earlier by the 10 respondents, an emulation of the conditions, methods, and procedures of the physical sciences. It reflects that period in the development of sociology in the 1930's when it moved from a social-progress orientation to an empirical one. The empirical sociology then conceived was to be a scientific venture in which a facsimile of the methods of the natural and physical sciences was required (Sussman, 1963).

Ogburn (1934) equated the experimental method with pure laboratory procedures. Since human beings could not be controlled as inanimate objects in the laboratory, he concluded that the experimental method was unusable in the study of human behavior. He asked if the social sciences would ever become a science without the laboratory.

The identification of experimental procedure with the physical laboratory is based upon a limited conception of the nature of experimentation. In this view, the experimental method presupposes creation of conditions of the laboratory type, in which reality is re-created, stimuli are introduced either singly or in combination, relevant variables are rigidly controlled, measurements obtained by instruments are available to gauge the effect of stimuli, and experiments are repeated with slight variations and recombinations of factors in order to determine the efficacy of the relationship originally found (Greenwood, 1945).

This narrow view of the nature of the experimental method and its identification with the laboratory of the physical and natural scientist is losing popularity among some students. It appears to be less and less required for or appropriate to the study of phenomena which concern the social sciences. Experiments, it will be recalled, involve manipulation of one group through the introduction of a stimulus, while a second group remains unmanipulated because the stimulus is withheld. The manipulated—i.e., stimulus-receiving group—is called the experimental group, while the nonstimulated group is called the control group. There is need to have a control group or other controls in order to study cause-effect or producer-product relationships. In an earlier period of science and statistics, when statistical analysis was relatively undeveloped compared to methods available today, it was appropriate and necessary to conduct only laboratory types of studies involving manipulation. Statistical know-how at that time was limited to simple tests of correlation and association. Today, in statistical analysis, one can use complicated techniques for handling multiple factors (Gee, 1950).

Paralleling the development of statistical theory and method is a new technology of computer systems, which permits the manipulation of complex sets of data and the further development of statistical methods. As a consequence of these developments, the social scientist now can approximate the conditions of control found in the laboratory type of study without using a research laboratory as such. He now can use advanced statistical procedures to meet the criteria of control. Consequently, to conceive of manipulation as the only method of control and therefore as necessary to the laboratory type of study is no longer tenable (Ackoff, 1953).

Nevertheless, although statistical controls permit a variety of experimental designs, the focus of this chapter is on laboratory types of experiments in which manipulation and randomization are principal processes.

EXPERIMENTAL RESEARCH

Experimental research in the social sciences is concerned with causality—that is, with the cause-effect relationships of phenomena. Given a group of individuals in a condition or situation of X, stimulus (S) is introduced which is presumed to affect or produce Y. Y is different from X but dependent upon X. Y is referred to as a dependent variable, while X is an independent one. If stimulus (S) is known to have an effect upon X to cause or produce Y, and if this relationship is established with appropriate controls and measurements, the investigator is thus brought one step closer to the development of his science.

The Nature of Science

The assumption of a science is that seemingly unrelated and disparate events and facts are logically organized into orderly patterns. Science is a way of ordering events into lawful patterns of relationships. The uniformity and lawfulness of events and facts are assumed, and the task of the scientist is to discover these laws. Bronowski (1953) has suggested that the scientist observes events and struggles to organize them in his mind so that they have order, consistency, and uniformity. A collection of facts which are ordered, consistent, and uniform provides scientific laws from which it is possible to make predictions. The goal of science is prediction and control based upon lawful relationships of events.

Prediction, as pointed out by Bachrach (1962), cannot be based on absolute certainty, since it is virtually impossible to have knowledge of all the variables operating in a given situation. Predictions are couched in probabilities. What is the probability that X, given stimulus (S), will produce Y? What are the chances, if X is given stimulus (S_1), that it will produce or not produce Y? Prediction, therefore, is a forecast within a known range of accuracy (with constant attempts to reduce the range of uncertainty) that under a lawful ordering of events a particular event will occur. Experimentation is the principal method for improving the accuracy of prediction and therefore is basic to the development of a scientific sociology of the family.

The Research Design

Research designs varying from the "shotgun" (Stouffer, 1950) to the four-group design (Solomon, 1949) and the posttest-only control group design (Campbell & Stanley, 1963) have been described by a variety of authors (Campbell, 1957; Campbell, 1959; Campbell, 1960; Chapin, 1947; Chapin, 1955; Edwards, 1960; Kempthorne, 1952; Kempthorne, 1961; Lindquist, 1953; Stanley, 1961a; Stanley, 1961b). Every one of these designs has been used by the family researcher. If one conceives of research designs arrayed on a continuum ranging from the shotgun or one-case study at one end to the experimental with controls at the other end, one concludes that the bulk of family research is at the shotgun pole. The reasons for this condition are the existence of a set of factors which confound the validity of good experimental designs, and of special problems confronting the researcher who uses the family and its members as units for study.

Campbell and Stanley (1963) have delineated the major factors which jeopardize the validity of experimental designs. An exposition of these factors indicates the general problems facing the scientist in undertaking quality experimental research, as well as those problems of special significance for the family researcher.

The investigator is concerned with the validity of his research. He begins with the basic question of whether his observations $O_1, O_2, O_3, \ldots, O_N$ actually occur. In experimental studies, the concern is whether changes in X are results of the introduction

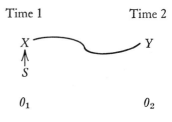

Fig. 1.

of stimulus S. Schematically, this is shown in Fig. 1. The crucial question of internal validity of the experimental design is whether O_1-O_2 differences are due to S or to some confounding variable. No experiment has meaning unless internal validity is established.

External validity is concerned with representativeness of experimental findings (Campbell & Stanley, 1963). Can the results of experiments be generalized to other populations? Can one expect, under appropriate conditions with another sample, to obtain the same difference O_1-O_2 as the result of stimulus S?

Most family researchers are concerned primarily with the internal validity of their studies, because, unless internal validity is established, it is fruitless to consider external validity. External validity is dependent upon internal validity, which, therefore, is the *sine qua non* of all experiments in family sociology.

An examination of different research designs used in family research provides the basis for discussing the factors which jeopardize the validity of findings derived from such undertakings. It is axiomatic to state that a particular problem requires a specific research design. Still, many researchers are unaware that properly conceptualized problems must be fitted to appropriate designs, and that each design must be assessed for the validity of prospective research findings. Some designs are more adequate than others in meeting the conditions of a valid study. Costs in energy and money, accuracy of measurements, and relevance of findings must be weighed in the selection of a particular design.

FREQUENTLY USED NONEXPERIMENTAL DESIGNS

The "Shotgun" Type of Design

The most frequently used pre-experimental design in family research is the study of a single group at a single given period of time. Stouffer (1950) has referred to this design as the "shotgun" type, shown in Fig. 2. Its chief utility is to obtain a "handle" on a problem as an exploratory or descriptive effort. Still, in an overwhelming

Fig. 2.

number of one-group, single-time studies, inferences and conclusions of existing relationships suggest that differences exist between the X and some other unknown group, or that conditions found within X, such as dating practices among high-school seniors, express the actual state of dating. One is never certain of what the researcher has found, unless some check is made on the absoluteness of the reported information. One principal method is to make comparisons among subgroups. Thus, one improvement in a single-group, one-time study design is to separate the study population into two or more groups in order to make comparisons. In a study of dating practices, differences found by social class, age, intelligence, and other factors give more meaning and provide bases for stating the findings of the one-shot study.

The Group-Comparison Design

Comparison among groups is another frequently used design in family research (Fig. 3). Deliberate selection of groups to be compared prior to beginning the undertaking differentiates this type of design from the single-group, one-time study. Such a design approaches but never quite achieves the results of a controlled study. The best one can achieve is correlation among selected variables. Correlation analysis often provides data on relationships which can be

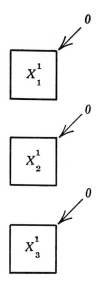

Fig. 3.

used in the formulation of hypotheses and then tested with more experimental designs.

In an area of inquiry devoid of exploratory and descriptive studies, the usual pattern is for the investigator to begin with the single-group and group-comparison models and to proceed to a more experimental design. Hill, Stycos, and Back (1959) used a progressive set of designs in a study concerned with factors accounting for the success or failure of Puerto Rican families to regulate their fertility in line with goals regarding desirable family size. Nye, in Chapter 7 of this Handbook, details the methods and problems of field studies, of which the Puerto Rican study just referred to is one type. Therefore, discussion is limited to illustrating progression in the selection of research designs.

Three basic designs were used in the Puerto Rican study. The first, identified as the exploratory or "stage of reconnaissance," as distinct from the one-group, one-time study, was used to look at a variety of variables believed to be related to fertility. Case studies were made, techniques of interviewing developed, interview schedules formulated, and hypotheses prepared.

The second design was a group-compari-

son one, sometimes identified as a cross-sectional design. A survey was conducted after instruments and techniques were developed and pretested, interviewers were trained in the administration of a questionnaire requiring probing in matters of family planning, and samples were drawn from a defined universe.

The researchers were unable to conduct a national survey on birth-control use and knowledge from which to draw comparison samples because of limitations of funds and staff. They were especially interested in studying a lower-class population, since this class group had the greatest difficulty in controlling family size, made up a large proportion of the population of the island, and—as the authors reported from Hatt's research—had the greatest discrepancy between ideal and actual family size (Hill, Stycos, & Back, 1959, p. 36).

The initial sample of lower-class respondents was selected from a population attending outpatient departments of nine regional health centers. The criteria of selection were that the couples be of proven fertility, live together, married five to 20 years, and have less than a sixth-grade education. The sample was stratified by rural-urban residence, whether contraception was practiced currently or in the past, and length of marriage. A shortage of cases in the "user" and "quitter" contraception categories required sampling of individuals in the premarital clinics of the health centers. Cases lost because of incomplete addresses and records were replaced from a reserve sample. The design used is shown in Fig. 4.

This design permits comparisons between groups of different fertility control states according to length of marriage and type of residence. Tests for association were made between these and other variables such as age, attitudes and preference regarding family size, intrafamily communication, and the like. The results indicate likely associations of factors relevant to fertility control and planning, but in no way do the findings establish the veracity of these re-

No. of Comparison Groups	Fertility Control Category	*Urban* By Years Married	*Rural* By Years Married
X^1_1	Never Users	5 – 9 10 – 14 15 – 20	5 – 9 10 – 14 15 – 20
X^1_2	Active Users	5 – 9 10 – 14 15 – 20	5 – 9 10 – 14 15 – 20
X^1_3	Quitters	5 – 9 10 – 14 15 – 20	5 – 9 10 – 14 15 – 20
X^1_4	Sterilized	5 – 9 10 – 14 15 – 20	5 – 9 10 – 14 15 – 20

Fig. 4. Comparison Groups with Stratified Characteristics.

lationships. How much of the difference between X^1_1, X^1_2, . . ., X^1_N groups on dependent variables such as preference regarding family size can be attributed to experience in a given clinic or to attributes which led each individual to seek out the particular clinic? Differential recruitment of respondents made it impossible to determine whether differences in dependent variables may have occurred regardless of differentials in clinical experience.

Establishing the causality of relationships such as these requires clearly formulated hypotheses before the research commences, with exposition of independent, dependent, and intervening variables; random selection of respondents; and controls able to account for variables which may confound the validity of the findings. The establishment of association among variables is not be confused with the establishment of a cause-effect relationship. For example, is use or nonuse of contraceptive devices a result of particular attitudes about family goals, or a consequence of more generalized attitudes and values? The best one can obtain from the group-comparison design is the discovery of an association of variables—a preliminary step to the formulation of hypotheses and to the testing of these hypotheses in a design with adequate controls. Several such designs are described later in this chapter.[2]

The Before-and-After Design

A third type of design, which has several experimental features but does not quite make the grade as a controlled experiment, is the before-and-after design involving just one group (Fig. 5). In this design, observations O_1 are made at the beginning of the

[2] The researchers in the Puerto Rican study on fertility control also used a quasi-experimental design when dealing with a problem concerned with the most efficacious educational program related to fertility planning for different types of respondents. They used matching of subjects, testing in order to complete quotas, and random assignment of subjects.

Time 1   Time 2

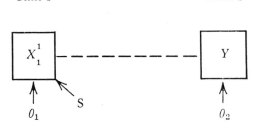

Fig. 5.

study; after this, stimulus S is introduced; then observations O_2 are made on the same group at time 2. The difference between O_1 and O_2 is then believed to be caused by the introduction of stimulus S. The before-and-after design represents one kind of longitudinal research, as does the controlled experiment. [Cf. pp. 247–249; 368–387; pp. 984–985.]

Evaluations of programs aimed to improve family life are usually desired by educators or at least by their critics. Such evaluations provide guidelines for changing curricula and approaches to education and for determining the worth of specific programs. Frequent use is made of the before-and-after design in such evaluations.

The following hypothetical example illustrates. During "Family Life Week" in one community, a family service agency decided to take advantage of the expressed community interest in family welfare by undertaking a before-and-after study of knowledge and attitudes toward family stability. The general aims were to assess the group programs in family life education conducted by the agency and to use findings, such as lack of knowledge or increment of knowledge, to interest the members of the community in participating further in the program.

Specific information was obtained on knowledge of family interpersonal processes and attitudes toward rearing of children. The staff considered these two variables to be importantly related to family stability. In the selection of these variables and construction of a questionnaire, the investi-

gators made a number of a priori judgments of what was important to the achievement and maintenance of family stability. Questions concerning the significance of the reported information for family stability were considered irrelevant. Important as these are, the investigators focused more on effecting change according to their own criteria of factors affecting family stability than upon establishing through empirical research the relatedness of particular knowledge and attitudes to family stability.

The main concern was to discover changes in level of information and attitudes believed to be important for family stability after introducing an educational program, stimulus S. The design resembles an input-output one commonly found in systems analysis. Members of a couples club of the agency were asked at the beginning of their weekly meeting to complete a form, giving "yes" and "no" responses to questions which measured the level of correct knowledge and proper attitudes regarding family stability. Following this administration, a panel discussion was conducted with staff experts of the agency serving as leaders. Problems of and prospects for family stability were the topics under discussion. Pamphlets were distributed, and each couple was urged to discuss between themselves the materials which supplied knowledge and appropriate attitudes for effecting family stability. Staff members indicated that they were available for consultation after the meeting and all during the week until the next meeting.

The input was a total effort in communication of knowledge and experience in order to effect an output of family stability. One week later, at the next meeting of the club, the tests previously used were readministered. The differences noted between O_1 and O_2 for the group X were found to be statistically significant. At O_2 observations made one week after the experiment, the group proved to have higher levels of knowledge and correct attitudes than before the experience. The conclusion was drawn that the experiment was a success. It indicated to the agency staff that group discussions, pamphlets, presentation of the facts, and similar educational endeavors would produce desired results and therefore justify these efforts.

It may be said that this hypothetical study is too contrived to be found in the real world. The reader must reach his own conclusion. The form of this presentation is deliberate, because it serves to demonstrate the variables which confound the validity of research findings and illustrates clearly that this before-and-after design involving just one group is not an experimental one.[3] Alternative explanations of findings are equally possible because of the lack of control of invalidating variables in this design.

FACTORS RELATED TO VALIDITY OF EXPERIMENTAL RESEARCH DESIGNS

Twelve factors jeopardizing the validity of various experimental designs have been outlined by Campbell and Stanley (1963). Eight pertain to internal and four to external validity. The internal factors are concerned with the question of whether the introduction of a stimulus causes some effect upon dependent variables. As explained above, internal validity is concerned with those factors which may produce "no difference" in a particular experimental treatment of a problem. External validity is related to questions of generalizability. Its principal concern is with the general applicability of findings from experimental research for other populations. Internal validity, at the moment, is more important than external, because if internal validity cannot be established for an experimental study, it is fruitless to talk about the generalizability of findings to other populations. [Cf. Straus' discussion of validity, pp. 364-368.]

---

[3] The same can be said of the one-group, one-time design and the group-comparison design described previously; both are nonexperimental.

Internal Validity

Eight variables relevant to the internal validity of experimental studies are: (a) history, (b) maturation, (c) testing, (d) instrumentation, (e) regression, (f) selection, (g) mortality, and (h) interaction of selection and maturation (Campbell & Stanley, 1963).

History and its control. History refers to those events which occur to samples after the introduction of a stimulus and between the times when the first and second measurements are made, and whether these events effect a change in lieu of the experimental stimulus. In the above-mentioned before-and-after study on effecting family stability through a crash program of education, it would be difficult to determine if differences between O_1 and O_2 were the result of the group sessions, pamphlets, consultation, and other educational strategies, or whether they resulted from the publicity connected with Family Life Week. This latter provides an equally plausible alternative hypothesis.

The effects of history are best controlled in such experiments when the time between O_1 and O_2 is very short, such as several hours. In the family stability project, retesting on the same day after the introduction of the stimulus would have controlled for the effects of history upon O_1 and O_2 differences. Still, in many family research projects such as the one described, the stimuli being introduced are far more complex and varied than is the single stimulus traditional with learning experimentation in psychology. The lesson to be learned is that, when possible, one should design simply and test for the effects of only one experimental variable at a time. But the wisdom of this does not modify the condition that learning complex systems of knowledge and changing encrusted attitudes takes a longer period of time than a few hours. Integration of knowledge and experience may be required before the necessary change in family behavior favoring stability can be produced.

Therefore, controlling for the effects of history by shortening the time between the test-retest period in projects concerned with cumulative and involved learning processes may be an error of magnitude equal to leaving the effects of history uncontrolled.

The biasing effects of history raise an additional problem of controlling for events which occur during an experiment. The order of presentation of stimuli, and extraneous and unintended happenings such as laughter, noise, or discussion while completing the tests, may contaminate the effects of stimulus S. This would be particularly important if more than one couples group had been studied in the family stability project.

The ideal condition required for control of "internal" events is a laboratory type of setting such as is used in the physical sciences. In family research, such settings are difficult to establish. Nevertheless, the investigator should insist upon and hope to obtain as complete control of the entire experimental situation as is possible.

Control of the experimental situation or process should not be confused with the use of control groups in experimental research. Control of the research process means having established and maintained the conditions under which a stimulus S is introduced and tested for its effect upon X to produce Y as measured by the difference between O_1 and O_2. The inability to control the research process as the result of confounding internal events (history) makes it virtually impossible to assess the strength or power of the stimulus S variable and how much of its power is vitiated by these confounding events (Deutsch, 1949; Festinger, 1953). The following is an illustration of this problem.

In a recent study concerned with the factors affecting the behavior of diabetic children, conditions and controls were established for the introduction of stimulus variables which were being studied for their effects upon behavior. The laboratory was established in a camp where the children participated in the usual program of camp activities. This camp differed from most others in one respect: the researchers were given control over the scheduling of activities during the period of the study. The study design was so conceived that the children performed all of the usual camp activities, but in a sequence determined by the researchers. This control over the order of activities was to permit introduction of S variables and to guarantee the conditions for carrying out an experimental study (Sussman & Weil 1960; Weil & Sussman, 1961).

Soon after the study commenced, the researchers discovered that the conditions for undertaking a study with controls, providing for the proper introduction of the S variable and for maintaining this variable's power, were not being met. At one stage in the study, boys in two cabins were given verbal instruction on an impending competition between them. They were to participate in a series of games and activities of skill called "the Camp Olympics." Members of the winning cabin were to receive very desirable rewards. The theoretical questions were concerned with the methods of organization used by these children to achieve victory in the competition. It was important to assess how the leadership utilized the group structure. Observations were to be made on the reactions of cabin members to success or failure in achieving this goal and the consequent effects of success or failure on the maintenance of control of their diabetes.

The two counselors assigned to these cabins were instructed that their roles would be as "consultants" rather than leaders. Since the study was on group structure and leadership and the effects of group interaction upon each boy's behavior and medical control of his diabetes, it was imperative that the group be permitted to function without an adult leading it. The counselor's task was to facilitate the achievement of the goals of each cabin after goals were formulated and courses of action effected by the children themselves. Counselors were instructed repeatedly to help where and when the boys were unable to accomplish what they set out to do. But under no circumstances were they to plan the program and direct the boys. They were to be the advisors and consultants.

In spite of repeated warnings to the counselors, confounding events were inadvertently introduced into this experimental situation. The two counselors were unable to maintain a consultant role and entered actively into planning and strategy sessions with their respective groups in preparation for the impending competition. Their behavior would have been inconsequential as an extraneous variable if the study had been concerned principally with the effects of success or failure in group competition upon control of diabetes—provided the counselors became involved to the same degree and in the same manner in their respective groups. But they participated unevenly and used such different techniques to incite their groups that even the relationship between competition in group activities and medical control of diabetes could not be studied. The counselors had internalized the goals and norms of the cabin subcultures so completely—a most laudable procedure for counselors in a camp uninvolved in research— that they "forgot" they were in a study. The strength of the introduced experimental S variable was unknown, because the counselors' precipitous behavior contaminated and dispersed the strength of the experimental variable in this situation.

The camp had been conceived by the researchers to be an ideal laboratory, since it seemed to provide unlimited possibilities to institute and maintain control of the research process. The possibilities may be present, but often they cannot be realized.

The lesson learned is that conditions for maintaining controls and introduction of experimental variables must be assured in order to give credence to findings derived from such studies. If the manipulation of the S variable is hindered in any significant way by extraneous events, it is more prudent to discontinue than to continue the study. The bias resulting from unintended events can be described, but not measured for its effect upon dependent variables.

The effects of history are best controlled in a design in which experimental and control groups are used, selection for member-

Selection	Time 1	Time 2	Type of Group
Random	X	Y	Experimental
	S		
Random	X_1	Y_1	Control
	O_1	O_2	

Fig. 6. Random-Selection Control Group Design.

ship in these groups is based upon random selection, and samples are taken from the same population. Both the experimental and control groups experience the same exposure to events in the cultural milieu and have the same probability of being affected by these events. The use of randomization in the selection of members for the experimental and control groups is predicated on the assumption that extenuating events operate on the dependent variable somewhat independent of the cause-effect ($X \sim Y$) relationship being studied.

Even with these improvements in design and technique, the similarity of conditions must be established in order to minimize the effect of internal events upon the power or strength of stimulus variable S. Members of each group are randomly selected and a stimulus is given to one group and withheld from the second. Observations are made, and the differences between O_1 and O_2 are attributed to the S variable. In the hypothetical family stability project, if this experimental design had been used as illustrated in Fig. 6, the historical events during Family Life Week could have been assessed for their effects upon the Y or dependent variable and for their relationship to the S

variable. One would anticipate that if the events during Family Life Week created an effect, it would have had an equal effect upon both groups. The "family treatment program" S, given to the experimental group X, should have created a greater change in Y compared to Y_1, since X_1 remained untreated. The effects of Family Life Week publicity on the dependent variables Y and Y_1 were independent of the cause-effect relationship introduced by S, as the result of randomization in the selection of membership for the two groups.

Maturation. Maturation refers to the individual's growth in physical and social competencies, a growth which occurs independently of specific events. In a family, one witnesses the growth of a child's awareness of self, roles of others, perception, sensitivity to phenomena, and utilization of skills. Maturation occurs with the passage of time and can be easily confounded with the S variable.

It is conceivable that results of maturation may be attributed to the introduction of S in a before-and-after study design in which a control group and the random assignment of respondents are absent. In studies on child development in which a control group is not used, behavior may result as a consequence of maturation—which is independent of the stimulus but which may be attributed to it. The child performed as he did because he was "ready" for the next step. He put together the bits and pieces of knowledge and experience of everyday living and remitted spontaneously.

Maturation as a confounding variable is adequately handled when a control group is included in the design and randomization of subjects occurs. It is particularly important to consider the effects of maturation in longitudinal studies, where systematic measures are made over long periods of time.

Testing. The administration of a test to a group creates an effect difficult to measure when the group is retested, unless a control group is used. Tests are devices for learning, and on a second test the respondent usually improves his score. In areas of social

disapprobation, such as race attitudes, the direction of the results is related to the conditions under which the test is presented. Prejudiced persons who can express their views under the veil of anonymity will exhibit higher prejudice scores; when less protected, they may present socially approved responses (Rankin & Campbell, 1955). And repeated testing for intelligence and achievement produces higher scores, a significant illustration of testing as a learning device (Cane & Heim, 1950).

Stanley and Campbell (1963) have indicated that a test introduced as a measurement may be functioning as a stimulus. This condition is known as the reactive effect of a test. It is well understood among medical researchers that measurements can easily be regarded by patients as part of the treatment process and therefore as therapeutic agents. In family research, equipment used as part of measurement procedures, such as tape recorders, may function as a stimulus. Since measurement can be confused with stimuli, all tests must be assessed for their possible effects upon measurement.

The individual's condition at the time of testing influences his response. Unique experiences occurring prior to the test situation, states of mind and the like, affect responses to tests. In a study conducted in a well-baby clinic on mother-child interaction, for example, if a test intended for research purposes were introduced at a time when the mother was quite upset over the behavior of her child, one could expect responses to be influenced by her fears and anxieties associated with her concerns.

The confounding effects of repeated testing can be diminished by careful selection and evaluation of tests, in which their function as stimuli is considered, and by using a research design in which selection of respondents for the experimental and control groups occurs in a random manner. This last procedure does not neutralize the effects of the test as a stimulus, but enables the investigator to measure the effects of the stimulus. For example, in the hypothetical family stability project, testing for knowledge and attitudes may have had a stimulating effect upon respondents, and respondents were probably in various states of readiness to respond. But in using a random-selection control group design (see p. 285), these effects are randomly distributed among participants of the experimental and control groups and are assumed to occur independently of the cause-effect relationship resulting from the introduction of S. Testing may be conceived as a stimulus for both groups. It is expected, however, that if the introduced S has created an effect upon Y, the O_1-O_2 difference for the experimental group will be significantly different from the O_1-O_2 difference for the control group. The O_1-O_2 difference for the control group is the result of testing and probably other factors such as maturation, history, and the like. In using the random-selection control group design, the specific effects of testing are understood and measured but are not eliminated. It becomes possible with this design to separate the effects of S from the effects of testing.

Instrumentation. In estimating the effects of S upon the difference between O_1 and O_2, the measure of change in the Y variable, it is important to evaluate how techniques of administering instruments, and the instruments themselves, may operate to produce this change in lieu of stimulus S. This confounding variable has been described as "instrument decay" (Campbell, 1957). Measuring instruments, with few exceptions, are imperfect and are unable in repeated administrations to measure precisely the same thing. Even under ideal laboratory conditions in which physical experiments are attempted, replication of exact measurements is virtually impossible because of slight changes in the environment and properties of the instrument. Error-free, automatically operated systems of measurement are being developed, but few of these are available or applicable to the work of the family researcher.

Attainment of precision, even with the assistance of some physical instrument, is difficult, because human beings administer these instruments. Observer bias results because no two individuals perceive or evaluate what they perceive in exactly the same fashion. In a study concerned with the effects of family interaction on the behavior of the diabetic child, physicians varied significantly from one another in their measurement of medical status of the child, an important dependent variable. Errors were of two types: a given physician varied in reported glucosuria for a child after making two urine analyses from the same urine specimen, and there were variations among physicians in making the same measurement of glucosuria from the same urine specimen (Sussman & Weil, 1960).

In certain types of problems, errors of this kind may have insignificant consequences for the measurement of dependent variables. Does an error of three or five points seriously affect the meaning when the state of control of the diabetic child is given? Variations found among physicians in taking blood-pressure readings when some prefer to round out dystolic and systolic measures, e.g., 160/80, while others prefer exact readings, 161.5/79.5, may also be insignificant in diagnosing and treating heart disease. The question of significance is not easily answered.

The issue of error deriving from the characteristics of instruments and their application is important to recognize, evaluate, and control. There are several principal methods of control. One is to use a random-selection control group research design. Another is to engage the same researcher for both the control and experimental groups. In longitudinal studies requiring many observations and probably many observers, e.g., studies in child growth and development, random assignment of observers may be made to both groups and for the particular periods of observation. Still another procedure is to use, whenever feasible, a "blind" approach in observation: the observer is unaware of which respondents are in the experimental or control groups. This latter practice is used extensively in medical research.

Regression. In before-and-after studies without the use of controls, statistical regression frequently interferes. It is a variable which often leads researchers to attribute to the effects of S results actually accountable by the selection of the groups specifically for their extreme performance on a particular parameter, which results in a concomitant low and imperfect correlation on performance of the test-retest scores (Campbell & Stanley, 1963; McNemar, 1958; Thorndike, 1942).

For example, the lowest scorers on the knowledge and attitude scales in the hypothetical family stability project may have demonstrated higher achievement upon taking the tests at O_2, and this improvement may have been attributed to the family program S carried on after the initial testing and until retesting occurred. This may be a statistical artifact, if the study group had been selected from either extreme, since low scores on retest are likely to scatter or regress upward toward the group mean. Progress on the posttest of extreme low to high or extreme high to low, toward the group mean, is a function of statistical law rather than of the introduction of S.

The regression phenomenon is best controlled in using the random-selection control group design. The anticipated regression toward the mean for both the control and experimental subjects has the same probability of occurring independently of the cause-effect relationship produced by stimulus S. Interpretations of change or lack of change in mean scores upon retest always need to be evaluated to decide whether they are results of the introduction of stimulus S or of regression effects. Frequently, the lack of change results from canceling out of changes in high and low score groups upon retest. Analysis for change of individual scores in extreme high and low categories for both control and experimental groups provides an explanation for differential gain in mean scores.

Selection and mortality. Two other factors confound validity of research findings in studies which omit use of controls and randomization in the selection of participants. These are *differential selection* of respondents for the study groups and *loss of participants* from the study before it is completed. Both of these problems are overcome if there is use of experimental and control groups and random selection of participants.

Randomization rules out the explanation that the difference between O_1 and O_2 is the result of selection of respondents rather than of the introduction of S. It establishes the equivalence of both groups and the basis upon which to state that O_1 and O_2 differences could not have occurred without the introduction of S.

The family stability project hypothesized above is particularly vulnerable to the invalidity of selection. The group to be tested, it should be recalled, was selected purposively. The couples club was active in the agency, and it can be assumed that its members were favorably disposed toward the goals and program of the agency. Could the improvements in knowledge and attitudes recorded at O_2 have resulted without the introduction of the family life program? A more efficacious test of the effects of such a program, involving control of the bias in selection, would have been to sample for participants from a population not known to the agency with randomization in sample selection and in assignment to control and experimental groups. Equivalence in groups would be the result, and hence selection as an invalidating variable would be ruled out.

Studies requiring repeated measurements at many different time periods, such as prospective-longitudinal ones, can be weakened by losing participants. This, referred to as experimental mortality (Campbell & Stanley, 1963), jeopardizes the validity of research findings. Results from comparisons made between groups at O_2, O_3, . . ., O_N become incomprehensible if there is uneven loss of participants from the experimental and control groups. It is vitally important, therefore, to assign subjects randomly to the experimental and control groups so that each group has the same probability of experiencing dropouts.

The choice of sample size of groups to be studied should be related to expected mortality of participants. The demands made upon respondents for their cooperation; characteristics such as age, socio-economic status, residential location, etc.; number of and time between follow-up tests and observations; and requirements for matching on selected characteristics are several of the factors to be considered in estimating mortality. The important requirement in any long- or short-term experimental study is to end up with two groups of sufficient size in which losses, if they occur, are about equally distributed in both groups. The two groups are similar in characteristics and differ only in relation to the introduction of stimulus S.

Relationship of Internal with External Validity

The problems of internal validity cannot be solved without considering those of external validity in which the generalizability of findings is the principal focus. Experiments in all fields and particularly in the social sciences are influenced by conditions and forces in the larger society. The researcher cannot control all the conditions to insure external validity but has the responsibility of accounting for these conditions and their possible effects upon the validity of his experiment. In this chapter, the factors jeopardizing the external validity of experiments are seen as being related to the internal validity of experimental studies.

How a population universe is selected before it is used for an experimental study affects internal validity, as already noted. This may be further illustrated in a proposed experimental study, being planned by the writer, to increase parents' ability to aid their children develop latent social and intellectual competencies. This study requires the cooperation of both many families and the school system. One feasible approach to obtain a population would be to select a school and then to solicit the cooperation of families. Schools have records of tests and measures of achievement, are interested in the problems of learning and achievement, and usually exercise considerable influence over families, an important condition for obtaining cooperation.

The schools in the district were listed. One school was selected after using the procedure of randomization. The officials at the selected school were lukewarm toward the project; they were interested but could not find the time to participate. A resample was made and the result was the same. Further study revealed that the degree of receptivity among the 45 schools in the system varied along a continuum ranging from 0 to 100 per cent. One helpful principal recommended that the researchers approach school A, because "they are always experimenting at that place." This example of choosing a site for undertaking research is closer to the usual occurrence than to fiction. The sampling of populations for experiments rarely occurs without the subjective element entering in.

A design in which controls are used can measure the influence of S—in this case, techniques to improve parental skills. However, the proneness "to try things" may have an effect upon the experimental variable S. The effect is to contaminate the introduced S, and to make it exceedingly difficult to decide whether to attribute the O_1-O_2 difference to S or to the school's characteristic of being experimentally prone. Parents of children in such a school are also likely to be experimentally oriented. Middle-class parents are particularly likely to seek out a residential area of the city where the school system reflects their educational values and desires for their children. Under these circumstances, it may be impossible to obtain a "neutral" or "normal" population to use in studying the effects of S. Random choice of a population for an experimental study is required to avoid invalidity resulting from interaction of selection with the S variable.

Random-selection, control, one-test design. The effects of initial testing have been viewed as producing change in subjects;

initial testing is not a usual process found in everyday life and therefore may be a threat to external validity. This concern led to further developments of experimental designs useful to the family researcher. The first was to omit pretesting of the two randomly selected control and experimental groups. This procedure is based on the assumption that random selection insures equality of the two groups. The degree of equality can be estimated statistically.

Many studies involving attitudes and values where the mere introduction of the issues in the pretest period produces an effect can successfully use this random-selection, control, one-test design (see Fig. 7). Samples are drawn from the population

Time 1   Time 2

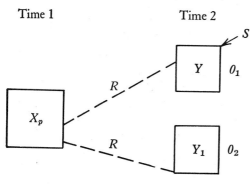

Fig. 7.   Random-Selection, Control, One-Test Design.

at time 1 and randomly assigned to Y and Y_1. At time 2 (usually immediately following time 1), stimulus S is introduced to Y and withheld from Y_1. Differences between O_1 and O_2 determine the effects of S. This design controls for the effects of testing and the interaction of the S variable but does not measure these effects.

In the hypothetical family stability project described earlier, the effects of the family life program upon changes in knowledge and attitudes related to family stability could be adequately studied with this design. The selection of couples for the experimental and control groups is done in a random manner, the intensive family life

program S is presented to the experimental group, and then testing determines the effects of S. Measurement of the amount of change induced by S in the predetermined levels of knowledge and attitudes about family stability is impossible with this design. Still, an important answer to the question of whether S caused an effect is possible.

This design is one of the most useful ones available to the family researcher. It is especially fitted for problems concerned with social processes and effecting change. Randomization of subjects for control and experimental groups and simple manipulation by introduction of the S variable provide the conditions for testing a cause-effect relationship.

This design becomes even more feasible if information on a given population is already known, does not have to be obtained by pretest, and can be used as baseline measures. In the proposed family and school project on strategies to improve parental competence, there may be available observations and tests on children and parents which are usable in measuring the effects of the S variable upon changes in levels of parental competence, while still enabling control for the effects of testing and interaction. Under these conditions, this less expensive and less time-consuming design has advantages which outweigh the two-test, random-selection, group control design, considered the standard of true experimental designs.

Solomon's modifications of the standard design. Concern with the effects of testing and interaction of variables led Solomon (1949) to propose extensive modifications in the standard design. Using three and even four groups on occasion, control for testing and interaction effects could be evaluated. Solomon studied three types of problems: the transfer of learning; experimentally induced changes in attitudes, opinions, and values; and the effects of controlled experience on existing behavior.

The usual control group design for the

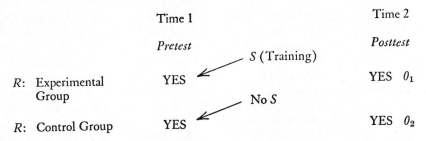

Fig. 8.

study of transfer of learning would be that shown in Fig. 8. Selection R is randomized, training is given to the experimental group but withheld from the control, pre- and posttesting takes place, and the difference between O_1 and O_2 measures the effect of S. Now compare this with Fig. 9.

This latter design enables assessment of the effects of the testing and the interaction of testing with the S variable. The effects of history, instrument decay, and maturation are also established.

If comparisons of O_3 and O_5 are in agreement, pretesting had no effect. Differences between O_1 and O_6 or O_2 and O_6 indicate that some uncontrolled effect, E, is confounding the validity of the experiment. Groups 2 and 3 actually use the one-test, group-control design for testing the effects of S while controlling for the effects of test-

ing. In Solomon's four-group design, these two groups have a replication function. If the differences found between O_5 and O_6 are similar to those found between O_3 and O_4, the inferences drawn concerning the impact of S are strengthened considerably. The effects of maturation and history are evaluated by comparing O_6 with O_1, and O_3 (O_6 should be similar to O_1 but different from O_3 if these variables are controlled).

The Solomon four-group design is best for controlling and measuring the effects of testing and stimulus S and for expanding the generalizability of experimental findings. It handles effectively one important question concerning external validity: how stimulus S is interacting with other variables and whether the effects attributed to S are actually those of extraneous variables. This design requires a population of suffi-

	Time 1		**Time 2**
	Pretest		*Posttest*
R: Experimental Group	YES O_1	S	YES O_3
R: Control Group 1	YES O_2	No S	YES O_4
R: Control Group 2	NO	S	YES O_5
R:[a] Control Group 3	NO	No S	YES O_6

Fig. 9.

[a] This fourth group is sometimes omitted in studies where time intervals between testing are short and there appears to be little need to account for uncontrolled events related to the passage of time.

cient size to allow samples to be drawn randomly in order to assign membership in the four groups. Careful supervision of experimental conditions, with rigid scheduling of observations, is also required.

Quasi-experimental designs. The presentation in this chapter of truly experimental designs applicable to the study of the family is to emphasize the problems and prospects for undertaking quality experimental research on the important process of cause and effect. In situations where full control over the selection of samples, introduction of stimuli, and testing and measurement is absent, it may still be possible to introduce some elements of an experimental design. Campbell and Stanley (1963, pp. 204–241) have outlined 10 partial or quasi-experimental designs in which degrees of control over confounding variables are obtained. The investigator choosing one of these designs must evaluate the conditions of his experiment and select a design which offers the best opportunity for control over invalidating variables. Quasi-experimental designs are used extensively in studies outside of the laboratory and in the field where laboratory conditions are impossible to maintain. A discussion of field studies approaching experimental conditions would include coverage of designs identified by Campbell as time series experiments, equivalent time samples, nonequivalent control group, separate-sample pretest-posttest designs, and several multiple-group experimental designs.

The ex post facto design, referred to in the literature as an illustration of the quasi-experimental type, deserves a brief comment (Chapin, 1947; Chapin, 1955; Greenwood, 1945). The most accurate description of ex post facto is that it is a simulated experimental design. The basic approach is to examine outcome (Y) variables and from these to deduce causality resulting from a condition or event (X) occurring some time previously. Chapin (1955, pp. 99–124) studied success and community participation as related to success in completing high-

school education 10 years prior to the study. Completing or not completing high school were the X and no-X variables, respectively (data obtained from interviews). A matching process was used on six variables, and an initial group of 1,194 interviewed (the initial universe was 2,127) shrank to 46 cases.

The basic deficiency of the ex post facto design is the choice of variables to be matched and the consequent undermatching of variables. Randomization of variables is impossible in this design, and selection of particular ones for matching presents a continuous uncertainty as to whether the right ones were picked. Some determinants of success or no success antecede the condition of X or no X, and these antecedents are probably related to the occurrence of Y at a later time. The probabilities are that more obvious factors such as age, class, and occupation are matched, while less obvious ones are ignored. The result is undermatching. The contribution of this study design is to provide some knowledge on possible cause-effect relationships which can then be substantiated by using one of the true experimental designs.

The specific problems in undertaking quality family experimental research have been described. For each problem there is a technical solution and a theoretical rationale which supports the efforts to validate that which is invalid. It is apparent that with careful selection and conceptualization of a problem, an adequate research design, and the means to meet the conditions of the design, study of the majority of issues, situations, and phenomena of concern to the marriage and family field is possible.

SPECIAL CONSTRAINTS UPON THE FAMILY RESEARCHER

There are a number of social constraints upon doing experiments with human beings. The researcher has to be sensitive to these and to develop strategies which blend the differences in perceptions and goals of the society and the researcher. These problems are presented with the assurance that common sense and good judgment can find ways to handle them.

One principal difficulty for the researcher is the hue and cry raised about the manipulation of human beings for the purpose of achieving research goals. Manipulation raises questions relative to ethical values (Baldwin 1960). Generally, the ethical values shared by the people of most cultures in Western society are inconsistent with the researcher's intent to manipulate individuals, particularly adults, in order to meet the conditions of his study. [Manipulation has many of the aspects of "disguise" as discussed by Straus; see pp. 368–370, 373–381.]

The researcher is faced with conflicting norms, those which conform with his role as a researcher charged with the responsibility of adding new knowledge to his field and those which guide his behavior as a respected and accepted member of society. Merton (1963) has indicated a set of institutionally defined pairs of conflicting norms of scientists today, and has pointed out the difficult task for the institution of science to integrate these inconsistencies in order to accomplish the goals of science. An example of a pair of norms in conflict is: New scientific knowledge is a prime goal of the researcher and is best obtained by methods capable of studying cause and effect relationships, the stipulation of hypotheses, and their subsequent testing; yet methods which may jeopardize the psyche or personality of the individual, or which are taboo in the culture, cannot be used to advance the frontiers of knowledge. As a result of norm inconsistency and stringent ethical values, many research problems cannot be studied successfully experimentally, but have to be investigated by other methods, such as ex post facto, historical, and survey.

Manipulation raises a fundamental question concerning the right of any human being to trifle with other human beings, to subject them to conditions of anxiety and fear which can threaten their physical and emotional well-being in a situation deemed unnecessary for living in a society. Manipulating human beings can be permitted in one situation but condemned in another. An unnecessary situation is one which is deemed unrequired for the maintenance of the society. It is noninstitutionalized and often believed to be nonessential and therefore subject to moral and ethical censure.

Manipulation of human beings occurs on a grand scale in a military system. It is used extensively to fit a human being into an organization capable of fighting a war. Complaints are often made regarding the effects of such manipulation, but these cries which raise moral and ethical issues are largely unheeded, because the military system is considered necessary and vital to the existence of a society. Moreover, it is usually a system which has power and influence and which can handle the critics who question the ethics involved in manipulation.

The social science researcher does not operate in a system which has such a "necessary and vital function"—not yet, anyway. His colleagues in the medical sciences are in a more vital system and have less of a problem in manipulating human beings. However, the controversy continues even in medical circles regarding informing patients of the research and receiving permission from them before beginning the experiment.

Manipulation is a generalized process in a society. Individuals are subjected continually to all varieties of purposive and nonpurposive manipulation, with very little thought given to the consequences. For example, the family in the low-income area of the central city is subjected to the uncontrolled manipulation of its environment, and the outcomes usually do not raise moral or ethical outcries. In our society, uncontrolled manipulation and its consequences are accepted as one condition of life. Spontaneous outcries about the unethical and immoral nature of such manipulation seldom occur. Only when the outcomes of uncontrolled manipulation are grossly in-human do reaction and action take place to control the process of manipulation and its consequences.

The objections to manipulation are less severe when animals and children are in-volved. The subjects brought into experi-mental situations are unaware that they are being studied and react uninhibitedly to the new situation. Frequently, the investigator attempts to make the alleged unethical study ethical by obtaining the cooperation and permission of the adults whose children are to be involved. Information concerning the study told to children, or their surro-gates, represents an extraneous variable which is difficult to measure or control for the bias it may introduce.

Child development researchers have been more successful in their experimental stud-ies than investigators working with adults. Children submit to manipulation more readily than adults. Nevertheless, the re-searcher cannot manipulate the child in the same way or to the same degree that his colleague can do in the animal laboratory (Baldwin, 1960). He cannot introduce stim-uli which may impair in any way the de-velopment of the child's character or personality. The effects of particular stimuli upon character development—whether per-sonality is molded by exposure to critical incidents or by long-term exposure to par-ticular stimuli in a social environment—are unanswered theoretical questions still sub-ject to debate and empirical testing.

The prevailing notion is that it is better for the researcher to accept any pattern of child-rearing found in the home, whether or not it is judged to be deleterious to the development of the child, than to impose an artificial pattern introduced experimen-tally, even though it qualifies on all counts as a desirable stimulus for improving a rearing pattern. The exception occurs with severely emotionally disturbed children, for whom in the course of therapy it is permis-sible to introduce planned changes in child-rearing patterns. Generally, it is taboo for the researcher to subject the child to situa-tions possibly fraught with excessive anxi-ety or frustration or which may produce conditions which conceivably could endan-ger the threshold of emotional tolerance. Such situations are considered to be in vio-lation of general standards and practices of child development. The stance is that such manipulation could possibly retard the child's growth in character and personality and his competence to function in society.

Manipulation of subjects can have curious effects upon the experimenters. Is it possible for experimenters to engage in the various forms of manipulation and control and still be unaffected by it? Most scientists abide by moral and ethical codes of conduct, self-derived and imposed. Their science stems from a humanistic tradition in which eth-ical principles are of paramount importance.

In research in child development, one recurrent question is the reliability of the commonly held notion that affection and love given by an adult to the child are prerequisite to the child's development as a social being capable of utilizing his innate potentialities as an active participant in so-ciety. For illustrative purposes, a random-selection, one-test, control-group design might be considered, in which the babies in one sample receive the usual love and affec-tion and those in the other sample do not. It would be highly desirable if one could separate identical twins and if parents could conduct the experiment. This arrangement establishes the homogeneity of the socio-cultural and physical environment of the subjects. One group of babies is given warmth and affection by being picked up and cuddled and by being involved in all types of interactions which make the infant feel that he is wanted, desired, and has a place in the family. The tissue needs of the second group of infants are met, they are fed and cared for and made comfortable, but they are denied those contacts with adults which produce love and affection.

The design can be less severely and rigidly conceived and perhaps made more acceptable on ethical grounds and more palatable emotionally if love and affection are not completely denied to infants in the control group. The theoretical question could be answered partially with this modification in design.

This problem is so emotionally laden that one could anticipate that the experimenter would experience extreme difficulty in treating the infants according to imposed conditions of the study. On an intellectual level, the researchers could envisage the need to maintain rigid controls, but these would fail, because enforcement of control is unacceptable on an emotional level. The gnawing thought that to withhold affection and love in any form or amount could result in improper socialization of the child and the development of an instable personality is too much of a stress for most researchers to handle. This is another example of conflict of norms and illustrates the difficulty, due to issues involving ethics and values, of undertaking experiments using adequate controls.

EARLY DEVELOPMENT
OF EXPERIMENTAL STUDIES

Interest in experimental studies on the family began in the field of social work. Practitioners were interested in how knowledge of the pretreatment condition of the individual could assist in solving the problem which the client brought to the social worker. Subsequent work followed on the dynamics of the treatment process. These inquiries, in which a laboratory approach was used to collect the data, contributed to understanding of the structure and function of the family.

Initially, the practitioners were uninterested in experimental studies. They wanted information upon which to base treatment strategies directed toward changing the individual's behavior according to the re-quirements of a therapeutic frame of reference. Information sufficient to make a judgment for a particular strategy was all that was necessary. The evaluation of outcomes of various strategies was something else, and few practitioners had the time, interest, or skill to undertake this type of research. The contribution derived from these studies was a delineation of role conflict, power arrangements, and decision-making as processes common to all family systems and important to understanding and treatment of the family (Deutsch & Solomon, 1958).

Another finding was that family behavior was complicated and difficult to understand, and that the usual instruments of questionnaires and interviews employed in surveys were insufficient to obtain the necessary data. A picture of actual role behavior and its effect upon family functioning was possible only through observation and depth interviewing, a situation in which the respondent could articulate freely on subjects divorced from the problem in question. Respondents were found to be incapable of responding to direct questioning as the result of "emotional blocking." Individuals with problems use various stratagems to protect their egos. Intellectual acceptance is dissimilar to emotional acceptance or to understanding of phenomena. Except for the extremely emotionally disturbed, a straightforward question posed to a respondent on love or acceptance of one's spouse and children tends to receive the usual affirmative answer. The subtleties, the if's, but's, and uncertainties raised by the question are left unrevealed. The response is an oversimplification of a complicated set of feelings. It is here that stereotypes are born, those convenient responses to handle many situations in which there are uncertainties and which may be upsetting to all parties involved.

Intensive case studies and subsequent analyses to determine the real meaning of behavior have been suggested as a technique for unraveling the complications of this problem. This approach received additional support, because in direct questioning the respondent was unable to give answers, since he did not have the information. In the clinical interview, respondents said many things, and a plausible explanation of family behavior resulted from piecing together the varied bits of information.

The clinical interview is an important research technique, if it becomes sufficiently standardized to permit quantification of findings. Bowman (1956) has indicated the need to have systematic "research clinic interviews" in order to build a series of case studies from which can be extracted hypotheses on conditions of structure and function which are associated with family problems.

Observation of the family in action was a necessary addition to the research clinic interview. The interplay among family members indicated the pattern of relationships. Restructuring the interaction as part of the therapy in problem-solving required accurate observation of verbal and nonverbal behavior in as many settings as possible. The clinic was the usual setting in which observations were made. Frequently, the clinician would observe various combinations of family members, such as child alone, father alone, mother alone, child and mother, and both parents and child together.

The clinician's urge to diagnose and treat, together with his inadequate training in research methods, worked against his undertaking well-designed research using controls. Use of controls sometimes presented an additional barrier to the clinician in undertaking research. In the experimental design, it involved withholding a service from individuals of one group, while the second group received service. In a field fraught with uncertainties and innumerable hypotheses, the thought of denying someone a service which has face validity and which sometimes works is untenable

even for the advancement of science. As clinicians became more successful in treatment through increased experience and knowledge, interest grew regarding the viability of different treatment strategies. With success, the likelihood of using controls should increase. A measure of success means confidence and a feeling that, while research is a luxury, it is one which now can be indulged in with ultimate profit to the field.

In the period after World War II, there emerged a coterie of researchers who viewed the small group as a social system. The efforts of the small-group researcher, together with those of the clinician, stimulated research on treatment processes and strategies.

The researcher of small groups began on the premise that human behavior can be observed systematically. Acts in group situations can be identified, typed, categorized, and given meaning. When these are analyzed completely, there follows an explanation of human behavior (Bales, 1950).

The applicability of methodologies developed by the small-group researcher to studies on family interaction precipitated a series of significant experimental researches. From these were derived tested hypotheses on decision-making and on the development of roles, especially leadership roles, in the family.

The family, as a small system, was found to possess some of the same characteristics of the experimental small groups studied by Bales (1950). The pattern of leadership formation and structure is similar to that found in experimental small groups, with some variations resulting from age and sex. Leadership tends to differentiate along an instrumental-expressive axis in which some roles are concerned primarily with achievement of tasks, while others are involved primarily with organizing social and emotional relationships among family members.

Research on decision-making in the family used the same theoretical stance and research paradigm as the small-group study. Successful completion of tasks oriented to commonly shared family goals is considered basic to the maintenance and perpetuation of the family as a social system. The experimental situation usually involved a presentation of problems or issues over which there was disagreement among marital partners. Problem-solving under varied conditions determined the process of decision-making and the role of each marital partner, and in some instances of other family members. The usual pattern of differentiation in the family is a sharing of leadership functions. Instrumental or task-oriented activities are directed by the father. Leadership in the more expressive and social-managerial types of activities is given by the mother. Role differentiation along this instrumental-expressive axis has been established in a series of studies by Kenkel (1963), Parsons and Bales (1955), and Strodtbeck (1951; 1952; 1954).

CONCLUSION

A complete review of marriage and family problems, or areas of study, in which true experimental designs are being used has not been possible within the space limitations of this chapter. Also, studies on learning, perception, motivation, socialization, and other basic processes relevant to family functioning which have been successfully researched with experimental designs are unreported here (although attention is given them elsewhere in this Handbook). The studies of role structure, decision-making, and leadership in the family were presented briefly merely as illustrations of types of experiment-like studies recently undertaken in the marriage and family field. Evaluation of their experimental "rigor" in terms of the problems of validity stated above might quench the thirst of experimentally minded researchers. The constraints upon doing experimental

family research are probably more annoyances than formidable obstacles for the motivated researcher to overcome. The objections, if not expressed overtly, are at least latent and are exercised on occasion, often by well-meaning people who view research, particularly experimental research involving manipulation, as violating the sanctity of the family, as being unethical, and as ultimately destructive of the family system. The researcher's awareness of these constraints makes him better prepared to handle them.

The view in this chapter is that marriage and family research using experimental designs is in a beginning stage of development. Nevertheless, the prospects for quality experimental research are considerable. The recent developments in family theory (Hill & Hansen, 1960), the increasing availability of funds for family research, and the multiplication of trained social scientists sophisticated in research methodology and statistics indicate a renaissance in experimental family sociology.

The mandate for the family researcher is to begin basic studies on cause-effect relationships using experimental designs in which the confounding variables affecting the internal and external validity of findings are controlled. Randomization in selection of populations and members of control and experimental groups; use of control groups; systematic testing for occurrence of change and, in some problems, the measurement of change; and introduction of stimulus S are the important characteristics of the true experimental design.

The choice of a particular design must be based upon the characteristics of the problem, how it has been conceptualized, and the degree of control over invalidating variables required for the problem and obtainable under given conditions. A variety of quasi-experimental designs providing some degree of control over extraneous variables are available. These, however, are used mostly in field studies in which laboratory conditions are absent and rigorous control of the experimental situation is impossible.

The family researcher should focus his work at the present time on cause-effect problems which enable use of true experimental designs. Such studies are the building blocks of any science and are vital to the development of an empirically tested family theory.

REFERENCES

Ackoff, R. L. *The design of social research.* Chicago: Univer. of Chicago Press, 1953.

Bachrach, A. J. *Psychological research.* New York: Random House, 1962.

Baldwin, A. L. The study of child behavior and development. In P. H. Mussen (Ed.), *Handbook of research methods in child development.* New York: Wiley, 1960. Pp. 3–32.

Bales, R. F. *Interaction process analysis.* Cambridge: Addison-Wesley, 1950.

Bijou, S. W., & Baer, D. M. The laboratory-experimental study of child behavior. In P. H. Mussen (Ed.), *Handbook of research methods in child development.* New York: Wiley, 1960. Pp. 140–200.

Bowman, C. C. Research in family dynamics: a criticism and a proposal. *Soc. Forces,* 1956, 34, 201–206.

Bronowski, J. *The common sense of science.* Cambridge: Harvard Univer. Press, 1953.

Campbell, D. T. Factors relevant to the validity of experiments in social settings. *Psychol. Bull.,* 1957, 54, 297–312.

Campbell, D. T. Methodological suggestions from a comparative psychology of knowledge processes. *Inquiry,* 1959, 2, 152–182.

Campbell, D. T. Recommendations for APA test standards regarding construct, trait, or discriminant validity. *Amer. Psychologist,* 1960, 15, 546–553.

Campbell, D. T., & Stanley, J. C. Experimental and quasi-experimental designs for research on teaching. In N. L. Gage (Ed.), *Handbook of research on teaching.* Chicago: Rand McNally, 1963. Pp. 171–246.

Cane, V. R., & Heim, A. W. The effects of repeated testing: III. further experiments and general conclusions. *Quart. J. exp. Psychol.,* 1950, 2, 182–195.

Chapin, F. S. *Experimental designs in sociological research.* New York: Harper, 1947.

Chapin, F. S. *Experimental designs in sociological research.* (Rev. ed.) New York: Harper, 1955.

Christensen, H. T. The method of record linkage applied to family data. *Marr. & fam. Living,* 1958, 20, 38–42.

Deutsch, M. An experimental study of the effects of cooperation and competition upon group process. *Hum. Relat.,* 1949, 2, 199–232.

Deutsch, M., & Solomon, L. Some methodological suggestions for research in a family counseling setting. *Marr. & fam. Living,* 1958, 20, 21–26.

Edwards, A. L. *Experimental design in psychological research.* (Rev. ed.) New York: Rinehart, 1960.

Festinger, L. Laboratory experiments. In L. Festinger & D. Katz (Eds.), *Research methods in the behavioral sciences.* New York: Dryden Press, 1953. Pp. 136–172.

Gee, W. *Social science research methods.* New York: Appleton-Century-Crofts, 1950.

Greenwood, E. *A study on methods.* New York: King's Crown Press, 1945.

Hill, R., & Hansen, D. A. The identification of conceptual frameworks utilized in family study. *Marr. & fam. Living,* 1960, 22, 299–311.

Hill, R., Stycos, J. M., & Back, K. W. *The family and population control.* Chapel Hill: Univer. of North Carolina Press, 1959.

Kempthorne, O. *The design and analysis of experiments.* New York: Wiley, 1952.

Kempthorne, O. The design and analysis of experiments, with some reference to educational research. In R. O. Collier & S. M. Elam (Eds.), *Research design and analysis: the second annual Phi Delta Kappa symposium on educational research.* Bloomington, Ind.: Phi Delta Kappa, 1961. Pp. 97–133.

Kenkel, W. Observational studies of husband-wife interaction in family decision-making. In M. B. Sussman (Ed.), *Sourcebook in marriage and the family.* Boston: Houghton Mifflin, 1963. Pp. 144–156.

Lindquist, E. F. *Design and analysis of experiments in psychology and education.* Boston: Houghton Mifflin, 1953.

McKinney, J. C. Methodology, procedures, and techniques in sociology. In H. Becker & A.

Boskoff (Eds.), *Modern sociological theory.* New York: Dryden Press, 1957. Pp. 186–235.

McNemar, Q. On growth measurement. *Educ. psychol. Measmt,* 1958, 18, 47–55.

Merton, R. The ambivalence of scientists. *Bull. Johns Hopkins Hosp.,* 1963, 112, 77–97.

Ogburn, W. F. Limitation of statistics. *Amer. J. Sociol.,* 1934, 40, 12–20.

Parsons, T., & Bales, R. F., with Olds, J., Zelditch, M., Jr., & Slater, P. *Family, socialization and interaction process.* Glencoe, Ill.: Free Press, 1955.

Rankin, R. E., & Campbell, D. T. Galvanic skin response to Negro and white experimenters. *J. abnorm. soc. Psychol.,* 1956, 47, 257–264.

Solomon, R. L. An extension of control group design. *Psychol. Bull.,* 1949, 46, 137–150.

Stanley, J. C. Analysis of a doubly vested design. *Educ. psychol. Measmt,* 1961, 21, 831–837. (a)

Stanley, J. C. Studying status vs. manipulating variables. In R. O. Collier & S. M. Elam (Eds.), *Research design and analysis: the second Phi Delta Kappa symposium on educational research.* Bloomington, Ind.: Phi Delta Kappa, 1961. Pp. 173–208. (b)

Stouffer, S. A. Some observations on study design. *Amer. J. Sociol.,* 1950, 55, 355–361.

Strodtbeck, F. Husband-wife interaction over revealed differences. *Amer. sociol. Rev.,* 1951, 16, 468–473.

Strodtbeck, F. The interaction of a "henpecked" husband and his wife. *Marr. & fam. Living,* 1952, 14, 305–309.

Strodtbeck, F. The family as a three person group. *Amer. sociol. Rev.,* 1954, 19, 23–29.

Sussman, M. B. The social problems of the sociologist. *Soc. Probl.,* 1964, 11, 215–225.

Sussman, M. B., & Weil, W. B. An experimental study on the effects of group interaction upon the behaviour of diabetic children. *Int. J. soc. Psychiatry,* 1960, 6, 120–125.

Thorndike, R. L. Regression fallacies in the matched group experiment. *Psychometrika,* 1942, 7, 85–102.

Weil, W. B., & Sussman, M. B. Behavior, diet, and glucosuria of diabetic children in a summer camp. *Pediatrics,* 1961, 27, 118–127.

CHAPTER **9** Demographic
Analysis
of Family Data

PAUL C. GLICK
United States Bureau of the Census

The demographer studies marriage and the family on the basis of statistics from vital records and census questionnaires. Although the source materials in themselves are impersonal, they yield penetrating insights into some of the most highly valued experiences in the lives of men, women, and children. Moreover, they bring to light many relationships and trends that have practical utility for governmental and business planning. Marriage, household formation, childbearing, changing ages of children in the home, adult care of the children, departure of grown children from their parental home, divorce, residential movements associated with changing family composition, productive activities of the members at different phases of the family's development, and living arrangements of the members during the retirement period are among the subjects which claim the demographer's attention.

The initial section of this chapter presents a brief summary of findings and conclusions from some of the studies of these subjects, to acquaint the reader with the content of family demography. The discussion turns, then, to the central problem, the description of major sources and methods employed by the family statistician in gathering, classifying, and interpreting his factual material. A closing section suggests ways to improve the quality of the data and ways to expand the quantity of the data to advantage.

DEMOGRAPHIC PROFILE
OF FAMILY LIFE

More of the people were married in 1960 than in 1940, and their marriages were taking place at a younger age, on the average; yet more of those who had married were currently living apart from their spouse because of marital difficulties. Thus, the number of persons in 1960 who were married was approximately 8 million larger than it would have been if the percentage married in each age group had remained the same as in 1940. This "excess" of married persons is the equivalent of more than the number of marriages that occur in two and one-half years. Most of the increase in married persons took place during the 1940's and resulted largely from higher first marriage rates, which made the number of single persons in 1960 far short of the number "expected" on the basis of the percentage single at each age in 1940. It also occurred to some extent from a decline in death rates among married persons, which kept the current number of widowed persons about 2.5 million below the expected level under mortality conditions and remarriage rates that prevailed up to 1940. The growth occurred, moreover, in spite of a substantial excess in 1960 (about 1 million) over the expected number who were divorced but not remarried. Sharply higher proportions of separated and divorced persons have been noted in recent years for nonwhite persons, whose indicators of marital instability were already far above those for whites.

During the 1950's and early 1960's, one-half of the women entered their first marriage by the time they were about 20 years old; in 1940, this figure was about 21.5 years. For men, the corresponding ages were between two and three years higher. Fifty per cent of the ages of women at first marriage were concentrated within a range of about four years around the median age at first marriage (18 to 21 years), and for men the corresponding range was about five years (20 to 24 years). Marriage rates for men were closely and positively correlated with the amount of income. For women, marriage rates were lowest for those with college education, but the differences in marriage rates by education have declined. Age for age, eligible persons with previous marital experience had a greater chance for remarriage than spinsters and bachelors had for a first marriage.

The annual number of births between the mid-1940's and the early 1960's was about half again as high as the number in 1940. As one consequence, the annual number of first marriages during the latter part of the 1960's and throughout the 1970's is expected to be about half again as high as the number in 1940. The median interval between marriage and the birth of the first child, currently about one and one-half years, is shorter by a few months than it was a decade or two ago. Women who are currently at the height of childbearing seem likely to have about three children during their lifetime, on the average, whereas a generation earlier the average number was closer to two. Fewer couples are having only one or no children, and more are having two or three (Grabill & Parke, 1961). The proportions of women with larger numbers of births have increased somewhat over the 1940 level but are still smaller than they were two or three generations ago. Infant mortality rates fell approximately 50 per cent in the two decades after 1940, while maternal mortality rates fell an amazing nine-tenths.

Differences between birth rates among higher and lower status groups tended to become narrower during the 1940's, but shifted irregularly in the opposite direction during the 1950's. Particularly notable have been the substantial increases in childbearing among college-educated women, a trend which reflects, in part, the larger proportion married among these women and, in part, the larger number of children per married woman. Despite this change, however, women with a college education still bear fewer children, on the average, than other women (Grabill, Kiser, & Whelpton, 1958, p. 201). The evidence indicates that there is no necessary contradiction between the tendencies for women to have more children now than a generation ago and for them to gain more education and to participate in the labor force. [Cf. Ch. 14, pp. 558–559 of this Handbook.]

The divorce rate hit an all-time peak in 1946, as an aftermath of World War II, when many marriages deteriorated. It then declined steadily until the late 1950's, at which time the number of divorces per 1,000 married persons under 55 years of age reached approximately the same level as that for 1940. By 1961, the divorce rate had risen again slightly, to about the 1950 level. Among nonwhite women, separation ratios in 1960 were seven times as large as those for white women; on the other hand, divorce ratios for nonwhite women were only half again as high as those for white women (Glick, 1963). To a large extent, no doubt, the high separation ratios computed from census data for nonwhite women are related to the high rates of illegitimacy for nonwhite births, which are 10 times as high as those for white births; the appropriate inference, it appears, is that many unwed mothers report themselves on their census questionnaires as separated. Research by Hillman (1962) has established that, among white men, there is a negative relationship between socioeconomic status (measured in terms of education, occupation, or income) and marital disruption (measured in terms of divorce or separation); the results are less clear and consistent for nonwhite men and for women.

Women who had remarried by the time they had reached middle age have been reported as two years younger at first marriage, on the average, than women who were still in their first marriages. These findings, together with findings by Christensen (1953) to the effect that divorce rates are higher among those with premarital pregnancies, lend support to the thesis that a part of the apparently younger age at first marriage of those whose marriages later failed may represent misreporting of the date of the first marriage as earlier than it really occurred, in order to conceal the fact that the first child was conceived (if not actually born) before marriage (Cf. Christensen, Andrews, & Freiser, 1953). Among persons who obtain divorces, about two-thirds of the women and three-fourths of the men eventually remarry (Glick, 1957, p. 139). More of the couples who have obtained divorces in recent years than formerly have had children (Pratt, 1959), yet remarriage rates—age for age—for women with children tend to be lower than those for childless women.

In 1960, one out of every eight married couples with the husband under 25 years of age had not established a home of their own. The ratio had been almost one out of three in the late 1940's, during the severe housing shortage. For married couples of all ages, only 2 per cent in 1960 were sharing the homes of others. Nearly one-third of the wives were in the labor force in 1960, twice the corresponding proportion in 1940. Most of the increase occurred among two groups, young wives who had not yet had any children and, especially, wives in later middle age whose children had become grown. The median family income in 1960 was $5,620, as compared with $4,063 in 1950 (in terms of 1960 dollars). During this period, the proportion of families with less than $3,000 income (in 1960 dollars) fell from 32 per cent to 22 per cent, and the proportion with $10,000 or more rose from 6 per cent to 14 per cent.

Although the couples who entered marriage around the turn of the century had less than a 50–50 chance of surviving jointly until their children had married, the couples of the current era have close to a third of their married life yet to live jointly, on the average, after their children have married.

There were 39.6 million husband-wife families in the United States in 1961. One means of describing these families according to stage of the family life cycle is as follows: In 20.1 million of the families, the head was under 45 years old. Of these 20.1 million families, 3.1 million had no sons or daughters under 18 of their own living at home, and 17.0 million of them had one or more. Of these 17.0 million, 5.6 million had children of preschool age only, 6.3 million had some of preschool age and some of school age, and 5.1 million had children of school age only. There were 14.7 million husband-wife families with the head 45 to 64; of these, 6.3 million had one or more sons or daughters under 18 at home, and 8.4 million had none. Only 4 per cent of the 4.9 million husband-wife families with the head 65 years old and over had any children of their own under 18 still at home.

The foregoing summary includes only a few of the many facts about marriage and family life that have been developed by demographic research. They reveal that a much larger proportion of adults in 1960 than in 1940 were marrying and participating in the bearing and rearing of children, but that some groups in the population have a more stable family life than others. Although the material well-being of families has been improving, some of this improvement has been taking the form of more separate living among adults, apart from parents and offspring. Some of the economic well-being has resulted from an increase in the average number of earners per family and, in particular, from the employment of a larger proportion of women who, under former circumstances, would have remained housewives. As more women gain work experience before marriage, a larger proportion will be qualified to obtain employment after their children are in or through school. Whether wives make use of their time beyond child-rearing to work outside the home or not, the span of years available to them in this later part of life is a bonus they have received for marrying younger and having fewer children, on the average, than their great-grandmothers, and for being born in an era when people tend to live longer, thanks to modern sanitation and medical science.

NATURE, SOURCES, AND USES OF DEMOGRAPHIC DATA

In the sections which follow, discussion is to be centered on the kinds of data family demographers produce, the unique methods they use in collecting, processing, analyzing, and evaluating their data, and selected references to the scientific literature where further details on demographic sources and methods can be found.

Most of the comprehensive demographic statistics on marriage and the family are of recent origin. An examination of the pages of *Historical Statistics of the United States,* *Colonial Times to 1957* (U. S. Bureau of the Census, 1960a) demonstrates that the variety of relatively comparable series with nationwide coverage back to 1930 or earlier is quite limited. Such subjects include several from census reports: marital status by age, color, and sex; median age at first marriage by sex; households by size, age, and sex of head, race of head, and farm-nonfarm residence; married couples with and without own household; and relationship to head of household. Although the subjects are limited in number, many of them are available by states and the larger urban areas and could, therefore, serve as the basis for analyses of historical trends according to various area classifications. Series of vital statistics and related rates of interest to readers of this Handbook which extend back to 1920 or earlier include the following: crude birth, marriage, and divorce rates; birth rates by order of birth, color, and age of mother; gross and net reproduction rates; number of children under five years old per 1,000 women 20 to 44 years old (back to 1800), by race, urban-rural residence, and geographic division; ever-married women by number of children ever born, by year of birth of woman (back to 1835–1839); marriage rate per 1,000 unmarried females; and divorce rate per 1,000 married females.

Mass data on marriage and the family are collected primarily because of their practical utility. Census and vital statistics data are useful in government and business planning in such areas of research as housing, marketing, employment, and finance. Marriage and divorce records which are centrally filed in state offices aid lawyers in their legal proceedings. Although the census and vital records are assembled largely to satisfy administrative and economic needs, it should not be overlooked that they are available for exploring subjects that are more exclusively of interest for their theoretical or informational purposes, such as differences in family formation, composition, and dissolution among ethnic and other social groups. As research workers in the fields of production, distribution, and investment become more sophisticated in their search for underlying factors in economic trends, however, they have turned in increasing numbers to the use of demographic statistics that, in an earlier period, might have been considered as outside their range of interest.

Most of the sources and methods of the family demographer are also those of other demographers, except that many aspects of family statistics involve data for groups of persons who live together, as contrasted with persons considered as units without respect to their living arrangements. These sources include facts from vital records (births, marriages, divorces, and deaths) and from household surveys (population distribution, composition, living arrangements, work experience, and socioeconomic status). Demographic methods relate to research design, collection of data, adjustment of observations, tabulation, analysis, and evaluation. These topics constitute the framework of the sections of this chapter which follow. Each substantive and methodological topic cannot be treated exhaustively; hence, the purpose will be to call attention to illustrative sources and methods that are especially pertinent to the family statistician.

The demographer's source materials are elementary external facts—births, marriages, migration, ethnic characteristics, age composition, and the like. These facts contrast with, but are nonetheless related to, other kinds of personal characteristics, such as attitudes, values, roles, temperament, intelligence, and aggressions. Each research area has its unique contributions to make. In many studies, demographic classifications serve as the scaffolding for elaborate nondemographic analyses, but in other studies they provide penetrating insights of their own, quite independent of nondemographic source material. To illustrate: "Pure" demographic research shows the components of population growth for an area in terms of

past, current, and probable future birth, death, and migration rates; phases in the life cycle of the family; trends in the spacing of children; seasonal variations in births, marriages, and divorces; and ratios of dependent young and old persons to persons of productive age.

Most demographers are primarily professional experts in other fields (sociologists, economists, or geographers), and their areas of professional training and experience tend to color their research output. Thus, sociologists interested in marriage and the family may be preoccupied with differences in family behavior among social strata; economists, in the family as an economic unit; and geographers, in the spatial distribution of various family patterns.

DEFINITION OF CONCEPTS

A full treatment of the preliminary steps in designing a demographic study of family behavior would cover a wide range of topics: formulation of hypotheses, selection of indicators of the behavior to be studied, definition of concepts, frequency of the survey, financing, staffing, and so on. For brevity, the treatment here is limited to only one of these topics, the definition of selected concepts.

The definition of a family which is used for census purposes in the United States was developed in 1947 with the help of an advisory group. According to this definition, a family is a group of two or more persons related to each other by blood, marriage, or adoption; the entire group of persons who are living together and related to each other is regarded as one family. By this definition, two sisters who live together as a two-person household constitute a "census family." So also would two married couples who are related to each other and live together as one household. This concept is intended to represent a unit of consumption, in that relatives who live together generally share the use of many items in common as a single household. Classification by type of family isolates the families that do not contain both head and wife. In recent years, the proportion of nuclear family groups (married couples and parent-child groups) which live doubled-up with relatives has become so small (about 3 per cent) that the total number of families would be affected little by counting all the nuclear family groups as separate families, as is done by the Dominion Bureau of Statistics in Canada. Special tabulations have been prepared by both countries, however, which make it possible to provide comparisons of distributions of family groups in the two countries.

An important bridge between the two approaches just described is the concept "subfamily," according to United States terminology, or "related secondary family," according to Canadian terminology. This concept relates to a nuclear family group which is sharing the living quarters of a relative (a primary family head) who maintains a household. Census figures in Canada show this unit as a separate family, but those in the United States do not. The bridge is incomplete, therefore, to the extent that data are published only in the form of the nuclear family (Canada) or of the "household" family (United States). For instance, in studying family size, family income, and family housing space, the nuclear family concept yields a larger number of smaller units (and usually therefore more units with smaller total incomes and smaller housing quarters) than the other concept. The difference is generally of minor practical significance, yet it is of theoretical interest and may actually be of some practical importance for selected age groups (especially for couples of young adult ages), for certain marginal areas with low average incomes, and for periods when there are housing shortages and doubling-up with relatives increases.

The stage of development of a family may be denoted in several different ways. Perhaps the most useful classification, as a rule, is one which describes the ages of the children in the home (preschool, school, postschool), with additional categories for the beginning family, the family in middle age, and the aging family (Duvall, 1957; Foote, 1961; Rodgers, 1962). To show developmental stages for families which remain childless, special treatment, such as classification by age of the head, may be required. Families in which one of the marital partners is missing, or in which one or both partners have remarried, likewise deserve special treatment. Subdivisions of families into a large number of separate types, however, may result in a classification which is too complex for most purposes.

Marriages may be studied on the basis of licenses issued or marriages performed. The latter usually constitute 2 or 3 per cent fewer than the former and often have a lag ranging from a day to several months, as compared with the date on the license. Divorce decrees may be "limited" or "final" and generally have a substantial lag between the date of separation and effective date of the decree, which tends to affect the results of studies of the relationships between divorce rates and associated factors.

COLLECTION OF BASIC DATA

The importance of exerting proper care in planning and executing the collection stage of a statistical study can hardly be overemphasized. Imperfect data may be adjusted, as shown in the next major section, but irreparable losses may be incurred if information on a key subject is not covered or is not obtained in a convenient form to be efficiently processed.

Data used in demographic studies of marriage and the family generally come from government records, in the form of birth, marriage, and divorce certificates or of census records, but during recent years numerous private research centers have made extensive surveys in this field with the purpose of delving into more penetrating factors associated with family building than government sources could provide. These private surveys are discussed below in the section on "Analysis of Tabulated Data."

Design of Basic Records

Vital documents are designed by the several states and revised every 10 years, following recommendations of national advisory committees and the staff of the Division of Vital Statistics, National Center for Health Statistics, United States Department of Health, Education, and Welfare [Cf. Ch. 23, pp. 960–967]. These records contain a limited number of items (age, sex, race, place of birth, present residence, etc.), nearly all of which are collected primarily for administrative uses but which have statistical uses as well. Few states include items that would serve exclusively statistical purposes, such as education or religion, largely because of the resistance of some persons to supplying the information. Many states have items such as occupation on their vital records but do not code and tabulate the results. The quality of data on occupation of parents on birth records, and of the person on death records, has been carefully investigated and found to be only partially satisfactory (Kaplan, Parkhurst, & Whelpton, 1961).

Census questionnaires contain questions on personal, social, and economic characteristics of the population and on characteristics of housing. Items on the questionnaires that are of special interest to the family statistician include relationship to head of household (which portrays family groups living together according to generations or lateral kinship, and persons not in families), marital status and times married (which reflects first marriage and remarriage patterns), date of first marriage (which may be combined with current age to determine age at first marriage and number of years since first marriage), duration of present marital status (which provides data on years in current state of marriage,

widowhood, or divorce), and number of children ever born alive (including those children who have died or left the home to be adopted by someone else or for some other reason).

Several devices have been developed in recent years to make the reporting on the vital and census records more precise and to make the forms clearer to those who fill them. Illustrations include the provision of "None" as a check box for items like number of children ever born, to discourage respondents from leaving the space blank on the quite erroneous assumption that no reply is needed if the quantity is zero; the provision of a special category for "separated" in the marital status distribution to describe those living away from their spouse because of marital discord but who are not divorced; and asking for month and year of first marriage rather than age at first marriage or duration of marriage in order to encourage greater exactness in reporting and to provide more analytical content. The form and content of the questionnaires are carefully pretested before final adoption.

Completeness of Basic Records

Vital records are completed by persons responsible for filing administrative reports on events such as births and marriages. Many of these persons are not greatly impressed with the importance of the documents as basic statistical documents and, accordingly, leave some of the questions unanswered or supply vague approximations without probing for exact responses. This is particularly true of items having no obvious administrative significance. Conscientious state registrars frequently return incomplete certificates to the persons who filed them to fill in the missing information.

The enumerators in a decennial census or interim sample survey receive training on interviewing methods, basic concepts, and a host of administrative details. Practice enumeration before completion of training provides enumerators with the opportunity to ask questions about troubles they encounter. Again, a review of the first day or two of work is an excellent device for correcting errors of omission and commission before much damage to the basic data has been done. Self-enumeration in a census, as in the 1960 Census, permits the conscientious respondent to give more accurate information on technical items such as the husband's occupation and industry than the enumerator might obtain from the man's wife in a direct interview. The use of self-enumeration is believed to have improved the data for those who properly filled their questionnaires but to have led to nonresponses on more items than the use of direct enumeration. Moreover, self-enumeration tends to eliminate clustering of errors, such as those arising from biases introduced by enumerators, and it provides an atmosphere of privacy in reporting which is believed to be conducive to greater accuracy of response on sensitive items, such as educational level (particularly among older persons) and marital status or date of marriage (where children were conceived out of wedlock), and on other items with low visibility, such as race of persons in mixed marriages or of persons living in a neighborhood where the predominant race is different from their own.

dents, who are generally at the ages when marriage rates reach the maximum. These students are counted in the census at their residences while attending college rather than at their parental homes, whereas they are counted in the Census Bureau's Current Population Survey at their parental homes, because this is a more stable year-round location where the sample panel can be reached on a uniform basis month after month. Moreover, for practical reasons, inmates of institutions are counted where they are in care or custody rather than in their place of origin, from which they may have been gone for many years. Still another factor with a distorting effect on the trend in number of adults in the family is the changing number of persons in the armed forces, who are counted as residing at their military post (in private homes or in barracks, according to their living arrangements).

The counting of divorces in the state where the divorce is issued tends to distort the rates upward where divorce is easily obtained and downward where it is hard to obtain. Classification of divorces by state of birth, or by state where the divorcing partners lived when they became separated, would provide a basis for correcting divorce rates by states for the effect of migration related to obtaining a divorce.

Coverage—Place of Residence

Where people should be counted is far from simple and differs according to the purpose, or purposes, of the records. When a couple marries, the ceremony may occur in a state different from the state of usual residence of either party. People may die in hospitals or rest homes in areas other than those where they spent most of their lives. Persons may live in suburbs and work in the city. These and other problems disturb relationships between the proper universe for numerator and denominator in computing birth, marriage, and divorce rates.

Additional technical difficulties arise in assigning place of residence to college stu-

Coverage—Household as Unit

In 1950, the census employed a sample design (every fifth person in order of enumeration) which made it impossible to obtain sample data (on migration, education, occupation, income, etc.) for each member of a given household. In 1960, the census employed a different sample design (every fourth household in order of enumeration), which corrected the weakness just cited. This change was made partly as the result of the strong need expressed for demographic data on all members of a particular family for cross-classification, and partly as a consequence of using self-enumeration in collecting data from about

80 per cent of the population (those in the thickly populated areas); in self-enumeration, the household is the logical unit of reporting.

Cross-Sectional Versus Longitudinal Survey

The conventional household survey or census asks for information about the current or recent situation, such as present marital status and income last year, but for certain purposes the same types of information may be desired *for the same persons* for several earlier dates. To illustrate: Cross-sectional data from successive censuses may be used to show changes in the stages in the life cycle of the family (marriage, childbearing, children leaving home, and death). In addition, longitudinal data from a given group of persons about their own family-building experience could also be used to show the same kinds of changes. The longitudinal data might come from a panel whose past years of experience are reported retrospectively, or from a panel which is followed through many years, or from some adaptation of these and related procedures. A comparative study of cross-sectional and longitudinal data on family building could be made to advantage, in order to demonstrate whether the two approaches yield essentially the same conclusions about patterns of change in the family life cycle or whether one approach is distinctly superior to the other.

On several bases of evaluation, the cross-sectional survey is preferable to the longitudinal survey from the operational viewpoint. Thus, the cross-sectional survey which deals with current characteristics involves a minimum of memory error and of distortion of reporting on remote events, some of which may be charged with unpleasantness. The questionnaire which covers current items can be shorter and less of a strain on the respondent than one which covers the same types of items for several retrospective dates. The complexi-

ties of reconstructing family composition at earlier dates, as required in a retrospective survey taken at one point in time, are magnified. The panel which is traced through time by successive interviews is hard and costly to follow without serious loss (and possible bias) by attrition due to death, long-distance moves, and changing family composition. The professional research organizers, as well as the respondents in longitudinal panels, may change. The panel which is followed may become self-conscious of its behavior because of repeated study, and so on.

The advantages of following a given sample over time by one device or another, however, are numerous. The aftereffects of earlier acts on subsequent acts can be traced directly (for instance, the effects of early versus late marriage on eventual size of family or on eventual socioeconomic status can be studied with maximum confidence when specific family groups are traced). Following the same groups introduces tighter controls on variables which might distort research findings if left uncontrolled, and so on.

Problems involved, and advantages gained, by the use of repeated observations from a fixed sample are discussed at length by Goldfarb (1960) and Downes (1952).

Efforts to reduce the complications in collecting retrospective data are exemplified in a study now in process of completion by two sociologists, Otis Dudley Duncan of the University of Michigan and Peter M. Blau of the University of Chicago. In their study of occupational changes in a generation, one of the chief features is the investigation of differences in the fertility behavior of couples where the husband's occupation is above, below, or the same as that of his father, and as that of his wife's father. Residential changes are measured by comparing present size of place with that where the husband lived most of the time up to 16 and with the actual place where he lived at the age of 16. Occupational mobility during the husband's lifetime is measured by comparing his present and first fulltime job. Intergenerational changes in occupation are measured with the additional use of questions on the husband's father's occupation when the husband was 16, and on the wife's father's occupation when the wife was 16. Also, intergenerational changes in educational level of the husband and of his father are obtained by questions on highest grade of school each completed. [Longitudinal design is also discussed elsewhere in this Handbook; see especially pp. 233–234; 267–268.]

Longitudinal Research by Use of Record Linkage

A rewarding supplement to questionnaire surveys in demographic studies of family behavior is the use of record linkage. Perhaps the most highly developed methodology in family research employing record linkage has been that relating to the linking of marriage records with birth and divorce records for members of the same family, to determine the outcome of marriages that are performed under varying conditions with regard to age, time when the first child is born, and other factors (Christensen, 1958; Christensen, 1963). By searching and matching vital records (marriage, birth, and divorce) for persons who continue to live in the locality, such as the county where they were married, light is also shed on circumstances under which residences before and after marriage are nearer to those of the bride or of the groom. The relationship between the sex ratio of first-born children and the time when the first child is born is also illuminated; this relationship is evidently significantly affected by more frequent attempts at induced abortion among those with premarital pregnancies, and such attempts are more successful, as a rule, when the unborn child is a boy.

Record linkage as a method of collecting family data has numerous advantages over the interview and observation methods

(Christensen, 1958; Christensen, 1963). The basic data are generally available in relatively uniform quality and may be less expensive to obtain than those involving field work. Cross-checks of reports on the different records provide corrections for errors of reporting on the part of the marital partners or others involved (such as obstetricians). Checks of vital (birth) and census records have been used by the United States Bureau of the Census (1953) and by the National Office of Vital Statistics (1956) to determine the completeness of the enumeration of infants in the 1950 Census and the completeness of registration of births in 1950, and by the two agencies to investigate the comparability of reports on occupation from vital records and the 1950 Census (Kaplan et al., 1961). Using matched vital records tends to avoid the distortions which arise in questioning persons directly about previous events of a sensitive nature, such as premarital pregnancy and other disturbing factors, including the rationalizing of unpleasant aspects of behavior or forgetting. There is no waiting for events to occur if the final step in the study (for instance, the divorce) has occurred, and the relationship between researcher and respondent is eliminated.

Two obvious limitations of record linkage are that available data are restricted to the items on the records and that data for persons who have moved from the study area may be lost (Christensen, 1958; Christensen, 1963). Some research workers have partially overcome this restriction in linking vital records by making follow-up studies with mail questionnaires to cover additional analytical items and to reduce bias from various sources, including selective migration; the latter purpose of follow-up studies is mentioned again in the next section of this chapter. Other limitations in using this technique in many parts of the country are the complete lack or inadequacy of vital records in some states and the absence of central files of vital records in others.

ADJUSTMENT OF BASIC DATA

After the basic data are collected, but before they are compiled into tables, they can almost invariably be adjusted in various ways to improve the usefulness and convenience (if not also the quality) of the tables that are eventually produced. The quality of the data on an item, such as marital status, is improved to the extent that the proper proportion of missing cases is assigned to each category. The convenience in use of the data is enhanced if the "unknown" categories are eliminated by acceptable means. The adjustments consist mainly of editing, assigning codes, and weighting.

Editing and Coding

Editing is used chiefly to replace nonresponses with specific entries on the records and to eliminate inconsistencies in the responses on related questions. Filling these gaps by editing is generally much easier to accomplish in an acceptable manner when the interest centers on gross classifications rather than on detailed cross-classifications. Thus, if the number of married persons with missing age at first marriage is relatively small, a crude method of assigning such ages to these persons may be quite adequate for gross distributions but very inadequate for some of the subgroups in a detailed cross-classification, where the ages at first marriage were not reported for a large proportion of the married persons.

The assignment of numerical codes is generally performed by hand for items with entries on the source documents made in verbal form, as in detailed descriptions of household relationships, place of birth, migration, occupation, and industry. Where the entries for a particular item are made by checking boxes or shading circles, that is, where "precoding" is used, the documents may move into the tabulation operation with no manual coding of that item.

Wherever editing and coding performed by mechanical methods are feasible, they are ordinarily preferred to those done by manual methods. Thus, the use of a tabulating machine or related electronic equipment to assign specified codes invariably under rigidly defined circumstances, which the equipment is capable of sensing, almost always assures a more uniform and higher quality of results than the use of hand methods, which are subject to "human" errors. In any large-scale project, however, some work units (counties, enumeration districts, etc., as defined by those who are in charge of the mechanical editing) are rejected because of substandard quality. The basic data for these work units must then be examined by clerical or professional reviewers to discover and correct the errors, generally by hand. In the 1960 Census, for example, basic data for inmates of certain types of institutions contained so many nonreports on several items that hand methods were deemed necessary to assign proper types of codes on these items (U. S. Bureau of the Census, 1962b, p. xlii).

A new method of mechanically assigning entries for missing or inconsistent responses was introduced in the 1960 Census. The key features of this method were the storing of reported values on an item and the assignment of one of these stored values to the next person of similar characteristics who did not have the item reported. Thus, the electronic computer stored the reported marital status of a man in a given group (according to age and relationship to the head of the household) while the record for that man was being edited. When the record for the second man in the same group was being edited, the computer erased the marital status category for the first man and replaced it by that reported for the second man with similar characteristics. This process was repeated until the record was reached for a man with information on marital status either not reported or inconsistent with other information on his record. The last man was thereupon assigned the marital status category (single, married –wife present, separated, other married–wife absent, widowed, or divorced) that had been stored in the matrix for the next preceding man in the same age-relationship group. This method tended to assure that the distribution of marital status categories assigned would closely resemble that for similar persons with marital status reported.

Manual coding is generally required in processing the written entries for detailed relationship that are made on the questionnaires by respondents or enumerators. In the 1960 Census, codes for head, wife, and child were assigned by the enumerator but, for persons in sample households, codes for child-in-law, parent of head or wife, sibling of head or wife, other relative of head, unrelated lodger (partner, other), and unrelated resident employee were assigned by clerks in the central office on the basis of field entries on the questionnaires. In like manner, type of "group quarters" was assigned by clerks to sample persons not in households; these codes included 38 types of institutions for inmates and other persons (mostly resident employees and members of their families) in institutions, and nine types of group quarters for group-quarters members not in institutions—rooming house, hotel or motel, mission or flophouse, general hospital including nurses' quarters, college dormitory, military installation, religious group quarters not elsewhere classified, ship, and workers' dormitory. For persons in households with one or more subfamilies or secondary families, clerks assigned each member of a particular subfamily or secondary family the same "family number." Thus, in a five-person household comprising a head, son-in-law, daughter, (wife of son-in-law), lodger, and lodger's infant son, family number 1 was assigned to each person in the subfamily (married couple), and family number 2 was assigned to each person in the secondary family (parent-child lodger group).

Research workers who conduct demographic studies of families from small-scale surveys without the benefit of electronic computers may find it advisable to prepare a "family transcription sheet," with one line of codes on the several items to be studied for each family, subfamily, and "unrelated individual" (heads of households with no relatives in the household being "primary individuals," and lodgers—including partners—and resident employees with no relatives in the household plus noninmates in group quarters being secondary individuals). Each line of data can be placed on a punchcard for tabulation.

Weighting the Data

The representativeness of distributions obtained from sample data can be increased if the sample figures are adjusted to totals within significant classes by use of "ratio estimates." For instance, a sample that was intended to represent 25 per cent of the universe (county, enumeration district, etc.) may actually be overrepresented in some strata and underrepresented in others because of sampling error, bias due to differential nonresponse, etc. If each stratum of the sample, however, is independently weighted to the "known" total in that stratum of the universe, the resulting distributions of data are improved. This type of adjustment was performed on 44 subgroups of the 1960 Census sample in each publication area (usually a census tract, small city or village, or balance of county). The subgroups consisted of a cross-classification of persons by age, color, and sex further subdivided as to whether head of a household and, if so, whether the head was the owner of his housing unit.

Assigning weights for sample persons rather than entire sample families means that some family members obtain greater weights than others in the same family. This fact arises because of sampling errors and biases, which are usually negligible for large areas but may be large for small areas where difficulties in obtaining sample data from a strictly representative cross-section of households are encountered. Where such discrepancies are substantial, follow-up enumeration on nonreporting households may be required, or substitution of a proper number of larger (or smaller) households for the same number of smaller (or larger) households may be made in order to yield the proper distribution of households by size.

As a final caution, it should be noted that if adjustments of the data are made in the several ways discussed in this major section, this should always be done with care lest the changes result in overadjustment for suspected errors or introduce distortions that are more troublesome and misleading than the original weaknesses in the data. Experience demonstrates, however, that these adjustments are usually relatively small and, if properly administered, increase the meaningfulness of relationships shown in the final tabulated results without unduly complicating the use of the data.

TABULATION OF ADJUSTED DATA

The final step in the processing of basic demographic data is to reduce the mass of detail for persons, families, or other units into statistical tables. These tables may contain simple inventory distributions (generally for smaller areas or parts of the universe) or detailed cross-classifications of substantive data (generally for major parts of the universe). Instead, however, the tables may consist of highly refined summary measures, exemplified in the next major section, together with the size of the base from which the measures are derived. Most of the tables are likely to be devoted to the presentation of details for use in substantive analyses, but some may be used to show the reliability or other evaluative aspects of the data (see section below on "Evaluation of the Data").

Classifications of Data

Demographic statistics on family behavior may be presented in terms of numbers of *events* (births, marriages, divorces, etc.), in terms of numbers of persons with specified *structural characteristics* (persons by age, sex, marital status, etc.), or in terms of summary measures related to these events or structural characteristics. The events may be thought of as constituting dynamic aspects and the structural characteristics as static aspects of family behavior. Cross-classifications of such events by the structural characteristics, or of one type of structural characteristic by another, account for most of the volume of demographic tables.

Figure 1 presents an illustrative list of the types of events and associated structural characteristics that are commonly used in demographic studies, with special attention to those relevant to family behavior.

The usual purpose of cross-classifying events and characteristics is to perform a simplified version of partial correlation (see section below on "Analysis of Tabulated Data"). The purpose of the cross-classification, stated otherwise, is to study differences between the frequency and dispersion of various subgroups of the population with potentially disturbing variables held constant. For example, consider a table on age at marriage. A simple distribution of all persons by age at marriage would disregard many important distinctions: whether the persons were men or women, whether they were entering their first marriage or a remarriage, and, if a remarriage, whether they had been previously widowed or divorced. Hence, a meaningful table would show marriages classified by previous marital status of bride and groom, further cross-classified by age at current marriage of bride and groom. This table permits a detailed analysis of age of grooms who are entering their first marriage, controlling on whether their brides are marrying for the first time or not and on age of the bride at current marriage. For men who are remarrying, separate data in similar detail are also shown for those who had been previously divorced and those who had been previously

Events	Closely related variables	Related structural characteristics
Births	Number of births, child-spacing, sex ratio of births, legitimacy, stock, religion, characteristics of parents	Age, sex, ethnic, and religious composition of the population
Entrance into school	Full- or part-time enrollment, regular or special school	School enrollment, public or private school, educational level
Participation in labor force	Full- or part-time employment, full- or part-year employment, place of work, transportation to work	Work experience, current employment status, occupation, income, socioeconomic status
Marriages and divorces	Number of marriages, divorces, and annulments, previous marital status, number of times married	Marital status, age at marriage, duration of marriage, years in present marital status
Household formation and dissolution	Number of households, families, and subfamilies, type of household or group quarters, living (housing) arrangements, generations together	Relationship to head of household (family, subfamily), children in family, characteristics of head and wife
Moving to different home	Number moving, date of move, distance of move, origin and destination	Internal and external migration, size of place, location (region, etc.), farm residence
Illnesses and handicaps	Number ill or handicapped, length and cause, chronic conditions, hospitalization	Various classifications relating to morbidity
Deaths	Number of deaths, causes of death, infant and maternal deaths	Various classifications relating to mortality

Fig. 1. Events, Variables, and Structural Characteristics Commonly Used in Demographic Studies.

widowed. If this table shows 10 groups with regard to age at current marriage for the bride, by 10 groups for age of the groom, and if previous marital status consists of three groups (single, divorced, widowed) for the bride and three for the groom, there would be a total of 900 (10 × 10 × 3 × 3) cells in the table for the basic data, that is, excluding totals and subtotals. If additional detail is added for two color groups, the basic cells are doubled. Further subdivision by size of place, state or region, and socioeconomic status could inflate the number of cells at a very rapid pace, unless judicious reductions are made in intervening variables, or unless parts of the detail are shown only in summary form.

Collation of Data from Different Sources

Family statistics on demographic characteristics may come from punchcards or electronic tapes with the person or the family (or subfamily) as the unit of measurement. As a means of adding an extra dimension to the analysis, the punchcards or tapes for these two types of units can be run through a machine simultaneously and matched (collated) so as to make tabulations of persons by their own characteristics cross-classified according to the characteristics of their families. In the resulting tables, each person is a unit of tabulation, but the information for the person is shown in his or her family context (Glick, 1961). Illustrative uses for this type of "person-family" tabulation are as follows: to show the age distribution and living arrangements of dependent children cross-classified by relevant family characteristics; to show the number of adult family members other than the head and wife (including aged persons) by their own income crossed by the total family income; to compare the characteristics of the head of the family with those of other adults in the family (including the chief earner); and to show how many family members of selected characteristics are in families chiefly dependent on a given industry (such as agriculture, mining, or manufacturing).

Record linkage, discussed in the preceding section, also provides two or more sets of collated records from different sources for comparison and analysis.

ANALYSIS OF TABULATED DATA

The climax of most statistical studies is the analytical phase. This is the place where the highlights of the tabulated data and their implications are set forth. This is the place where the reader is told whether the basic hypotheses which were to be tested by the study were borne out or not, and where the evidence for the conclusions of the study is presented. Methods of distilling such evidence from tabulated data constitute the central content of the present section. [Cf. Ch. 10 below for complementary treatments.]

Most of the attention of basic data-gathering agencies, such as those engaged in compiling and publishing vital statistics and census data, is focused on the statistical methods which lead up to but largely exclude the more refined analytical methods. These agencies usually provide massive cross-classifications of data which can serve as general-purpose sources from which research workers can make detailed analyses of narrowly defined problems. Along with the massive data tables, these sources generally contain, at most, rather elementary statistical measures, such as averages and percentage distributions. During intervals between major censuses, analysts in these agencies and outside prepare numerous interpretive papers, articles, and monographs which bring the essence of the data to the users of demographic statistics in various walks of life.

Analytical variables used in demographic studies of the family were outlined in the preceding section of this chapter. The principal analytical methods customarily used in studying these variables could be classified equally effectively in several different ways, but those treated here are grouped more or less arbitrarily into *four* broad types: measures of central tendency, measures of dispersion, correlation, and trend analysis.

Measures of Central Tendency

The measures of central tendency which are probably most frequently used by family demographers may be described as averages, rates and ratios, indexes, and attrition tables. The central purpose of these measures is to give a "probability statement" of an event's occurrence or of a structural characteristic's existence. The median age at marriage, the birth rate per 1,000 inhabitants, the cost-of-living index for the average urban family, the chances that a 30-year-old spinster will ever marry—all of these may be regarded as measures of central tendency. They all tell the reader what happens "on the average." Ways of refining the measures so as to improve the probability statements they can provide are included in the following presentation. In numerous instances, methods relevant to various types of vital events are described only in relation to one type, usually births.

Averages. Averages may be shown in terms of the mode, mean, or median of a distribution. The mode is the value which occurs most frequently in a distribution. The mean (often referred to loosely as the "average") is the sum of the values in a distribution divided by the number of values. Thus, the number of children per family represents the total number of children (of specified age and relationship) divided by the total number of families (of specified type, location, age of head, socioeconomic grouping, etc.) The more precisely the kinds of children (numerator) and families (denominator) are defined, the more meaningful, the more closely controlled, and usually the more variable from group to group, the mean number of children becomes.

The median age at first marriage can be obtained by direct or indirect methods. Computing the median involves the location of the point which divides the distribution of ages at first marriage into two equal groups, one-half being older and one-half being younger than the median. The median age at first marriage is computed in a straightforward manner according to procedures found in standard textbooks on statistics when the direct method is used, with distributions of age at first marriage obtained from marriage records or from census or survey records. An indirect method may be used to estimate the median age at first marriage from a classification of marital status by age and sex. In brief, the median is computed by the indirect method as follows: (a) Estimate the expected proportion of young people who will ever marry during their lifetime—a practical estimate being the current proportion 45 to 54 years old who have ever married. (b) Calculate one-half this expected proportion. (c) Compute the current age of young people who are at this halfway mark. The date of the survey is the approximate date, on the aver-

age, when this halfway mark is reached. Further details about how to refine the computation of the median by the indirect method are given in various publications (Jaffe, 1951; U. S. Bureau of the Census, 1962a).

Both the direct and indirect methods of computing the median age at first marriage yield very similar results for most groups of persons. The indirect method is generally reserved for application, however, where data required for use of the direct method are lacking. Thus, marriage records showing age at first marriage are not available for all 50 states; hence, unless census or survey data are available from questions on age at first marriage, the only way to obtain comparable median ages at first marriage for all states is to employ an indirect method. Caution is urged in comparing median ages at first marriage from marriage records for a long series of successive years (computed by the direct method) for available states combined, because the number of states with detailed marriage records has increased over time, and the underlying characteristics of the states with such records have changed considerably from one time to another. In using the medians obtained from data on marriage records, the problem of comparability over time can be minimized if a uniform set of states is included for all years. This approach leaves open the question of how representative of the entire United States those particular states happen to be.

Median ages at entering remarriage, widowhood (or widowerhood), divorce, or separation can ordinarily be computed only by direct methods. Marriage records provide information on age at current marriage for those previously widowed or divorced but rarely, if ever, show age at time of becoming widowed or divorced. Likewise, divorce records show age at one phase of the divorce proceedings or another but usually do not show age at the time of the marriage that is being dissolved. Death records ordinarily do not show age of surviving spouse, if any, from which age at becoming widowed could be readily computed. Distributions and, therefore, medians for all the above-mentioned ages (and also median age at first marriage) can be obtained from census or survey questions on present age, length of time in present marital status, and whether married more than once (as was done in the 1950 Census); for example, the difference between present age and duration of widowhood is age at widowhood. Median ages at entering current marital status that are computed from this source are approximations, because they involve the use, generally, of whole years of age and of duration of current marital status (Hauser & Duncan, 1959, pp. 585–586). By using months or quarters of a year (as in the 1960 Census) in tabulating present age and date of first marriage, the area of overlap in deriving related measures (year of or age at first marriage) is correspondingly reduced.

In computing median size of family, the choice of the limits of the interval containing the median is noteworthy. According to census practice, these limits are placed at equal distances from the whole number, for instance, the limits of three-person families are 2.50 and 3.49, with 3.00 as the midpoint. This choice can be defended on several grounds, including the fact that the distribution of family size is such that the median size should usually be smaller than the mean size, whereas it would often be larger if the limits of the intervals were one-half person higher to correspond with conventional class intervals.

Ratios and rates. Ratios and rates are similar in that one quantity is expressed as a proportion of another quantity of related or similar nature. Thus, the number of males divided by the number of females in a given population (times 100) is called the sex ratio, and the number of births divided by the number of women of childbearing age is called a birth rate. These examples demonstrate that demographers use the word "ratio" to describe a relationship in which the universe covered by the numerator does not ordinarily "come from" the universe covered by the denominator, whereas demographers use the word "rate" to imply that the numerator did "come from" the universe in the denominator. There are, however, some exceptions. Thus, a crude divorce rate (divorces divided by total population) might have been more properly called a ratio because unmarried persons—who cannot obtain divorces—are included in the denominator. Likewise, a crude marriage rate includes married persons in the denominator, although such persons are not subject to getting married. Regardless of efforts to refine the bases of rates, however, whenever the rates apply to large population groups, they almost always contain irrelevant persons to some extent.

Among the most commonly used ratios in demographic literature (which are called "ratios") are dependency ratios; these are usually expressed as ratios of young and old persons to persons in the middle age range. According to interest and available data, the numerator may include children under 15 or under 18 years of age and persons 60 or 65 years old and over, with the denominator including those in the intermediate ages. The ratio can be refined, where data permit, by transferring all economically active persons, regardless of age, from the numerator to the denominator, and all economically inactive persons to the numerator. Another example of ratios is the disrupted marriage ratio (Glick, 1963). The numerator of this ratio contains separated and divorced persons and the denominator contains married (including separated) persons. The ratio actually consists of the sum of a separation rate (separated persons divided by married —including separated—persons) and a divorce ratio (divorced persons divided by married—including separated—persons). Having a common base, the separation rate and the divorce ratio are additive.

Birth rates appear in numerous degrees of refinement, generally with each one having a unique title. To give an exhaustive treatment to the various forms of birth rates would introduce a gross imbalance into the presentation. Brief descriptions of several are presented, however, with references to publications where further details can be found.

Crude birth rates (births divided by total population) are generally used in presenting preliminary indications of recent changes in fertility, before more detailed tabulations by characteristics, such as age of mother, have been received. They are also used for making comparisons of birth rates for countries, some of which have meager vital statistics available, and for showing trends over long periods of time within a country, where the only relevant measures available for early dates are crude birth rates (which, in themselves, may have been estimated on the basis of age distributions of the population from census data). Although crude birth rates lack refinement, they are widely used by competent demographers in situations where differences between countries or other groups are sufficiently great that essentially the same general conclusions about the relative magnitudes of the rates would be drawn from rates based on simple as well as complex methods.

Crude rates of natural increase are obtained by subtracting crude death rates (deaths divided by total population) from crude birth rates.

The fertility ratio is usually presented as the number of children per 1,000 women and is obtained by dividing the number of children under five years old by the number of women who were of childbearing age when these children were born, commonly 15 to 49 years old. If children under one year old are used, the upper limit of the women is generally lowered to 44, and the lower limit is sometimes raised to 20. In preparing fertility ratios for groups with many children born to teenage mothers, it is advisable to keep the lower limit at 15, if feasible.

An effective fertility rate is the number of sons and daughters under five years old per 1,000 women of childbearing age. This rate is a refinement of the fertility ratio in that the children are known to be associated with their own mothers, who may be classified by nativity or other characteristics. Like the crude birth rate and the fertility ratio, the effective fertility rate describes the *current* rate of reproduction. The last two measures have several added features: They are less subject to variation due to fluctuations from year to year in the fertility level; they reflect the effect on population growth potential of differences between groups in infant mortality; and, when based on children under five, they are roughly five times as large as crude birth rates and, thus, are more likely to show substantial, hence more reliable, group differences in fertility.

Cumulative fertility rates are rates with the total number of live-born children of the women up to the present time included in the numerator and the corresponding number of women in the denominator. A substantial majority of the women who have reached the age of 30 years have produced all of the children they will bear in their lifetime. Cumulative fertility rates have the advantages and disadvantages associated with their inclusion of children who are no longer living or who no longer live in their parental home for other reasons.

Completed fertility rates are cumulative fertility rates for women who have finished childbearing. This group of women is generally construed, for most practical purposes, as including women 45 years old and over. The youngest five-year age group for which completed fertility can be shown is the group 45 to 49 years old. Often, research workers make estimates of future childbearing for women over 30 or 35, on the reasonable assumption, in most cases, that estimates of additional children born after those ages are subject to only minor error, as compared with the number of children born prior to those ages. These estimates permit analysis of estimated trends in completed fertility rates up to a point 10 or more years beyond the time when final figures become available.

Specific birth and fertility rates are rates that are controlled by relevant factors. For example, age-specific rates show separate figures for each age group of women; parity-specific rates show figures for women who have already borne a specified number of children (with zero parity referring to women with no previous children); and age-parity-specific rates show figures controlled for both age and parity.

A gross reproduction rate represents the number of daughters a cohort of 1,000 female infants beginning life together would have during their lives, if the cohort were subject to the birth rates at each age level which prevailed at the time specified, and if none of the females in the cohort were to die before the end of the childbearing period. Augmentation or diminution by migration is not taken into account.

A net reproduction rate differs from a gross reproduction rate by adding the stipulation that death rates at the age level which prevailed at the specified time also are applied, by use of life tables. For replacement in the next generation, each cohort of 1,000 female infants should eventually give birth to 1,000 daughters. The net reproduction rate, unlike the gross reproduction rate, makes allowance for the fact that not all women live to the end of the childbearing period. A comparison of the two rates shows how much fertility is diminished because of deaths occurring to the infant females before they pass the childbearing ages.

For the method of computing gross and net reproduction rates see Kuczynski (1929; 1931); United States Bureau of the Census (1944); Volume I, for any recent year, of *Vital Statistics of the United States,* published by the Division of Vital Statistics, National Center for Health Statistics in the United States Department of Health, Education, and Welfare; or a standard textbook on vital statistics or demography. Spiegelman (1955) discusses several variations of the gross and net reproduction rates, with controls on marital status, number of previous children, and other relevant variables.

Gross and net reproduction rates provide, in a sense, a static description of long-run future population growth. Actual future population growth will be affected by past and future changes in births, deaths, and migration, and resultant changes in age structure. In countries with relatively unchanging levels of population growth, the gross and net reproduction rates tend to give a reliable indication of future population totals if no new factor is introduced to alter current growth patterns. More caution in using the rates is appropriate for countries, like those in Western society, where birth rates are more responsive to changing economic and social conditions.

Other elaborate methods of analyzing vital rates that were developed by Dublin and Lotka (1925) and other statisticians are described in demographic textbooks. Among these are the intrinsic birth rate, intrinsic death rate, intrinsic rate of natural increase, and mean length of a generation. These measures indicate conditions which would exist in the "stable" population of the remote future if present vital rates continued unchanged at each age level and if migration had no net effect on the population of each age level. Recent research by Ryder (1959) shows impressively the cumulative effect on the eventual population of an area after a long period of time, such as a century, if the length of a generation is increased by means of radically delayed childbearing.

Standardized rates (birth, fertility, marriage, divorce, death, etc.) show what the rates for a group of persons would be if the base population had the same distribution as a standard population, that is, a population having a fixed distribution with respect to one or more specified characteristics (age, color, urban-rural residence, etc.), taken singly or in combination. For example, differences between birth rates for women with husbands in farm and non-farm occupation groups may reflect age differences in the adult female population as a consequence of movement of young adults—in particular, the movement of young nonwhite persons—from rural to urban areas. If the relationship between birth rates and occupational level is studied with the age of the women "held constant" by use of standardization, the disturbing factor of age is eliminated.

Birth rates for women in the United States by occupation of husband standardized by age of woman are calculated as follows: For women in the first occupation group, the birth rates for women in each age group are multiplied by the proportion of women in the United States who are in the corresponding age groups. The sum of the products over all age groups gives the birth rate for women whose husbands are in the first occupation group, standardized for age. The same process is then applied to the women whose husbands are in the other occupation groups, each time using the same percentage distribution of women by age as is found in the United States as a whole without regards to husband's occupation. The standardized birth rate for each occupational level shows in an abstract manner what the rate would be if the wives of husbands in each occupation group had the same age distribution. The procedure for standardizing data is described in detail by Jaffe (1951, Ch. 3) and by Grabill, Kiser, and Whelpton (1958, Appendix B).

Comparing a standardized rate and an unstandardized rate shows the effect of the standardized factor on the rate. Thus, in the above example, the comparison shows the effect of differences in ages of women on the birth rate for women with husbands in the several occupation groups, that is, it shows the effect on the birth rate resulting from the deviation of the age distribution of women in each "husband's occupation group" from the national average age distribution of women. Standardization may be performed on two or more factors as well as on one, but age is probably the factor most often standardized, because of its pervading influence on demographic variables. The use of simple and multiple

standardization is one form of the analysis of variance, described below in the section on "Measures of Dispersion."

Used properly, standardization may be a very powerful analytical tool. If, however, the factor being standardized is closely related to the factor being studied, extreme caution must be exercised in interpreting the results. For instance, birth rates by occupation of husband standardized by residence (urban places by size; rural nonfarm; rural farm) may yield some unusual results because the rural-farm residents in certain occupations other than farm work may be highly selected, or because farm workers living in the largest cities may be very highly selected or nonexistent. Thus, standardization may "control out" the variable that is being studied.

Generation analyses and other cohort analyses of vital events provide highly sophisticated and valuable results. Birth, marriage, and divorce rates of this type may be used to trace the lifetime experiences of a "generation" of women with respect to childbearing and of adults with respect to marriage and divorce. Rates computed for entire generations are generally expressed in terms of cohorts, or groups of persons who pass through life together. A birth cohort is the group of persons who were born in the specified period, and a marriage cohort is the group of persons who were married in the specified period. Differences between fertility levels of birth cohorts and approximately corresponding marriage cohorts throw light on the effect on fertility of the proportion in the group who never marry. Representative studies of cohort fertility include the pioneering work of Whelpton (1954); useful summaries of Whelpton's data are presented by Grabill, Kiser, and Whelpton (1958) and by Petersen (1961, pp. 236–239). The more recent work of Grabill and Parke (1961) shows retrospective marriage and fertility data that were developed by the Bureau of the Census and makes use of a cross-section of women from the August 1959 Current Population

Survey to show distributions by age at first marriage and cumulative numbers of children for successive past dates, with current survivors augmented by use of life tables to reconstruct total numbers of persons at earlier dates.

The computation of joint marriage rates for men and women has been attempted by Ryder (1961) with only limited success. Age-specific marriage rates for men produce levels that differ from those for women because of differences in the numbers of men and women who are eligible for marriage. The problem is to attempt the development of joint probabilities of marriage among groups of eligible men and women. A similar hiatus arises in the computation of birth rates for men and women, where the coverage is not limited to those married and living with their spouse. Conventional practice, as a rule, is to use rates based on women and not to compute rates for men. The differences in the results for men and women are generally of more theoretical than practical significance, except where the numbers of men and women at risk of having children, marrying, or obtaining a divorce differ greatly.

Infant mortality rates are useful as indexes of health conditions and of economic well-being of the population in areas with limited statistical systems. They are of interest to family demographers in that lowering these rates means that the population will tend to increase more rapidly. They are usually computed by dividing the number of deaths of infants under one year of age by the number of births in the same year.

Other types of rates of interest to family statisticians are discussed in later sections. These include household formation rates, which are covered in the subsection on "Trend Analysis"; and death rates by marital status, adoption rates, and orphanhood rates, which are covered in the section on "Evaluation of the Data." Rates of institutionalization because of dependency, ill health, old age, impairment of mind or body, infraction of the law, and the like are also of interest to the family demographer,

because of the fact that commitment of persons to institutions depletes household size and because commitments fall unequally among families of different structural types and economic statuses, among other reasons. (See the discussion of rates of admission to mental hospitals later in this section.)

Indexes. Indexes of social and economic behavior relating to the family may be simple or complex. Percentages of married couples who are living doubled-up (that is, couples who share the home of relatives as husband-wife subfamilies or of nonrelatives as husband-wife secondary families) are widely used by housing research workers as a simple index of housing potential that remains unsatisfied, generally with the realistic assumption that there is a "hard core" of doubling which no reasonable expansion of available housing would ever erase. Intermarriage rates have been used by Price and Zubrzycki (1952) as an index of assimilation. The percentage of women ever married, the percentage childless among ever-married women, the percentage of young children not living with both parents, the percentage of children with working mothers, the percentage of family heads engaged in manufacturing, and endless additional simple measures are regularly used as indexes of one aspect of family behavior or another.

Three indexes used in social area analysis have been developed by Shevky and Bell (1955). These indexes—social rank, urbanization. and segregation—are used to study variations among census tracts within metropolitan areas. The fertility ratio is among the measures from which the index of urbanization is derived.

A new index of socioeconomic status (SES) has been developed by Nam and associates at the United States Bureau of the Census and will be described in a forthcoming issue of *Supplementary Reports* of the 1960 Census of Population, Series PC (S1). A special report containing detailed classifications of data from the 1960 Census on marriage, fertility, and other subjects by socioeconomic status of the family will probably be published in 1965. This index provides a single summary value for a family, which is ascribed to each member of the family. It consists of the average percentile ranking of the family on three measures: education of the chief income recipient in the family, detailed occupation of the chief income recipient, and total income of the family members. The ranking of occupation is based on the average educational and income levels of persons in each occupation in 1950. Measures such as the SES index are in no sense a substitute for detailed cross-classifications of the component factors, but serve a different set of purposes. For a description of other socioeconomic indexes and their uses in studying social stratification, see Duncan (1961) and Hatt (1950).

Another relevant index that may prove useful for direct study or for correlation with data on vital events is the consumer price index, which provides comparable data on standard urban families for several decades. The index is shown by type of consumer product and is prepared by the United States Bureau of Labor Statistics.

Attrition tables. Attrition tables show probabilities that persons will continue in a given condition for specified periods of time, usually single years or groups of years. Life tables show probabilities of death and of survival and are standard tools of demographers who compute such derived measures as net reproduction rates (Kuczynski, 1926; Kuczynski, 1931), retrospective birth and marriage rates (Grabill & Parke, 1961), and chances of joint survival of husband and wife (Glick, 1957; Myers, 1959).

Attrition tables for the single population as of 1940 have been developed by Grabill (1945). The "double decrement" tables show attrition because of nuptiality and mortality for men and women, in terms of such measures as the percentage of persons of each single year of age who will ever marry, the average number of years remaining before death or marriage, and first mar-

riage and death rates at each age in the stationary population (that is, in a hypothetical cohort of persons passing through life as if they were subject to current mortality conditions).

Nuptiality (marriage) tables by sex for single persons as of 1948 and for widowed and divorced persons as of 1940 have been published by Jacobson (1959). Problems encountered in developing such tables and some of the implications of the values in the tables are discussed in the reference cited. These tables are not only valuable to social scientists but also are often cited by lawyers in assessing damages resulting from premature deaths of heirs.

Other attrition tables of interest to family demographers are to be prepared from research currently in progress under sponsorship of the National Institutes of Health. One set is being developed by Evelyn M. Kitagawa and Philip M. Hauser of the University of Chicago and is expected to show national life-table values for persons in different social and economic strata, based on family characteristics. Another set may be developed from research which is being conducted by Earl Pollack, Richard W. Redick, and colleagues at the National Institute of Mental Health. This project is expected to yield rates of admission to mental hospitals between mid-1960 and mid-1961, classified by characteristics of the families of which the patients were members at the time of the 1960 Census. Still another project in the exploratory stages, under the direction of Jon Simpson and Maurice Van Arsdol of the University of Southern California, would show rates of juvenile delinquency according to the characteristics of the youths' families as shown in the 1960 Census. All three of these studies involve record linkage.

Measures of Dispersion

Standard statistical tools for showing the extent to which distributions of variables show deviations from the central tendency are called measures of dispersion. Perhaps the simplest of these measures is the range between highest and lowest values. Other commonly used measures of dispersions are percentiles, deciles, quintiles, quartiles, tertiles, and medians, all of which imply locations of values in terms of cumulative distances from the top or bottom of the range (in hundredths, tenths, fifths, fourths, thirds, and halves, respectively), in accordance with the manner in which the data are arrayed. Average deviations show the mean of the deviations (without regard to positive or negative sign) of values in a distribution from the mean itself. Standard deviations show the square root of the mean of the squared deviations from the mean itself, and thus accentuate the weight of extreme variations from the norm. Further discussion of these relatively simple statistical measures can be found in any standard textbook on statistics. The purpose of mentioning them here is to call them to the attention of those beginning work on family demography without any formal training in statistics.

Analysis of variance. A more complex standard technique, analysis of variance, can be used to great advantage in summarizing the relative contributions of two or more factors in explaining variations in the distribution of a demographic variable. An example of the application of this method is found in a study of the relative importance of size of place and region in explaining variations in marriage instability (Glick, 1963). In this study, instability of marriage is inferred from separation and divorce ratios (see section above on "Measures of Central Tendency").

The underlying method of performing analysis of variance is presented in standard textbooks on statistics and involves several computational steps. First, compute the value of the variable (for example, separation ratio) for each cell of a table which cross-classifies two factors (such as size of place and region). Second, find the deviation of each detailed value from that for the universe as a whole. Third, square each

deviation. Fourth, weight each squared deviation by an appropriate base (here, the number of married females in the cell). Fifth, sum the weighted (squared) deviations for all rows and columns. Repeat these five steps, using deviations of each detailed value from the value for the total in the relevant category of the first factor (here, for example, for the total rural farm, as a category of size of place); repeat, again using deviations from the total in the relevant category for the second factor (here, for example, for the Northeast, as a category of region). Next, subtract the combined sum of the weighted variances for the first and second factors from the sum of the weighted variances for the total of the universe to determine the interaction (or error of closure) factor. Finally, add equal shares of the interaction factor to the weighted variance of the first and second factors.

Without further clarification, the foregoing description of analysis of variance is intended to communicate the essence of the measure to persons not previously familiar with it, namely, to summarize the share of the squared deviations that can be accounted for statistically by each of the variable factors. In the example used here, the results showed that knowledge of size of place tends to aid the demographer much more than the knowledge of region in evaluating the circumstances under which married couples tend to become separated or divorced.

Several techniques for describing dispersion that are more or less unique in the demographic analysis of family behavior deserve special mention. These include graphic techniques, such as the population pyramid; the measurement of intervals between events, such as the spacing of children and of other stages in the life cycle of the family; and the measurement of the degree of consistency among the components of the family's socioeconomic status.

Population pyramid. The population pyramid is a graph which consists of horizontal bars for successively older age groups, with the youngest group at the bottom and oldest at the top. A vertical dividing line is drawn in the center of the pyramid. Each bar to the left of this line shows the number of males, or the percentage of all males in the entire universe (such as the percentage of males of all ages) who are in the age group. Each bar to the right of the center shows corresponding information for females. The unique feature of population pyramids on family data is that each bar may be further subdivided to show a family characteristic, such as the number or percentage of persons who are in each of the marital status categories or who are in each category by relationship to head of household.

Child-spacing. Child-spacing studies are of relatively recent origin, on a nationwide basis. Pioneering work on child-spacing in an elaborate survey of social and psychological factors affecting fertility was sponsored by private foundation grants and conducted in Indianapolis in the early 1940's. Numerous reports based on this survey have been published in the *Milbank Memorial Fund Quarterly* and reproduced in five volumes edited by P. K. Whelpton and Clyde V. Kiser (1946; 1950; 1952; 1954; 1958). Research reported by Christensen and Meissner (1953) on a study of child-spacing in Tippecanoe County, Indiana, serves as an example of a local study in which record linkage was a central feature, and a later report (Christensen, 1963) summarizes this and related studies; references in the sources cited here provide leads to earlier research on this subject. A carefully designed study of the timing of births in Great Britain, with emphasis on the importance of knowing the eventual number of children the woman will bear, was made by Glass and Grebenik (1954).

Recently, the results of elaborate foundation studies on family planning and other aspects of child-spacing in relation to social background factors including religion, biological factors including sterility, and efforts to control fertility including contraceptive practices, have been published by Freedman, Whelpton, and Campbell (1959); Hill, Stycos, and Back (1959); and Westoff et al. (1961). These studies were concerned less directly with establishing levels of fertility than in the investigation of nondemographic factors which throw light on group differences in fertility and in the extent and effectiveness of family limitation devices and practices. Summaries of these and many other studies, including the Indianapolis study mentioned above and studies of family planning throughout the world, are presented in a book edited by Kiser (1962). A classic analysis of factors related to fertility generally, and to fertility in Africa and Latin America in particular, has been published by Lorimer (1954).

The first official statistics for the United States as a whole on the spacing of young children in the family were based on data from the March 1954 Current Population Survey, conducted by the Bureau of the Census under the sponsorship of the National Office of Vital Statistics and published by Schachter (1958). A highly informative study of child-spacing, with retrospective data for several past decades, was made by the Bureau of the Census in 1959 (see Grabill & Parke, 1961). One of the reports in Volume II of the 1960 Census reports on population is to present data on child-spacing in relation to social and economic factors. It will probably be published in 1965.

In child-spacing studies, the interest may center on the length of time from marriage to the birth of each succeeding child, or on the periods between succeeding children. The former approach is used in tracing the life cycle of family growth and is simpler in some respects to measure and summarize. The latter approach, however, provides measures with less dispersion for orders of birth above the first child. For instance, variations from woman to woman in the interval from marriage to the second birth are obviously going to be much greater than variations in the interval from the first to the second birth; this smaller dispersion of intervals between births means that projections of future numbers of children of second and higher orders can be made with more confidence on the basis of knowledge about when the preceding child was born than on knowledge about when the mother was married.

Life cycle stages. Statistics on stages in the life cycle of the family—and on differences in family composition, socioeconomic status, housing, and other characteristics of the family during successive stages of this cycle—are considered here as indications of dispersion in family behavior. These statistics demonstrate the need for recognizing that references to *the* family are references to an abstraction. Families, as separate entities, are in a continuous process of change throughout their existence. Moreover, patterns of family behavior in modern societies, and in societies which are becoming modern, are likewise in the process of change over the decades. So, the life cycle of family behavior is variable in two aspects.

Measures of the stages in the family life cycle are generally stated in terms of medians and may be assembled from various sources (Glick, 1955; Glick, 1957; Sussman, 1963). Thus, the median age at first marriage may be obtained from vital statistics or census data on marriage. Likewise, the median age at having the first and last child may come from vital or census data on births by age of mother and father. Median ages of the marital partners when their children marry and leave home may be approximated by assuming that the children will marry at a certain age in relation to the age when their parents married; one variation which has been used is to assume that the children will marry at the same age as their parents. The median age of the wife at the death of her husband, if the wife is the survivor (and of the husband if he is the survivor) may be computed from life tables by multiplying the survival rates for men and women from marriage age

onward to the point where half the couples have survived jointly. The median ages obtained for each of the stages will vary somewhat, depending on the source of the data and the exact procedures that are used, but the variations generally do not seriously affect the general inferences drawn from the values obtained. Suggestions for improving the conceptual framework relating to the family life cycle have been proposed by Coughenour and Gladden (1960), and research by Reuben Hill and associates designed to improve the construction and analysis of the life cycle categories has been published by Rodgers (1962; see also Ch. 5 of this Handbook). The cycle concept has been used in population analysis for business research purposes by Tella (1962) and Linden (1961).

Status consistency. Status consistency types represent a recently developed way of showing dispersion and have been developed as an adjunct to the index of socioeconomic status (SES) of family members, discussed above in the section on "Measures of Central Tendency." A family may rank consistently high, intermediate, or low on all components of SES, or it may deviate from a consistent pattern in as many different ways as there are permutations and combinations of the components. These types of status consistency or inconsistency constitute a very useful means of studying the factors underlying differences in marriage, fertility, and divorce rates, and in other aspects of family behavior. For example, the data on SES in one study were found to yield the highest correlation with fertility rates when the women with inconsistent components of SES were arranged in an order which gave priority to any indication of low status (U. S. Bureau of the Census, 1958). A special report in Volume II of the 1960 Census reports is to show socioeconomic status groups of family members classified by the family's status consistency type and further cross-classified (in separate tables) by stage of the family life cycle, percentage childless, fertility rate, age at first marriage, education and occupation of chief income recipient, family income, and selected indexes of the quality of housing. This report may be published in 1965.

Correlation Methods

Until recent years, studies of mass data on marriage and the family obtained from vital statistics and census reports have made relatively little use of simple, partial, and mutiple correlation techniques, which are described in standard statistics textbooks. An example of the use of correlation in the analysis of census data is to be found, however, in the report on socioeconomic status mentioned in the preceding paragraph. Here, the SES scores for chief income recipients are correlated with occupation rating, education rating, family income rating, and pairs of the three items taken jointly.

Multivariate analysis of the influence of numerous social and psychological variables on fertility behavior is reported by Westoff et al. (1961). The technique of factor analysis was employed to isolate the components of variables which were mathematically independent. By this technique, it was found that the 25 variables used for Protestants and Jews, and the 26 used for Catholics (including extent of Catholic education), could be reduced to 11 independent dimensions or factors. Analyses such as this demonstrate the degree to which variables form clusters and to which a particular cluster measures something unrelated to the content of other clusters.

Another form of multivariate analysis, the multiple regression technique, is being used by the United States Bureau of the Census in determining which demographic variables are most closely related to the occurrence of a birth in a particular family or group of families during a specified period, such as a year or a quarter of a year. (See discussion of demographic model in the section below on "Trend Analysis.") The same technique can be used, of course, to establish which variables are associated most closely with the occurrence of a marriage, a divorce, or other demographic event.

Still another measure, whereby the significances of difference between fertility rates for adjacent categories of closely controlled demographic variables were calculated, has been used quite effectively by Ruggles and Ruggles (1960).

Trend Analysis

Just as correlation techniques deal with the measurement of joint dispersion of two or more variables, trend analysis deals with the same phenomena where time is one of the variables. As more and more data on demographic events are cumulated on a comparable basis over a long period of time, the more meaningful the studies of sequences of events can become. Thus, if annual, quarterly, or monthly data on vital events (such as marriages, births, and deaths) are carefully studied along with other simultaneous events (such as business fluctuations) and with related personal characteristics (age, marital status, and household relationship) and employment characteristics of participants in the vital events, the results can be used with a certain amount of confidence in projecting the numbers of events into the future. In general, the longer the period for which historical data on the events are available, and the sharper and more relevant the measures of the variables, the greater the likelihood that future fluctuations in the number of events can be approximated within reasonably narrow limits. Historical series are often beset with many difficulties, however, because of gaps in the data, changing concepts and coverage, sequences of unusual periods (depression, war, prosperity), and changes of research directors who generate the data.

Past trends in vital events show seasonal variations, reflecting preferences for marrying and for having children at some parts of the year rather than at others, or domestic court calendars for handling divorces, or periods of extreme temperatures when fragile persons are more likely to die. These variations can be "adjusted out" by taking the average experience of the last several years as a means of estimating how atypical the events of a given month (such as June marriages) tend to be as compared with the average for the entire year.

Relationships between cyclical fluctuations in business conditions and in marriage and birth rates have been analyzed by several demographers, a noteworthy recent study being that by Kirk (1960).

Estimating missing data for past dates can often be done with an acceptable degree of accuracy by one of several methods. For example, the reproductive experience of cohorts of women has been estimated by Whelpton (1954) for dates back into the 1800's by judicious use of census data on women by number of children ever born for 1940 and 1910 and available birth statistics. These retrospective data make use of life tables for "younging" the original female population back to earlier dates (the reverse of "aging" the surviving population forward to future dates). Other gaps in the data can be filled by routine methods of interpolation, if data are available for dates on both sides of the gap.

Projecting the population into the future has obvious practical utility and has become a standard demographic operation (Zitter & Siegel, 1958). Population projections constitute an essential element in the complex of factors that are taken into account in planning future needs in many fields, including production, marketing, finance, education, housing, and recreation. They are also of great interest to those academicians who are concerned with the underlying economic and social processes which account for past, current, and probable future trends in population growth (Freedman et al., 1959). The projections are made more valuable when they include subdivisions of the future population by marital status, and when the population projections are used as

bases for projecting the numbers of marriages, numbers of households, and numbers of related family units (Glick, 1957; Parke & Glick, 1963). These supplemental projections of family units are prepared by extrapolating past trends in the proportions of persons in each age group who are in each broad marital status category, further subdivided by family status, and then multiplying these extrapolated proportions by the population projected for corresponding future dates. Results are at various levels, reflecting differing assumptions about the degree to which past trends in the parameters will continue into the future.

In making projections, the technician may wish to use quite a different procedure from that of making basic assumptions about the continuation of past trends. He may choose, instead, to assume that certain levels of the components will be reached at specified future dates. Thus, in projecting birth rates for a developing country, the future trend of the rate may be assumed to fall to the level of that in a more advanced country as of a specified past or current date.

Demographic models of the future population are being developed by the United States Bureau of the Census, taking into account research in this field done previously by others, notably Orcutt et al. (1961). As a point of departure, these models start with a "one-in-one-thousand" sample of the 1960 population and are designed to show the future levels and distributions of the population by personal and family characteristics. In developing these projected statistics, elaborate arrays of probabilities of the occurrence of marriages, births, deaths, changes in household composition, etc., are applied to the 1960 base population as input to electronic computers, and the future population levels and distributions constitute the output. A lengthy process of refining the probabilities and the operational procedures may be required before the results become acceptable. Extensions of this technique of projection, however, hold great promise for the eventual development of a wide range of data on interrelationships between social, economic, personal, and family characteristics of the population for future dates, according to varied assumptions about forthcoming changes in the probabilities of the occurrence of demographic, social, and economic events. Reasonably accurate predictions, based on such projections, may well become one of the means whereby the social sciences become a full-fledged partner with the natural sciences in promoting scientific advancement.

EVALUATION OF THE DATA AND NEXT STEPS

This concluding section suggests ways to improve the quality and quantity of demographic data on family behavior and calls attention to the merits of orienting the interpretation of these data to a theoretical framework. Numerous steps have already been taken along these lines in recent years, and many others are currently being taken, as earlier sections have shown. However, there is still much room for improvement.

Improving Quality of the Data

Some of the weaknesses in family data are much more amenable to repair than others. Obviously, the best place to start is to eliminate avoidable faults in the collection and processing of the data, insofar as time, staff, and means permit, so that the analyst can start his job with "clean" material. Many of these faults, however, are only partially subject to elimination or can be removed only by slow steps in enlightening those in control of public funds about the need for more and better data on marriage, divorce, and other aspects of family statistics. Some of the shortcomings, unfortunately, have little prospect for being solved, either because of the decentralized system under which the nation operates (with state rather than federal control over the collection and processing of marriage

and divorce records), or because the content is inherently complex and therefore defies relatively simple yet adequate solution.

Sensitivity of some people to some of the items that are of central importance to demographic analysis in general, and to the demographic analysis of family behavior in particular, is one of the major sources of weakness in the data. This observation is universally true but has special relevance to data from public records. Sensitive respondents often leave questions unanswered or answer the questions in an inaccurate manner to cover embarrassment. Sensitive interviewers and recorders of vital events often "cooperate" by not probing for complete and truthful answers when they meet resistance, or they avoid asking "delicate" questions even though the respondents would readily provide the correct answers without objection. This problem is by no means unique in population studies; research studies on social and psychological factors in human behavior perhaps more often delve into intimate subjects. In studies which involve collecting demographic data alone, however, the respondent is probably asked fewer questions, on the average, and hence the interviewer may not take the time required to prepare the respondent to give answers freely and correctly. Zeal on the part of social scientists to overcome problems arising from this source can be carried a great distance with propriety, but its application has recognizable limits.

Illustrations of shortcomings in marriage and divorce data, not already discussed in earlier sections, are given here. In marriage records, numerous brides and grooms who are younger than the legal age for marriage are misreported as of legal age (Christensen, Andrews, & Freiser, 1953). On the other hand, in census records, many women with premarital conceptions are misreported as having entered their first marriages before the conceptions occurred. Possibly a majority of the young mothers who are reported as separated are actually unwed and misreport their marital status to cover up the fact. Many people who should be reported in censuses and surveys as divorced are reported in some other category; there is evidence, however, that this type of error is diminishing (Jacobson, 1959).

A study currently being made by the National Center for Health Statistics and the United States Bureau of the Census is designed to show what marital status was reported in the 1960 Census for persons in five states who obtained a divorce just prior to the census date. The results of this study are expected to be useful in estimating the extent of underreporting of "divorced" as a census category for persons of various ages and other social and economic characteristics. The study will also provide a variety of census data on population characteristics of recently divorced persons. An important by-product of such estimates of misreported marital status will be improved bases for the computation of marriage and death rates for divorced persons. Without improved bases, an adequate assessment cannot be made of marriage rates for divorced persons alongside those for otherwise statistically comparable single and widowed persons, and of death rates for similarly comparable persons of each of the marital statuses.

Illustrations of weaknesses in data on births and young children are likewise abundant (Schachter, 1956). On birth records, some mothers who bore illegitimate children before marriage fail to include those children in determining the order of birth of children born later on in wedlock. Other mothers "forget" to include children who have died or left home under other painful conditions. A special study of infant enumeration in the 1950 Census, made jointly from birth and census records, showed the surprising fact, however, that 82 per cent of the infants under three months of age who were missed in the census were not the only ones in their families to be missed—their parents also escaped enumeration (U. S. Bureau of the Census, 1953). A series of evaluation reports on the 1960 Census was being printed by the United States Bureau of the Census (1963) at the time of this writing. The underlying research was similar in many respects to that in the Post-Enumeration Survey conducted in 1950 by the United States Bureau of the Census (1960b). In the more recent study, a sample of women answered a series of questions which were designed to reveal whether any of their children had been stillborn, had died, had been adopted, had left home for other reasons, etc., or whether any of the children reported as children she had borne had actually been borne by omeone else. Counts of adopted children are seldom, if ever, complete, and attempts to count orphans and half-orphans are hard to make (Fisher, 1950; Orshansky, 1960).

Current fertility statistics from census reports for Negroes are notoriously weak unless they are corrected for the substantial proportion of children under five years old (amounting to about one out of every five, on the average) who have died or who are actually or reportedly not living with their mothers for one of several reasons. This proportion undoubtedly varies from one status group to another, though estimates of such variation can hardly be made. The corresponding proportion for white children is only about one out of 20, but it is undoubtedly much higher for some subgroups of white children. Changes in family patterns or improvements in collecting and processing methods for a recent date may affect the comparability of the current figures with those for earlier dates, unless those for the earlier dates are adjusted by judicious means. This fact reinforces the need for obtaining complete and accurate data at the original source.

The failure of numerous states to qualify for entrance into the Marriage Registration Area and the Divorce Registration Area is a continuing handicap to those interested in analyzing marriage and divorce statistics [cf. Ch. 23, pp. 961–963]. A laudable move to provide at least a temporary stop-gap, however has been initiated by Carter (1960), Ortmeyer (1962), and associates at the Division of Vital Statistics, National Center for Health Statistics. This program will supplement the data available from the MRA and the DRA by securing and tabulating nationwide samples of marriage and divorce records for 1960. Plans call for a repetition of this program annually for states in the registration areas and nationally at less frequent intervals. Additional steps to improve the coverage and content of the divorce statistics program have been suggested in replies made to a questionnaire that was sent to users of the data on divorce by the United States Department of Health, Education, and Welfare (1962).

Moreover, problems inherent in the data may create unavoidable difficulties in attempts to make meaningful classifications. For example, data on residence for marriage and divorce analysis are complicated by out-of-state events. For birth and death statistics, where the coverage is nationwide, events that occur outside the state of residence can be allocated to the state of residence, but for marriage and divorce statistics, where the coverage is not nationwide, the same kind of allocation cannot be made. Also, in the absence of specific information on divorce records about the place where the couple lived when they separated, the sociologically proper base for computing divorce rates according to place of residence is lacking.

Expanding Quantity of Data

As interest in family statistics has increased, ways have been sought to expand the quantity as well as the quality of the data. Such an expansion can be made in part by more intense exploitation of data that have already been collected. Some kinds of expansion can be realized, however, only by gathering data on new topics or by gathering data on familiar topics but with a new orientation.

New types of data currently being developed from vital records were cited in the preceding section (Carter, 1960; Ortmeyer, 1962). Thus, statistics will soon be available for a few states on several items which have not previously appeared in the regular reports on marriage and divorce statistics. These items include educational attainment, religious denomination, and detailed ethnic categories of both marital partners. The results from this program should permit analysis of personal characteristics of the partners and aspects of intermarriage. Hopefully, the usefulness of these data for a few states will encourage additional states to include these and other items of statistical interest on their records. Ideally, of course, such data should be nationwide in order to eliminate doubts about their representativeness.

New types of data for the United States as a whole, and in some instances for regions and states, which are to be published from the 1960 Census of Population will help to fill the gaps in vital statistics by making available several kinds of data on characteristics of recently married persons (age at marriage, number of times married, migration, education, occupation, income, ethnic features, etc.) and to increase the data already available from censuses and surveys on child-spacing, family composition by stages of the family life cycle, and economic characteristics of families, such as care of children of working mothers, acquisition of housing durables, and quality of housing (Glick, 1962). From one-in-a-thousand and one-in-ten-thousand samples of the 1960 Census of Population, which are purchasable for the first time from the Bureau of the Census, almost endless tabulations of data can be made to throw light on marriage and family topics. Tentative plans call for expanding the information on the 5 per cent sample of the 1960 Census records by inserting on the electronic tapes summary measures for each community (census tract or other small identifiable area) in such a way that this information can be cross-classified by the characteristics of each family and each person in the area (Glick, 1961). These summary measures may include such indicators as median education of adults, median family income, an index of housing quality, an index of housing conveniences (to reflect "style of life"), ethnic concentrations, and mean length of time in present residence for adults.

More intensive analysis of family data currently available, or in process of preparation, can yield important contributions in many ways: increasing knowledge about mate selection, including clearer appraisals of the strengths of dividing lines across which few persons cross in choosing marital partners; exploiting marriage data by counties, with the counties classified by degree of concentration of population in selected ethnic and status groups; using census data on marriage and the family to study the relationship between family stability and socioeconomic status and to make specialized analyses of childless families, one-child versus medium-size and large families, families in depressed areas or areas of depopulation, families in which the head is not the chief earner, low-income versus middle- and extremely high-income families, migrant versus nonmigrant and mixed families, and so on.

Augmenting family statistics by the collection of data on new subjects is at least theoretically feasible with either vital or census records as the source. Adding new subjects to marriage and divorce records has met with considerable resistance in many states but will undoubtedly be attempted at regular intervals in the future. For immediate results, however, vital statisticians look with more hope to the collection of statistics on new subjects by making follow-up interviews with a sample of those who recently became married or divorced (Ortmeyer, 1962). Mail-in questionnaires could be used as an alternative. These supplemental sources would throw light on the etiology of changes in marital status by relating these changes to work experience, living arrangements, residential movement, and marital histories of the marital partners and of their parents and siblings.

Performing record linkage by use of electronic computers (Newcombe et al., 1959) and a uniform system of registration numbers assigned to all persons would open up a new era in the joint analysis of marriage, birth, divorce, and death records and Social Security work records when these records have universal coverage.

Attempts to add new subjects in censuses and surveys have met with obstacles in some instances, as in the effort to include a question on religious preference in the 1960 Census. (See Ch. 23, "Religious Affiliation," in Bogue, 1959.) The introduction of new questions could permit the exploration of the extent to which persons are closely integrated to their family of origin but not residing at their home; these persons include students away at college, members of the armed forces in barracks, residents of institutions, and breadwinners whose work requires them to live apart from their families. These new items could also show the extent to which substitutes are used for maternal care of children, such as adoption or "farming out" children to grandparents while the mother moves to another place to obtain employment. Surveys of retrospective marital histories and associated behavior (children of each marriage, work and residential histories, and related experiences of parents and siblings) would provide valuable longitudinal data for analysis of the family life cycle and for use in the demographic models which were discussed in an earlier section. New subjects to investigate through census and vital records can be found in reports of private research workers in the field of marriage and the family (Bernard, 1956; Goode, 1956; Heer, 1958; Monahan, 1958; Morgan, 1961; Tietze, 1962; Wallace, 1959).

Orienting Analysis to Theory

Demographic studies of family behavior differ widely in the degree to which self-conscious attempts are made to relate hypotheses and findings to underlying theoretical principles. As demographers make headway in their attempts to expand the volume and improve the quality of their basic data, they may be expected to become less preoccupied with problems of collection and adjustment of data and more preoccupied with manipulation of the data in new ways to answer fundamental questions about the manner in which different parts of the population mosaic fit together and how these parts are changing through the decades (Hauser & Duncan, 1959, p. 11; see also Davis & Blake, 1962).

The central feature of demography is its emphasis on external distributive aspects of people in the context of time and place (Lorimer, 1959; Moore, 1959). Theory in the demographic analysis of family life, therefore, consists of explanatory principles for use in analyzing distributions of births, marriages, divorces, and family groups chronologically in space. These principles include factors explaining differences and changes in the cohesion of family groups, and in the roles of the family members in the productive and protective activities related to home life (Coughenour & Gladden, 1960; Goode, 1959; Parsons & Bales, 1955). In investigating these factors, the demographer has the responsibility to make his "hypotheses researchable," in the words of Winch, McGinnis, and Barringer (1962, p. 6), and either to integrate his research findings into existing theory or to show how this theory should be modified in the light of his results.

REFERENCES

Bernard, Jessie. *Remarriage.* New York: Dryden, 1956.

Bogue, D. J. *The population of the United States,* with a special chapter on fertility by W. H. Grabill. New York: Free Press, 1959.

Carter, H. Plans for improved statistics on family formation and dissolution in the United States. *Soc. Forces,* 1960, 39, 163–169.

Christensen, H. T. The method of record linkage applied to family data. *Marr. & fam. Living,* 1958, 20, 38–43.

Christensen, H. T. Childspacing analysis via record linkage: new data plus a summing up from earlier reports. *Marr & fam. Living,* 1963, 25, 272–280.

Christensen, H. T., Andrews, R., & Freiser, Sophie. Falsification of age at marriage. *Marr. & fam. Living,* 1953, 15, 301–304.

Christensen, H. T., & Meissner, Hanna H. Studies in child spacing. III. premarital pregnancy as a factor in divorce. *Amer. sociol. Rev.,* 1953, 641–645.

Coughenour, C. M., & Gladden, J. W. Toward a dynamic concept of family stages: an evaluation of family life cycle theory. Paper read at S. Sociol. Soc., Atlanta, April, 1960.

Davis, K., & Blake, Judith. The general theory of factors governing age at marriage. Paper read at Population Ass. Amer., Madison, Wis., May, 1962.

Downes, J. The longitudinal study of families as a method of research. *Milbank mem. fund Quart.,* 1952, 30, 311–340.

Dublin, L. I., & Lotka, A. J. On the true rate of natural increase. *J. Amer. stat. Ass.,* 1925, 20, 305–339.

Duncan, O. D. A socioeconomic index for all occupations. (Ch. 6). Properties and characteristics of the socioeconomic index (Ch. 7). In A. J. Reiss, Jr., et al., *Occupations and social status.* New York: Free Press, 1961.

Duvall, Evelyn M. *Family development.* Philadelphia: Lippincott, 1957.

Fisher, J. Orphans in the United States: number and living arrangements. *Soc. Security Bull.,* 1950, 13, 13–18.

Foote, N. N. (Ed.) *Consumer behavior.* Vol. 4. *Household decision-making.* New York: New York Univer. Press, 1961.

Freedman, R., Whelpton, P. K., & Campbell, A. A. *Family planning, sterility, and population growth.* New York: McGraw-Hill, 1959.

Glass, D. V., & Grebenik, E. *Summary chapter from the trend and pattern of fertility in Great Britain: a report on the family census of 1946.* London: H. M. Stationery Office, June, 1954.

Glick, P. C. The life cycle of the family. *Marr. & fam. Living,* 1955, 17, 4–9.

Glick, P. C. *American families.* New York: Wiley, 1957.

Glick, P. C. Joint analysis of personal and family characteristics. Paper read at Int. Population Conf., New York, Sept., 1961.

Glick, P. C. The 1960 census as a source for social research. *Amer. sociol. Rev.,* 1962, 27, 581–585.

Glick, P. C. Marriage instability: variations by size of place and region. *Milbank mem. fund Quart.,* 1963, 41, 43–55.

Goldfarb, N. *Longitudinal statistical analysis.* New York: Free Press, 1960.

Goode, W. J. *After divorce.* Glencoe, Ill.: Free Press, 1956.

Goode, W. J. The sociology of the family. In R. K. Merton, L. Broom, & L. Cottrell, Jr. (Eds.), *Sociology today.* New York: Basic Books, 1959. Pp. 178–196.

Grabill, W. H. Attrition life tables for the single population. *J. Amer. stat. Ass.,* 1945, 40, 364–375.

Grabill, W. H., Kiser, C. V., & Whelpton, P. K. *The fertility of American women.* New York: Wiley, 1958.

Grabill, W. H., & Parke, R., Jr. Marriage, fertility, and childspacing: August 1959. *Current population Reports, Series P-20, No. 108.* Washington, D.C.: U.S. Bureau of the Census, 1961.

Hatt, P. K. Occupation and social stratification. *Amer. J. Sociol.,* 1950, 55, 533–543.

Hauser, P. M., & Duncan, O. D. *The study of population,* with Ch. 24, Family statistics, by P. C. Glick. Chicago: Univer. of Chicago Press, 1959.

Heer, D. M. Dominance and the working wife. *Soc. Forces,* 1958, 36, 341–347.

Hill, R., Stycos, J. M., & Back, K. W. *The family and population control.* Chapel Hill: Univer. of North Carolina Press, 1959.

Hillman, Karen G. Marital instability and its relation to education, income and occupation: an analysis based on census data. In R. F. Winch, R. McGinnis, & H. R. Barringer (Eds.), *Selected studies in marriage and the family.* New York: Holt, Rinehart & Winston, 1962. Pp. 603–608.

Jacobson, P. H. *American marriage and divorce.* New York: Rinehart, 1959.

Jaffe, A. J. *Handbook of statistical methods for demographers.* U. S. Bureau of the Census. Washington, D.C.: U. S. Government Printing Office, 1951.

Kaplan, D., Parkhurst, Elizabeth, & Whelpton, P. K. The comparability of reports on

occupation from vital records and the 1950 census. National Office of Vital Statistics (later National Vital Statistics Division), *Vital Statistics–special Reports,* 1961, 53, 1–44.

Kirk, D. The influence of business cycles on marriage and birth rates. In National Bureau of Economic Research, *Demographic and economic change in developed countries.* Princeton: Princeton Univer. Press, 1960.

Kiser, C. V. (Ed.) *Research in family planning.* Princeton: Princeton Univer. Press, 1962.

Kuczynski, R. R. *The balance of births and deaths.* Vol. 1. *Western and Northern Europe.* New York: Macmillan Co., 1926. Vol. 2. *Eastern and Southern Europe.* Washington, D.C.: Brookings Institution, 1931.

Linden, F. Consumer profiles: I. the six ages of family. National Industrial Conference Board, *Bus. Rec.,* 1961, 18, 40–42.

Lorimer, F. *Culture and human fertility.* Zurich, Switzerland: Berichthaus, for UNESCO, 1954.

Lorimer, F. The development of demography. In P. M. Hauser & O. D. Duncan (Eds.), *The study of population.* Chicago: Univer. of Chicago Press, 1959. Ch. 6.

Monahan, T. P. The changing nature and instability of remarriages. *Eugenics Quart.,* 1958, 5, 73–85.

Moore, W. E. Sociology and demography. In P. M. Hauser & O. D. Duncan (Eds.), *The study of population.* Chicago: Univer. of Chicago Press, 1959. Ch. 33.

Morgan, J. N. Household decision-making. In N. N. Foote (Ed.), *Consumer behavior.* Vol. 4. *Household decision-making.* New York: New York Univer. Press, 1961.

Myers, R. J. Statistical measures in the marital life cycles of men and women. In *International Population Conference, Vienna, 1959.* Vienna: Christoph Reisser's Sons. 1959. Pp. 229–233.

Nam, C. B. *Methodology and scores of socioeconomic status.* Working Paper No. 15. Washington, D.C.: U. S. Bureau of the Census, 1963.

National Vital Statistics Division, Department of Health, Education, and Welfare. *Vital Statistics of the United States.* Washington, D.C.: U. S. Government Printing Office (annual volumes).

Newcombe, H. B., Kennedy, J. M., Axford, S. J., & James, A. P. Automatic linkage of vital records. *Science,* 1959, 130, 954–959.

Orcutt, G. H., Greenberger, M., Korbel, J., & Rivlin, Alice M. *Microanalysis of socioeconomic systems (a simulation study).* New York: Harper, 1961.

Orshansky, Mollie. Money income sources of young survivors, December, 1959. *Soc. security Bull.,* 1960, 23, 10–13.

Ortmeyer, C. E. Marriage and divorce statistics programs of the National Vital Statistics Division—current developments and research potentials. *Amer. sociol. Rev.,* 1962, 27, 741–746.

Parke, R., & Glick, P. C. Illustrative projections of the number of households and families: 1960 to 1980. *Current population Reports,* Series P-20, No. 123. Washington, D.C.: U. S. Bureau of the Census, 1963.

Parsons, T., & Bales, R. F., with Olds, J., Zelditch, M., Jr., & Slater, P. *Family, socialization and interaction process.* Glencoe, Ill.: Free Press, 1955.

Petersen, W. *Population.* New York: Macmillan, 1961.

Pratt, W. P. Profile of American families, 1940–57. National Office of Vital Statistics (later National Vital Statistics Division), *Publ. hlth Reports,* 1959, 74, 189–194.

Price, C. A., & Zubrzycki, J. The use of intermarriage statistics as an index of assimilation. *Population Stud.,* 1952, 16, 58–69.

Rodgers, R. H. *Improvements in the construction and analysis of family life cycle categories.* Kalamazoo: Western Michigan Univer., School of Graduate Studies, 1962.

Ruggles, R., & Ruggles, Nancy. Differential fertility in United States census data. In National Bureau of Economic Research, *Demographic and economic change in developed countries.* Princeton: Princeton Univer. Press, 1960. Pp. 155–209.

Ryder, N. B. Time as a demographic variable. Paper read at Amer. Ass. Advancem. Sci., Chicago, Dec., 1959.

Ryder, N. B. Bisexual marriage rates. Paper read at Population Ass. Amer., New York, May, 1961.

Schachter, J. Birth registration completeness in the United States and geographic areas, 1950. Part III. data for detailed characteristics. National Office of Vital Statistics, *Vital Statistics–special Reports,* 1956, 45, 113–152.

Schachter, J. Child spacing as measured from data enumerated in the Current Population Survey: United States, April 1950 to April 1954. National Office of Vital Statistics, *Vital Statistics–special Reports,* 1958, 47, 75–126.

Shevky, E., & Bell, W. *Social area analysis.* Stanford, Calif.: Stanford Univer. Press, 1955.

Spiegelman, M. *Introduction to demography.* Chicago: Society of Actuaries, 1955.

Sussman, M. *Sourcebook in Marriage and the Family,* with Ch. 1, Section 5, Family formation and family composition: trends and prospects, by P. C. Glick, D. M. Heer, & J. C. Beresford. Boston: Houghton Mifflin, 1963.

Tella, A. Marriages: trend and cycle. National Industrial Conference Board, *Bus. Rec.,* 1962, 19, 24–28.

Tietze, C. Pregnancy rates and birth rates. *Population Stud.,* 1962, 16, 31–37.

U. S. Bureau of the Census. *Sixteenth Census, differential fertility, 1940 and 1910–standardized fertility rates and reproduction rates.* Washington, D.C.: U. S. Government Printing Office, 1944.

U. S. Bureau of the Census. Infant enumeration study: 1950. *Procedural studies of the 1950 Censuses,* No. 1. Washington, D.C.: U. S. Government Printing Office, 1953.

U. S. Bureau of the Census. Fertility of the population: March 1957. *Current population Reports,* Series P-20, No. 84, 1958.

U. S. Bureau of the Census. *Historical statistics of the United States, colonial times to 1957.* Washington, D.C.: U. S. Government Printing Office, 1960. (a)

U. S. Bureau of the Census. *The post-enumeration survey: 1950.* Tech. Paper No. 4. Washington, D.C.: U. S. Government Printing Office, 1960. (b)

U. S. Bureau of the Census. Marital status and family status: March 1961. *Current population Reports,* Series P-20, No. 114, 1962. (a)

U. S. Bureau of the Census. *U. S. Census of population: 1960, general social and economic characteristics, United States summary.* Final Rept PC(1)-1C. Washington, D.C.: U. S. Government Printing Office, 1962. (b)

U. S. Bureau of the Census. *Evaluation and research program of the U. S. Census of Population and Housing, 1960.* Series ER 60. Washington, D.C.: U. S. Government Printing Office, 1963.

U. S. Department of Health, Education, & Welfare, Public Health Service. Improving national divorce statistics (a report of the Subcommittee on National Divorce Statistics of the U. S. National Committee on Vital and Health Statistics). *Vital Statistics—special Reports,* 1962, 47, 401–426.

Wallace, K. M. An experiment in scientific matchmaking. *Marr. & fam. Living,* 1959, 21, 342–348.

Westhoff, C. F., Potter, R. G., Jr., Sagi, P. C., & Mishler, E. G. *Family growth in metropolitan America.* Princeton: Princeton Univer. Press, 1961.

Whelpton, P. K. *Cohort fertility: native white women in the United States.* Princeton: Univer. Press, 1954.

Whelpton, P. K., & Kiser, C. V. *Social and psychological factors affecting fertility.* New York: Milbank Memorial Fund, 1946–1958. 5 vols.

Winch, R. F., McGinnis, R., & Barringer, H. R. (Eds.) *Selected studies in marriage and the family.* New York: Holt, Rinehart & Winston, 1962.

Zitter, M., & Siegel, J. S. Illustrative projections of the population of the United States, by age and sex: 1960 to 1980. *Current population Reports,* Series P-25, No. 187. Washington, D.C.: U. S. Bureau of the Census, 1958.

CHAPTER **10** **Measuring Families**[1]

MURRAY A. STRAUS
University of Minnesota

MEASUREMENT: ITS NATURE AND RELATION TO THE TOTAL RESEARCH PROCESS

Although the focus of this chapter is on measurement, it is appropriate first to locate the position of measurement in the context of the total research process. Probably the two most difficult and important steps in empirical research on the family come either *before* or *after* the measurement process. As Merton (1959) and many others have noted, the difficult and really crucial step is the development of a research focus and *design*. This is the process of *deciding*

what to do. The operations needed to carry out the design, i.e., the "doing" of the research, is largely a process of measurement. It consists of observing and recording the phenomena under study, expressing the data in numerical form, and measuring the relation between variables or difference between groups.

This middle phase of research demands a high order of ability and poses problems of great technical complexity, some of which are dealt with in this chapter. Nevertheless, the problems involved are typically not as abstract and do not demand as high an order of intellectual ability as those involved in either research design (i.e., in deciding what to do) or research interpretation and writing (i.e., determining what the research shows). This is something of an oversimplification, but it conveys a necessary perspective if the reader is to keep the total research process in balance while reading the strictures concerning the inadequacy of existing techniques for measuring family properties and the pleas for more systematic work on measurement which occur throughout this chapter.

[1] The preparation of this chapter and the abstracting and tabulation of measurement instruments were supported by grant M-5147A from the National Institute of Mental Health, U.S. Public Health Service; and by project 2027 of the University of Minnesota Agricultural Experiment Station. This is miscellaneous Journal Series Paper No. 1171.

I would like to express my appreciation to Professor Reuben L. Hill for his careful reading of the manuscript and many suggestions, not all of which could be incorporated in the chapter, and to Anne-Marie Hare for editorial assistance.

Meaning of Measurement

Having broadly located measurement in the research process, it is time to define more formally and explicitly what is meant by the term and to specify those aspects of the phenomenon which are treated in this chapter. Since this is not a theoretical treatise, it is not necessary to present and analyze critically the many definitions of measurement which have been offered. The reader interested in historical and theoretical considerations of this issue should consult works such as Cohen and Nagel (1960), Woolf (1961), or Churchman and Ratoosh (1959). In the present context, it is sufficient to note that these definitions can be arrayed on a continuum of increasing strength or restrictiveness.

The most restrictive definitions require that the units of measurement be additive, equal, start from an absolute zero, etc. The most liberal definitions simply require a system of rules for unambiguously assigning numbers to phenomena. The definition which is followed in this chapter is close to the liberal end of the continuum. However, in addition to number-symbol isomorphism, for the present it seems advisable to add the requirement that the process identified as measurement should also serve to place these phenomena in some kind of sequential order. Consequently, the definition put forward by Caws (1959) is closest to the usage implicit in this chapter: "Measurement is the assignment of particular mathematical characteristics to conceptual entities in such a way as to permit (1) an unambiguous mathematical description of every situation involving the entity, and (2) the arrangement of all occurrences of it in a quasi-serial order" (p. 5).

Unfortunately, having just accepted one definition of measurement, it is now necessary to introduce another, or, more properly, to add a restriction to the liberal definition presented. This necessity grows out of the fact that at various points in the chapter, findings from a survey of existing family measurement techniques are reported. In order to restrict the materials surveyed to a reasonable figure, it was arbitrarily decided that instruments to be included must meet the following criteria:

1. The technique must provide a classification or numerical score based on the use of three or more "indicators" or determinations of the property being measured, that is, three or more questions, observations, events, etc.
2. The behavior measured must refer to interaction, or disposition to interact, in a family role (or proto-family role, as in the case of courtship measures).

The findings to be reported are based on analysis of 263 instruments published between 1923 and 1962.[2]

Interrelation of Definition and Measurement

The processes of definition and conceptualization are intimately related to the process of measurement, and one desirable feature of Caws's definition of measurement is its explicit inclusion of "conceptual entities."

The process called *definition* relates one entity or phenomenon to other different phenomena or entities. Definition serves to relate and differentiate concepts. The process of *measurement,* on the other hand, relates different manifestations of the particular phenomena or defined entities to each other. Measurement serves to make concepts amenable to mathematical manipulation. Thus, as Margenau (1959) has noted, measurement stands at the critical junction between theory and sensory ex-

[2] The search for instruments to be included involved a check of all volumes since 1935 of the major journals publishing family research, such as *Marriage and Family Living, Child Development,* and the *American Sociological Review,* together with *Psychological Abstracts, Sociological Abstracts,* and whatever leads could be uncovered in other sources. Although considerable effort has been put into this search, it is undoubtedly incomplete. It is nevertheless felt to be representative. (For a partial preliminary report see Straus, 1962c.)

perience or data. Moreover, regardless of one's theoretical position in relation to operationalism, there is no avoiding the fact that once a researcher has chosen the measurement procedures for his investigation, these procedures constitute, for that study, a "working definition" of his concepts.

Ideally, measurement presupposes definition. As with so many other aspects of empirical science, however, the actual process does not always follow the ideal model. Much significant work has, in fact, been done the other way around. That is, a system of measurement has been evolved first and conceptualization has followed, as investigators struggled with the process of understanding what they measured. Perhaps the most familiar example of this is the measurement of mental ability which, even half a century after Binet, is not yet adequately defined and conceptualized (Liverant, 1962). Surely, it would have been a vast mistake to have rejected Binet's work simply because the phenomena measured by his techniques were inadequately defined and conceptualized. Whatever the merits of operationalism as a philosophical or methodological system, the many instances of measurement occurring before definition or conceptualization cannot be ignored. In short, empirical science in this aspect, as in so many others, has achieved important results while violating what seemed to be elementary and basic rules of procedure.

The same point may be made in relation to the restrictive definitions of measurement. Stevens (1959) has noted that, just as earlier mathematicians had to modify their most basic theories in order to admit what they had first disdainfully called "irrational" and "imaginary" numbers—today restrictive definitions of measurement—"have toppled as the practice of measurement, outrunning legislation, has forced us to broaden and generalize our concepts" (p. 18). Increasingly, it is being found that mathematical treatments supposedly inappropriate to the type of measurement applied to the phenomena under study can be successfully used. The situation is similar to that prevailing in relation to the restrictive assumptions underlying the use of parametric statistics. It is now being found that parametric statistics are at least as efficient as nonparametric, even when the data do not meet the assumptions inherent in the mathematics of the statistic (Anderson, 1961; Boneau, 1960; Boneau, 1962).

Deficiencies in Measurement

Anyone who thinks that quantification is in dispute only in the social sciences will come to quite different conclusions after only a brief perusal of the numerous and often heated debates among philosophers, physicists, and mathematicians during the past two decades. Indeed, it is only slightly stretching the point to say that the *conceptual* status of measurement is not greatly more primitive in the social sciences than in the physical sciences. The key difference lies in the vastly more primitive state of measurement *technology* in the social sciences. Even this difference is commonly exaggerated, for the physical and biological sciences are constantly struggling with purely technological as well as conceptual problems in attempting to measure their objects of study.

While this chapter was being written, for example, a plant physiologist friend was trying to trace the movement of phosphorous from plant leaves to the pod. He put radioactive phosphorous on the leaf and placed the measurement probes at the base of the leaf and at the junction of the leaf stem with the main stem. He was puzzled when the reading at the base of the leaf was about 620, whereas farther down at the main stem it was 2,400 units. If he had taken this at face value, it would have required reformulating the theories concerning translocation of minerals within a plant. After two days of struggling with the problem, it was discovered that the supposedly identical instruments used at the base of the leaf and at the main stem were made by different companies and gave different readings. But imagine if the placement of the instruments had been reversed. The observations obtained would have indicated tremendous differences in phosphorous count at the two points. They would have provided the basis for a major journal article but, due to errors of measurement unreliability, an erroneous one.

Among the many famous examples of technical problems and errors in basic physical measurement is the work on the speed of light. The experiments to measure this basic quantity were a model of care and precision. Yet, for almost a generation, astronomical calculations were rendered inaccurate by an error in the original experiment. Finally, it should not be forgotten that two recent Nobel prizes were awarded primarily for achievements in measurement technique.

Perhaps, then, the key difference accounting for the inadequacy of measurement in the social sciences is not to be found in either particularly unique or difficult problems of conceptualization or technology, but rather in a simple failure to expend sufficient time and thought on the problem. This is especially true of sociology. With some notable exceptions, sociologists have devoted remarkably little attention to the problem of measurement. It is true that there are several general works on research methods which include attention to measurement technique. However, with the exception of interest in cumulative scaling as represented in Volume 4 of *The American Soldier* (Stouffer et al., 1950) and Riley and associates (1954), there is no comprehensive work on measurement in sociology. This is in part a reflection of the very meager amount of research on measurement and is in striking contrast to the sister discipline, psychology.

Psychologists have for years devoted a large part of their energies to theoretical development and empirical research on measurement, including numerous texts and monographic studies. To select only a few

from the better recent works, one could cite Edwards' *Techniques of Attitude Scale Construction* (1957), and his *The Social Desirability Variable in Personality Assessment and Research* (1957); Gulliksen's *Theory of Mental Tests* (1950); and Torgerson's *Theory and Methods of Scaling* (1958). These are not mere "how to do it" compendia for testers, but sophisticated analyses, drawing on a large body of measurement theory and empirical research evidence.

Not only is relatively little attention devoted to the development of measurement technique and theory by sociologists, but a large proportion of what has been done is carried out in apparent ignorance of or disregard for the relevant findings from research on the measurement of individual properties by psychologists. At the same time, there have also appeared in the literature a number of techniques for measuring family properties. Some of these are worthy of continued use and development, but they are widely scattered in the literature. Consequently, applicable existing techniques are often overlooked by the investigator.

Chapter Focus

This chapter is intended to contribute to the solution of some of these problems. First, paradigms are specified for classifying and constructing family-measurement instruments which it is hoped will provide an impetus to systematic efforts in the quantification of family behavior. At the very least, the chapter should help to provide structure and clarity in the assessment of existing techniques. Whether it will be fruitful for the development of new techniques, of course, remains to be seen.

Second, emphasis is placed on the use of multi-indicator measurement, and on the need to demonstrate the validity and reliability of such measures. In part, this emphasis is built into the chapter since, for purposes of the survey of existing techniques, the operational definition of what is counted as a "measurement technique" contains the requirement of multiple indicators. The emphasis on validity and reliability is also intended to be heavy, even though less direct, since neither validity nor reliability forms one of the criteria for inclusion. If they did, the number of instruments to be described would be slim indeed.

Third, it is hoped that the author's forthcoming volume of *Family Measurement Abstracts* (for a partial draft, see Straus, 1962a) will facilitate comparability and continuity in family research where appropriate. Or, as is more frequently the case, where the existing techniques are inadequate, it is hoped that these abstracts will encourage investigators to build on the original work either by refinement and improvement, or by a completely new approach to the particular measurement problem.

At the same time, there is a danger with such a compendium, for although it is desirable to call attention to previously developed techniques, this may encourage blind use of instruments whose validity has not been demonstrated. Even worse is the possibility—indeed, the likelihood—that the volume of abstracts will encourage use of inappropriate instruments just because they are conveniently available. There are already many examples in the sociological and psychological literature of the use of inappropriate measures resulting simply from the fact that the instrument exists. Somehow, a test or scale with an attractive label seems to invite use, almost irrespective of other considerations.

It is in part to meet problems of this type that the present chapter is organized on the basis of techniques of measurement. The chapter, therefore, differs from Hoffman and Lippitt's (1960) treatment of "The Measurement of Family Life Variables" in that the latter is organized according to the properties of the family for which measures have been (or should be) developed.

A methodological rather than a substantive framework is used here because of a belief that existing measures are only the crudest beginning and are primitive and inadequate. Although a number of specific measures are noted, it is hoped that one of the effects of this chapter will be to encourage the development of new instruments which will eventually make descriptions of existing instruments for the most part obsolete.

Despite this objective, space limitations preclude attempting to describe the specific steps needed to make use of each of the numerous quantification techniques which can be applied to the family. Although quantification techniques, such as cumulative scaling and paired comparison, are discussed, only their general features are described, together with existing or suggested applications to the family. References in which the specific steps and procedures for each technique are described are, of course, given throughout.

RELATION OF CONSTRUCT TO OPERATIONAL INDICATORS

The close relationship of conceptualization to measurement has already been indicated in general terms. But for the practicing researcher it is essential to be far more specific about the operations involved in this crucial linkage.

The Rational Approach

For convenience in exposition, this process is described in terms of five steps, but it should be recognized that on both logical and empirical grounds either more or fewer steps could be specified. Moreover, this outline is in terms of what Guilford (1954) has called a "rational" or theoretical approach, as compared to an approach which starts with empirical regularities (to be discussed later).

1. *Conceptual definition.* Sometimes an investigator is fortunate enough to be concerned with a concept which is already clearly defined and differentiated from other properties of the family. At the other

extreme is the situation occurring when a new concept is developed, based on the researcher's informal observation or derived from an existing body of theory or substantive findings. There is also the situation in which it is necessary to deal with a variable in fairly wide use, but which on close examination turns out to be poorly defined and differentiated from other similar concepts. In this latter and most usual case, the researcher must be prepared, in the absence of prior consensus and specification, to choose or impose the definition which seems to him to be most adequate, either generally or in terms of his particular research problem.

2. *Specification of components.* Almost all the concepts with which the family researcher deals will be found on a close examination to consist of a number of presumably interrelated, but still distinct, component dimensions. This specification of the various "aspects," "components," or "dimensions" is, as Lazarsfeld and Rosenberg (1955) have pointed out, a continuation of the first step. It is essential because the concept to be measured is almost never a simple and directly observable item. It is only the component elements which are specific enough to permit discovery of observable indicators.

Suppose, for example, one were interested in measuring the extent to which a certain sample of families is "patriarchal." Kirkpatrick's analysis of this concept (1963) resulted in three dimensions:

I. Traits favoring male dominance;
II. Family organizational characteristics; and
III. Traits pertaining to the status of women.

Each of these three major dimensions was in turn subdivided into a total of 22 different elements. For example, under family organization, Kirkpatrick listed such items as a double standard of sexual morality and male representation of the family group in the community, and under traits favoring male dominance are such items as patri-

lineal inheritance and patrilocal residence. Furthermore, it is unlikely that Kirkpatrick would consider this list of 22 as in any way exhaustive.

3. *Selection of indicators.* By *indicator* is meant simply a specific observation, the presence of which is taken as reflecting presence of the concept being measured.[3] Like the specification of the component dimensions, the choice of appropriate indicators is in part an intuitive process and in part a matter of logical deduction and knowledge of previously discovered relationships. There are a number of different types of indicators and a number of criteria by which their adequacy may be judged. These are described in a subsequent section.

4. *Index construction.* Following Lazarsfeld and Rosenberg (1955), the term *index* is used in this chapter in a very broad sense, to signify any combination of indicators to form a measurement instrument, for example, paired comparison, equal-appearing interval, rank order, forced choice, and cumulative scaling.

5. *Standardization and validation.* No matter how carefully designed the instrument is up to this point, there is no way of knowing whether or not it will work, i.e., whether it will measure the concept which the investigator originally intended. Indeed, given the history of social measurement up to now, the chances are more than likely that the instrument will *not* work. Thus, in the case of a major research project in which large resources will be expended in using the instrument, or in the case of an instrument designed for general use by other researchers, it is imperative to carry out methodological investigations designed to determine, among other things, the concurrent, predictive, and/or construct validity of the instrument. In addition, if the test is to be used for individual diagnosis, normative data based on a population similar to that with which the test will be used

---

[3] The term *item* is synonomous with indicator, except that, historically, it has been used to refer to indicators in tests or questionnaires.

is essential for determining the validity of the instrument.

In introducing this outline of steps in quantification, it was noted that it is given in terms of a so-called rational approach, that is, the steps outlined started with a consideration of the concept. It proceeded to specify the concept, select indicators for the elements specified, and finally combine them into some type of index. By contrast, the "empirical" approach starts with the selection of indicators, goes on to the formation of an index, and only then seeks to determine the nature of the concept measured by the index.

The Empirical Approach

Instruments developed in the empirical tradition are designed to evaluate the performance of families in a particular type of situation. The best-known example of the empirical approach are the marital success prediction tests developed by Burgess and his co-workers. The procedure used by Burgess was to assemble a large pool of items, all of which had only one common element: the hope that they would differentiate between happily and unhappily married couples. The resulting test consists of those items which did in fact differentiate between the criterion groups. Burgess and Cottrell's test has by now been cross-validated on a number of different populations in both cross-sectional and longitudinal studies. The validity coefficients revealed by these studies tend to be in the .40 to .50 range, which makes them among the highest in the entire sociological and psychological literature. [Cf. pp. 218–221.] What, then, accounts for the uneasiness which students of the family have increasingly expressed concerning these marital success prediction instruments? Essentially, it is the lack of conceptual underpinning. Here is an instrument which "works," but no one knows why. (See, however, the factor analysis of Locke & Williamson, 1958.)

By contrast, in the rational approach, the researcher starts with a concept, such as "role differentiation." He seeks to develop a measure of this property because it is judged to be of theoretical importance. The question of whether the resulting variable will have any practical importance (for example, whether it influences marital happiness), is left for later investigation, just as the researcher who takes the empirical approach leaves for later investigation the question of the conceptual structure of his measure.

The great majority of instruments developed to measure some property of the family seem to belong, more or less, under the heading of "rational" measures. They are concerned, however inadequately, with the measurement of a concept.

Ideally, if the quantification process is carried through to completion, both the rational and the empirical approach end at the same point. The problem, however, is that devotees of the rational approach usually fail to proceed on to empirical validation, and devotees of the empirical approach usually fail to proceed on to conceptual specification.

QUANTIFICATION OF GROUP PROPERTIES

Family research is primarily interested in the properties of a social *group*. A discipline concerned with groups cannot depend on measurement of the characteristics of *individuals*, or, in most cases, on the summation of the properties of individuals making up the group. Instead, it is necessary to move to the next level of abstraction and develop ways of measuring *group properties*, as that term is used by Lazarsfeld and his colleagues (Lazarsfeld, 1959; Lazarsfeld & Menzel, 1961; Lazarsfeld & Rosenberg, 1955).

Although a number of other distinctions have been proposed, the purposes of the present chapter can probably best be served by restricting consideration to what seem to be the three most important types of group-property indicators: those which Lazarsfeld has called "analytical," "structural," and "global."

Analytical Indicators

Perhaps the most readily perceived technique for quantifying the properties of a social group, including, of course, the family, is *aggregation of the characteristics of individuals* making up the group. Thus, if a measure of family "religiousness" is desired, a religious-interest scale can be given to each member of the family and the results summed to provide a family score. Similarly, if a measure of family "maladjustment" or "neuroticism" is needed, one of the many of the adjustment inventories can be administered. The average for the group may then be taken as a measure of the family's position on this dimension.

Structural Indicators

The second of the two examples just given was deliberately chosen to highlight the inappropriateness of analytical measures for many purposes. If one wishes to quantify such concepts as family wealth or family religiosity, analytical measures are meaningful, because these properties are in large part dependent upon the aggregate performance or status of family members. However, concepts such as "adjustment," "neuroticism," or "cohesion" deal with properties which largely reflect the *interaction* of family members. Assuming for the moment that a valid personality inventory were available, it would be perfectly possible for all members of the family to have normal scores and yet constitute a "neurotic family." Conversely, all could have relatively high scores on neuroticism but constitute an adequately functioning and supportive social group, perhaps even by virtue of sharing a common disability. But family maladjustment, disorganization, or pathology—in the sense used by analysts such as Ackerman (1958) or Haley (1959)—is an interactional concept which can only be measured by the

use of indicators consisting of interactional events. Such indicators are termed "structural" because they deal with the basic elements of social structure: regularities in the interaction of members of the social unit.

Returning to the example of family maladjustment, a structural measure might consist of the number of times (during the course of a standardized problem-solving task) in which the overt communication of one family member to another was at variance with a meaning inferred from subsequent actions and statements. The summation of the number of such contradictory "metacommunications" would provide a measure of the type of neurotic interaction which Bateson (Bateson et al., 1956) and others believe to be important in the etiology of schizophrenia.

The example just given uses indicators consisting of interaction observed in a standardized laboratory situation. However, most family structural data (like the data in other areas of sociology) are based on self-report rather than on observed performance, that is, the indicators commonly utilized to form a structural measure consist of interview or questionnaire statements concerning interaction within the subject's family. The many measures of parent properties, such as Blood's Traditional-Developmental Parent Scale (1953), are examples of such measures.

Global Indicators

This type of indicator consists of a *collective product,* irrespective of its relation to any one specific member of the social group. Examples include the proportion of a family budget spent on food, a cleanliness rating of the household, or a family-group-produced TAT, as in the work of Hess and Handel (1959).

Property-Space Position Measures

Lazarsfeld and Menzel (1961) have discussed a number of different ways in which these three types of group-property indicators, together with various types of individ-ual-property indicators, can be combined to form a variety of additional types of meas-ures. Of these, the most generally useful is the notion of property-space position. The basic idea is simply an extension of the Cartesian coordinate system. If one thinks of each index as a system of locating fami-lies in geometrical space, there is no reason to confine consideration to a single dimen-sion. In fact, there are examples in the litera-ture of the use of two- and three-dimen-sional positions.

A generalized mathematical treatment of the concept and procedures may be found in the literature on "multidimensional scaling" (Abelson, 1954–1955; Coleman, 1957; Tor-gerson, 1958). Closely related are the theory and techniques of "profile" and "pattern" analysis (Cronbach & Gleser, 1953; Gaier & Lee, 1953; Helmstadter, 1957; Mosel & Roberts, 1954; Zubin, 1950), as applied to multiscore psychological tests. Such a test profile can be considered as a series of points in a set of property-space vectors represented by the test scores. Profile simi-larity is measured by determining the "dis-tance" between these points for any one subject or group of subjects and another subject, group, or norm.

The separate indexes used to form prop-erty-space position measures may be either analytical, structural, or global; or any com-bination of these; or in some cases, combina-tions of individual-property measures.

Suppose, for example, one wishes to classify families according to their social-mobility or occupational-achievement poten-tialities. It would be possible to measure the husband's occupational aspiration level and the wife's aspirations and combine these to form an analytical measure. It seems likely, however, that a more powerful measure would result by locating the families in the two-dimensional property space formed by the coordinates of these two properties. In the simplest case, quadrants formed by dichotomizing the variables permits identi-fication of four distinctive types of families: (a) achievement-oriented, (b) achievement-

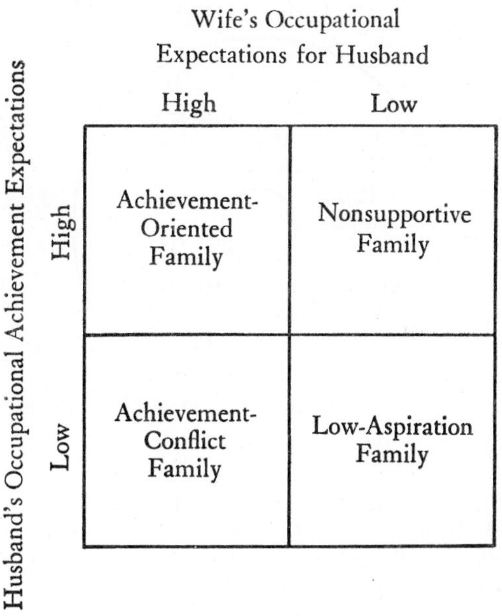

Fig. 1. Family Mobility Potential Types.

conflict, (c) nonsupportive, and (d) low-aspiration. These are illustrated in Fig. 1.

Alternatively, a simple multidimensional scale can be computed to measure the extent to which a given family exemplifies any one of the four types by the use of a measure of profile similarity, such as Osgood and Suci's "D" (1952).

The PALS test (Williams, 1958) uses two structural measures—the extent of parental love and parental authority—to identify four family socialization types, as specified in Fig. 2. Similarly, Straus (1962a) used the power-assertion attempts of husband and wife to delimit four family power types as shown in Fig. 3.

In short, property-space measures are based on the idea that the several indicators forming an index represent successive posi-tions on a single vector or dimension in geometrical space. By the use of two or more indexes, it is possible to represent posi-tions in a multidimensional geometrical space. The unique positions located by these coordinates constitute distinctive properties of the family, or types of families.

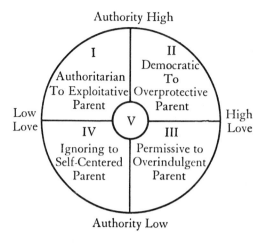

Fig. 2. Family Socialization Types of Williams (1958). Type V (Center Region) Represents Unknown, Unpredictable, or Inconsistent Parent Roles.

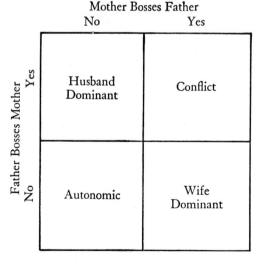

Yes = "Very often," "Often," or "Sometimes."

No = "Seldom," or "Never."

Fig. 3. Family Power Types of Straus (1962a).

SYSTEMATIC INDICATOR GENERATION

Besides an awareness of the various types of group-property indicators which may be used to quantify the properties of the family, it is important to specify a number of general characteristics of indicators. Awareness of these characteristics, and in particular the systematic consideration of them during the process of creating sets of indicators, is essential to a consistent and theoretically meaningful measure.

The indicator properties which are considered are: prescriptive versus performance indicators; predictive versus directly expressive indicators; the role system to be measured; the behavioral fields in which the property to be measured is manifest; and judgmental versus objective indicators. In addition, a number of relatively minor, but still important, details of item format are mentioned.

Prescriptive and Performance Indicators

In both the design of family research and the construction of measures to quantify the concepts employed in the research, it is essential to specify whether one is dealing with the *prescriptive* or normative aspects of family interaction or the actual role performance of members of the family. As Brim (1957) has noted, the prescriptive aspects of role are those that state what is correct or appropriate for a person occupying a certain status in the system. This must be distinguished from descriptions of actual role performance of members of the system.

The prescriptive and performance aspects of roles must in the long run approximately coincide if the social system is to persist without major change. However, it is clear that individuals and families differ in the extent to which role performance is congruent with role prescription. In fact, Ryan and Straus (1954) hold that the extent to which performance coincides with prescription is a theoretically crucial aspect of social structure which may be used to differentiate between families and also between societies, and Straus (1954) and Straus and Straus (1957) have found that certain of the distinctive aspects of Sinhalese personality may be traced in part to the wide discrepancy between role prescriptions and role performances within the Sinhalese family system. Thus, by maintaining the conceptual separation of prescription and performance, and by locating societies or families within the two-dimensional property space formed by these two distinct aspects of role, an important area of family research is both clarified and methodologically facilitated.

Similarly, recognition of the prescription-performance distinction both suggests and clarifies the analysis of either aspect considered separately. Brim (1957), for example, has suggested that an important area for investigation is the question of *why* different groups or individuals vary in their family role prescriptions:

So far as we know, differences in role prescriptions between different sub-cultural groups, between mother and father, or parent and child, have not been examined as to whether the differences arise from different theories of how to reach the same ends, or different ends, or some mixture of both. . . . There is some indication that conflict in prescriptions between various special interest groups, such as the preventive mental health movement and the society at large, arise from differing conceptions of competency in adulthood. Where the general prescription for the parent and child roles are tuned to the production of persons competent to perform in the society *as it exists,* requiring perhaps a moderate amount of anxiety, high achievement drive, etc., the prescriptions of special interest groups may be unrealistic in the sense that they are not directed to the existing societies' demands (pp. 346–347).

Although it should be clear from the preceding discussion that study of family role prescriptions is an important area in its own right, there are many research situations in which either role prescriptions or performance of these roles could, with equal logic,

constitute the appropriate variable to be measured. This is particularly true of studies of the relationships between parent practices and child personality. In such cases, the relative value (in terms of efficiency in explaining development of the child's personality) of knowing the normative prescriptions held by parents, as compared with knowing the actual performance, has not been determined. There are almost no studies in which prescriptive and performance data are compared in terms of efficiency in predicting a dependent variable. Nevertheless, at this stage of development of family research, it may be better strategy to concentrate on actual performance measures, because such a focus may help avoid preoccupation with moral judgments of family behavior.

In the survey of family measurement techniques, approximately half of the instruments studied quantified some aspect of role performance, about one-quarter made use of prescriptive indicators, and another quarter intermixed both prescriptive and performance indicators. Particularly common in the latter group are many of the "parent-attitude" instruments. A frequent type of instrument in this group contains mostly prescriptive indicators asking what parents or children should or should not do, but also contains items asking if a given behavior characterizes a subject or her child. Although it is true that prescriptions can be inferred from performance, it would seem inefficient to do so and, in any case, from the point of view of conceptual clarity, unwise to intermix the two types of indicators.

The pervasive ethical concern with the family, and the corresponding preoccupation with family improvement, leads to certain scientific difficulties and limitations. Thus, a disproportionate amount of the literature on the family is concerned with prescriptions. Although prescriptive material may be handled scientifically, as in the example from Brim, this has not usually been the case. Consequently, trends in the frequency with which prescriptive measures

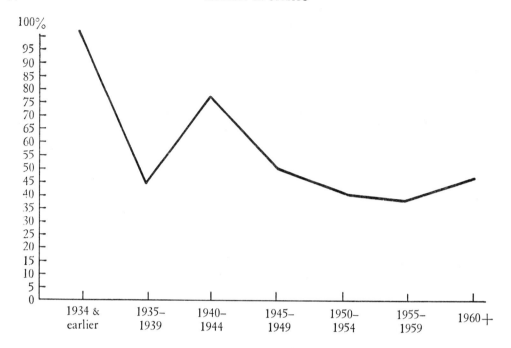

Fig. 4. Trends in Proportion of Prescriptive Measures.

are used can provide an indirect yardstick of the progress of family research. The data shown in Fig. 4 suggest that it has indeed been moving away from preoccupation with right and wrong.

The three main disciplines carrying out quantative research on the family differ in the extent to which they make use of prescriptive measures. As might be expected from the melioristic orientation of home economics, almost three-quarters of the instruments developed in that field are prescriptive. At the other extreme, psychologists have used mostly role-performance measures with less than one-quarter classified as prescriptive, and sociologists fall between with 44 per cent prescriptive.

Predictive and Expressive Indicators

Predictive indicators may be used to form indirect measures of family properties. They are events or attributes which are conceptually or empirically *correlated with* the family property to be measured. Consequently, presence of the predictive indicator also constitutes presence (or future presence) of the family property being measured. Perhaps the best known example of an instrument making use of predictive indicators is the *F* scale (Adorno, Frenkel-Brunswik, Levinson, & Sanford, 1950). Although this instrument can be used to identify racially prejudiced individuals, it contains no items dealing with racial prejudice. The items which it does contain, such as "Obedience and respect for authority are the most important virtues children should learn," are elements in the authoritarian personality syndrome which the theory holds lies at the root of racial prejudice in societies where prejudice is not part of the normative structure.

The term *expressive* is a convenient short-hand to signify indicators which are relatively direct expressions of the variate being quantified. Thus, to measure role differentiation within the family, it is possible to observe (or ask questions) concerning which members of a family carry out various tasks. A set of predictive indicators for the same variate might also be assembled. For example, predictive indicators of role differentiation might be items which deal with equality of sexes, religious conservatism, and emphasis on parental discipline, after the fashion of Levinson and Huffman's Traditional Family Ideology Scale (1955).

Predictive indicators are characteristic of the "empirical approach" to quantification discussed previously. However, they may also be used in the rational approach when, for purposes of controlling a social-desirability response set or preserving the naivete of subjects, an indirect measure is needed. It should be noted that although the term *predictive* may refer to correlation over time, the more usual meaning is cross-sectional or concurrent, as it is used below in discussing types of validity evidence.

Role-System Specification

For some purposes, it is desirable to measure family properties at a very general level. For example, one can measure family cohesion or morale without specifying whose morale. At the next level of specificity, one can deal with parental roles generally, or child roles such as obedience to parents. But, as Brim has noted, it is clear

that there are specific roles associated with sex differences of both parents and children; that is, in addition to the general parent and child roles, there are also roles in the system for father and mother, son and daughter. These four roles are fundamental in the monogamous nuclear family characterizing our society (1957, pp. 351–352).

Even more specific are the sexual role systems formed by the combinations of these four basic statuses in the nuclear family system. Thus, the father-*son* role is both theoretically (Parsons & Bales, 1955) and empirically (Bronfenbrenner, 1961b) differ-

ent from the father-*daughter* role. In fact, one of the significant findings from Bronfenbrenner's research is that parents interact differently with children of the same and opposite sex, and the same type of interaction has different consequences depending on the specific role system within which the action is carried out.

Basic advances in the study of the family seem more likely to occur if there is careful specification of the role system being measured. This does not mean that it is always necessary to measure at the most specific level; but it does mean that when a more general pattern of role behavior is being measured, this should be done explicitly, and the indicators comprising the role should *systematically* sample each of the more specific constituent roles.

Behavioral Field Specification

Many family behavior variables can be expressed in a variety of different situations or behavioral fields. In the *Family Patterns Profile* (Straus, 1963c), for example, one of the variables measured is affective neutrality. If it were possible to assume that the degree of control of affectivity expressed in child-care activities is the same as the amount of affectivity expressed in the course of recreational, economic, and household-task activities, it would not be necessary to be concerned with the behavioral field in which the affective neutrality is expressed. In the absence of willingness to make such an assumption, two alternatives are open: either the indicators can be phrased in a general form without reference to the behavioral field (for example, "yells at his wife"), or systematic attention can be given to sampling relevant fields in which the behavior being quantified may be expressed. Thus, it might be possible to have an item concerning "yelling" in relation to money matters and others in relation to household-task performance and the way children are brought up.

There are several advantages to specifying

behavior fields and attempting to have each field represented in the set of indicators constituting the measure being developed. First, and perhaps least consequential, is the fact that such specification greatly aids in thinking of suitable items for the pool of indicators. It is a map which shows the investigator where to look for relevant behavior. For example, in developing the *Family Patterns Profile,* it became apparent that almost all the items thought of for the affectivity-neutrality variable referred to control of emotion in relation to child care and guidance. On the other hand, the items for the role-differentiation variable were all concerned with occupational versus household-task roles. Had the author continued with this procedure for generating items, the resulting item pool for each variable would also have tended to coincide with a specific area of family behavior. Thus, any instrument built from such an item pool would confound measurement of the pattern variable with measurement of the behavior field which happened to occur as a result of this unsystematic procedure.

A second reason for systematic sampling of behavior fields is that the greater specificity of the resulting items probably makes them easier to answer. Third, and most important, items which do not specify a behavior field in effect require the respondent to generalize his behavior over the relevant fields. This violates the principle that it is preferable to have the subject report specific acts or behaviors rather than generalizations about his behavior. The specific indicators are then used as a basis for generalization about his behavior *by the investigator.*

On the other hand, behavioral accuracy may not be the object of investigation. If the concept which is being quantified is the subject's self-*perception,* then, of course, items which require the subject to generalize about his behavior are appropriate.

There are difficulties with systematic sampling of behavior fields. In the case of a multivariate instrument, it will often be found that one of the variables measured is not usually expressed in all of the behavior fields being sampled. The *Family Patterns Profile* seeks to measure affective neutrality, achievement orientation, self versus familistic orientation, and role differentiation. The indicators were selected to sample the concepts in the fields of child care, recreation, economic activities, and household tasks. It proved difficult to find meaningful items expressing achievement orientation in the field of household tasks performed by the husband.

Another difficulty with systematic representation of a set of behavior fields is that the items can become repetitious to answer, particularly if the instrument is designed to measure only one variable. However, this problem is minimal with a multivariate instrument. For example, in the case of a four-variable instrument, a parallel item cannot occur more frequently than every fourth item, and will more usually occur only every eighth, twelfth, or sixteenth item.

Judgmental and Objective Indicators

One of the most fundamental distinctions to be made in considering the characteristics of indicators is that between what can be called (for want of better terms) judgmental as compared to objective indicators. A *judgmental* indicator is one in which the basic unit of data employed to quantify the family property consists of a human judgment or evaluation. An *objective* indicator is one in which the basic unit consists of some directly observable phenomenon such as number of unmade beds or volume of sound produced by a family attempting to solve an experimental task as registered on an oscillograph.

There has been some empirical investigation of relationship between judgmental- or rating-data and objective- or performance-data measurements. A study by Jack (1934) found ratings of "ascendance" by nursery-school teachers to be correlated .81 with scores based on observations of the child's specific acts on the playground. However, most correlations have been substantially lower. For example, Peters and Campbell

(1955) found a correlation of only .35 between supervisors' ratings of job knowledge and knowledge as measured by a formal test. A study by Stockford and Bissell (1949) found even a lower correlation (.22) between ratings given by department heads to foremen and objective records of the work performance of the foremen's crews. This same study also illustrates the type of bias to which judgmental indicators are subject. The correlation between how long the department head knew the foreman and his rating of the foreman was .59, and between efficiency ratings and liking of the foreman, .65. Similarly, studies of self-rating inventories (i.e., the usual personality test) have generally shown correlations in the .20 to .30 range with peer judgments or with teachers' ratings. However, in these latter cases it is difficult to know which measure should be taken as the criterion.

Other Indicator Characteristics

In dealing with a topic such as sampling of behavior fields, the language used may have given the impression that the points made apply only to measurements based on questionnaire or interview items, but the discussion was intended to, and does, apply to observed-performance and projective as well as self-report indicators. Structuring the discussion in terms of interview and questionnaire items was primarily a matter of simplicity and exposition and also reflects the fact that this is the predominant type of data with which family researchers work. However, the indicator characteristics to be mentioned in the present section do refer primarily to self-report questionnaire or interview data. Some of these are mundane and obvious, others are more subtle; but all must be taken into account in the process of devising verbal instruments to measure family properties.

Wording. The many small details which go into adequate wording of interview and questionnaire items have been so well covered in such standard works as Payne's *The Art of Asking Questions* (1951) and the sections on questionnaire and interview design in Selltiz and associates (1959) that it seems best merely to list here a few of these considerations. These references include discussions of such wording problems as item length and vocabulary, the use of second as compared to third person or passive voice, and bias and emotional loading of items.

It should be noted that it is generally preferable to have all items worded in the positive form. This avoids the confusion of double negatives when the subject responds "no" to an item. This does not mean that all items should be scored in the same direction. On the contrary, it is frequently advisable to alternate scoring direction systematically.

Alternate scoring direction. Cronbach (1950), McGee (1962), Webster (1958), and others have shown that some subjects have a tendency to acquiesce consistently (i.e., respond "true" or "agree") and others to dissent consistently (i.e., respond "false" or "disagree"). A partial control for this type of *response set* can be achieved by wording the items in such a way that a response of "true" or "agree" is required to receive a positive score on approximately half the items and a response of "false" or "disagree" is needed to receive a positive score on the other half.

The acquiescence tendency is only one of a whole class of response biases and sets. One of the most important of these is the social-desirability response set, which is discussed in detail later in this chapter. For systematic discussion of the other types, the reader is referred to Anastasi (1961), Cronbach (1960), or Guilford (1954, pp. 451–459).

Time-period referent. In accordance with the principle of avoiding asking the subject to generalize about himself, it is preferable to choose indicators which sample a specific time period, such as "yesterday" or "last week," rather than asking what has been done "during the last year" or, even more extreme, what is "usually" done. This principle, however, conflicts with the fact that many types of family behavior do not occur with regularity and hence may be missed in a limited time-period-referent indicator. If, for example, data on physical punishment of children is needed, should it be asked in the form, "Did you have to spank your son for anything last week?" as compared to the form "Do you find that you have to spank your son from time to time: (1) Never; (2) Once or twice a year; (3) About once a month; (4) About once a week; (5) Almost every day; (6) Every day or oftener?" The advantage of the latter form of question is that even though the parent may not have spanked the child during the last week, if the last week was not a typical period, the parent could choose alternative (4) or (5).

One consideration which can help in deciding between these two types of indicators is whether the data are to be used primarily to derive aggregate estimates of frequency, or whether they will be used primarily to classify individual families. In the former case, the specific time-period indicator is preferable, since the greater specificity and shorter time span covered are likely to produce more accurate data. The individual errors due to an atypical week are balanced out in the total population by virtue of including those whose atypical week involved more and those whose week involved less spanking than usual. But if the primary purpose is location of specific families on the physical-punitiveness property-space continuum, it may be preferable to run the risk of conscious or unconscious distortion to which the more general type of item format is subject in order to avoid the temporal unrepresentativeness of a specific time-period referent.

Factorial Designs for Systematic Item Generation

Although the preceding discussion of item characteristics is by no means complete, the reader who is thinking in terms of his own measure must by this time have realized that it is impossible to keep even part of these characteristics systematically in mind during the process of thinking up indicators relevant to the concept being quantified. Procedures which have proven useful in dealing with this problem are offered here in the form of sequential steps.

1. *Specification of the* fixed *characteristics of the indicators which will comprise the completed instrument.* For example, in constructing an instrument to measure intrafamily support patterns (Straus, 1963b), it was decided that the instrument should consist entirely of *structural* indicators, directly *expressive* of *performance* in a supportive role.

2. *Specification of the* variable *characteristics of indicators.* The second step involves those indicator properties for which the systematic *variation* is required. In the case of the support measure above, it has just been noted that *all* indicators were to be structural, directly expressive, and of the performance type. On the other hand, systematic variation in indicators was desired in role system, behavioral field, and support modality, as follows:

a. Role system. It was decided that the completed measure should provide scores for the full matrix of each of the possible two-person interactional networks in a three-person family (i.e., husband to wife, wife to husband, father to son, son to father, mother to son, son to mother).

b. Support modality. Previous conceptual specification of "support" (Straus & Cytrynbaum, 1962a; Straus & Cytrynbaum, 1962b) identified a number of subdimensions or modalities by which support could be expressed. In order to produce an instrument which would truly sample intrafamily support patterns, it was felt necessary to have the indicators represent five of these modalities: companionship, help, nurturance, affection, and praise.

c. Behavior field. Finally, in order to have the instrument sample these behaviors in representative situations, the following behavior fields were specified: half of the items were to represent support in the course of instrumental activities and half expressive or social-emotional activities.

3. *Item matrix.* With three different sources of item variation, some mechanical aid is necessary to assist in obtaining and keeping track of the desired variations. A procedure which can provide this aid is to block out a matrix of each of the variables, as shown in Fig. 5.

A complete factorial design such as the one illustrated is usually appropriate. However, there are situations in which an incomplete design such as a *latin square* (Lindquist, 1953) may be necessary.

4. *Item generation.* With the equivalent of Fig. 5 drawn on much larger paper, it is possible to proceed toward systematically creating indicators to fill each of the cells. A single item in each cell would, in this case, result in a 30-item instrument, two items per cell in a 60-item instrument, and so on. To maintain comparability of indicators within each of the role systems, the procedure followed was to create a husband item and then write a parallel item for the wife as recipient of the support act, and also a parallel item for the child as recipient of the support. The same was then done for the wife column and finally for the child column.

5. *Refinement of items.* The item-generation process discussed above concentrates on the substantive content of each indicator. In the course of this process, it will generally be found difficult to pay much attention to other characteristics of the indicators, that is, to keep in mind details of grammatical form (such as present or past tense, or positive versus negative statement), to say nothing of having all items consistently in a performance rather than a prescriptive form, and the like. Once the rough form of the item pool has been created, the items can then be systematically edited to insure, for example, that all items refer to specific role performance (rather than "should" or "ought"), that all are in the tense desired, and that other aspects of wording and format fit the design specified in step 1. In short, the creation of a pool of indicators is a complex task which can be efficiently and accurately accomplished only

Behavior Field	Support Modality	Recipient of Support Act:		
		Husband	Wife	Child
Instrumental	Affection			
	Companionship			
	Help			
	Nurturance			
	Praise			
Expressive	Affection			
	Companionship			
	Help			
	Nurturance			
	Praise			

Fig. 5. A Three-Variable Factorial Design for Generation of Intrafamily Support Items.

by differentiation of the process into the component parts to enable careful and systematic treatment of each aspect.

INDEX CONSTRUCTION

The process of generating the pool of indicators described in the previous sections is closely interrelated with the method by which indicators will be selected from the pool, and the method of combining these into an index which will express varying degrees of the property being measured.

This is because different modes of index construction require differing types of indicators. Consequently, the type of index to be formed constitutes an additional specification of indicator characteristics which, optimally, must be determined before or during the process of indicator generation.

Rating Scales versus "Summation" Scales

Probably the most widely used technique of quantification in family research is the rating scale. The typical rating scale makes use of a single judgmental item. (See the previous discussion of judgmental versus objective indicators.) There are three major types of situations in which rating scales are used: (a) assessment of a family or individual by an observer; (b) assessment of written interviews, life history, or documentary protocol; (c) self-assessment.

Methods of constructing and using rating scales to quantify the properties of the family do not differ importantly from rating-scale methods as applied to individual properties. The reader is, therefore, referred to Cronbach (1960) or Guilford (1954) for discussion of these matters, and to the Fels Parent Behavior Rating Scales (Baldwin, Kalhorn, & Breese, 1949) or to Sears, Maccoby, and Levin's *Patterns of Child Rearing* (1957) for examples of the careful use of rating scales.

In rating scales, the numbered position on the continuum where the family is judged to fall constitutes the quantity locating that family's position in the property space being measured. In summation scales, on the other hand, various techniques are used to combine *mathematically* a series of indicators. For example, to measure "neatness of household," the rating-scale method would require the observer to inspect the house and, on the basis of his over-all observation, designate a position on a neatness continuum. In the summation-scale approach, by contrast, there might be a list of indications of untidiness for each room (dishes on dining-room table, food lying around kitchen, beds not made, etc.). The observer checks each of the indicators he notices. The family's position on the neatness property-space vector may then be determined by some mathematical operation, such as summing the number of items checked.

The rating scale has the advantage of simplicity and presumably also the ability to take into account subtle variations and combinations which the observer may note but which are not included in the items to be observed in the summation-scale approach. On the other hand, the summation scale has greater freedom from the many sources of bias which have been revealed in two generations of research on rating scales. A prudent rule of thumb would seem to be to use summation or point scales whenever this is possible and to reserve rating scales for those properties for which it does not seem practical to devise a summation measure.

The distinction between rating scales and summation scales is somewhat confused by the fact that judgmental items (i.e., ratings) of specific indicators are frequently summed to provide a measure of some more general property. In fact, a synonym for the Likert scale, which consists of the summation of a series of self-assessment ratings on a one-to-five scale, is the method of "summated ratings."

The discussion which follows is concerned with techniques of constructing indexes by performing various mathematical operations over a set of indicators. In most cases, these methods apply to both judgmental or rating indicators as well as to performance or objective indicators.

Arbitrary Summation Scales

In the example of measuring household neatness, a number of indicators were arbitrarily given scores of zero to one. The resulting index was formed by summing these arbitrarily weighted indicators. Similarly, the index for measuring "oral frustration" in a test of certain Freudian theories (Straus, 1957a) consisted of summing points for such events as being fed on schedule, early weaning, sudden weaning, and so on.

Arbitrary summations of this type are open to a number of objections. First, they appear to treat all items as of equal importance, whereas it may be that leaving dirty dishes on the dining-room table is either of greater or lesser importance as an indicator of family neatness than is leaving beds unmade. In fact, however, the items are not equally weighted but only appear to be so. This is because the contribution of any one item to the variance in total test score is proportional to the variance of that item. The weighting thus introduced may or may not reflect the theoretical importance of the indicator. Second, even if differential weights are selected on the basis of the investigator's judgment, there is still no assurance that this weighting in any way improves the extent to which the resulting measure reflects the property which it is designed to measure. Third, some indicators may be completely unrelated, or even negatively related, to the property being measured. In the latter case, retaining the item as part of the index lowers validity. Fourth, the scores resulting from arbitrary summation are at best ordinal. Consequently, the use of most of the standard parametric statistical tools becomes open to question, to say nothing of their use in a research which is concerned with measuring absolute difference in scores or *amount* of change. To meet these and other problems, a variety of more complex systems for combining indicators into indexes have been developed.

Differential Scaling

Differential scales represent an attempt to produce an instrument having the characteristics of an interval scale, that is, a measurement device in which the distances between points on the scale are known, and in which equal numerical distances represent equal distances along the continuum being measured.

Differential scales, as developed by Thurstone and his co-workers, use judges to select items from the item pool. The judges essentially assign ratings to each item on the basis of the extent to which they feel the item reflects the property being measured. The average value of each item in the pool is then computed. Finally, items are selected from the pool to produce a test in which each item is separated from its neighboring items by the same amount, expressed in average scores assigned to the item by the judges. The various techniques of securing these judgments, such as *paired-comparison, equal-appearing-interval,* and *successive-interval* techniques, are described in Edwards (1957b), Guilford (1954), and Thurstone and Chave (1929).

When used for attitude scaling, the resulting test usually consists of about 20 statements expressing varying degrees of favorable or unfavorable attitude toward a social group, institution, or activity. The instrument is completed by having the subject check statements with which he agrees, or the two or three items closest to the subject's views. The average of the scale values of the items the subject checks is used to locate him on the attitude vector being measured.

The popularity of differential scaling has fallen off sharply since the 1930's. This is in part because the technique does not provide any real assurance of creating an interval scale, and in part because social psychology has become interested in more specific variables than extent of positive or negative attitude toward some object. However, in this connection it is important to note that although Thurstone's work was focused on the development of attitude measures, these same techniques may be also applied to items which are indicators of family role performance.

Item-Analysis Scales

Like the methods developed by Thurstone, item analysis is also a method for selecting indicators from the pool and assigning them values in a completed instrument. In the Thurstone differential scales, the criterion for selection and weighting is equality in the number of units separating indicators. In item-analysis techniques, the criterion is either the extent to which the item is consistent with whatever trait is measured by the total pool of items (internal-consistency item analysis), or the extent to which the indicator is correlated with an external criterion (external item analysis).[4]

Item analysis first came into use in sociology on the basis of Likert's work on attitude scaling (1932). The technique, however, can be (and has been) applied to many types of variables in addition to attitudes, for example, to design tests measuring knowledge of contraceptive techniques (Hill, Stycos, & Back, 1959), socioeconomic status (Sewell, 1940), and to family role performance (Straus, 1963c).

External item analyses. This technique is dependent on the availability of a criterion group or variable with which each item in the pool may be correlated. Items having the highest correlation with the criterion are selected for inclusion in the completed instrument. For example, external item analysis was used in developing the Settler Self Inventory (Straus, 1958). This instrument was intended to identify families likely to be successful settlers in the Columbia Basin irrigation project. First, a large pool of indicators consisting of everything which might conceivably be related to a family's ability to deal with the difficulties of new land settlement was assembled. Second, a sample of settler families was interviewed.

The families were divided into low, middle, and high groups according to the adequacy with which they met the problems of new land settlement. Finally, the performance of the low- and high-success groups was compared for each item in the pool. Items which significantly differentiated the high- from the low-success group were retained to form the Settler Self Inventory.

A major defect in the procedures just outlined is that the family characteristics found by the item analysis to be significantly related to successful settlement may be a *consequence* of having had this experience rather than characteristics which existed prior to settlement in the project. Moreover, if a large number of items are correlated with the criterion variable, by chance alone a certain proportion will be found "significant," even though there may be no relationship in the universe (Sakoda, Cohen, & Beall, 1954). The only way to rule out both of these possibilities is by a *cross-validational prediction study*. This requires administering the test developed on the basis of item analysis to a new population prior to settlement. Subsequent variations in success in settlement may be correlated with scores on the test. Obviously, such a procedure is difficult, expensive, and above all, slow to produce needed results. That it is nonetheless possible has been demonstrated in the longitudinal studies of prediction of marital success by Kelley (1939) and Burgess and Wallin (1953).

The more important problem with external item analysis has already been mentioned in the discussion of empirical versus rational approaches to family measurement. More specifically, the properties of the family of greatest scientific interest are not molar conglomerations such as "marital happiness" or "successful settlement," but rather relatively abstract concepts, for which it is rarely possible to find a criterion group. Typically, in fact, the measurement device being developed is either the only empirical technique available, or is judged

---

[4] Readers interested in a comparison of the characteristics of instruments developed by Thurstone (differential methods) with those developed by Likert (internal-consistency summated-rating methods) will find a careful analysis in Edwards (1957b).

to be the best available. Thus, it is either impossible or unwise to base the instrument on an external item analysis.

Internal-consistency item analysis. By far the most frequent application of item-analysis procedures is to determine the internal consistency of the set of indicators comprising the measure. The objective is to produce an instrument which is as pure a measure as possible of a given construct. Essentially, internal-consistency item analysis provides a basis for rejecting items which are not correlated with the other items in the scale.

The most efficient procedure for carrying out such an analysis is to assign each subject a score on the basis of the total pool of items from which the final set will be selected. High- and low-scoring 27 per cent groups are then identified, and the two groups are compared on each item. Division of the sample into the low-scoring 27 per cent group, a middle group, and the highest-scoring 27 per cent (as compared to, say, the top and bottom deciles or terciles) is based on Kelley's demonstration (1939) that the most accurate determination of item validity or internal consistency is obtained with these cutting points. In addition, Flanagan has prepared a table for estimating the product-moment correlations from the percentages in the upper and lower 27 per cent groups "passing" the item. This table, which is quick and convenient to use, is available in Thorndike's *Personnel Selection* (1949). Items which do not significantly differ in the extent to which they characterize the low and high group are rejected. If a test of a specific length is required, for example, 20 items, the 20 with the highest *t* ratios are retained for the final instrument.

In summary, internal-consistency item analysis is used to increase the *reliability* of an instrument, whereas external-criterion item analysis is used to establish or improve *validity.* Under certain conditions, internal and external analysis may lead to opposite results. This would occur in the case of an instrument developed using a strictly empirical approach. Instruments of this type contain a wide variety of indicators sampling various behaviors. The indicators have in common only the fact that they are related to the criterion. The items in such an instrument are likely to have only low correlations with each other. In fact, the greater their intercorrelation, the *less* useful they are as additional predictor variables. Thus, elimination of the internally discrepant items would result in the loss of those with the greatest predictive utility. The objectives of the two forms of item analysis may be reconciled if the instrument is divided into groups of relatively homogeneous items, that is, into separate subtests, each of which would be internally consistent or homogeneous. One technique for accomplishing this is factor analysis, described below.

Factor-Analysis Derived Scales

The availability of large-capacity electronic computers has made possible a new method of index construction. These procedures have been known for many years, but they were not practical until computers with a capacity for generating and factor-analyzing large matrixes became available. Assuming that a machine rather than the researcher and his assistants does the computing, factor-analysis methods combine tremendous ease and convenience with the possibility of integrating the objective of both external- and internal-consistency item-analysis procedures.

The first step is to administer the pool of items to an appropriate population. In the case of dichotomous items, presence of the indicator is scored as 1, whereas absence is scored as 0. The matrix of intercorrelations for the complete pool of items is then calculated. Next, the matrix is factor-analyzed. The resulting machine print-out lists the "loading" of each item on each of the resulting factors. If a general factor is revealed by the analysis, items with the highest loading on this factor may be selected as the ones to constitute the final instrument. If, as will usually be the case, there are a number of factors, each item may be assigned to the factor with which it has the highest loading. The result is a set of measures rather than a single one. Sometimes, these separate factor-derived dimensions are correlated with each other. If the factors are correlated, it may for some purposes be advisable to calculate a total score by summing each of what would then be considered "subscores." If the factors are "orthogonal," that is, not correlated with each other, they should, of course, be kept separate. However, orthogonal subscores may be combined when the focus of the research is on a practical problem, as in the example of predicting success in new land settlement.

It is sometimes appropriate to take advantage of the capacity of a computer by including both the item pool and one or more criterion variables (or theoretically related variables) in the matrix which is factor-analyzed. Inspection of the resulting factor loadings permits both selection of sets of relatively homogeneous items and also identification of items and factors which are correlated with the criterion variable or variables.

As in the case of all factor analyses, the investigator will be faced with the problem of identifying and labeling the resulting factors. This is customarily done by examining the content of the items included in each factor. An additional advantage of including criterion variables in the matrix is that it may facilitate the process of identifying the concept measured by each of the factors.

Cumulative Scales

Since cumulative-scaling procedures were first introduced by Guttman (1944), there has been a tendency among sociologists to overestimate what they accomplish. This chapter takes its cue in this matter from Guttman's own statement, which is simply that the scalogram procedures which he developed are designed to produce a "unidimensional" scale.

Conceptually, unidimensionality means that all items represent varying intensities or amounts of the same construct, or, as Guttman put it, they are all drawn from the same "universe of content." Operationally, unidimensionality means that an individual or family characterized by the second item in a scale must also be characterized by the first item; an individual or family characterized by item 3 must also be characterized by items 2 and 1, and so on.

It is this cumulative nature of the item arrangement that constitutes the unique element in Guttman's method. Cumulative properties were incorporated in two well-known social-psychological measurement techniques early in the century: the Bogardus Social-Distance Scale and the Binet Intelligence Scale. But it was Guttman who generalized the rationale and developed generally applicable procedures for this property of a measurement instrument. The Guttman scale, then, has a cumulative structure or arrangement of items, and it is presumed that this cumulative structure is evidence of unidimensionality. Unidimensionality, in turn, is a formal property of the instrument most similar to internal-consistency reliability. At best, the cumulative nature of a scale is only indirectly related to validity.

Provided one does not confuse unidimensionality with other aspects of measurement, the cumulative property introduced into a scale by Guttman's techniques represents an important addition to measurement theory and technology. Cumulative scaling has been applied to such varied concepts as adoption of improved home-making techniques (Abell, 1952), delinquency (Nye & Short, 1957), achievement tests (Davidoff & Maslow, 1950), role conflict (Gullahorn, 1956), personality as measured by the Thematic Apperception Test (Auld, Eron, & Laffal, 1955), and group interactional structure (Riley et al., 1954).

The work of the Rutgers group, as reported in the volume by Riley and her associates, is particularly important for family sociologists, because it is almost entirely focused on the use of cumulative scales to measure group rather than individual properties. The authors provided a theoretical rationale and examples of a number of different types of group-property scales. They started with the distinction between scales used to order a population of groups rather than the more usual use of cumulative scales to order a population of individuals. The major part of the work, however, is devoted to the application of cumulative scaling to measure the internal structure of groups, including "object," "subject," "consensus," and "reputation" scales. Each of these types aggregates indicators for members of the group to form a "synthetic" item, and it is these synthetic group-property items which are ordered into cumulative scales.

A number of different methods have been developed for arranging items into the hierarchical pattern characteristic of a cumulative scale and for measuring the extent to which a given set of items constitutes a perfect hierarchy. If a set of items selected by these procedures is completely cumulative, then the scale would have a "coefficient of reproducibility" of 1.00. It is customary to require that a scale have a reproducibility of at least .90 to be regarded as approximating the model of the cumulative scale. But other criteria must also be satisfied before .90 is a meaningful figure, and this is often overlooked (see Edwards, 1957b, or Green, 1954, for a discussion of these factors). In fact, under certain conditions, a coefficient of reproducibility of .90 is the *minimum* that is possible with a given set of items.

Assuming, however, that a scale meets all of the necessary criteria, what does the co-efficient of reproducibility tell? Take as an example the Rejection of Parents Scale used in a study of relationship between conjugal power structure and adolescent personality (Straus, 1962b), based on the earlier work of Nye (1958), and containing the following items:

1. I have felt ashamed of my parents.
2. If it were possible to change real parents into ideal parents what would you change about your mother?
3. If it were possible to change real parents into ideal parents what would you change about your father?
4. I have more fun away from home than at home.

The scale formed by these items has a coefficient of reproducibility of .94. The items above are arranged here in scale order (even though they were not that way in the questionnaire). The coefficient of reproducibility of .94 therefore means that, on the average, almost everyone who had a score of 2 gave the response of "nothing" to item 3 and "seldom" or "never" to item 4, but answered items 1 and 2 indicating some degree of feeling ashamed of parents and some desire to have a mother with different characteristics. More specifically, the figure of .94 means that 94 per cent of the responses fell into the cumulative pattern, and only 6 per cent were "errors" in the sense that they did not follow this pattern.

In the original Cornell technique of scalogram analysis, a table is constructed in which the rows represent individuals or families and the columns represent the response category for each item being considered. The resulting tabulation is then inspected, and operations of an iterative nature are carried out to rearrange and eliminate items so as to produce a set and an arrangement of items which meet the characteristics of a cumulative scale. More efficient techniques, particularly for use with dichotomous items, have been developed (Green, 1956; Stone, 1958). Once the data are punched on cards, the use of these procedures permits the coefficient of reproducibility to be computed for a set of items in from 15 minutes to, at most, an hour.

Since the coefficient of reproducibility provides important evidence on the internal structure of the measure, and since it can be computed so readily, it should, as Borgatta (1957) has suggested, become a routine procedure. Unfortunately, it does not now seem to be even a frequent one. A tabulation of trends in the use of the coefficient of reproducibility shows that it jumped from 5 per cent of instruments published in the period 1950–1954 (the first five-year interval when its use was widely known in sociology) to 19 per cent of instruments published during 1955–1959. But for the most recent period, the percentage of researchers who have applied this test to their instruments has dropped to only 8.

The stylish thing now seems to be factor analysis. It is likely that a similar cycle of boom and bust with factor-analysis techniques will also occur, and the causes will be similar. That is, the boom in Guttman scaling during the mid-1950's and the present boom in factor analysis reflect a tendency to view these techniques as virtually guaranteeing a good measurement device. Unfortunately, when the bubble bursts there is also a tendency to forget that even though these techniques are not panaceas, they are extremely useful steps in the inevitably complex process of developing reliable and valid measuring techniques.

Intensity Scales and Zero Point

Cumulative scales (and, indeed, almost every other measure a sociologist is likely to work with) only meet the measurement criteria of ordinal scales. With them, one knows only the rank order of the family. He does not know which point in the scale constitutes a zero intensity (that is, which point divides families into groups possessing some degree of the attribute, as compared to those who have a deficit in relation to this attribute), nor does he know how much of the attribute being measured separates families occupying different points on the scale. For example, in Bowerman's Marital Adjustment Scale (1957), one can assume that those low in scale scores are deficient in marital success. But if one wished to divide a population of families into successfully versus unsuccessfully married groups, where would the cutting point be set? Usually, this is done in some purely arbitrary fashion, such as dividing the distribution at the median. An alternative rationale is based on the theory of the "second component" in scale analysis (Guttman, 1950).

The use of this technique requires an independent indicator or set of indicators to measure how strongly the subject feels about the substantive item or items in the scale. These are used to form an intensity index. When such intensity scales are plotted against *content* scale scores, a U-shaped or J-shaped curve usually results. The inflection point on this curve represents the least intensity and is regarded as the "zero point," or point of neutrality which divides the positive from the negative part of the scale (Guttman, 1954). This seems intuitively reasonable, since, as Torgerson (1958) has noted, it uses as a dividing line the point where subjects are most indifferent.

Intensity analysis therefore offers an opportunity to locate the zero point with Guttman scales and also with scales developed by other techniques at least somewhat objectively. In addition, it is possible to use intensity as a content variable in its own right. For example, Brim, Glass, and Lavin (1962) developed a Parent Motivation Test which is designed to measure drive strength or affect in 10 child-rearing areas, such as obedience, sex, behavior, etc. The test consists of items to be rated on a five-point scale from strongly agree to strongly disagree. The assessment of motivation strength or affect is based on the extremity of the subject's agreement or disagreement with the item and not on the direction of the response. Thus, items answered either strongly agree or strongly disagree are scored 2. Those answered agree or disagree are scored as 1, and those answered as uncertain or not answered receive a score of 0.

The scoring technique used by Brim is known as the "fold-over technique." It has been used as an alternative to the "two-part technique" described by Empey (1957) and others. Instruments set up to use the "method of controlled marginals" (Willis, 1960; Willis, 1961) are especially amenable to this procedure. Although the fold-over technique permits considerable economy in interview of questionnaire time, since it requires only half as many items, it is suspect because of its inherent lack of experimental independence of the content and the intensity observations. Furthermore, Suchman (1950) has reported that fold-over techniques sometimes fail to yield a U-shaped curve in situations where the two-part procedure does produce such a curve. Nevertheless, according to Suchman, different measures of intensity tend to produce curves and zero points which are very similar. Unfortunately, the writer knows of only one other empirical study comparing different measures of intensity (McDill, 1959), and that leaves the issue still open, since the two measures which McDill compared with the fold-over technique seem to reflect the "involution," or third principal component (Guttman, 1954), more than they do the intensity component.

Concluding Comments

Although the preceding sections have discussed what are probably the major techniques of index construction, these by no means exhaust the possibilities. For example, rank-order agreement indexes such as Farber (1957) used to measure "value consensus," and which Hurvitz (1960a; 1960b) and Kirkpatrick and Hobart (1954) used to measure marital role conflicts have not been discussed. Q-sort technique, which is essen-

tially a highly developed elaboration of rank-order methods, has also been omitted for lack of space. This extremely arbitrary exclusion is made somewhat permissible by the excellent methodological literature on Q-sort techniques (Block, 1961; Edwards, 1955; Jackson & Bidwell, 1959; Stephenson, 1953; Wittenborn, 1961). Finally, a glance through the chapter in Zeisel (1957) on index construction or at Barton's work on organizational measurement (1959) will soon convince the reader that the main limit on types of indexes is the ingenuity of the investigator.

Which of the many techniques should be used in any particular research? This depends primarily on the nature of the data it is possible to gather, the nature of the problem to be investigated, and the time and resources available for development and standardization of measures. At one extreme one can throw together a collection of indicators intuitively felt to represent the concept of interest. At the other extreme would be the "scale-discrimination" technique developed by Edwards and Kilpatrick (1948) which combines differential, internal consistency and cumulative scaling into a grand package.

It is true that indexes which have met the rigors of the Thurstone, Likert, *and* Guttman methods of item evaluation are likely to have a higher validity as well as reliability than those developed by any one (or none) of these techniques. But, granting that, there is still no specific evidence of validity. To establish validity requires an entire additional series of investigations.

It follows from this discussion that family research is in a difficult position in respect to instruments. Most substantive investigations are not budgeted for the time necessary adequately to develop and validate measures of the key family properties of interest. Yet few carefully developed and standardized instruments exist, to be pulled off the shelf for use. One can only hope that some of the well-funded research projects can afford the time to develop adequate measures and will be directed by men who are capable of tolerating the long delays in getting to the substantive problem.

Alternatively, but less immediately on the horizon, would be the growth of a measurement tradition among family sociologists, such as exists among personality and differential psychologists. In such a tradition, the development of new measurement techniques and tests is in its own right a scientific activity with high prestige. It thereby encourages at least some researchers to devote a substantial part of their career to the development of tests, and makes available to the entire scientific community an essential set of tools.

THE ADEQUACY OF A MEASURE

The two most general and basic considerations in evaluating the adequacy with which a particular family property has been quantified are subsumed under the terms *reliability* and *validity*. Measures of reliability estimate the consistency of a series of measurements. Measures of validity estimate the extent to which scores reflect the property for which quantification is desired.

It is perfectly possible to have high reliability (that is, complete consistency in measurement), together with zero validity (that is, complete irrelevance to the property of concern to the investigator). On the other hand, if a technique is completely unreliable, that is, if it gives different results on each application, then it obviously must also have zero validity. But even a little reliability goes a long way. A more accurate statement of the interrelation of these two basic aspects of measurement adequacy is that "the validity coefficient cannot exceed the square root of the reliability coefficient" (Cronbach, 1960, p. 129). Thus, an instrument with a very high validity coefficient, such as .70, could have a reliability as low as .49. There are, in fact, many examples of useful instruments of low reliability. Nevertheless, both research and clinical uses demand reliable measure-

ment. The larger the chance variation, the harder it is to find a significant difference between groups, or the less confidence one can place in the technique's appraisal of an individual family. Research carried out with a reliable instrument requires fewer subjects than would the same research if a less reliable instrument had to be used.

Reliability

The term *reliability* covers several different aspects of measurement consistency. This section deals with only the three aspects which are most likely to be of concern for the family researcher: temporal consistency, internal consistency, and examiner, observer, or scorer consistency.

Temporal consistency. Assuming that the family itself does not change, it is obviously desirable to have a measure which yields the same score when applied on two different occasions. All measurements are, of course, subject to minor variations and errors. No two galvanometers will give exactly the same reading, for example, and Geiger counters can vary widely, as in the example given earlier. In addition to such instrument-located sources of unreliability, some variation may be expected from random fluctuations in the characteristics of the objects being measured. Iron bars are longer on a hot day than on a cold day. Similarly, families vary from day to day due to factors such as fatigue or recent pleasant or unpleasant experiences. Measurement of temporal stability consists of estimating the extent to which scores yielded by a technique reflect such random daily fluctuations in the environment or in the family.

The procedure for estimating temporal stability is simply to apply the same measure on two different occasions. Usually, this will be a fairly short interval, perhaps successive days or successive weeks. If a longer interval occurs, differences between the results of the two measurements may reflect permanent changes in the family rather than random fluctuations. The correlation between the two measurements is known as the *coefficient of stability* (APA, 1954).

This is certainly the most obvious and generally applicable aspect of reliability, but it is not without some difficulties. For example, the measurement technique may be "reactive" (Campbell, 1957b). A reactive measure modifies the phenomena under study by the very act of its use. Campbell feels that "any measurement procedure which makes the subject self conscious or aware of the fact of the experiment can be suspected of being a reactive measurement. Whenever the measurement process is *not* a part of the normal environment, it is probably reactive" (p. 299).

Internal consistency. This aspect of reliability refers to the consistency of performance *among the indicators* which comprise an instrument. It is measured by the extent to which items in a test are correlated with each other, or, more simply, by the extent to which a random half of the items are correlated with the other half of the items. It should be noted that lack of internal consistency represents "error variance" only when the property being measured is itself a homogeneous, unitary characteristic. If, on the contrary, the focus is on the measurement of a heterogeneous property of the family, then one should expect corresponding heterogeneity in the indicators comprising the measure of this property. The reader should remember in this connection the distinction between "empirical" and "rational" approaches and the discussion of item-analysis scales earlier in this chapter.

Reliability in the internal-consistency sense is very close to unidimensionality in the Guttman-scaling sense. Hence, in plotting trends in the use of methods for increasing and for measuring instrument reliability, the coefficient of reproducibility should be included with other measures of reliability.

Scorer consistency. Rating scales of various kinds are frequently used in family measurement. Sometimes rating scales are used to quantify an interviewer's over-all impression of a family. Sometimes ratings are used to quantify a self-appraisal by family members, and sometimes they are used to obtain quantitative and standardized judgments of interview protocols or tape recordings of observed interaction sessions. In all such cases, the investigator is concerned with the extent to which variations in the ratings represent the characteristics of the family being rated rather than the characteristics of the person doing the rating. Even when the unit of data consists of objective rather than judgmental indicators, it is still important to assess reliability in observing and recording these supposedly objective indicators empirically. There are many examples of apparently objective items being observed and recorded differently by different scorers. For example, when intelligence tests are given, examiners differ in the extent to which they establish rapport, and consequently the extent to which they elicit optimum performance from the subject. Examiner or scorer consistency is even more important when projective techniques are employed.

Before proceeding to make use of scores based on the work of a single scorer, the prudent investigator will have at least two individuals observe and record or score the same set of materials. If the measurements obtained by the different scorers are highly correlated with each other (say, .85, .90, or above), the efficiency in time and cost of using a single scorer may, if necessary, be made. If, however, scorer reliabilities are low, and remain so after attempts to locate and correct the difficulty, the usual procedure is to average the two scorings.

Reliability of existing family measures. Certainly, the minimum that one should expect from an instrument is some evidence of its reliability. Reliability in the sense of internal consistency is so easy to ascertain that there is almost no excuse for an investigator not computing and reporting it. Indeed, some wasted effort might be saved

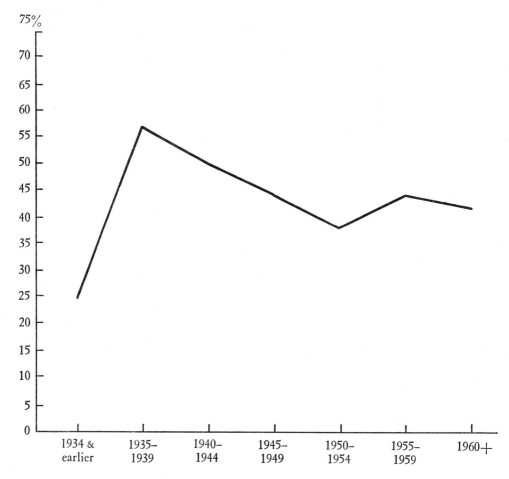

Fig. 6.   Trends in Percentage of Studies Reporting Internal-Consistency Evidence.

if this were uniformly done, since there is little point to basing a major analytical effort on instruments of very low reliability.

For the sample of 263 instruments analyzed by the present writer, slightly over half—56 per cent—were presented without mention of any tests for reliability. The 44 per cent for which reliability evidence was available were divided as follows: 21 per cent reported split-half reliability, 10 per cent reported coefficients of reproducibility, 12 per cent reported agreement between observers or coders, and 2 per cent reported alternate-forms correlations.

Of course, it is possible to look at these data optimistically and note that almost half of the instruments were backed up by some evidence of reliability. Unfortunately, however, Fig. 6 reveals that the percentage of test developers reporting internal-consistency evidence shows no trend during the 25-year period under study. This is particularly disappointing in view of the point previously made concerning the ease of computing such internal-consistency measures as split-half correlations and coefficients of reproducibility.

Turning to reliability in the sense of *stability* over time, a similar situation prevails. Only 15 per cent of the instruments analyzed in this chapter are backed up by information on test-retest reliability, and again the trend is sharply in the wrong direction, as shown in Fig. 7.

In some cases, the researcher may take steps to insure an internally consistent test but not actually measure the over-all reliability of the completed instruments. At the simplest (and least dependable) level, the items or observational categories may be submitted to a panel of expert judges so as to eliminate those items which the judges do not agree belong to the universe of content which it is desired to measure. This is an excellent beginning, but it guarantees nothing, since consensus among the panel of half a dozen or so judges may be nothing more than a shared cultural error. In any

case, 18 per cent of the techniques analyzed went at least this far.

A more objective procedure is the use of item analysis as described earlier in this chapter. Some 10 per cent of the tests reviewed were constructed with the aid of an internal-consistency item analysis, and another 7 per cent with external-criteria item analysis. Finally, 2 per cent of the instruments used loadings from a factor analysis as a basis for item selection, and 1 per cent used Thurstone's equal-interval technique.

Altogether, only about 4 out of 10 tests were reported as having been developed with the aid of one or more of these techniques; and if a panel of judges is not counted as an adequate technique, the figure becomes only 23 per cent of the instru-

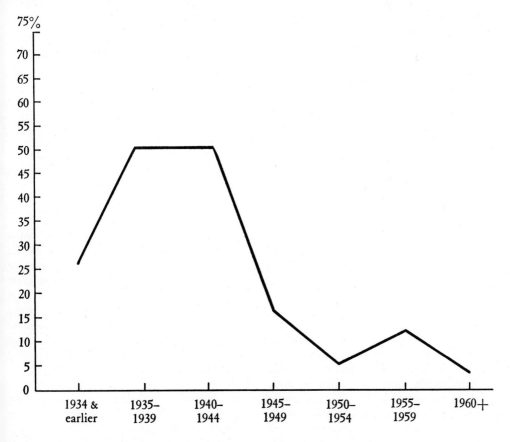

Fig. 7.   Trend in Percentage of Studies Reporting Test-Retest Reliability.

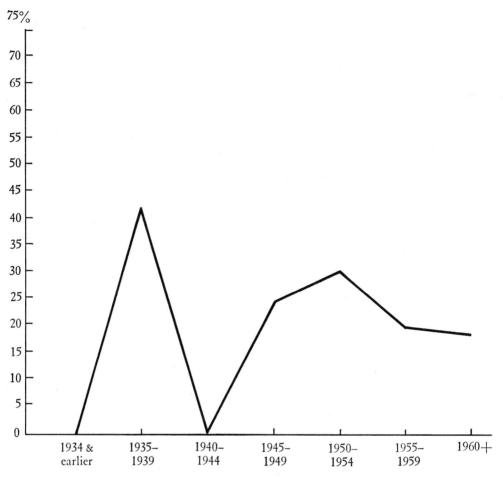

Fig. 8.   Trends in Use of Technique to Determine Internal Consistency of Item.

ments reviewed. Again, this cannot be attributed to omissions made by early family researchers, because Fig. 8 shows essentially no change over the 25-year period surveyed.

Validity

Validity has previously been defined as the extent to which variations in scores produced by the measurement technique reflect variations in the property which it is designed to measure. This is a conceptual definition. It does not provide much aid in the actual process of maximizing the extent to which the scores represent "trait" variance as opposed to error variance. When the operations involved in such a process, or the actual measurements used to estimate validity, are examined, it will be found that these procedures always involve relating some independently observable phenomena to performance on the instrument being validated. There are several ways of doing this. The analysis of different types of validity measures in this section is in terms of the American Psychological Association classification (1954). [Cf. Sussman's discussion of validity, pp. 283–292.]

Even this scheme, which distinguishes among four types of validity (content, concurrent, predictive, and construct), has been subject to dispute (Bechtoldt, 1959) and amplification, as in Campbell and Fiske's subdivision of construct validity into "trait" validity and "nomological" validity and the addition of the idea of "discriminant" validity (Campbell, 1960; Campbell & Fiske, 1959).

Predictive validity. The most readily understood types of validity are concurrent and predictive validity. The *Technical Recommendations* (APA, 1954) states:

Predictive validity is evaluated by showing how well predictions made from the test are confirmed by evidence gathered at some subsequent time. The most common means of checking predictive validity is correlating test scores with a subsequent criterion measure. Predictive uses of tests include long-range prediction of intelligence measures, prediction of vocational success, and prediction of reaction to therapy (p. 13).

Predictive validity is rare in family research. Only 10 per cent of the instruments surveyed report this type of evidence and, as might be expected, most of these are the various marital success prediction instruments. The correlation of the prediction test given to the Burgess sample during engagement with their subsequent marital adjustment (Burgess & Wallin, 1953) is the best-known example.

Concurrent validity. Not all correlations of marital prediction instruments with marital happiness scores (or with divorce) are evidence of predictive validity. In fact, most such correlations fall under the heading of "concurrent" validity, which is defined as follows in the *Technical Recommendations:*

Concurrent validity is evaluated by showing how well test scores correspond to measures of concurrent criterion performance or status. Studies which determine whether a test discriminates between presently identifiable groups are concerned with concurrent validity.

Concurrent validity and predictive validity are quite similar save for the time at which the criterion is obtained. Among the problems for which concurrent validation is used are the validation of psychiatric screening instruments against estimates of adjustment made in a psychiatric interview, differentiation of vocational groups, and classification of patients. It should be noted that a test having concurrent validity may not have predictive validity (p. 14).

Thus, the correlation between the prediction scores of Burgess and Cottrell's (1939) original sample and their marital adjustment scores is an example of concurrent rather than predictive validity, because the measurement of the predictive items was made after marriage. Campbell (1960) succinctly expressed the relationship of predictive and concurrent validity when he noted that "the latter is usually but an inexpensive and presumptive substitute for the former, and together they might be called *practical* validity" (p. 547). Of the 263 instruments analyzed, one-quarter reported this type of validity evidence, and there has been essentially no change over the 25-year period surveyed.

This one-quarter, however, is one of the better records among family measurement attempts, because practical validity (i.e., predictive and concurrent validity) is only applicable where there is a clear external criterion, such as success or failure in marriage. Most properties of the family (for example, degree of dominance of husband) are constructs or abstractions from behavior for which there is no adequate criterion. Typically, in fact, the measurement device under consideration is either the only empirical technique available, or is judged to be the best one available. Thus, the investigator could relate his measure of dominance of husband to self-ratings on this aspect of family structure. However, since the investigator probably decided to develop a measure of dominance of husband because he felt that self-ratings lacked adequate validity or reliability, or both, he would be unlikely to accept presence or absence of such a relationship as validating evidence.[5] In short, the family researcher is usually interested in obtaining a measure of a hypothetical internal process, system, or structure of the family and cannot expect to find a clear behavioral criterion.

Construct validity. The type of validation effort applicable under the circumstances just mentioned is termed "construct" validity in the APA *Technical Recommendations*. This type of validity and the method for its determination are described as follows:

Construct validity is evaluated by investigating what psychological qualities a test measures, i.e., by demonstrating that certain explanatory constructs account to some degree for performance on the test. To examine construct validity requires both logical and empirical attack. Essentially, in studies of construct validity we are validating the theory underlying the test. The validation procedure involves two steps. First, the investigator inquires: From this theory, what predictions would we make regarding the variation of scores from person to person or occasion to occasion? Second, he gathers data to confirm these predictions (p. 14).

How does construct validation proceed in practice? To continue with the example of a husband-dominance measure, theoretical considerations or informal observation might lead the investigator to expect that dominance of husband increases as socioeconomic level increases. If the investigator computed the correlation between these two variables and found it to be positive, he would simultaneously have evidence for his theory and for his measure of dominance of husband. Of course, if no relationship were found, it would be impossible to determine from this one finding whether the inadequacy lies in the theory or in the measure.

This problem is the reason the process of construct validation is focused on *integrating evidence of various types* rather than on finding the perfect criterion. Thus, if the same investigator also found that families which scored somewhat above the mean but not extremely high on his measure of dominance of husband tended to have a more pronounced sex division of labor, and to have more stable and satisfying marriages, he might be inclined to conclude in favor of the measure and against the theory of positive correlation with socioeconomic level, since the majority of results are consistent with prior theory and empirical findings. But if he found no relationship in these instances as well as in his correlation with socioeconomic level, there would be good reason to suspect the validity of the measure.

It should be clear that in the process of devising techniques to measure family properties, the main reliance is necessarily on the operations and the judgments summarized under the heading of construct validity. In fact, as family researchers become less tied to the immediately practical and value-determined types of research, such as are represented by the marital success prediction tradition, one can expect that more and more reliance must be placed on construct validity.

Construct validity of existing family measures. What, then, is the present status? As expected, the most frequent type of validity evidence recorded for the 263 instruments surveyed is evidence of construct validity. Exactly two-thirds of the techniques have at least some entry recorded under this heading. However, this finding is much less reassuring than it seems. First, in recording the characteristics of these in-

[5] Actually, the studies reviewed by Campbell and Fiske (1959) suggest that simple self-ratings are often as efficient measurement devices as personality tests. This is one of the considerations which led to their recommendation that "discriminant" validity be added as a fifth type to the APA classification of types of validity. Thus, they urged that the validation of a test include the demonstration that the test scores predict independent measures better than do self-ratings. If not, they argued, why bother with the more complex and time-consuming test?

struments, the idea of construct validity has been grossly stretched. Thus, all empirical relationships between scores on the instrument and other variables with which these scores might reasonably be expected to be associated if both measures were in fact valid, have been counted as tests of construct validity. Perhaps a fifth of these tests resulted in a finding of no relationship, thus reducing the figure to about 50 per cent with evidence of construct validity.

In one sense, the problem of discovering and evaluating evidence of validity for these family measurement techniques is the reverse of the problem usually encountered in evaluating the validity of psychological tests. To oversimplify somewhat, one might say that the key problem in evaluating psychological tests consists of deflating the excessive validity claims made in test manuals and other sources. The authors of these family measurement instruments are clearly innocent of any such charge.

By and large, the term *validity* seldom occurs in the research reports surveyed. More specifically, almost none of the evidence classified as construct validity was reported by the test author as evidencing validity. Rather, it represents the present writer's own inference or judgment that an empirically tested relationship could contribute to establishing the construct validity of the instrument. Thus, if an author reported that girls have higher scores on his parent-child adjustment inventory than boys, it was counted as a construct validity "prediction." The author need not have been thinking about validity when reporting this finding. But because of the theoretical and empirical weight behind the expectation that boys are less well integrated into their families of orientation than girls, this can be interpreted as evidence of construct validity. Unfortunately, a number of the "predictions" which were counted as evidencing construct validity are much less plausible than the example just cited. Hence, the need for caution in interpreting the 50 per cent figure.

Finally, the most important reason for being skeptical of the apparent finding that half of the instruments surveyed are supported by at least some evidence of construct validity stems from the necessity of interpreting construct validity evidence in a theoretically guided matrix of findings, rather than from a relationship with a single-criterion variable. Most of the instances tabulated consist of a single relationship, whereas, at the very least, construct validity must be inferred from more than one theoretically predicted relationship of the instrument with relevant variables. Greater confidence in the instrument will be generated if this matrix is constructed along the lines of the "multitrait-multimethod" matrix (Campbell & Fiske, 1959).[6]

Content validity. Finally, there is *content validity,* which the *Technical Recommendations* (APA, 1954) describes as being

evaluated by showing how well the content of the test samples the class of situations or subject matter about which conclusions are to be drawn. Content validity is especially important in the case of achievement and proficiency measures.

In most classes of situations measured by tests, quantitative evidence of content validity is not feasible. However, the test producer should indicate the basis for claiming adequacy of sampling or representativeness of the test content in relation to the universe of items adopted for reference (p. 13).

Instances of content validity are relatively rare in family measurement attempts. Using a very liberal standard in judging its presence results in 26 per cent of the instruments being classified as having some evidence of content validity. Most of these

---

[6] The "multitrait-multimethod" matrix is simply a method of ordering the matrix of correlations in a logical and consistent fashion in order to answer systematically such questions as whether the instrument under consideration is more closely related to dependent variables than are alternative methods of measuring the family property under consideration, or such confounding variables as socioeconomic level, intelligence, and various response sets.

represent instances in which a panel of judges was used to assess the items of an instrument in terms of their conceptual unity. Another type of evidence is represented by some of the family-problem check lists which have been made up by selecting items from free-response lists of family problems collected as a step in the test-development process.

What, then, can be said over-all about the validation of family measurement techniques? It can be summarized by noting that if proper allowance is made for the inflation factor in the counting of evidence of construct and content validity, and if the large class of reasonably carefully developed but theoretically unimportant instruments structured in terms of good versus bad (such as the marital prediction and adjustment tests) is eliminated, all but a few of the 263 instruments surveyed were conceived without benefit of validating procedures. They are retained because family researchers do not discriminate against bastard offspring. One hopes that, like the human illegitimate, despite the inadequacy of their origins, a number of these instruments will in the long run turn out well. But at present, they are mostly accepted on faith, or from lack of alternatives.

Measurement Norms

In view of the lack of evidence of validity just discussed, the urgency of presenting adequate norms for each instrument is minimal. The reporting of normative data is, however, even more minimal than the need. Only 5 per cent of the instruments are presented with standard score or percentile distributions. Since the majority of the instruments surveyed were developed for use in a specific investigation rather than as general-purpose instruments, this is understandable. However, even a simple frequency distribution of scores is rare. For only 22 per cent of the instruments is it possible to determine this crucial information. Consequently, approximately three out of four techniques developed to measure a family property have no normative data at all with which other researchers can compare their findings, or at best a measure of central tendency such as the mean or median.

Evidently, there is a symmetry between the intentions of those who develop techniques for measuring family properties and those who use family measurement techniques. New techniques seem to be generated only as by-products of a particular substantive investigation without concern for developing a standardized instrument, and there is a corresponding failure to use existing techniques in other investigations. Thus, 80 per cent of the instruments surveyed have to the writer's knowledge never been used beyond the original study for which they were designed, and the few which have escaped this oblivion have mostly been used by only one additional investigator.

This is an unfortunate state of affairs, because only by cumulative use can the validity of an instrument be established or rejected. It reflects a combination of circumstances. Outstanding among them is the vicious circle set up by failure to see the need for, and devote time to, developing standardized general-purpose instruments. Instead, the family researcher develops an *ad hoc* technique for measuring the variable needed by his study and presents it with an apologetic disclaimer footnote such as the present writer did in a recent article (Straus, 1962a). Why, then, should another researcher make use of a technique in which even the original author lacks confidence?

THE CONTROL OF MEASUREMENT DISTORTION

The fact that the family is an institution of great structural importance, ethical concern, and personal saliency leads to difficulties both in the design of family research and in the measurement of family properties. In this section, the measurement distortions introduced by this social sensitivity of the family form the focus. Specifically, because of the great importance to both the individual and the society of "good families," all measurement techniques based on *self-report* are suspect. This is because individuals asked to report on or describe their own families in interviews or questionnaires are likely to give information which largely reflects the normative prescriptions or "social-desirability" value of the response.

Edwards (1957a), in a series of devastating empirical and theoretical analyses of the social desirability effect in personality assessment, has shown that from 70 to 90 per cent of the variation in personality test scores reflects differences in individual subjects' tendencies to give socially desirable answers. Thus, only 10 to 30 per cent of the variance in personality test scores reflects differences in the trait which the test is designed to measure.

There have been no similar empirical studies of family self-report measures, but there is every reason to believe that family measures are at least as sensitive to differences in the subject's motivation to present a socially correct appearance as are personality tests. Moreover, family self-report measures often exaggerate the social-desirability effect by asking the subject to make a generalization or evaluation of whether or not a certain type of behavior characterizes his family. Such self-evaluative instruments are even more suspect than are instruments asking for report of a specific action or event.

Distrust of self-evaluative data arises out of several considerations. First, as already noted, self-evaluations probably have the highest vulnerability to conscious or unconscious social-desirability distortion. Second, they may require a mode of cognition or verbalization beyond the capacity and vocabulary of the subject. Finally, because of the socially sanctioned privacy of the family and the importance attached to not introducing elements which may disturb the solidarity of the family, the very act of measurement by self-evaluative techniques may be rejected.[7] [Cf. Ch. 7, pp. 000–000.]

Voluntarism and Disguise

The analytical framework of this section makes use of two of the axes used by Campbell (1957a) and Straus (1957b) to classify social-measurement techniques. These two axes are of particular importance for the problem of social-desirability distortion. The first axis is *voluntarism,* and the second is *disguise.*

By voluntarism is meant the degree to which the measure is dependent on the subject's self-report. Voluntary measures may be identified by instructions to the subject which stress that "there is no right answer; we would like to find out what you do, and how you feel about this," etc. They may also be termed subjective measures.

Nonvoluntaristic measures are called *performance* measures in this chapter. In Campbell's (1957a) classification, they are termed "objective" measures. The salient feature of performance measures is that they present a task to the subject with the instruction that he (or the family) is to try to achieve some correct solution. Thus, from the viewpoint of the subject, performance measures refer to the external world rather than to self-description, as do voluntaristic measures.

The second axis, disguise, refers to the extent to which the true purpose of the measurement is concealed from the subject. At one end of the continuum are instruments which attempt to conceal their purposes completely, and which in this chapter are called disguised measures. Such measures make use of indirect indicators (Campbell, 1957a), or predictive indicators (Lazars-

[7] For example, a recent study (Straus, 1964a) required giving a questionnaire concerning certain aspects of family structure to a sample of school children. The most important objection raised by school officials to this questionnaire was that it might introduce disturbing elements into the family relations of the subjects. As one school official put it, "Why, some of these kids have never even thought about things like that."

feld, 1959). At the other end are what both Campbell and the present writer call direct measures. In Lazarsfeld's terminology, direct measures are based on "expressive" indicators, i.e., indicators which are direct expressions of the property. [Cf. the disguise procedures outlined in this section with Sussman's discussion of manipulation; pp. 293–295.]

The combination of these two axes yields four types of measures, as shown in Fig. 9. Existing family measures, and potential new measures, are classified in this typology, after the next sections deal more specifically with the voluntarism axis and then the disguise axis. Finally, modes of controlling social-desirability distortion with direct-voluntary measures are described.

Voluntaristic versus Performance Measures

In one sense, the ideal solution to response-set distortion is to avoid all voluntaristic or self-report measures and to use instead strictly observed performance data. However, performance measures have been rarely used in the study of the family. This

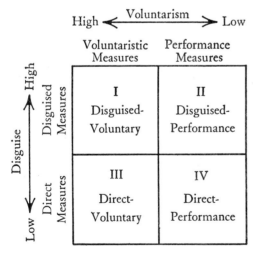

Fig. 9.   A Typology of Measurement Techniques Based on Degree of Disguise and Voluntarism.

is in part because of inherent limitations of observed performance data, but also in part because of the historical accident that empirical sociological research has primarily made use of self-report interviews and questionnaire data. At the same time, there is a modest recent trend in the direction of laboratory research in sociology, and the next decade of family research is likely to see a growth in performance as compared to self-report types of measurement. [Cf. Ch. 8.]

A few examples may serve to illuminate what is involved in measures lying at varying points on the voluntarism continuum. Consider as a first example measurement of the power structure of the family. Starting at the most voluntaristic end of the continuum are instruments which require the subject to make a generalization or an evaluation about his family. For example, to assess parental power as perceived by the child, Nye (1958) asked a series of questions such as: "When I date, father gives: 1. Too much freedom, 2. About right, 3. Too little freedom." This is probably the most voluntaristic type of item possible, since it requires the subject both to make a generalization about the behavior of his father and to evaluate that behavior. Only slightly less voluntaristic are items such as the one used in a study by Straus (1962a) which ask for a generalization but no evaluation: "Father bosses mother: 1. Never, 2. Seldom, 3. Sometimes, 4. Often, 5. Very often."

Much less voluntaristic is the type of questionnaire item introduced by Herbst (1954) to measure power. The child is first asked who in the family does a series of tasks. Then comes a parallel of items asking who decides about these tasks. One item, for example, is: "Who fixes father's breakfast?" The parallel item is: "Who decides what father is to have for breakfast?" Herbst's use of these items is based on a definition of social power as ability to control the behavior of others. The method of computing power scores follows from this definition. If father prepares the breakfast but mother decides what is to be served for breakfast, this is counted as $+1$ for mother power. If, on the other hand, mother fixes breakfast but father decides what will be served, this is counted as $+1$ for father power. The present chapter is not concerned with this theory of social power and whether or not it is adequately operationalized by Herbst's technique. Rather, the important points to note are, first, the simplicity and specificity of the behavior which the child is asked to report, and, second, the way in which these specific behaviors are utilized *by the investigator* to form a generalization about the power structure of the family. The latter feature introduces an element of disguise which is discussed later.

Least voluntaristic of all would be observation of family interaction, either in the natural or in a laboratory setting. It should be noted that, even in the case of directly observed behavior, the element of voluntarism is not absent unless the family does not know they are being observed or thinks they are being observed for another purpose (i.e., disguised measurement); or unless the task presented to the family is "objective" rather than self-descriptive (i.e., performance measurement). If the family is aware of the observation, it can choose to display certain patterns of interaction before the investigator. Thus, Vidich (1956) asked families to discuss four topics (such as how they would spend a particular sum of money if they were given it) and arrive at a decision as a family. Vidich considered the measurement a failure. He felt that the norms prescribing correct family behavior, and particularly those requiring family unity, led the subjects to minimize differences, disagreements, and tensions while being observed. He concluded that the observed interaction was not an accurate representation of the day-to-day interaction of the husband and wife.

In addition to attempting to maximize disguise and performance, two other strategies have been employed to minimize the socially expected "front," and presumably,

therefore, to maximize the degree to which the laboratory observation represents the family's usual patterns of interaction. The first of these, which requires the family group to deal with an existing or artificially created breach in group solidarity, is Strodtbeck's "revealed-difference" technique (1951; 1958). In this technique, family members *separately* complete an opinion questionnaire. Items on which there is a difference of opinion are then presented one at a time to the subjects with the request that they reach a family decision. Thus, the family cannot suppress the revelation of internal differences. Faced with the "revealed difference" and the necessity of resolving rather than denying a difference, the likelihood of representative interaction is much higher. Strodtbeck's published reports show that the families do concentrate on the experimental task, and leave the impression that this technique is successful in eliciting representative interaction among family members.

The revealed-difference technique depends on pre-existing differences among family members, and thus obviously imposes limits on the type of problems which it may be used to investigate. However, there is no reason why the experimenter cannot *create* differences needed for his particular research. For example, different members of the family may be provided with discrepant types of information needed for solution of the experimental task, as in Goodrich and Boomer's Color Matching Test (1963). Similarly, they may be provided with conflicting or discrepant norms or rules for proceeding in the experimental task. This has apparently not yet been done in family research, but there are no technical or theoretical reasons for expecting that it cannot be done. On the contrary, the actors in normal family interaction frequently operate with both divergent information and norms, for example, those growing out of age and sex differences inherent in the composition of the nuclear family. Closely related is the ingenious technique devised by Haley (1962) for eliciting and observing coalition formation among family members.

Another procedure for reducing self-report bias in observational studies can be termed the "absorbing situation" strategy. The essential point is simple and obvious: The experiment or performance being observed must be sufficiently engrossing and demanding of attention that the actors will, at least temporarily, forget about the presence of an observer.

The problem with this "simple and obvious" strategy is the ingenuity required to devise such situations. Although it is difficult, it is important not to create a self-fulfilling prophecy by assuming that it cannot generally be done. As a matter of fact, there are examples from the small-group research tradition of such engrossing tasks. One is the shuffleboard game used by Hamblin for a study of leadership and crisis (1958). In this experiment, the groups were required to infer the method of scoring this particular variation of shuffleboard from red and green lights which flashed if they scored positively or negatively. These procedures, plus ego-involving instructions, were evidently successful for "the average group behaved as though they were in a tournament" (Hamblin, 1958, p. 70), and have also proved successful in a recent study of the way families deal with a crisis (Straus, 1964).

Another example of a structured-performance situation which is likely to be interesting and demanding enough to distract the family from the fact that they are being observed is a station-wagon loading problem. This can be used to measure variables such as power, support, role differentiation, and communication. A large crate painted to represent a station wagon is in a room with camping gear strewn about. The family is required to pack the wagon in a specified time period. As in normal station-wagon loading, there is more camping equipment than can be placed in the wagon. Although this procedure has not yet been

tried, it seems promising. In advance of actual trials, the number of other games, tasks, or problems which might be used is almost infinite. Attempts to use such techniques will certainly narrow the list, but this experience is not yet available, except by transference from experimental studies of *ad hoc* small groups.

Trends. The overwhelming majority of family measurement techniques are voluntaristic in nature. In fact, only 10 per cent of the techniques analyzed by the present writer are methods for quantifying observed interaction between family members. Most of these are mother-child interaction measures developed by child psychologists. Another 10 per cent are projective techniques which could reflect the subject's actual performance, his prescriptions of correct roles, or either of these. The majority of the instruments—68 per cent—are self-reporting in the sense of being based on what the subject says about his family. An additional 18 per cent require a self-generalization, and some are based on both self-report and self-generalization, making a total of 86 per cent clearly voluntaristic in nature.

There has been a slight downward trend in the percentage of measures based on voluntaristic sources of data, and especially the self-generalization type. However, the replacement has been projective techniques rather than observed-performance measures. Projective techniques do offer some promise, but they are low in reliability, and less is known about their validity than any other type of measurement technique applicable to the family.

In summary, the more the data to be quantified depend on voluntary self-description by the subject, the more likely is the measurement to be influenced by irrelevant sources of variance, such as social-desirability response set. Consequently, from the viewpoint of control of such response-set distortion, objective or performance measures are to be preferred. On the other hand, (a) relatively few performance measures have so far been developed for family research,

(b) not all performance measures are free of response-set distortion, and (c) data of this type may be relatively expensive to obtain. Nevertheless, the almost exclusive reliance of family sociology on voluntaristic data constitutes a major soft spot in the discipline. There is, consequently, an urgent need to add performance measures to the repertoire of family researchers.

Direct versus Disguised Measures

Perhaps the most widely used technique for attempting to control deliberate or unconscious distortion is to conceal the true purpose of the measurement from the subjects. The rationale is that if the subjects do not know what is being measured, they will find it difficult to alter their responses or performance along the dimensions being measured. Personality tests, for example, almost never reveal the names of the traits which the test is designed to measure. Similarly, in most interview situations, the subject is given only a vague and general description of the research. The specific variables to be measured on the basis of interview data are seldom revealed. However, the element of disguise in withholding the names of the variables being measured is so minimal that it seems best to consider the usual personality test and the usual interview as direct rather than disguised measurement. This is because the intent of the investigator is apparent from the nature of the specific questions asked.

The dividing line between what constitutes a direct and what constitutes a disguised measure is a matter of judgment. Although personality tests generally are direct measures, under certain conditions they may be disguised. The necessary condition is that the item not reveal the nature of the variable being measured. Many of the empirically derived Minnesota Multiphasic Personality Inventory scales meet this condition. The MMPI scales developed by Gough to measure intelligence (1953) and status (1948) can be classified as disguised measures. It is true that the MMPI is a self-descriptive inventory. However, the manifest content of the items in these two scales is unrelated to the dimension being measured. But Taylor's manifest anxiety measure (1953), which is also a MMPI scale, is a direct measure, since the manifest content of the items clearly coincides with the variable being measured.

The classic projective tests such as the Rorschach and Thematic Apperception Test (TAT) may be considered disguised measures. By now, most literate subjects probably realize that the purpose of the test is to assess some aspect of personality. However, it is almost impossible for the layman to guess the specific variables being measured. On the other hand, sentence completion inventories, with stems such as "I sometimes worry . . ." or "My wife and I . . .," reveal the nature of the variables being measured in the manifest content of the sentence stem. Nevertheless, a study by Getzels (1951) shows that under some conditions even the minimal reduction in voluntarism achieved by sentence completion items may be effective. Getzels found that his sentence-completion items discriminated better between the criterion groups of his study than did matched direct questions, *if* the topic under study was subject to clearly perceived norms or pressure. He found little or no advantage for sentence completions over direct questions when the topic permitted a variety of socially acceptable answers.

Getzels' work also shows that if sentence completions are put in the "Most people . . ." form, the subjects often do not project. Instead, they attempt a realistic estimate of popular opinion. This finding suggests that sentence completions should be phrased in terms of, for example, "A wife . . . ."

As in the case of the voluntarism continuum, the need to control response set and other measurement distortion leads to a preference for measures occupying one end of the continuum rather than the other. However, although disguised measures are to be preferred, limitations similar to those pointed out for performance measures are applicable: (a) relatively few disguised family measures are available; (b) disguise of the variable to be measured (even when successful) by itself provides no assurance that the instrument measures what it is intended to measure; (c) the cost of obtaining and analyzing disguised data is often high, as in the case of the TAT.

Having described and briefly illustrated the voluntarism and the disguise axes, it is time to return to the classification presented in Fig. 7, in which these two axes are interrelated to form a four-position typology of measures. In the following paragraphs, each of these four types of measures is discussed and examples are given of existing and theoretically possible family measures falling into each type.

Disguised-Voluntary Measures

Instruments in this category are dependent on the subject's willingness to provide some sort of self-description either verbally or in terms of overt performance. However, an essential characteristic of the disguised-voluntary technique is that the manifest content of the indicators is unrelated to the variable which the instrument is actually designed to measure. As was previously indicated, the most widely known instruments falling into this type are the classic projective techniques.

Projective technique. Projective technique is the name given to a wide variety of attitude and personality measurement devices which roughly correspond to the following formula:

1. Stimulus materials ranging from the completely unstructured "cloud pictures" or the Rorschach ink blots to the fairly definite structure of uncompleted sentences are presented to the respondent.

2. The respondent is asked to describe or to tell a story about what he sees, or in some other way complete and give structure to the material presented.

3. The respondent's replies are then analyzed on the basis of the theoretical premise that his structuring of the stimulus material is a sample of his mode of reacting to the world in general or to those areas of it tapped by the stimulus material.[8]

Projective techniques were originally designed for and are still primarily used in psychiatric diagnosis. The literature on clinical use of projective techniques is well summarized in the work of Abt & Bellak (1950), Anderson and Anderson (1951), and Bell (1948), and need not be repeated here. The present discussion concerns applications and modifications of these techniques for social-psychological research.[9]

A technique such as the Rorschach clearly belongs in the disguised category. Techniques like the TAT can shift back and forth across the disguise-direct dividing line, depending on the instructions given the subject and the context in which the research is carried out. Straus and Cytrynbaum (1962b) analyzed TAT's given to university students as part of a series of tests given to all entering freshmen. The test was given immediately following an intelligence test and was described to the students as another kind of intelligence test. Since the Straus and Cytrynbaum analysis is concerned with the intrafamily support and power structure depicted in the stories, and since it is not likely that the subjects anticipated such a use of the data, it may be considered a disguised measurement. If, however, the TAT is given to

---

[8] There is considerable evidence in support of this assumption (e.g., Borgatta, 1955; Calogeras, 1958; Davids & Pildner, 1958). But as Lindzey (1952) has noted, at most this evidence can demonstrate that projective test interpretation is not in direct conflict with experimental evidence. Thus, although the plausibility of projective testing is supported by the evidence, the need to demonstrate the validity of specific scoring systems remains.

[9] For references which deal with the application of projective techniques to social psychological research, see Anastasi, 1961; Brower and Weider, 1950; Campbell, 1950; Cobliner, 1951; Cronbach, 1960; Selltiz, 1959; Maccoby and Maccoby, 1954; Proshansky, 1950; and Rose, 1949–1950.

clients of a family service association, or if it is given as part of a research which the subjects know to be focused on the family, almost no disguise is present, and the TAT would in this context be considered as a type III or direct-voluntary instrument.

It should be noted that projective techniques may take an almost infinite variety of forms and offer great flexibility of adaptation to family research. Thematic apperception of pictures need not be confined to the original set of TAT cards developed by Murray. Pictures depicting particular family situations or groups of actors may be developed in order to maximize production of the type of content material in which the investigator is interested. For example, in a study of cross-sex relationships of fifth-, sixth-, and seventh-grade boys and girls, Broderick and Fowler (1961) used a variation of the picture interpretation technique called the "cartoon fill-in technique." This method was introduced by Rosenzweig (1945) for measuring modes of dealing with frustration. This technique requires the respondent to fill in a blank "balloon" or to answer questions concerning each of a series of cartoon drawings. One of the cartoons employed by Broderick and Fowler is shown in Fig. 10.

Although Broderick and Fowler have not yet published methodological information on their application of this technique, previous uses of cartoon fill-in to study such variables as leadership and authoritarianism have given coefficients of stability ranging from .54 to .78 (Sanford, 1950–1951; Sanford & Rosenstock, 1952), and coding reliabilities were about .90.

A study by Graham (1954) demonstrates the feasibility of a self-administered questionnaire containing projective pictures. Sayles's study of factory grievance procedures (1954) and Hess and Handel's (1959) study of families illustrate the use of picture interpretation as a basis for a group interview. Sayles's study also demonstrates the technique's ability to elicit information on emotionally charged topics without antag-

What is happening in this picture?

Why?

How does the girl feel?

How does the boy feel?

Fig. 10. Broderick & Fowler (1961) Cartoon Item.

onism or the lengthy preparatory work to establish the rapport needed to obtain the same data by direct questioning.

Finally, it is important to bear in mind the distinction between the use of projective techniques to delimit individual personality, as compared to uses in which the purpose is to measure role relationships and group structure. For example, the Straus and Cytrynbaum study previously cited used the TAT to measure the *interactional* aspects of power, while the scoring system developed by Veroff (1958) was designed to measure individual power *motivation*. Projective techniques were originally designed to secure personality rather than social-structural data, and most of the literature is oriented toward personality measurement. Even when the focus of the research or scoring system is explicitly familial (Friedman, 1957; Meyer & Tolman, 1955a; Meyer & Tolman, 1955b; Singer, 1954), the scoring is still designed to elucidate the personality characteristics of the subject or other family figures. There are, however, a few examples of interactionally focused applications (Meadow, 1956; Mussen & Kagan, 1958). Since it is social structure which is most central to family sociology, the family sociologist needs to emphasize adaptations of projective techniques to measure interactional rather than personality variables.

Proverbs and humor. The use of cartoons in the example just presented does not necessarily involve humor. But there is a group of techniques which are based on the principle that like or dislike for various types of humor is closely related to the subject's personality and social-interactional network. This rationale has been applied to the development of tests employing lists of jokes and to others which use lists of proverbs or famous sayings.

Fromme's "cartoon test" (1941) consists of a series of cartoons, for each of which the subject is asked to choose a caption from four possibilities. Questioning on the reasons for choices follows. Still another variation occurs in the work of Strother, Barnett, and Apostolakos (1954). Their method was to have the subjects rate 46 Steig cartoons as funny or not. Given the large number and wide variety of family-situation cartoons published annually, it should prove possible to select a group of cartoons relevant to a great many dimensions of family behavior. Similarly, it seems likely that the techniques employed in the humor and proverb tests described below could be applied to develop measures of family role behavior.

Cattell and Luborsky's IPAT Humor Test of Personality (1952) has two forms.

Form A contains 91 pairs of jokes. The respondent is asked to choose the one from each pair which he prefers. In Form B, 112 jokes are presented. The respondent is asked to rate each on a two-point scale. Ten personality variables are scored.

In the Famous Sayings Test developed by Bass (1956b), the respondent is asked to state whether he likes or dislikes 130 famous sayings. The test was developed from an original 300-item list. The four scales for which the test is scored are based on the findings of a factor analysis which revealed the following four factors: conventional mores, hostility, fear of failure, and social acquiescence.

Word association. Word association is the oldest and simplest projective technique and one which offers considerable promise for family research. If family-relevant stimulus words are intermixed with other stimulus words, and if the list is administered in a context which the subject does not perceive as designed to elicit family data, the technique can be considered disguised. To the extent that scoring is based on family-relevant *responses* to stimulus words having no manifest family content, even greater disguise is achieved.

Play situations. Doll play has been widely used in the study of socialization, and it is one of the few techniques adapted to obtaining data from children. Although doll play has been most frequently used to assess the personality of the child, the technique is of particular importance for family research because it has also been used to measure interactional patterns among the family actors represented in the set of dolls given the child to manipulate. Child psychologists have made considerable use of the technique, but to the writer's knowledge, no family sociologist has published data on family interaction based on doll-play projection. Despite a number of methodological difficulties, the technique is so inherently suited to study of family interaction that it deserves to be tried. Fortunately, the task of adapting the technique to the needs of family sociology has been greatly facilitated by the publication of a comprehensive review and analysis of the research uses of doll play by Levin and Wardwell (1962).

A bold investigator might also wish to explore the use of play situation and techniques with adults. Obviously, dolls would be considered childish by adults, but it is possible that puppets might be intriguing. A completely unstructured approach would present the subject with a table full of puppets labeled "father," "mother," "son," "daughter," etc. The only requirement would be to "put on a play with these puppets." In a more structured approach, the subject might be given a puppet for a father and one for a teen-aged son. He would then be asked to put on a show which starts with the son coming home at one in the morning. Obviously, however, in most contexts this would not be a disguised measure.

Disguised-item questionnaires. Most personality inventories are designed on the implicit (and questionable) assumption that the responses are a substitute for an outside observer's ratings of the respondent. They are therefore "direct" measurements. But the literal self-report assumption of these instruments is not a necessary feature. Meehl (1945) pointed out some years ago that the scoring system for the MMPI does *not* assume a valid self-rating in response to the test items. Instead, the manifest content of both the items and the response is ignored. Scoring is based solely on the empirical determination that one criterion group of respondents tends to answer the questions in one way and another group in a different way. Many of these differentiating items have no obvious relation to the characteristics of the criterion groups. The most extreme examples of this are the MMPI scales already mentioned which consist of items differentiating between high and low intelligence groups in one case and high and low socioeconomic status groups in the other.

Although it is possible for MMPI and similar test items to be faked in a socially acceptable direction (Edwards, 1957a), it is almost impossible to guess on which specific scale any item will appear. Consequently, even such apparently direct tests may be considered disguised techniques when the scoring keys and interpretation are based on external-item analysis. There is every reason to believe that these procedures may also be used to develop measures of family properties. Following the analogy of the MMPI, this would involve creating a large and diverse pool of items covering many different aspects of family interaction. The growth of the MMPI has demonstrated that once such an item pool is established, a large number of diverse keys or scales can be developed to meet either general research needs or the requirements of a specific investigation.

The possibilities of this approach are suggested by the fact that when the MMPI was first published, only about 300 of the 550 items in the test were used for scoring the original nine scales. However, the entire 550-item test was routinely given to all those tested. Subsequently, various investigators have drawn on almost the entire pool of items to develop a total of about 100 additional scales!

Among the better designed (in the sense of being based on item-analysis comparisons of criterion groups) of these new scales are measures of introversion, socioeconomic status, anti-Semitism, dominance, and intellectual efficiency. An investigator who has retained the answer sheets for his subjects can rescore them for any of the new scales which pertain to his research. Moreover, the fact that the MMPI is a multivariate test makes possible a configural, profile, or pattern analysis (Cronbach & Gleser, 1953; Gaier & Lee, 1953; Nunnally, 1962), thus making available a powerful mode of analysis.

Applications for family research. To follow the example of the MMPI in the development of family behavior measures requires in the first instance creation of a large and diverse item pool. The only requirement for inclusion in the pool would be that the item refer to some aspect of family interaction. After creation of the pool, scales can be developed by use of criterion groups. For example, if a scale to measure schizophrenia-prone family behavior is desired, the parents of a sample of children hospitalized for schizophrenia can be given the test and their responses to each item compared with a sample of parents of children hospitalized for appendicitis. Items which significantly differentiate the two groups would constitute the "schizophrenia-proneness" scale. Similarly, such a multiphasic family inventory could be given to a large cross-section sample together with a variety of other materials. On the basis of these other materials (such as the ratings by the subject himself, by the other members of his family, and by his kin), it might be possible to identify a husband-dominant subsample. Items which differentiate this subsample from the rest of the population would then constitute a "husband-dominant" scale. Over a period of years, it is conceivable that a wide variety of scales could be developed for such an inventory. The same procedures can, of course, be applied to word-association responses and to a family adjective check list.

It is also possible to develop disguised-voluntary instruments starting with an a priori or construct-based selection of items. A widely known example of this type of instrument is the *F* scale. Scores on this scale are highly correlated with measures of racial prejudice, even though none of the items mentions race. Instead, the items were selected because, in the investigator's judgment, they reflected various aspects of the authoritarian personality. Despite the success of the *F* scale, a strictly empirical rather than a rational approach seems to be preferable in the development of disguised-voluntary questionnaire inventories. In fact, Berg (1959), in a paper on "The Unimportance of Test Item Content," makes a strong theoretical case for a completely empirical approach which starts with a pool of apparently irrelevant items.

In part to demonstrate this point, Berg developed a Perceptual Reaction Test (Berg, Hunt, & Barnes, 1949). It consists merely of 60 abstract designs drawn with ruler and compass. For each design, the subject checks either Like much, Like slightly, Dislike slightly, or Dislike much. In a series of empirical comparisons, Berg and his coworkers have shown that this simple test can measure certain aspects of personality in the same way as personality inventories using traditional verbal content.

Disguised-Performance Measures

Measurement techniques of the disguised-performance type differ from those of the disguised-voluntary type in the nature of the task and the explanation of the task to the subject. In contrast to the disguised-voluntary instrument, the disguised-performance situation presented to the subject is not even ostensibly self-description. Instead, the subject is asked to carry out some objective task or to describe some aspect of the external world. His instructions are not to describe himself, but to produce some objectively correct performance.

Campbell (1950) has given the following formula for the construction of this type of instrument:

A plausible task, (a) which your respondents will all strive to do well, (b) which is sufficiently difficult or ambiguous to allow individual differences in response, (c) which can be loaded with content relative to the attitude you seek to measure. Test the responses of individuals for persistent selectivity in performance, for correlated or nonrandom error (pp. 33–34).

The rationale for this type of instrument derives from the theoretical and experimental evidence for the concepts of balance (Heider, 1946), congruity (Osgood & Tannenbaum, 1955), and dissonance (Festinger, 1957). These concepts have in common the notion that thoughts, beliefs, attitudes, and behavior tend to organize themselves in consistent ways. Thus, there is considerable experimental evidence to show that individuals tend to learn and perceive in ways which are consistent with and nonthreatening to their personality and social networks, including (one may assume) the family.[10]

Free response. The borderline between disguised-performance measures and disguised-voluntary measures is not always clear. Word-association techniques were classified as disguised-voluntary on the assumption that in modern urban societies a large proportion of the population will recognize word association as some kind of personality test. On the other hand, if a situation can be presented as designed to measure some variable external to the subject, it becomes a disguised-performance measure. For example, the stimulus words can be presented with the aid of a tachistoscope, and the situation described to the subject as an experiment designed to measure the readability of various sizes and styles of printer's type. With school children, it may be possible to present the situation as a vocabulary test.

The same basic strategy may be applied to a number of other kinds of stimulus materials. In the tautephone or verbal-summator technique (Grings, 1942), indistinct words or sentences are presented. The task for the subject is to attempt to recognize as many of the words as possible. In the picture-judgment technique (Campbell & Burin, 1956), a series of pictures is presented to the subject as an experiment to determine if it is possible to judge character on the basis of appearance. Production of family-relevant materials may be maximized when using this technique by having the subject try to estimate not only the character of each person pictured but also "what sort of husband or father he is" and "what kind of employee he is." Closely related is the "insight test" developed by French (1958).

[10] It is important, however, to bear in mind Zajonc's caution (1960) that, historically, these concepts resemble "the concept of vacuum in physics—a useful doctrine for organizing knowledge, although full of exceptions and contradictions" (p. 280).

Brief behavior descriptions are presented, and the subject is asked to explain the motives of the persons in the description. The test is presented as a measurement of ability to guess the motivation of people, but is actually used to measure achievement and affiliation motivation of the subject.

All the examples of disguised-performance measures discussed up to this point have involved free-response data. It should be recognized that all of them can be presented in multiple-choice or other structured-response format. However, in doing so care must be exercised that the manifest content of the alternatives presented does not rob the technique of the disguise feature. There are also a group of disguised-performance measures which are inherently structured rather than free-response in format. Examples of such techniques are described below.

Error-choice. One of the most intriguing of the disguised-performance techniques is the "error-choice" test developed by Hammond (1948). It is described to the respondents as a test of information. The respondents, however, are required to choose between two alternatives which are equally wrong, but in opposite directions from the correct answer.

For example, the following two items are taken from Hammond's error-choice test to determine attitudes toward labor. "Average weekly wage of the war worker in 1945 was (1) $37, (2) $57." "Financial reports show that out of every dollar (1) 16 cents, (2) 3 cents is profit." By the use of 20 such items, Hammond was able to differentiate between a labor group and two business clubs with almost no overlap.

The error-choice technique was further validated in a study by Kubany (1953) of attitudes toward national health insurance, and by Weschler (1950) in a study of the labor attitudes of several populations, including a group of labor mediators. In Weschler's study, the presumably unbiased mediator's scores were, as predicted, near the mean for the total sample. In addition, it was found that mediators who were rated high in ability by their colleagues obtained scores closest to the sample mean. Those who were rated poor by their colleagues scored in either the "pro-management" or "pro-labor" zones of the attitude range.

Bernberg (1951; 1961) has pointed out that error-choice questions need not have any factual basis. He has argued that it is better if they do not, since a respondent who knows the correct answer cannot become suspicious. Moreover, if there are no factual data, answers must necessarily be based entirely on existent attitudes. Bernberg used such a test in a study of employees in a large aircraft factory. He obtained 88 per cent returns and general acceptance of the test by the respondents.[11]

The possible applications of the error-choice technique to family sociological studies are numerous, especially when, as Bernberg has demonstrated, it is not necessary to restrict the choice of items to those for which factual data are available.

Family relations is a topic where known or perceived social values are very likely to influence the response to direct questioning. By the same token, family relationships are a relatively private area about which most people have little objective knowledge of other people's behavior. Hence, people are most likely to project onto others their own pattern of family attitudes and behavior. Items such as the following could be included in an instrument presented to the respondent as a "test of knowledge of family relations":

1. Recent surveys have shown that today most husbands
   a. do very little housework
   b. do housework but resent it
   c. do housework and enjoy it to a considerable extent

2. Sexual incompatability is a major cause of marital discord for
   a. less than a tenth of those seeking divorce
   b. about half of those seeking divorce
   c. three-fourths or more of those seeking divorce

The second of these two hypothetical illustrations well illustrates the value of the indirect approach, since it refers to an aspect of family relations to which it may be difficult to apply direct questioning.

Public opinion estimate. Work on change in perception during psychotherapy by Rogers (Rogers & Dymond, 1954) and others has shown that change in self-perceptions and attitudes is associated with change in perceptions of others. The counterpart in normal behavior is the often-observed tendency to perceive another's or a group's opinion as corresponding to one's own. Several tests using this principle are reviewed in Campbell's survey of indirect techniques (1950), and are called public-opinion estimate tests. The Family Opinion Survey (Elias, 1952) applies this technique to an aspect of family behavior. The objective of this test is to measure the respondent's feelings of "homelessness." However, respondents are instructed to answer all 132 items in terms of their estimate of families in general. The test has been found to differentiate between a group of juvenile delinquents and a partially matched group of children from normal families.

Proverbs and humor. Most of the existing measurement techniques which involve humor or proverbs involve expressions of the subject's liking for, or ranking of, the set of jokes, cartoons, or proverbs. They were therefore classified with the disguised-voluntary measures. However, at least one of these, Baumgarten's Proverb Test (1952), is presented in an objective or performance framework. The respondent is asked to choose proverbs which he feels are correct and those which he feels are incorrect, and to tell why he thinks so.

[11] Although Bernberg obtained 88 per cent returns, it is possible that error-choice and other "information" tests may not always be well received. There is some evidence that certain groups become defensive when their knowledge is being tested. See the discussion of the true-false format below.

It seems entirely possible to modify the existing voluntaristic humor and proverbs tests (or to create new ones) to provide the subject with an objective rather than a self-evaluative task. Another possibility is to relate proverbs or humor items to physiological processes. The subject could be shown a series of family-relevant cartoons or jokes on a screen and asked to rate the adequacy of the joke on a seven-point scale, while at the same time his psychogalvanic response, blood pressure, or other physiological reactions are recorded.[12]

Recall distortion. One additional approach to disguised-performance measurement needs to be mentioned. This is the *recall-distortion* technique illustrated by Horowitz's Aussage Test (Horowitz & Horowitz, 1938). Horowitz showed a sample of Southern white children a complex picture for two or three seconds. They were then asked, "What is the colored man doing in the corner?" The older the age group, the larger the proportion of children who perceived this nonexistent Negro as engaged in menial activities.

Many variations are possible for use in family research. For example, sets of four pictures could be shown for two seconds. The four pictures within each set could be chosen to represent different intensities of a variable of interest to the researcher, such as display of affection between family members. After each exposure, the respondents would be asked to describe as many of the pictures as they can. The test could then be scored for: (a) saliency, as indicated by the order in which the pictures are described; (b) the accuracy with which pictures representing each point on a continuum are described; (c) the nature of the distortions and omissions.

Considerable care would have to be taken to structure the situation so that it is perceived as one involving an objective task rather than self-assessment. It might be

possible to present the pictures as part of a study being carried out by a magazine or advertising agency to identify the characteristics of illustrations which will stick in the minds of readers.

Direct-Voluntary Measures

By far the overwhelming proportion of measurements in family sociology are based on voluntaristic self-report data obtained in a situation with little or no disguise of the fact that the purpose of the interview, questionnaire, or observations is to assess some aspect of family behavior. Like the other three types of measures, the direct-voluntary type may either prestructure the permissible responses or permit free responses. Measurements based on free-response data include all forms of open-ended interviews, essays, autobiographies, and most examples of sentence-completion instruments. It should be noted that this is a classification in terms of the mode of eliciting and recording the data to be quantified. Various techniques may be used to quantify such data, the most common being the use of rating scales which permit a coder who has read the protocol to assign a numerical value, Q-sorts (Block, 1961), or the use of "point scales" in which magnitude of the variable is indicated by the frequency with which predefined statements or events are depicted in the protocol.

Among structured direct-voluntary instruments are to be found most of the multitude of tests and questionnaires dealing with the family. Descriptions of a large number of such instruments will be found in the *Family Measurement Abstracts* (Straus, 1962c & forthcoming). These range from such standardized and widely used instruments as the Burgess-Cottrell Marital Adjustment and Prediction Indexes (Burgess & Cottrell, 1939; Burgess & Wallin, 1953) and the Schaefer and Bell (1958) *Parent Attitude Research Instrument*, to ad hoc collections of questionnaire items which the investigator feels will measure a variable

[12] See, in this connection, Martin's review of physiological correlates of anxiety (1961).

and which are seldom tested for reliability or validity and seldom used in another investigation.

In introducing this section, a preference was expressed for measures which are based on objective performance rather than voluntary self-report and also for measures in which the purpose cannot be discerned by the subjects. Despite these preferences, there is still vast scope for development and improvement of direct-voluntary measures. It is by no means certain that well-designed instruments of this type will turn out to be inferior to instruments falling into the other three categories. This question can only be answered by empirical investigations in which the reliability and validity of a direct-voluntary instrument are compared with disguised and/or performance instruments measuring the same variable. In fact, examination of the few such empirical studies available (e.g., Burwen & Campbell, 1957; Westfall, Boyd, & Campbell, 1957) provides little evidence in favor of the theoretical preference for disguised or performance measures.

Assuming the importance of continued development of direct-voluntary measures, what directions need to be taken in the course of such development? Of the many possible recommendations and needed improvements, three are mentioned here: (a) construct-centered rather than evaluative measures; (b) standardization and validation studies; and (c) control of response sets, particularly the social-desirability effect. The first two have been emphasized earlier in this chapter, and the third is discussed in a subsequent section.

Direct-Performance Measures

The prototype of the direct-performance measure is the classroom examination in both its free-response (i.e., essay exam) and its structured-response (i.e., so-called objective-test) forms. Instruments of this type have been rare in family research. There are, however, some significant examples,

and the number of such instances is likely to increase as research uncovers specific knowledge and specific skills associated with varying family patterns. Hill, Stycos, and Back (1959), for example, made use of a direct-performance test to measure the extent to which the subjects of their investigation had knowledge of contraceptive techniques; and Slocum, Brough, and Straus (1958) tested knowledge of modern homemaking practices in a study of factors related to the utilization of the agricultural extension service. Studies in which the effectiveness of parent-education campaigns has been measured by knowledge tests are reported in Brim's review of parent education (1959).

Skill in actually carrying out specific family roles has been assessed by role-playing technique and by investigators in the "interpersonal-competence" tradition (Karlsson, 1958; Stanton, Back, & Litwak, 1956; Stanton & Litwak, 1955). Closely related is the *improvisations* technique (Bronfenbrenner & Newcomb, 1948) being used in a longitudinal study of newly married couples by Goodrich and co-workers at the National Institute of Mental Health. Their procedure is to create an interpersonal or a role conflict in a scene which the husband and wife must act out. For example, in the first improvisation of the series currently being used in the NIMH study, both husband and wife are told that the setting is their first anniversary. However, the husband is separately instructed to make believe that he has arranged everything for a dinner out at a fancy restaurant of sentimental value to the couple. He has ordered the best table in the house, a meal he knows his wife relishes, and has even paid for the meal in advance so that there will be no fumbling with money to mar the occasion. In the meantime, the wife is instructed to make believe that she has just prepared an elaborate meal containing the things which she knows her husband most enjoys. Everything is prepared, and it only remains for her to put the meal on the table when the husband arrives home. The scene begins with the husband knocking on the door and greeting his wife.

It is fairly common in social psychological experimentation to make use of a confederate to provide a standardized element needed in the course of the experiment. There is one experiment in which a child was employed as a confederate (Sears, Alpert, & Rau, 1963). This suggests the possibility of making use of a child actor in a direct-performance measure of skill in carrying out certain elements of the parent role.

CONTROL OF SOCIAL-DESIRABILITY EFFECT IN DIRECT-VOLUNTARY MEASURES

Although disguise and/or performance may in the long run offer the best possibilities for control of the social-desirability effect, techniques which can achieve varying degrees of control of this interfering variable are available for direct-voluntary measures.

Item Style

It is likely that some degree of control of variation due to social-desirability response set can be achieved by reducing the normative saliency and threatening elements in the test format and item style. Attempts can be made to phrase questions or to structure the interview so that respondents do not feel personally threatened by the need to express socially disapproved opinions. Steps which will achieve this end are difficult to specify, since the technique needed depends on the nature of the variable being measured and the situation in which it is measured. But a few examples illustrate the point.

The homemaking-practices test used by Slocum, Brough, and Straus (1958) is parallel to an ordinary classroom examination. However, agree-disagree response categories were presented to the subjects rather than true-false as would be customary in an examination, because pretesting revealed greater acceptance of the interview in this form. Apparently, the true-false format threatened the respondent by emphasizing that her knowledge was being tested. In contrast to the testing connotation of the true-false form, the agree-disagree format may have been perceived as a subtle kind of compliment, and may have carried the connotation that the respondent's views are valuable and that she is on an equal plane with the people who designed the questionnaire.

Maller (1932) used the third person for the items in his personality inventory. In responding, the subject indicates whether he is the same or different from the person described in the item. Maller has presented some evidence to show that this format arouses less annoyance than does the more usual first person or passive voice. It seems possible (although there is no evidence) that this type of wording arouses less defensiveness on the part of the respondent and, therefore, less tendency to respond in terms of the social desirability of the item.

Another approach which attempts to reduce the tendency to respond in terms of the social norms rather than in terms of one's own behavior might be called the "we all do it approach." A series of questions designed to secure data on husband-wife quarrels might start out: "Most couples disagree sometimes about important things. What are some of the things on which you and your husband sometimes disagree?"

It should be emphasized that the case for this and the other approaches mentioned is largely intuitive. There are countless examples of such intuitive judgments being proved wrong when subjected to empirical test, and the "we all do it" approach may be a case in point.

Buss (1959) investigated the frequency of endorsement and the social-desirability rating of the same set of items phrased in seven different styles, one of which was a format which began "Like most people...." Contrary to expectations, this item style only slightly (and not significantly) decreased the social-desirability rating assigned by his sample of university students. The item format which had the greatest effect is one which expresses guilt over the action and begins "I am concerned about . . ." or "I am guilty about. . . ." In considering Buss's findings, it should be noted that his data are confined to the social-desirability ratings and frequency of endorsement of items, and do not include any data on the comparative validity of the different styles. This question is particularly important when it is realized that the "guilt" style ("I am concerned about sometimes getting into fights") may tap a different class of phenomena than the "like most people" style or the unelaborated style.

Forced-Choice Technique

A more direct method of controlling the tendency to respond to self-report items in terms of their social desirability rather than in terms of the traits which the item is intended to measure is known as the "forced-choice" technique (Edwards, 1957a; Rundquist, 1950).

Attitude and personality tests employing this technique have proved resistant to such distortions (Gordon & Stapleton, 1956; Highland & Berkshire, 1951; Rusmore, 1956). Despite the unfortunate name, the forced-choice format seems to arouse no greater, and sometimes less, respondent resistance than the same questions in the usual personality or attitude inventory, and it may provide a more valid measurement (Gordon, 1951; Highland & Berkshire, 1951; Perry, 1955).

Instead of asking the respondent to agree or disagree (or indicate the intensity of his agreement or disagreement) with a series of separate questions, forced-choice technique presents sets of items (usually pairs or tetrads). From these, the respondent must choose in the case of pairs, only the one which is most like himself. In the case of tetrads, he chooses the item which is most like himself and the item which is least like himself.

Forced-choice is in some ways a variant of the well-known paired-comparisons technique. But there is one important difference: each description in a forced-choice pair has previously been assigned a "social-desirability" score. Only items with approximately equal desirability scores are included in a pair. However, although equally acceptable in terms of the social norms for the group on which the test will be used, the items are also chosen so that each represents a different substantive variable. The following pairs are taken from the Maryland Parent Attitude Survey (Pumroy, 1959).

46. A. Parents should clean up after their children.
    B. Children need their natural meaness taken out of them.
91. A. Children should be taught to follow the rules of the game.
    B. Parents should do things for their children.

This test is designed to measure the extent to which parent roles are oriented toward (a) discipline, (b) indulgence, (c) protectiveness, (d) rejection. Each pair is made up of items which are equal in social desirability (empirically determined as part of the test-construction process), but each item represents a different variable. The first pair illustrates matching of negatively valued items. If the subject selects the first item in pair 46 as being most similar to his point of view, he gets $+1$ on the *indulgence* scale. If he chooses the second item he gets $+1$ on the *discipline* scale. The second pair illustrates matching of positively valued items. Similar pairs are made up for all possible combinations of items representing the four variables.

Since each item in the pair is equally flattering or derogatory, the theory of the forced-choice instrument is that the subject will select the item which in fact best describes himself. Forced-choice technique thus deals with the basic problem of social-desirability response set which gave rise to disguised techniques.

Forced-choice technique also deals with another type of response set—the tendency of some subjects to answer all questions "yes"—known as acquiescence response set (Bass, 1956; Chapman & Campbell, 1959; Jackson & Messick, 1958). Acquiescence response set is, of course, ruled out by the format of the forced-choice instrument. Closely related is the theoretical advantage that forced-choice measurement places each item in a specific choice context rather than leaving the context to the varying definitions of the subjects.

Like many of the techniques described in this chapter, almost the only limit upon variables which forced-choice technique can be used to measure is the investigator's responses and ingenuity. In addition to measuring individual personality traits (the use for which forced-choice was originally designed), the technique has been used to measure values (Straus, 1959), family role structure (Straus, 1963c), and, as just noted, by Pumroy (1959) to measure parent role prescriptions.

Ipsatized Scores

If the matching of items comprising the pairs, triads, or tetrads of a forced-choice instrument has been successful, the scores resulting from its administration essentially provide data on the rank order with which the variables measured characterize the subject. This type of measurement has been called an ipsative score by Cattell (1944). It is not necessary to employ the forced-choice format in order to obtain ipsative scores. It can be achieved by arithmetical operations, as indicated by Horst and Wright (1959):

essentially a forced-choice set of scores for an individual may be regarded as a set of normative scores expressed as deviations from the person's own mean . . . . One might, therefore,

construct sets of items for each postulated dimension and present them in conventional format, scoring them so that a person's score on a dimension is derived from his responses to the individual items for that dimension. The scores for each dimension for a group of subjects could then be appropriately scaled such as by conversion to standard scores. For each person, then, the standardized measures could be expressed as deviations from his own mean of standard scores. Such scores might then again be standardized over persons (p. 389).[13]

The advantages of arithmetically ipsatized scores are: (a) their use avoids the laborious task of empirically establishing the social-desirability value of items and matching these items in the forced-choice sets; (b) they can be used with any existing multivariant instrument; (c) in the forced-choice technique, the control for social desirability is dependent on the similarity of the standardizing populations to the population utilized in the research. In addition, the conditions of administration must insure a similar motivational pattern or set on the part of the research population. It is one thing to control for social desirability in a population completing the instrument as part of an experiment in which they have little or no interest and involvement, and another thing to assume that similar motivation and response sets will occur when the instrument is administered as part, for example, of an employment selection procedure.

However, arithmetically ipsatized scores do not yield the same results as the experimentally ipsatized forced-choice method (Wright, 1961). Moreover, among the disadvantages of arithmetically ipsatized scores may be listed: (a) the time cost of computing the scores for each subject; (b) the fact that the procedures are questionable unless there are sufficient subtests or scores to allow enough range for the T-score con-

[13] A simple but less adequate mode of arithmetical ipsatization was used by Chance (1955), who merely rank-ordered each person's set of scores.

version to have meaning; (c) finally, it should be remembered that ipsatized scores (whether of the forced-choice or arithmetical variety) provide only a measure of intrafamily ranking or variation in the variables measured. If such intrafamily scores can in fact be freed from the factor of social desirability, this alone is sufficient justification for the use of ipsatized scores; provided, of course, the researcher is aware of what is and what is not being measured.

Social Desirability (SD) Indexes

To carry out his investigations of the social-desirability effect, Edwards (1957a) constructed indexes designed to measure the SD effect in as pure a form as possible. One such index was constructed by administering the MMPI with instructions to rate each item along a continuum expressing the extent to which it is desirable or undesirable to be characterized by that item. That is, the subjects were not asked to rate the extent to which they were in fact characterized by the item, but rather how much they would like or not like to be characterized by the item. Using these scores, Edwards was then able to select a group of items which had in common only the fact that they were rated high in social desirability. The social-desirability index (SDI) score consists of the number of such items which a subject taking the MMPI under normal conditions marks as characteristic of himself.

Use of correction scales. In the case of the instruments with which Edwards was working (particularly the MMPI), the correlation between this SDI and the substantive scores was so high that he felt it necessary to abandon the original instruments and construct new forced-choice ones, such as his *Personal Preference Schedule* (Edwards, 1954). However, it is also possible to retain the original instrument and correct arithmetically for the social-desirability loading. To a limited extent, this has been done with the MMPI. The MMPI K scale

is similar to and correlated with Edwards' SD scale. On the theory that a subject's score on any of the substantive scales will be artificially depressed if he has a strong set to respond in a socially desirable manner, a value representing score on the K scale is added to certain of the substantive scale scores in order to counteract this factor (Hathaway & McKinley, 1951).

Partial correlations. Another method for controlling the social-desirability effect with a SD index is the use of partial correlation and analysis of covariance. This procedure has the advantage that it can be used with almost any instrument without prior methodological research. All that is required in addition to the substantive instruments is for the subjects to answer a series of questions constituting a SD index.

Assume that a measure of spousal affection is desired, and that this variable is inherently high in social desirability in the society or subsection of the society under study. Granted this assumption, it is necessary to control for the fact that the scores yielded by the instrument represent not only variation in the extent of affection shown between husband and wife, but also variation in the extent to which subjects are inclined to answer such items in terms of the norms of their social group. Control of the latter source of variation is possible if SDI scores are available to provide information on the extent to which each subject responds in terms of item SD.

Suppose the researcher is interested in testing the idea that the greater the degree of spousal affection, the greater the variety of topics of conversation (as measured by a score consisting of the number of different topics discussed by the couple during the last week). Then, suppose the correlation between the affection and the communication score is .50, indicating substantial support for the hypothesis. This may be entirely a reflection of the covariance which both the affection and the communication scores share with the SDI. For example, the correlation of the affection score with the

SDI might be .63 and the correlation of the communication score with the SDI, .55.

If the SD variance is partialed out, is there any residual relationship between affection and range of communication? The usual partial-correlation formula, which can be computed quite simply with the three zero-order correlations just presented, may be used to answer this question. For the hypothetical example given, the correlation between affection and communication, with SD response set held constant, is .22. This could be interpreted as meaning that if subjects all had the same degree of set to respond in social-desirability terms, the correlation between affection and communication would more likely have been .20 than .50. Assuming a sample of about 100, this would indicate a statistically significant, but much less impressive amount of association between the two variables.

Analysis of variance. Partial correlation techniques can be employed only if all three variables have at least ordinal characteristics. But suppose one wishes to test the hypothesis that affectional patterns differ in husband-dominant, wife-dominant, autonomic, and syncratic families? It is not possible to compute a correlation coefficient between affection scores and this set of nominal categories. However, it is possible to compute the mean affection score for each of the four conjugal power types and to test the significance of the difference by analysis of variance. The social-desirability effect may be dealt with by using either a randomized blocks model or an analysis of covariance model. In the former case, the conjugal power types are considered "treatments," and the division of the sample into low and high social-desirability set groups may be thought of as blocks or replications. The advantage of the randomized blocks model is that it permits consideration of interaction effects. However, the interaction effects may be uninterpretable, as in Straus's study of the relationship between conjugal power and adolescent personality (1962b).

Use of analysis of covariance, on the other hand, retains the simplicity of interpretation of the partial correlation approach, since it yields mean scores adjusted for variation in social-desirability response set. One can, therefore, interpret the results as approximating what would be the case if the subjects did not differ in social-desirability set.

Ad hoc SD scales. Among the disadvantages which should be noted in connection with using a separate SD index are, first, the fact that this procedure requires the administration of an additional instrument. Since interview or questionnaire time is usually limited, researchers will be reluctant to devote this precious time to an SDI. A second disadvantage is that these procedures cannot be applied if the data for the study have already been gathered and if reinterview or retesting is not practical. For both these reasons, an alternative procedure may be worth while in some studies. This alternative is to have the SD of the substantive items rated by a population similar to the one studied. A large group of raters is not necessary, since Edwards has found that the SD ratings are highly reliable, and almost identical results are achieved with as few as 15 raters and with a much larger sample.

Items with high SD scores, but representing as many different kinds of behavior as possible, may then be selected to constitute the SD index for the study. The resulting index consists of items which are heterogeneous in content and homogeneous only in social-desirability value. Each subject is given a score representing the extent to which he endorses these items. The resulting scores can then be employed in a partial correlation or analysis of variance or covariance to control for social desirability effects.

TRENDS AND FUTURE OF FAMILY MEASUREMENT

A tabulation of the number of instruments measuring family properties pub-

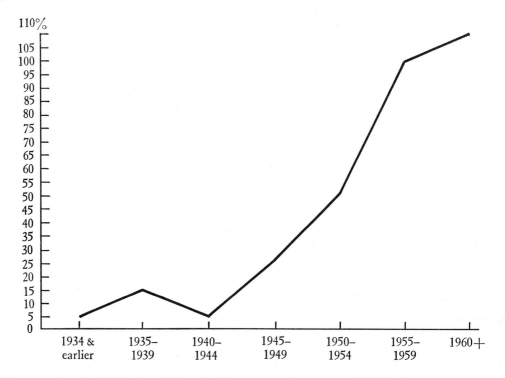

Fig. 11.   Trends in Number of Family Measurement Instruments Published.

lished during each five-year period since 1934 is graphed in Fig. 11.

It is clear that there has been a continuous and, indeed, an accelerating growth in the number of instruments developed to express properties of the family quantitatively. The minor exception is the period 1940–1944, which reflects the general curtailment of scholarly activity due to World War II. The last section of the graph is a dotted line because it represents an estimate based on the years 1960–1962, rather than the full five-year period.

This is an encouraging picture, because it shows that family researchers are increasingly using the quantitative modes of expressing family properties, necessary for the growth of any empirical science. However, this rapid growth in numbers is not paralleled by a growth in the *quality* of these instruments, as was indicated by the figures

presented earlier on trends in reliability, validity, and presentation of normative data, and by the continued preoccupation with evaluative concepts.

Evaluative versus Descriptive Measures

The material in the next few paragraphs concerns a distinction of great importance for family sociology, but at the same time one for which there is no accepted terminology, and which is often difficult to maintain in practice. In the absence of better terms, measures falling on one side of the continuum will be termed "evaluative" and those on the other end "descriptive."

An evaluative measure is one based on some determination (usually a priori assumption) of what constitutes desirable, adjustive, satisfactory, or in some way "good" family behavior, as compared to undesirable, maladapted, unsatisfactory, or in some way "bad" family behavior. The indicators in such an evaluative measure are chosen in terms of the good-bad criteria. By contrast, a descriptive instrument aims to measure a neutral construct. Whether or not the social meaning of low versus high amounts of this construct are good or bad is either irrelevant or left to later empirical research. This distinction between evaluative and descriptive measures largely overlaps the distinction between empirical and rational approaches to index construction discussed earlier, except that for most of the instruments classified as evaluative, the mode of item selection was the investigators' judgment rather than criterion-group differences.

The preoccupation of family research with evaluative moral and ethical rather than with conceptual and theoretical issues is reflected in the findings of the survey of published instruments. Some 40 per cent of the 263 instruments abstracted are classified as evaluative.

Illustrative of evaluative measures, and also of the problems which they introduce into family research, are the instruments designed to measure a so-called developmental approach to child-rearing or to husband-wife relationships. In neutral scientific terms, there seem to be two main components to what has been called a developmental approach. First, this particular style of family interaction is characterized by a symmetrical power distribution among the family members. Second, it is characterized by a high level of personally supportive actions and affectional demonstration. These "developmental versus traditional family" instruments *assume* that this particular combination is an optimum for human development. But is this assumption correct?

Power and support are probably the two most central axes for describing families (Schaefer, 1961; Straus, 1964b; Straus & Cytrynbaum, 1962a). Theoretical considerations, as well as the empirical findings of

socialization research by Bronfenbrenner (1961a; 1961b), Hoffman (1960), and Mussen and Distler (1959), all suggest that quite different and important effects are to be expected from different positions in the two-dimensional property space formed by these two variables. Thus, the concentration on the particular quadrant evaluated as "developmental" has obscured attention to the consequences, both good and bad, of other ways of ordering these two key elements of family structure.

Compounding these problems is the tendency in some of the evaluative instruments to lump together theoretically inconsistent items because they happen to be deemed indicative of good family life by the researcher. One recent example of this is the Kell-Hoeflin Incomplete Sentence Blank (Hoeflin & Kell, 1959). The scoring procedures for this test include with "developmental" all responses indicating warmth, closeness, and understanding, as well as statements reflecting positive affect or satisfying intrafamilial relations. Similarly, they score as "traditional" responses indicating negative affect, coldness, lack of understanding, and unsatisfying intrafamilial interaction. Thus, permissive families with unsatisfactory interpersonal relations are scored as "traditional." With such a scoring scheme, it would be strange indeed if research using this instrument were to reveal any inadequacies for "developmental" as compared to "traditional" family relationships. Furthermore, it is clear that this instrument has no conceptual consistency, except possibly as a measure of positive and negative affect towards one's family of orientation.

The above discussion is not intended to suggest that evaluative measures are inherently poor measures. The *technical adequacy* of evaluative measure may be very high indeed. The Burgess-Cottrell-Wallin marital prediction and adjustment tests are among the best standardized and validated instruments to be found in family sociology. Nor is it meant to imply that even when technically adequate, evaluative measures are worthless. Technically adequate evaluative measures are needed for individual guidance and service programs, and there are some research situations where they can serve a useful purpose. However, for research purposes, whether aimed at immediate application or the general building of scientific knowledge, the number of such situations is limited.

As a general principle of research strategy, a strong skepticism is in order for any research design employing an evaluative instrument. Concentration on measurement of, and research making use of, abstract descriptive variables does not mean that family research will thereby become impractical. Quite the contrary, in some ways practical knowledge is like happiness: it tends to elude those who seek it too directly. The desire for knowledge leading to family amelioration is likely to be more readily achieved through the apparently devious route of focusing on concepts and their nomological network than by concentration on problems and their correlates. It is to be hoped, therefore, that the trend in instrumentation from this point on will be more heavily on the side of descriptive, conceptually oriented variables than has been true up to now.

A glance at Fig. 12 shows that the trend

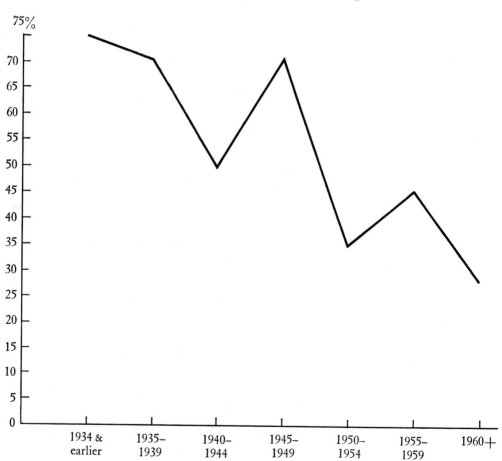

Fig. 12.   Trends in Proportion of "Evaluative" Measures.

is in this direction. During the first two of the five-year periods covered by the survey, over 70 per cent of the measurement instruments were evaluative rather than descriptive. The figure has since fallen to just over a third of the instruments checked.

Concepts in Search of Measures

Several pages could be filled with lists of concepts and properties of the family for which no adequate measures exist. In fact, it does not take a very stringent definition of "adequate" to come to the conclusion that there are few properties of the family which have ever been adequately measured.

If there were even half a dozen sociologists in the United States actively engaged in the development, standardization, and validation of almost any of the properties on this hypothetical list, they would make an immense contribution to the growth of scientific knowledge of the family. Historically, periods of rapid progress in both the physical and the social sciences have occurred under two conditions. The first is the one which usually comes to mind: the creation of a new theory or conceptual scheme which opens whole new areas of investigation. Thus, modern physics made tremendous strides with introduction of such concepts as the quantum theory by Planck and relativity by Einstein.

The second general condition producing a surge of new scientific developments is less widely appreciated. It is the development of new instrumentation and measurement techniques. To use the example of physics again, tremendous advances have been made possible by the development of the electron microscope and atomic accelerators. Large blocks of modern physics would not even have been thought of as possibilities for investigation if the availability of these instruments had not suggested them.

Where to begin? Out of the hundreds of possibilities, which should be selected for intensive analysis and the development of adequate measures? For the researcher whose interests are primarily substantive rather than methodological, the answer is obvious: he must develop measures appropriate to his particular substantive interest. Such a research will forever face a dilemma. Since he is primarily interested in the substantive problem, he is unlikely to be willing to delay the main research the one, two, three, or more years required to develop, standardize, and validate new measures. Instead, he will have to combine the development and validation of the new measures with his research on the substantive problem. If the research results are "positive," this is a satisfactory procedure; both the measure and the theory are validated. But if the results are "negative," it is hard to know if the theory or the measure, or both, are invalid.

Unfortunately, the solution to this dilemma will not be found by waiting for methodologically oriented family researchers to develop adequate instruments. Even assuming a great upsurge in measurement-technique research in the future, the growth in concepts and theory will always outdistance the growth in instrumentation. In one sense, therefore, the hypothetical list of concepts in search of measures is infinite in length. Consequently, for many investigations it will always be necessary to make do with *ad hoc* instruments of unknown validity because they are the only ones appropriate to the issue or theory under investigation; and this will always be preferable to making use of instruments of known validity, but which are tangential or inappropriate to the substantive issues of the investigation.

Even for methodologically oriented researchers, that is for those interested in developing new measures which can be used in a wide range of investigations, there is no simple answer to the question of which specific variable or variables should be the focus of his attention. An approach which seems most likely to advance the theoretical adequacy of family sociology starts from the theoretical orientation in which the researcher has the greatest confidence. Next, the propositions concerning the family which stem from this theory are identified. Finally, the central concepts embodied in these propositions are identified, and a choice of the variables to be measured is made from among them. Presumably, it was by some such process, starting with symbolic interactionist theory, that Buerkle and Badgley (1959; 1961) developed their Yale Marital Interaction Battery.

At the present state of theoretical development in family sociology, there are severe limitations to such an approach. Consequently, many researchers will simply wish to single out a concept or set of concepts which they judge to be major properties of the family needing measurement, irrespective of whether these properties are central to any one theoretical schema. For example, Hemphill's measurement of group dimensions (1956) can be adapted to the family. This consists in part of an instrument designed to measure 13 "group dimensions" such as autonomy, control, and flexibility, most of which are also important dimensions for understanding and differentiating families. Consequently, it would seem desirable to modify Hemphill's instrument so that the items have a specific family referent and so that the resulting scores yield measurements of family group properties.

Measures in Search of Concepts

Since a substantial portion of this chapter has been devoted to outlining types of indicators, types of measures, and modes of index construction applicable to family properties, one can say that the entire chapter has been devoted to outlining techniques which need to be applied to the measurement of family behavior. Consequently, in these concluding remarks it is not necessary to list again these types. Although definite preferences have been expressed (for example, for performance-based measures rather than those which depend on

voluntaristic self-description), all of the techniques outlined have a legitimate place in family research. A tremendous amount of methodological research is called for in attempting to apply these techniques to the central dimensions of the family. The researcher who singles out a particular measurement technique and applies it to a particular property of the family with care and precision will be making a singular contribution to the advancement of family sociology.

But in the long run, there must be a multimethod approach. Only if two or more methods are applied to quantification of the same property will it be possible to carry out really adequate validation studies.

The ideal situation would be if a single investigator were to develop measures for two or more properties using two or more different methods for each of the properties. The intercorrelation of this minimum set of four variables, together with their correlation with one or more criterion variables, will enable questions such as the following to be answered: (a) Is the correlation between the two variables intended to measure the same property higher than the correlation between the two variables intended to measure different properties but using the same method of measurement? If it is not, then there are grounds for suspecting that the major source of variance in the test scores is inherent in the measurement technique rather than the properties supposedly being measured. (b) Is the correlation between the two measures of the same trait sufficiently large to provide evidence of mutual validation? (c) If not, is one correlated with the theoretically relevant outside variable to a greater degree than the other? If it is, it may be possible to decide that the reason for the low correlation between the two measures of the same variable is that one is a valid and the other an invalid measure.

The type of analysis just described has been termed by Campbell and Fiske (1959) "convergent and discriminate validation by the multitrait-multimethod matrix." Behind this formidable terminology lies an elegant simplicity and a high degree of analytical power for dealing with the complex and controversial issues of measurement validation. It need hardly be said, therefore, that consideration of Campbell and Fiske's technique is essential for those seriously concerned with measurement.

As great as the advantages of the multitrait-multimethod analysis may be, it is unrealistic to expect that many investigators will develop two or more methods for measuring each of two or more family properties. The task of developing a single measure for a single property is demanding enough. Fortunately, as in most other scientific endeavors, a number of investigators can and will work on varying parts of the problem. Thus, when and if two or more methods are each used to measure two or more properties of the family, it only remains for another investigator to apply these measures to a single population, compute the multitrait-multimethod matrix, and carry out the type of analysis outlined by Campbell and Fiske.

It is not unrealistic to expect that a number of such analyses will be possible in the next few years. Even now, to measure, for example, the relative power position of family members, there are available the self-report technique developed by Herbst (1954), the projective technique developed by Straus and Cytrynbaum (1962a), direct observation making use of categories such as those developed by Bales (1950) and, of course, self-ratings. Similarly, intrafamily support patterns can be measured by means of the self-report technique now being developed by Straus, by the Straus and Cytrynbaum projective technique, by the Bales categories, and by self-rating.

With the power and support variables each currently capable of being measured by four different techniques, it is to be hoped that it will not be long before a multitrait-multimethod matrix analysis is published to provide information on the important and baffling question of the relative validity of these measures. Even then, the answer will be only partial, since few will wish to depend on only a single analysis. Moreover, the two-variable and four-method matrix just outlined by no means exhausts the applicable methods. It leaves out, for example, all the disguised-performance instruments such as the error-choice technique, and direct-performance measures such as role-playing. Also omitted are self-report measures with control for social-desirability response set, such as the forced-choice technique. Clearly, it will be some time before measures making use of some of these techniques to quantify the support and power structure of the family are available, and even more time until these measures are employed in a multitrait-multimethod matrix. It is to be hoped that the time will not be too long, for adequate instrumentation is prerequisite to major growth in empirical knowledge of these or of any other aspects of the family.

REFERENCES

Abell, Helen C. The use of scale analysis in a study of the differential adoption of home-making practices. *Rural Sociol.*, 1952, 17, 161–165.

Abelson, R. P. A technique and a model for multi-dimensional attitude scaling. *Publ. opin. Quart.*, 1954–1955, 18, 405–418.

Abt, L. E., & Bellak, L. (Eds.) *Projective psychology; clinical approaches to the total personality.* New York: Knopf, 1950.

Ackerman, N. W. *The psychodynamics of family life.* New York: Basic Books, 1958.

Adorno, T. W., Frenkel-Brunswik, Else, Levinson, D. J., & Sanford, R. N. *The authoritarian personality.* New York: Harper, 1950.

American Psychological Association, American Educational Research Association, & National Council on Measurements Used in Education, Joint Committee. *Technical recommendations for psychological tests and diagnostic techniques.* Washington, D.C.: American Psychological Association, 1954.

Anastasi, Anne. *Psychological testing.* (2nd ed.) New York: Macmillan, 1961.

Anderson, H. H., & Anderson, Gladys L. (Eds.) *An introduction to projective techniques.* New York: Prentice-Hall, 1951.

Anderson, N. H. Scales and statistics: parametric and non-parametric. *Psychol. Bull.,* 1961, 58, 305–316.

Auld, F., Jr., Eron, L. D., & Laffal, J. Application of Guttman's scaling method to the TAT. *Educ. psychol. Measmt,* 1955, 15, 422–435.

Baldwin, A. L., Kalhorn, Joan, & Breese, F. H. The appraisal of parent behavior. *Psychol. Monogr.,* 1949, 63, No. 4 (Whole No. 299).

Bales, R. F. *Interaction process analysis: a method for the study of small groups.* Cambridge: Addison-Wesley, 1950.

Barton, A. *Organizational measurement.* Princeton: Educational Testing Service, 1959.

Bass, B. M. Development of a structured disguised personality test. *J. appl. Psychol.,* 1956, 40, 393–397.

Bateson, G., Jackson, D. D., Haley, J., & Weakland, J. H. Toward a theory of schizophrenia. *Behav. Sci.,* 1956, 1, 251–264.

Baumgarten, F. A. proverb test for attitude measurement. *Personnel Psychol.,* 1952, 5, 249–261.

Bechtoldt, H. P. Construct validity: a critique. *Amer. Psychologist,* 1959, 14, 619–629.

Bell, J. E. *Projective techniques: a dynamic approach to the study of the personality.* New York: Longmans, Green, 1948.

Berg, I. A. The unimportance of test item content. In B. M. Bass & I. A. Berg (Eds.), *Objective approaches to personality assessment.* Princeton: Van Nostrand, 1959. Pp. 83–99.

Berg, I. A., Hunt, W. A., & Barnes, E. H. *The perceptual reaction test.* Evanston, Ill.: Author, 1949.

Bernberg, R. E. The direction of perception technique of attitude measurement. *Int. J. opin. & attitude Res.,* 1951, 5, 397–406.

Bernberg, R. E. The measurement of two personality traits within a socio-cultural framework. *Educ. psychol. Measmt,* 1961, 21, 349–395.

Block, J. *The Q-sort method in personality assessment and psychiatric research.* Springfield, Ill.: Thomas, 1961.

Blood, R. O., Jr. A situational approach to the study of permissiveness in child-rearing. *Amer. sociol. Rev.,* 1953, 18, 84–87.

Boneau, C. A. The effects of violations of assumptions underlying the *t* test. *Psychol. Bull.,* 1960, 57, 49–64.

Boneau, C. A. A comparison of the power of the *U* and *t* tests. *Psychol. Rev.,* 1962, 69, 246–256.

Borgatta, E. F. Analysis of social interaction: actual, role playing, and projective. *J. abnorm. soc. Psychol.,* 1955, 51, 394–405.

Borgatta, E. F. Cumulative scaling as a routine procedure. *Sociometry,* 1957, 20, 317–325.

Bowerman, C. E. Adjustment in marriage: over-all and in specific areas. *Sociol. soc. Res.,* 1957, 41, 257–263.

Brim, O. G., Jr. Parent-child relations as a social system: I. parent and child roles. *Child Develpm.,* 1957, 28, 342–364.

Brim, O. G., Jr. *Education for child rearing.* New York: Russell Sage Foundation, 1959.

Brim, O. G., Jr., Glass, D. C., & Lavin, D. E. *Personality and decision process; studies of the social psychology of thinking.* Stanford, Cal.: Stanford Univer. Press, 1962.

Broderick, C. B., & Fowler, S. E. New patterns of relationships between the sexes among preadolescents. *Marr. & fam. Living,* 1961, 23, 27–30.

Bronfenbrenner, U. Some familial antecedents of responsibility and leadership in adolescence. In L. Petrullo & B. M. Bass (Eds.), *Leadership and interpersonal behavior.* New York: Holt, Rinehart & Winston, 1961. (a)

Bronfenbrenner, U. Toward a theoretical model for the analysis of parent-child relationships in a social context. In J. C. Glidewell (Ed.), *Parental attitudes and child behavior.* Springfield, Ill.: Thomas, 1961. Pp. 90–109. (b)

Bronfenbrenner, U., & Newcomb, T. M. Improvisations—an application of psychodrama in personality diagnosis. *Sociatry,* 1948, 4, 367–382.

Brower, D., & Weider, A. Projective techniques in business and industry. In L. E. Abt & L. Bellak (Eds.), *Projective Psychology.* New York: Knopf, 1950. Pp. 437–461.

Buerkle, J. V., Anderson, T. R., & Badgley, R. F. Altruism, role conflict, and marital adjustment: a factor analysis of marital interaction. *Marr. & fam. Living,* 1961, 23, 20–26.

Buerkle, J. V., & Badgley, R. F. Couple role taking: the Yale marital interaction battery. *Marr. & fam. Living,* 1959, 21, 53–58.

Burgess, E. W., & Cottrell, L. S., Jr. *Predicting success or failure in marriage.* New York: Prentice-Hall, 1939.

Burgess, E. W., & Wallin, P. *Engagement and marriage.* Philadelphia: Lippincott, 1953.

Burwen, L. S., & Campbell, D. T. The generality of attitudes toward authority and nonauthority figures. *J. abnorm. soc. Psychol.,* 1957, 54, 24–31.

Buss, A. H. The effect of item style on social desirability and frequency of endorsement. *J. consult. Psychol.,* 1959, 23, 510–513.

Calogeras, R. C. Some relationships between fantasy and self report behavior. *Genet. psychol. Monogr.,* 1958, 58, 273–325.

Campbell, D. T. The indirect assessment of social attitudes. *Psychol. Bull.,* 1950, 47, 15–38.

Campbell, D. T. A typology of tests, projective and otherwise. *J. consult. Psychol.,* 1957, 21, 207–210. (a)

Campbell, D. T. Factors relevant to the validity of experiments in social settings. *Psychol. Bull.,* 1957, 54, 297–312. (b)

Campbell, D. T. Recommendations for NAPA test standards regarding construct, trait, or discriminant validity. *Amer. Psychologist,* 1960, 15, 546–553.

Campbell, D. T., & Burin, L. S. Trait judgements from photographs as a projective device. *J. clin. Psychol.,* 1956, 12, 215–221.

Campbell, D. T., & Fiske, D. W. Convergent and discriminant validation by the multitrait-multimethod matrix. *Psychol. Bull.,* 1959, 56, 81–105.

Cattell, R. B. Psychological measurement: ipsative, normative, and interactive. *Psychol. Rev.,* 1944, 51, 292–303.

Cattell, R. B., & Luborsky, L. B. *The IPAT humor test of personality.* Champaign, Ill.: Institute for Personality and Ability Testing, 1952.

Caws, P. Definition and measurement in physics. In C. W. Churchman & P. Ratoosh (Eds.), *Measurement: definitions and theories.* New York: Wiley, 1959. Pp. 3–17.

Chance, Erika. Measuring the potential interplay of forces within the family during treatment. *Child Develpm.,* 1955, 26, 241–265.

Chapman, L. J., & Campbell, D. T. The effect of acquiescence response-set upon relationships among the F scale, ethnocentrism, and intelligence. *Sociometry,* 1959, 22, 153–161.

Churchman, C. W., & Ratoosh, P. (Eds.), *Measurement: definitions and theories.* New York: Wiley, 1959.

Cobliner, W. G. On the place of projective tests in opinion and attitude surveys. *Int. J. opin. & attitude Res.,* 1951, 5, 480–490.

Cohen, M. R., & Nagel, E. Measurement. In E. H. Madden (Ed.), *The structure of scientific thought.* Boston: Houghton Mifflin, 1960.

Coleman, J. S. Multidimensional scale analysis. *Amer. J. Sociol.,* 1957, 63, 253–263.

Cronbach, L. J. Further evidence on response sets and test design. *Educ. psychol. Measmt,* 1950, 10, 3–31.

Cronbach, L. J. *Essentials of psychological testing.* (2nd ed.) New York: Harper, 1960.

Cronbach, L. J., & Gleser, G. C. Assessing similarity between profiles. *Psychol. Bull.,* 1953, 50, 456–473.

Davidoff, M. D., & Maslow, A. P. Application of Guttman's scale analysis to objective test analysis and construction. *Amer. Psychologist,* 1950, 5, 356.

Davids, A., & Pildner, H., Jr. Comparison of direct and projective methods of personality assessment under different conditions of motivation. *Psychol. Monogr.,* 1958, 72, No. 11 (Whole No. 464).

Edwards, A. L. *Edwards personal preference schedule.* New York: Psychological Corporation, 1954.

Edwards, A. L. Social desirability and Q sorts. *J. consult. Psychol.,* 1955, 19, 462.

Edwards, A. L. *The social desirability variable in personality assessment and research.* New York: Dryden, 1957. (a)

Edwards, A. L. *Techniques of attitude scale construction.* New York: Appleton-Century-Crofts, 1957. (b)

Edwards, A. L., & Kilpatrick, F. P. Scale analysis and the measurement of social attitudes. *Psychometrika,* 1948, 13, 99–114.

Elias, G. A measure of "homelessness." *J. abnorm. soc. Psychol.,* 1952, 47, 62–66.

Empey, L. T. An instrument for the measurement of family authority patterns. *Rural Sociol.,* 1957, 22, 73–77.

Farber, B. An index of marital integration. *Sociometry,* 1957, 20, 117–133.

Festinger, L. *A theory of cognitive dissonance.* Evanston, Ill.: Row, Peterson, 1957.

French, Elizabeth G. Development of a measure of complex motivation. In J. W. Atkinson (Ed.), *Motives in fantasy, action and society*. Princeton: Van Nostrand, 1958. Pp. 242–248.

Friedman, I. Objectifying the subjective—a methodological approach to the TAT. *J. proj. Tech.*, 1957, 21, 243–245.

Fromme, A. On the use of qualitative methods of attitude research. *J. soc. Psychol.*, 1941, 13, 429–460.

Gaier, E. L., & Lee, Marilyn C. Pattern analysis: the configural approach to predictive measurement. *Psychol. Bull.*, 1953, 50, 140–148.

Getzels, J. W. The assessment of personality and prejudice by the method of paired direct and projective questions. Unpublished doctoral dissertation, Harvard Univer., 1951.

Goodrich, D. W., & Boomer, D. L. Experimental assessment of modes of conflict resolution. *Fam. Process*, 1963, 2, 15–24.

Gordon, L. V. Validities of the forced choice and questionnaire methods of personality measurement. *J. appl. Psychol.*, 1951, 35, 407–412.

Gordon, L. V., & Stapleton, E. S. Fakeability of a forced choice personality test under realistic high school employment conditions. *J. appl. Psychol.*, 1956, 40, 258–262.

Gough, H. G. A new dimension of status: I. development of a personality scale. *Amer. sociol. Rev.*, 1948, 13, 401–409.

Gough, H. G. A nonintellectual intelligence test. *J. consult. Psychol.*, 1953, 17, 242–246.

Graham, M. D. The effectiveness of photographs as a projective device in international attitude surveys. *J. soc. Psychol.*, 1954, 40, 93–120.

Green, B. F. Attitude measurement. In G. Lindzey (Ed.), *Handbook of social psychology*. Cambridge: Addison-Wesley, 1954. Pp. 335–369.

Green, B. F. A method of scalogram analysis using summary statistics. *Psychometrika*, 1956, 21, 79–88.

Grings, W. W. The verbal summator technique and abnormal mental states. *J. abnorm. soc. Psychol.*, 1942, 37, 529–545.

Guilford, J. P. *Psychometric methods*. (2nd ed.) New York: McGraw-Hill, 1954.

Gullahorn, J. T. Measuring role conflict. *Amer. J. Sociol.*, 1956, 61, 299–303.

Gulliksen, H. *Theory of mental tests*. New York: Wiley, 1950.

Guttman, L. A. A basis for scaling qualitative data. *Amer. sociol. Rev.*, 1944, 9, 139–150.

Guttman, L. A. The problem of attitude and opinion measurement. In S. A. Stouffer, et al., *Measurement and prediction*. Princeton: Princeton Univer. Press, 1950. Pp. 46–49.

Guttman, L. A. The principal components of scalable attitudes. In P. F. Lazarsfeld (Ed.), *Mathematical thinking in the social sciences*. Glencoe, Ill.: Free Press, 1954. Pp. 216–257.

Haley, J. An interactional description of schizophrenia. *Psychiatry*, 1959, 22, 321–332.

Haley, J. Family experiments: a new type of experimentation. *Fam. Process*, 1962, 1, 265–293.

Hamblin, R. L. Group integration during a crisis. *Hum. Relat.*, 1958, 1, 67–76.

Hammond, K. R. Measuring attitudes by error-choice. *J. abnorm. soc. Psychol.*, 1948, 43, 38–48.

Hathaway, S. R., & McKinley, J. C. *Minnesota multiphasic personality inventory: manual*. (Rev. ed.) New York: Psychological Corporation, 1951.

Heider, F. Attitudes and cognitive organization. *J. Psychol.*, 1946, 21, 107–112.

Helmstadter, G. C. An empirical comparison of methods for estimating profile similarity. *Educ. psychol. Measmt*, 1957, 17, 71–82.

Hemphill, J. K. Group dimensions: a manual for their measurement. *Ohio Stud. Personnel*, Res. Monogr. No. 87. Columbus: Ohio State Univer., Bureau of Business Research, 1956.

Herbst, P. G. Family relationships questionnaire. In O. A. Oeser & S. B. Hammond (Eds.), *Social structure and personality in a city*. London: Routledge & Paul, 1954. Pp. 316–321.

Hess, R. D., & Handel, G. *Family worlds*. Chicago: Univer. of Chicago Press, 1959.

Highland, R. W., & Berkshire, J. R. A methodological study of forced-choice performance ratings. *Hum. Resour. Res. Inst. res. Bull.*, 1951, No. 51–9.

Hill, R., Stycos, J. M., & Back, K. W. *The family and population control: a Puerto Rican experiment in social change*. Chapel Hill: Univer. of North Carolina Press, 1959.

Hoeflin, Ruth, & Kell, Leone. The Kell-Hoeflin incomplete sentence blank: youth-parent relation. *Monogr. soc. Res. child Develpm.*, 1959, 24, No. 3 (Whole No. 72).

Hoffman, Lois W., & Lippitt, R. The measurement of family life variables. In P. H. Mussen (Ed.), *Handbook of research methods in child development.* New York: Wiley, 1960. Pp. 945–1014.

Hoffman, M. L. Power assertion by the parent and its impact on the child. *Child Develpm.,* 1960, 31, 129–143.

Horowitz, E. L., & Horowitz, Ruth E. Development of social attitudes in children. *Sociometry,* 1938, 1, 301–338.

Horst, P., & Wright, C. E. The comparative reliability of two techniques of personality appraisal. *J. clin. Psychol.,* 1959, 15, 388–391.

Hurvitz, N. The marital roles inventory and the measurement of marital adjustment. *J. clin. Psychol.,* 1960, 16, 377–380. (a)

Hurvitz, N. The measurement of marital strain. *Amer. J. Sociol.,* 1960, 65, 610–615. (b)

Jack, Lois M. An experimental study of ascendant behavior in preschool children. *Univer. Iowa Stud. child Welf.,* 1934, 9, No. 3.

Jackson, D. M., & Bidwell, C. E. A modification of Q-technique. *Educ. psychol. Measmt.,* 1959, 19, 221–232.

Jackson, D. N., & Messick, S. Content and style in personality assessment. *Psychol. Bull.,* 1958, 55, 243–252.

Karlsson, G. A reliability test of the Foote observational technique for studying interaction in the family. In N. Anderson (Ed.), *Studies of the family.* Vol. 3. Gottingen: Vandenhoeck & Ruprecht, 1958. Pp. 151–158.

Kelley, E. L. Concerning the validity of Terman's weights for predicting marital happiness. *Psychol. Bull.,* 1939, 36, 202–203.

Kirkpatrick, C. *The family: as process and institution.* (2nd ed.) New York: Ronald Press, 1963.

Kirkpatrick, C., & Hobart, C. Disagreement, disagreement estimate, and non-empathetic imputations for intimacy groups varying from favorite date to married. *Amer. sociol. Rev.,* 1954, 19, 10–19.

Kubany, A. J. A validation study of the error-choice technique using attitudes on national health insurance. *Educ. psychol. Measmt,* 1953, 13, 157–163.

Lazarsfeld, P. F. Problems in methodology. In R. K. Merton, L. Broom, & L. S. Cottrell, Jr. (Eds.), *Sociology today.* New York: Basic Books, 1959. Pp. 39–78.

Lazarsfeld, P. F., & Menzel, H. On the relation betwen individual and collective properties. In A. Etzioni (Ed.), *Complex organizations: a sociological reader.* New York: Holt, Rinehart & Winston, 1961. Pp. 422–440.

Lazarsfeld, P. F., & Rosenberg, M. (Eds.) *The language of social research: a reader in the methodology of the social sciences.* Glencoe, Ill.: Free Press, 1955.

Levin, H., & Wardwell, Elinor. The research uses of doll play. *Psychol. Bull.,* 1962, 59, 27–56.

Levinson, D. J., & Huffman, Phyllis E. Traditional family ideology and its relation to personality. *J. Pers.,* 1955, 23, 251–273.

Likert, R. A technique for the measurement of attitudes. *Arch. Psychol., N.Y.,* 1932, 22, No. 140.

Lindquist, E. F. *Design and analysis of experiments in psychology and education.* Boston: Houghton Mifflin, 1953.

Lindzey, G. Thematic apperception test: Interpretive assumptions and related empirical evidence. *Psychol. Bull.,* 1952, 49, 1–25.

Liverant, S. Intelligence: a concept in need of reexamination. In N. F. Washburne (Ed.), *Decisions, values and groups.* Vol. 2. New York: Pergamon Press, 1962. Pp. 66–85.

Locke, H. J., & Williamson, R. C. Marital adjustment: a factor analysis study. *Amer. sociol. Rev.,* 1958, 23, 562–569.

Maccoby, Eleanor E., & Maccoby, N. The interview: a tool of social science. In G. Lindzey (Ed.), *Handbook of social psychology.* Cambridge: Addison-Wesley, 1954. Pp. 449–487.

McDill, E. L. A comparison of three measures of attitude intensity. *Soc. Forces,* 1959, 38, 95–99.

McGee, R. K. Response style as a personality variable: by what criterion? *Psychol. Bull.,* 1962, 59, 284–295.

Maller, J. B. *Character sketches.* New York: Columbia Univer., Teachers Coll., Bureau of Publications, 1932.

Margenau, H. Philosophical problems concerning the meaning of measurement in physics. In C. W. Churchman & P. Ratoosh (Eds.), *Measurement: definitions and theories.* New York: Wiley, 1959. Pp. 163–176.

Martin, B. The assessment of anxiety by physiological behavioral measures. *Psychol. Bull.,* 1961, 58, 234–255.

Meadow, L. A study of dyadic relationships in the French family. *J. proj. Tech.*, 1956, 20, 196–206.

Meehl, P. E. The dynamics of structured personality tests. *J. clin. Psychol.*, 1945, 1, 296–303.

Merton, R. K. Notes on problem finding in sociology. In R. K. Merton, L. Broom, & L. S. Cottrell, Jr. (Eds.), *Sociology today.* New York: Basic Books, 1959. Pp. ix–xxxiv.

Meyer, M. M., & Tolman, R. S. Correspondence between attitudes and images of parental figures in TAT stories and in therapeutic interviews. *J. consult. Psychol.*, 1955, 19, 79–82. (a)

Meyer, M. M., & Tolman, R. S. Parental figures in sentence completion test, in TAT and in therapeutic interviews. *J. consult. Psychol.*, 1955, 19, 170–172. (b)

Mosel, J. N., & Roberts, June B. The comparability of measures of profile similarity: an empirical study. *J. consult. Psychol.*, 1954, 18, 61–66.

Mussen, P. H., & Distler, L. Masculinity, identification, and father-son relationships. *J. abnorm. soc. Psychol.*, 1959, 59, 350–356.

Mussen, P. H., & Kagan, J. Group conformity and perceptions of parents. *Child Develpm.*, 1958, 29, 57–66.

Nunnally, J. The analysis of profile data. *Psychol. Bull.*, 1962, 59, 311–319.

Nye, F. I. *Family relations and delinquent behavior.* New York: Wiley, 1958.

Nye, F. I., & Short, J. F., Jr. Scaling delinquent behavior. *Amer. sociol. Rev.*, 1957, 22, 326–331.

Osgood, C. E., & Suci, G. J. A measure of relation determined by both mean difference and profile information. *Psychol. Bull.*, 1952, 49, 251–262.

Osgood, C. E., & Tannenbaum, P. H. The principle of congruity in the prediction of attitude change. *Psychol. Rev.*, 1955, 62, 42–55.

Parsons, T., & Bales, R. F., with Olds, J., Zelditch, M., J., & Slater, P. *Family socialization and interaction process.* Glencoe, Ill.: Free Press, 1955.

Payne, S. L. *The art of asking questions.* Princeton: Princeton Univer. Press, 1951.

Perry, D. K. Forced-choice vs. L-I-D response items in vocational interest measurement. *J. appl. Psychol.*, 1955, 39, 256–262.

Peters, R., & Campbell, J. T. *Diagnosis of training needs of B-29 mechanics from supervisory ratings and self-ratings.* Air Force Personnel and Training Research Center, Tech. Memo. No. 55-12, 1955.

Proshansky, H. M. Projective techniques in action research: disguised diagnosis and measurement. In L. E. Abt & L. Bellak (Eds.), *Projective psychology.* New York: Knopf, 1950. Pp. 462–485.

Pumroy, D. K. *Preliminary manual for the Maryland parental attitude survey.* College Park: Univer. of Maryland, 1959. (Mimeographed.)

Riley, Matilda W., Riley, J. W., Jr., Toby, J., et al. *Sociological studies in scale analysis: applications, theory, procedures.* New Brunswick, N.J.: Rutgers Univer. Press, 1954.

Rogers, C. R., & Dymond, Rosalind F. (Eds.), *Psychotherapy and personality change.* Chicago: Univer. of Chicago Press, 1954.

Rose, A. W. Projective techniques in sociological research. *Soc. Forces*, 1949–1950, 28, 175–183.

Rosenzweig, S. The picture-association method and its application in a study of reactions to frustration. *J. Pers.*, 1945, 14, 3–23.

Rundquist, E. A. Personality tests and prediction. In D. H. Fryer & E. J. Henry (Eds.), *Handbook of applied psychology.* New York: Rinehart, 1950. Pp. 182–191.

Rusmore, J. T. Fakeability of the Gordon personal profile. *J. appl. Psychol.*, 1956, 40, 175–177.

Ryan, B. F., & Straus, M. A. The integration of Sinhalese society. *Res. Stud. State Coll. Washington*, 1954, 22, 179–227.

Sakoda, J. M., Cohen, B. H., & Beall, G. Test of significance for a series of statistical tests. *Psychol. Bull.*, 1954, 51, 172–175.

Sandford, F. H. The use of a projective device in attitude surveying. *Publ. opin. Quart.*, 1950–51, 14, 697–709.

Sandford, F. H., & Rosenstock, J. Projective techniques on the doorstep. *J. abnorm. soc. Psychol.*, 1952, 47, 3–16.

Sayles, L. R. Field use of projective methods: a case example. *Sociol. & soc. Res.*, 1954, 38, 168–173.

Schaefer, E. S. Converging conceptual models for maternal behavior and for child behavior. In J. C. Glidewell (Ed.), *Parental attitudes and child behavior.* Springfield, Ill.: Thomas, 1961. Pp. 124–146.

Schaefer, E. S., & Bell, R. Q. Development of a parental attitude research instrument. *Child Develpm.,* 1958, 29, 339–361.

Sears, R. R., Alpert, R., & Rau, Lucy. Identification in preschool children. Unpublished monogr., Stanford Univer., 1963.

Sears, R. R., Maccoby, Eleanor E., & Levin, H. *Patterns of child rearing.* Evanston, Ill.: Row, Peterson, 1957.

Selltiz, C. Data collection: I. observational methods. In C. Selltiz, Marie Jahoda, M. Deutsch, & S. W. Cook, *Research methods in social relations.* (Rev. ed.) New York: Holt, 1959. Pp. 200–234.

Selltiz, C., Jahoda, Marie, Deutsch, M., & Cook, S. W. *Research methods in social relations.* (Rev. ed.) New York: Holt, 1959.

Sewell, W. H. *The construction and standardization of a scale for the measurement of the socio-economic status of Oklahoma farm families.* Tech. Bull. No. 9. Stillwater: Oklahoma Agricultural Experiment Station, 1940.

Singer, J. L. Projected familial attitudes as a function of SES and psychopathology. *J. consult. Psychol.,* 1954, 8, 99–104.

Slocum, W. L., Brough, O. L., Jr., & Straus, M. A. *Extension contracts, selected characteristics, practices, and attitudes of Washington farm families.* Bull. No. 584. Pullman: Washington Agricultural Experiment Station, 1958.

Stanton, H. R., Back, H. W., & Litwak, E. Role-playing in survey research. *Amer. J. Sociol.,* 1956, 62, 172–176.

Stanton, H. R., & Litwak, E. Toward the development of a short form test of interpersonal competence. *Amer. sociol. Rev.,* 1955, 20, 668–674.

Stephenson, W. *The study of behavior: Q-technique and its methodology.* Chicago: Univer. of Chicago Press, 1953.

Stevens, S. S. Measurement, psychophysics, and utility. In C. W. Churchman & P. Ratoosh (Eds.), *Measurement: definitions and theories.* New York: Wiley, 1959. Pp. 18–63.

Stockford, L., & Bissell, H. W. Factors involved in establishing a merit rating scale. *Personnel,* 1949, 26, 94–116.

Stone, Carol L. *A machine method for scaling as many as twelve dichotomies.* Circular No.

329. Pullman: Washington Agricultural Experiment Station, 1958.

Stouffer, S. A., Guttman, L., Suchman, E. A., Lazarsfeld, P. F., Star, S. A., & Clausen, J. A. *Measurement and prediction.* Princeton: Princeton Univer. Press, 1950.

Straus, M. A. Childhood experience and emotional security in the context of Sinhalese social organization. *Soc. Forces,* 1954, 33, 152–160.

Straus, M. A. Anal and oral frustration in relation to Sinhalese personality. *Sociometry,* 1957, 20, 21–31. (a)

Straus, M. A. *Direct, indirect, and disguised measurement in rural sociology.* Tech. Bull. No. 26. Pullman: Washington Agricultural Experiment Station, 1957. (b)

Straus, M. A. *Matching farms and families in the Columbia basin project.* Tech. Bull. No. 588. Pullman: Washington Agricultural Experiment Station, 1958.

Straus, M. A. *A technique for measuring values in rural life.* Tech. Bull. No. 29. Pullman: Washington Agricultural Experiment Station, 1959.

Straus, M. A. Conjugal power structure and adolescent personality. *Marr. & fam. Living,* 1962, 24, 17–25. (a)

Straus, M. A. Deferred gratification, social class, and the achievement syndrome. *Amer. sociol. Rev.,* 1962, 27, 326–335. (b)

Straus, M. A. Family measurement abstracts, preliminary series, part 1. Minneapolis: Minnesota Family Study Center, 1962. (Ditto.) (c)

Straus, M. A. Family measurement series, preliminary statement. Minneapolis: Minnesota Family Study Center, 1963. (Ditto.) (a)

Straus, M. A. The family interaction schedule. Minneapolis: Minnesota Family Study Center, 1963. (Mimeographed.) (b)

Straus, M. A. The family patterns profile. Minneapolis: Minnesota Family Study Center, 1963. (Mimeographed.) (c)

Straus, M. A. Family support and power structure in experimentally induced crisis. Progress report to National Science Foundation on research in progress. Minneapolis, 1964. (Ditto.) (a)

Straus, M. A. Power and support structure of the family in relation to socialization. *J. Marr. & Fam.,* 1964, 26. (b)

Straus, M. A., & Cytrynbaum, S. A scoring

manual for intrafamilial power and affective support. Minneapolis: Minnesota Family Study Center, 1962. (Ditto.) (a)

Straus, M. A., & Cytrynbaum, S. Support and power structure in Sinhalese, Tamil, and Burgher student families. *Int. J. comp. Sociol.*, 1962, 3, 138–153. (b)

Straus, M. A., & Straus, Jacqueline H. Personal insecurity and Sinhalese social structure: Rorschach evidence for primary school children. *East. Anthropologist*, 1957, 10, 97–111.

Strodtbeck, F. L. Husband-wife interaction over revealed differences. *Amer. sociol. Rev.*, 1951, 16, 468–473.

Strodtbeck, F. L. Family interaction, values, and achievement. In D. C. McClelland, A. L. Baldwin, U. Bronfenbrenner, & F. L. Strodtbeck, *Talent and society*. Princeton: Van Nostrand, 1958. Pp. 135–194.

Strother, G. B., Barnett, Margaret M., & Apostolakos, P. C. The use of cartoons as a projective device. *J. clin. Psychol.*, 1954, 10, 38–42.

Suchman, E. A. The intensity component in attitude and opinion research. In S. A. Stouffer et al., *Measurement and prediction*. Princeton: Princeton Univer. Press, 1950. Pp. 213–276.

Taylor, Janet A. A personality scale of manifest anxiety. *J. abnorm. soc. Psychol.*, 1953, 48, 285–290.

Thorndike, R. L. *Personnel selection*. New York: Wiley, 1949.

Thurstone, L. L., & Chave, E. J. *The measurement of attitude*. Chicago: Univer. of Chicago Press, 1929.

Torgerson, W. S. *Theory and methods of scaling*. New York: Wiley, 1958.

Veroff, J. Development and validation of a projective measure of power motivation. In J. W. Atkinson (Ed.), *Motives in fantasy, action, and society*. Princeton: Van Nostrand, 1958. Pp. 105–116.

Vidich, A. J. Methodological problems in the observation of husband-wife interaction. *Marr. & fam. Living*, 1956, 18, 234–239.

Webster, H. Correcting personality scales for response sets or suppression effects. *Psychol. Bull.*, 1958, 55, 62–64.

Weschler, I. R. An investigation of attitudes toward labor and management by means of the error-choice method. *J. soc. Psychol.*, 1950, 32, 51–62.

Westfall, R. L., Boyd, H. W., Jr., & Campbell, D. T. The use of structured techniques in motivational research. *J. Marketing*, 1957, 22, 134–139.

Williams, W. C. The PALS tests: a technique for children to evaluate both parents. *J. consult. Psychol.*, 1958, 22, 487–495.

Willis, R. H. Manipulation of item marginal frequencies by means of multiple-response items. *Psychol. Rev.*, 1960, 67, 32–50.

Willis, R. H. An empirical test of the method of controlled marginals. *Educ. psychol. Measmt*, 1961, 21, 39–52.

Wittenborn, J. R. Contributions and current status of Q methodology. *Psychol. Bull.*, 1961, 58, 132–142.

Woolf, H. (Ed.) *Quantification: a history of the meaning of measurement in the natural and social sciences*. Indianapolis: Bobbs-Merrill, 1961.

Wright, C. E. A factor dimension comparison of normative and ipsative measurements. *Educ. psychol. Measmt*, 1961, 21, 433–444.

Zajonc, R. B. The concepts of balance, congruity, and dissonance. *Publ. opin. Quart.*, 1960, 24, 280–296.

Zeisel, H. *Say it with figures*. New York: Harper, 1957.

Zubin, J. Symposium on statistics for the clinician. *J. clin. Psychol.*, 1950, 6, 1–6.

PART **III** The Family
in Its
Societal
Setting

CHAPTER 11

Family Forms
and Variations
Historically Considered

PANOS D. BARDIS
University of Toledo

ORIGIN AND EVOLUTION

In *Themistocles,* Plutarch asserted, "So very difficult a matter is it to trace and find out the truth of anything by history." And in *Sertorius,* he added, "It is no great wonder if in long process of time, while fortune takes her course hither and thither, numerous coincidences should spontaneously occur. If the number and variety of subjects to be wrought upon be infinite, it is all the more easy for fortune, with such an abundance of material, to effect this similarity of results." On the other hand, Thucydides, in his *Historia* (I, ii, 2), expressed an opinion which generated the well-known phrase, "History repeats itself," namely, "I shall be content if those shall pronounce my *History* useful who desire to give a view of events as they did really happen, and as they are very likely, in accordance with human nature, to repeat themselves at some future time—if not exactly the same, yet very similar."

These or other analogous controversial statements will undoubtedly come to mind whenever an effort is made to determine the origin of the family and reconstruct its more or less recondite evolutionary stages. Indeed, as the following discussion indicates, there is very little agreement among the scholars who, with impressive indefatigability, have explored this subject. [This chapter essentially follows the institutional approach discussed above in Ch. 2. Of necessity it is selective, focusing upon the chief precursors of the contemporary Western family.]

Bachofen

Johann Jakob Bachofen (1815–1887), for example, the famous Swiss jurist, philologist, and classicist who in 1861 published *Das Mutterrecht,* believed that human society began with *promiscuity* (sexual communism or extreme sexual permissiveness), which was succeeded by *gynecocracy* (a society ruled by women), which was finally superseded by the *patriarchate* (a culture in which the male has higher social status, and in which descent, inheritance, and succession are usually reckoned through the father, while residence is patrilocal and women and children are subordinated to the ruling male).

That our earliest ancestors actually lived in a state of promiscuity is indicated, Bachofen contended, by the fact that fatherhood was originally unrecognized—all children belonged to the entire group—as well as by what he considered survivals of a transition period from sexual communism to pair marriage. These survivals were temple prostitution and the *jus primae noctis.*

Of these, the first, which is also known as religious prostitution and sacred harlotry, refers to the practice of having women function as religious prostitutes in the temple. In this way, according to Bachofen, the favor of the gods was believed to be won anew, since temporary prostitution expiated the breaking of natural law by entering marriage, which is characterized by sexual exclusiveness.

The *jus primae noctis* (law of the first night), on the other hand, which is sometimes referred to as *droit de seigneur* (right of the lord), is a practice found in various primitive societies and probably in medieval Europe. This law gave the chief of the tribe, the priest, the lord, or some other leader the right to sleep with the bride on the first night after her marriage.

The theory concerning the second stage, that of *Mutterrecht* (mother right), was based on a reinterpretation necessitated by accumulating anthropological research which indicated that certain folkways and mores among primitives were incompatible with patriarchal theory. After asserting that mother right was typical of some societies, Bachofen theorized that matriarchy everywhere preceded patriarchy. His main arguments were as follows: (a) There is no conclusive anthropological evidence that patriliny was succeeded by matriliny. (b) Many patrilineal societies include features that seem to constitute vestiges of earlier matrilineal cultures. (c) Analogous patrilineal vestiges are quite uncommon among matrilineal societies. (d) Patrilineal cultures in general appear more advanced than matrilineal ones, thus indicating that the latter preceded the former. (e) Primitives must

have been unfamiliar with the nature of biological paternity. (f) The association of mother and child has always been physically obvious. And (g), among early nomadic peoples, the father seems to have been excluded from the family group.

Believing that social evolution consists in transcending the material or animal-like aspects of the human race, or in increasingly dominating the laws of matter, and thus gradually spiritualizing and humanizing mankind, Bachofen concluded that the matriarchate was superseded by the patriarchate. According to him, the most genuinely spiritual power of the male family head was attained in ancient Rome. There, and only there, was found the ideal of *potestas* over wife and children, the highest type of human law, which facilitated the prevalence of the corresponding concept of a unified political *imperium* so relentlessly and unremittingly pursued in the Eternal City.

Maine

In the same year that Bachofen's *Das Mutterrecht* appeared, Sir Henry J. Sumner Maine (1822–1888), an English lawyer and historian, published his classic study, *Ancient Law.*

In this work, Maine cautioned scientific researchers against attributing antiquity and universality to certain primitive customs and averred that a matriarchal stage in social evolution never existed; on the contrary, the patriarchate has always been prevalent. The establishment of private property and mother right, he added, are positively incompatible.

With reference to evidence concerning the patriarchal theory, he stated:

The effect of the evidence derived from comparative jurisprudence is to establish that view of the primeval condition of the human race which is known as the Patriarchal Theory.... this theory was originally based on the Scriptural history of the Hebrew patriarchs . . . its connexion with Scripture rather militated than otherwise against its reception as a complete theory, since the majority of the inquirers who till recently addressed themselves with most earnestness to the colligation of social phenomena, were either influenced by the strongest prejudice against Hebrew antiquities or by the strongest desire to construct their system without the assistance of religious records.... indeed the difficulty, at the present stage of the inquiry, is to know where to stop, to say of what races of men it is *not* allowable to lay down that the society in which they are united was originally organized on the patriarchal model (n.d., p. 101).

Maine's theory of family evolution is also presented in his tracing of the development of cultures from those with group relations and tradition determining rights and obligations to those in which legal power and contract were the dominant forces. This is the classic "Mainean shift," epitomized in his own phrase, "from status to contract." According to Maine, the shift is especially noticeable after the period of urbanization, when kinship bonds become less strong. "The contrast may be most forcibly expressed by saying that the *unit* of an ancient society was the Family, of a modern society the Individual" (p. 104). More specifically, when social evolution began, kinship and the family constituted the foundation of social organization. The most ancient legal systems, therefore, were concerned with the collectivity and not with the individual, whose life constituted a mere continuation of the existence of his ancestors. In this way, the ideal of liberty became reinforced as human society moved from status to contract, or as the individual gained power at the expense of the family group. When, for instance, the family was powerful in relation to the state, woman's social status was extremely low. But when familism declined and the state became stronger, her position was improved considerably. In other words, civil law now began to take account of the individual, the family no longer being considered the unit. Adding that marriage had

its origin in the family and not vice versa, Maine also predicted further encroachments on the family by the state, as the latter grew in power and as individualism became a more popular ideology.

Morgan

Lewis Henry Morgan (1818–1881), a lawyer of Rochester, New York, became a prominent ethnographer and social evolutionist through his firsthand acquaintance with the Iroquois and other American Indians. His studies of their family customs enabled him to collect kinship data on more than 200 different societies, which he discussed in *Systems of Consanguinity and Affinity of the Human Family,* published in 1870. The first work of its kind and one of the most brilliant and original anthropological achievements, this treatise established the study of kinship as a branch of comparative sociology. Morgan distinguished between two basic types of kinship nomenclature, the classificatory and descriptive systems. The former represents a kinship system in which main emphasis is placed on kin solidarity rather than on exact genealogical relationships. The remoteness of a blood relationship, therefore, does not diminish its importance. The term *father,* for example, may refer not only to the male parent, but also to his brothers. On the other hand, the descriptive system, as is typical of Western cultures, includes specific kinship terms to designate specific individual relationships.

Another important treatise by Morgan is *Ancient Society* (1877), which constituted a synthesis of the social history of Oceania, the Indians of America, and classical Greece and Rome. Believing in uniform laws of social evolution, and beginning with the Australians and Polynesians, Morgan divided all human history into three great stages of "human progress," savagery, barbarism, and civilization. As he wrote, "So essentially identical are the arts, institutions, and mode of life in the same status upon all continents, that the archaic form of the principal domestic institutions of the Greeks and Romans must even now be sought in the corresponding institutions of the American aborigines" (1877, p. 18).

Influenced by Charles Darwin, he developed his evolutionary scheme sufficiently to include various social institutions. The family, for instance, Morgan asserted, followed these stages: promiscuity, punalua, polygamy (commencing with matriliny and ending with patriliny), and monogamy. This is what Morgan himself called "Sequence of Institutions Connected with the Family," referring to the first stage as "Promiscuous Intercourse."

That promiscuity had actually existed, Morgan was never certain. He merely claimed that such an assumption was made quite logical by the stages that followed later, confessing that he deduced "Promiscuous Intercourse" at the theoretical level, since it lies concealed in mankind's misty antiquity beyond the reach of certain knowledge.

He did claim, however, to have found conclusive evidence of the punaluan family among the Indians of North America. This family system, which is also known as group marriage, involves a group of brothers sharing their wives in common or a group of sisters sharing their husbands. At this stage, the clan becomes the domestic institution and the basic unit of social structure.

Matriliny, on the other hand, must have preceded patriliny, since paternity was at first uncertain. But later, as fatherhood became more certain, and as economic progress led to the accumulation of property, the male parent must have resented the exclusion of his offspring from inheriting his goods. The rules of descent and inheritance thus became patrilineal.

Westermarck

Edward A. Westermarck (1862-1939), a Finnish sociologist and brilliant student of the types and history of human marriage,

rejected primitive promiscuity and declared that, by nature, man has always been monogamous. His theories were presented in his classic work, *The History of Human Marriage,* published in 1891, which, although rather outdated, still constitutes a valuable source of descriptive information regarding the family systems of innumerable cultures around the world.

In the first volume of this treatise, Westermarck wrote:

It is often said that the human race must have originally lived in a state of promiscuity, where individual marriage did not exist, where all the men in a horde or tribe had indiscriminately access to all the women, and where the children born of these unions belonged to the community at large. This opinion has been expressed by Bachofen, McLennan, Morgan, Lord Avebury, Giraud-Teulon, Lippert, Kohler, Post, Wilken, Kropotkin, Wilutzky, Bloch, and many others (1922, Vol. I, p. 103).

Such an assumption, however, was completely unjustifiable, Westermarck asserted uncompromisingly.

I shall not merely endeavour to show that the supposed survivals of ancient promiscuity really are no such survivals at all, but also indicate how the customs in question may be explained.

The evidence adduced in support of the hypothesis of promiscuity flows from two different sources. First, there are in books of ancient and modern writers notices of peoples who are said to live or to have lived promiscuously. Second, there are certain customs which are assumed to be relics from an earlier stage of civilisation when marriage did not exist (pp. 104–105).

In one of his most interesting passages, he attacked the first source of evidence in this manner:

Considering how uncertain the information is which people give about the sexual relations of their own neighbours, we must be careful not to accept as trustworthy evidence the statements made by classical writers with reference to more or less distant tribes of which they evidently possessed very little knowledge. In the very chapter where Pliny states that among the Garamantians men and women lived in promiscuous intercourse he tells us of another African tribe, the Blemmyans, that they were said to have no head and to have the mouth and eyes in the breast. I have never seen this statement quoted in any book on human anatomy, and can see no reason to assume that our author was so much better acquainted with the sexual habits of the Garamantians than he was with the personal appearance of the Blemmyans (p. 110).

Concerning the second source of evidence, Westermarck contended that the customs considered survivals from an earlier state of sexual communism were actually due to other causes. The *jus primae noctis,* for example, was not really accorded to a king, chief, priest, or other leader because the sexual exclusiveness of marriage had put an end to promiscuity, but because, in certain cultures at least, the bridegroom wished to protect himself from pollution by hymenal blood, to which the king, chief, or priest was believed to be unsusceptible. In other cultures, where the priest functioned as a substitute, the common belief was that the marriage would thus be sanctified and fertility would be ensured. And, of course, it would be a great honor if the king himself performed the rite.

An additional argument, of a biological nature, was inspired by Darwin, who had stated that the extreme jealousy of the male among the most highly developed apes made sexual communism quite unlikely.

Regarding Morgan's hypothesis of the punaluan stage, Westermarck objected that "so far as I can see, this hypothesis is not only unfounded but contrary to all reasonable assumptions. Among other things it presupposes unrestricted sexual intercourse between brothers and sisters, which is found nowhere among existing savages and is utterly inconsistent with the strict exogamy

which prevails among most peoples who have a classificatory system of relationship terms" (p. 240). His additional argument was that housemates feel a natural repugnance to coitus between each other. Incest tabu, of course, is not instinctive, he explained, since the sexual appetite is merely diminished as a result of constant and prolonged association, especially when such association begins in childhood.

He was equally critical of the matrilineal interpretation of various family customs. "Nor must we take for granted," he maintained, "that a certain prominence given to the maternal uncle by a people with patrilineal descent is an indication of the former prevalence of maternal descent. The reckoning of descent either through the father or through the mother does not imply that the nearest blood-ties on the other side are ignored" (p. 277).

Among his arguments for his own theory of natural monogamy were selected examples involving the anthropoids (1936), as well as his assertion that peoples at the stage of food-gathering and hunting, who were considered economically most primitive by the social evolutionists, were predominantly monogamous. In the last volume of his *History,* he also concluded that if "the causes to which monogamy in the most progressive societies owes its origin will continue to operate with constantly growing force, if especially the regard for the feelings of women, and the women's influence on legislation, will increase, the laws of monogamy are not likely to be changed. It is certainly difficult to imagine a time when Western civilisation would legalise the marriage of one man with several women simultaneously" (1922, Vol. III, p. 106).

Spencer

Herbert Spencer (1820–1903), an English liberal who dealt extensively with the concepts of evolution and the organic state, applied biological theories to social phenomena. He was uncompromising concerning the theory of primitive promiscuity. In his great work, *The Principles of Sociology,* he declared: "I do not think the evidence shows that promiscuity ever existed in an unqualified form, and it appears to me that even had it so existed, the name 'communal marriage' would not convey a true conception of it" (1897, Vol. I, p. 644). On the contrary, influenced by Darwin's theory of the transmission of acquired traits, he asserted that monogamy, especially in the more advanced societies, was innate. This form of family organization, he explained, is appealingly definite and simple. Besides, it has been dictated by nature itself, which has created an approximately equal number of males and females. And he added:

The same marital relation occurs in the simplest groups and in the most compound groups. A strict monogamy is observed by the miserable Wood Veddahs, living so widely scattered that they can scarcely be said to have reached the social state; and the wandering Bushmen, similarly low, though not debarred from polygyny, are usually monogamic. Certain settled and more advanced peoples, too, are monogamic; as instance those of Port Dory (p. 686).

Spencer also maintained that the evolution of Homo sapiens has rendered propagation a less dominant task in the life of the individual. More specifically, the reasons are three: The number of offspring has declined; the period of youth has become considerably longer; the period between the cessation of propagation and death is also much longer. Consequently, the development and advancement of the individual are more feasible at the present time.

However, although Spencer identified the ancient social unit with the family, which has recently been replaced by the individual, and although he accordingly predicted the gradual decline of the family institution, he rejected the political emancipation of woman, asserting that her activities should be confined to the home. He also theorized that woman's social status is inversely pro-

portional to the degree of militarism in a given society.

Briffault

Finally, Robert Briffault, in his famous treatise, *The Mothers,* published in 1927, attacked Westermarck's theory of primitive monogamy, maintaining that this form of marriage constitutes the fourth stage in the evolution of the family, the other three being original group marriage, matriarchy, and patriarchy. "It would be difficult," he wrote, "for any hypothesis to be so uniformly and directly in contradiction with the facts upon which it may be supposed to depend for evidence than the theological doctrine of primitive monogamy. Whatever the variability of the practice of polygyny among uncultured peoples, no monogamous primitive society is known" (Vol. II, p. 303). Besides, he added, as far as nature is concerned, the function of the male in both the plant and animal kingdoms is to impregnate as many females as possible, and monogamy limits this function. He also asserted that, if, unlike Westermarck, one does not confine research to a few cases, he will find that anthropoids are not actually monogamous. Then, he explained that primitive monogamy is not genuine monogamy, since it is determined by economic, not moral, factors. Finally, he pointed out that wife hospitality (the practice of a host's permitting a guest sexual access to his wife), the levirate (the practice of permitting or requiring a man to marry the widow of his brother, or of another close relative), and the sororate (a man's marrying his wife's sister, on either a mandatory or permissive basis, after the wife's death) are indicative of an early stage of group marriage.

Polyandry and polygyny, on the other hand, are not distinct forms of family organization, but merely phases of group marriage. In other words, depending on the particular circumstances, group marriage may develop into polyandry or polygyny.

Polyandry, for instance, usually evolves in matriarchal cultures, which were organized both matriarchally and gynecocratically, as in certain parts of Tibet. In brief, group marriage is the source, not the result, of polygamy.

Regarding matriarchy, Briffault stated that one should not conceive of this stage as the opposite of patriarchy, with the male having low social status similar to that of the female in patriarchy.

The characteristics of societies of a matriarchal type are by no means a simple inversion of the parts respectively played by the sexes in a patriarchal society. In the most primitive human societies there is nothing equivalent to the domination which, in advanced societies, is exercised by individuals, by slaves, by one sex over the other. The notion of such a domination is entirely foreign to primitive humanity; the conception of authority is not understood.... A social order involving such a domination . . . can exist only in advanced economic conditions where private property has acquired a paramount importance; to impute that organisation to primitive society, where private property scarcely exists, is an anachronism. The development of durable private property, of wealth, the desire of the constitutionally predatory male to possess it and to transmit it to his descendants, are, in fact, the most common causes of the change from matriarchal to patriarchal institutions (1927, Vol. I, pp. 433-434).

Briffault also argued that, in the animal kingdom, patriarchy is completely nonexistent. Moreover, the maternal instinct typical of the more advanced mammals led to the development of maternal love among primitive women, which became a permanent force long before the periodic sex drive generated heterosexual love. The mother-child bond was further intensified by the long period of dependence on the part of the young, resulting from the prolonged immaturity of the human offspring. In this way, the mother and her children formed a relatively strong and permanent social unit, while a corresponding father group was nonexistent. The unity of the mother group was first threatened when the male child reached puberty and began to make sexual approaches to his sisters. Such behavior was strongly discouraged by the jealous mother, who forced her sons to seek mates outside their mother group, while the male outsiders that mated with her daughters were required to become loyal members of her cohesive social unit. According to Briffault, however, when the mother's authority expanded and finally included property rights, it became the Achilles' tendon of matriarchy, which was thus superseded by patriarchy and, ultimately, by monogamy.

Theory Evaluation

In brief, the above theories of family evolution dealt with systems primarily presented in three ways. (a) The various evolutionary stages were conceived of as actual deviations from the Christian ideal of monogamy. (b) On the basis of atypical existing primitive family systems, earlier stages were reconstructions of which present examples are not in existence. And (c), beginning with the "family" life of the anthropoids, various Homo sapiens family stages were constructed.

These theories dominated anthropology, sociology, and other social sciences until Franz Boas, the father of American historical anthropology, and his students began to combat unilinear evolutionism by means of extensive ethnological research. Because of such investigation, these theories were soon rejected by virtually all serious social scientists.

In the present section, some of the limitations of unilinear evolutionism, which inevitably led to its downfall, are briefly discussed.

Bachofen, for instance, relied on mythology so extensively that, quite frequently, *Das Mutterrecht* sounds like a work of art rather than a scientific treatise. Moreover, he often attributed social consequences to biological phenomena in rather uncritical fashion, as in the case of ignorance of paternity among primitives. First of all, this argument, even if such ignorance ever prevailed, is not exactly relevant. Then, ethnological research has demonstrated that descent is associated primarily with group membership, not with recognition of kinship. Certain Australian primitives, who are completely unaware of biological fatherhood, still emphasize patrilineal descent. Additional field work in anthropology has also indicated that the father's membership in the human family is practically universal. Many of the so-called survivals of matrilineal cultures have been rather satisfactorily explained by means of arguments different from those presented in *Das Mutterrecht*. Bachofen's presentation, however, seemed so logical that his theory was long accepted.

Like Bachofen, Maine often presented arguments from mythology, as if the ancient tragedies, epic poems, and other literary works were objective ethnological treatises. It has already been mentioned that part of Maine's evidence concerning primitive patriarchy was based on a few Homeric verses dealing with the legend of the Cyclopes. For many reasons, however, the legend itself cannot seriously be cited as an adequate source of anthropological evidence, especially because it presents innumerable inconsistencies and contradictions in its appearances in the body of classical literature.

Westermarck's assertion concerning incest is equally unreasonable. First of all, ethnographic data demonstrate that marriage with a housemate is often favored, as among the Angmagsalik Eskimo, who permit marriage between children who have been reared together. This assertion is also contradicted by the fairly common preference for sororate and levirate unions, which may involve members of the same extended family. Then, the enduring attachment between spouses is not an unusual occurrence. Finally, innumerable clinical studies prove not only that incestuous inclinations are often present in the nuclear family, but also that such inclinations are constantly combated by both individual repression and social control.

Similarly, Briffault's arguments are not always logical. His contention, for instance, that the natural function of the male, in both the plant and animal kingdoms, is to impregnate the largest possible number of females, and that this function is limited by monogamy, is unreasonable. In monogamy, as in polyandry, polygyny, hetaerism, and so forth, the period of gestation is always nine months and remains the same even when the female has coitus quite frequently. Briffault's other conclusion, that polyandry is generated by group marriage, is not supported by anthropological research; for if group marriage were universal in the past, as Briffault asserted, why should the remnants of polyandry be so uncommon at the present time? Moreover, if it could prevail only in cultures in which matriarchy was dominant until recently, why is it nonexistent in most societies that seem to have been matriarchal in the past?

At any rate, "All of these attempts to reconstruct the earlier forms of organization of the family remain at best only elaborate hypotheses" (M. Mead, 1931, p. 65). And, in brief, the reasons may be outlined as follows:

1. The postulation of the evolutionary stages is arbitrary.

2. Because of the bias of our own social norms, the evolutionists have often concluded that the earlier forms of family organization constituted the exact antithesis of modern family systems—for example, primitive promiscuity.

3. Conclusive evidence concerning such evolutionary stages is not available.

4. The argument of survivals is unacceptable, since, according to recent ethnological research, these customs are functioning institutions.

5. Ethnological research has also demonstrated that matrilineal cultures are not always less advanced. Among primitive societies are

the patrilineal Witoto of Amazonia, the matrilineal Kutchin of northern Canada, and the bilateral Andamanese pygmies. On the other hand, in the civilized areas of the world, are the patrilineal Chinese, the matrilineal Brahman Nayars of India, and the bilateral Syrian Christians. It is true, of course, that matrilineal cultures in general are more primitive than patrilineal ones. But it is also true that the difference is not considerable, that the similarities are very great, and that the difference may indicate nothing more than the fact that the patrilineal and bilateral Europeans and Asians have recently influenced the rest of the world extensively.

6. Combinations of family systems are anything but uncommon.

7. Not infrequently, the social status which accompanies polygamy is considered more important in various cultures than the relationship between the two spouses.

8. Not all inferences from the anthropoids can be accepted unquestioningly, since, if one defines instinct as "inherited invariable predisposition to perform certain *complex* acts," one must conclude that, unlike lower species, Homo sapiens has no instincts.

THE ANCIENT HEBREW FAMILY

Among the Hebrews, the concept of family was quite broad. In the Holy Scriptures, for instance, the family is usually represented by such Hebrew words as *bayith* (house) and *mishpachah* (clan). In Genesis 7:1, Jehovah commanded Noah, "Come thou and all thy house into the ark." A "house," then, might consist of a man, his mother, his wives and concubines as well as their children, his sons-in-law and daughters-in-law with their offspring, his illegitimate sons, and his slaves of both sexes.

The importance of the family among the Hebrews is indicated by the fact that, in Genesis, human beings are first mentioned as members of a family. Moreover, "The Fifth Commandment sanctified the family, as second only to the Temple in the structure of Jewish society" (Durant, 1935, p. 333).

Engagement

Even engagement was considered very important, and was more binding than in the Western nations at the present time. During this early period, the bride still depended on her father, who was expected to assemble her property within one year, as the community disapproved of a longer interval.

Numerous Old Testament passages reveal the seriousness of engagement. "And they called Rebekah, and said unto her, Wilt thou go with this man? And she said, I will go. And they sent away Rebekah their sister, and her nurse, and Abraham's servant, and his men. And they blessed Rebekah, and said unto her, Thou art our sister; be thou the mother of thousands of millions, and let thy seed possess the gate of those which hate them" (Genesis 24:58–60). The groom himself, during his engagement, enjoyed many privileges, including exemption from military service: "And what man is there that hath betrothed a wife, and hath not taken her? let him go and return unto his house, lest he die in the battle, and another man take her" (Deuteronomy 20:7).

Dowry

One of the elements that made engagement so serious was the *mohar,* or dowry, which was given by the groom to the prospective bride's father. After defiling Dinah, Jacob and Leah's daughter, Shechem, the son of Hamor the Hivite, said to Jacob and his sons: "Let me find grace in your eyes, and what ye shall say unto me I will give. Ask me never so much dowry and gift, and I will give according as ye shall say unto me: but give me the damsel to wife" (Genesis 34:11–12).

Of course, the *mohar,* which was offered as a compensation for the loss of the bride, not quite as a purchase price, and which usually consisted of 50 shekels (the chief Hebrew silver coin), might assume various forms. Jacob, for example, served Laban 14 years for his daughters Leah and Rachel (Genesis 29). And Saul, the son of the Benjamite Kish and first king of Israel, offering his elder daughter Merab to David, said to his servants: "Thus shall ye say to David, The king desireth not any dowry, but a hundred foreskins of the Philistines" (I Samuel 18:25).

The bride herself might bring considerable means to her husband's home. Abigail, the wife of "Nabal the fool," soon after the death of her apoplectic spouse, "hasted, and arose, and rode upon an ass, with five damsels of hers that went after her; and she went after the messengers of David, and became his wife" (I Samuel 25:42).

Marriage

The dowry system, however, did not imply the prevalence of materialistic considerations in marriage and the complete exclusion of romance. Although love seems at that time to have played a secondary role in mate selection, there was often sufficient tenderness between the sexes to lead to love affairs. Shechem's "soul clave unto Dinah the daughter of Jacob, and he loved the damsel, and spake kindly unto the damsel" (Genesis 34:3). Dinah's father "served seven years for Rachel; and they seemed unto him but a few days, for the love he had to her" (Genesis 29:20).

Marriage among the Hebrews was commonly arranged by the parents, although child marriage was absent. Abraham, when "old, and well stricken in age," commanded his eldest servant: "go unto my country, and to my kindred, and take a wife unto my son Isaac" (Genesis 24:4; cf. Genesis 21:21; 28:1–2; & Judges 14:1–3). Occasionally, the consent of the prospective groom and bride was sought by their parents, as is indicated by Abraham's suggestion to his servant: "And if the woman will not be willing to follow thee, then thou shalt be clear from this my oath" (Genesis 24:8). The children themselves might disregard

their parents' wishes, as in the case of Esau, who, when he was 40 years old, "took to wife Judith the daughter of Beeri the Hittite, and Bashemath the daughter of Elon the Hittite: Which were a grief of mind unto Isaac and to Rebekah" (Genesis 26:34–35).

Such control by the parents was a private matter not based on any legal regulations, since marriage in general required no religious or state sanction; it was merely a sanctification and not a contract.

Nevertheless, this does not mean that religion and the state considered marriage of secondary importance. On the contrary, "The Seventh Commandment recognized marriage as the basis of the family, as the Fifth had recognized the family as the basis of society; and it offered to marriage all the support of religion" (Durant, 1935, p. 335).

One of the forms which such support assumed was disapproval of celibacy. In fact, "celibacy was looked upon as a religious crime, equivalent to murder and to diminishing the image of God" (Briffault, 1927, Vol. III, p. 362). It "was not tolerated for any man over twenty, not even for the priests" (Sait, 1938, p. 80). Only the Essenes, a brotherhood constituting the first organized monastic order in the Mediterranean basin, placed extreme emphasis on celibacy. The Hebrews in general, being a small and insecure nation that needed numbers, made marriage compulsory and virtually ostracized marriageable virgins and childless women. And, according to the Talmud, a compilation of Jewish tradition, "Any Jew who has not a wife is no man."

Forms of marriage. In the beginning, this popular institution seems to have been of the matrilocal type. In this system, which prevailed until the establishment of the monarchy, the husband left his parents and became part of the bride's tribe.

In one form of this, the husband merely visited his wife occasionally in her own home. This differed from prostitution in two ways: the wife's group recognized her children, and no disgrace was attached to the relationship. Samson's marriage to the Philistine woman of Timnath probably was of this type (Judges 15:1).

The other form was characterized by the groom's more extensive incorporation into the bride's group; the children belonged to her tribe, and descent was matrilineal. In the case of Jacob's marriage, for instance, Laban, his father-in-law, asserted: "These daughters are my daughters, and these children are my children, and these cattle are my cattle, and all that thou seest is mine" (Genesis 31:43; cf. Exodus 2:21–22 & Judges 16:4).

As the matrilocal form declined, the patriarchal, patrilocal, and patrilineal form of marriage became prevalent among the Hebrews. In this system, the husband was the wife's *Baal* or owner (Hosea 2:16), while she was *Beulah* or owned (Isaiah 62:4). Like the wife, the children were incorporated into the husband's tribe. This form of marriage was established in one of the following three ways:

First, in more ancient times, by capture: according to Judges 5:30, "Have they not sped? have they not divided the prey: to every man a damsel or two." (For a more detailed description, see Deuteronomy 21: 10–14.)

Second, by contract between the spouses and their respective families.

And third, which was more common, by purchase: for example, the case of Boaz and Ruth. Hosea, also, who lived during the reign of Jeroboam II (786–746 B.C.), and who married an adulteress—perhaps an allegorical parable of God's continued love for an unfaithful Israel—mentions that he bought her "for fifteen pieces of silver, and for a homer of barley, and a half homer of barley" (Hosea 3:2).

The wedding ceremony. Not much is known about the wedding ceremony, but it seems certain that the religious element was virtually absent, and that, in some cases, there was no other ritual besides the betrothal (see Genesis 24:63–67). In other cases, a brief wedding ceremony followed immediately after the betrothal, while in later times a more formal ceremony was adopted, which could not be postponed for longer than one year.

The festivities included a marriage supper that usually took place at the groom's home. Such festivities might last seven days, as in the case of Jacob's marriage to Leah: "Fulfil her week," said Laban, "and we will give thee this also for the service which thou shalt serve with me yet seven other years" (Genesis 29:27).

Another part of the festivities was a wedding procession, a description of which is found in Psalm 45:13–15. This passage, besides suggesting an element of vestigial capture, speaks of magnificent rejoicing, which Jeremiah (640–587 B.C.) described as "the voice of mirth, and the voice of gladness, the voice of the bridegroom, and the voice of the bride" (7:34). Similarly, the Trito-Isaiah mentioned that the "bridegroom decketh himself with ornaments" and the "bride adorneth herself with her jewels" (Isaiah 61:10). The scattering of flowers and nuts and the use of torches and lights at night were also part of the festivities. Then, according to Deuteronomy 24:5, "When a man hath taken a new wife, he shall not go out to war, neither shall he be charged with any business: but he shall be free at home one year, and shall cheer up his wife."

Monogamy. As to the number of women a man was permitted to marry, it seems that, at least according to Genesis 2:24, monogamy was the ideal: "Therefore shall a man leave his father and his mother, and shall cleave unto his wife: and they shall be one flesh." In the fifth century B.C., Malachi, the "messenger of the Lord," took monogamy for granted in his short and didactic book: "Because the Lord hath been witness between thee and the wife of thy youth, against whom thou hast dealt treacherously: yet is she thy companion, and the wife of thy covenant" (2:14). The same was true of the New Testament times.

The fact that monogamy was not always

practiced may be explained by the peculiar philosophy of worldly asceticism, which prevailed among the Hebrews and influenced their family life. Unlike early Christianity's absolute asceticism, this philosophy subjected the material world to the spiritual one only partially, thus limiting sensual pleasure without denying it completely. Monogamy, therefore, was accepted as the only form of marriage much later. In the Middle Ages, it was finally included in the family code known as *Ebenhaze* (the body of the house), which considered marriage a duty, stressed early marriage for both sexes, emphasized a religious wedding ceremony, allowed divorce to both sexes (although the husband had certain privileges), and idealized patriarchal family life.

Polygyny. Polygamy, then, of the polygynous type was not uncommon among the Hebrews, its origin being Asiatic. Polyandry, however, although the levirate type of marriage appears as one of its vestiges, was never practiced. Similarly, harems were tabu; the harem of Solomon (960–922 B.C.) was exceptional.

At least three factors led to the adoption of polygyny. (a) The existence of slavery facilitated the introduction of concubinage. (b) The need for numerous alliances with neighboring states necessitated international marital unions. Solomon, for instance, a cosmopolitan-minded king who adopted many international political and business policies, married an Egyptian princess (I Kings 3:1), whose dowry consisted of the stronghold of Gezer and who remained his favorite queen. In addition, he had many other foreign wives and consorts, including Naamah, perhaps an Ammonite princess, whose child Rehoboam was Solomon's only son (according to certain rabbis, this was the king's punishment for violating monogamy). (c) The desire for prolific reproduction forced the first wife, when she was barren or unable to bear any more children, to encourage her husband to take a concubine—for instance, Abraham with Sarah

and Hagar, and Jacob with Leah, Rachel, and their maids.

In such cases, the wife's status was not the same as the concubine's. To begin with, the former's birth was higher and, unlike the concubine, the wife was usually defended by her relatives. Also, concubinage had to be approved by the wife, as in the case of Sarah, who said to Abraham, "Behold now, the Lord hath restrained me from bearing: I pray thee, go in unto my maid; it may be that I may obtain children by her" (Genesis 16:2). Furthermore, the wife often considered the concubine's children as her own and had the right to claim the inheritance for her own offspring (see Genesis 21:10).

Of course, polygyny, being expensive, "was largely confined to the wealthy, who had the means of purchasing several wives" (Groves & Groves, 1947, p. 93). Such men were Abraham, Jacob, David, Solomon, and others. Many common people, however, did practice polygyny (see I Samuel 1:2).

But polygyny created many domestic problems, including jealousy (see Genesis 30:1–13). It is no wonder that such problems gradually led to the disapproval of polygyny. It is significant that the Hebrews believed that bigamy was introduced by Lamech, who was one of the descendants of Cain, a vagabond and fugitive murderer (Genesis 4:19). Later laws limited a common citizen to four wives and a king to 18—the king could not "multiply wives to himself" (Deuteronomy 17:17). Moses himself had "endeavored to check this institution by narrating the original institution of marriage, and showing the evils resulting from a plurality of wives" (Clare, 1898, Vol. I, p. 384). Hosea and other prophets also stressed monogamy. After all, the first and second founders of the human race, Adam and Noah, had one wife each, and so did some other great Hebrews, such as Isaac and Joseph. In the Bible, domestic happiness is always typical of monogamous unions. Nevertheless, it was only after

Christ that polygyny was formally and completely eliminated.

Levirate. According to this practice (from the Latin *levir:* brother-in-law), if a man died, his wife was often taken by his brother, even if the latter was already married. If the deceased husband had no brother, this obligation fell upon the nearest surviving male relative (see Deuteronomy 25:5–10).

The levirate was aimed at prolific reproduction, the prevention of the division or alienation of property, and the preservation of the family name. That is why, although later laws declared that, "if a man shall take his brother's wife, it is an unclean thing" (Leviticus 20:21), the custom seems to have persisted among the Jewish people until the Middle Ages. At the time of Christ, the Sadducees, a group of wealthy and intellectual Jews who did not believe in resurrection, spirits, and angels, said to Jesus: "Now there were with us seven brethren: and the first, when he had married a wife, deceased, and, having no issue, left his wife unto his brother: Likewise the second also, and the third, unto the seventh" (Matthew 22:25–26).

The Father

As has already been mentioned, the Hebrew family was patriarchal. Indeed, the father was the family's guardian, business manager, judge, priest, and even teacher. This last was exceedingly important, since, for the common people, the family was the only educational institution up to the time of Christ. The father also owned the land, which rendered a child's survival practically impossible without filial obedience. The wife herself was instructed by Jehovah, "Thy desire shall be to thy husband, and he shall rule over thee." Similarly, "he that smiteth his father. . . . And he that curseth his father . . . shall surely be put to death" (Exodus 21:15, 17).

In addition, the father arranged his children's marriage and had the right to sell his daughter as a concubine or servant. But, through Moses, God ordered the father: "Do not prostitute thy daughter, to cause her to be a whore" (Leviticus 19:29). Before and after her husband's death, a daughter-in-law was also controlled by her spouse's father, who might even condemn her to death if she were wicked (see Genesis 38:24). In general, judging by the various sacrifices to Molech—a Semitic deity that, in very early times, seems to have had a sanctuary in the Jerusalem Hinnom Valley at Topheth—the father had powers of life and death over his children (see Leviticus 18:21; Jeremiah 32:35).

In the same way, the Hebrews' genealogical practices are indicative of a definite association between power and paternity. Genealogy was of the individual and national types. In the days of Ezra, the Jewish priest and reformer who returned to Jerusalem when Artaxerxes was king, and who organized the celebrated pilgrimage of 1,496 families across the desert, the Jews emphasized purity of national descent and discriminated against non-Jews. Consequently, as they did with their own Abraham and his nation, they assigned to every tribe and nation of the world, as known to them, a *father.* The entire tenth chapter of Genesis deals in detail with this form of genealogy, beginning with Noah's sons, Shem, Ham, and Japheth. Moreover, among the Hebrews, the term *father* often represented the founder of a city. And, according to Genesis 4:20, *father* also stood for the person who introduced a given occupation: "And Adah bare Jabal: he was the father of such as dwell in tents, and of such as have cattle."

Still, the Hebrew father enjoyed less influence than his Roman counterpart. "He had the power of life and death over his wife only in case she committed adultery. And the death penalty once pronounced, the sentence had to be carried out by some other person" (Nimkoff, 1934, p. 143). Furthermore, he does not seem to have abused his authority. On the contrary, he is pictured "as zealously devoted to his wife and his children. And though love did not determine marriage, it often flowered out of it" (Durant, 1935, pp. 336–337).

Women

Unlike men, women had low status in the ancient Hebrew society. Although polygyny was fairly common, polyandry was tabu. Moreover, remarriage on the part of a widow was often disapproved, since she was her husband's property; widowers, however, could easily remarry. Then, men were often considered as "the sons of God," while women were merely "the daughters of men" (Genesis 6:2). Accordingly, even during the second century, the devout Jew repeated three benedictions, including: "Blessed art thou, Lord our God, who has not made me a woman." The Talmud also stated that the "testimony of one hundred women is equal only to the evidence of one man."

One of the reasons for such discrimination was the alleged impurity associated with woman's sex functions, since "The Jews were distinguished above all other peoples for the importance they attached to the state of ritual undefilement" (Briffault, 1927, Vol. III, p. 360). At childbirth, for instance, a woman became unclean, especially if the child were female, when the period of uncleanness was twice as long (Leviticus 12:2, 5). Numerous biblical passages reveal that, during menstruation, coitus was forbidden, while anything a woman touched became unclean (see Leviticus 15:19–20; 20:18; I Samuel 21:4–5).

A childless woman was especially unhappy, since the small Hebrew nation placed great emphasis on numbers. Concerning Abraham, Sarah, and Hagar, it is said: "And he went in unto Hagar, and she conceived: and when she saw that she had conceived, her mistress was despised in her eyes" (Genesis 16:4). This and other verses indicate that barrenness, being considered as punishment by God, often led to conflict (see Genesis 30:1; I Samuel 1:6).

Additional problems were created by the Hebrews' man-centered code of ethics. Although men enjoyed considerable freedom, women were expected to be virtuous. For instance, the death penalty was imposed much more frequently on the adulteress than on the adulterer.

But more than mere equality for women is suggested by the older Hebrew writings. It seems that in very ancient times women had a great deal of power. Indeed, "vestiges of a maternal order are to be found imbedded in Semitic speech, which is said to be dominated by forms distinctly indicative of mother kinship" (Messer, 1928, p. 115). Matronymy, for instance, that is, deriving a name from the mother or a maternal relative, is much more common in early Hebrew writings than in later ones. Something similar is indicated by the feminine clan names Leah and Rachel, as well as by Abraham and Sarah's marriage, which was possible because they had the same father but different mothers. Marriages such as Samson's and Gideon's involved a definite matrilocal element.

Woman's lower status in later times did not prevent some Hebrew women from becoming prominent. Sarah, a beautiful, virtuous, and wise woman, became the first Hebrew matriarch and the only one to be buried beside Abraham in the Cave of Machpelah (Genesis 49:31). Rebekah, the daughter of Milcah and Bethuel, was a respected woman in the Beer-sheba region, and her grave is still honored today at Hebron. Rachel, Laban's daughter, who led a prosperous life with Jacob at Succoth, Shechem, and Bethel, was so highly regarded that the elders of Bethlehem hoped that Ruth would emulate her (Ruth 4:11); Jeremiah spoke of her "weeping for her children" in Ramah (31:15); the Crusaders built a Moorish tomb for her in Bethlehem of Judaea in the twelfth century; and many Moslems adopted her as a sacred person. Deborah (Lepidoth's wife) was a gifted judge, prophetess, and leader in peace and war, who became famous for her victories against Sisera's Canaanites, held court wisely, and diminished tribal isolationism. Abigail's sagacity and beauty enabled her to become David's wife, after her husband Nabal's death. Huldah, a prominent prophetess ranking with Hannah and Deborah, contributed considerably to King Josiah's reforms by confirming the authoritativeness of "the book of the law" which the high priest Hilkiah had found accidentally in the Temple (II Kings 22). And Esther, unusually beautiful, charming, and courageous, delivered her race from Haman's violent anti-Semitism, as a result of which the Feast of Purim was instituted.

Less important women also had sufficient authority and power to make valuable contributions to the Hebrew family. "While the family was patriarchal, the wife played a most important part in the family organization, and much of the family activity centered around her. Her position and her privileges brought her into contact with all phases of life" (Elmer, 1945, p. 79). For instance, although her role in public worship was quite limited, at home she was a prominent participant in religious ceremonial. Such participation was of great importance, since the Sabbath and Passover were observed mainly at home, religion permeated virtually every aspect of family life, and traditional ceremonies facilitated the survival of the Jewish family, despite conquest, dispersion, and captivity. In view of the fact that the household was fairly self-sustaining —at least up to the time of Solomon—the wife's direction of domestic productive activities also made her rather important. Some of these activities have been described as follows:

She seeketh wool, and flax, and worketh willingly with her hands. She is like the merchant's ships; she bringeth her food from afar. She riseth also while it is yet night, and giveth meat to her household, and a portion to her maidens. She considereth a field, and buyeth it: with the fruit of her hands she planteth a vineyard. . . . She layeth her hands to the spindle, and her hands hold the distaff. . . . She maketh herself coverings of tapestry; her clothing is silk and purple. . . . She maketh fine linen, and selleth it; and delivereth girdles unto the merchant (Proverbs 31:13–16, 19, 22, 24).

Children

But since, in general, woman's status was rather low, one would expect female children to be considered less desirable than male ones. Indeed, poor parents sold their daughters to wealthy Jewish families and even to foreigners (Exodus 21:7). Moreover, although infanticide was commonly disapproved, "female infants could be exposed up to Ezekiel's time" (Dorsey, 1931, p. 496). The Hebrews' genealogical lists seldom included girls. After all, the Israelites believed, girls were products of the left testis, which was considered weaker and smaller than the right one, from which boys came. So, according to the Talmud, "luckless is he whose children are daughters."

Such biological misconceptions, however, did not render a boy's life much easier than that of his sister. Even when he was married, a son was under his father's control. In general, child discipline was exceedingly stern. The author of Proverbs wrote: "He that spareth his rod hateth his son: but he that loveth him chasteneth him betimes" (13:24); similarly, "The rod and reproof give wisdom: but a child left to himself bringeth his mother to shame" (29:15). Not infrequently, the unworthy son was stoned to death (see Deuteronomy 21:18–19, 21; 27:16; Leviticus 20:9). The extreme emphasis placed on filial duty is also indicated by the fact that, in the Ten Commandments, this subject follows immediately after the duties to Jehovah. The author of Proverbs added: "Hearken unto thy father that begat thee, and despise not thy mother when she is old" (23:22).

Concerning the illegitimate child, Deuteronomy says, "A bastard shall not enter into the congregation of the Lord: even to his tenth generation shall he not enter" (23:2). And if a man died before paying his debts, his orphan might be taken as a slave. That is why a widow complained to Elisha, "the creditor is come to take unto him my two sons to be bondmen" (II Kings 4:1).

All this, of course, does not mean that Hebrew children were unloved, for their complete rejection would be at least inconsistent with the small, insecure nation's need for numbers. In fact, children were thought of as divine gifts, as is indicated by Eve's words after Cain's birth: "I have gotten a man from the Lord" (Genesis 4:1). Some degree of parental love was also rather typical: for instance, David's reaction to the sickness of the child that he had by Bath-sheba, the wife of Uriah the Hittite, was fasting and weeping and lying "all night upon the earth" (II Samuel 12:15-16, 21).

As far as the education of the child was concerned, up to the time of Christ, the home played the most important role. The mother herself assumed a great deal of responsibility in this area, instructing both boys and girls, especially the latter, who were taught housekeeping, including the preparation of food according to Hebrew law. The father, on the other hand, when boys were five years of age, began to instruct them in Mosaic law and to supervise their occupational training.

Divorce

The double standard mentioned previously is further reflected by the Hebrews' divorce policies. Indeed, "The right of the husband to divorce his wife at his pleasure is the central thought in the entire system of Jewish divorce law" (Westermarck, 1922, Vol. III, p. 307). Moreover, "divorce was neither a civil nor a religious concern. It was strictly a ceremonial matter in charge of . . . the husband" (Nimkoff, 1934, p. 453). The procedure merely consisted in the husband handing his wife a bill of divorcement containing the statement, "Be thou divorced (or separated) from me."

Nevertheless, the husband's freedom in this area was not complete. In some cases,

the barrenness of the wife had to be established first. In addition, in the seventh century B.C., the Deuteronomic Code attempted to protect the wife by requiring a legal document that made divorce much less hasty.

In the final book of the Pentateuch, it says that one of the grounds for divorce was the wife's "uncleanness" (Deuteronomy 24:1). The meaning of this term was debated for centuries and, at the time of Christ, two rabbinical schools gave diametrically opposed interpretations. On the one hand, Hillel's disciples asserted that "uncleanness" referred to virtually anything that displeased the husband, and, on the other, Shammai's followers believed that the term meant adultery or something analogous—it was because of such confusion that the question of which interpretation was acceptable was put before Christ.

Another restriction concerned premarital intercourse between the spouses: "she shall be his wife; because he hath humbled her, he may not put her away all his days" (Deuteronomy 22:29). Similarly, if a husband accused his wife of not being a virgin, but her parents proved that she was, the elders "shall amerce him in a hundred shekels of silver, and give them unto the father of the damsel, because he hath brought up an evil name upon a virgin of Israel: and she shall be his wife; he may not put her away all his days" (Deuteronomy 22:19).

The Mishnah, a collection of oral laws made by Rabbi Judah ha-Nasi (A.D. 135-220) which became the basis of the Talmud, added three new restrictions: a man could not divorce his wife if she were in captivity, if she had become insane, or if she were too young to take care of the bill of divorcement. The Mishnah further made the divorce procedure so complex that the husband was compelled to consult a legally trained person, who was expected to attempt the reconciliation of the spouses if their divorce did not appear justifiable.

When a divorce was secured, the children

remained in the woman's "custody at least until they were weaned, and after that time it was optional with her to retain the custody of them; but the custody of the boys could be claimed by the father after their sixth year" (Westermarck, 1922, Vol. III, p. 310).

Regarding the wife's remarriage, Deuteronomy 24:2 says, "And when she is departed out of his house, she may go and be another man's wife."

As has already been indicated, divorce laws gradually became less man-centered and, by the time of Christ, divorce was reciprocal. The Talmud itself later permitted a woman to divorce her husband if he had a loathsome disease, as well as for other reasons. The new laws also protected the wife by means of her dowry, which was returned to her when she was divorced, if she were innocent.

Inheritance

"In the days of the patriarchs, individual ownership was restricted to cattle and movable possessions" (Sait, 1938, p. 110). By the time of King Ahab (869–850 B.C.), however, as his covetous demand for the vineyard of Naboth the Jezreelite indicates, individual land ownership was well established (I Kings 21).

The laws concerning the inheritance of these possessions were not always the same. At first, especially in nomadic times, primogeniture was the rule, the oldest heir or son inheriting almost all of the father's property as well as patriarchal leadership. It was this birthright that Jacob, with subtlety and Rebekah's assistance, took away from his brother Esau, Isaac's eldest son (Genesis 27). Even when a man had "two wives, one beloved, and another hated," and both had offspring, the firstborn son being the hated woman's child, the father "shall acknowledge the son of the hated for the firstborn" (Deuteronomy 21:15–17). That is why, although the father had the authority to transfer his property to a younger child,

he rarely did so. Cases such as those of Ishmael and Isaac, Reuben and Joseph, Manasseh and Ephraim, Eliab and David, and Adonijah and Solomon are so exceptional that one cannot conclude that they constituted vestiges of ultimogeniture or junior right (leaving the property to the youngest child).

Later, when agriculture was prevalent, all of the sons inherited the property, a double portion being transferred to the eldest. Failing sons, the daughters became the heirs, and if there were no children, the property was passed to the next of kin or, sometimes, to the slaves (Numbers 27:8–11). In Ruth 4, Boaz announced to the elders that he purchased Ruth the Moabitess, Mahlon's widow, and the property of Elimelech, her father-in-law, only after a nearer kinsman had relinquished his rights.

Morals

In very ancient times, incestuous unions were sometimes approved and practiced (see Genesis 20:12; 24:1–4). However, the Hebrews, although they emphasized endogamy, later generally considered incest a serious sin and occasionally punished the offenders by death. The father, the mother, the father's wife, a sister, a son's daughter or a daughter's daughter, an uncle, an aunt, a daughter-in-law, a sister-in-law, and so forth were unapproachable (Leviticus 18:6–18).

Hebrew law was equally strict concerning other forms of questionable behavior. Numerous offenses were considered sacrilegious and the concern of the entire society, which, according to the Israelites, was punished by God for the sins of its members. A short time before the walls of Jericho fell "down flat," and while the Jews, led by the Ark of the Lord, were compassing the city for the seventh time as their priests were blowing trumpets of ram's horns, Joshua advised his people: "keep yourselves from the accursed thing, lest ye make yourselves accursed . . . and make the camp of

Israel a curse, and trouble it" (Joshua 6:18). Such strictness, which was uncommon among the surrounding nations, was partly due to the fact that the Hebrews often associated sin with the licentious cults of their hostile neighbors. Oriental zoogamy, for example, was forbidden. It is needless to add that marriage between a Jew and one of the Girgashites, Ammonites, Moabites, Amorites, Canaanites, Perizzites, Hivites, Jebusites, and other outsiders was strictly forbidden (see Nehemiah 13:23-25).

Prostitution was also disapproved. One of the statutes declared: "Do not prostitute thy daughter, to cause her to be a whore" (Leviticus 19:29). Another stated: "And the daughter of any priest, if she profane herself by playing the whore, she profaneth her father: she shall be burnt with fire" (Leviticus 21:9). In addition, a prostitute's children were not allowed to inherit their father's property (see Judges 11:2).

Nevertheless, the people did not always disapprove of prostitution, which was rather common. On his way to Timnath, Judah met Tamar, to whom he said, "Go to, I pray thee, let me come in unto thee . . . and she said, What wilt thou give me, that thou mayest come in unto me?" (Genesis 38:16). And Amos complained that "a man and his father will go in unto the same maid" (2:7). Even religious prostitution was practiced occasionally. When Eli, a weak judge and priest in Shiloh, was very old, he heard that his wicked sons, Hophni and Phinehas, "lay with the women that assembled at the door of the tabernacle of the congregation" (I Samuel 2:22).

The law itself appeared more liberal regarding relations with foreign prostitutes, the so-called strange women, who were often seen along the highways, living in tents and sometimes working as peddlers. Solomon later liberalized the laws further, allowing foreign harlots to enter Jerusalem. Such harlots perhaps constituted the majority of Israel's prostitutes, as the phrase "strange woman" suggests (Proverbs 6:24; 7:6-18).

Sodomy was also common. When two

angels visited Lot, the men of Sodom (one of the "cities of the plain" in the "vale of Siddim") gathered around his home, begging, "Where are the men which came in to thee this night? bring them out unto us, that we may know them" (Genesis 19:5). In other parts of the land "there were also sodomites . . . and they did according to all the abominations of the nations which the Lord cast out before the children of Israel" (I Kings 14:24). And although the law declared that "there shall be no whore of the daughters of Israel, nor a sodomite of the sons of Israel" (Deuteronomy 23:17), this form of sexual behavior remained rather common even after the destruction of Sodom and Gomorrah.

Another type of sexual behavior, fornication, "was forbidden to women, but was looked upon as a venial offense in men" (Durant, 1935, p. 336). A bride, for instance, was stoned to death if she were not a virgin.

An adulteress, too, was occasionally burned or stoned to death, although the more usual penalty was divorce and loss of dowry. And although the law stated that "the man that committeth adultery with another man's wife . . . the adulterer and the adulteress shall surely be put to death" (Leviticus 20:10), the male was actually considered much less guilty. The reason is obvious: since the woman, who had low status, had essentially been purchased by her spouse, she was guilty of an offense against her husband, while the adulterer's behavior constituted an offense against another man's property.

Summary

In brief, the main characteristics of the ancient Hebrew family were as follows: (a) engagement was more binding than it is now in the West; (b) a dowry, usually 50 shekels, was given by the groom to the bride's family; (c) marriage was ordinarily arranged by the groom's and bride's families; (d) celibacy was considered a religious crime; (e) the main forms of marriage were the matrilocal (visiting and residential) and the patriarchal (by capture, by contract, and by purchase); (f) although monogamy was regarded as ideal, polygyny and concubinage flourished; (g) great emphasis was placed on large families; (h) the father was exceedingly powerful; (i) at first, women had high status which later declined considerably; (j) divorce was common and usually man-centered; (k) in nomadic times, primogeniture was stressed, but when agriculture became dominant, all sons inherited their father's property; (l) unlike the Egyptians, the Hebrews condemned incest, especially in later centuries; (m) although the law disapproved of immorality most strongly, prostitution, sodomy, and similar practices were rather common.

THE ANCIENT GREEK FAMILY

Four different groups were involved in ancient Greece's family life: male citizens, legitimate wives, prostitutes, and slaves. Through the interaction among these groups, as well as through the influence of changing conditions, the Hellenic family evolved constantly, thus assuming a variety of more or less distinct forms. According to Zimmerman, "Homer gave witness to the death of the trustee family. Hesiod and Herodotus described the domestic type. We still possess the documents which describe the atomistic type, from Pericles to Polybius" (1947b, p. 173).

Marriage

Such heterogeneity is seen, for instance, in Greece's marriage customs.

First of all, it seems that in ancient times marriage by capture was typical. As Dionysius of Halicarnassus stated in *Antiquitates Romanae* (II, xxx, 5), when Romulus wished to comfort a group of virgins seized in this manner, he merely asserted "that this was an ancient Hellenic practice and that this method of contracting marriages for women was the most illustrious one."

Later on, complex legal systems were de-

veloped which regulated virtually every aspect of marriage, since "the ancient Greeks regarded marriage as a matter not merely of private, but also of public interest" (Westermarck, 1903, p. 142). Such interest is indicated by the laws of Solon (638 B.C.), the Athenian legislator, which required that the state inspect marriage. Similarly, Sparta's officials often prosecuted those who remained single or married quite late.

In general, three major marriage systems evolved in ancient Greece: the Homeric, the Athenian, and the Spartan.

Homeric marriage. Of these, the Homeric ordinarily involved a preliminary meeting between the groom's and the bride's representatives, who discussed the gifts—usually cattle—with which the wife was bought. This custom, which was later abandoned, explains why Homer, in the *Odyssey,* described Penelope as a richly endowed wife (XXIV, 294; see also *Iliad* VI, 394). Concerning the gifts, Westermarck wrote that "the father did not always keep the wedding presents for his own use, but bestowed them, wholly or in part, on the daughter as her marriage portion" (1903, p. 406).

Instead of such gifts, the groom sometimes offered his services to the bride's father. This practice constituted a desirable alternative, in view of the frequent wars during the Homeric age.

At other times, the groom was selected through a contest. Danaus, for example, after giving Hypermnestra, one of his 50 daughters, to Lynceus, proclaimed athletic games in which the winners were to receive her sisters as prizes. Similar stories deal with Antaeus and his daughter, as well as with Icarius and his daughter Penelope, whom he gave to Ithaca's King Odysseus.

Athenian marriage. Solon appears to have made marriage compulsory in Athens. In *De Amore Prolis* (2), Plutarch of Chaeronea averred that "animals do not wait for laws against celibacy or late marriage, as did Solon's citizens."

Moreover, extreme emphasis was placed on endogamy, marriage with an alien constituting a criminal offense. In *Pericles*

(37), Plutarch spoke of "a law that only those whose parents on both sides were Athenians should be regarded as Athenians."

In addition, marriage was usually arranged by the families involved. Due to Asiatic influences, romantic love was reserved for mistresses only. After the age of 20, however, a man was ordinarily allowed to marry without his father's consent. On the other hand, innocent and docile girls of 15, who lacked adequate training in practically all areas, were often given to husbands at least 30 years old.

In general, there were two main types of marriage in Athens. The more common was the giving of a young woman to her prospective husband by her father or guardian. The second type involved an heiress who lacked a guardian. Such cases were brought before the archon, and the next of kin, usually a relative on the father's side, became the woman's husband. Naturally, as is indicated by Demosthenes' *Contra Macartatus,* if the heiress were poor, the next of kin was ordinarily unwilling to marry her. The archon then forced the relative to do so, or, at least, compelled him to facilitate her marriage to another person by portioning her.

Spartan marriage. In Sparta, the officials "punished not merely him who did not marry, but even the man who married late" (Duruy, 1889, Vol. IV, Sec. 2, p. 541, n. 1). In *Lycurgus,* Plutarch also reported that, at first, marriage took place secretly, the husband visiting his wife only at night. Since such relations often lasted for years, it is no wonder that children were sometimes born before such secrecy came to an end.

In the same work Plutarch revealed that marriage by capture persisted as a symbolic feature:

For their marriages women were carried off by force when they were mature and quite ripe, and not when they were too young and unfit for marriage. After a woman was carried off in this way, the so-called bridesmaid took her in charge, cut her hair close to the head, dressed her in a man's cloak and shoes, and left her alone on a pallet, on the floor, in the dark. Then the bridegroom, composed and sober, and not flown with wine or influenced by excesses . . . walked stealthily into the room where the bride was lying. There he loosed her virgin's zone and carried her in his arms to the marriage bed (15).

Marriage Ceremonies

A vestige of marriage by capture was also included in the Athenian marriage ceremony.

In general, marriage in Athens was contracted in a temple, but the services of a priest were not always necessary. The entire ceremony was usually spectacular, except in cases where the groom was not marrying for the first time. Then, one of his friends merely brought his future wife to him from her house. Equally unimpressive was the procedure in very ancient times, when the simple ceremony was accompanied by a brief wedding feast. Later, however, two major features were distinguished: the betrothal, involving the financial aspects and a legal document, and the elaborate ceremony of the nuptials.

The ceremonies began with a sacrifice to some god or gods. Part of the sacrifice consisted in dedicating the bride to the gods by offering a few locks of her hair. Before leaving her house, the bride further dedicated her maiden girdle and toys to Artemis or another deity. Another sacrifice by her father included a formula by means of which his daughter was transferred to the control of her husband and the worship of his own family gods.

On the wedding day, the doors of the couple's houses were decorated with colorful garlands. The bride and bridegroom were themselves crowned with beautiful wreaths and, like their families and guests, wore gay and festal clothes, a long veil being added to the bride's attire. On the same day, the groom and his bride were bathed in water carried from the famous fountain Callirrhoe or Enneacrunus, situated in the southeastern part of Athens. Because this water was often carried by a girl, there developed an Athenian practice of placing the image of a maiden carrying water on the graves of persons who died unmarried.

The nuptial procession was equally joyous. In front went the nuptial torches, which had been lit by one of the mothers-in-law. Behind the torches came the bridal chariot, drawn by horses and carrying the bride, next to whom sat the groom and the best man. (In Boeotia, as soon as the procession was over, the axle of the chariot was burned, thus emphasizing the irreversibility of marriage.) All the while, according to the *Pax* of Aristophanes (1316–1356), the musicians played their flutes and the people sang joyfully, "Hymen, Hymen, Ho!"

When the procession arrived at the groom's house, he and his bride stopped in front of the main entrance and engaged in a mock fight. The groom then indicated his future control over the bride by taking her in his arms and carrying her over the threshold.

One of the most important parts of the entire ceremony was the wedding feast, which took place in the groom's house. Its importance was due to the fact that, in reality, the guests were witnesses who might be asked later to prove the validity of the marriage, since no emphasis was placed on documentary evidence. In *Contra Onetor* (20), Demosthenes stated: "I asked Onetor and Timocrates whether, when the dowry was being paid, any witnesses were present . . . and they all replied severally that there were no witnesses present. . . . But can any of you believe that . . . Onetor and Timocrates gave so much money to Aphobus not in the presence of witnesses?"

To insure fertility on the part of the couple, the feast included the eating of sesame cakes. To achieve the same goal, the bride ate a quince, as Plutarch wrote in *Solon* (XX, 3), where he mentioned "the requirement that the bride eat a quince and be shut up in a chamber with the groom."

Lucianus of Samosata, in the *Convivium* (8), wrote that, for reasons to be discussed later, it was customary for the women who were present at the wedding feast to occupy different tables from the male guests.

After the feast, a chorus of beautiful maidens gathered before the bridal chamber, where they danced and sang the epithalamion. This form of composition was of two types, one sung in the evening and another sung in the morning to wake the groom and his bride.

On the third day after the wedding, the bride received various gifts from her relatives. On the same day, she appeared without her veil for the first time.

An additional custom involved Athena's goatskin aegis, which was taken by a priestess to the bride's home. It seems that contact with the aegis was believed to insure fertility on the part of the bride.

Polygamy

Monogamous unions were not always typical. In fact, the Athenians believed that, many centuries earlier, some form of group marriage, or even matriarchy, prevailed until Cecrops, a Pelasgic hero who founded Athens and became Attica's first king, introduced monogamy. In the *Deipnosophistae* (XIII, 2), Athenaeus mentioned that Clearchus the Solensian wrote the following in his treatise on *Proverbs:* "But Cecrops was the first man in Athens to marry one male to one female only; before then, random unions were common." He also added that Cecrops was called double-natured, "since, before his time, people didn't know their fathers, as there were many men who might have been so."

Accordingly, monogamy became so common that ancient authors mentioned very few cases of bigamy (certain tyrants in some Hellenic colonies) or polygyny (Priam, Troy's last king). In his *Historiae,* however, Polybius stated that the other form of polygamy, polyandry, was not unusual in Sparta, where a few men, especially brothers, often married the same woman.

Dowry

In Homer's time, a marriageable woman did not need a dowry. On the contrary, it was the suitor who was expected to present her father with gifts, sometimes in installments, usually in the form of cattle.

Later, however, the dowry, which was rather small at first, became customary, although not required by formal law. According to Westermarck, the Greeks then "regarded a union into which the woman entered without dowry as concubinage, rather than as marriage" (1903, p. 429).

When this custom prevailed in Athens, the dowry of a daughter was discussed at the time of her betrothal. If her father were dead, her oldest brother supplied the dowry. This financial arrangement was aimed at the bride's future welfare, since, under Athenian law, she had no claims on the property of her spouse. Indeed, the husband, who was required to give a guarantee for its return, merely administered the dowry during the couple's married life. Moreover, if his wife died, he was expected to pass the dowry to their children or, if they were childless, to the wife's family.

These securities did not prevent the Athenian father from regarding female children as a liability. Plato himself disapproved of the dowry with vehemence, as he considered it conducive to avarice.

Housing

The Homeric house usually had three main parts: the courtyard, the men's hall, and the women's hall. Apparently, as indicated by the *Odyssey* (XX, 258), the threshold in front of the main entrance was of stone. The entrance itself consisted of colossal folding doors.

The men's hall, a structure of gigantic dimensions supported by towering pillars, included the hearth in its upper part, where cooking took place. According to Homer (*Odyssey,* XX, 123), the maidens "gathered together and were kindling on the hearth untiring fire." In the women's hall, where they engaged in various domestic activities, was the bridal chamber, while the women's common sleeping rooms were on the upper floor (XXIII, 192). This architectural design, therefore, necessitated the inclusion of a stairway: Penelope "climbed the high staircase to her chamber" (XXI, 5).

In general, even during the Golden Age, the Greek house was small and exceedingly simple, with plain walls which were sometimes covered with stucco or plaster. The walls consisted of bricks of unbaked clay, which explains why few Greek houses have been found by archaeologists. The nature of the walls also explains why Plato (*Leges,* 831e) referred to burglars as wallbreakers, as it was much easier for a thief to enter through the wall than through the door or windows.

The interior was equally plain. In the *Republic* (II, 372e–373a), Plato derogatorily spoke of wall-painting as a sign of a luxurious city, and Xenophon was furious when Alcibiades became the first Athenian to paint the walls of his house. "Regarding painting and decorations," objected Xenophon, "they rob us of more delights than they give" (*Memorabilia,* III, viii, 10). Like the walls, the floors of the house were simply covered with plaster—the introduction of mosaics has been associated with the kings of Pergamus. The roof was usually flat, and people used to walk on it, as is indicated by the *Lysistrata* of Aristophanes, where the *Probulus* speaks of the Adonis dirge on the roof (389). On the other hand, doors between rooms often consisted of a curtain which might be dyed or embroidered, while windows were ordinarily found in the upper floor. Simplicity was also typical of the furniture: a variety of kitchen utensils; chairs, couches, and beds, which were often made of bronze; adjustable tripods that functioned as tables; chests for the clothes; and water clocks and sundials.

The furniture also included portable stoves or chafing dishes for artificial heating. It seems that the chimney was always in the kitchen, and that the *capnodoce* mentioned by Herodotus in his *Historiae* (VIII, 137) was merely an opening in the roof and not a real chimney.

The Father

The father in Greece's patriarchal family system was the sole lord of his legal wife, children, concubines, and slaves. His functions included various priestly duties, as well as the direct or indirect management of all nonreligious affairs of his household. He even "had the right to accept or reject his child at birth, and could expose any child which he did not wish to rear" (Elmer, 1945, p. 80).

During the Homeric age, the patriarch seems to have remained master of his household as long as he was mentally and physically able. Later on, as Greece reached higher peaks of progress, his power declined to some extent. In general, it is doubtful whether the Greek father had as much authority as his Roman counterpart. Even in Homeric times, as the case of Ithaca's King Laertes indicates, a patriarch might occasionally be deposed by his son.

Still, the male citizen, who controlled both the household and society, succeeded in avoiding manual labor almost completely. He thus was able to climb the Olympian heights of the sublime Hellenic civilization, but at the expense of his women's and slaves' welfare.

Women

Indeed, the Greek woman's status, unlike that of the Hebrew woman, began virtually equal to the man's position, but soon declined considerably and remained quite low. Therefore, although in prehistoric Greece some form of matriarchy seems to have prevailed, during the Golden Age *woman* became practically synonymous with *slave*.

The Homeric woman. Even as early as Homer's time, women were not equal to men. Yet, according to ancient epic poems, they enjoyed extensive freedom, respect, and men's dignified love. As single women, although chastity was emphasized quite strictly, they were allowed to converse and dance with young men, both inside and outside the home.

During this period, married women were usually confined to the house, but such seclusion was not of the strict Oriental type. At home, they supervised the female slaves, engaged in weaving and spinning, and washed the family's clothing. It is interesting to note that even the daughters of kings participated in such domestic activities.

Sappho and the women of Lesbos. During the seventh century B.C., the women of Lesbos, a large Greek island in the Aegean Sea, were still free. One of them, Sappho, the great poetess of the Aeolian school, organized a literary club for women, the members of which asserted their rights and mixed freely in general society. It was such liberty that led later writers to conclude, perhaps incorrectly, that immorality was one of the literary club's characteristics (homosexuality between women is now known as Lesbianism or Sapphism).

The freedom of the Lesbian women is also partially indicated by the fact that Sappho, who was only six years old when her father died, and who had three brothers, upbraided one of them in a poem because he spent a fortune to ransom a courtesan.

The Athenian woman. In Athens only two or three centuries later, however, women were no longer free. Aristocratic young men who had visited Asiatic cities adopted many of their customs, including female seclusion, which, through Greece's influence, later became part of Rome's culture also.

As a result, the Athenian woman was confined to her special apartments, where she led a monotonous life with her sons under seven, her daughters, and her female slaves. If she ever went out, she was accompanied by a trusted person and covered with a large veil. Moreover, she was not even introduced to her husband's male guests, who ate by themselves. Demosthenes said in his *Contra Neaera* that the wife might dine and converse with her spouse, if he were alone.

Her activities at home included weaving, making clothes, managing supplies, supervising cooking, and controlling the slaves. Needless to add, these activities no longer constituted sources of prestige for the wife, since, in view of the development of various industries in Athens, the household had ceased to be economically autonomous.

As if this loss were not enough, the wife was usually forced to remain illiterate, could not inherit property, and was not permitted to function as her own children's guardian. As a widow, said Pausanias in the *Periegesis,* she was further expected to remain loyal to her deceased husband by not remarrying and by accepting a new master selected by her spouse. Even the selling of women as slaves or concubines was common during the Attic period.

The greatest geniuses in Greece did not object to such injustice. Demosthenes ignominiously declared that the wife had two functions, to be a loyal housekeeper and to produce legitimate children. Menander considered her a necessary evil. Thucydides ignored women with infinite contempt. Plato, the greatest Athenian philosopher, thought them weak: "Do you know, then," he wrote in the *Republic,* "of any human activities in which the males do not surpass the females in all these respects? Must we make a long story of it by alleging weaving and the watching of pancakes and the boiling pot, whereupon the sex plumes itself and wherein its defeat will expose it to most laughter? You are right, he said; one may assert that one sex is far surpassed by the other in all things. Of course, many women are better than many men in many respects, but, in general, you are right . . . the woman is weaker than the man" (454–455). His pupil Aristotle carelessly attributed to nature feminine characteristics actually caused by social injustice, adding, "for the free

rules the slave, the male the female, and the man the child . . . for the slave does not have the deliberative part at all, while the female has it, but without full authority" (*Politics,* 1260a). Aristophanes, on the other hand, was ambivalent, sometimes satirizing the feminism of Euripides (his *argumentum ad hominem,* employed repeatedly, was that Clito, the tragedian's mother, was a lowly herb-seller!), while at other times, longing for a breeze of progress, he displayed supreme disgust with the vegetating conservative woman.

Only Euripides, the celebrated tragic poet and painter, imparted importance, emotions, and intelligence to his female characters. In the *Medea,* for instance, he exposes smug, weak, and selfish Jason's injustice to an emotional woman. Even he, perhaps because his first and second wives made him exceedingly unhappy, filled his 120 tragic and satiric plays with sayings about the inferiority of women and the superiority of men.

Still, the Athenian woman was not completely neglected. According to Plutarch's *Solon,* at least one law prohibited the ill treatment of wives. It was with this subject that Cratinus (519–422 B.C.), the Athenian comic poet, dealt in his comedy *Pytine* (The Wine Flask). Cratinus presents an unfortunate woman who takes her husband to court because he devotes most of his time to the wine flask, constantly neglecting his wife.

In general, after considering all of the extant Greek classics, the modern reader will agree that the most fascinating and most comprehensive picture of the ancient Athenian wife is found in Xenophon's *Oeconomicus,* where Ischomachus speaks to Socrates about his young wife's wool spinning and other duties:

She was not quite fifteen when she came to me, and up to then she had been sheltered, seeing, hearing, and saying as little as possible. If, when she came, she only knew how to take wool and make a cloak out of it, and only how the spinning is given out to the servants, is not that as much as one should expect? . . . Well,

Socrates, as soon as she became obedient and sufficiently domesticated to converse with me, I questioned her, speaking in this way: "Tell me, darling, have you realized why I married you?" . . . My wife, Socrates, then replied to me: "How can I possibly help you? What is my power? All depends on you. My mother told me my duty is to be discreet." "Yes, by Jupiter," I said to her. "Yes, darling. My father told me the same." . . . "And what do you see," said the woman, "that I can possibly do to help in the improvement of our household?" "Why, by Jupiter," I said, "try to do as well as possible whatever the gods made you capable of doing and the law approves." "And what are these things?" she said. . . . I replied . . . ."It seems to me, God from the beginning made the woman's nature for the indoor and the man's for the outdoor tasks and cares. For he created the body and soul of the man more capable of enduring cold and heat and journeys and campaigns; and so he commanded him to do the outdoor tasks; but the woman's body he made less capable of these tasks, and so I believe that he commanded her to do the indoor work. And, knowing that to the woman's nature he gave and assigned the rearing of the infants, he gave to her more affection for babies than to the man. And because he also assigned to the woman the protection of the stores, knowing that for protection a fearful soul is no disadvantage, God gave to the woman a larger share of fear than to the man. And, knowing that he who has the outdoor tasks will have to defend them against any offender, he gave him a larger share of courage. . . . Now, darling, since we know what God has imposed on each of us, we must each try to do our respective duties as well as possible" (VII, 4–42).

After many additional comments of this nature, Ischomachus says:

Well, Socrates, one day I saw that her face was made up, as she had rubbed in white lead in order to appear whiter than she was, and alkanet juice to make her cheeks rosier than they were in reality; and she was wearing high heels to seem taller than she was by nature. "Tell me, darling," I said, "when would you consider me more lovable as a partner in our possessions, if I showed them to you as they actually are, without boasting of having more than I do or concealing some of the goods, or if I tried to trick you by telling that I have more than I actually do, showing you counterfeit money and necklaces that are wooden inside, and telling you that clothes which soon fade are genuine purple?" "Hush!" she broke in immediately; "I beg you, never be like that; for I would not be able, if you were like that, to love you with all my heart and soul." "Then, darling," said I, "are we not joined together by another tie to be partners in our bodies?" "Well," she answered, "that's what people say." "Then, when," I said, "would I seem more lovable in this partnership of the body, if I tried to keep my body healthy and strong and give it to you in this condition and present it to you when its complexion is really beautiful, or if I smeared my cheeks with red lead and painted myself under my eyes with rouge and showed myself to you like a statue and took you in my arms, cheating you and offering you to see and touch red lead instead of my real skin?" "Oh," she said, "neither red lead would I prefer to touch instead of you, nor a statue's color would I prefer to see instead of yours, nor your eyes would I prefer greasy rather than healthy." "Then, my darling . . . remember that I, too, prefer your own color to that of white lead and alkanet; for just as the gods made horses to delight in horses, cattle in cattle, sheep in sheep, so human beings believe that the pure human body is most delightful. These tricks may easily help to deceive outsiders, but those who live together are necessarily caught, if they try to deceive each other. For they are caught while leaving the bed in the morning, before they have a chance to make up their faces; or while they perspire; or while tears betray them; or while a bath shows them exactly as they are. . . ." And she asked me . . . how she could really become beautiful, instead of only appearing such. And I advised her, Socrates, not to sit about for ever . . . but to go around and see if everything is in its place. For I thought that this would give her occupation and a walk. I also said it was excellent exercise to mix flour and knead dough and to shake and fold cloaks and mattresses. With such exercise, I said, she would eat better and keep healthier, while her complexion would actually become more beautiful (X, 2–11).

The Spartan woman. Such subservience and docility were diametrically opposed to the liberalism of Sparta's women. In the

city of Lycurgus, wives were virtually equal
to their husbands, and it was not uncommon to see them walking unattended even
in Sparta's main streets. In view of the
state's militaristic ideology, which defined
the male as a potential warrior, this form of
emancipation was necessary, women being
regarded as mothers of warriors.

Besides this eugenic motive, the residential arrangements imposed on the male by
the state explain woman's freedom. Since
men were required to reside in barracks,
their continual absence necessitated their
wives' freedom.

Another explanation given by Plutarch
was that Lycurgus (ninth century B.C.),
Sparta's great legislator, was influenced by
Crete's matriarchal customs. Herodotus further stated that the culture of the Lycians,
who lived between Caria and Pamphylia in
Asia Minor, and who were of Cretan origin, also had certain matriarchal characteristics. Crete itself seems to have been influenced by its propinquity to the Egyptian
society, whose female members enjoyed a
great deal of freedom.

Unfortunately, in view of the prevailing
militarism, regimentation, and eugenics,
which involved both males and females, this
form of equality often became synonymous
with the reduction of both sexes to healthy
subhuman beings. It is also significant that
eugenics did not actually prevent the de-
generation of the Spartans.

Children

Naturally, this militaristic ideology rendered fertility on the part of Spartan
women most desirable. For both military
and nonmilitary reasons, parents in other
parts of ancient Greece also valued it.

One of the ways in which fertility was
believed to be reinforced was the ritualistic
employment of blows, that is, the beating
of women worshipers at the festival of the
Thesmophoria. This festival, which was
celebrated in November throughout Greece,
but especially in Athens, and in which only

married women participated, was dedicated
to Demeter as the founder of the civic rite
of marriage and as the goddess of fair children.

Another ritual against barrenness included water from certain springs and
streams in various parts of Greece. Some
of them were the Elatus, a river in Arcadia,
a spring near Aphrodite's temple on Mount
Hymettus, and the Thespian spring on
Helicon.

Homeric children. Certainly, this emphasis on fertility was especially typical of the
Homeric times. Since, at this stage, the
economy was primarily agricultural and
pastoral, additional workers were most valuable and desirable. Women, therefore,
achieved their highest status upon becoming mothers. Even illegitimate children
were accepted. Needless to add, the loss of
a child was regarded as an unbearable misfortune.

As a result, the bonds between parents
and children were strong and affectionate.
The conqueror Achilles, moved by Priam's
entreaties and tears, restored Hector's body
to the old king and, respectfully and sym-
pathetically, permitted him a 12-day truce
for the funeral. As among the Hebrews,
caressing and kissing were also quite common. And when parents were old, their son
was expected to live with or near them so
that he might supply them with the necessary care and protection.

Athenian children. In Athens, the production of heirs was of paramount importance.
According to Plutarch's *Solon* (XX, 2),
there was a law "which permits an heiress,
in case the man under whose power and
authority she is placed by law is himself
unable to consort with her, to be married
by one of his next of kin. Some say . . . this
was a wise provision against those who are
unable to perform the duties of a husband,
and yet, for the sake of their property,
marry heiresses."

The newly born infant, however, was
not always accepted, as child exposure did
not constitute a crime. The father, when

the midwife brought his child to him, had the power to decide whether it was to be abandoned before a temple or on a hillside. Of course, in view of woman's lower status, female infants were exposed more frequently than male ones.

The newborn infant was bathed in oil and water and wrapped in long, narrow bands of woolen cloth. Then, after its neck had been decorated with charms, it was placed in a cradle, usually made of twigs woven together. On the fifth day, a ritual around the hearth placed the child under the aegis of the household gods. Finally, 10 days after its birth, the father officially recognized his child and named it.

If its parents were wealthy, the child was virtually taken away from its mother and given to a nurse to rear for some time. Even its food did not come from the mother, since it was customary to employ slaves and sometimes Spartan women to function as wet nurses.

As boys and girls grew older, they were allowed to play together until the age of seven. Among their toys, according to Aristotle, was a rattle created by Archytas, the ancient Da Vinci whose inventions included a wooden pigeon that could fly. Lead and clay models were also common. Additional amusement was provided by pets, particularly dogs, ducks, tortoises, and cockchafers. The cockchafer, a large beetle whose grubs live in the ground for three years, was tied to one end of a string, while the child held the other end and ran.

Athenian children were expected to respect and obey their parents. As Plato stated in the *Protagoras* (325d), "and if he readily obeys, well and good; if not, they straighten him with threats and blows like a piece of warped and twisted wood."

Of course, there were significant differences between the rearing of boys and of girls. The former, when very young, were encouraged to spend many hours in the courtyard, amusing themselves with balls and the games of tug of war and blindman's buff, as well as with inflated wineskins on which they engaged in juvenile acrobatics. Moreover, their education, as in the case of Sparta, emphasized the development of citizenship, but while the Spartans stressed militarism, the Athenian ideal was the Homeric man, who was both intellectual and athletic.

Unlike boys, who attended school, girls were trained mainly at home. First of all, when they were very young, they were taught singing and dancing, as well as games involving dolls, clay dishes, knucklebones, balls, swings, and seesaws, which they played in the courtyard. Most of their serious training was confined almost exclusively to embroidering, spinning, weaving, and, if the family were not wealthy, cooking.

Spartan children. In Sparta, main emphasis was placed on the production of healthy children. Eugenics, therefore, even in its most extreme forms, was a dominant program. Husbands were encouraged to promote the production of physically superior children by lending their wives to men healthier than themselves.

The purposes of the state were also realized by eliminating the sentiment of motherhood. Accordingly, a mother became exceedingly happy when her son died in battle. Daementa, for instance, who lost eight sons in this way, instead of shedding tears, was stirred to stentorian rapture: "Victory! Sparta, I bore them but to die for thee!"

Another eugenic measure consisted in destroying all defective infants by throwing them into the cavern Apothetae, near Mount Taygetus. All other infants were washed with wine, since the Spartans believed that the sickly ones would die in the process, while those who were born healthy would both survive and become stronger.

Children that succeeded in surviving the wine test were never swaddled. The freedom which the limbs and the body thus enjoyed usually led to the development of a strong and beautiful human being. The nurses further trained the little Spartans to face danger without crying, not to be afraid when left alone for long periods of time, and, similarly, to stay in the dark without fear. Many years of severe physical training followed for both boys and girls, which led Aristotle to remark (*Politics*, 1338a): "today some of the states reputed to be extremely interested in their children produce in them athletic habits that harm the body's form and growth, while the Spartans, who have avoided this error, brutalize their children through laborious exercises which, they believe, will make them very courageous." In Sparta, unlike the rest of Greece, except for Crete, this training and all other forms of education were controlled by the state.

For the boys, the brutalization mentioned by Aristotle began at the age of seven, when they "left their homes . . . to live in barracks" (Cunningham, 1940, p. 62). There, as Plutarch wrote, all training emphasized absolute obedience. At the age of 12, a much more severe type of physical and military education began. During this period, which lasted until he was 30, the young Spartan wore only a light upper garment that was replaced every 12 months. At 18 he entered the class of youths, and at 20 he commenced a 10-year course in brutal military training. It was only when this course had been completed that the young Spartan was considered a man and was permitted to marry and attend the public assembly.

The training of the Spartan girls did not differ much from that of the boys. As Grote wrote, "the Spartan damsels underwent a bodily training analogous to that of the Spartan youth" (1857, Vol. II, p. 384). Stripped of their clothes, they took part in public games, contests, and gymnastics. Even their ordinary clothing was simple and liberal, consisting of a short and sleeveless tunic that exposed the knees as well as, through two vertical side slits, the thighs.

Abortion

Regarding abortion, which, as is indicated by Lysias' *Contra Antigonus,* was not unknown in ancient Greece, and which was often performed by midwives, Plato wrote (*Republic,* 461c): "when the men and the women have passed the age of legal reproduction . . . we must admonish them preferably not even to bring to light what is conceived in this way, but to dispose of it, if they cannot prevent the birth." His pupil Aristotle added (*Politics,* 335b), "there should be a law forbidding the rearing of misshapen children . . . there should be a limit fixed to the production of children, and if, through coitus and despite these regulations, any people have a child, abortion must be procured before the child develops sensation and life; for the distinction between legal and criminal abortion will be based on having sensation and being alive."

Adoption

Adoption was also common in classical Greece. However, only respected citizens who had no male heirs were allowed, while still living or by will, to adopt a son for the sake of insuring the family's continuity. Moreover, if a man had daughters only, it was common for one of them to be betrothed to the adoptive son, whose rights were equal to those of the male heir who might be born later. In such cases, the other daughters were provided with dowries. Again, when a citizen died childless, a male relative was selected by the state to function as adopted son and heir.

Inheritance

It seems, then, that great emphasis was placed on property and family continuity. In fact, this was the main goal of Athenian inheritance law. And, since an illegitimate child could not inherit his father's property, the wife's chief function was to produce a legitimate heir.

In general, the law stated that the "oldest son alone could inherit the family estates, while movable property was inherited equally among the sons" (Sait, 1938, p. 112). But if a citizen died childless, his nearest male relative inherited his property, and if there were no male relatives, a female one became his heiress.

The wife herself could never inherit her deceased husband's estate. In fact, she was not even permitted to reside in her deceased spouse's house, unless she was pregnant. Even then she was required to leave as soon as her child was born. In Demosthenes' *Contra Macartatus* (75), when the orator asks the clerk to read the law, the latter begins as follows: "The archon should protect orphans, heiresses, and families becoming extinct, as well as women remaining in the houses of their deceased spouses, declaring that they are pregnant."

Spartan law was much more liberal. Indeed, women were allowed by the state to inherit both family estates and movable property. With some degree of amazement, Aristotle reported (*Politics,* 1270a): "almost two fifths of the entire country is owned by women, because of the number of women who inherit estates and the custom of large dowries."

Divorce

Not much is known concerning the divorce laws of ancient Greece. The few passages in classical writings dealing with this subject refer mainly to Athens. It is known, however, that in Homeric times great emphasis was placed on the indissolubility of marriage.

In general, divorce was regarded as a private affair in Athens, especially when it was secured on grounds such as mere dislike or the wife's barrenness. In the case of adultery, however, the state interfered to some extent, although even then the husband was allowed to punish the offenders himself. In Demosthenes' *Contra Neaera* (87), the court clerk reads the law regarding adultery, mentioning the following: "When he has caught the adulterer, it will be unlawful for the person who has caught him to continue living with his wife, and if he does so, he will lose his civil rights." It must be remembered, however, that the husband did not always seek a divorce with eagerness, since the law required him to return his divorced wife's dowry to her family.

The wife was also allowed by the state to divorce her husband. As Plutarch stated in *Alcibiades,* no legal procedure was required for this purpose, as long as the husband gave his consent. But if he refused to do so, the wife was expected to appear before the archon and supply evidence of her spouse's cruelty. She was further permitted to secure a divorce when her husband lost his freedom in war or by being sold as a slave. In all such cases, the wife's property was returned to her family.

Two additional features characterized divorce in ancient Greece: the husband was required to pay alimony, and the presence of witnesses was absolutely necessary. As Lysias reported in *Contra Alcibiades* (I, 29), "Hipponicus assembled a number of witnesses and put away his wife, saying that this man had been entering his house, not as her brother, but as her spouse."

Adultery, Incest, and Homosexuality

As has already been mentioned, adultery usually led to divorce, for Athenian law emphasized endogamy and the purity of the citizens' lineage. Severe measures were, therefore, taken to prevent adultery. Accordingly, when the law was violated, the husband might kill both the adulterer and the adulteress, his wife or concubine. The adulteress was not permitted to enter the temple, and if she did, any person was allowed to offend her in any way, as long as he did not mutilate or kill her.

Like adultery, incest was forbidden. Indeed, in Homeric Greece, there were very few marriages between close relatives, while brother-sister unions were found only among mythological figures.

Homosexuality, on the other hand, was not uncommon, and it seems that its prevalence in Greece "owes its origin chiefly to the immemorial mimicry of the female sex by male priests" (Briffault, 1927, Vol. III, p.

208). In Sparta, homosexuality between boys and men in the military barracks was very common. In fact, it was encouraged so much that boys often competed with one another for the love of their officers, who, in their turn, devoted a great deal of time and energy to the educational success of the boys they loved. It was equally honorable for young virgins to seek lovers among Sparta's most respected matrons. As Plutarch wrote in *Lycurgus* (XVIII, 4), "this kind of love was so approved by them that even young girls sought lovers among good and noble women."

Prostitution

Prostitution was also prevalent. In Homeric times, for example, concubines were often given as prizes or even bought like animals to live in the same house as their master's family.

Later, as woman's status declined, and as the domestic relationship became less important, the male felt forced to seek among prostitutes the companionship and sex appeal which he was denied in his home. Few of these women were citizens. Most, especially those belonging to the lower classes, were foreign. Since the state taxed them rather heavily, it was usually unwilling to deprive itself of much of its revenue by allowing prostitutes to return to their home countries. Such women, therefore, were both tolerated and protected by the state.

At least part of this protection seems to have resulted from a definite association between prostitution and the worship of Aphrodite, the goddess of love. Indeed, in Corinth and other cities, the sacred slaves, mentioned by Philo, Strabo, Pindar, and others, were public courtesans and votaries of this goddess. In other words, religious prostitution was prevalent in certain ancient Greek communities (Dreikurs, 1946, p. 53).

The terms employed with reference to the unconventional women were *porne, pallace, auletris,* and *hetaera*. Of these, *porne* referred to the common prostitute (cf. por-

nography), who was usually bought (*pernemi:* to sell). The *pallace,* on the other hand, was a captive or bought slave kept by a married man. The *auletris* (flute girl), like the Japanese geisha, was a professional dancer and singer who entertained men in their homes or in public. Finally, the *hetaera* (companion) was similar to the French courtesan—highly trained and educated, respected, and associating with the noblest men of Greece (the term itself, however, often referred to the concubine and even to the lawful wife).

Perhaps the most famous comparison between these women and wives is found in Demosthenes' *Contra Neaera* (122): "Harlots we keep for the sake of pleasure only, concubines for daily service, but wives for bearing us legitimate children and acting as loyal guardians of our households."

Summary

In brief, the ancient Greek family system was characterized by the following main features: (a) although concubinage was fairly common, a man usually had only one lawful wife at a time; (b) a union without dowry was regarded as concubinage; (c) the typical house consisted of a courtyard, the men's hall, and the women's apartments; (d) the father was the sole lord of his legal wife, children, concubines, and slaves; (e) at first, women were equal to men, but their status later declined considerably; (f) child-rearing stressed citizenship, but Sparta emphasized eugenics and militarism more than Athens did; (g) adoption laws were aimed at family and property continuity; (h) the same goals were also achieved by inheritance law; (i) both men and women could secure a divorce, but the former had more privileges in this area; (j) adultery on the part of a woman was punished severely, since much emphasis was placed on endogamy and pure lineage; (k) incest was usually forbidden; (l) homosexuality was prevalent both in Athens and in Sparta; and (m) there were several socially accepted forms of prostitution, the highest being that of the celebrated hetaerae.

THE ANCIENT ROMAN FAMILY

The Roman family consisted of the *pater familias* (father), his wife, his sons, his unmarried daughters, his sons' wives, sons, and unmarried daughters, and his slaves.

The main features of this family system were as follows:

Engagement

Engagement was known as *sponsalia,* as Seneca's *De Beneficiis* (1, 9, 4) indicates; for, at this stage, the official parental response was *"Spondeo!,"* that is, "I promise in marriage!" (Plautus, *Aulularia,* 2, 2, 75; *Trinummus,* 5, 2, 34). Not infrequently, according to the *Codex Justinianeus* (5, 71, 8), which was compiled in A.D. 530, the same term was employed by the ancient Romans to designate the betrothal gift, as well as the betrothal feast (Cicero, *Epistulae ad Q. Fratrem,* 2, 6, 1).

An additional feature of the engagement ceremony was the placing by the groom of a ring on the fourth finger of his bride's left hand. As Aulus Gellius wrote in *Noctes Atticae* (X, 10), this finger was selected because, according to the Romans, a mysterious nerve connects it with the heart.

Many ancient authors indicated that girls were often engaged when they were still quite young. They also reported that, at least in later times, engagement was rather long. Tullia, the daughter of Cicero, for instance, was betrothed when she was only 10 years old, while her marriage occurred at the age of 13.

Dowry

An important consideration at the time of the *sponsalia* was the dowry or marriage portion. This was the bride's contribution, but, according to Roman law, the husband was not permitted to have complete control of it later on. In fact, particularly in later times, although the husband had the right to dispose of the income of the dowry, he was not allowed to attach it to his estate. On the contrary, if he died, or if he divorced his wife, the marriage portion was usually returned to the bride's father, who had remained its legal owner.

Marriage

Such financial arrangements, together with political deals, constituted the main considerations in the typical union, for marriage in Rome was ordinarily arranged, professional marriage brokers with well-organized bureaus functioning as intermediaries. That courtship was not emphasized is further indicated by the fact that the Latin language lacks verbs corresponding to the English *to court* or *to woo*—the verbs *ambio, colo, blandior,* and *proco* or *procor* do not exactly mean *to court.* An additional goal of marriage, commonly the most important one, was the procreation of children. Since it facilitated the continuity of the family's religious traditions, it was regarded as a patriotic and religious duty. Accordingly, as Cicero stated in *De Legibus* (III, 3), the state taxed rather heavily those men who remained unmarried. The famous *Lex Papia Poppaea* considered as enemies of the state persons who had not married by the age of 25. The same law was equally critical of widowed and divorced Romans who refused to remarry. Nevertheless, only Roman citizens enjoyed the right to contract a valid civil marriage.

Regarding age at first marriage, ancient authors reported that women ordinarily married at about 15. This, of course, was not too early, since in this southern part of Europe women matured when quite young, and no advanced education forced them to postpone matrimony. Still, marriage between children, which has been very common in the Orient, was extremely rare in ancient Rome. The men were usually much older than their wives, and this was so common that the public tended to disapprove of men who married at a very early age. Moreover, waiting was not difficult for them, since they were not expected to emphasize chastity before marriage.

Concerning the legal aspects of marriage, Roman law included certain terms to describe various matrimonial arrangements. The most important ones were the following:

Matrimonium justum: true marriage, between persons with the same social status. In later times, however, "intermarriage was allowed between patricians and plebeians" (Thorndike, 1934, p. 178).

Matrimonium non justum: a form of legalized concubinage, involving a citizen and a woman of lower social status. Children resulting from a union of this type were regarded neither as heirs nor as members of the citizen's family.

Sine in manum conventione: in such cases, the wife remained under the authority of her father, her husband having no control over her.

Cum conventione uxoris in manum viri: as Cicero indicated in *Topica* (3, 14), this union placed the wife under the authority of her husband, or under that of his father. Its forms were three, *confarreatio, coemptio,* and *usus.*

Confarreatio or *farreum:* this form, which is mentioned in the *Aeneis* of Vergil (4, 374), was a patrician marriage. Being of a religious nature, it included an important sacrifice to Jupiter Farreus and required the presence of the *flamen Dialis,* Jupiter's patrician priest. Ten witnesses were also present.

Coemptio: this plebeian form later became a mixed marriage between a patrician and a plebeian. Its name, meaning "joint purchase," indicates that, as Cicero wrote in *Oratio pro L. Flacco* (34, 84), this union involved a pretended purchase of the bride. The "sale" was conducted by the *libripens,* a person holding the "balance," in the presence of five witnesses.

Usus: this, too, was ordinarily a plebeian marriage, requiring the consent of the bride. Being similar to the English common-law unions, or to the canonical *matrimonium per verba de praesenti* (marriage by words of the present), it was valid only when the spouses had cohabited for a year, the wife having never been absent for three days.

Contubernium: this, as Quintus Curtius Rufus, a Roman historian, stated in *Historiarum Alexandri Magni Libri Decem* (5, 5, 20), was a marriage of slaves, but the term also applied to unions between slaves and free persons.

Concubinatus: this form of cohabitation involved two unmarried free persons or a single free man and a maidservant; it differed from legal marriage.

Imparia matrimonia: these were mixed marriages between pagans and Christians that became quite common during the fourth century A.D. (Dill, 1910, p. 13).

Polygamy was one of the unlawful forms of marriage. Indeed, the Romans never legalized such unions, since they stressed monogamy more than the Greeks did.

The Wedding Ceremony

As in most ancient civilizations, the wedding ceremony was rather elaborate, but many Roman families often omitted certain of its features. In general, its main component elements were four: the marriage contract, the giving away of the bride, the wedding procession—usually at dusk, which led to the custom of including torches—and the wedding feast at the house of the bridegroom.

According to Cicero's *De Divinatione ad M. Brutum* (I, 16, 28), the festivities began with a religious ceremony by means of which the two families consulted the omens. On the day before the wedding, a special sacrifice was also made to the lares, the deified spirits of ancestors, who protected and guarded the Roman household. In addition, the bride wore a beautiful dress, which, together with a bright veil, constituted her attire on the wedding day, too.

On the following day, the ceremony was continued with a mock fight during which the bride fled to her mother's arms, from which she was taken with pretended force by the groom and his companions. Perhaps this fight was a vestige of the ancient marriage by capture. The Romans themselves asserted that it was a survival of the Sabine marriage in the time of Romulus.

The aforementioned veil, unlike that of the Greek bride, was red. To her dress, on the other hand, was added a woolen belt encircling the hips, which symbolized marital stability—it also seems to have been the precursor of the "true lover's knot." Moreover, the bride wore an iron ring on her fourth finger, as well as other ornaments given to her by her husband to be. Her hair was parted by means of a spear, which, like the mock fight mentioned previously, was another vestige of the ancient marriage by capture. As Plutarch reported in *Pompeius* (55), an additional decorative feature was flower wreaths for both the bridegroom and his future wife.

The wedding procession included, among many other things, the distaff and the spindle of the bride, which were carried rather conspicuously after her. Vergil added in *Eclogae* (VIII, 30) that the bridegroom himself, joyously and merrily, scattered nuts—the symbol of fertility and prosperity —for the cheerful lads who participated in the procession. (In many countries rice is now preferred.)

When the procession reached the groom's house, the bride continued this symbolism by rubbing ointment on the door to insure future prosperity. She also placed a bit of wool on the same door, perhaps to indicate that, in the future, the welfare of her new family would be promoted through her unceasing labor.

Then, as Plautus reported (*Casina*, VI, 4, 1), the bride was carried over the threshold by the groom, which seems to have been an additional vestige of the old marriage by capture. At the same time, according to Cicero's *Oratio pro L. Murena* (12, 27), the bride saluted her husband with these words: *"Quando tu Gaius, ego Gaia"* ("When thou art lord, I am lady").

At the house of the groom, the festivities were continued joyously. One of the features of the ceremony was the laurel cake or wedding cake, which was eaten by the guests (Cato, *De Re Rustica,* 121).

On the following day, as Aulus Gellius said in *Noctes Atticae* (II, 24, 14), the bridegroom invited friends and relatives to a drinking party. Incidentally, this form of feast was quite common in ancient Rome, since it followed many other festive occasions, such as the birth of a child and the like.

Needless to add, such ceremonies, particularly when their major phases were not omitted, were extremely expensive. Still, the typical Roman was eager to spend as much money as possible on such occasions. It is no wonder, therefore, that Augustus was not exactly successful later on when he adopted measures aimed at making weddings less lavish and extravagant.

Housing

Few Romans could afford to be similarly extravagant regarding their houses. Most segments of the typical Roman house consisted of wood, which explains why fires were exceedingly common in the Eternal City. In fact, as Aulus Gellius stated (*Noctes Atticae,* XV, 1), such catastrophes prevented many Romans from investing in buildings, although owning houses was unusually lucrative. It was Nero's famous Building Act that made fires less frequent, since the use of materials that were not fireproof now became illegal.

Another significant characteristic of early Roman housing had resulted from the typical family's passion for privacy—a passion that was prevalent throughout Roman history. This characteristic was the absence of "windows on the ground floor of houses" (Heitland, 1923, Vol. III, p. 489).

In later times, when Rome was a more populous city, houses were built taller, but the law imposed certain limits on height. Under Augustus, for example, the limit was

70 feet. Houses, however, seemed much higher than they were in reality, since the typical street was extremely narrow.

The Father

Another feature of the Roman family system was the high status which the father enjoyed. Being even the priest of the family, he made arrangements for the worship of the household gods as well as of his ancestors, thus insuring both religious and family continuity.

His *manus* was also impresssive. Although this term often referred to the legal power of the master of the household over all family members, usually, as Cicero implied in the *Oratio pro L. Flacco* (34, 84), it was confined to the husband's power over his wife, which was almost unlimited. Nevertheless, "*manus* implied not only the wife's subordination to the husband, but also the husband's obligation to protect the wife" (Westermarck, 1903, p. 17). In later times, this form of power declined considerably, as woman's social status became higher.

An additional characteristic of the Roman father's position was the *patria potestas* (paternal authority). This type of authority "was perhaps more developed among the Romans than among any other western people" (Flugel, 1939, p. 128). The father arranged his children's marriages; he also controlled their earnings, and, "Although a grown-up son might establish a separate household of his own, all his property, however acquired, belonged legally to his father" (Mommsen, 1910, Vol. III, p. 11). Then, the father had the right to scourge, banish, and even sell his children as slaves. Furthermore, according to the fourth of the *Duodecim Tabulae* (Twelve Tables), which discusses paternal authority, he was sometimes permitted to kill his children. Roman historians, however, described such cases in a manner indicating that this right was seldom exercised. Besides, like *manus,* the *patria potestas* was in later times limited considerably.

Women

The social status of the Roman woman was much lower than that of the man. Indeed, the law often referred to her as a creature characterized by weakness. Her property was controlled by her husband, who, in addition, was allowed by law to sell or kill his spouse.

But, since this right was seldom exercised, and since women enjoyed many privileges, it is correct to assert, as Sait (1938) did, that, in general, "the position of the Roman matron was one of dignity" (p. 148). Similarly, Woody (1949) stated: "Despite numerous restraints, Roman women enjoyed a more dignified status than did those of Greece" (p. 504). To a great extent, the wife was the mistress of the household and was not confined to anything analogous to the Greek women's apartments. Her husband not only took his meals with her, but also consulted her concerning various issues, except for serious social, political, and intellectual matters. Furthermore, she was free to nurse her children and, to a certain degree, control their rearing. Even the inheritance laws gave her a share equal to that of the legitimate child. When a woman went out, however, she was expected to have her husband's permission as well as an escort.

In later times, woman's status rose. In the second century B.C., for example, marriages *cum manu* were extremely rare, the wife and her property remaining under her father's authority. But, since the father seldom functioned in an authoritarian manner, his married daughter gained freedom, power, and some wealth. This trend had already been generated by the first and second Punic Wars (264–241 B.C. and 218–201 B.C.), for the absence of men, many of whom had died fighting the Carthaginians, had left women free to control their households and to secure important outside positions. When the wars were over, the Eternal City emerged wealthier and its women more independent. Such emancipation, however, was accompanied by licentious habits and some degree of masculinization on the part of the women. When the patriarchal barbarians finally conquered Rome, its female population was again subordinated to the authority of fathers and husbands.

Children

In ancient Rome, children, too, were subordinated to their fathers, who often treated them as subhuman beings, despite the Romans' strong desire for offspring. Infanticide, for instance, was fairly common and was practiced even after the third century A.D., when, for the first time, the law attempted to abolish it. If the father wished to rear his child, however, he indicated his desire merely by taking it in his hands immediately after birth. After this, a small amulet was placed around the infant's neck, in an effort to protect it from evil forces.

On the ninth day after a boy's birth—the eighth for a girl—the day of purification was observed, which involved a sacrifice, a feast, and the naming of the child. By now, the mother had assumed a great deal of responsibility for the child's rearing, which she controlled rather extensively. Nevertheless, in later centuries, many women preferred to employ barbarian wet nurses and to leave child care primarily to slaves.

In early times, child-rearing, which was supervised mainly by the mother, stressed such ideals as health, courage, prudence, obedience, modesty, piety, and religiousness. In addition, girls were taught spinning and weaving, while boys were instructed by the father in reading, writing, arithmetic, agriculture, and law. Religious training was emphasized so much that both "boys and girls served as acolytes in the worship of the Lares and Penates, the household gods" (Cunningham, 1940, p. 63).

Education was home-centered, although much of it was the responsibility of the school. Ancient authors reported that education at school lasted eight months a year, the period between June and November constituting a vacation. Unlike the Greeks, the Romans did not stress gymnastics beyond what was included in military training.

In later times, as Rome grew more powerful and cosmopolitan, education became more extensive. Both boys and girls were now taught not only the works of Latin writers, such as Terence, Vergil, and Horace, but also those of Greek authors. Homer was especially popular, his *Iliad* and *Odyssey* being two of the most common textbooks in Rome. To facilitate such instruction, innumerable Greek slaves were employed as professors. In addition, many young Romans were sent to Greece to complete their education. There, the most popular universities were Plato's Academy, Aristotle's Peripatetic School, the Stoic School, and the university of the Epicureans.

Adoption

The male-centeredness of the Roman society was reflected in its adoption laws: Women were not permitted to adopt, whereas men, as long as they were childless, could easily do so.

The main types of adoption were two, *arrogatio* and adoption proper. The former involved an independent person adopted by a man unlikely to have children of his own at any time in the future.

Those adopted under the second form were previously dependent on their own fathers. The natural father merely sold his son, thus transferring him to the *patria potestas* of the adopter. This was accomplished by means of a legal transaction.

Abortion

Although some Romans were eager to acquire children through adoption, others were equally eager to rid themselves of potential offspring through abortion. In vain did the law define the distribution of abortive medicines as a serious crime. Unavailing were the efforts of Severus and Caracalla, who decreed that women seeking abortion would be banished. Abortion was quite common, as is indicated by Cicero's mention of the Oppianicus case, as well as by other Latin authors' numerous comments, for example, Juvenal in his satires (II, 32) and Plautus in the *Truculentus* (202).

Inheritance

Other laws were aimed at family and property continuity by protecting Roman heirs. Fathers, however, often evaded their duties in this area. The law, therefore, finally became quite explicit by requiring a testator to leave at least one-quarter of his property to his heir—this was the *Lex Falcidia* of 40 B.C. Three previous legal experiments had failed to protect Roman heirs. The first of these was the *Duodecim Tabulae*—Rome's first code—of 451 B.C., which gave a testator almost complete control. The second was the *Lex Furia Testamentaria* (183 B.C.), which forbade the giving of more than 1,000 asses to one individual, unless he was related to the testator in one of the ways designated by the law. The third experiment, the *Lex Voconia* of 169 B.C., declared that the heir should not receive less than any other person.

In general, when a citizen died, the group of his heirs included his wife and children—except for daughters under the authority of their husbands and children not under the *patria potestas* of the deceased at the time of his death. If the citizen were unmarried and childless, relatives on the male side became his only heirs, and if such relatives did not exist, his clan inherited a patrician's property.

The law also dealt with relatives on the female side who were at first ignored by Rome's civil law but were given several inheritance privileges under later codes. Much later, Justinian rejected the philosophy of civil law and introduced the idea of blood relationships.

Not all Romans had the right to make a will. Only a Roman citizen who was also a *pater familias* enjoyed this privilege. Although the law did not specifically require that wills be written, such documents were usually engraved on wax or wood, and only a few of them were made orally. When a will was written, witnesses were required to mark the document, often with a ring, and also to sign their names. The will was then kept in a friend's house or in a temple. The estate of a freedman who had left no children was inherited by his liberator, that is, his former master, or by the patron's relatives.

Divorce

Unlike inheritance, divorce was often a private affair. Indeed, unless the spouses disagreed about their children or property, a judicial procedure was unnecessary. Instead, since both parties wished to secure a divorce, one of them, in the presence of seven witnesses, merely gave the other a statement concerning the dissolution of their marriage without even referring to the reasons.

The result was *divortium*, by which the Romans meant *separation*. The same term was employed with reference to what is now meant by *divorce,* but in Rome *divortium* was confined to cases of mutual consent. *Repudium,* on the other hand, meant compulsory divorce by either party. According to Cicero, *divortium* originally referred only to the wife (*Oratio pro Cluentio,* 5, 14), but it later included both spouses (*Epistulae ad Atticum,* 12, 52, 2).

In ancient times, as Aulus Gellius pointed out (*Noctes Atticae,* IV, 3), there was no divorce in Rome. It was as late as 233 B.C. that, according to certain authors, S. Carvilius Ruga secured the first divorce, because of his wife's barrenness. The Roman historian Valerius Maximus asserted in *Factorum et Dictorum Memorabilium* (II, 1-4) that Ruga's fellow citizens regarded this action as inadvisable. But, even in earlier times, husbands perhaps divorced wives of whom they disapproved. In his *Romulus* (22), Plutarch wrote: "Romulus introduced several laws. One of them, which was quite severe, forbids a wife to leave her spouse, but gives a husband the right to divorce his wife for poisoning her children, for falsifying his keys, and for adultery." Then, according to the *Duodecim Tabulae,* a husband might divorce his spouse for drinking wine, for adultery, and for other forms of wicked behavior. In such cases, he also kept her dowry. But, if he divorced an innocent wife, he was expected to return the dowry with these words: *"Tuas res tibi habeto"* ("Keep your property for yourself").

In later centuries, divorce was exceedingly common. As soon as conjugal affection between two spouses disappeared, it was considered desirable to dissolve their union. Even in small towns, as Cicero's comments on Cluentius and Sassia indicate, divorces were secured quite frequently and for the most insignificant reasons. The dissolution of aristocratic unions was especially common. Tertullian observed that "the fruit of marriage is divorce," while Juvenal spoke contemptuously of a woman who had eight spouses in five years. Similarly, St. Jerome mentioned a lady who married 23 men, the last of whom had already had 20 other wives. Accordingly, Seneca stated that women no longer measured time in terms of the administrations of Roman consuls, but in terms of their husbands' names!

Adultery

Like divorce, adultery became so prevalent that, as Livy wrote in *Ab Urbe Condita Libri* (X, 31), even as early as 285 B.C. the Romans were able to build a temple to Venus out of the fines paid by adulteresses. Besides fines or other forms of economic punishment, the penalty imposed upon an adulteress might be banishment or death. Since adultery threatened the purity of lineage, the husband was not always required to consult the family council before killing his guilty wife. In practice, however, the death penalty was rather uncommon.

The man caught with a Roman's wife was also fined and banished. If he were caught in the very act by the husband, the latter was permitted by the law to detain the adulterer for 20 hours in order to secure witnesses.

Perhaps the most famous Roman law dealing with adultery was Augustus' *Lex Julia de Adulteriis* of 17 B.C. According to this law, the husband who refused to punish his adulterous wife and the adulterer, although he was aware of their offense, was regarded as a procurer. He was, therefore, expected to take legal measures against the adulteress within two months. At the end of this period, such measures might be taken by any other person, if the husband had not acted. The law further imposed inhumanly severe penalties on the adulteress, although a husband who committed adultery was not considered guilty.

Incest

Another aspect of family life regulated by Roman law was incest. At first, in very ancient times, blood relations within the seventh degree were not allowed to marry each other. Later, however, only closer relatives were included in this prohibition.

When Claudius married his beautiful niece Agrippina—his brother's daughter and Nero's notorious mother—the law became more liberal, thus permitting uncle-niece unions. Still, as Suetonius remarked in *Claudius* (26), the public refused to accept incest of this form. Nevertheless, as long as child exposure prevailed, incest remained more common than it was believed to be, since those who reared and sold slaves were not aware of, or did not wish to reveal, the identity of their human merchandise.

Prostitution

It seems that the world's oldest profession was first introduced into the Eternal City from the land west of the Tiber and the Apennines, Etruria. Prostitution was further reinforced by two forces, slavery and the influence of Oriental corruption.

Still, the state did not approve of this vice completely. The praetors, for instance, were authorized to punish harlots in various ways without a trial. In addition, the law did not permit prostitutes to wear the *stola,* the Roman ladies' outer garment. Like disgraced wives, harlots were required to wear a dark toga.

At the same time, the state officially recognized prostitution in certain ways. One of them was the concession of various freedoms to women practicing this profession, as long as they paid a tax. Another was the harlots' participation in an important Roman festival dedicated to Flora or Chloris, the goddess of flowers and wife of Zephyrus, which was introduced in 238 B.C. According to Seneca's *Epistulae* (96), lewd, licentious, and lascivious activities were prevalent during the festival, and they constituted one of its main parts. Even in small towns—but rarely in rural areas—the public demanded that the actresses perform nude during it.

In later times, prostitution was so popular that even some daughters of aristocrats left their homes to become harlots. Tacitus, in his *Annales* (XI, 26–38), and the great satirist Juvenal (VI, 115, 638; X, 333) mentioned that Empress Valeria Messalina frequently left the palace at night to practice prostitution under the name of Lycisca. Still, although the Eternal City was buzzing with sensational whispers about the lusty and libidinous empress, Emperor Claudius alone seemed blissfully unaware of his third wife's wanton activities.

Summary

In brief, the main features of the ancient Roman family were as follows: (a) early engagement for women; (b) a dowry brought by the wife, but not completely controlled by the husband; (c) usually arranged marriage; (d) extensive concubinage; (e) greater emphasis on monogamy than among the ancient Greeks; (f) elaborate and expensive wedding ceremonies; (g) housing which gave emphasis to privacy; (h) almost unlimited paternal authority; (i) rather low status for women, but higher than that of the Athenian matrons; (j) children's almost complete subordination to their fathers; (k) adoption, often by purchase; (l) widespread abortion, although Roman law disapproved of it; (m) inheritance laws stressing family and property continuity; (n) divorce, which was rare at first, but extremely common in later centuries; (o) male-centered and often barbarous adultery laws; (p) prohibition of incestuous unions; and (q) extensive prostitution after the Punic Wars, introduced from Etruria and reinforced by slavery and Oriental corruption.

THE CHRISTIAN FAMILY

Christianity, which has influenced our family system even more extensively than have Hebrew, Greek, and Roman thought, was introduced as a Jewish sect. The term *Christianity,* which is not included in any of the New Testament books, seems to have been first employed by Ignatius (A.D. 50–116), who, according to Eusebius Pamphili's *Historia Ecclesiastica* (III, 36, 2), was the third bishop of Antioch. The term *Christian,* on the other hand, appeared for the first time in Acts 11:26, where the "man of Macedonia" wrote: "And the disciples were called Christians first in Antioch."

Concerning one of the forces that determined the nature of this religion, Groves (1934) has stated: "It has been chiefly through the impression its intellectual achievement made upon the leadership of the Church during the first twelve centuries that Greek culture has influenced the Christian doctrine regarding marriage and the family" (p. 51). Three centuries before Christ, Zeno of Cyprus (340–265 B.C.), who founded the school of Stoicism in Athens, spoke of a cosmic Reason, a purposive and immanent Logos animating the entire world. This Logos was later identified with Jesus Christ, the second person of the Christian Trinity. The same Greek philosopher, in a pantheistic manner, conceived of cosmic unity, which led to the concept of universal brotherhood, and which influenced the Romans considerably. In less abstract fashion, the founder of Christianity taught the brotherhood of man, one of the basic Christian doctrines, by asserting that God was the Father of all people.

Two other cultures exerted some influence upon the Christian family. One was the Roman civilization, whose decadence often caused the Church Fathers to advocate a family system diametrically opposed to that of the Eternal City. The other was the constellation of barbarian customs that influenced certain aspects of the Christian family throughout the Middle Ages.

Christ himself was extremely interested in the family. As Bogardus (1955, p. 157) has stated, "the social institution which Jesus supported above all others, even above the church and the state, was the family." Similarly, Truxal and Merrill (1947, p. 52) have written: "With the possible exception of Confucianism, few religions maintain as intimate a connection between family values and religious teachings as Christianity." This is indicated by at least three facts: (a) Christ emphasized God's fatherhood and man's brotherhood—Christianity's two fundamental principles—also employing innumerable metaphors and similes derived from family life ("For whosoever shall do the will of God, the same is my brother, and my sister, and mother" [Mark 3:35]). (b) Jesus devoted most of his life to his earthly family, working as a carpenter at Nazareth. (c) Even while on the cross, he was concerned with his mother's welfare ("Woman," he said, "behold thy son! Then saith he to the disciple, Behold thy mother!" [John 19:26–27]). Thus, Christianity "succeeded in reinvigorating the family, which subsequently became one of the dominant powers in western Europe from the tenth century onward, well into the Reformation" (Anshen, 1949, pp. 3–17).

Marriage

In addition, Jesus took monogamy for granted, regarding both polyandry and polygyny as sinful.

Criticism of marriage. Many of the leaders of Christianity, however, often condemned marriage even in its monogamous form. In fact, marriage was considered the lowest of the three types of sex purity which they distinguished, the highest being virginity, and the second highest denial during widowhood.

St. Paul wrote: "For I would that all men were even as I myself. But every man hath his proper gift of God, one after this manner, and another after that. I say therefore to the unmarried and widows, It is good for them if they abide even as I. But if they cannot contain, let them marry: for it is better to marry than to burn" (I Corinthians 7:79).

Clement of Alexandria (A.D. 150–213), the great theologian of the Logos and a Christian Platonist and Stoic, was equally unenthusiastic about marriage. To him, even an infant's wail was a heartbreaking jeremiad, a lugubrious protest against this institution. "Why, O mother," he thought that the helpless child complained, "didst thou bring me forth to this life, in which prolongation of life is progress to death?"

Tertullian (A.D. 160–240), who coined the Latin ecclesiastical terminology and whose works are replete with quotations from the *Itala,* a Latin translation of the Bible, often spoke violently against marriage. In his *Liber de Exhortatione Castitatis* (IX), for instance, he referred to such a relationship as synonymous with fornication.

St. Jerome (A.D. 340–420), one of the greatest Church Fathers, who composed a Latin translation of the Bible (the celebrated Vulgate), and, during his residence in Bethlehem, administered four convents founded by two Roman ladies, was also critical of marriage. There is nothing marvelous about a crying brat, he asserted. Nevertheless, he did see something desirable in marriage, the production of virgins (*Epistola* XXII).

St. Augustine (A.D. 354–430), who became bishop of Hippo and established Tertullian's Latin ecclesiastical terminology, regarded reproduction as the only goal of marriage (*De Genesi ad Litteram,* IX, 5).

Second marriage. Such attitudes toward

matrimony, one would expect, could easily lead to a more intense and vehement disapproval of second marriages.

Indeed, according to Athenagoras, a Christian apologist of the second century, "a second marriage is merely a specious adultery" (*Legatio pro Christianis,* 33). Similarly, as is asserted in the *Apostolic Constitutions* (III, i, 1), an early Christian manual of discipline, doctrine, and worship, a second marriage is wicked, a third one indicative of unbridled lust, and one after the third, synonymous with fornication. St. Jerome added that young widows weep as follows:

"My little estate is wasting every day, the property I have inherited is being scattered, my footman has spoken insultingly to me, my maid pays no attention to my orders. Who will appear for me in court? Who will be responsible for my land tax? Who will educate my little children and bring up my houseslaves?" . . . Why these pretexts of property and arrogant servants? Confess your vileness. No woman marries with the idea of not sleeping with a husband. If you are not spurred on by lust, surely it is the height of madness to prostitute yourself like a harlot merely to increase your wealth, and for a paltry and passing gain to pollute that precious chastity which might endure forever (*Epistola* LIV).

Mixed marriage. Unions between Christians and nonbelievers were also tabu. In *Ad Uxorem* (II, 3), Tertullian described such marriages as identical to fornication. In addition, he asserted that mixed marriages created numerous problems. A pagan husband, for example, might forbid his Christian wife to take part in church activities, and even compel her to adopt his own faith.

In A.D. 306, the Synod of Elvira, Spain, declared that Christians giving their daughters to Jews or heretics in marriage would be excommunicated for as long as five years. If, however, an infidel were willing to be converted to Christianity, such a union would be recognized by the church.

Constantine the Great (A.D. 280–337), the first Christian emperor of Rome, who issued the famous Edict of Toleration in 313, made Christian-Jewish marriages illegal. Half a century later, in A.D. 388, a Roman law described such unions as adulterous.

Nevertheless, mixed marriages were rather common among early Christians. The reasons were at least two: the believers hoped to convert Jews and other infidels by means of such unions, and, since the Christian group was still very small, endogamy was not always feasible.

Marriage as a sacrament. Despite the Church Fathers' attacks on matrimony, Christianity defined marriage as a sacrament.

In 1164 the church distinguished the seven sacraments—baptism, confirmation, penance, holy eucharist, holy orders, *holy matrimony,* and unction.

Four centuries later, the Council of Trent (1545–1563), which, as a reply to the Protestant Reformation, attempted to reunite Christianity and establish sounder moral principles, anathematized various Protestant beliefs concerning the seven sacraments and re-emphasized the sacramental nature of marriage.

Luther (1483–1546), the author of the 95 theses on indulgences (1517), who married a former nun, contributed to the conception of marriage as a civil contract. This doctrine became one of the forces that gradually led to a higher divorce rate in modern times.

Another aspect of marriage, debated for many centuries, was the time at which its sacramental nature began. Certain theologians averred that this occurred at the time of the betrothal, others when marriage itself was established, and others when sex consummation took place.

Mutual loyalty. Concerning love between spouses, St. Paul wrote: "Husbands, love your wives, even as Christ also loved the church, and gave himself for it. . . . So ought men to love their wives as their own bodies. He that loveth his wife loveth himself" (Ephesians 5:25, 28).

Further, "For this cause shall a man leave his father and mother, and cleave to his wife; And they twain shall be one flesh: so then they are no more twain, but one flesh" (Mark 10:7–8).

Arrangement of marriage. At first, influenced by the Hebrews and Romans, Christians considered marriage a private matter. When its sacramental nature was accepted, it was also emphasized that even the families concerned should not arrange the union, but should permit the young people to exercise their free will, thus making the sacramental relationship possible. Engagement was especially private and free, and its breaking did not result in any form of punishment.

In practice, however, due to the influence of various Christian leaders, marriage was often arranged. Tertullian, for instance, preached that, on earth, no marriage was valid without the father's consent. Ignatius, on the other hand, advocated some church control. In his famous letter to Polycarp (A.D. 69–159), the martyr and bishop of Smyrna, he wrote: "It becomes both men and women who marry to form their union with the approval of the bishop, that their marriage may be according to the Lord, and not after their own lust" (V).

In feudal times, marriages were also arranged by the overlord. Needless to add, such control was usually aimed at the promotion of the overlord's socio-economic security and not at his ward's welfare. Widows were particularly helpless, their remarriage being virtually impossible without the overlord's permission.

The wedding ceremony. Another way in which the church attempted to control marriage was through the introduction of a wedding ceremony.

At first, the Christian Fathers were not concerned with this matter. The customs followed, therefore, were those of a given place, time, and social class. Perhaps the first religious element adopted in this area was a priestly benediction. In A.D. 398, one of the many Synods of Carthage, a city which had become Africa's Christian center, added the rule that, in view of this benediction, virginity should be maintained on the wedding night. Later it was ruled that the couple should abstain from sex relations for three days and three nights. Soon, however, more moderate regulations allowed the newlyweds to have coitus on the first night after marriage, as long as they paid a fee to the Church.

Ecclesiastical control was further reinforced by means of the bride mass, which was fairly common between the fourth and tenth centuries. This mass became the prelude to the more formal and elaborate marriage liturgy which was adopted in later times. After the tenth century, marriages usually took place in church, under the direction of the clergy.

Women

Christianity advocated women's spiritual equality to men, although it recognized a certain degree of male superiority in the temporal sphere. St. Paul, for instance, believed that men and women were one in Christ. Clement of Alexandria, in his *Paedagogus* (IV), spoke of the spouses' common food and equal yoke. In A.D. 399, St. Jerome wrote to Oceanus, "It cannot be that an adulterous wife should be put away and an unfaithful husband retained. . . . Among the Romans, men's unchastity goes unchecked" (*Epistola* LXXVII).

Great women. Such equality was reinforced to some extent by the influence of Christianity's great women, a few of whom were:

Elizabeth of the house of Aaron, the wife of the prophet Zacharias and the mother of John the Baptist. Elizabeth's importance is indicated by the fact that she has been associated with three of the most sublime poems in the New Testament: a beautiful psalm (Luke 1:42–45), the "Magnificat" or "Song of Mary" (1:46–55), and the "Benedictus" of Zacharias (1:68–79).

The Virgin Mary, Joseph's wife and

Christ's mother, a spiritual figure and not an Oriental-like goddess, to whom the angel Gabriel announced: "Hail, thou that art highly favored, the Lord is with thee: blessed art thou among women" (Luke 1:28). Jesus himself was constantly devoted to his mother, and perhaps his late entrance into his public ministry may be explained in terms of Joseph's death and Christ's desire to support his mother and younger brothers and sisters (Mark 6:3).

Christians, who feared eternal damnation and needed an influential mediator, gradually accorded Mary a sort of special veneration that led, among other things, to the creation of magnificent cathedrals dedicated to her. Moreover, Roman Catholic Mariolatry now includes Mary's presentation, annunciation, visitation, purification, and assumption. In December 1854, Pope Pius IX, in his famous bull *Ineffabilis Deus,* also proclaimed the doctrine of the immaculate conception—the belief that, in view of Christ's merits, Mary was in the first instant of her conception in Anne's womb preserved exempt from original sin. Even in the Middle Ages, this doctrine was supported by the Franciscans and Duns Scotus, although the Dominicans rejected it. In 1431, the Council of Basle adopted this belief as a Catholic dogma, and the eighth day of December was decreed a festival of its commemoration.

St. Catherine of Siena, Italy (1347-1380), whose 300 letters are of great literary and historical value, and who was canonized in 1461. Catherine easily became a great political leader who was respected by popes and statesmen and who often settled conflicts, including that between the Florentines and Pope Urban VI.

St. Elizabeth of Hungary (1207-1231). Elizabeth, the daughter of Hungary's king and the wife of a Thuringian prince, devoted herself to asceticism and charitable works as a Franciscan Tertiary, which led to her canonization by Gregory IX only four years after her death.

Women's roles. Despite a limited number of great women and the fact that the husband was no longer a powerful patriarch, women in reality remained less influential and free than men. Perhaps this was one of the results of the Christians' reaction to the almost complete emancipation of Rome's aristocratic ladies. At any rate, in I Corinthians, St. Paul preached: "Let your women keep silence in the churches: for it is not permitted unto them to speak; but they are commanded to be under obedience, as also saith the law. And if they will learn any thing, let them ask their husbands at home: for it is a shame for women to speak in the church" (14:34-35). In the same epistle he declared:

But I would have you know, that the head of every man is Christ; and the head of the woman is the man; and the head of Christ is God. Every man praying or prophesying, having his head covered, dishonoreth his head. But every woman that prayeth or prophesieth with her head uncoverd dishonoreth her head: for that is even all one as if she were shaven. For if the woman be not covered, let her also be shorn: but if it be a shame for a woman to be shorn or shaven, let her be covered. For a man indeed ought not to cover his head, forasmuch as he is the image and glory of God: but the woman is the glory of the man. For the man is not of the woman; but the woman of the man. Neither was the man created for the woman; but the woman for the man. For this cause ought the woman to have power on her head because of the angels (11:3-10).

In another epistle, Paul described women's duties as follows: "That they may teach the young women to be sober, to love their husbands, to love their children, To be discreet, chaste, keepers at home, good, obedient to their own husbands, that the word of God be not blasphemed" (Titus 2:4-5). In his *Paedagogus* (III, 10), Clement of Alexandria included cooking, spinning, and weaving among women's roles.

Virgins. The duties of a distinct group of girls and women, known as "virgins" or "brides of Christ," were different. These Christians were both unmarried and chaste, and their position, which was regarded as extremely important, "involved the most minute precautions against the entering in of any temptation whatsoever" (Langdon-Davies, 1927, p. 284). The main function of these virgins was Christian social service, including administrating relief, visiting prisoners, caring for the sick as well as needy orphans and widows, and the like. The necessity for such services was usually great, in view of the many persecutions that broke up innumerable Christian families.

The widow. Between the highly respected virgins and the wives, who enjoyed low status, were the widows, whose prestige was intermediary. Like the "brides of Christ," women who had lost their husbands also played an important role in church social service. Concerning such women, Paul advised:

Let not a widow be taken into the number under threescore years old, having been the wife of one man, Well reported of for good works; if she have brought up children, if she have lodged strangers, if she have washed the saints' feet, if she have relieved the afflicted, if she have diligently followed every good work. But the younger widows refuse: for when they have begun to wax wanton against Christ, they will marry; Having damnation, because they have cast off their first faith. And withal they learn to be idle, wandering about from house to house; and not only idle, but tattlers also and busybodies, speaking things which they ought not. I will therefore that the younger women marry, bear children, guide the house, give none occasion to the adversary to speak reproachfully (I Timothy 5:9–14).

Regarding a widow's remarriage, St. Paul added, "The wife is bound by the law as long as her husband liveth; but if her husband be dead, she is at liberty to be married to whom she will; only in the Lord" (I Corinthians 7:39).

Women and sex. One of the reasons women were often criticized—sometimes quite violently—by various Christian leaders was the tendency to identify them with carnal love. Accordingly, as the Church Fathers' disapproval of sex was reinforced, woman's status declined. (In Rome, as decadence was intensified, her position improved.) One of the arguments employed to justify such a critical attitude was based on Eve's disobedience. According to St. Paul, "Adam was not deceived, but the woman being deceived was in the transgression" (I Timothy 2:14).

Other leaders were more passionately vehement. In his *Stromata* (VII, 12), Clement of Alexandria called woman the organ of the devil, and, in his *Paedagogus* (II, 2), he exclaimed, "every woman ought to be filled with shame at the thought that she is a woman." In his *De Cultu Feminarum* (I, 1), Tertullian screamed, "You are the devil's gateway." And John Chrysostom of Antioch (A.D. 347–407), the "golden-mouthed" patriarch of Constantinople, described woman as a "necessary evil," while others spoke of her as a scorpion, a viper, and the like.

As a result, many choir leaders in Christian churches preferred eunuchs to women as chanters and choristers. Moreover, in A.D. 578, the Council of Auxerre forbade women to receive the holy sacrament with uncovered hands. Seven years later, the Council of Macon seriously debated the nonexistence of souls in human females, but women won by one vote! In Russia, until the time of Peter the Great (1672–1725), the church considered women subhuman, while even today the Orthodox Church does not permit their presence behind the altar.

To diminish temptation, the church also attacked the use of cosmetics and erotic clothing by women. Clement of Alexandria averred that elaborate headdresses were typical of completely shameless, immoral, and lascivious females. In *De Cultu Feminarum,* Tertullian advocated the obliteration of feminine beauty.

The lady. Later in the Middle Ages, despite feudalism, women gained various freedoms as a result of certain new conditions. For instance, men often left home to take part in long military expeditions. Naturally, during their absence, women were forced to assume a great deal of responsibility for the management of the castle. Participation in community activities became equally necessary, and this soon led to some improvement in the medieval lady's position.

The witch. The woman with the lowest status in Christian times was perhaps the witch. Although witchcraft was practiced by both males and females, since the latter were accused of such behavior more frequently, the belief that witches are female has now become dominant.

In a way, witchcraft and demonology were invented by St. Augustine, whose writings dealt with the devil quite extensively, as did those of St. Thomas Aquinas. Both saints ardently disapproved of such practices, and the church, to make sin less attractive, depicted witches as hideous, revolting, and malevolent creatures.

After A.D. 900, the church, which considered most witches heretics, punished them with excommunication. The Council of Treves (1310) also condemned witchcraft in all its forms. At the end of the Middle Ages, Luther, who asserted that he had quite a few personal conversations with the devil, referred to witchcraft as a most serious sin.

In A.D. 1258, when the Inquisition asked for permission to prosecute witches, Pope Alexander IV gave a negative answer, adding, *"nisi manifeste hearesim saperent"* (unless they were real heretics). Although witches had been executed in earlier times, it was in 1320 that Pope John XXII allowed Carcassonne's Inquisition to prosecute them. Thus, the first witch trials began, and, in Carcassonne and Toulouse alone, by A.D. 1350, 1,000 persons had been tried, most of whom were executed.

Children

As in the case of women, Christianity was inconsistent regarding children. It is true, of course, that this new religion "seems to have been the first to succeed in reconciling family unity and stability with a liberty for the children that enables them to display plenty of initiative. Everywhere else . . . children were emancipated only through the breakdown of the family" (Leclercq, 1949, p. 366).

It is also true that Jesus said, "Suffer little children, and forbid them not, to come unto me; for of such is the kingdom of heaven" (Matthew 19:14). And at Capernaum, "he took a child, and set him in the midst of them: and when he had taken him in his arms, he said unto them. Whosoever shall receive one of such children in my name, receiveth me. . . . And whosoever shall offend one of these little ones that believe in me, it is better for him that a millstone were hanged about his neck, and he were cast into the sea" (Mark 9:36–37, 42).

Still, since children were produced through sexual intercourse, Tertullian and others could not see why some people were eager to bear offspring. Needless to add, if the production of children in marriage were virtually a sin, illegitimacy constituted a more serious offence. As a result, during the Middle Ages, illegitimate children were usually outlaws without inheritance rights.

Once children were born, however, the church urged them to attach themselves to the religious institution rather than to their families. After all, the Church Fathers argued, the Apostles John and James, when they met Jesus, "left their father Zebedee [who was a fairly wealthy fisherman] in the ship with the hired servants, and went after him" (Mark 1:20). And when one of the disciples asked Christ to permit him to go and bury his father, "Jesus said unto him, Follow me; and let the dead bury their dead" (Matthew 8:22). Accordingly, in one of his letters (LIV), St. Jerome concluded: "Great is the reward for forgetting a parent." All this, of course, does not mean that respect for one's mother and father was not encouraged. On the contrary, Matthew 15:4 commands: "Honor thy father and mother: and, He that curseth father or mother, let him die the death."

The church's interest in the child's welfare is further indicated by its disapproval of infanticide, which was also due to the belief that no infant should die unbaptized. Even selling children into slavery was regarded as a serious sin. Constantine the Great permitted child sale only when the parents were unable to support their offspring. And Valentinian I, in A.D. 374, introduced a law defining infanticide as a criminal offense and declared that violators would be punished by death. Still, throughout western Europe, both infanticide and the sale of children were rather common until about A.D. 1000, particularly whenever war and famine were raging.

Abortion

The destruction of the fetus was also considered sinful, since Christians conceived of all forms of life as sacred. In his *Apologeticum* (9), Tertullian argued that abortion was synonymous with murder because of the presence of a soul in the fetus. St. Basil (A.D. 330–379), the great advocate of monasticism, also regarded the destruction of an unborn child as murderous. At about the same time, St. Augustine asserted that an embryo *informatus* lacked a soul, while an embryo *formatus* definitely had one. Consequently, in the former case, abortion should be punished by a mere fine, but in the latter by death.

Inheritance

As to the economic welfare of children, the church declared that primogeniture was unjust, and that the family estate should be divided equally among all sons. Perhaps this was due to the church's desire to cause the fragmentation of such estates, thus facilitating the giving of lands to various religious institutions. Indeed, in a later period, this policy of religious endowment became one of the main reasons why the power of the feudal lord began to decline, while that of the church increased.

Although Christian leaders also spoke in favor of females with reference to inheritance, they were less successful in this area; for, in feudal times, land ownership and military service were very closely associated. Accordingly, even when a daughter or a wife inherited land, she was soon deprived of it, since she was not capable of military service.

Divorce

Typical of the New Testament passages dealing with divorce are the following:

"What therefore God hath joined together, let not man put asunder" (Matthew 19:6).

"Whosoever shall put away his wife, except it be for fornication, and shall marry another, committeth adultery: and whoso marrieth her which is put away doth commit adultery" (Matthew 19:9; cf. Matthew 5:32 and I Corinthians 7:10–15).

In general, unlike Luther, who placed less emphasis on the indissolubility of marriage, the early Christian Fathers condemned absolute divorce. A few of them, however, accepted grounds such as apostasy, covetousness, idolatry, and the like. This lack of agreement is also indicated by the fact that Christian leaders debated the possible recognition of divorce for 300 years and took 800 more to complete the ecclesiastical code dealing with this matter. But, despite the church's opposition, a special form of divorce became quite common during the Middle Ages. This was the dissolution of marriage by asserting that a previous clandestine union had been contracted.

More specifically, in A.D. 140, Hermas, one of Rome's most famous Christians, contended that a divorce should be obtained when a spouse was guilty of apostasy, covetousness, fornication, or idolatry. A century later, Origen (A.D. 185–251), one of the most brilliant Christian scholars of all time, permitted husbands to divorce their wives, if the latter had committed fornication or any other equally or more serious crime. The Council of Elvira, on the other hand, in A.D. 306, threatened with excommunication women who put away their guilty husbands and then remarried. In A.D. 314, the Council of Arles, which was the first general synod of the Western church, despite its emphasis on the indissolubility of marriage, suggested that a divorced husband be advised not to remarry before his former wife's death. In other words, the council stressed advice, not prohibition. In A.D. 331, Constantine further declared that no divorce should be secured for insignificant reasons. The emperor added that serious grounds were adultery, poisoning, and procuring on the part of the wife, and murder, poisoning, and violation of sepulchers on the part of the husband. A husband might also be divorced by his wife, if he had not communicated with her during four years of military service.

Constantine's laws, however, were repealed in A.D. 363 by Julian the Apostate. A few decades later (A.D. 400), St. Jerome accepted the philosophy of Hermas concerning divorce, and John Chrysostom of Antioch taught that, in case of adultery, absolute divorce was definitely justified. At about the same time, the Council of Carthage (A.D. 407) ruled that marriage was strictly indissoluble. In the same way, St. Augustine spoke of the indissolubility of marriage, but also recognized divorce in case of "unlawful lusts" on the part of either spouse.

In A.D. 449, Theodosius II restored Constantine's divorce law, adding the following grounds: a husband's association with harlots, cruelty to his wife, fraud, conspiracy against the government, and robbery; and a wife's analogous offenses as well as staying out at night or visiting public places without her husband's permission. Another Byzantine emperor, Justinian the Great (A.D. 483–565), forbade divorce by mutual consent. The main grounds that he recognized were either spouse's entering a monastic order and a husband's impotence or absence for at least five years because of captivity in a foreign land.

A thousand years later, the Council of Trent distinguished between *divortium a vinculo matrimonii* (annulment) and *divortium a mensa et thoro* (separation). Of these, annulment resulted from the belief that the original marriage was not genuine, the most serious impediments being a previous verbal contract of marriage expressed in the present tense, that is, "I take thee," not "I will take thee"; consanguinity to the seventh degree; and spiritual affinity, such as having sponsored the same confirmation ceremony. Separation, on the other hand, involved only bed and board, the grounds being adultery, apostasy, cruelty, and heresy. Needless to add, since the tie of matrimony was not broken, remarriage was forbidden in such cases.

Incest

Christianity also dealt with incest quite extensively. St. Paul wrote: "It is reported commonly that there is fornication among you, and such fornication as is not so much as named among the Gentiles, that one should have his father's wife. And ye are puffed up, and have not rather mourned, that he that hath done this deed might be taken away from among you" (I Corinthians 5:1–2).

After the Forged Decretals (A.D. 850), a collection of works on canon law which became the basis of Gregorianism and Ultramontanism, ecclesiastical regulations concerning incest were particularly strict. Even remotely related royal houses were not allowed to intermarry without the church's permission. But, since prohibition within the seventh degree of consanguinity seemed exceedingly stringent, in A.D. 1215, the Fourth Lateran Council permitted marriage beyond the fourth degree.

Unlike the church, the feudal system placed great emphasis on incestuous unions for the sake of maintaining and extending the property of the family. But Christianity's condemnation of incest, which included both biological and spiritual ties, and which St. Thomas considered a serious sin—although less serious than bestiality, pederasty, and sodomy—gradually led to the abolition of such unions as well as to the fragmentation and dissipation of feudal estates.

Morals

Finally, in the area of sexual morality, the Christian religion was so spiritually oriented that its early teachings placed celibacy above marriage. It was stressed, for instance, that there is no matrimony in heaven, and that the spiritual elite should become attached to the church, leaving family life, with its children, fidelity, and sacrament, to the common people. As a result, the Roman laws condemning childlessness and celibacy were soon repealed.

St. Paul himself declared, "It is good for a man not to touch a woman. Nevertheless, to avoid fornication, let every man have his own wife, and let every woman have her own husband" (I Corinthians 7:1-2). Similarly, in *Ad Uxorem* (I, 3), Tertullian concluded that it is much better neither to marry nor to burn, adding the following in *Adversus Marcionem* (I, 29): "not as if we superseded a bad thing by a good, but only a good thing by a better; for we do not reject marriage, but simply refrain from it." In one of his letters (XXII), St. Jerome complained about the "negative" aspects of matrimony, including pregnancy, wailing infants, the agony of jealousy, housekeeping chores, and the wife's devotion to her husband's welfare, unlike the virgin, who dedicated herself to Christ. In the same way, in *De Virginitate* (IX), John Chrysostom wrote that "marriage is good, but virginity is better than marriage. . . . I consider virginity to be as high above marriage as the heavens are above the earth." Equally enthusiastically, St. Augustine averred that in the next life unmarried people would beam like brilliant stars, while married ones would be similar to less bright heavenly bodies.

Some of the reasons for such beliefs were the following: (a) the influence of the Essenes, a Jewish sect of monastically minded healers, who, according to Josephus' *Ioudaicos Polemos* (II, viii, 2), considered pleasure as evil and thus rejected marriage; (b) the partial acceptance of philosophical systems such as Neoplatonism, a dualistic ideology regarding the spirit as good and the body as wicked; (c) the tendency to compete with non-Christian faiths that placed great emphasis on self-control; (d) the new sect's reaction to the decadence of the Eternal City; (e) the Roman cry, *"Christianos ad leonem!"*, which caused Tertullian and others to advise the followers of Jesus not to marry and create new martyrs; (f) certain practices of the martial barbarians, whom, in *De Civitate Dei,* St. Augustine described as morally superior to the Romans; (g) the conviction that the Last Judgment was near, which made preparation for the next life more important than matrimony; and (h) the penitence, or perhaps contrition, of various Christian leaders for their youthful sins, which led them to the most violent rejection of sex.

Sex was thus condemned with boundless fanaticism. Even the kiss, which primitive Christianity adopted as a ritualistic type of salutation, was frequently suspected as a highly erotic act. In *Legatio pro Christianis* (XXXII), Athenagoras stated that it was exceedingly immoral to kiss for the second time, after having enjoyed the first kiss. In *Ad Uxorem* (IX, 3, 5), Tertullian added that the human race should prefer extinction to reproduction by coitus. And John of Damascus, in the eighth century A.D., asserted that Adam and Eve had been created sexless, but their sin in Eden led to sexual reproduction. He further averred that, if the two protoplasts had obeyed God, human reproduction would now take place in a less sinful manner (*De Fide Orthodoxa,* IV, 24).

Adultery and prostitution were considered especially wicked. With reference to the former, Jesus, who attacked the double standard of morals, "introduced a new test of inward loyalty that transcended any attempt to translate it into legal codes or social customs" (Nash, 1955, p. 93). Prostitution, on the other hand, was often regarded as a means of protecting the honor of non-prostitutes. In his *Summa Theologica* (II–II, 10, 11), for instance, St. Thomas agreed with St. Augustine that, if prostitution were absent, lust would dominate the world.

The diametrical opposite of such offenses, virginity, was praised with enthusiasm. Cyprian of Carthage (A.D. 200–258), the great theoretician of ecclesiastical administration, spoke of it as the ornament of morality and the crown of concord. Methodius (A.D. 300) referred to the same state as something supernaturally great, wonderful, glorious, as well as the noblest manner of life. St. Thomas further derived the word *virginity* from the Latin *viror* (verdure, freshness), implying that a virgin has not been burnt by the blazing fire of sexual passion—Thomas always stressed the life of reason. In the New Testament, St. Paul stated, "For to be carnally minded is death; but to be spiritually minded is life and peace" (Romans 8:6). Therefore, I Peter 2:11 advises: "Dearly beloved, I beseech you as strangers and pilgrims, abstain from fleshly lusts, which war against the soul." And John, the prophet of Ephesus, explained the fall of Babylon as follows: "Babylon is fallen, is fallen, that great city, because she made all nations drink of the wine of the wrath of her fornication" (Revelation 14:8).

It is no wonder, therefore, that Tertullian, in *Monogamia* (III), exclaimed, "The Kingdom of Heaven is thrown open to eunuchs." And, as Eusebius wrote in *Historia Ecclesiastica* (VI, 8)—because of Matthew 19:12, which states, "For there are some eunuchs, which were so born from their mother's womb: and there are some eunuchs, which were made eunuchs of men: and there be eunuchs, which have made themselves eunuchs, for the kingdom of heaven's sake"—Origen actually castrated himself. Physicians were besieged by countless other Christians who were equally eager to be castrated.

Clergymen, particularly those belonging to the higher orders, were further required to practice celibacy, on which no other culture has ever placed greater emphasis. In fact, the church presented "celibacy as an imitation of the angels" (Saltus, 1906, p. 119). It was Pope Siricius who, in A.D. 385, introduced this rule. But, since many clergymen disapproved of the new policy, the Trullan Council of A.D. 680 permitted members of the lower orders to marry. The *digami* (those married twice), however, were excluded from the hierarchy. Still, for about three centuries, clergymen demanded additional freedoms with reference to marriage and even concubinage. Then, in A.D. 1073, Pope St. Gregory VII, the famous "Monk Hildebrand" who excommunicated Emperor Henry IV of Germany, once more introduced celibacy, which, through the influence of the Lateran Council of 1215, became definite and official in the West.

The Eastern Orthodox Church, on the other hand, has never been quite as enthusiastic about celibacy. The rule since the time of Leo VI (865–912), the Byzantine emperor known as "the Wise," has been that priests, unlike monks, are permitted to marry. This privilege, however, prevents them from achieving higher ecclesiastical positions, since bishops are always former celibate monks.

Another way in which Christianity combated temptation was asceticism. This practice, before Christ's time, was found in Greece, Egypt, India, and, especially, among the Essenes, who influenced Jesus' thought considerably. Christian monasticism itself first appeared in Egypt, where St. Anthony, the hermit of Coma (A.D. 251–356), introduced it by living alone in the mountains for two decades. From Egypt, Christian monasticism traveled to Syria, then to Greece, and later to Rome. In Greece, the movement was founded by Basil the Great (A.D. 330–379), and in Rome by St. Jerome and St. Athanasius (A.D. 293–373), the brilliant bishop of Alexandria and defender of the Nicene faith. In general, it may be asserted that one of the most important consequences of this movement was the creation of a religious occupation for women who remained unmarried. Such women were of course countless, since the many wars often led to a low sex ratio.

More moderate were the ideas of Jovinianus (A.D. 390), a famous monk who advocated both celibacy and matrimony, as well as fasting and eating, and who was excommunicated because of his strong disapproval of Christians attacking the family. Similarly, Vigilantius, one of his followers, was afraid that monasticism's immense popularity in Europe would lead to the extinction of mankind before Christ's return. St. Jerome, therefore, wrote a violent treatise against Vigilantius in A.D. 406, calling him "Gaul's monster" and "Dormitantius" (sleepy or stupid).

Between the ninth and eleventh centuries, thousands of clergymen also disapproved of celibacy and even engaged in scandalous licentiousness. In addition, many priests in Europe "would take wives without the benefit of wedlock, have children by them, and then just before death be legally married in order that they might pass on their property to their children" (Feucht, 1961, p. 63). The church itself often augmented its revenues "by means of taxes paid by clergy for the privilege of keeping concubines" (Sait, 1938, p. 155). In A.D. 1563, however, the Council of Trent abolished all forms of concubinage.

It is interesting to add that Christianity's condemnation of sex was one of the main forces that gradually led to the development of a vastly complex system of demonological beliefs regarding carnal love. St. Anthony, for instance, like innumerable other saints, was convinced that he was tempted at night by voluptuous and lascivious succubi, or female demons that tormented him by gesturing and beckoning erotically. Equally seductive and alluring was the incubus, a fallen angel. Nuns and other Christian women often asserted that this male demon visited them at night and had coitus with them. Even great religious leaders accepted the existence of incubi and succubi. Pope Innocent VIII took them for

granted; Pope Benedict XIV discussed them in *De Servorum Dei Beatificatione;* St. Augustine dealt with them extensively in *De Civitate Dei;* and St. Thomas Aquinas, in the *Summa Theologica,* wrote seriously about the possibility of offspring resulting from the union between a human being and a succubus or incubus!

Summary

In brief, the main characteristics of the Christian family, especially in early times, have been as follows: (a) emphasis on the importance of a more or less spiritualized family institution; (b) God's fatherhood and man's brotherhood; (c) monogamy; (d) marriage as a sacrament; (e) ecclesiastical control of the wedding ceremony; (f) loyalty on the part of both spouses; (g) woman's spiritual equality to man; (h) interest in children's spiritual and physical welfare; (i) indissolubility of marriage; (j) condemnation of sex; (k) disapproval of abortion; (l) prohibition of incest; and (m) glorification of celibacy and monasticism.

THE CHANGING AMERICAN FAMILY

In *Marriage Analysis,* Christensen (1958, pp. 48–65) stated that the American family has been undergoing these main changes: more and earlier marriages, greater family disorganization, acceptance of remarriage, declining birth rates, partial loss of family functions, changing sex roles, and increasing individualism. Burgess and Locke (1960, p. 450) added that "the family is changing from the institutional to the companionship form."

In the present discussion, emphasis is placed on certain of the changes in the American family, from colonial times to the present day.

The Early American Family

In colonial times, in view of the pioneer conditions that prevailed in the typical community, young men and women were permitted to associate with one another rather freely. Parents, however, expected their children's courtship to be fairly short. In addition, romantic love was usually discouraged. At least three forces led to the disapproval of romantic love affairs: the strict Puritan morality, the fierce struggle for existence, and the realistic stress on the economic aspects of marriage contracts.

Bundling. An unusual form of courtship was bundling, introduced from Europe by the Dutch and the English and practiced mainly by the lower social classes in New England. This custom, which became dominant chiefly in the second half of the eighteenth century, consisted in permitting lovers to court in bed, at least partly dressed and often in the presence of other family members.

This type of courtship was accepted for several reasons: the prevailing hospitality in pioneer times; the predominance of one-room cabins, resulting in a relative absence of privacy; and the fact that sitting up at night was inadvisable, in view of the very limited supply of candles and fuel. Indeed, according to a poem dealing with bundling:

> Since in a bed a man and maid
> May bundle and be chaste,
> It does no good to burn out wood,
> It is a needless waste.

But, obviously, not every couple could both "bundle and be chaste." Washington Irving has observed, "wherever the practice of bundling prevailed, there was an amazing number of sturdy brats annually born . . . without the license of the law, or the benefit of clergy" (1880, p. 210).

Later, bundling began to decline, and this "is to be attributed largely to the increase of wealth which made possible larger houses and less rigorous conditions of life" (Calhoun, 1945, Vol. I, p. 132). Its decline was further accelerated by the intemperance and excesses that accompanied this

practice, as well as by the protests of numerous respected leaders.

Mate selection. The same pioneer conditions were partly responsible for the relative freedom that characterized choice of mates. Indeed, despite "the seeming parental tyranny that prevailed in colonial days young women seem to have exercised considerable independence in love affairs" (Calhoun, 1945, Vol. I, p. 55).

Still, parents and masters, who usually placed main emphasis on the economic aspects of marriage, often influenced mate selection extensively.

Miscegenation, in spite of the absence of restrictions on interclass unions, was definitely forbidden. In 1698, for instance, Pennsylvania's Chester County court prohibited marriage between Negroes and whites. Similarly, a Massachusetts law of 1705 imposed a fine of 50 pounds on those officiating at white-Negro or white-mulatto unions. In general, white-Indian marriages were also tabu. Needless to add, this does not mean that persons of racially mixed ancestry, born of illicit unions, were nonexistent.

An additional restriction dealt with incest. The laws specified certain degrees of affinity and consanguinity within which marriage was prohibited. Offenders were commonly punished most severely, one of the penalties consisting in wearing a capital I, which represented incest.

Colonial laws further required the publication of matrimonial intention. This was usually done by reading an announcement at a public meeting or by posting a written notice in a public place.

Emphasis on marriage. Another feature of the early American family was the colonial village's emphasis on marriage. Bachelors and maids were often rejected and penalized in various ways. Plymouth and Hartford, for example, taxed single men much more heavily than married ones. To render bachelorhood ludicrous, the government of Eastham, Massachusetts, also ordered the following in 1695: "Every unmarried man in the township shall kill six blackbirds or three crows while he remains single; as a penalty for not doing it, shall not be married until he obey this order." It is no wonder, therefore, that such attitudes, combined with the many needs generated by the prevailing conditions, often led to hasty marriages. Not infrequently, a lonely man merely proposed to a woman whom he had just met for the first time, thus securing a desperately needed mate and housekeeper on the very same day!

Such attitudes further made early marriage desirable. Thus, one "finds unmarried women of twenty-five referred to in the literature as 'ancient maids' " (Nimkoff, 1947, p. 77). Even at 20 a woman was regarded as a "stale maid." Both sexes, therefore, usually married when quite young—girls very often at the age of 13—as a result of which, in places such as North Carolina, one could find many grandmothers of 27! Of course, in view of the scarcity of women and the abundance of free land, this practice was not unwise.

The predominant form of marriage in colonial days was not the sacramental, but the civil type. "This was owing partly to the fact that certain colonists had resided in Holland, where civil marriage existed, and others had come at the time of the Cromwell Civil Marriage Act. Hostility to papism was keen in the English colonies" (Kirkpatrick, 1955, p. 114). Accordingly, it was the magistrate, not the clergyman, who officiated at marriages. In fact, a Boston clergyman who dared perform a wedding ceremony was taken to court and tried for his offense.

Countless marriages involved widows and widowers, since the death rate was exceedingly high. Moreover, because of their property and experience, widows were among the most desirable potential spouses. In Plymouth, the widow Susanna White married Edward Winslow only seven weeks after his wife's death, and Isaac Winslow, needing a spouse urgently, proposed to a certain woman a few hours after burying his wife.

Decline of patriarchy. Not many years after the wedding, households, which started with small groups of parents and children, "often grew by the addition of indentured or wage-earning servants, unattached female relatives, and sometimes married sons with their wives and children" (Queen, Habenstein, & Adams, 1961, p. 272). But these were not households of the patriarchal type found in Europe. Since, in numerous cases, "young people never returned to the paternal home or even saw their families again, after they had set out toward the frontier on horseback or by wagon" (Truxal & Merrill, 1947, p. 99), the father's authority was undermined considerably. In other words, social and geographical mobility, resulting from the Protestant ethic, individualism, political democracy, and the frontier environment, led to the gradual decline of patriarchy. The individual thus replaced the family as the basic unit of society in the New World.

Woman's status. Women's position tended to improve as a result of the spirit generated by such forces. According to Groves and Groves (1947, p. 144), the "new conditions on this side of the ocean made it difficult from the first to maintain the patriarchal control of daughters." Her companionship, hard work, and the creation of additional workers through reproduction rendered a wife most useful. Women's high death rate, usually caused by childbirth and backbreaking labor, made them scarcer, thus raising their status further. Such scarcity was especially prevalent in the western regions of the country. That is why, occasionally, heroic efforts were made to supply men in this area with unattached women from the eastern sections of the New World. At any rate, these conditions led to many freedoms for women. The economic rights of daughters, for instance, were virtually identical to those of their brothers. Moreover, not only husbands, but also wives were in general permitted by the law to divorce their spouses. A few women, like Salem's Mrs. Goose, even worked outside the home, operating shops or stores of various types (cf. Calhoun, Vol. I, p. 169).

Still, women's emancipation was not complete. In the sphere of religious matters, men continued to be dominant. Fornication and adultery led to the imposition of more severe penalties on females than on their male partners. The practice of witchcraft among women was punished inhumanly. And in 1699, Virginia formally forbade its female population to vote.

In general, women functioned primarily as diligent and industrious housekeepers. The making of clothes, the preparation of food, the rearing of children, and the like constituted their chief activities. Not infrequently, they also worked in the fields, helping their men and servants.

It was only in the South that chivalry became dominant, and even there, romance, courtesy, and respect for women were typical of only the upper classes, not of Negroes and poor whites. The reasons for the rise of this unusual phenomenon were at least three: the shortage of women, which made them more valuable; the presence of slavery, which freed women from manual labor; and the plantation system, which created wealth and leisure for the South's aristocracy.

Family size. Regarding family size in early America, Bossard (1954, p. 623) has stated: "Families of ten or twelve were quite common; twenty or twenty-five children in one family were not rare enough to occasion comment." Benjamin Franklin, for instance, came from a family of 17, and Boston's Green, a printer, produced 30 children. Also prolific was Sara Thayer, who died in 1751, and who was eulogized as follows (quoted in Bossard, 1954, pp. 623–624):

Also she was a fruitful vine,
The truth I may relate,—

Fourteen was of her body born
And lived to man's estate.

From these did spring a numerous race,
One hundred thirty-two;
Sixty and six each sex alike,
So I declare to you.

This characteristic, resulting from limited knowledge of birth control and the importance of children as potential workers, tended to reinforce the family members' security. Ordinarily, no individual depended exclusively on one or very few relatives. Thus, the death of a person seldom constituted a major psychological or economic catastrophe for the rest of the family. Nevertheless, in view of the rather primitive medical conditions that prevailed at that time, one should not conclude that the early American family was much larger than the one which is typical of the United States today.

Indeed, child mortality was quite high. The specific reasons for this were: (a) rigorous geographical conditions; (b) inadequate housing; (c) the rule of baptizing children on the first Sunday after birth, even if the water and the church were exceedingly cold; (d) the small number of available physicians; (e) the often charlatanic methods of treating children's diseases; (f) poor sanitation; (g) certain curious practices, such as the effort to toughen children's feet by keeping them wet as long as possible, for instance, by wearing shoes with thin soles; and (h) widespread child labor.

Child training. This last began at a very early age, since there was a great deal of hard work to be done in the rather forbidding and inhospitable new environment, and since the Puritans conceived of work as a virtue. Two other reasons were the influence of the Hebrew tradition and the tendency among the aristocrats to utilize child labor. Especially unfortunate were children coming from very poor families, who were often sold as apprentices. In the South, one of the organizations making extensive use of child labor was Virginia's London Company, some of whose workers were children that had been kidnapped in Europe.

The home, like the school and the law, also placed extreme emphasis on discipline. Corporal punishment was usually administered generously. This, of course, is not surprising, since most early Americans agreed with preacher John Robinson, who asserted: "there is in all children . . . a stubberness and stoutness of minde arising from naturall pride which must in the first place be broken and beaten down" (quoted in Calhoun, 1945, Vol. I, p. 112). Respect for one's parents and grandparents was further stressed in every possible way. Accordingly, a Long Island lass of 11 considered it necessary to open one of her letters in this way: "Ever Honored Grandfather: Sir." And she closed thus: "Your most obedient and Duty full Granddaughter Pegga Treadwell." Moreover, a New York law stated: "If any Child or Children, above sixteen years of age . . . shall smite their Natural Father or Mother, unless provoked . . . that Child, or those Children so offending shall be put to Death" (Earle, 1896, p. 16).

The religious training of children was equally strict. According to the diary of Boston's Judge Sewall, one day his little daughter began to cry, as "she was afraid she should goe to Hell, her Sins were not pardon'd. . . . Her Mother asked her whether she pray'd. She answered yes but fear'd her prayers were not heard because her Sins were not pardon'd" (quoted in Bossard, 1954, p. 633). Sam, the judge's 10-year-old son, however, was less receptive at first, when his father began to give him a rather morbid and macabre lecture on religion and death. The little boy, complained Sewall in frustration, "seemed not much to mind, eating an Aple" (quoted in Bossard, 1954, p. 632). Cotton Mather's daughter had a similar experience when she was only four. In her father's words: "I took my little daughter Katy into my study and there told my child that I am to dy shortly

and she must, when I am dead, remember everything I now said to her. I sett before her the sinfull condition of her nature, and charged her to pray in secret places every day" (quoted in Calhoun, 1945, Vol. I, p. 108).

At least two factors explain the emphasis placed on this sort of religious training. To begin with, the prevalent belief was that children were wicked by nature—Jonathan Edwards called them vipers, and Whitfield described them as rattlesnakes. The other belief was that children were miniature adults.

The educational training of children was more advanced in the North, where there were many more public and private schools than in the South. By 1649, with the exception of Rhode Island, all New England colonies had made a certain amount of education compulsory. It was in the South, then, that the educational role of the home was more extensive. Among the upper classes, it was not the parents themselves, however, but nurses, governesses, and tutors who were responsible for the child's training. In general, boys in early America were taught the three R's, Euclid, and Latin, while girls were usually given much less training, most of which consisted of sewing, dancing, and the like.

In the area of manners, innumerable manuals supplied children with detailed instructions such as the following: "Sing not, hum not, wiggle not. Spit nowhere in the room but in the corner, and wipe it with thy foot." Boys and girls were also advised: "When any speak to thee, stand up. Say not I have heard it before. . . . Snigger not; never question the Truth of it" (quoted in Bossard, 1954, p. 629). And a didactic poem suggested

Defile not thy lips with eating much,
As a Pigge eating draffe;
Eate softly and drinke mannerlye,
Take heed you do not quaffe.
Scratche not thy head with thy fyngers
(pp. 629–630).

Divorce. During this period, divorce was

much less common than at the present time. In Connecticut, the grounds for dissolving marriage were desertion, adultery, and fraudulent contract. Those in Massachusetts were similar: cruel treatment of the wife, desertion, and adultery committed by the female spouse, but not by the male.

Self-sufficiency. Another difference was the emphasis which early Americans placed on the family as an economic unit. According to Hart and Hart (1941, p. 244), "The home was the factory during the first two centuries after our ancestors began to settle America." And it was the household rather than the family which, particularly in the South, functioned as an economic unit. Furthermore, in the plantation system, the size, isolation, and self-sufficiency of the household were greater than in New England. Southern male heirs also enjoyed more inheritance privileges than their northern counterparts, since primogeniture and other male-centered property rights in New England were soon abandoned almost completely. Concerning a typical southern estate of the self-sufficing type, Calhoun (1945, Vol. I, p. 229) wrote that George Washington "had a smithy, charcoal-burners, brickmakers, carpenters, masons, a flour-mill, coopers, and a vessel to carry produce to market. He also employed shoemakers and operated a weaving establishment." Needless to add, kinsmen often co-operated extensively, not only in economic matters, but in others as well, in view of the relative absence of agencies that might deprive the family of its functions.

Morals. In another passage, dealing with morality in early America, Calhoun (1945, Vol. I, p. 132) stated that, according to Groton church records, "until 1803 whenever a child was born less than seven months after marriage a public confession had to be made before the whole congregation." Obviously, the faithful found such confessions most interesting and fascinating, since church attendance increased considerably whenever sinners confessed their offenses. One may further conclude that

sexual immorality may have been promoted rather than diminished by this sort of sensationalism. Other penalties were fines, imprisonment, whipping, branding, the wearing of the scarlet letter (A), and the use of pillories and stocks. One of those punished by confinement to the stocks was a captain who, in public and on Sunday, dared kiss his wife upon his return from a three years' voyage! Women, of course, were ordinarily punished more severely. And adultery, especially when it was committed for the second time, was considered a most serious crime— much more serious than fornication. In fact, in very early times, it was often punished by death in virtually all New England colonies. Such was the Puritan moral code.

In the South, however, the laws dealing with immorality were much less strict. One of the reasons for such liberalism was the presence of Negro women, whom white men were usually tempted to exploit. In this part of the country, wrote Mowrer (1932, p. 259), before the Civil War, concubinage involving colored women "was a common, if not a sanctioned, practice." White mistresses were also common. In fact, several governors kept paramours quite openly, while it was not unusual among upper-class men to recognize their illegitimate offspring.

Forces Shaping the Modern American Family

Marriage in the United States at the present time is ordinarily based on romantic love and individual choice of mate through dating. Moreover, the average age at first marriage is lower for both sexes than it was a few decades ago, though probably not lower than in early America. And interethnic, interclass, and interreligious unions are much more numerous now than in the past.

Parents, too, have become more democratic. Their authority, even that of the father, has declined extensively. Thus, decisions are commonly made, not by the father alone, but through discussions involving the husband, his wife, and, not infrequently, their more mature offspring.

Emancipation of women. As a result of the feminist movement and other forces, one of the most spectacular changes may be seen in the social status of women. Although Thomas Jefferson, despite his liberal convictions, believed that women should not participate in the world of politics, men such as Thomas Paine, Ralph Waldo Emerson, John Greenleaf Whittier, and others supported feminism with enthusiasm. In 1848, the first American women's rights convention took place at Seneca Falls, New York, where it was called by Elizabeth Cady Stanton and Lucretia Mott. Through the "Declaration of Sentiments" drawn up by this convention, women complained: Man has made woman, "if married, in the eye of the law, civilly dead"; "He has taken from her all right in property"; and "He has so framed the laws of divorce . . . as to be wholly regardless of the happiness of woman—the law in all cases going upon a false supposition of the supremacy of man, and giving all power into his hands" (quoted in Calhoun, 1945, vol. II, p. 119).

Such protests led to the gradual emancipation of women. For instance, "The first woman in government service was Clara Barton, who became a clerk in the Pension Office in 1854" (Sait, 1938, pp. 421–422). Previously, in 1833, the first institutions of higher education had opened their doors to female students. Then, in 1837, the first measures were taken to remove women's property disabilities. Another economic freedom consisted in their gainful employment outside the home, which, even for married women, was accelerated dramatically by both world wars. Moreover, as early as 1868, the territory of Wyoming permitted its women to vote. But it was President Woodrow Wilson who, in spite of his rather antifeminist attitudes, in September 1918 recommended a constitutional amendment that would give the female population the right to vote. The amendment, which the President believed would help win the war, was adopted in 1920.

All this, of course, does not mean that complete equality between the sexes has now been attained. On the contrary, this is still a man-centered world, and, strangely enough, even at the present time there are many women who seem to approve of a certain degree of discrimination against their own sex.

Women's emancipation constitutes one of the main reasons why family size has declined. As the birth rate decreases and childlessness increases, although infant mortality has diminished appreciably, the small nuclear family becomes more dominant. Needless to add, the extended type cannot be maintained in our society, in view of the prevailing geographical mobility and the higher educational and occupational achievements of the younger generation.

The birth-control movement. The freedom gained by the female population is only one of the factors explaining the modern birth-control movement and the resulting limited family size. More specifically, the reasons for expanding birth control may be outlined as follows:

1. The emancipation of women, which has rendered them much less reproduction-minded.

2. The economic insecurity generated by industrialization.

3. The often exorbitant expenses involved in child-rearing. The passing of the frontier and the adoption of laws against child labor have changed preadolescent and, to some extent, adolescent children into liabilities. Even childbirth itself has become more expensive, since it now usually takes place in a hospital.

4. The prevailing budgeting complex, because of which even children must be budgeted through planned parenthood.

5. The educational and other advantages enjoyed by children coming from small families.

6. The vertical social mobility which parents ordinarily emphasize at the expense of having children.

7. The decline of religiosity and the corresponding prevalence of secularism, due to which a child's birth is no longer regarded as an act of God. In 1931, even the Federal Council of Churches expressed its approval of birth control.

8. Recognition of birth control by the medical profession: the American Medical Association recognized this practice officially in 1937.

9. The increase in the number of birth-control clinics.

10. The legal approval in all states, except for Connecticut and Massachusetts, of medical advice concerning contraception for reasons of health.

11. More extensive education, which tends to liberalize the population in many respects, including acceptance of birth control.

12. The philosophy of individualism.

As a social movement, modern birth control began in England in 1823. Francis Place, a worker, in that year distributed for the first time his so-called diabolical handbills. These were leaflets advocating the reduction of family size as a panacea for the problem of poverty.

Five years later, under Place's influence, the birth-control movement reached the United States. Then, in 1832, appeared the first American work on the subject, written by a physician, Charles Knowlton's *Fruits of Philosophy*. In 1914, another controversial work on contraception was published, Margaret Sanger's *Family Limitation*. This brave public-health nurse also established the American Birth Control League and, in 1916, the first birth-control clinic. Moreover, she was one of the leaders who organized the Geneva World Population Conference of 1927. Part of the history of the movement is presented in her famous autobiography, *My Fight for Birth Control,* which appeared in 1931. Two other developments were the founding of a monthly journal, the *Birth Control Review,* in 1917, and the organization of the Voluntary Parenthood League, in 1919.

The child-welfare movement. As far as children are concerned, one of the most important developments has been the child-welfare movement. In 1899, the National Conference of Charities and Corrections suggested numerous ways of promoting the welfare of children. Ten years later, Theodore Roosevelt called the first White House Conference, which emphasized the principles of prevention, foster homes, adequate record-keeping, and so forth. It also recommended the following: "A bill is pending in Congress for the establishment of a Federal Children's Bureau to collect and disseminate information affecting the welfare of children. In our judgment the establishment of such a Bureau is desirable." This measure was adopted in 1912. The Children's Code movement, aimed at the unification, coordination, and improvement of laws dealing with child welfare, was first organized in Ohio, in 1911.

Loss of family functions. The family's economic, educational, religious, recreational, and protective tasks have been reduced considerably. For instance, while the early American household functioned as a unit of production and consumption, today virtually all economic goods are manufactured outside of the home. The making of clothes, baking, canning, preserving, and the like are no longer prevalent domestic activities. Even consumption—as in the case of meals—often takes place outside. The typical housewife's work has been rendered much easier by the use of innumerable modern household appliances.

Next, the educational function has been taken over by the school, since social complexity necessitates highly specialized training. The time element alone reveals the immensity of this change: in colonial days, children ordinarily attended school for about three months, not nine or 10, as they do at the present time; now education typically begins at an earlier age and ends at a later one; and children nowadays spend a greater part of the day in school. Furthermore, a larger proportion of young people are now enrolled in high schools and institutions of higher education.

Similarly, religious activities have become much less common, especially among the urban and Protestant segments of the population. For example, saying grace at meals, reading the Holy Scriptures, attending church, and the like are emphasized less today, in view of the influence of war, modern economic conditions, and the spirit of secularism and hedonism. Religious training usually takes place, not at home, but in churches and Sunday schools.

World War II, by partially dissolving the family, also led to the development of new recreational habits among lonely soldiers, working wives, and neglected children. Extended leisure time has further contributed to this change, and recreational pursuits, even among members of a family, are becoming more and more heterogeneous. Therefore, the government and private business have responded by organizing many facilities and activities: city parks, picnic areas, baseball diamonds, tennis courts, swimming pools, skating rinks, bowling alleys, drama, music, dancing, crafts, and so forth. Even schools and churches have, to a certain extent, become recreational centers.

In addition, the protective functions of the family have been transferred, at least partially, to the government, as well as to various private social agencies and insurance companies. To illustrate, it is the police and fire departments that now protect the family. The sick are treated in hospitals. And the juvenile court system, introduced in 1899, assumes responsibility for child discipline.

Personal and family disorganization. Finally, immorality, divorce, and other forms of individual and social disorganization have become more extensive. The anonymity of the urban community now "is an invitation to prostitution and illicit unions that offer temporary, and sometimes permanent, substitutes for marriage and family life" (Baber, 1939, p. 11). War, economic crises, crowding in the city, the emancipation of women and young people, commer-cialized recreation, the automobile, modern methods of contraception, Freud's theories, certain types of literature, and countless other forces have also reinforced the prevailing disorganization.

Summary

In brief, some of the main changes in the American family are as follows: (a) individual choice of mate based on romantic love; (b) decline in parental authority; (c) emancipation of women; (d) reduced family size; (e) emphasis on child welfare; (f) decline in the economic, educational, religious, recreational, and protective functions of the family; and (g) prevalence of various forms of disorganization.

CONCLUSION

When dealing with changes in the family, it seems necessary to add a few words regarding the past, present, and future of this institution.

1. It appears that, at the present time, there is a lack of data whose synthesis would facilitate the construction of satisfactory supersystems concerning family evolution. This, however, does not mean that regularity, which renders scientific research meaningful, is not present in this area. On the contrary, as in other social spheres, a certain degree of regularity or recurrence is typical of family phenomena.

2. It seems that, in view of man's nature, as well as of the conditions prevailing on our planet, the family is a virtually indestructible institution, which, throughout history, has been capable of resolving seemingly insoluble problems, and surviving cataclysmic catastrophes. In addition, even during periods of decadence, it remains exceedingly influential in numerous respects.

3. The concept of *social telesis* (the conscious choice and achievement by society of desirable objectives), as Lester F. Ward, America's pioneer sociologist, would suggest, constitutes an indispensable tool, if the

world of the family is to be transformed consciously, intelligently, creatively.

4. Needless to add, such telesis would be incomplete and ineffectual if not based on the cooperation of all social institutions.

5. Undoubtedly, family life education is a most valuable instrument, and it will be rendered more valuable and efficacious if greater emphasis is placed on its more serious, objective, scientific aspects. [Cf. Ch. 21.]

6. Stressing some knowledge of the history of the family would diminish parochialism and provincialism in this area, while at the same time it would supply invaluable insights into familial phenomena.

7. The often meaningless debate between "old-fashioned sentimentalists" and "Plutarchian types" (Zimmerman, 1947a, pp. 786 *et passim*), rather fashionable among family experts at the present time, should be discouraged, since it is primarily based on a priori arguments. Instead, main emphasis should be placed upon an objective evaluation of each family characteristic, which should then, and only then, be reinforced or combated, depending on its unemotionally and empirically ascertained merits. After all, change is inevitable. In an industrial society, for instance, it is futile and unavailing to attempt the resurrection of familism, with all of its ramifications. But its complete rejection, without scientific justification, also seems unwise.

8. Objective, extensive, and sufficiently coordinated family research may easily lead to the construction, at least for each social system, of an ideal-typical *Homo domesticus,* characterized by attitudes and behavior regarded as highly desirable by scientific investigators. This construct or abstraction may then be presented to the members of the social system as a goal to be pursued and approximated.

9. Finally, the author is convinced that research and teaching emphasizing the discovery and internalization of fundamental principles of the "A causes B" type would achieve much more than mere description or value-laden polemics. And this can be employed in probing both historical and cross-sectional phenomena.

REFERENCES

Anshen, Ruth N. The family in transition. In Ruth N. Anshen. (Ed.), *The family: its function and destiny.* New York: Harper, 1949.

Baber, R. E. *Marriage and the family.* New York: McGraw-Hill, 1939.

Bachofen, J. J. *Das mutterrecht: eine untersuchung über die gynaikokratie der alten welt nach iherer religiosen und rechtlichen natur.* Stuttgart: Krais & Hoffman, 1861.

Bogardus, E. S. *The development of social thought.* (3rd ed.) New York: Longmans, Green, 1955.

Bossard, J. H. S. *The sociology of child development.* (Rev. ed.) New York: Harper, 1954.

Briffault, R. *The mothers: the matriarchal theory of social origins.* New York: Macmillan, 1927. 3 vols.

Burgess, E. W., & Locke, H. J. *The family.* (2nd ed.) New York: American Book, 1960. 3 vols. in 1.

Calhoun, A. W. *A social history of the American family.* New York: Barnes & Noble, 1945. 3 vols. in 1.

Christensen, H. T. *Marriage analysis: foundations for successful family life.* (2nd ed.) New York: Ronald Press, 1958.

Clare, I. S. *Library of universal history.* New York: Peale & Hill, 1898. 12 vols.

Cunningham, Bess V. *Family behavior.* (2nd ed.) Philadelphia: Saunders, 1940.

Dill, S. *Roman society.* (2nd ed.) London: Macmillan, 1910.

Dorsey, G. A. *The story of civilization.* New York: Halcyon House, 1931.

Dreikurs, R. *The challenge of marriage.* New York: Duell, Sloan & Pearce, 1946.

Durant, W. *The story of civilization.* Vol. 1. *Our oriental heritage.* New York: Simon & Schuster, 1935.

Duruy, V. *History of Rome.* Boston: Dana Estes, 1886.

Duruy, V. *History of Greece.* Boston: Dana Estes, 1889.

Earle, Alice M. *Colonial days in old New York.* New York: Scribner, 1896.

Elmer, M. C. *The sociology of the family.* Boston: Ginn, 1945.

Feucht, O. E. (Ed.) *Sex and the church.* St. Louis: Concordia, 1961.

Flugel, J. C. *The psycho-analytic study of the family.* (6th ed.) London: Hogarth Press, 1939.

Grote, G. *History of Greece.* New York: Harper, 1857.

Groves, E. R. *The American family.* Philadelphia: Lippincott, 1934.

Groves, E. R., & Groves, Gladys H. *The contemporary American family.* Philadelphia: Lippincott, 1947.

Hart, H., & Hart, Ella B. *Personality and the family.* (Rev. ed.) Boston: Heath, 1941.

Heitland, W. E. *The Roman republic.* Cambridge: Cambridge Univer. Press, 1923.

Irving, W. *Diedrich Knickerbocker's a history of New York.* New York: Putnam, 1880.

Kirkpatrick, C. *The family.* New York: Ronald Press, 1955.

Langdon-Davies, J. *A short history of women.* New York: Literary Guild of America, 1927.

Leclercq, J. *Marriage and the family.* (4th ed.) New York: Pustet, 1949.

Maine, H. J. S. *Ancient law.* New York: Dutton, n. d.

Mead, Margaret. Family: primitive. In R. A. Seligman (Ed.), *Encyclopedia of the social sciences.* Vol. 6. New York: Macmillan, 1931. Pp. 65–67.

Messer, Mary B. *The family in the making.* New York: Putnam, 1928.

Mommsen, T. *The history of nations: Rome.* Chicago: Snow, 1910.

Morgan, L. H. *Systems of consanguinity and affinity of the human family.* Washington, D.C.: Smithsonian Institution, 1870.

Morgan, L. H. *Ancient society, or researches in the lines of human progress from savagery, through barbarism to civilization.* New York: Holt, 1877.

Mowrer, E. R. *The family.* Chicago: Univer. of Chicago Press, 1932.

Nash, A. S. Ancient past and living present. In H. Becker & R. Hill (Eds.), *Family, marriage & parenthood.* (2nd ed.) Boston: Heath, 1955.

Nimkoff, M. F. *The family.* Boston: Houghton Mifflin, 1934.

Nimkoff, M. F. *Marriage and the family.* Boston: Houghton Mifflin, 1947.

Queen, S. A., Habenstein, R. W., & Adams, J. B. *The family in various cultures.* (2nd ed.) Philadelphia: Lippincott, 1961.

Rostovtzeff, M. *The social and economic history of the Roman empire.* (2nd ed.) Oxford: Clarendon Press, 1957.

Sait, Una B. *New horizons for the family.* New York: Macmillan, 1938.

Saltus, E. *Historia amoris.* New York: Brentano, 1906.

Spencer, H. *The principles of sociology.* New York: Appleton, 1897. 3 vols.

Thorndike, Lynn. *A short history of civilization.* New York: Crofts, 1934.

Truxal, A. G., & Merrill, F. E. *The family in American culture.* New York: Prentice-Hall, 1947.

Westermarck, E. A. *The history of human marriage.* London: Macmillan, 1903.

Westermarck, E. A. *The history of human marriage.* (5th ed.) New York: Macmillan, 1922. 3 vols.

Westermarck, E. A. On primitive marriage, a rejoinder to Mr. V. F. Calverton. *Amer. J. Sociol.,* 1936, 41, 565–589.

Woody, T. *Life and education in early societies.* New York: Macmillan, 1949.

Zimmerman, C. C. *Family and civilization.* New York: Harper, 1947. (a)

Zimmerman, C. C. *The family of tomorrow.* New York: Harper, 1947. (b)

CHAPTER 12 Cross-Cultural Analyses of Family Structure

MORRIS ZELDITCH, JR.
Stanford University

This review is limited to examining data from non-Western societies that bear on theories about the structure of the family. The limitation is severe in several respects. First, investigations from the United States and Canada, Europe (including the whole of the Soviet Union), and any colonial nations that are to all intents and purposes Western (e.g., nonaboriginal Australia), are excluded even where the evidence is relevant to whatever hypothesis is reviewed. This refers both to historical and to contemporary evidence. For example, in examining evidence relevant to effects of industrialization on the family, all the recent results in England and the United States, as well as pertinent developments in the Soviet family, are omitted.[1]

Second, the large amount of purely descriptive ethnography of the family that does not bear on any particularly significant theoretical issue is given scanty or no treatment. Nor are certain fairly general issues discussed—such as the determinants of

polygamous marriage—which are not at the moment of much theoretical import.

Third, a theory, or part of a theory, on which no comparative data bear is omitted. Thus, much of the theory of role differentiation cannot be tested with the available evidence, and only that part for which one can provide evidence is developed here.

Finally, among other topics, theories about complementary needs in mate selection, factors that determine happiness in marriage, the social psychology of sexual relationships, or child-rearing practices are omitted as not bearing on problems of structure. The attention in this review is given mostly to the range of family structures, the properties of different kinds of family structure, and some of the characteristics of society that correlate with the occurrence of different kinds of structure.

The one limit not stipulated is that the relevant theories do not have to originate in problems of the kind found in Western societies. A great deal of attention is given to theoretical issues that arise only where there are corporate descent groups, preferential marriage systems, multifunctional kinship systems, and so on. Ordinarily, the

---

[1] This evidence is reviewed elsewhere in this volume. See also Zelditch (1964), where historical and Western data are the main focus of attention.

contrast with the West will prove to illuminate our own family structure, but that is not the justification for inclusion in this review. The justification used here is only whether a general theoretical issue is concerned; the Western world is only a special case, no matter how important to us. [This chapter follows the structural-functional approach presented in Ch. 3, and although with a necessary minimum of substantive overlapping, it is essentially complementary to both that chapter and Ch. 13.]

METHODOLOGY AND CONCEPTS

Sources of Data

Three sorts of materials are available. First, there is an extensive library of descriptive ethnographies; although a given example may or may not have data relevant to a given theoretical question, and the data may or may not be complete and accurate. An excellent example of a useful ethnography is Firth's *We The Tikopia* (1936).

Second, there are analytic investigations of one, two, three, or more, but always a very few, carefully (and nonrandomly) selected societies that are intensively documented, or even represent primary field work of the investigator. Classic and early examples are Durkheim's *Elementary Forms of the Religious Life* (1915) and Radcliffe-Brown's *Andaman Islanders* (1922). The so-called functional school tends to produce monographs of this sort.

Third, there are analytic investigations that compare many (say, 250) societies, representing either all that are available with relevant information or else some random sample of the available body of monographic information. The classic early example is Tylor's "On a Method of Investigating the Development of Institutions: Applied to Laws of Marriage and Descent" (1889), which, despite its evolutionary biases, sets many of the problems that still concern students of family structure. Since

that time, Hobhouse, Wheeler, and Ginsberg's *Material Culture of the Simpler Peoples* (1915) and Murdock's *Social Structure* (1949) have represented the principal advances in method.

Critique of the Methods

The intensive and the extensive comparative study represent two somewhat opposed traditions; when the heirs of one tradition face the heirs of the other, great heat is sometimes produced by their friction (see Leach, 1960). That they have something in common is easily demonstrated. For example, both have the purpose of extending the possible states of affairs encompassed by a theory by taking advantage of naturally occurring variations in social arrangements from society to society. And both tend to regard society, rather than individuals, as their natural unit of investigation. But each can muster very severe criticisms of the other, and the fact is that neither alone is wholly satisfactory.

The extensive statistical study is examined first, on the grounds that it looks at first sight the more impregnable of the two. Among the defects for which the extensive statistical study has been criticized are:

1. *The quality of its data.* The finest ethnography is usually treated as no better evidence than the sloppiest amateur effort, and a case that is much studied with a wealth of documentation by many different observers is treated as no better evidence than a case described in a single account. If only the best cases were used, there would not be enough for statistical analysis.

2. *The definition of its units.* The Cheyenne and the Arapaho are two North American Indian tribes. It happens that they are virtually identical, however, because of their historical relationship. Do two names make two societies? Put more technically, are they independent cases? Application of tests of statistical significance, at least the kind used in most current studies, presumes independent cases. More recently, distributional safeguards are in

use to guard against such error; that is, an attempt is made to obtain cases from widely separated geographical areas. But there is a second problem: there are perhaps six or eight studies of Chinese villages, and perhaps one study of one Kaska village. Do the six or eight Chinese villages count as one case and the Kaska as one? Is China one society?

3. *The homogeneity of its units.* Even technically sophisticated sociologists and anthropologists talk about the "simpler" societies. Their simplicity is a fiction. But if they are not homogeneous, what is it scholars are really interested in comparing? Are they comparing group averages? Are they comparing only rules, regardless of how far individuals deviate from the rules? While the latter view is frequently expressed, the amount of deviation is often important, yet completely unknown.

4. *The meaningfulness of its comparisons.* Earliest efforts at large-scale comparisons fell into errors because of the way comparisons were made: superficially similar traits were compared regardless of what they meant to different people in different societies. Tylor (1889), for example, interpreted customs such as marriage by capture and matriliny as "survivals" of earlier customs, without regard to their present meanings. This gave rise, in reaction, to somewhat misleading methodological rules applied in functional studies (such as the "unity" of the parts of a system) that were sometimes thought of as empirical generalizations or, worse, as theoretical postulates. The problem is not to confuse abstraction with trait atomism. Every study abstracts, but trait atomism, instead of abstracting properties of systems, abstracts parts from their context. This is legitimate only where the context has no bearing on the properties of the trait, an unlikely situation. Whiting (1954) has insisted that current investigations do not suffer this defect, since only comparable meanings, not just superficially similar traits, are used. Indeed, he believes, traits superficially very different can be compared if shown to have the same meaning.

5. *Its inattention to time trends.* In 1930, the Japanese divorce rate was 98 divorces for each 1,000 marriages made in that year, while the United States divorce rate was 173.9 per 1,000 marriages. Someone is bound to claim that the more stable, more familistic society had the lower divorce rate. But this is sheerest nonsense. In 1890, the Japanese divorce rate was 335 divorces per 1,000 marriages, while the United States rate was 55.6 per 1,000 marriages. Since that time, the Japanese rate has steadily declined, while the United States rate has steadily risen. Two comparisons are legitimate: (a) a comparison of the two time trends; (b) a comparison of two points in that trend that are either both in equilibrium or both represent some equivalent stage in the same process. But this problem in comparison is very often ignored, although occasionally great efforts at reconstructing time paths are made (see Murdock, 1949).

6. *The completeness of its enumeration.* Neither random sampling nor the standard kinds of enumeration of cases guard against the danger that rare events are missed. The size of the sample gives a false sense of security. This is partly what has happened in the controversy over the universality of the nuclear family: If 250 societies have a nuclear family, is it not universal? No.

Aside from all this, one of the supposed virtues of the extensive statistical study is no virtue at all. Even well-trained students sometimes confuse random sampling with randomization. Random sampling ensures that one has an unbiased, representative selection of available cases in some specifically defined universe. Randomization is a procedure used in experimentation whereby a subject in the experiment is assigned by some chance procedure to one of the manipulations in the experiment. Randomization ensures that many characteristics of the subjects that might confound the experimental manipulations have, in the long run, approximately zero correlations with the experimental manipulations. The effects of these randomized factors appear as "error" in the analysis of the results. A statistical significance test compares this error to the difference produced by the experimenter's manipulations and provides a test of the hypotheses that the error is at least as great as the difference obtained. If this hypothesis is rejected, then one is moderately confident that the result is due to the experimenter's manipulations rather than the uncontrolled (but randomized) properties of the subject. The statistical significance test applied to a *random sample* provides no such information. It ensures that differences are true differences, but says nothing about how the differences arise. Hence, from the point of view of explanatory hypotheses, the critical question is still unanswered: are the differences due to the factor to which they have been attributed, or to some other factor correlated with it? Care in interpreting the statistical paraphernalia, in other words, is required so as not to be misled by the amassing of .0001 probability levels.

Not that the alternative is without striking defects of its own. These are:

1. *Its possibilities of confusing the particular and the general.* The fewer the cases, the more likely that properties of the particular instance are confounded with properties of the type it is supposed to represent. Hence, such studies are often either undergeneralized or overgeneralized.

2. *Its limited control over confounding factors.* The danger of spurious correlation is acute, because there are too few cases to control for many factors. Thus, at best, any explanatory causal hypothesis is tested inconclusively.

Both defects are partially alleviated by careful selection of cases, as well as gradual accumulation of information if it is collected in the light of some question of continuing interest. The intensive comparative study samples "purposively," as distinct from randomly. Cases are chosen to satisfy certain specific criteria of the investigator, and accordingly can be chosen so that they are the most strategic, and also so that cases compared are matched on characteristics known at the time to be relevant. [Compare Sirjamaki's treatment of the comparative method in Ch. 2, above.]

The Meaning of the Family

If the family is universal, as most scholars believe, it ought to be possible to say just what property universally characterizes all families and only families; yet Leach (1955, p. 183), who is an eminent scholar of the subject, has claimed that there is no such property. Murdock has shown that sexual access, for example, is not universally confined to the family (1949, p. 5): only 39 per cent of societies for which he could collect relevant evidence disapproved of sexual relations between unrelated partners before marriage (see Table 1); 24 societies permitted great sexual freedom even after marriage (p. 270).

TABLE 1

SEXUAL ACCESS TO UNRELATED PARTNERS BEFORE MARRIAGE[a]

Freedom Permitted	Qualified Consent	Disapproval	N
47%	14%	39%	139

[a] Adapted from Murdock (1949), p. 5.

Not even the biological facts of parenthood can be universally identified with the family. In some societies, it has been necessary to distinguish the *genitor,* the agent of conception, from the *pater,* the role in society concerned with transmitting jural bonds, rights, and obligations (Radcliffe-Brown, 1930). The attitude of the Tallensi toward illegitimate children illustrates the importance of the distinction (Fortes, 1949). Among the Tallensi, all persons are grouped into patrilineal descent groups, that is, legal rights and one's position in society are determined by descent in the male line, from father to son. If a woman is married, any child she bears is the property of, and a member of, the descent group of her husband. Hence, if she has an adulterine child, it is easily absorbed into a legal status. The genitor does not feel any fatherly emotions at all, but the pater, who is the woman's husband, does feel the emotions of a father, even though he knows he is not the genitor. He also receives all the credit that is given to a father in that society, and the child is not stigmatized or deprived of any legal rights. The illegitimate child of an unwed mother, however, is not so easily absorbed. It must be given to the mother's patrilineal descent group (which is her father's group), in which it receives only part of its legal rights and is stigmatized as inferior in status (see Fig. 1).

Nor, finally, can the "family" be identified with some particular concrete group that always performs some particular functions (Gough, 1959; Levy, 1955; Levy & Fallers, 1959; Spiro, 1954). There is no single group that universally performs the same set of functions (see the discussion of the universality of the nuclear family below).

Nevertheless, there is always some institution in a society that scholars intuitively identify as a family. Malinowski (1930) has argued that this institution is always somehow involved in placing the "barbarian invasion" into appropriate jural relations with members already functioning in the society, that is, they normatively regulate the sociological process of inducting members into society (cf. Davis, 1939a; Davis,

1939b). This he called the "legitimacy" principle. It implies that a family exists if and only if there is a pater role in a society. And a pater role is one that is: (a) the determinant of the jural status, rights, and obligations of a child specifically recognized as the pater's child, whether or not he was involved in its conception; (b) specifically charged with "responsibility" for the child's behavior in society, whether or not the pater actually directly supervises that behavior. Two comments are required. First, the use of "he" in the definition is irrelevant; pater may occasionally, although never regularly, be a female. Second, the pater role may be split into two roles without violating the definition, but both must exist in some determinate relation to each other.

The legitimacy criterion is open to objection on the grounds that in certain societies the illegitimacy rate is very high, and that in these societies apparently no premium is put on either legal union or legal birth. Goode (1960), for example, has assembled the data on Caribbean illegitimacy rates

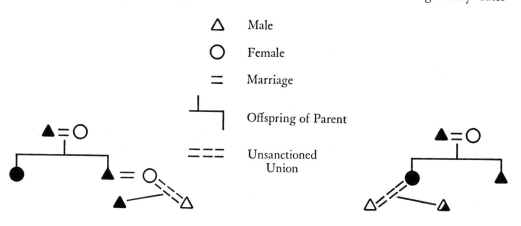

Δ   Male

O   Female

=   Marriage

⊥   Offspring of Parent

≡   Unsanctioned Union

Case 1. Jural Father Exists   Case 2. Jural Father Does Not Exist

Fig. 1. Jural Status of Tallensi Child Born Out of Wedlock. In Case 1 in Which Father's Descent Group Is Shown in Black, the Adulterous Child Is a Full Legal Member. In Case 2, in Which Mother's Descent Group Is Shown in Black, the Illegitimate Child is an Inferior and Stigmatized Member of This Group. Diagram Conventions Used in This Figure Are Followed in All Succeeding Figures.

(see Table 2), many of which exceed 50 per cent.

TABLE 2

Illegitimacy Rates in Selected Caribbean Political Units[a]

Political Unit	Year	Per Cent
British Guiana	1955	35
French Guiana	1956	65
Surinam (Excluding Bush Negroes and Aborigines)	1953	34
Barbados	1957	70
Bermuda	1957	30
Dominican Republic	1957	61
Guadeloupe	1956	42
Jamaica	1954	72
Antigua	1957	65
Martinique	1956	48
Trinidad and Tobago	1956	47
Grenada	1957	71
Puerto Rico	1955	28
Haiti	–	67–85

[a] From Goode (1960), p. 22.

Goode has argued, however, that these rates are more correctly interpreted as signs of family disorganization than as normatively approved births. They arise because family instability produces a courtship situation in which partners are anonymous and isolated from others, so that the usual family protections of Caribbean societies (chaperonage, family supervision) do not function. At the same time, the economic position of males is marginal, so that they do not wish to marry. Themselves in no position to bargain successfully, females gamble on eventually converting consensual unions into marriages. Ultimately (sometimes late in life), nearly all do marry. Middle- and upper-class marriages do not follow the same pattern, because these classes have more to lose in prestige, a less marginal economic foundation, and a stable family structure capable of sustaining the traditional courtship institutions (Goode, 1960).

When father, mother, and child form a recognizable unit within a society, this unit is referred to as a *nuclear family*. They are a "recognizable" unit when: (a) they are an acting unit with respect to some task or function; (b) they are treated as a single unit by persons outside the nuclear family, such as the father's father, for at least some, although not necessarily all, purposes. *Compound* nuclear families are formed if polygamy is permitted in a society. In that case, the *polygynous* family is one in which a man has two or more wives at the same time; a *polyandrous* family, which is relatively rare, is one in which a wife has two or more husbands at the same time. Polygynous families often bring together several sisters as co-wives, which is referred to as *sororal* polygyny; the corresponding case for husbands is *fraternal* polyandry.

Other Definitions and Distinctions

Larger units may be built up out of parent-child genealogical relationships. Where such groups are found, they are called *descent* groups. A *patrilineal* descent group is one in which membership is determined solely through male genealogical relationships; a *matrilineal* descent group is one in which membership is determined through the female line. A *bilateral* descent group, also called a *kindred,* is one in which the two lines are not distinct and both are counted. *Double descent* occurs where two distinct sets of groups are formed, one through females and one through males. Where descent is counted through one line only (male or female), the rule is called *unilineal* descent, and if the genealogical relationships can be actually traced the descent group is called a *lineage,* either a patrilineage or a matrilineage. If the links are believed to be there but cannot be traced, the group is called a *clan.*[2] If the lineage or clan actually acts in concert with respect to some

[2] In most of these definitions, Murdock (1949) is followed in order to encourage standard usage, at least in the United States. The writer has departed in the use of "clan," because its earlier use seems more common, some term of the sort is necessary, and another term is easily found for what Murdock calls a clan, namely, the "localized descent group" described below.

task or function, and has an authority structure of some sort, it is called a *corporate descent group* (see below, pp. 486–489).

The descent group, however, is never a *residential unit;* because it is *exogamous* (marriage is outside the group), either males or females must leave the group at marriage. A rule of residence is a rule that determines where a newly married couple lives after marriage. *Patrilocal* residence requires that a man live with his father and bring his wife home with him; *matrilocal* residence requires that a woman live with her mother and bring home her husband; *matri-patrilocal* residence requires first the one, then the other. If there is a choice between the two parental families, the rule is *bilocal.* If the nuclear family lives independently, the rule is *neolocal.* Finally, if the couple go to live with the husband's mother's brother, the rule is *avunculocal.*

Each residence rule except the neolocal creates an *extended family,* which is a group of relatives greater than the nuclear family living together and subordinate to the same authority.[3] Extended families are classified according to the rules of residence, e.g., *patrilocal extended family, matrilocal extended family, avunculocal extended family,* and so on.

In an extended family, the core of members that remain in their natal home is linked by descent, and those that marry into it are called the *affines.* It is possible to build an entire community by localizing a descent group in some manner, bringing in affines through a consistent rule of residence. For example, in China, a whole village will often be dominated by a single *Tsu* (patrilineage or patriclan), which, through a patrilocal residence rule, gives up its women in order to keep all the men together. These men then bring home their own wives. Authority in the community

will be in the hands of the males of the descent group. In this way, a *localized descent group* is formed. It differs from an extended family only in that it is a whole community.[4] Although patrilineages with patrilocal residence are the most common localized descent groups, two others are also sometimes found: matrilineages with matrilocal residence, and matrilineages with avunculocal residence.

So far, various *kinship units,* that is, concrete groups that act together in some capacity, have been defined. A *kinship system* is never such a unit in itself. A kinship system is a system of statuses (socially recognized categories) constructed of putative or real genealogical relationships. Social recognition of a genealogical link is required; biological links are not. Every kinship system ignores some biological links (as we ignore the difference between mother's brother and father's brother), and many kinship systems invent others, that is, use putative links to form groups where the links do not actually exist.

The various statuses are labeled by *kinship terms* that show how they are organized with respect to each other. There are two functions of such terms (Schneider & Roberts, 1956): They *classify,* in the same way that words are used to classify plants, animals, and other stimuli, in order to be able to talk about them and respond to them; and they *designate roles,* different roles being indicated by different terms. In some societies, all roles are allocated to kinship statuses, so that the roles designated may be economic, political, and ritual as well as kinship roles. In such societies, it is almost impossible for two persons to interact unless they are able to place people in the right kinship role with respect to themselves.

A knowledge of these different kinds of units is assumed in the review that follows.

---

[3] This usage is consistent with that of almost all comparative studies, but many American sociologists misuse it to designate *any* kind of kinship outside the nuclear family. See the discussion of industrialization and the family.

[4] Usage here follows Leach, 1951, although he called it a "local" descent group. It is this unit that Murdock called a clan.

It is particularly important to recognize the difficulties in simply referring to "the family" in comparing two or more societies, or in talking of "the family" in respect to two or more functions in the same society. If one wants to focus on the authority structure of the nuclear family, for example, it is important to keep this structure clearly distinct from the authority structure of the extended family. One may talk about the great authority of the "father," only to discover that it is the authority of the oldest male generation over affairs of the extended family that is being described. Because it is the father of the adult, married, but younger males who wields this authority, this "father" is easily confused with the "father" of the young, unmarried children of the nuclear family. The latter's authority may be very much less because of the incorporation of the nuclear family in the extended family.

If distinguishing the nuclear family and the extended family is difficult, distinguishing descent-group functions from extended-family functions may be even more difficult. Both, for example, may have economic functions: the descent group will regulate inheritance, own property, acquire wealth, and at the same time the extended family will be the unit of production, consumption, and distribution. The descent group may "lose" its economic functions (and wither away) without the extended family losing *its* economic functions—and perhaps vice versa.

Thus, even within the same society, one cannot refer to the "family" without specific knowledge of just what unit is meant. Many of the "simpler" societies are undifferentiated in the sense that economic, political, and ritual functions are performed by some form of kinship unit. But it is seldom the case that all are performed by exactly the same unit. And it is particularly the case that the *domestic* functions of child-rearing, preparing food, sleeping, eating, and the like, are not necessarily performed by the same units as the economic,

political, ritual, even educational functions. Some family units, such as the corporate descent group, can behave more like a business corporation than a "family." They can be impersonal, have a strict authority structure, be task-oriented, have restricted channels of communication, have problems of succession, develop elaborate rules, have conflicts among subunits, be elaborately stratified, and so on. These will affect, but not be the same as, the problems and processes of the more domestic units.

MARRIAGE AND DIVORCE

The Institution of Marriage

The elders of an African tribe, discussing the problems of "runaway" marriages and illegitimacy, complained to the 1883 Commission on Native Law and Custom: "It is all this thing called love. We do not understand it at all. This thing called love has been introduced . . . " (Gluckman, 1955, p. 76). *Romantic love* implies three things. It implies an intense affective involvement with a particular person, so that no other person will do as well. It implies freedom to choose that person without regard to the wishes of anyone else, and certainly not the wishes of parents. And it implies that instrumental considerations—money, power, calculated advantage, social rank—do not play a part in the choice. To the African elders, struggling with new social problems, marriage implied no particular attachment for the chosen partner, the marriage was not the free choice of the couple marrying, and instrumental considerations played a paramount part in the choice.

Arranged marriage is found where the consequences of marriage concern whole groups of kinsmen. The consequences are of two kinds: first, the choice of a mate itself has an effect on the kinship group. Where extended families and descent groups are prominent, marriage is conceived as an alliance between two lineages, not simply as a relation of two individuals, and both sides are concerned to select their allies with great care. Furthermore, significant economic interests are involved. Not only is there an exchange of goods at the time of the marriage, but the marriage affects the dispersal or concentration of inherited property, wealth, and resources. Where the kinship unit is a unit of stratification, so that a "poor" marriage reflects on the honor of the whole family, a powerful incentive is added to protect the family name. Of course, even if the descent group and/or extended family is a prominent feature of the social structure, freedom of choice is greatly increased where not much wealth or property is at stake or not much reputation is to be lost. Hence, freedom of choice is correlated with class status within societies and subsistence level between societies (Driver & Massey, 1957, p. 394).

A second consequence follows from the apparently universal conflict between the solidarity of the parent-child versus the husband-wife bond. The interests of the larger kinship group are organized around and embodied in the solidarity of parent and child after marriage; the greater the solidarity of the husband and wife, the more are the interests of the larger kinship group threatened. In Africa generally, as Gluckman (1955, p. 60) has observed, the bonds of conjugal solidarity are suspect. Among the Barotse, for example—and they are typical in this respect—if a man becomes too devoted to his wife, his family claims that his wife and her family used illegitimate magic to bewitch him out of his senses (see also Schapera, 1940). Hence, where the corporate descent group is important, so is arranged marriage, because it ensures that too strong a personal attachment will not destroy the lineal bond. At the same time, the unilocal extended family has an interest in the kind of working relationship it will be able to develop with in-marrying strangers—an interest that they will usually not leave to the whims of their younger, less responsible members.

That arranged marriage is correlated

with the inheritance of property and wealth is illustrated by Richards' (1940) comparison of the Central African Bemba with Southeastern Bantu tribes. The Bemba are close to the subsistence level, do not have permanent, inheritable possessions, and are seminomadic shifting cultivators—they move every four or five years, so that no hereditary claim to any particular plot of land is established. No extensive bridewealth is exchanged. Hence, when a man marries, no great economic involvement of his kinsmen is entailed, and he is relatively free to choose his wife as he wishes so far as they are concerned. In any case, since they do not provide him with bride-wealth, they cannot enforce authority over him even if they wished to do so. The pastoral Bantu have much more inheritable wealth and extensive exchanges of economic goods accompany marriage. There is, therefore, created between the marrying kin groups a network of credits, debts, future obligations, and instrumental concerns, and the system of payment and repayment binds individuals together for two to three generations (Richards, 1940, p. 14).

The roles of extended family and descent group solidarity after marriage are also illustrated in Richards' study. The Bemba are matrilineal and matrilocal. Therefore, although the husband's kinsmen care rather little about his choice, the wife's kinsmen care a good deal. As a result, the man may marry without his parent's consent, but the woman may not. According to Richards, Bemba women are famous for rebelling and even succeed in their rebellion some of the time; they are, however, much more restricted than men, because their fathers and their mothers' brothers (the latter are the authority figures in Bemba matrilineworking partner or who is going to ages) care who is going to become their threaten the solidarity of the descent group, respectively.

Where the exchange between kinship groups becomes very important, it is usually expressed in marriage payments or *bride-*

wealth. The bride-wealth represents two things: the cement of an instrumental alliance between groups and the exchange of wealth for the rights to a woman's offspring, and hence the heir necessary to perpetuate the descent group. It is not viewed as payment for chattel or for rights to treat the wife as a slave—indeed, the wife's family often views it as insurance of good treatment, since in the event of divorce the bride-wealth must be returned (see the discussion of bride-wealth and divorce below). In patrilineal societies, the association of bride-wealth with jural rights to a woman's offspring is indicated in the importance of bride-wealth as a criterion of legitimacy. If a woman bears a child to a man who has not paid bride-wealth, often the child is considered not legitimate and payment is required to validate it as heir to the father. Bride-wealth is most likely when residence is patrilocal and does not occur at all when residence is neolocal (see Table 3).

There are a number of mechanisms by which societies "contain" the danger of love relationships in the conjugal bond (see Goode, 1959).

1. *Child marriage.* Choice is absolutely controlled in this way. A well-known example is India. The Hindu idea, however, does not preclude the development of solidarity after marriage, since love and respect between husband and wife are supposed to grow gradually into a rather idealized relationship.

2. *Seclusion of women.* Everything is done to prevent possible marriage partners from meeting before marriage. A go-between or a family representative makes the contracts between the mates. Affective involvements remain for some time closer with parents than with husband or wife.

3. *Supervision.* Couples are not allowed to meet alone, and, if possible, whom one meets is determined by the parents. Hence, control over the courtship is in the hands of the parents or chaperones. If a couple is seen alone, it is taken as a sign that they are engaged, so that little preliminary exploration of a casual nature is possible before commitment is required—a contrast to the dating pattern always associated with romantic love.

4. *Preferential marriage.* Choice is stipulated with some particular person or class of persons. This is examined in detail in the next section.

The relation to romantic love of the contrasting mechanism of "dating" is made clear by Marsh and O'Hara's (1961) study of "modern" family ideas among Chinese students on Taiwan. They found that undergraduates in two Taiwan universities favored love marriages almost as much as did undergraduates at the University of Michigan. Ninety-two per cent believed marriage should be based on love, compared to 98 per cent at Michigan, and 87 per cent of the Taiwanese wanted to choose

TABLE 3

BRIDE-WEALTH AND RESIDENCE RULES[a]

Rule of Residence	Bride-Price	Exchange of Women	Bride-Service	Marriages without Consideration	Total
Patrilocal	103	10	2	25	140
Matri-patrilocal	6	0	13	2	21
Avunculocal	2	0	4	2	8
Bilocal	6	2	1	10	19
Neolocal	0	0	2	15	17
Matrilocal	4	0	8	24	36
Total	121	12	30	78	241

[a] From Murdock (1949), p. 20.

their mates independently. But only 58 per cent expected to do so (compared to 98 per cent of Michigan students), and more striking is the fact that 75 per cent of unmarried female government employees did not know a "suitable" partner to date, although there were 81,000 unmarried males aged 25–29 in Taiwan, compared to only 17,000 unmarried females in that age group. Despite the desire to choose independently and fall in love, dating as an institution was absent. There was no way for the market to gather; introductions could not be found; and casual early phases of courtship could not be chanced because a couple seen alone, as in the old pattern, was assumed to be engaged.

Preferential Marriage Systems

No effort is made here to give an exhaustive treatment, but enough will be said to suggest the range and type of problems associated with discussions of *cross-cousin marriage*. Actually, there are several kinds of preferential marriage systems. The *sororate,* for example, is a preference for marrying the sister of a dead wife. The *levirate* is a preference for marrying the brother of a dead husband. Both are very common institutions. These, however, are preferred *secondary* marriages. Among preferred *primary* marriages, the most important case is marriage of a cross-cousin. A *cross-cousin* (*CC*) is the child of a parent's sibling opposite in sex to the linking parent. A daughter of a mother's brother is a cross-cousin; so is a daughter of a father's sister. (It is the sex of the parent's sibling, not the sex of the child, that counts.) The remaining cousins are called parallel cousins, and in many societies they are called brothers and sisters rather than cousins.

There are three kinds of *CC* marriage. Bilateral *CC* marriage permits male ego to marry either his fasida[5] or his mobrda. The effect of this is to permit the formation of two divisions or marriage classes (technically, dichotomous divisions are called *moieties*), which exchange wives. An example is shown in Fig. 2. Moiety A gives wives to moiety B, who give their own women, in return, to moiety A. The effect is to repeat generation after generation an economic and political alliance created by a marriage in the first generation.

More complicated systems exist among the Australian aborigines. These systems can be conceived in several different ways, but the exposition is simplest if they are thought of as the result of two, cross-cutting, systems of descent. Let ego's fa belong to two different unilineal moieties, A and α; and let ego's mo belong to B and β. Ego's own affiliation is determined by the rule that Roman letter descent is through males and Greek letter descent is through females. Ego, then, is $A\beta$. He is not allowed to marry into his own descent groups (either A or β). The marriage can only be into marriage class $B\alpha$, which will mean

[5] In referring to kinship relations, it is necessary to state some point of reference, which is called *ego*— meaning simply "I" and having no psychoanalytic connotations. Since this chapter must refer often to complicated relationships, certain conventions in abbreviation are adopted here that are common in comparative studies of kinship systems. Nuclear family roles are abbreviated *fa* (father), *mo* (mother), *so* (son), *da* (daughter), *si* (sister), *br* (brother), and all other relatives are *descriptively* designated. That is, other relatives are specified as those combinations of the six nuclear terms that exactly describe how they are related to ego.

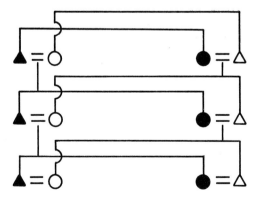

Fig. 2. Bilateral Cross-Cousin Marriage in a Patrilineal Society. Moiety A Is Shown in Black, B in White.

he marries a *CC*. His own children will be Aα; and so on. This system is often called the Kariera system, after an Australian tribe in which it is found. Figure 3 shows how it operates.

The result is a marriage "ring" of four sections linked perpetually either by marriage or descent, as in Fig. 4.

In *patrilateral CC* marriage, male ego may marry only fasida and female ego only mobrso. The distinctive features of patrilateral *CC* marriage are that there cannot be symmetrical exchange in a given generation, as there is in bilateral exchange. But a complete "transaction" can be made in two generations, so that no necessary perpetual link occurs as occurs in bilateral exchange. Finally, the system requires three descent groups for an exchange to be made. The system is shown in Fig. 5.

Matrilateral CC marriage marries a male ego to his mobrda and a female ego to her fasiso. Just as in patrilateral *CC* marriage, no two lineages can symmetrically exchange women. But matrilateral *CC* marriage has the distinctive property that the same groups remain in the same relationship—either wife-giver or wife-receiver—from generation to generation. In Kachin marriage, for example (the society for whom the system is sometimes named),

. . . if a man of patrilineage A marries a woman of patrilineage B, it is proper and expected that at a later date there will be a further marriage between another man of lineage A and another woman of lineage B. Furthermore, a marriage between a man of lineage B and a woman of lineage A would be a breach of customary law.

The relationship between the two lineages A and B is thus specific and has structural continuity. With respect to persons of lineage A, lineage B is *mayu* (wife-giver); with respect to persons of lineage B, lineage A is *dama* (wife-receiver) . . . (Leach, 1951, p. 40).

Observing the exchange properties of various types of *CC* marriage, Lévi-Strauss (1949) has attempted to account for them

Ego (Male) Is	He Marries (Female)	His Child Is
Aα	Bβ	Aβ
Aβ	Bα	Aα
Bα	Aβ	Bβ
Bβ	Aα	Bα

Fig. 3. The Kariera Marriage Class System.

as due to the following principles:

1. A marriage is a part of a series of marriages between unilineal kinship groups.
2. Each marriage is an exchange, and exchange requires reciprocity.
3. Bilateral *CC* marriage is *restricted* in scope, in the sense that the minimum number of descent groups required to complete an exchange is two.
4. Patrilateral *CC* marriage is *discontinuous* in the sense that, although the minimum required to complete exchange is three, the exchange is completed in two generations and need not involve perpetual reciprocity.
5. Matrilateral *CC* marriage is the most *general* exchange, because the minimum number of required descent groups is three and the relationship is perpetual.
6. The more general the exchange, the greater the organic solidarity in Durkheim's sense, that is, the greater the number of parts in a society linked by mutual dependence.
7. Societies tend to greater rather than less organic solidarity.

Hence, Lévi-Strauss sees matrilateral *CC* marriage as more "progressive" than other forms, and expects it more frequently.

Leach (1951) has pointed out that Lévi-

Marriage

Descent $\left\{ \begin{array}{ccc} \nearrow\text{A}\alpha & = & \text{B}\beta \\ \downarrow\text{A}\beta & = & \text{B}\alpha \end{array} \right.$

Fig. 4. The Kariera System as a Ring.

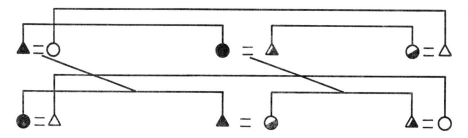

Fig. 5. Patrilateral CC Marriage in a Patrilineal Society. Descent Group A Is Shown in Black, B in Half-Black, and C in White. In the First Generation, A Gives a Wife to B and B Gives to C, While C Gives a Wife to A. In the Next Generation the Cycle Is Completed, Since B Gives a Wife Back to A, C Gives a Wife to B, and A Gives a Wife Back to C.

Strauss, in common with Murdock and others, assumes that matrilateral systems necessarily "marry in a ring." Analyzing Kachin field data, he showed that a ring is not necessary, and that exchange can be completed by other goods and services, not simply by returning women. The Kachins themselves use this form of marriage to perpetuate a feudal, lord-vassal relationship that corresponds to the *mayu-dama* (wife-giver, wife-receiver) relationship. Such a marriage relationship is also, in that society, synonymous with a landlord-tenant relationship, a chief-retainer relationship, and a wealth-receiver–wealth-giver relationship. (This refers, of course, not to the conjugal bond but to the relationship between larger kin groups established by the marriage.) It is linked with hypogamy (husbands marry wives of higher social rank than themselves), which is rather a rare institution. It is inherently an asymmetrical structure from the point of view of social stratification, and the preservation of that structure is its function. At least, if the present writer has understood him correctly, this is what Leach has said. The only thing, incidentally, that prevents the wife-receivers —who give in return an elaborate bride-price—from becoming an impoverished group is that wealth in itself does not give prestige to the wife-giver (wealth-receiver) unless he spends it on feasts, at which the *dama* is present.

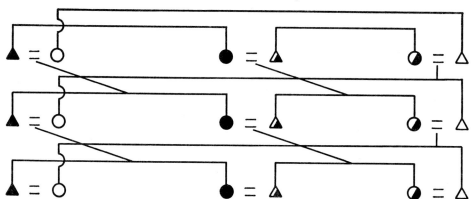

Fig. 6. Matrilateral CC Marriage in Patrilineal Society.

Homans and Schneider (1955) objected to the teleological structure of Lévi-Strauss' argument and attempted to account for the motives that would actually lead members of a society to marry CC's. They also observed that patrilateral and matrilateral CC marriage is correlated with the *type* of descent group in a society. Matrilateral CC marriage occurs more often with patrilineal descent groups, and patrilateral CC marriage occurs more often with matrilineal descent groups (bilateral CC marriage is omitted from the argument). They attributed this correlation to the role structure associated typically with the two forms of descent (see below for greater detail concerning this role structure). In patrilineal societies, the father's family represent authority and respect, while the mother's family, and especially her brother, represent affection and close sentimental ties. Hence, marrying mobrda is "sentimentally appropriate," both for the mobr and ego. What is more natural than that a man should ask his closest intimate for the hand of his daughter? Even the deviant cases—those that do not show the expected correlation—turn out also to diverge from the usual role structure in such a way that the argument itself is sound: there are reasons inherent in interpersonal relations for the direction CC marriage takes.

This review cannot do justice to the elegance, from an aesthetic point of view, of the argument and exposition. However, the argument has certain limitations. The patrilineal complex is very common. Matrilateral CC marriage is rare. It occurs in only 34 of the 247 patrilineal societies in Murdock's World Ethnographic Sample (Eyde & Postal, 1961, p. 749).[6] One can properly ask what accounts for the few cases that develop matrilateral CC marriage that differentiates them from other patrilineal societies. It can also be objected that

the argument depends substantially on what the boy wants to do, whereas it is the boy's father, surely, who will have the greatest influence over the decision. If sentimental appropriateness matters, it must be sentimental appropriateness of the fa and mobr relationship. Perhaps more important —this remains to be seen as more work is done—is the kind of authority structure that is produced in the extended family by CC marriage. CC marriage has the effect, of course, of bringing in as subordinate members of the family persons already in a subordinate role to the family into which they marry.[7]

Divorce

About 60 per cent of the societies of the world exceed the United States rate of divorce (Goode, 1961; Murdock, 1950, p. 197). For example, in traditional Japan, and formerly also in most of the Arab countries, divorce rates were over six times that of the United States, although since 1900 their rates have mostly decreased sharply, while United States rates have increased sharply, so that now, except for Egypt, the United States rate is greater. That traditionally Japan and the Arab countries had strong patrilineal descent groups may partly account for their high divorce rates in the nineteenth century. But Gluckman (1950), in one of the most influential papers on the subject, has suggested that strong patrilineal descent groups are in fact correlated with lower divorce rates. Having observed that expensive and complex bride-price is often found with low divorce rates, Gluckman has concluded that this is due to the spurious correlation of bride-wealth and family stability, independently, with strong patrilineages (see also Gluckman, 1953). In fact, the strength of the patrilineage, in his view, produces family stability, which in

---

[6] Murdock (1957) has published data on an expanded sample of 565 societies that have already been used for several important investigations.

[7] See also Eyde and Postal, 1961, for a more complex argument depending on cooperative relations among members of the extended family household.

TABLE 4

Divorces Per 1000 Marriages in Selected Countries, 1890–1956[a]

Country	Year								
	1890	1900	1910	1920	1930	1940	1946	1950	1956
U.S.	55.6	75.3	87.4	133.3	173.9	165.3		231.7	259 (1959)
Germany		17.6	29.9	40.7	72.4	125.7		145.8	89.2
England & Wales				8.0	11.1	16.5		86.1	74.5
Australia		13.6	12.4	20.4	41.2	41.6	90.0	97.3	85.5
France	24.3	26.1	46.3	49.4	68.6	80.3		106.9	100.5
Sweden		12.9	18.4	30.5	50.6	65.1		147.7	175.4
Iran						194		211	185 (1952–53)
Egypt					269 (1935)	273		273	288 (1953)
Japan	335	184	131	100	98	76		100	
Algeria	370 (1897)	352	288	396	286	292			161 (1955)

[a] From "Family Disorganization" by William J. Goode in *Contemporary Social Problems*, p. 406, by Robert R. Merton and Robert A. Nisbet, © 1961 by Harcourt, Brace & World, Inc., and reproduced with their permission.

turn makes the elaboration of bride-wealth possible. And there are many patrilineal societies, like the Zulu, in which the divorce rate is negligible.

In response to Gluckman's paper, both Fallers (1957) and Leach (1954; 1957) have advanced the hypothesis that there are two kinds of patrilineal societies, one with high and one with low divorce rates, and that the difference depends on the relation of the wife to her husband's lineage. In some societies, the wife is completely assimilated into the husband's patrilineage. Her legal and even many of her social ties to her own lineage are severed, and she belongs solely to her husband's family. This is true, for example, of the Zulu, where the divorce rate is very low. But in some patrilineal societies, even though all her child's legal rights are with the husband's lineage, the wife herself retains membership in and important ties with her own. This is true among the African Soga, for example, where between 25 and 50 per cent of all

marriages end in divorce, despite the fact that bride-wealth must be repaid (Fallers, 1957).

Leach (1957) has carefully compared three South Asian marriage systems, in one of which there is a high divorce rate, in one permissible but uncommon divorce, and in one no divorce at all—despite the fact that in all three there is an extensive and complicated bride-price. The three have in common matrilateral CC marriage, hypogamy, the lord-vassal relation of fa-in-l to so-in-l (see previous section), the levirate, and strong patrilineages. But, contrasting only the two extremes, the Gumsa Kachins, among whom divorce is not permitted, absorb a woman wholly into her husband's patrilineage. That is, her own lineage ceases to have any rights over her, and the sibling bond, which essentially expresses the tie to the descent group, is weaker than the marriage bond. Among the Lakher, where divorce is frequent, although a woman's children are legally the husband's lineage property, the wife herself is not. She remains legally a member of her fa's lineage, and the sibling tie remains strong.

The same hypothesis accounts for the high rates of divorce usually found in matrilineal societies. A matrilineage cannot, unlike a patrilineage, ever completely sever its legal claims on *either* males or females (Schneider, 1961). Females are the line through which descent is counted; males are the line through which authority in the matrilineage is exercised. Husbands are always a threat to their wives' matrilineage and always strongly rooted in their own matrilineage. Divorce is almost always very easy—a man just walks off one morning, or a woman puts her husband's few personal possessions outside the door.

A high divorce rate does not necessarily mean that a marriage *system* is unstable. One must distinguish clearly three kinds of instability: (a) instability of the personal relationship between husband and wife; (b) instability of the jural bond of marriage; (c) instability of the marriage system (Schneider, 1953). Divorce reflects only the instability of the jural bond. Some societies that have no divorce have frequent separation, for example. But divorce in such a society is a matter mostly of jural relationships, of legal rights to a woman's offspring, and a couple can separate openly without disrupting these. In other societies, the jural bond itself may be frequently broken, particularly where the fundamental social relationships of that society are not disrupted in the process, without any tendency for the system itself to change.

On the other hand, both Japan and the United States are examples of unstable marriage systems; that is, their history reflects an actual change in the kind of system that they have had. Probably, the changes in both cases are due to increasing industrialization and modernization. If this is so, the implication is that industrial societies have an intermediate-level equilibrium divorce rate, toward which both societies are tending. The Japanese, on this hypothesis, must be moving away from a system that resembles the Soga and toward a system that gives greater importance to the conjugal bond; while the United States must be moving away from a system in which the marriage bond is of great legal and instrumental significance and toward one in which greater importance is given to personal and affective bonds. On this hypothesis, both trends must be correlated with industrialization. But the entire argument is largely conjecture. [Cf. pp. 76–80.]

THE NUCLEAR FAMILY

Is It Universal?

Murdock has claimed that among the 250 societies sampled in his *Social Structure,* there is no case in which the nuclear family is not found. This he attributed to the advantages it has over other units in performing four basic functions: (a) control of sexual access, (b) control of procreation, (c) education of children, (d) economic cooperation. Levy and Fallers (1959) have objected that for no other institutional sphere has anyone discovered either a universal concrete structure or one which invariably performs the same functions, and they do not believe such a structure exists among family institutions either. They believe that sexual access, procreation, socialization, and economic cooperation are universal, that they are universally functions of some kinship-based unit, and that this kinship unit is universally relatively small. What they object to is the view that this unit is universally the nuclear family. The nuclear family roles, fa, mo, so, da, hu, wi, br, si, are, so far as is now known, universally found; the question is, Do they always form a recognized, acting unit distinct from other units, and do they always perform at least the four Murdock functions?

In the case of the Nayar, Gough (1959)

has reported that the intact household unit is made up of the br-si-siso or sida roles; husbands only "visit" their wives. At a very young age, a woman is ritually married to a man chosen by her family, and within days is ritually divorced from him; the woman is then free to take "lovers," although these may be more or less regular. These lovers give her gifts, but do not provide her support. If a child is born, one of the woman's lovers—not necessarily the genitor—pays a fee that legitimates the child and is thereby legally recognized as the father. But socialization, economic cooperation, and household composition are structured around the brother-sister relation.[8]

In an Israeli kibbutz—meaning collective farm—Spiro (1954) has reported that the acting units are: (a) the hu-wi unit, where again sexual access and legitimation of the child are regulated; (b) nurseries of children who live apart from their parents, where socialization is regulated; and (c) the kibbutz as a whole, which is the unit of economic cooperation. Thus, although the children have some of the same feelings that most children do for their specific parents, they only "visit" them in their room, much as Nayar husbands visit their wives. And the economic activities of hu and wi are in and for the kibbutz itself, not for the "family." In return, the kibbutz provides meals, allowances, clothes, and so on. The children in the nurseries, furthermore, come to think of themselves as like siblings in the same family; for example, an incest taboo spontaneously develops among them (see below, p. 485).

Because the Nayar and kibbutz families actually live apart, they are relatively easily recognized as exceptions to Murdock's rule. But Levy (1955) has claimed that the Chi-

nese family, too, is an exception, although husband, wife, and child all live in the same household. Levy has argued that the nuclear family unit is not the unit of economic cooperation; rather, hu and wi contribute services to the extended family, within which the nuclear family is completely (for economic purposes) unidentifiable. In socialization, furthermore, for many phases of that process the relevant units are the females of the extended family as a whole and the males of the extended family as a whole. Except for sexual relations, in fact, Levy did not see any set of nuclear family bonds as an acting unit distinct from the extended family.

The counter-example that Levy has offered raises issues of conceptualization more delicate even than those raised by Gough or Spiro. Probably many cases that in his work Murdock has classified as having the nuclear family would have been classified differently by Levy. Murdock views the extended family as an aggregate of distinct subunits in which, no matter how subordinated, the conjugal solidarity is never quite obscured. Levy, on the other hand, refuses to think of extended families, at least in societies like China, as aggregates of component nuclear families because, in his view, the extended family is so paramount that the nuclear family cannot be said to function at all (see Fig. 7). It is not entirely clear whether Levy meant to say that the nuclear family in China was not an acting unit for *any* purpose, except procreation, that for *most* purposes it was not an acting unit, or only that, although it was sometimes a relevant unit of action, it was never of *paramount* importance—but probably he meant that for most purposes it was not the acting unit. It is even less clear what Murdock intended, but probably he would dispute Levy's point. What is beyond dispute is that the nuclear family in many societies is so subordinated to the extended family that it is for many purposes not the paramount acting unit, and for some purposes not even relevant at all. But

[8] There is always a misleading aspect to such a statement, because the *status* "brother" may be occupied by someone who is not biologically the woman's actual brother. What counts is that some male member of the matrilineage exercises authority over the female's household.

it has yet to be demonstrated that, except for the Nayar, the kibbutz, and perhaps the Minangkabau (De Jong, 1951), there is not at least *one* purpose, aside from sex, with respect to which in most societies the nuclear family is at least *sometimes* the relevant acting unit. [For additional discussions of the universality of the nuclear family, see pp. 88–90, 508–510.]

Internal Role Structure

Where the nuclear family is an acting unit, it has been said to have a number of relatively constant properties that are referred to here as the "Parsons-Bales role structure" (Blood & Wolfe, 1960; Herbst, 1952; Parsons & Bales, 1955). The most important features of this role structure are:

1. There is differentiation of the authority of husband, wife, and child with respect to family decision-making.
2. There is differentiation of more "instrumental," or task-oriented, roles from more "expressive," or social and integrative roles.
3. Because of the age-sex structure of the nuclear family, roles are allocated in such a way that[9]

[9] It is important to keep in mind that the focus is the nuclear family. This means that the same role structure may or may not be found in: (a) male and female roles in the larger society; (b) male or female roles in the extended family; (c) male or female roles in the descent group; (d) male or female roles in the occupational structure, where that structure is differentiated from kinship structures. Thus, the very great authority of an old patriarch is often confused with the authority of the "father" in the nuclear family, whereas in fact it is authority in the extended family. The hu-fa's authority may be much less in the nuclear family, particularly when he is young, has only unmarried children, and is not head of an extended family household.

These analytic distinctions, however, make it difficult to interpret the role structure of a nuclear family in a highly differentiated society such as the United States. The nuclear family itself, in such a case, may be a predominantly "expressive" structure, with the activities that provide its support, and perhaps other instrumental activities, exercised beyond its concrete boundaries. In that case, either the external role is called the instrumental role *in* (because *for*) the family, or such a family looks relatively undifferentiated. The American hu-fa,

a. The hu-fa role is more instrumental and has more authority,
b. The wi-mo role is more expressive,
c. The so and da roles are subordinate to both mo and fa roles.

This is intended to describe roles in *decision-making* rather than *task execution,* and, as a matter of fact, there seems to be somewhat less regularity in differentiation of task execution. Although there are several tasks that are universally masculine, virtually no role is always feminine (Murdock, 1937, p. 553; see, for North American cultures, Driver & Massey, 1957, pp. 363–371). There are also a substantial number of tasks that, although differentiation is the rule, are either done jointly by both hu and wi or can be done indifferently by either (see Table 5).

That the decision-making structure of the family is so regular is due, in the Parsons-Bales theory, less to its age-sex structure than to features of social interaction common to social systems that

1. Are responsible for physical care of children,
2. Are responsible for socialization of children,
3. Act as a unit in task behavior requiring that decisions be made.

Where the nuclear family is engaged in tasks requiring that decisions be made,

for example, observed only at home, is probably at least as "expressive," and possibly more expressive, than the wi-mo observed only in the home. Only the fact that many societies have household economies and educate their children almost entirely in the household makes the instrumental-authority role so easily located within the concrete boundaries of the nuclear family. In the research reported here (based on Zelditch, 1955), the nuclear family was *not* defined as existing only when concretely joined together in the household. Rather, it was an analytic concept. That is, concrete boundaries were less important than "functional" boundaries. This does not, incidentally, violate the rule that nuclear-family roles are not necessarily the same in pattern as male and female roles in the occupational structure; a female occupational role, for example, may be more or less instrumental as a contribution *to her family* and quite independently seen as more or less instrumental from the point of view of the *occupational* system.

Murdock

Levy

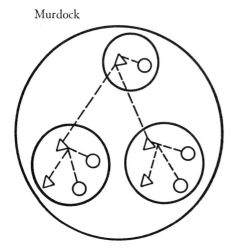
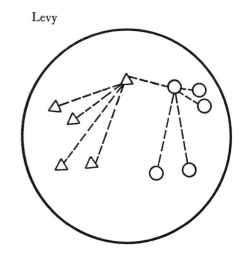

Fig. 7. Nuclear Families in the Extended Family: Murdock's View Versus Levy's View. Single Broken Lines Represent Lines of Authority and Joint Action in the Extended Family. Murdock's Conception of the Extended Family Is that It Is Built up out of Distinct Component Nuclear Families. Levy's Conception Is that the Nuclear Family Roles Are not Organized into a Distinct Acting Unit, and the Extended Family Cannot Be Seen as Simply an Aggregation of Such Units. Unbroken Lines Represent Solidarities.

differentiation of control over the inter-action process regularly develops and tends to become institutionalized in a stable au-thority structure. Furthermore, where it confronts such fundamentally different problems as, say, managing an estate and socializing children, in which different kinds of abilities and different kinds of attitudes are probably required, relatively seldom will a single person combine the required abilities and attitudes into a single leadership role (Bales & Slater, 1955, pp. 300, 302). It is sometimes overlooked that two distinct arguments are involved: one con-cerns the differentiation of authority with respect to a single dimension of activity; the other concerns the differentiation into more than one leadership hierarchy, so that a given person may have authority with re-spect to some spheres of behavior which he does, not exercise in others.

In a sample of 56 societies for which the required information was available, 46 were found to have a Parsons-Bales role structure

(Zelditch, 1955, p. 320). Broadly, the most universal property was the subordination of children to their parents. The next most universal was the expressive content of the wi-mo role. The principal variations in nu-clear family structure were due to variations in the role of the hu-fa.

There are two sources of variation in the hu-fa role, both having to do with the way the nuclear family is related to comprehend-ing, external structures: (a) the relation to larger kinship groups; (b) the relation to the economic and rank structures of the larger society.

In patrilineal descent groups, the line of authority and the line of descent are coor-dinate, that is, descent is from father to son, and authority is of father over son. The effect is to increase the authority of hus-bands and fathers when the nuclear family is patrilocal and descent is patrilineal, be-cause to authority in the nuclear family is added the authority inherent in extended family headship. When younger, the hu-fa

TABLE 5

ROLE-DIFFERENTIATION IN TASK-EXECUTION[a]

Task	No. Undifferentiated[b]	% Masculine[c]
Metal working	0	100.0
Weapon making	0	99.8
Pursuit of sea mammals	0	99.3
Hunting	0	98.2
Manufacture of musical instruments	0	96.9
Boat building	4	96.0
Mining and quarrying	1	95.4
Work in wood and bark	5	95.0
Work in stone	2	95.0
Trapping or catching of small animals	4	94.9
Work in bone, horn and shell	3	93.0
Lumbering	3	92.2
Fishing	19	85.6
Manufacture of ceremonial objects	13	85.1
Herding	4	83.6
House building	25	77.0
Clearing of land for agriculture	17	76.3
Net making	4	74.1
Trade	20	73.7
Dairy operations	3	57.1
Manufacture of ornaments	40	52.5
Agriculture–soil preparation and planting	33	48.4
Manufacture of leather products	9	48.0
Body mutilation, e.g., tattooing	44	46.6
Erection and dismantling of shelter	5	39.8
Hide preparation	4	39.4
Tending of fowls and small animals	8	38.7
Agriculture–crop tending and harvesting	35	33.9
Gathering of shellfish	8	33.5
Manufacture of non-textile fabrics	9	33.3
Fire making and tending	25	30.5
Burden bearing	33	29.9
Preparation of drinks and narcotics	13	29.5
Manufacture of thread and cordage	11	27.3
Basket making	10	24.4
Mat making	6	24.2
Weaving	2	23.9
Gathering of fruits, berries and nuts	15	23.6
Fuel gathering	10	23.0
Pottery making	6	18.4
Preservation of meat and fish	10	16.7
Manufacture and repair of clothing	8	16.1
Gathering of herbs, roots and seeds	11	15.8
Cooking	9	8.6
Water carrying	5	8.2
Grain grinding	5	7.8

[a] From Murdock (1937), p. 552.
[b] Number out of 224 societies in which roles are either joint (both male and female together) or could be performed indifferently by either a male or a female.
[c] The per cent masculine is obtained as a weighted average of the per cent of cases falling into the classes: only male, mostly male, equal, mostly female, only female, with weights = 100, 75, 50, 25, and 0 respectively.

is actually subordinate to his own father and very often exercises less authority even over his own family than the head of the extended family; but because he will be the successor, his authority is still great.[10] In patrilineal, patrilocal cases, the hu-fa is ordinarily an instrumental authority figure, regardless of the degree of strength of the larger kinship group.

[10] Brothers, if they live together, will of course be differentiated in their authority according to their probable succession. Many societies have *primogeniture,* in which the eldest brother succeeds to headship and inherits the entire family estate; he will obviously have greater authority in the extended family than his younger brothers. Some have *ultimogeniture,* in which the youngest son inherits, which fundamentally alters the authority structure of brothers in the extended family.

But in matrilineal descent groups, the line of authority and the line of descent are not coordinate (Richards, 1950; Schneider, 1961), because, within their own lineages, males are as much in authority in matrilineal societies as in patrilineal societies, yet descent is traced through females. The result is what Richards has called the "matrilineal puzzle" (1950, p. 246), the problem of reconciling authority of hu-fa versus br-mobr. The effect on the hu-fa's role depends on how strong the matrilineage is and how completely the nuclear family is subordinated to it. In the Trobriands (Malinowski, 1927; Malinowski, 1929), for example, the content of the hu-fa role is almost as expressive as the mother's role, with most authority and instrumental functions allocated to the wife's brother; but there are other solutions to the puzzle.

Comparing a number of matrilineal tribes in Central Africa, Richards found three common solutions, although this still does not exhaust the possibilities. Among the Mayombe, for example, the residential unit is the avunculocal extended family. This means that typically the matrilineal descent group is localized around its male members, maximizing their authority. These men bring their wives into their households, and at puberty receive also the children of their sisters—of course, sending their own children away at puberty to live with the brothers of their wives. The effect is to subordinate wives to husbands, but to divide the authority of fa and mobr over children. The fa tends to have substantial domestic authority, exercised over his children when they are at home, while the mobr has the overriding jural rights over those activities that are important to the descent group, such as regulating mate selection or determining inheritance and succession, and when the si's children are transferred to his household, he acquires also the primary domestic authority over them.

Among the Bemba, the residential unit is described by Richards as the "father-daugh-ter-grandfamily," that is, the typical household consists of a grandfather, his married daughters and their husbands, and their unmarried children. This structure develops out of matri-patrilocal residence, or perhaps more exactly out of bride-service. A young man lives in the compound of his wi, until gradually he validates his position as a hu, after which he moves, with his wi, back into his own village. The domestic authority of the grandfather is great, and that of the hu-fa gradually increases as the marriage stabilizes. But the overriding jural rights are still the mobr's.

Among the Ila, residence is patrilocal, so that the typical household consists of a grandfather, his married sons, and their children. The wife is very subordinate to her husband—domestic authority resembles that of a patrilineal, patrilocal household. The jural rights over the child are divided between fa and mobr. The fa, for example, legally may keep his children if he is divorced by his wi, even though they belong still to her descent group. The Ila differ from both the Bemba and Mayombe in having substantial inheritance through fathers to sons, although they have matrilineal succession to offices; cattle and homesteads may both be inherited from fathers.

Thus, there is a pattern of divided authority rights, in which the following must be distinguished from each other: (a) a hu's authority over his wi; (b) a fa's domestic authority over his own children; (c) a mobr's jural rights over his si's children; (d) not described very much in Richards, but often found elsewhere, the mobr's rights to discipline, direct, and socialize his sisos. In 18 of 19 matrilineal societies for which data on role differentiation have been examined (Zelditch, 1955, p. 331), the hu role was more important than the br role in economic support of the household; in 19 out of 19, hu was more instrumental in this respect than wi; in 15 of the 19, however, mobr had greater *jural* authority than fa, although, in 10 of these 15, fa had the greater *domestic* authority (see Tables 6 and 7).[11]

TABLE 6

ROLES OF FA AND MOBR IN ECONOMIC (PRODUCTION) TASKS AND SOCIALIZATION IN MATRILINEAL SOCIETIES[a]

Jural Control of Socialization	Economic Production		
	Hu-Fa	Br-Mobr	Total
Hu-Fa	3	0	3
Br-Mobr	15	1	16
Total	18	1	19

[a] Adapted from Zelditch (1955), p. 331.

TABLE 7

JURAL VS DOMESTIC AUTHORITY OF FA AND MOBR IN MATRILINEAL SOCIETIES[a]

Domestic Authority over Children	Jural Rights Over Child		
	Fa	Mobr	Total
Fa	4	10	14
Mobr	0	5	5
Total	4	15	19

[a] Adapted from Zelditch (1955), p. 331.

In bilateral societies, the line of descent does not so enhance the authority of the hu-fa as in patrilineal societies, but it does not conflict with it as in matrilineal societies. The Caribbean family, which is most often bilateral, shows great variations in the hu-fa role which must be accounted for in a different way. The extreme instability of the conjugal bond, frequent desertion, early mortality of males, with a resultant "matrifocal" family, have been described by Henriques (1953), by Herskovits and Herskovits (1947), and others. The old mothers become the dominant authority in the household. Careful analysis of quantitative data (R. T. Smith, 1956) for British Guiana

[11] Strodtbeck, however, found that Navaho husbands lost more decisions to their wives than they won in a forced-decision task (1951).

Negro communities shows that actually the momo-mo-da family is not the typical family type; nevertheless, there is a family type that can be called "matrifocal" in which, even where the hu-fa is present in the household, he is not the dominant authority. The matrifocal family, Smith showed, is actually one phase in a cycle that begins with a couple setting up a household, having children, the sons and daughters beginning various extra-residential unions that might or might not become stable, the husband sometimes dying or deserting, the da's children from extra-residential unions becoming part of the household, until finally more stable unions are formed, and they leave the household to begin the cycle again. For most of a woman's childbearing career, once she has set up a new household, the hu-fa is in that household. He is the primary source of its support, although he may gradually be replaced either by sons or, if he deserts, by new lovers of the mo (who do not necessarily live in her house). Fa is also active in early socialization. But, "Whether they leave or not, the focus of authority and control gradually shifts to the wife-mother, so that irrespective of whether there is a husband-father present, the household at this stage can be referred to as 'matrifocal'" (R. T. Smith, 1957, p. 70).

This family pattern is not prevalent throughout the society in which it is found, however. It is predominantly determined by class and color. Smith's interpretation is that:

1. Among lower-class Negroes there is little internal differentiation in rank, no property, no upward mobility, and uncertain wages.
2. Therefore, the male is "marginal" in the sense that he contributes nothing to the social status of the family and his support of it cannot be counted on.
3. Therefore, one can interpret variations in the authority of the hu-fa as due to his position in the economic and rank structures of the larger society. The more marginal he is, the weaker his authority.

Smith supports this argument further by observing that the hu-fa role is more important where ecology or class increases his contribution to the status and support of his family. Among middle-class Negroes in British Guiana, there is more differentiation of status, and the husband's occupation can increase (or decrease) the family's status. "So long as the man's income provides the basis for the style of life that is important in maintaining the whole group, then there is a point beyond which his position in the family is unlikely to deteriorate" (R. T. Smith, 1957, pp. 72–73). Among Negro families in Orange Grove, Jamaica (Clarke, 1953), the hu-fa is the manager of a medium-sized farm which confers status on the family, and the hu-fa role is correspondingly greater in authority.[12] [Family role structure is also discussed in Ch. 3.]

The Incest Taboo

Incest taboos are institutionalized norms that prohibit sexual relationships within certain classes of kin. Basic empirical regularities in their application are (Murdock, 1949):

1. They universally apply to all persons of opposite sex within the nuclear family, except hu and wi.
2. They never apply only to the nuclear family.
3. They apply with diminished intensity outside the nuclear family.
4. There is no class of roles outside the nuclear family to which they universally apply.
5. Tabooed classes of kin do not correlate with nearness of their biological relationship.
6. Application of the taboo does correlate with

[12] R. T. Smith's interpretation has been challenged by M. G. Smith. He believes that R. T. Smith has erred in the way he treats extra-residential unions, and that the correct interpretation of the Caribbean family is that it depends on alternate forms of mating; these, in turn, depend essentially on particular past histories of different communities. The present writer cannot find the objection convincing, but the reader should consult the very detailed and complete data provided by M. G. Smith (1962) on five Caribbean communities.

conventional groupings of kin, such as the type of descent group found in a society.

Most theories of the incest taboo make it depend on the role structure of the nuclear family. Its extension to statuses outside the nuclear family is then explained as a secondary phenomenon, by accounting for extension of nuclear family statuses to other relatives (see Murdock, 1949).

Analysis of the taboo is complicated by the fact that it is easily confused with *exogamy*, a norm which has to do with marriage rather than sex. Exogamy prohibits marriage within certain classes of kin; but explaining exogamy, which is what some theories of incest actually accomplish, does not necesarily explain the incest taboo (Seligman, 1929). Moreover, many explanations of parent-child taboos are not sufficient to account for br-si taboos, and conversely.

Perhaps the best-known and most general sociological theories are those that see the incest taboo as an institution maintaining either the stability or effectiveness of the role structure of the nuclear family. For example, if it is taken for granted that socialization requires children to be subordinate to their parents and parents to cooperate in raising them, then either fa-da or mo-so incest would disrupt the socialization of the child (Parsons, 1954). In an incestuous relationship, the child would become more equal to the parent, so that it would become more problematic who was to socialize whom; and one parent would have to compete with the child for the favor of the other parent, disrupting the coalition on which parental cooperation in child-rearing is based. In the case of sibling incest, this would not be true, but critical problems would arise if a child were conceived. If the child were actually born, its brother would be its fa and mobro; its sister would be its mo and fasi. To the degree that these are statuses the roles of which are different, the result would be confusion (Davis, 1949, pp. 401–404). Often they are different, particularly in the relative distribution of affection and respect. Thus, the Parsons-Davis theory of incest might be summarized as follows:

1. Sexual relations of parent and child tend to make parent and child more equal.
2. Sexual relations of brother and sister tend, if a child is born, to put one or the other in a role which simultaneously involves both affection and respect.
3. A role that is both superordinate and subordinate is incompatible.
4. A role that is both affective (based on affection) and neutral (based on respect) is incompatible.
5. Incompatible roles are unstable.

Such a theory is extremely difficult to disprove. Appeal is usually made to the universality of the incest taboo, but what is required is some evidence of the actual effects of incest on roles in the family. Cross-cultural data on this point are scarce. However, since the theory is so dependent on processes in the nuclear family, it should be useful to examine incest taboos in cases where the nuclear family (in the Murdock sense) does not occur.

Gough has reported on incest taboos among the North and South Malabar Nayars (1952a). The North Malabar Nayars are matrilineal but patrilocal, paternity is important, the fa brings up the children. Incest with either fa or mo is regarded as a horrible idea, and incest taboos are extended to the father's kin, such as his si and his brda. The South Malabar Nayars have the "visiting husband" union described earlier, are polyandrous with relatively unstable conjugal bonds, and mobr raises siso. Mo-so incest and br-si incest are regarded as horrible, but fa-da incest, although prohibited, is regarded only as amusing. It is prohibited, according to Nayars, because it would make mo and da co-wives, which would contradict their asymmetrical relation. Nor is the incest taboo extended to the fa's relatives. In more recent times, though, as pa-

ternity has become increasingly important, and the fa raises the child, fa-da incest has excited more sense of horror.

Fox (1962) has made use of Spiro's observations on incest in the kibbutz, where again the nuclear family in the Murdock sense does not exist, in raising objections to the teleological structure of the Parsons-Davis argument. Fox, who concentrated entirely on sibling taboos, preferred to discover their causes in early childhood experiences. He distinguished a "Westermarck" effect, in which constant early contact leads to aversion, which leads to br-si indifference, from a "Freud" effect, in which early separation of br and si leads to repression of desire, which leads to great horror at the thought of incest and strong taboos. He found evidence that both effects exist. In the kibbutz (Spiro, 1958), for example, children of a number of families are raised in coeducational dormitories, take mixed showers, and are permitted considerable sexual freedom from birth through adolescence. But Spiro found no evidence of actual sexual intercourse within groups of peers that grow up together, and no desire to marry each other. Rules of incest and exogamy spontaneously developed. When asked why, they reported that they felt like siblings. There are, however, societies in which great horror does accompany the idea of br-si incest—not just indifference—and these are also societies in which br and si are early separated. Unfortunately, there is a certain circularity in this argument, since it is usually also argued that the purpose of separation is to prevent sibling sexual attraction. It is still not clear why the thought of their sexual attraction should frighten parents in these societies.

Middleton has objected to the Parsons-Davis theory, on the grounds that incest taboos are not universal. Reviewing evidence on br-si marriage in Egypt, he pointed out that historians now have strong indications that br-si marriage was not only a royal affair, but, at least in Roman Egypt, commoners, too, sometimes, possibly often, resorted to it (1962). Thus, in Arsinoe during the Roman period, out of 52 marriages for which documentary evidence has been discovered, 20 were consanguine (p. 607). In other Egyptian communities, the rate was less, but of 124 marriages, 38 were consanguine. The most plausible conjecture, Middleton believes, is that because das inherited family property as well as sos, br-si marriage developed as a way of maintaining property and estate intact. Thus, he argued, although role confusion may be a problem, incest taboos should be seen as part of the total balance of forces in a family system. Marriage is a matter of the preservation of interests and privileges of kinship groups, and these interests may combine to override the interests in nuclear family stability. It ought to be observed, of course, that Middleton confuses incest and exogamy, but that hardly seems to matter to his argument. If Middleton is right, and Fox not conclusive, it remains an open problem why the br-si incest taboo is so nearly universal.[13] [The incest taboo is also discussed on pp. 64-66, 502-503.]

KINSHIP AND DESCENT

Kinship Corporations

The birth of a new child in any society inevitably effects the rights and privileges of other members. Some are compelled to assume new obligations. Others may gain new rights. The prospects of others are altered with respect to such matters as inheritance, succession, and marriage. In short, jural relations are modified in various ways, and everyone must know how his own are affected (Murdock, 1949, p. 43).

One knows how his rights and duties are affected by applying a rule of descent. A rule of descent affiliates ego with a group

[13] Middleton also argued that Egypt is not exceptional, that a number of other ancient societies existed in which incest was common, and he is presently surveying the evidence for this. However, the only thing approaching it today is parallel-cousin marriage among the Bedouins.

of relatives who have certain rights and obligations with respect to him. That the various rules of descent are matters of social recognition of rights and not different theories of biology was shown very early by Rivers (1924).

The rights that are transmitted are (Radcliffe-Brown, 1935):

1. *Rights in personam,* or duties that are imposed on ego.
2. *Rights in rem,* or duties that are imposed on other persons in their behavior toward ego.
3. *Rights over things,* fundamentally right *in rem,* but which specifically establish the behavior of other persons toward objects in which ego has a vested interest.

The three classes of rights, taken together, form an *estate,* transmission of which is called *succession.* The idea of an estate comprehends not only property rights in the usual sense but also one's "status." Exercise of the rights in an estate can be:

1. *Divided,* so that with respect to some part of the estate, say C, one class of rights is exercised by person A, while another is exercised by person B. For example, a tenant may have the right of use of a property without having the right to alienate it.
2. *In common,* so that A and B each has equal, though independently exercised, rights in C. For example, two hunters might enjoy equally the use of the same hunting ground.
3. *Jointly,* so that A and B together form a single entity, D, to which is attributed the rights over C and in the name of which A and B act. For example, the board of directors of a modern company make decisions to commit their organization to some action which is then legally the action, not of the directors, but of the company. It is therefore the company that is legally responsible, that is sued by injured parties, that earns income, that pays salaries, that is taxed, and so on.

When rights are jointly exercised, one speaks of a *corporation,* so that a kinship group in which the estate is in this sense held jointly may be called a *corporate kinship group* (Radcliffe-Brown, 1935).

Current usage of the term corporate group follows either Maine or Weber, or sometimes both (see Fortes, 1953; Fried, 1957). Maine (1861) meant by a "corporation" a group capable of acting as, and being treated as, a single legal person which could have rights defined independently of any particular members of the group. Such a group can be perpetual in that death of members does not imply extinction of the rights-exercising "person." Weber meant by a corporate group (a *Verband*) a group capable of acting together as a unit and having a differentiated authority structure, a "leader" who directs its activities (1947).

Of particular interest has been the study of the corporate descent group, the principal properties of which are:

1. All members are jurally equivalent before the law—they have collective responsibility. This follows from their legal identity.
2. Boundaries of the descent group are unequivocal, do not overlap other descent groups, and are the same for all members. The result is the *segmentation* of society into concrete, mutually exclusive groups each with structurally unchanging rights over estates.
3. Although the exercise of control over production, distribution, and similar economic activities requires the localization of the lineage, many activities of the lineage as cult, as property owner, and as marriage regulator can be carried out even if the lineage is dispersed.
4. Because rights are vested in the corporation itself, not simply transmitted to particular members, the rights *lapse* if the "ancestors" are not fertile, rather than simply gravitating to other groups linked by affinal ties. The lapse of rights is usually regarded with horror and despair, and various fictitious devices exist to recruit members into the group if procreation itself fails.

The legal identity of the corporation (called by Radcliffe-Brown the *unity of the lineage,* or the *lineage principle*) is reflected in the way statuses are defined with respect to it. For example, what looks at first like a rather peculiar terminology for referring to cross-cousins sometimes develops, called *Omaha* cousin terms (associated with patrilineal descent) and *Crow* cousin terms (associated with matrilineal descent). In both cases, parallel cousins are called si and br, and in both cases mobrda and fasida are distinguished from each other by different kinship terms. In Omaha terminology, the fasida is called by the same term as sida, while the mobrda is called by the same terms as mosi. In Crow terminology, the fasida is called by the same term as fasi, while mobrda is classified with brda. This is shown in Fig. 8.

The reason for this usage is brought out more clearly if the structure of the lineages as they are related to ego is examined (Radcliffe-Brown, 1941). Figure 9 shows Fox kinship terms for ego's own lineage. (The Fox are a patrilineal society having Omaha cousin terms.)

Statuses within the lineage are differentiated, since various members play different kinds of roles in the activities of the kinship group. But note that all in-marrying males are called "brother-in-law," and their children are all sisos and sidas, regardless of generation. The outside world is a common group in the way it is attached to one's own lineage. This is even more clear in the terminology for ego's mother's patrilineage, shown in Fig. 10. There, except for mo, all females in mo's generation and below, are mosi, all their hus are fa, all the males of the lineage are mobr, and all the sos and das of the mosi are br and si. The lineage principle applied to famo's lineage has the effect that all the men are grandfathers and all the women grandmothers, whatever their generation. The children are fas and fasis, whatever their generation. In the lineage of ego's wi, not only the wifa, but also his sons and their sons, are "father-in-law," all the women are "mother-in-law," and the sons of these are "brother-in-law," again whatever their generation. The struc-

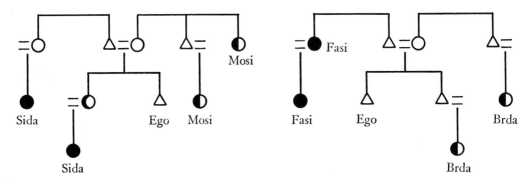

Omaha Cousin Terms   Crow Cousin Terms

Fig. 8. Omaha and Crow Terms for Cross-Cousins.

tural principle is similar in Crow terminology. Thus, the crossing of generations peculiar to Omaha and Crow terms arises essentially from the fact that lineages, looked at from the outside, are legally one.

The corporate descent group, however, may be stronger or weaker, in the sense either that it encompasses more or less of the life of its members or is more or less solidary (Schneider & Roberts, 1956). The strength of the descent group, as has already been seen, correlates with the ease of divorce, the significance of marital ties, the conflicts and tensions within a society (between the descent group and other groups), and the structure of both the extended family and the nuclear family. The range of functions it performs, however, depends

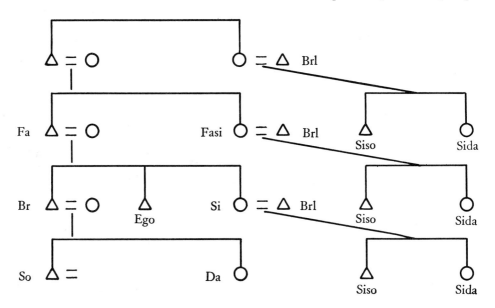

Fig. 9. Fox Kinship Terms: Ego's Patrilineage. The Diagram Is Altered in Terms for Sida from Radcliffe-Brown's Original (1952, p. 71) in Order to Show the Omaha Cousin Terms More Clearly. Brl Means Brother-in-Law.

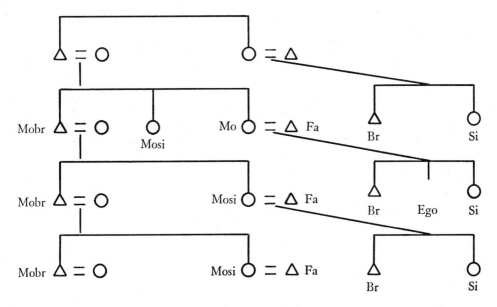

Fig. 10. Fox Kinship Terms: Ego's Mother's Patrilineage
(Radcliffe-Brown, 1952, p. 72).

partly on its localization. Although not all localized descent groups are strong (see Kroeber, 1917; Schneider & Roberts, 1956), most descent groups that are not localized are relatively weak (Fried, 1957, p. 17). If they are not localized, conflicts over transmission of the estate between descent group and residential kinship units are greater, and acting as a single decision-making unit is more difficult.

Murdock has found that localized descent groups with a definite organization and corporate activities are present in 87 societies and absent in 131 out of 218 for which he was able to assemble definite information. Of the 131 societies which do not have organized local descent groups, 56 have unilinear descent (1949, p. 71). There are 33 matrilineal societies with either matrilocal or avunculocal residence (p. 59), but only 15 with matrilocal or avunculocal localized descent groups (p. 71). There are 92 patrilineal societies with patrilocal or matri-patrilocal residence (p. 59), but only 72 localized patrilineal descent groups. Of the 56 societies that have unilinear descent

but no localized descent groups, 30 are matrilineal and 23 are patrilineal—the remaining 3 have double descent (p. 75).

Matrilineal and Patrilineal Complexes

Radcliffe-Brown, to whom the most fundamental early work on unilineal descent is due, tended to think of the patrilineal and matrilineal descent groups as "mirror images" of each other. More recent work has made it clear that they are not simply mirror images, because in patrilineal descent groups authority and descent lines are coordinate, while in matrilineal descent groups they are not (Richards, 1950; Schneider, 1961). As a consequence (Schneider, 1961):

1. In *patrilineages,* females can be totally severed from legal rights in their own descent group and totally assimilated into their hus' descent group. The stronger the descent group, the more they are assimilated. In *matrilineages,* females are as important as males to the continuity of the

group, and neither females nor males can be given up to other descent groups.

2. *Patrilineal descent groups* depend on in-marrying affines for continuity, and the wis are stable members of the group. *Matrilineal descent groups* require males as genitors only, and the hu-fa role need not be important or permanent.

3. In *patrilineal descent groups,* no special institutions are required to ensure that authority of the descent group's officials is not impaired by authority of inmarrying affines. In *matrilineal descent groups,* authority of the inmarrying affines is a threat to the descent group, and special institutions are required to limit and circumscribe the authority of hus and fas over wis and children.

4. In *patrilineal societies,* monolineage communities (communities with a single localized descent group) are stable. In *matrilineal societies,* they are not.

5. In *patrilineal societies,* fa is a figure of respect, mo is a figure of warmth and love, and these attitudes are extended to their siblings so that fasi is a figure of respect also, while mobr is a figure of warmth and love (a "male mother"). In *matrilineal societies,* mo is a figure of warmth and love, but often fa is also (where he is least important as instrumental authority and inheritance and succession are least dependent on him); mobr is a figure of great respect. In *patrilineal societies,* strong affective bonds of mo and so do not threaten the descent group. In *matrilineal societies,* strong affective bonds of fa and so do threaten the descent group.

Bilateral Kinship

About a third of the societies of the world are bilateral, but only recently have the concepts necessary to analyze bilateral kinship been developed, or its properties been examined with any care. There appear to be two fundamentally distinct forms of bilateral kinship group. One is the *kindred,* in which descent is counted *from ego* through any connection, male or female, up to some stipulated collateral range. The other is the *ambilineage* (or *ramage* or *nonunilineal de-*

scent group), in which descent may be through either a male or female, but the focus on which the group is defined is *an ancestor* rather than ego. The difference is quite fundamental, the ambilineage having more in common with unilineal descent groups than with the kindred.

A kindred, because it is structured around ego, has the following properties (Freeman, 1961; Murdock, 1960):

1. It is never the same for any two individuals except full siblings. Ego and his fa, for example, have different kindreds (see Fig. 11).

2. Hence, kindreds of different persons overlap, so that discrete, united collectives are not formed, and they have no common sense of identity, no collective interests, and no well-developed structure of authority common to all members.

3. Although never a regular corporate group, a kindred can be activated on specific occasions for specific purposes. It may, for example, be active at weddings, funerals, and other rites of passage. But again, these are always focused on a specific ego. They are not corporate activities of a distinctive descent group.

The kindred seems everywhere to be correlated with a small, bilateral, domestic family, but never with uniformly unilocal residence. Murdock has identified three domestic family types associated with it: (a) the *independent nuclear* family (including the polygamous family); (b) the *stem* family, in which one child remains in the household at marriage but the others leave; (c) the *lineal* family, in which several brothers remain in the household after marriage, but the household is split up when the parents die (1960). Where children do remain in the house of their parents, residence is bilocal—usually depending on the relative economic needs or resources of the hu and wi's parents. The usual range of kindreds, Murdock found, is between second and fourth cousins. Kindreds are known which count collaterals in the sixth-cousin range and some, such as the Ifugao

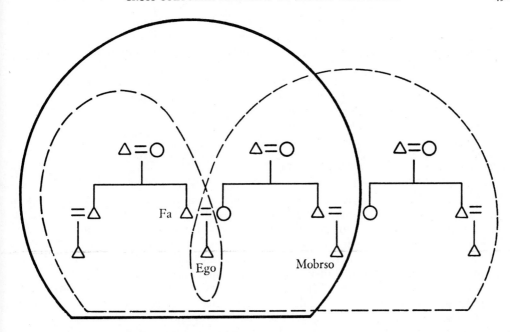

Fig. 11. Structure of the Bilateral Kindred. Ego's Kindred (a Part Only) Is Shown Enclosed by an Unbroken Line. His Br's Kindred Would Be the Same. His Fa's Kindred Excludes Some of the Members of Ego's Kindred—Ego's Mofa, for Example. His Cousin (Mobrso) also Has a Different, Though Overlapping Kindred (Enclosed by Broken Line). It Includes the Cousin's Own Mofa and Momo who Are Not in Ego's Kindred. Thus, for Every Individual Except Siblings, the Kindred Is Different, Although Two Kindreds May Overlap; and in Every Generation Old Kindreds Disappear and New Ones Appear.

kindred, can include as many as 2,000 persons (Barton, 1919).

The ambilineage, because it is based on descent from a common ancestor, has many properties of the corporate descent group, differing from the unilineal type mainly in the flexibility with which membership is determined. By emphasizing the founder rather than ego, it is possible to construct discrete collectivities all of whose members have the same descent group in common. Such a group can be named, own land in perpetuity, transmit status and titles, and otherwise act as a single entity (Firth, 1929; Goodenough, 1955; Solien, 1959). There is a considerable range of types possible (Davenport, 1959; Murdock, 1960), depending on:

1. *The range of choice permitted:* A child (a) may be assigned at birth by his parents to one or the other of their groups; (b) may choose at the time he is married from groups to which his parents belong; (c) may choose any group to which parents, grandparents, sometimes even great-grandparents have belonged.

2. *Exclusiveness of membership:* A person (a) may be required to choose one and only one ambilineage, giving up rights in other possible choices; or (b) may be allowed to retain claims on and membership in more than one at a time.

A kindred, although fundamentally different in structure from an ambilineage, can approach it in form under certain conditions. Davenport (1959) has pointed out that if landholding rights are separated into rights of use and control versus rights of alienation, use and control of land can be vested in a *title* which is inherited by a member of the title-holder's kindred. So long as there is any patterned rule of succession, the ownership of the land will be continuous, and action with respect to it may be collective. Davenport referred to this as the *stem kindred*. The stem kindred will always have certain rights in the land that the title-holder must respect: for example, it has the right to forbid him to alienate any part of the estate. Title, of course, will not be allowed to pass out of the kindred. However, those persons born outside the recognized collateral range in any given generation will lose their rights and their claim to the title. The stem kindred will resemble a single genealogical line for many generations in the past, but be a kindred in the present. Like the ambilineage, such a group is not ego-centered. Its focus is clearly governed by the present and past title-holders. [Additional discussions of kinship and descent systems are found on pp. 86–88, 504–506.]

INDUSTRIALIZATION AND THE FAMILY

Evidence for the hypothesis that industrialization is sufficient to change a family system into a bilateral kindred with independent nuclear families is reviewed in this section, and an attempt is made to discover what it is about industrialization that produces this effect, if it exists at all. The results are inconclusive, since nothing is said about historical data or about contemporary Western societies, but that is not the most difficult problem; the real problem is to understand what the hypothesis means to assert.

There is great confusion currently, particularly among sociologists with a limited comparative perspective, as to just what is changing into what, if anything. Everything from the prominence of kinship in

society, to unilineal corporate descent groups, to extended families (in the technical sense), to any kind of interpersonal contacts among members of a kindred have been mentioned by various writers as possible units of analysis.

Theory

It is assumed here that the fundamental papers are by Ogburn (1928) and Parsons (1943), and that most of the rest are misreadings of these. The first describes a process of differentiation in society, in which formerly multifunctional kinship units—either a large nuclear family or a small extended family is meant—change into monofunctional kinship units. There are corresponding changes in power structure, including the emancipation of women and youth and more equalitarian hu-wi relationships based on more purely affective bonds (cf. Burgess, 1926; Ogburn & Tibbitts, 1933). The second is partly a technical account of the properties of a bilateral kindred—any kindred, not just that of the United States—which observes that in such a system the nuclear family is "structurally isolated," in the sense that it is not incorporated into larger descent groups or extended families which have greater parent-child than conjugal solidarity. Partly it is also an argument that, because the hu-fa role of the nuclear family is the status-giving role in the family, because this status is based on the occupational role, because the occupational role in such a system is not strictly hereditary, and because a bilateral kindred cannot maintain perpetual succession to a landed estate, the social and geographical mobility that are therefore possible facilitate industrialization. In the absence of such a system, either industrialization is retarded, or whatever other system exists must be broken down (see also Levy, 1949).

Is industrialization a necessary condition? That industrialization is not *necessary* to produce either bilateral kindreds or the independent nuclear family was shown in

Steward's work on the Basin Shoshone (1938). The Shoshone live in small, independent nuclear families, occasionally gathering into larger (bilateral) groups for ceremonial purposes; they live this way because they are an economically marginal hunting-gathering tribe which, since the per capita productivity of their resources decreases as the population density increases, would starve if they lived in extended families.

A complete and conclusive demonstration has been reported by Nimkoff and Middleton (1960). They tested only the hypothesis that the extended family is correlated with type of subsistence, ignoring the kindred, but that hardly matters for the present purpose. Table 8 shows that almost half of the societies in their sample (45.2 per cent) have independent nuclear families, and that there is a substantial correlation of this family type with hunting-gathering cultures. (See Driver & Massey, 1957, p. 402, for the distribution of the independent nuclear family in aboriginal America.)

The extended family, on the other hand, is associated with settled agriculture and rights in land. Following Steward, Nimkoff and Middleton attributed this correlation to the stability of food supply and geographical mobility. They showed each to be independently related to extended family structures. Evidence on geographical mobility is fairly direct; evidence for stability of food supply depends on supposing that food supply is correlated with elaborate stratification, which is then shown to be positively correlated with the extended family.

Is industrialization a sufficient condition? But will industrialization lead to changes in the family system if it does occur? First, evidence that the loss of functions of the descent group brings about a change into a bilateral kindred—independent nuclear family structure will be examined. The classic

TABLE 8

FAMILY TYPE AND SUBSISTENCE PATTERN[a]

Subsistence Pattern	Family Type			
	Independent		Extended	
	N	Per Cent	N	Per Cent
Agriculture and animal husbandry codominant	2	11.1	16	88.9
Agriculture and fishing codominant	4	22.2	14	77.8
Agriculture and hunting codominant	1	33.3	2	66.7
Fishing dominant	15	37.5	25	62.5
Agriculture dominant, animal husbandry important	72	39.8	109	60.2
Agriculture dominant, animal husbandry absent or unimportant	73	45.6	87	54.4
Animal husbandry dominant or codominant with fishing	21	48.8	22	51.2
Fishing and hunting codominant	7	50.0	7	50.0
Hunting and gathering dominant; agriculture or animal husbandry important	10	55.6	8	44.4
Hunting and gathering dominant; fishing important; agriculture or animal husbandry absent or unimportant	22	73.3	8	26.7
Hunting and gathering dominant; agriculture, animal husbandry, and fishing absent or unimportant	20	83.3	4	16.7

[a] From Nimkoff & Middleton, "Types of Family and Types of Economy," *Amer. J. Sociol.,* 1960, 66, 217. Copyright © 1960 by The University of Chicago.

monograph is Spoehr's (1947), which analyzes changes in kinship terminology and
camp organization of the Creek, Cherokee,
and Choctaw Indians (see also Spoehr,
1944, on the Seminole). All three once had
important multifunctional matrilineages.
With the decline of the vengeance group,
the loss of educational functions to mission
schools, the increasing control of inheritance by United States courts, and the loss
of descent-group functions in the ancient
town organization, the matrilineage had
become mostly a matter of ideological interest to the more conservative members of
the tribes. As a result, the authority of the
mobr was very much weaker, the effective
kinship units were the nuclear family and
a kindred of rather narrow range, and kinship terms for the immediate family had
shifted to a bilateral pattern. More distant
terms had not changed, since, Spoehr argued, they were not used. He also found
changes in the residence rule and extended
family.

The net result has been a shift from a
consanguine to a conjugal type of family organization. The matrilineal lineage, with a
close tie between brother and sister, and
mother's brother and sister's child, has been replaced by an elementary family unit of parents
and children with perhaps a relatively stronger
emphasis on the husband-wife tie. The extended family of the Creeks has broken down
into elementary family units, with the abandonment of matrilocal residence. This process
of change has brought Creek, Cherokee, and
Choctaw family organization to a form generally similar to our own (Spoehr, 1947, p. 204).

Because these three tribes are in direct
contact with a bilateral system, it might be
argued that contact alone accounts for the
change; and Spoehr was not able to show
conclusively whether it is diffusion or economic change that produces these effects.
Gough, however, was able to disentangle
the two in analyzing changes in the Nayar
kinship system (1952b). The Nayar taravad
has been disintegrating for some time.

Since 1933, for example, the law has permitted individual claims to the family estate
and required that husbands support their
wives and children. The descent group is
less important as a corporate, multifunctional unit, and there is increased importance of paternity, increased independence
of the nuclear family, and a change from
matrilineal to bilateral inheritance. Gough
attributed these changes, first, to political
change—eliminating the functions of the
warrior caste and opening civil service occupations—and, second, to an expanding economy and social mobility. She concluded that
these changes were due more to political
and economic changes than diffusion, because other evidence showed minimal diffusion from the British, and where there was
more diffusion—from Brahmanical influences—it was not in the direction of bilateral kinship or independent nuclear families.

Similar evidence is available for Japan.
Reporting on a sample of 100 families in a
Tokyo ward, Dore found that the conjugal
bond is increasingly important in Tokyo,
and that kinship ties there are less the traditional ties of economic dependence and
subordination to family authority and more
simply "personal affective links" between
individual relatives (1958, pp. 126, 157).
For example, 75 per cent of respondents in
his sample felt that if there were a conflict
between wife and mother-in-law, the husband should not divorce his wife, and 60
per cent felt that the husband and wife
should move from the mother-in-law's
household (p. 126). These are not the traditional norms.

*Is it industrialization itself that produces
change?* It remains to show that it is industrialization that has produced these changes.
But that is not so easy. In the first place, the
Cherokee, Choctaw, and Creeks are not
particularly industrialized; in the second
place, the alterations in Nayar lineages began with political rather than economic
changes, and were accelerated by commercial rather than industrial expansion; in the
third place, the changes in the Japanese

family in Tokyo could be due to urbanization rather than industrialization. Nor is it clear what process really takes place where it is industrialization that is correlated with changes in family system.

At least the role of urbanization can be settled conclusively. Comparing accounts of a large number of nonindustrial cities, Sjoberg (1960) was able to show that most of them had extended families and corporate descent groups, although in some cases the latter was an ambilineage rather than a unilineal descent group. This is in agreement with reports by Agarwala (1955), Comhaire (1956) and Lewis (1952).[14]

Nor is it geographical mobility alone that is important, despite Nimkoff and Middleton's findings, since the descent group seems able to retain the loyalties and contributions of its members, if it retains ritual or economic functions, no matter how far away they move. For example, the Chinese *Tsu* apparently retains a good deal of its hold over members who migrate to cities or who live in distant parts of China (Hu, 1948). Comhaire also describes some of these ties:

In Léopoldville, the capital of the Belgian Congo, the growth of the nuclear family and of a native middle class is impeded by low wages as well as by the absence of private property for African residents. The extended family thus remains a necessary institution for security and for educational and religious purposes. The newcomer in town and the unemployed both expect from their cousins some help, which

they will be prepared to return when fortune changes. Children born in town are often sent to relatives in the rural home who can more easily take care of them and who educate them in customs which include the recognition of kinship ties up to the level of ancestor worship .... Urban social life centers around *matanga,* week-long funeral proceedings which include both rites and entertainment, and to whose considerable cost distant relatives must contribute (1956, p. 47).

It is instructive to examine a case in which the kindred and independent nuclear family are found, despite the fact that the economy is based on agriculture. Greenfield (1961) reported on the independent nuclear family in Barbados, the economy of which is based on commercial export agriculture. He himself interpreted his data to show that any connection between industrialism and the independent nuclear family is fortuitous; but it is clear from his description that commercial agriculture is associated with an open-class, achievement-oriented, socially mobile stratification system, a separation of kinship and occupational contexts, wage labor, and the determination of a nuclear family's status in society by the hu-fa's occupational status and his wages.

Dore's analysis of the Japanese *doozoku* is also instructive. His conception is that the traditional large kinship unit had severe internal strains, such as the mo-in-l, da-in-l conflict, and was only held together because of the economic dependence of so on fa, or younger so on eldest so, which in turn depended on occupational inheritance and a household economy. When the family ceases to be the unit of production, when the so ceases to be apprenticed to the fa, when there are other ways to earn an income than to depend on *doozoku* resources, the authority structure of the traditional family breaks down and only affective ties are left.[15]

[14] Kahl (1959), reviewing evidence on social effects of industrialization and urbanization, attributed development of the nuclear family apparently to urbanization; but, in the first place, in every case, what is described is a migration of labor to cities rather than a stable preindustrial city of the type Sjoberg dealt with, and, in the second place, he believes the effect of urbanization is due to its correlation with wage labor ("an individualistic affair," p. 66) and geographical mobility. The present writer believes the latter correlation is spurious, but see Kahl (1959), particularly pp. 65–69. Kahl reviewed a very extensive literature, including several studies not mentioned here, and provides an annotated bibliography.

[15] In view of the fact that affective ties are always bilateral, unlike instrumental organization, it is plausible that such a system would eventually develop into a kindred.

Families . . . in which the main family still retains its economic stranglehold are now a rarity. . . . as soon as the economic implications of the traditional main-branch family relations cease to hold good, main and branch status are mutually recognized and visiting is continued only so long as there are personal affective links between members of the two families, and the implications of super- and subordination in the traditional main-branch family relationship tend from the very beginning to be very much modified. The stress is now on personal links whereas it was formerly essentially a question of relations between family units (Dore, 1958, pp. 148–149).

Some common elements begin to emerge if one compares changes in Japan with changes in India. Gough, it was noted, attributed changes in the Nàyar taravad first to political developments, which were then accelerated by commercial expansion. The effects of political and economic change, in her view, were to open new occupations, to destroy the homogeneity of occupation within the taravad, to reduce the dependence of taravad members on its estate, and to differentiate kinship from occupation. All this, of course, was associated with social mobility as well. She regards the development of sources of individual wealth and reputation that are independent of the taravad and beyond its control as particularly important (1952b). Ross (1962), who also attributed changes in India to political and economic changes that came before anything one could properly call industrialization, saw their effects as altering the prestige of occupations (so that sons want different occupations than fathers), raising the level of aspiration because of the rising standard of living, decreasing the homogeneity of occupations within the family, and reducing the dependence of sons on fathers or younger brothers on elder brothers. All of these took place as the family became less self-sufficient, as opportunities arose elsewhere, and as the interests of the members in a single estate in land or a single productive enterprise

disappeared (see particularly Ross's Ch. 6). [Interrelationships between industrialization and the nuclear family are also discussed in other parts of this Handbook; see especially Chs. 2, 3, 11, 13.]

Conclusions

It is difficult to come to any definitive conclusions, even ignoring the necessity of examining historical and contemporary Western data, but one fact stands out, that certain conditions are required to sustain the authority of the extended family over the nuclear family, and the authority of the descent group over the extended family. The conditions are:

1. The extended family must be a basic task unit in the society.
2. The "estate" of the descent group must be the basic source of economic wealth and social status in the society.
3. The "estate" must be indivisible, first, in the sense that one does not mark out particular sons or brothers as each making his own individual contribution of income or status to it, nor can it easily be divided among members— thus, frequently, the correlation is with estates in land, although an undivided estate of money should have the same effect.
4. The occupational differentiation of the task unit must be basically a kinship differentiation; so far as the external world is concerned all members are engaged in the same occupation.

Apparently, any kind of nonsubsistence, expanding economy, or even political changes can destroy these conditions, and hence destroy the authority structure on which the descent group and extended family depend. Any process by which kinship and occupational structures become differentiated, income and status come to depend on factors not controlled by the extended family, particularly where they can be acquired without inheriting them, where sons can begin to contribute more status and income to the family than their fathers, and where the self-interests of the members are not identified with the interest in continuity of the family estates, already creates the conditions of change—whether or not industrialization is involved.

There are, of course, some additional conditions that are not necessary, but may be sufficient to preserve the extended family and the descent group, such as cult or political functions. If the family is also the cult group, or if the kinship group is localized and village power structure is determined by kinship status, or if more generally political and religious activities in a society are structured through kinship, then the interests of nuclear family members are centered in the extended family and the descent group, and the authority of these structures is sustained. But these, too, seem to erode with differentiation of economy and kinship structure, with increasing opportunities for occupation outside the extended family and its estate, and with the proliferation of specialized occupational statuses—in which usually political and religious, as well as economic statuses are involved. What is left after such changes is the sense of personal obligation to kin and the sense of affective attachment to them. The former seems to pass in two or more generations, or more precisely, to take in fewer and fewer kin after two or more generations; the latter seems inherently bilateral.

The writer does not like to say "seems," or to end with the conclusion that a great deal remains to be done, but hardly any other is possible.

REFERENCES

Agarwala, B. R. In a mobile commercial community. *Sociol. Bull.,* 1955, 4, (2).

Bales, R. F., & Slater, P. E. Role differentiation in small decision-making groups. In T. Parsons, & R. F. Bales, with J. Olds, M. Zelditch, Jr., & P. Slater, *Family, socialization, and interaction process.* Glencoe, Ill.: Free Press, 1955. Pp. 259–306.

Barton, R. F. *Ifugao law.* Berkeley: Univer. of California Press, 1919.

Blood, R. O., & Wolfe, D. M. *Husbands and wives: the dynamics of married living.* Glencoe, Ill.: Free Press, 1960.

Bohannan, P. *Justice and judgment among the Tiv.* London: Oxford Univer. Press, 1957.

Burgess, E. W. The family as a unity of interacting personalities. *Family,* 1926, 7, 3–9.

Busia, K. A. *Position of the chief in the modern political system of the Ashanti.* London: Oxford Univer. Press, 1951.

Clarke, Edith. Land tenure and the family in four selected communities in Jamaica. *Soc. & econ. Stud.,* 1953, 1, 81–118.

Comhaire, J. L. Economic change and the extended family. *Annals Amer. Acad. pol. & soc. Sci.,* 1956, 305, 45–52.

Davenport, W. Nonunilinear descent and descent groups. *Amer. Anthropologist,* 1959, 61, 557–572.

Davis, K. Illegitimacy and the social structure. *Amer. J. Sociol.,* 1939, 45, 215–233. (a)

Davis, K. The forms of illegitimacy. *Soc. Forces,* 1939, 18, 77–89. (b)

Davis, K. *Human society.* New York: Macmillan, 1949.

De Jong, P. E. De J. *Minangkabau and Negri Sembilan.* Leiden: E. Ijdo, 1951.

Dore, R. P. *City life in Japan.* Berkeley: Univer. of California Press, 1958.

Driver, H. E., & Massey, W. C. Comparative studies of North American Indians. *Trans. Amer. phil. Soc.* (New Series), 1957, 47, Part II.

Durkheim, E. *Elementary forms of the religious life.* New York: Macmillan, 1915.

Evans-Pritchard, E. E. *The Nuer.* Oxford: Clarendon Press, 1940.

Eyde, D. B., & Postal, P. Avunculocality and incest: development of unilateral cross-cousin marriage and Crow-Omaha kinship systems. *Amer. Anthropologist,* 1961, 63, 747–771.

Fallers, L. A. Some determinants of marriage stability in Busoga: a reformulation of Gluckman's hypothesis. *Africa,* 1957, 27, 106–123.

Firth, R. *Primitive economics of the New Zealand Maori.* New York: Dutton, 1929.

Firth, R. *We the Tikopia.* London: Allen & Unwin, 1936.

Firth, R. *Primitive Polynesian economy.* London: Routledge, 1939.

Fortes, M. *The dynamics of clanship among*

the Tallensi. London: Oxford Univer. Press, 1945.

Fortes, M. *The web of kinship among the Tallensi.* London: Oxford Univer. Press, 1949.

Fortes, M. The structure of unilineal descent groups. *Amer. Anthropologist,* 1953, 55, 17–41.

Fox, J. R. Sibling incest. *Brit. J. Sociol.,* 1962, 13, 128–150.

Freeman, J. D. On the concept of the kindred. *J. royal anthropol. Inst.,* 1961, 91, 192–220.

Fried, M. H. The classification of corporate unilineal descent groups. *J. royal anthropol. Inst.,* 1957, 87, 1–29.

Gluckman, M. Kinship and marriage among the Lozi of Northern Rhodesia and the Zulu of Natal. In A. R. Radcliffe-Brown & D. Forde (Eds.), *African systems of kinship and marriage.* London: Oxford Univer. Press, 1950.

Gluckman, M. Bridewealth and the stability of marriage. *Man,* 1953, 53 (223).

Gluckman, M. *Custom and conflict in Africa.* Oxford: Blackwell, 1955.

Goode, W. J. The theoretical importance of love. *Amer. sociol. Rev.,* 1959, 24, 38–47.

Goode, W. J. Illegitimacy in the Caribbean social structure. *Amer. sociol. Rev.,* 1960, 25, 21–30.

Goode, W. J. Family disorganization. In R. K. Merton & R. Nisbet (Eds.), *Contemporary social problems.* New York: Harcourt, Brace, 1961.

Goodenough, W. A problem in Malayo-Polynesian social organization. *Amer. Anthropologist,* 1955, 57, 71–83.

Gough, E. Kathleen. A comparison of incest prohibitions and the rules of exogamy in three matrilineal groups of the Malabar Coast. *Int. Arch. Ethnogr.,* 1952, 46, 82–105. (a)

Gough, E. Kathleen. Changing kinship usages in the setting of political and economic change among the Nayars of Malabar. *J. royal anthropol. Inst.,* 1952, 82, 71–87. (b)

Gough, E. Kathleen. The Nayars and the definition of marriage. *J. royal anthropol. Inst.,* 1959, 89, 23–34.

Greenfield, S. Industrialization and the family in sociological theory. *Amer. J. Sociol.,* 1961, 67, 312–322.

Henriques, F. *Family and colour in Jamaica.* London: Eyre & Spottiswoode, 1953.

Herbst, P. G. The measurement of family relationships. *Hum. Relat.,* 1952, 5, 3–35.

Herskovits, M. J., & Herskovits, Frances S. *Trinidad village.* New York: Knopf, 1947.

Hobhouse, L. T., Wheeler, G. C., & Ginsberg, M. *The material culture and social institutions of the simpler peoples.* London: Chapman & Hall, 1915.

Homans, G. C., & Schneider, D. M. *Marriage, authority, and final causes.* Glencoe, Ill.: Free Press, 1955.

Hu, H. C. The common descent group in China and its functions. *Publ. in Anthropol.,* No. 10. New York: Viking Fund, 1948.

Kahl, J. A. Some social concomitants of industrialization and urbanization. *Hum. Organ.,* 1959, 18, 53–74.

Kroeber, A. L. Zuni kin and clan. *Amer. Museum natural Hist. Anthropol. Papers,* 1917, 18, Part II.

Leach, E. R. The structural implications of matrilateral cross-cousin marriage. *J. royal anthropol. Inst.,* 1951, 81, 23–55.

Leach, E. R. Bridewealth and the stability of marriage. *Man,* 1953, 53 (279).

Leach, E. R. Polyandry, inheritance, and the definition of marriage. *Man,* 1955, 55 (199).

Leach, E. R. Aspects of bridewealth and marriage stability among the Kachin and Lakher. *Man,* 1957, 57 (59).

Leach, E. R. Review of S. Udy, *Organization of work. Amer. sociol. Rev.,* 1960, 25, 136–138.

Lévi-Strauss, C. *Les structures élémentaires de la parenté.* Paris: Presses Universitaires de France, 1949.

Levy, M. J., Jr., *Family revolution in modern China.* Cambridge: Harvard Univer. Press, 1949.

Levy, M. J., Jr. Some questions about Parsons' treatment of the incest problem. *Brit. J. Sociol.,* 1955, 6, 277–285.

Levy, M. J., Jr., & Fallers, L. A. The family: some comparative considerations. *Amer. Anthropologist,* 1959, 61, 647–651.

Lewis, O. Urbanization without breakdown: a case study. *Sci. Monthly,* 1952, 75, 31–41.

Maine, H. J. S. *Ancient law.* London: Murray, 1861.

Malinowski, B. *Sex and repression in savage society.* London: Paul, 1927.

Malinowski, B. *The sexual life of savages in Northwestern Melanesia.* New York: Liveright, 1929.

Malinowski, B. Parenthood—the basis of social structure. In V. F. Calverton & S. D. Schmalhausen (Eds.), *The new generation.* New York: Macaulay, 1930. Pp. 113–168.

Marsh, R. M., & O'Hara, A. R. Attitudes toward marriage and the family in Taiwan. *Amer J. Sociol.,* 1961, 67, 1–8.

Middleton, J., & Tait, D. Introduction. In J. Middleton & D. Tait (Eds.), *Tribes without rulers.* London: Routledge & Paul, 1958.

Middleton, R. Brother-sister and father-daughter marriage in ancient Egypt. *Amer. sociol. Rev.,* 1962, 27, 603–611.

Murdock, G. P. Comparative data on the division of labor by sex. *Soc. Forces,* 1937, 15, 551–553.

Murdock, G. P. *Social structure.* New York: Macmillan, 1949.

Murdock, G. P. Family stability in non-European cultures. *Annals Amer. Acad. pol. & soc. Sci.,* 1950, 272, 195–201.

Murdock, G. P. World ethnographic sample. *Amer. Anthropologist,* 1957, 59, 664–687.

Murdock, G. P. Cognatic forms of social organization. In G. P. Murdock (Ed.), *Social structure in South East Asia.* Chicago: Quadrangle Books, 1960.

Nimkoff, M. F., & Middleton, R. Types of family and types of economy. *Amer. J. Sociol.,* 1960, 66, 215–225.

Ogburn, W. F. The changing family. *Publ. Amer. sociol. Soc.,* 1928, 23, 124–133.

Ogburn, W. F., & Tibbitts, C. The family and its functions. In President's Research Committee on Social Trends, *Recent social trends in the United States.* New York: McGraw-Hill, 1933.

Parsons, T. The kinship system of the contemporary United States. *Amer. Anthropologist,* 1943, 45, 22–38.

Parsons, T. The incest taboo in relation to social structure and the socialization of the child. *Brit. J. Sociol.,* 1954, 5, 101–117.

Parsons, T., & Bales, R. F., with Olds, J., Zelditch, M., Jr., & Slater, P. *Family, socialization, and interaction process.* Glencoe, Ill.: Free Press, 1955.

Radcliffe-Brown, A. R. *The Andaman islanders.* Cambridge: Cambridge Univer. Press, 1922.

Radcliffe-Brown, A. R. The social organization of Australian tribes. *Oceania Monogr.,* No. 1. 1930.

Radcliffe-Brown, A. R. Patrilineal and matrilineal succession. *Iowa law Rev.,* 1935, 20, 286–303.

Radcliffe-Brown, A. R. The study of kinship systems. *J. royal anthropol. Inst.,* 1941, 71, 1–18.

Radcliffe-Brown, A. R. *Structure and function in primitive society.* London: Cohen & West, 1952.

Richards, Audrey I. *Hunger and work in a savage tribe.* London: Routledge, 1932.

Richards, Audrey I. Bemba marriage and present economic conditions. *Rhodes-Livingstone Papers,* No. 4. 1940.

Richards, Audrey I. Some types of family structure amongst the central Bantu. In A. R. Radcliffe-Brown & D. Forde (Eds.), *African systems of kinship and marriage.* London: Oxford Univer. Press, 1950. Pp. 207–251.

Rivers, W. H. R. *Social organization.* New York: Knopf, 1924.

Ross, Aileen D. *The Hindu family in its urban setting.* Toronto: Univer. of Toronto Press, 1962.

Schapera, I. *Married life in an African tribe.* London: Faber & Faber, 1940.

Schneider, D. M. A note on bridewealth and the stability of marriage. *Man,* 1953, 53 (75).

Schneider, D. M. The distinctive features of matrilineal descent groups. In D. M. Schneider & E. Kathleen Gough (Eds.), *Matrilineal kinship.* Berkeley: Univer. of California Press, 1961. Pp. 1–29.

Schneider, D. M., & Roberts, J. M. Zuni kin terms. *Note book,* No. 3. Lincoln: Univer. of Nebraska, Laboratory of Anthropology, 1956. Pp. 1–23.

Seligman, Brenda Z. Incest and descent: their influence on social organization. *J. royal anthropol. Inst.,* 1929, 59, 231–272.

Sjoberg, G. *The preindustrial city.* Glencoe, Ill.: Free Press, 1960.

Smith, M. G. *West Indian family structure.* Seattle: Univer. of Washington Press, 1962.

Smith, R. T. *The Negro family in British Guiana.* London: Routledge & Kegan Paul, 1956.

Smith, R. T. The family in the Caribbean. In V. Rubin (Ed.), *Caribbean studies: a symposium.* Jamaica: Univer. Coll. of the West Indies, Institute of Social & Economic Research, 1957. Pp. 67–75.

Solien, Nancy. The nonlineal descent group

in the Caribbean and Central America. *Amer. Anthropologist,* 1959, 61, 578–583.

Spiro, M. E. Is the family universal? *Amer. Anthropologist,* 1954, 56, 839–846.

Spiro, M. E. *Children of the kibbutz.* Cambridge: Harvard Univer. Press, 1958.

Spoehr, A. The Florida Seminole camp. *Field Museum of natural History Anthropol. Series,* 1944, 33 (3).

Spoehr, A. Changing kinship systems: a study in the acculturation of the Creeks, Cherokee, and Choctaw. *Field Museum of natural History Anthropol. Series,* 1947, 33 (4).

Steward, J. H. *Basin-plateau aboriginal sociopolitical groups.* Bull. No. 120. Washington, D.C.: Bureau of American Ethnology, 1938.

Strodtbeck, F. Husband-wife interaction over revealed differences. *Amer. sociol. Rev.,* 1951, 16, 468–473.

Tylor, E. B. On a method of investigating the development of institutions; applied to laws of marriage and descent. *J. royal anthropol. Inst.,* 1889, 18, 245–269. See also Discussion, pp. 270–272.

Weber, M. *The theory of social and economic organization.* Trans. A. M. Henderson & T. Parsons. London: Oxford Univer. Press, 1947.

Whiting, J. W. M. The cross-cultural method. In G. Lindzey (Ed.), *Handbook of Social Psychology.* Vol. 1. Reading, Mass.: Addison-Wesley, 1954. Pp. 523–531.

Zelditch M., Jr. Role differentiation in the nuclear family: a comparative study. In T. Parsons & R. F. Bales, with J. Olds, M. Zelditch, Jr., & P. Slater, *Family, socialization and interaction process.* Glencoe, Ill.: Free Press, 1955. Pp. 307–352.

Zelditch, M., Jr. The family. In R. E. L. Faris (Ed.), *Handbook of Modern Sociology.* Chicago: Rand McNally, 1964. Pp. 680–733.

CHAPTER 13 Family and Community in Urban-Industrial Societies

JOHN MOGEY
Boston University

This chapter considers theories which link the type of family to community structure, and the ways in which social scientists have sought to explain the consequences for the functioning, formation, and continuity of the family unit in a particular type of community. [It is complementary to Ch. 12, and these two together represent further expansion of the structural-functional method discussed in Ch. 3.]

This is a complex area of inquiry, still dominated by descriptive and anecdotal material. Its successful exploration requires both a typology of families and a typology of communities. Since none of the classifications in use fulfills the requirements of a scientific typology—to employ only well-grounded concepts in such a manner that hypotheses, which can be tested against data, are derivable—the discussion begins with an attempt to derive concepts that might be meaningfully used in such a typology. The discovery of the elements of the community structure, within which the modern Western family has emerged, is one goal for such an exploration, and this quest is pursued in the first part of the chapter. The second part is essentially a review of what is known about community factors in family functioning within such societies.

RELEVANT ELEMENTS OF COMMUNITY STRUCTURE

All societies rely upon the interdependence of status holders regularly interacting in a predictable series of encounters. The word *interdependence* is chosen in place of other concepts because it allows a variety of theoretical approaches. *Interaction*, the word common in many textbooks on the family, has as its normal referent individuals or personalities rather than statuses or roles; *reciprocity* implies some equivalence in the interdependence between statuses; and *exchange*, with its overtones of a market situation and the appropriate attitudes of *caveat emptor*, introduces the notion of the exploitation of status prerogatives by the members or holders of other statuses. A predictable and regularly recurring series of encounters is here called a *social structure* or a *social system*.

501

An Introductory Overview

The principles, or rules, or norms, which establish the interdependence of statuses and constrain the holders or occupiers of these positions to engage in social intercourse are still perceived in a cloudy fashion, but those that are basic to family sociology can fortunately be stated fairly simply and concisely. These are the norms that govern legitimacy and sex in any society; sexual relations between full members of the society, or adults, are expected to follow the patterns so delimited. Actual, empirical, observed behavior may show a considerable variation from normative, or expected, or approved behavior, but no society could continue with a purely random, uncontrolled pattern of sexual encounters.

Norms of sexual behavior. Biologically, human beings are so constituted that sexual gratification is available to everyone at all times. The human animal knows no rutting season: satiety or exhaustion may turn biological drives away from sex and toward other basic needs such as food or shelter, and deprivation may lead individuals to prefer food or body warmth to sexual expression, but the universality of sex and its power to compel action always lead to its social control.

Interdependence between the sexes logically requires three norms before it can be stabilized, and these norms must be both internalized as part of the personality and controlled by social regulations of disapproval, or sanctions. All societies seem to disvalue autoeroticism and homosexuality in the sense that none approves these forms of sexual expression above the heterosexual type.

The norms are:
1. Autoerotic sexual acts are not satisfying and are improper.
2. Homosexual acts are not satisfying and are improper.
3. Heterosexual acts are satisfying and are proper.

These three principles constitute an ideal construct for one expression of the division of labor. If enough individuals share the norm that heterosexual relations are the most satisfying form of sexual behavior, one can say that a society already exists.

Such a society will, of course, be a very rudimentary social structure until rules for other essential activities are formalized. It can have at most four statuses or positions for individuals to occupy: immature male, immature female, mature male, mature female. The distinction between immaturity and maturity need not fall at puberty, since quite small children are capable of giving and receiving sexual stimulation either with other children or with adults.

For understanding how families emerge within such a rudimentary society, one consequence of sex, reproduction, has to be singled out for special attention. The norm is that random reproduction is less satisfying than legitimate reproduction. Once this norm exists, legitimate fatherhood and motherhood come into being as social roles. The recognition of these statuses is formalized through the marriage ceremony, so one may say that marriage, which establishes legitimate parenthood, is the origin of the family as a social group. Legitimacy establishes continuity through inheritance: what is inherited is the status of son or daughter recognized and attached to two parents. Societies around the world show considerable variation in the degree to which they link heterosexual acts with legitimate descent: several make a distinction between *genitor* and *pater,* that is, between biological and sociological fatherhood.

Family continuity. Up to this point, individuals and single families of parents are provided for by the two basic principles of heterosexuality and legitimacy. The next logical step is to provide for continuity of the family rather than simply of the individual members and their statuses. The rule for this must provide for the interdependence of the families, in accordance with the basic assumption that social life consists of interdependence within a set of rules.

One social rule which leads to interdependence between families is called the *incest taboo*. Incest is not a biological crime; it is a social one. Sexual gratification between a man and his mother, his sister, or his daughter would disrupt the family through sexual rivalry and jealousy. Additionally, because forbidden, the product of such a union would disrupt completely the terminology which assigns rights and obligations to members of the society: parental and sibling obligations would become confused, and such an individual could not be fitted into the statuses available. He would be more than illegitimate, he would be, socially speaking, incapable of fitting into the approved patterns of interdependence, for he could combine statuses which society has decreed shall be kept apart (Davis, 1949; Middleton, 1962; Parsons, 1954).

In some societies, incest is a fairly regular and acceptable occurrence. References to the Old Testament and to Egyptian texts document both attitudes and occurrence (Middleton, 1962; Patai, 1959). Yet the incest taboo is a more nearly universal social rule than any other. An analysis of the social structures where its violation is tolerated is needed before any more definite statements can be made.

Although incest is known to occur, one must distinguish between sexual relations and marriage. Marriage legitimizes sexual relations between the partners and, in all societies, family exogamy is normal. Where the family is defined as the conjugal group of husband-wife and their children, incest prohibitions need to be involved in controlling the marriage of children who share one parent. Marriages between half-brothers and half-sisters are known as a minority type in such societies. Parent–own child marriages are apparently much rarer and universally subject to disapproval, except in the case of persons who are both royal and divine. Since the interest of this chapter is in marriage and interdependence between roles, rather than in sexual relations as such, this section has given prominence to the sociological explanation of incest. Alternative theories for this taboo, whether based on the psychoanalysis of emotional development or on interaction and avoidance, need not be pursued here (Flügel, 1921; Goody, 1956; Weinberg, 1955; Westermarck, 1922).

It is simplest to think of the exchanges enforced through the operation of the incest rule as applying to women. Females alone through their fertility have the capacity to build new families (Leach, 1951; Lévi-Strauss, 1949). The absolute minimum size for any society, therefore, is two families who agree to exchange daughters, that is, eight individuals. These individuals would, however, have to be distributed equally among the statuses: husband-wife, father-mother, brother-sister, parent-child, uncle-nephew, and aunt-niece. For the purposes of sociology, this distribution of status prerogatives is more important than the mere number of persons.

Community formation. Such a group would become a complete community only if there were a rule against marriage to outsiders. Consequently, to the rules of heterosexuality, legitimacy, and incest there should be added rules which specify the available partners among those positions that exist beyond the limits of incest. Such rules of *exogamy* or *endogamy* create community or society boundaries, for they provide for the roles of member and nonmember in the social group. That is to say, while incest rules force families toward interdependence, marriage rules of exogamy or endogamy establish limits within which a nonincestuous exchange may take place, and thus create communities.

From this standpoint, the community is a subsystem of the society, rather than just a territorial social unit. As such, it is the group within which marriage and avoidance rules work themselves out in observable behavior within the limits established for age, sex, and generation by the society.

Nevertheless, the rules of a society have to embrace many other activities as well, so this simple model will never build a completely functioning social system.

When these four norms operate to establish within a population a sense of heterosexuality, legitimacy, incest avoidance, and membership, the primacy of society over the family follows, and within the society the existence of residential groups, descent groups, domestic groups, community groups, and status differentiation is made possible. Only the existence of domestic groups and their analytical separation from family groups has been stressed thus far. However, if stable heterosexual relations between individuals are established, so that children are legitimately produced and descent assured, then food, affection, and sustenance are subsumed, and, consequently, domestic groups emerge as a necessary unit in society.

This opening section should not be construed as giving a hypothetical evolutionary sequence to the origin of either society or families. The principles are simply logical statements which seem to be necessary for the existence and continuity of social structures with families. Before they can be taken as factual statements, they would have to be tested against empirical reality. Many refinements will, in all probability, be needed, since as they stand the statements are very sweeping. But they seem to derive logically from anthropological and sociological studies. The richness and detail in anthropological case studies is a tremendous intellectual treasure, still inadequately exploited by family sociology.

Family and Descent

The recognition of legitimate descent provides every child at birth with a set of relatives. The rules of descent distinguish two logical possibilities for attaching the child to a set of relatives: (a) unilateral descent assigns the child to relatives of one parent, patrilineal to the father, matrilineal

to the mother; (b) bilateral descent assigns the child equally to both parents.

Descent systems are vitally important because they establish for all members of a society the kinds and extent of social interdependence that may be expected. Ties in a kin group thus established are primarily of an economic or political kind, rather than affectional, educational, or sexual: they provide rights to sustenance or to support and establish obligations of a like nature. These are corporate rights attached to membership in a corporate group. As in all sociological analysis, the existence of a strict unilineal descent system, for example, a patrilineal one, does not completely free other relatives from obligations of social interdependence. In a patrilineal society, a child will have some rights from its mother's people, although these are often of a grace-and-favor kind rather than strictly enforceable jural or legal rights (Lévi-Strauss, 1958).

Unilateral descent. In patrilineal societies, the establishment of paternity is a major sociological problem, and institutional devices which unequivocally establish the *pater* of every child are essential to the survival of the society. Consequently, in patrilineal societies, marriage is a most important institution. Its function is to determine economic and political rights between a child and its father's people.

By contrast, motherhood does not pose the same problem, so the marriage ceremony has a different emphasis in matrilineal societies. Further, in these social systems, what are transferred to the husband are sexual rights only and not both sexual and reproductive rights. The child of a woman in a matrilineal society belongs to *her* kinsmen. Marriage is still essential to distribute sexual rights, but not rights over the issue. Many of the disciplining, nurturing, and child-rearing duties of the husband, if he is patrilineal, are carried out by the mother's brother. The matrilineal peoples of South India phrase the distinction well when they say that in their society husbands and wives are playmates rather than partners in a family enterprise.

In general, patrilineal societies have highly formal marriage ceremonies, matrilineal societies fairly informal ones. This distinction reflects the importance of the rights transferred from one kindred to another at marriage.

Unilineal descent systems have been intensively studied by social anthropologists, and the rules for them have been given in Chapter 12. This discussion may turn, then, to an examination of bilateral descent in its effect on community structure and on family structure.

Bilateral Descent. Bilateral kinship systems, such as our own, have a completely different structure from unilateral ones. In them, a child may expect to share equally in its formal relations with both its father's and its mother's relatives. Such a social group is called a *kindred* rather than a *lineage.* Kindreds differ from lineages in being endlessly different for each individual in each generation; only siblings share all members of the same kindred. Consequently, as a form of social structure, they are unsuited to several functions performed by lineages. In particular, they are never corporate groups in their own right, although corporate groups may be formed from individuals within them. For example, in the formation of corporate work groups, affinal kin may be commonly used as well as consanguineal kin, since the distinctions between relations by marriage and those by descent are blurred (Blehr, 1963). As a consequence of these structural disabilities, the kindred is a group that can only operate sporadically. It is particularly involved when an individual member faces a special crisis, as in the case of birth, marriage, death, migration, or physical disaster.

Societies with bilateral descent are called *cognatic* societies. In them, the social structure is best regarded as the probabilistic outcome of multiple individual choices, rather than as a direct reflection of the rules. Many more variations in social organization are found in them than in unilineal systems. Combinations of structural elements seem more easily formed to meet changing situations in cognatic societies, and it may be that, in over-all terms, they are less solidary.

In spite of this variability, an analysis of existing cognatic societies has put forward eight predominant tendencies, common to all:

1. Small domestic unit, never extended families;
2. Monogamy, polygamy very limited in occurrence;
3. No fixed residence rules, neolocal residence common;
4. Descent groups not functionally important;
5. Bilateral kindreds;
6. No distinctive terms for cousins, such as parallel or cross;
7. Marriageability of first cousins is equal;
8. Parental terms not extended to uncles and aunts (Murdock, 1960).

Societies with these characteristics are distributed around the world from Southeast Asia to Tierra del Fuego. They range in their technology from simple hunters and gatherers, through agricultural peoples with *swidden* (slash and burn) practices, to complex societies like that of Java. All of these eight criteria distinguish our own civilization, and that of modern Europe, from that of the Iroquois, or that of the Yao of Southern Rhodesia. They do not, however, permit discrimination between the present residents of Illinois and the Eskimo of Alaska. These criteria are shared by the hill people of Tennessee and the urban dwellers of New York. Around the world, 44 out of every 100 societies are patrilineal, 15 are matrilineal, 5 have bilineal descent, and 36 are ambilineal or bilateral (Layard, 1954; Murdock, 1959; Pehrson, 1954).

Our society, with its prominence of bilateral kindreds and small domestic groups, may thus be seen as one of a numerous class. The independence of the nuclear family domestic group from technology, or the economic structure, in all this literature adds a new dimension to sociological reports linking the family with urbanization, industrialization, and technological change.

Differences in group structures between these societies do exist, but it would appear that bilaterality leads to neolocal residence groups, help patterns between members of a kindred that are sporadic rather than regular and voluntary rather than obligatory, and a set of kinship terms that makes few distinctions. To account for the presence of the nuclear family as a neolocal domestic group in our society, the rules of bilaterality are necessary; however, taken in isolation from other factors they are not both a necessary and sufficient explanation. Their explanatory power is increased by combining them with an analysis of corporate group structure, which is done in the next section.

Bilateral kinship as a structural principle does account for occasionally operative kindreds. The rediscovery of the functions of the kindred, and the disappearance of the fiction of the isolated nuclear family as a structural unit, is adequately explained by the rules of kin relations. Recent accounts of the details of the operation of kindreds add new depth to understanding (Axelrod, 1956; Bell & Boat, 1957; Litwak, 1960a; Litwak, 1960b; Sussman & Burchinal, 1962).

Earlier attempts to explain the presence of neolocal residence and of nuclear family units by reference to urbanization or industrialization, or both, erred in two particulars. First, they neglected the kin as a community principle which affects family structure; and, second, they derived the modern family from a type of extended family or lineage which has a dubious historical existence.

In continuing to build a model of the relation between community or society factors and family systems, the next set of problems is to work out the conditions within bilateral descent systems under which *neolocal domestic corporate groups,*

with the love and affection of the intending mates as the prime determinant in marriage choices, can emerge. This social group —one type of family in sociological research—has certain prerequisites before it can become the dominant locus for conferring status in a society.

Family and Corporate Group

Historically, a central problem in family sociology has been to account for the emergence in modern, urban, industrial societies of the small domestic group which is also a conjugal, nuclear family. Arguments about the distribution of types of societies around the world show 64 per cent of them to have unilineal descent systems, often with accompanying structural features of lineages, clans, and prescriptive marriage rules. The remaining 36 per cent are bilateral systems, with frequent neolocal residence, small domestic corporate groups, and preference marriage systems (Murdock, 1949).

These propositions are not likely to be very reliable, since they are only one drawing from a universe of societies which show individual transitions from one type to the other over time. If one assumes that the proportions are roughly correct, however, it follows that the European origins of our American family are unlikely to be all of one kinship type.

Some "clan" organized groups of patrilineal lineages survived in eighteenth-century Scotland. The "mir" of Russia, and the "zadruga" of Yugoslavia are other examples of extended patrilocal lineages which survived into the twentieth century in remote places. Latin and early forms of German distinguished between matrilateral and patrilateral uncles, aunts, and cousins. Some forms of French now distinguish between the extended family and the nuclear family, as does modern Dutch, in which *familie* is the extended family and *gezin* the nuclear family of husband, wife, and unmarried children (Kooy, 1958). A study of the composition of households in modern Holland as reported in the census found that some provinces had households of the extended-family type, while others had nuclear families as the general rule. These types were not distributed according to the degree of urbanization or industrialization. Thus, the tentative conclusion was that nuclear families in some provinces were the aboriginal type. In these provinces, the nuclear family antedated urbanization and industrialization (Kooy, 1963). If this analysis is correct, they should have had bilateral descent systems, with partible inheritance.

Over a century ago, Le Play (1855) had already documented in great detail the families of Europe. From his research notes on the family budget, on inheritance, and on the contribution of each member of a domestic residential group to the sum total of its possessions and services, he recognized three great family types: (a) the patriarchal or extended family, (b) the stem family, and (c) the unstable family. From the standpoint of this chapter, the patriarchal family would occur in a society with lineages. The distinction between the stem family (*la famille souche*) and the unstable family turns on one point only: the father in the stem family had the right to determine which son would inherit all of the family possessions, that is to say, he could make one decision affecting a nonpartible inheritance.

Corporate groups are units of social organization concerned with the production, distribution, and consumption of economic and political resources. Three sets of rules are important to their functioning and continuity: task and authority, inheritance, and residence.

Societies with unilineal descent normally have some form of extended family as their unit of production. Extended family corporations persist as long as their authority structure maintains control of (a) the production of wealth and (b) the inheritance of authority over the corporation. In practice, this means nonpartible inheritance, together with an absence of alternative sources of subsistence, and often a clear distinction between ownership and usufruct.

In bilateral societies, neolocal family units may be independent corporate groups. Examples of this are guild types of organizations and family farms. In all such cases, because of the small size of the unit and its variable capacities at different stages of the family cycle, community-wide organizations to support the nuclear family are essential. Such community organizations may be based on kinship, as in the *meihel* of County Clare, Ireland (Arensberg & Kimball, 1940), on the neighbors, as in Northern Ireland (Mogey, 1947), or on the *kith,* as in the Hebrides or Faroes (Blehr, 1963). Furthermore, both neighboring and kinship may be combined, as in closed corporate peasant communities (Wolf, 1957). In early industrial organizations, the family, not the individual wage earner, continued to be the unit of employment (Smelser, 1959).

Given bilateral reckoning of kinship obligations, meaningless numbers of kin in each generation accumulate, even within a farming population of a few hundred conjugal families. Three solutions for this problem have been discovered in empirical studies: (a) the number of kin is reduced by disregarding genealogical depth; grandparents are rarely known and great-grandparents are always ignored; (b) kin relations are reduced by selection among those available, either in terms of social class or in terms of personal attributes; (c) kindred are reduced by endogamy, and in particular by a preference for a double collateral bond at marriage (Firth, 1956; Wolf, 1957). In the latter case, the sons in one family marry first cousins who are sisters in another; the children of these monogamous unions share grandparents; and in a community of such marriages, individuals may refer to each other as either close kin or distant kin, since the same individuals occupy both positions (Matthews, 1964).

The effects of inheritance on corporate family structures have been best illustrated by reference to the feudal communities of medieval England. Where inheritance is limited to a single person, as in primogeniture, ultimogeniture, or in *la famille souche,* the community is stabilized through control of family access to subsistence.

Economists insist that, given partible inheritance and a fixed amount of land, there is a tendency toward an egalitarian productive system. The larger farms successfully rear larger families than the smaller ones; but in the next generation, thanks to partition among sons, farm sizes and consequently family sizes revert to the mean for the village as a whole (Mukerjee & Girling, 1950; Stys, 1957).

Partible inheritance also has other consequences for the social structure. The above-mentioned inheritance patterns lead to a fossilization of the class structure in the society. The son of a medieval yardlander inherited a yardland, the son of a cotter a cotsetle patch of land. Yardlanders were eligible for high manorial community offices like reeve or sheriff; cottiers were not. By contrast, partible descent, or gavelkind, leads to an increase in the mobility of families among the offices or positions of the community. Gavelkind inheritance is conducive to movement in land ownership, since some of the inheritors are more interested in their land than are others. A market in land develops, both for this reason and because certain fathers have more sons than others, so that what some sons in each generation inherit is inadequate to support them. In a rural society where status and land ownership are linked, partible inheritance of a fixed amount of land leads inevitably to a fluid or open class system (Homans, 1953). Inheritance systems are therefore closely linked both to family formation and to the social opportunities available to families in the community.

Changes in residence rules disturb all existing patterns of social interdependence, because they alter for a lifetime the political, economic, and affectional ties of society members. This is to say that residence rules are one key to membership in corporate groups; they subsume inheritance of possessions and facilities and distribute rights in both to various statuses (Barnes, 1960; Ehrenfels, 1956; Goodenough, 1956).

Emergence of the Nuclear Family

Murdock (1949) defined this family type as a coresidential group fulfilling four explicit functions for its members: sexual, reproductive, economic, and educational. Coresidence is not common amongst the Nayar, nor indeed can the Israeli kibbutz be easily assimilated to this feature. In this latter community, while sexual cohabitation is common, children are often reared in communal nurseries rather than with the parents (Eisenstadt, 1954; Spiro, 1956; Talmon-Garber, 1956). The kibbutz family has lost both its child-rearing or educational functions and its economic functions.

In unilineal descent systems with corporate lineages, the family unit has few productive functions, although it may operate occasionally as a principal mechanism for distribution and more frequently as a mechanism for consumption. Economic functions in production are dominant in extended families and in stem families, but not in the individual nuclear families within these corporate groups. Consequently, one must distinguish within economic activities between production, distribution, and consumption in order to deal meaningfully with the variety of data available (Arensberg, 1960).

There is a conflict in the evidence between the effects of major economic changes and the effects of mobility in itself on the emergence of the nuclear family from extended family systems. On the one hand, Smelser (1959) has shown that, historically, most disturbance and confusion arose when the role of the husband-father as head of a productive unit was threatened. When families moved from being units of economic production under the "putting-out" system into factories, few family dissatisfactions arose so long as the conjugal family worked as a corporate unit. Once the husband's role as foreman was taken over by another person, then came instant outbursts of machinery-smashing and riots. The developed industrial family, fitted to survive in a world of factories and wage-giving occupations, thus differed significantly in inheritance, authority, and role structure from the domestic manufacturing family, and from the rural subsistence farm family which preceded it.

While this particular family transformation is amply documented by economic historians and sociologists, the fact that neolocal nuclear families are a constant element in European history should not be overlooked. The Le Play unstable family type was common all over middle Europe, a zone where the agricultural system involved mobility in the colonization of vacant lands, a medieval version of the moving frontier. In addition, this whole area was swept constantly by wars and political upheavals, so that many social groups were agglomerations of refugees. Extended families seem to have been a product of power, wealth, and stability and were always a minority type in the population. However, they dominate recorded history and so appear very important. They were probably important politically, but in an account of relations between family types and social structures, this over-emphasis obscures the record.

Settlement studies show wide areas of Europe where single-family homesteads were the rule. This includes all of the Atlantic coast lands from Galicia through Ireland and Scotland to Norway, large segments of the North German Plain, all of the foothill zone of the Alps from Carinthia to the Savoy, and about two-thirds of the area of France (Demangeon, 1927). These areas were some of the earliest to be industrialized and also furnished the bulk of the settlers in the United States until 1890. Since they came from stem-family or isolated-nuclear-family cultures, the prevalence of this type under conditions of industrialization or migration may be an ex-ample of persistence rather than of change.

The distinction between the nuclear family as a corporate or productive unit and as a unit of consumption, affection, and socialization needs to be made clearly. The urban-industrial family is not a corporate unit, since the key to status (or access to the resources of the society) rests in parental occupations, and these are normally found in specialized productive organizations. This point was the pivot of the loss-of-functions argument put forward by Ogburn (1928). Subsequent work has added detail to the process of differentiation by which the family lost some functions, but the basic argument remains sound.

The Nuclear Family as a Dominant Type

Around the world today, societies formerly practicing nomadic or subsistence-agricultural systems of production are changing slowly toward more complex economies. Indices of this change are urbanization and industrialization. Everywhere, it seems, these forces induce population mobility, which affects residential patterns and lessens the controls exerted by community and kinship. One consequence of this change is that the Western-style nuclear family unit becomes the desired way of life, and cooperation in production among kinsmen becomes an occasional rather than a regular feature of family living.

The modern ideal nuclear family consists of a distinctive combination of functions: sexual gratifications for both spouses, free choice for future spouses at the point of entry into marriage, neolocal residence, reproduction-conferring inheritance, and status, consumption, and education. Evidence for the recognition of the desirability of such a family group can be found in constitutional amendments and in acts of the United Nations. The Declaration of Human Rights (UN, 1948) seeks to assure freedom of choice at marriage, parental freedom in selection of education, and guarantees of subsistence to individual family members.

Beginning with the constitution of the Weimar Republic (1919) in Germany, a movement has spread to write into the fundamental law of the state special protection for the family, in addition to rights granted to individual citizens. This movement has been particularly evident in Catholic countries and in the Communist constitutions written since 1945 (UN, 1954). What these constitutional phrases mean in terms of actual behavior within families raises a number of questions that have still to be explored.

A parallel constitutional movement has been the outlawing of polygamy. Examples of this are the 1955 Hindu Marriage Act covering all of India; the Women's Equal Rights Act of 1951 in Israel; Tunisia in 1957 prohibited polygamy, although this is permitted by Islamic law; decrees of 1951 and 1952 in the Belgian Congo declared polygamous unions void, but made no provision for the compulsory registration of marriages. Some countries, while permitting polygamy, lay down that if the spouses declare at the marriage ceremony that their union is to be monogamous, this can be enforced in the law courts; these rules applied widely throughout former colonial territories in Africa, and in the Moslem states of Syria, Iran, and Pakistan. In Africa, marriages had to take place in the civil courts of the occupying power, not under the village native courts, however, and were consequently expensive and rare. The position since independence has not been ascertained.

Another legal compromise in some Moslem countries is to impose extra obligations on those who wish to take a second wife. The consent of the first wife and a financial obligation to treat all wives with exact equality are common conditions for the registration of a plural marriage. In Africa, polygamists may be banned from government service or have to pay extra taxes for each additional wife or hut. One or two governments, however, permit polygamists to take office and give equal allowances for wives and children to Europeans and indigenous workers. This practice encourages polygamy (UN, 1957).

As in the case of constitutional statements, the effects of amending the legal rules for marriage are not known. A study now under way may throw some light on the consequences for families of changes in marriage laws. The laws concerning marriage in Greenland are now being rewritten from the present Danish code so that they correspond to the norms and practices of the native population. Sociologists and psychologists from Copenhagen are conducting research on family formation and processes before and after the enactment of this new set of laws (Torben Agersnap, personal communication, 1962).

If the United States is any guide, one may surmise that legal requirements surrounding marriageability are easily breached. They have a restraining effect, of course, especially for those individuals who accept their validity and who raise no questions in the courts.

Section Summary and Evaluation

From this excursion into the literature available on the family as a structural unit, it is evident that relations between the social structures of family, marriage, community, and society are close and interdependent. The family as a social group has to accommodate its structure and processes to those norms of the society that govern marriage, sexual gratification, reproduction, inheritance, residence, production, distribution, consumption, and, to a lesser extent, education.

It may be concluded that the emergence of the nuclear family in its conjugal form, as it is to be found in Western society, requires the presence of a community with rules favoring

1. Patrilineal descent, to account for the emphasis on the marriage ceremony and the concern felt about marital stability.
2. Bilateral kindreds, to account for the

occasionally operative kin groups, the lack of generational depth, and kin-group exogamy.

3. Partible inheritance, or no inheritance, or inheritance by individual testament, to account for intergenerational social mobility, the presence of a market system for property transfers, and the potential of geographical mobility.

4. Neolocal residence, to account for the dominant values placed upon the conjugal family as the unit of socialization and consumption, and propinquity as an element in mate selection.

5. Specialized productive organizations, to account for the absence of lineages or affinal or consanguinal alliances as work and ownership groups, the absence of parental choice in mate selection, and love as a value in mate selection.

6. Open societies, to account for residential segregation, interaction with neighbors rather than kinsmen, propinquity among eligibles at mate selection, socialization for achievement rather than for ascription, inheritance by individual testament rather than by ascription.

Finally, methodologically speaking, it is believed that this discussion may have opened up types of data new to family sociology and shown something of its richness and variety. Quite apart from the serious problems raised by the lack of comparability from author to author, the tendency for the nuclear family to change over time through its own developmental processes raises issues in the interpretation of survey or descriptive data. Social anthropologists now in the field no longer classify families once and for all into types by sexual rights, residence, legitimacy, descent, kin obligations, or production, distribution, and consumption. They recognize that neither a simple recording of normative patterns nor a single census of a village group provides adequate data for testing general propositions. Many families change residence from matrilocal to patrilocal, once a bride price has been paid in labor services—as Jacob

did in Biblical Palestine. In matrilineal societies, control of children sometimes passes from their father to their maternal uncle once infancy is over (Fortes, 1949; Goodenough, 1956; Goody, 1958; Gough, 1959; Leach, 1954). Field data about family structure need to take into account such social regulations at each point in the developmental cycle. In fact, family sociologists, whether their source of data is from preliterate or literate industrial societies, need to collect material covering all stages of the family cycle, and to develop from this indices for families akin to the standardized age and sex distributions of the demographers, if they are to handle adequately problems of theory and prediction. This task has still to be begun.

THE MODERN FAMILY IN ITS COMMUNITY SETTING

This section discusses studies within family sociology which document changes in some structural aspect of the nuclear family and relate these to changes in community social systems within the society. This chapter has already shown that a family typology has to consider the family group as it is affected by social norms or regulations governing marriage, sexual gratification, affection, reproduction, legitimacy, residence, production, distribution, consumption, and education. The nuclear family, now emerging as a world type of domestic group from many different antecedent types, combines sexual gratification, affection, reproduction, inheritance, conferring of status, residence, consumption, and education as its constituent functions.

The rest of this chapter seeks explanations for the effects on the family of its residence in particular modern communities. Such interchange involves, first, a consideration of the social positions available within community structures for family members to occupy, and, second, family participation in these positions as it is influenced by the kindred, social class, and stage in the family developmental cycle. Social systems which are subordinate to the community will be next to occupy attention. The data on the consequences for the family of membership in a network of neighbor and friendship relations are examined. Finally, information is sought about the influence on family members of the house and of social and geographical mobility within the physical and social structures outlined in these paragraphs.

The Community as a Social System

Nowhere is the lack of consensus in the use of terms more evident than among sociologists using the word *community*. [The discussion which follows may be compared with Sirjamaki's conceptionalization of community found on pp. 41–42 of this Handbook.] Well over 100 different definitions have been reported, and a search of the literature could add new ones to the list (Arensberg, 1955; Arensberg, 1961; Hillery, 1955; McGuire, 1951; MacIver, 1928; Parsons, 1956). For present purposes, such confusion is unfortunate but not an insuperable obstacle. Families have often indicated that the boundaries of their community or neighborhood are well established, so one may say that clusters of families exist that are conscious of community membership (Davies, 1943; Lee, 1954; Sanders, 1940).

The minimum common elements discovered by comparative analysis of the usages of the term *community* are territoriality, culture, and social interaction (Hillery, 1955). The major analytical problem raised by such definitions is to separate clearly society and community. Murdock (1955) has claimed that families and communities are the only truly universal forms of human social organization. Parsons (1951), on the other hand, has argued for the primacy of the society as a universal social system and saw two subsystems within it: (a) families plus kin groups combine to make ethnic groups; and (b) ethnic groups when local-ized form one type of community. From this standpoint, community and society always coexist in the same territory. As a contribution to their separation, Parsons (1956) proposed to confine the term *community* to the territorial aspect of every recognized social system. This reduces community to a single factor to be used in the analysis of ecological systems. For the effective use of this concept, a whole new area of social theory, the relations between spatial, or ecological systems and normative, or sociological systems, would have to be developed.

The reduction of the functions of community to adaptive problems in the ecological environment is inadequate for the purposes of this chapter. One fact emerges clearly from the welter of case studies of individual communities: they vary in the goals they set for their members and in their degree of integration. The literature on communities, that is to say, considers that as social systems they solve more than merely adaptive problems, and, furthermore, these sociological phenomena are very loosely related to ecological variables.

Arensberg (1955) placed central emphasis on the cultural aspect, seeing a community as the "basic unit of organization and transmission within a culture . . . and the essential base for high specialization of the society" (p. 1143). If *culture* is to be understood as an anthropological term, and therefore include all the knowledge and beliefs of a community social group, this usage is too broad. Considering community as a subculture within a society, as Arensberg did in the paper quoted, helps to separate community and society, but still leaves untouched the detailed operations for making this distinction in specific cases.

Attempts to base a typology of the term *community* on social interaction have been rare (Kaufman, 1959; Sutton & Kolaja, 1960). They concentrate their analysis on the degree to which locality is important, on the residence patterns of the participants, and on the type of problem that is at issue;

the social interaction pattern as a single factor appears as one of several modes of classification.

The model discussed earlier showed that to understand family structure and functioning, the social rules and patterns based on age, sex, generation, inheritance, and status are essential. The community is the field within which these become manifest. Age, sex, and generation usually correspond to residence or domestic groups; kindreds represent generational and status groups. Within the community, productive groups have apparently most impact on the family. In the literature of sociology, access to corporate groups comes primarily through membership. In turn, membership may be based upon inheritance or upon achievement. Other aspects of community organization recognize different categories of membership, that is, make manifest a status hierarchy. In the political arena, leaders and representatives have to be distinguished, although both roles may be filled by the same individual. Associations, and participation in them, are one mechanism for the creation of leaders and representatives out of members. One should also consider neighbor-neighbor relations and friendship cliques, which are groups based in part on propinquity. Reference groups are an additional analytical tool for understanding the relations between society, community, and the family.

From the standpoint of sociology, corporate groups are those with tasks and an authority structure. Since membership in them assures access to property, to goods, and to services, they are here called productive organizations. The rules for membership may be given by inheritance or descent. Partible inheritance, as seen, leads to exchanges of property rights, the creation of a market, and social mobility. Where inheritance loses its importance, rational-legal rules for membership and achievement processes arise. The family, under these conditions, loses some of its functions to the society.

The major function of productive organization is to produce resources and distribute them: such distribution may be done directly according to status prerogatives or indirectly through a market. The consumption of these resources, however, depends upon the community. This approach would limit the function of the community to setting "styles of life." Style of life is also an index of social class, which in the study of modern society is an important explanatory variable. It is usually indexed either by income, education, and occupation, which are appropriate to society as a social system, or by residence, furnishings, acceptance by others as social equals, or the proportional division of the family budget between housing, food, display, and entertainment. These latter derive both from territorial attachments and from subcultural preferences which are basic to the existence of communities. Insofar as the resources available to domestic groups permit a choice between differing styles of life, reference groups become important side by side with membership groups. One may say they act to distribute styles of life within and between communities, as a market acts to distribute the resources that make possible the styles of life.

A glance at the theory of consumption in economics shows that the approach given in the above paragraph is in line with recent thinking about the classical model of consumption. The trend is to conceptualize consumption as family decision-making, guided not only by income and assets, but also by the subculture of the community. One theory, for example, incorporates the weight applied to the consumer by the expenditure of other individuals (Duesenberry, 1949). A study of the ownership of four specific items of equipment found highly significant variations between area of residence and ownership of automobiles and television sets (Cramer, 1962). The influence of community and reference groups on family life-style is an area where family sociologists and economists could both profit by collaboration (Clark, 1955; Clark & Carney,

1958; Clarkson, 1963; David, 1962; Norris, 1952; Parsons & Smelser, 1956; Zimmerman, 1936).

The communities dealt with here are classified as those with patrilineal descent, bilateral kindreds, neolocal residence, free or partible inheritance, noncorporate structures as a community, nonhomogeneity in cultural influences, and nonisolation from other parts of the society. The isolated and completely homogeneous subculture probably does not exist as a pure type; most actual descriptions of small isolated communities record the presence of strangers, or in-migrants, often with skills vital to the survival of the community as a productive organization. Equally common in modern societies is the village where the men work elsewhere, so that the community has become a residential group rather than a productive one (Dennis, Henriques & Slaughter, 1956; Frankenberg, 1957; Mogey, 1947; Rees, 1950; Williams, 1956).

Not all families live in communities. For some, the social ties of the locality and the social controls of the residential group are so weak that a community social system is absent. This appears to be the case in Jamaica where, as a consequence, there is an emphasis on individual amassment of wealth and intense individualistic status rivalry. Absence of consensus and local leadership under these conditions is followed by an individualistic resort to sorcery and by a weakening of kin solidarity. Family groups are extremely unstable; the men move from one liaison to another with little feeling of responsibility for their consorts or their children (Blake, 1961; Cohen, 1956).

This "family" system, formed of unstable common-law unions, is the type case of the matricentric family. Failure to attach the *genitor* firmly to the family residential group and induce him to fill the role of *pater* (Davis, 1949) has also been reported among Negroes of the southern states of the United States, among Negro families in British Guiana and Brazil, among lower-lower-class whites in urban areas in the United States and western Europe, and among a variety of ethnic groups engaged in migrant farm labor in the United States (Cohen, 1956; Gans, 1962; Kerr, 1958; Michel, 1959; Mogey, 1962; Schorr, 1963; Smith, 1957).

This matricentric quasi-family has been variously explained as a survival of cultural inheritances from slave societies, as a consequence of personality defects or moral weaknesses of the individuals concerned, and as a consequence of poverty due to the reduction of employment opportunities for the male, so that he cannot earn an income sufficient to support a wife and family over the full range of the family cycle. None of these propositions is substantiated by other than descriptive studies. It may be that the causal factor is lack of a community structure, so that these families exist with casual day-to-day connections. Individual violence and family instability could result from the absence of a community social system, and, in turn, the absence of community is indicated by the repudiation of kin and the substitution of neighbors (Michel, 1959). Distinctions made between working-class families that are kin-connected and those that are not emphasize the family stability of the former and the family disorganization of the latter (Gans, 1962). This is elaborated later in the discussion of the structure of neighbor relations and the cultural distinctions between "roughs" and "respectables."

Community, Kindred, and Family

The simplest division made is into families born in the community and strangers born elsewhere, that is, into mobile and nonmobile families. This distinction is fundamental to the structure of village communities and even to certain cities, where however long you live you cannot in one generation gain acceptance by the high-status native-born (Arensberg & Kimball, 1940; Fei, 1939; Warner & Lunt, 1941; Warner & Srole, 1945). The point at issue here, however, is not community exogamy or the assimilation of individual strangers (women and men) into families, but the assimilation of families of strangers into a community organization.

The most extreme institutionalization of this feature is the caste division in Indian villages (Srinivas, 1955). The Mysore village of Rampura, with a population of 1,523, has 22 caste divisions, and this is not atypical. Each caste forms a neighborhood within the community. Each caste has a monopoly on certain occupations, and one consequence of this is the organic solidarity of the village community, since it fosters interdependence within that group. However, friendships between caste members are rare, since these members are rivals in production. This, again, fosters village solidarity. Caste groups are endogamous, but the village is exogamous. The rules of marriage are complex, but in effect they mean (a) you must marry a member of your own caste; (b) you must marry out of your village; (c) you must not marry into a village whose land touches your village; (d) you must not marry into a village whose dominant lineage or sib is the same as your own, or your father's, or your mother's, or your father's mother's. The operation of these rules leads to long marches by the men of the village in search of suitable brides for their sons. They also ensure that any village is linked through the mothers and the daughters to hundreds of other villages within a 40- to 50-mile radius (Lewis, 1955). Strictly speaking, this territorial region may be the community rather than the village as such.

This situation contrasts markedly at every point with conditions in European or Western agricultural villages, where the single important rule is not to marry close relatives; in practice, this means nonmarriage of first cousins, although the rule is often broken. A Mexican village, forming a local solidary agricultural community, like the Indian one in the example above, had 90 per cent of its marriages within the village and almost half within the neighborhoods (*barrios*) of the village (Lewis, 1955).

A similar endogamous group is reported from Prince Edward Island. There were three marriage classes in this community, depending on ownership of land: class A, with 10 families with average holdings of 150 acres; class B, eight families of 100 acres or less; and class C, seven landless families. Daughters of class B could marry into A or into C, but no marriages between A and C took place. To maintain stability over time, this means that either class B regularly produces a surplus of daughters or else nonmembers become brides more frequently in A and C (Charles & Anthony, 1943). An intermarrying community of this type can remain stable over time because there is a high tolerance of bachelorhood, and perhaps some local woman is sexually available to the single men.

If the distinction between the local-born and migrants has any social significance, its importance to the family may be checked by comparing intermarriage rates. An English study permits this; the comparison is suggestive only, however, for the migrants tended to be in higher occupational and income groups than the locals. Published data do not permit control for social class but, since marriage across class lines in England appears to be infrequent, perhaps one may assume that class endogamy is operating Of the local-born, two-thirds married wives who were also local-born, and, among migrants, two-thirds married another migrant. Individuals who came to the town as children and those who came from surrounding villages tended to marry the local-born rather than migrants. The local-born proportion of the total population was 41 per cent, and migrants made up 45 per cent, so child migrants and people from the surrounding district had about the same choice between locals and immigrants. If anything, they had wider choices among migrant families, for these tended to be slightly younger. About one-third of marriages in the town involved a local-born and a migrant, so a certain amount of intermarriage did occur. Nevertheless, the distinctions between the groups remain marked: the value of *P* on the chi square test was beyond 0.005 for local-migrant marriage (Stacey, 1960).

Modern urban-industrial societies are not simple congeries of congruent social systems. They encapsulate many folk elements surviving from preindustrial periods (Kooy, 1958). Studies of rural villages of farmers and craftsmen indicate a further independence of family and kindred. These villages are inhabited by class-conscious people, yet kinship ties and obligations cut across the class system. Farmers' sons become wage laborers for uncles or more distant kinsfolk until they amass enough capital or experience to get their own farm. Some cousins begin as high-status owner-farmers but because of market fluctuations become unskilled wage earners in rural factories. These facts do not interrupt the pattern of obligations among the kindred for, as shown, such obligations are functionally defined as being occasional and permissive (Brown, 1953; Kosa, Rachiele, & Schommer, 1960; Litwak, 1960a; Litwak, 1960b; Mogey, 1947; Rees, 1950; Sussman, 1954; Williams, 1956).

Typical of rural societies is the importance of the family as a production team, the mother producing from eggs and stock-rearing and the father from his field husbandry. The ideology central to this family type is "children owe a debt to their parents," and the tendency is for postponed marriages and the stem family to arise. Farmers' children marry slightly later than urban children of similar social-class background. In patrilineal European peasant families, the bridegroom depends on his family for the bulk of the goods he requires to begin an independent nuclear household (Arensberg & Kimball, 1940; Rosenfeld, 1958; Williams, 1956).

Even among wage-earning families, local residence reinforces the bonds of kinship (Firth, 1956; Mogey, 1956; Young & Willmott, 1957), and so stem families tend to arise. This is particularly true when the father can vouch for his son as responsible in unskilled occupations like dockers in London, porters in the major London markets, or college servants in Oxford. Even among the skilled trades, like printing composition, where entry to an occupation is strictly controlled by union locals or branches dominated by a few family lines, the right of entry to an occupation may in this fashion become almost a family inheritance.

The more typical family in urban-industrial societies has moved its residence away from the families of orientation of the spouses. Several recent studies have shown that, even in those societies where family mobility is great, the kindred form a functional group. Families spend their vacations with kinfolk. The parents help the new couple establish themselves with loans and gifts. At every emergency of the family life cycle—birth, marriage, sickness, divorce, death—kinsfolk are invoked or offer assistance. Only unstable families isolated in inadequate housing repudiate their kindred. However, mobility and independence are associated with a change in family ideology; this now becomes "parents owe a debt to their children"—a debt which must be discharged subtly, so that the children's independence is not undermined once they have established their own nuclear family unit (Litwak, 1960a; Litwak, 1960b; Sussman & Burchinal, 1962).

Dependence on kindred in emergency is also shown by a study of matched samples of broken and stable families in England. The original study included all women who had a child within one week of April 1946. Those who continued to live in Britain, whose child survived to be four years old, and who continued to cooperate with the inquiry (97 per cent of the total) produced the data in the study. For broken families, the proportion living with grandparents, usually the wife's mother, was five times greater among the widowed, four times greater among the separated, and two and a half times greater among the divorced than was found in a matched sample of stable families where both parents lived together. Differences between these proportions were found to be highly significant. Furthermore, because of kin support, broken-family mothers were much more often out at work than was true in the rest of the population (Rowntree, 1955; Young & Willmott, 1957).

In their capacity to call on kindred for help, siblings have equal rights and may call on either the husband's or the wife's kindred. This equivalence among siblings has been noted mainly in anthropological studies of preliterate cultures, but it appears to hold for modern industrial societies, too. Since, in urban-industrial societies, calls are sporadic and are generally made to meet emergencies, the choice of kinsman on whom to make demands is important. Bilateral kindreds have little depth, and, with mobility of residence, relatives beyond the third degree (first cousins) are little known. Social-class divisions are influential in this process of winnowing the kindred, and it may be necessary to distinguish between acknowledged kin and actual kin (Blood & Wolfe, 1960; Chapin, 1934; Dyer, 1956; Firth, 1957; Garigue, 1956; Hayner, 1933; Marsh & Coleman, 1954; Mogey, 1956; Nakano, 1949).

Open and Closed Communities

One theoretical framework relates community structure and marital behavior in the family. It contrasts closed and open communities. A *closed community* is one where the members share many reciprocal roles in kinship networks, in work groups, and in recreation, and, as a consequence, have developed a distinctive subculture of their own. Communities of this type are scenes of intense interfamilial cooperation and are cohesive, homogeneous in cultural values, and closed against nonmembers. Reports in the research literature emphasize the mood of warmth, security, and identity of these areas (Bott, 1957; Campleman, 1951; Chombart de Lauwe & Couvreur, 1958;

Curle, 1952; Fried & Gleicher, 1961; Fried & Lindemann, 1961; Gans, 1959; Hole, 1959; Mogey, 1955; Mogey, 1956; Riemer, 1951; Young & Willmott, 1957). *Open communities,* by contrast, are those where members have selective attachments to a variety of associations or secondary groups. In these, they interact with individuals from other areas as well as from their own (Bott, 1957; McGuire, 1951).

The closed community has been found in rural areas—where one variety is called the closed corporate peasant community (Wolf, 1957)—as well as in the working-class areas of cities in Europe and the United States. Its effects in rural areas on marriage choices under conditions of endogamy have already been mentioned.

In closed communities, two types of social structure have been identified. In one, there is a clear hierarchy of roles within which a group of specialists devote their time to maintaining the distinctive subculture, leaving others free for extra-community contacts. The type case of this sort of community is the small-town Jew of Europe. In the second type, all adult members are responsible collectively for perpetuating the culture. The type case is the Old Order Amish (Freed, 1957). The closed communities of the urban areas in the modern world are more like the collective than the hierarchical type.

The principal effects of these community structures on the family apparently are found in socialization, or parental tasks. This whole area of inquiry promises well for future understanding. Up to the present, however, work has been directed toward identifying and describing the community variables, and little or no work as yet relates community variables to the socialization process.

The effect of a closed community on marital roles is better documented. Closed communities are inhabited by "open" families, that is, by families in which the husband and wife each performs a separate set of household tasks. Working at tasks independently, help for husbands and wives must come from other families in the area, if the household is to survive emergencies. Under these conditions, the man need never do what is considered woman's work, nor the woman, man's work. Leisure time finds husbands interacting with men in the area, wives with other wives. In such areas, a woman entering a family house and finding children in need of correction will discipline them without consulting either parent, and this will be acceptable behavior. Within families with segregated role patterns, mother-daughter relations tend to be stronger than father-son relations, particularly when the men have moved residence at marriage to the street of the wife's mother (Bott, 1957; Chombart de Lauwe & Couvreur, 1958; Mogey, 1956; Young & Willmott, 1957).

The conjugal-nuclear family within which husband and wife share many tasks and often work together cannot survive in such a social structure. It requires an open community structure, and probably a community structure with secondary as well as primary groups. Family mobility, whether caused by decisions of the family or forced by slum clearance or urban redevelopment, also leads to the abandonment of segregated family patterns. One should add to the community structure that permits the presence of the nuclear family, therefore, a specification of openness—that is, the presence within the area of associational attachments based on the society rather than on the territorial community. It will be remembered that the earlier discussion of the emergence of the nuclear family called for communities that have patrilineal descent, bilateral kindreds, partible or free inheritance, and occupational structures not based on consanguinity or affinality.

Community, Association, and Family

In view of the prevalence of the notion that participation in organizations is a topic that concerns individuals rather than families, it is good to be able to begin this section by reporting a study which tests this assumption. The data collected fully supported the conclusion that individual participation in social organizations is associated closely with participation by other family members: participation as a form of social behavior was found to be, to a considerable degree, a family characteristic (Anderson, 1944).

Participation in associations is also highly related, both in urban and rural open communities, to the composition of the family as a domestic group. At the child-rearing stage of the family cycle, participation is least; and it should be noted that households of spouses, children, and another adult, where parents presumably could engage in outside activities, do not rate high in participation (Schmidt & Rohrer, 1956). Social-class differences do not enter into this interpretation. The post-child phase of family life is also marked by "considerably lessened participation in formally organized activities" and by a restriction of such activities as are maintained to the immediate locality of residence (Mayo, 1951). These were rural families whose rates of participation are low at any stage of the family cycle, but, presumably, a similar trend applies among urban populations.

Studies of participation in cities have found, as have the rural sociologists, that the higher the educational, income, and occupational classification of the family, the more likely are its members, adults and children alike, to be members of more than one organization (Anderson, 1946; Foskett, 1955; Hay, 1950; Komarovsky, 1947; Reissman, 1955). Moreover, formal membership is not an alternative to interaction within a kindred or informal groups of neighbors; formal and informal participation vary together positively (Axelrod, 1956). Participation in organizations does not necessarily mean a different quality of attachment; the warmth of informal relations in primary groups has been contrasted too strongly with the instrumentality of secondary-group interaction. One urban study comparing residents from areas of very different family status found that 51 per cent of members in formal organizations had nine or more close friends in the same organization (Bell & Boat, 1957).

The presence of kindred as an informal group in these urban studies was apparently not incompatible with associational participation (Hollingshead, 1950a). In the village of "Pentrediwiath," a fictitious Welsh place name signifying a settlement where the men had to find wage-earning occupations outside the village, Frankenberg (1957) distinguished native and stranger families in terms of cultural background—the natives being Welsh in speech and Nonconformist in religion; the strangers speaking English and belonging to the Episcopalian church. These distinctions were paralleled by class divisions, for the Welsh were wage earners in nearby cities and the English were salary earners or retired. Community issues involved these families differentially, and the background factors seemed to determine the roles of family members in voluntary organizations. The chairman or president role was always filled by a resident stranger. One reason for this was that meeting the community-wide interests which the organization existed to promote could lead to fission among kindred based on particularistic obligations. Another reason was that strangers were expendable, so that decisions taken in the organization tending to fission among kindred could be thwarted by forcing the resignation of the chairman. This effectively prevented the action being pursued.

Communities like this resemble the bi-cultural groups common in many parts of the United States. One observer in Colorado has noted that informal leaders of kin groups will be repudiated if they enter into negotiations with the other culture. Anglos and Spanish in the Southwest maintain the boundaries between their cultures by such devices (Watson & Samorra, 1954).

One may tentatively say that open communities, with associations as an integral element of their structure, provide three types of roles for their populations. Apart from rare families who are completely isolated from local contacts, one may recognize (a) members, who are conscious simply of some identification with the community; (b) informal leaders, who are those local influentials generally looked up to and consulted about issues; and (c) representatives, who have acquired or assumed the right to speak for the community in associations or outside groups. These correspond, in some contexts only, to "cosmopolitan" roles (Gouldner, 1957; Greer & Orleans, 1962; Katz & Lazarsfeld, 1955; Merton, 1957; Mogey & Morris, 1960).

Criss-crossing these community positions as variables intervening between them and family participation are social classes, kindreds, and neighborhoods. Both kindreds and neighborhoods, as membership groups, are often the sources of influence explaining the behavior of different community role players.

Community, Neighborhood, and Family

Mobility, together with neolocal residence rules, creates neighbors for families. Conversely, stability of residence turns neighbors into kinfolk. No anthropologist has ever considered neighborhood factors in tribal groups practicing shifting (*swidden*) agriculture; the village moves and families reassemble on a new site in the same relationship to each other. The active explanatory principle in such societies is assumed to be kinship, not neighborship. Among stable farming families in Tennessee, these two principles, kinship and neighborship, account for almost all marriages.

There is a Texan saying that "poor people marry conveniently," and, as noted in other societies, the poor are least involved with kinship reckoning, so that convenience (neighborhood) is the prime factor. Studies of English working-class populations find that husbands generally come to reside in the neighborhood of the wife and of the wife's relatives; this happens because often it is the mother who finds the house for her newly married daughter. Among newly established housing-project populations, marriages can be explained by propinquity alone, and the house where the new family will live is determined by the housing manager, not the mother (Durant, 1939; Hodges & Smith, 1954; Mogey, 1956).

Now that it has been shown that in modern urban-industrial societies the kindred is an active sociological system, one may expect some revision of the studies showing that residential propinquity—in one sense, the neighborhood, or perhaps the residential community, if the area used as a base is a census tract rather than a single street— is the prime operant factor in mate selection. Residential propinquity studies have shown that a major explanation for marriage choices is the distance between the doors of the two intending spouses; the probability of marriage between two persons of eligible status in terms of race, sex, age, education, and social class is proportional to the distance separating their homes (Katz & Hill, 1958). Significantly, this formula is the same as the intervening-opportunities formula used to explain the distance traveled by migratory individuals seeking an occupation (Stouffer, 1940).

Mobility, in the terminology of this chapter, creates neighbors, and when neighbors intermarry kindreds emerge and kinship prescriptions may in time take priority over mere propinquity in the choice of mates.

Three explanations are current to explain neighboring relations among families: the phase hypothesis, the status hypothesis, and the siteing hypothesis (Mogey, 1958).

The *phase hypothesis* says that among an agglomeration of newly settled families, neighbor-neighbor interaction among them is extensive at first. After a short period of a month or two, however, families withdraw from general participation, either restricting their neighbor relations to next-door neighbors only or practicing complete isolation (Chombart de Lauwe & Couvreur, 1958; Durant, 1939; Mogey, 1956; Newcomb, 1959). The explanation rests on the proposition that once families find that their neighbors do not share the same beliefs about housekeeping, child-rearing, or property acquisition, they cease to interact.

The *status hypothesis* divides families of working-class origin into "respectables" and "roughs." "Respectability" is a family characteristic or ideology independent of occupation (Mitchell & Lupton, 1954). "Respectable" and "rough" are naturally ideal types at either end of a continuum, but, in the absence of more refined measures of family ideologies, the scheme is useful as a research tool. "Respectable" families acted as if they wished to maintain social distance between themselves and their neighbors: none expressed attitudes of mutual help and approval of neighbors; their statements referred to unwanted contact with, and criticism of, their neighbors; they took an unfavorable view of neighborhood life in their area and participated significantly less in organizations of the locality than the "rough" families did (Mitchell & Lupton, 1954; Mogey, 1958).

If this family ideology is strong, "respectable" families should control the play activity of their children. Children, being ignorant of adult rules about status, are naturally a problem for these families. Two-thirds of respectable families reported serious disturbance with neighbors over children; two-thirds of rough families did not mention disagreements over children at all. "Respectables," when asked to name a friend tended to choose each other; "roughs" gave the neighbor as the friend (Jaco & Bellknap, 1953; Kuper, 1953).

With the *siteing hypothesis,* the explanation of neighbor-neighbor relations turns again to propinquity. Several studies have reported that, in communities of homogenous families, relations between families are based on distance (Festinger, 1951; Festinger, Schacter, & Back, 1950; Kuper, 1953; Wilner, 1955). To a question about the "good neighbor" in Coventry, Kuper (1953) found that 32 per cent named the most accessible next-door neighbor, as compared with 15 per cent who named the alternate next-door family.

Neighbor relations are important in building a sense of community membership. An unpublished monograph by Mogey, Morris, and Mogey demonstrates that a principal component of both house satisfaction and community satisfaction is a sense of cohesion among next-door neighbors. The practice of housing officials of placing a "rough" family between two "respectable" families, to raise the housekeeping and child-rearing standards of the community, is not effective; these families usually refuse to interact socially, after the initial phase of getting acquainted is over. The consequence is that families are isolated from neighbor interaction, and a sense of community membership does not develop. The alternate fear of housing-project directors, that one "rough" family will lower standards all around them, does not stand up to critical examination either (Drewery, 1957).

Neighboring has been found to be an active force in explaining participation in community organizations within the United States. The most powerful explanation rests on social class, but neighborhood factors add to it independently (Devereux, 1960; Hollingshead, 1950a; Lundberg & Lawsing, 1938). Among middle-class urban families, the neighbor is an alternative kinsman; he may be counted on for help to the family in emergency, for daily exchanges of mutual aid as in shopping, child-minding, or home repairs, and as a respectful community colleague who keeps up the appearance of his yard and property and does not intrude on family privacy (Useem, Useem, & Gibson, 1960).

In the United States, propositions about the effects of neighboring on family living are complicated by problems introduced through racial segregation. The proposition that a neighborhood mixture of families promotes a change in attitudes toward Negroes has been supported by some field research. The alternate hypothesis that segregation by neighborhoods leads to better social relations is supported only by anecdotal evidence. The great number of variables in these research studies—race, social class, family ideology, relations within kindreds, etc.—effectively prevents any firm conclusions being reached. Before such field research becomes productive, knowledge of the distribution of rights and obligations in the whole series of social structures should be available; only then will attempts to relate classificatory variables to attitude changes become meaningful.

Neighbor-neighbor relations, being a series of two-family groups, are subject to a structural strain. Inherent in the nature of a two-role social system is a demand for intimacy (Simmel, 1902). Yet in all industrial societies, neighboring carries the overtone that the families must not get too close. Neighbor, kindred, and friend roles all have distinctive rights and obligations attached. The exact distinctions have not yet been adequately explored, but the difference is implicit in the existence of the words and in their common-sense usage. If neighbor relations form a series of two-role social systems with intimacy barred by the culture, the fragility of such relations is a direct consequence of the structural strains built into the roles (Goode, 1960).

In the more usual meaning, a neighborhood is a "cluster of families with a sense of territorial identification and unity" (Davies, 1943, p. 52). Such a loosely structured social group functions as occasion demands to help its constituent families with child socialization, the development of life styles, and in meeting occasional emergencies. Looked at in this light, it is closely analogous to the kindred in a society having low geographical mobility.

In all this discussion of family and neighborhood, the neighborhood is seen as the social system within which relations called "neighboring" take place. The difference between this usage and that given the term by city planners must be emphasized. A planning neighborhood is defined as an agglomeration of families sufficiently great to support a range of community institutions, like a school or a row of stores, for day to day needs; such a unit may include as many as 3,000 families. The neighborhood as viewed here cannot exceed the normal size of a primary face-to-face group, around 15 to 20 families. Moreover, since family mobility is an essential consequence of the social structure of industrial societies, the sociology of neighbor relations offers virtually untrodden ground for the testing of propositions about family roles, behavior, and belief.

Community Values and Family Values

A cultural aspect of participation in community organizations, much used in England, divides families of working-class status into "respectables" and "roughs." The "roughs," as described above, correspond in some measure to Warner's Lower-Lower social class. The "respectables" insist on their dignity as respectable and proper citizens and disassociate themselves mentally from the indignities of the working-class label in our societies: they would correspond to Warner's Upper-Lower class (Mogey, 1956; Stacey, 1960; Warner, 1941; Warner, 1949; Warner & Srole, 1945).

The cultural characteristics of the "roughs" lead them to dependence on neighbors for friends, to avoidance of participation in community-wide or society-based organizations, and to a lack of support for individuals (respectables) who can negotiate with local government departments (Kuper, 1953; Mitchell & Lupton, 1954; Mogey, 1956; Mogey, 1962; Stacey, 1960). Among those families who live in one-room furnished apartments in Paris, and who presumably belong to the "rough" category, similar rejection of kindred and dependence on neighbors has been reported (Michel, 1959). Attempts by housing officers to

change families in the "rough" category into "respectables" have been mentioned already in this chapter.

A parallel distinction within an Italian working-class community in Boston recognizes "routine seekers," who search for a quiet, respectable way of life, and "action seekers," who emphasize thrills, toughness, and daring and who show a lack of respect for all types of authority above that of a neighborhood peer group (Gans, 1962). The same general recognition of two ideal types among the life styles of urban working-class families is placed in a purely ecological context by labeling them "block dwellers," that is, those whose range of contacts is strictly limited, and "city dwellers" (Schorr, 1963).

A practical aspect of this academic discussion arises when it is desired, as a matter of national or community policy, to promote certain values among families. The values to be promoted are normally those held by "respectables," such as independence, hard work, success, capacity to plan for the future, and those social skills and attitudes which foster the voluntary combination with others in the pursuit of approved community goals. At least three theories are in use in these practical attempts at sociological intervention: (a) the melting-pot approach; (b) the community approach; and (c) the mixture of neighbors by housing officials. This third theory is taken up in the next section.

The *melting-pot approach* is based upon the belief that children, through a common school controlled by a local community committee, will repudiate the values of their parents, act as principals in their own choice of mates, and acquire the language, social skills, and attitudes that make for success in the wider society. Insofar as this affects families, the greatest impingement is in mate selection. Tests of how accurately this theory describes empirical reality show that racial beliefs effectively prevent intermarriage between whites and Negroes in the United States. Further, intermarriage across religious divisions is not frequent: about 97 percent of the Jews marry other Jews, 94 per cent of the Catholics marry Catholics, and 75 per cent of the Protestants marry Protestants. There is some disagreement about the exact proportions, particularly with regard to intermarriage between Catholics and Protestants, and it is generally assumed that religiously exogamous marriages are increasing. Whether this is the case or not, the idea of a single "melting pot" for the United States is not tenable. Assimilation at the point of marriage proceeds in at least six "melting pots" (Burchinal, 1960; Cavan, 1959; Golden, 1958; Hollingshead, 1950b; Locke, Sabagh, & Thomes, 1957).

The *community approach* in its most sophisticated form has developed to enable Jewish families to assimilate quickly and effectively the values necessary for survival in modern Israel. European Jewish refugees posed few problems, since their own ancestors had originated the Israeli nation state, but Jewish groups from Kurdistan, Yemen, Morocco, or Cochin India failed to assimilate in the neighborhoods in which they were housed as individual families. The community approach keeps a unit of about 80 families with the same background together in one hamlet or neighborhood, instead of sending them out in twos or threes to a wide diversity of settlements. These 80 families of one ethnic background are assigned tasks collectively by the regional authorities, given full-time assistance from social workers in understanding these tasks, and rewarded by regional recognitions when they succeed. Tasks are mostly economic—for example, to produce a crop for processing in the regional urban center—but this type of life is foreign to these people's experience. The interaction of social workers, sanitary advisers, local prestige groups in the urban center, and the cohesive refugee group has apparently had an excellent record since 1955, when the new policy was adopted (A. Ben Ari, Mayor of Lakhish, personal communication, 1961;

Ajzenstadt, 1951; Danhof, 1943; Talmon-Garber, 1956).

The *"caretaker"* type of community approach involves an outside group taking action to change community and family value systems. Studies in the United States and England have found that neither volunteers nor professionals have had much success; the persistence of lower-class communities in spite of attempts to "improve" them represents a challenge to sociology. One index of the community is the presence of a local vocabulary and a local accent. The persistence of local accents in England, despite its cohesive society, the social rewards that go with "received pronunciation," and the models given by radio and television, is a remarkable phenomenon (Dennis, 1961; Gans, 1962).

The above paragraph should not be construed as saying that settlement houses and other types of caretaking have had no effects. In areas of great cultural diversity, they have prevented, or resolved, intergroup conflict; and always they provide a stimulus to mobility for that minority of families who identify with the settlement goals (Gans, 1962; Schorr, 1963).

Community, Housing, and Family

As a separate domestic group, the family in our society is peculiarly the nuclear family; but where there are lineages, extended families, or stem families, the family social group and the coresidential group do not coincide. Granted, then, a society where nuclear families are the predominant or the preferred form, the relationship between a family and its physical shelter begins with marriage, or as soon thereafter as a separate dwelling can be found. The allocation of families to housing is affected, therefore, first by the community rules of residence and subsequently by the conditions of entry to the house. Wherever the supply of houses is limited, for whatever cause, it follows that marriage will have to be postponed, and those houseless families which do emerge will have low satisfaction and possibly low stability. Factory towns and corporations, like universities, which provide housing should therefore be expected to experience direct consequences on the formation and stability of families.

Housing is, of course, through the effects of location, intimately related as an intervening variable to neighbor relations, to mate selection, to community relations, and to many general features of the society as an over-all social system. Such gross measures as social class, occupation, hours and conditions of work, urban-suburban-rural residence, all are in part measures of housing or are reflected in housing. Over and above these relational or structural features, the operation of normative forces is apparent. The norm of "one family—one house" is an important source of social motivation and of identity satisfaction for the sexually active male in the family. Most European societies accept this norm as a matter of social policy, and English law specifically lays on local authorities the duty of providing a house for every family that "needs" one. The concept of housing "needs" is defined by law, too, largely in terms of overcrowding, age, and structural condition of the existing shelter.

Low-rent housing, subsidies, tax exemptions, political encouragement of rehousing schemes by private builders, and a host of special rules and regulations, both physical and financial, surround the provision of housing in modern urban-industrial societies. These may be taken as indicators of certain structural strains in a vital area of family living.

Sociologists of the family and others have meandered into this problem area, as if by accident, over the past quarter of a century. Contributions with sociological implications have also come from social psychologists concerned with loneliness or privacy, and from engineers and planners concerned with noise in buildings, with family complaints, and with discovering standards of livability. Recent literature concerned with rehousing and urban renewal is full of propositional assumptions about the goals of family living (Abrams & Dean, 1949; Brunsman, 1948; Chapin, 1940; Chapin, 1951; Chombart de Lauwe et al., 1959; Dean, 1949; Frazier, 1937; Hager, 1960; Henry, 1953; Johnson, 1952; Lundqvist, 1955; McGuire, 1952; Riemer, 1945; Robinson, 1914; Rossi, 1955; Schorr, 1956; Schorr, 1963; Seeley, 1959; Wilner, 1962; Wirth, 1947).

Although causal relations rarely appear in this literature, certain conclusions have acquired some respectability. Families with less than about $5,000 per annum at 1960 United States values cannot buy decent, safe, and sanitary housing on the open market. (This figure should be read as applying to a two-child family, and be raised to $6,000 for a metropolis or lowered to $4,000 for a small town.) This is about the average figure for family income, and studies show that 88 per cent of families with a lower income are inadequately housed.

Seriously inadequate housing, whether overcrowded or lacking essential sanitary facilities, certainly affects family living. Social relations tend to spread out into the streets and lots of the neighborhood, rather than deepen within the family; there is a high degree of sexual stimulation, without adequate outlet; and such families become "block dwellers" and resist moving, even if a better job demands it (Schorr, 1963).

Most of these studies deal descriptively with the interaction of economic, political, and jural forces with the goals of families and not strictly with community forces. The discussion now turns to family phenomena on the level of community, focusing upon two problems: (a) the house as a physical entity, and (b) mobility from house to house.

The physical house. In 1954, the International Council on Building Research (CIB, 1954) came to the conclusion that the family's judgment of its home was an over-all assessment and not a summation of separate satisfactions felt about its size, room arrangement, bathrooms, internal decorations, windows, external architecture, and so on. This conclusion was amply supported by reference to studies of attitudes toward housing in all countries of Europe. Studies in the United States also gave general support to this important development.

The implication for family scholars is clear: the physical shell of the house, so easily manipulated by the mechanical power of our civilization, has only an indirect relation to sociological facts. Intervening between the house and attitudes toward it comes the world of social judgments. These are normative elements which are assumed to arise out of interaction in varying social structures. Physical aspects of the building, too—its location or its noise-carrying potential—are very indirectly related to social behavior (Brockman, 1952; Dahlström, 1951; Moss, 1956; Myllymäki, 1954; Plant, 1937; Rosow, 1961).

One significant study produced a factor analysis of variables related to complaints about the house by tenants. The major finding was an explanation of the level of complaints according to the number of children next door—the investigator having failed to find much loading on the factors for noise, the frequency of breakdown in services, etc., which are directly related to the quality of the house as a physical shelter (Moss, 1956). Family satisfaction over its housing, in all this research, is more closely related to adequacy of space for family functions and to neighborly or community relations than to design or physical standards of the house as a shell for living (Gans, 1961a; Gans, 1961b). A still unpublished study of family satisfaction with house and with community by Mogey, Morris, and Mogey has found these two sorts of satisfaction closely related and largely independent of satisfaction with work, social class, education, and membership in organizations—that is, with general social satisfactions. Other attempts

to relate family satisfaction, job satisfaction, and satisfaction with the home have also given inconclusive results (Dahlström, 1951; Gadourek, 1956; Myllamäki, 1954; Siipi, 1954). The house in this unpublished English study accounted for about 5 per cent of the variance explained, while satisfaction with the spouse, by contrast, accounted for almost 25 per cent of house satisfaction. The total variance explained was 46 per cent, and additional contributions (12 per cent) come mostly from the neighbor-neighbor relationships.

If these results stand up under repetition, therefore, it might be concluded that building good houses in and of itself has little chance of building good family relations or good communities (Rosow, 1961). However, since families entering houses controlled by public authorities or obtained in the open market are selected by varying criteria from those desiring houses, the influence of the house as a physical entity is difficult to isolate satisfactorily. In the English study above, the majority of an existing village community of industrial workers was rehoused without movement except to a new dwelling unit across a street.

The internal arrangements of rooms in the house and the degree of overcrowding are assumed to affect both health and family relations. Incest is much more common in overcrowded dwellings. This, however, may not be attributed to the dwelling itself, for it may be that husbands and wives prone to incestuous practices for other reasons happen to be inadequate in their capacity to provide a roomy house for their nuclear family (Kaufman, Peck, & Taguiri, 1954; Middleton, 1962; Perry, 1959).

If father and mother share a bedroom and exclude the children from it, will this practice affect the personality of the child? A comparison between societies where the practice is to exclude the child from the mother's bed with those where the practice is to exclude the father suggests that it may not only affect the child but also its fate as it enters the status of adulthood. The severity of community initiation ceremonies in some societies has been related to the desire of the group of adult men to whisk the child away from the world of women and make a man of him. Empirical evidence supports this proposition. But an alternate explanation is also substantiated. The degree of severity of the initiation ceremony is significantly related to the solidarity of the male group. It may be that the solidarity of the males in any society is related to the frequency and circumstances under which they interact with their wives, and sleeping arrangements may be an index of this (Whiting, 1958; Young, 1962).

This elegant attempt to link ecological patterns of house use directly with personality, and with community structure, once again leaves an uncertainty about the power of the physical environment alone to effect sociological structures. The presence of the "good" family in a street of delinquent families, of the "good" child in the delinquent family, or of the single delinquent child in the otherwise law-abiding family, lead to doubt about the adequacy of this type of explanation.

Residential mobility. Mobile families contrast with static families in husband-wife relations and perhaps also in parent-child relations. Bott's work (1957) in London noted that family mobility led to changes in community networks as well as to changes in marital roles. A test for this in England, where families changed houses but stayed in the same community, found that change from a substandard house to a good house was followed by changes in marital role relations. However, these changes were not all in the same direction; moving house, as such, is an inadequate explanation of change, for all families moved in the same direction to a better-quality residence. A suggested explanation for the direction of change in family roles was the nature of neighbor-neighbor relations in the new house. A group of families which kept the same neighbors after the change had no changes in family roles (Mogey & Morris, 1960).

The social relations on which satisfaction with the house are based change in highly mobile areas. The general level of satisfaction in the community goes down, and in the level that remains, the contribution of neighbor-neighbor relations ceases to be important. These studies have involved public housing; and in mobile communities where more than a third of the families change every six months, satisfaction is best explained by a sense of dependence on the housing authority (Mogey, 1956; Mogey & Morris, 1960).

The effects of mobility on children have been inadequately explored. One result reported is that children of broken homes suffer more from migratory conditions than children from stable homes (Abrams & Dean, 1949; Tiller, 1957). Many more studies are needed in this area. The effect on marital and parental roles of "transient" life, of father-absent families as among sailors, and of personnel movements in bureaucracies like the army, offer opportunities for research still unexploited. Many descriptive accounts are available, but few research studies which seek to test hypotheses (Grønseth, 1957).

CONCLUSIONS
Family Typology

Implicit in much of the foregoing has been a family typology for societies of the Western world. The basis for this are the social rules for attaching the family to its community and its society. The categories in the typology are:

1. extended family, stem family, or joint family;
2. corporate nuclear family;
3. conjugal family, a noncorporate nuclear family;
4. unstable family, or matrifocal family.

These families differ principally in the degree and the type of their access to the resources of food, shelter, property, and power provided by the society as a productive organization. A secondary method of distinguishing them is by inheritance:

1. Nonpartible inheritance is characteristic of the various types of extended family.
2. Partible inheritance is characteristic of the nuclear corporate family group.
3. No inheritance or free testament by individuals typifies the conjugal family. This is the normal family of sociology: various names for it include nuclear family, immediate family, family of procreation, conjugal family, small family. The term *conjugal family* seems particularly appropriate because of the importance of the marital bond to its inception and continuity.
4. Lack of strength in this bond turns conjugal families into unstable or matrifocal families. The absence of anything to inherit is characteristic and follows from the inability of the *pater* to claim enough resources from the society to support his family throughout its full cycle.

Community Typology

As the literature was reviewed, a first approach to a typology of communities became apparent. This rested on three dimensions called, variously:

1. Closed or open, isolated or nonisolated, corporate or noncorporate.
2. Homogeneous in values or heterogeneous in values, and within heterogeneous communities, the "roughs" and "respectables"; the "routine seekers" and the "action seekers"; the "block dwellers" and the "city dwellers."
3. Social structure based on a hierarchy of statuses or based on collective action. The universals of status distinction—age, sex, and generation—naturally and necessarily apply to every community and cannot therefore be used as a major classification device.

Community and Family

The coincidence of extended families with closed, corporate, homogeneous community systems is generally supported. Nuclear corporate families appear most frequently in communities that are open and homogeneous. If the community is closed through endogamy, within the family the sibling bond may become dominant over the conjugal one.

Communities with associations present as a structural entity are mainly inhabited by conjugal families and have a moderate rate of family mobility. They are characterized by divisions between kindred or ethnic groups and associational interests.

Unstable families seem to be typical of social areas where community structures, other than the domestic group and the peer group, are absent. It is doubtful if in these areas anything properly called a community exists. Mobility rates tend to be high. This generic type is the slum of much of the literature of social reform.

But it has to be carefully distinguished from the working-class area with low mobility, stable families, and much kindred interaction. These working-class areas are closed, homogeneous, collective communities. Marital roles within their families are segregated, and socialization practices rest on sanctions for action rather than for intent (Kohn, 1963). This latter statement is established for the working class in general rather than for the community type. A test of this hypothesis, using community structure as an intervening variable, would be very desirable. Socialization based on sanctions for deed rather than thought probably constitutes a good preparation for ascriptive roles; and perhaps it is also common both in rural societies with corporate nuclear families and among stable middle-class people generally.

On the other hand, socialization based on sanctions for intent should prepare children for places in an achievement society.

It is associated with middle-class values but might be found if sufficiently detailed studies were made among the "respectables" in working-class communities.

Community, Mate Selection, and Marital Satisfaction

Selection of a mate among families living in communities seems to follow two patterns: either the parents choose or the future spouses choose each other. Corporate nuclear families and extended families favor mate selection by parents; conjugal families and unstable families favor self-selection by the spouses. Associated with this patterning is a change in the importance attached to marital satisfaction as compared to marital stability. Also, parental attitudes to children change from "children owe a debt to their parents" to "parents owe a debt to their children."

From the standpoint of society, marital relations take precedence over parental relations as reasons for family breakup. Divorce for adultery is widely approved by legal systems, divorce for maltreatment of children by parents is not so widespread, and no legal system known permits divorce because of malfunctioning sibling relations. Much of social welfare used to consist of removing children from the deleterious effects of inadequate parents, but parental rights to their children are now strongly guarded.

Marital satisfaction for both spouses becomes important only when affection and sexual outlets are not sanctioned outside the marital relationship. Self-selection by love, combined with exclusive sexual possession in each other, gives maximum weight to marital satisfaction as a basis for family continuity. "Love" is not simply, as Goode holds, a universal psychological drive; it is a series of normative standards for choosing a mate, learned slowly by teaching and by experience with age mates in the adolescent peer group, in a specific community area. A marital choice based on love is the culmination of a long winnowing process

among eligibles, defined in the first instance by parental or community standards, secondly by age mates, and only thirdly by individual psychological predispositions (Jacobsohn & Matheny, 1962; Karlsson, 1962; Kerckhoff, 1962; Winch, 1958).

Thanks to studies of mate selection, the structural constraints and the processes of allocation to marital roles in our society are now known in some detail. It is the subsequent norms of marital interaction, and the transformation of marital into parental roles, that should occupy the attention of family sociologists in the coming decade.

Reproductive Social Systems

Community controls over reproduction specify allocation to the roles of legitimate child and parent. Two complicating forces are at work in Western societies in these areas: (a) There is a tendency to erode the privileges of legitimacy and to treat all children as equally desirable. This is endemic in children's allowances within certain political systems, since from the point of view of the state all children are desirable recruits to citizenship. Legal complications about property transfer have been avoided, since in societies where occupations and current income are the keys to social status, property transfers affect only a minority of citizens, and individual testaments can provide for them. (b) Technical advances in medicine, such as artificial insemination, pose an unsolved problem about the entry into legitimate status. Traditionally, any child born to a married pair has been regarded as legitimate, unless adultery is clearly proved.

Filiation rules are much less vital to the continuity of a productive system based on achievement than of systems where ascription governs the productive world. Family may confer birth status in our society, but more and more educational achievement confers occupational status. The consequence is that reproductive rules and legitimacy are less important sociologically.

Naturally enough, when one considers the

identity of the children produced in the family, the strains introduced by ambiguity in the rules of reproduction and legitimacy may become very crucial. The fact remains that sociologists still have much research to do before an understanding is reached of the regularities in family living which stem from the norms surrounding legitimacy and reproduction.

Family and Consumption Systems

The major sociological variable at this point is social class. Inheritance plays little part in an achievement society such as characterizes the modern urban-industrial world. One significant index of social-class position is the house and its contents. Since consumption is an interest of industry and advertising, many studies give detailed descriptions of the housing and purchasing of durables of families by social class and stages of the domestic developmental cycle. The best explanation of why families move is to get a bigger house to meet the needs of an expanding domestic group. The effects on the family of upward and downward social-class mobility require much more adequate documentation than exists today.

Patterns of domestic household purchases certainly vary by social class. The territorial aspect of this is community. Community, however, provides the family with more than a physical location. Through interaction as neighbors, as community members, and through participation in voluntary organizations in a local setting, sociological interdependence between certain aspects of family roles and the society as a whole are established. Changes in the structures of society, toward bureaucratic groups applying universal norms to individuals collected into publics, have to some degree led to neglect of the community attachments of families. Yet every bureaucracy learns that "local attachments" have to be taken into account when its rules are applied. So the community persists as an important part of the structure of every society. [For an expanded treatment of consumption systems as related to the family, see Ch. 3, pp. 105–108.]

Community effects on family behavior should be as important in studies of consumption as in the field of eligibles for mate selection, in marital role behavior, and in child-rearing practices.

REFERENCES

Abrams, C., & Dean, J. P. Housing and the family. In Ruth N. Anshen (Ed.), *The family: its function and destiny.* New York: Harper, 1949. Pp. 463–487.

Ajzenstadt, S. N. *Absorption of immigrants into Israel.* Jerusalem: Hebrew Univer., 1951.

Anderson, W. A. The family and individual social participation. *Amer. sociol. Rev.,* 1944, 8, 420–424.

Anderson, W. A. Types of participating families. *Rural Sociol.,* 1946, 11, 335–361.

Arensberg, C. M. American communities. *Amer. Anthropologist,* 1955, 57, 1143–1162.

Arensberg, C. M. The American family in the perspective of other cultures. In E. Ginsberg (Ed.), *The nation's children.* Vol. 1. New York: Columbia Univer. Press, 1960. Pp. 50–75.

Arensberg, C. M. The community as object and as sample. *Amer. Anthropologist,* 1961, 63, 241–264.

Arensberg, C. M., & Kimball, S. T. *Family and community in Ireland.* Cambridge: Harvard Univer. Press, 1940.

Axelrod, M. Urban structure and social participation. *Amer. sociol. Rev.,* 1956, 21, 13–18.

Bell, W., & Boat, M. D. Urban neighborhoods and social participation. *Amer. J. Sociol.,* 1957, 62, 391–398.

Blake, Judith. *Family structure in Jamaica: the social context of reproduction.* New York: Free Press, 1961.

Blehr, O. Action groups in a society with bilateral kindreds. *Ethnol.,* 1963, 2, 269–275.

Blood, R. O., & Wolfe, D. M. *Husbands and wives: the dynamics of married living.* Glencoe, Ill.: Free Press, 1960.

Bott, Elizabeth. *Family and social network: roles, norms, and external relationships in ordinary urban families.* London: Tavistock, 1957.

Brockman, O. *Livsform og Boligsform*. Oslo: Grundt, 1952.

Brown, J. S. The conjugal family and the extended family group. *Amer. sociol. Rev.*, 1953, 17, 297–306.

Brunsman, H. G. Current sources of sociological data in housing. *Amer. sociol. Rev.*, 1948, 12, 150–155.

Burchinal, L. Research on young marriage. *Fam. life Coordinator*, 1960, 10, 6–24.

Campleman, G. Some sociological aspects of mixed class neighborhood planning. *Sociol. Rev.*, 1951, 43, section 10.

Cavan, Ruth S. *American marriage*. New York: Crowell, 1959.

Chapin, F. S. Degrees of kinship intimacy. *Sociol. & soc. Res.*, 1934, 19, 117–125.

Chapin, F. S. Social effects of good housing. *Amer. sociol. Rev.*, 1940, 5, 868–879.

Chapin, F. S. Some housing factors related to mental hygiene. *Amer. J. publ. Hlth*, 1951, 41, 839–845.

Charles, Enid, & Anthony, Sylvia. The community and the family in Prince Edward Island. *Rural Sociol.*, 1943, 8, 37–51.

Chombart de Lauwe, P., & Couvreur, L. Ménages et catégories sociales dans les habitations nouvelles. *Informations sociales*, 1958, 5, 1–138.

Chombart de Lauwe, P., & Chombart de Lauwe, M. J., Couvreur, L., Dubois-Taine, D., Fichet-Poitrey, F., Labat, P., Madaule, P., Marcu, L., Miret O. *Famille et habitation*. Paris: Centre National de la Recherche Scientifique, 1959–1960. 2 vols.

Clark, L. (Ed.) *Consumer behavior*. New York: New York Univer. Press, 1955.

Clark, L., & Carney, J. B. (Eds.) *Consumer behavior*. New York: Harper, 1958.

Clarkson, G. P. E. *The theory of consumer demand*. Englewood Cliffs, N.J.: Prentice-Hall, 1963.

Cohen, Y. A. Structure and function: family organization. *Amer. Anthropologist*, 1956, 58, 664–686.

Conseil International de Batiment (International Council on Building Research). *Report on needs and desires in housing*. St. 11/6/1. Paris: Author, 1954.

Cramer, J. S. *The ownership of major consumer durables*. Cambridge: Cambridge Univer. Press, 1962.

Curle, C. T. W. A. Kinship structure in an English village. *Man*, 1952, 52, 100.

Dahlström, E. *Trivsel in Söderort* (Satisfaction in a southern suburb). Stockholm: Esselte Aktiebolag, 1951.

Danhof, R. The accommodation and integration of conflicting cultures in a newly established community. *Amer. J. Sociol.*, 1943, 48, 14–43.

David, M. H. *Family composition and consumption*. Amsterdam: North Holland, 1962.

Davies, V. Neighborhoods, townships and communities in Wright County, Minnesota. *Rural Sociol.*, 1943, 8, 51–61.

Davis, K. *Human society*. New York: Macmillan, 1949.

Dean, J. P. The myths of housing reform. *Amer. sociol. Rev.*, 1949, 14, 281–288.

Demangeon, A. Settlement patterns in Europe. *Annales de géographie*, 1927, 36, 1–17.

Dennis, N. Changes in function and leadership renewal. *Sociol. Rev.*, 1961, 9, 55–84.

Devereux, E. Neighborhood and community participation. *J. soc. Issues*, 1960, 16, 64–84.

Drewery, J. L. The selection of tenants: unsatisfactory tenants. *Housing*, 1957, 18, 119–120.

Duesenberry, J. *Income, saving and the theory of consumer behavior*. Cambridge: Harvard Univer. Press, 1949.

Durant, Ruth. *Watling, a social survey of a housing estate*. London: King, 1939.

Dyer, W. G. The interlocking of work and family social systems among lower occupational families. *Soc. Forces*, 1956, 34, 230–233

Ehrenfels, U. R. Some observations on American kinship. *Amer. Anthropologist*, 1956, 58, 918.

Eisenstadt, S. N. *The absorption of immigrants: a comparative study based mainly on the Jewish community in Palestine and the state of Israel*. London: Routledge & Paul, 1954.

Fei, H. T. *Peasant life in China*. New York: Dutton, 1939.

Festinger, L. Architecture and group membership. *J. soc. Issues*, 1951, 7, 152–163.

Festinger, L., Schacter, S., & Back, K. *Social pressures in informal groups*. New York: Harper, 1950.

Firth, R. *Two studies of kinship in London*. London: Athlone Press, 1957.

Flügel, J. C. *The psychoanalytic study of the family*. London: International Psychoanalytical Library, 1921.

Fortes, M. Kinship and marriage among the Ashanti. In A. R. Radcliffe-Brown & C. D. Forde (Eds.), *African systems of kinship and marriage*. London: Oxford Univer. Press, 1949. Pp. 254–284.

Foskett, J. M. Social structure and social participation. *Amer. sociol. Rev.*, 1955, 20, 431–438.

Frankenberg, R. *Village on the border*. London: Cohen & West, 1957.

Frazier, E. F. Impact of urban civilization upon negro family life. *Amer. sociol. Rev.*, 1937, 2, 609–618.

Freed, S. A. Suggested type societies in acculturation studies. *Amer. Anthropologist*, 1957, 59, 55–68.

Fried, M., & Gleicher, Peggy. Some sources of residential satisfaction in an urban slum. *J. Amer. Inst. Planners*, 1961, 27, 305–315.

Fried, M., & Lindemann, E. Sociocultural factors in mental health and illness. *Amer. J. Orthopsychiat.*, 1961, 31, 87–101.

Gadourek, I. *A Dutch community*. Leiden: Institute for Preventive Medicine, 1956.

Gans, H. J. The human implications of current redevelopment and relocation planning. *J. Amer. Inst. Planners*, 1959, 25, 15–25.

Gans, H. J. Planning and social life: friendship and neighbor relations in suburban communities. *J. Amer. Inst. Planners*, 1961, 27, 134–140. (a)

Gans, H. J. The balanced community: homogeneity or heterogeneity in residential areas? *J. Amer. Inst. Planners*, 1961, 27, 176–184. (b)

Gans, H. J. *Urban villagers*. New York: Free Press, 1962.

Garigue, P. French-Canadian kinship and urban life. *Amer. Anthropologist*, 1956, 58, 1090–1101.

Golden, J. Social control of negro-white intermarriage. *Soc. Forces*, 1958, 36, 267–269.

Goode, W. J. A theory of role strain. *Amer. sociol. Rev.*, 1960, 25, 483–496.

Goodenough, W. H. Residence rules. *Sw. J. Anthropol.*, 1956, 12, 25–26.

Goody, J. A comparative approach to incest and adultery. *Brit. J. Sociol.*, 1956, 7, 286–305.

Goody, J. The developmental cycle in domestic groups. *Cambridge Papers in Social Anthropology*. No. 1. Cambridge: Cambridge Univer. Press, 1958.

Gough, E. Kathleen. Changing kinship usages in the setting of political and economic change among the Nayars of Malabar. *J. royal anthropol. Inst.*, 1959, 89, 23–24.

Gouldner, A. W. Cosmopolitans and locals: towards an analysis of latent social roles. *Admin. sci. Quart.*, 1957, 2, 281–306.

Greer, S., & Orleans, P. The mass society and parapolitical structure. *Amer. sociol. Rev.*, 1962, 27, 634–646.

Grønseth, E. The impact of father absence in sailor families upon the personality structure and social adjustment of adult sailor sons. *Recherches sur la famille*, 1957, 2, 97–119.

Hager, D. J. Housing, social conflict and the law. *Soc. Probl.*, 1960, 8, 80–87.

Hay, D. G. The social participation of households in selected rural communities of the North-East (U.S.A.). *Rural Sociol.*, 1950, 15, 141–148.

Hayner, N. S. The family spatial pattern. *Sociol. & soc. Res.*, 1933, 18, 37–42.

Henry, A. F. Residential turnover and family composition of home owners in four subdivisions of Natick, Mass. *Soc. Forces*, 1953, 31, 355–360.

Hillery, G. A. Definitions of community: areas of agreement. *Rural Sociol.*, 1955, 20, 111–123.

Hodges, M., & Smith, C. The Sheffield Estate. In *Neighbourhood and community: an enquiry into social relationships on housing estates in Liverpool and Sheffield*. Liverpool: Liverpool Univer. Press, 1954. Pp. 79–133.

Hole, Vere. Social effects of planned rehousing. *Town planning Rev.*, 1959, 30, 161–173.

Hollingshead, A. B. Class and kinship in a middle-western community. *Amer. sociol. Rev.*, 1950, 14, 469–475. (a)

Hollingshead, A. B. Cultural factors in the selection of marriage mates. *Amer. sociol. Rev.*, 1950, 15, 619–627. (b)

Homans, G. C. The rural sociology of medieval England. *Past & Present*, 1953, 4, 32–43.

Jaco, E. G., & Bellknap, I. Is a new family form emerging in the urban fringe? *Amer. sociol. Rev.*, 1953, 18, 551–557.

Jacobsohn, P., & Matheny, A. P. Mate selection in open marriage systems. *Int. J. comp. Sociol.*, 1962, 3, 98–163.

Johnson, E. H. Family privacy in a multi-unit building. *Marr. & fam. Living*, 1952, 14, 219–225.

Karlsson, G. On mate selection. *Int. J. comp. Sociol.*, 1962, 3, 91–97.

Katz, A. M., & Hill, R. Residential propinquity and marital selection: a review of theory, method and fact. *Marr. & fam. Living,* 1958, 20, 27–35.

Katz, E., & Lazarsfeld, P. F. *Personal influence.* Glencoe, Ill.: Free Press, 1955.

Kaufman, H. Towards an interactional conception of community. *Soc. Forces,* 1959, 38, 8–17.

Kaufman, I., Peck, A. L., & Taguiri, C. K. The family constellation and overt incestuous relations between father and daughter. *Amer. J. Orthopsychiat.,* 1954, 24, 266–277.

Kerckhoff, A. D., & Davis, K. E. Value consensus and need complementarity in mate selection. *Amer. sociol. Rev.,* 1962, 27, 295–303.

Kerr, Madeline. *The people of Ship Street.* London: Routledge & Paul, 1958.

Kohn, M. L. Social class and parent-child relationships: an interpretation. *Amer. J. Sociol.,* 1963, 68, 471–480.

Komarovsky, Mirra. The voluntary associations of urban dwellers. *Amer. sociol. Rev.,* 1947, 11, 686–698.

Kooy, G. The traditional household in a modernized rural society. *Recherches sur la famille,* 1958, 3, 183–204.

Kooy, G. Household size and composition in the Netherlands. *Current Sociol.,* 1963–1964, 12, 13–24.

Kosa, J., Rachiele, L. D., & Schommer, C. O. Sharing the home with relatives. *Marr. & fam. Living,* 1960, 22, 129–131.

Kuper, L. (Ed.) *Living in towns.* London: Cressett Press, 1953.

Layard, J. The family and kinship. In E. E. Evans-Pritchard (Ed.), *The institutions of primitive society.* Oxford: Blackwell, 1954. Pp. 50–65.

Leach, E. R. The structural implications of matrilateral cross-cousin marriage. *J. royal anthropol. Inst.,* 1951, 81, 23–55.

Leach, E. R. *The political system of highland Burma.* Cambridge: Cambridge Univer. Press, 1954.

Lee, T. A study of urban neighbourhood. Unpublished doctoral dissertation, Cambridge Univer., 1954.

Le Play, F. *Les ouvriers européens.* Paris: Imprimerie Royale, 1855.

Le Play, F. *L'organisation de la famille selon le vrai modèle signalé par l'histoire de toutes

les races et de tous les temps. Paris: Tequi, 1871.

Lévi-Strauss, C. *Les structures élémentaires de la parenté.* Paris: Presses Universitaires de France, 1949.

Lévi-Strauss, C. *Anthropologie structurale.* Paris: Plon, 1958.

Lewis, O. Peasant culture in India and Mexico. *Amer. Anthropologist,* 1955, 57, 162–163.

Litwak, E. Geographic mobility and extended family cohesion. *Amer. sociol. Rev.,* 1960, 25, 385–394. (a)

Litwak, E. Occupational mobility and extended family cohesion. *Amer. sociol. Rev.,* 1960, 25, 9–21. (b)

Locke, H. J., Sabagh, G., & Thomes, Mary M. Interfaith marriages. *Soc. Probl.,* 1957, 4, 333–340.

Lundberg, G. A., & Lawsing, M. The sociography of some community relations. *Amer. sociol. Rev.,* 1938, 2, 318–335.

Lundqvist, Agnes. *An passing i helmoch samhalle* (Adjustment of individuals to their home and community.) Stockholm: Norstedt, 1955.

McGuire, C. Family backgrounds and community patterns. *Marr. & fam. Living,* 1951, 13, 160–164.

McGuire, C. Family life in lower and middle class homes. *Marr. & fam. Living,* 1952, 14, 1–6.

MacIver, R. M. *Community, a sociological study.* New York: Macmillan, 1928.

Matthews, E. Family and community: a study of the social structure of an endogamous community with bilateral kindreds. Unpublished doctoral dissertation, Vanderbilt Univer., 1964.

Mayo, S. C. Social participation among the older population in the rural areas of Wake County, North Carolina. *Soc. Forces,* 1951, 30, 53–59.

Merton, R. K. *Social theory and social structure.* Glencoe, Ill.: Free Press, 1957.

Michel, Andrée. *Famille, industrialisation, logement.* Paris: Centre Nationale de la Recherche Scientifique, 1959.

Middleton, R. Brother-sister and father-daughter incest in ancient Egypt. *Amer. sociol. Rev.,* 1962, 27, 603–611.

Mitchell, G. D., & Lupton, T. The Liverpool Estate. In *Neighbourhood and community:*

an enquiry into social relationships on housing estates in Liverpool and Sheffield. Liverpool: Liverpool Univer. Press, 1954. Pp. 15–77.

Mogey, J. M. *Rural life in northern Ireland.* London: Oxford Univer. Press, 1947.

Mogey, J. M. The contribution of Frédéric le Play to family research. *Marr. & fam. Living,* 1955, 17, 310–315.

Mogey, J. M. *Family and neighbourhood.* Oxford: Oxford Univer. Press, 1956.

Mogey, J. M. Social aspects of English family housing: from poverty to privacy. *Recherches sur la famille,* 1958, 3, 225–248.

Mogey, J. M., & Morris, R. Causes of change in family roles. *Bull. fam. Develpm.,* 1960, 1, 1–10.

Moss, L. Sample surveys and the administrative process. In F. Edwards (Ed.), *Readings in market research.* London: British Market Research Institute, 1956. Pp. 175–187.

Mukerjee, R. K., & Girling, F. K. Breton family and economic structure. *Rural Sociol.,* 1950, 15, 49–62.

Murdock, G. P. *Social structure.* New York: Macmillan, 1949.

Murdock, G. P. Statistical relations among community characteristics. In P. F. Lazarsfeld & M. Rosenberg (Eds.), *The language of social research.* Glencoe, Ill.: Free Press, 1955. Pp. 305–311.

Murdock, G. P. World ethnographic sample. *Amer. Anthropologist,* 1959, 59, 669–687.

Murdock, G. P. (Ed.) *Social structure of Southeast Asia.* Chicago: Quadrangle Books, 1960.

Myllymäki, P. Asukkaiden viihtyryys Käpylässa. *Väestöliiton Vuosikirja,* 1954, 4, 77–95. (Helsinki.)

Nadel, S. F. *The theory of social structure.* London: Cohen & West, 1958.

Nakano, T. The extended family and kinship in the city. In E. Hayashi (Ed.), *Problems of modern sociology.* Tokyo: Yuhikaku, 1949.

Newcomb, T. M. The study of consensus. In R. K. Merton, L. Broom, & L. S. Cottrell, Jr. (Eds.), *Sociology today.* New York: Basic Books, 1959. Pp. 277–292.

Norris, Ruby. *The theory of consumer's demand.* New Haven: Yale Univer. Press, 1952.

Ogburn, W. F. The changing family. *Publ. Amer. sociol. Soc.,* 1928, 23, 124–133.

Parsons, T. *The social system.* Glencoe, Ill.: Free Press, 1951.

Parsons, T. The incest taboo in relation to social structure and the socialization of the child. *Brit. J. Sociol.,* 1954, 5, 101–117.

Parsons, T. The principal structures of community: a sociological view. In C. J. Friedrich (Ed.), *Community.* New York: Liberal Arts Press, 1959.

Parsons, T., & Smelser, N. J. *Economy and society.* Glencoe, Ill.: Free Press, 1956.

Patai, R. *Sex and family in the Bible and Middle East.* New York: Doubleday, 1959.

Pehrson, R. N. Bilateral kin groupings as a structural type. *J. East Asiatic Stud.,* 1954, 3, 199–202.

Perry, M. Relationship of space in housing to attitudes towards family life. *Dissertation Abstr.,* 1959, 19, 2334.

Plant, J. S. *Personality and the cultural pattern.* Cambridge: Harvard Univer. Press, 1937.

Rees, A. D. *Life in a Welsh countryside.* Cardiff: Univer. of Wales, 1950.

Reissman, L. Class, leisure and social participation. *Amer. sociol. Rev.,* 1955, 19, 76–84.

Riemer, S. Maladjustment to the family home. *Amer. sociol. Rev.,* 1945, 10, 642–648.

Riemer, S. Villagers in metropolis. *Brit. J. Sociol.,* 1951, 2, 31–43.

Robinson, C. M. The sociology of a street layout. *Annals Amer. Acad. pol. & soc. Sci.,* 1914, 51, 192–200.

Rosenfeld, H. Processes of structural change within the Arab village extended family. *Amer. Anthropologist,* 1958, 60, 1127–1139.

Rosow, I. The social effects of the physical environment. *J. Amer. Inst. Planners,* 1961, 27, 127–133.

Rossi, P. H. *Why families move: a study in the social psychology of urban residential mobility.* Glencoe, Ill.: Free Press, 1955.

Rowntree, Griselda. Early childhood in broken families. *Pop. Stud.,* 1955, 8, 247–263.

Sanders, I. T., & Ensminger, D. Alabama rural communities. *Alabama Coll. Bull.,* 1940, 33 (1).

Schmidt, S. F., & Rohrer, W. C. The relationship of family type to social participation. *Marr. & fam. Living,* 1956, 18, 224–230.

Schorr, A. L. Mobile family living. *Soc. Casewk,* 1956, 37, 178–180.

Schorr, A. L. *Slums and social insecurity.* Res.

Rept No. 1. Washington, D.C.: Social Security Administration, 1963.

Seeley, J. R. The slum: its nature, use and users. *J. Amer. Inst. Planners,* 1959, 25, 7–14.

Siipi, J. *Pulkaty ovaen Viihtyryys.* Helsinki: Author, 1954.

Simmel, G. The number of members as determining sociological form of a group. *Amer. J. Sociol.,* 1902, 8, 1–46, 158–196.

Smelser, N. J. *Social change in the industrial revolution: an application of theory to the Lancashire cotton industry, 1770–1840.* London: Routledge & Paul, 1959.

Smith, R. T. *The negro family in British Guiana.* London: Routledge & Paul, 1957.

Spiro, M. *Kibbutz: venture in utopia.* Cambridge: Harvard Univer. Press, 1956.

Srinivas, M. N. Social system of a Mysore village. In M. McKim (Ed.), *Village India: comparative studies of cultures and civilizations.* No. 6. *Amer. Anthropologist,* 1955, 57, Memoir No. 83.

Stacey, Margaret. *Tradition and change: a study of Banbury.* Oxford: Oxford Univer. Press, 1960.

Stouffer, S. Intervening opportunities: a theory relating mobility and distance. *Amer. sociol Rev.,* 1940, 5, 845–867.

Stys, W. The influence of economic conditions on fertility of peasant women. *Pop. Stud.,* 1957, 11, 136–148.

Sussman, M. B. Family continuity: selective factors which affect relationships between families at generational levels. *Marr. & fam. Living,* 1954, 16, 112–120.

Sussman, M. B., & Burchinal, L. Kin family network: unheralded structure in current conceptualizations of family functioning. *Marr. & fam. Living,* 1962, 24, 231–240.

Sutton, W. A., & Kolaja, J. Elements of community action. *Soc. Forces,* 1960, 38, 325–331.

Talmon-Garber, Yonina. The family in collective settlements. *Trans. III World Congr. Sociol.,* 1956, 4, 116–126.

Tiller, P. O. Father absence and personality development of children in sailor families. *Recherches sur la famille,* 1957, 2, 115–137.

United Nations. *Universal declaration of human rights.* Doc. A/777. General Assembly: Official Records, 3rd Session, Pt 1, Vol. 2, 535–542. Paris: Palais de Chaillot, 1948.

United Nations. *Yearbook on human rights for 1952.* New York: Author, 1954.

United Nations. Doc. E/CN6/295. New York: Author, 1957.

Useem, R. H., Useem, J., & Gibson, D. L. The function of neighboring for the middle-class male. *Hum. Organ.,* 1960, 19, 68–76.

Warner, W. L. The measurement of social class. In M. Fortes (Ed.), *Social structure: studies presented to A. R. Radcliffe-Brown.* Oxford: Clarendon Press, 1949. Pp. 1–17.

Warner, W. L., & Lunt, P. S. *The social life of a modern community.* New Haven: Yale Univer. Press, 1941.

Warner, W. L., & Srole, L. *The social systems of American ethnic groups.* New Haven: Yale Univer. Press, 1945.

Watson, J. B., & Samorra, J. Subordinate leadership in a bicultural community: an analysis. *Amer. sociol. Rev.,* 1954, 19, 413–421.

Weinberg, S. K. *Incest behavior.* New York: Citadel Press, 1955.

Westermarck, E. *The history of human marriage.* New York: Macmillan, 1922. 5 vols.

Whiting, J., et al. The function of male initiation ceremonies at puberty. In Eleanor Maccoby, T. M. Newcomb, & E. L. Hartley (Eds.), *Readings in social psychology.* New York: Holt, 1958. Pp. 359–370.

Williams, W. M. *The sociology of an English village: Gosforth.* London: Routledge & Paul, 1956.

Wilner, D. *Human relations in interracial housing.* Minneapolis: Univer. of Minnesota Press, 1955.

Wilner, D., et al. *Housing and family life.* Baltimore: Johns Hopkins Press, 1962.

Winch, R. F. *Mate selection.* New York: Harper, 1958.

Wirth, L. Housing as a field for sociological research. *Amer. sociol. Rev.,* 1947, 12, 137–143.

Wolf, E. Closed corporate peasant communities. *Sw. J. Anthropol.,* 1957, 13, 1–13.

Young, F. W. The function of male initiation ceremonies: a cross-cultural test of an alternative hypothesis. *Amer. J. Sociol.,* 1962, 67, 379–396.

Young, M., & Willmott, P. *Family and kinship in East London.* London: Routledge & Paul, 1957.

Zimmerman, C. C. *Consumption and standards of living.* New York: Van Nostrand, 1936.

CHAPTER 14 Subcultural Variations and Mobility

RUTH SHONLE CAVAN
Rockford College

The family is deeply embedded in the total social and cultural organization of society, in a reciprocal relationship. The family transmits the culture to its children, teaching them the values, attitudes, techniques, and roles that are part of the culture and that enable them to function in the social organization. The family is also controlled by the social organization. It functions well only when it adapts to the social organization. It is also subject to stresses when social changes occur, or when the social organization permits mobility that may carry certain units of the family away from the total family matrix. In the United States and other complex cultures, the total social organization is divided into subcultures to which the family must adjust, as well as adjusting to certain aspects of the total culture.

CULTURE AND SUBCULTURE

The total culture of a society is of two general types: component elements accepted by virtually the total population, and elements accepted only by some portion of the population.

Commonly Accepted Family Culture

Certain values, attitudes, and behavior patterns are commonly accepted and practiced by families in the United States. These common elements include professed belief in and actual practice of monogamy, legal marriage, legal dissolution of marriage prior to remarriage, limitation of sex relations to the spouse, legitimacy of children through birth in wedlock, joint residence of husband, wife, and dependent children, financial and personal responsibility of parents for the rearing of their children, and preparation of children for their adult roles. Individual denials of such values and deviation from the related norms do not destroy the basic social pattern that is given support by law and the mores. Punishment such as legal penalties, public condemnation, or social ostracism tends to hold the most flagrant major deviations to a minimum. Organized group deviations from the basic pattern are of more significance. However, only in the case of extreme defiance of sacredly held values and norms is formal punishment applied.

535

Not all deviations are of a kind that threatens the basic culture. Another order of deviation is subordinate to the basic culture and gives a quasi-organization to aggregates of people who accept the basic culture but are distinctive in ways in which they implement it, or in less fundamental phases of culture. These aggregates are subcultural groups.

Subcultures

A subculture assumes that there is a basic general culture, whose characteristics permeate all groups in the society. Upon this basic culture different groups erect distinctive subordinate cultures that characterize only the one type of group; the basic culture plus the distinctive features constitute the subculture. In some societies one particularly influential subculture may come to be regarded as the basic culture, from which all other groups deviate in subcultural fashion. For example, in the United States, the white, middle-class, Protestant ethic or culture is often assumed to set the dominant pattern of culture. If this point of view is accepted, all cultural patterns that deviated markedly from the white, middle-class, Protestant pattern would be subcultures. However, if one considers that certain cultural traits characterize all the varying subcultures, then the peculiar characteristics of the white, middle-class, Protestant culture would place it in the ranks of the subcultures. In this discussion, the point of view is that there is a basic set of cultural values generally accepted by all groups, but that the entire society is subdivided loosely into many subcultural groups, one of which is the middle class.

The term *subculture* has been loosely used by many writers to refer to peripheral or transient aspects of the way of life of some segmental group. Thus one reads of adolescent subculture, delinquent subculture, old-age subculture, and male and female subcultures. As used in this chapter, however, subculture does not refer to age or sex variations in interests or activities, but to cohesive patterns of culture that encompass many aspects of life. The concept is of a group, not a category. The unit of a subculture is not the individual, but the family, which transmits the subculture to its children. Children are born into the subculture of their parents and escape from it only under favorable conditions and usually with conscious effort.

Usually, families of one subculture live in proximity to each other, making possible interaction and membership in the primary groups of family, peer group, and neighborhood. On a national basis, subcultures are maintained through mass communication and the drawing together of individuals through occupational organizations. This drawing together and sharing of values and behavior patterns results in a sense of identification among members of a given subculture that prevents its fading away into other subcultures.

Another element that sustains subcultures is the mutual sense of difference and perhaps hostility between the groups that prevents or hinders acculturation or social integration. Subcultures may change, but as a rule the change comes slowly.

SUBCULTURES IN THE UNITED STATES

Subcultures in the United States differ greatly in the degree to which their members interact among themselves and isolate themselves from other subcultures. Certain subcultural groups achieve almost complete and relatively permanent isolation, for example, the Amish, Doukhobors, and Hutterites, and, in the past, the Shakers and the Oneida Community. However, ease of transportation and the need of these small communities to sell and buy outside their community have tended to reduce isolation. Some such communities have tended to modify their distinctive subcultures to bring them into harmony with other, less distinctive subcultures. In contrast, others expel the members who seek outside contacts or cultural changes. These small, exclusive subcultures are not to be included in the discussion which follows.

Sometimes urban, suburban, and rural ways of life are spoken of as subcultures. In remote, isolated pockets, rural communities may be properly referred to as subcultural. However, the degree of mobility back and forth among nonisolated communities and the easy interchange of culture by mass media signify simply minor and shifting variations that do not justify placing urban, suburban, and rural ways of life into subcultural categories. But within each of the three types of communities can be found cohesive cultural clusters that do justify the term *subculture*.

Three subcultural groups stand between the isolated communities and the merging urban, suburban, and rural communities. These are social classes, ethnic-religious groups, and racial groups. The way of life of each such group is sufficiently distinctive to set it apart from others; at the same time the common cultural elements hold all of them together. Interaction is most intense on a personal level within the subcultural group, but is sufficient between the groups that all function as part of the total social organization. It is these three groups that are to be discussed here. Of the three, social class gives the basic framework.

Social Classes

According to one point of view, social classes do not exist as cultural entities; the term *social class* is artificially applied to what is only a segment of a continuous stratified scale (Cox, 1948; Cuber & Kenkel, 1954; Haer, 1957; Lenski, 1952). The scale of stratification is based on such individual attributes as income, education, or the prestige ranking of occupations, each of which falls into a continuous scale, or a combination of these attributes. These attributes can be measured objectively, and they tend to be correlated. It is difficult to

find marked breaks in the continuum that might justify the concept of discrete social classes (Landecker, 1960).

Opposed to those who support the theory of stratification based on objective individual attributes is another array of sociologists who offer evidence to support the theory of discrete social classes, whose most distinguishing characteristics are not individual attributes but group attitudes, norms, and behavior patterns. Individual attributes are not overlooked; in fact, some scale based on attributes often is used as a tool to classify individuals or communities into classes. From a cultural point of view, however, the significant feature of the scales now in use is not the hierarchical continuity of individual characteristics such as education or occupational prestige, but the fact that, community by community, individuals with the same or similar characteristics tend to hold the same values and to follow essentially the same patterns of conduct. Warner and his associates (Warner, 1949; Warner & Lunt, 1941; Warner, Meeker, & Eels, 1949) have identified many characteristics of the social-class system. Davis, Gardner, and Gardner (1941) have analyzed social-class subcultures in a southern city; Hollingshead (1949) made an exhaustive study of a small city, and with Redlich (Hollingshead & Redlich, 1958) of New Haven. The cultural clustering rather than the stratification conception of social class is used in this chapter.

In this context, social class has been defined as a large number of families that are, and consider themselves to be, approximately alike and equal to each other and that are differentiated from other groups of families (Kahl, 1957, pp. 12–14). Class members regard themselves more or less as equals and interaction tends to flow freely on an intimate, personal basis. Davis and Dollard (1940) stated that the crucial tests of class position, true for all class systems, are the normal practice of eating and drinking together as a social ritual, talking intimately in a social clique, visiting freely in each other's homes, and having cross-sexual access to one another outside the kinship group. It is important to note that the basic unit is the family rather than the individual and that the concept of class is of a group, not of individuals who just happen to have similar characteristics.

Social class meets the qualifications for a subculture. Most important are the fundamental values and common behavior patterns that hold the members together. Members also interact with each other more than with members of other social classes. For example, informal clubs, small associations, as well as many large, well-organized institutions, are class-linked (Ellis, 1957; Lantz, 1958, pp. 222ff; Warner & Lunt, 1941, pp. 87–91, 110–126, 301–354). Class members tend to live in the same or similar neighborhoods, where they see, hear, and talk with each other. Many studies, old and new, have pointed up the residential segregation of social classes in towns ranging from a few thousand people to the giant cities of Philadelphia and Chicago (Baltzell, 1958; Ellis, 1957; Lantz, 1958; Schmid, 1950; Shaw & McKay, 1942; Warner, 1949; Warner & Lunt, 1941).

The routine of life differs from one social class to another. In the workingman's area lights go on in the windows at an early hour, as the man of the house prepares to be at his machine at 7 A.M.; in the upper-class area, lights do not appear until several hours later, but burn later at night. The workingman carries his lunch or eats at a factory cafeteria; the professional or business man lunches at his private club. Dress, speech, manners, recreation, interests, and many other cultural traits differ.

The similarity of life pattern and the high degree of interaction within the class produce a sense of class consciousness. Centers (1949, p. 33) has defined class consciousness as having "the meaning both of a feeling of membership in a class and the possession of certain attitudes, interests, ideas, etc., typical of some class." People recognize not only their class likenesses but class differ-

ences. Several studies (Centers, 1949; West, 1945) have shown that people tend to describe their own class in favorable terms; conversely, they tend to describe other classes, both higher and lower than their own, in less favorable or distinctly unfavorable terms—a characteristic of in-group ethnocentric identification and out-group animosity.

Social classes fall into a hierarchy that is functional for the economic organization of the society as a whole. Virtually all writers on social class agree that its basis is a complex of occupation, income, and education (Centers, 1949; Gordon, 1958; Parsons, 1953; Sorokin, 1953; Warner, Meeker, & Eels, 1949). The significance of the occupation-income-education complex is indirect. The prestige ranking of occupations is an important factor in the way in which people characterize their own social-class position and that of other people. The amount of income helps to determine where people can afford to live and hence with whom they will normally associate; more important is the way in which money is spent and thus the style of living that may be maintained. Amount of income does not itself open the door to a social class. Higher education, in Europe traditionally a mark of the gentleman, in the United States is a mark of the bright and ambitious person as well as of a member of the higher class levels. Regardless of these limitations, the occupation-income-education complex is the principal foundation stone of class placement. It creates a similarity of activities and interests, of values and goals, that tends to integrate the class members.

Although social classes represent subcultures, they are not discrete in the sense that one class is set off *completely* from another class. For one thing, the common cultural traits join them. Moreover, some families or their members are in transition from one ·social class to another. Some may still be considered as members of their original class; others are marginal between two classes and at least temporarily belong to neither.

Ethnic-Religious Groups

According to the *Dictionary of Sociology* (Fairchild, 1955), an ethnic group is one characterized by unity of both race and nationality and is the logical outcome of relative isolation and segregation. Race is the more inclusive term; within each race are many ethnic groups with distinctive cultures.

In the United States the origin of ethnic groups (exclusive of the Indians) is the free and slave immigration of past decades. During the years when, in free immigration, the foreign-born formed the adult group in the immigrant colony, the culture usually was more foreign than American. Work contacts of adults and especially public-school attendance of children carried the immigrant family toward Anglo-American culture. (The term *Anglo-American* is here used to refer to the dominant strain in our national culture which was established when the United States were still colonies and which has continued to shape the pattern of integration of ethnic cultural elements into a common culture.) For some, the transition from foreign to Anglo-American culture was completed in one generation. Many, however, required another generation for acculturation, and then often with a residue of the original foreign culture. Eventually, Caucasian ethnic groups are integrated into the Anglo-American culture and social groups.

However, one ethnic trait tends to resist change—religion. Religion may become modified, but tends to retain distinctiveness. In areas other than religion, the process of integration tends to be first into a specific social-class level. The working-class immigrant usually becomes the working-class ethnic, who in turn becomes (or his sons become) the working-class Anglo-American. At the last stage, the person may be upwardly mobile.

Foreign-culture and ethnic groups tend to become subcultural groups, with the qualities already described. They overlap on social-class subcultures. In the working-class levels, ethnic groups fragment the subculture into many distinctive complexes; in higher levels, they create variations in the class through different religious affiliations.

Racial Groups

Racial groups enter the United States with distinctive native cultures which they lose slowly. The exception is the Negroes, who were stripped of their native culture when they first entered the United States as slaves (Frazier, 1939). They perforce adopted the American culture as it seeped down to them through their limited contacts with white people. Since they were not fully integrated, many remnants of the peculiar slave culture remained long after the end of slavery. Some cultural traits from slavery still characterize the lower-class Negroes, who are most completely segregated from contacts with Caucasians and have limited access to the typical Anglo-American culture. A marked contrast exists between these lower-class Negroes and the middle- and upper-class Negroes who have access to Anglo-American culture through education and other entrances into cultural life, even though there is little social integration.

Oriental racial groups have arrived with a variety of cultures, depending upon the country from which they came. Each group has tended to retain many elements of its culture. The peculiar attitude of white Americans toward people of darker skin has hindered social assimilation even after acculturation has reached a high point. The Oriental groups, distinctive in race and culture, represent ethnic groups in the strict meaning of the term.

To the degree that racial groups have been excluded from full cultural and social participation in American life, each has tended to develop a social-class system restricted to its own people. The extent to which this system reflects the original culture is related to the degree of exclusion from the Anglo-American culture and from free social interaction. The extent to which it resembles the Anglo-American culture is related to the degree of participation in that culture. In some instances a distinctive type of subculture has resulted.

Distribution of the Population in Subcultures

The distribution of the population into subcultures is important to a clear understanding of the relation of subcultures to family life. Only approximations can be made, and the overlapping of social class with ethnic subcultures is difficult to assess.

From the data of the 1940 Census, McGuire (1950) made an estimate of the distribution of the entire population into social classes, by collating various status indices. His classification follows: upper class (upper-upper and lower-upper classes combined), 3 per cent; upper-middle, 9 per cent; lower-middle, 36 per cent; upper-lower, 35 per cent; and lower-lower, 17 per cent. Individual cities differed in class composition, partly in terms of size, partly in terms of dominant occupations.

It is almost impossible to estimate the percentage of the population that is ethnic, since the term goes beyond foreign-born to include partially assimilated groups. According to the *Statistical Abstract of the United States* (1962), the Caucasian population in 1960 was composed of 79 per cent native-born of native parentage (assumed to be Anglo-American in culture), 15 per cent native-born of foreign or mixed parentage (ethnics in the process of assimilation), and 6 per cent foreign-born. On the basis of these figures, about a fifth of the white population is foreign or ethnic in culture.

The situation is vastly more complicated than these figures suggest. The ethnic population breaks down into numerous cultural groups which are unevenly distributed over

the United States. For example, in Yankee City (Warner & Lunt, 1941, pp. 211–226) 45.55 per cent of the population was ethnic, representing eight different nationality groups. In addition, the English, North Irish, and Scotch, even though foreign-born, had been assimilated into the native population and were considered natives. In Coal Town, an Illinois mining community of 2,300, immigrants had come from 16 different European countries, all within a short span of time (Lantz, 1958).

The ethnic distribution overlaps the social-class distribution. Ethnics may spread out over a number of social classes, but each ethnic group tends to cluster heavily on one or two levels. In Yankee City, the longer the ethnic group had lived in the community, the higher some of its members had climbed. The Irish, the oldest ethnic group, spread from lower-upper to lower-lower class; however, 27.52 per cent were lower-middle class and 53.75 upper-lower. The Poles, who arrived much later, had 89.48 per cent in the lower-lower class. Other ethnic groups fell into intermediate positions.

In Coal Town, social ranking of immigrants and ethnic groups did not depend upon length of time in the community but upon the positions held in the mining operations. The upper class of immigrants was composed of English-speaking miners from England, Scotland, Wales, and Ireland, who held supervisory positions. The ethnic middle class consisted of skilled and semiskilled miners and small merchants from eight European countries. The lower-class ethnics were irregularly employed persons from central and southern Europe and disorganized individuals without family or church connections. Equivalent social class position did not unify the ethnic groups, however; each tended to live in isolation from the others, to speak the native language, to follow national patterns of thought and behavior, and to regard all other groups with suspicion. The native-born, regardless of their status in their own social-class hierarchy, regarded all foreign-culture people with suspicion.

The racial distribution is also complex. In 1960, whites constituted 88.6 per cent of the total population of the United States, Negroes 10.5 per cent, and other nonwhites (that is, Mongoloids) 0.9 per cent (U. S. Census of Population, 1961). The small proportion of nonwhites other than Negroes consisted of the following groups, in descending order of numbers: American Indians, Japanese, Chinese, and Filipino, with smaller groups lumped together as "all other." As with the ethnics, the distribution of each group is unevenly spread over the United States.

The Composite Subcultural System

The subcultural system of the United States is a composite of social classes and of ethnic-religious and racial groups. They are combined into a vertical hierarchy according to general principles of relative status and along a horizontal spacing according to the degree of mutual acceptability. When groups are unacceptable to each other, they tend to form parallel social-class systems.

Religion clings to each group, and the different religions represented in the United States therefore have their own social-class distribution. This distribution is not independently achieved but depends upon the social position of the followers of each faith. For example, in Yankee City, the Episcopal Church was most highly representative of the upper class, whose members were chiefly of English ancestry (Warner & Lunt, 1941, pp. 356–359). Various other Protestant churches represented the middle class, while the Catholic Church was most characteristic of the lower classes, since many of the lower-class ethnic groups were traditionally Catholic. A finer analysis showed that the different Protestant churches each catered to a narrow range of social classes.

Nonwhite groups experience little integration along horizontal lines, no matter how long they have lived in the United States nor how thoroughly acculturated they are. Therefore they develop independent social-class systems. The largest nonwhite group, the Negro, has a social-class distribution that is very different from that of the whites, with a higher proportion in the lower class and smaller proportions in the upper ranks. Drake and Cayton (1945, p. 522) estimated that in Chicago in the early 1940's, 65 per cent of Negroes in contrast to 50 per cent of whites (including ethnics) were lower class, 30 per cent of Negroes and 40 per cent of whites were middle class, and 5 and 10 per cent, respectively, were upper class. In 1941, in Old Town, a southern city, three-fourths of the Negroes but only one-third of the whites were lower class (Davis, Gardner, & Gardner, 1941, pp. 79, 221). Due to the improved status of Negroes since 1940, it seems probable that a higher proportion of Negroes is in middle-class status, but that in most communities they are still heavily concentrated in the lower classes.

In analyzing the relationship of subcultures to the family, it is necessary to consider the composite subculture to which the family belongs. Race, ethnic-religious affiliation, and social-class placement all enter into the subculture in which the family lives.

GENERAL CHARACTERISTICS OF SOCIAL CLASSES

Each social class and, at least in the lower levels, each ethnic and racial group has its own peculiar characteristics, including differences in family structure and roles and in child rearing. General characteristics underlie family differences. They are presented here as of the middle of the twentieth century and are based on studies of New Haven, population about 160,000 (Hollingshead & Redlich, 1958); Yankee City, population 17,000 (Warner & Lunt, 1941); Old City in the South, population 10,000 (Davis, Gardner, & Gardner, 1941); and Elmtown or Jonesville (the same city), population 7,000 (Hollingshead, 1949; Warner, 1949).

Special studies contributed to the understanding of specific subcultures.

Upper-Upper Class
(Amory, 1947; Baltzell, 1958)

The upper-upper class is smallest numerically of the social classes but has the highest prestige and influence. Ancestors have resided in the United States for a number of years and are primarily of English and northwestern European origin. The class tends, therefore, to have a high degree of unity of culture and, alone of the social classes, forms a national and in some respects international elite, who may feel more unity with and seek more companionship among geographically separated elite groups than with members of other social classes in their own communities.

Members of the upper-upper class are college educated and firmly established in professional and major business operations. Not only is income ample for a well-rounded material and cultural way of life, but much of it has been inherited.

Since this class is at the apex of the social-class hierarchy, certain values related to its position distinguish it from other social classes. The members seek to maintain their position and to preserve its ancient symbols of status. Therefore genealogies, records of ancestral achievements, journals and autobiographies of ancestors, and heirlooms are all important symbols.

Although money alone does not fix class position, it is important that inherited or currently acquired money should not be dissipated. Therefore family trust funds and businesses preserve wealth regardless of the desires of certain deviating members who may wish to spend it beyond the accepted level of living of the class.

A worthy position of prestige in the community is of great importance. Acceptable positions vary, but within a narrow range. Certain members may become responsible for the financial management of the family fortune; others may enter a learned profession; still others may devote themselves to general cultural pursuits or to public welfare. Devotion to recreation as a full-time pursuit is also found but is contrary to the generally held upper-class veneration for industriousness, good health, social leadership, and a balanced life.

Because of the national origin of the class, the Protestant church predominates, although in different communities the denomination differs. In certain cities with an old, well-established Catholic population, the upper-upper class contains Catholics.

The upper-upper class is self-protective. It trains children into the class precepts and behavior, shields errant members from public censure, and excludes aspiring social climbers.

Lower-Upper Class

The lower-upper class resembles the upper-upper in many ways, but its members lack the long history of prestige and suffer from the reluctance of the upper-upper class to accept them as equals. For example, in Philadelphia, where many families established their status in the colonial period, families moving into the upper-upper class after the Civil War are still regarded as new families (Baltzell, 1958, pp. 9–10). In Yankee City, upper-upper-class members referred to lower-upper-class people as *nouveau riche* and as social climbers. Nevertheless, the two upper classes tend to fuse, first in secondary business and professional associations, and finally in primary groups and through intermarriage. The lower-upper class may be thought of as replenishing the upper-upper class, which tends to lose members through low birth rates and downward mobility.

Although lower-upper-class persons are no longer ethnic, they represent a somewhat greater diversity of national background than does the upper-upper class and often are less far removed from the ethnic stage of transition. Their remote ancestors rarely have held positions of prestige, although the grandfather of the currently adult lower-upper-class man may have started the upward climb through successful business maneuvers (Lipset & Bendix, 1959, p. 118; Warner & Abegglen, 1955a, pp. 289ff). The father added greater success and consolidated his position, and the adult son strives to maintain his position and to move upward. Absorption in business success tends to prevent achievement in other areas. Artistic activity, recreation, and some family activities are sacrificed for financial success.

Income in the lower-upper class is ample and may be larger than in the upper-upper class. Income lacks the stability of some types of inherited or long-established fortunes. The chief difference in financial status, however, is in what the money buys. The lower-upper-class person, concerned with status and without old family homes or heirlooms, surrounds himself with modern equipment, buys fashionable clothes, and indulges in expensive recreation, sometimes overstepping the bounds of good taste and good manners as defined by the upper-upper class.

The lower-upper class is primarily Protestant, although the denominations represented do not coincide completely with those patronized by the upper-upper class in the same community.

The educational level is not lower than high-school graduation and usually includes college education, although not necessarily in the prestige preparatory schools and colleges from which upper-upper-class members graduate.

Upper-Middle Class

The upper-middle class is made up largely of native-born whites but includes a small contingent of the total ethnic population (in Yankee City, 15 per cent), chiefly those with a long period of residence in the community, and a still smaller proportion of the Negro population, which is not, however, socially integrated. Occupationally, it is characterized by professionals, managers of large businesses, and proprietors of smaller but substantial businesses. Education typically includes college attendance at one of a wide variety of colleges. Since the professions are well represented in the upper-middle class, many men have professional education. Income is adequate for a comfortable way of life, with such cultural attainments as travel during vacations and support of local cultural projects. Magazines and books are bought and read. Children receive private lessons in music or dancing and attend summer camps. Money is spent but not squandered, and some is saved, although there is only a slight tendency to build a large financial estate. The adult members pride themselves on community leadership and form the dedicated working core of many boards and committees devoted to education, welfare, and civic improvement.

Although the upper-middle class does not have marked upward mobility as a major goal, it values its position in the social-class hierarchy and stresses personal and social assets that help to maintain and strengthen that position. Thus occupational success is a major value.

Religious affiliation reflects the background of the family, and the class has a higher proportion of non-Protestants than does the upper-upper class. Moreover, a wider spread of Protestant denominations is represented.

Lower-Middle Class

In the lower-middle class, national backgrounds are varied, although usually the ancestors of the members of this class arrived in the United States a generation or more ago. In old industrial cities, as much as a third of the class may be classified as ethnic. These people tend to be descendants of the so-called old immigration, that is, from northern and western Europe, whose members arrived prior to 1910. All levels of occupations are found, with a predominance of the white-collar, skilled, and semiskilled. Religious affiliation tends to resemble that of the upper-middle class, although the predominance of Protestant or Catholic faith rests to some degree on the makeup of the ethnic population. Education typically ended with high-school graduation.

Income is sufficient for some of the amenities of life, and these amenities plus minor savings often are all that older people anticipate as symbolic of success. Upward mobility is valued by the younger people, although usually it is conceived in narrow terms as perhaps a better position than the father had, but in the same occupation. Downward mobility is feared and is a major dread in periods of economic recession or depression.

Upper-Lower Class

In the upper-lower class, the typical occupation is some form of semiskilled labor. The median education for the young adults of this class in New Haven (Hollingshead & Redlich, 1958) was the eleventh grade. In industrial cities, ethnic groups tend to outnumber fully assimilated persons. In Yankee City (Warner & Lunt, 1941, p. 225) 62 per cent of the upper-lower class were ethnic, and in New Haven only 7 per cent were of old Yankee stock. Many of the New Haven ethnics had ancestors who had been in the United States for two or three generations but were still in process of assimilation. This fact was evidenced by continued attendance at ethnic instead of parish churches by the Catholics who constituted a high percentage of the ethnics.

Lower-Lower Class (Davis, 1948, pp. 1–38; Miller, 1958; Miller, 1959)

The lower-lower class is the bedrock level of the social-class system. It differs both in degree and in kind from the other social classes. It has a stable population but also is the recipient both of new immigrants and internal migrant groups and of certain economic failures and personally disorganized persons who drift down from classes higher up in the scale. Occupationally, unskilled labor is typical. At all times, unemployables are on relief, and during a depression the proportion on relief soars.

The educational median for men is about six years. The ethnic groups are predominantly Catholic, except for the Negroes who are heavily concentrated at this class level.

The lower-lower class leads a precarious existence, not only economically, but in other ways. Its members are regarded with aversion by those of higher class levels. Especially when the lower class includes people of foreign culture or a nonwhite race, they are misunderstood and unfavorably stereotyped.

Life is lived in unpleasant surroundings in the least desirable parts of a community, from which the inhabitants see little possibility of escape. Their efforts are directed toward meeting daily needs and enjoying life as it comes. Although insecurity is a constant threat, their inability to save from meager earnings leads them to spend any extra money for immediate pleasures, such as food or the down payment on a television set.

Disputes are settled immediately by direct combat with fists or some weapon. Husbands and wives often battle at home, children fight on the streets, men fight over disputes at work, girls fight to stave off overzealous youths. This ability to care for themselves is a valued attribute which shows itself in other ways than combat, such as the acquisition of money or goods by trickery or thievery.

The lower-lower class in industrial cities includes large segments of the newest arrivals to urban culture. In this class the first shocks of a different way of life are felt, the first disruption of family relationships occurs, and the first steps toward acculturation are taken. In the early stages the process seems to be one of family and personal disorganization.

Since the 1940's, Negroes have moved in large masses into certain northern industrial cities. Poorly educated and unsophisticated, they are not prepared for the pressures of urban industrial life, nor does the community usually facilitate their adjustment through special educational or social programs. Although they have the rudiments of Anglo-American culture, they are handicapped by the barrier of skin color.

FAMILY STRUCTURE AND ROLES

The family is closely incorporated into the subculture. Ideally, the family carries out certain functions in each subculture, specifically passing on the subculture to each child reared in the family and thus continuing and stabilizing the subculture. Through this transmission the family molds the child to his subculture and prepares him for his future subcultural roles. The family also insulates the child from contacts with members of other subcultures.

However, in a period of rapid change, when new groups introduce new subcultures into a community and when personal and family mobility from one subculture to another is frequent, the family often is the victim rather than the supporter of the subcultural system. The tendency of parents to perpetuate the past often unfits the child for the trend toward mobility. The family may make itself vulnerable to intergenerational disruption. Even when the family desires upward mobility for a child, the disruptive results may not be foreseen.

The function of the family in a stable situation is discussed first, with the family relationship to mobility reserved for later sections.

The structure and composition of the family group is important to internal life. Roles, lines of interaction, and a hierarchy of responsibility and authority are closely related to the structure. Family structure and roles, in turn, are closely related to the total social-class structure as described in the preceding section.

The Upper-Upper-Class Family (Amory, 1947; Baltzell, 1958; Davis, Gardner, & Gardner, 1941)

The upper-upper class, especially in the older parts of the United States where the social-class structure has its fullest development, tends to include in the family circle of influence a kinship group. This kinship group is held together by proximity and stability of residence, a desire to protect itself from intrusions from lower classes, and often by a common fund of inherited wealth invested in a trust fund or a common business from which all draw income. In some large kinship groups, intermarriage between relatives is not uncommon. The American upper-class families of the Lowells, the Lees of Virginia, and the Roosevelts all have had some kinship marriages. In Yankee City, one couple found great satisfaction in learning that the husband's great-grandfather and the wife's great-grandmother were brother and sister.

Within the kinship group, the nuclear family has its own household, but usually related nuclear families live close together. The husband is the head of his nuclear family, but he also owes deference and allegiance to the older members of the family, as do his wife and children. In financial matters, especially, the eldest male or his widow who has inherited his money maintains a strong position of power. A typical hierarchy of authority places the grandfather (or his widow) at the top, sons in the order of age, their wives slightly below them, then sons and daughters. This hierarchy suggests the structure of the traditional extended patriarchal family, for instance, in China in the premodern period. However, it is a mere shadow of the Chinese family, in which roles were rigidly prescribed and the large family lived in one household (Lee, 1953). The upper-upper class family has elements of the extended family, but permits greater freedom among the nuclear units, the use of independent households, and more flexibility of behavior.

In general, wives are regarded as belonging to their husband's kinship group and are expected to accept the cultural elements of this group and to provide sons to carry on the name. The wife's loss of individual identity is furthered by the desire of upper-upper-class men to find wives who are not career minded and who do not necessarily have college degrees, although they require intelligence (Baltzell, 1958, pp. 53ff). If the wife's family is of somewhat higher status than the husband's, the wife and children keep a sense of identification with it (Warner & Lunt, 1941, p. 100).

Children fit into the kinship group as links in the chain of lineage (Davis, Gardner, & Gardener, 1941). Their role is to carry on the family name and to maintain the prestige of the family. Therefore sons have special significance. Children tend to take their social class identification from the kinship group as represented by its head. The ancestral family, especially on the father's side, may be more influential than the nuclear family, especially if the parents are downwardly mobile.

Lower-Upper-Class Family

Members of the lower-upper class are sometimes recent arrivals in the community as well as to their social class. As is often true of upwardly mobile people, they tend to detach themselves from their families of procreation which represent a lower level that they are intent upon leaving behind. The family therefore tends to be nuclear and to act independently of kin. As head of the family, the husband establishes and consolidates his economic position; the wife establishes and consolidates the social posi-

tion of the family, especially seeking membership in informal cliques of the upper-upper class. The position of the family is less secure than that of a family in the upper-upper class, and misfortune may send it back to its former class position. It also lacks the financial protection and guidance of an older generation of kin.

Children are attached to the nuclear family and are charged with the role of maintaining and improving upon the family position. The child is often in an anomalous position, with his parents pushing him into contacts with upper-upper-class children who tend to reject him.

Upper-Middle-Class Family

In the stable upper-middle class, the nuclear family is typical. It is not isolated as the lower-upper-class family tends to be, nor is it deeply enmeshed in a kinship group, as in the upper-upper class. Nuclear families of siblings and their parents maintain a web of friendly social relationships, especially when they live in the same community. In times of stress they assume special responsibilities in a definite mutual assistance pattern, which end with the resolution of the stress (Sussman, 1953a; Sussman, 1959; Sussman & Burchinal, 1962). Each nuclear family maintains its autonomy, but is strengthened by the informal relationships and by the assurance of assistance when needed. Typically, the husband is regarded as head of the family. Even when his wife is employed, he is the chief earner and has the more influential voice when major expenditures are made (Blood & Wolfe, 1960, pp. 24–34).

The child is born not only into a nuclear family but into a kinship web that may gently pressure him into position, but is without the powerful authority of the upper-upper class with its ability to disown or disinherit—for in the upper-middle class there is not great wealth to be inherited. Moderate upward mobility may be a goal of the family but for many upper-middle-class families their way of life is satisfactory and is what they wish to pass on to their children. Pride in the child is based on his conformity to upper-middle-class standards and on his ability to achieve middle-class goals.

Lower-Middle-Class Family

It was noted earlier that the northern urban lower-middle class had a wide variety of occupations and ethnic backgrounds. However, whatever traces of the original immigrant patriarchal family may have existed at one time, the current family is nuclear in structure (Rainwater, Coleman, & Handel, 1959).[1]

The husband is clearly the head of the family in the sense that the wife accepts his decisions and caters to his wishes; the wife, however, tends to control the purse on household expenditures (pp. 82–85). Since little money is saved, she is really the financial agent for the family.

The kinship group is socially close; most social activities are with close relatives on either side of the family, and in many families a large group of relatives and inlaws regularly gathers at one or another home as often as once a month (pp. 103–108). The nuclear families do not live as neighbors, however, and the wives strongly assert that a little physical distance between homes makes for good relationships.

Children "belong" to the nuclear family

[1] Rainwater and his associates do not specifically identify their subjects as lower-middle class. Their description of their group indicates that it is a combination of lower-middle and upper-lower class. The husbands are referred to as blue-collar skilled workers, who comprise from 60 to 75 per cent of the population in various cities. They are contrasted with white-collar lower-middle-class individuals and with upper-middle-class members. Obviously, there is a social class that is lower than the workingman category. What is cited from the Rainwater book therefore applies also to the upper-lower class (Rainwater, Coleman, & Handel, 1959, pp. 15–25, 225).

and are expected to uphold the respectability of the family.

Upper-Lower-Class Family

As was noted earlier, the upper-lower class includes many partially assimilated ethnic groups. In New Haven (Hollingshead & Redlich, 1958, pp. 104–114) the structure of the family often included three generations living in one household: the original immigrants, old and with few family ties of their own generation, living in the home of a married son or daughter; the adult couple; and their children. This type of family is sometimes referred to as an extended family (McGuire, 1950). The gap in degree of assimilation between the children and their grandparents is very wide and conflicts are frequent. In other ways, also, the family is weak. In New Haven it was found that 18 per cent of the homes with children under age 17 were broken. The type of break was not stated, but unless the mother was dead, the household probably consisted of the mother as head of the family, her children, and whatever relatives lived in the home. Many homes had roomers. Thus, although the family basically is nuclear with the father as head, there are many variations.

Children are subject to the strains created by the contrast between low family status and the expectation for them set by such American institutions as the mass media, school, community center, or church. Often the children's status seems to be set less by their families than by their failure to reach these institutional expectations.

Lower-Lower-Class Family

The lower-lower class is more likely than any other to include families that are disorganized or broken. Even under conditions of partial acculturation, the family structure of many ethnic groups resembles the traditional one. Two of the most recently arrived ethnic groups are the Mexican and the Puerto Rican. In both cultures the traditional family is patriarchal (Humphrey, 1944; Jones, 1948; Opler, 1955), and in neither group is it able to function adequately under the conditions imposed by the industrial city. Unable to support his family adequately, the father loses status. Employment of the wife and older children, with their own pay checks, further destroys the father's role. Sometimes he deserts the family entirely. Children, poorly supervised, adopt the street life of the city, or, if they attend community-center functions, adopt habits of American teenagers that are alien to their native culture.

In other ethnic groups, also, broken homes are a commonplace. In New Haven (Hollingshead & Redlich, 1958), 41 per cent of lower-lower-class children under age 17 lived in broken homes of various types. Tensions were rife. The family typically did not function as a unit. Activities spilled over into the street and alley.

In the lower-lower class, the family structure varies from one subcultural group to another, and from family to family. In New Haven, 44 per cent of the families were nuclear in structure, with father, mother, and children living in one household; 23 per cent consisted of three generations, in some cases including remnants of a broken family; 18 per cent consisted of one parent and the children. The remainder were various types of childless families. In cities other than New Haven, the father with the nonresident or transient status seems to be especially typical of the lower-class Negro family. The dominant role in the family varies with its structure; roles of children are not clearly defined.

The Negro Variant

As has been noted earlier, Negroes crowd the lower-class levels. Middle- and upper-class Negroes tend to fall into much the same pattern of family structure as do the equivalent white classes. The lower-class Negro family has some of the same char-

acteristics as the lower-class white family, but also has some historical precedents that set it apart.

During the period of slavery, the Negro husband had little opportunity to carry out the role of the white American husband; he was relieved by his master of authority and responsibility for his family's welfare (Frazier, 1939, Chs 3, 6, 7, 8, 15, 16). On many plantations little emphasis was placed on marriage of the slaves, and on others husband and wife, whether united legally or in a common-law marriage, might be separated at the will of the master. The mother therefore became the functioning head of the family unit, whose stable elements were composed of a grandmother, one or more daughters, and their dependent children. Husbands might or might not be present. This basic form of family carried over into freedom and still is present in a large proportion of lower-class Negro communities. Many lower-class Negro families therefore resemble matriarchates. When the children's father is present, the mother, through tradition, assumes a dominant role; when there is a succession of men, not all children have the same father, and the mother alone plays the parental role. The illegitimacy rate is high among Negroes; unlike many white unwed mothers, the Negro mother typically retains the custody of her baby and unprotestingly becomes responsible for it, sometimes taking it to her mother's home, or in time setting up a household of her own.

FAMILY ROLES
OF HUSBAND AND WIFE

The discussion up to this point has indicated the roles of husband and wife with reference to the total family structure. A further discussion of husband-wife roles, especially in relation to each other, follows.

Interpersonal Roles

In general, satisfaction with love and marriage tends to increase for the wife from lower to upper class. This conclusion is based on a study of wives made by Blood and Wolfe in Michigan (1960, pp. 228–230, 253). The differences were not extreme but were fairly consistent. The authors gave several tentative explanations. Members of the higher classes are better educated than those in the lower classes; therefore they are better able to communicate with each other. They are more secure in many areas of life, including emotional security, and hence can give more love. Also, it is part of the value system of the higher classes that love is important and needed; therefore men and women expect to give and to receive love.

It is consistent with the concept of love that satisfaction with companionship also tends to increase for the wife, though irregularly, from lower to higher class status (Blood & Wolfe, 1960, p. 171). Rainwater's (1959, Ch. 4) study of the workingman's wife revealed that there was little companionship between husband and wife, except in such passive activities as looking at television. The husband disliked to talk about his work at home, and the wife had few contacts outside the home to serve as topics of conversation. The husband's recreation—fishing and sports—was with men friends. The wife's free time was spent at home or with close relatives. In fact, in the working class, husband and wife seemed to meet on a rather superficial level of exchange of services—the wife created a home, the husband provided the income. Sexual intercourse, primarily on a physical level, was also a strong tie (Rainwater & Weinstein, 1960b).

In contrast to the lack of companionship among the working-class husbands and wives, the middle-class wives (upper-middle class and white-collar lower-middle class) included in Rainwater's study (1959, Ch. 4) maintained a companionable relationship with their husbands. They had a more highly developed sense of inner security and therefore depended less on their husbands. They felt less compulsion to cater slavishly to them, and they expected and received more consideration for their own wishes. The exchange between husband and wife was less utilitarian than in the working class and was characterized by companionable exchange of services and sharing of experiences.

Although throughout all subcultures except the Negro lower class, the husband tends to have somewhat more power and authority than the wife, nowhere does the truly patriarchal family typify a subculture, according to the study by Blood and Wolfe (1960, pp. 24–26). Ethnic families, generally thought to be patriarchal, may have been so in the years immediately following immigration, but this type of family organization has faded under the strain of urban industrial life and the acculturation of immigrants and their children into the prevailing patterns of Anglo-American culture. Rural families, also stereotyped as patriarchal, have moved into similarity with urban families.

In the Michigan study by Blood and Wolfe (1960, pp. 32–35), power within the family was measured by the predominance of husband or wife in making decisions on eight items. By constructing a scale of dominance, the authors were able to compare decision-making among families at different levels of social status. The middle-status (roughly middle-class) group showed the highest degree of equality between husband and wife. In high-status groups the husband made more decisions than the wife, especially in matters involving income and the handling of money. In low-status groups, the wife tended to be more dominant than in either the high- or middle-status families. Similar findings resulted from a study in Omaha (Olsen, 1960). Among lower-class Negro families, husbands had the least power of all.

When wives are employed, they gain power in decision-making, and may become dominant over their husbands (Blood & Wolfe, 1960, pp. 32–34; Heer, 1958). Since a higher percentage of lower-class wives work than wives in other classes, the loss of power of lower-class husbands is explained at least in part by the increased power of working wives (Blood & Wolfe, 1960, pp. 98–99). Heer's study (1958), however, showed that nonworking wives in the lower class also have more power than middle-class wives.

Roles of husband and wife in the home also show some variation by subcultural groups. Responsibility for the performance of household duties rests more heavily on low-status wives and least heavily on high-status wives (Olsen, 1960). Husbands are most active in the middle status. The high-status wife transfers about 10 per cent of household duties to servants, whereas middle- and low-status wives have little outside help. Although middle-class husbands and wives tend to share responsibility for household tasks in slightly greater degree than do couples in other classes, the study does not imply that they actually carry out tasks together.

Economic Roles of Husband and Wife

Economic role suggests employment, which indeed is part of the economic role but not all of it. An important part of social-class economic roles is type of employment, together with its prestige and income. These items have already been discussed.

Security of employment varies with social class. In the depression years of the 1930's, in Yankee City (Warner & Lunt, 1941, pp. 277–279) 90 per cent of the upper-upper class and 94 per cent of the lower-upper class had full employment. The percentage with full employment decreased until in the lower-lower class only 28 per cent had full employment; 46 per cent at this level had part-time employment, and 26 per cent total unemployment. Since the lower-lower class typically includes some men who are unemployable, even in periods of full employment, the upper-lower class, typically employed, furnishes a more realistic contrast to the upper classes as to the ravages of an economic depression. Among upper-lower-class men, 42 per cent were fully employed, 36 per cent had part-time employment, and 22 per cent were unemployed. Unemploy-

ment not only brings financial privations to the family, but a sense of insecurity and failure, disturbance of family roles, and, if long continued, permanent downward mobility. The results are more fully discussed in a later section on downward mobility. These personal and family disturbances are more severe and long-lasting the lower the social-class position.

Employment of the wife also varies from one class to another. The Women's Bureau (1960) has made detailed studies that showed the percentage of wives living with their husbands who were employed, according to the income of the husband and the number of children under age 18. When income alone was considered, about a third of wives whose husbands had an income of less than $5,000 a year worked, as compared with about a fourth of those whose husband's income was between $5,000 and $10,000, and only 15 per cent of those whose husband's income was $10,000 and over. A finer classification at the top of the scale would probably show that no wives worked in the highest income groups. When both income and children were considered, the highest percentage of working wives fell into the group with children between the ages of 6 and 17 with an income from the husband of less than $1,000; 58 per cent of these wives worked. The presence of children under 6 years in the low-income group reduced the percentage of working wives to about 25. The lowest percentage of working wives fell into the group having children under age 6 with income from the husband of $10,000 or over.

The results for the family of employment of the wife vary from class to class. Previous discussion showed that when the wife is employed her influence in family decision-making increases. The husband therefore suffers some loss of status relative to his wife. Ethnic families in which the original structure was patriarchal may suffer serious disorganization when the husband is unable to support his family and the wife and older children become employed.

The threat to the husband's superior role

is mitigated by several factors. Many wives work only before the birth of the first child, and when this arrangement is part of the family plan—as is likely to be true in middle-class families—the advantages of the wife's income in improving the home offset any implied threat to the husband's status. Other middle-class wives work only part-time or seasonally, fitting their work around their major responsibility of child rearing. What they earn is a minor part of the total income.

In the lower classes the income of the wife often is necessary, and tends to be accepted realistically by the husband. In the higher-class levels, where there is no implication of need, the few wives who are employed are tolerantly regarded as doing so because of some special talent or personality need.

Economic roles are not limited to employment of the wife and husband. Since the husband usually is the only or chief earner, his position as an employed person is regarded as more important than his wife's position, either as worker or as homemaker. It is anticipated on all class levels, except perhaps the very lowest, that the wife will give her husband needed personal support in holding his job or improving his status.

In the upper classes the wife's identification with her husband's family indirectly supports his position. Her civic activities on committees and boards also indirectly contribute to her husband's status in the business world. Entertainment is in the hands of the wife and is not only for pleasure but often to consolidate or improve the business status of the husband.

Without an attempt to place them in a specific social-class category, the roles of wives of executives have been subjected to analysis (Helfrich, 1961; W. H. Whyte, 1948; W. H. Whyte, 1951a; W. H. Whyte, 1951b). Within the family, the wife is expected to run a well-organized household and care for the personal needs of her children, as well as save some time for her husband. Entertaining and being entertained by her husband's business associates are consid-

ered important parts of her role. Personally considered, the ideal is a woman who is generally well-educated, who can understand the general aspects of her husband's occupation (but not the technical details), who is affable, discreet, well-dressed, and well-mannered. Since many executives are transferred from one place to another, the wife should be adaptable; she should not become so dependent on one locality or group that she cannot easily pull up roots and move physically and socially.

In Rainwater's (1959, Ch. 4) report on the workingman's wife, the wife had virtually no role to play with reference to her husband's employment. He did not discuss it with her and resisted her efforts to enter into such a discussion. Her role was a general one of catering to her husband's wishes.

In the lower classes, the wife enters directly into her own employment with little effort to support her husband in his job.

The personal and economic roles of husbands and wives differ greatly among the subcultures, but not in haphazard fashion. The variations are related to the special features of the subculture and to the position of the couple in the social-class hierarchy. Within the family, the roles of husband and wife are closely interrelated, and the resulting coordination supports the subculture of the family.

UNCOMPLETED AND DISINTEGRATED FAMILIES

Incomplete families are those in which the couple have children although they have never married and do not regularly live together; disintegrated families are those in which divorce, annulment, desertion, or other types of separation have destroyed the family as a functioning unit. Remarriage is a move to re-establish the family unit.

Uncompleted Families

As used here, the uncompleted family consists of one parent (almost invariably the mother) and her children. It does not refer to the unmarried mother who places her child for adoption and thus does not assume a familial role toward it. The most fully developed uncompleted families include more than one child, sometimes with a succession of fathers.

These families have variously been termed female-based families (Miller, 1959) and matrifocal families (Freilich, 1961). The dominance of the wife in lower-lower-class families has already been noted; dominance is especially high in families in which the man is an intermittent, marginal, or transient member of the matrifocal family, a situation that frequently occurs in lower-class Negro families (Frazier, 1939, Chs 6, 15).

The dominance of the mother—sometimes of the grandmother—and absence of the father create a distortion of family roles. The child tends to accept as normal the family life that he finds. Girls pattern themselves after their mother and build up a self-concept of the dominant person who must in the future fend for her children, either through employment or relief payments. The boy also accepts this concept of women and for himself a concept of the irresponsible, transient male.

Husband and wife, if they can be called that, expect little of each other except sexual satisfaction.

Disintegration of Marriage

Disintegration of marriage also seems to be more prevalent in lower than in upper classes. Goode (1956) not only presented his own data but summarized other studies that showed an increase in the divorce rate with decrease in various indices of socioeconomic status, such as occupation, income, and the ranking of ecological areas (cf. Kephart, 1955; Monahan, 1955; Schroeder, 1939). Goode, in his study of divorce among a sample of Detroit women ever divorced, developed an index of proneness to divorce which he applied according to the occupational level of the husbands of the divorced

women. A consistent increase in divorce proneness was found from professional and proprietary occupations, through clerical-sales-service, skilled-foremen, semiskilled-operatives, to unskilled. The unskilled group had 2.6 times as great proneness to divorce as the professional-proprietary group. Although some other studies have shown an irregular increase with decreased social class status, in general the progression is clear.

The significance of the relation between divorce rates or proneness and social class does not lie in the mere fact that the lower the class the greater the tendency toward divorce, but in the significance of the difference in proneness to class and family. Different subcultures have different attitudes toward divorce. Catholics are opposed to divorce. Lower-class Negroes are prone to marital disintegration of various sorts. Middle- and upper-class people often seek counseling when they face marital problems. The higher education of the upper classes may facilitate communication and enable husband and wife to talk out their problems. Divorce is only indirectly a reflection of the prevalence of marital problems in different subcultures. It is closely related to attitudes toward marriage and divorce.

Remarriage

The rate of remarriage, after all types of marital dissolution, is higher among the poorly educated than among people with high-school or college education. Moreover, the poorly educated remarry successively more than college graduates, a consequence of repeated divorces or some mixture of divorce and death. More than a fourth of persons with elementary-school education had been married twice or more, compared with approximately a tenth of college graduates, according to Census data (Glick & Carter, 1958). The poorly educated were also more likely to have been married three or more times than were college graduates. These figures indicate the greater instability of lower-class marriages, the frequent changes in family members, and the necessity of adapting and readapting roles, especially where the husband is concerned.

MARRIAGE AS A SUBCULTURAL FUNCTION

From a personal point of view, marriage is the uniting of a man and woman for the development of a common life together. Endogamous marriage contributes to the stability of the subculture and exogamous marriage to its dissolution or in some circumstances to the merging of subcultures. Subcultures with a firm system of values usually are opposed to exogamous marriages; nevertheless, many such marriages occur.

Exogamous Marriages

The attitude toward different types of exogamous marriages differs in a way that is related to the social structure. When cultural or racial merging of one group with another is tolerated or approved by both groups, the attitude toward intermarriage is permissive. When such merging is objected to by one or both groups, permissiveness declines, and when merging is regarded as a major threat to the very existence of the group, intermarriage is proscribed. The following attitudes toward merging and intermarriage prevail among the various subcultures discussed.

Among social classes, a slow transition is approved, especially at all levels below the upper-upper class. Interclass marriages between adjacent social classes therefore are permissible, but between members of widely separated levels, unapproved or opposed. The opposition comes primarily from families or friends and may be unevenly applied by the two groups involved.

Attitudes tend to be neutral toward intermarriage between ethnic groups when the groups consider themselves to be mutually assimilable. This stage usually is reached only after a certain loss of ethnicity and after a common language is in use. In the United States this stage may be found more often among native-born ethnics who have attended a public school and learned some common values. When there is opposition, it tends to come from older members of the family and their friends, who still look with some suspicion on other ethnic groups.

Among religious denominations, attitudes toward exogamy differ with official policies. Since the Constitution of the United States grants freedom of religious belief, religions are not under public pressure to merge. When differences of creed and practices are minor, as among some Protestant denominations, intermarriage generally is permissible. However, when differences are regarded as irreconcilable, intermarriage is proscribed. Of the religious groups in the United States, opposition to exogamous marriages is strongest among Jews. Catholics oppose exogamous marriages but provide a halfway position for the non-Catholic which permits the marriage to take place under the conditions prescribed by the Church. Protestants differ by denomination but in general are permissive.

The position of each religious group is made clear in institutional rules, supported by penalties for violations.

Marriage between racial groups is generally disapproved. It is opposed by different races as a social policy, although it occurs on an individual basis. Caucasians seem especially sensitive to interracial marriages. In many states interracial marriage is proscribed by laws passed by white legislators. Racial exogamy is the only type forbidden by law.

Intermarriage may involve several different types of subculture and bring into play opposition from different groups or several types of penalty. An example of multiple subcultural differences exists in the marriages between American servicemen and Japanese women. These marriages united two persons different in race, culture (often including language), and sometimes religion and social class. Opposition could and sometimes did come from many disapproving groups.

Intermarriages tend to occur only under certain conditions when the identification of one or both persons to his own subculture or race is weak. Intermarriage often occurs when the bride and groom are isolated physically from the parental family and subcultural group. Interracial marriages may involve a foreigner, as was true of the American-Japanese marriages. Work or education may draw a person away from his own group and place him in contact with persons of other subcultures. These contacts may call for courtesy and cooperation on a secondary level (Glaser, 1958) but may not change the original unfavorable stereotypes. In time, however, a man and woman of different subcultures may become personally interested in each other and then redefine the situation. The white man no longer defines the woman as nonwhite or as of a different religion or social class. Instead, he defines her in terms of appearance, intelligence, or common interests. Intermarriage may also occur when one subcultural group is very small in number and lives in close proximity to a larger subcultural group; a member of the smaller group, unable to find a mate to his liking in his own group, may explore the possibilities of the larger group.

When members of different subcultures marry, they may be ostracized by their groups, including their parents. When this rejection occurs for only one, the rejected member may identify with the subculture of the spouse. However, if both subcultures disapprove, the couple may be without subcultural roots, their only chance for group identification coming through association with other similarly exogamous couples.

Problems of exogamous couples seem to exceed those of endogamous couples. Usually it has been assumed that the problems are the result of cultural differences. However, other possibilities may be mentioned. The person who detaches himself from his earlier subcultural identification may have been seeking release from close family relationships and therefore may find the close association and reciprocal adjustments of marriage difficult, whereas he had anticipated freedom. Or the opposite may be true. At the time of marriage, personal attachment may override subcultural identification. Later, rejection by family, friends, and sometimes institutions such as a church or club may cause dissatisfaction with the marriage. The birth of children may arouse a longing to rear them in the original subculture even when, as in Catholic–non-Catholic marriages, the non-Catholic had pledged himself to rear the children in the Catholic faith.

It should not be overlooked, however, that many intermarriages seem as well adjusted as endogamous marriages. In many of these marriages it seems probable that the formal subcultural classifications do not have real meaning for the couple. The Jew and the Protestant may be emancipated and find themselves more compatible religiously than an Orthodox and a Reformed Jew, or a member of a fundamentalist and a liberal Protestant denomination.

Intermarriage is sometimes regarded as a measure of and means to assimilation, especially when it is permissible (Marcson, 1950). However, between subcultures where merging is desired or approved, merging may occur without intermarriage; where merging is disapproved, intermarriage will not bring it about. Endogamous marriage plays an important role in preserving the subcultural group physically, since children of the marriage "belong" to the subculture, and in transmitting the subculture to another generation. Exogamous marriages tend to destroy the group and to dissipate the subculture. The way in which this threat is met differs from one subculture or race to another.

Racial Exogamy

Racial endogamy is taught to most American children as a policy to be followed without exception. Exogamous marriages are forbidden by law in more than half the states, so far as white people are concerned. Not only is marriage between a white person and a Negro forbidden, but sometimes between whites and various branches of the Mongolian race. So great is the opposition that some states define a Negro as a person with one-fourth, one-eighth, or one-sixteenth Negro ancestry. Penalties are severe; examples are fines of $100 to $5,000 or one to five years in prison. When laws have not been passed, opposition is strong in the mores, with social penalties such as rejection by family and friends, loss of job, or difficulty in finding adequate housing.

As a consequence of these measures, few interracial marriages occur, even in states without laws forbidding them. Available studies show that approximately 2 to 5 per cent of northern Negro marriages are with white people (Klineberg, 1944, pp. 277–278). Since whites outnumber Negroes, the percentage of whites involved is much lower. In California in the first 30 months after the repeal in 1948 of all laws forbidding various types of interracial marriages, only 0.56 per cent of marriage licenses were issued to a white and a nonwhite couple (Burma, 1952).

Since interracial marriages are most strongly opposed, the penalties are most severe and extend to the children. Children usually resemble the nonwhite race sufficiently to be identified as of that race. The white parent may attempt to place the child in white groups, but this movement usually results in rejection and eventually the child is either marginal to both groups or seeks his identification in the nonwhite group, where he suffers from whatever limitations are placed on that group by the dominant whites.

Religious Exogamy

Religious exogamy is not forbidden by civil law. Each religious group sets its own policy regarding exogamy and fixes its own penalties.

The Jewish religion in the United States, in all three of its branches, is extremely restrictive and adamant about refusing to sanction or recognize the marriage of a Jew to a non-Jew. The traditional Orthodox position was that the Jew who married a non-Jew was religiously and socially dead; he was exiled from the synagogue and from his family. Although this position has been softened to some extent, individual Orthodox parents sometimes refuse to have any further contact with a child who has married outside the faith.

Typically the rabbi refuses to perform a marriage ceremony for an exogamous couple. In 1958, the Executive Secretary of the Rabbinical Council of America (Orthodox position) supplied the author with the following statement:

Marriage is an expression of human living according to Judaism and must be governed always by our religious faith and practice. Marriage is a religious ceremony and religiously in a Jewish sense can take place only between two members of the Jewish faith. Marriage between a Jewish person and a non-Jewish person is not sanctioned in a religious sense and might be said to be nonexistent.

The Conservative branch of Judaism holds the same view on marriage as does the Orthodox branch, according to a 1958 statement from a member of the Committee on Marriage and the Family of the Rabbinical Assembly of America. The Reform branch of Judaism, the most liberal of the three branches, rests its position on a statement made in 1909 by the Central Conference of American Rabbis: ". . . mixed marriages are contrary to the tradition of the Jewish religion and should therefore be discouraged by the American Rabbinate" (Central Conference of American Rabbis, 1909, pp. 170, 174–184). The importance of the family in the Jewish religion makes it especially important that the husband and wife should be united in faith. A non-Jew may be converted to Judaism prior to marriage and thus establish this unity, but it has been emphasized by Jewish leaders that the conversion must be sincere and not merely an expedient to facilitate the marriage. In the intensity of its desire to maintain the Jewish faith, the risk is run of losing exogamous Jews entirely.

Roman Catholics, opposed to marriage of their members to non-Catholics, nevertheless have made a compromise with reality that retains the Catholic member. A valid exogamous marriage requires a dispensation from the bishop, which rests in part upon pledges made by both the Catholic and the non-Catholic, known as the antenuptial agreement. The Catholic pledges that all children of the marriage will be baptized and educated in the Catholic religion alone; that only the Catholic ceremony will be used for the marriage; and that he will do all that he can to lead the non-Catholic to the Catholic faith through prayer, example, and frequentation of the Sacraments. (This is taken from the form used in the Archdiocese of Washington, D.C.) The non-Catholic makes the first two pledges stated above and in addition pledges not to hinder the Catholic party in practicing the Catholic religion. Through this compromise the exogamous marriage is accepted, but at the same time the solidarity of the Church in this generation and its extension into the next are safeguarded.

Most Protestant denominations are less rigidly opposed to exogamous marriages than are either Jews or Catholics. Therefore most exogamous marriages of Jews or Catholics are with nominal Protestants. Those Protestant denominations that are strongly opposed warn their young people against interreligious marriage and point out that they will not be able to rear their children in their own faith but will be expected to rear them in the non-Protestant faith of the spouse (Bossard & Boll, 1957). Some Protestant denominations discourage their members from marrying into other Protestant denominations, although severe penalties are not usually imposed (Bossard & Letts, 1956).

The proportion of exogamous marriages in any given religious faith seems related to the degree of opposition to such marriages on the part of the religious group in question. Jews have a very low rate of exogamous marriages. In New Haven in 1940, 93.7 per cent of marriages involving a Jew were endogamous (Kennedy, 1944), and in 1948, 97.1 per cent (Hollingshead, 1950). A study of Jews in a small eastern city also emphasized the infrequency of exogamous marriages (Barron, 1946).

Catholics tend to have a higher rate of exogamous marriages than Jews. For the United States as a whole, sanctioned mixed marriages for 1930–1950 equalled 30 per cent of all Catholic marriages, with perhaps an equal percentage of nonsanctioned mixed marriages (Thomas, 1951). Percentages vary widely from one community to another, depending apparently on the relative size of the Catholic community. For example, in the dioceses of Raleigh, Charleston, and Savannah-Atlanta, with small Catholic populations, as many as 70 per cent of sanctioned Catholic marriages were exogamous, while in El Paso, Corpus Christi, and Santa Fe, with large Catholic populations, the percentage was only about 10 (Thomas, 1951).

Since both Jews and Catholics usually marry Protestants when they marry exogamously, and since Protestants intermarry among themselves, the proportion of exogamous marriages that are Protestant exceeds the proportion that are Jewish or Catholic.

Religious exogamy does not seem to further merging of religious faiths either ideologically or in social participation. One spouse may become converted to the religion of the other, each may retain his own religion, or the couple may avoid all religious observances. None of these constitutes merging. The Jews attempt to preserve their faith by refusing to admit the non-Jew (until converted), and thereby lose members. The Catholics attempt to keep their members and children born to the marriage, provided that the non-Catholic spouse actually makes the promised concessions. Nevertheless, they also lose members who marry non-Catholics through a civil ceremony and without making pledges. The Protestants in general are neutral and both lose and gain members through inter-marriage.

Ethnic Exogamy

Interethnic marriages within the same race and religion encounter chiefly family or other primary-group opposition. Inter-marriages increase in number with length of residence of the ethnic group in this country, its degree of acculturation into the Anglo-American way of life, and its social participation with other groups. For example, in New Haven in 1870, 86.67 per cent of marriages involving one person of German origin also involved another person of the same national origin; in 1900, the intra-German marriages had declined to 55.26 per cent, and by 1940 to 27.19 per cent (Kennedy, 1944). Other ethnic groups also showed a decline in endogamous marriages, although less extensive in the amount of change. The author noted, however, that when endogamous ethnic marriages declined, endogamous religious marriages tended to continue; for example, the Irish Catholic who married outside the Irish group nevertheless tended to marry another Catholic. Endogamous ethnic marriages may be said to be a passing characteristic of the early phase of ethnic adjustment in the United States and to decline as acculturation occurs. Religious endogamy, however, is a more permanent part of the national culture.

Social-Class Exogamy

Interclass marriages are not forbidden by law but arouse various emotional reactions of opposition or approval on the part of parents and of both informal and formal associations. To the degree that established members of a social class wish to preserve their status, they tend to encourage endogamy. However, if the individual or family is upwardly mobile, marked approval may be given to an upward exogamous marriage. Hence, the same marriage may be approved by the family and entourage of relatives and friends of one spouse and opposed by those of the other. The upwardly mobile person receives the approval, but it is into the social world of the spouse of higher class that he hopes to enter—the class that is opposed to the marriage.

Studies show three types of social-class marriage—endogamy, downward exogamy, and upward exogamy. The two upper classes and the two lower classes have the highest percentage of endogamous marriages—from 52 to 68 per cent for different classes, according to a New Haven study (Hollingshead, 1950). In the two middle classes, only slightly over a third of marriages were endogamous. In the upper and middle classes, downward exogamy exceeded upward, while the reverse trend was true of the two lower classes. This trend of exogamous marriages suggests a tendency for married couples to move toward middle-class status, and thus may indicate a trend toward unification of the subcultures into the middle-class pattern.

Pressures Toward Endogamous Marriage

Within each subculture are various forces that influence young people toward endogamous marriages. It is part of the general culture that individuals make a personal choice of a mate, regardless of the amount of direct pressure for or against a specific mate that may be exerted by family, friends, or institutions. This personal choice necessitates person-to-person contacts. The tendency of members of a given subculture to live near each other and to have their earliest contacts with others of the same subculture in neighborhood and school sets the basic friendships.

The counterpart is the tendency of each subculture to exclude members of other subcultures. However, the physical isolation of a given subculture is rarely complete. Teenagers and young adults have many more out-group contacts than have younger children. If they leave home to work or attend college, outside contacts may exceed those within the subculture. Social distance between the subcultures may still continue, but if increased association causes the social distance between the two individuals to decline, the way is opened for exogamous marriage.

A more direct influence on endogamous marriages is provided by parental pressure. Indirect pressure comes from deliberate control of parents over their children's social contacts. The upper-upper class has the most complete indirect control achieved through confining their children to exclusive class-oriented institutions. Children become so thoroughly socialized into the upper-upper-class subculture that they find it difficult or impossible to communicate with children of other subcultures. The debut of the girl is to introduce her as a marriageable young woman to the eligible young men and their parents.

More direct influence may be exerted by parents through interference in the dating or courtship of their child with persons of other and disapproved subcultural groups (Sussman, 1953b). Parental pressure may force the couple to elope—a method of escape. After the marriage, parents may refuse to meet the couple or even their own child (Golden, 1954).

[A somewhat parallel, though differently oriented and expanded, treatment of endogamous-exogamous marriage will be found in Ch. 16, pp. 645–658.]

CHILDREN IN THE SUBCULTURES

In the discussion of "Family Structure and Roles" differences in the significance of children in the various subcultures were noted. These differences are reflected in a number of ways in the birth rate and the training of children.

Number of Children Desired and Born

Almost all married women, regardless of subculture, desire some children. Moreover, the difference in average number of children desired differs only slightly from one social-class level to another. The study by Blood and Wolfe (1960) showed that among Michigan wives the smallest average desired number of children, 2.8, was specified by wives in the lowest status, the largest average number, 3.5, by the second rank from the top. The difference is less than one child. Other studies show little difference in expected family size according to social class or rural or urban residence (Freedman, Whelpton, & Campbell, 1959, pp. 318ff; Rainwater & Weinstein, 1960b).

Actual birth rates, however, differ widely among social classes, with the greatest number of children at the lower end of the scale. *The Statistical Abstract of the United States* (1962, p. 58) reported on the number of children ever born per 1,000 women aged 45 and over who had ever been married. For 1957, with the women classified by amount of education, the average number of children per woman showed a regular decline from 3.8 for the woman with eight years of education to 1.6 for the woman with four or more years of college. When the women were classified by occupation of the husband, the average number of children born to the wives of laborers was 3.3 per wife, contrasted with an average of 1.9 per wife in the category of professional, technical, and kindred workers. The intermediate levels of occupations fell between these two rates. [Cf. Ch. 9, p. 302, of this Handbook.]

The comparison of such rates with the desired number of children shows a wide discrepancy. Lower-class women would appear to have more children than desired, and higher-level women fewer. Several factors seem to be involved. The number of children born to women aged 45 and over expresses the experience of a past generation. The desired or expected number of children cited above tends to be the expression of contemporary young women. There are various indications that urban middle- and upper-class women are now more favorable to having two to four children than was the preceding generation, and that lower-class and rural women wish to limit the number of children. However, even for women now in the childbearing period, more children are born in a given period of married life to lower-class than to middle-class or upper-class women.

Former explanations of the lower birth rate in upper than lower classes included the belief that urban living or psychosomatic effects of tensions of white-collar types of work reduced fertility (Freedman, Whelpton, & Campbell, 1959, pp. 48–56). Recent studies, however, indicate that the real difference is in the effectiveness of the use of contraceptives. The high birth rate of the lower class (especially the lower-lower class) is closely related to their failure to use reliable contraceptives consistently (Rainwater & Weinstein, 1960a, pp. 28–29; Rainwater & Weinstein, 1960b). Poorly educated wives and their husbands do not understand that contraceptives must be used systematically—one omission may lead to pregnancy—hence the use of contraceptives tends to be sporadic or carelessly carried out. Wives object to certain types of contraceptives as messy, or they fear mechanical appliances may become "lost" in their bodies. Husbands object to other methods as interfering with their pleasure. In contrast, people in the upper social levels have a better understanding of the physiological processes involved in conception and the need for consistent use of contraceptives. They tend to plan ahead as to how many children they want and when they want them, sometimes from before the birth of the first child, sometimes after they have had the number of children desired (Boek, Sussman, & Yankauer, 1958).

The basic attitudes of subcultural groups toward children, of course, cannot be overlooked—the acceptance of children as natural among lower-class groups, the ideology of certain religious faiths that producing many children is a sacred duty, and the ideology of other subcultures that the number and spacing of children are matters for individual decision. The differences in birth rates among religious groups are shown in the United States Census figures for 1957 (*Statistical Abstract of the United States,* 1962, p. 115). For women aged 45 and over, who had ever been married, the number of children born per wife was as follows: Catholic, 3.1; Protestant, 2.8; Jewish, 2.2; and other or no religious affiliation, 2.7. In addition to religion, differences in education, ethnicity, and social-class level also affect the rates.

Goals and Methods of Child Rearing

The values and goals that parents have for their children are related, first, to the subculture, and second, to whether or not the parents hope that the child will eventually occupy a more favorable status than they do, either through upward mobility or through acculturation and assimilation into a different subculture. Individual families, of course, may have special goals but in general goals for children are related to subcultural values. [Cf. Ch. 18, p. 8.]

According to the subcultural values summarized earlier in this chapter, the following points seem especially pertinent in socialization of the child into his subculture.

Upper-upper-class child rearing (Amory, 1947; Baltzell, 1958; Davis, Gardner, & Gardner, 1941; Warner & Lunt, 1941). The emphasis on lineage and the maintenance of the family position make children significant for the entire kinship. Married couples are expected to have children; sons are very highly valued, since they will carry on the name. Commenting on the Philadelphia social elite, Baltzell stated that as many children are desired as can be privately educated, that is, educated into the upper-upper class through attendance at private schools. Training of children to identity with the family and class position is carried out in several ways. More so than with children of other subcultures who are less completely insulated by their subculture, upper-upper-class children are subjected to a uniformity of cultural impact. Their peer associates are of their class. When governesses are employed, they represent the class subculture, although not of it themselves. In the South, Negro mammies have prided themselves on training their young charges in the upper-class ideals and manner of living (Davis, Gardner, & Gardner, 1941, pp. 84–99).

Parents are the most immediate source of training; not the parents alone but the kinship is concerned with the training of each child. Various units of the kinship may live near each other, or may have a common summer home. Anniversaries bring large segments of the kinship together. The child is thus exposed to contacts with many adult relatives. Family legends are passed on to the child. Rituals of courtesy and respect for older people are carefully followed, impressing upon the child the superior status of the elders. Heirlooms link the child with the past. Thus, through many avenues, each child learns his role in the kinship group.

The conformity implied is offset to some extent by the variety of the activities in which the upper-upper-class child and youth engages, such as music and dancing lessons, sports, travel, and organized recreation groups. They also enjoy certain freedoms not open to many public-school, lower-level children. A study (Cramer, 1949–1950) of upper-level students at a private day school in Erie, Pennsylvania, showed that 80 per cent were absent from school during one year from one to 60 days, presumably spent in travel or vacations, with an average of 10 to 15 school days each. Such absences would be regarded as a serious interference with the school program in most public schools. Family influence also often protects the upper-upper-class child when he is guilty of minor or even major misdemeanors. Restitution for damages is made privately. If necessary, the child is removed by his parents from the community to attend a boarding school, or he is provided with psychiatric treatment.

In general, the upper-upper-class child holds a secure position socially and economically. In case a parent dies or the family disintegrates for some other reason, relatives step in to assume care of the child. The orphanage and the paid foster home are not for the upper-upper-class child. For example, Eleanor Roosevelt (1939), writing of her own childhood, mentioned five different relatives who assumed responsibility for her at different times after the death of her mother.

The child may feel, however, that family pressures are very heavy and that he cannot live up to family expectations. For example, Mrs. Roosevelt spoke of her shyness and lack of self-confidence; she especially felt her inability to play the role of social belle as her mother and grandmother had done.

Lower-upper-class child rearing. Little information is available on children in the lower-upper class. Few members of this class have written autobiographies or been the subject of biographies, both valuable sources of information on the upper-upper class. Empirical studies tend to be limited to the formal processes of occupational mobility of the men. Comments therefore are necessarily general.

Since the lower-upper class is generally upwardly mobile, it seeks to instill into children the goals and ways of life of the upper class. With inadequate experience in the upper-upper class, lower-upper-class parents often are unable to pass on to their children the upper-upper-class way of life. The tendency is strong, therefore, to place children in situations where they will have extra-familial contacts with upper-upper-class children. Such opportunities are presented by private schools and summer camps that accept both upper-upper- and lower-upper-class children. A chief contribution of the lower-upper-class parents who wish their children to enter the upper-upper class is to instill in them a desire to be upper-upper and a dissatisfaction with their parents' way of life. It seems probable that lower-upper-class children feel less secure in their family and class position than do upper-upper-class children. They also lack strong kinship ties to give them emotional and, if needed, financial support.

Upper-middle-class child rearing (Davis, Gardner, & Gardner, 1941; Hollingshead, 1949; McGuire, 1952). The emphasis on good behavior and success in the upper-middle class calls for careful consideration of each child's potentialities and training. The number of children is limited, not to those who can be privately educated, as in the upper-upper class, but to the number who can be given education sufficient to maintain or improve moderately upon the family standard of living. Some children attend private schools, but more are in public schools, within which they form an important social group with its own cliques and customs.

Children are inducted into the class subculture primarily by their parents. They are taught to value education as a means to success as well as to cultural development. They are also taught to avoid personal aggression and to exert self-control. They are placed in contact with other upper-middle-class children in play groups and organized youth groups. Although upper-middle-class children are rewarded for conformity by special privileges, they are also taught to look ahead toward adult success. Immediate restraint in order to achieve future goals therefore is a constant objective in child rearing, and involves inducing the child to internalize the goal of future success.

Attempts have been made to discover differences in methods of child rearing between middle class and lower class. Davis and Havighurst (1946) compared certain methods used by middle-class (primarily upper-middle) families and upper-lower-class families living in Chicago. White and Negro mothers were separately compared. For white mothers, the authors found that middle-class children as compared with lower-class children were less often breast fed only, were weaned approximately two months earlier, and were started on toilet

training earlier, although the training was not necessarily completed as early with middle-class as with lower-class children. The middle-class mothers also restricted the community activities of their children and demanded assistance in the home to a greater extent than did lower-class mothers. The differences were interpreted to mean that middle-class mothers were training their children in restraint and self-discipline, whereas lower-class mothers were more permissive.

Since the Davis-Havighurst study appeared, other studies (Havighurst & Davis, 1955; Littman, Moore, & Pierce-Jones, 1957; Maccoby & Gibbs, 1954; Sears, Maccoby, & Levin, 1957; White, 1957) have followed that show less wide differences between the two classes and indicate more leniency and less strictness on the part of middle-class mothers; in other words, child-rearing practices of middle-class and lower-class children tend to be the same or similar. Several explanations have been offered to account for the differences between the early study and these later studies. The samples used in the different studies may fall within the same social class but represent differences in ethnic or religious subgroups. Regional and suburban versus urban differences in the samples may also account for part of the difference. It is also possible that the cult of permissiveness that was popular among middle-class parents in the 1950's may have modified the restrictive practices of middle-class mothers between the time of the early and the more recent studies.

Another approach to the effect on the child of middle-class patterns of child rearing was made by Green (1946) in an analysis of Anglo-American and ethnic practices, based on observation rather than empirical research. Green regarded the situation of the ethnic child, despite family conflict and harsh treatment, as preferable to that of the middle-class child. He stated that the middle-class child is a source of frustration to his parents. The expense of his rearing interferes with his father's desire for increased training and better clothing to further upward mobility. His care interferes with his mother's desire for a career. He also hampers his parents' pursuit of recreation. Nevertheless, middle-class values call for a relationship of love between parents and children. The close association between the mother and child causes her to absorb the personality of the child. Her method of discipline becomes a threat to withdraw her love. To avoid this threat, the child learns to be submissive. He then faces another problem, for middle-class culture calls for him to be competitive and assertive with his peers, in preparation for later adult competition. The boy feels these various conflicts keenly and, according to Green, develops a neurosis.

Green's statement was accepted rather uncritically and was widely quoted. Later research by Sewell and Haller (1956; 1959) seems to contradict Green's sweeping generalizations. Their research shows that anxieties are relatively mild among middle-class children, but prevalent among lower-class children, although for different reasons than those posited by Green as the basis for middle-class neurosis.

Middle-class parents tend to be self-conscious about their parenthood and attempt to make a rational approach to training their children for approved goals in the present and future. They read books on child psychology and attend child study classes. When they feel that they are failing in their objectives, they resort to psychiatrists and other counselors. Child rearing tends to become a semiprofession for middle-class parents, and especially so for mothers. At the same time, their close emotional ties with their children and their intense desire that their children be successful prevent a truly rational approach. They thus tend to be ambivalent and insecure in their relationship with their children.

The pressure on middle-class children to reach future goals by way of education and conformity is alleviated by some youths through a judicious bypassing that provides superficial conformity but saves the youth from all the rigors of effort and conformity. This bypassing may be engineered or condoned by parents. Parental pressure on high-school principals and teachers may induce them to pass a reluctant learner through to graduation (Hollingshead, 1949). The tolerant attitude toward cheating in order to pass courses has become part of upper-middle-class culture (Cavan, 1962). The emphasis on delay of marriage until education is completed, and on chastity until marriage, has also led to bypasses whereby these middle-class goals may outwardly be delayed to the proper future time, without complete denial of present satisfactions. Heavy petting with sexual climax but without intercourse is an evasion of strict chastity. Sexual relations of upper-middle-class boys with lower-class girls is a way to maintain the chastity of the middle-class girl by taking advantage of the traditional double standard of morals for men (Ehrmann, 1955; Ehrmann, 1960; Hollingshead, 1949). The proportion of middle-class girls who engage in premarital intercourse is presumably increasing, a movement away from the socially prescribed chastity that they carefully rationalize by adopting a romantic ideology which regards premarital intercourse as an expression of love and therefore acceptable (Reiss, 1960).

Lower-middle-class child rearing. Some of the studies on child rearing discussed in the preceding section have dealt with the lower-middle-class child, others have merged lower-middle and upper-middle class into a generalized middle-class category. As stated above, the trend of these studies has tended to establish concern with the training of children, combined with a permissive attitude. Other studies suggest that lower-middle-class parents and children look to the upper-middle-class as a model and reject the upper-lower class; the children are not, however, readily accepted by the upper-middle-class children (Hollingshead, 1949). Parents are concerned about the education and future of their children and with their public behavior (Hollingshead & Redlich, 1958).

As has been observed previously, the lower-middle class has a wide variety of ethnic group and occupational classifications. It is probable that the position of children in the family and the methods of child rearing show the influence of these differences, even though the general goals and trends may be more or less uniform.

The lower-middle class also includes upwardly mobile people from lower levels. The mobile child undoubtedly suffers many stresses. Bohlke (1961) has suggested that some middle-class delinquency may be the result of displacement of lower-class boys when their parents move into the middle-class position financially but not culturally. Marginal to their new subculture, the mobile boys are often rejected by lower-middle-class boys and in turn express their resentment through delinquent behavior.

Upper-lower-class child rearing. Upper-lower-class people are aware of their lowly status in the social-class hierarchy. According to a New Haven study (Hollingshead & Redlich, 1958), approximately a third of upper-lower-class people were upwardly mobile from the lower-lower class. In search of material comforts and security, approximately half of the mothers as well as the fathers are employed after the youngest child is in school (Women's Bureau, 1960).

Employment of the mother reduces the supervision that she may have over her children and may contribute to the permissiveness in child training found by Davis and Havighurst (1946) and others cited in the preceding section. The lenient methods of child training were interpreted to mean that the children were free of anxieties and frustrations. However, Sewell and Haller (1959) pointed out that stresses exist for these children and seem to originate in the contrast between the lenient family standards and the middle-class expectations that they encounter in public schools.

In contrast to the middle class, the upper-lower class is less concerned with instilling principles of good behavior in children and more concerned with immediate respectable overt behavior. A comparative study by Kohn (1959) made in Washington, D.C., showed that upper-lower-class parents more often used physical punishment than did middle-class parents. Of more importance was the fact that the upper-lower-class parents were concerned chiefly with respectable behavior, whereas middle-class parents sought substitutes for physical punishment that would help the child internalize principles that would guide him in future behavior.

Lower-lower-class child rearing. The relationships between parents and children are a result of the general subcultural aspects of the lower-lower class, with its many foreign-culture, ethnic, and nonwhite racial members. The immediacy of needs leaves little opportunity for future planning or holding remote goals. The hardness of life strips the family of niceties in family relationships. Children are expected as the result of sexual intercourse, in or out of marriage, and in either case often are a source of satisfaction to their parents. In a very real sense life is lived in the present on a day-by-day basis. "Now is for now" is the way one anthropologist (Freilich, 1961) has phrased the outlook on life of certain Negro groups.

The limited education and low job status of lower-class parents prevent their conceiving of upward mobility, or they visualize only limited improvement in status of their children. In surveys (Barber, 1957, pp. 309–311; Hyman, 1953), lower-class teenagers may express a desire for higher education or for prestige occupations but rarely do they attempt realistically to prepare for either. Parents are unable to give support to these poorly formulated aspirations. They may visualize their children as simply repeating their own lives, or as moving a small step upward into a better-paying job, perhaps within the same occupational rank as that in which the father stands. Parents therefore do not hold out as a goal academic success or continuance in school past the age of compulsory attendance. Sometimes they are not disturbed by persistent truancy or academic retardation. The school itself has little influence on the children. The divergence between the actual patterns of living in the lower-class subculture and the preachments of the middle-class school is so great that school has little significance to the child, and his chief aim is to avoid school as much as possible, put forth no more effort than is necessary, and drop out as soon as he can.

The rigors of life have often led lower-class parents to cut corners on strict honesty, defining their acts as necessary in terms of their needs. Children follow the same policy, gaining status in their peer groups through cleverness in petty stealing or by outwitting someone (Miller, 1958). Parents condone and sometimes benefit from the begging, petty thievery, or quasi-delinquent acts of their children. "Getting by" is a positive value, taught at home and learned on the street.

Children are taught early by parents and in their peer groups to defend themselves. They are not expected to maim or kill anyone but are expected to look out for themselves and their own safety in the rough life of the streets. The boy or girl who is not molested or exploited often is the one with the greatest physical strength.

In discipline, parents are not inclined to appeal to reason or love as a way to induce a child to obey. The problem is settled quickly on the basis of physical strength or punishment.

As was noted earlier, the lower-lower class is also the subculture with the highest proportion of incomplete or disintegrated families. Fathers are especially likely to be absent, with the mother and children forming the functioning unit. Children almost literally "belong to the mother." Various observations have been made as to the probable effect of the "female-based" family on children (Miller, 1959; Opler, 1955). With-

out a father for a model, the boy may continue his attachment to his mother, normal for infancy, and find it difficult to develop a masculine self-concept. Another possibility is that he will find a substitute father model, and a third is that he may turn to a street gang for his concept of an adult male. As a rule, he does not find a model that conveys the concept of the stability and responsibility of the husband. He therefore often becomes in his turn the transient husband his father was before him. The girl in the female-based family finds it relatively simple to model her role after her mother, to accept transient mates, and to assume in her turn responsibility for her children. [Cf. Ch. 18, pp. 759–762.]

In spite of the dead-level aspects of the lower-lower class, it must be recalled that some families are able to move out of it. As stated in the discussion of the upper-lower class, as many as a third of that class (New Haven) may be upwardly mobile from the lower-lower class. Their places in cities are soon filled by newcomers from other countries and the poorly prepared rural population that exists in some regions in our own country.

Passage of Children into Adulthood

The passage of children into adulthood differs from one subculture to another both with reference to age and to the criteria of adulthood. In general, adulthood may be said to be achieved with the completion of basic education, attainment of self-support, and marriage.

Basic education. The highest grade of schooling achieved often is used as one of the indices of social class. Some degree of college education is typical of the upper classes and the upper-middle class. Hollingshead and Redlich (1958) found that in the lower-middle class in New Haven, high-school graduation was typical. In the upper-lower class the median education for older males was 9.4 years and for women 10.5; for young adults the median for men was 11 years and for women 11.4. In the lower-

lower class, the educational median for men was 6 years and for women 8 years. Studies (Bledsoe, 1959; Davie, 1953) of school dropouts prior to graduation from high school shows an increasing proportion as the social-class level of pupils declines.

When release from school is used as the criterion, adulthood comes in the mid-teens for the lower-lower class, the later teens for the upper-lower class and lower-middle class, and the early twenties for the upper-middle and upper classes.

The expectation, class by class, is that with completion of education each person will enter into the adult occupations and pursuits of his class. Moreover, higher classes expect adulthood from lower-class individuals when they drop out of school, although they expect only adolescent behavior from upper-middle-class and upper-class children of the same age who remain in school—and sometimes from young adults who are college students (Hollingshead, 1949). For example, the out-of-school youth in the lower-lower class who creates a public disturbance may be arrested, tried, and either placed on probation, fined, or given a short jail sentence. The middle-class high-school boy for the same behavior may be referred by police to his parents or to the high-school principal. The rioting college student on campus or in a summer resort typically is dealt with by his university or is arrested but released without penalty; only more serious disturbances with property damage or personal injury become police and court cases. Prolonged adolescence and prolonged education seem to go hand in hand. The lower-class youth, the least well educated, is expected to exhibit the most adult behavior.

Attainment of self-support. Attainment of self-support is related to the educational level achieved and the standard of living expected by the subculture and anticipated by the individual. It is also related to stability of employment and to the sources of support.

The higher-class levels are secure in the present and have savings for the future.

Members of these classes are not concerned with minimum standards of living, but with the maintenance of the high standards that have become traditional. Education is a matter of status rather than of ability for self-support.

The middle classes strive for savings for the education of children, for comfort in old age, a better residence, and similar future goals. Satisfactory self-support includes provision for the education of children through high school or college.

The upper-lower class values self-support at a comfortable level, without recourse to relief except temporarily during some great emergency.

The lower-lower class, more intent on survival than on a high standard of living or savings, may be content with a low level of income from a relief agency. The husband may regard himself as providing satisfactory support for his family when he has established himself as eligible for one or more types of relief. Minor thefts of cash, food, or clothing are justified, especially if they are from the rich or from stores instead of individuals.

The criteria of adequate self-support are different for each social class. What the lower levels regard as satisfactory, the higher levels would regard as pauperism. Whatever the level of support sought, it is closely related to the amount and kind of education.

Marriage. In the sequence of steps toward adulthood, typically completion of school comes first, finding means of self-support second, and marriage third. It follows that the age at marriage varies widely from one social class to another. In Yankee City in the 1930's (Warner & Lunt, 1941, p. 255), the median age at marriage, class by class, was as follows: upper-upper, 27.9 years; lower-upper, 26.6; upper-middle, 26.1; lower-middle, 25.1; upper-lower, 24.4; and lower-lower, 23.2, indicating a difference of almost five years between upper-upper and lower-lower. In the small city of Elmtown (Hollingshead, 1950), upper- and upper-middle-class brides and grooms were usually in their mid-twenties; lower-middle-class brides and grooms were in their early twenties; upper-lower-class brides were in the late teens and their grooms in the early twenties; lower-lower-class brides were in their mid-teens with grooms in the early twenties.

Ethnic groups often follow a similar progression in average age at marriage as they become acculturated to Anglo-American life and move upward in the social-class scale. For example, in the peasant community of southern Italy, marriage took place in the early teens; in the partially acculturated Italian group in the United States, marriage shifted to the late teens or early twenties; in the fully acculturated group (grandchildren of the original immigrants), marriage occurred in the early or middle twenties (Campisi, 1948).

Caution should be used in comparing ages at marriage in different communities. The character of the community and the socioeconomic conditions of the times influence age at marriage. In the 1950's the age at marriage decreased generally in the United States. It seems certain, however, that the ranking of ages by social classes remains. [Cf. Ch. 16, pp. 648–649.]

Early adulthood of lower class. The coordination between the age of leaving school, finding an income of some kind, marriage, and social definition of adulthood catapults the lower-class youth into adult status five or more years before the upper-class youth is categorized as an adult. The lower-class boy or girl has a brief adolescence, the upper-class boy or girl a leisurely one.

The early achievement of social adulthood in the lower classes has several consequences for marriage and family life: less educational training with which to cope with adult problems; less cultural training and therefore a restricted conception of the personal development and fulfillment that the culture makes possible; less facility to communicate with other family members; less vocational and professional training and therefore restricted job opportunities and lowered probability of job advancement; less ability to direct the education of children.

Encapsulation of the Child in the Subculture

Whether children are deliberately planned for or accepted in any number as the natural outcome of marriage, they have significance for each subculture in terms of its values. The evidence is that married people in all subcultures want children, but the meaning and function of these children differ.

From upper-upper to lower-lower class the significance of children as elements of the subculture declines, and the attitude toward children as belonging simply to the nuclear family (or the mother) increases. The goals set for children are in agreement with subcultural values. At the highest level children must meet standards set by their ancestors. In the middle levels children must struggle to maintain the level of their parents through individual competition and success. A little lower, the child must uphold the respectability of the family. At the lowest level, where few positive goals are set, the child must avoid causing trouble for the family.

Methods of child care differ. From upper levels to lower there is a decrease in dependence on specialists and the use of counseling. Emotional aspects of training differ, with emotional appeals to the child most often made in the middle class where child rearing often is the mother's chief function in life. In the upper class, child rearing is shared with nursemaids, governesses, and private schools. In lower-class levels the employment of mothers causes them to depend on neighbors, relatives, and day nurseries for assistance in child care.

Methods of child care are related to the above social-class attributes. The upper-class child has close adult supervision mixed with recognized, protected outlets for aggression. In the middle ranges child training is a mixture of love and discipline, as the parent seeks to induce the child to internalize middle-class values, in the face of his knowledge of other class values. The middle-class child finds escapes from repression through subterfuges. In the lower ranges the methods of child training are direct and immediate with little regard for the internalization of values. The child's contacts go beyond the family to the community center, the tavern, and the street, where he mingles with many types of people and has a choice of values, some beneficial, some detrimental.

In general, child training perpetuates the subculture of the parents, but in each subculture nonfamily factors exist that pull some children away from strict inclusion in the subculture.

SOCIAL MOBILITY

In the United States, more than in most other cultures, the social organization provides not only for stable social classes and permits the existence of other types of subcultures, but also provides for transition from one subculture to another and from class to class, although not with equal ease and approval throughout the possible range of possible types of transition.

Transition may be horizontal, from one ethnic subculture to another or from an ethnic subculture into the main stream of Anglo-American culture at the same status level. Transition may also be vertical, from one social class to another. According to abstract principles, our open class system operates equally in all parts of the social system. Actually, there is inequality based on such factors as the degree of acceptability of a mobile group by the group into which it is moving; the class position of the parents of the upwardly mobile members; the education of the mobile persons; and certain personal qualities.

Most mobility is from ethnic to Anglo-American and from lower to higher levels.

These two directions of movement tend to improve both the social and economic advantages of the mobile persons or families. Downward mobility or enforced exclusion from Anglo-American culture are resisted.

Degree and Direction of Vertical Mobility

Various studies show that in normal economic periods large proportions of people are upwardly mobile, small proportions are downwardly mobile, and the majority remain in the same class position from one generation to another. In a study of stability and vertical mobility from childhood to adulthood in the small city of Jonesville, McGuire (1950) computed the amount of mobility in a sample from each social class. In the upper classes, all persons in his sample were stable. They could not move up and none had moved down. In the upper-middle class 88 per cent were stable, 6 per cent were upwardly mobile, and 6 per cent downwardly mobile. In the lower-middle class, 73 per cent were stable, 21 per cent upwardly mobile, and 6 per cent downwardly mobile. The upper-lower class had 68 per cent of members who were stable, 26 per cent upwardly mobile, and 6 per cent downwardly mobile. The lower-lower class, unable to sink lower, had 75 per cent of members who were stable and 25 per cent who were upwardly mobile. For Jonesville, and by estimate for the total population, McGuire placed upward mobility at about 25 per cent and downward mobility at about 5 per cent for each generation.

Upward mobility is a slow process for all except an exceptional few. The study of New Haven by Hollingshead and Redlich (1958), covering only the three lowest classes, showed that 50 per cent of lower-middle-class people were descendants of the "old immigration" from western and northern Europe that arrived in the United States two or three generations ago, with the first class placement usually in the lower class. A third of the upper-lower class had moved up from the lower-lower class where they started life, some families having required several generations to accomplish the move.

"Rags to riches" mobility is rare. A study (Warner & Abegglen, 1955a) of the origins of 8,300 chief executives of the largest firms in certain businesses and industries in the United States showed that 63 per cent were the sons of owners or major executives of large businesses, the sons of owners of small businesses, or the sons of professional men. These executives had made no, or only moderate, change in social-class position. From lower business levels (approximately lower-middle class) came 11 per cent. Farmers' sons constituted 9 per cent and laborers' sons 15 per cent.

A similar study (Newcomer, 1955) of the presidents and board chairmen of 1,262 large corporations confirms the findings that few top-level business men come from lower-class levels. The parental families of 36 per cent of these business men were wealthy, 52 per cent had "middle" incomes, and only 12 per cent were poor.

The middle-class boy, intent on reaching the top, has a shorter distance to climb and better equipment than the lower-class boy. College education is a commonly accepted goal for middle-class boys; in the upper-middle class, many parents are college-educated. Boys accept the goal of college education as a normal part of growing up. Their fathers also are in businesses or professions that may provide openings for their sons or serve as stepping stones for the sons to reach occupations of greater prestige and income. Studies (Warner & Abegglen, 1955b) show that the quickest climb to the top in business comes to the man who has both family influence and education, but that the lower-class boy with education and advantageous personal qualities also may reach the top, though more slowly. A comparison of 1952 with 1928 shows that direct family influence has tended to decline and education to gain in importance as factors in upward mobility in business. Lipset and Bendix (1959) concluded that only college education will enable the sons of manual workers to enter the labor market in a middle-class occupation. Otherwise they lack knowledge, have vague plans, and take the first available job, usually in manual labor. Newcomer's study (1955) showed that the chance of becoming a big business executive is almost completely absent for the foreign-born person. Only a few people have been able to overcome the handicap of a foreign background.

Rural and small-town boys are variously handicapped, according to Lipset and Bendix (1959). Few highly successful business men are sons of farmers. The process of upward mobility covers several generations, beginning with a movement from farm to city, with only 41 per cent of this generation achieving nonmanual positions, usually at a low level. Small-town boys have a slightly better record of upward mobility. Boys born in the city have a better opportunity for education and for knowledge of occupational openings. They can also more easily escape from the tight family control that may keep the boy in the rural area or small town in his parents' social class.

These studies clearly show that vertical mobility is both upward and downward, with upward mobility exceeding downward in normal times. The average degree of mobility in any one generation is slight. "Rags to riches" stories are notable only because they are so rare.

Primary and Secondary Aspects of Upward Mobility

Janowitz (1956) has called attention to the different effects of upward mobility on secondary and primary groups. Upwardly mobile people may be successfully integrated into secondary groups, such as large-scale businesses or community organizations, at the same time that their primary groups are disrupted. As a consequence they suffer certain psychological tensions and deprivations. This discussion is concerned chiefly with the primary group known as the family, and its relation to mobility.

Mobility involves two general processes:

acculturation into the new subculture and personal acceptance into the primary groups of the new subculture. Acculturation often is carried on in secondary groups to which the upwardly mobile person is admitted. Such contacts are more easily established than the personal contacts in informal cliques, social events in a person's home, or (the final act of successful mobility) marriage into the higher social level.

Mobility is a function either of the family or of an individual. In either case the immediate results for the family may be disruptive. If the family survives the process of adjustment and becomes an accepted unit of the new class, it reorganizes along the lines and with the ideals decreed by the new class.

In individual mobility, the family of procreation remains in the original subculture, whether social class or ethnic. Stated concretely, a son or daughter usually moves away from the parents and sometimes from siblings. Siblings who are mobile often move individually along different lines and at different paces.

"Going to is away from," according to Warner and Abegglen (1955a). Acculturation into the new subculture is only half the process; the other half is rejection of the subculture of earlier socialization. On the personal side, acceptance into the primary groups of the new subculture is linked to withdrawal from and at least partial rejection of the primary groups of the original subculture.

Relation of Parental Family to Upward Mobility

Various studies have brought out several very different types of relationship of the family of procreation to upward mobility of its members. The attitude that the parents take toward the future of their children is important. Studies of high-school students show a difference by social class in the mobility aspirations of boys, with the highest aspirations among boys whose parents are in the higher social classes. However, Barber (1957, pp. 309-311) reported from one study that 45 per cent of the children of the lowest social class aspired to high-level occupations. Lower-class boys usually do not carry through on the preparation that would be necessary to fulfill such aspirations. Unlike middle- and upper-class children, who take college preparatory courses, the lower-class boys elect industrial arts or a general curriculum and do not plan to attend college. Actual preparation for high-level occupations seems to depend not only on the expressed desires of high-school students or on the opportunities for higher education, but also on the attitude of the parents. Lower-class boys tend to develop a steady motivation for upward mobility and to prepare for it rationally when the parents set this as their goal. Since the parents themselves are not college-educated, the boys do not identify with the parents directly, but with the ambition of the parents for them. Attaining this goal requires withdrawal from the original subculture even in childhood, since the time spent in study or extra-curricular school activities leaves less time to spend with a free-roaming, pleasure-bent peer group.

Even when the parents do not set the goal for their children, lower-class boys may acquire such a goal from other adults, chiefly such middle-class people as an encouraging teacher or a leader in a settlement house or community center. One writer has termed boys who withdraw from their street-corner pals and follow an academic path "college boys" (W. F. Whyte, 1955), even though they have not yet entered college. In Whyte's study the motivation for college came from a teacher and leaders at a community center. Such identification with a nonfamily adult involves eventual withdrawal from peer groups and refusal to accept the limited expectations of their parents.

Another study (Douvan & Adelson, 1958) shows that upwardly mobile lower-class boys, although they retain a friendly relationship with their parents, do not have a strong personal identification with their fathers; they are thus free to choose a different pattern of life without the emotional strains of first breaking a strong identification with their fathers.

Still another study (Warner & Abegglen, 1955a) indicates that men who have reached a high position in business from a lower-level background have tended to have dominant mothers who taught them to be upwardly mobile rather than to emulate their weaker fathers. In adolescence or early adulthood such men may find a successful father-figure to emulate. Successful upward mobility demands, however, that they do not remain attached to this father-figure but later discard him for a more independent existence.

The contention that the mobile individual detaches himself from his parental family has been challenged by Litwak (1960) in a study of family contacts of stable and of mobile persons, among native-born, white, middle-class people. He found that the kinship web, typical of middle-class nuclear families, seemed to function regardless of upward mobility. He concluded that one factor in favor of maintenance of family contacts was the urban environment of his group (Buffalo) which made it possible for the upwardly mobile person to maintain family contacts separately from the secondary contacts involved in occupational upward mobility. He noted that middle-class parents often urge their children to prepare for upward mobility and look with admiration on those who succeed. This deference and admiration helps to offset the effects of possible rejection by the higher class into which the mobile person is moving. Also, parents of upwardly mobile children often aid them financially in maintaining a standard of living suitable to their new status.

Litwak's study does not refute the findings that upward mobility of the lower-class boy may create a schism in the parental family. The cultural difference between a middle-class family and the higher destination of the son is much less than the difference between the culture of the lower-class and perhaps ethnic parent and the same final destination.

Influence of the Wife in Upward Mobility

Disruption within the mobile family may occur if the husband moves upward at a faster pace than the wife. Higher education among lower-class people is more likely to be viewed as a means to occupational advance than as the opportunity for cultural and personal development. Higher education for the girl often is not regarded as necessary, since it is assumed that her husband will set the standard of living and make the income. The man in his youth may expect little more from a wife than that she be personally pleasing and equipped to become a good wife and mother. Only later does the importance of the wife's role become apparent as he moves from the lower to the higher levels of his occupation. Whether or not the wife of the upwardly mobile man can meet the requirements for being a gracious hostess and an effective community leader, as described earlier in this chapter, may be important in the advance of the husband and in his passage into the primary groups of the higher class.

The tendency among top business men to marry within their social class or into a higher class differs from one class of origin to another. According to the Warner and Abegglen study (1955b), successful men who were originally either upper or lower class tended to marry within their class or only slightly out of it. For the upper-class men, endogamous marriage solidified their position. For the lower-class men, it was a handicap. Middle-class men more often tended to marry above their own rank. Men whose fathers and grandfathers had also been upwardly mobile, as well as those with college educations, had a better chance to marry upward than men who were making the first break from a lower-class level or who lacked college education. The lower-class men, starting from bedrock, and lacking the full quota of higher education, were most likely to marry into their own class, and therefore less likely to receive aid in upward mobility from their marriages or later from their wives.

Several studies show that wives at all social levels help their husbands, but in different ways. Blood and Wolfe (1960) designated four ways in which Michigan wives helped their husbands get ahead. One way was collaborative, and applied only to families with small, self-owned businesses in which the wife as well as the husband worked. A second way was by employment of the wife in some other business; this was common among blue-collar workers, including Negro families, in which the wife worked to help her husband accumulate enough money to start a small business. A third way was termed supportive, and applied to the young, high-status house-wives who gave emotional support and encouragement to their husbands and entertained business associates and prospective customers. In this situation the role of wife was paramount to that of housewife; also, this wife was not gainfully employed. The fourth type referred to old and low-status couples, whose opportunities for getting ahead were slight. The wife fulfilled a housekeeper role for the husband's comfort. Referring to men who have advanced to top positions in business, Warner and Abegglen (1955a) identified the following roles of wives.

1. The wife-mother role, perhaps carried over from a lower social level. The husband usually forges ahead of his wife. If the wife can manage to keep pace with her husband, even though she does not change her role, the husband may enjoy relaxing in the home atmosphere that she creates.

2. The wife may be essentially a hostess to guests whose entertainment contributes to her husband's advancement. She is often active in community activities and usually fulfills the wife and mother role as a subordinate function.

3. A few wives participate directly in the husband's advance by discussing his problems with him. She may not fulfill roles 1 or 2.

4. The wife infrequently is a professional woman in her own right; this role may be of disservice to her husband in his advancement, since it prevents her from adopting the supportive hostess role that is expected in high status levels.

The most frequent and presumably most helpful role is number 2.

The role of the wife of the successfully upwardly mobile man runs counter to the movement that has been developing over some decades for the husband and wife to form a partnership, with the wife perhaps employed and in any case in an equalitarian role with reference to planning and decisions. The wife who is best able to help her husband in upward mobility apparently is not the equalitarian wife. Instead, she plays an adjustive role to her husband. His goals and needs take precedence over her own; her success and satisfaction come through helping him gain success, from which she benefits financially and in improved social status. One may argue that the husband and wife roles are complementary in nature and therefore that an equal partnership prevails; actually, the wife is less a partner with equal influence than a subordinate.

Speed of Mobility

All studies emphasize the slowness with which upward mobility usually takes place. It may easily be a three- or four-generation span of time from the starting point in lower or lower-middle class to the top echelons of business—and this position may not include full social participation in the upper class. Upward mobility progresses generation by generation through successively slightly better occupational positions, better education, and ability of the second- or third-generation man to marry into a slightly higher class level than the one into which he was born.

Strains increase with the speed of upward mobility. Adjustment into an adjacent class level, where the family stabilizes itself, is easier than adjustment over an intervening class or successive adjustments within a few years (Roth & Peck, 1961). At some class levels the speed of upward mobility has tended to increase over the years. At workingman- and lower-middle-class levels, increased income and buying power have created a pseudo-upward mobility. The family is able to buy the same brands and styles of goods as people in the class above them and often to move into neighborhoods occupied by the higher class. Using the term *nouveau bourgeoisie,* Bohlke (1961) discussed the situation of families that are lower class in origin but middle class in income. Although they move into middle-class neighborhoods, they cannot readily discard the lower-class beliefs, attitudes, and behavior patterns in which they were reared. They therefore experience "stratification inconsistency." Bohlke was especially concerned about delinquency among youth in this rapidly upwardly mobile group. He hypothesized that some middle-class delinquency is attributable to the marginal status of boys reared in lower-class values, but living in middle-class communities where another set of values is current. The youth and his family may be rejected by the middle class, a situation that creates intrafamily and interfamily stresses. Boys in this position may band together into a marginal peer group, whose behavior offends their middle-class peers. The misbehavior of the marginal group may increase, whereupon they may be further rejected.

Frazier (1957a; 1957b) has noted the difficulties of rapid upward mobility among Negroes. Through the advanced education that has been more readily available in recent years, lower-middle-class Negroes have gained business or professional positions in the Negro community and have demanded entrance to the older, stable upper- and middle-class Negro groups. Their behavior, however, lacks the older elements of thrift, industry, and strictly moral—even Puritanical—behavior. They pattern their behavior on a superficial knowledge of the flamboyant behavior of upwardly mobile whites and neglect the more disciplined ways of established Negroes and whites. The superficial behavior pattern is then passed on to their children.

A slow rate of upward mobility permits the family to become acculturated into the higher-class subculture slowly while income is also slowly increased. The affluence since World War II has made possible financial without cultural upward mobility.

Intrafamily Results of Upward Mobility

Intrafamily tensions arise not only when the wife is unable to play a supportive role, but when the husband fails to meet the expectations that his upward mobility has created in his wife and children. The income and standard of living may exceed those of earlier years, but inability to reach an aspired height may be defined as failure on the part of the husband (Winch, 1952). Since the husband's status sets the status for the entire family, he is in an extremely vulnerable position. If a man lacks self-confidence, he may be unable to withstand the pressures and feeling of failure and retrogress to his earlier, or even a lower, status (Warner & Abegglen, 1955a).

The relation between the upwardly mobile business man and his sons may not be a happy one. He seems to have little time for personal contacts with his sons, although he provides education and other advantages made possible by his income and position (Warner & Abegglen, 1955a). Sons may feel a pressure to equal or exceed their fathers. If they fear they cannot do this, they may sidestep the problem by entering a profession instead of business, or some other less demanding type of work (Kahl, 1957).

Another study (LeMasters, 1954) pertains to moderate upward mobility displayed by college students and the resulting discontinuity of social-class positions between parents and children. In a limited sample from one college, 65 per cent of students were upwardly mobile. In about 10 per cent of the cases the entire family was upwardly mobile; in the remainder, the child or several children were mobile, with the parents remaining in a stationary position. In these families, a gulf developed between parents and children, sometimes with reduced communication or feelings of guilt on the part of the upwardly mobile student. In other cases parents attempted to keep pace with the students, perhaps reading their textbooks. Correspondence and frequent visits also helped to prevent disintegration of the family unity.

Downward Mobility

Downward mobility is most widespread during an economic depression. On a local basis, the closing of a large industry in a one-industry town may create extensive downward mobility in that community. Individual downward mobility may accompany chronic alcoholism of a family member, especially the husband. Other individual causes are failure of a man to hold a personally achieved status, or failure of either a man or woman to meet expectations of the parental family, perhaps in moral behavior. Many people experience downward mobility in old age, especially when income declines. The effect of each type of downward mobility on the family varies according to the social class in which it occurs. [In addition to the material of this section, see Hansen and Hill's discussion of stressful situations for the family, Ch. 19 of this Handbook, especially pp. 806–810.]

The economic depression of the 1930's. In 1933, at the depth of the great depression, approximately a third of the normally gainfully employed persons were unemployed (Leiserson, 1939). The Yankee City study (Warner & Lunt, 1941) showed widespread differentiation among social classes of full- and part-time unemployment, from 6 per cent in the upper classes to 72 per cent in the lower-lower class.

Unemployment is not synonymous with downward mobility. Lowered income may cause curtailment of luxuries and even some comforts without disturbing intrafamily relationships or the social status of the family. Sources other than earned income as well as the degree of firmness of social-class position are stabilizing factors. The effect of prolonged unemployment on families of different social classes has been summarized by Cavan (1959) in an article based on a number of studies.

The upper class in general suffered least disturbance, and most upper-middle-class families were required to make only slight readjustments (Morgan, 1938). However, severe loss of income in the upper-middle class wrought serious damage on some families. An analysis (Angell, 1936) of such families that had suffered a decrease of at least 25 per cent showed that the greatest damage was not to social-class placement but to intrafamily relations. The families studied did not lose their homes or have to apply for relief. Husbands lost status within their families, since they were no longer able to carry out their roles as chief or sole wage-earner. The greatest damage was done when roles were reversed, and some other member of the family, often the wife, became the chief wage-earner. The family structure was often disrupted, and the husband became personally disorganized. However, the disruptive effects were not uniformly experienced by all the families studied. The predepression organization and characteristics of the family were also important. Well-integrated, adaptable families made the best adjustment to changes in roles. Adaptability increased with a non-materialistic philosophy of life, freedom from traditionalism, and responsibleness of the parents.

The lower-middle and upper-lower class (the working class or common man) tended to suffer from lowered social status when unemployment was long continued (Bakke,

1940a; Bakke, 1940b; Cavan & Ranck, 1936; Komarovsky, 1940). Families that were upwardly mobile and had succeeded in "getting ahead" were especially hard hit. With few savings and heavy mortgages on their homes, they were soon destitute, compelled to move into less desirable neighborhoods, and eventually forced to apply for relief. In a marginal position between the class they had left and the one toward which they were moving, the material symbols of house, car, telephone, club memberships, and clothing were of great importance. Loss of these symbols was proof of downward mobility.

Within the working-class families, men had previously prided themselves on being able to provide support. Their admission of loss of this ability came slowly. Men at first regarded unemployment as temporary or as providing a needed vacation. When they were not recalled to their former jobs, they sought the same type of work, then less specialized types of work, and finally any type, including odd jobs. The final step in their sense of personal failure came with application for relief.

Employment by other members of the family eased the financial strain but emphasized the lowered status of the husband. If he had no work at all, he often had no role to play. Some men became personally disorganized, had "nervous breakdowns," or sought comfort in drunkenness. The period of greatest tension seemed to be just prior to applying for relief, considered a proof of failure in the 1930's when each family was expected to support itself. Wives shared their husbands' feeling of degradation.

For some families the period of unemployment and relief status was short, and the family was able to readjust to its old pattern. For others, however, a long period of downward mobility began. Emotional disturbances tended to continue until the family reached a level of stability, however low. When the family was able to accept this level as probably permanent, reorganization began. Often the husband did not regain his former personal status but was forced to yield to a different hierarchy of roles within the family. The wife, especially if she became the chief wage-earner, was accorded the higher status with higher authority than that of her husband. Old plans for the education and future of children were abandoned, and new realistic ones were developed. If the various family members were able to accept the new roles and integrate them with each other, the family again became a cohesive unit. Readjustment was complete when the family stopped comparing its current situation with the better times of the past, rationalized its decreased status, and accepted the new way of life as normal and beneficial. Children in the family might then renew the movement toward upward mobility.

Unemployment and downward mobility did not often destroy the family. Disintegration was most likely to occur among families already poorly organized; cohesive families remained together in spite of tensions (Cavan & Ranck, 1936). The status of the husband was best maintained in families in which the authority of the husband was based on love and respect or on the traditional semipatriarchal organization of the working-class family (Komarovsky, 1940). When the authority of the husband rested on fear or on utilitarian services, loss of employment tended to be followed by collapse of the husband's position.

Lower-lower-class families suffered less from the depression than did the working-class families (Cavan & Ranck, 1936). Accustomed to being on and off relief in prosperous times as well as during depressions, they had little to lose from prolonged unemployment. Relief payments did not greatly lower their esteem or their standard of living. In some cases the regular relationship with the relief agency and the case worker brought added security and direction to the family.

Individual downward mobility. Downward mobility of an individual occurs when he is unable to meet the expectations of either his subculture or his family or both, a common situation, since the two sets of standards are closely entwined. Types of deviation are violations of the moral code of the subculture or family, disapproved criminal behavior, and chronic alcoholism. These and similar types of overt behavior result from less obvious sociological or psychological factors whose origin lies somewhere in the past experiences of the individual. The overt deviation and the underlying problem develop a cyclical relationship: maladjustment leads to overt deviation, which in turn contributes to further maladjustment, and so on. During the depression of the 1930's, a not uncommon situation was found when the man who lost his job began to drink steadily; he thus lowered his chances of employment; this failure led to more drinking, which contributed to increased unemployability.

These cyclical trends lower the individual's social-class status as he becomes less and less able to meet the expectations of his class. Even in the lower class the downward spiral takes place. The origin of the majority of a group of police-case inebriates studied by Pittman and Gordon (1958) was lower class; they were nevertheless alienated from their families and debased to a status below that of the lower-lower class.

Different subcultures react differently to their downwardly mobile individuals. The higher social classes often seek to protect their deviating members, not for their sakes alone but to protect the class from social disgrace. A companion may be provided for a troublesome person by his family or he may be semi-institutionalized—if young, in certain types of private schools; if older, in a sanitarium or nursing home. If he is sufficiently deviant in behavior, he is disowned and disinherited. He may be placed on an allowance and encouraged to move to another part of the country or abroad.

Farther down the social scale, the downwardly mobile member of a family may be rejected. The family may disclaim relationship with him, discourage visiting, or cut off all contacts. Another pattern is to retain him within the family circle and try to rehabilitate him.

Intrafamily relationships are severely strained by a deviating individual. A study (Jackson, 1958) of alcoholism of the husband shows that at first the family tries to conceal the problem from friends and neighbors. As the alcoholism continues, with unemployment and impoverishment, concealment becomes increasingly difficult. The husband may begin to desert the family periodically; he may be arrested and imprisoned for public misconduct; he may become guilty of infidelity to his wife. As the situation becomes known, the family is forced to appeal to various types of social agencies and further concealment is impossible. The family members tend to lose their original sense of shame and guilt and seek rationalizations to explain the alcoholism. Subsequent steps somewhat resemble those that accompany downward mobility because of economic depression. Roles are reassigned to place responsibility and authority in the hands of the wife. Especially if the husband leaves home, the family circle closes to exclude him. The wife and children accept the husband's alcoholism as chronic and begin to establish new family plans that are realistic in terms of their new condition and status. If the husband becomes cured and returns home, further adjustment of roles is necessary to include him again in the family circle as a functioning member.

Social Mobility, the Class Structure, and the Family

In a culture with a philosophy of an open class system and a fluctuating economy, individuals and families move up and down the social-class scale. The movement serves the purpose of keeping a realistic relationship between the social structure and the economic position of individuals and families. The adjustment between the new economic position and the subculture comes more slowly than that between the social structure and economic position. The old subculture clings to people as they move into new economic positions, either up or down. Perhaps for years they remain in a marginal position before they acquire the subtleties of the new subculture and are accepted into full personal participation. In the interim, intrafamilial relationships may be strained, both within the mobile family and between it and the parental family still on the lower or upper level. During any period of rapid change, these primary-group disturbances must be accepted as normal.

CONCLUSION

The social and cultural organization of the United States has been presented as a complex of subcultures held together in part by certain commonly accepted elements, and in part by the place that each plays in the total organization. The subcultures are distinctive in many ways but are functionally interdependent. The cultural complex breaks down into several types of subcultures. A massive social-class system is occupied by Caucasians, and several smaller parallel systems are occupied by various numerically small, nonwhite racial groups. The social organization is further complicated by the splintering of the social classes, especially at the lower levels, into numerous ethnic-religious groups. Since these various types of subculture overlap, each family has a position in a social class, an ethnic-religious group, and a race. The three are closely intertwined in the family's pattern of living.

The family is a strong, conservative repository of its several interrelated subcultures. An important function of the family is to pass on to children the subculture of the parents. Since the parents have been reared in the subculture, they tend to accept its sacred connotations. Therefore to the best of their ability they pass on to their children not only overt behavior patterns

but also the deepest values. The transmission of the subculture plays two functions: it fits the child for present and future life in the subculture, and it stabilizes the social organization.

Too great a measure of success on the part of parents in insulating their children in the family's subculture, however, is dysfunctional for both the child and the society. In order for the society to have unity, avenues of communication exist through public schools, community contacts, and many forms of mass media. The family that attempts to pass on the subculture in complete traditional form works against the pull of these many secondary integrating forces that facilitate acculturation and in some situations social assimilation. The child is the family member who is most likely to pass from one subculture into another. Training for his parents' subculture often unfits him for his eventual emergence into another subculture.

Two forces then operate against each other, those that conserve and transmit the subculture, and those that encourage mobility from one subculture to another. Most families are subjected to both pulls. Some families respond most strongly to one set of forces and remain within their subculture from one generation to another with little change; other families are caught up in the processes of mobility, either horizontally from an ethnic group into the Anglo-American subculture, or vertically from one social class to another.

The conserving forces are lodged in the subcultural definitions of the family, marriage, and children; in the roles of family members that correspond to their functions in the subculture; and in the training of children into specific values and behavior patterns, by methods that fit the children into the subculture. Emphasis by some subcultures on endogamous marriages is a measure for conserving the subculture.

The forces for mobility are usually based outside the family, in education, occupational opportunities, and the selective use of income. The family reacts strongly to these forces. It may resist them or it may make use of them for its own mobility or that of its children. If the parents resist, parents and children may be torn apart. If the entire family enters into mobility, it is subject to strains created by differences between the original subculture and the new subculture into which it is entering. A slow speed of mobility for limited numbers of the population at any one time maintains a social balance and permits the mobile persons to acquire the new culture and be assimilated into new groups.

SUGGESTED RESEARCH

When W. Lloyd Warner and his associates began to publish their studies of social class in the early 1940's, interest in social classes, ethnic and racial groups, and mobility was greatly stimulated. Research in the general field caught the imagination of many people in the social sciences, from the candidate for a master's degree to the mature specialist who could launch a massive research program whose execution covered years of work. Since the field was virtually untouched and there was little coordination among researchers, the result has been a flow of articles and books, revealing in themselves but leaving large gaps and sometimes duplicating each other without fruitful cooperation. Many of the suggestions listed below arise from this basic situation.

1. More complete integration of research is needed. Each discipline that undertakes research has its own philosophy of motivations of behavior, whether economic, sociological, or psychological. These philosophies help to shape the objectives of the research and the methods employed. Many techniques have been used, but rarely in connection with each other. Some commonly used techniques are objective indices of status, participant or objective observation, surveys and interviews, and psychological and psychiatric analyses. Focusing all these philosophies and techniques on one research

project should widen understanding of the problem involved and also clear up some of the controversies that seem to have arisen from the use of different methods; for example, stratification versus social class, or sociological patterns of conduct versus individual psychological traits as the explanation for subcultural differences.

2. More attention needs to be paid to the overlapping of different subcultures. Almost the only subculture that approaches uniformity of race, ethnic background, religion, and social-class status is the upper-upper class. Certainly from the lower-middle class downward, any study of social class should take into account differences in race, ethnicity, and religion.

3. Comparative studies of social classes, for example, upper-middle and upper-lower, should be limited to persons of the same race and ethnic-religious affiliation, thus controlling these variables.

4. Studies should differentiate between the commonly accepted cultural values and those that have a subcultural aspect. It seems probable that some of the failure to find sharp differentiation between family roles and methods of child rearing between classes is because common elements that run through all subcultures have not been identified and eliminated, thereby leaving true class differences.

5. Useful studies might be made contrasting the place of the family in cohesive conservative subcultures, such as the Orthodox Jews, the Polish Catholics, or the Mormons, and in unaffiliated groups, such as the unchurched or freethinkers, keeping the social-class placement constant.

6. Most studies emphasize majority situations, for instance, upward mobility, endogamous marriages, or the success of the middle-class boy. More attention needs to be given to the conditions under which the minor situations occur or exist. What has been the function of the family in downward mobility? In exogamous marriage? In the upward mobility of the poor boy?

7. Very little is known by firsthand re-

search about the upper-upper-class family and its methods of child rearing. More is known about their occupational and public status, but a curtain of concealment envelops their primary groups. This should be studied.

8. With the exception of the Gluecks' (1959) study of prediction of delinquent behavior according to family characteristics, little has been done to attempt to predict the future outcome of different methods of child rearing in different subcultures by following up individual cases to determine whether predicted outcomes actually occurred. Did the middle-class boys for whom Green predicted neuroses actually become more neurotic in number and severity than lower-class boys?

9. At present the trend of research seems to have concentrated on public aspects of social class. Other types of subcultures and the functioning of the family in all of them, including social class, are attracting less research than their importance merits.

REFERENCES

Amory, C. The proper Bostonians. New York: Dutton, 1947.

Angell, R. C. The family encounters the depression. New York: Scribner, 1936.

Bakke, E. W. Citizens without work. New Haven: Yale Univer. Press, 1940. (a)

Bakke, E. W. The unemployed worker. New Haven: Yale Univer. Press, 1940. (b)

Baltzell, E. D. Philadelphia gentlemen, the making of a national upper class. Glencoe, Ill.: Free Press, 1958.

Barber, B. Social stratification: a comparative analysis of structure and process. New York: Harcourt, Brace, 1957.

Barron, M. L. The incidence of Jewish intermarriage in Europe and America. Amer. J. Sociol., 1946, 11, 6–13.

Bledsoe, J. C. An investigation of six correlates of student withdrawal from high school. J. educ. Res., 1959, 53, 3–6.

Blood, R. O., & Wolfe, D. M. Husbands and wives, the dynamics of married living. Glencoe, Ill.: Free Press, 1960.

Boek, W. E., Sussman, M. B., & Yankauer, A. Social class and child care practices. Marr. & fam. Living, 1958, 20, 326–333.

Bohlke, R. H. Social mobility, stratification inconsistency and middle class delinquency. Soc. Probl., 1961, 8, 351–363.

Bossard, J. H. S., & Boll, Eleanor S. One marriage, two faiths. New York: Ronald Press, 1957.

Bossard, J. H. S., & Letts, H. C. Mixed marriages involving Lutherans. Marr. & fam. Living, 1956, 18, 308–310.

Burma, J. H. Research note on the measurement of interracial marriage. Amer. J. Sociol., 1952, 57, 587–589.

Campisi, P. J. Ethnic family patterns: the Italian family in the United States. Amer. J. Sociol., 1948, 53, 443–449.

Cavan, Ruth S. Unemployment, the crisis of the common man. Marr. & fam. Living, 1959, 21, 139–146.

Cavan, Ruth S. Juvenile delinquency. Philadelphia: Lippincott, 1962.

Cavan, Ruth S., & Ranck, Katherine H. The family and the depression. Chicago: Univer. of Chicago Press, 1936.

Centers, R. Psychology of social classes, a study of class consciousness. Princeton: Princeton Univer. Press, 1949.

Central Conference of American Rabbis. Yearbook, 1909, 19, 170, 174–184.

Cox, O. C. Caste, class and race: a study in social dynamics. Garden City, N.Y.: Doubleday, 1948.

Cramer, M. W. Leisure time activities of economically privileged children. Sociol. & soc. Res., 1949–1950, 34, 444–450.

Cuber, J. F., & Kenkel, W. F. Social stratification in the United States. New York: Appleton-Century-Crofts, 1954.

Davie, J. S. Social class factors and school attendance. Harvard educ. Rev., 1953, 23 (3), 175–185.

Davis, A. Social class influences upon learning. Cambridge: Harvard Univer. Press, 1948.

Davis, A., & Dollard, J. Children of bondage. Washington, D.C.: American Council on Education, 1940.

Davis, A., Gardner, B. B., & Gardner, Mary R. Deep south. Chicago: Univer. of Chicago Press, 1941.

Davis, A., & Havighurst, R. J. Social class and color differences in child-rearing. Amer. sociol. Rev., 1946, 11, 698–710.

Douvan, Elizabeth, & Adelson, J. The psychodynamics of social mobility in adolescent boys. *J. abnorm. soc. Psychol.*, 1958, 56, 31–44.

Drake, St. C., & Cayton, H. R. *Black metropolis, a study of Negro life in a northern city.* New York: Harcourt, Brace, 1945.

Ehrmann, W. W. Influence of comparative social class of companion upon premarital heterosexual behavior. *Marr. & fam. Living,* 1955, 17, 48–53.

Ehrmann, W. W. *Premarital dating behavior.* New York: Holt, 1959.

Ellis, R. A. Social stratification and social relations: an empirical test of the disjunctiveness of social classes. *Amer. sociol. Rev.,* 1957, 22, 570–578.

Fairchild, H. P. (Ed.) *Dictionary of sociology.* Ames, Iowa: Littlefield, Adams, 1955.

Frazier, E. F. *Negro family in the United States.* Chicago: Univer. of Chicago Press, 1939.

Frazier, E. F. *Black bourgeoisie, the rise of a new middle class in the United States.* Glencoe, Ill.: Free Press, 1957. (a)

Frazier, E. F. The Negro middle class and desegregation. *Soc. Probl.,* 1957, 4, 291–302. (b)

Freedman, R., Whelpton, P. K., & Campbell, A. A. *Family planning, sterility and population growth.* New York: McGraw-Hill, 1959.

Freilich, M. Serial polygyny, Negro peasants, and model analysis. *Amer. Anthropologist,* 1961, 63 (Part I), 955–975.

Glaser, D. Dynamics of ethnic identification. *Amer. sociol. Rev.,* 1958, 23, 31–40.

Glick, P. C., & Carter, H. Marriage patterns and educational level. *Amer. sociol. Rev.,* 1958, 23, 294–300.

Glueck, S., & Glueck, Eleanor. *Predicting delinquency and crime.* Cambridge: Harvard Univer. Press, 1959.

Golden, J. Patterns of Negro-white intermarriage. *Amer. sociol. Rev.,* 1954, 19, 144–147.

Goode, W. J. *After divorce.* Glencoe, Ill.: Free Press, 1956.

Gordon, M. M. *Social class in American society.* Durham, N.C.: Duke Univer. Press, 1958.

Green, A. W. Middle-class male child and neurosis. *Amer. sociol. Rev.,* 1946, 11, 31–41.

Haer, J. L. Predictive utility of five indices of social stratification. *Amer. sociol. Rev.,* 1957, 22, 541–546.

Havighurst, R. J., & Davis, A. A comparison of the Chicago and Harvard studies of social class differences in child rearing. *Amer. sociol. Rev.,* 1955, 20, 438–442.

Heer, D. M. Dominance and the working wife. *Soc. Forces,* 1958, 36, 341–347.

Helfrich, Margaret L. The generalized role of the executive's wife. *Marr. & fam. Living,* 1961, 23, 384–387.

Hollingshead, A. B. *Elmtown's youth: the impact of social classes on adolescents.* New York: Wiley, 1949.

Hollingshead, A. B. Cultural factors in the selection of marriage mates. *Amer. sociol. Rev.,* 1950, 15, 619–627.

Hollingshead, A. B., & Redlich, F. C. *Social class and mental illness.* New York: Wiley, 1958.

Humphrey, N. D. The changing structure of the Detroit Mexican family: an index of acculturation. *Amer. sociol. Rev.,* 1944, 9, 622–626.

Hyman, H. H. The value systems of different classes: a social psychological contribution to the analysis of stratification. In R. Bendix & S. M. Lipset (Eds.), *Class, status and power.* Glencoe, Ill.: Free Press, 1953. Pp. 426–442.

Jackson, Joan K. Alcoholism and the family. *Annals Amer. Acad. pol. & soc. Sci.,* 1958, 315, 90–98.

Janowitz, M. Some consequences of social mobility in the United States. *Trans. 3rd World Congr. Sociol.* Vol. 3. London: International Sociological Association, 1956. Pp. 191–201. Also Reprint 135, Indianapolis: Bobbs-Merrill.

Jones, R. C. Ethnic family patterns: the Mexican family in the United States. *Amer. J. Sociol.,* 1948, 53, 450–451.

Kahl, J. A. *American class structure.* New York: Rinehart, 1957.

Kennedy, Ruby J. R. Single or triple melting pot? Intermarriage trends in New Haven, 1870–1940. *Amer. J. Sociol.,* 1944, 49, 331–339.

Kephart, W. M. Occupational level and marital disruption. *Amer. sociol. Rev.,* 1955, 20, 456–465.

Klineberg, O. (Ed.) *Characteristics of the American Negro.* New York: Harper, 1944.

Kohn, M. L. Social class and the exercise of parental authority. *Amer. sociol. Rev.,* 1959, 24, 352–366.

Komarovsky, Mirra. *The unemployed man and his family.* New York: Dryden Press, 1940.

Landecker, W. S. Class boundaries. *Amer. sociol. Rev.,* 1960, 25, 868–877.

Lantz, H. R. *People of Coal Town.* New York: Columbia Univer. Press, 1958.

Lee, S. C. China's traditional family, its characteristics and disintegration. *Amer. sociol. Rev.,* 1953, 18, 272–280.

Leiserson, W. M. A balance sheet of benefits. *Survey Graphic,* 1939, 28, 214–218ff.

LeMasters, E. E. Social class mobility and family integration. *Marr. & fam. Living,* 1954, 16, 226–232.

Lenski, G. E. American social classes: statistical strata or social groups. *Amer. J. Sociol.,* 1952, 58, 139–144.

Lipset, S. M., & Bendix, R. *Social mobility in industrial society.* Berkeley: Univer. of California Press, 1959.

Littman, R. A., Moore, R. C. A., & Pierce-Jones, J. Social class differences in child rearing: a third community for comparison with Chicago and Newton. *Amer. sociol. Rev.,* 1957, 22, 694–704.

Litwak, E. Occupational mobility and family cohesion. *Amer. sociol. Rev.,* 1960, 25, 9–21.

Maccoby, Eleanor E., & Gibbs, Patricia K. Methods of child rearing in two social classes. In W. E. Martin and Celia B. Stendler (Eds.), *Readings in child development.* New York: Harcourt, Brace, 1954. Pp. 380–396.

McGuire, C. Social stratification and mobility patterns. *Amer. sociol. Rev.,* 1950, 15, 195–204.

McGuire, C. Family life in lower and middle class homes. *Marr. & fam. Living,* 1952, 14, 1–6.

Marcson, S. A theory of intermarriage and assimilation. *Soc. Forces,* 1950, 29, 75–78.

Miller, W. B. Lower class culture as a generating milieu of gang delinquency. *J. soc. Issues,* 1958, 14 (3), 5–19.

Miller, W. B. Implications of urban lower-class culture for social work. *Soc. serv. Rev.,* 1959, 33, 219–236.

Monahan, T. P. Divorce by occupational level. *Marr. & fam. Living,* 1955, 17, 322–324.

Morgan, Winona L. *The family meets the depression.* Minneapolis: Univer. of Minnesota Press, 1938.

Newcomer, Mabel. *The big business executive: the factors that made him, 1900–1950.* New York: Columbia Univer. Press, 1955.

Olsen, M. E. Distribution of family responsibilities and social stratification. *Marr. & fam. Living,* 1960, 22, 60–65.

Opler, M. K. The influence of ethnics and class subcultures on child care. *Soc. Probl.,* 1955, 3, 12–21.

Parsons, T. A revised analytical approach to the theory of social stratification. In R. Bendix & S. M. Lipset (Eds.), *Class, status and power.* Glencoe, Ill.: Free Press, 1953. Pp. 92–128.

Pittman, D. J., & Gordon, C. W. *Revolving door, a study of the chronic police case inebriate.* Glencoe, Ill.: Free Press, 1958.

Rainwater, L., Coleman, R. P., & Handel, G. *Workingman's wife.* New York: Oceana Publications, 1959.

Rainwater, L., & Weinstein, Karol K. *And the poor get children.* Chicago: Quadrangle Books, 1960. (a)

Rainwater, L., & Weinstein, Karol K. A qualitative exploration of family planning and contraception in the working class. *Marr. & fam. Living,* 1960, 22, 238–242. (b)

Reiss, I. L. *Premarital sexual standards in America.* Glencoe, Ill.: Free Press, 1960.

Roosevelt, Eleanor. *This is my story.* Garden City, N.Y.: Garden City, 1939.

Roth, J., & Peck, R. F. Social class and social mobility factors related to marital adjustment. *Amer. sociol. Rev.,* 1961, 16, 478–487.

Schmid, C. F. Generalizations concerning the ecology of the American city. *Amer. sociol. Rev.,* 1950, 15, 264–281.

Schroeder, C. W. *Divorce in a city of 100,000 population.* Peoria, Ill.: Bradley Polytechnic Institute Library, 1939.

Sears, R. R., Maccoby, Eleanor E., & Levin, H. *Patterns of child rearing.* Evanston, Ill.: Row, Peterson, 1957.

Sewell, W. H., & Haller, A. O. Social status and the personality adjustment of the child. *Sociometry,* 1956, 9, 114–125.

Sewell, W. H., & Haller, A. O. Factors in the relationship between social status and the personality adjustment of the child. *Amer. sociol. Rev.,* 1959, 24, 511–520.

Shaw, C. R., & McKay, H. *Juvenile delinquency and urban areas.* Chicago: Univer. of Chicago Press, 1942.

Sorokin, P. A. What is a social class? In R. Bendix & S. M. Lipset (Eds.), *Class, status and power.* Glencoe, Ill.: Free Press, 1953. Pp. 87–92.

Statistical Abstract of the United States, 1962. Washington, D.C.: U.S. Government Printing Office, 1962.

Sussman, M. B. The help pattern in the middle class family. *Amer. sociol. Rev.,* 1953, 18, 22–28. (a)

Sussman, M. B. Parental participation in mate selection and its effect upon family continuity. *Soc. Forces,* 1953, 32, 76–81. (b)

Sussman, M. B. The isolated nuclear family: fact or fiction. *Soc. Probl.,* 1959, 6, 333–340.

Sussman, M. B., & Burchinal, L. Kin family network: unheralded structure in current conceptualizations of family functioning. *Marr. & fam. Living,* 1962, 24, 231–240.

Thomas, J. L. The factor of religion in the selection of marriage mates. *Amer. sociol. Rev.,* 1951, 16, 487–491.

U.S. Census of Population, 1960. *United States summary, general population characteristics.* Washington, D.C.: U.S. Government Printing Office, 1961.

Warner, W. L. *Democracy in Jonesville.* New York: Harper, 1949.

Warner, W. L., & Abegglen, J. C. *Big business leaders in America.* New York: Harper, 1955. (a)

Warner, W. L., & Abegglen, J. C. *Occupational mobility in American business and industry, 1928–1952.* Minneapolis: Univer. of Minnesota Press, 1955. (b)

Warner, W. L., & Lunt, P. S. *Social life of a modern community.* New Haven: Yale Univer. Press, 1941.

Warner, W. L., Meeker, Marchia, & Eells, K. *Social class in America.* Chicago: Science Research Associates, 1949.

West, J. *Plainville, U.S.A.* New York: Columbia Univer. Press, 1945.

White, Martha S. Social class, child rearing practices, and child behavior. *Amer. sociol. Rev.,* 1957, 22, 704–712.

Whyte, W. F. *Street corner society, the social structure of an Italian slum.* (2nd ed.) Chicago: Univer. of Chicago Press, 1955.

Whyte, W. H., Jr. *Is anybody listening?* New York: Simon & Schuster, 1948.

Whyte, W. H., Jr. Corporation and the wife. *Fortune,* 1951, 44, 109–111. (a)

Whyte, W. H., Jr. Wives of management. *Fortune,* 1951, 44, 86–88. (b)

Winch, R. F. *The modern family.* New York: Holt, 1952.

Women's Bureau, U.S. Department of Labor. *1960 handbook on women workers.* Women's Bureau Bull., No. 275. Washington, D.C.: U.S. Government Printing Office, 1960.

PART IV Member Roles and Internal Processes

CHAPTER 15 Marital and Nonmarital Sexual Behavior[1]

WINSTON EHRMANN
American Association of University Professors

This presentation is to focus upon the social significance of sexual behavior, particularly heterosexual behavior, in our own society. The primary and most pervasive sexual interest of our society, as well as of virtually all societies, has been with heterosexual behavior, both marital and nonmarital. The social regulation of sexual relations between the sexes has been by prescriptions and proscriptions which have taken into consideration the erotic and reproductive interests of males and females. The actual patterns of sexual behavior that exist at any time also reflect the degree to which the traditional mores are obeyed or violated.

TERMINOLOGICAL DISTINCTIONS

The term *sexual* as used here includes overt acts, individual attitudes, and social values. *Sexual* is also categorized according to the person or persons involved, the acts performed, the social situation encompassed, and the emotions experienced. Un-

less indicated otherwise by the context in which it appears, *sexual,* as well as *heterosexual,* means sexual behavior with a person of the opposite sex, and *homosexual* with a person of the same sex regardless of the nature of the experience. Masturbation includes all autoerotic activities. Heterosexual activities include both coitus, more frequently referred to as sexual intercourse, and petting, erotic activities not immediately followed by coitus. Light petting usually means holding hands, kissing, and embracing without greater intimacies; heavy petting connotes all other more intimate fondling without coitus.

Further distinctions are made in many societies among relationships classified as marital and nonmarital, and, especially, premarital and extramarital. Among many peoples, being bethrothed permits the couple to engage in greater physical intimacies, including coitus. Our own society is somewhat unique in having developed several degrees of socially sanctioned relations for the premarital period: random dating, going steady, and being engaged. And even a fourth stage is now in the process of development, "engaged to be engaged."

[1] Grateful acknowledgment is made to Mary Stelmak for assistance in the preparation of this chapter.

Each of these, as well as similar, although not identical, relations in other societies, carries with it an increasing delineation of progressively greater personal involvement, including sexual, between the couple as it moves from stage to stage. A basic characteristic of these relationships in our society is that they provide a socially sanctioned relationship in which the sentiment of friendship and especially love can be expressed with reciprocal rights and duties. These identify and define the relationship and protect each partner to some degree from exploitation by the other and from abuses from the community.

Extramarital relations also have varying social meanings. Where they are forbidden, as in our own society, great effort is made by the persons involved to keep the relation secret or to disguise its true nature by various subterfuges. The keeping of a mistress among some groups represents a quasi-institutionalization of the relationship. Frequently, no attempt is made to keep its existence a secret, except perhaps from the man's and, more especially, from the woman's family, although it is not openly publicized. The system of concubinage among some eastern and a few primitive cultures is a fully institutionalized extramarital sexual union in which, however, the woman has fewer rights—even though she may enjoy greater personal attention from the man—than he bestows upon his wife or wives.

That marriage plays a decisive role in the patterning of sexual, as well as other, relations between males and females is indicated even by the connotation of sexual activities with reference to the socially sanctioned union of male and female as premarital, marital, extramarital, and postmarital. The term *premarital sexual intercourse* is generally used to indicate the experience of coitus by an individual who is single and not previously married with a person of the other sex. Strictly speaking, it should be used to denote only the premarital coitus of persons who eventually

marry. A single act of coitus can be premarital for one partner, extramarital for the other, and adulterous for both, as in the case of a single person who has sexual intercourse with a married person. Most premarital coitus in our society, however, and apparently in many other cultures as well, involves partners who are both single. The sexual experiences of divorced and widowed persons, even though they are single in a social and legal sense, are usually referred to as postmarital (Ehrmann, 1961b).

CULTURAL AND HISTORICAL SETTING

Man and Other Animals

The difference between the sexual behavior of man and other animals is both of degree and of kind (Ehrmann, 1957; Ford & Beach, 1951; Leuba, 1954). The overt sexual behavior patterns of animals, like the organisms themselves, reflect a regular evolutionary sequence through the various phyla from the one-celled organisms to the mammals. Except for the asexual fission among some lower orders, the most typical form of reproduction is heterosexual.

The transition from the invertebrates, to fishes, to amphibia, to reptiles, to birds, to mammals reveals, in general, the increasing significance and specificity of the male-female relation, not only in sexual, but in all associations. Among the vertebrates, for instance, fish tend to be with other fish as fish, irrespective of sex except during brief periods for reproduction, whereas mammals tend to associate more specifically as males and females, as well as with other members of the same species. This closer association of the sexes from fish to mammals and from the lower order of mammals to man is evidenced in physical and psychological reactions, and in man in social relations as well.

Male and female mammals, generally speaking, with their highly developed copulatory organs, must come into a physically more intimate relation in the sexual union than most other forms of animal life. In addition, the female is viviparous and nurses her young, and among many species, especially those most closely related to man, as well as man himself, she needs the protection or cooperation of the male in order to survive. The psychological interrelations of males and females in general and of their sexual activities in particular also undergo a significant transition. In ascending the mammalian class to man, there is a change from an instinctual and periodic to a learned and continuous pattern of sexual behavior (Leuba, 1954).

The sexual behavior of the subhuman primates is in some respects more like that of man than is that of nonmammalian species, and in other ways it is not (Ford & Beach, 1951). Most of the subprimate mammals and nearly all of the lower vertebrates are fertile for only one or two relatively short periods in each year, and it is only during these periods that the female is in heat, or estrus, and that copulation takes place. The female of the primate species, including the human, has a series of regular ovarian cycles throughout the year, during any one of which she might conceive. Although the female of the subhuman primates is in estrus usually only during a few days around the time of ovulation, there are occasions among some species when sexual behavior occurs at other times.

The human is the only animal in which sexual behavior is not integrally related to the cycle of fertility. Although cycles of sexual desire have been reported among some women, the peak of their erotic interests was not found to be coincident with their fertile periods (Davis, 1929; Terman, 1938). Even among women who experience this rhythm of desire, coitus may occur at any time, first, because the desire of the male exerts considerable control over the occurrence of intercourse and, second, because the female is usually sexually respon-

sive even when not at the peak of her cycle (Ford & Beach, 1951).

Thus, generally speaking, because the subhuman primate females are in estrus several times a year, whereas the submammalian species only once or twice, and because the human female may be sexually receptive at any time, the frequency of sexual intercourse is higher among subhuman primates than among subprimates, and it is highest among humans.

Patterns that are common to man and the [other] primates are sex play in childhood, masturbation, homosexual behavior, heterosexual foreplay preceding coitus, and, of course, heterosexual coitus. Although practiced by both sexes, masturbation, homosexual acts, and heterosexual exploration of the partner's body by means of the mouth and hands occurs more frequently among males than females. Humans, however, are more individually discriminating than the primates in their choice of sexual partners, and the primates in turn more so than the other mammals (Ehrmann, 1957, p. 18).

The sexual responses of humans and of some other primates, particularly the chimpanzee, have another similarity which sets them apart from other mammals. In most subhuman mammalian species, the sexual receptivity of the female and the copulatory advances of the male appear to be determined more by internal body chemistry, so that the sex act has a standardized pattern that changes little with experience. The patterns of sexual behavior among humans, since they are acquired and not innate, belong more to the art than to the instinct of love. Even the chimpanzees, when they are deprived of the opportunity for learning, do not know what to do sexually when they are first in the presence of the opposite sex after puberty (Leuba, 1954).

Even though humans and other primates, particularly the chimpanzees, are alike in that their total behavior is subject more to learning experiences than to innate physiological mechanisms, man differs from the subhuman primates, and, of course, even more so from all other species, in that his behavior is controlled, patterned, and channeled by customs, and in that this behavior is greatly influenced by symbolic thought and by the contemplation and evaluation of his own ideas and actions (Ehrmann, 1957). These distinctions have been so well established within the last half-century by anthropological, psychological, and sociological studies that there is no need to elaborate them. An illustrative comment will suffice to bring these contrasts into focus. Males and females among humans and the chimpanzees, for example, pair off into monogamous or polygamous associations which endure for a much longer period of time than is required for the reproduction of the species. Although the establishment of these relationships is a learning experience for both groups, the mating of humans, but not of any other form of life so far as we know, is established and patterned by the folkways and mores. Thus, man has the social institution of marriage, and various other socially sanctioned arrangements for nonmarital associations, which other animals do not.

Man also is the only creature, as far as we can determine, who not only uses symbols, primarily through language, but whose culture, and hence his very existence, is absolutely dependent upon this usage. Symbols are words, signs, gestures, and objects which have meanings given to them which usually have little or no relation to the inherent qualities of the actions or objects themselves. Through their use man is able to store things within himself and also in external forms, such as books, paintings, and figures, and to communicate with others an infinite variety of ideas which other animals cannot.

These symbols convey knowledge, influence the emotions, and establish values in accordance with the social usages of a particular culture. Words such as "love," "coitus," "petting," "adultery," and "prostitution" describe a social condition or action about which we have complex emotional feelings and for whose meaning and significance we have personal and social values. To one who does not understand our language, however, they are meaningless sounds or marks on a paper. They would mean something slightly or even vastly different to a foreigner who had learned English, but who had not had the opportunity to understand their full significance by living in the social setting in which they are used. The same partial or complete incomprehensibility of the symbols of another culture applies, of course, equally well to ourselves.

Cross-Cultural Comparisons

All societies control heterosexual behavior, primarily through marriage and its preliminaries. Other forms of sexual activity are also often regulated through other institutional means, but sometimes in conjunction with the husband-wife and parent-child relations. There are, however, a few codes of sex conduct which are found among all peoples. One of these is the expectation and right of sexual intercourse between married partners, and another is the prohibition against incestuous relations between a parent and a child. Although certain matters are of universal concern—such as impotency, infertility, sexual jealousy, sexual attractiveness, adultery, premarital coitus, availability of sexual partners within and outside marriage, and other considerations—they have been evaluated and treated quite differently from society to society and from age to age.

Adultery, for instance, which is frequently viewed as a violation of a proprietary right rather than a sin, is, among some people, summarily punished by death to the guilty. Among the Todas, by contrast, wives have freedom of sexual relations with men other than their husbands (and they are by our standards, but not by theirs, quite "promiscuous"); the concept of adultery, or even a word to identify this relationship, does not exist. Hence, adultery is not a social problem among these people. This example is cited to illustrate the general principles that the social reaction to specific sexual acts varies considerably, and that sexual as well as nonsexual behavior becomes a matter of concern when it violates or comes in conflict with cherished social expectations and values.

Although masturbation, premarital coitus, and homosexual practices probably occur in most societies, their social significance takes a variety of forms. They may be encouraged, permitted, condoned, ignored, condemned, or suppressed (Ehrmann, 1957; Ford & Beach, 1951; Murdock, 1949). Furthermore, as Ford and Beach (1951) and other writers have indicated, there is among known societies at one extreme a relative coincidence and at the other extreme a considerable variance between actual behavior and the idealized standards of sex conduct. Sexual transgressions of the formal mores are among some peoples invariably and summarily punished, and among others condoned.

Most cultures have been more lenient than ours in permitting nonmarital intercourse. In fact, ours is one of the few that has had, during certain periods in our history, a general prohibition of all sexual activities outside the marriage relation. Murdock (1949, pp. 260–283), on the basis of evidence compiled from a world-wide sample of 250 societies, maintains that, except for a few societies, sex itself is not the focus of regulation, as might be assumed with the existence of a generalized sex taboo. The control of sexual intercourse is with respect to one or more other considerations to which sex is pertinent, such as marriage, kinship, social status, and reproduction, rather than a prohibition of sex expression itself. In the other societies, the prohibition is directed mainly at the female and seems to be primarily concerned with preventing out-of-wedlock births.

There are many societies in which child sex play and postadolescent sexual intercourse are formally forbidden, but are tacitly accepted by the adults, who either ignore them or fail to punish those who are caught. A majority of societies have tolerated or permitted sex expression in childhood, such as masturbation and mutual fondling, and some have even permitted children to observe adult sexual intercourse. In a minority of societies, the prevention of premarital sexual intercourse among postadolescent youths is accomplished by attempting to instill in the individual the idea that these acts are wrong; to reinforce self-restraints by threats of adverse public opinion, ostracism, disgrace, or punishment; and by making these prohibitions effective by preventing young males and females being together either by chaperonage of girls or segregation of the sexes (Murdock, 1949). Even threats of disgrace and severe punishment including death, however, have not always been effective in preventing young people from engaging in premarital coitus (Ehrmann, 1961b; Ford & Beach, 1951; Murdock, 1949).

Among a majority of known societies, premarital sexual coitus has been permitted (Murdock, 1949). This arrangement has usually been accompanied by rigorous safeguards which protect the parties concerned, the male and female and their kin, from exploitation, and which insure eventual marriage for members of both sexes. Thus, the idea that permitting premarital coitus inevitably leads to unbridled promiscuity and the ruination of women is a myth. Examples of societies which permit premarital coitus are the Samoans of Polynesia and the Scandinavians of northern Europe, and of those which prohibit it are the Cheyenne Indians of North America and the Irish of Ireland.

The most typical form of heterosexual coitus among all known peoples is between husband and wife in a monogamous relationship. Nevertheless, in most societies, sexual activities are not formally limited to this relationship, as is the case in American society, in that usually males and females may engage in premarital sexual intercourse, and frequently the male may have, in addition to his first wife, one or more concubines or other wives, if he can support them. Among the groups for which there were these data, Ford and Beach (1951) found that about four-tenths approved of some type of extramarital liaison, and less than one-third wholly disapproved of both premarital and extramarital liaisons. Every society in this sample which approved of extramarital liaisons specified and limited these relationships in one way or another. Among the majority of peoples in this study (about six-tenths), extramarital relations were prohibited for women, and in some of them males were likewise restricted, but in others they were not.

Thus, summarizing from the existing data, the generalization can be made that most people have permitted premarital sexual relations for both sexes, but that a majority have expected sexual relationships of married persons to be limited to spouses. Even though a few cultures have allowed both husbands and wives to have extramarital relations, more have permitted husbands, but not wives, to establish liaisons (Ford & Beach, 1951).

Western Culture

Scholarly commentaries on the significance of sex in the Western world began to appear in some numbers during the Victorian period (Howard, 1904; Lea, 1867; Lecky, 1859; and others), and they have witnessed a recent revival (Biegel, 1951; Cole, 1955; Cole, 1959; de Rougemont, 1940; Malinowski, 1929; Mead, 1949; Reiss, 1960; and others). The many works of the incomparable Sigmund Freud, which spanned these two periods, contain innumerable insightful observations upon the relationship between sex and civilization. His writings and those of his followers are of even greater significance because they have played a meaningful role in changing our whole concept of sex in our total life.

The principal themes which run through the writings of all of these authors, past and present, are the relation of sexual behavior and codes to the rights of women, to romantic love, and to morals, particularly those influenced by Christianity.

Actual sexual practices have shown much greater variations from time to time, place to place, and among various groups within a society from the ancient Greeks and Hebrews to the present than have the sexual patterns formally established by the mores of the Judaic-Christian traditions (Ehrmann, 1961a; Ehrmann, 1961b). The early Christians, for instance, apparently adhered generally to a taboo on all sexual activity except marital heterosexual coitus, and even this was considered less noble than celibacy, while some upper-class Romans were relatively liberal or even licentious in their sexual conduct. That the early, as well as the later, Christians did not always obey the strict canons of sexual morality is evidenced by the innumerable exhortations of the Church fathers against sexual transgressions and by various commentaries, plays, law cases, and biographies which have come down to us.

The ten centuries of the Middle Ages also witnessed great extremes in sexual practices among different groups, from promiscuity to celibacy. The Elizabethan English, who were extremely liberal in their outlook, treated sex with a frankness and frequently with a ribaldry that has no parallel in Western history. By the Victorian period, however, sex was treated with such great circumspection that among some groups of these very same Englishmen one would hardly have known that coitus ever took place, and every effort was made to conceal violations of the formal mores, which, if they became known, were the cause of great scandal and disgrace.

Today, even though there has been a marked liberalization in both formal codes and actual sexual practices, there still remain great variations between and within countries of the Western world. The Irish of Ireland and some religious groups in the United States and elsewhere maintain a strict general taboo on all sexual activities outside of the marital relation within a relatively strong (for the modern period) patriarchal family structure. By contrast, the Scandinavians and other northern European groups maintain a liberal, permissive, premarital code of sexual behavior with adequate social safeguards for the protection of all parties concerned, particularly the female. Within the contemporary United States, sex codes and practices of various groups seem to span the range from the restrictive standards of the Irish to the permissive ones of the Scandinavians. These extreme variations within our society represent in part different adjustments to incongruous life philosophies of sexual behavior.

The history of Christendom since the Middle Ages has been marked by a growing conflict between the contradictory values that sex as eroticism, particularly outside the marital relation, is sinful and that romantic love, the mystical and irresistible force between male and female, justifies and is consummated by sexual expression. Curiously enough, and contrary to the emphasis given to this pervasive idea, eroticism itself was not initially the fundamental concern in Christian doctrine. The original sin of man which corrupted all facets of human life, sex among them, is called by Catholic theologians "concupiscence," the ravages of lust. This malady makes him discontented with whatever he has—money, power, knowledge, or sexual pleasure (Cole, 1961). By the events of history, however, rather than by the tenets of this theological concept, eroticism became to an increasing extent the core issue, so that this specific manifestation of the basic sin rather than the basic sin itself became a central concern of the Christian mores. The conflict over sex was heightened because, while the worship of motherhood and the bearing of children were considered noble, the basic human motivation of eroticism surrounding conception was not.

Another anomalous condition also arose during the development of romantic love (Howard, 1904). Its initial form in the early Middle Ages was characterized by a glorification of women—that is, women of the nobility, not the peasantry—and by a denial of consummation of this love in the sex act, which created extreme fantasies about the qualities of love and the loved one. During the course of the Middle Ages, however, romantic love became increasingly the rationale for illicit sexual relations, very frequently adulterous ones, while at the same time there continued to exist many love affairs that remained unconsummated. Thus, the element of fantasy was enhanced even in those liaisons in which sexual intercourse occurred, as well as those in which it did not, because by being illicit the emotional tensions surrounding these relations were further dramatized.

Throughout the centuries leading from the Middle Ages through the modern era to the present, the ideal of romantic love went through a great transformation. It became the ideal of the common man, and instead of being separated from marriage, it became the basic motive for falling in love and getting married (Beigel, 1951; de Rougemont, 1940; Kirkpatrick, 1955). This new ideal evolved along with—or was produced by, or was a product of—the dramatic emergence of individualism and the growing equality of women. This romantic love contained two new principles: one, that any individual might fall in love with any other individual of the opposite sex; and, two, that marriage not only might, but should, be a free choice of the individuals involved on the basis of their love for one another in an equalitarian relationship. These revolutionary ideals, along with other great social changes, helped destroy the highly structured patriarchal family which was based in part upon the supremacy of the father and the family over the individual.

Throughout the history of the Western world, there have existed not one, but three distinct codes of sex conduct. The religious traditions of our culture have prescribed a strict single standard of sex conduct which has forbidden premarital coitus or any sexual activity other than marital coitus for both males and females. The other two codes are the liberal or permissive single standard, which permits some premarital sexual expression for both males and females, and the double standard, meaning a different standard for each sex, which has permitted the premarital sexual expression of males but prohibited it for females (Ehrmann, 1959a; Reiss, 1960).

The double standard would, of course, be merely a matter of intellectual speculation if its tenets, as stated, were strictly obeyed, because males would have no females with whom to have sexual activities. This code was made a reality by having two classes of females, "good women" and "bad women." Males had premarital relations with bad women who, by entering into sexual liaisons, disqualified themselves for consideration for matrmiony; the females who resisted the males' advances, or who were not subjected to the test of sexual susceptibility because they were considered above reproach or approach, were made eligible for consideration for, but not assured of, matrimony.

Since the days of the ancient Hebrews, even though the strict single standard has been the dominant code, with certain notable exceptions, there have existed even in the religious traditions, as well as in the folk culture, strong undertones of the double standard. Although this has formally prohibited premarital intercourse for both sexes, more subtle interpretations have meant in fact the condemnation of female sexual transgressions, but only a milder disapproval, and even at times the encouragement, of male sexual exploits. At other times, a more permissive attitude toward sexual expression of both sexes has given rise to a wider acceptance among some groups, and even among a majority, as in Scandinavia today, of a liberal, single stand-

ard (Ehrmann, 1961a; Ehrmann, 1961b). Thus, the many variations in actual sexual practices throughout history, and especially at the present time in our society, have been caused, first, by individual violations of the code of sex conduct dominant in the particular group at the time, and, second, and perhaps of greater historical significance, by differential adherence to each of the three standards. Only one code has been for all intents and purposes the standard of a people at a given time, but more frequently two and usually all three have coexisted simultaneously, although the relative importance of each has varied considerably.

United States in the Twentieth Century

The remarkable changes in sexual behavior, attitudes, and values in the United States, as well as in many other parts of the world, during the first part of the twentieth century and especially since World War I, may with justification be called a sexual revolution (Ehrmann, 1961a). The changes in sexual customs were, of course, a part of a more general social revolution affecting every phase of our lives: psychological, social, technological, and religious. [Relevant to the concerns of this section are certain discussions in Burchinal's chapter to follow; see especially, pp. 332–336.]

Individual freedom of choice in many aspects of life, including sexual behavior and the choice of a spouse, increased, while the traditional dictates of family, community, and church declined. Women became less dependent, economically speaking, upon men, and they achieved greater equality with men than had ever existed before in the history of the West. The opportunity for nonmarital sexual expression contrary to the traditional mores was made possible by the anonymity of the city and the use of the automobile and by increasing scientific and folk knowledge of ways of avoiding the embarrassment and stigma of an out-of-wedlock pregnancy through the techniques of conception control and the social invention of petting. New theories about the nature of man, either implicit in the evolving human scene or explicit in intellectual formulations—political speculations on the rights of man and woman, psychoanalytical and behavioristic concepts of human personality, social action theories of social interrelations, existential philosophies on the nature of being, and the resurgence of the ideals of romantic love—encouraged sexual expression and experimentation. The advocates of free love of the 1920's epitomized and set in bold relief the characteristics of the sexual revolution at its extreme. Yet the pervasive feelings of guilt about sex so characteristic of the Christian world throughout its history continued to persist, although guilt was less potent than in some historic periods, including the one just past.

In consequence of the social and personal demands of the situation, American youth began, after the turn of the century and especially after World War I, to evolve a set of social values and practices which served the dual purposes of bringing males and females into a more individualistic and intimate companionate relationship, both outside and inside marriage, and of resolving "the great sex dilemma" created by the proscription "sex is sinful" and the prescription "romantic love justifies erotic expression." The two principal social inventions which were evolved by youth for premarital relations were dating and petting (Ehrmann, 1959a). Couples had some opportunity for being alone during the preceding latter half of the nineteenth century, but usually these occasions were rigorously circumscribed by effective social conventions of the patriarchal family or traditional community. Taking a stroll after church, going for a buggy ride—in broad daylight—or having some precious moments alone in the parlor or on the porch swing were traditional examples of the privacy allowed couples during the Victorian period. This sanctioned privacy, however, was usually allowed only older youth and young adults who had "serious intentions," and lovemaking was generally limited to "spooning." Clandestine episodes and long-standing illicit relations occurred, but were rare or better-kept secrets than they are now.

Dating as it developed after World War I, as compared with the restrained and constrained privacy accorded couples of serious intention of the previous age, was an activity that rapidly became the setting for the weekly, or even daily, relationship of virtually all postadolescent youth. The involvement in a dating relationship, the decision of the male to extend the offer and the female to reject or accept it, and the choice of where and when to go and come and what to do, within limits which expanded rapidly to make more and more conditions and circumstances socially acceptable which formerly were not, became to an increasing extent a matter of individual determination. Petting enabled the couples to engage in the now expected and accepted pleasures of eroticism, while maintaining the traditional female symbol of purity.

At the same time, the rapid spread of knowledge of practical and usually effective contraceptive techniques among youths, as well as adults, enabled those who wished to violate the core of the premarital sex taboo, the prohibition against coitus, to do so with only a slight risk of suffering the most severe stigma for violating the sexual mores, a known out-of-wedlock pregnancy. And even this penalty could often be avoided by an abortion, or a visit to relatives whose existence had never been mentioned before, or even a trip abroad for educational or health reasons.

The great personal "freedom" of males and females in the dating situation was and is, however, in a very real sense a social mirage, because couples were still not supposed to go "too far," and the feeling of guilt was and is still an effective force in human motivation. The development of promiscuous petting was actually only one aspect, although the most apparent and spectacular manifestation, of a complex set of codes of sexual behavior to deal with this new-found freedom which did not permit, personally or socially, a complete abandonment to lust. These codes include a variety of interpersonal modes of behavior to control, channel, and rationalize the presence or absence of sexual acts (Ehrmann, 1959a; Kirkendall, 1961). An example is the "line," in which usually the boy attempts to seduce the girl into a kiss or coitus. If she does not wish to give in, she parries his advances by indignation, aloofness, or humor; if she does, she can sometimes be forward and candid in her assent, but, particularly in a developing relationship, she must more often convey by expressions and gestures, if not words, that somehow he has overwhelmed her against her better judgment (Ehrmann, 1959a).

Other aspects of these codes are frequently more explicit and well understood, even though there are often great differences and hence conflicts between individuals and couples as to which code should be followed (Ehrmann, 1959a). The maxim of some girls, "Don't kiss until the third date!" is a good illustration of a simple code, which, however, is more complex than it appears because it contains three essential elements: a proscription, a prescription, and an implicit rationalization. If he does not appear a kissable candidate, the third date is refused; if he appears to be, the maxim gives sanction to the kiss on the third date. Should he prove not desirable after the kissing test or tests, however, the fourth, fifth, or sixth date is refused and the relation terminated. The male code is, of course, to a considerable extent complementary or supplementary or a combination of both to the female's. These codes also include the complex answer to how far to go sexually and with whom.

Patterns of dating underwent a profound change between the ends of World War I and World War II. After World War I, young people developed a form of promiscuous petting in which popularity was sought by having as many different partners as possible. This trend was manifested even at dances with the stag lines and the custom of "breaking in," whereby success and failure were measured by the frequency of changes of partners during a single dance and in the course of an evening. The continuous flow of gossip from partner to partner, from male to male in the stag line, and from female to female in the powder room continuously characterized and evaluated individuals as to their dancing, conversation, dress, looks, personality, and directly or indirectly their sexual desirability or undesirability. Dating and petting had the same turbulent qualities as the whirlwind of the dance with ever changing partners. The new-found freedom of male-female association became both the basis for boisterous and rollicking equalitarianism and an arena for the heightened battle of the sexes. The cartoons and novels of the day reflected, even if in caricature, the tragic and comic aspects of the social relations of the sexes.

Although the vivid description of Waller (1937) is specifically of a campus setting, dating even for noncollegians, including high-school students, became more a means for striving for status, prestige, and self-gratification than for companionship, and hence a relationship in which exploitation of one sex by the other frequently occurred. Usually, the male tended to take advantage of the female for sexual gratification and the female of the male for prestige and material gain. Sometimes, of course, the relationship was the other way around. The female might use sex to entice the male into a relation, even including marriage, which he might otherwise have avoided; and the male might hold the female (who otherwise might find him undesirable or even repugnant) by the prospect of a secure and exalted position. Within this setting, the number of couples engaging in premarital petting and coitus increased greatly. Some, or even much, of this sexual activity was undoubtedly a genuine expression of affection and love. Nevertheless, the antagonism between the sexes was much in evidence in the sexual, as well as in other, relations. The stigmatization of the girl as a "tease" by the frustrated and often irate male, and the girl walking home in disgust as her defense against the unwanted advances of the male were much more characteristic of that period than this one.

Marriage also underwent a profound change during the period, as an adjustment to the new individualism, by becoming more of a companionship with emphasis upon affection, comradeship, equalitarianism, and happiness rather than a status—stressing respect, obedience, authority, and duty (Burgess & Locke, 1953). The search for personal happiness included also an increasing stress upon the expectation of sexual adjustment and satisfaction for females, as well as males, in marriage. That sex was playing a more crucial role in marriage was attested by the rapid increase in the frank discussion of these matters in the folk culture, previously an unheard-of occurrence among females in the Victorian period; and in the appearance of and great demand for "marriage manuals"—a euphemism for instructions in sexual techniques and the psychology of sexual adjustment—and for similar discussions in the respectable organs of the mass media (Ehrmann, 1957).

The new individualistic goals for marriage produced two distinct results. On the one hand, probably more couples achieved a greater degree of satisfaction and self-fulfillment than was possible previously, but, on the other hand, ideals and expectations of the marriage relation led to greater frustration and disillusionment if these goals were not achieved (Kirkpatrick, 1955). Hence, more marriages ended in divorce as the only solution, in many instances, for the failure to achieve the new ideals, including, frequently, a satisfactory sexual adjustment.

The great depression and World War II brought an end to the extremes in the social whirl and the "battle of the sexes" of the twenties. Dating and marriage became more the basis for companionship in which couples sought understanding, friendship, love, and emotional security. Thus, going steady became a common custom among all ranks of adolescents and young adults, by which males and females learned to understand and to have more confidence in themselves and in one another (Ehrmann, 1961a). Going steady and the pre-existing, but changing, engagement compact also marked another step in the greater institutionalization of premarriage. This was evolving in a social setting of greater freedom, coupled with the necessity of providing adequate guidelines and constraints for a highly emotionally involved interpersonal relationship. The great increase in the number of teenage marriages was and is yet another manifestation of the search for the social security offered by the institutionalization, and in this instance also the legal sanction, of the male-female relation. In addition, and of great personal and social significance, was the fact that youth was desperately trying to achieve both the independence of adulthood and the security of a protected emotional and social relation, and that marriage offered, or appeared to offer, a solution to both of these quests.

Marriage also underwent a profound though more subtle change. Married couples, although retaining many aspects of the romantic tradition, tempered this idealism with more realism, which resulted in the establishment of a more secure equalitarian relationship with complementary male and female roles that were well adapted to fulfilling the companionship form of marriage (Burgess & Locke, 1953). Thus, marriage became a more satisfactory human relationship by changes occurring both in premarriage, specifically, and in all male-female relations, generally. Sex, too, by inference from research findings and from changed social attitudes and values, seemed to become more of a positive force for solidifying male-female relations and less of an antagonistic, exploitative, and disruptive element in both premarriage and marriage.

Contemporary Heterosexual Values

A characteristic which, analytically speaking, pervades the social system, with respect to the sexual relations of men and women in our contemporary society, is an elaborate and intricate means for resolving the dilemma between two coexisting and conflicting values or philosophies: that sex, as eroticism, is sinful or wrong, and that romanticism, as love, justifies or makes mandatory erotic expressions (Ehrmann, 1959a; Ehrmann, 1961b). The statements of these great values in these short phrases are, of course, gross oversimplifications, because social adjustments to them, speaking both in a historic and a contemporary sense, run the gamut from an acceptance of the first and a denial of the second, through innumerable variations with greater and lesser emphasis given to one or the other, to a denial of the first and an acceptance of the second. Celibacy, as a commitment, is a rejection of eroticism, whereas "free love" within a romantic, rather than an antiphilosophical, context is a denial of the sinfulness of eroticism.

Some intermediate positions between these extremes with respect to marriage are: erotic satisfaction is justifiable only as a consequence of sexual intercourse which is engaged in solely for the reproduction of children within the marriage relation; marital sexual pleasure is a goal to be sought within marriage, but the failure to achieve it does not justify a divorce; satisfactory sexual relations are an indispensable condition of marriage which, if not achieved, justifies a divorce or—as a variant on this theme—extramarital relations while maintaining the marriage as a formal, legal relationship.

Because of the social invention of petting, which provides for erotic pleasures without the social stigma of being nonvirginal and without the fear, usually, of an out-of-wedlock pregnancy, a greater variety of behavior adjustments are available in premarital relations. This range is increased even further through the use of contraception, so that intercourse can be engaged in with or without the thought of subsequent marriage in the indefinite or definite future.

The various combinations and permutations of values in sexual interrelations are far more numerous in the premarital than the marital relation. This statement does not carry the implication that sexual values are either more or less significant for single than for married persons, but rather that they form a more complex social array for the former than the latter. Marriage is a socially sanctioned relationship between a man and a woman which, among other things, sanctions coitus between them as an exclusive relation. The value issue for marital relations, therefore, as far as sex is concerned, revolves around the extent to which eroticism influences, or is influenced by, the whole relationship between husband and wife, including the possibility of terminating their sexual activity only or their marriage as well. Premarital relations in our society, by contrast, allow of a greater variation in the expression of values both with reference to the type of heterosexual activity and to the social interrelation between the companions. Premarital heterosexual relations range from dating without petting, through holding of hands, kissing, and embracing, to more intimate fondling, and to coitus. These activities are furthermore structured within a series of social relations: random dating, going steady, "engaged to be engaged," and engaged. The propriety of sexual conduct in premarital relations may range from a set sexual response with all categories of companions (from no petting with any companions at one extreme to coitus with all companions at the other, both of which are exceedingly rare) to a variation in sexual activities according to the nature of the interpersonal relation. The more usual progressions are from random dating to being engaged and from not being in love to being in love.

The great attention which has been given in the folk culture and in academic, welfare, religious, and philosophical writings and discussions to the question of "violations" of the traditional sexual mores since the turn of the century has frequently obscured the fact that the sexual revolution includes the development of a new social system with respect to the erotic relationships of men and women. We might advisedly speak either of a system or of systems. There are certain elements, including values, behavior, and emotions, which are pervasive enough in our society to constitute a system; whereas variations among groups within our society are sufficiently distinct to set apart visible systems. Part of the task of research into the social significance of heterosexual expression, past and present, is to delineate and to understand, conceptually speaking, the system and the systems.

RESEARCH INTO HUMAN SEXUAL BEHAVIOR

Development of Scientific Studies

The scientific study of human sexual behavior began with the appearance of descriptive anthropological reports and clinical studies about 80 years ago and with systematic analyses of sample populations less than 50 years ago, even though anecdotal, moral, philosophical, religious, and literary commentaries about this basic human phenomenon have been prolific throughout history (Aberle & Corner, 1953; Ehrmann, 1957; Sears, 1943).

The appearance within this century of systematic research into human sexuality has witnessed, not an abeyance or lessening, but rather a virtual deluge of nonscientific utterances on this subject, which have far outnumbered the scientific offerings. They have covered almost every conceivable aspect of sex: birth control, abortion, sexual techniques, sexual rights of women, free love, sexual restraint, romance, promiscuity, frigidity, impotency, morals, religion,

and advice to the lovelorn. And they have appeared by the thousands in every type of publication imaginable, from scholarly and religious tomes to "girlie" and "confession" magazines. They are anecdotal, hortatory, polemic; they make bold assertions as to what is true (which, of course, may or may not be true in spite of the conviction or positiveness of the assertion); and they are especially concerned with pleas as to what should or should not be done about what is thought to be true. Although they are part of the regular fare for millions of readers and have become an integral part of our civilization, in that they bolster and maintain particular opinions and values or change them, they are not scientific.

On the other hand, the reliable and systematic studies of human sexuality are very few in number, and are published in less than 20 major research monographs with a few dozen articles in various professional journals. But they form a core, a beginning, of a respectable body of verifiable knowledge. These scientific writings have fallen into three major categories: first, the anthropological, comparative, and historical studies which have given us knowledge of the extent and variety of human sexual customs. Second, clinical reports by psychoanalysts and other psychotherapists have described the role of sex in the dynamics of human personality, but these have been almost entirely confined to people with emotional problems and disorders. To what extent their findings and theories apply to the general population is not known. Third, the systematic studies of segments, or "samples," of population which have been carried on in our own country have recorded the incidence, or occurrence, and frequency of specific sexual behavior and of concomitant beliefs, attitudes, and values. It is the latter group of studies that has given us some idea of what a representative group of people do, and what they think about their sexual behavior.

The factual data presented in this present chapter are necessarily highly simplified and generalized. While the data are drawn from the systematic sampling studies described above, their interpretations make use of the anthropological, clinical, and all other available sources (Ehrmann, 1963).

The scientific study of sex as a human problem was greatly facilitated in the nineteenth century by the writings of romantic poets and novelists and by the action programs of the advocates of modern conception control and of equal rights for women. In Europe and in America other incentives to the original systematic research into sex were public concern with the social and moral problems of divorce, illegitimacy, prostitution, and sexual aberrations and maladjustment. Many of the initial studies were made in Germany, and they were closely followed by ones in America, England, and elsewhere. Krafft-Ebing's famous *Psychopathologia Sexualis* (*Psychopathology of Sex*) was first published in Germany in 1886 and Albert Moll's *Die Konträre Sexualempfindung* (*The Perverse Sexual Feeling*) in 1891. Even in these early days, however, the scientific interest in sex was not limited to the "abnormal." Europeans also led the way in the comparative anthropological study of sexual behavior. Ploss's great work (later Ploss and Bartel's) *Das Weib in der Natur und Völkerkunde* (*Woman in Nature and Ethnology*) was published in 1885, Mantegazza's *Gli amori degli Uomine* (*Sex Relations of Mankind*) in 1886, and Westermarck's *History of Human Marriage* in 1891.

After the turn of the century, impetus was given to the study of human sexuality by the psychoanalytical studies of the incomparable Sigmund Freud, the commentaries of Havelock Ellis, and the rise of behaviorism in psychology. Another series of events which encouraged public interest and support of sex research was the enormous popularity and continuing influence of so-called "sex manuals" on the art of love, beginning with the publication of Marie Stopes' *Married Love* in England in 1918; the great public effort given to combating venereal diseases as a result of the shocking revelation of their exceedingly high incidence among American soldiers in World War I; and the emancipation of women, and in fact, the great growth of individualism

among both men and women with the development of the new urban-industrial society.

In spite of the fact that Europeans led the way in clinical and anthropological studies, systematic sex research based upon the organized collection of data according to a prearranged qualified and quantified scheme and their logical and statistical analyses is essentially an American development. Its beginning may be reckoned from the publication of Exner's excellent little study of the sexual behavior of one thousand students in 1915. Probably because of World War I, no major work appeared after his for almost a decade and a half. Beginning with 1929, however, the years immediately preceding World War II marked a most productive period. Seven of the eleven major monographs in this field appeared during that time. Research again came almost to a standstill during World War II. The period since then has seen the publication of a few large-scale studies and an increasing number of small-scale research. History might reveal that the publication of the two great works of Kinsey and his associates in 1948 and 1953 marks the end of the pioneering period, which began in 1915 with Exner, and the beginning of a second period of systematic sex research (Ehrmann, 1957, pp. 16–17).

Most of the systematic research into human sexual behavior has been made in the United States. The investigators have included sociologists, psychologists, psychiatrists, journalists, and others. The principal studies published prior to World War II are those of Exner (1915) of 948 college men; Davis (1929) of 2,200 women; Hamilton (1929) of 100 married couples; Terman (1938) of 792 married couples; Bromley and Britten (1938) of 1,300 college students; and Carney Landis and associates (1940) of 153 normal women and 142 female psychiatric patients. Although all of these works are highly suggestive, the study of Terman contains the most extensive and the most systematically analyzed data.

Since World War II, there have appeared seven major studies which present systematically collected data on social determinants of sexual behavior. Three of these works are by the members of the Institute of Sex Research, Indiana University: Kinsey, Pomeroy, and Martin (1948) on the male, from a sample of 5,300 white males of diverse educational background; Kinsey, Pomeroy, Martin, and Gebhard (1953) on the female, from a sample of 5,940 white females of diverse educational background; and Gebhard, Pomeroy, Martin, and Christenson (1958) on pregnancy, birth, and abortion, from a sample of 6,193 white and 881 Negro females. These volumes contain more data on sexual behavior than all other published works combined. The study by Locke (1951) gives data on premarital sexual intercourse and marital sexual adjustment for 525 divorced and 404 happily married persons. Burgess and Wallin (1953), in their analysis of factors influencing the engagement and marriage adjustments of 1,000 engaged couples, and of 666 of these after they had been married, include considerable data on sexual behavior and attitudes. The research of Ehrmann (1959a) on the youthful sex expressions of 841 college students in the dating situation is an extensive study of premarital sexual behavior in terms of social variables including sex codes of conduct and the love relationship. Reiss (1960), utilizing the empirical data of Burgess and Wallin, Ehrmann, Kinsey and associates, Terman, and others, makes a systematic analysis of premarital sex standards.

A study by Kirkendall (1961) is an analysis of the attitudes of 200 college-level males about their premarital coital experiences. Although his research concerns a consequence of sexual behavior rather than the behavior per se, a study by Vincent (1961) of several hundred unwed mothers contains extensive data on the social situations and characteristics of his subjects. Some of the most promising developments are reported in journal articles (Christensen, 1960; Christensen & Carpenter, 1962a; Christensen & Carpenter, 1962b; Kanin, 1957; Kanin, 1960; Kanin & Howard, 1958; Kirkpatrick & Kanin, 1957; and others).

Principal Correlates with Sexual Behavior

The three conditions within our own society which are related to heterosexual behavior to a greater extent than any others thus far studied are so commonplace that their significance might easily be overlooked. They are being male or female, being single or married, and the aging process. Other conditions which are markedly correlated with variations in patterns of sexual behavior are social group identifications, such as social class, educational level, ethnic group, and age generation; social values, such as degree of religious devoutness and sex codes of conduct; and intimacy relations, such as going or not going steady, being or not being engaged, and being or not being in love. Several other social variables which show some, but a less consistent, relation with sexual behavior are such items as age at puberty, age at first date, home discipline and punishment, source and adequacy of sex information, rural-urban residence, military service, and other matters (Bromely & Britten, 1938; Burgess & Wallin, 1953; Davis, 1929; Ehrmann, 1959a; Hamilton, 1929; Hohman & Schaffner, 1947; Kinsey et al., 1948; Kinsey et al., 1953; Locke, 1951; Terman, 1938; and others).

These considerations, although spoken of as if they were discrete entities, are, of course, interrelated. For instance, the sexual behavior of one group differs from another because there are variations among the premarital sex codes of conduct, the social status of women, and the age of marriage. In this connection, the task of research, speaking conceptually and with over-simplification, is twofold: first, the single relations are established, and then their interrelations are determined, which process in turn leads to other considerations and a revision of the theoretical scheme.

Male and female. All studies which include both sexes reveal that male and female patterns of sexual behavior differ significantly, but that this difference is much greater, as might be expected, for premarriage than for marriage. This difference seems to be real even though women apparently tend to understate their premarital and to overstate their marital sexual activities (Ehrmann, 1959a; Kinsey et al., 1948; Locke, 1951). More males than females engage in premarital, extramarital, and postmarital petting and coitus and in nonheterosexual activities, and the typical male has higher frequencies and is engaged more continuously in these activities than the typical female (Kinsey et al., 1948; Kinsey et al., 1953).

Most males and from one-third to one-half of all females in our society experience coitus prior to marriage (Ehrmann, 1959a; Kinsey et al., 1953). Since premarital coitus is a heterosexual experience involving a male and a female in each act, the *total* frequencies for all males and for all females must be equal, though of course there may be differences in frequency between single males with married, widowed, or divorced females and single females with married, widowed, or divorced males. Discounting the possible effects of these latter considerations, the only way that the typical male can have more premarital coital experiences than the typical female is for some females to have very high frequencies with a large number of males. Although there is no systematic verification of this conclusion, there is strong support for it on logical grounds and because of the existence of prostitutes and nonprostitutes who have reputations for phenomenally high activities (Ehrmann, 1954; Ehrmann, 1959a).

Males and females are more nearly equal in their premarital petting experiences without coitus. All but a few individuals of both sexes engage in petting, and this activity has become an almost universally socially acceptable activity among peers (Ehrmann, 1959a; Kinsey et al., 1953). Some of the variations between the sexes probably occur because a few females have petting activities with a large number of males. Observed sex differences at any given time within a specific social category or group may represent variations in age, intimacy relations, and partners rather than an average difference between all males and all females. For example, most petting activity, as well as sexual intercourse, is confined to partners within the same social class, but among those who cross social-class lines for partners, males have more sexual activities with girls of a lower social class and females with boys of a higher social class. For this reason, as well as the tendency for females to understate their sexual experiences, the data from middle-class respondents, the ones used most often as subjects for research, indicate higher frequencies and incidences of sexual activities for males than females (Ehrmann, 1959a).

There are, however, moderate to marked differences between males and females with respect to certain attitudes about and practices connected with premarital heterosexual activities (Burgess & Wallin, 1953; Ehrmann, 1959a; Kinsey et al., 1953; Rockwood & Ford, 1945; Terman, 1938). Generally speaking, females tend to be more conservative in their attitudes and more passive in their behavior. Although females, both married and single, have become much more forward in this respect in the last few decades, males more often initiate the sexual activity, and females more often set the limits to which it goes. Females are more conservative and males are more liberal in their judgment as to the propriety of sexual activity for themselves and for the opposite sex. Females, although they are more conservative than males, are, however, more equalitarian in the codes they set for themselves and for males. Thus, females in general tend to have a single standard of sex conduct (Ehrmann, 1959a; Ehrmann, 1959b), whereas males tend to follow either a single or a double standard.

Another way of seeing both the difference between and the convergence of the premarital sexual expression of males and females is through the changes which have occurred in recent generations. The studies of Hamilton (1929), Terman (1938), Locke (1951), and Kinsey (1953) indicated that premarital sexual experience has increased some for males and markedly for females. The major increase in sexual experience occurred among females born after the turn of the century, i.e., those who reached sexual maturity around World War I or later. There were more nonvirgins among the younger generation of females because of a marked increase in the number who had experienced coitus with the future spouse and a moderate, though proportionately greater, increase in the number who have had sexual intercourse with other males. Although males, too, have increased their coital experience with both categories of partners, proportionately more men in the later generation had intercourse with their future wives. The abrupt increase in the number of nonvirgins occurred around World War I and shortly thereafter. Thus, the patterns of premarital sexual experiences of the typical male and female are converging.

The social situation places different constraints and goals upon males and females from childhood through adulthood. Females to a greater degree than males are oriented in the family, peer group, community, and larger society toward marriage and motherhood. Greater constraints and controls are placed upon their relationships with males and especially upon their sexual expression. The female is continuously inculcated to a far greater extent than the male with the idea that self-respect and the respect of others for her are dependent upon decorum and discretion in sex matters. In adolescence and then in adulthood, the male, who is less specifically and less persistently oriented to future marriage and parenthood or to the need for constraints of sexual expression, is inculcated by the pervading male culture to express himself sexually as the mark of the man. Indirectly, and sometimes directly, the expression of male eroticism is tacitly and even overtly encouraged by the female. As the relationship between couples be-

comes more intimate and stabilized, in going from random dating, to going steady and being in love, to being engaged, the practices and attitudes of males and females tend to converge in the heterosexual peer relation. Females become more free in their sexual expression, and males limit their sexual interest to an increasing degree to one female (Ehrmann, 1959a). In marriage, and especially with passage of time, the sexual desires and interest of males and females tend to become more alike, although significant differences remain. Actual sexual behavior is more nearly alike as the dominant sexual expression becomes marital coitus (Kinsey et al., 1953).

Premarriage. Although the differences between the sexual behavior of males and females briefly described in the foregoing section involve premarital, as well as marital, behavior, here we shall chiefly be concerned with the sexual characteristics of two developing institutional aspects of premarriage. One is the social relationships of random dating, going steady, and being engaged which are usually related directly with the emotion of not being or of being in love. The other is the sex codes of conduct, the single and double standards of sexual behavior. Variations in sexual behavior related to other social and cultural characteristics will be discussed in a later section.

The premarital relation of males and females has become institutionalized, that is, established in socially accepted and expected patterns of behavior running over several stages of increasingly involved commitments in interpersonal relations. These usually are referred to as random dating, going steady, and being engaged. Furthermore, these intimacy relations are closely associated with the emotion of love in that usually only a few persons dating at random are in love, but many going steady are, and all engaged couples are expected to be, even though a few may not be. These premarital relations form an essential part of our highly developed individualistic social system by providing for leisure-time activities, socializing the individual to his sex role including learning to live with, or adjust to, the opposite sex, and the selection or rejection of a dating partner, a steady, and eventually a spouse. Sex, of course, plays a significant, and sometimes a crucial, role in this process through the expressing of a basic human emotion in a creative or destructive way, or both.

These intimacy relations are, however, influenced by the pre-existing sex codes of conduct of the couples concerned. In fact, one of the most promising trends for the exploration of the relationship between sexual behavior and the social structure is the current research interests in the love relationship, sex codes of conduct, and the comparative social class of companion (the last to be discussed later) as they are related to premarital heterosexual experiences. The work of Ehrmann (1959a; 1959b) was the first to treat these matters systematically and interdependently in an empirical manner; and the study of Reiss (1960) was the first to analyze conceptually the premarital sex standards in our society using historical data and the research data of other investigators.

The researches of Terman (1938) and Burgess and Wallin (1953) for both males and females, and of Kinsey et al. (1953) for females, showed that, although more males than females had premarital coitus, a greater proportion of females than males had this experience with the future spouse only. Kinsey et al. (1953) also found that premarital petting and coitus were definitely correlated with nearness to marriage among females but not among males. These findings suggest, but do not confirm, that the premarital sexual behavior of the female is more closely correlated with being in love than is that of the male.

The study of Ehrmann (1959a; 1959b) confirmed this inference and also demonstrated the relationship between considerations of love and sex codes of conduct. Whether measured by going or not going

steady or by being or not being in love, the premarital sexual experiences, either petting or coitus, of the female, but not the male, were consistently related to ideas of love. The reason for this sex difference stems from variations in the degree of adherence to a single or a double standard of sexual behavior. All of the females in this sample adhered to a single standard: a majority to a conservative, or restrictive, standard which prohibited premarital coitus; and a minority to a liberal, or permissive, standard which permitted premarital sexual intercourse. Among both groups, the females tended to have the same or greater sexual intimacies with a steady than a nonsteady or with a lover (loved one) than a nonlover. This correlation was consistent whether measured by not petting and petting, light petting and heavy petting, or no coitus and coitus.

The lack of a correlation between love and sexual experience among males occurred because, first, the males with a single standard, in many instances, were not able to go as far sexually with a lover as with a nonlover; and, second, a substantial minority of males followed a double standard of sex conduct which permitted them to have intercourse with girls they would not marry (nonlovers) but not with girls they would marry (lovers). Love is, however, directly related to the sexual experiences of the males with a conservative single standard, in that they engaged more often in heavy petting with a lover than a nonlover. Love is inversely related to the sexual experiences of males with a liberal single standard and of males with a double standard, but for quite different reasons. Although males with a liberal standard desired to have coitus with both lovers and nonlovers, they were somewhat more successful with females they did not love than with females they did love. The inverse relation between love and erotic experiences among males with a double standard is a direct manifestation of their sex code of conduct. They did not attempt to have coitus with loved ones, but they did, and were often successful, with females they did not love (Ehrmann, 1959a; Ehrmann, 1959b).

Another significant element in this interplay of ideas of love and sex codes of conduct is that the male tends to initiate and press his sex advances, whereas the woman tends to resist and limit these advances until she has established the nature of her thoughts and feelings toward him and of his toward her. She will either reject him, or he her, or the sexual relationship will become established at light or heavy petting or coitus according to the intricate interplay of feelings of love and sex codes of conduct. As the relationship becomes more emotionally intimate in terms of going steady or being in love, the female becomes freer in initiating the love-making activities, and she will usually go farther than she had before, but she usually, though not always, sets the limits of sexual activity. In consequence, the love relation tends to equate the sexual expression of males and females. This conclusion is confirmed in this research by the convergence among males and females in love, as compared to those not in love, in the extent and frequency of actual heterosexual behavior and attitudes toward sexual expression (Ehrmann, 1959a; Ehrmann, 1959b).

Since dating in our society usually occurs in a situation not under the scrutiny of a chaperon, couples could, if they so desired, engage in petting or in coitus almost at will. That they do not always do so means, of course, that the control of sexual activity is primarily in the hands of the couples involved. The limitation, as well as the initiation of sexual activities, reflects their individual wishes and desires, their likes and dislikes of their partners and of sexual activities, and their sex codes of conduct.

The earlier studies by Bromley and Britten (1938) and of Rockwood and Ford (1945) cite "fear of pregnancy" as being one of the most important reasons given by their subjects for not engaging in premarital coi-

tus, but the more recent researches of Kinsey and associates (1948; 1953), Burgess and Wallin (1953), Landis and Landis (1953), Reevy (1954), and Ehrmann (1959a) indicate that this reason for restraint was of negligible significance among their subjects. All of these studies are similar in that "morals," "religious precepts," "fear of adverse public opinion," "self-respect," "fear of endangering future marriage relations," and related matters are cited among the important reasons for self-imposed restraints.

The decrease of fear of pregnancy, as well as the small place given to the fear of venereal diseases, as a reason for not engaging in premarital coitus probably represents a true change in cultural attitudes. The marked reduction in the incidence of venereal diseases since World War I and the widespread dissemination of the knowledge of effective contraceptive techniques among the youth culture since then, and especially among females since World War II, along with the increased acceptance of premarital sexual activities, have no doubt played a crucial role in these changed attitudes.

Of the more recent researches, data were systematically reported for "lack of opportunity" as a reason for not engaging in sexual intercourse only by Burgess and Wallin (1953), Kinsey and associates (1953), Reevy (1954), and Ehrmann (1959a); and for "no desire" by Kinsey and associates, Reevy, and Ehrmann. The studies of Kinsey and associates and of Ehrmann suggest further that lack of sexual responsiveness of the young female is one of the most significant deterrents, but the analysis of Ehrmann shows in addition that this is a primary reason for the sexual restraints of females with males they do not love (nonlovers), but not with loved ones (lovers).

According to Ehrmann (1959a), the patterns of heterosexual behavior, both petting and coitus and its control and attitudes about these activities, are perhaps more sharply defined by the sex codes of conduct —the conservative and liberal single standards and the double standards—and by the intimacy relation of being or not being in love (or of going or not going steady, or of being or not being engaged) than by any other matters considered thus far in systematic researches. Furthermore, as discussed previously, although these considerations are significant for both sexes, the sexual behavior of the female seems to be influenced more, comparatively speaking, by her intimacy relation of being or not being in love, and that of the male by his sex code of conduct.

The limitation is determined primarily by the female in that the male is restrained either by her overt refusal, or anticipation of her refusal, or by his "respect" for her, or secondarily by his own moral code, the ideal that one ought not to engage in certain activities, or by his timidity in initiating sexual advances even though he would like to do so. The female tends to limit her sexual behavior with a male she does not love because of no desire and lack of interest, and with the loved one because of moral considerations. The point of limitation varies, of course, considerably. It may be at no petting, light petting, or heavy petting, or at the frequency at which a sexual activity, including coitus, as well as petting, takes place.

Females with a conservative single standard cited "morals" more frequently and females with a liberal single standard "no opportunity" as a control in their sexual activities with a loved one. The males with a liberal single standard cited "girl refusal," both for girls they were and were not in love with, as the overwhelming reason for limitation of their sexual activities; whereas males with a double standard, as might be expected, gave as the principal reason for not going farther with the loved ones "morals" and "respect for girl," and "girl refusal" for the others. The conservative males, by contrast, tended to cite as proportionately of greater significance "timidity," "no desire," and "respect for date" (Ehrmann, 1959a).

The isolation of the dating situation creates a condition in which offensive male sexual aggression may occur, or in which either male or female may become involved in unwanted sexual activity, through either duress or a sense of obligation. A majority of the females in the studies of Kirkpatrick and Kanin (1957) and of Kanin (1957) reported one or more episodes of offensive male aggression, and a majority of the females and a substantial minority of males in the research of Ehrmann (1959a) reported one or more occasions on which they had engaged unwillingly in some sexual behavior. Contrary to the popular notion that dating with one man offers security against erotic aggression, Kirkpatrick and Kanin (1957), and Kanin (1957) found that offensive sexual advances at the more advanced levels of eroticism—such as petting below the waist, attempted sexual intercourse with and without violence—were more characteristic of couples dating regularly, pinned, or engaged.

Using a somewhat different frame of reference, the study of Ehrmann (1959a) indicated that undesired sexual activities for both sexes occurred more among those not in love than those in love, and that being physically forced by the male into sexual activities occurred more frequently among females with nonloved ones than with loved ones; whereas both males and females more frequently engaged in an unwanted erotic activity (or at least unwanted at the moment) to please a loved one than a nonloved one.

The presence of an older brother, and specific parental warnings about male sexual aggression, were found by Kanin (1957) to be related to the female not being offended. Older brothers may play the same role as parents in cautioning females against male sexual aggression, or their presence in the family may give their younger sisters a better understanding and hence tolerance of male sexual aggression. The studies of Kirkpatrick and Kanin also indicate some of the ways girls respond to offensive male sex aggression: usually by terminating the relationship or discussing the episodes with, and receiving warnings from, peer groups and, less often, by appeals to parents and other authorities or by keeping the matter secret.

It should be emphasized that on most dates no offensive or unwanted sexual behavior occurs, and as a corollary most males and females desire and are pleased with the erotic activities in which they are engaged (Ehrmann, 1959a). The system of testing, rejecting, accepting, and adjusting to the sexual and other aspects of the male-female relation forms an integral part of the newly evolved sex codes of conduct of the youth culture, which serves to give some stability to the premarital relations of the sexes and to help them select a future spouse.

Marriage.[2] The development of the philosophy within the last half-century that a satisfactory sexual relation for females, as well as males, is not merely a desirable but an expected condition of marriage has undoubtedly increased the significance of the sexual element in marriage in many ways. Whether people are happy or not, or whether they seek divorces or not, is frequently decided by the degree to which they have been able to achieve this ideal. That an unsatisfactory sexual adjustment in marriage may be a symptom rather than a true cause of marital unhappiness does not lessen the importance of the sexual aspect. The mere fact that people ascribe their difficulties to sex, even though this may not be the "real" cause of their troubles in many instances, is in itself significant. In another age, the ascription of marital failure, even though divorce was not per-

mitted or recourse to it was rare, was to insobriety, irresponsibility, or irreligiousness, reflecting certain dominant values of the times. That failure to achieve happiness in marriage now justifies a divorce introduces a strong sexual element into the termination of a marriage, for sexual incompatibility is frequently the ascribed reason for the dissolution.

Marriage today, however, apparently creates a situation, especially for the female, which is highly conducive to sexual adjustment. This is because marriage carries with it the traditional approval of coitus between spouses and especially of children born of the union, as well as the new goal of sexual satisfaction for both parties. Although marriages may now be dissolved by divorce with relatively little social stigma as compared with the past, most couples enter into it with the idea that it will be permanent; hence, the sexual relation, as well as the marriage itself, has in consequence a security not present in other sexual unions, until the prospects of a divorce are seriously considered. On the other hand, the traditional ideal that premarital sexual intercourse is detrimental to marital happiness, which still persists, although its prevalence is waning, may pose a threat to marital happiness.

It is not surprising, therefore, that most of the studies of the sexual element in marriage, with notable exceptions, have been concerned with the correlation of premarital sexual experiences with marital adjustment, and of a satisfactory marital sexual adjustment with an over-all marital adjustment.

An interesting and significant sidelight on the social consequences of research findings which go contrary to the prevailing mores was the reaction to the works of Kinsey and his associates (1948; 1953) by their scholarly peers, to say nothing of laymen. Some of the voluminous criticism of the Kinsey studies, for example, those compiled by Geddes (1954) and Himelhoch and Fava (1955), tended to be scholarly and provocative in delineating both the

---

[2] Dr. Jessie Bernard, in Chapter 17, pp. 711–721, also discusses the findings of research into human sexual behavior, but from a frame of reference different from that used in this discussion. Her treatment stresses interpersonal relationships, whereas this one emphasizes patterned behavior, attitudes, and values. Particular attention is called to her discussion of the provocative work of Rainwater and Weinstein (1960), which is not covered in this chapter.

contributions and the limitations of these great works. On the other hand, the violent attacks, rather than criticism, of these works seemed to stem from the fact that these studies examined human sexual behavior in such massive and appalling detail, and also that they stated explicitly or implicitly that having sexual outlets, or orgasms, was a good thing. Apparently, the most offensive finding to those who attacked the Kinsey findings on moral grounds was that females who experienced orgasm in premarital coitus were more prone to have orgasm in marital coitus, and, hence, by implication, better marriages.

Irrespective of the controversy over moral issues in research into human sexual behavior, marriage is the social condition which appears to influence, or determine, sexual behavior more than any other studied thus far. Although we are here concerned with our own society, it is probable that this generalization has universal, or almost universal, application. The male in our society has higher frequencies of sexual activities of all kinds than the female in premarriage, as indicated previously, and also in marriage.

Marriage tends to equalize the sexual interest and responses of males and females in two crucial ways. The most obvious is that, since marriage is by custom and law an exclusive monogamous sexual relation in our society, and since couples usually marry because of love, including a strong sexual attraction, coitus is the dominant sexual expression between marital couples. At the beginning of marriage, the male's interest in sexual activities is usually much greater than the female's. With the passage of time, however, the husband's desire for coitus tends to decrease, whereas the wife's tends to increase, so that by age 40 and later they are more nearly equal; and as they grow older, their sexual activities tend to decrease at about the same rate (Kinsey et al., 1953). Furthermore, as Kinsey and his associates (1953) have shown by their data, marital coitus provides for both males and females

a larger proportion of their total sexual experiences than does any other single type of activity.

Certain sex differences involving sexual techniques which may occur in any heterosexual relation are perhaps more readily observed in marriage because coitus is usually a regular, periodic occurrence in this relationship (although married couples may make, on the average, a better resolution of possible difficulties because of their prolonged personal relation). Most females prefer to be caressed and to have other parts of their bodies fondled to a greater or lesser degree prior to coitus, whereas males are more interested in genital manipulation or in coitus without extended preliminaries. Men are also more sexually stimulated vicariously by erotic objects and words, whereas women by romantic and sentimental love stories and personal situations. Although true of only a minority of both groups, fewer women than men prefer to have sexual activities where there is at least some light. Women are also more easily distracted during petting and coitus by extraneous sights and sounds. Although involving an appreciable minority of both sexes, more males than females engage in extramarital relations (Kinsey et al., 1953).

Perhaps the most surprising and unanticipated findings in the history of sex research, as measured by the popular folkways and mores, were two made by Terman (1938): first, the proportion of women virgin at marriage was decreasing rapidly; and, second, marital happiness and adjustment were only slightly correlated with virginity. The most important factors found by Terman to be correlated with marital adjustment and sexual expression were, first, the orgasm adequacy of the wife, and, second, equality or near equality of sex desire or drive between the mates. He concluded that although sex was not the single most important determinant of marital happiness, it was among the most important ones. He, Burgess and Wallin (1953), and Thomason

(1955a) found that sexual adjustment is correlated with marital adjustment. Other investigators (Davis, 1929; Ferguson, 1938; Hamilton, 1929; Landis & Landis, 1948; Locke, 1951) have reached similar conclusions, particularly with reference to equality of sexual desire and interest, sexual satisfaction, orgasm adequacy, and absence of desire for extramarital intercourse.

One of the most significant and consistent findings of the researches which have included a consideration of this item is that satisfactory sexual adjustment, as measured either by self-evaluation or by the experience of orgasm, is more of a learning process for women than men. Although perhaps a majority of all women experience orgasm or a satisfactory degree of pleasure during their initial experience or shortly thereafter, a significant minority acquires the ability to experience orgasm in coitus only after months and sometimes years of sexual experience (Davis, 1929; Ferguson, 1938; Hamilton, 1929; Kinsey et al., 1953; Landis, 1946; Terman, 1938; Thomason, 1955a; Thomason, 1955b). This capacity of the female is exceedingly important to the marriage, as the inability of the female to experience orgasm is related both to the husband's, as well as to the wife's, chances of having an unsatisfactory over-all marriage relationship (Terman, 1938; Thomason, 1955a; Thomason, 1955b).

Other than ascertaining the patterns of sexual outlet in marriage, the principal orientation of the research of Kinsey et al. (1953) with respect to marital coitus is to experience, frequency, orgasm, and techniques. Little or no correlation was found between experience and frequency of coitus except for age. There was found to be more variation in sex techniques and an increase in sex techniques and in nudity in coitus in the younger generation. The frequency of orgasm was proportionately higher among the better educated. There was a marked increase in coitus ending in orgasm among females born after, as compared with those born before, 1900, although there was little variation in frequency of intercourse. These findings, as well as those of Terman (1938) and others, suggest that the "democratization" of the sexual interest to include all females has been highly effective in increasing the sexual reaction of married women, and this influence has been greater among the better-educated groups. The easing of sexual taboos, the positive search for sexual satisfaction in marriage, the greater concern by husbands for the sexual satisfaction of their wives, especially among the better educated, and the general reduction of sexual inhibitions among women seem to have been the immediate instruments for producing these changes.

Parent-child relations. Among the behavioral sciences, there is virtual consensus that the relationship between the child and its parents is the principal, or at least one of the principal, determinants of the personality of the individual. Furthermore, the clinical literature is resplendent with case histories using this postulate as an unquestioned assumption, or demonstrating this relationship without questioning its validity. It is surprising, therefore, that so little attention has been given to attempting to establish systematically the influence of the parents upon the subsequent sexual development of the individual. This hiatus is even more curious in view of the fact that some of the pioneers in the study of human sexual behavior, particularly Davis (1929), C. Landis and associates (1940), and Terman (1938) for our own society, and Malinowski (1929) and others among primitive peoples, addressed themselves to this as well as to other problems.

There are undoubtedly many reasons why the early attempts of these pioneering investigators have not been pursued. First, the investigation of human sexuality, particularly outside the clinical situation, is exceedingly difficult because of the assumed opposition of public opinion. Second, the investigation of sexual behavior is not yet considered among the academicians themselves as a subject worthy of serious scientific effort. Third, until more is known about what people actually do sexually or about the patterns and subtleties of the sexual content of the parent-child relation, little can be done to try to establish the relationship between personality development and subsequent sexual behavior. One fact which does, however, emerge from these early works is that violation of the mores of heterosexual behavior cannot be ascribed wholly, or even principally, to psychopathological personalities. The scholarly review of Sears (1943) contains many stimulating suggestions which might be pursued with excellent results.

The limited, though suggestive, systematically assembled data which we do have deals in part directly and in part indirectly with this topic. For example, marital success has been shown to have a slight to moderate positive correlation with these childhood experiences of the married persons studied: source of sex information and instruction from parents and teachers rather than from children or books (Davis, 1929; King, 1951; Terman, 1938; Terman & Oden, 1947); adequacy of sex instruction (Terman, 1938); wholesome sex instruction (Burgess & Wallin, 1953); and a frank rather than an evasive or false parental response to the child's sex curiosity (Terman, 1938; Terman & Oden, 1947). These findings certainly tend to confirm innumerable clinical observations and to give support to the general orientation and rationale of current sex-education programs. The study of Ehrmann (1959a), the only research which analyzed the source of sex information with actual premarital behavior, found no correlation between the two.

The assumed interrelationships, which could be systematically verified by future research, stated in an oversimplified form, are as follows: a frank, though non-threatening and nonseductive, parental attitude toward the child's developing sexuality, with adequate guidance, strengthens the child's personality and orientation toward interpersonal relations in general and hetero-

sexual relations in particular, which in turn facilitates both a more adequate choice of a mate and a more satisfactory relationship, including sexual adjustment, with the spouse. A perhaps strategic finding by both Terman (1938) and Ehrmann (1959a), which has otherwise been overlooked, is that premarital coital experience of the female, but not of the male, is associated more with "irregular" than with either "firm" or "lenient" parental discipline.

The data on the correlation between the individual's attitude toward sex and his or her premarital sexual behavior and marital adjustment suggest a heretofore unexplored area of parent-child relations which may have a crucial bearing on subsequent marriage relations. The research thus far has shown a correlation between the individual's attitude toward sex and (a) general marital adjustment and (b) premarital sexual behavior. Interestingly enough, however, no attempt thus far has been made to demonstrate any relationship between attitudes toward sex and (a) marital sexual adjustment and, perhaps of greater importance, (b) parental influence upon the child's sex attitudes. The interrelations that apparently should be established are first between the parent-child relation and the child's attitudes toward sex, and then the individual's attitude toward sex and his or her premarital and marital general, as well as sexual, adjustment.

The researches of Burgess and Wallin (1953), Ehrmann (1959a), and Terman (1938) reveal both significant similarities and dissimilarities in the premarital attitudes of males and females toward sex. Although a majority of both sexes in these studies had an attitude of "interest and pleasant anticipation" toward sex, the remainder tended to have opposite attitudes, in that the females cited "indifference" or "disgust" and the males "passionate longing." Ehrmann found, however, that although more females than males had unfavorable attitudes toward sex, there was a much closer correlation between sexual attitudes and sexual experiences among males than females.

The inference drawn from these and other findings by Ehrmann leads to the supposition that, although this consideration is important for both sexes, a favorable attitude is a more significant motivation for participation, or an unfavorable attitude for nonparticipation, in premarital sexual activities—usually petting although sometimes coitus—for the male than the female; whereas other considerations, particularly being or not being in love, are more important for the female than the male. Although he did not give his findings on this topic for marital sexual behavior, Terman reported the same kind of variation among his subjects with reference to marital adjustment, in that unfavorable attitudes toward sex among women were only slightly, but among men markedly, related to marital happiness.

These limited, though provocative, findings suggest that the exploration of the relationship between the family structure and function and the sexual attitudes and behavior of children, and subsequently of their sexual and general adjustment in premarital, marital, and family relations, has scarcely begun.

Social groups. The review of research on sexual behavior in premarriage and marriage in the preceding sections dealt with findings of general significance without focusing upon variations observed between social groups. It was decided to treat this question separately in this section for a definite reason. Several recent studies, particularly those by Christensen (1960), Christensen and Carpenter (1962a; 1962b), Ehrmann (1955; 1959a; 1959b), Gebhard et al. (1958), Kanin (1960), Kanin and Howard (1958), Kinsey et al. (1948; 1953), and Vincent (1961), suggest that one of the most useful approaches for obtaining scientific insights into the significance of human sexual behavior is through a study of that behavior in terms of the social structure in its various manifestations. Interestingly enough, most of the studies which have thus far attempted to ascertain the place of sexual behavior in the social structure have, wittingly or unwittingly, been in terms of premarital behavior. A possible reason for this focus is that variations in patterns of sexual activities appear to be much greater in premarriage than in marriage, and hence more readily recorded.

Observation of sexual variations by social categories have in the history of sex research tended to precede those by social groups, although frequently in the more recent studies analyses in terms of both of these perspectives have occurred simultaneously. Two categories, age and particularly sex, which are significantly related to patterns of sexual behavior, have been dealt with throughout this chapter. Three others which have been examined at length in various studies need also to be mentioned. They are rural-urban residence, particularly in childhood; religion by the identification of Protestant, Catholic, and Jewish; and regularity of church attendance. The rural-urban difference is slight or negligible (Ehrmann, 1959a; Kinsey et al., 1948; Kinsey et al., 1953). The reason for this unanticipated similarity is probably that rural life is becoming more like city life in its social values and practices.

Of the other social variables which have been used in research, the degree of religious devoutness as measured by regularity of church attendance appears most consistently related to premarital sexual expression, both petting and coitus. The religious inactives, males and females alike, are sexually more experienced and active than those who attend church more regularly (Burgess & Wallin, 1953; Ehrmann, 1959a; Kinsey et al., 1948; Kinsey et al., 1953). By contrast, the research has revealed to date no consistent and reliable relationship between the three major religious groups (Protestant, Catholic, and Jewish) and premarital sexual behavior (Burgess & Wallin, 1953; Ehrmann, 1959a; Kinsey et al., 1948; Kinsey et al., 1953; C. Landis et al., 1940). Further-

more, the researches of Kinsey and associates (1953) indicated that the patterns of
marital coitus among females were essentially the same, regardless of their religious
identification or their level of devoutness.
Whether regular church-attenders are less
sexually active in premarriage *because* of
church teachings, or whether these people
are primarily social conformists to the traditional mores, and in consequence engage
less in sexual activities as well as go to
church more regularly, irrespective of theological considerations, has not been determined.

The studies which have demonstrated
important correlations between sexual behavior, primarily premarital, and the social
structure have come from studies of social
classes, ethnic (Negro-white) groups, and
cross-cultural comparisons.

One of the principal contributions of
Kinsey and associates (1948; 1953) was
their analysis of sexual behavior in terms of
educational achievement, which probably
gives the same results as would an analysis
by social class. Their findings revealed that
significant differences existed between the
sexual practices of the members of the various educational levels, and further that variations in the patterns for males and females
are not the same. They found that an increase in premarital sexual experience, particularly coitus, was related primarily to age
at marriage and secondarily to educational
level among females, but among males to
educational level but not to age at marriage.
The order of heterosexual and autoerotic
experiences in the late teens for the noncollegiate males, i.e., those who eventually
did not go beyond grade or high school,
was coitus, masturbation, and nocturnal
orgasm; whereas for the collegiate male it
was masturbation, nocturnal orgasm, and
coitus. For the same age group, the variation among the females was much less
pronounced, although there was a reported
difference by educational level. The order of
sexual activity in which orgasm was reached
was, for noncollegiate females, masturba-

tion, coitus, and petting; and for collegiate
females, masturbation, petting, and coitus.

When the criteria of whether the individual experienced premarital coitus is used,
the same pattern for males, but a diametrical one for females, emerges in the data of
Kinsey and associates (1948; 1953). About
two-thirds of the collegiate males and
nearly all of the noncollegiate males, and
more than half of the collegiate females, but
less than half of the noncollegiate females
had had sexual intercourse by the time of
marriage. The reason for this difference in
pattern among females is that females in
the lower educational levels marry at an
earlier age, and the sexually most active
period of the single female is the one or
two years prior to marriage, irrespective of
educational level. The consequence is that
girls in the lower educational levels are
sexually more active at an earlier age and
those in the higher levels at a later age.
Eventually, therefore, the collegiate females
equal, then surpass, the noncollegiate females in the proportion who have had premarital coitus.

It should be noted that the patterns of
premarital sexual behavior of males and females in the college-level group are much
more alike than are those of the noncollegiate males and females. A possible explanation (Ehrmann, 1954) is that there is a
greater male-female equality and, especially
after the age of 20, an increasing acceptance
of female sexual expression by both males
and females in the collegiate group. Among
the noncollegiate group, however, males
apparently have greater resort to prostitutes
or to other categories of highly promiscuous
females.

Although the tendency of some males in
our society to descend the social ladder in
their search for willing sexual partners is
legend, the observation by Hollingshead
(1949) that some Elmtown young males
considered girls from a lower social class as
"fair game" was one of the first empirical
observations of the influence of the crossing
of class lines for sex partners. In a later

study, Hollingshead (1953) made a systematic analysis of marriage partners by social class in an eastern city. This research confirmed another folk legend. Although persons usually marry within their own social class, the men who cross class lines in marriage are more likely than women to select a spouse from a lower social class. It must be added parenthetically that this phenomenon is one of the two principal ways social classes are kept fluid. Some women raise their status by marriage, since the husband usually establishes the social position, and many men, as well as some women, by economic or professional activities. Although Hollingshead did not draw the analogy, this pertinent question suggests itself: To what extent does the male's search for sex partners help to maintain a fluid social structure? (Ehrmann, 1955; Ehrmann, 1959b). Although there is as yet no scientific answer to this question, two other studies are germane to this general topic.

The comparative social class of the companion was found by Ehrmann (1955; 1959a) to be markedly associated with the premarital sexual behavior of the male, but only slightly with that of the female. Most members of both sexes limit their dating to companions of the same social class, and, in consequence, have all their experiences with these companions. Male crossers of class lines were sexually more active than noncrossers, and their extreme experiences were more often with girls of a lower social class. Kanin and Howard (1958) also report that the comparative social-class position of husbands and wives, but not the social-class position of the husband, was correlated with premarital coitus with future spouse. The incidence of premarital sexual intercourse with spouse was highest for couples when the husband was of a higher social class than his wife, intermediate when husband and wife were from the same social class, and lowest when the wife was from a higher social class than her husband.

The study of the actual and assumed differences between the sexual mores and practices of Negroes and whites is an excellent lesson in cultural history and social change. Under the conditions of slavery wherein the Negro was unable to develop any semblance of marriage stability or of a family unit with a father at its head, sexual activities became transitory, and the family became centered on the mother. Although the Negroes became Christians, and in many ways among the most devout of all people, they never acquired the deep guilt about sex being sinful which was prevalent among the whites. The limited research data on this subject tend, however, to confirm the common observations, first, that Negroes have more premarital sexual experiences than whites, but, second, that Negroes and whites are converging in their patterns of sexual behavior. Hohman and Schaffner (1947) found among a large sample of male Army inductees that a great majority of whites but nearly all of the Negroes had experienced premarital coitus. Gebhard and associates (1958) reported that although the Negro females had higher incidence rates of premarital sexual intercourse than the white females, the more educated had lower rates than the less educated, and hence the better-educated Negro females were more like their white counterparts than were the less educated.

The greater sex guilt of the white as compared to the Negro woman also shows up in a very objective way in some of the data of the Kinsey researches as reported by Gebhard and associates (1958). Out-of-wedlock births were much higher among Negro than white females, but induced abortions were much higher among white than Negro females. Thus, seemingly, the greater sex guilt of the white woman drives her to undergo an abortion, which many consider to be a greater sin than an illegitimate birth, rather than face the consequences of an irrefutable proof of her illicit sexual act.

The cross-cultural studies of premarital sexual behavior and values among collegians in Denmark, the Midwest, and a

Mormon culture of the Intermountain West by Christensen (1960) and Christensen and Carpenter (1962a; 1962b) are also pathfinders in the search for sociological interpretations of the interrelation between sex and the social order. They found higher rates of premarital coitus and higher scores on sex permissiveness in Denmark as compared with the two samples from the United States, and the Midwestern students showed higher permissive scores and higher coital rates than did the students in the Mormon culture (1962a). In all three samples, males showed higher permissiveness scores and coital rates than females, but these sex differences were relatively small in the permissive culture of Denmark. In the study of premarital pregnancy by the "record linkage" method in Denmark, Indiana, and Utah, Christensen (1960) determined that Denmark shows the highest incidence of premarital pregnancy and Utah the lowest, but the premarital pregnant couples in Denmark tended to take their time about getting married, and tended not to let the pregnancy affect them negatively to the point of divorce in comparison with those from the other two cultures. Thus, cultural sexual permissiveness was found to be associated with higher incidences of but lower divorce rates from premarital pregnancy.

IMPLICATIONS FOR FUTURE RESEARCH

In these concluding remarks, it would seem appropriate to speculate upon the nature and condition of research into the social aspects of human sexual behavior. As a point of departure, we might consider the following perennial questions, without the expectation of answering them, but with the reminder of their never-ending relevance, for they summarize the basic issues which need to be faced by future researchers.

What role does sex play in contemporary human social relations?

What basic contributions have been made and, perhaps, should be made to the study of these aspects of human existence?

What are the limitations imposed upon the scholarly pursuit of these studies?

The Role of Sex in Social Relations

It would also seem appropriate to reiterate a basic theme of this chapter: sex does play an extremely critical role in both the non-marital and marital aspects of our culture. This conclusion is worth repeating, even though it appears patent. The crux of the problem is that eroticism has become an integral part of romantic love, and romantic love is to an increasing degree the basis for male-female relations in premarriage and marriage alike, as well as even in extramarital affairs. That the erotic emotions and acts of humans are still viewed in our society, although to a lesser extent than in the recent past, as sinful, or indecent, or improper and as a perennial source of guilt and anxiety has necessitated the development of elaborate social arrangements for reconciling these two pervasive value systems, and for providing, however imperfectly, greater protection for males and females in their relationships. These considerations alone, to say nothing of all others, make the sexual component of contemporary human relations an issue of vital significance.

The principal social arrangements which have emerged to enable all individuals in our society, but primarily the adolescent and the young adult, to cope with these conflicting demands of our cultural heritage are the emerging premarital sex codes of conduct and the now well-established value of marriage based on love and a satisfactory sexual adjustment. The essential feature, or social structure, which has made these new customs effective, or "functional"—to use the appropriate scholarly jargon—is the institutionalization of male-female relations generally and of heterosexuality specifically, so that erotic expression tends to be linked to an increasing degree with personal ideas and feelings of affection and love.

Furthermore, this institutionalization provides safeguards through reciprocal individual commitments and social acceptance for both sexual expression and sexual restraint. There are, of course, individuals at each extreme: those who deny themselves any expression, probably for an infinite variety of reasons, and those who attempt to give unrestrained play to their sexual desires. But even the latter are usually unable to behave entirely in accordance with their purely personal wishes because of restrictions imposed by their partners and by the social setting generally.

Another aspect of these arrangements which has contributed equally to their success, and one which is certainly not accidental, is that, whereas they offer a common frame of reference within which these adjustments can be made, and, hence, they are socially integrating in this respect, they also allow for great group and individual variations. Thus, we can say with equal justification that the sex codes of conduct and the romantic union of sex and love in marriage are a reflection of the pluralistic society within which we live, and that they provide for both unity and diversity, the essential ingredients for a social organization of partially disparate but wholly interdependent groups.

Accomplishments and Further Requirements

The second question would seem to be the easiest one to answer. The main requirement in this area is the same as that for any systematic inquiry into phenomena, that is, the constant construction and reconstruction of a theoretical frame of reference which by experience provides, insofar as we are humanly able to determine, a more accurate "fit," or understanding, of the "reality" which we are studying. We are here, of course, not speaking about statistical or other research techniques, for these have probably been taken to points of refinement in the behavioral sciences far beyond anything needed for the foreseeable future in sex research. What we are talking about is the need for formulating propositions about the interconnection between the sexual and other components of human social relations which can be verified or recast by the time-tested means which have been developed over the centuries by scientists and scholars.

When one views the history and the present status of research into the social aspects of human sexual behavior from a substantive aspect, he finds an interesting—and one might say even a curious—unevenness in development. The most significant contributions have been made in the study of the premarital relations of adolescents and young adults. By contrast, the systematic studies of eroticism and marriage, which were initially highly promising, have subsequently not been pursued as energetically as those of premarriage, and the ones which have been made seem to have produced inconclusive results, generally speaking. Only meager attempts have been forthcoming in the analysis of the sexual component of parent-child relations, and these efforts have been largely, although not entirely, sterile.

It is recognized, of course, that those dealing in the study of the human personality, particularly those concerned directly with psychotherapy in the broad sense of the term—clinical psychologists, psychoanalysts, and psychiatrists—have made great strides in understanding the erotic aspects and components of the psychodynamics of human behavior. Their efforts would appear to have produced findings and orientations which are remarkably effective in treating an enormous variety of emotional ills. These contributions, however commendable in their own right, are nonetheless not primarily concerned with the study of the social patterns of human relations, nor do they purport to be. Hence, although they have been suggestive to the area of concern of this paper, and will certainly continue to be so, they do not, we believe, offer the fundamental theoretical framework for its scholarly understanding.

The earlier studies of premarriage began with the simple description of premarital sexual behavior, a prerequisite to developing a more analytical and theoretical study of this phenomenon, to which subsequent researches have continued to make substantial contributions. The more recent studies have taken a distinct step forward by describing not simply the patterns of sexual behavior, speaking in a limited sense of the word, but also the associated social elements, such as the sexual codes of conduct, within which this behavior takes place: how sexuality is patterned and channeled, given expression or nonexpression through an interrelated system which includes emotions, behavior, and values. These researches have also entered into still a third stage in the development of a theoretical understanding of premarital heterosexuality by examining the way in which the patterns of heterosexuality are related to other aspects of the total social system, such as those characteristics associated with class, ethnic, and religious groups. In a very real, although limited, sense, therefore, this discussion can be concluded with the remark that an adequate groundwork has been laid for future research into the social aspects of heterosexual relations—provided, however, that we are speaking solely of premarriage.

With reference to marriage, the meager results achieved thus far can probably be attributed to three quite different considerations: one has to do with the nature of marriage itself; another with the manner in which its sexual component has been studied heretofore by the experts; and a third with the pervasive resistance of the mores to undertaking in a "purely objective" fashion the study of these matters. The third consideration has, of course,

hindered advances in the study of all areas of human sexuality. Hence, its significance in this regard will be discussed later on in its over-all implications for research, past and future.

Other things being equal, it is usually more difficult to determine the relative significance of an element (such as sex) in a social situation which appears more uniform (such as marriage) than in one which appears less so (such as premarriage). As mentioned previously, the relation of male and female in our society has been to a far greater extent institutionalized in marriage than in premarriage, but we can add here that its institutionalization within marriage has taken place in a more standardized or uniform manner throughout the population. The distinction between these two considerations should be clearly noted. For example, it might well be that marriage is thoroughly institutionalized in each of two groups, but its form in one is quite different from the other. The point to be made is that although the new forms of premarital relations are becoming to an increasing degree institutionalized, they are not as institutionalized as marriage, and, furthermore, they show more variation.

It may be, therefore, that while eroticism has become a more significant item in marriage generally—an observation which appears well substantiated by historical events —it has been incorporated into the expected and accepted ways of a husband-wife relation—i.e., institutionalized—in a more uniform way than it has been in premarriage. Although this uniformity may in fact be much more characteristic of marriage than premarriage, there is good reason to believe also that it is not as uniform as it appears to be. The net result is the same, however, because determining the consequences of sexual considerations in marriage is actually more difficult or is thought to be more difficult.

This research problem appears also to have been compounded by the scholarly precedents established through the great pioneering studies of marital happiness. Subsequent adherence to their general theoretical orientation and research technique may have led us into a blind alley from which we have not yet extricated ourselves. This comment is made with no intent to derogate or to be hypercritical of the works of Terman, Burgess and Wallin, and the other pioneers in this area. Quite the contrary is true, for we owe these men a great and lasting debt for their contributions. Furthermore, great strides in one direction which were not productive in creating new knowledge beyond a certain point are a common occurrence in the history of all sciences. In this specific instance, the blame lies not with these scholars, for they did their task extraordinarily well, but rather with those of us who followed, because we failed to build creatively upon what they had done. We merely parroted their ways, which is fatal in any creative scholarly endeavor. [Cf. Ch. 6 of this Handbook.]

The first pitfall, a theoretical one, was created by an assumed or conceived connection between sex and marriage based upon the mores, which was compounded by a methodological device, the second pitfall, that led, not to a clarification of their interdependence, if any actually existed, but into a morass of greater obscurity. Here again a word of explanation is in order. There is nothing amiss with studying interdependencies assumed in the mores of the folk culture. In fact, a considerable portion of the study of human relations deals precisely and with scientific fruitfulness with these issues. But to limit scholarly inquiry just to these problems or to assume, after a few or even many dedicated efforts, either that there is no real connection between the phenomena studied or that the interdependence between them indicated by the mores is the only significant one is a serious and grievous error.

Historically, the two insistent questions which were paramount in our society, and the ones to which the researchers rightly turned their attention at the time systematic studies of male-female relations were being initiated, were: Does nonvirginity at marriage, particularly among females, really contribute to marital unhappiness? and, Is a satisfactory sexual adjustment essential to marital happiness?

As mentioned previously, perhaps the most surprising and unanticipated findings in the history of research into the social aspects of heterosexual behavior were two by Terman (1938). The one was that the proportion of women who were virgins at marriage was decreasing in succeeding generations with great rapidity, and the other was that marital happiness and adjustment appeared only slightly correlated with virginity. Another highly significant finding of Terman was that eroticism as measured by the orgasm adequacy of the wife and by equality or near equality of the sex desire of the spouses was an exceedingly important correlate of general marital adjustment. Although some investigators anticipated Terman to a slight extent, and others since then have tended to confirm his findings, his research into these questions was undoubtedly the most original and the most convincing.

The surprising facts are, first, that so little has been done to examine more extensively and intensively these findings as they may relate to a variety of social conditions and considerations and, even more important, to explore other aspects of the sexual components of marriage; and, second, that the studies which have made these attempts have not gone very much beyond the point where Terman left off. The basic limitation to further advances in these areas would appear to be that subsequent researchers have made no substantial effort to use any other frame of reference than that of Terman—in other words, the obvious and apparent orientation suggested by the mores. It should be noted parenthetically that although Kinsey and his associates in their studies published to date were not greatly concerned with the interrelation between sexual behavior and other aspects of marriage, their extensive data and method of analysis are highly suggestive for future research into this area. The same thing can, of course, be said about many of the recent studies into premarital behavior.

The second limitation is inherent in the method of analysis used by Terman and those who followed in his footsteps. These investigators attempted to determine the interrelation between sex and marriage by correlating marital adjustment "scores," or "indices," with sexual items. The marital adjustment scores were compiled from a variety of attitudinal and behavioral items concerning the marriage. Although this device produced some fruitful results in the Terman and a few other studies, its potential except for some further refinements seems to have been virtually exhausted. The limitation of this method is that the marital adjustment score is a conglomerate of items, each of which undoubtedly has a difference of degree and kind in social-sexual relations. It is not merely conceivable but quite probable that this method obscures the importance of individual items and, of much greater importance, it also obscures, or may even make impossible, a consideration of fundamental patterns of interrelationship. This problem, however, being of a technical nature, is one that the specialists, once they focus attention on it, could resolve without undue difficulty. [For amplification and a somewhat different point of view, see Ch. 6 of this Handbook.]

Outside Resistance to Sex Research

In the history of sex research, the basic and most effective limitation imposed upon the pursuit of the study of human sexuality, whether marital or nonmarital, has come not primarily from scholarly considerations in and of themselves, even though these have sometimes been, and still are, formidable. During almost every age in which scholarly and scientific advances have been made which appeared to have challenged cherished traditional beliefs, they and their chief creators have been vigorously and even savagely attacked. A few of the famous among the long list who have been persecuted in this socially significant way in the strand of modern scientific effort (to which, of course, could be added many of the great names of the ancient world, such as Socrates) are Galileo, Pasteur, Darwin, Freud, and Kinsey. That the two most recent members of this list were the centers of great controversy in part at least because of their interest in sex is particularly germane to our present discussion.

It would seem fitting in this context to call attention to the famous "Koch case." Dr. Leo F. Koch, Assistant Professor of Biology at the University of Illinois, was suspended and then discharged from his position on the faculty in April, 1960, because of a letter written by him and published in the campus paper (AAUP, 1963). In that letter Professor Koch was severely critical of contemporary mores. Upon an appeal from Professor Koch, the American Association of University Professors authorized an *ad hoc* committee to investigate the case and to report to the Association's Committee on Academic Freedom and Tenure (Committee A). Committee A authorized the publication of the report in this case, which appeared in the Spring, 1963, issue of the *AAUP Bulletin*. The Annual Meeting of the AAUP in April, 1963, upon the recommendation of Committee A, censured the administration of the University of Illinois, including the Board of Trustees, for the "improper manner" in which Professor Koch was dismissed. In other words, censure was invoked over the procedural, not the substantive, issue in the case. The published report on the Koch case (AAUP, 1963), it should be noted parenthetically, carries implications which go far beyond the scope of our discussion, because in the addenda to the Report of the *Ad Hoc* Committee the issue of what constitutes "academic responsibility" is discussed by that committee and by individual members of Committee A. "Academic responsibility" in this context pertains to the rights and obligations of a faculty member in his public utterances as a citizen.

The Koch report is of immediate concern to our current discussion, however, because it is an exceedingly well documented "case study" of the reaction of an important segment of the academic community to the expression of unpopular views on sex. In censuring the administration of the University of Illinois, the AAUP was neither accepting nor rejecting Professor Koch's views or the reaction of the university officials to them. His views are, however, discussed in the report of the case and in the addenda. Although Professor Koch's letter and the documented reaction of Dr. David D. Henry, president of the university, and the Board of Trustees to it are too extensive to be cited here in full, a few extracts will reveal their tenor.

In his letter to the student newspaper, which was published on March 18, 1960, Professor Koch stated:

With modern contraceptives and medical advice readily available at the nearest drugstore, or at least a family physician, there is no valid reason why sexual intercourse should not be condoned among those sufficiently mature to engage in it without social consequences and without violating their own codes of morality and ethics (AAUP, 1963, p. 26).

President Henry, in his letter to the dean of the college of April 7, directing him to suspend Professor Koch from his duties, observed:

With you, I consider Professor Koch's letter a grave breach of academic responsibility. The views expressed are offensive and repugnant, contrary to commonly accepted standards of morality and their public espousal may be interpreted as encouragement of immoral behavior. It is clear that Mr. Koch's conduct has been prejudicial to the best interests of the University (p. 28).

One of the basic findings adopted by the Board of Trustees of the University of Illinois after a hearing on June 14 was that the Koch letter of March 18

... was not a reasoned statement, marshalling evidence in support of views held by him, but was one in which, through the use of overstatement and ridicule, he denounced society as depraved, condemned as inhumane and obsolete the widely accepted moral standards derived from the Christian code of ethics and the commonly accepted moral standards then prevailing in the community ... (p. 30).

The investigating committee in its discussion of academic responsibility stated that

Generally speaking, it seems clear to us that, had the letter dealt with any subject other than sex mores, religion, or some other acutely sensitive area, its language and tone would have passed unnoticed. We do not believe that a faculty member writing on these subjects should be held to higher standards of responsibility than one writing on less controversial topics. In any event we are convinced that fundamentally the objections of the Board of Trustees are directed against the "offensive and repugnant" views expressed, rather than the style of composition. This would appear to have been the reaction also of President Henry, as conveyed in his letter of April 7. Once one excludes from consideration the "offensive" nature of the substantive ideas in Professor Koch's letter, as it is conceded the principles of academic freedom require, the finding of a breach of academic responsibility because of language and tone seems to us wholly untenable (p. 39).

The committee might well have added that if Professor Koch had used precisely the same forceful language in *support* of the traditional sex mores, it is inconceivable that those in authority would have raised the question of its propriety or of Professor Koch's "academic responsibility" in making it.

One might, of course, properly ask why reference is made to the Koch case in this discussion when he was not a specialist in the study of human sexual behavior—and he never portrayed himself as such—and he was expressing an *opinion,* not the results of objective research findings. The point is that even a cursory examination of the history of scientific inquiry into the social aspects of human sexual behavior demonstrates that there is a tendency to view researches which have reported sexual practices, attitudes, and values contrary to the prevailing mores—and, of course, this includes virtually all research of this kind—as being merely "opinions," not substantiated findings, and as "irresponsible," not the considered judgment of professional scholars. The Koch case is, therefore, of immediate interest to our discussion because it contains elements which are analogous to those used in criticisms by laymen and scholars alike of research into human sexuality.

In the contemporary scientific ethos, it is usually not considered proper to impugn the motives of a researcher, but it is eminently correct to criticize his theoretical orientation and his techniques of investigation. In fact, scholarly and scientific criticisms are essential elements in the advancement of knowledge. Critics of sex research have, therefore, frequently attacked the theoretical frame of reference and the method of sex research so that its validity is questioned, and hence its "findings" are reduced to 'opinions." Thus, the so-called researcher is in the minds of his critics—however unconscious the process—removed from the brotherhood of "sound" scholars or scientists, and can thereby become the subject of some rather unscholarly attacks. A portion of the voluminous critical literature on the Kinsey reports appears to be of this kind.

This system of discrediting scholars whose findings go contrary to the received opinions of dominant groups has, of course, characterized all intellectual history. The bitter historic conflicts in philosophy, theology, politics, economics, the natural sciences, and other disciplines can all be told in these terms. The aspect which may be temporarily characteristic of the battle of

issues in sex research is that the antagonists may still be in a state of "pre-Machiavellian" consciousness about what they are doing.

There are at least two other considerations which should be mentioned as having a bearing upon the nature and direction of research into the social aspects of human sexual behavior: the first may have and the second certainly has had an effect. Scholars—researchers, teachers, and clinicians—who deal in the area of the family and of male-female relations in general, and especially in their sexual aspects, are considered even by their peers a peculiar lot. It need hardly be added that laymen in general view scholars, particularly college professors, in this very same light, sometimes with aversion but, happily for those in the academic profession, more often with affection. The crucial fact, however, within the academic community is that, generally speaking and with notable exceptions, those who deal in male-female relations and especially in sex are not held in as high esteem as those who are concerned with most other aspects of human affairs, to say nothing of those who deal in molecules and atoms and greater and lesser manifestations thereof. Whether scholars of male-female relations are less competent in this field than the others are in theirs is, of course, completely moot. The significant consequence, however, is that the former do not usually receive as much personal prestige and resultant moral support as do scholars generally, when they are frequently the very ones who need it most in order to carry on their work. Then, too, it should be remembered that this field is not one which now receives any substantial research support from either private or public sources. [Cf. this and the following sections with Kerckhoff's discussions, pp. 898–903.]

Handicaps from Within the Family Life Movement

A more serious limiting condition to the advancement of sex research may be the doctrinal quarrels which have been endemic among those who are involved in the social phenomenon called the "family life movement." The unifying element in it, the improvement of family life in its broadest aspects, is certainly considered among the most noble in our culture. The groups which compose the movement are a motley array, however. They include those who are interested in all manifestations of male-female relations, including their aberrations. Many of them are, however, concerned primarily with educating, helping, or indoctrinating—according to one's frame of reference—young and old alike to become "better" parents and husbands and wives. They are, therefore, as a whole not greatly interested in research per se—although each faction within the movement might very well be, especially in some cases if the findings from research support their goals. This statement is not a criticism, but an observation; and of course there are exceptions to it. It is characteristic of all proselytizing groups—whether religious, political, economic, or other—to use that which aids the "cause" and to ignore or minimize that which does not. The members of the movement include teachers, social workers, psychotherapists, marriage counselors, clerics, lawyers, and others of virtually all religious commitments whose philosophies in sex range from "free love," although there are precious few of these, to the most strict puritanism, here used in its generic sense.

Nevertheless, the adherents of this movement, primarily through several formal organizations and particularly the National Council on Family Relations, would appear to have done much over all to enhance the general quality of male-female relations. Furthermore, there is a solid core within the movement well committed to the research point of view.

Because of the great heterogeneity of the groups within this movement, conflicts about ways and means of achieving its goals are inevitable. That a substantial consensus has been reached on certain basic issues in the face of extremely basic differences is remarkable. Furthermore, having this open forum for considering different points of view, actually a lay-academic market of ideas, should lead to even greater creativity in dealing with male-female relations.

These doctrinal conflicts within the movement may have deleterious effects upon research, however. The reason for this, of course, is that a clear distinction in these discourses has not been maintained between what is research and what is indoctrination, or to put the question more broadly, "what is" and "what ought to be." Therefore, research results have frequently been supported or attacked in terms of doctrine rather than considered on their scholarly merits. Furthermore, the formulation of research has too frequently used as a basic frame of reference the value system of a particular partisan group—although this has unquestionably been done quite unconsciously by the investigator—rather than one based upon purely scholarly, i.e., theoretical, considerations.

In view of the many obstacles thus far encountered in the history of sex research, there is little wonder that so few have chosen this subject as their field of scholarly inquiry. But mavericks and pioneers occur in every condition of life, and especially in the field of the intellect, and this one appears to be no exception. Whether there should be a greater or smaller number of individuals in the field of sex research is a debatable question. The reason that it is moot is that the criteria for deciding such an issue depend upon one's system of values. One set might dictate that no investigation is justified, whereas another might establish the need for a far greater effort than we have seen thus far. In view of the great demand among large segments of the general public and professional groups for answers to problems of sex, however, even though its full force is greatly weakened by the handicaps previously discussed, there appears every expectation that research into this subject will continue at least at the present rate. Even though we may not be able to agree that there should be greater research efforts in this area— although most of us who are engaged in it believe, of course, that there should be—we can at least make a justifiable plea of another kind.

If we grant that it is desirable to adhere to the "ethos of scientific and scholarly inquiry," then we can at least ask that investigators into the social aspects of human sexual behavior be given a fair and full opportunity to be heard. It would then follow that their contributions would be properly tested within the arena of scholarly discourse. Worthwhile theoretical advances could then follow, which, in turn, would offer some solutions for the practical problems of everyday life. If this were done, it would also seem reasonable to believe that even a small number of investigators might make exceedingly worthwhile contributions. In fact, throughout the history of scholarly thought and scientific enterprise, most of the basic contributions to the fund of knowledge have been made in each generation by a relative handful of dedicated "searchers" and "researchers." There is no reason to doubt that this same thing can happen in this particular branch of intellectual endeavor, provided those in it are given a reasonable opportunity to carry on their work.

REFERENCES

Aberle, Sophie D., & Corner, G. W. *Twenty-five years of sex research.* Philadelphia: Saunders, 1953.

American Association of University Professors. Academic freedom and tenure: the University of Illinois. *AAUP Bull.,* 1963, 49, 25–43.

Beigel, H. Romantic love. *Amer. sociol. Rev.,* 1951, 16, 326–334.

Bromley, Dorothy D., & Britten, Florence H. *Youth and sex: a study of 1300 college students.* New York: Harper, 1938.

Burgess, E. W., & Locke, H. *The family.* New York: American Book, 1953.

Burgess, E. W., & Wallin, P. *Engagement and marriage.* Philadelphia: Lippincott, 1953.

Christensen, H. T. Cultural relativism and premarital sex norms. *Amer. sociol. Rev.,* 1960, 25, 31–39.

Christensen, H. T., & Carpenter, G. R. Timing patterns in the development of sexual intimacy. *Marr. & fam. Living,* 1962, 24, 30–35. (a)

Christensen, H. T., & Carpenter, G. R. Value-behavior discrepancies regarding premarital coitus in three western cultures. *Amer. sociol. Rev.,* 1962, 27, 66–74. (b)

Cole, W. G. *Sex in Christianity and psychoanalysis.* New York: Oxford Univer. Press, 1955.

Cole, W. G. *Sex and love in the Bible.* New York: Association Press, 1959.

Cole, W. G. Protestantism and sex. In A. Ellis & A. Abarbanel (Eds.), *The encyclopedia of sexual behavior.* Vol. 2. New York: Hawthorn Books, 1961. Pp. 883–888.

Davis, Katharine B. *Factors in the sex life of twenty-two hundred women.* New York: Harper, 1929.

de Rougemont, D. *Love in the western world.* Trans. M. Belgion. New York: Harcourt, Brace, 1940.

Ehrmann, W. Non-conformance of male and female reports on premarital coitus. *Soc. Probl.,* 1954, 1, 155–159.

Ehrmann, W. Influence of comparative social class of companion upon premarital heterosexual behavior. *Marr. & fam. Living,* 1955, 17, 48–53.

Ehrmann, W. Some knowns and unknowns in research into human sex behavior. *Marr. & fam. Living,* 1957, 19, 16–22.

Ehrmann, W. *Premarital dating behavior.* New York: Holt, 1959. (a)

Ehrmann, W. Premarital sexual behavior and sex codes of conduct with acquaintances, friends, and lovers. *Soc. Forces,* 1959, 38, 158–164. (b)

Ehrmann, W. Changing sexual mores. In E. Ginzberg (Ed.), *Values and ideals of American youth.* New York: Columbia Univer. Press, 1961. Pp. 53–70. (a)

Ehrmann, W. Premarital sexual intercourse. In A. Ellis & A. Abarbanel (Eds.), *The encyclopedia of sexual behavior.* Vol. 2. New York: Hawthorn Books, 1961. Pp. 860–868. (b)

Ehrmann, W. The variety and meaning of

premarital heterosexual experiences for the college student. *J. nat. Ass. women Deans & Counselors*, 1963, 26, 22–28.

Exner, M. J. *Problems and principles of sex education: a study of 948 college men.* New York: Association Press, 1915.

Ferguson, L. W. Correlates of woman's orgasm. *J. Psychol.*, 1938, 6, 295–302.

Ford, C. S., & Beach, F. A. *Patterns of sexual behavior.* New York: Harper, 1951.

Gebhard, P. H., Pomeroy, W., Martin, C., & Christenson, Cornelia. *Pregnancy, birth, and abortion.* New York: Harper, 1958.

Geddes, D. P. (Ed.) *An analysis of the Kinsey reports on sexual behavior in the human male and female.* New York: Dutton, 1954.

Hamilton, G. V. *A research in marriage.* New York: Boni, 1929.

Himelhoch, J., & Fava, Sylvia F. (Eds.) *Sexual behavior in American society.* New York: Norton, 1955.

Hohman, L. B., & Schaffner, B. The sex lives of unmarried men. *Amer. J. Sociol.*, 1947, 52, 501–507.

Hollingshead, A. B. *Elmtown's youth: the impact of social classes on adolescents.* New York: Wiley, 1949.

Hollingshead, A. B. Cultural factors in the selection of marriage mates. *Amer. sociol. Rev.*, 1953, 15, 625–626.

Howard, G. E. *A history of matrimonial institutions.* Chicago: Univer. of Chicago Press, 1904. 3 vols.

Kanin, E. J. Male aggression in dating-courtship relations. *Amer. J. Sociol.*, 1957, 63, 197–204.

Kanin, E. J. Premarital sex adjustments, social class, and associated behaviors. *Marr. & fam. Living*, 1960, 22, 258–262.

Kanin, E. J., & Howard, D. H. Postmarital consequences of premarital sex adjustments. *Amer. sociol. Rev.*, 1958, 23, 556–562.

King, C. Factors associated with the marital adjustment of Negro couples. Unpublished doctoral dissertation, Univer. of Chicago, 1951. (Cited in Burgess & Wallin, 1953.)

Kinsey, A. C., Pomeroy, W. B., & Martin, C. E. *Sexual behavior in the human male.* Philadelphia: Saunders, 1948.

Kinsey, A. C., Pomeroy, W. B., Martin, C. E., & Gebhard, P. H. *Sexual behavior in the human female.* Philadelphia: Saunders, 1953.

Kirkendall, L. A. *Premarital intercourse and interpersonal relationships.* New York: Julian Press, 1961.

Kirkpatrick, C. *The family: as process and institution.* New York: Ronald Press, 1955.

Kirkpatrick, C., & Kanin, E. J. Male sex aggression on a university campus. *Amer. sociol. Rev.*, 1957, 22, 52–56.

Landis, C., et al. *Sex in development.* New York: Harper, 1940.

Landis, J. T., & Landis, Mary G. *Building a successful marriage.* New York: Prentice-Hall, 1948.

Lea, H. C. *An historical sketch of sacerdotal celibacy in the Christian church.* Philadelphia: Lippincott, 1867.

Lecky, W. E. H. *History of European morals from Augustus to Charlemagne.* London: Longmans, 1859. 2 vols.

Leuba, C. *The sexual nature of man.* Garden City, N.Y.: Doubleday, 1954.

Locke, H. J. *Predicting adjustment in marriage: a comparison of a divorced and a happily married group.* New York: Holt, 1951.

Malinowski, B. *The sexual life of savages in northwestern Melanesia.* New York: Liveright, 1929.

Mead, Margaret. *Male and female: a study of the sexes in a changing world.* New York: Morrow, 1949.

Murdock, G. P. *Social structure.* New York: Macmillan, 1949.

Rainwater, L., & Weinstein, Karol K. *And the poor get children.* Chicago: Quadrangle Books, 1960.

Reevy, W. R. Marital prediction scores of college women relative to behavior and attitudes. Unpublished doctoral dissertation, Pennsylvania State Univer., 1954.

Reiss, I. L. *Premarital sexual standards in America.* Glencoe, Ill.: Free Press, 1960.

Rockwood, L. D., & Ford, Mary E. N. *Youth, marriage, and parenthood: the attitudes of 364 university juniors and seniors toward courtship, marriage, and parenthood.* New York: Wiley, 1945.

Sears, R. R. *Survey of objective studies of psychoanalytic concepts.* New York: Social Science Research Council, 1943.

Terman, L. M., with Buttenwieser, P., Ferguson, L. W., Johnson, W. B., & Wilson, D. P. *Psychological factors in marital happiness.* New York: McGraw-Hill, 1938.

Terman, L. M., & Oden, Melita H. *The gifted*

child grows up: twenty-five years follow-up of a superior group. Stanford: Stanford Univer. Press, 1947.

Thomason, B. Extent of spousal agreement on certain non-sexual and sexual aspects of marital adjustment. *Marr. & fam. Living,* 1955, 17, 332–337. (a)

Thomason, B. Marital sexual behavior and total marital adjustment: a research report. In J. Himelhoch & Sylvia F. Fava (Eds.), *Sexual behavior in American society.* New York: Norton, 1955. Pp. 153–163. (b)

Vincent, C. *Unmarried mothers.* Glencoe, Ill.: Free Press, 1961.

Waller, W. The rating and dating complex. *Amer. sociol. Rev.,* 1937, 2, 728–729.

CHAPTER 16 The Premarital Dyad and Love Involvement

LEE G. BURCHINAL
United States Department of Health, Education, and Welfare

Dating and courtship in the United States usually occur early in life and cover, on the average, approximately six to eight years. Most boys and girls begin to date between their fourteenth and sixteenth birthdays. The median age for women entering first marriages in 1961 was just over 20 years of age, and the comparable median for men was just under 23 years of age. This chapter focuses on research related to dating, courtship, and mate selection during these early years of life between initial dating and marriage.

The research literature consists almost exclusively of sociological studies and, although its roots reach back into the early part of this century, the bulk of the research is less than two decades old. Despite the fact that hundreds of investigations have been conducted on various aspects of courtship and mate selection, there is no comprehensive theoretical conceptualization of the courtship process.

The well-established endogamy-homogamy and residential-propinquity generalizations are not theoretical propositions, they are empirical generalizations. Winch's theory of complementary needs (1954), the masterful theoretical analyses of residential-propinquity data by Katz and Hill (1958), or, in a modest way, Coombs' (1961) value theory of mate selection represent movements toward a theoretical understanding of mate selection in the United States. Further research employing a wide range of variables capable of broad conceptual generalization is needed before a comprehensive theory of the courtship process can be developed. At present, however, available data can be reviewed and integrated. This is the objective of the present chapter.

Research on courtship and mate selection is impressive for its richness and diversity, apart from its substantive content in certain areas. Five areas of research concentration and continuity emerge from the mass of investigations: residential propinquity, rating and dating, endogamy-homogamy and assortative mating, love and romanticism, and complementary needs. In addition, there is an accumulating body of descriptive and analytical data on numerous other facets of dating and courtship and, particularly in recent years, on dating, courtship, and marriage during the high school and immediate post-high school years. Generalizations emerging from these latter varied studies are discussed first and, following this, attention is given to the five areas previously mentioned.

ADOLESCENT DATING ATTITUDES AND BEHAVIOR

The conceptual relationships between dating and courtship have never been fully agreed upon by most American students of the phenomena.

Following the lead of Waller (1937), some students of family behavior have maintained a distinction between dating and courtship. One set of norms supposedly applied to dating roles, whereas another applied to courtship roles. More recent students of dating and courtship have abandoned this distinction and, instead, speak of a courtship continuum. The crux of the problem is that dating is a social relationship capable of wide variation in its meaning and functions, not only to family sociologists, but also to participants in the dating system, even between two persons who comprise a dating dyad. As more knowledge has become available, previous conceptual differences over "aim-inhibited" dating versus courtship have lost their meaning. Instead, the impressive features of American dating patterns have been their diversity and versatility in coping with changes in sex roles. Terms such as "playing the field," "favorite date," "competitive dating," "noncommitment steady dating," or "committed steady dating" (E. A. Smith, 1962) are used to describe the varied patterns.

Although sociologists have written much about courtship and mate selection, careful study of dating began only after World War II. Prior to this time, much of the thinking about dating was dominated by the conceptions of Waller (1937). As recently as 1948, for instance, Lowrie (1948) could publish a paper rightly entitled, "Dating: A Neglected Field of Study." Since then, at least several dozen studies of high school dating patterns have appeared. Still more studies on the dating and courtship of college students are available, but there is little direct research on the dating and courtship behavior of post-high school and noncollege youth.

Dating, as an American innovation, developed in the urban areas and among college students in the 1920's in response to the emancipation of women, increased leisure time, greater emancipation of youth, higher real incomes, commercialized recreation, and the extension of coeducational institutions. During the late 1930's and the 1940's, dating moved to the high school level. In these few decades, norms have been evolving to guide dating behavior. To some extent, these norms are perceived differently by adults and by adolescents, although they are not shared equally by all persons in either age group.

Some of the important norms and related generalizations pertaining to the earlier phases of dating in the United States are summarized in seven major areas.

Initial Ages at Dating

Contrary to popular opinion, boys and girls begin to date and go steady at approximately the same ages. Girls may begin and attain physical maturity earlier than boys, but recognized sex differences in physical development appear to have little relation to ages at initial dating. Dating is a social relationship which is defined by cultural norms, not by biological developments per se. Apparently, only a minimum level of physical development is necessary for initiating dating.

Lowrie (1952) provides the most conclusive evidence for the similarity of mean or median ages for first dates or first steady dating among boys and girls. Bardis (1958), Cameron and Kenkel (1960), and Bock and Burchinal (1962) provide supplemental support for Lowrie's generalization.

Median ages for initial dating among the high school males and females in Lowrie's samples ranged between 14.1 and 14.9 years; medians for the college samples ranged between 14.7 and 15.7 years. On the average, these students began dating in the ninth and tenth grades. The averages reported by Bardis (1958), Cameron and Kenkel (1960), and Bock and Burchinal (1962) were toward the lower end of the ranges reported by Lowrie. These data for beginning ages at dating do not support the cries of alarm, especially in the press, about preteen dating. Some preteen dating undoubtedly occurs. Cameron and Kenkel, for instance, reported that the range in ages at first dates was from 11 to 18 in their population of high school seniors in Mason City, Iowa. But it appears that most students are not dating, in the usual sense of the word, during elementary school years or the first years of junior high school.

Although boys and girls begin to date at the same ages and generally date classmates initially (Crist, 1953; Lowrie, 1952), both sexes recognize female social precocity. For instance, Bardis (1958) found that females would like males to begin dating at older ages, and males would like females to begin dating at younger ages.

These attitudinal differences probably are reflected in behavior. Long-established differences in ages at marriage and in various levels of courtship suggest that, while girls are first interested in boys their own ages, they soon turn to older boys for attention and dates, and older boys, in turn, interest themselves in younger girls.

Transition to Dating

The transition from single-sex associations to association in heterosexual groups or paired-heterosexual association probably is less abrupt and less traumatic today than previously. Casual and friendly relations between the sexes in later adolescence and adulthood appear to have drifted downward into late childhood and early adolescence, periods which generally are assumed to be characterized by mutual antagonism between boys and girls. Broderick and Fowler (1961), for instance, found norms which

encourage and sustain cross-sex interaction among children in the fifth through seventh grades. A majority of the children claimed to have a sweetheart, and most expected reciprocation. Their claims did not seem to be wishful thinking, nor were they kept as hidden loves from afar; most of their classmates knew of and were able to identify various pairs.

Data reported by Broderick and Fowler for dating in these grades are not in agreement with data reported by Lowrie and others. About 45 per cent of the boys and 36 per cent of the girls in the Broderick and Fowler sample who were 10 and 11 years old claimed to have had at least one date. Still higher percentages were reported among the 12 and 13 year olds: 70 per cent of the boys and 53 per cent of the girls claimed they had dated. These percentages require means or medians well below the levels reported in other studies. It is possible that the youth from the middle class, southern, urban community studied by Broderick and Fowler began dating earlier than other youth in the northern or midwestern urban centers included in the studies previously discussed. Other data by Lowrie (1961) indicated that Texas youth begin dating earlier than youth in Ohio or California, which may suggest regional differences in ages at initial date. On the other hand, the sizes of the differences between the Broderick and Fowler results and other research on ages at initial dating suggest that the respondents in the sample they studied probably defined or interpreted dating in a less restrictive sense than respondents in other studies.

Insecurity in Dating

Although the transition to dating may be easier today than before, many youth still report considerable anxiety and unhappiness about their dating relationships. A national sample of high school students reported common feelings of inadequacy in dating and feelings of shyness, self-consciousness, or being ill at ease (Christensen, 1952; Christensen, 1958, pp. 231–245). Furthermore, large percentages of each sex were anxious for the other sex to assume more initiative in making dates. In another study, one-half of the high school students reported fears and anxiety over their first dates (Crist, 1953). The anxiety of the youth may be related to the fact that most of these ninth-grade students said they dated primarily because the group expected it, not because they wanted to. Breed (1956) found that two-thirds of the boys and girls in two social status levels, from business and working-class families, agreed they were "pretty scared" that they would do "something wrong" on their first dates.

Frustration is not limited to initial dating experiences. Williams (1949) surveyed approximately 1,500 high school students in comparable urban and rural communities in Michigan and Georgia. One-fourth of the males and one-third of the females felt that they were failures in dating and courtship. Over half wanted to date more frequently, and one-third reported they did not know how to act on dates. One-third reported that dating was not a pleasurable experience and that they experienced fear while on dates. Their personal insecurity was reflected in their need for material possessions to give them status in dating, particularly among boys.

Dating Norms

The normative structures that control dating have not been described clearly. Norms emanate from different and sometimes conflicting reference groups, particularly the parent-adult and the peer group; and, for individuals, dating norms change over time with greater dating experience and progressive commitment leading toward marriage. Changes in dating norms also occur from one generation to another, as reflected in the decline of ages for initial and more serious dating relationships and marriage. Not only do gaps exist in our

understanding of the dating norms, but there are inconsistencies among some of our present findings as well.

Broadly speaking, dating behavior among youth at any given time represents the dynamic synthesis of previous experiences and the interplay of the influences of parental and other adult reference groups and peer reference groups. In some areas, the two sets of influences appear to reinforce one another; in other areas, adult and peer influences are less harmonious or are in conflict. But peer reference groups also show wide variations in permitted, desirable, or disapproved behavior.

Several areas in which general agreement is found among adult and peer reference groups include the desirable characteristics sought in a date and in male-female status and role relationships. Considerable agreement has been found for the ratings of boys and girls for several kinds of characteristics desired in a date. Christensen (1952) reported a correlation of .73 between the rankings of boys and girls for the importance of things looked for in a date, a correlation of .93 for ratings of conduct patterns characteristic of each sex, and a correlation of .83 for the degree of self-criticism applied to dating situations by boys and girls. The characteristics judged to be important in a date reflected evaluations congruent with adult values for dating and mate selection. These included being physically and mentally fit, being dependable, taking pride in manners and personal appearance, being clean in speech and action, having a pleasant disposition and a sense of humor, being considerate of one's date and others, acting one's age, and not being childish. (Cf. Christensen, 1958, pp. 231–264.)

Sex reference groups differed, however, in the fact that boys gave greater emphasis to the domestic skills of the female and her attractiveness, whereas girls attached greater importance to the man's financial position and his attitudes toward intimacy. Additional differences between the sexes occurred in the degree to which boys and girls accepted criticism or projected blame for things which went wrong on dating. Boys assigned about two-thirds of the blame to females. Projection of blame on boys was less true of females; they attributed more to their own sex (Christensen, 1952; Christensen, 1958, pp. 231–243).

Family and adult reference groups appear to be stronger for girls than for boys and seem to influence the behavior of the former more than the latter. Crist (1953) reported that parents influenced the behavior of girls more than boys, younger children more than older children, and farm students were influenced more by their parents than rural nonfarm or urban students. Mothers had closer relationships than fathers with both boys and girls, but the relationship was more intimate between mothers and daughters than between mothers and sons. P. H. Landis (1960) also observed that girls felt closer to their parents and felt that they could discuss their dates more with their parents than could boys.

Crist (1953) noted that most of the parents of the youth he interviewed used democratic control techniques; only a few were authoritarian. As parents became better acquainted with dating and other practices of their adolescents and friends, they became more lenient, and family dominance gave way to peer-group norms. Where conflicts occurred between parental and peer norms, though, farm children more frequently continued to accept family norms, whereas rural nonfarm and urban children tended to accept peer norms.

Other data indicate that rural youth begin to date later and have more doubts and fears about dating than urban youth (W. M. Smith, 1952). Smith found that 73 per cent of the urban females in his university sample had their first date before 15 years of age, whereas 67 per cent of the rural females had their first date when they were 15 years of age or older. Fifty-eight per cent of the rural men first dated when they were 16 or younger, in contrast to 70 per cent of the urban men.

Adult and peer reference-group norms continue to provide more freedom for boys and to maintain greater control over girls. P. H. Landis (1960) reported that boys less frequently sought parental permission for first dates, had greater freedom in their time limits, were allowed to date more frequently than girls, and were subject to parental vetoes regarding dating partners less frequently than girls. These normative differences are reflections of the double sexual standard, one of the basic norms that structures dating behavior from the most casual to the most intimate sexual relationships.

Because a separate chapter is devoted to sexual relationships (Ch. 15), sexual behavior is not discussed at any length in this chapter. However, data from two studies relevant to the operation of the double sex standard in high school dating patterns are presented to provide a more complete description of high school dating. First, Breed (1956) observed that chivalry as well as prowess was institutionalized in male reference groups. A larger percentage of girls than boys agreed that boys should stop further sexual advances if a female said no, whether the boy thought she meant it or not. But the percentage of boys agreeing that boys should stop increased from 41 per cent for the situation where the boy thought she didn't mean it to 89 per cent when the boy knew she meant him to stop. This difference in attitude reflects the value of respect for the female—especially a female of whom the male is fond and from whom he also wants affection—and represents the institutionalized basis for idealization in love.

Second, the results of the national sample reported by Christensen indicated that females more frequently favor the double sexual standard for dating behavior than males. The females were more critical of their own sex than were men. Females apparently accept male-dominated dating, courtship, and marriage norms and recognize that masculine values have priority (Christensen, 1952). Yet, while accepting these conditions, females function effectively in the male-dominated heterosexual milieu.

Among those who were not going steady or were not engaged, females from 16 to 21 years of age dated more frequently than males. And, as might be expected, with those who were going steady or were engaged, differences in the frequency of dating between males and females were nonsignficant (Lowrie, 1956).

Some of the influences of the adolescent peer reference groups on dating and other adolescent behavior are well known. However, it is easy to overemphasize the influence of peer groups in contrast to family or adult reference groups in establishing dating norms. It was observed that student values in dating generally reflected accepted adult values for interpersonal relationships. And, with a few additional years beyond high school, young persons seem to conform to some of the endogamous norms.

Positive attitudes toward religiously endogamous dating can be used to represent internalization of adult mate-selection norms of religious endogamy. Burchinal (1960) found that positive attitudes toward religiously endogamous dating increased from the high school to the university level, even after the socioeconomic status of the youth was controlled. This finding suggests that as youth became older and approached marriage, they internalized adult mate-selection norms more strongly.

The Burchinal investigation also showed that farm students were more favorably disposed toward religiously endogamous dating than nonfarm students. This observation reinforces the earlier finding that farm students adhered more strongly than nonfarm students to family or adult norms when these conflicted with peer norms. Higher-status students and those who were frequent church attenders held more positive attitudes toward religiously endogamous dating, and girls favored religiously endogamous dating more than boys. Age, farm-nonfarm residence, sex, family status, and degree of church attendance each were

related to the religiously endogamous norm independent of the other four variables. Data also have been presented by Burchinal and Chancellor (1962a; 1962b) for relationships between the ages of spouses, farm-nonfarm occupations of husbands, and the occupational status of husbands and interreligious marriage rates. Where analyses were comparable, the results based on the attitudes of high school and college students were consistent with the marriage results: interreligious marriage rates were inversely related to status and age and were greater among couples that included grooms employed in nonfarm in contrast to farm occupations.

Other data reveal an interesting variation from the generalization that youth probably grow into conventional dating and marriage norms as they enter young adulthood. Leslie and Richardson (1956) and Coombs (1962) found that adherence to the status and religious endogamous norms occurred more frequently among college youth who lived at home during courtship, or who courted their spouses prior to coming to college, as compared with college youth who did not live at home or who met or courted after coming to campus. In these studies, campus norms, in contrast to family or hometown norms, appeared to provide less support for endogamous mate selection.

Dating as a Dynamic Process

Dating is a dynamic process that starts with the first prearranged heterosexual meeting and continues until the last such meeting of an engaged couple before marriage. As a process for developing and maintaining heterosexual association before marriage, dating relationships generally move toward deeper commitments, acceptance of greater obligations for the other party, and greater mutual agreement on the range and type of intimacy in which the couple engages. Initially, for any couple, dating is begun with relative freedom and with no obligation on the part of either party to carry the association further. Somewhere, at some time, greater obligations of each member toward the other may emerge, as in circumstances associated with steady dating or being pinned. Engagement is the formal acknowledgment of a mutually binding obligation to proceed toward marriage.

Some of the dynamics of high school dating may be inferred from conditions that influence the age at which dating begins and the frequency with which it is practiced. Lowrie (1961) investigated factors which influenced the ages of initial dating among youth in Ohio, Texas, and California. Ages at which dating began were related to the national origins of the parents of the youth, the parents' educational levels, sizes of the families, their socioeconomic status, and the region of the country. Also, some of these factors were related to the youths' dating practices. Two broad patterns are suggested by Lowrie. In one group were children from families that are throughly American, with above-average education, a relatively high socioeconomic status, and fewer siblings. Children in this group dated early and comparatively frequently; after considerable experience in dating they tended to go steady relatively early, but they returned quickly to playing the field. The second group of children came from families of more recent foreign origin, of lower education, lower socioeconomic status, and more siblings. Children of these families tended to begin dating later and to begin going steady relatively quickly without much experience in dating. The ages of initial dating for girls were affected more by variations in the variables than were those of boys.

Three studies agree that age is the most important variable influencing the frequency of dating. In all, frequency of dating rose with increased age (Cameron & Kenkel, 1960; Heiss, 1960b; Lowrie, 1956). Heiss used a seven-point continuum, from not having gone steady to public announcement of the intention to marry, to measure the courtship progress of a sample of high

school students in Connecticut. Courtship progress increased with age or class standing, and, consistent with the results of other studies, boys had made less courtship progress than girls.

Lowrie has published the most complex analyses of factors influencing the frequency of dating (1956). Age and sex lost much of their predictive power when dating status was controlled. At each age level, youth who were going steady or who were engaged dated about twice as frequently as those who were playing the field. Earlier ages at dating also were associated with more frequent dating during later high school and college years, but among those who were going steady or were engaged, variations in the mean frequency of dating by ages of original dating were small and irregular.

Further complications among ages at which dating begins, dating status, and the frequency of dating were reported by Lowrie (1961). Ages at initial dating and going steady were related, but not in the same manner for all students. As dating began earlier, there was a larger delay before going steady, and as dating began later, there was a corresponding shorter delay before initiation of steady dating. Early dating was related to a relatively broad and lengthy experience in paired-sex association before steady dating, whereas later introduction of dating was associated with a relatively short experience in intersex association before going steady began.

Lowrie's comprehensive data pertaining to high school dating patterns leave two problems unsettled. First, his data suggest that going steady is only a phase through which many students pass who then revert to playing the field, especially if they started dating earlier than most youth. This conclusion is contrary to the findings of studies that reveal the importance and preferential status of going steady among both high school and college students. Second, Lowrie's data lead to the conclusion, which he recognized, that the late daters who rush into steady dating without much previous experience should be the ones to whom youthful marriage would appeal most highly.

The one study which he cited (Burchinal, 1959) pointed to a contrary pattern. Burchinal found that girls who married while still in high school had begun dating earlier, dated more frequently, dated more boys, had gone steady earlier, and felt that they had been in love with a greater number of boys than a control group of girls. Lowrie cited several reasons why these data should be qualified in relation to his relationship between earlier initial dating and later playing the field. However, results comparable to those reported by Burchinal have been found by Moss and Gingles (1959) and by Inselberg (1961; 1962) both of whom used different kinds of control samples and ones which would not be subject to the limitations Lowrie felt were inherent in Burchinal's precision-matched sample design. The agreement of three studies on the relationship among younger-than-average ages for initial dating, accelerated heterosexual development, and younger ages at marriage cannot be dismissed lightly. Obviously, considerably more research is needed on the correlates and consequences of variations in initial ages of dating and going steady.

Going steady, as one status in the dating relationship, is only partially understood. Herman's study (1955) helped to clarify the concept. His sample consisted of university students, but he asked them about their high school dating as well as about their current dating behavior. Dating increased in frequency and moved from playing the field in the sophomore year to going steady in the senior year in high school. Going steady also was the most frequent form of dating among the most popular students, but steady dating did not represent the same kind of relationship to all youth.

Herman distinguished between two types of steady dating. One was marriage-oriented, and the dating of students with this view represented courtship. The other type

implied no thought of marriage and represented a relationship maintained for recreation, fun, education, or other reasons. This twofold nature of going steady is reflected in the fact that of the 52 per cent who went steady in any high school year, only about one-third thought about marriage before high school graduation. Furthermore, two-thirds of those who went steady in high school had done so with at least two persons, and most youthful steady relationships are ultimately broken, generally with few traumatic results (Kirkpatrick & Caplow, 1945a; Kirkpatrick & Caplow, 1945b).

Heiss (1960b) likewise substantiated Herman's view of two kinds of going-steady relationships. He found that courtship progress was slightly related to the belief that marriage was possible soon after high school. Nevertheless, this study introduced a needed view, that of interpreting high school dating and courtship behavior not only in terms of its antecedents, but in terms of expected contingencies as well.

Dating Functions

Dating fulfills many important functions in the socialization of youth and, as such, may best be considered as a gradual developmental process based on progressively greater experience, all of which ideally should help youth to make more intelligent selection of marriage partners. Lowrie (1948) has listed 11 functions of dating which, in general, may be summarized as contributions to the socialization, educational, or developmental processes of the individual in general and as preparation for courtship and marriage in particular. The nondater, Lowrie insisted, misses experience vital to his personality development. Lowrie emphasized that dating is associated with extracurricular activity and mixing and contributes to normality and prestige ratings, both important for adequate interaction in high school peer groups. In fact, he questioned whether there can be an adequate substitute for dating and its effects, given our type of social system with its marriage requirements and forms of adult interaction as they are.

Lowrie (1951) also tested various theories of dating. These included Waller's idea of the competitive, aim-inhibited relationship dominated by the quest for thrills, Burgess and Locke's idea that dating is a distinct yet preliminary phase of courtship, and a view that dating is a gradual process whereby youth obtain the training and experience needed for sensible selection of mates. The latter represents Lowrie's view of high school dating and is called an educational process by him. Data from high school and college students were analyzed to test the validity of the three views. In general, the students rejected dating as courtship interaction. To them, it was primarily a social relationship. Over one-third of the students gave educational reasons as their chief interest in dating. Reasons associated with obtaining educational experience, developing poise or ease, were cited more frequently by girls than by boys, and, in both groups, tended to decrease with age. By far, the chief reasons given by the students for dating were not competitive or exploitative, but broadly educational.

Steady dating also may be viewed in an "educational" framework and not as courtship-oriented. Random dating permits only superficial association, because of the lack of personal attachment and lower feelings of responsibility. Steady dating, by permitting the development of personal security, enhancing peer recognition and acceptance, increasing symbolic status in the peer group, and lessening the competitive and possibly traumatic quest for a date, offers an opportunity to act at a deeper, more revealing, and, frequently, more creative level. In this sense, steady dating provides anticipatory socialization for courtship and later marital adjustment.

Data pertaining to dating norms and dating as a dynamic developmental process have been discussed separately, although such a distinction can be made only for analytical or heuristic purposes. Full understanding of dating requires that the two sets of conditions be combined by viewing dating behavior as role behavior in a social system influenced by the status of the two participants. Dating may be competitive, in which the interaction pattern is limited in time and depth, or dating may reflect progressively greater involvement, as the members of the couple attribute greater unity to their dyad, and as such unity is attributed to their relationship by others, particularly by their peers.

Greater commitment during adolescence may occur by means of noncommitted versus committed steady dating (E. A. Smith, 1962). These terms are reminiscent of Herman's original distinction between two orientations toward steady dating, although the two sets of distinctions are not identical. Precise distinctions between these and other conceptions of dating statuses become lost in a jungle of definitions and semantics. For different purposes, different conceptions of dating statuses are appropriate. Terms such as "random dating," "playing the field," "favorite date," "going steady" or "noncommitted steady," "going steady" or "committed steady," each has value depending on the aspect of dating under discussion. The underlying conceptual view is that dating norms and roles are defined by the status between the members of the dyad, as they and others see it. The general term *date* is too broad to cover all types of dating relationships.

E. A. Smith (1962) and others recognize the contribution dating makes to the emancipation process, particularly more serious dating. However, Smith's view that steady dating encourages withdrawal from adult and youth institutions is difficult to reconcile with the role dating plays in enhancing or maintaining peer-group status. And assertions (E. A. Smith, 1962) that steady dating appeals most strongly to the unpopular, frightened, and relatively unchosen youth is impossible to reconcile with the demonstrated popularity, even modality, of this form of dating, especially among the most popular youth. More likely, the nondaters, who comprise only a minority of youth after their sophomore year in high school, are among the less competent youth. Research is needed to test Lowrie's view that dating is a necessary part of adolescent development. To what extent can adolescents bypass high school dating and, at a later age, acquire the poise, skill, confidence, and knowledge needed to pursue courtship successfully and to develop reasonably competent marital relations?

Dating Outcomes

Different views exist about the possible outcomes of preadolescent and adolescent cross-sex interaction. Data are not available to clarify certain issues. For instance, Broderick and Fowler (1961) suggest that increased cross-sex interaction at preadolescent or early adolescent ages may lead to greater romantic attachment, earlier sexual experimentation, an increase in early marriage rates, and greater difficulty in finding clearly defined and generally acceptable social sex roles. The relationship between young marriage and younger-than-average ages for initial dating offers a basis for some of these apprehensions. On the other hand, an introduction to dating by means of a heterosexual gang may better be accomplished by earlier cross-sex association and lead to better early dating adjustment than direct movement from a single-sex group into paired-heterosexual association (Crist, 1953). Furthermore, although ages for initial dating have declined greatly since World War II, and going steady has become a more common experience, young marriage rates, after a sharp increase between 1940 and 1950, have remained relatively stable for the last decade. At this point, we simply need more comprehensive and, preferably, longitudinal studies to de-

termine the various outcomes of different dating histories and patterns.

COLLEGE DATING AND COURTSHIP

Numerous attitudes toward campus dating and courtship, and norms associated with these practices, have been studied at many campuses, beginning mainly in the 1930's.

Three broad generalizations emerge from the studies of norms and values that influence students' attitudes toward dating and courtship: (a) The dominant values in campus dating and courtship are diffused widely and are generally accepted by both sexes, in all but the lowest socioeconomic levels, and among different racial, religious, or other groups. These values cluster around basic themes directing cross-sex interpersonal relations in the United States today. (b) The dominant themes are not the competitive-prestige or trivial norms, but seem to be based on norms that are functional for current courtship and marriage. (c) Although there is general agreement on the values directing dating and courtship, some important differences emerge for some groups of youth.

Campus Values and Norms

Campus dating and courtship values and norms are widely diffused and reflect basic themes of heterosexual association in contemporary United States. Substantial agreement exists between males and females in what they value in a date or mate. Hill (1945) found that men and women at the University of Wisconsin had similar opinions regarding the six most important factors in the choice of a mate. These factors included dependable character, emotional stability and maturity, pleasing disposition, mutual attraction, good health, and a desire for home life and for children. Men and women at Brigham Young University, primarily Mormons, also emphasized these same qualities in the selection of a mate

(Christensen, 1947), as did high school and university students included in later investigations by Christensen (1958, pp. 239–264). These values gave greater emphasis to personality traits such as dependability, pleasantness, and emotional maturity than to competitive or materialistic values in the selection of a date or mate. Christensen (1948; 1958, pp. 235–239) reported that men and women showed high agreement on the ranking of 20 traits considered undesirable in courtship. University of Colorado students were asked to specify in their own words those traits, qualities, or characteristics desired most in a mate (Smith & Monane, 1953). Responses of males and females were similar for the importance of companionability, desirable physical attraction or appearance, social graces, intelligence, and education.

Blood (1956) asked students at the University of Michigan to choose from among 37 traits or characteristics those items which formed the bases of campus norms governing the popularity of students as dates, the students' preferences when choosing a casual date, and their preferences when choosing a date with serious possibilities of marriage in view. Six characteristics received virtually unanimous approval in respect to all three questions: being pleasant and cheerful, having a sense of humor, being a good sport, being natural, being considerate, and being neat in appearance.

Negro and white college students express similar evaluations. Sussman and Yeager (1950) compared the responses of white college students attending several colleges in Connecticut with those reported for Negroes by Himes (1949). For 14 of the 20 factors, similar ratings were observed among the Negroes and the white students.

Dominant Values Are Functional

The dominant values underlying dating and courtship represent anticipatory socialization for marriage. In summarizing their results, various researchers have observed that those factors desired in a date or mate also are highly functional for marriage in the United States. Hill (1945) found little evidence for the "Hollywood" notion of dating and courtship. Student preferences for dates or mates are more consistent with mature and realistic conceptions of marriage than with the "frothy and frivolous trivia" assumed to go with dating today (Smith & Monane, 1953). Blood (1956) maintained that college dating is more functional than it is given credit for; personal characteristics are sought which promise to provide a relaxed and satisfying human relationship, one that should "wear well in marriage." College dating is dominated by friendly, nonexploitative, relaxed relationships between the sexes, with emphasis on an easygoing, informal interaction. Casual friendships are strengthened by the emphasis of emotional maturity, intelligence, and affection. All of these characteristics should be conducive to functional courtship relationships and, later, to competence in marital relationships. The differences which exist among subgroups of students are reflections of the social pluralism of United States society, of which the campus is a small-scale replica, and form secondary sets of norms within the broader context of norms that emphasize companionship, maturity, and nonexploitative exchanges of affection.

Some norms are controversial. While general agreement exists relative to dominant dating and courtship values among college students, multigroup memberships give rise to differential values attached to some characteristics desired in a date or mate. The other side of the coin of general male-female agreement on dating and courtship values is a set of male-female differences relative to some characteristics. Typically, men place greater emphasis than women on attractiveness, youthfulness, or popularity of their dates or mates, her cooking or housekeeping ability, and her desire for home and children. In contrast, women put more emphasis on the ambition or industriousness of their date or mate, his ability and general intelligence, his financial prospects, on similar backgrounds for the partners, on chastity, and on his social graces or refinement (Blood, 1956; Christensen, 1947; Christensen, 1958; Hill, 1945; Himes, 1949; Neely, 1940; Smith & Monane, 1953).

Male-female differences in dating attitudes seem to diminish as students progress through college. Compared to underclassmen, senior men and women placed less emphasis on ambition and industriousness as desirable traits and devalued chastity as a prime consideration in the selection of a mate (Hill, 1945). Smith and Monane (1953) found that as educational attainment increased from the freshmen level through to graduate school, date preferences were less restricted by conservative or conventional norms, and the criteria for dates became more varied. Blood (1956) noted that while the double standard persists, there was increased rapprochement between the sexes as students moved to higher class levels and became more serious in their dating relationships. Students gradually became disenchanted with the competitive dating world of the first several years of college and replaced this "whirl" with more individualized pair activities.

Some norms are more controversial than others. For instance, Blood (1956) discovered five controversial norms which differentiated males from females, Greeks from nonaffiliated students, and underclassmen from upperclassmen. These were: having no reputation for petting, being good looking or attractive, being popular with the opposite sex, willing to drink socially, and having access to a car. In the social ferment of the university community, students can find support both for their present norms and for norms which differ markedly from their present ones. The freedom and diversity of university associations and dating provide students ample opportunities to select dating partners whose norms either agree or differ from their own. In this setting, there is an opportunity for the emergence of individualized patterns of be-

havior that may differ from previous conceptions of what is right or proper. Some data suggest that changes in norms probably occur more frequently in the direction of greater sexual permissiveness, with affection and choice of partners based on fewer conventional restrictions associated with the student's social or religious background. The convergence of the preferences of males and females during four years of college, for instance, represents the emergence of more mutually compatible preferences between the sexes and, for women, adoption of more permissive sexual standards.

Dating norms also may vary among types of campuses. Several decades ago, change appeared to occur more rapidly and was further advanced at larger state-supported universities than at smaller denominationally related colleges. Neely (1940) found differences in the ratings of traits desirable in a mate between state-university and private-college students in Iowa, both in 1929 and 1936. In all samples, there was a rise, over the eight years, in the importance attached to traits associated with companionship interaction. Among all students, traditional values associated with sexual purity and religious attendance slumped, but not to the same extent: both the college men and women in 1936 rated sexual purity at the level university students placed it in 1929. More recent comparisons between university and college students have not been reported. However, it probably can be assumed that both groups of students share the dominant values approximately equally, and that the university students, as a group, probably adhere to a wider range and less traditional set of values than students attending the smaller, denominationally related colleges.

Some norms are changing. After a lapse of 17 years, McGinnis (1958) found no evidence of any marked change in evaluations of desirable characteristics in a date among students attending the University of Wisconsin. The few differences which emerged replaced traditional values in mate selection and family life with values associated with companionship.

Another study compared the courtship behavior of three generations of Ohio women (Koller, 1951). For these three groups, courtship norms had changed toward a freer, personal-centered relationship and away from the institutional-centered or traditional pattern. Over the three generations, there was an increase in the frequency of dating males of whom parents had disapproved, in the frequency of daughters trying to change their parents' minds about the desirability of the daughters' dating partners, in the number of dates per week, in the frequency of gift exchanges between engaged men and women, and in the amount of discussion of problems with their fiancé before marriage. On the other hand, there was a decline in community control over courtship, in the length of engagement, and in the age differences between the spouses. Nonsignificant differences were observed for the number of persons seriously considered as potential husbands, the daughters' mean ages at the time they first dated their present husbands, the frequency of visiting both sets of relatives before marriage, the proportion of either set of relatives visited before marriage, or the total time spent in courtship, the latter being one and one-half years.

In summary, dating and courtship norms, as primarily reported by college students, are a function of our present marriage system. The major values have remained relatively similar over the past several decades. Changes that have occurred over the longer run have strengthened those aspects of the dating and courtship system which should contribute to increased competency in marriage. Modern youth, it seems, acquire more experience in heterosexual association before engagement and marriage than was true for youth several generations ago. And this association is governed by norms that permit a wider range of activities and types of interaction conducive to more functional selection of mates, at least in terms of modern criteria for marital competency. The freedom, the social and cultural diversity, and the anonymity of university campuses or modern urban life provide youth the opportunity to explore highly valued personal-centered and affectionate heterosexual dating and courtship relationships.

Dating and Courtship Behavior

Love, intimacy, and courtship stages. Kirkpatrick and Caplow (1945a; 1945b) studied numerous aspects of courtship behavior among University of Minnesota students. For both sexes, there was a movement toward "love" in their more recent relationships as compared with earlier ones, and there was some evidence of conflict and confusion between the sexes. For instance, males more frequently than females reported they were worried over their degree of involvement. Males were the more jealous of the two sexes, and they expressed greater fear of being trapped in their relationships. Perhaps the burden of finding and maintaining the interest of the female leaves men more uncertain and ambivalent about their dating roles than is generally true for females.

The 141 males in this sample reported 230 broken love affairs, and the 258 women reported 414. The modal cause for the breaks, 47 per cent for men and 38 per cent for women, was mutual loss of interest. Females more frequently reported unilateral breakups because of their interest in another male (32 per cent) than males (15 per cent). On the other hand, 30 per cent of the males' breakups were attributed to their partners' interest in another male, but only 15 per cent of the females attributed their breakups to their dates' interest in another female. The combined unilateral reasons accounted for 45 per cent of the broken love affairs for men and for 47 per cent for women.

These differences suggest that once a love affair has begun, men shift to a more conservative role, whereas women may enjoy the role of being sought after and more frequently take the initiative in breaking love affairs. Regardless of the motives for their termination, the data for all love affairs suggest that about one-half of these students had no major adjustment problems following the broken love affair. Pleasant memories were retained more frequently than unpleasant ones. About half of the boys and girls reported they readjusted immediately, and another third of the males and a fifth of the females reported they recovered in several weeks' time. Only about 7 per cent of the males and 11 per cent of the females reported they required a year or more to readjust.

Sexual relations among couples at different dating and courtship stages are treated in detail in the previous chapter. Yet brief discussion of this topic is necessary here. Movement from random dating to engagement and finally to marriage generally occurs by means of changes in status relationships between the members of the couple. Sets of roles and norms associated with each status position allow or encourage different forms of behavior. The progressive identification of the couple with one another, and corresponding public recognition of the couple as a pair, encourage progressively increased emotional involvement and greater sexual intimacy, the level of greatest intimacy being determined by the values and desires of the couple.

Norms for intimacy levels differ among various groups of our society. Males generally desire and expect to attain greater physical involvement than females, at least up to engagement. Bell and Blumberg (1960) reported that among students at an eastern urban university, norms at dating were necking for women and petting for men. At steady dating and engagement, petting became acceptable for both. The Kinsey data indicate that intimacy beyond petting varies inversely with the family status, educational levels, and with the frequency of church attendance. A composite of the results of another study (Bell &

Blumberg, 1959) suggests that differences in intimacy levels are greatest between Catholics and Jews, with Protestants occupying an intermediate position. Jewish students began to date relatively early, tended to play the field and, once a decision was made, moved directly to engagement. When it occurred, steady dating was further along the continuum toward engagement for Jewish students than for Protestant or Catholic students. The Protestant students began dating later than Jewish students and moved from random dating into the security of steady dating sooner than the Jewish students. Steady dating among Protestants lacked the overtones of permanency that Jewish students attached to it. Catholic students also began dating relatively late, and males more than females sought to play the field, perhaps seeking to maximize sexual achievement as early as possible at any of the stages—random dating, going steady, or being engaged.

It is not known how these differences in ages at initial dating and levels of courtship intimacy among members of the three religious groups affect ages at marriage and other mate selection patterns. The data came from one sample where most of the students were living at home in an eastern metropolitan area. However, in Iowa (Burchinal, 1963), Catholic spouses averaged nine months to more than a year older than Protestant spouses, even after socioeconomic status was controlled. These data suggest that, for Iowa, spouses' religious affiliation operates as a reference group that influences courtship progress. Clarification of the way in which religious systems influence ages at marriage as well as other courtship norms and relationships must await further research.

Parent-youth relations and courtship progress. Winch pioneered in the studies of relationships between students' attitudes toward their parents and their courtship progress. His first publication in this area (1943) dealt with the relationships between courtship behavior and attitudes toward parents among college men. Courtship behavior was measured along an eight-point continuum from no dating to marriage. The parent-youth variables, considered as the independent factors, included several measures for each parent such as love, hostility, intensity of love, fluctuations between love and hostility, parental dominance, submission of the child, and a measure of the direction of the love-hostility feelings for fathers and mothers.

Winch hypothesized that excessively strong attachments of children to parents inhibited what might be called "normal" courtship behavior. Although correlations among the variables were generally low, Winch drew two major observations from his analyses of relationships among the parent-youth variables and the courtship progress of the college youth. (a) There was little relationship between the males' feelings toward fathers and their degree of courtship behavior. (b) To the extent that the small correlations permitted interpretation, the role of the mother was clearly more important in the son's courtship progress than that of the father. More advanced courtship behavior was associated with less love for the mother and with more intense feelings toward her.

Winch (1946) subsequently enlarged his study of the courtship behavior of the college men he investigated in 1941 by including certain social-background data as additional independent variables. These additional analyses showed that the degree of courtship behavior was positively and significantly correlated with the favorability of early dating, wish to be married, and the son's age, but was negatively associated with his career drive. Less significant, though of possible marginal importance, were the positive relationships between the son's courtship progress and his parents' marital happiness and their economic and social status. The wish to have children, physical appearance, size of college attended, and the sex ratio at the college were unrelated to courtship behavior.

Factor analysis of the original 1941 data (Winch, 1947) led to more succinct organization of the generalizations previously discussed. Winch identified seven independent factors derived from the 456 courtship, parental-relations, and social-background variables. These factors included social adjustment, degree of courtship behavior, social maturity, submission to parents, fluctuations in feelings toward parents, socioeconomic status, and family harmony. Degree of courtship behavior among men remained an independent factor and did not load highly on any other factors.

The loadings for the socioeconomic and family-harmony factors provided data for speculating how matrices of family variables influenced the males' courtship behavior. For instance, the socioeconomic factor included an empirical type with these characteristics: high socioeconomic and social status with inherited status, families in which the mothers were the breeders and rearers of children and where, by satisfying the son's wants, the mothers received love from them; but the blessings in the family flowed from the father's success, and while the father was the master against whom the son could not rebel directly, the son could rebel indirectly by expressing his domination over women whom he dated and ultimately over his wife and children. Males from this background exhibited a high frequency and range of courtship behavior and had strong wishes to be married and have children.

The family-harmony type included families where harmony was not related to socioeconomic or social status, and families in which the parents' marriage happiness was followed by the son's love for his father, which was based on harmony and not upon monetary success. Love for mother was there, but it was lower than love for father. There were no loadings on wish to marry, to have children, or any measure of courtship behavior. Presumably, in these harmonious families, there was an absence of any extraordinary drive or stimulus for the son to progress in courtship, to marry, or to get ahead.

Analyses of the courtship behavior of college women were initially undertaken by Winch (1949) to test two competing hypotheses: (a) For both sexes the mother is the most important parent in accounting for the courtship progress of children. (b) The parent of the opposite sex is the more important influence in the courtship progress of the youth.

The mother-son results were not repeated in the mother-daughter analyses for college women, nor was age correlated with courtship progress among females as it was with males. These data failed to support the hypothesis that one parent was more important than the other in relation to courtship progress among females. Courtship progress among females, however, was related to their appearance, wish to be married, absence of career drive, and favorability of early dating.

The difference in the male-female results may mean four things (Winch, 1949): (a) Females are emancipated earlier and break family ties before college. (b) Females retain home ties and become emancipated after college. (c) Female emancipation occurs by a different process than that for males and was not adequately measured by Winch. (d) Females are not emancipated to the same extent or in the same manner as males. Further research (Winch, 1951) suggests that the last explanation and, to a lesser extent, the second explanation as well are the most valid.

Differential cultural expectations for the emancipation of males and females also are clear in Komarovsky's research (1950). Girls who had older brothers testified that in various ways parents tended to accelerate, sometimes unwittingly but also deliberately, the emancipation of boys from the family, whereas they retarded the emancipation of the daughters. A consequence of these differences in expectations for sons and daughters is that daughters are more

closely identified with their family and, correspondingly, retarded in their emancipation. These data represent further explanations of the pattern found by Winch. The progress of men in courtship was related to loosening their attachments to their mothers, whereas for women, courtship behavior was not dependent upon emancipation from either parent. The women could transfer dependence from their parents to their husbands, whereas men had to achieve independence from parents to pursue courtship.

The role of the mother relative to the father in the dating progress of children also is evident in data reported by Kirkpatrick and Caplow (1954a). Fathers disapproved or prohibited first dates for daughters more frequently than for sons. In contrast, mothers encouraged their daughters more than their sons in their initial dating experiences, although they encouraged the first dating of both sexes considerably more frequently than fathers. Rather than becoming involved in elaborate Oedipal interpretations, these data are more easily and probably more appropriately interpreted in terms of the primary role of the mother in the socialization of children. Furthermore, the mothers' desires to enhance the social status of their daughters while attaching less importance to the social-sexual development of sons may explain their greater encouragement of daughters than sons in dating.

Hobart (1958b) tested the hypothesis that emancipation from the parental family is accompanied by increased involvement in the peer subculture. Emancipation from the home was measured in terms of the degree respondents were willing to criticize their parents' marriages. Three indexes of participation in the adolescent subculture were used: courtship status, romanticism as measured by a 10-item scale, and previous going-steady or engagement status. Criticism of parents' marriages and courtship status were related positively, as predicted, for males, but no relationship between these two variables was found for females. Romanticism was not related to criticism of parental marriages for either sex. Having gone steady or having been engaged also was related to greater emancipation for males but not for females.

These data agree with the findings of Winch and Komarovsky, who suggested that courtship progress is preceded or accompanied by greater family emancipation for men than for women. Further analyses by Hobart (1958b) show that the influence of courtship status on emancipation is not independent of age, but is more significant than age. This finding refines the relationship reported by Winch (1946) between increasing age among men and greater criticism of their parents' marital happiness. Older respondents (22 or older) in Hobart's investigation were more critical of their parents' marriages only when they were advanced in courtship. The transition from going steady to engagement represented the greatest step in emancipation during courtship.

A neglected article (Bates, 1942) provides some important data for understanding the role of parents in their children's courtship. Direct or indirect actions by parents affected both the courtship behavior and the final decisions of the children. Mothers were more involved in their children's courtship than were fathers. Females reported greater action by both fathers and mothers than males. Parental roles included indirect and direct forms of control. Indirect techniques included all of those associated with the development of the complex interaction associated with socialization in the family. Direct intervention ranged from such things as giving advice, discussing the potential mate and, in extreme cases, attempting outright domination. Domination included a range of actions from wise interference to parental despotism. Indirect or moderately direct parental roles achieved results satisfactory to the parents more frequently than did authoritarian or dominating behavior. All secret marriages, for instance, came from the authoritarian families with extreme parental domination over the children's courtship. Bates suggested that parental behavior in the courtship of children is less a function of cultural norms than it is of the over-all personal adjustment of the parents.

Sussman (1953) has provided detailed descriptions of how parents influence the mate selection of their children. Intensive interviews were obtained from parents in 97 families, from which there were 195 married and departed children. In 166 of the 195 cases, parents sought to influence the marital choices of their children. Methods used to exert influence were summarized as: (a) providing a proper milieu for dating and courtship, and (b) using persuasion and, where necessary, threatening to withdraw economic support, if the child married outside of his socioeconomic class. Procedures used to create a proper social milieu for the children included selecting a proper neighborhood in which to live, teaching the children to honor family and clique expectations regarding mate choice, developing the importance of rituals such as the engagement and its announcement, showers, and the wedding itself, and planning activities for the children, including inviting friends for weekends or holiday visits.

Eighty-one per cent of the parents admitted using persuasive techniques, including the threat of economic reprisal, when their children were courting a person of whom the parents did not approve. In 36 cases, parents successfully dissuaded their children from an imminent marriage of which the parents disapproved. Only eight children were reported to have resented parental intrusions. Class endogamy, assumed as a desired parental objective, occurred in 145 of 166 marriages, which suggests that the parents were relatively successful in helping to direct the courtship of their children.

Furthermore, intergenerational class endogamy was related to stronger intergenerational marital relationships. Similarity of backgrounds between the inlaws and the parents was related to fewer disagreements, easier solution of difficulties that arose, and more joint family activities between the two generations. Disagreements among parents and inlaws with dissimilar backgrounds seemed to exaggerate and elaborate original antagonisms and make subsequent relationships more difficult.

Other data suggest that family continuity patterns may play an increasingly important role in the courtship behavior of young people in the future. Considerable evidence documents the strength of a modified extended family system in urban as well as rural United States. Despite geographical and social mobility, widespread and important help patterns and reciprocal social obligations and relationships exist among nuclear family units (Sussman & Burchinal, 1962a; Sussman & Burchinal, 1962b). Theories of mate selection will be inadequate if they do not include parental participation in children's mate choices.

Personality factors and courtship. A variety of studies may be included under this heading. Studies of complementary needs by Winch and others are reserved for separate treatment, as are studies of love, romanticism, and empathy processes in courtship.

Several studies included among investigations of personality or subjective factors in courtship report measurements between personality ratings and courtship behavior. Nimkoff (1948) found that the emotionally adjusted as well as the maladjusted, and the socially aggressive as well as the socially retiring, participated in dating. However, social and emotional adjustments were related to the dating and courtship behavior of his respondents. College students who seldom or never dated, who started to date late in high school and who did not have over one steady dating relationship, were predominantly socially retiring and showed slight tendencies to be emotionally maladjusted. Those who had several dates during two weeks' time, who started dating in junior high school, had several steadies, and went steady in college approximated the emotional and social adjustment norms. The frequent college daters, four to six times in the two-week period in this sample, were predominantly socially aggressive and moderately emotionally maladjusted. Emotional adjustment was associated with having gone steady during some year in high school, but going steady before high school or against parental wishes and having had four or more steadies was associated with social aggressiveness and emotional maladjustment. In another study, satisfaction with dating was associated with personal happiness among University of Minnesota students (Kirkpatrick & Caplow, 1945a).

Straus (1947) also studied relationships between personality characteristics and mate selection. Respondents checked their major personality needs from a long list. Later in the questionnaire, they were asked to recheck the list of their needs and to indicate the degree to which their mate or fiancé filled each need. Aside from the overwhelming 90 per cent who agreed that no one could better fill their needs than their mate or fiancé, there was as much evidence against the need-fulfillment hypothesis as there was for it.

The importance of this investigation, however, lies in the detailed interview data which suggested the diversity of the processes by which need patterns may influence mate choices. Straus cited seven sets of needs which may influence marital choice. Three cases can be used to illustrate several types of need influences: (a) Mate choice is influenced by needs for attention and prestige derived from family affectional relationships. (b) Mate choice is influenced by needs for trust and sympathy derived from family and school relationships. (c) Mate choice is influenced by needs derived from critical emotional experiences in early adult life.

Straus emphasized that needs are developed from nonfamily interaction as well as and together with earlier and continuing family interaction. Personality needs also are linked to other factors in mate selection, as illustrated by the relationship between personality needs and one's ideal images of a mate or parent images sought for in a mate. The latter two areas also have been investigated by Straus.

In one study, Straus (1946b) tested hypotheses from general theory pertaining to the influence of parental images upon mate choice. Mates resembled parents in physique, opinions, beliefs, personality, and in temperament. None of the relationships was marked, but all exceeded chance. Men's wives resembled men's mothers more closely than women's husbands resembled their fathers. However, there was no general support for the hypothesis that one's mate is like or unlike the opposite-sex parent. Straus provided 12 concrete illustrations to describe ways in which parental images influenced mate choice. A brief description of five of these shows the range of such influences: (a) choice resembles the father; (b) choice is influenced by unsatisfactory relationships with the father; (c) choice is influenced by violent reaction against the father and by friendly feelings toward the mother; (d) the resemblance between the mate and the mother is linked with a satisfactory mother image and an unsatisfactory father image; and (e) choice is influenced by reaction against both parents.

Relationships between ideal-mate images and the actual chosen mate were reported by Straus in another article (1946a). An ideal image is one which a person of marriageable age has for the kind of person he or she would like to marry. Eighty per cent of both the males and the females reported they had some ideal image before they met their mate or fiancé. Only 14 per cent felt their ideal was rooted in their unconscious. Most reported their ideal conceptions were uppermost in their minds when they chose their mate or fiancé. And about half said they made concrete comparisons of the characteristics of the potential mate to their ideal-mate image. However, the content of the images among respondents varied from clear and well-defined images to vague formulations.

Personality resemblances between the ideal and real exceeded those between the physical ideal and real. Correspondence between the latter characteristics was judged close or identical by 59 per cent of the respondents, as compared with similar agreement between personality characteristics as reported by 74 per cent of the respondents. Further analyses of the case data suggested how ideal-mate images influenced the actual selection of mates. Another study (Prince, 1961) suggested that college youth are aware of ideal-mate conceptions. Ninety-one per cent of the men and 93 per cent of the women, most of whom were enrolled in marriage classes at the University of Wisconsin (Milwaukee Branch), had some image of the ideal characteristics of the person they wished to marry. Over half of the students reported that their ideal images were based primarily on their observations of both of their parents or of the opposite-sex parent. Dating experiences were a close second source of the students' ideal-mate images. Other sources of considerably lesser importance included observations of married couples, friends, and people in general.

MAIN AREAS OF MATE-SELECTION RESEARCH

Theory building with reference to mate selection, as in other substantive areas, requires pulling together relevant concepts and research findings with the goal of conceptual synthesis. Recent articles by Karlsson (1962) and by Jacobsohn and Matheny (1962), especially the latter, which is accompanied by a 250-item bibliography, represent major steps in this direction.

Residential Propinquity

Residential propinquity in the context of mate selection refers to the tendency for the proportion of marriages in a population to be inversely related to the distance between the residences of the contracting parties. In their review of theory and research pertaining to residential propinquity, Katz and Hill (1958) reported that at least 13 studies were published between 1932 and 1958. Because of their excellent review, only brief attention needs to be devoted to this topic in this chapter.

One study, however, deserves separate discussion because of the innovation introduced. In addition to obtaining residence at the time of marriage application, Clark (1952) also obtained residence at the time of the first date. For a sample of 281 persons obtaining marriage licenses in Columbus, Ohio, in July and August, 1949, 53 per cent of the couples resided within 16 blocks of one another at the time of marriage-license application, and 54 per cent did so at the time of their first date. Although residential propinquity was evident at each successive courtship stage—at first date, at engagement, and at marriage-license application—several differences were noted: the number who lived at the same residence, or within four blocks of each other, was proportionately greater at the time of application than at first date or subsequent engagement. The process of courtship seems to increase residential propinquity.

The notable feature of the Katz and Hill (1958) review is their codification of the residential-propinquity data and their development of a theoretical explanation of residential propinquity. The norm-segregation theory has been the most frequently advanced explanation of residential propinquity. Hill and Katz used this theory in their attempt to conceptualize residential propinquity. They pointed out that the norm-segregation theory rests upon two assumptions: (a) Generally, marital selection occurs within a field of eligibles that are defined by cultural norms, and (b) cultural groups that form fields of eligibles also tend to be segregated by neighborhoods. Residential segregation of cultural groups increases the probability of endogamous marriage which, upon subsequent investigation, also reveals low residential-propinquity distances. Persons who deviate from marriage norms may be expected to have relatively higher residential-propinquity distances.

Although the norm-segregation theory had some explanatory value in relation to available data, its limitations led Katz and Hill to introduce a second scheme which focussed more on behavior than on the normative factors related to residential propinquity. The second scheme is called an interaction-time-cost theory. Three assumptions underlie this theory: (a) Marriage is normative and occurs within normative fields of eligibles; (b) the probability of marriage varies directly with the probability of interaction; and (c) the probability of interaction is proportional to the ratio of opportunities at a given distance over intervening opportunities.

Further review and codification of research based on the interaction-time-cost theory led to the development of a final and more generalized theory for conceptualizing residential propinquity. Katz and Hill call this the norm-interaction theory. Its basic assumptions are that: (a) Marriage is normative; (b) within a normative field of eligibles, the probability of marriage varies directly with the probability of interaction; and (c) the probability of interaction is proportional to the ratio of opportunities for interaction at a given distance over the intervening opportunities for interaction. They summarized their theory in the following way:

. . . the basic mechanism leading to the choice of a mate for any *mass* sample whose members share the same marriage norms is the same for all groups, whether of high or low socio-economic status, of whatever ethnic group, or of whatever age class. The differences in propinquity of these groups are due to differences in their prior geographical distribution of opportunities. If this hypothesis is correct, then the propinquity tables that we work with are seen to be the complex summing up of these various distribution differences (Katz & Hill, 1958, p. 33).

The theoretical analyses of Katz and Hill lead from the empirical study of residential propinquity to a more general theory of mate selection, of which residential propinquity emerges as an empirical by-product.

Rating and Dating

Waller's essay on rating and dating (1937) greatly influenced sociological conceptions of dating and courtship. In his conceptualization, dating and courtship are separate activities, governed by greatly different norms, and engaged in for different purposes, although courtship may emerge from dating. Dating is largely dominated, in his view, with the quest for thrills, and becomes a frank and admitted barter in thrills, usually leading to exploitation of one of the parties. This cultural complex was identified as the "rating and dating complex" by Waller. Competition for dates was keen at college X (Pennsylvania State College) in the late 1930's, and this competition determined a rank order of persons in each sex group from the most desirable to the least desirable date. One's rating was determined by campus values. Top men belonged to the best fraternities, were prominent in campus activities, had money, were well dressed, had a smooth line, could dance well, and had access to an automobile. Top women had good clothes, a smooth line, could dance well, and were popular as a date or at least could give that impression. Whom one dated depended on one's position in the prestige system and one's bargaining power in relation to the position of the opposite sex in the system. Numerous additional norms regulated when and whom one asked for a date.

The rating and dating system encouraged brittle relationships and, because of the thrill-seeking and exploitation associated with them, enhanced hostilities between men and women. Varying degrees of trauma were experienced by the nondaters. These persons, however, apparently became accustomed to their lot and developed rationalizations for not dating.

Waller's rating and dating thesis allows little opportunity for love or sentiment development. To him, dating was dysfunctional, a dalliance before courtship, during which functional preparation for marriage would more likely occur. Yet Waller recognized that courtship may emerge from the dating process as periodic crises redefine the dating relationship at deeper levels. To Waller, courtship proceeds on a directional trend as contrasted to dating and is based upon mutually reinforcing idealization of one another. But idealization leads to departure from reality: positive features of the beloved are enhanced and negative characteristics are minimized. A person "falls in love" when he reaches the point where sentiment formation overcomes objectivity (Waller, 1937, p. 734). Mutual idealization is reinforced by social situations in which others treat the pair as a social unity.

The substance of Waller's rating and dating complex has been presented in some detail because of the influence his views have had on theories of dating and courtship. To some extent, dating and courtship have remained separate areas of discussion. The rating and dating complex has been ritualistically repeated in marriage and family textbooks, and the dysfunctional elements of the dating system are emphasized. Yet little direct research was done on dating and courtship practices until the late 1940's. On the other hand, Lowrie (1951) has called attention to the discrepancies between theories about dating and student responses for this activity. He found that motivation for dating was dominated by educational and socialization aims, and that aims associated with the rating and dating complex were negligible. In addition to

Lowrie's approach, there have been at least three attempts to retest elements of Waller's thesis for current generations of college youth.

The first of these (W. M. Smith, 1952) was based on responses from students at Pennsylvania State University in the 1950's. At that time, the sex ratio at the university was only three to one, in contrast to six to one when Waller observed dating practices at the same institution. At the time of Smith's study, dating was no longer a privilege (as Waller claimed) of fraternity men and sorority women. Smith also failed to substantiate the rating and dating system as described by Waller. Competitive-materialistic characteristics included in Waller's description of the rating system were intermixed with personality-companionship items on Smith's questionnaires. The students rejected the rating factors suggested by Waller and attached greater importance to the personality-companionship factors.

However, Smith reported some support for Waller's thesis in the selection of dating partners: dating among fraternity men exhibited status homogamy. By itself, however, evidence that the fraternity men and sorority women selected dates on an equal prestige basis does not mean that their dating was characterized by the rating and dating complex; more on this point later.

Blood (1955) tested four hypotheses derived explicitly from Waller's rating and dating concept:

1. The items listed in Waller's rating complex are the most generally supported campus criteria for dating popularity.
2. Students are extremely conscious of these social distinctions based on a scale of campus values which is generally recognized by the student body.
3. Generally students follow these campus norms in their casual dating.
4. A sharp break exists between dating and courtship or what Blood calls casual dating and serious dating. This differentiation occurs because casual

dating is governed by the rating complex, whereas serious dating is based on another set of values.

Data were obtained from a random sample of single undergraduate students at the University of Michigan in 1953. In general, little or no support was found for the four hypotheses. Popularity was based more on personality items than on those derived from Waller's complex. The data questioned Waller's complex at every point insofar as it applied to the University of Michigan students in 1953. If the rating and dating formulation was applicable earlier, it was not typical among these students.

The most recent investigation of rating and dating practices was based on a random sample of unmarried undergraduate students at Iowa State University in 1956 (Rogers & Havens, 1960). Prestige ratings were established for fraternities, sororities, dormitories, and off-campus housing. Sorority women concentrated their dating on students, especially fraternity men. Dating of sorority pledges was more endogamous in relation to prestige than was the dating of actives. Dormitory girls dated nonstudents more frequently, but otherwise dated more evenly across prestige levels than sorority girls.

Dormitory men concentrated their dating on dormitory women and nonstudents. Fraternity men generally dated sorority girls. Dating choices of fraternity pledges living at the fraternities resembled those of actives more than those of pledges who lived elsewhere. Men who lived off campus were most likely to date nonstudents, less likely to date dormitory women, and more likely to date off-campus women. In short, endogamous dating following prestige lines of the living units was observed for both men and women.

Generally, pinning and engagements also followed prestige endogamy patterns. Men from high-prestige fraternities pinned women from high-prestige sororities more frequently than women from middle- or low-prestige sororities.

Rogers and Havens concluded that students date, pin, and become engaged within their own prestige groups, and contrasted their findings with the conclusions reached by Blood, namely, that the rating and dating complex no longer is valid among college students. As a means of clarifying differences between the two studies, they noted that Blood's data were based upon students' attitudes, whereas their findings were based on dating and courtship behavior.

There need not be any quarrel between these two sets of data. Data reviewed later in this chapter show that mate selection is endogamous with regard to most measures of status. Rogers and Havens' data for Iowa State University and Smith's data for Pennsylvania State University, as well as numerous other studies, indicate that dating and courtship follow these norms. But this does not mean that the dating and rating complex motivates students to select dating partners in conformity to status-endogamy norms. Dating may be endogamous with regard to the prestige of residence units but still be characterized by the norms described by Blood and Lowrie. The data from Blood, Smith, and Lowrie are formidable. Dating appears to be based on the educational-personality-companionship norms described by these researchers. Yet, at the same time, dating generally is endogamous with regard to race, religion, status, and other sociological variables.

The endogamous and companionship norms are neither mutually exclusive nor necessarily mutually reinforcing. They probably tend to operate at different stages in the selection of dates or mates, and do not reflect elements of the rating complex. The educational-companionship-affectionate norms become operative by means of dyadic interaction, usually after the "filtering effects" of endogamous norms have provided some selection-rejection probabilities.

The Rogers and Havens data and the Smith data are especially valuable in showing the influence of residence groups upon college dating patterns. These data suggest ways in which group norms are internalized and become operative in behavior. Pledges, who are conscious of their status and desirous of becoming members in good standing in their fraternities, conformed more highly to the status-endogamy patterns than actives whose status in the group generally is beyond question. Pledges living at fraternities conformed more closely than pledges living elsewhere. Men living in off-campus housing probably were least integrated into college life. They also were most likely to depart from the general endogamy norm of dating college girls. Residence units seemed to provide reinforcement for endogamy norms to the degree that the status of the unit may have been enhanced or endangered by the dating behavior of its members. In turn, the members' behavior reflected the saliency of the norms and the reference groups represented by their residence units.

Endogamy, Homogamy, and Assortative Mating

Homogamy refers to the observation that, in general, husbands and wives in American families resemble one another in various physical, psychological, and social characteristics. *Assortative mating* has been used by some writers to describe the same empirical generalization. Aside from being a violation of parsimony in scientific research and communication, having two terms with relatively similar meaning may be confusing. The issue becomes even more confused when *endogamy* is added to the other two concepts.

Homogamy and assortative mating are based upon empirical observations, and both result from the operation of mate-selection norms. One set of norms prescribes or requires selection of mates from within specified sociological categories. These are called endogamous mate-selection norms. Because of the importance of the family unit, selection of mates, which serves as the basis of the family institution, is never left completely to the whims of the inexperienced youth or to chance factors of selection. In all societies, endogamous norms prescribing selection of mates from within defined sociological categories guide choice.

The number and relative saliency of mate-selection norms vary among different societies. Certain exogamous norms requiring selection of mates outside of specified groups coexist alongside endogamous norms. However, apart from legal requirements prohibiting incestuous marriages or those among certain types of more distant relatives or between guardians and children for whom they have had legal custody, exogamous mate-selection requirements are practically lacking in American society. In varying degrees, endogamous norms provide one of the two main normative structures for selection of mates. The other main normative structure is the companionship-romantic-affectionate complex.

As with all norms or values, direct measurement of the saliency of endogamous norms is extremely difficult, if not almost impossible. However, inferences about the saliency of endogamous norms may be drawn from the degree to which mate-selection choices follow the expected patterns. Adherence to the endogamous norms results in homogamous or assortative mating for those social attributes selected for endogamous control. In the main, these include race, status, religious affiliation, and ethnic background. However, adherence to endogamous norms for these variables also may help produce husband-wife similarity in values and preferences, intellectual ability, or other personal attributes for which endogamous norms do not exist. Homogamy in characteristics not specifically included in endogamous norms is enhanced when: (a) differences in the other sociological or social-psychological characteristics exist among racial, socioeconomic, religious, or ethnic groups subject to endogamous norms; and (b) mate-selection choices generally conform to the endogamous norms for these groups.

Apart from adherence to endogamous norms, selection of marriage partners on the basis of the companionship-affectionate norm complex also should increase the probability of husband-wife similarity in personal attributes. The operation of both the endogamous and the companionship-affectionate norms, in varying levels of interdependence, should contribute to similarity in personal attributes between husbands and wives. Some writers (Burgess & Wallin, 1944) have referred to this kind of similarity as "personal homogamy." "Social homogamy" was used by Burgess and Wallin (1943) to refer to adherence to endogamous norms. On the other hand, Kephart (1961) restricted the use of "homogamy" to the tendency to select a mate having physical or psychological characteristics similar to one's own, whereas "assortative mating" was used to refer to any similarity in broader sociological variables such as race, age, socioeconomic status, religion, or ethnic background.

In this chapter, no distinction is made between homogamy and assortative mating. Both represent empirical generalizations resulting from the endogamous, or companionship-affectionate norms, and possibly other mate-selection norms. However, for simplicity, "homogamy" generally is the only term used in describing similarity in husband-wife characteristics, whether these characteristics reflect physical, psychological, or group-membership variables.

A massive body of research documents the operation of endogamous norms in the American marriage system. This evidence is reviewed in relation to race, age, religious affiliation, status, ethnic background, and previous marital status. In addition, homogamy has been observed for certain attitudes, values, and other social-psychological characteristics of married couples. Data for these types of homogamy also are reviewed.

Race. Race is still the most rigidly enforced endogamous norm and reflects almost 100 per cent homogamy. Burma (1952) found that approximately 0.6 per cent of all marriages conducted in Los Angeles between November, 1948, and April, 1951, were interracial marriages. By 1959, interracial marriages in the Los Angeles area constituted approximately 1.6 per cent of all marriages (Burma, 1962). Although the rate of interreligious marriages in the Los Angeles area more than doubled in the decade, adherence to the racially endogamous norm remained virtually unbroken. And Los Angeles may have the highest rate of interracial marriage in the United States. It has a greater variety of racial and ethnic groups than most metropolitan areas in the United States, as shown by the variety of interracial marriage combinations in Burma's findings.

Knowledge about those who depart from the racially endogamous norm may suggest changes in the saliency of this norm among different social groups. Unfortunately, because of the extremely small incidence of interracial marriages, it is difficult to obtain sufficient cases for statistically reliable analyses. However, some data are available. Interracial marriages predominantly involve nonwhite males and white females (Burma, 1962; Golden, 1953). Contrary to earlier assertions, Burma (1962) found that sex ratios were not causal factors in interracial marriages. Instead, the size of the racial group or its proportion to the total population was inversely related to the frequency of interracial marriages. This relationship has been well demonstrated for the probability of Catholic interreligious marriages (Burchinal & Chancellor, 1962c; Locke, Sabagh, & Thomes, 1957).

When interracial marriages occur, they tend to follow broad lines of social and cultural homogamy (Burma, 1962; Golden, 1953). Except for persons who were products of interracial marriages themselves, those entering such marriages in the Los Angeles area generally were older, on the average, than those who married endogamously with regard to race (Burma, 1962). And median age differences between husbands and wives were significantly greater in interracial marriages than in racially endogamous marriages. Interracial marriages including Negroes in the Los Angeles

area were most likely to include previously divorced persons, whereas most other interracial marriages were less likely to include divorced persons than were homogamous white marriages.

In most other communities in the United States, Negro-white combinations generally are the major type of interracial marriages (Golden, 1953). In the Southwest, Mexican or Anglo-white marriages, or in some Eastern metropolitan areas, marriages of white United States citizens and Puerto Ricans, may be defined locally as interracial marriages. But, because of the more limited possibilities of interracial combinations, it is likely that the national interracial marriage rates are less than those reported for Los Angeles, and may be considered to constitute approximately 1 per cent or less of all marriages.

Otherwise, little is known about the characteristics of the extremely small group of persons who enter interracial marriages. Because of their small numbers, interracial marriages must be extremely highly selective with regard to personal, psychological, and social characteristics. Golden (1953; 1954) documented the strong pressures against Negro-white marriages. Friends and relatives in both racial groups, particularly among whites, discouraged such marriages. As a result, courtship was conducted sub rosa and marriages often were kept secret. These impediments probably created further selectivity in choice of marriage partners.

An insightful study by Freeman (1955), based on interracial and interethnic marriages in Hawaii, suggested ways in which persons who enter interracial marriages may differ from those who marry endogamously with regard to race.

Intraracial or intraethnic marriages are still the preferred type in Hawaii. Freeman found that students who deviated from these norms reported feelings of early rejection within their own ethnic group, poor parent-child relationships, and poorer adjustments in school. Their feelings of rejection led to some form of deviation, which brought further sanctions from members of their ethnic group, and began a cycle of mounting interdependence between rebelliousness, hostility, and further rejection. Exposure to other ethnic groups led to identification with a new group and an attempt to develop a new pattern of life which rationalized their rejection of their own group and their present deviation. Members of the opposite sex in the new group were idealized, and potential mates were sought within that group.

Relationships between two rebels, though, may be superficial and often short lived. Successive partners were frequently sought, and, if disillusionment with the new group and a potential marriage partner from that group was sufficiently delayed, and, at the same time, if mutual idealization was maintained, marriage followed. However, the marriages observed by Freeman followed a long and difficult adjustment process in which the rebelliousness of one or both parties had to be moderated. Although ethnic and sociologically heterogeneous marriage partners were sought, the resulting unions were homogamous in one way: each partner shared a common psychological characteristic and social adjustment pattern —both were rebels from their ethnic or racial groups.

Aside from this social isolation and rejection hypothesis, it may be that interracial marriages are disproportionately represented among a very different class of youth. In American urban centers, particularly among the intellectually-oriented university students and younger professionals, racial equalitarianism and integration are leading causes with which youth can identify and to which they can lend support. Interracial dating and, consequently, the possibility of interracial marriage may occur more frequently among these students. Some of the previous barriers to interracial heterosexual association, and, therefore, marriage, due to segregation in urban centers, especially in higher education, are rapidly disappearing.

Currently, equalitarian interaction among members of different races can occur more easily. Research on interracial dating attitudes and behavior of college students with varying ideological orientations and reference groups may produce some clues to alterations in the saliency of racially endogamous norms. Oddly enough, more is known about dating relations between American coeds and foreign students than interracial dating of American youth. Data on international dating experiences are reviewed later, in the section dealing with ethnic background.

Age. Homogamy in age is characteristic of American marriages, although the male typically is two and one-half years older than the female. Several studies by Hollingshead provide correlation estimates of the relationship between the spouses' ages for different types of marriages for Negro and white couples. Correlations for four types of marriages—first marriages for both parties, first marriages for males and remarriages for females, the reverse arrangement, and remarriages for both parties—ranged from .64 to .84 (Hollingshead, 1951).

Norms seem to limit marriage choices of men and women of a particular age and marital status to individuals of the opposite sex in the same approximate age range. These norms appear to be binding on all marriage types and on both races to the same extent. However, other research has identified some interesting variations in ages at marriage by previous marital status.

Marriages and remarriages are, naturally, a function of age. Ages at marriage have been moving downward since 1900, but little change occurred during the past decade. In 1961, as in 1950, the median age at first marriage for females was 20.3 years and that for males was 22.8 years.

Glick (1950) has reported age differences by socioeconomic levels. The smallest husband-wife age gap occurred among men employed at the professional level. The median age difference for these couples was 2.5 years. Typically, these men married relatively late and selected women near their own ages. At the other extreme, laborers were among the youngest at marriage and showed the largest age differences, having a median husband-wife age difference of 3.2 years.

Hollingshead (1951) studied age characteristics for the four types of marriages listed earlier. For first marriages for both parties, the predominant ages for brides were between 16 and 25 years. After 25, a woman's chances for marriage became restricted, unless she was willing to marry a previously married male. A man's chances for marriage with a previously unmarried female, however, remained about as high after as before 25 years of age.

Bowerman (1956) used a 50 per cent sample of marriage-license applications in King County (Seattle), Washington, from July, 1939, to December, 1946, to study relationships among ages at marriage and previous marital status. He reached five main conclusions: (a) Single persons selected as mates were younger, on the average, than those who were previously married, and the median age of widowed mates was higher than that of divorced mates. Brides and grooms selected mates in this rank order— single, divorced, and widowed—on age regardless of their own age or marital status. (b) As men grew older, they married women who were increasingly younger than themselves. Increased age differences were largest when men married single women and least when men married widows. (c) As women grew older, they tended to marry men nearly their own age. The greatest difference was found for women who married widowed men, and the least difference occurred when they married single men. (d) There was more variability in ages of mates selected by older people than by younger people. (e) Variability in age differences between spouses was greater for males than for females.

The foregoing data on age patterns relating to marriage support several inferences: (a) Selection of mates is normative with respect to age. (b) However, the saliency of this norm is moderated by contingencies associated with the ages of persons at the time of marriage. (c) Age-endogamous norms become less operative for remarriages than for first marriages and for older persons, regardless of previous marital status, than for younger persons. (d) The lower saliency of age-endogamous norms and other mate-selection norms among persons 30 or older is probably due to a combination of at least two sets of conditions: After age 30, age as a measure of experience, achievement, and potential for greater growth and development becomes relatively meaningless, and as one's field of eligibles of previously unmarried persons near one's age becomes increasingly restricted, age and sometimes other endogamous considerations must be given lower priority if a person desires to marry. However, because of their original differences in ages at first marriage, the initiation and dominance of courtship by males, perhaps the greater interest of males in the physical attractiveness of females relative to the corresponding interest of females in males, and the probable greater income and security advantages of older males, older males possess an advantage in being able to marry women considerably younger than themselves. On the other hand, women must be content to marry men older than themselves or closer to their own ages, and more likely, men who have been previously married.

Religion. Hollingshead (1950) stated that next to race, religion is the most decisive factor in the segregation of males and females into fields of eligibles for marriage. In New Haven, 97 per cent of the marriages involving Jewish persons were religiously endogamous, as were 94 per cent of the marriages involving Catholics and 74 per cent of the marriages involving Protestants.

Thomas (1951) challenged the alleged high religious endogamy among Catholics in the United States. Using data for Catholic dioceses in various parts of the country which included only Catholic church marriages, he found that interreligious marriage rates among Catholics varied from 70 per cent in Raleigh and Charleston to 10 per cent in El Paso. For one-half of the Catholic dioceses in the United States, the interreligious Catholic marriage rate was approximately 30 per cent and had averaged so for the past several decades. Furthermore, 41 per cent of all Catholic-sanctioned marriages in Connecticut in 1949 involved a non-Catholic partner. If all marriages involving Catholics, including those not married with the blessing of the Catholic church, were included in the population, Thomas estimated that at least one-half of all the marriages involving Catholics in Connecticut probably would not have been religiously endogamous.

Other data show that the religious-endogamy norms exist, but the rates of religious endogamy or homogamy vary greatly, being dependent upon many factors. In Iowa (Burchinal & Chancellor, 1962a), interreligious marriage rates for first marriages were lower among brides or grooms who identified with any Protestant denomination than among Catholic brides or grooms. Approximately 13 per cent of the brides identifying with a Protestant denomination and 24 per cent of the Catholic brides entered interreligious marriages. This also was true of about 9 per cent of the grooms who identified with a Protestant denomination and 21 per cent of the Catholic grooms.

Heiss (1960a), who used data from a midtown Manhattan sample, found that approximately 21 per cent of the Catholics were married interreligiously, as were 18 per cent of the Jews and 34 per cent of the Protestants.

National estimates of religious homogamy have been provided by Glick (1960). Slightly under 93 per cent of the marriages including Jewish spouses were religiously homogamous, as compared with slightly over 91 per cent of the marriages including Protestant spouses and slightly over 78 per cent of the marriages including Catholic spouses. The variations in interreligious marriage rates among the several studies just reviewed point to the limited value of general interreligious marriage rates. Rather, attention should be directed to the correlates of religiously endogamous or interreligious marriages as conditions which differentiate these two marriage patterns. Recent research has moved in this direction, both in the study of attitudes of single persons toward interreligious or religiously endogamous dating and marriage and in the study of differences among persons in the two types of marriages.

These data are not clear as to which sex most frequently is involved in interreligious marriages. In Jewish-Gentile marriages, generally it is the Jewish male who marries a Gentile female (Hollingshead, 1950), but there is no consistent agreement among findings for which sex most frequently is involved in Catholic-Protestant marriages (Burchinal & Chancellor, 1962a; Hollingshead, 1950; Thomas, 1951).

Most interreligious marriages in the United States involve Catholic-Protestant combinations, which is not surprising in view of the small proportion of Jewish persons in the population of most areas. When Jews enter interreligious marriages, they appear to select Catholics or Protestants with approximately equal frequency.

Research based on all marriages in Iowa for 1953 to 1957 show that interreligious marriage patterns were considerably more frequent among persons involved in remarriages than among persons entering first marriages. And increments in interreligious marriage rates between first marriages and remarriages were greater among Catholics than Protestants (Burchinal & Chancellor, 1962b).

Other analyses of the Iowa data revealed a differential relationship between ages at marriage and interreligious marriage rates. Interreligious marriage rates were greatest at the extreme ends of the age distribution used, at ages 16 or younger and 30 and older. Contrary to studies which reported high interreligious marriage rates among samples of marriages of high-income or high-status persons (Thomas, 1951), the Iowa analyses based on first marriages showed an inverse relationship between status levels and interreligious marriage rates. Age and status each remained associated with interreligious marriage rates as described when the other factor was controlled. And when the two factors were used jointly to predict interreligious marriage rates, the highest rates were found among the youngest or oldest spouses with low-status grooms, and lowest interreligious marriage rates were found among couples in their twenties with high-status grooms (Burchinal & Chancellor, 1962a).

The size or direction of age differences between husbands and wives who married endogamously with respect to religion in Iowa were not different from similar characteristics for the intrareligiously married couples. But differences between the two types of marriage were found for other characteristics. Interreligious marriages were more frequently characterized by an out-of-state residence of the bride and by civil weddings (Burchinal & Chancellor, 1962b). The Iowa findings suggest that the saliency of the religious-endogamy norm varies among reference groups associated with status levels, ages at marriage, and with more generalized attitudes toward marriage, as represented by the likelihood of marrying outside one's own community and of having a civil ceremony.

There is strong evidence that the proportion of a religious body in a community is probably the single most influential factor for predicting interreligious marriage rates (Burchinal & Kenkel, 1962; Locke, Sabagh, & Thomes, 1957). In the former study, Iowa counties were used as the units of observation in place of the more heterogeneous Catholic dioceses or archdioceses used in previous investigations. The correlation between the proportions of Catholics in county populations and Catholic endogamous first-marriage rates was .66; with Catholic endogamous remarriage rates, it was .44, and

both rates were based on state-reported marriage data. A correlation of .60 was observed between the proportions of Catholics per county and the Catholic endogamous marriage rates based on diocese records. Diocese records did not differentiate between first marriages and remarriages.

The cohesiveness of the ethnic group is related to religious-endogamy norms, and, consequently, to interreligious marriage rates among Catholics. Cizon (1954) noted that 70 per cent of the interreligious marriages over a 30-year period in one Catholic parish were interethnic marriages as well. Ethnic bonds appeared to weaken first, resulting in a subsequent increase in interreligious marriages. Variations in the ethnic composition of the Catholic populations in different-sized cities may account for fluctuations in interreligious marriage rates among Catholics living in these cities. For instance, Thomas (1951), found that interreligious marriages are more frequent in cities of 5,000 to 100,000 than in cities of less than 5,000 or more than 100,000 persons.

And, finally, socialization experiences are related to interreligious marriages. Among the couples of a mid-Manhattan sample (Heiss, 1960a), persons who entered interreligious marriages, as compared with those who entered religiously endogamous marriages, were characterized by having: (a) nonreligious parents, (b) greater dissatisfaction with their parents when young, (c) early family strife, (d) more tenuous ties with their families when young, and (e) greater emancipation from their parents at the time of marriage. These relationships were supported for total sample comparisons as well as for the Catholic sample. For the Protestant sample, the differences for all five tests were generally in the direction described, but only the first and fourth received strong support. Only the last two relationships received strong support from the Jewish sample.

Another set of studies has attempted to estimate relationships between various personal and social factors and attitudes toward interreligious dating and marriage. Although there are wide variations in attitudes, most appear tolerant or accepting of such behavior. Landis and Landis (1958), for instance, reported that approximately 50 per cent of the 2,000 students in one sample were willing to marry a person of another faith if other things were equal. Even more favorable responses have been reported by Prince (1956) among University of Idaho students: 97 per cent were favorable toward interreligious dating; 80 per cent of the males and 72 per cent of the females were not opposed to going steady with a person of another faith; and 62 per cent of the males and 52 per cent of the females were willing to consider an interreligious marriage. Catholic students in the sample were more favorable toward interreligious marriage than Protestant students—a result common to several studies on this topic—but they held more strongly to certain requirements for such marriages than did Protestant students. These requirements included the assurance that one's mate would change to the respondent's faith or let the children be brought up in the respondent's faith.

In contrast, considerably less favorable attitudes toward interreligious dating and marriage have been observed among students at Iowa State University. Approximately 38 per cent of the males and 18 per cent of the females included in a probability sample of the students at this university provided favorable attitudes toward interreligious marriage.

Present research has produced some findings having sufficient reliability to allow the following tentative generalizations:

1. Attitudes toward interreligious dating are more favorable than attitudes toward interreligious marriage, the difference probably reflecting the degree of commitment involved in the two types of relationships (Burchinal, 1960; Prince, 1956).

2. Considerable interreligious dating occurs among college youth and probably among nonstudents as well. Kirkpatrick and Caplow (1945a) found that 42 per cent of the Catholic males and 62 per cent of the Catholic females of the University of Minnesota dated non-Catholics. About 62 per cent of the Catholic males and 51 per cent of the Catholic females attending four Catholic universities in the Midwest, two of which were coeducational, one of which was an all-male university, and one of which was an all-female university, dated non-Catholics at least occasionally (Barta & O'Reilly, 1952).

3. Although results differ on the proportion of Catholic males and females who dated non-Catholics, males have less opposition to interreligious dating or marriage than females (Hoover, 1950). This finding has been confirmed for attitudes toward going steady and for marriage by Prince (1956), and for Protestant high school and college students in Iowa (Burchinal, 1960). Differences in favorability of attitudes toward interreligious dating and marriage between Iowa males and females remained after controls were imposed for frequency of church attendance, age, farm residence, or family status for nonfarm youth.

4. Differences exist among findings for the relationships between family status and attitudes toward interreligious marriage. The relationship between these two variables was nonsignificant for the sample of Catholic youth included in Hoover's study (1950). In contrast, Burchinal (1960) found inverse relationships between family status and favorability of attitudes toward interreligious dating or marriage. Youth from lower-status homes, as measured by their fathers' occupations, had more favorable attitudes toward interreligious dating or marriage. Also, a slight inverse relationship was observed between interreligious marriage rates and status of grooms during a five-year

period in Iowa (Burchinal & Chancellor, 1962a; Burchinal & Chancellor, 1962b).

5. Several studies agree on finding an inverse relationship between frequency of church attendance and attitudes toward interreligious dating or marriage (Burchinal, 1960; Hoover, 1950; Prince, 1956).

6. Acceptance of the religious-endogamy norm may be related directly to age. In Iowa, young marriages more frequently were interreligious than were marriages of persons who were at least 20 years of age (Burchinal & Chancellor, 1962a; Burchinal & Chancellor, 1962b). Comparisons of attitudes of high school and college students toward interreligious dating supported the same generalization. After controls were imposed for the frequency of church attendance, sex, farm residence, or nonfarm social status, high school students endorsed more favorable attitudes toward interreligious dating than did college students (Burchinal, 1960).

7. Experiences associated with interreligious dating or marriage probably contribute to more favorable attitudes toward them. Notable among the findings of Hoover were the relationships between deviation from the religious-endogamy norms by relatives of the youth and the youths' attitudes toward interreligious marriages. Also, Barta and O'Reilly (1952) observed that among Catholic students the belief that interreligious marriage had a good chance of succeeding was related to current dating with non-Catholics. [Cf. the above discussion with Ch. 14, pp. 555–557.]

Social status. Status endogamy is well established (Burgess & Wallin, 1943; Centers, 1949; Hollingshead, 1950). Another investigation (Sundal & McCormick, 1951) not only found the usual evidence of status endogamy, even during the early years of World War II, but also found that among those who were employed, the status levels of the occupations of the brides were more closely related to those of the grooms than were those of the brides' fathers. The coefficient of contingency between the employment status of brides and grooms was .66, whereas that between the occupations of the grooms and those of the brides' fathers was .41, and that between the fathers of both brides and grooms was .48. Yet little attention in mate-selection research has been given to the employment and occupation of females before marriage. With rising rates of employment among women, acquaintanceship through occupational propinquity may become an increasingly important selective factor.

Some evidence suggests that status endogamy has been too greatly emphasized. For instance, Hunt (1940), while finding general support for status endogamy among all marriages conducted in Norwood, Massachusetts, from 1872 to 1937, failed to find much evidence for status endogamy in the selection of husbands by females. In each of five occupational groups—professional, semiprofessional, white collar, skilled, and unskilled workers—men most frequently selected females whose fathers' occupations were on the same status level as the males. The next most frequent choices involved contiguous occupational levels, and choices between more remote status levels occurred least frequently. Among females, however, most of those from only the lowest status level married endogamously. Females from other status levels showed no uniform tendency for selection for partners from any other status level. It would be just as accurate to speak of status exogamy as status endogamy for these females.

Data from a study by Leslie and Richardson (1956) clearly dispute the status-endogamy generalization. These researchers failed to discover status endogamy among marriages of Purdue University students who came predominantly from the middle status level. There was a slight tendency toward homogamy in the total sample and for those who met before attending college, but no homogamous tendency was observed among those who met and married while on campus. Because there was no apparent difference between the students who met their spouses at home and those who met them on campus, Leslie and Richardson inferred that different environmental pressures operating on the two groups accounted for the differences noted. Campus norms for association may favor heterogamy with regard to status, whereas community norms continue to favor status endogamy.

More recent findings by Coombs (1962) support this interpretation. Nearly 88 per cent of the couples when both spouses lived at home during the courtship were homogamous in regard to religion. In contrast, 64 per cent of the couples when neither was living at home during courtship were homogamous in religious affiliation. Homogamy in social status was observed for 83 per cent of the couples when both lived at home, compared with 61 per cent for those when neither lived at home during their courtship.

Distinctions in place of first acquaintanceship, and in early dating and courtship, may be important variables in considering the importance of status endogamy on subsequent courtship and mate selection.

Most of the studies just reviewed also included data on two related questions: (a) Do men tend to marry women with lower status than their own more frequently than the reverse? (b) What differences exist in the saliency of the status-endogamy norms among different groups in our society?

The bulk of the data support the generalization that when status heterogamy occurs, men tend to marry down and women tend to marry up—a phenomenon known as the mating gradient. Centers (1949) found that all men, except those in the semiskilled and unskilled occupations, more frequently married down than up. In contrast, more females married up than down. In terms of the positions of their parents, the greater proportion of the sons married down than

up, except at the lowest status level. When class lines were crossed in New Haven, men married women of lower status than themselves more frequently than was true for women, and men generally had a wider choice of mates than females (Hollingshead, 1950). Among the couples married in Madison, Wisconsin (Sundal & McCormick, 1951), one-third of the women who married sons of professional or business men were daughters of skilled or semiskilled workers. Only the study by Hunt (1940) did not support the generalization that men married down more frequently than women: he found that men and women married down the status system with about equal frequency.

Few data are available concerning the relative saliency of the status-endogamy norms in various groups. Hollingshead (1950) reported that status endogamy was equally present in all three major religious groups in New Haven. Otherwise, aside from the unsystematic observations of high-status endogamy among persons in the well-established and recognized upper classes, little is known of the relative adherence to the status-endogamy norm in different strata or residential groups. Centers (1949) suggested that for both males and females, adherence to the status-endogamy norm is greater at the higher than lower status levels. In contrast, Hunt found greater status endogamy for males than for females in all five occupational classes, and, for females, status endogamy was evident only at the lowest status level. Obviously, additional research is needed to establish the relative saliency of status-endogamous, religious-endogamous, and other mate-selection norms among different social groups in the United States.

One study, unique of its kind, completes this review of data pertaining to status endogamy. Using marriage data over a period of 25 years for Columbus, Ohio, Dinitz, Banks, and Pasamanick (1960) tested the hypothesis that there was a decline in cross-class marriages from 1933 through 1958.

One basis of this hypothesis was the finding that college students in 1949 and 1957–1958 were more critical of cross-class marriages than were students in two previous decades. Although the authors treated their study as more provocative than conclusive, several interesting findings emerged: (a) In 1933, 1939, and 1949, most marriages were characterized by relative class endogamy. (b) Systematic decline over time, though, occurred both in the selection of marriage partners from the same socio-equivalent census tracts and in the range of mates from widely disparate classes. (c) At the same time, an increasing proportion of marriages during the periods covered were contracted between persons whose residences were in socioeconomically comparable, although not geographically identical, tracts. Increasing geographic mobility in selection of mates was accompanied by selection from a proportionately narrower socioeconomic range of tracts. (d) Persons responsible for most of these fluctuations lived mainly in the middle-range tracts. Persons from average to above-average tracts were comparatively the most endogamous in all time periods and were becoming increasingly more endogamous in the later periods. In contrast, disparate marriages occurred with increasing frequency in the poorest tracts and in an undulating and less predictable manner in the most desirable tracts.

Ethnic background. Only a few mate-selection studies have dealt with ethnic status. The strength of ethnic background as a mate-selection factor is related to other characteristics of the groups, such as language, religion, and other cultural differences, the cohesiveness of the group, its size in relation to the total community, and the length of time the group has resided in an area. Thomas (1954) and Cizon (1954) described ethnic marriage patterns among Catholics in several urban centers. Interethnic marriages were not frequent among long-established ethnic centers in large cities, but were much more common among migrants from these stable ethnic communities.

Both studies agreed in finding that interethnic and interreligious marriages were interrelated, with interethnic marriages occurring first and, in a sense, helping to create the circumstances which promoted interreligious marriages. Cizon found that both types of marriages had been steadily increasing from 1929 to 1949 in the midwestern city he studied, a city which included a large proportion of Polish descendents. And both studies agreed in finding that females more frequently than males entered interreligious or interethnic marriages. Thomas interpreted this sex difference as resulting from the greater freedom of choice in mate selection enjoyed by the males, whereas females, if they want to marry, cannot afford to be as selective as males.

Otherwise, for youths who represented at least the third generation, unless they lived in an ethnic community such as the cultural islands in urban centers described by Thomas (1954), ethnic background probably is relatively meaningless and does not operate as a strong mate-selection variable. Religion and possibly socioeconomic status remain as the vestiges of former ethnic background.

Blood and Nicholson (1962a; 1962c) have called attention to a recent and interesting variation in the dating attitudes and practices of college students regarding ethnic or, in this case, international endogamous norms. In their first study (1962a) they surveyed the attitudes of a random sample of students at the University of Michigan in the spring of 1957. International acquaintanceships were almost universal on this campus, and almost half of the women had dated a foreign student. Among the women who had not, the majority thought they would accept a date if asked. While a permissive climate of student opinion existed toward dates of American women with foreign men, campus norms discouraged promiscuous international dating. The norms tolerated selective dating with emphasis upon compatability and the personal qualifications of the foreign student. Group differences between religious and nonreligious students, males and females, and between younger and older students existed. In this atmosphere, coeds had substantial freedom of self-determination to date internationally and freedom from sanctions if they chose to do so.

The second report was based on interviews with 99 American coeds who had dated at least one foreign student (1962c). International dating, even among those who dated foreign students most frequently, was not related to parental rebellion or a crusade against prejudice. The coeds were overwhelmingly satisfied with their experiences. Moreover, their girl friends were sympathetic; in contrast, their parents and American boy friends typically were neutral. The girls were almost universally agreed that international dating did not impair their ability to get American dates. International dating was viewed by these girls as an interesting and enjoyable part of the total university experience.

A third study by Blood and Nicholson (1962b) reported experiences of foreign students who dated coeds at the University of Michigan. Despite a wide range of problems, the foreign students were enthusiastic about their dating experiences. Except for Latin Americans, the majority reaction was extremely favorable—a tribute to the adaptability of the foreign students to our dating norms and to the American coeds involved.

Previous marital status. Previous marital status generally is not considered as a variable influencing selection of mates, because most marriages include first marriages for both parties. However, as a result of present high divorce and remarriage rates, previous marital status becomes a theoretically important variable for understanding mate selection among persons past 30 or 35 years of age.

Studies by Sundal and McCormick (1951) and Hollingshead (1951), among others, support the generalization that persons select marriage partners whose previous marital status is similar to their own.

Bowerman (1953) has provided the most comprehensive data on selection of marriage partners by previous marital status. Five generalizations can be drawn from the results of this investigation: (a) At all ages persons selected as marriage partners persons whose previous marital status was similar to their own far more frequently than would have been expected by chance. (b) When age groups were combined into a total sample, marriage of two widows occurred comparatively more frequently than any other type, and marriage of two single persons occurred less frequently. However, when age was introduced as a control variable, this ranking held only up to age 30 for brides and 35 for grooms. After these ages, similarity with respect to previous marital status was greater for single persons, and, after age 50 for brides and age 60 for grooms, the widowed-widowed combination had the least rate of similarity. (c) At all ages, marriages of single and previously married persons occurred less frequently than would have been expected by chance. Widowed and divorced persons, however, married each other more frequently than would have been expected due to chance, but only up to ages 30 or 40. Thereafter, the frequencies for this combination were below the chance expectancy and remained similar to that of the single–previously married combination. (d) General trends were relatively comparable whether analyzed by the ages of grooms or by those of brides. (e) In marriages involving single persons, there was an increase in the selection of single persons with increasing age at marriage, but among marriages involving previously divorced persons, similarity in previous marital status decreased with increasing age.

Physical and psychological characteristics. Numerous studies attest to homogamy in physical, psychological, and social-psychological characteristics such as height, weight, appearance or attractiveness, intelligence, memory, emotional stability or neuroticism, religious, political, economic, and family values, conceptions of marriage, conceptions of child-rearing and attitudes toward children, and marital happiness or satisfaction ratings. Only several of the more recent studies need to be considered in this discussion.

The Burgess-Wallin investigation (1943; 1944) is important because their data were obtained from engaged couples, whereas most other studies were based on data from couples who had been married for varying lengths of time, some for 20 or more years. Correlation measures of assortative mating based on couples who have been married for some time may be spuriously high because of the modification of the characteristics through marital interaction and mutual reinforcement. The Burgess-Wallin data should minimize the confounding influence of marital interaction upon measurements of variables that may have been instrumental in contributing to mate selection. However, this still leaves the question of possible convergence in social-psychological variables as a result of dating and courtship interaction. Nevertheless, the Burgess and Wallin results do provide support for homogamy in psychical and personality characteristics as well as for homogamy related to group memberships normally subject to endogamous norms.

Several recent studies complicate the interpretation of psychological or social-psychological homogamy between couples as resulting from assortative mating in relation to those characteristics. Data from these studies suggest that when homogamy in these characteristics occurs, it is partly a by-product of the filtering effects of endogamous norms and the influence of the companionship norms in mate selection.

Schellenberg (1960) studied the similarity in values between mates in engaged- and married-couple groups. One member of each couple was a student at the University of Kansas. The data were derived from the Alport-Vernon-Lindzey study of values. Convergence scores based on the responses of 64 married couples and of 36 couples who were engaged or going steady differed significantly from chance, thus indicating homogamy in the values measured. The convergence scores for the values among the two sets of couples also showed significantly greater homogamy than observed for 80 artificially matched couples who were used as a control group and who had background characteristics similar to the study groups. Convergence scores for the control group, however, also showed a significant degree of homogamy, probably as a result of the matching on common background factors. This portion of the results discredits the interpretation of homogamy in personal characteristics—in this case values as measured on the Alport-Vernon-Lindzey scale— as a function of assortative mating only. Instead, these results suggest that such homogamy occurs partially from underlining similarity in characteristics that are affected by endogamous norms. On the other hand, additional results from Schellenberg's study suggest that assortative mating occurred in relation to personality-related variables, apart from the operation of endogamous norms. The convergence scores of the married and premarried couples were significantly higher than the scores for the artificially matched couples. This finding indicates that a portion of homogamy in values between the married and the premarried couples was left unexplained by controlling on common background characteristics. These data suggest that endogamous norms, by creating pools of eligibles, also partially match individuals on value characteristics. However, homogamy in relation to other personality characteristics may or may not follow the patterns observed for the value characteristics he studied.

Data from another study (Kerckhoff & Davis, 1962) suggest that value consensus and personality homogamy or heterogamy between members of a couple do not necessarily follow from adherence to social-endogamy norms. Finally, a longitudinal study that began with the investigation of 300 engaged couples in 1934 and continued for 20 years provided data for the degree of husband-wife similarity in numerous variables (Kelly, 1955).

The results of the latter study require adjustment of many ideas held about husband-wife similarity in characteristics as a function of length of marriage. Test-retest data were analyzed for 103 widely different psychological, social-psychological, and sociological variables. In general, little change occurred between the husbands' and wives' scores over the 20 years. Cross-spouse comparisons of change scores from test to retest showed low correlations, indicating little tendency for wives to change toward the original scores of their husbands or vice versa. Few of the correlations were significant, and about three-fourths were negative, indicating a slight tendency to change away from the score of one's spouse. Correlations between the scores of husbands and wives at both time periods ranged from —.02 to .58, most of them being positive, thus supporting the homogamy generalization.

The initial similarity between husbands' and wives' scores became neither greater nor less with length of marriage. This initial similarity apparently was adequate enough for most men and women to have established and maintained a reasonably cohesive relationship without the need to become more alike. Although sociologists may have emphasized factors and relationships that should increase congruence between mates, these results indicate that attention also should be given to centrifugal forces in relationships associated with differences in husbands' and wives' roles throughout the years of adulthood.

Love and Empathy Relationships

Although they may be unable to articulate what they feel and their reasons for feeling that way, most persons in love have an approximate idea of how they *should* feel toward those they want to marry, and

that feeling is expressed in one word—love. For understandable reasons, the literature on love is immense. Probably the largest body of literature on this subject is that of the poet, essayist, and novelist, all of whom use humanistic devices to arouse and communicate feelings. More recently, analytical views of love have been appearing. Sociologists, anthropologists, psychologists, and psychiatrists have been attempting to understand the development of love, its functions for individuals, and its structural importance in society.

As the analytic study and discussion of love have developed, the emphasis given to the dysfunctional elements of romantic love has been partially replaced by a greater appreciation of the positive consequences of love in heterosexual relationships, not only in Western society, but in other societies as well.

In this section, two main areas of data are reviewed: (a) studies and some analytic essays dealing with love, and especially romantic love, in the United States; and (b) studies dealing with a closely related concept, the development and expression of empathy as the function of dating and courtship.

Analytic views of love. The dysfunctional view of love in American society, usually referred to as "romantic love," has been evident in many discussions of this topic by family sociologists from Waller (1937) to the present. Kolb (1950) and Beigel (1951) directly challenged this view, and, more recently, Foote (1953) and Goode (1959) have sought to broaden the sociological conception by re-examining the relationships between expressions of love and the structure of society.

Kolb (1950) rightly pointed out that persons who attack romantic love also are attacking fundamental values inherent in the family system and our larger society. These include the fundamental obligation of the family and other social systems to encourage personal freedom and growth and the integrity of democratic values and freedom in human relationships. Furthermore, Kolb argued that the attack on romanticism is based on a false dichotomy between freedom and order, the society and the individual, and self-love and love of others. If carried to its logical conclusion, denunciation of romantic love would result in rigid conformity to the endogamous norms, mate selection would become congruent with the views of one's parents, and by reflecting extreme conventionality and conforming behavior, probably would stifle further personality growth or creativity in human relationships.

Beigel (1951) joined the attack on criticism of romanticism by reconciling elements of courtly love, from which romantic love has evolved, and the requirements of modern marriage. Love, Beigel argued, is an expression of a social-psychological process that attempts to reconcile basic human needs and frustrating social conditions. In this function, love or so-called romantic love is not a harmful relationship between the sexes, but has helped to raise the status of the female and to soften the impact of factors which might endanger the marital union. In this way, love not only serves as a final and powerful catalytic agent in mate selection, but it also helps persons to adjust to frustrating situations. Currently, love provides the single most pervasive basis of integration in our monogamous marriage system, a system which now lacks the economic, political, or religious bases of organization that it formerly had, before the rise of our metropolitan-dominated society.

All definitions of love have their shortcomings. No definition has nor probably ever will satisfy everyone. All definitions of love involve value judgments, reflecting what the author wishes to emphasize. Nevertheless, increased understanding of this varied and volatile emotion may be attained by examining several of the current approaches.

Foote (1953), for example, offered no concise definition of love; instead, he presented a conception whereby persons can detect the "real article" beneath the "babble of spurious affirmations." Foote's conception of love is stated in terms of human development. Love is that relationship between two persons which is most conducive to the optimum development of both. This optimum development is measured in terms of their gross competency in interpersonal relationships. Foote's dynamic conception of love is almost opposite to the earlier views of romantic love. Conceptions of romantic love generally emphasize a fluctuating emotion which can be controlled or stabilized only by a ritual or pretense, usually including sublimation of sexual desires by intense idealization. Instead, Foote argues, one commits himself to another, not on the basis of forced delusions, but on his expectations of real possibilities which can emerge with proper cultivation and trust.

The relationship which is most conducive to development of mutual personal development is like that between the artist and the audience. The ideal audience (the loved object) expects the artist to work hard at his performance and is disappointed only when he does less than his best. Thus, the relationship most conducive to Foote's conception of love is social equality and reciprocity. In turn, reciprocity can occur only when persons are relatively equally matched in their development, creativity, and interdependence. Persons who insist on affection from dependents whom they cannot let go cannot develop further or contribute to the others' growth. Hierarchy and unilateralism are static and hinder the development of love in its contribution to the potential to which a person can rise.

Goode (1959), in contrast to Foote, provided a brief and concise definition of love, one he admitted probably would not satisfy critics any better than others. Goode viewed love as "a strong attachment, a cathexis between adolescents or adults of opposite sexes, including at least components of sex desire and tendencies." Goode's main interest was in developing relationships between love and social structure. Therefore, he avoided the implied dichotomy between romantic love and the other expression of love, the latter type generally being considered as conjugal love with its settled, domestic, familistic, and child-centered foci. Instead, Goode conceptualized love as a range on a continuum between two polar types. At one pole, a strong love involvement may elicit negative social sanctions, whereas at the other position, almost mandatory social approval exists for love as a basis for marriage.

Correspondingly, the institutionalization of love in a society may range from high to low. Thus, differences may occur between the intensity of individuals in a love relationship and the cultural expression of love as a basis for marriage. For this reason, Goode differentiated between a love pattern, where love is permissible and may be an expected prelude to marriage and the usual element in courtship, and the romantic complex, which includes the elements of the love pattern, but with an ideological prescription of their necessity and a highly institutionalized complex of values and roles.

Love patterns and the romantic complex may exist along separate continua, and deep love attachments do not necessarily reflect extreme romanticism. Concepts such as *rational love* have been advanced to describe the love pattern among some persons in American society, particularly the better-educated members of the middle classes who do not reflect extreme romanticism in their courtship behavior.

Reiss (1960) presented an interpretation of love that emphasizes the social aspects and suggested appropriate sociological research pertaining to this phenomenon. The task for the sociologists, Reiss argued, is to identify the social and cultural background factors that make a couple capable of feeling rapport with one another. Rapport, to Reiss, is the basic element of love. Rapport develops as a feeling of ease and relaxation, whereby persons are willing and eager to talk about themselves and learn more about the other person. According to Reiss, the feeling of rapport is the first step in the development of a heterosexual relationship. Following rapport comes a second process that Reiss called self-revelation. Through self-revelation, a third process occurs, the development of mutual dependencies or, more technically, of interdependence between habit systems. Habits can perpetuate the relationship, and the type of habits that are established are culturally determined. And, finally, the fourth process, building upon the foregoing ones, is personality need fulfillment. Reiss saw these four processes as part of a broader process; while building rapport, one reveals himself and becomes more dependent upon the other, thereby fulfilling his personality needs. Because of the circularity of this process, Reiss called the conceptualization a *wheel theory of love.*

The wheel can move indefinitely in a positive direction as long as the four processes continue to be active. Throughout his discussion, Reiss emphasized cultural or social factors only and avoided psychological variables. Thus, he saw the wheel turning positively as long and as intensely as the cultural backgrounds of the people involved allow. Of course, the wheel can turn backwards as well, and unwind. The relationship can be weakened and ultimately dissolved when any of the elements is decreased. Events that lessen rapport or decrease self-revelation, mutual dependency, or need fulfillment will decrease the love experienced. Thus, love represents the development and elaboration of one type of primary relationship.

Considerable harmony exists between Foote's conception of mutual development and Reiss's conception of the wheel theory moving in a positive direction. Reiss emphasized the cultural aspects of love and its development. Foote cast his formulation more in a social-psychological framework. Both emphasized the developmental characteristic of love. Reiss recognized a reversal in direction, and Foote also developed this point in other sources. However, Reiss's classification of types of love does not add greatly to an understanding of the phenomena. He speaks of (a) ultraromantic love—at first sight; (b) sexual love, when the sex factor is dominant; (c) rational love, where the intellectual appraisal of the affair is important; and (d) several mixed types.

Goode's idea of a continuum ranging between polar types provides a better basis for conceptualizing love, although this approach does not specify what continuum or continua should be employed. Reiss's classification suggests that the obvious sexual factor, impulsiveness of commitment, and rational assessment should be considered as three separate continua.

Criticisms of romantic love, frequently derived from Waller's observation and interpretation of the fragile heterosexual relationships among Pennsylvania State College students during the middle and late 1930's, abound in most textbooks written for marriage-preparation courses. Research on the incidence or correlates of romantic love, on the other hand, has a much shorter history.

Wallin (1952) focussed on the relationships between love and idealization in contemporary American middle-class courtship. Idealization was defined as the imputation of desirable qualities to a person lacking them, or as an exaggeration of their proportions and/or the denial or underestimation of unfavorable attributes. Love was considered as a state of feeling characterized by powerful drives to be with a particular person of the opposite sex, a sense of happiness and well-being in their presence, and an intense desire for exclusive rights to affection and sexual response from that person. The research problem became: Does love impair lovers' perceptions of one another? At least two theoretical propositions have been advanced to answer this question.

First, Waller and those who more or less followed his arguments believed that extensive idealization is a necessary component of love in our society. The elements of romantic love and especially the romantic-love complex—an important distinction made by Goode—are considered evidence for the extreme importance of idealization in relation to love. The development and expression of idealization in love, it is asserted, result from the frustration of sexual drives, leading to the development of sublimation and to the idealization of the love object. In contrast, another position holds that college-level lovers are friends and acquaintances first, and know each other to some extent before they are seized by the "commanding emotion of romantic love." Freedom of association and lack of supervision facilitate physical intimacy, including varying levels of petting and, less frequently, intercourse; but regardless of the level of physical expression, these conditions help reduce the frustrating circumstances on which Waller's theory was based.

Nevertheless, Wallin (1952) argued that some idealization remains present in love affairs. Its basis, however, is not sexual frustration, but rather a consequence of the importance of maintaining self-esteem. Persons with whom we identify closely involve our self-esteem, what we think of them influences how we evaluate ourselves and vice versa. And what one thinks the loved object thinks of him also influences one's self-conception. Views of self and the other become interdependent, affecting images of one's self and others.

Wallin developed three hypotheses for relationships between idealization and love in courtship and marriage: (a) Individuals who idealize in courtship also tend to do so in marriage. (b) Individuals differ in the degree to which they idealize; some do not idealize at all, others do so to a great extent. Lack of idealization, he hypothesized, may occur when one's standards are not met and, hence, there is no need to idealize. Also, those who idealize most may be individuals who are insecure or inadequate. (c) Idealization in most cases is not extreme.

A wide variety of data from couples included in the Burgess-Wallin (1943; 1944) study of engagement and marriage were used to test these hypotheses. In general, they were supported and, on the basis of these results, Wallin suggested: (a) There is no evidence of extreme idealization in middle-class American courtship behavior. (b) There is strong evidence of moderate idealization in courtship, and this can be accounted for adequately by the theory of identification of self-esteem. (c) Waller's theory, if correct in part, is not generally applicable in current middle-class courtship.

Hobart has reported studies on relationships between romanticism and disillusionment in marriage (1958a), some effects of romanticism during courtship on marital-role opinions (1958c), and the incidence of romanticism in courtship (1958d). In a fourth article, Hobart (1960) reported data for the relationship between romanticism and marital-role opinions for his original college-couple sample and for 76 per cent of these couples for whom marital-role data were obtained four years later.

Four hypotheses were advanced for the incidence of romanticism in courtship (1958d): (a) The romanticism of adolescents changes according to different courtship stages. As adolescents occupy different statuses, they experience different tensions, and their tensions are reflected in their idealization and romanticism. (b) There is a cyclical movement in romanticism in relation to courtship stages: students at the beginning and the end of courtship (marriage) are least romantic, whereas those in the middle stages are most romantic. Romanticism is assumed to vary directly with courtship tensions. Tensions during the middle stages of courtship are assumed to be greater because of greater parent-youth conflict, which, it is assumed, reaches its peak during steady dating and declines after engagement and marriage. (c) Separated couples have higher romanticism scores than members of couples who are not separated. Again, it is assumed that romanticism is heightened by strain and tension. (d) Romantic tendencies of unmarried persons who previously had gone steady or were engaged are more pronounced than those of unmarried persons who never had these experiences.

None of the four hypotheses was supported for females. Hypotheses (a), (c), and (d) were clearly supported for males, and partial support was observed for the second hypothesis as well. For males, romanticism increased up to going steady, but the predicted decline from going steady to marriage did not occur.

Other data from Hobart's study show that the greatest criticism of their parents' marriage came from males in advanced courtship and least from nondaters. For females, no relation was observed between courtship stages and criticism of their parents' marriages. As noted in the analyses by Winch over a decade earlier, emancipation from home and movement toward marriage do not occur in the same manner or at similar rates for the two sexes. Hobart's findings suggest that for females, progress in courtship is not related to emancipation as it may be for males. And for females, romanticism was not related to courtship stage or presence of one's partner as it was for males.

Hobart's study of relationships between romanticism and disillusionment in marriage (1958a) was based on comparisons between scores for disagreements and disagreement estimates between couples in four courtship stages: among persons in relation to their favorite dates, those going steady, engaged couples, and married couples. Disagreement was measured by comparisons of males' and females' responses to a series of items in a marital-role inventory. Disagreement estimates represent disagreements between personal responses of a person and the responses he or she ascribed to his or her partner. Disillusionment was operationally defined as the discrepancy between disagreement and disagreement-estimate scores. Cross-sectional, not longitudinal, data were employed in this first investigation.

Postmarital disillusionment was observed

for both males and females, but it was stronger for males. There was little evidence of disillusionment during premarital courtship transitions, and there was no clear relationship between disillusionment and romanticism for either males or females.

Two hypotheses were tested by Hobart (1960) in his longitudinal study of romanticism and marital attitudes during courtship and marriage: (a) Romanticism follows a cyclical movement with regard to courtship stages; it is low during the initial stages, reaches its peak during steady dating and engagement, and declines again after marriage. (b) Marital-role opinions follow a similar cyclical pattern with respect to courtship stages. Scores for opinion changes were based on a comparison of the original 1954 scores and the follow-up scores obtained in 1958.

The first hypothesis was not supported. Changes from casual dating to advanced dating suggested a relative increase in romanticism, but the number of subjects was too small to provide an adequate test. However, it was clear that when students left the college subculture, romanticism declined, unless they changed from casual to advanced courtship if they were males or changed from casual to advanced courtship and/or marriage if they were females. Changes in romanticism associated with departure from college and integration in the noncollege world appeared to be more severe for males than for females, probably because males were originally more romantic than females and, thus, more vulnerable at the onset.

The second hypothesis also was not supported. However, marital-role opinions changed differentially at different courtship stages. They seemed to follow a straight-line trend with regard to courtship status. Maximum change occurred between casual dating and marriage, and minimum change occurred between advanced courtship and marriage. There was no evidence of romantic disturbance of marital roles during advanced courtship. This finding flatly contradicted the finding of Hobart's earlier study (1958c), which showed that for both males and females, romanticism disturbed marital-role opinion scores among persons in advanced courtship.

Because this section's interest is primarily in romanticism, no further discussion is given to Hobart's contradictory findings on marital-role opinions. The two important results from this investigation are: (a) the lack of support for the cyclical relationship between romanticism and courtship status; and (b) the influence of leaving the college environment upon both romanticism and marital-role opinions. These findings suggest that some aspects of courtship and, more important, certain aspects of marital-role adjustments differ between college youth and young adults whose lives are integrated with the world of work.

There are few direct comparisons of courtship and marriage adjustment between these two classes of youth. Research is needed to identify in what ways they are similar and in what ways they are different.

The assumed relationship between strain or tension and romanticism, upon which Waller's formulation was based and which was critical to Hobart's analyses, was included, at least in part, in Dean's (1961a) investigation of relationships between romanticism and emotional maladjustment. Correlations between romanticism scores and adjustment scores were low and ranged between .02 and .19.

In subsequent research, Dean (1961b) developed 14 subscales for measuring emotional maturity. These and his romanticism scale were administered to 160 freshmen women at a small, church-related, liberal arts college in Ohio. The 14 correlations ranged from —.10 to .06, none being statistically significant, and, consequently, provided no support for his hypothesis of a negative relationship between maturity and romanticism. These findings support his earlier results. Because Dean did not report the ranges or sigmas for his romanticism scores or specify what proportion of the females could be defined as extremely romantic, we cannot judge how common romanticism was among his subjects. But his data are valuable in suggesting that romanticism among college-level females—and here we generalize far beyond his sample—is not a function of their personal maturity or adjustment, but probably is a reflection of the internalized peer-group norms.

Empathy in courtship. It is unfortunate that research on emotional trends during courtship begun by Kirkpatrick and Caplow (1945b) has not been developed further by these or other researchers. Their interesting and valuable study stands alone. Using graphic techniques of data collection, they found that the majority of their college students reported an uncomplicated pattern of emotional involvement, with a rise and then a decline during the love relationship. In broken love affairs, emotional involvement generally rose from attraction to love and then declined to indifference, and, in a minority of cases, terminated in dislike. Approximately 80 per cent of the broken love affairs ended near the indifference level, and only 9 per cent ended at the love level. In about one-half of the cases, students reported no serious emotional trauma following a broken love affair. The other half were about equally divided among three adjustment patterns: an upsurge of love following the break, hostility, and ambiguous emotional reactions that fluctuated between love and dislike. Males and females had approximately similar patterns of adjustment.

Several researchers recently have begun investigating disagreements between couples and empathy relationships during courtship. Some of the major problems investigated include sex differences in couple disagreement, sex differences in empathy, relationships between courtship status or duration of association and disagreements, disagreement estimates, and empathic responses of couples.

Consistent or theoretically meaningful sex differences in disagreement, disagreement estimates, or empathy scores have not been found. Kirkpatrick and Hobart (1954) used five scores for analyzing disagreements and nonempathic predictions of partner responses and disagreement estimates at four stages of courtship—favorite date, going steady, engaged, and married. Consistent sexual differences in trend scores for the four groups were not found. However, men had higher disagreement-estimate scores at engagement than females. In another investigation (Hobart, 1956), nonsignificant differences were observed for differences in the disagreement scores of males and females. And Hobart (1956) reported that males and females expressed the same relative disagreement for the same areas.

The Kirkpatrick and Hobart (1954) and Hobart (1956) studies also agreed in finding a decline in disagreement scores with advanced courtship status. The largest drop in the sample studied by Hobart occurred between the favorite-date and going-steady stages; the second largest occurred between engagement and marriage. Kirkpatrick and Hobart (1954) reported a slight variation in the pattern between disagreements, disagreement estimates, empathy scores, and courtship status. While there was no particular trend toward lower scores with increasing intimacy among the couples in their sample, the means for married couples were significantly lower than those for couples in the favorite-date stage. Also, pair scores differed significantly from random scores at every courtship stage. In his separate investigation, Hobart (1956) observed that courtship status, not length of association, was related to disagreement, disagreement estimates, and empathy scores.

Additional data supporting the generalization that empathy is related to courtship status or degree of intimacy come from Vernon and Stewart (1957). Besides being related to the degree of involvement with one's partner, Vernon and Stewart found that empathy was related to greater frequency of dating the person used in developing the empathy measure, and with greater frequency of dating in general. The authors recognized that the latter two relationships probably were confounded: higher frequency of dating and more intimate involvement are interrelated. When involvement was controlled, there was no association between the amount of dating and empathy, indicating that frequent daters per se do not show greater empathy, unless they are also more highly involved with their partners.

These findings led Vernon and Stewart to suggest that empathy in dating results from the interplay of situational and personality factors. This conclusion is developed in greater detail in their second report (Stewart & Vernon, 1959). Empathy was not considered as a trait or capacity, but conceptualized as a process. Four sets of relationships were used to test this conceptualization, with the following results: First, empathy among 52 dating couples was highly associated with dating satisfaction. Second, only tenuous support was observed for the relationship between empathy and the type of date. Greater empathy occurred between couples who had more serious dates than those who had casual dates. Third, there was no relationship between empathy and degree of campus leadership. And fourth, empathy was related to middle-range scores on the Kuhn 20-statement test for self images. Persons with higher or lower locus scores had lower empathy scores.

What conclusions can be drawn from these data on disagreement, disagreement estimates, and empathy scores? First, as Vernon and Stewart maintained, it is clear that empathy is an emergent concept, reflecting both personality characteristics and the nature of the interaction between a person and others. But such a statement does not go much beyond the obvious interdependence of most social-psychological variables upon both biological and social systems.

The relationship between satisfaction with dating and empathy observed by Vernon and Stewart can be harmonized with a tentative inference about empathy in dating drawn by Kirkpatrick and Hobart (1954). The latter writers suggested that empathy in dating results more from selective-rejection factors than from the dyadic association by itself. At any time, dating a person is based on the selection. Many factors operate at this stage, including varying degrees of adherence to the endogamous norms and the expectation that an individual tentatively selected will contribute to one's feelings of self-esteem and personality development. Lack of satisfaction in dating a particular person generally leads to the rejection of that person, whereas satisfaction leads to greater involvement and, as shown in several studies, to greater empathy, and possibly to marriage.

Complementary Needs

In 1953, Winch and the Ktsaneses began publishing a series of papers on the "Theory of Complementary Needs" in mate selection. The core of this theory, presented in a later paper (Winch, Ktsanes, & Ktsanes, 1954), combines need-motivation theory and endogamous mate-selection norms. All human behavior is viewed as activity oriented to the gratification of needs. Certain important needs are organized by the formation of the ego-ideal. The organization of these needs gives pattern to behavior and makes it selective. Because needs may be experienced consciously or unconsciously, a person may be completely aware, partially aware, or quite unaware of the motivation for his behavior. But individual needs are learned and become operative within social groups, into which behavior is directed by cultural norms as well as by individual needs. Therefore, Winch added to his theory a set of postulates regarding the impact of cultural norms upon mate selection. Every culture contains principles of endogamous mating which give rise to what Winch called a person's field of eligibles. For any person, the field of eligibles is defined by the endogamous norms (and generally a few exogamous ones) and by the differential opportunities for heterosexual association under which he lives. In all societies, the congeniality group is an important source for gratification of social needs. In the subculture of the American middle class, the heterosexual dyad is a singularly gratifying congeniality group.

From these postulates, Winch deduced a definition of love and a principle of mate selection in the American middle class. Love is the positive emotion expressed by one person in an interpersonal relationship in which the second person either meets certain important needs of the first or manifests or appears to manifest personal attributes highly valued by the first; or, of course, meets both criteria. The basic hypothesis of the theory of complementary needs may now be stated: In mate selection, each individual seeks within his or her field of eligibles for that person who gives the greatest promise of providing him or her with maximum need gratification. A second hypothesis follows from the first: In mate selection, the need pattern of each spouse will be complementary rather than similar to the need pattern of the other spouse. Complementariness may be of two kinds: (a) The needs of A which are being gratified are different in kind from the needs being gratified for B; and (b) the needs which are being gratified by the members of the dyad differ in intensity.

The tests of these hypotheses and additional ones elaborated from the basic theory rest upon data obtained from 25 native-born, recently married couples who were undergraduates at Northwestern University in 1950. All were childless. The data-gathering devices included responses to a need interview, a case history interview, and selected TAT cards. These data were subjected to a specific need-content analysis, analysis of the need interview as a whole, analysis of the case history interview, TAT

interpretation, and a final conference among the investigators, from which ratings were established on the basis of a summary of all of the data.

The first report of this complex research project described the process and results for testing hypotheses that the assertive-receptive dimension of needs was important in mate selection (Winch, Ktsanes, & Ktsanes, 1953). The authors concluded that this dimension was important in mate selection and that high assertives tended to marry high receptives, although some qualifications of this tendency were noted.

Winch, Ktsanes, and Ktsanes (1954) used correlation analyses to test the two types of complementary needs. Type 1 referred to a difference in degree, whereas type 2 referred to a difference in kind. Negative correlations were expected for each of the 44 sub-variables included in the analysis of type 1 needs. Males' abasement, for instance, should correlate negatively with females' abasement. Positive correlations were expected for the 344 interpersonal correlations based on type 2 needs. For example, males' hostility scores should correlate positively with females' abasement scores, or males' deference scores should correlate positively with females' dominance scores.

The previous report by Winch, Ktsanes, and Ktsanes (1953) was accepted as providing evidence for type 2 complementary needs. The analyses for type 1 complementary needs consisted of computing Q-type correlations for the need-interview ratings and final conference ratings of the 25 husband-wife dyads, as compared with 25 randomly matched pairs, and of comparing the Q-type correlations of the 25 husband-wife pairs with 600 Q correlations of men and women not married to one another. When the Q correlations for the husband-wife dyads were compared with those for the 25 random pairs or with the results for the 600 men and women, the mean differences in the Q correlations based on both the need interviews and the final conference ratings were in the expected direction. The difference from the need-interview data was significant at the 5 per cent level, whereas that from the final conference data approached significance.

Neither the results of the Winch, Ktsanes, and Ktsanes study (1954) nor the separate results of Winch (1955a) supported the view of motivational or needs homogamy. Although Winch admitted the results were "not as compelling as might be wished," he felt that the burden of evidence supported the hypothesis of complementary needs within the group sampled.

The most elaborate test of the theory of complementary needs (Winch, 1955b) was based on an analysis of 388 correlations for which the direction of association was hypothesized, being either type 1 or type 2 relationship. Analyses were based on five sets of correlations involving ratings derived from the need-content analysis, holistic analysis of the need interviews, holistic analysis of the case history interviews, holistic analysis of the TAT responses, and holistic analysis of the final conference study. Winch's statistical criterion for testing the significance of his predictions was based on the proportion of the correlations which were in the expected direction.

On the basis of chance, 19 correlations could have been expected in the predicted direction. Seventy-one correlations based on the need-interview content analyses, 107 correlations based on the holistic need-interview analyses, and 56 correlations based on the final conference ratings were in the expected direction and exceeded the .001 level of departure from chance. Only 11 of the correlations based on the case history analysis and 12 of those based on the TAT analysis were in the predicted direction, both being less than expected by chance. However, the 377 correlations based on the case history and the 376 based on the TAT results that were opposite from the predicted direction did not depart significantly from the 369 that were expected in this direction due to change alone.

Detailed analysis of the deviant correlations showed that most clustered around zero, and few were statistically significant. On this basis, Winch concluded that the bulk of the data suggested that mates tended to select each other on the basis of complementary needs. Results which failed to support the complementary-needs theory did not support the contrary hypothesis for homogamy in needs, but rather showed little relationship among variables.

T. Ktsanes (1955) reasoned that patterns or configurations of need scores might offer a better opportunity to test the theory. He used factor analysis to allow for simultaneous variation in the total number of variables being studied and to provide a more general test of the complementary-needs theory. His hypothesis was that persons who showed high loading on a factor tended to select a mate who showed low or negative loading on the same factor. The factor analysis of the 44 variables derived from the needs interview yielded four types: yielding dependence, hostile dominance, mature nurturance, and neurotic self-depreciation. Eight combinations of these types accounted for 44 of the 50 persons in the sample.

The results were consistent with the theory of complementary needs. No husband and wife team showed the same personality type. Also, the proportion of couples showing homogamous matching was .17, whereas the proportion showing heterogamous matching was .83, the difference being significant at the 5 per cent level. Rank-order correlations for husband and wife loadings on the same factor were all negative, as predicted, and two were significant: $r = -.43$ for the hostile-dominance factor, and $r = -.29$ for the mature-nurturance factor.

These results offer additional support for the basic premise of the theory of complementary needs. However, Ktsanes observed that the complementary-needs hypothesis is more complicated than the hypothesis that "opposites attract." Polar attraction seems to operate only in the case of some specific need patterns.

Despite the comprehensive and detailed codification, quantification, and statistical analysis of these data, the various reports by Winch and his colleagues are based upon a very small sample. Moreover, they do not represent independent tests of the hypothesis, because the data were derived from the same basic sample. Regardless of the size or selectivity of the sample, or elegance of analysis performed upon these data, a certain consistency among the findings should be observed. It is not surprising, therefore, that other researchers have attempted to retest the complementary-needs hypothesis.

Bowerman and Day (1956) obtained scores from the Edwards Personal Preference Schedule for 60 college couples who were formally engaged or considered themselves regular dating partners. Fifteen scores are derived from this test. Following the lead of Winch, Bowerman and Day predicted that the 15 intercorrelations between scores for the same need should be negative, and the 210 intercorrelations among scores involving different needs should be positive. Two of the 15 predicted negative correlations were negative, and, while neither of these was significant, four of the correlations that were in the opposite direction were significant. One hundred of the predicted 210 positive correlations were in the hypothesized direction, five of which were significant. However, 110 of the predicted positive correlations were negative, and of these, 10 were significant. Further comparisons based on 32 needs which were more directly comparable to the needs tested by Winch produced only three significant results.

The results of the Bowerman and Day study failed to support Winch's theory of complementary needs. Not only were most of the correlations between couple scores low, but among those large enough to be significant, there was no consistent support for either complementary needs or emotional homogamy. Furthermore, Bowerman and Day argued there is no reason to believe all needs should be either complementary or homogamous. Very likely, there will be little support for any theory of motivational selection that is stated in terms of uniform direction of relationships between needs. Instead, they suggested that we need to start with a general theory of mate selection and not with the theory of complementary needs. The general theory would specify relationships among variables, including emotional characteristics of spouses, some of which might be complementary and others homogamous.

Schellenberg and Bee (1960) also used the Edwards Personal Preference Schedule in an attempt to resolve differences in findings between Winch and associates and Bowerman and Day. They administered the Edwards PPS to 18 couples who were going steady, 18 engaged couples, and 64 recently married couples. In addition to using correlations among pair scores, they developed a convergence score that measured the extent to which patterns of manifest needs were similar. In general, their results showed emotional homogamy rather than complementariness: positive correlations existed among the need patterns. The mean convergence score of the married couples was 112.4, which differed considerably and significantly from chance as represented by a score of 100. Scores above 100 indicated a homogamous tendency. The mean convergence score of 106.9 for the unmarried couples, although in the homogamous direction also, was not significantly different from chance. Additional tests of the dominance-submissive or nurturance-receptive dimensions failed to provide evidence of need complementarity.

Important methodological differences exist between the Winch investigation and the other two studies. These include differences in the marital status of some members of the sample and in the use of greatly different data-gathering and analytical procedures. All of these studies are based on extremely small samples, with the usual bias of college attendance. Adequate empirical testing of the hypothesis requires larger samples and ones based on random designs.

However, there are theoretical grounds

for questioning the theory of complementary needs. Winch's formulation of the concept of complementariness must assume that needs do not necessarily operate at the conscious level. This theoretical postulate contrasts sharply with that of role theory, which suggests a process of interaction and the development of mutually reinforcing values and interaction patterns, all at a conscious level. From a sociological perspective, the premise of unconscious motivation limits the scope of the operation of complementary needs in the total process of mate selection. Homogamy studies provide greater predictive power for selection of mates than do studies based on complementary needs. Perhaps the chief value of the complementary theory is to account for some of the residual variations in mate selection that are not first accounted for by the operation of endogamous norms, adherence to the affectionate-companionate norms, and other mate-selection norms.

Both retest investigations used paper-and-pencil procedures for measuring complementary needs. It is difficult to compare their negative or inconclusive results with those obtained by .Winch, whose research was based on careful codification and quantification of detailed interview and projective data. Certainly, Winch has not conclusively demonstrated the operation of complementary needs in mate selection, but it is just as true that the results of the two retest investigations in which an "instrument-centered approach" was used have not demolished the support Winch and associates have put forth for the theory.

It is fortunate that one additional team of researchers have addressed themselves to the problem of complementariness in mate selection. Kerckhoff and Davis (1962) introduced an innovation by conducting a longitudinal study to examine the relationship between progress in mate selection and measures of homogamy and complementariness. In October, 1959, 103 women students at Duke University who were engaged, pinned, or seriously attached completed a questionnaire. Questionnaires were

also completed by their partners. In May, 1960, the couples were asked to complete a second questionnaire. Usable forms were returned by 94 couples. The dependent variable was movement toward a permanent union between October and May. This was measured by a dichotomy: closer in May than in October (56 cases) versus all other cases (38). The two independent variables were value consensus, as measured by the Farber Family Values Index, and need complementarity, as measured by the FIRO-B scales for inclusion, control, and affection. Each of these scales is concerned with either the desire to have others act in some way toward one's self or the desire to act in some way toward others. Length of time the couples had been going together was introduced as a control variable. Long-term couples had been going together 18 months or more; short-term couples, less than 18 months.

The original hypotheses were that value consensus and need complementarity were independently related to progress toward a permanent union. These hypotheses were neither clearly confirmed nor denied by the data, although value consensus was significantly related to progress toward permanence for the total sample. The relationship between value consensus and permanence was evident for the short-term couples as well, but not significantly. On the other hand, when the relationships between permanence and the three measures of complementarity were examined, a different pattern was found. No relationship was observed between permanence and the three measures of complementarity among the short-term couples. But for the long-term couples, the relationship was significant for the inclusion and control variables, and, though not significant, the results based on the affect variable also supported the hypothesis.

These results led Kerckhoff and Davis to generate a series of hypotheses concerning homogamy, need complementarity, and courtship progress. High homogamy was found for social attributes such as education, religion, and father's occupation. Although homogamous tendencies were noted for the value-consensus variable as well, there was much clearer discrimination among the couples for more individualized expressions of values. Thus, Kerckhoff and Davis speculated, different kinds of homogamy are represented by value consensus and by similarity in social-background variables. The couples had limited their fields of eligibles in relation to the usual homogamous social attributes, but they were far from having limited their choices in relation to value consensus.

These authors suggested that "filtering factors" operate during mate selection. It would be convenient if the various factors fit into a neat order of social attributes first, followed by value consensus, and finally by complementary needs; but the data obtained by Kerckhoff and Davis do not follow this pattern. What they found was that the couples who survived the earlier stages of courtship, even those having low value consensus, were more likely than short-term couples with low consensus to move toward permanent unions; and this greater probability was explained largely by complementary values. But the filtering actions of need complementarity were not noticeable until the later stages of courtship.

Additional data, based on Farber's index of role tension, showed that short-term couples were less likely to attribute negative characteristics to each other than were long-term couples (Kerckhoff & Davis, 1962). An increase in negative evaluations was noticeable between October and May, even when original scores were held constant. It seemed that short-term couples were responding more frequently to an idealized image of their partner. In turn, this would make the effectiveness or appeal of personality complementarity less likely. After this idealization has been tempered, interaction at more realistic levels can occur, and only then can need complementarity begin to affect the relationship.

This valuable study by Kerckhoff and Davis reinforces present knowledge about mate selection and extends it in three ways: (a) Not only does it give support to both theories of homogamy and complementarity, but it provides a tentative formulation of the relationships between these two concepts during the mate-selection process. (b) It has demonstrated more conclusively than the original test by Winch and associates that complementarity makes a difference in the actual selection process. (c) It is the first study in which measures derived from pencil-and-paper tests have made a significant contribution to the understanding of complementarity in mate selection.

Winch pioneered in suggesting complementary-need relationships. Kerckhoff and Davis have extended this area of research, but many problems remain. The concept of needs itself is a difficult one and involves many dimensions. It is obvious that there is a necessity for conceptual clarity among these dimensions before statistical measures can be developed. Saliency of needs for individuals has not been determined, nor do we have much knowledge about the organization of needs in subjects or the hierarchy of needs satisfied by intimate heterosexual association. Furthermore, needs change over time with personal growth and development. Different needs attain prominence in different life stages and perhaps in different situational relationships.

It is clear that we cannot speak of complementarity as an inclusive concept. Just as there are different kinds of homogamy, there probably are different kinds of complementariness. Need complementariness is only one kind. However, need relations in the marital dyad should be useful for predicting other marital and family relationships. In addition, the use of need concepts in small-group research argues for attempting to resolve present limitations of the concept.

REFERENCES

Bardis, P. D. Attitudes toward dating among students of a Michigan high school. *Sociol. & soc. Res.*, 1958, 42, 274–277.

Barta, R., & O'Reilly, C. T. Some dating patterns and attitudes toward marriage of 174 Catholic college students. *Amer. Catholic sociol. Rev.*, 1952, 13, 240–249.

Bates, A. Parental roles in courtship. *Soc. Forces*, 1942, 20, 483–486.

Beigel, H. G. Romantic love. *Amer. sociol. Rev.*, 1951, 16, 326–334.

Bell, R. R., & Blumberg, L. Courtship intimacy and religious background. *Marr. & fam. Living*, 1959, 21, 356–360.

Bell, R. R., & Blumberg, L. Courtship stage and intimacy attitudes. *Fam. life Coordinator*, 1960, 8, 61–63.

Blood, R. O. A retest of Waller's rating complex. *Marr. & fam. Living*, 1955, 17, 41–47.

Blood, R. O. Uniformities and diversities in campus dating preferences. *Marr. & fam. Living*, 1956, 18, 37–45.

Blood, R. O., & Nicholson, S. O. The attitudes of American men and women students toward international dating. *Marr. & fam. Living*, 1962, 24, 35–41. (a)

Blood, R. O., & Nicholson, S. O. The experiences of foreign students in dating American women. *Marr. & fam. Living*, 1962, 24, 241–248. (b)

Blood, R. O., & Nicholson, S. O. International dating experiences of American women students. *Marr. & fam. Living*, 1962, 24, 129–136. (c)

Bock, E. W., & Burchinal, L. G. Social status, heterosexual relations and expected ages of marriage. *J. gen. Psychol.*, 1962, 101, 43–51.

Bowerman, C. E. Assortative mating by previous marital status: Seattle, 1939–1946. *Amer sociol. Rev.*, 1953, 18, 170–177.

Bowerman, C. E. Age relationships at marriage, by marital status and age at marriage. *Marr. & fam. Living*, 1956, 18, 231–233.

Bowerman, C. E., & Day, Barbara. Test of the theory of complementary needs. *Amer. sociol. Rev.*, 1956, 21, 602–605.

Breed, W. Sex, class and socialization in dating. *Marr. & fam. Living*, 1956, 18, 137–144.

Broderick, C. B., & Fowler, S. E. New patterns of relationships between the sexes among preadolescents. *Marr. & fam. Living*, 1961, 23, 27–30.

Burchinal, L. G. Adolescent role deprivation and high school marriage. *Marr. & fam. Living*, 1959, 21, 378–394.

Burchinal, L. G. Membership groups and attitudes toward cross-religious dating and marriage. *Marr. & fam. Living*, 1960, 22, 248–253.

Burchinal, L. G., & Chancellor, L. E. Ages at marriage, occupations of grooms and interreligious marriage rates. *Soc. Forces*, 1962, 40, 348–354. (a)

Burchinal, L. G., & Chancellor, L. E. Factors related to interreligious marriages in Iowa, 1953–1957. *Iowa agr. & home econ. exp. sta. res. Bull.* No. 510, 1962. (b)

Burchinal, L. G., & Chancellor, L. E. Proportions of Catholics, urbanism, and mixed-Catholic marriage rates among Iowa counties, *Soc. Probl.*, 1962, 9, 359–365. (c)

Burchinal, L. G., & Chancellor, L. E. Social status, religious affiliation and ages at marriage. *Marr. & fam. Living*, 1963, 25, 219–221.

Burgess, E. W., & Wallin, P. Homogamy in social characteristics. *Amer. J. Sociol.*, 1943, 49, 109–124.

Burgess, E. W., & Wallin, P. Homogamy in personal characteristics. *J. abnorm. soc. Psychol.*, 1944, 29, 475–481.

Burma, J. Research note on the measurement of interracial marriages. *Amer. J. Sociol.*, 1952, 57, 587–589.

Burma, J. Interethnic marriages in Los Angeles, 1948–1959. Paper read at Amer. Sociol. Ass., Washington, D.C., Aug., 1962.

Cameron, W. J., & Kenkel, W. F. High school dating: a study in variation. *Marr. & fam. Living*, 1960, 22, 74–76.

Centers, R. Marital selection and occupational strata. *Amer. J. Sociol.* 1949, 54, 530–535.

Christensen, H. T. Student views on mate selection. *Marr. & fam. Living*, 1947, 9, 85–88.

Christensen, H. T. Courtship conduct as viewed by youth. *J. home Econ.*, 1948, 40, 187–188.

Christensen, H. T. Dating behavior as evaluated by high school students. *Amer. J. Sociol.*, 1952, 57, 580–586.

Christensen, H. T. *Marriage analysis: foundations for successful family life.* (2nd ed.) New York: Ronald Press, 1958.

Cizon, F. A. Interethnic and interreligious marriage patterns in Parish X. *Amer. Catholic sociol. Rev.*, 1954, 15, 244–255.

Clark, A. C. An examination of the operation of residential propinquity as a factor in mate selection. *Amer. sociol. Rev.,* 1952, 17, 17–22.

Coombs, R. H. A value theory of mate selection. *Fam. life Coordinator,* 1961, 10, 51–54.

Coombs, R. H. Reinforcement of values in the parental home as a factor in mate selection. *Marr. & fam. Living,* 1962, 24, 155–157.

Crist, J. R. High school dating as a behavior system. *Marr. & fam. Living,* 1953, 15, 23–28.

Dean, D. G. Romanticism and emotional maturity: a preliminary study. *Marr. & fam. Living,* 1961, 23, 44–45. (a)

Dean, D. G. Romanticism and emotional maturity: a further exploration. Paper read at Nat. Counc. on Fam. Relat., Univer. of Utah, Salt Lake City, Aug. 1961. (b)

Dinitz, S., Banks, F., & Pasamanick, B. Mate selection and social class: changes during the past quarter century. *Marr. & fam. Living,* 1960, 22, 348–351.

Foote, N. N. Love. *Psychiatry,* 1953, 16, 245–251.

Freeman, L. Homogamy in interethnic mate selection. *Sociol. & soc. Res.,* 1955, 39, 369–377.

Glick, P. C. Intermarriage and fertility patterns among persons in major religious groups. *Eugenics Quart.,* 1960, 7, 31–38.

Glick, P. C., & Landau, E. Age as a factor in marriage. *Amer. sociol. Rev.,* 1950, 15, 517–529.

Golden, J. Characteristics of the Negro-white intermarried in Philadelphia. *Amer. sociol. Rev.,* 1953, 18, 177–183.

Golden, J. Patterns of Negro-white intermarriage. *Amer. sociol. Rev.,* 1954, 19, 144–147.

Goode, W. J. The theoretical importance of love. *Amer. sociol. Rev.,* 1959, 24, 38–47.

Heiss, J. S. Premarital characteristics of the religiously intermarried in an urban area. *Amer. sociol. Rev.,* 1960, 25, 47–55. (a)

Heiss, J. S. Variations in courtship progress among high school students. *Marr. & fam. Living,* 1960, 22, 165–170. (b)

Herman, R. D. The going steady complex: a re-examination. *Marr. & fam. Living,* 1955, 17, 36–40.

Hill, R. Campus norms in mate selection. *J. home Econ.,* 1945, 37, 554–558.

Himes, J. S., Jr. Mate selection among Negro college students. *Sociol. & soc. Res.,* 1949, 33, 204–211.

Hobart, C. W. Disagreement and nonempathy during courtship. *Marr. & fam. Living,* 1956, 18, 317–322.

Hobart, C. W. Disillusionment in marriage and romanticism. *Marr. & fam. Living,* 1958, 20, 156–162. (a)

Hobart, C. W. Emancipation from parents and courtship in adolescence. *Pac. sociol. Rev.,* 1958, 6, 25–29. (b)

Hobart, C. W. Some effects of romanticism during courtship on marriage role opinions. *Sociol. & soc. Res.,* 1958, 42, 336–343. (c)

Hobart, C. W. The incidence of romanticism during courtship. *Soc. Forces,* 1958, 36, 362–367. (d)

Hobart, C. W. Attitude changes during courtship and marriage. *Marr. & fam. Living,* 1960, 22, 352–359.

Hollingshead, A. B. Cultural factors in mate selection. *Amer. sociol. Rev.,* 1950, 15, 619–627.

Hollingshead, A. B. Age relationships and marriage. *Amer sociol. Rev.,* 1951, 16, 492–499.

Hoover, H. F. Attitudes of high school students toward mixed marriages. *Catholic Univer. of America educ. res. Monogr.,* No. 15, 1950.

Hunt, T. C. Occupational status and marriage selection. *Amer. sociol. Rev.,* 1940, 5, 495–504.

Inselberg, R. M. Social and psychological factors associated with high school marriages. *J. home Econ.,* 1961, 53, 766–772.

Inselberg, R. M. Marital problems and satisfactions in high school marriages. *Marr. & fam. Living,* 1962, 24, 74–77.

Jacobsohn, P., & Matheny, A. P. Mate selection in open marriage systems. *Int. J. comp. Sociol.,* 1962, 3, 98–123.

Karlsson, G. On mate selection. *Int. J. comp. Sociol.,* 1962, 3, 91–97.

Katz, A. M., & Hill, R. Residential propinquity and marital selection: a review of theory, method and fact. *Marr. & fam. Living,* 1958, 20, 27–34.

Kelley, E. L. Consistency of the adult personality. *Amer. Psychologist,* 1955, 10, 659–681.

Kephart, W. *The family, society and the individual.* Boston: Houghton Mifflin, 1961.

Kerckhoff, A. C., & Davis, K. E. Value consensus and need complementarity in mate selection. *Amer. sociol. Rev.*, 1962, 27, 295–303.

Kirkpatrick, C., & Caplow, T. Courtship in a group of Minnesota students. *Amer. J. Sociol.*, 1945, 51, 114–125. (a)

Kirkpatrick, C., & Caplow, T. Emotional trends in the courtship experience of college students as expressed by graphs with some observations on methodological implications. *Amer. sociol. Rev.*, 1945, 10, 619–626. (b)

Kirkpatrick, C., & Hobart, C. Disagreement, disagreement estimate and nonempathic imputations for intimacy groups varying from favorite date to married. *Amer. sociol. Rev.*, 1954, 19, 10–20.

Kolb, W. L. Family sociology, marriage education, and the romantic complex. *Soc. Forces*, 1950, 29, 65–72.

Koller, M. R. Some changes in courtship behavior in three generations of Ohio women. *Amer. sociol. Rev.*, 1951, 16, 366–370.

Komarovsky, Mirra. Functional analysis of sex roles. *Amer. sociol. Rev.*, 1950, 15, 508–516.

Ktsanes, T. Mate selection on the basis of personality type: a study utilizing an empirical typology of personality. *Amer. sociol. Rev.*, 1955, 20, 547–551.

Landis, J. T. & Landis, Mary G. *Building a successful marriage*. Englewood Cliffs, N.J.: Prentice-Hall, 1958.

Landis, P. H. Research on teen-age marriage. *Marr. & Fam. Living*, 1960, 22, 266–267.

Leslie, G. R., & Richardson, A. H. Family versus campus influences in relation to mate selection. *Soc. Probl.*, 1956, 4, 117–121.

Locke, H. J. Sabagh, G., & Thomes, M. M. Interfaith marriages. *Soc. Probl.*, 1957, 4, 329–333.

Lowrie, S. H. Dating, a neglected field of study. *Marr. & fam. Living*, 1948, 10, 90–91, 95.

Lowrie, S. H. Dating theories and student responses. *Amer. sociol. Rev.*, 1951, 16, 335–340.

Lowrie, S. H. Sex differences and age of initial dating. *Soc. Forces*, 1952, 30, 456–461.

Lowrie, S. H. Factors involved in the frequency of dating. *Marr. & fam. Living*, 1956, 18, 46–51.

Lowrie, S. H. Early and late dating: some conditions associated with them. *Marr. & fam. Living*, 1961, 23, 284–291.

McGinnis, R. Campus values in mate selection: a repeat study. *Soc. Forces*, 1958, 36, 368–373.

Moss, J. J., & Gingles, R. The relationship of personality to the incidence of early marriage. *Marr. & fam. Living*, 1959, 21, 373–377.

Neely, W. C. Family attitudes of denominational college and university students, 1929 and 1936. *Amer. sociol. Rev.*, 1940, 5, 512–522.

Nimkoff, M. F., & Wood, A. L. Courtship and personality. *Amer. J. Sociol.*, 1948, 53, 263–269.

Prince, A. J. Attitudes of college students toward interfaith marriage. *Fam. life Coordinator*, 1956, 5, 11–23.

Prince, A. J. Factors in mate selection. *Fam. life Coordinator*, 1961, 10, 55–58.

Reiss, I. L. Toward a sociology of the heterosexual love relationship. *Marr. & fam. Living*, 1960, 22, 139–145.

Rogers, E. M., & Havens, A. E. Prestige rating and mate selection on a college campus. *Marr. & fam. Living*, 1960, 22, 55–59.

Schellenberg, J. A. Homogamy in personal values and the field of eligibles. *Soc. Forces*, 1960, 39, 157–162.

Schellenberg, J. A. & Bee, L. S. A re-examination of the theory of complementary needs in mate selection. *Marr. & fam. Living*, 1960, 22, 227–232.

Smith, E. A. *American youth culture: group life in teenage society*. New York: Free Press, 1962.

Smith, Eleanor & Monane, J. H. G. Courtship values in a youth sample. *Amer. sociol. Rev.*, 1953, 18, 635–640.

Smith, W. M., Jr. Rating and dating: a restudy. *Marr. & fam. Living*, 1952, 14, 312–316.

Stewart, R. L., & Vernon, G. M. Four correlates of empathy in the dating situation. *Sociol. & soc. Res.*, 1959, 43, 279–285.

Straus, A. The ideal and chosen mate. *Amer. J. Sociol.*, 1946, 52, 204–208. (a)

Straus, A. The influence of parental-images upon marital choice. *Amer. sociol. Rev.*, 1946, 11, 554–559. (b)

Straus, A. Personality needs and marital choice. *Soc. Forces*, 1947, 25, 332–335.

Sundal, A. P., & McCormick, T. C. Age at marriage and mate selection, Madison, Wisconsin, 1937–1943. *Amer. sociol. Rev.*, 1951, 16, 37–48.

Sussman, M. B. Parental participation in mate selection and its effects upon family continuity. *Soc. Forces,* 1953, 32, 76–81.

Sussman, M. B., & Burchinal, L. G. Kin family network: unheralded structure in current conceptualizations of family functioning. *Marr. & fam. Living,* 1962, 24, 231–240. (a)

Sussman, M. B., & Burchinal, L. G. Parental aid to married children: implications for family functioning. *Marr. & fam. Living,* 1962, 24, 320–332. (b)

Sussman, M. B., & Yeager, H. C., Jr. Mate selection among Negro and white college students. *Sociol. & soc. Res.,* 1950, 35, 46–49.

Thomas, J. L. The factor of religion in selection of marriage mates. *Amer. sociol. Rev.,* 1951, 16, 487–491.

Thomas, J. L. Out-group marriage patterns of some selected ethnic groups. *Amer. Catholic sociol. Rev.,* 1954, 15, 9–18.

Vernon, G. M., & Stewart, R. L. Empathy as a process in the dating situation. *Amer. sociol. Rev.,* 1957, 22, 48–52.

Waller, W. The rating and dating complex. *Amer. sociol. Rev.,* 1937, 2, 727–734.

Wallin, P. Two conceptions of the relationship between love and idealization. *Res. Stud. State Coll. Washington,* 1952, 20, 21–35.

Williams, M. J. Personal and family problems of high school youth and their bearing upon family education needs. *Soc. Forces,* 1949, 27, 279–285.

Winch, R. F. The relation between courtship behavior and attitudes toward parents among college men. *Amer. sociol. Rev.,* 1943, 8, 164–174.

Winch, R. F. Interrelations between certain social background and parent-son factors in a study of courtship among college men. *Amer. sociol. Rev.,* 1946, 11, 333–341.

Winch, R. F. Primary factors in a study of courtship. *Amer. sociol. Rev.,* 1947, 12, 658–666.

Winch, R. F. Courtship in college women. *Amer. J. Sociol.,* 1949, 55, 269–278.

Winch, R. F. Further data and observations on the Oedipus hypothesis: the consequences of an inadequate hypothesis. *Amer. sociol. Rev.,* 1951, 16, 784–795.

Winch, R. F. The theory of complementary needs in mate selection: a test of one kind of complementariness. *Amer. sociol. Rev.,* 1955, 20, 52–56. (a)

Winch, R. F. The theory of complementary needs in mate selection: final results on the test of the general hypothesis. *Amer. sociol. Rev.,* 1955, 20, 552–555. (b)

Winch, R. F., Ktsanes, T., & Ktsanes, Virginia. Empirical elaboration of the theory of complementary needs in mate selection. *J. abnorm. soc. Psychol.,* 1953, 51, 508–513.

Winch, R. F., Ktsanes, T., & Ktsanes, Virginia. The theory of complementary needs in mate selection: an analytic and descriptive study. *Amer. sociol. Rev.,* 1954, 19, 241–249.

CHAPTER 17

The Adjustments
of Married Mates

JESSIE BERNARD
Pennsylvania State University

Lest the emphasis on conflict and manipulation in this chapter leave a wrong impression, it must be emphasized at the outset that adjustment behavior constitutes only a part of all marital interaction. In a large proportion of most ongoing marriages, there is a great deal of interaction which is playful, complementary, and joyous (see Ch. 4), as well, of course, as interaction which is hostile (Waller & Hill, 1951). The title of this chapter, further, is "Adjustments of Married Mates" rather than, as it might have been, "Conflicts of Married Mates." The fact that most marriages survive and are judged to be happy (Ch. 6) indicates that most adjustments succeed in achieving a relatively satisfying goal.

THE INEVITABILITY OF CONFLICT

The process of mate selection in most societies is endogamous and hence guarantees a certain degree of similarity in the partners with respect to class background, religion, and education. Such similarity reduces the necessity for marital adjustments in many areas.

But too great similarity in personality, if not in background—homogamy—may itself require adjustments, for differences as well as similarities are essential to marital functioning. If the partners are too much alike in their aims and goals, if, for example, both want to be decision-makers, the conditions of competition may arise, since the conditions under which marital adjustments must be made often demand a choice among competing alternatives.

Differences Differ

Differences may vary all the way from those which are essential to the functioning of any given system (living organism or complex organization) through those which, while not essential, are nevertheless pleasant, through those which, while not actually disintegrative, are unpleasant, to those which are positively disintegrative.

Some differences are essential for the division of function which is basic to the operation of all complex organisms and organizations. Such differences are fundamental for any form of life beyond the most primitive. In the human body, the same heredity exists in every cell, but cells become specialized to perform different tasks, so that a mature neurone differs greatly from a mature blood cell, and both differ from a mature muscle cell or mature bone cell; the body could not function without such differences. An analogous differentiation and specialization underlie the functioning of task-oriented groups and organizations. If, for example, neither spouse is willing to assume responsibility for making decisions, difficulties may arise; one or the other, or both, must learn to perform this function if the union is to function effectively. Or, contrariwise, if both wish to make all the decisions, again some sort of adjustment will be called for. If both spouses are overly dependent—or independent—they may have difficulty. One school of thought holds, in fact, that people seek mates who are different enough from them in personality to complement them, each supplying to the other what the other lacks (Winch, 1958). In brief, unless there is a modicum of differences in personality and in preferences for performing family functions, the effective functioning of the marriage will be impeded. As the popular aphorism has it, it takes all kinds of people to make a world. It takes at least two kinds to make a marriage. The absence of differences may require adjustments.

Some differences are not necessarily integrative in nature, or essential for the successful functioning of the marriage, but merely pleasant. This fact is reflected in the popular saying that opposites attract, which recognizes the fact that people find differences attractive as well as essential. There may be no functional advantage in having a variety of different interests represented in a marriage, but it may be more interesting to have both music and art as avocations. Variety, in brief, as folklore well recognizes, is the spice of life, even when it is not essential to functioning. And in marriage, such differences in interests and personality may be the source of great delight. If so, obviously, they do not call for adjustments.

Some differences, however, are unpleasant, even if they are not positively divisive. People can live and work together even though they dislike one another's taste in clothes or food or entertainment. So long as they do not attempt to change one another and force their own tastes on others, such differences have merely nuisance value and do not demand adjustments.

But some differences are not only unintegrative and unpleasant, but actually divisive. They are so incompatible that they constitute disintegrative forces. Differences in goals, values, or objectives are often of this nature. The specifications of the marital relationship, to be discussed below, make such differences especially likely to be divisive, because the conditions which render differences incompatible are those which demand a choice among or between alternatives, so that if one is chosen the others are rejected, or so that what one wins the other loses. Because, that is, the marital relationship is defined as a union, there are frequent occasions when the success of one partner in enforcing a choice means that the other partner must give up his (her) preference. They must face the world as a unit (Bernard, 1942).

Even within the union, apart from the outside world, the specifications of the marriage impose choices. The partners cannot have sex relations and not have them at the same time; they cannot go to the party and to the concert together at the same time; they cannot rear the children as Catholic and as Protestant; they cannot spend the same money for slipcovers and for the power mower. Such are among the kinds of differences which call for adjustments.

Substantive Areas of Adjustment

The substantive areas in which differences are likely to be divisive and hence to call for adjustments in marriage have been variously classified. Landis (1946) classified them as religion, social life, mutual friends, in-laws, money, and sex relations. Kirkpatrick (1963) spoke of 10 "dilemmas," including family freedom versus order and efficiency; free expression of age, sex, and individual potentialities versus specific and stable goal expectations; personal self-expression versus child-rearing; work achievement versus the love-reproduction function; family loyalty versus community loyalty; extensive casual association versus restricted intensive association. Goode (1956) found numerous "themes of complaint," such as drinking; desertion; relatives; triangles; "the complex" of drinking, gambling, and helling around; nonsupport; consumption behavior, that is, the management of money; lack of affect for home life; value differences with respect to style of life, education, manners, entertainment, the arts, and religion; authority; and idiosyncratic characteristics. Farber (1962) found four "predicaments": social-emotional versus instrumental values and norms; short-run versus long-run considerations; family versus community commitments; and emphasis on parents' versus emphasis on children's needs and desires. Blood and Wolfe (1960) reported eight areas of "stress" in the marriages they studied: money, children, recreation, personality, in-laws, roles, religion-politics, and sex. Herndon and Nash (1962) found physicians reporting sex, fear of pregnancy, money, affection (too much or too little), inability to discuss problems, in-laws, failure to express appreciation, and inability to conceive as problems among their patients. Although there are constantly recurring issues in all studies of marital adjustments, it may be said that anything may become an issue demanding adjustment. Our discussion in this chapter is limited, therefore, with the exception of sex, primarily to the processes involved in adjustments, whatever the nature of the issue, rather than including the substantive areas in which the adjustment occurs.

THE CONCEPT OF ADJUSTMENT

Adjustment, Adaptation, and Accommodation

The concept of adjustment is sometimes contrasted with the concept of adaptation. Although both refer to functional changes in the organism, adaptation implies a body change, genetic or acquired. It might, that is, be a change selected into the heredity of the species, or it might be a change in the individual organism in response to exposure to certain stimuli, such as tanning of the skin in response to sunlight or addiction in response to drugs. In the case of human beings, biological sex differences have evolved adaptively; the reproductive organs of each sex are anatomically adapted to those of the other. And so, in fact, are many of the concomitant biological differences. So far as living in today's world is concerned, it may be argued that the two sexes are no longer biologically well adapted to one another, that they are, in fact, maladapted to one another, that biological sex differences have even become maladaptive to the functioning of our society as a whole. Individual marital adaptations may occur, as when one spouse's gastrointestinal system adapts to the dietary of the other, but they are not a major concern in our discussions here.

"Adaptation" is also used in a psychological sense. Negative psychological adaptation is said to result when a sensory stimulus no longer evokes a conscious response. It is no longer felt or heard or seen. An analogous "psychological adaptation" may be said to occur in marital relationships. The bride may be said to be "psychologically adapted" to her marital status when it no longer excites or thrills or delights or surprises her to be called Mrs. Jones. She doesn't even notice it. Such "psychological adaptation" is common in the marital relationship; the spouses become so used to one another that they are scarcely aware of one another's presence. It is only when one or the other is absent that either becomes conscious of the relationship. Again, such "adaptations" are not a major concern to us here.

"Accommodation" is used primarily by sociologists to describe the processes by which groups achieve and maintain a modus vivendi. An accommodation may vary along a continuum all the way from a highly cooperative and even friendly relationship to a hostile and exploitative one (Bernard, 1962). In our discussion below, we shall speak of models of adjustment at three such levels, namely, at the assimilative level, where there is an attempt to get rid of differences; at the optimizing level, where each partner attempts to do the best he (she) can without destroying common interests; and at the stalemate or standoff level, where the gains of one are canceled by the losses of the other. At the lowest level, the accommodation breaks down and the relationship is destroyed.

Uses of the Concept "Adjustment"

The term "adjustment" is used in several ways. In a dynamic sense, the term refers to the process of making functional changes in a relationship. "They are adjusting to the situation." That is, they are making the functional changes called for by the situation. But the term also refers to the more or less stable end results of such changes. "They have arrived at an adjustment." Since other chapters of this volume deal with the large research literature on marital adjustment as end result, the emphasis in the discussion here will be on adjustment, or functional change, as process. What are the processes by which spouses interact to achieve the best possible—not the best imaginable—relationship with one another? The image is not of a static *fait accompli,* but rather of an ongoing interaction between partners, an interaction determined by the institutional specifications of the relationship, by the nature of the partners themselves, and by the quality of the relationship between them. [Cf. Bowerman's discussion above, pp. 237-245.]

The Concept of Maladjustment

The usage of the term "adjustment" is further complicated by the fact that both the process and the results of change are often evaluated as good or as bad. Thus, the concept of maladjustment is introduced. When some unit or system—mechanical, biological, or social—is not functioning successfully in terms of some criterion, the term "maladjustment" is applied, the implication being that the change or the results were not functional.

The term "maladjustment" probably can apply only to the end result of change. We do not ordinarily speak of maladjustive processes, although we might speak of processes which lead to maladjustments. A change which proves to be malfunctional rather than functional might be called maladjustive. Studies of personality disturbance have tended to blur the concept of maladjustive processes; they seem to indicate that what looks like a maladjustive process to the outsider may be quite adjustive to the person involved. On a more rational level, also, game-theory concepts suggest that a change which seems maladjustive may be the best possible under the circumstances and in this sense, if in no other, adjustive.

Individual, Social, and Marital Adjustments of Married Mates

As functional change, "adjustment" may refer to a variety of phenomena. Thus we speak of adjusting a mechanism such as a screw or valve, for example, or of adjusting temperature, speed, and the like. Plants adjust to the conditions of light or water available to them by means of tropisms. Animals adjust to their circumstances, as well as to one another, by learning. And, of course, human beings themselves are in constant process of adjustment, individually, in informal groups, or in formal organizations.

Our concern here is with only a limited, albeit fundamental, area of human adjustment, namely, adjustments involved in marriage. (The peculiar set of specifications for marital relationships which determine the nature of the adjustment processes available will be elaborated in more detail below.)

But not all the adjustments even of married people concern us here, for not all are marital in the strictest sense. Some, that is, are individual, determined by age, and are marital only in the sense that they occur in people who are also marital partners. The individual, married or not, has to learn to adjust, for example, to the limitations which age imposes upon his activities in whatever area. He must also adjust to the succession of roles and statuses which constitute a career (Strauss, 1962). These adjustments must occur regardless of marital status.

Still other adjustments are individual, but marital also. They are marital, however, only in the sense that they are determined by the marital status of the person involved. The wife as an individual has to adjust to the restrictions placed upon her by marriage; so does the husband. Behavior suitable to the unmarried girl is no longer permissible; "helling around" which might have been acceptable in the bachelor is viewed with disfavor in the married man.

Some adjustments of married people are social, but not directly marital. As a social system, for example, married people must adjust together to other systems or to other individuals: to children, to in-laws, to a social set, to a church, to a job, to community demands (see Chs 13 & 14). Or, again as a unit, they may have to adjust to poverty, misfortune, calamity, retirement, illness, bereavement, hospitalization, incarceration, unemployment, war, depression, disaster, or other kinds of crisis (Ch. 19). Since these are discussed in other chapters, they will not be included here. Our present concern is limited to the adjustments of husbands and wives to one another.

ADJUSTMENT AS FUNCTIONAL CHANGE

Among the questions to be asked with respect to any adjustment as a process of functional change are these: (a) What end or goal is involved; that is, "Why" is the change or adjustment made? (b) Who, or what, adjusts to whom, or what? (c) What are the targets, limits, and probabilities of change? And, finally, (d) What are the processes by which it is effected?

Without entering into the philosophical implications involved, or into the problems of motivation, cause, reason, or function (MacIver, 1942), we may say that adjustment is telic, that is, goal-oriented. Not all behavior or personality changes are adjustive in nature; some may even be fortuitous or accidental. But our concern here is only with goal-oriented changes, or adjustment behavior.

The End or Goal of Adjustment

The end or goal of adjustment as applied to a mechanism is very simple: it is to make the mechanism operate with maximum efficiency; we adjust or change the carburetor in order to get a better mixture of gasoline for the car. Although we cannot legitimately say that a plant has a goal or end when it grows toward the light, it does adjust itself in such a way that the end result is better exploitation of its source of light. Animals, similarly, adjust to the demands of their trainers in ways that avoid punishment or achieve rewards.

Among human beings, however, the goals or ends of adjustment are more complex. The goal may be immediate, to get rid of some irritation or to achieve some reward, as in the case of animals; or it may be distant, as when the young couple pare their expenditures to the bone in order to finance the husband's professional training. At one extreme, the goal may be something as primitive as sheer survival; the wife adjusts to her husband to forestall physical assault. At the other extreme, the goal may be something as esoteric as the achievement of salvation; the husband adjusts to religious demands for continence in order to avoid sin. The preservation of the marriage, "peace" or the avoidance of bickering and quarreling, smooth functioning, presenting a good front to friends and relatives, "happiness," are among the goals or ends of marital adjustments.

Although the characterizing adjective "functional," as applied to change, implies that the change is oriented toward some goal or end, it does not imply that the change is necessarily purposive or deliberate or conscious. In the case of plants or lower animals, it is obviously not. Two puppies sleeping together adjust to one another; the change of position is functional in the sense that they both feel more comfortable now, but it is not conscious or deliberate, certainly not planned.

Among human beings the functional change, or adjustment, may or may not be purposive, deliberate, or conscious. People are sometimes surprised, in fact, when they become aware of the changes which have occurred in their relationship over a period of time; they have been adjusting to one another without even recognizing the fact. Often, however, the goal is not only conscious, it may even be articulated. There is a verbalized level of aspiration which guides the adjustment. The spouses know what they want, and this level of aspiration or goal becomes a fundamental variable in marital adjustments. "We'll never be able to afford a second car if you spend so much on drinking" or "You'll never get anywhere if you don't take better care of your looks." One can call for change in the other to implement a common goal.

A great deal of marital interaction is not adjustive in nature, not goal-oriented. The husband and wife quarreling at the breakfast table are not adjusting their differences; each is merely venting hostilities or frustrations on the other. Neither believes the quarreling will achieve reform in the other; both may, in fact, know from past experience that the bickering merely impedes reform. (It is true, of course, that quarreling may be used as a strategic move by one partner in such a way that the other gives in; the costs of conceding are less than the costs of continuing the fight. This point is discussed below under "Stra-

tegic Models.") If or when the interaction changes character and is designed to achieve a goal, it becomes adjustive, and the nature of the situation is wholly altered.

The difference of opinion among students of marriage with respect to the function of quarreling in marital relationships is probably traceable to differences in the referents involved. Those who see no adjustive function are probably thinking of one kind of situation; those who do see an adjustive function, another (Duvall & Hill, 1960; Waller & Hill, 1951).

Who, or What, Adjusts to Whom, or What?

A second basic question in any adjustment situation has to do with the question: Who, or what, adjusts to whom, or to what? In the physical and biological sense, adjustment may be either transitive or intransitive. In the transitive sense, human beings adjust objects or plants: they adjust mechanisms by turning screws or valves; they adjust plants by turning them to get more sun. In the intransitive sense, entities adjust themselves. The sophisticated computer is programmed to adjust itself to new conditions; the plant adjusts itself to the source of light.

Among human beings, the question often arises as to whether the individual should adjust to his environment or attempt to adjust the environment to his wishes. As related to groups and institutions, this question raises the whole problem of conformity versus nonconformity, acquiescence versus rebellion, resignation versus reform or revolution. Even Jesus was concerned with this question, asking whether institutions were made for men or men for institutions. If marriage as now instituted leads to hardships, should one adjust to it anyway, or should one attempt to change it, adjusting it to people rather than people to it? Or should one merely defy it?

Within the limits of our concern in this chapter, however, the problem takes on a different form. In interpersonal relationships, adjustment is likely to be intransitive; that is, individuals do not adjust other individuals, as to the Procrustean bed. It is true that counselors and psychiatrists may help individuals to adjust, but the adjustment is usually intransitive; the individual changes himself rather than being changed by someone else. (The point has been made that the person who comes to the counselor for help in a marital situation is usually the one on whom the weight of adjustment ultimately falls. He, or she, is often the one who has to make the adjustment to the other spouse. The reason for this will become clear later in our discussion.)

But adjustment—functional change—is sometimes unpleasant, if not actually painful. There may be a jockeying to see who can force the other to change or to "give in," that is, make the adjustment. One tries to manipulate the other. Because of the structure of the marital relationship, "something has to give," and each may try to shift the onus of "giving" to the other. Petruchio, for example, manipulates Kate in such a way that she adjusts to his demands rather than he to hers.

Where there are no differences there will, obviously, be no need for either to give in to the other. A study of 731 Detroit families found, for example, that in areas of major concern to husbands—his job and the car—the men tended to make the decisions, and in areas of major concern to wives—family food—the women did. But in areas of common concern—vacation and house—both husband and wife had exactly the same voice in decisions (Blood & Wolfe, 1960).

But sometimes there are differences. Marriage may become an arena in which each spouse is attempting to make the other do the changing or adjusting rather than having to do the changing himself or herself. The Christian model is one in which, as Paul commanded, wives submit to their husbands. And it has been stated (Burgess & Cottrell, 1939; Goode, 1956) that by and large it is wives who are most likely to do the adjusting. Evidence for

this conclusion was presented in the Detroit study referred to above. In reply to the question, "When you and your husband differ about something, do you usually give in and do it your husband's way, or does he usually come around to your point of view?" about one-third of the wives (34 per cent) said that they usually or always gave in under these circumstances, about one-fourth (24 per cent) said their husbands did, and about two-fifths (40 per cent) gave equalitarian responses (Blood & Wolfe, 1960, p. 23).

With respect to the religious rearing of children, the mother usually prevails, whether she is Catholic or Protestant (Landis 1949). But in Jewish–non-Jewish marriages, it is the father who usually prevails, except where the father is Catholic, and even here the Catholic father prevails in only the ratio 6 to 5 (Baber, 1953).

So far as sex is concerned, data will be presented below which suggest that wives may impose adjustments on husbands, as Rainwater and Weinstein conclude (1960).

There is some evidence that the costs to wives of having to make adjustments when there are differences may be fairly high. It has been hypothesized that wives may

. . . tend to be more vulnerable psychologically than the husbands to conflicts generated in their relationship to each other. In that case, and other factors being equal, it could be hypothesized that marital strains are potentially more unbalancing for women than for men, a situation that might conceivably register on the former by swinging their [mental health] impairment rates higher and their Well proportions lower than before marriage (Srole et al., 1962, p. 177).[1]

Empirical data tending to corroborate this hypothesis were reported a generation ago in a study which found that married women tended to be somewhat more neurotic than unmarried women (Willoughby,

[1] From *Mental Health in the Metropolis*, by L. Srole, T. S. Langner, S. T. Michael, M. K. Opler, and T. A. C. Rennie. Copyright 1962. McGraw-Hill Book Company, Inc. Used by permission.

1938). More recently, in a survey of American mental health, single women were reported to have experienced an approaching nervous breakdown less often than other women had (Gurin, Veroff, & Feld, 1960, p. 234); and, finally, a report on the mental health of mid-Manhattan found that, although not statistically significant, there was a tendency, except at ages 40–49, for married women to show a larger proportion with impaired mental health than single women (Srole et al., 1962, p. 178).

But wives do have some bargaining power, and clever women use it to "buy" changes in their husbands, a process hilariously though realistically portrayed by Clarence Day in *Life with Father*.

Targets, Limits, and Probabilities of Change

Whatever the goal of adjustment, whether the changes are transitive or intransitive, and whatever the policy may be with respect to who should adjust or change, there are limits to changes that are possible. There are some things which, regardless of theory, cannot be changed. Physique and height, for example, are among the things which cannot be "adjusted." There are certain natural physiological rhythms that may be changed, if at all, only with the greatest difficulty; they are dependent on body type. Sleep, for example, comes easily to some people, and so does waking. Others, different in fundamental physical type, find both falling asleep and waking up difficult. The lark who jumps out of bed wide awake in the morning ready for the day, but who begins to droop early in the evening, can only with great effort, if at all, be changed into the owl who takes many hours to wake up in the morning but who, once awake, warms up and is at his best toward midnight. To what extent rhythms of sex desire can be changed is by no means clear, although change in sex behavior is usually quite possible.

Even when aspects of personality cannot be changed, however, the evaluation placed on the trait, whatever it is, can be changed or "adjusted to." Physique cannot be changed, but we can adjust to it by learning either to ignore it or actually to like it. One of the most basic tenets of Alcoholics Anonymous is that one should change what it is possible to change and learn to accept what it is not possible to change. In effect, the burden of adjustment is shifted from an area in which change is not possible to one in which it is, with resulting reduction of frustration.

As a matter of fact, it is habits, tastes, attitudes, and values that are the usual targets of change or adjustment. Some are changeable without too much difficulty. The husband learns to break the annoying habit of tipping his soup dish toward instead of away from him, thus adjusting himself to his wife's standards; the wife learns to enjoy fishing, adjusting herself to her husband's recreational tastes. Both may change their attitudes and opinions with respect to intellectual issues.

There is by no means unanimity, however, with respect to the degree of fixity or plasticity of personality. To those with a genetic bias, the personality is fixed at conception and thereafter nothing can change it; for those who hold this position, only the most superficial kinds of adjustment or functional changes are possible. If the individual does not find a suitable social "habitat," he will be forever doomed to failure in his relationships, since he cannot change his personality "spots" to fit the world outside. Others hold that personality is set at birth or, at latest, at the age of five or six. To them, the fundamental structure of personality is determined by the play of forces operating in the early years in the family; thereafter change is possible, if at all, only by years of re-education by means of psychoanalysis (Bergler, 1948). Others grant greater plasticity to personality, holding that there is really no time in life when change is absolutely impossible (Bossard & Boll, 1960).

That some things cannot be changed

after conception has already been conceded above. But that there ever comes a time when change in the nongenetic aspects of personality is impossible is by no means demonstrable. The fact that people are "converted," "reborn," or succeed in a remarriage is documentable in many lives. It must be conceded, however, that some changes or adjustments are more difficult than others, that changes become more difficult with age, and that there are great individual differences in ability to change.

Even the ability to change does not, of course, guarantee that it can be motivated. Since any change, whether of habit or basic personality structure, involves some cost, marital adjustments may be easy or difficult according to the degree of change involved and the relative rewards for such change. If the personalities of two people dovetail fairly completely—in a manner suggested by the theory of complementary needs (Winch, 1958)—relatively little change may be demanded of them; marital adjustments will therefore be easy. If two people do not dovetail in their personality structures, a great deal of change may be required on the part of one or both partners. Adjustment might be difficult under these circumstances. Only if the rewards are sufficiently great will the changes seem to be worth the cost. Sometimes the change called for in a marital adjustment is so drastic, involving such a deep-rooted defense mechanism, that making it would destroy the personality (Spiegel, 1957).

Probability of change, in brief, is as important in analyzing an adjustment situation as is possibility of change. It is possible for an alcoholic to achieve remission of his illness, but whether it is probable is another matter. The girl who confidently marries a man hoping to reform him soon learns that the possible is not necessarily the probable in marital adjustments. Mentally and emotionally ill people, or those who have ill "spots" in their makeup, may find marital adjustments possible but too costly to be worth while.

The possibility of change may or may not be related to genetic makeup. It may be possible to change an inherited trait (such as shape of nose) and impossible to change an acquired one (destruction of the optic nerve).

How Change Is Effected

Some of the functional changes in marriage are the result of growth and maturation. The disparity in sexuality, for example, which characterizes the marriage in its earliest years, declines as the wife's sexual capacity (for whatever reason) grows and that of her husband tapers off. Sexual differences in interests are also maximal in the younger years; they tend to converge in maturity (Strong, 1931). Sheer maturation, in brief, tends to dissipate some of the differences between the sexes, reducing the need for adjustment.

Some functional changes are intransitive and the result of learning. Each spouse learns to perform roles; the wife learns to cook so that burned food is no longer an issue, and the husband learns to keep a job so that financial problems are no longer an issue. Each spouse learns the way the other operates and how to mesh gears with it. Much of this learning is impersonal; it is like learning to adjust to the weather or some other natural phenomenon. No attempt is made to change the other.

Both maturation and learning may be viewed as individual processes of change, and individual models are adequate to explain them. But some adjustment processes are the result of interaction between the spouses. The changes result from the interplay between them. Ego may try to change Alter by winning him or her over to his way of thinking (assimilative models); or there may be a bargaining process involved; or one may manipulate the other; or there may be a standoff (strategic models). In these situations, changes can be explained or interpreted only in terms of behavior determined not by Ego himself (or herself) but by both Ego and Alter, joined in a unique kind of relationship in which neither has complete control but in which both have some, and in which the behavior of each is limited by that of the other.

Sometimes differences snowball or escalate; they grow rather than decline (escalation model). The result may be that the only functional change is to destroy the relationship (schismatic models). Divorce is the preferred adjustment.

These several models will be discussed and illustrated in more detail in later sections.

SPECIFICATIONS OF THE MARITAL RELATIONSHIP

The relationships between husband and wife occur in a very specific context and the adjustment processes between them can be understood only if these specifications are understood. The nature and number of the adjustments called for in any relationship—partnership, team, jury, cruise, theatrical cast, committee, parliament—depend on a large number of variables, including, among others, the function of the relationship, the age and sex composition of the membership, the duration of the relationship, the intensity of the relationship, and the institutional specifications defining the roles involved. A transitory relationship among acquaintances who see one another very infrequently requires one kind of adjustment; a long-enduring relationship between business partners who work together in the same office every day demands another. A relationship that can be broken easily, without hurting anyone, will have a characteristic pattern of adjustment; one that can be broken only with great difficulty and at great emotional cost will have another.

Although marital relationships share some characteristics with other kinds of relationships, they are unique among all forms which human relationships may take with respect to the peculiar combination of specifications and conditions which characterizes them. Marriage shares some of the functions of friendship—companionship, for example—but it transcends friendship. It shares bisexual composition with some play and work groups, but it defines the relationships differently. Marriage shares long duration and legal control with business or professional partnerships; but, again, the role definitions of the partners differ greatly. Marriage shares with the jury the requirement that consensus be reached; but the relationship among jurors, unlike that of spouses, is transitory and detached from the major concerns of their lives. And so on. There is no other human relationship just like the marital relationship; it is *sui generis*.

Sex Differences Between Partners

The absolutely characterizing aspect of marital relationships is that they always involve two sexes. This obvious fact conditions every adjustment. Despite the similarities which assortative mating—endogamy and homogamy—tends to produce in married partners, basic underlying sex differences pervade all aspects of their relationship. Some of the differences, of course, as noted earlier, are complementary and hence integrative and do not demand adjustments on either side. But some are so basically divisive as almost to guarantee conflict and the necessity of adjustment. The sexes are more different from one another anatomically than either is from the same sex of another race. The differences are basically biological, but on this biological structure are based a host of other kinds of differences. Many were once functional but, in a modern cultural setting, have become dysfunctional. The nature of these differences and their impact on marital adjustments are discussed in more detail in a later section.

Public and Binding Nature of the Marital Relationship

A second characteristic of marriage which colors the nature of the adjustments involved is its public and binding nature.

Marriage is always a publicly recorded relationship. Even if it is secret in the sense that friends and family are not told about it, it is public in the sense that someone knows of it; there is a record of it. And usually, of course, it is public in the sense that friends and relatives also know about it. This has important bearing on the nature of the relationship and on the adjustment strategies available to the partners. Clandestine relationships do not have the support of institutions, but neither do they restrict as much as sanctioned ones. There are no scientific studies of clandestine liaisons; we do not, therefore, know how they compare with marriages in courtship practices, duration, processes of adjustment, methods of reconciling differences, and the like. Fictional studies—*Anna Karenina, Back Street*—suggest that liaisons which endure take on many of the characteristics of sanctioned marriages; but we do not know how many endure, how long they endure, or what the "divorce" rate is among them.

Marriages, being publicly sanctioned, are difficult to break. Other sexual ties may also be difficult to break, but not in the same way. The difficulty varies from one time to another, from one culture to another, from one nation to another, from one region to another, from one community, social class, neighborhood, and family to another. But formal and official breaking of marital ties for most human beings (as distinguished from violation of the specified terms for the relationship) involves legal permission and, for a large proportion of human beings, religious permission as well.

For these reasons, the marital relationship between people holds them in a kind of vise. They are "a unity of interacting personalities" (Burgess, 1927). They are members of a union. The existence of this vise exerts a profound—perhaps even the profoundest—influence on the relationship. The members must act as a unit; the public holds them accountable as a unit. Their decisions must be interdependent. The relationship is analogous to that among jurors: they must finally agree. Just as this specification for the jury demands certain adjustments, so does this union-specification of marriage similarly demand certain adjustments. The partners are bound to one another in a way that makes certain models (mixed-motive) of relationship especially suitable. They cannot easily break the relationship; they *must* adjust somehow or other. Some married persons view this specification of the relationship as a trap; they rebel against the restrictions it imposes on them, against the concessions it forces upon them. They resist the fact that every decision they make must take into account the will and wishes of their spouse. Others are glad that they have the security of the tie that binds the other to them. They are glad that they have at least veto power over the decisions of their spouses. However it is valued, the binding nature of the marital relationship is one of the most influential forces determining the adjustment processes.

Physical Propinquity

Another specification of the marital relationship is that the partners live together. Individual as well as sex differences become important here. Intimacy, infringement on privacy, confusion of identity, enforced interaction, as well as cold cream and curlers, unshaved stubble, body odors, halitosis, and deshabille may be involved as a concomitant of living together. The self must be presented under less than auspicious circumstances (Goffman, 1959).

Popular literature is full of references to the shock resulting from the contrast between the relationship before marriage when each presented a self to the other which was ready for the performance, and the relationship after marriage when each was behind the scenes and disillusioned.

Some of the changes which husbands and wives have to make in themselves are identical with changes or adjustments which any two people living together must make if they want to continue living together, whatever their sex or age or class or race. In order to free themselves for preferred contacts, they have to work out accommodations that require them to make changes in their habits. The untidy one, for example, has to learn to tidy up, the early riser has to learn to be quiet, the late-hour-keeper has to learn not to bother the early-to-bed, and so on. Studies of the way in which roommates adjust to one another on a college campus are suggestive, but their relevance is limited by the absence of other restraints which characterizes marital relationships. The same might be said of adjustments between travelers sharing the same cabin on a ship or between people sharing a common apartment or prisoners in the same cell. How do people forced to live together reconcile themselves to the messy toothpaste tube, the singing in the shower, slovenly disorder, or compulsive neatness? There may be demands on them to talk when they don't feel like talking, to participate when they want to withdraw. Such adjustments may seem trivial, but they may also be fundamental. Sheer physical propinquity demands adjustments.

Propinquity influences the nature of the process of adjustment available as well as the problems involved. It influences communication; tacit as well as explicit communication is possible. It intensifies the involvement—whether of love or of hate—of the relationship.

Children

And, finally, marriage is likely to result in children. This fact greatly complicates the relationship. Where only the partners themselves are involved, a wider latitude in adjustments might be permitted. The fact that other lives must be taken into account restricts the limits within which adjustments must be made. This characteristic, along with the others, is so fundamental as to set marital relationships off from any and all others. The implications are far-reaching and, in some respects, almost de-

terminative of the nature of the relationship.

The marital relationship is, then, without parallel or even analogue. The specifications of the marital model of human relationship may vary in detail from place to place or class to class, but in general they always call for a relationship between a male and a female, which must have community sanction, which is unbreakable without legal permission or at least community sanction, which requires them to live together (except under unusual circumstances), and which may result in children for whose care they will be held responsible.

The net effect of this unique combination of specifications is that (because the partners are of different sex) there are bound to be conflicts which (because of the binding nature of the relationship) cannot be dealt with easily by dissolving the relationship. There are, similarly (because they are dealt with as a unit), certain to be common interests which exert braking effects on conflicts or which modify the kinds of behavior likely to occur. There are bound to be limits on the freedom of action of both partners, each having some control of his actions but each also having some control over the actions of the other. These inevitable concomitants of marital relationships constitute the specifications demanded of any models for the study of marital adjustments.

Because of the uniqueness of marital relationships, there is some doubt whether research on other forms of human groups can be legitimately used to interpret or explain the adjustments involved in marriage (Udry, Nelson, & Nelson, 1961). Fortunately, there are several which may be used, especially those derived from modifications of the theory of games of strategy, to be presented below.

ARCHETYPICAL PATTERNS OF MARITAL RELATIONSHIPS

The specifications just outlined which define the nature of the marital relationship give the limits within which the relation-ship must operate. But even within these confines, the ways in which men and women can relate to one another are ex-tremely varied. And the way in which they do both reflects and influences the nature of the processes of adjustment operating in the marriage.

Several archetypical patterns of family, and hence of marital, relationships have been delineated. On the basis of the control of family behavior, Burgess and Locke dis-tinguished two patterns, institutional and companionship. In the first, control of fam-ily behavior lies in tradition, custom, mores, and other institutional norms outside the nuclear family itself; in the second, mutual affection is the controlling force (Burgess & Locke, 1960). In applying this typology to a study of families with retarded chil-dren, Farber found it necessary to add a third type and to make room for residual cases which did not fit any of the three. On the basis of the way in which families faced four predicaments—(a) social-emo-tional versus instrumental values and norms, (b) short-run versus long-run con-siderations, (c) family versus community commitments, and (d) emphasis on par-ents' versus emphasis on children's needs and desires—Farber found three combina-tions of solutions which made for integra-tion and stability. He called them the child-oriented, the home-oriented, and the parent-oriented (1962). In general, the child-oriented family corresponds to the institu-tional pattern and the other two to the companionship pattern, with this difference: in the home-oriented pattern the husband is the central figure in the family, whereas in the parent-oriented family an equali-tarian relationship is characteristic.

Since our concern here is primarily with the marital interaction aspect of family organization, only two types are distin-guished: the one corresponding to the Burgess-Locke companionship family is called the *interactional pattern,* and the one corresponding to their institutional family is called the *parallel pattern.* In Farber's typology, the interactional pattern includes both the home- and the parent-centered family and the parallel, the child-centered family. The characterizing criterion is the relative emphasis on instrumental and on social-emotional norms and values.

The Parallel Pattern

In the parallel pattern, emphasis is on the role aspects of the marriage, and these roles are defined by tradition. This is, in fact, a tradition-oriented pattern. If the man is a good provider, not excessive in his sexual demands, sober most of the time, and good to the children, this is about all a woman can reasonably ask. Similarly, if the woman is a good housekeeper and cook, not too nagging, a willing sex partner, and a good mother, this is all a man can really expect. Each lives his or her own life primarily in a male or a female world. There are some-times even strong mystic barriers between the sexes in such a pattern, and neither violates the boundaries of the other's world. In some backwoods communities where this pattern prevails, women do not even refer to their husbands by name; they refer, rather, to "him." Spouses refer to "my wife" or "my husband" rather than casually to "Mary" or "John." The wife does not interfere in her husband's life, nor he in hers. She has her social life primarily with other women or with her family or in her church; he has his with fellow-workers, or with hunt-ing, fishing, or drinking companions at the tavern. Companionship in the sense of ex-change of ideas or opinions or the enhance-ment of personality by verbal play or conversation is not considered a basic com-ponent in this pattern.

There are, of course, standards within this archetypical pattern. How good, for example, must a man be before he "passes" the good-provider test? How much sex is "passing"? Standards vary. A man might be considered a good provider according to one woman's standards but not another's, sober enough of the time according to one woman's standards but not another's, good to the children according to one woman's standards but not to another's. And so, conversely, standards of housekeeping, cooking, nagging, sexual complaisance in women vary from man to man, group to group, class to class, culture to culture. But whatever the standards might be within the pattern, the essential characteristic is strong emphasis on certain roles and little emphasis on personality interaction, on instrumental rather than on emotional-expressive norms. Duty, not spontaneity, is a key word. Tradition, not personality, is the decisive factor.

For marriages of this pattern, the individuals do not have to know one another in any intimate way before marriage; parents, in fact, may select partners with the required qualifications. Or men in the West might send for a boatful of women with confidence that if the women had the specified role qualifications, marital adjustments would not be difficult.

Marital adjustments in this tradition-directed or parallel pattern tend to conform to learning models. If the spouses learn their roles and perform them adequately, adjustments—i.e., functional changes—tend to occur in the process. They change in the direction of conformity to role specifications, and a satisfactory marital relationship is the result.

The Interactional Pattern

The interactional pattern of marital relationships demands a great deal more involvement in the relationship on the part of the participants. Personal involvement refers to:

the degree to which the person's "self" is invested in [the relationship], how important it is in a person's life. . . . A high degree of personal involvement implies that he expects to gain from it an expression of the self and the satisfaction of personality and interpersonal

needs. . . . The degree of personal involvement implies how limited or broad is the person's conception of the role, how limited or broad are the gratifications derived from it. In this sense, a high degree of personal involvement has sometimes been viewed as reflecting a "healthy" adjustment, an indication that one is getting "more" out of the role (Gurin, Veroff, & Feld, 1960, p. 86).

Emphasis is placed on personality interaction. The role qualifications specified in the parallel pattern are taken for granted; they may even be added to. But whatever they are, they constitute only a minimum; far more is demanded. Companionship, expressions of love, recognition of personality (as distinguished from mere role performance) are among the other and characterizing specifications of this pattern.

Personal involvement has been found to be positively related to marital happiness.

People who report very happy marriages are more likely to concentrate on relationship sources of happiness, while those reporting less happiness in marriage tend to concentrate on the situational aspects of marriage (home, children, social life) as sources of their marital happiness. Conversely, in the association with sources of unhappiness, we see that those happier in marriage—when they give any reasons for unhappiness—tend to focus on situational sources, while the less happy stress difficulties in the relationship (or the spouse). Thus, feelings of happiness in marriage bear a clear relationship with the extent to which a person is satisfied or frustrated in the relationship aspects of his marriage. When he is happy with the relationship aspects of the marriage he tends to feel generally happy in the marriage; when unhappy with this aspect of the marriage, he tends to be unhappy. . . . To a considerable extent happiness in marriage implies happiness in the *relationship* (Gurin, Veroff, & Feld, 1960, p. 98).

Marital adjustments in this relational pattern are more likely to be the result of interaction; the spouses adjust to one another primarily and to the role secondarily. The processes are somewhat different from the processes of adjustment in tradition-directed or parallel relationships.

Class Differences in Marital Patterns

There is some evidence that there are class differences in characteristic marital patterns, the parallel or tradition-directed tending to occur more frequently in low-income marriages and the interactional in high-income families:

A couple faced with economic privations is likely to direct its energy toward overcoming them or at least toward learning to "make-do;" but these efforts may deplete their investment in the marital relationship itself, an investment which would have led both to efforts to achieve greater marital satisfaction and attempts to acknowledge and cope with personal problems or inadequacies.

Further evidence of this difference in involvement among income groups may be found in relationships between *sources* of inadequacy feelings and income. There is a high concentration of concern with economic provision among people with low incomes, but a focus on the inadequacies manifest in the marital relationship (particularly . . . inconsiderateness, impatience, etc.) among those at the higher income levels. A similar distribution of emphasis is found in relationships between income level and sources of both current dissatisfactions and past problems in marriage (Gurin, Veroff, & Feld, 1960, p. 219).

Further evidence of class differences in patterns of marital relationships has been forthcoming from a study of working-class as contrasted with college-educated wives. The working-class couples accept the traditional sexual division of labor and the roles assigned each sex without question. But the marriages are less satisfying, especially to the women.

Although the working class housewife may have more favorable attitudes toward *housekeeping* activities than her college-educated sister, it is my impression, which cannot be documented here, that she is less satisfied with marriage and less satisfied with life in general (Komarovsky, 1962, p. 229).

Sex Differences in Marital Pattern Preferences

There appear to be sex, as well as class, differences, at least in preferred marital patterns. By and large, women tend to prefer the interactive pattern of marital relationship, even within the lower socio-economic classes, while men tend to prefer the traditional. One study of marriage in the lower socio-economic levels, for example, found that "husbands emphasize functions which, while complementary, are parallel—the husband goes to work, the wife works at home; the husband relates to the children as a father, the wife as a mother. Women highlight the importance of such interactive functions as love-making and friendship" (Rainwater & Weinstein, 1960, p. 68).[2]

The significance of these sex differences in preferred pattern of marital relationship is that they greatly influence the strategic "chips" each spouse has in the adjustment processes. The husband is at a strategic advantage.

. . . it is probably easier for the wife to go along with her husband than it is for her to persuade him to interact more affectionately—both because it is difficult for one person to force affection from another and because the wife already is persuaded that the parental and work roles are important, while the husband may be quite insensitive to the wife's affectional needs (Rainwater & Weinstein, 1960, pp. 68–69).

Patterns May Change

Patterns may change. Thus, even husbands and wives in the higher socio-economic levels who begin their marriage at a

[2] From *And the Poor Get Children* by Lee Rainwater and Karol Kane Weinstein. Copyright © 1960 by Social Research, Inc. Published by Quadrangle Books, Inc., Chicago.

level of intense interaction and involvement in their relationship may later be drawn into separate orbits, each living his or her own life, but performing the basic marital functions to keep the marriage stable (Blood & Wolfe, 1960, p. 264). There is a minimum of interaction, although what there is may be polite, if not pleasant, or at least not hostile. These may even be the "comfortable as an old shoe" relationships which make little demand on the members, or, conversely, they may be only alternative or even preparatory to physical as well as emotional separation.

The trend in marriage in our day is in the direction of the interactional pattern (Blood & Wolfe, 1960). This fact helps to explain the increasing preoccupation with the interpersonal relations in marriage and the greater strain put on marriage, since it is more difficult to adjust to the demands of an intensely interactional relationship than it is to learn how to deal with more technical role requirements, such as homemaking or vocational skills (Bernard, 1942, pp. 17–18). It is easier for most women to be good housekeepers than it is to be equally successful in the more demanding role of companion, sex partner, comforter, playmate, and other interacting relationships.

One result is that in most working class families sharing experience tends to be limited. Each partner becomes a specialist in certain tasks and sees the other in specialized roles. This emphasis on formal, impersonal roles results in a sense of distance, an attitude of "O.K., you stick to your job and I'll stick to mine." Still, the affectional needs of the wife are not met and less conscious needs of the husband for intimate contact are also unmet. . . . In such a situation there is much room for conflict; each partner may operate at cross-purposes to the other, and misunderstandings may arise in whatever efforts are made to establish common family goals (Rainwater & Weinstein, 1960, p. 69).

Whether the pattern is parallel or interactional, then, the need for adjustments is likely to be present. And the general nature of the process of adjustment, that is, of the variables involved, is likely to be the same, however different the specific issues and however different the most suitable models for interpreting the process may be.

THE DIMENSIONS OF MARITAL ADJUSTMENTS

The major dimensions of any human adjustment problem are: (a) the degree or extent or nature of the differences between or among the parties involved; (b) the degree or extent or nature of the communication between or among the parties; and (c) the quality of the relationship between or among them, that is, its positive or negative affectivity, friendliness, or hostility. If the differences are so extensive or so deep that no rapprochement is possible, that is one thing; if they are relatively minor, that is another. If they are matters of principle, that is one thing; if they are matters of degree, that is another. If communication is open and free, that is one thing; if it is blocked or if it is meant to deceive or mislead, that is another. If the quality of the relationship is one of love and affection, that is one thing; if it is one of hatred and hostility or enmity, that is another. And so on. Each of these dimensions is therefore important for understanding the processes of adjustment.

Degree or Extent of Difference

Any of the kinds of differences referred to above may be categorical or matters of degree. Matters of principle are usually categorical: such-and-such is wrong, period. No exceptions. No mitigating circumstances. No leeway. If this is the nature of the differences between people, adjustments are difficult, if possible at all. They are particularly likely to occur with respect to sexual behavior, tending to complicate adjustments in this area, as noted below. Differences which are matters of degree on the other hand, may be amenable to "bargaining," as discussed below. But they may also be subject to so-called salami tactics, by which rights and privileges are nibbled away. The phenomena of limits come into play (Schelling, 1960). No one case seems significant enough to make an issue of, but slices add up. Just how far can the partner be pushed? There comes a time when he (she) can stand it no longer. There is a breaking point. There is a last straw. The spouse may be completely surprised at the result. All of a sudden, it seems, the wife (husband) packs up and leaves. "I'm fed up. I just can't stand it any longer. I can't take it any more." The difference was too great to be bridged by one partner alone; "bargaining" might have worked.

Communication

The responsibility for failure in such cases may rest on the partner who did not protest, who did not warn, who did not put up the storm signals as the limits of patience or endurance approached. For communication is essential in arriving at satisfactory relationships.

Interaction implies—indeed, consists of—communication. Communication may be explicit or tacit. Explicit communication is usually verbal, although it may also use other conventional symbols. It may be used to convey correct or incorrect information, to clarify or to mislead, to enlighten or to deceive. The importance of information is fundamental in all human adjustments, but especially in those which conform to the specifications of strategic models. Explicit communication is basic to any form of adjustment which seeks to persuade or cajole or bargain.

Tacit communication—by way of body movements or "strategic moves"—is peculiarly important in sexual adjustments because, for so many people, verbal communication in this area is impossible (Rainwater & Weinstein, 1960). A vast amount of communication in the field of sex consists of gestures. But tacit communication is not at all precise: the message is hard to read. Misreading is common. The rejected swain hotly accuses the indignant miss of "leading him on." She rejects the accusation; she did not lead him on! The husband and the wife, each hungry for the loving caress of the other, lie side by side immobilized by their inability to communicate or fearful that an advance by one may be rejected by the other.

In some situations, tacit communication takes on the aspect of a cat-and-mouse game of move and countermove. There is often an intent to confuse, to create uncertainty. What does he mean by that? Why did she do that? What is he up to? What's her idea? Often the tacit move is designed deliberately to arouse such fears and suspicions in order to humiliate the partner when the true nature of the "move" is later made clear. What was the meaning of the lipstick on his handkerchief, which he was at great pains to leave where she would find it? After suffering as long as she can, she breaks down and asks him, accusingly. With obvious pleasure and enjoyment, he offers an innocent and perfectly plausible explanation, backed by incontrovertible proof. Strange as it may seem, some couples seem to enjoy this cat-and-mouse game of tacit move and countermove: it is intense; it is interesting; it adds excitement to their essentially dull lives (Lantz & Snyder, 1962).

The importance of communication in marital relationships highlights the seriousness of breakdowns or failures in communication. These may take many forms. At one extreme they may result from general inarticulateness: one or both partners do not have the verbal skills to express themselves. The result is tacit or behavioral communication, by acts rather than by words, and the chances of misinterpretation are great.

At the other extreme, however, is an aberration resulting from too great articulateness. This difficulty is more commonly reported or commented upon in women than in men; it may be pancultural, not necessarily because of biological differences in the sexes—although they may be involved, since the vocal cords of women have greater innervation than those of men —but perhaps because of inevitable relational conditions. The stock figure here is the nag, the scold, the woman who talks incessantly at, rather than to, her husband. This phenomenon has not been subjected to scientific inquiry, but it appears constantly in folk culture, and it is observable in the social circle of many people. This is the woman to whom others are primarily objects to talk at or against; she is little interested in what the other person has to say or even in how he (or she) reacts to what she herself is saying. She is, in effect, talking to herself in the presence of another person. The contents of her talk may be pleasant or hostile; it is nearly always boring after a few minutes, if not actually antagonizing. It is to escape this barrage of noncommunicatory articulateness, allegedly, that men sometimes seek refuge in the club or tavern, if not in desertion.

Communication between spouses is often honestly blunted because of sex differences. "I just can't understand women (men)," says the baffled spouse who has failed to communicate or to receive communication. "I just don't know what he (she) expects of me," is a common complaint of spouses, even those with the best of intentions.

Refusal to be communicated with, that is, "to get the message," is another form, this time deliberate, which communication failure may take. It is a powerful defense. The spouse becomes deaf, or inaccessible. Or pretends not to understand or shakes his (her) head incredulously. The strategic use of such blocking of communication will be discussed below in connection with mixed-motive models.

Women appear to be especially dependent on sympathetic communication with their spouses. "Striking differences in marital satisfaction," for example, are reported "between marriages in which the wife's problems are understood by the husband and those in which she is unable to communicate her troubles to him or is rejected for doing so" (Blood & Wolfe, 1960, p. 261).

Quality of the Relationship

Adjustments may not be any easier when the parties involved are friendly or loving. They may, indeed, be more difficult than when the parties are unfriendly or hostile. But they are more likely to be motivated in the direction of a suitable accommodation. The rewards for success are likely to be greater. If the partners in a marital relationship love one another, the costs or sacrifices demanded of them in adjusting their differences seem slight. It may not be true that love conquers all, but it goes a long way in making changes palatable.

Hostile people held within the vise which marriage imposes may also adjust their differences, but the resulting relationship is more likely to be a standoff than a victory for both.

The kinds of models suitable for interpreting or understanding marital adjustments will differ according to the quality of the relationship. Assimilative models and mixed-motive models fit relationships in which there is affection; zero-sum and schismatic models, those in which there is not.

MODELS OF MARITAL ADJUSTMENT

The incompatible differences which demand adjustments in marriage, as in other relationships with similar interlocking of parties, may be handled on several levels: (a) the differences may be eliminated and similarities substituted; (b) each partner may attempt to optimize his or her position vis-à-vis the other; (c) the degree of interaction may be reduced to a minimum so that there is relatively little influence of one on the other, each arranging his (her) life in such a way that no matter what the other does, the effect is slight; or, finally, (d) the relationship may be destroyed, each going his or her separate way; conflict is avoided, if not resolved, by getting rid of the relationship. Processes at the first level are assimilative in nature, those at the second and third, strategic, and those at the fourth, schismatic.

Level 1: Assimilative Models

Several techniques have been distinguished for achieving change in one or both partners so that they are no longer different: (a) brainwashing, based on the theory of conditioned response; (b) explaining away an opponent's image of the situation, based on Freudian theory; and (c) removing the felt threat associated with alternative images, based on Carl Rogers' theory of understanding and permissiveness (Rapoport, 1960).

Brainwashing. Brainwashing is a subtle use of the carrot-and-stick method of manipulating responses. For maximum effectiveness, it requires isolation of the subject, removing him or her from competing stimuli. It requires alternate punishment and reward in a way that creates willingness to accept control as an alternative to the anxiety of uncertainty. It seems to work best when carried out in a spirit of ostensible friendliness. The best-known applications of brainwashing techniques were those used by communists in prisoner-of-war camps; but in less sophisticated ways they are commonly used in everyday life, even in marriage. The husband manages to cut his wife off from contacts with her family or friends so that his definition of any situation cannot be counteracted by theirs. To the outsider, the spouse seems to be in thrall. "He has her hypnotized." "She doesn't dare to call her soul her own." The taming of the shrew, Kate, by Petruchio, as described by Shakespeare, is an illustration of change by brainwashing using the conditioned response. A wife

might, similarly, make certain behavior on the part of her husband so painful that he would cease to indulge in it in order to avoid the punishment she inflicted; we say he is "henpecked." Either spouse may be so conditioned in the direction of compatibility with the other. The punishments may take many forms: weeping, sex refusal, beating, coldness, withdrawal, money deprivation, brawling, or what have you. Whatever it is, the spouse comes in time to prefer to concede whatever is under issue rather than endure the punishment, and finally the very anticipation of the punishment is enough to make him avoid the situation. A change has been effected; the difference has been removed. The entire cost has been borne by one of the partners. The resulting relationship may or may not be stable.

Explaining away. The "explain away" technique is often used by therapists, but it can be used by anyone. It is especially likely to be used by articulate people with a smattering of Freudian theory. The wife tries to change her husband by telling him he has an Oedipus complex; or the husband tries to change his wife by telling her she is a compulsive housekeeper. The general idea is that if the underlying origin of the offending behavior can be explained, the behavior itself will stop. In a sense, the adverse labeling of unwanted behavior is a subtle form of punishment; it defies the opponent to change in order to escape the onus of the explanatory factor. The husband has to prove he does not have an Oedipus complex by not going to visit his mother; the wife has to prove she is not a compulsive housekeeper by never mentioning the husband's slovenliness about the house. Otherwise, the "I-told-you-so" tactic can be used: "See, what I said about you is true; your behavior proves it."

Threat removal. The threat-removing technique is an application of the theory of permissiveness in human relationships. It has three components: (a) it conveys to the opponent a feeling that he is understood but not judged; (b) it delineates clearly the area of validity of the opponent's position; and (c) it induces an assumption of similarity (Rapoport, 1960).

(a) One of the commonest characteristics of verbal conflict is the failure of one or both parties to listen to or even to hear the other. Each is so busy stating his or her own case in the most forceful manner that the time during which the other is talking is used merely to regroup forces for further assault. The opponents are unwilling or unable to listen to one another. There is no communication. A basic condition for changing people, however, is that they be assured that the opponent understands what their position is. Thus, the spouse who is eager to change a partner by persuasion must learn first of all to be able to state the partner's position to the partner's own satisfaction. By so doing he, or she, demonstrates that at least he understands the other's position. He not only can take the other's role, put himself in the other's position; he can also convince the other that he has done so. This is the first step in removing a sense of threat.

There is no guarantee that the opponent will continue to listen after you have presented his case and gone on to present your own. But there is at least hope, indeed on two counts. First, having had the experience of listening and agreeing (when his own case was being presented), the opponent may carry some of his responses over at least for a while to listening to another point of view. Second, he too has a job of presenting your case to your satisfaction. He will want to do it well, because getting an admission from you that he has succeeded is a minor victory in the debate. Listening to your case will make the job easier for him. He therefore has some motivation for listening (Rapoport, 1960, p. 291).[3]

This is a form of role-taking; it teaches each one how the situation looks to the other. It gives each one the experience of

viewing himself as he looks to the other. By proving that each understands the other, each mollifies the other. Change becomes easier.

(b) A second step in the threat-removal technique is to grant that the opponent's position may be justified under certain conditions. "It is hard to find a statement in ordinary language without *any* region of validity. There are, roughly speaking, no absolutely false assertions. If one tries hard enough, one can usually think of circumstances under which any given assertion might be true" (Rapoport, 1960, p. 292). Sometimes differences that are incompatible result from differences in definition of the situation, or in perception, or in interpretation. Establishing the extent of validity of both points of view is itself cooperative, and hence itself tends to reduce felt threat; but, in addition, it also clarifies the boundaries of the differences and thus offers a transition to a recognition of the area of disagreement, related to the now recognized differing frames of reference. "You hate me!" "Why, yes, I can see how you think so if you think my absorption in my work is a sign of hatred. But couldn't it also be a sign that I love you because I want to get ahead to do more for you?" "The idea . . . is to steer the debate away from polarities and toward the examination of contexts. If both parties do this (if one starts, the other may follow—imitation is a surprisingly widespread principle of human conduct), progress may be made toward the resolution of the issue" (Rapoport, 1960, p. 302). The idea is to avoid charge and countercharge or accusation and defense, both of which are threatening. The idea is, rather, to accept the charge or the accusation but to show its limitations or to reinterpret it in a different context.

(c) The third phase of the threat-removal technique is to induce an assumption of similarity rather than to emphasize the differences. Usually, we attribute bad qualities to our opponents; the threat-removal technique suggests that we look for these bad

[3] Reprinted from *Fights, Games and Debates* by Anatol Rapoport by permission of The University of Michigan Press. Copyright © 1960 by The University of Michigan Press.

qualities in ourselves. Usually, similarly, we attribute good qualities to ourselves; the threat-removal technique suggests that we look for these good qualities in our opponents.

Our ultimate purpose in raising questions about ourselves is to induce the opponent to raise similar questions about himself. We see ourselves as intelligent, honest, and considerate. It will often serve us well to imagine that the opponent possesses these qualities to some degree. Maybe he does not, but maybe this "delusion" of ours will induce a similar delusion in him about us (Rapoport, 1960, p. 306).

Again, this is an exercise in role-taking. By seeing ourselves as we look to the other, we begin to understand his, or her, fear or resentment. We know better how to behave in order to dissipate it. We come to see that both of us share good as well as bad qualities.

The net effect of brainwashing, explaining away, and threat removal is, presumably, to change the spouse in such a way as to get rid of differences and foster similarities. They may be used in either the parallel or the interactional form of marital relationship, but inasmuch as they depend on explicit communication, they are probably more likely to occur in the interactional form. If they are used manipulatively only, that is, if the change is only in the way differences are interpreted, the change or adjustment may last only a short time. If the quality of the relationship is one of basic hostility and resentment, it may not be amenable to any of these techniques.

It should be pointed out that even if and when such techniques succeed in changing a spouse, the result may not be what was anticipated. It has been noted in the literature, for example, that the wives of alcoholics who have learned to control their illness by abstention are sometimes greatly disappointed in the result. Some found that they preferred the man who, however difficult he might have been when intoxicated, was more lovable when sober than the man

who is sober always. The serious husband who finally succeeds in muting his wife's exuberance sometimes finds that he has lost something he much loved in his wife; the difference he has erased was not divisive in the first place.

Levels 2 and 3: Optimizing or Strategic Models

[Descriptions to follow are based upon recent developments in game theory. The reader will note certain similarities with role theory discussed in Ch. 4; see especially pp. 133–142.]

The assimilative models just described are straightforward; they embody fairly simple principles of conditioning, analysis, and persuasion. There is control, in varying degrees, by one person in the situation; he is acting on or "adjusting" the other. It is a transitive kind of adjustment.

But in many marital situations, as in other kinds, it is not a matter of independent action. In most organizational or systemic situations, and most especially in marriage (as we noted in discussing the specifications for marital relationships) decisions are interdependent. The success or failure of Ego's policies depend on Alter's policies. Decisions must therefore always be made with the probable behavior of someone else in mind. What if Alter decides to do this? or that? Ego has to know how to select his own alternatives of behavior in terms of what Alter may do. Such situations, sometimes known as interdependent decision situations, are usually explored by means of strategic game models. Marriage fits the specifications very well, especially with modifications introduced by T. C. Schelling (1960).

The components of strategic models. The components of strategic game models are the following: (a) there are players—in our case, husbands and wives—who have conflicting goals; (b) each has alternative courses of action available to him from which he can choose; (c) each combination of alternatives of the players has an antici- pated outcome; and (d) each outcome has a certain value or payoff to the players. It is specified that each player has some control over the situation, to the extent, at least, that he can decide his own behavior; but he does not have complete control, because he is tied into this relationship with the other players whose decisions also affect the situation. Decisions with respect to what course of action to follow have to be made bearing in mind that the success or failure of any course of action depends on what the other player also is going to do.

The components are usually presented for analysis in the form of a matrix, although, of course, the people involved in the situation are not always aware of the existence of such a matrix.

Ego's Alternatives			Alter's Alternatives	
	A	B	C	D
1	A-1	B-1	C-1	D-1
2	A-2	B-2	C-2	D-2
3	A-3	B-3	C-3	D-3
4	A-4	B-4	C-4	D-4

Fig. 1.

Each outcome (A-1, B-2, etc.), or result of combination of strategies, has a value for each player. When these values are speci- fied, the result is called a payoff matrix. By convention, the sign used in the matrix refers to Ego's payoff. In some situations, to be noted below, the payoff for Alter is the same, but with reversed signs. If the payoffs are different for Ego and Alter, the payoff for Ego is given at the lower left corner and that for Alter in the upper right.

In real life, of course, people rarely eval- uate alternatives in any such neat and for- mal way; nor are evaluations as precise as implied by the use of specific numbers. But in a nonverbal way, a "calculus" is posited, and a value is arrived at. There *are* ranked preferences among outcomes. Some *are* considered more desirable than others; some *are* feared more than others. "I'd rather die than. . . ." "It's better to . . . than to. . . ." We are always expressing such sets of preferences. It is in this sense that the use of specific numbers is justified; their use does not imply that a true metric has necessarily been imposed on the outcomes, although such a metric is feasible under laboratory conditions (Siegel, 1956).

Adjustment situations under strategic models. Games of strategy may be classified in a great many ways; for our purposes here, two salient criteria are (a) the pres- ence or absence, or the degree, of commu- nication between the partners, or, in other words, the amount and accuracy of infor- mation available to them, and (b) the de- gree of conflict or the extent of the differ- ences or divergences between the partners. On the basis of these two criteria, the adjustment situations may be viewed as in Table 1.

For our purposes here, Situations A and B may be disregarded; they do not involve divisive interspousal differences.

Situations E and F fall at Level 3. They are zero-sum models and, while not suitable for many ongoing marriages, may fit a marriage in which each partner fences him- self (herself) off from the other and, in effect, reduce the other to a thing, behaving in such a way that no matter what the other does, he (she) is safe. There is only as much interaction as the expectation that each will behave in a way to maximize gains or minimize losses. Beyond this, the other becomes a natural phenomenon, like the weather, which one cannot influence but which one must take into account in one's own behavior. The situation reflects a stalemate or standoff. Neither can improve the situation by his (her) own efforts. Strictly speaking, there is no process of ad-

TABLE 1

CATEGORICAL CLASSIFICATION OF STRATEGIC
ADJUSTMENT SITUATIONS

Nature or Degree of Differences	Nature or Degree of Communication	
	Communication Is Absent or Tacit in Nature	Communication Is Present or Possible
There are no differences, or the differences are integrative; common interests predominate	Situation A: Coordination game involved. For some reason or other there has been a breakdown in communication. Each must behave according to the expectations of the other to achieve the common goal without communicating with the other.	Situation B: No interspousal adjustments are necessary. The pair may have to adjust as a unit to other systems—in-laws, friends, church, school, job, etc.—but no marital adjustments, as here defined, are necessary.
Both conflicting and common interests are present. (Level 2)	Situation C: Coordination game involved, as above. See Matrix 1, Appendix, for illustration.	Situation D: Bargaining game involved; strategic moves to manipulate partner are important. See Matrixes 2, 3, and 4, Appendix, for illustrations.
"Pure conflict" is present; that is, there are no common interests. (Level 3)	Situation E: Secrecy, bluff, deception are important; the classic zero-sum game of strategy without saddle point. See Matrix 5, Appendix, for Illustration.	Situation F: Communication is not important one way or another here; knowing what an opponent is going to do does not help. The outcome which maximizes the gains of one also minimizes the losses of the other. (A "saddle point" is said to be present when this occurs.) The classic zero-sum game with saddle point; a "standoff" or "stalemate." See Matrix 6, Appendix, for illustration.

justment here. It is a static situation in which any change must be for the worse. It may be a very stable relationship, even though unfair to one party. Alienated or estranged partners may find themselves in such a relationship; so also may hostile partners in a parallel relationship. The distinction between E and F lies in the fact that communication makes no difference in F; in E secrecy is so important that, mathematically speaking, the player himself does not know which strategy he is to use until he is ready to use it. There are techniques to tell him how often to use one and how often another (Williams, 1954).

At Level 2, Situations C and D—called cooperative or mixed-motive games—do fit the specifications of marriage and are useful models for explaining or interpreting marital adjustments.

The mixed-motive model uses the same conceptual equipment as does the zero-sum model, but it changes the specifications. In the zero-sum model, neither player attempts to change the payoff or values of the several outcomes; both accept the matrix as given. In the mixed-motive model, however, one player, or both, may attempt by his own behavior to change the payoff or value of the several outcomes for his opponent. He behaves in such a way (to be elaborated presently) as to make it more or less rewarding for his opponent to select certain alternatives rather than others. In the zero-sum model, the gains and losses of the two players cancel out; what Ego wins, Alter loses, so only one set of figures in the payoff matrix is called for. In the mixed-motive model, the payoffs may be different, not only in terms of gains and losses, but also in terms of amount. It is characteristic for mixed-motive models that it is possible for both players to win or for both to lose.

Because the mixed-motive model fits so many marital adjustment situations and is so illuminating when it does fit, it is elaborated in some detail below. It is merely introduced here. In order to complete our description of the models at the several levels of adjustment, however, escalation and schismatic models are presented before continuing with the discussion of the mixed-motive model.

Level 4: Escalation and Schismatic Models

Useful as they are, strategic concepts do not explain the processes by which situations change. They are dynamic only in the sense that they explain how in any given situation one player manipulates the other to make him select one alternative rather than another. But each situation requires a new "frame." Game concepts are useful dynamically, that is, in a given situation, but not for changes in the situation over time. For changes over time, "moving pictures" rather than separate "frames" are needed. Escalation and schismatic models, with parameters moving the partners either farther and farther apart, or closer and closer together, provide such a "moving picture."

The escalation model. The mathematical model for this process—designed originally to explain arms races, psychological epidemics, and the like—is useful also for understanding marital adjustments. In general, this model refers to a situation in which the rate of increase or decrease in a certain kind of behavior of one party is related to (a) the rate of increase or decrease in certain kinds of behavior on the part of the other party, (b) costs or inhibitions which brake the increase or decrease, and (c) permanent grievances between them which keep the process going. In the equations for this model, the interdependence variable and the braking variable are as-

sumed to be positive; but the permanent grievance variable may be either positive or negative. If negative, it refers to the opposite of a grievance, to something, that is, which holds the parties together, like love or friendliness.

Applied to marital relationships, this model states that the rate of increase of hostile acts by Ego is positively dependent on the amount of hostile behavior on the part of Alter, negatively on the cost involved in engaging in such hostile behavior, and positively on some stable issue, such as the "permanent grievances" which are present (Rapoport, 1960). The equations for these statements are:

$$dx/dt = ay - mx + g,$$
$$dy/dt = bx - ny + h.$$

Here dx/dt refers to rate of change; x and y refer to the amount of hostility present in the two partners; m and n stand for the effort or cost involved in pursuing the hostile behavior; and g and h stand for the "permanent grievances." The parameters a and b stand for the degree of mutual dependence of one party's behavior on the other party's behavior. For understanding the relationships to which such a model applies, it is not necessary to solve the equations which represent it. The chief purpose the model serves, in fact, is simply to help see how marital relationships function.

Since the parameters a, b, m, and n may sometimes have the value of zero, and g and h may be negative as well as positive (the opposite of a grievance as well as a grievance), this model explains how partners may move toward, as well as away from, one another; it also explains stability. Rapoport summarizes four situations which may result from his model, according to the relationship among the parameters.

1. If the product of the braking forces or costs in the two parties (mn) is greater than the product of the degree of mutual dependence (ab), and if there is an underlying griev-

ance (*g* and *h* are positive), there will be stability in the relationship; there will be no escalation, one way or another.

2. If, as above, the braking force (*mn*) is greater than the mutual dependence (*ab*), and there is the opposite of a grievance present (*g* and *h* are negative), hostile behavior will cease.

3. If the braking force (*mn*) is less than the mutual dependence (*ab*) and there is an underlying grievance (*g* and *h* are positive), there will be runaway escalation; the partners will move farther and farther away from one another.

4. If the braking force (*mn*) is less than the mutual dependence (*ab*) and there is the opposite of a grievance present (*g* and *h* are negative), the situation will be equivocal, depending on the initial level of hostility. If the initial level is above a certain point, there will be upwardly escalating hostility; if it is below that point, there will be declining hostility.

We shall have more to say about escalation in our discussion of divorce below.

Rapoport summarizes the interpretation of the escalation model as follows, but here the application to marital adjustments is substituted for his application to an arms race:

What can we learn from this analysis? Let us review what we have done. We have contrived an extremely artificial situation, a model, which bears *some* resemblance to what we can abstract from the dynamics of [marital interaction]; that is, we have put into the simplest type of mathematical equations the usual arguments given about the causes of [hostile behavior in marriage], namely, underlying grievances and mutual resentment, and the limiting factors, such as the constraints of [difficulties in the way of hostile behavior]. So long as these factors were discussed in conventional language, not much could be concluded as to what would happen, for example, whether the [hostile behavior] could be stabilized, whether a runaway race would result, or whether total [ending] was thinkable. Once a translation was made into quantitative relations, at least theoretical conclusions about the "fate of the system" could be made. The truth of these conclusions depends, of course,

entirely on the accuracy of the model. It goes without saying that the model here depicted is grossly inaccurate and oversimplified. Note, however, that the "would-be" conclusions are in accordance with common sense, to a degree. The presence of grievances would prevent total [ending of hostile behavior]. Balance of power is possible if the degree of mutual [hostility] is sufficiently tempered by constraints on the [extent of hostile behavior]. Underlying good will can insure [cessation of hostile behavior], provided mutual [hostility] is not too great or provided the level of [hostile behavior] had already been brought down below a certain critical level or had not risen above it, etc.

What the model gives us that common sense conclusions do not is a neat quantitative way of expressing these results. So far, these results are little more than shorthand notation for the common sense conclusions although it can be argued that being rigorously deduced they deserve more confidence as conclusions (Rapoport, 1960, pp. 29–30).

As in the case of other models, the major contribution of this one is not necessarily in determining measures for the parameters but rather in showing that there are processes at work which, under certain circumstances, can lead inevitably and even irreversibly to stepped-up hostility and widened breaches. Adjustment involves somehow or other changing these parameters at the most feasible point. If *x* and *y* cannot be changed, perhaps *m* and *n* can; perhaps the "permanent grievance" can be reduced or eliminated; if nothing else, perhaps *a* and *b* can be reduced to zero by temporarily separating the spouses.

Perhaps other variables must be inserted into the model to make it fit marital adjustments. But in any event, the concept of escalation and the formulation of a model to describe it is a useful one in thinking about marital adjustments.

Other schismatic models. Schismatic models refer to situations where the differences between or among parties are so great that no accommodation is possible. The relationship must be destroyed. Conflict is not resolved in this way but it is avoided. The parties go their separate ways. One partner leaves or divorces the other. Schismatic models attempt to explain how such social systems fall apart.

One such model, not further elaborated here, is in terms of the relative costs and/or rewards involved in remaining within the system as opposed to destroying it. ". . . the increased attainment of a given end entails increased utility [rewards] to the system up to a certain point, though with decreasing increments of utility [rewards] as that point is approached. Beyond that point, at first with small decrements but with progressively increasing decrements as the given end is further pursued, utility decreases" (Firey, 1948, pp. 21-22).

The statement of this model is purely theoretical and general; the application varies, of course, according to the specific situation. That is, the costs and the rewards have to be determined specifically in each case. What constitutes a cost or a reward would be different in different marriages, according to personality variables as well as institutional variables. Where, for example, beatings are defined as a form of attention, they might be evaluated as rewards; where they are defined as cruelty, contrariwise, they would certainly be evaluated as costs.

Another model not elaborated here which may be classed as schismatic refers to groups characterized by four variables, all of which apply to marriages: (a) intensity of interaction; (b) level of friendliness; (c) amount of activity carried on by partners; and (d) amount of activity imposed by the external environment. In addition, there are three postulated sets of relationships among these variables: (a) intensity of interaction is dependent upon and increases with the level of friendliness and the amount of activity within the group; (b) the level of friendliness will increase if or when the actual level of interaction is greater than the amount appropriate at the existing level of friendliness; and (c) the amount of activity will tend to increase if the actual level of friendliness is higher

than necessary and if the externally imposed amount of activity is higher than the existing amount of activity (Simon, 1952). This model can derive the conditions of stability and of instability in a relationship. It finds that if a group is dissolved, as one of the parameters is reduced, it cannot necessarily be restored by once more increasing that parameter; that is, a group—in this case a marriage—may be destroyed by reducing one of the parameters so irretrievably that attempting to restore it by increasing the parameter becomes impossible. There is a point, in brief, when marriages are so severely strained that mending them becomes impossible.

All these models may be useful in interpreting or explaining marital adjustments, although with varying degrees of frequency. Models which specify explicit communication will not fit marriages in which communication tends to be tacit; models which specify verbal interaction will be more appropriate for the interactional pattern of marital relationships than one which does not. For a relationship as diverse and as complex as marriage, a variety of models is necessary.

One family of models, based on the theory of games of strategy, especially as modified by Schelling, is of such special interest that it is discussed now in greater detail.

THE MIXED-MOTIVE MODELS

There are few if any marital adjustment situations which conform to *all* of the following specifications of classic zero-sum game theory: (a) one which states that what one wins the other loses; (b) one which states that the payoffs for all outcomes are identical, signs opposite, for both players; and (c) one which requires the existence of uncertainty and/or risk.

There are, to be sure, some kinds of situations which might fit the first of these specifications, such as one in which the wife wished to rear the children in one religious faith, the husband in another. Or one in which the wife wanted the husband to reject the proffered job that would require the family to move away from the home community and in which the husband wanted to accept it. Indeed, the specification of the marital relationship as a unit often imposes this zero-sum characteristic on it; there is an either-or choice. In such situations only one partner can win.

There may also be, perhaps, situations in which the second specification holds, the payoffs for all outcomes being identical, signs reversed, for both players. The loss "means" as much to one as the concomitant "gain" does for the other. If money has exactly the same value for both of the spouses, this specification of classic game theory is met in situations involving the expenditure of family income. The "loss" to the husband in not getting the power mower exactly balances the "gain" to the wife in getting the new drapes for the living room. But even so, we are, as all students of the subject recognize, on perilous ground when we come so near to comparing the utilities or values of one person with those of another.

So, also, is the third specification for the application of classic game theory—the existence of either uncertainty or risk—uncharacteristic of the marital relationship. A major idea in game theory, viewed normatively, is to guide the players when they do not really know what they are up against; it is designed to help them decide what to do when they do not have all the information they need about the probable behavior of their opponents. It is a gambler's tool. Such uncertainty is not a major characteristic of marriage. There will, of course, be some day-by-day adjustment situations of most marriages in which uncertainty and/or risk are involved. What kind of mood will John be in when he gets home from work today? Mary doesn't know exactly. If he is in a good mood, strategy A will yield her the highest payoff; but if he is in a bad mood, strategy B is her best bet. She has to decide before he gets home. She

might try "espionage," that is, have one of the children telephone him to see if she can judge from his reaction what his frame of mind is; or she might depend on her past observations or knowledge of his behavior. Monday is the day he has to make a report to the committee; he was uncertain about it when he left; he will probably feel frustrated and depressed. Conclusion: don't try strategy A. He will say "no," and once having committed himself, he won't feel like changing when his mood lifts. Or, Monday is the day he gets his citation for best performance in his department this year; he will probably feel elated and on top of the world. Conclusion: strike while the iron is hot; he will be in an expansive mood tonight and ready to concede anything. And once having promised, he won't be in a position to renege. In such situations, there is an element of uncertainty and/or risk involved in a marital adjustment. But here, again, as in the other game-theory specifications, the most characteristic aspect of marital adjustment situations is not the presence of uncertainty and/or risk, but rather, in fact, the opposite. "Winning" often depends on "making known" one's behavior.

Although any one, or even two, of the specifications of the zero-sum situation may be present in marital relationships, it is not likely that all of them will be. For this reason, the model that perhaps best fits the usual marital situation is the so-called cooperative or mixed-motive game in which (a) if one wins the other does not automatically lose, that is, in which both may win—or lose; (b) the payoffs or values for all outcomes may be different for husband and for wife rather than identical with reversed signs; and (c) in which there is little or no uncertainty and/or risk. Strange as it may seem, the model which least well fits the specifications of classic game theory appears to be the most useful one in explaining or interpreting marital adjustments.

Schelling (1960), by shearing or peeling away many of the basic specifications of game theory—especially the specification of uncertainty and/or risk—has given us a valuable way of looking at marital adjustment situations. Perhaps it is no longer game theory, but it is based on concepts borrowed from game theory.

The cooperative game, as Luce and Raiffa (1957) call it, or the mixed-motive game, as Schelling (1960) calls it, is one in which (a) there are both conflicting and common interests in the relationship, a situation characteristic of marriage; (b) there is not a zero-sum situation but one in which both partners can either win or lose; (c) the values of all outcomes may differ for both spouses not only in sign but also in magnitude; and (d) the strategic use, not of secrecy and misleading information, but of precisely the opposite—information convincingly communicated—is important. It is this last-named specification which is of major importance.

There is probably no contrast more striking, in the comparison of the mixed-motive and the pure-conflict (zero-sum) game, than the significance of having one's own strategy found out and appreciated by the opponent. Hardly anything captures the spirit of the zero-sum game quite so much as the importance of "not being found out" and of employing a mode of decision that is proof against deductive anticipation by the other player. Hardly anything epitomizes strategic behavior in the mixed-motive game so much as the advantage of being able to adopt a mode of behavior that the other party will take for granted (Schelling 1960, p. 160).

In his analysis of the so-called coordination game, Schelling makes a great deal of expectations and in his analysis of bargaining he shows how the payoffs—since there is no longer uncertainty and/or risk present perhaps the term should be value instead of payoff—of opponents can be changed by proclaiming loudly one's own strategies and thus forcing opponents to do something they would originally have preferred not to do.

Referring back to Table 1, two relevant situations will be described here. One is the so-called coordination game characterized by the presence of both common and conflicting interests and the absence of communication (Situation C); here *expectations* are the key elements. It is, of course, true that expectations are fundamental in all strategic games; but there is a difference. In the classic game, strategies do not change the incentive structure of an opponent; the payoffs are not altered by the expectations. Each player expects his opponent to select a strategy which will maximize his gains or minimize his losses; he bases his own strategy on this expectation. But in the coordination situation, the players can change the incentive structure of their opponents. In Matrix 1 (See Appendix), for example, it is Mary's expectation that John will expect her to come to the prize fight that gives this outcome so much value to her. If, however, the nature of their relationship were such that she could expect him to expect her to go to the concert and therefore to go there himself, outcome 1A would have a higher value.

The other relevant situation is the bargaining game, characterized by the presence of both common and conflicting interests and the presence of communication (Situation D); here a convincingly communicated *commitment,* which nails down the expectation, is the basic element.

Coordination

No conflict present. Problems of coordination may arise even though there is no conflict present; if for some reason or other communication is impossible, how should each spouse act in order to achieve a common goal (Situation B)? A husband and wife, for example, get separated in a crowded department store; they want to locate one another in the shortest time. They have this common interest and no conflicting interests. What should they do? How do they "adjust" to one another in such a situation? Each has to "read the other's mind." Success depends on each acting in a way that will conform to what each expects the other to expect of him or her. By accurate expectations of what each will expect the other to do, and by acting in accord with these expectations, they coordinate their behavior and achieve their common goal.

Conflict present. More difficult are coordination adjustments when there are conflicting, as well as common, interests present (Situation C). How, in the absence of communication, does adjustment take place? "The problem is to develop a modus vivendi when one or both parties either cannot or will not negotiate explicitly or when neither would trust the other with respect to any agreement explicitly reached" (Schelling, 1960, p. 53). This kind of situation might arise in a marriage during a quarrel in which communication has broken down. Neither one wishes the breach to proceed to the point of divorce; this much they have in common. But neither one wishes to recognize the other to the extent of open interaction and explicit communication.

Coordination under these circumstances can be achieved on the basis of mutual knowledge of expectations. A trivial example will illustrate. John and Mary quarreled at breakfast over how to spend the evening. John wanted to go to a prize fight, Mary to a concert. This is the conflicting interest. But neither wanted to go anywhere alone, and neither wanted to stay home, together or alone. This is the common interest. In the absence of communication, how can they coordinate their activities to attain the most satisfactory result? John would rather go to a concert with Mary than to a prize fight alone; Mary would rather go to a prize fight with John than to a concert alone; both would rather go to either event than stay home.

If Matrix 1 (see Appendix) accurately reflects the values for both John and Mary of the several outcomes in this situation,

the choice narrows down to outcome concert–concert or outcome prize fight–prize fight. Thus Mary, on the basis of her knowledge of her husband, might reason as follows: "John knows I know how much he enjoys a prize fight; he'll take it for granted that I'll give up the concert tonight, so he'll expect me to meet him at the prize fight. I might as well go. It's worth more being with him there than either with him at home or alone at the concert." John might, on the basis of his knowledge of his wife, reason like this: "Mary knows how much I enjoy a prize fight and she wouldn't stand in the way of my seeing this one, so I'll go ahead and meet her there." On the basis of their knowledge of one another they know what to expect— "to take for granted"—and hence what to do to optimize their payoffs or values. The situation might, of course, have been reversed: he might have said, "She knows I know how much she wants to go to the concert tonight so she'll expect me to go there; I'd rather go there with her than to the prize fight alone." And she might have said, "He knows how much I want to hear the concert tonight and he wouldn't stand in the way of my going, so I'll go and meet him there."

As a matter of empirical fact, however, in a satisfactory marriage, the chances are greater that Mary will coordinate her behavior to adjust to John's expectations rather than the other way round, for it has been found that congruence between a wife's perception of her husband and his perception of himself is related to satisfactory marriage whereas the reverse was not found. The author concluded that "if it is the wife who does the adjusting [as Burgess and Locke and as Goode contend], it is to the benefit of the relationship if she knows what she's adjusting to! If she sees the husband as he sees himself, she is better able to make adjustments which bring more satisfaction to the marriage" (Luckey, 1960, p. 157).

The above situation, whoever expects the

other to conform to his (her) preferred outcome, assumes a good relationship between the spouses. But expectations can also be used negatively. In reverse coordination, one spouse can use expectations to reduce the satisfaction of the other. For it is always possible for one or the other to "cut off his nose to spite his face." In such a case, the values in the above matrix change so that Mary, let us say, now derives more satisfaction from going to the concert alone or staying home, either alone or with John, than she does from being with him either at the concert or the prize fight. Reducing his pleasure rather than enhancing her own is her objective (Matrix 1A, Appendix). "I'll show him" by acting contrary to his expectations, by disappointing him, reflects her attitude. It is worth being miserable herself to make him miserable. People who know one another well know best how to hurt, as well as how to please, one another. Now, both can lose.

Ordinarily, however, if the situation in Matrix 1 rather than Matrix 1A is a true reflection of the situation, each optimizes his payoff or satisfaction by acting on the expectations of the other, for an

. . . odd characteristic of . . . [this type of situation] is that neither . . . can gain by outsmarting the other. Each loses unless he does exactly what the other expects him to do. Each party is the prisoner or the beneficiary of their mutual expectations; no one can disavow his own expectation of what the other will expect him to expect to be expected to do. The need for agreement overrules the potential disagreement, and each must concert with the other or lose altogether (Schelling, 1960, p. 60).

The precise decision will depend, of course, on the satisfaction resulting from each outcome for each player. The end result is that conforming to the expectations of the other yields the maximum satisfaction or payoff.

There is, of course, no assurance that coordination without communication will succeed, or that it will yield results as favorable as or more favorable than those achievable by explicit interaction. A set of experiments has convinced Schelling that in most such situations, "the outcome is determined by something that is fairly arbitrary. It is not a particularly 'fair' outcome, from either an observer's point of view or the points of view of the participants" (1960, p. 65). He concludes also that "when agreement must be reached with incomplete communication, the participants must be ready to allow the situation itself to exercise substantial constraint over the outcome; specifically, a solution that discriminates against one party or the other or even involves 'unnecessary' nuisance to both of them may be the only one on which their expectations can be coordinated" (p. 75). In explicit interaction a wife might be able to "bargain" for the husband's going to the concert; but in the absence of communication, this is not possible, and her best bet is to do what she expects her husband to expect her to do.

The possibility of error in coordinating behavior without communication highlights the importance of keeping the channels of communication open. "At a minimum," says Schelling, "this might mean assuring that a surrender offer could be heard and responded to by either side" (p. 78). After a quarrel it is important that channels for communication be open enough at least to send apologies and an "I'm sorry, let's kiss and make up."

Schelling, speaking of war, says that practice in the use of referees and mediators might be a useful prior arrangement to serve as a coordinating mechanism in a serious crisis. There is thus established a precedent which both parties might be expected to recognize and which would thus coordinate their behavior in a situation where communication has broken down. An analogy in marital adjustments would be prior agreement on a trusted mutual friend or even professional counselor to whom both would be expected to turn when communication broke down.

In the coordination situation, each spouse is manipulating or influencing the behavior of the other by an "unseen hand" or by "remote control," so to speak. Each is adjusting his (her) own behavior to the expected expectations of the other. The matter of expectations is related no doubt to the phenomenon of social or interpersonal perception, on which a fairly large literature of empirical research has developed in recent years.

The bulk of theory and interpretations of research findings indicate that interpersonal behavior is closely related to, if not dependent upon, the way in which individuals perceive themselves, others, and the situation of the moment. Both the role theorist and the phenomenologist would agree that where individuals perceive similarly, and frames of reference are thus shared, communication is easier, and the relationship existing between the individuals concerned is more satisfactory (Luckey, 1960, p. 153).

In general, marriages in which the wife perceives her husband as he perceives himself tend to show higher marital satisfaction scores than those in which she does not (Luckey, 1960). The implication is that she knows what he expects of her and can therefore coordinate her behavior with his on her expectations of his expectations.

In a bargaining type of situation, these expectations become explicit. Ego knows exactly what to expect from Alter, not on the basis of social perception, but because Alter has committed himself to a certain course of action and has communicated it convincingly to Ego.

Bargaining

Popular wisdom has long recognized that marital adjustments are a matter of give and take. The conception of the relations between the sexes as a bargaining situation is very old. Quite aside from the patent form of bride purchase or the dowry, the psychological give and take between men and women has long been viewed as essentially a duel of wits for advantage. The

courts of love in the twelfth century dealt with the nature of such bargains: who owed what to whom and why. A knight must perform certain feats in order to obligate his lady to become his love. ". . . in the service of love, pain and sorrow were necessities; . . . there was never a joy which was not purchased at the expense of a hundred griefs" (Rowbotham, 1895, p. 240). The courtly give and take or bargain was highly conventionalized; its rules were enforced in the so-called courts of love.

It was Willard Waller who formulated most elaborately and insightfully the bargaining model of relations between the sexes. His application was primarily to the premarital period, but the fundamental processes are the same, although the specific "goods" involved in the exchange may vary greatly—love, mink coats, sex relations, approval, "freedom," etc.

The kind of bargaining which has to do with marriage has had a long history, and folk wisdom recognizes its importance. As in dating, so in marriage, one gets about what he deserves according to the accepted standards of the group. In the simple, homogenous group, this is very clear. In modern society, groups are confused, and cultural imperatives are in conflict, and therefore the nature of the bargaining process is more complex and its outlines are confused. Further, the current emphasis upon marriage for love causes the bargaining element to be concealed, and yet no thoughtful person will contend that it is not present (Waller & Hill, 1951, p. 160).

These intuitive insights have been refined and incorporated in the mixed-motive model. It is specified that some bargain or exchange is considered preferable to none at all by both parties; this guarantees a common interest. If one partner does not feel this way, he is not likely to enter the relationship; or if he does, to remain long in it. The bargaining model is suitable in any situation "in which adversaries watch and interpret each other's behavior, each aware that his own actions are being interpreted and anticipated, each acting with a view to the expectations that he creates" (Schelling, 1960, p. 21).

These expectations are established now not by social or interpersonal perception, as in the coordination game, but rather by convincing and explicit commitments, clearly communicated. Commitment is thus a central core in Schelling's analysis of bargaining. One of the players makes a commitment to a specified line of action rather than to any other; he convinces his opponent that he is committed to this line of action. There must be no uncertainty about this; the commitment must be binding. It is precisely the lack of uncertainty, the complete conviction on the part of the opponent, that renders the commitment effective.

In Matrix 2 (Appendix), for example, the usual solution would be for Ego to select strategy A, knowing that Alter would expect him to do so and hence would himself select 1 rather than 2, even though 2 would yield him a higher payoff. That is, under classic game theory, each would expect the other to expect his opponent to behave in a way to minimize expected losses or to maximize expected gains. But suppose that Alter makes it unequivocally clear that no matter what Ego does he is going to select strategy 2. Ego now has no better alternative than B. Alter has changed Ego's expectations with respect to his behavior. By such a commitment, one party can manipulate the other.

Manipulation may permeate any bargaining situation, as, indeed, any interactional one. In manipulation (Situation D as shown in Table 1) there is an attempt to place the burden of change or adjustment on the other partner. The object is to change the opponent's payoff or satisfaction matrix by removing all uncertainty from the alternatives, so that his problem becomes one of simple maximization, in one's own favor. The manipulating party removes any uncertainty from his own behavior by committing himself unequivocally to a certain course of action.

But a commitment is useless unless the opponent knows what it is: a threat, for example, cannot be made if the opponent does not hear it or understand it or believe it; a promise has no effect if it is not received or if it is not believed. Serious strategic errors in choice of behavior may result from lack or defects in the system of communication. So communication becomes extremely important; it is of the essence. Not secrecy and surprise, not deception and misrepresentation but, on the other hand, convincing proof of what one is going to do is the important characteristic of this situation.

Basic, then, to the strategic moves about to be presented, is a firm commitment persuasively communicated; this commitment eliminates uncertainty. Once Ego has committed himself and convinced Alter of his commitment, Alter is in no doubt about what will happen. He is no longer making a decision in the face of uncertainty; the probability is 1.00 that Ego will behave in a certain way. His choice is now between the alternatives which net him most; and Ego's behavior has predetermined this by means of his strategic moves.

Three basic strategic moves are: "first move," strategic threat or "second move," and strategic promises. All depend on commitments:

If the essence of a game of strategy is the dependence of each person's proper choice of action on what he expects the other to do, it may be useful to define a "strategic move" as follows: A strategic move is one that influences the other person's choice, in a manner favorable to one's self, by affecting the other person's expectations of how one's self will behave. One constrains the partner's choice by constraining one's own behavior. The object is to set up for one's self and communicate persuasively to the other player a mode of behavior (including conditional responses to the other's behavior) that leaves the other a simple maximization problem whose solution for him is the optimum for one's self, and to destroy the other's ability to do the same (Schelling, 1960, p. 160).

"First move." If one party can commit himself irrevocably to a certain position as described above, and convince the other party that his position is indeed irrevocable no matter what, he has won. The other party can only take it or leave it and, by definition, any solution is preferable to a breakdown in the relationships. In order to make first move effective, the commitment must be so convincing that there can be no question about it; preferably there is a penalty attached to nonfulfillment.

The *fait accompli* is a form of first move. "I've already bought the tickets to the concert; we'll have to go," says the spouse who did not want to go to the prize fight. Or a situation is created in which the commitment is validated by putting the onus on some third party. "I can't go to the party with you tonight, dear, much as I'd like to because I promised the boss I'd work tonight; if I don't he'll fire me." She cannot bargain against such a commitment; he has won.

Strategic threats. Strategic threats, like "first move," depend on commitments, but they are characteristic of situations where the opponent has "first move." They are, in fact, an attempt to gain the advantage of "first move."

The threat differs from the ordinary commitment . . . in that it makes one's course of action *conditional* on what the other player does. While the commitment fixes one's course of action, the threat fixes a course of reaction, of response to the other player. The commitment is a means of gaining *first move* in a game in which first move carries an advantage; the threat is a commitment to a strategy for second move (Schelling, 1960, p. 124).

A theoretical distinction is made between a warning, which is also conditional, and a strategic threat. The essential characteristic of a warning is that it reminds the other party what will happen if he does, or does not do, something or other; it conveys information. In this sense it may be mutually beneficial; it prevents an inadvert-

ent outcome by improving the warned person's understanding. In a warning, there is a clear incentive on the part of the warning person to do what he is warning the other that he will do. "If you continue to charge so many things, I'll refuse to pay the bills," is a warning. The husband has an incentive to do what he warns the wife he will do.

A strategic threat, however, is a more complex phenomenon. The person who makes a strategic threat surrenders choice, renounces alternatives; more important, he changes his own incentive structure in such a way as to constrain his opponent. He commits himself to a course of action which he, as well as his opponent, wishes to avoid, a course of action, further, which has no necessarily logical relationship to the action of his opponent.

In a warning, there is a logical and understandable relationship between the action of Ego and the reaction of Alter. There is a tit-for-tat situation. It is easy to see why the husband will refuse to pay the bills if the wife continues to overspend. His incentive is clear; he will save money. In a strategic-threat situation, however, there is no necessarily logical relationship between the action of Ego and the threatened reaction of Alter, such, for example, as going through bankruptcy. Alter must therefore create an incentive. He can do this by making the threatened behavior preferable to any alternative. In both warning and strategic threat, there are dire consequences; but in the strategic threat they are made relatively less dire for the threatener than alternatives and more dire for the threatened than alternatives. Matrix 3 (Appendix) illustrates the strategic threat.

A strategic threat places on the threatened person the responsibility for the dire consequences to the threatener himself. It shifts blame. "If you continue to run home to your mother, I'll go back to drinking," says the husband as he brings home a fifth of whiskey. In order to be even more convincing, he tells her he has told his cronies what he will do. Neither he nor she wants him to go back to drinking; the strategic threat now puts her in the position of having to save him from doing something he doesn't want to do anyway in order to save his face vis-à-vis his friends and herself. He has changed the game. He has given himself an incentive (face-saving) to do something he prefers not to do (return to drinking). "If you don't stop running around with other women, I'll divorce you," says a wife, "and I have told mother so." Neither wants a divorce. She has given herself an incentive (again, face-saving vis-à-vis her mother) to do something she prefers not to do. She is putting him in the position of being to blame for the divorce, for ruining the marriage which neither wants to end. The threatened person must, in effect, protect the threatener in order to protect himself.

To be effective, of course, strategic threats must be credible. "If you don't get home for meals on time I'll kill myself" is an empty, meaningless threat for which it would be difficult to create a credible incentive. But "if you don't get home for meals on time I'll simply not eat at all" might be a credible threat; in order to keep himself from the onus of responsibility for her hunger and malnutrition, he must get to meals on time. In order to be credible, the strategic threat must make carrying out the threat the only alternative; reneging must be more painful than carrying it out. Otherwise, it may be taken as a bluff and called.

The strategic threat is especially interesting for interpreting marital relationships because its effectiveness is often based on love, pity, forbearance rather than—as in classic game theory, especially zero-sum game theory—on fear and hostility. The strategic threat is effective against people who care. One coerces an opponent by presenting him with an alternative that he just can't bring himself to select unless he is inhuman. It uses coercion by the self. It is the kind of thing that Gandhi exploited so successfully. The Hindus who chained

themselves to railroad tracks knew that the engineer would not run over them; he couldn't, not because his engine was incapable of doing it, but because his self was. They won because their opponent was unable to select so horrible an alternative. Hunger strikes represent another example. The strategic threat puts both parties in a situation where, in order to save himself— literally "his self"—the threatened person must also save the threatening person.

Strategic promises. Strategic promises differ from conventional promises in that they are designed to induce or prevent behavior in an opponent. "If you promise to give up drinking, I'll promise to be more careful about keeping the house in order" is a bilateral commitment, similar to a bargaining situation. Sometimes unilateral promises may be used to get the opponent to do something good for both partners. "I promise to take you to the theater tonight" is reassuring to the wife; she doesn't have to promise to stay home. Being home and ready to go to the theater is more rewarding to both her and her husband than going out to play bridge with the girls.

To be effective as strategic moves, promises must truly commit. A person who offers no guarantee that he will fulfil his promise will find it hard to convince people; he must prove that he will fulfil it. He must also, if he wishes future promises to be effective, carry out his commitment. If he welshes on a promise, he will find it difficult to use it again; he cannot induce anyone to act in his favor, no matter what he promises. There is hardly anything more devastating than to find oneself faced with a dishonored promise after one has based his own choice of action on confidence in its fulfilment. The young man promises to marry the girl; she has sex relations with him. He reneges on his promise. "But you promised!" He replies cynically, "What are you going to do about it?" The promise to marry is usually validated by publishing banns or by getting a license or by wearing an engagement ring; there is now some penalty for reneging on the promise. "I want it in writing," or "Let's tell the family," or "a legal contract" are ways of giving promises genuine commitment value. Within the marriage relationship, such shoring up of promises is more difficult. Success in the strategic use of promises is more likely to rest on previous behavior, confidence, and trust.

Strategic release from commitments. Important as strategic commitment is—whatever form it may take—there is always a "risk of establishing an immovable position that goes beyond the ability of the other to concede, and thereby provoking the likelihood of stalemate or breakdown" (Schelling, 1960, p. 28). So some provision must be made for tactfully permitting an opponent to get out of commitments without loss of face. One must, in effect, reduce his losses and one's own gains by not "rubbing it in" or gloating over his capitulation.

Or sometimes one party may wish to make a concession and hesitate, not because of the loss of face involved, but because openly making a concession may lead an opponent to misinterpret his position. It may not only be construed as capitulation, but it may also "mark a prior commitment as a fraud, and make the adversary skeptical of any new pretense at commitment. One, therefore, needs an 'excuse' for accommodating his opponent, preferably a rationalized reinterpretation of the original commitment, one that is persuasive to the adversary himself" (Schelling, 1960, p. 34). The wife, that is, must persuade her husband that he is not really committed; or that he is not really giving in; or that his original commitment was genuine and he is acting on it; or that he has miscalculated his commitment; or that no precedent is being established; etc. She saves not only his face but also his reputation for use in future commitments. This verbal use of strategy has been called "casuistry." She also protects him from his friends or family by making it impossible for them to determine whether he has held to his commitment or not.

. . . when the opponent has resolved to make a moderate concession one may help him by proving that he *can* make a moderate concession consistent with his former position, and that if he does there are no grounds for believing it to reflect on his original principles. One must seek, in other words, a rationalization by which to deny oneself too great a reward from the opponent's concession, otherwise the concession will not be made (Schelling, 1960, p. 35).

There is no "I told you so," no gloating, no emphasis on the concession; but rather, face-saving and casual understatement.

Refusing communication. A major defense against strategic moves is simply not to permit oneself to be communicated with. It is often to Alter's advantage to be stupid, uncomprehending. This characteristic of the mixed-motive model helps to explain why it is that the weaker or the stupider partners in a marriage often seem to have the upper hand. They refuse to listen or they cannot understand, and thus cut off communication; this gives them, in effect, the advantage of first move. The partner must take it or leave it, and, often, he takes it. Or, if they listen, they fail to understand and thus cut themselves off from having to give. Marriages of this kind may last for years; they illustrate for the mate who cannot "get through" to the other the quiet desperation that Thoreau noted in the lives of many people. These marriages last as long as the rewards of remaining married exceed the costs, or as long as there is no preferable alternative. The time may come, of course, when the payoff or value of this outcome changes: it is no longer worth the costs to remain married; alternative outcomes seem preferable. Desertion or divorce may result. The spouse who has refused for years to accept communication may, in all sincerity, be surprised to find that the marriage has failed. "I just don't understand," he might say, after never having permitted himself to be enlightened.

Extortion and blackmail. A spouse who "has something" on a mate is in a position to exact blackmail. He (she) must pay to keep her (him) quiet. A spouse who is in a position to do a great deal of damage to a mate can use extortion. If a man's position in the community or his career would be greatly damaged by a divorce, his wife is in a strategic position to demand payment for being discreet. The time may come, of course, when he may feel that it is no longer worth while to protect his position at the expense of bribing his wife. The problem of limits would become involved. How far can she go before his value structure changes?

Despite the fact that the mixed-motive model is useful to explain and interpret hostile and fear-motivated behavior, however, it is most useful because it explains and interprets manipulative behavior based on love or compassion or pity or forbearance, as noted above. A spouse may win because he or she knows that the other "just can't" do what is required to win. The wife accepts an invitation in public, knowing that her husband "just can't" embarrass and humiliate her before others by rejecting the invitation she so obviously wishes to accept. Or the wife puts herself in a situation that will end in great embarrassment unless the husband does something or other, knowing that he "just can't" do this to her. Or the wife bails her husband out of a situation because she "just can't" let him down. A characteristic of the mixed-motive game, in brief, and one that makes it especially relevant for understanding marital adjustments, is that the preferred alternatives of an opponent may be changed by manipulating the matrix, by making the payoff or value of one alternative too costly in terms of pity, self-acceptance, self-image, self-conception, or what have you. One player makes a sacrifice of his gain because he "just can't" pursue his advantage. The loss of winning is greater than the loss of

losing. He would hate himself if he won under these circumstances; he has to lose. The payoff for a strategy which demands giving in may be greater than for a strategy which demands winning. The wife may get a higher return for making a sacrifice than for insisting on her rights.

The Detroit study referred to above concluded that power in the sense of decision-making tended to gravitate toward those who were competent to exercise it.

. . . the balance of power . . . is determined by the comparative resourcefulness of the two partners and by the life circumstances within which they live. . . . Husbands can no longer take for granted the *authority* held by older generations of men. No longer is the husband able to exercise power just because he is "the man of the house." Rather, he must prove his right to power, or win power by virtue of his own skills and accomplishments in competition with his wife (Blood & Wolfe, 1960, p. 29).

Yet in situations where decision-making involves conflict, it is sometimes noted that the less competent, the less able spouse wins. Strategic models help to explain this illogical situation when it occurs.

The mixed-motive model is valuable also because it highlights the fact that fairness or justice is not a necessary attribute of a marital adjustment. There are some situations in which men have an intrinsic advantage, others in which women do. Since, for example, sexual deprivation appears to be harder on men than on women, women have an advantage here. Women can use sex rejection as a strategic "chip" more successfully than men can. Contrariwise, men are usually the breadwinners; control of the pocketbook may give the husband an advantage in other areas. The double standard is not "fair" either; women are more likely than men to be condemned in extramarital affairs. Even within the relationship itself, it is by no means "fair" that the person who values the marriage more should be at a strategic disadvantage vis-à-vis the spouse who values it less. It is not at all "fair" that the rigid, unyielding spouse should dominate in the relationship, or that the stupid one should have his (her) way. It is not "fair" that the more compassionate one, the more understanding one, the more generous one should yield to the less compassionate, understanding, or generous one. The mixed-motive model helps us understand why it is so difficult to achieve a "fair" adjustment in marital relationships.

Although we noted earlier that our concern would not be with the substantive areas in which marital adjustments took place, pointing out that they might be required in any area of human life, there is one area so universal and so basic that no discussion of the adjustments of marital partners would be complete without including it, namely, sexual relations. We turn, therefore, to a consideration of this area of adjustment.

SEXUAL ADJUSTMENTS IN MARITAL RELATIONSHIPS

The area of sex has received more attention than almost any other in the study of marital adjustments. Because of its intense emotional significance and the powerful sanctions regulating it, it has been the subject of great controversy, so that much of the research is polemical in nature. There are, for example, those who find a sexual difficulty at the root of every problem of marriage. There are others who, although recognizing the existence of such difficulties in problem marriages, argue nevertheless that they may be the result rather than the cause and, further, that sexual difficulties may and often do occur in nonproblem marriages also (Terman, 1938). Sexual adjustment, in brief, is not the same as marital happiness. [For a somewhat parallel, though for the most part complementary, discussion of marital sexual behavior to that found in this section see pp. 605–607 of this Handbook.]

Sexual adjustment, as measured by orgasm capacity in women, has been found

to be related to premarital sexual experiences which resulted in orgasm (Kinsey et al., 1953), but no relationship, one way or another, has been found between sexual adjustment, again as measured by orgasm, and premarital sexual experience per se (Hamblin & Blood, 1957). And if marital happiness rather than sexual adjustment is the dependent variable, there is little if any relationship with premarital experience (Burgess & Wallin, 1953; Davis, 1929; Locke, 1951; Terman, 1938).

The above discussion referred primarily to premarital sex relations of women; some claim that premarital sexual experience hinders sexual adjustment in marriage because it accustoms the male, at any rate, to a casual relationship which is dysfunctional in marital adjustments.

Although the three dimensions of adjustment situations—differences, communication, and quality of the relationship—apply to sexual, like any other, adjustments, they operate within the limits of powerful cultural restraints. The sexual adjustments of husbands and wives are greatly influenced by the institutional or cultural ambience in which they occur.

Institutional Factors

In the nineteenth century, the Victorian definition of the sexual situation specified that normal women were nonsexual. They dutifully submitted to their husbands, however, and found their satisfaction in his. Female sexuality, especially orgasm, was never discussed by decent people, in private or in public. If a man was not a good sex partner, no one was ever the wiser: his wife had no standard to judge him by and other men had no way of knowing. Under these circumstances, women were protected from frustration, and men were protected from feelings of failure. A good sexual adjustment was one in which a wife was dutifully submissive to her husband and in which the husband was moderate and considerate in his demands. With such modest criteria of success, sexual adjustment was not too difficult to achieve. Women expected little; little was what they got.

At the turn of the century, however, a new definition of sexual adjustment began to appear. It now became standard doctrine for writers of marriage manuals that a woman should share in the pleasures of sex; that if she did not, it was the fault of her partner, for it was his responsibility to waken her responses, to play upon her body as upon a musical instrument, to give her pleasure, and hence to enhance his own.

The results of this change in orientation were profound for both men and women (Sapirstein, 1948). For women it raised great expectations; they were no longer to be merely submissive subjects but active participants in sex; they, too, were to know what this ecstasy was. When they found that sex was not what they had been led to believe, or when they found themselves not responding as they had expected or as the books prescribed, and when psychiatrists began to label them neurotic if they differed in response from the psychiatrists' norm, they became dissatisfied, frustrated, resentful. Many blamed their husbands, as the marriage-manual doctrine had taught them to do.

For men, also, the new definition was traumatic. The full responsibility for successful response in their wives was now placed squarely on their shoulders; if their wives failed to achieve sexual ecstasy, they felt it was their fault; they had failed. There must be something wrong with them as sex partners. They even felt guilty if they achieved orgasm and their wives did not. The stage was set for serious disturbance.

It is only recently that scientific research has begun to illuminate the biological similarities and differences between the sexes; many of them are contrary to both the theory of natural female frigidity of the nineteenth century and that of identical sexuality in men and women of the early twentieth century.

The Difference Dimension

Frequency of sex desire. Although the two sexes may be well adapted to one another for reproductive purposes, some of these differences may have become maladaptive and, indeed, be among the differences most requiring adjustment. Before the advent of culture, or when culture was still primitive and reproduction a major life task, it was adaptive to have the male sexually ready and responsive at all times to ensure coitus whenever the female was receptive. This disparity in sex drive—estimated on the basis of data by Kinsey to be about seven to one at the time of marriage (Bernard, 1956)—is no longer functional. In an elaborate cultural setting in which reproduction is no longer a major life preoccupation, the constant sexual readiness of males may actually be maladaptive. Reproduction is no longer necessary on so prodigal a scale as in earlier times, yet male sexual readiness remains. It is distracting to the males themselves and may even be annoying to the females. It remains one of the central problems in sexual adjustment.

The greater frequency of sex desire, as measured by frequency of "outlet," in men than in women was documented in Kinsey and associates' (1948; 1953) two reports. At the time of marriage, in fact, the difference in frequency is at a maximum. The men remain more active than women throughout their lives, although the difference declines. Thus, the ratio between the sexes is reduced to one-and-a-half to one in the later years. This difference in frequency of desire, once adaptive, is one of the most commonly reported problems in the sexual adjustments of marriage.

Sexual stimulability. Closely related to frequency of sex desire—in fact, perhaps one aspect of it—is the greater sexual stimulability of men than of women. Women are better able than men to tolerate abstinence; they are less driven, therefore, to seek release of tension through orgasm. The genital organs of women are more protected from stimulation than are those of men. Kinsey found only one area of stimulation —verbal—in which women equalled men. Thus, although there are more erogenous zones in women, they are more protected from excitation than are the bodies of men.

Orgasm experience. With respect to orgasm, the findings of recent research highlight both similarities and differences between the sexes. It was only in the 1930's that a research literature on the nature of female orgasm began to develop. What was it like? How did it compare with male orgasm? Why did some women experience it and others not? Female orgasm began to be one of the common variables in studies of marital adjustments. The nature of female orgasm became a mooted scientific question. There were some who argued that it must be vaginal in order to be normal; clitoral orgasm was infantile (Bergler, 1948; Deutsch, 1944-1945). There were others, however, who argued that orgasm must be clitoral, since the vagina was very poorly supplied with nerve endings—surgery could be performed upon it without anesthesia— whereas the clitoris was as well supplied with nerve endings as the penis (Kinsey et al., 1953). Recently, Masters has shown that orgasm can result from breast stimulation, so that neither the exclusively vaginal nor the exclusively clitoral school of thought with respect to female orgasm is correct (personal communication, January 8, 1962).

First Kinsey and then Masters were the major contributors to a solution of the problem of the nature of female orgasm. Kinsey in 1953 argued that orgasm, with the exception of ejaculation, was physiologically identical in women and in men, as shown by bodily reactions, and Masters in laboratory studies showed conclusively that Kinsey was correct. His laboratory studies of female orgasm showed it to be similar to male orgasm, again, of course, with the exception of ejaculation (Masters & Johnson, 1961). Even more surprising, in view of popular belief, was the fact that once the method of producing orgasm was learned, women had greater orgasmic capacity than men. Among Kinsey's thousands of subjects, the person with greatest orgasmic experience was a woman, and Masters found women better subjects than men because they could experience multiple orgasm more readily than men (paper presented before American Anthropological Society, Philadelphia, November 17, 1961).

There are differences, however. Males early become aware of the nature of orgasm: they experience it at a fairly young age; they do not have to be taught how to bring it about; the penis is open to stimulation. Women more rarely experience orgasm spontaneously during waking hours; most of them have to learn how to bring themselves to climax. Many do not even know what they are supposed to be experiencing until they learn from observing their husbands or male partners. Some may live their whole lives without ever learning how to bring orgasm about. Unless an active learning effort is made, some women do not experience climax. And whether or not the learning effort will be made depends on a complex of personal, cultural, and interpersonal factors.

It was once held that orgasm capacity was a physiological trait: some women did not have it; they were frigid by genetic makeup (Terman, 1938). Others held orgasm inadequacy to be the result of cultural training and inhibition. Some women could not bring themselves to the point of learning how to achieve orgasm; if they could bring themselves to that point, orgasm capacity could be taken for granted. This point of view appears to be validated by the fact that most women can, by proper coaching and motivation, bring themselves or be brought to orgasm (Dickinson & Beam, 1931).

Another significant difference is that orgasm is not really functional in women, as it is in men. Women can conceive without orgasm; indeed, they can conceive in their sleep. But, although orgasm may occur without ejaculation, ejaculation is not likely to occur without orgasm. Thus, orgasm is functional in men but only of peripheral significance in women. Women may be very happily married without orgasm; it is doubtful if many men could be.

Maturation and aging. The two sexes age in somewhat different ways. In the earliest years, for example, the bones of girls ossify sooner than those of boys; the spurt of preadolescent growth occurs earlier in girls than in boys. And reproductive capacity ceases at an earlier age in women than in men. On the other hand, orgasmic sexuality tends to occur earlier in boys than in girls, and the circulatory system deteriorates about a decade earlier in men than in women. Corresponding to these physiological differences are psychological differences. Despite a somewhat later maturing of active sex desire in girls, they appear to be ready for dating and marriage at an earlier age.

In terms of processes and rates of maturation and aging, it would be suitable for women to be somewhat older than the men they marry. Such a mating pattern would reduce the difference in sex desire in the early years, and it would leave fewer women widowed in the later years. By and large, however, it is customary in most societies for the husband to be older than the wife. This difference may vary as greatly as in traditional India, where a child might have been affianced to an older man at birth and become his wife at the age of 10 or 12. It may be very small, or even reversed, as in our society where the differential has been declining until now it is less than three years.

As in all group comparisons, there is overlapping between the sexes with respect to all these differences. There are some women with greater frequency of desire than most men; there are some women more stimulable than many men; there are some women with greater orgasmic intensity than that of most men; there are girls who are sexually as mature as boys at adolescence, and there are men who have lost reproductive capacity before some women of the same age have. The differences reported above are statistical in nature and not identical in all marriages.

The Communication Dimension

The "language" of love is one of the oldest in human—or, for that matter, prehuman—history. The mating call, the strutting of the male, the elaborate sexual "courtship" of lower animals might legitimately be viewed as tacit communication. Among human beings, tacit communication in the area of sex is far more elaborate even than verbal communication. There are limited ways of communicating love by way of words. But tacit ways are almost unlimited. Facial expression, tone of voice, stance, posture are among the many techniques used.

Despite a general inarticulateness, the subjects in the study by Rainwater and Weinstein (1960)—all of them of lower educational levels—had no difficulty "reading" their husbands; they got the message:

"I am very aware of his desires because he always starts loving me up and playing around" (Rainwater & Weinstein, 1960, p. 16); "I always know he wants to do it" (p. 102); "we can usually tell when we kiss each other goodnight" (p. 105); "I can always tell what's on his mind" (p. 104); "I can tell, believe me!" (p. 113); "I can tell as soon as he walks in the room when he wants it" (p. 114); "I am quite aware of his desires; I couldn't help but be; he lets me know right away when he gets home" (p. 116); "I know when my husband is hot" (p. 134); "He lets me know he wants it in different ways, usually he begins pulling at me" (p. 137).

Such tacit, as opposed to explicit, communication is less commonly successful with women in conveying their message. Either they want to be approached but are not successful in conveying this desire, or they do not especially want to be approached but convey the idea that they do. "Sometimes I'd like to, but once or twice I tried and he acted like he was deaf" (Rainwater & Weinstein, 1960, p. 110). Conversely, the playful coquetry of a woman may be misinterpreted as a "come-on" by a man, but when he gets the supposed message she is indignant and denies that she was leading him on. The dress of women is often designed cleverly to convey sexual complaisance; the wearers are not always aware of the message these clothes are broadcasting. This is especially true in young and inexperienced women.

Because tacit communication is so open to misinterpretation, refusal to be communicated with is a feasible defensive strategy. Even among Rainwater's subjects, women sometimes resorted to refusal to get the message: "Sometimes I tell him not to do it, but mostly I get the older kids around and keep them with me until he gets over it or goes out" (Rainwater & Weinstein, 1960, p. 137). The wife interposes extraneous conversation between her husband's advances and her acceptance of his message. She refuses to be communicated with on the subject of sex.

For some married couples, communication is almost wholly tacit. There may be little verbal interaction in the lower socioeconomic classes, because they are inarticulate and unskilled in language or, in the higher, because there is so much hostility in the relationship that neither trusts himself to talk. In the first type of situation, the relationship may be a good one if both understand the language of tacit communication and accept one another's messages accurately. In both types of situation, however, it *may* be a bad one.

By and large, women prefer a good deal of explicit communication; they like to be made love to verbally as well as physically. They are sensitive to verbal stimulation (Kinsey et al., 1953). A few well-chosen words of tenderness may have greater stimulation value than many minutes of silent physical advances.

Men often find obscene words, especially spoken by women, highly stimulating

sexually. Such use of words, however, can hardly be called explicit communication.

Neither explicit nor tacit communication alone is sufficient to guarantee a successful adjustment in every case; a judicious mixture of the two, different for every marriage, would seem to be the goal. Too much talking without physical expression of affection may result in a cold, clinical approach, chilling rather than endearing; too great dependence on tacit communication without loving words may reduce the relationship to a merely physical one, a level which most women reject. Without the endearing words, women interpret the behavior of men as "wanting me only as a body, not as a person." Words, further, help to integrate sex into the total relationship.

The Quality Dimension

If there is a warm and loving relationship between husband and wife, chances are improved for a successful sexual adjustment. They are motivated to reduce differences and to improve communication, tacit and/or verbal. Contrariwise, if the relationship is hostile, differences escalate and barriers to communication mount, reducing the chances for a successful sexual adjustment.

Conversely, a successful sexual adjustment reverberates throughout the total relationship and tends to improve its quality. Erikson (1963) has defined what he calls a healthy sexual relationship as follows:

Genitality . . . consists in the unobstructed capacity to develop an orgastic potency so free from pregenital interferences that genital libido (not just the sex products discharged in Kinsey's "outlets") is expressed in heterosexual mutuality, with full sensitivity of both penis and vagina, and with a convulsion-like discharge of tension from the whole body. . . . The total fact of finding, via the climactic turmoil of orgasm, a supreme experience of the mutual regulation of two human beings in some way takes the edge off the hostilities and potential rages caused by the oppositeness of male and female, of fact and fancy, of love and hate. Satisfactory sex relations thus make sex less obsessive, overcompensation less necessary, sadistic controls superfluous (p. 265).

The nature of orgasm may be the same, physiologically speaking, for everyone. But there are great individual differences, regardless of sex, in its intensity and meaning. For some individuals, both men and women, orgasm is a convulsive experience, involving almost violent thrashing about of the body. For others, again both men and women, it is a far less turbulent experience—"a quake, a spasm, and a quiver," as one woman described it. As in other areas of sensory experience, there are great individual differences in the enjoyment involved in the experience. There are some people to whom taste is a source of supreme pleasure; they refine their taste and appreciate subtleties with sophisticated gusto. Other people find no such pleasure in eating; they eat to keep themselves alive and one dish tastes much like another. Similarly, there are people to whom music is a source of profound ecstasy; they are moved to the depths of their being by a sequence of chords. Others find nothing at all in music but a lot of sounds, even noises, from which they derive no particular pleasure. Color and line and design, similarly, give enormous sensory satisfaction to some people, little, if any, to others. So, also, with odors and touch. The smell of perfume and the feel of silk are pleasant to some; olfactory and tactual feeling are matters of indifference to others. In every sense department, in brief, there are in both sexes enormous individual differences in pleasureableness. So also with respect to sex. Some people find enormous satisfaction in orgasmic experiences; others find it merely pleasant; some find it indifferent, they can take it or leave it. Some men profess to find orgasm a necessary release but not necessarily a pleasureable one; and Kinsey describes the expression of persons in orgasm as one not of pleasure but of very great strain (Kinsey et al., 1948).

In view of the wide range of individual as well as of sex differences with respect to all the variables involved, the chances of a precise matching in any mating are not high, especially since our institutions forbid any experimentation to determine the extent of sexual congeniality before marriage. The odds against "matching" of most of the variables cannot be determined from the research now available; but Kinsey's data do give frequency of desire as measured by frequency of orgasm in unmarried populations. For the two sexes the distributions he found were as given in Table 2.

TABLE 2

MEDIAN FREQUENCY OF ORGASM IN UNMARRIED MALES AND UNMARRIED FEMALES, BY AGE

Age	Median Frequency of Orgasm in Unmarried Males[a]	Median Frequency of Orgasm in Unmarried Females[b]
16–20	2.90	0.3
21–25	2.70	0.4
26–30	2.65	0.5
31–35	2.40	0.4
36–40	2.12	0.5
41–45	1.85	0.4
46–50	2.04	0.5
51–55		0.3
56–60		0.4

[a] From Kinsey et al. (1948), p. 226.
[b] From Kinsey et al. (1953), p. 549.

Even among persons of similar orgasmic intensity, the significance of the experience may vary. If sex is only one of many interesting and absorbing experiences, it will have relatively less salience than if it is one of very few. The man or woman who enjoys reading, theater, music, the arts, even work, who has, in brief, many competing or at least alternative interests and escapes, will be relatively less dependent on sex than one with few or no competing or alternative interests and escapes.

Theoretically, a good sexual relationship would be one in which frequency of desire, stimulability, orgasmic response, and pleasureableness were identical in both partners or one in which differences were minimal. In such relationships, neither partner would be deprived or overexerted; neither would feel that the other was getting more out of the relationship; both would be equally satisfied with the experience.

Empirical Findings

In view of the nature of the differences between the sexes and the difficulties of communication in this area, it is not surprising that the sexual aspect of marriage is often the most difficult to succeed in and takes the longest to adjust to (Landis, 1946). With respect to the distribution of success in this area, the most valuable piece of research so far has, unfortunately, been limited to subjects from the lower-socioeconomic class and the number of subjects has been small, only 46 men and 50 women. But these defects have been compensated in part by the depth of the interviewing, which makes even limited sampling rewarding (Rainwater & Weinstein, 1960).

On the basis of these interviews, three major patterns of relationship in sex were delineated, two with subtypes, as follows:

    I. Mutual genitality, including not quite half of the subjects, but more common among the upper-lower class (three-fourths) than among the lower-lower class (one-fourth)
      A. "Sexy" spouses
      B. "Loving" spouses
  II. Anxiety-inhibiting relationships, including less than one-third of the subjects
 III. Rejecting relationships, including less than one-third, but more common among lower-lower (40 per cent) than among upper-lower (10 per cent)
      A. Active rejection
      B. Repressive compromise

Mutual genitality may be the result of maturation, learning, or any of the assimilative processes which reduce differences; it may depend on either tacit or explicit communication. In any event, the result is a relationship in which both parties find optimum satisfaction for themselves in the optimum satisfaction of their mates. Those labeled "sexy," both men and women, were those to whom orgasmic experience in and of itself was important; those labeled "loving" were those to whom the nonphysical aspects and the after effects of sex relations were more important. For the "loving" spouses, sex relations are closely linked to other aspects of the marriage.

In the anxiety-inhibiting relationship, the wife is ambivalent. She both wants and yet rejects sex relations. The rejection may be related to fear. The situation is equivocal for the husband; at any particular confrontation is she likely to be receptive or rejecting? She may be motivated to say "no" when she means "yes." She may wish to project the responsibility of the relationship on him in order to blame him if, for example, she becomes pregnant against her will. The matrix of outcome evaluations may be complex.

Active rejecters are the frigid women, women who feel disgust and insult in the act; they condemn their husbands for even wanting sex relations. The repressive compromisers are not so actively rejecting; they submit to their husbands as a wifely chore. But they make it clear to their husbands that they do not derive pleasure from the act.

The rejecting wife, active or compromising, conforms to a very old archetype. The conflict is between the desirous male and the rejecting female. Since in all sexual interaction the possibility, if not always the probability, is that the male, being greater in size and kinetic strength, can overpower the woman and get his way by force, the female is more likely to resort to strategic ploys than the male. Two of the oldest folk masterpieces—the *Arabian Nights* and the *Odyssey*—illustrate the kinds of strategies women may use to put off unwanted sexual advances from lovers. It is true that educated men prefer not to resort to force. Women may even use this fact against them. They may, more or less deliberately, precipitate force in order to put men in an inferior moral position. Having maneuvered them into resorting to force, they can then fling "you brute" or "you beast" at them, filling the men with guilt and remorse. The man must then apologize for doing what she baited him into doing. Rainwater and Weinstein (1960, p. 113) describe women who achieve aggressive pleasure from such opportunities to frustrate and anger their husbands.

Models of Sexual Adjustment Processes

Any phenomenon as complex as sexual relations requires a variety of models for explanation or interpretation. Sex, for example, may be the "permanent grievance" in the Rapoport escalation model; it may, however, be the brake on hostility; it may be the dependence variable. Sex may be a blue chip in a husband-wife "game" situation. It may be an outcome; it may be used as a strategy. It is not, in brief, a simple variable. Many models for sexual adjustment processes may be useful.

Maturation and learning. In some cases, sexual adjustment is in part a process of physical, social, or psychological maturation. The young wife may not be physically ready for orgasm; more likely, she may not be socially or psychologically mature enough for the experience. The relatively late—in the middle or later twenties—achievement of orgasm by a large proportion of women as reported by Kinsey has been interpreted by some students as the result of delayed weaning from maternal control; it may take several years for women to cut the social and psychological ties to their mothers and free themselves for uninhibited sexual relationships.

Another useful model for sexual adjustment is a rather simple learning one. For the most part, women learn from men what the nature of orgasm is like. Many of the subjects in Rainwater's study made this clear. "I didn't know anything when I got

married." "I didn't know *anything* about sexual relations before I was married. I was green as grass." "I knew what married people did before I was married, but I had no experience." "I learned it's something pretty wonderful—I learned from my husband, of course." "My husband taught me all I know about sex." "I knew very little about sex when I got married." These were kinds of comments that occurred again and again in the reported interviews (Rainwater & Weinstein, 1960).

As in other learning situations, if the teacher is considerate and understanding, the pupil learns to the best of his ability; rewards and penalties operate much as in all learning situations. "Finding gratification requires that the husband be solicitous of his wife's state of mind, and the loving attention that this implies is gratifying to the wife on non-sexual grounds as well" (Rainwater & Weinstein, 1960, p. 105). But if the teacher is incompetent for the job, the result may be an inferior learning experience.

The educational role of the husband, which is so apparent in the cases of mutual participation, is manifested . . . [in cases of rejection] in a negative way. Whereas for . . . those with mutual genitality, the wives feel that their husbands have guided them toward mutual enjoyment, . . . [rejecting women] feel that their husbands have educated them only in the bare essentials necessary to perform the act (Rainwater & Weinstein, 1960, p. 110).

Learning on the husband's part, as well as teaching, is also part of a good sexual adjustment: " . . . The first year we were both young and didn't know too much, but now he knows what I like and what makes me happy. It took a few years to adjust . . ." is the way one wife put it (Rainwater & Weinstein, 1960, p. 105).

Sometimes it is a matter of both learning: "I guess we both know a lot more than we did, and it's better now than before. We know more different ways and positions . . ." (Rainwater & Weinstein, 1960, p. 133).

Assimilative models. Learning may take place by either tacit or explicit communication or by both. Assimilative models—brainwashing, explaining away, and threat removal—operate very largely, although not wholly, by way of explicit or verbal communication. Depending so largely on words, they are probably available only to a fairly sophisticated class. The adjustment problem here is usually one of changing the woman's conception of sex as filthy, nasty, dirty and reorienting her in the direction of defining it in a more acceptable manner. Rainwater reports women who remain prisoners of points of view inculcated in them as children by their mothers, who feel disgust even after years of marriage. Whether or not such image-changing processes can be mediated by words alone is doubtful; accompanied by nonverbal persuasion they may succeed.

Bargaining models. The concept of the relations between the sexes as a bargaining situation is a very old one. Men "buy" sex from women in exchange for whatever it is the women are in a position to demand. Ordinarily, the one who gets relatively more out of the relationship would be at a bargaining disadvantage vis-à-vis the person who cares relatively less, according to the principle of lesser involvement ("least interest") referred to above. But there is an anomaly here. Although men usually seem to their partners to "get" more out of the sexual aspect of the relationship and hence should, theoretically, be at a disadvantage, in other aspects of the relationship women seem to care more. Marriage as a status appears to be more important to them than to men. So women are at a disadvantage here. Bargaining therefore is between parties who have differential advantages in different areas. Each must use his (her) advantage to buy off the penalties or costs of the disadvantages. She trades sex for security; he trades his freedom for assured sex.

The resulting relationship will be stable or precarious according to the relative values placed upon the outcomes, weighted for probabilities. If the wife feels that she is only a little better off, if at all, by remaining married to her unloved husband, any slight change in the situation which adds to the value of alternatives to remaining married will lead to a break. So, also, if the husband comes to feel—by meeting another more sexually complaisant woman, for example—that he is getting too little out of his marriage, his evaluation of outcomes will change and he will switch to a different course of action. If, contrariwise, the alternatives to the current payment for security for the wife or for sex for the husband are far less desirable than the present situation, the relationship will be a stable one, regardless of its quality. The wife submits to her husband even though she loathes him because the alternative—giving up the luxuries he provides her—is so much worse. The husband resigns himself to sexual frustration because the alternative—scandal which would make him lose his respected position in the community—is even less acceptable (Bernard, 1956).

In carrying out the sex-security and sex-freedom bargain, either partner may give good measure or short measure. For most men, much of the pleasure derived from sex depends on the manner of the woman's giving. If she gives herself grudgingly, she is carrying out the letter of the implicit contracted bargain, but not the spirit. If she gives herself graciously, generously, and enthusiastically, she enhances her contribution to the bargain. Similarly, if the man is niggardly in his support, she may feel cheated. If he is generous, she may feel she has made an excellent bargain. Some women can be neither giving nor even accepting in the sexual relationship. They cannot admit that men have something to give them sexually that they value.

Who adjusts to whom. We noted above that the consensus among writers on the subject is that in general wives tend to adjust to their husbands more than husbands to their wives. This would be in line with the principle of least interest, since the status of marriage appears to be a more important value to women than to men. With respect to frequency of sex relations, however, the findings are not unequivocal.

Where there is mutuality in sex, no adjustment is needed. It is called for only among the marriages in which the wives are ambivalent or rejecting. And it is Rainwater's opinion that "in the day-to-day lives of these couples frequency is determined by the degree of the wife's acceptance of sexuality; [for] regardless of her husband's desires, she has ways of reducing the number of times they have relations if she does not desire them" (Rainwater & Weinstein, 1960, p. 97).

Some help in interpreting the situation is available from data reported by Kinsey and his associates. If we assume that married men would prefer to have orgasm in marital intercourse rather than by other "outlets," comparison of frequency of marital coitus and frequency of orgasm in married men gives a rough index of the "damp-

ing effect" of wives. Table 3 reports the relationship among certain specified variables for the "middle" man, that is, among medians. It suggests that in the early years of marriage, wives cut down the frequency of intercourse by about one-fifth (20 per cent); this "damping effect" declines until middle age, when it rises again. But even at the lowest level, the "damping effect" reduces coitus by a seventh. There is no measure of the extent to which husbands step up the frequency of coitus in wives beyond a most-preferred level, since there is no logically deducible "most-preferred level" to serve as a base. If Rainwater's opinion is correct, the actual frequency of coitus may reflect the wives' preference, and the frequency of orgasm in married men may reflect the husbands' preference. Under these assumptions, it is, indeed, the husband who adjusts to the wife so far as frequency of coitus is concerned.

The escalation model. The escalation model may also be useful for interpreting the course which sexual adjustments may take. Aggression on the part of the husband may stimulate increased resistance on the

TABLE 3

"DAMPING EFFECT" OF WIVES IN FREQUENCY OF COITUS[a]

Age Bracket	Frequency of Orgasm of "Middle" (Median) Married Man Per Week (1)[b]	Frequency of Coitus of "Middle" (Median) Married Man (2)[c]	Difference (1)–(2) (3)	"Damping Effect" of Wives (3)/(1) (4)
16–20	3.21	2.56	.65	20%
21–25	2.81	2.28	.53	19
26–30	2.47	1.98	.49	20
31–35	2.08	1.76	.32	15
36–40	1.89	1.59	.30	16
41–45	1.61	1.28	.33	20
46–50	1.20	.88	.32	27
51–55	1.04	.76	.28	27
56–60	.81	.68	.13	16

[a] Assumption: Married men would prefer to have orgasm in marital intercourse rather than by other "outlets."
[b] Kinsey et al. (1948), p. 226.
[c] Kinsey et al. (1948), p. 252.

part of the wife which, in turn, stimulates more aggression on his part, then more resistance on hers, with ramifications in all other aspects of the relationship. A bad sexual relationship may constitute the grievance factor which is one of the variables in Rapoport's model. Contrariwise, loving consideration on the part of each may stimulate greater tenderness and appreciation, and the escalation may be in the direction of greater love rather than in the direction of schism.

It is evident, however, from this brief overview of the several models as applied to sexual relationships, that schismatic models are often relevant. Sexual deprivation may so greatly reduce the rewards of remaining in a marital relationship as to make a break relatively attractive as an alternative. The nonsexual rewards must be great to compensate for the deficit in sexual satisfactions. If not, divorce may be the most rewarding alternative.

DIVORCE AS OUTCOME, AS STRATEGY, AND AS PROCESS

Early in this chapter, we pointed out that since the topic under discussion was marital *adjustments,* the emphasis was on the processes by which spouses come to terms with one another, not on the processes by which they fail to do so. The terms they arrive at, we have noted, are not necessarily the happiest possible, but they are good enough to keep the marriage viable; most marriages, that is, endure until death separates the spouses.

But not all do. The members of some marriages—perhaps one in four of all marriages as of 1955 (Jacobson, 1959), or one in six of all first marriages (Blood & Wolfe, 1960, p. 252)—find it impossible for one reason or another to make the necessary adjustments, or the marriage does not seem to one or both to be worth the effort of such adjustments. The fourth level of dealing with incompatible differences referred to

above is resorted to, namely, destruction of the relationship. Divorce ensues. It is to consideration of this level of dealing with incompatible differences that we now turn.

A major difficulty in developing theoretical models for the understanding of breakdowns in marital relationships lies in the fact that we do not always know exactly what it is we are trying to explain or interpret, and even when we do, objective data on the phenomenon we want to study are lacking. We speak, for example, of trends in the divorce rate as though we knew quite well what the divorce rate was.

There are several rates, and not all of them are always identical in trend. One rate is the number of divorces per 1,000 total population; another is the number of divorces per 1,000 existing marriages; still another is the number of divorces in any given cohort of marriages, giving the chances of divorce. The first two rates are especially vulnerable. Since divorce is related to age, any change in the age composition of the population will reflect itself in the divorce rate; since it is also related to the proportion of the population married, any change in the marital composition of the population will also reflect itself in the divorce rate. In 1938, for example, the rate per 1,000 marriages declined, but the rate per 1,000 total population remained the same. Similar discrepancies were notable in 1939, 1951, 1952, and 1955. We do not even have complete and accurate data on the number—let alone rates—of divorces, since not all states are included in national reports. In general, the number of divorces per 1,000 total population reached a high point (4.4) in 1946 and declined thereafter; in the late fifties and early sixties it appeared to be fluctuating around half that number (2.2). The number of divorces per 1,000 existing marriages (18.2) also reached a peak in 1946; it, too, fell to a level about half this size in the late fifties (Jacobson, 1959, p. 90).

It is, however, elementary knowledge

that divorce is by no means a unitary phenomenon. Some divorces merely formalize a breakdown in marital relationships which occurred years ago; nothing new except legal recognition has occurred. Others formalize a breakdown that has barely occurred. The divorce, furthermore, of a high dignitary without small children (a Rockefeller, a Stevenson, a Douglas) with circumspection and decorum, is not the same as that of a vindictive shrew who is out to "show" someone, or the glamorous star who moves from one husband to another almost without pause. Nor is desertion, another form of breakdown in marital relationships, a unitary phenomenon. The gentleman's agreement of the urbane couple not to bother one another is not at all the same as the disappearance of the husband and father of several children. Even the breakdown which takes the form of psychological schism or withdrawal or estrangement rather than legal divorce is a complex phenomenon, by no means identical in every case.

Marriages may break down, in brief, in many different ways and in varying degrees. Our concern here, however, is only with divorce, which may be viewed as (a) an outcome, (b) a strategy, or (c) the end result of the process of escalation. [Complementary treatments of divorce and divorce rates will be found in Chs 9 and 23 of this Handbook.]

Divorce as Outcome

Some marriages are, in effect, doomed at the outset. The partners are mismated, they have little in common, even the desire to remain married. Soon they may have in common only the desire to be divorced. Explaining divorce in such cases involves explaining only the timing and the procedure.

Some marriages are nonviable because the partners are, as we saw above, neurotic or poorly socialized or unsuited for the discipline imposed by marriage.

But there are many divorces which seem inexplicable in ordinary terms. They occur, not because the partners are in any fundamental way unsuited to marriage, for they prove themselves capable of successful marital adjustments in second marriages. Such divorced persons sometimes admit, in fact, that if they had known as much in their first marriages as in their second, they might never have divorced.

Such divorces may in many cases be interpreted as strategic failures. For some reason or other, one or the other partner "played his cards wrong" or became "cornered" or "boxed in" or was maneuvered into a position where divorce seemed to be the only alternative. Many divorced persons wonder themselves how it happened. These are the marriages that might be most salvageable. Divorce in such cases is almost accidental, in the sense that a modern war might come about by accident, neither side really wanting it.

Sometimes only one partner wants a divorce. He may deliberately maneuver his spouse into a situation where there is no alternative for her. He makes her life so miserable that the payoff for accepting divorce as outcome is higher than the payoff for fighting it. Goode (1956) has analyzed what he calls the "strategy of divorce" by which a husband brings his wife to the point of wanting a divorce. He makes the price of remaining together so costly in terms of self-respect, mental peace, and even the ordinary amenities that she is willing to pay even divorce for an escape. Any outcome is better than remaining married under the circumstances.

This "strategy of divorce" illustrates both the rationale and the futility of the theory underlying most divorce legislation in our country. Legally, divorce in most jurisdictions cannot be granted if both partners want it; there must be a fight. There are several justifications made for this provision. One is that if mutual consent were acceptable as a basis for divorce, one party could maneuver or badger the other into accepting it, even against his (her) will by means of

Goode's "strategy of divorce." Actually, the law cannot prevent this strategy in any event; it merely glosses over collusion, however achieved.

Divorce, in brief, may be the outcome of strategies of either or both parties; it may, further, be either "engineered" by one party or it may be the inevitable, though unanticipated, result of "playing one's cards wrong."

Divorce as Strategy

Folsom was one of the first to point out that divorce was only one of several alternative courses of actions, or strategies, for persons who found themselves in an unhappy marriage (1943). Other alternatives might include absorption in work, in travel, in entertaining, in clothes, in community service, in children, in church work; or retreat through alcohol; or illicit alliances; or separation.

If both partners want a divorce, there is no conflict, at least on this issue. The chances are that the only problems will be those associated with implementing the common decision. Negotiations and bargaining may be required to decide who gets what in the settlement, but that is only after the decision to seek a divorce has been agreed upon. In reaching the common decision to divorce, each one might well have canvassed the value or payoff for the outcomes of alternative strategies. "If we stay together we'll drive one another crazy"; "If we get a divorce he'll not receive a promotion"; "If we get a divorce I'll have to leave town." These are among the outcomes of divorce as a strategy that have to be evaluated in arriving at a decision for or against it. The outcome with the highest feasible, not the highest imaginable, value is the one that is sought.

Values change. A marriage in which divorce as an alternative did not have high probability for many years because the outcome was not highly valued as compared with the status quo may suddenly be rocked by the introduction of a third person. There was no incentive to terminate an unsatisfactory marriage before; but now that one or the other spouse or both have fallen in love with other partners whom they wish to marry, the probability of divorce becomes very high (Bernard, 1956). The "cause" of the divorce is the change in the relative value its outcome now has. The outcome of divorce as strategy is now a—hopefully—happy remarriage. Nothing has changed in the situation so far as the spouses are concerned; it is the same marriage that yielded the highest payoff in the past. But with the possibility of a happy remarriage in the offing as an outcome, divorce becomes a more probable strategy.

Sometimes the subjective probability of a happy remarriage influences strategies even before the third person has appeared on the scene. The spouse contemplating courses of action in an unhappy marital situation may, in effect, be in a so-called game against Nature, not against the spouse. He, or she, must make a decision in the presence of uncertainty. "If I divorce John (Jane) and find a new congenial mate, the outcome would be a happy marriage. If I divorce him (her) but fail to find a new congenial mate, the outcome will be loneliness and frustration. If I divorce him (her) and remarry, the outcome might be worse than my present condition." The evaluation of these outcomes, weighted by assessment of their probabilities, will influence her (him) in her choice of strategy. As of the present time, the chances of remarriage—and even of successful remarriage—are fairly high (Bernard, 1956).

Divorce is always one available alternative course of action, or strategy, in a marital adjustment situation. This is especially true in a society that provides many grounds for divorce or, what amounts to almost the same thing, makes slight procedural demands in seeking divorce. It may have very low priority, but the fact that it is possible at all means that it is always part of the adjustment picture.

Divorce as Process

It is a frequent observation that emotions tend to have a snowballing effect. A disagreement may begin with only a moderate amount of hostility present; but each parry or thrust adds to the hostility of the other and leads him, in turn, to increase his own hostility, and so on, in a process which has come to be known as escalation. Contrariwise, good will may also snowball, one good turn deserving another, so that friendly behavior escalates also.

The general model for escalation was presented earlier. As applied to marriage, the parameters a and b (see above, pp. 698–699), which specify the degree of dependence on mutual stimulation between the parties, would tend to be large because of the specifications of the marital relationship. They would tend to be especially high in the interactional pattern of relationship, in which the behavior of one partner is relatively highly influenced by the behavior of the other; it would tend to be relatively lower in the parallel pattern. But in any marriage where there was any sensitivity of one partner to the other, a and b would be more than zero. Only where alienation was complete, where each spouse was living a life of his own, would a and b be zero.

The braking forces, m and n, may be any of the constraints—internal anguish or external sanctions—which hold hostile behavior in check in a relationship with the specifications of marriage. The individuals may feel that the hostile behavior is just not worth while; it may interfere with sexual relations, with social life, with recreation. It may be frowned upon by family and friends. By and large, m and n would tend to be greater in marriages of higher than of lower socio-economic levels. Manners as well as morals put more constraints on hostility.

The permanent grievance parameters of the escalation model—g and h—if positive, may refer to such things as: a poor sexual relationship, alcoholism, infidelity, in-law difficulties, nagging, resentment with respect to money and expenditures, or, in brief, differences in any of the standard marital problem areas referred to earlier in this chapter.

If, as noted earlier, the parameters for the constraints which operate as brakes on hostile behavior (mn) are less than the parameters for the degree of mutual dependence (ab), and there is an underlying grievance present (g and h are positive), the conditions exist for runaway escalation. There is nothing in the model which states at what point, if any, legal divorce will take place. All it does is specify the conditions under which psychological separation escalates.

It has been noted that grounds for divorce which some court somewhere or other would accept as valid exist at some time or other in practically every marriage (Bernard, 1956). We know, for example, from Kinsey's findings that adultery, which all jurisdictions in the United States will accept, occurs in a large proportion of marriages; it is quite likely that cruelty on the part of one or the other spouse occurs at some time in most marriages also. The existence of grievances (parameters g and h), however small, may therefore be taken for granted. The existence of at least some dependence of one on the behavior of the other spouse (parameters a and b) may also be taken for granted, given the specifications of the marital bond. This leaves the size of the parameter for the braking influences (parameters m and n) of major significance in interpreting hostile escalation. Church, state, community, social set as well as class patterns will be important determinants in the influence of braking forces.

Intervention to save a marriage from the runaway escalation of hostility might be made at any feasible point in the process. An effort might be made to increase m and n, the braking effect, by sanctions or threats of ostracism if the hostility increases. Or an effort might be made to reduce g and h, the underlying grievance, or, if possible, to transform it into a negative value, i.e., an "anti-grievance." Divorce itself stops the escalation by reducing a and b, mutual dependence, to zero. Temporary separation might serve the same function.

The best empirical data on the divorcing process are those of Goode (1956), and they refer only to women. He found that the median number of months between first serious consideration of divorce to the final decision was 4.6 months; the median time between the final decision and the actual filing of the divorce suit was 3.2 months; the elapsed time between first serious consideration to filing of the suit averaged more than the sum of the above two medians, namely, 12.0 months. The total process was somewhat longer for rural-bred women than for urban-bred; and it appeared that the longer the marriage lasted, the longer it took for the wife to complete the divorcing process, suggesting that age may have had a braking effect, slowing down the process.

The actual incidence of divorce, therefore, as outcome, as strategy, or as process, will depend to a large extent on the values of the individuals concerned, and these, in turn, will reflect the importance assigned to stability by the society as a whole as manifested in the costs assessed to divorce or the braking effect exerted by anticipated sanctions.

DETERMINANTS OF PARAMETERS AND PAYOFFS

Models do not give us empirical information. All they do is tell us that if or when such and such a set of specifications is met, then such and so can be expected to follow. They are suitable for any set of relationships that conforms to their specifications. But the specific parameters and payoffs in any individual marriage are peculiar to that marriage and differ from those of any other. The problem then becomes one of determining what the specific parameters and payoffs are and why they are what they are.

Why, for example, is the strategy of divorce more probable at one time than at another? in one community than in another? in one marriage than in another? Why does it have a higher payoff value as an outcome in one marriage than in another? for one spouse than for the other? Why is the escalation effect high in one marriage, low in another?

Christensen has distinguished three sets of factors on which marital adjustments depend, namely, "(1) the situation that provides the setting; (2) the persons who are members; and (3) the relationships that exist" between them (1958, pp. 20–21). The first of these may be subsumed under institutional influences, the second under individual personal influences, and the third under interactional or team factors. The influences which come to bear, directly or indirectly, on the determination of parameters and payoffs may then be classified under these three headings.

Institutional Influences

Some differences in the evaluation of outcomes result from the institutional setting in which the marriage functions. If, for example, the social costs of divorce in the form of social ostracism, religious excommunication, job discrimination, and the like, are high, divorce as strategy will have low probability, and any other strategy likely to have divorce as an outcome will also. The parameters m and n will be large. Contrariwise, where divorce is common, not condemned, not a handicap socially, religiously or occupationally, it will have a higher evaluation relative to other adjustments; it will be a preferred alternative more often. The parameters m and n will not be large. Such institutional influences help to explain long-term trends, rural-urban differences, regional differences, racial, religious, and ethnic differences in the incidence of divorce.

In a similar way, institutional background factors will influence the relative availability of different strategies. The status of women at any given time or place, for example, will have a profound effect on the parameters and payoffs in marital adjustments. In a society in which employment outside of the home is almost impossible, so that financial independence is out of reach for all but a few wealthy women, the alternatives to submission to a husband, whatever his character, are few, and their probable outcomes have low value. However bad a woman's marriage might be, it would still seem preferable to the penalties of leaving him. In a society which makes independence possible, on the other hand, the values for alternatives to remaining married to an unloved husband are relatively high. The wife who is in a position to earn her own living is less vulnerable to threats; she does not have to take whatever her husband "dishes out." She has alternatives that do not demand prohibitive costs from her. Knowing this, her husband must select his own behavior in such a way as not to trigger a break; restraints are imposed upon him.

The clarity and specificity of institutional norms, as well as their contents, influence parameters and the relative value assigned to outcomes. Where there are clear-cut specifications for the roles of husband and wife and strong sanctions enforcing them, there will be less variety in the alternatives available to either spouse, greater predictability, and alternatives associated with much-desired outcomes will be rejected simply because the probability of achieving them is less.

There is one set of institutional factors—those associated with familism and hence with in-laws—that is so important in influencing marital adjustments in ongoing marriages that it warrants more detailed consideration. It is characteristic of our society

that we see the family as resulting from marriage, rather than seeing marriage as an incident in the life of the family.

In the old familistic setting, usually patriarchal in Western society, the nuclear family was an important but subsidiary unit in a much larger web of relationships. [See pp. 465–469.] The relationship between the husband and wife may not have been any simpler then than now, but it was different in many ways. In-laws were important in a different way; they had more effect on alternatives available to each spouse and on the values assessed to the outcomes. The traditional Chinese family of the gentry, for example, lived together in a large compound, and the wife of the head ruled her daughters-in-law with an iron hand. Women could hardly wait until they, too, became mothers-in-law, to have young women at their beck and call. In the West there was less such domination, but the parents-in-law who controlled property and supervised family industries were great centers of power. Marital adjustments were made under the actual or potential scrutiny of parents. Since young married couples tended to live with or near his, rather than her, family, he was more likely than she to have support in any conflict with her. He was at an advantage. The presence of his family could greatly influence the value of any outcome for her.

In modern American society, marriage tends to split couples off from the consanguineal family. Although family ties remain (Litwak, 1960a; Litwak, 1960b; Townsend, 1957), they are greatly attenuated as compared with the past. The evaluation of outcomes of alternatives is less influenced by what parents think. Popular lore pokes fun at the expression "After all, you have not lost a son (daughter) but gained a daughter (son)." As a matter of fact, neither event has occurred. The child has not been lost, but neither has the child's spouse been gained. It is because of the equivocal relationship between family and marriage as institutions that in-law problems so called take the form they do in our society and that in-laws exert the kind of influence they do on parameters and evaluations of outcomes.

The influence of in-laws on marital adjustments is complicated by the current trend toward young marriages. When it was customary for young men and women to wait until they were ready to set up an establishment of their own before they married, there were fairly clear-cut institutionalized patterns of responsibility. The young man was given a parcel of land to farm, or the young woman was given a substantial dowry, and they were then presumably on their own. At the present time, many young people marry before they have achieved independence from their families, a fact which complicates their relationships and hence adjustments to one another, especially in the younger years. "I can't do that, honey, much as I would like to, because it would make Dad mad and he might cut down on our allowance." In effect, the disadvantages of both the old *Grossfamilie* and the new *Kleinfamilie* are present, with the advantages of neither.

Further, in-laws may be substantive issues —the "permanent grievance" of the escalation model, or the incompatible differences of other models. One study of over 5,000 men and women reported that the commonest complaint by young people about their in-laws was that they were meddlesome and dominating. But the second most frequent complaint was, contrariwise, that they were distant, indifferent, thoughtless, and unappreciative (Duvall, 1954). Wives complained about in-laws more than did husbands. Sisters-in-law were sources of complaint more often than brothers-in-law. And mothers-in-law—especially mothers of husbands—were complained about more frequently than fathers-in-law. Whatever the nature of the influence might actually be, too much or too little attention, the institutional pattern of the family which now prevails does seem to make in-laws a potential issue in marital relationships.

The institutionalization of divorce, the status of women, and the anomalous position of in-laws are only a few among the many examples of the way marital adjustments are influenced by the normative matrix within which they must occur. They never take place in an institutional vacuum.

Personality Influences

Institutional influences operate upon individuals, but it is the individuals who make them manifest. The same institutional influences may operate differentially upon different individuals. Most empirical researchers have therefore concluded that personality factors are more important than any others in determining the nature of marital adjustments. "Marital success is dependent upon both people and circumstances—upon the quality of the persons who enter it and upon the nature of the environment that surrounds it. But the most crucial of these two is people . . ." (Christensen, 1958, p. 20). There are people who, however adverse the institutional background, work out a satisfying relationship; there are others who, no matter how favorable the institutional setting, do not.

Even among those who emphasize the importance of personality factors, however, there are wide differences of opinion with respect to the operation of such factors. It is agreed that some people succeed better than others in achieving a satisfactory marital relationship. But there is not consensus with respect to what it is that leads to this result. Some students emphasize intrinsic personality traits, whether hereditary or acquired early in life; others emphasize social factors in personality, such as community participation and institutional conformity.

It is undoubtedly true that marital adjustment processes are sometimes determined by pathological or near-pathological traits in one or both of the spouses. One party is obsessive or compulsive or for some reason or other incapable of exerting control over his behavior. In such cases, models which imply an ability to fit means to ends are not suitable. Parameters and payoffs for such individuals are bizarre; they select alternatives which lead to seemingly self-defeating outcomes.

Psychiatrists distinguish a number of ways of adjusting to life which are resorted to by individuals which they label neurotic, such, for example, as schizoid, paranoid, hysterical, manic, depressive, anxious, compulsive, and obsessive. In extreme form, these ways may become psychotic. Since in milder forms they are fairly common and widespread, they have long since been recognized in popular lore. The schizoid is labeled apathetic, withdrawn, out of touch; the paranoid is said to have a chip on his shoulder, to suspect the worst of everyone; the hysterical is said to be putting on an act; the manic is said to be excitable; the depressive is said to be pessimistic, seeing the worst in everything; the anxious person is said to be a chronic worrier; the compulsive is said to be a fussy housekeeper or a particular boss; and the obsessive is said to have whatever it is he is obsessed with "on the brain." Such traits can, of course, exert profound influence on marital adjustments. They deflect the processes of interaction and produce strange and improbable results, such, for instance, as wives who, despite the fact that their husbands may even have attempted to kill them, still refuse to leave them, or the wives of alcoholics who cling to their husbands no matter what. The values assigned to the outcomes of alternative lines of action are heavily weighted by their unusual personality structures.

Some people, in brief, no matter what the setting and no matter who the mate, are incapable of adjustment to the conditions of marriage. Studies of divorced people show a high incidence of both mental and physical illness as well as of suicide. That some of this difference may be the result of divorce rather than the "cause" is suggested by the fact that among those in the status of widowhood such pathologies also tend to be higher than among those in the status of marriage. But the incidence is higher among those in the status of divorce than among those in the status of widowhood. For those so handicapped, it has been suggested that only profound emotional re-education, if that, can render it possible for them to succeed in marriage. They are incapable, for whatever reason, of controlling their own behavior or of making suitable choices among alternative courses of action. As a result, they get much less than it is possible to get out of any marital relationship (Bergler, 1946; Bergler, 1948).

There are some people, however, neither neurotic nor psychotic, who still find marital relationships uncongenial. For them, almost any outcome is preferable to remaining married; or divorce is the most highly preferred strategy, regardless of the outcome. They may be capable, intelligent, even talented people in other respects, but they do not have what Terman and Wallin (1949) have called marital aptitude. They do not, that is, have the interests and values which go with domesticity. They chafe at the restrictions which go with marriage. The costs in loss of freedom seem high to them in terms of the rewards. The reasons for such interests and values would have to be determined in each specific case. Terman looked for them in such factors as interests which would be not only predictive but also amenable to change.

Two great classics, published by Terman and by Burgess and Cottrell, uncovered the background factors which appeared to be associated with personalities capable of making good marital adjustments. [For a methodological treatment of these pioneer researches see Ch. 6, pp. 218–224.] Terman (1938) found that persons with happy family backgrounds were likely to succeed in marriage, success being measured in terms of self-reported happiness. He found the 10 most predictive items for marital success, defined as happiness, to be: (a) superior happiness of parents, (b) childhood happiness, (c) lack of conflict with mother, (d) home discipline firm but not harsh, (e) strong attachment to mother, (f) same to father, (g) lack of conflict with father, (h) parental frankness about sex, (i) infrequency and mildness of childhood punishment, and (j) premarital attitudes toward sex which were free from disgust or aversion. In brief, happy homes which produced happy children and happy adults made for happy marriages. The alternatives available to such people assured high payoffs in marital satisfaction. They could select courses of action among these alternatives which optimized payoffs.

Burgess and Cottrell (1939) found, in effect, that conventional people—as measured by conformity behavior—were more likely to have good marital relationships than nonconformists. These authors, like Terman, emphasized "a harmonious and understanding family environment," and such traits as optimism, emotional balance, and sympathetic attitudes, but they made much more of group and institutional factors such as similarity of cultural backgrounds, a socialized personality as evidenced by number of friends, participation in organizations, keeping of religious observances, a job with a high degree of social control, self-confidence, especially in the husband, and emotional dependence, reasonable security, and little mobility (pp. 64–65).

By and large, all studies show that social status is an important determinant of success in marital relationships. A recent study by Blood and Wolfe confirms earlier findings to this effect (1960).

Some people, in brief, can "live happily ever afterward" because of the kind of people they are, almost independently of the person they marry. Happy people, that is, make happy marriages. This is obviously an exaggeration, although it is implicit in any study which looks to the personalities of the spouses as individuals for an explanation of the success or failure of marital adjustments. But even happily married people might have been happier if married to someone else. The team factor must always be considered; marital adjustment is not an additive phenomenon.

Team Factors

By and large, endogamous marriages tend to show up better than heterogamous ones; that is, when both spouses have similar educational and religious backgrounds, their scores on marital satisfaction tests tend to be higher than when they have different backgrounds (Blood & Wolfe, 1960, pp. 256–257). Homogamous marriages—with exceptions noted above—also show higher scores. But of greater significance is the fact that team-related functions—decision-making patterns, sharing of household tasks, type and degree of companionship, and especially the kind of response husbands give their wives when they have problems to solve—are all related to marital satisfaction. Women married to men who help them solve their problems show high marital satisfaction scores; those married to men who are critical or who dismiss their problems show low scores (Blood & Wolfe, 1960). If the women whose husbands helped them solve their problems had been married to men who criticized or dismissed them, their scores might also have been low. In brief, marital satisfaction is a team as well as an individual or personality matter.

Studies of remarriage after divorce and bereavement throw some light on both the institutional and the personality factors in marital adjustments (Bernard, 1956), but especially on the latter. One study of about 2,000 cases of such remarriages reported that although personality factors did seem to be involved in success—marriages of two divorced persons tending to have lower chances of success and any marriage in which there was a remarried divorced woman also having lower chances of success—still the team factor did seem to be extremely important also. That is, many people who failed in marriages with one mate were quite capable of succeeding in marriage with a different mate. There was, that is, nothing intrinsically deficient in them which made marital adjustments impossible. Interaction with one mate led only to frustration and defeat; interaction with another, to fulfillment and success.

The team factor was also noted above in the discussion of mixed-motive games. The French have a saying that in every love relationship between a man and a woman, one person loves and the other condescends to be loved. E. A. Ross was not the first to point out the principle of least interest, namely that the one who cares more in any relationship is at a disadvantage vis-à-vis the one who cares less (1921, p. 136). The person who cannot tolerate quarreling and bickering will give in to the person who can. The spouse to whom the marriage means more will make more concessions than the spouse to whom it means less. The person to whom the marriage means less is more independent; he has more strategic weapons in his armory. He can threaten; he can extort. Justice is not at all a necessary component in marital adjustments; exploitation is inherent in a relationship which one values more than the other (Waller & Hill, 1951).

In brief, no matter how happy the background of one of the spouses and no matter how conventional he (or she) is, his (her) personality alone cannot guarantee satisfactory marital adjustments. A marriage is not the sum of two individual and separate persons; it is a "unity of interacting personalities," neither one of which alone determines the success of the relationship. An outcome which has an extremely low value for the wife married to one man may have a high value for her if married to another, and vice versa. Conceding an issue to one woman may be much more rewarding than the same concession to another. And so on. The parameters and payoffs in any marriage are determined by neither spouse alone or independently of one another; they are always the result of interaction.

CRITERIA FOR EVALUATING MARITAL RELATIONSHIPS

As we have been using the term "adjustment" here, that is, as a process of functional change rather than as the result of that process, it cannot be judged good or bad but only successful or unsuccessful, correct or incorrect, according to whether it does or does not achieve a certain kind of result. At this point, therefore, a brief statement is in order on the criteria applicable to the marital relationship itself and thus, indirectly, to the processes which relate to it. [Cf. Ch. 6, especially pp. 239-245.]

A number of criteria have been applied in research attempting to evaluate marital relationships, including (a) how well a marriage meets the needs and expectations of society; (b) its permanence or endurance; (c) the degree of unity and/or agreement or consensus developed between the members; (d) the degree to which it facilitates personality development; and (e) the degree of marital satisfaction or happiness it achieves (Burgess & Cottrell, 1939; Burgess & Locke, 1960; Farber, 1962; Foote & Cottrell, 1955; Terman, 1938). The specific criteria applied in evaluating the quality of marital relationships have different weights, of course, from one society to another and from one researcher to another. In some, the claims of the society take precedence over those of the partners; in others, more weight is attached to the goals and values of the individuals involved. It is universally preferred that husbands and wives be fond of one another, that they live without quarreling and bickering, and that they find satisfaction in their relationship; but if a choice has to be made between this desideratum and stability, stability is given precedence in some societies, marital happiness and satisfaction in others.

The kind of marital relationship which is functional will depend to some extent on the demands made on the partners by other systems in that society. If, for example, the economic system depends on a high degree of individual mobility, marital stability will not be at a premium. Thus, it has been pointed out that stable unions were not encouraged under slavery since they would militate against the free sale of the separate spouses (Frazier, 1948). Conversely, the so-called domestic or prefactory system of manufacturing in Europe depended on stable families that could be relied upon to do the spinning, weaving, knitting, and other manufacturing tasks which the market called for. The kind of marital relationship which is functional will depend also on the relationship of the spouses to the larger kinship group. It will depend, too, on the demands made by the state. In the Soviet Union, for example, and in Nazi Germany, spouses were once encouraged to inform on one another; a close relationship which would interfere with such an exigency would be nonfunctional to the state. (It was found later in the USSR, however, that unstable marriages were dysfunctional for the economy; people who were irresponsible in their marital relationships tended to be irresponsible in their industrial relationships also. A so-called discipline theory of marriage underlay the radical revolution in marriage and divorce laws of the 1930's which transformed the Soviet family into one of the most stable, conservative, not to say puritanical, among industrial nations.)

In general, a good marital relationship from the point of view of society is one in which there is stability, in which children are provided care and affection, and the partners are kept well and efficient. In addition, it is usually also considered desirable for the relationship to be satisfying in itself. Indeed, since marital problems may spill over into all other relationships and may even adversely affect health, the societal criterion implies the others. But if a choice between personal satisfaction and stability has to be made, emphasis usually will be placed on stability. Any adjustment which is schismatic in nature will be judged bad; any strategy or course of action which has desertion or divorce as an outcome will be discouraged. Societal criteria for evaluating marital relationships are associated with the parallel or tradition-directed or the child-, home-oriented, or institutional pattern of marital relationship.

The mere continuance of a marriage, that is, refraining from divorce, is sometimes taken as a criterion of success. So long as a marriage remains a legal entity, regardless of the quality of the relationship, it is assumed to be successful. This is the implicit criterion in studies which use divorced persons as controls in studies of marital relationships. The fact that a marriage has ended in divorce does not, however, necessarily imply that it has failed all along the way. Some marriages that end in divorce have had periods in which they were successful. And many marriages endure which are failures if judged by other criteria than mere continuance.

The individual-oriented criteria (categories [c], [d], and [e] above) apply more intimately to the members of the marriage themselves and are likely to go with interactional, companionship, or parent-oriented patterns of marital relationship. Measures of agreement and disagreement between spouses were used as criteria of success in marriage in one of the first empirical studies (Burgess & Cottrell, 1939); consensus on domestic values is a major component in a recent measure of marital integration (Farber, 1960). But agreement in and of itself need not be "good." What if it results from brainwashing? intimidation? resignation? Is a relationship "bad" because it is challenged by one or the other party? Questions like these led some researchers to add the facilitation of personality development as a criterion of a good relationship. If one partner has paid all the costs of change to achieve agreement, the relationship resulting from the adjustment is not usually considered "good," at least according to middle-class standards in our society.

Marital happiness, either as self-rated or as rated by others, has been a commonly accepted criterion (Gurin, Veroff, & Feld, 1960; Terman, 1938); but sometimes the term is qualified: "When we say that marriage is successful if it is happy, we mean long-range or 'net' happiness, the kind that comes by understanding, cooperation, and self-effort" (Christensen, 1958, p. 19).

Happiness is, of course, a logical criterion in our society; but even when modified as above, it has defects. The Gurin, Veroff, and Feld study (1960), for example, found that whereas older people tended to be better "adjusted," they were also less "happy" than younger people. It is usually found that happiness ratings decline with age; but the relationships resulting from "adjustments" are usually reported as improved. The happiest years of a marriage may come in the young age periods, even though there are many marital adjustment problems present (Blood & Wolfe, 1960, p. 264). The marital relationship that comes with age may, therefore, reflect resignation rather than happiness.

It should not be assumed that happiness in marriage means an absence of adjustment problems. In one study, it was found that although fewer of those who reported their marriage as happy tended to report personal problems in their marriage—as expected—still, even a third of the very happy marriages reported problems, and half of the above-average marriages did (Gurin, Veroff, & Feld, 1960). Feelings of happiness in a marriage, in brief, did not mean that there were not adjustment problems present; or, conversely, the presence of adjustment problems did not necessarily militate against the happiness of the spouses.

Critique of the Happiness Criterion

Another important aspect of the relationship between happiness and marital adjustment must be noted here. A criterion for evaluating a marital relationship could be set up in terms, not of the best imaginable relationship, but in terms of the best possible one. If we specify as a criterion of suc-

cess of marital adjustments that in the resulting relationship each partner must achieve the best goal he can dream of, the standard is, obviously, impossibly high. A marriage may be said to be successful to the extent that it provides the highest satisfaction possible, not the highest one imaginable.

However unsatisfactory it may be from the point of view of happiness, it may still be judged to be better than the alternatives. Given the people involved and the setting they are functioning in, even Thoreau's "quiet desperation" may be the best relationship possible. It may not be a happy one. In brief, the payoff of the strategies which hold the partners in marriage may not be high, but it may be higher than that of any alternative.

From this relativistic point of view, two criteria may be set up: (a) a marital relationship is successful if the satisfaction is positive, that is, if the rewards to both partners are greater than the costs; and (b) a marital relationship is successful if it is preferable to any other alternative. In the first situation there is a positive gain, however slight, in the existing relationship. The gain will be slight if the costs are exorbitant and the rewards just barely sufficient to compensate for them; the gain will be great if the costs are slight and the rewards great. In the second situation, the marriage is not likely to be happy—the costs may be greater than the rewards—but the deficit is less than it would be for any other alternative.

An example of the first situation, where the margin between costs and rewards is small, would be this: A and B do not like one another; they get on one another's nerves; the costs of remaining married are great in frustration and loneliness. But the rewards are great also: together they can afford a lovely home; they have high status in the community; the children are protected from scandal; the Church approves of them; etc. This relationship is "successful" or "good," not because it is the best imaginable, but only because it is the best possible in the sense that the satisfactions are greater than the costs. At the other extreme is the marriage in which the satisfactions are enormous in appreciation, security, responsiveness, financial success, and the costs, in restrictions on freedom to come and go at will, an independent income, a job, very low.

An example of the second criterion, in which a marital relationship is successful only because it is better than any alternative, would be the marriage of a dependent woman to, let us say, an alcoholic, in which the costs in misery were much greater than the rewards in security or status; but the spread between costs and satisfactions would be much greater if she left him. She would then be alone; she would not have the protection of the status of marriage; she would not have even the occasional sober companionship of a husband; etc. Bad as it is, therefore, her marriage seems better to her than any alternative she has.

In brief, the criteria for judging a marital relationship successful or unsuccessful must be not in terms of the best imaginable situation—a maximum—but in terms of the best possible, given the specific parameters and payoffs of the situation—an optimum.

APPENDIX:
ILLUSTRATIVE MATRIXES

The following matrixes[4] are purely illustrative in nature. Even so, several caveats must be offered in order to prevent misunderstanding:

[4] No illustrative matrixes are offered for Situations E and F (zero-sum situations without and with a saddle point) because of their improbable occurrence in marital situations. The text reference to the religious rearing of children as Catholic or as Protestant is abstractly zero-sum, since a child cannot be reared as both; if the Catholic parent wins, the Protestant parent loses. But in real life, as T. C. Schelling points out (in a personal communication, August 28, 1962), this situation seems "unlikely to be truly zero-sum, partly because conflicting sales efforts might be perceived by both as doing some damage, partly because these issues could probably not be isolated from other issues on which threats could be based or on which compromise or compensation

1. The numbers have no significance except that of describing a scale of preference of the players with respect to the several anticipated outcomes. They do not imply that a metric has been imposed on them. In Matrix 1, the numbers mean only, for example, that Mary prefers to be at a prize fight with John (B2) to being at a concert with him (A1) or to being home with him (A3), and that she prefers being anywhere with him (A1, B2), except at home (C3), to being apart from him anywhere, etc.

2. The two numbers in any cell are never compared with one another. The comparisons are always among either the upper righthand numbers (Alter's values) or the lower lefthand numbers (Ego's values). If Mary's scale of preferences, as described in Matrix 1, were set along a linear scale, they might look like Fig. 2.

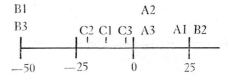

Fig. 2.

John's might look like Fig. 3.

The units are not the same; John has greater capacity for enjoyment than Mary; he enjoys things more than she does. But their satisfactions are never compared with one another's, always with their own.

might be based. . . ; once two games can be made conditional on each other, it is most unlikely that the enlarged game will be zero-sum." Furthermore, in real life, the child's religion would likely "mean" more to the mother than to the father and more to the Catholic parent than to the Protestant parent. Similar considerations apply to other theoretically possible zero-sum situations. Since marital relationships are in fact so unlikely to be zero-sum in nature, whatever the theoretical possibilities, it is almost impossible to illustrate zero-sum situations with credible instances. They are therefore omitted here.

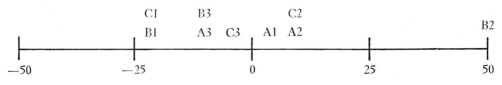

Fig. 3.

3. It is not necessary to assume that people think as precisely about their preferences as the payoff matrix seems to imply. But it must be assumed that people do prefer certain outcomes to others. If all outcomes have equal value, there is no problem, chance can determine the outcome without regard to the players.

Illustrative Matrix 1.
Coordination Game: Common and Conflicting Interests Present, No Communication
(Situation C)

Problem: John and Mary have quarreled at the breakfast table; they are not talking to one another when he leaves. How can they coordinate their behavior so that they can have the most enjoyable evening?

Preferences: The following matrix describes the relative value which each possible outcome has for each one.

Possible outcomes without communication:

A1. Both go to the concert. Mary enjoys the music but John is restless, looks bored, and thus detracts from her enjoyment. All he gets out of it is the pleasure of being with Mary. This outcome is "worth" 20 to Mary but only 5 to John, as shown in the cell for outcome A1.

A2. Mary goes to the concert and John goes to the prize fight. She doesn't get much enjoyment from the concert because John is not with her. John goes to the prize fight and enjoys it only moderately because Mary is not with him. This outcome has a value of zero for Mary and only 10 for John, again as shown in the cell for outcome A2 above.

A3. Mary goes to the concert and John stays home. She doesn't get any enjoyment because John is not with her. John is very bored and lonely without Mary.

B1. Mary goes to the prize fight and John goes to the concert. Both are miserable,

Mary's Alternatives	John's Alternatives		
	Go to Concert (1)	Go to Prize Fight (2)	Stay at Home (3)
Go to Concert (A)	5 20 (A1)	10 0 (A2)	−10 0 (A3)
Go to Prize Fight (B)	−20 −50 (B1)	50 25 (B2)	−10 −50 (B3)
Stay at Home (C)	−20 −10 (C1)	10 −20 (C2)	−5 −5 (C3)

Matrix 1.

Mary's Alternatives	John's Alternatives		
	1	(2)	(3)
(A)	5 0 (A1)	10 10 (A2)	−10 20 (A3)
(B)	−20 −50 (B1)	50 0 (B2)	−10 0 (B3)
(C)	−20 20 (C1)	10 10 (C2)	−5 0 (C3)

Matrix 1A.

not only because they are alone, but because neither enjoys the performance.

B2. Both go to the prize fight. Mary doesn't care for the performance but John enjoys it so much that she enjoys his pleasure and she enjoys being with him.

B3. Mary goes to the prize fight and John stays home. Both are miserable.

C1. Mary stays home and is lonely and miserable; John goes to the concert and is both bored and lonely.

C2. Mary stays home and John goes to the prize fight. She is lonely and miserable; he gets only moderate enjoyment from the prize fight because Mary is not with him.

C3. Both remain home and are bored and resentful because each missed a performance he (she) would have enjoyed.

Illustrative Matrix 1A.
Negative or Reverse Coordination Situation: Mary Uses John's Expectations to Frustrate Him

Mary now gets more satisfaction out of deliberately disappointing John's expectations than by fulfilling them. She knows, as in Matrix 1, that he expects her to meet him at the prize fight (outcome B2), because he expects her to prefer being with him at the prize fight to being alone either

Ego's Alternatives	Alter's Alternatives	
	1	2
A	8 7 (A1)	3 4 (A2)
B	1 2 (B1)	10 5 (B2)

Matrix 2.

Ego's Alternatives	Alter's Alternatives			
	1		2	
A	6	0 (A1)	1	−6 (A2)
B	−3	8 (B1)	2	12 (B2)

Matrix 3.

at the concert or at home. So, knowing he will go to the prize fight, she deliberately disappoints his expectation that she will also go there by going to the concert or staying home (A2 or C2), thus reducing his satisfaction. She has reduced her own satisfaction also (as compared with Matrix 1), but this seems worth while to her in order to reduce his as well. She has "cut off her nose to spite her face."

Illustrative Matrix 2.
Advantage of First Move
(Situation D)

If Ego had first move, he would select A, assuming that Alter would select 1 and the outcome would be A1. But if somehow or other Alter can manage to appropriate first move, he will select 2 and Ego will have to

settle for B. The outcome would then be B2.

Illustrative Matrix 3.
Manipulative Use of Strategic Threat by Alter When Ego Has First Move
(Situation D)

In this situation Ego prefers alternative A. This leaves for Alter the choice between 0 and −6, according to whether he selects 1 or 2. He could select 1, and the result would be outcome A1. If, however, he can threaten Ego with selecting 2 and convince Ego that he will carry out this threat, then Ego will prefer B to A, since the payoff is greater. Outcome B2 results. If Ego is not deterred by Alter's threat, both lose with outcome A2.

Ego's Alternatives	Alter's Alternatives			
	1		2	
A	6	11 (A1)	1	11 (A2)
B	−3	11 (B1)	3	12 (B2)

Matrix 3A.

Ego's Alternatives	Alter's Alternatives	
	1	2
A	5 3 (A1)	0 6 (A2)
B	12 —6 (B1)	10 6 (B2)

Matrix 4.

Illustrative Matrix 3A.
Warning Distinguished from Strategic Threat (Situation D)

Ego, in the absence of information about the probabilities of Alter's choice of 1 or 2, might be tempted to select A, taking a chance that Alter will select 1, leading to outcome A1. Alter's warning supplies the information Ego needs to make a better selection. When Alter "warns" that he will select 2, Ego changes his mind and selects B, leading to outcome B2. Alter's warning is not a threat, because 2 is preferable to him. He is not coercing Ego. If Ego had had all the necessary information in the first place, he would have known that B2 was as good a solution as he could expect; Alter's warning has clarified the outcomes and helped him select the one he would have selected in the first place.

Illustrative Matrix 4.
Manipulative Use of Strategic Promise by Alter
When Ego Has First Move (Situation D)

Ordinarily Ego, to avoid the possibility of losing 6, selects A. This leaves for Alter the choice between gaining 5 or 0, according to whether he selects 1 or 2. He would select 1, and the result would be outcome A1. If, however, Alter can promise Ego

that he will select 2 if Ego will select B, both can double their payoffs with the outcome B2. If Alter should renege on his promise and select 1 in order to raise his payoff from 10 to 12, leaving Ego with a loss of 6, the basis of trust between them would be shaken if not destroyed, and Alter would lose his ability to promise in the future.

REFERENCES

Baber, R. F. *Marriage and the family.* New York: McGraw-Hill, 1953.

Bergler, E. *Unhappy marriage and divorce: a study of neurotic choice of marriage partners.* New York: International Univer. Press, 1946.

Bergler, E. *Divorce won't help.* New York: Harper, 1948.

Bernard, Jessie. *American family behavior.* New York: Harper, 1942.

Bernard, Jessie. *Remarriage, a study of marriage.* New York: Dryden, 1956.

Bernard, Jessie. *American community behavior.* (Rev. ed.) New York: Holt, Rinehart & Winston, 1962.

Blood, R. O., Jr., & Wolfe, D. M. *Husbands and wives; the dynamics of married living.* Glencoe, Ill.: Free Press, 1960.

Bossard, J. H. S., & Boll, Eleanor S. The sociology of child development. New York: Harper, 1960.

Burgess, E. W. The family and the person. *Publ. Amer. sociol. Soc.,* 1927, 20, 133–143.

Burgess, E. W., & Cottrell, L. S. *Predicting*

success or failure in marriage. Englewood Cliffs, N.J.: Prentice-Hall, 1939.

Burgess, E. W., & Locke, H. J. *The family.* (2nd ed.) New York: American Book, 1960.

Burgess, E. W., & Wallin, P. *Engagement and marriage.* Philadelphia: Lippincott, 1953.

Christensen, H. T. *Marriage analysis: foundations for successful family life.* (2nd ed.) New York: Ronald Press, 1958.

Davis, Katharine B. *Factors in the sex life of twenty-two hundred women.* New York: Harper, 1929.

Deutsch, Helene. *Psychology of women.* New York: Grune & Stratton, 1944–1945.

Dickinson, R. L., & Beam, Lura. *One thousand marriages.* Baltimore: Williams & Wilkins, 1931.

Duvall, Evelyn. *In-laws: pro and con.* New York: Association Press, 1954.

Duvall, Evelyn, & Hill, R. *Being married.* Boston: Heath, 1960.

Erikson, E. H. *Childhood and society.* (2nd ed.) New York: Norton, 1963.

Farber, B. Family organization and crisis: maintenance of integration in families with a severely mentally retarded child. *Monogr. Soc. Res. Child Develpm.,* No. 25, 1960.

Farber, B. Types of family organization: child-oriented, home-oriented, and parent-oriented. In A. M. Rose (Ed.), *Human behavior and social processes.* Boston: Houghton Mifflin, 1962. Pp. 285–306.

Firey, W. Informal organization and the theory of schism. *Amer. sociol. Rev.,* 1948, 13, 15–24.

Folsom, J. K. *The family and democratic society.* New York: Wiley, 1943.

Foote, N. N., & Cottrell, L. S., Jr., *Identity and interpersonal competence: a new direction in family research.* Chicago: Univer. of Chicago Press, 1955.

Frazier, E. F. *The Negro family in the United States.* New York: Dryden Press, 1948.

Goffman, E. *The presentation of the self in everyday life.* New York: Doubleday Anchor, 1959.

Goode, W. J. *After divorce.* Glencoe, Ill.: Free Press, 1956.

Gurin, G., Veroff, J., & Feld, Sheila. *Americans view their mental health.* New York: Basic Books, 1960.

Hamblin, R., & Blood, R. O. Premarital experiences and the wife's sexual adjustment. *Soc. Probl.,* 1957, 4, 122–130.

Herndon, C. N., & Nash, Ethel M. Premarriage and marriage counseling. *J. Amer. med. Ass.,* 1962, 180, 395–401.

Jacobson, P. H. *American marriage and divorce.* New York: Rinehart, 1959.

Kinsey, A. C., Pomeroy, W. B., & Martin, C. E. *Sexual behavior in the human male.* Philadelphia: Saunders, 1948.

Kinsey, A. C., Pomeroy, W. B., Martin, C. E., & Gebhard, P. H. *Sexual behavior in the human female.* Philadelphia: Saunders, 1953.

Kirkpatrick, C. *The family: as process and institution.* (2nd ed.) New York: Ronald Press, 1963.

Komarovsky, Mirra. The homemaker: a comparative view. *AAUW J.,* 1962, 55, 226–229.

Landis, J. T. Length of time required to achieve adjustment in marriage. *Amer. sociol. Rev.,* 1946, 11, 666–677.

Landis, J. T. Marriages of mixed and nonmixed religious faith. *Amer. sociol. Rev.,* 1949, 14, 401–407.

Lantz, H. R., & Snyder, Eloise C. *Marriage: an examination of man-woman relationships.* New York: Wiley, 1962.

Litwak, E. Geographic mobility and extended family cohesion. *Amer. sociol. Rev.,* 1960, 25, 385–394. (a)

Litwak, E. Occupational mobility and extended family cohesion. *Amer. sociol. Rev.,* 1960, 25, 9–21. (b)

Locke, H. *Predicting adjustment in marriage: a comparison of a divorced and a happily married group.* New York: Holt, 1951.

Luce, R. D., & Raiffa, H. *Games and decisions.* New York: Wiley, 1957.

Luckey, Eleanore B. Marital satisfaction and congruent self-spouse concepts. *Soc. Forces,* 1960, 39, 153–157.

MacIver, R. M. *Social causation.* Boston: Ginn, 1942.

Masters, W. F., & Johnson, Virginia E. Orgasm, anatomy of the female. In A. Ellis & A. Abarbanel (Eds.), *Encyclopedia of sexual behavior.* New York: Hawthorn Books, 1961.

Rainwater, L., & Weinstein, Karol K. *And the poor get children.* Chicago: Quadrangle Books, 1960.

Rapoport, A. *Fights, games, and debates.* Ann Arbor: Univer. of Michigan Press, 1960.

Ross, E. A. *Principles of sociology.* New York: Century, 1921.

Rowbotham, J. M. *Troubadours and courts of love*. New York: Macmillan, 1895.

Sapirstein, M. *Emotional security*. New York: Crown, 1948.

Schelling, T. C. *The strategy of conflict*. Cambridge: Harvard Univer. Press, 1960.

Siegel, S. A method for obtaining an ordered metric scale. *Psychometrika*, 1956, 21, 207–216.

Simon, H. A formal theory of interaction in social groups. *Amer. sociol. Rev.*, 1952, 17, 202–211.

Spiegel, J. P. The resolution of role conflict within the family. In M. Greenblatt, D. Levinson, & R. H. Williams (Eds.), *The patient and the mental hospital*. Glencoe, Ill.: Free Press, 1957. Pp. 545–564.

Srole, L., Langner, T. S., Michael, S. T., Opler, M. K., & Rennie, T. A. C. *Mental health in the metropolis: the midtown Manhattan study*. New York: McGraw-Hill, 1962.

Straus, A. Transformation of identity. In A. M. Rose (Ed.), *Human behavior and social processes*. Boston: Houghton Mifflin, 1962. Pp. 63–85.

Strong, E. K. *Change of interests with age*. Stanford: Stanford Univer. Press, 1931.

Terman, L. M., with Buttenwieser, P., Ferguson, L. W., Johnson, W. B., & Wilson, D. P. *Psychological factors in marital happiness*. New York: McGraw-Hill, 1938.

Terman, L. M., & Wallin, P. Marriage prediction and marital adjustment tests. *Amer. sociol. Rev.*, 1949, 14, 497–504.

Townsend, P. *The family life of old people*. London: Routledge & Paul, 1957.

Udry, J. R., Nelson, H. A., & Nelson, Ruth. An empirical investigation of some widely held beliefs about marital interaction. *Marr. & fam. Living*, 1961, 23, 388–390.

Waller, W., & Hill, R. *The family, a dynamic interpretation*. New York: Dryden Press, 1951.

Williams, J. D. *The compleat strategyst*. New York: McGraw-Hill, 1954.

Willoughby, R. R. The relationship of emotionality to age, sex, and conjugal condition. *Amer. J. Sociol.*, 1938, 43, 923.

Winch, R. *Mate selection*. New York: Harper, 1958.

CHAPTER 18 Socialization and Personality Development in the Child[1]

EDWARD Z. DAGER
Purdue University

Beginning with the treatment of the psychodynamics of the human mind by William James (1890), "theories" about personality and the development of personality have flooded the behavioral sciences. With variable sets of assumptions, hypotheses, and differentiated frames of reference, and sometimes without the benefit of these, the proponents of each of these theories have attempted to study and understand the nature of human nature. Hall and Lindzey (1957), in their excellent survey of the field, were able to include over a dozen of these "theories" and still did not encompass the entire field.

Whatever the theoretical bent of the investigator, however, personality formation has been viewed universally as taking place during the early years. Since the first years of life are spent primarily within the family, it is our intention to focus upon the family and to attempt to assess its impact upon the developing personality.

[1] The author wishes to acknowledge the critical evaluations of G. R. Leslie and E. J. Kanin and the helpful comments of Kathryn Johnsen, James Moore, and Esther Dager.

CONVERGENCE OF THE THEORETICAL APPROACHES

In the past few decades, especially, we have witnessed the development of many "theories" of personality, each with its own emphasis. But the forerunner of practically all personality theorists and the man most responsible for the proliferation of theories of personality has been Freud (1949). Freud, although his influence on subsequent theorists has been variable, was the first to elucidate systematically the impact of infantile experiences on the development of the personality, its functioning, and its disorders. Thus, Freud set the pattern for the study of personality and the twin problem of personality, socialization.

Socialization, in addition to biological and hereditary makeup, is the common meeting ground of all the sciences dealing with man; for here biology, psychiatry, psychology, sociology, and anthropology come together (Davis, 1948). Although each of these intellectual traditions has had its own frame of reference and often has been convinced of the correctness of its own point of view, there has recently developed, in social psychology, a convergence of interests which incorporates extant knowledge and research into a unified and sophisticated study of human behavior.

Contributions to the study of socialization and personality by each of the disciplines mentioned above have not always been oriented toward the understanding of how the newborn infant is molded into a social being per se, but each discipline has studied some aspect of the problem and has thereby contributed to a greater understanding of the over-all process.

Anthropologists, although traditionally concerned with cultures, kinship systems, and artifacts, have more recently devoted a great deal of time to culture and personality studies. Prior to the 1920's, anthropologists dealt with few, if any, psychological elements, and the culture and personality approach was virtually unknown (C. Kluckhohn, 1944). Since then, however, the studies of Margaret Mead (1928; 1930) and Ruth Benedict (1928), coupled with the writings and influence of Edward Sapir (1932) and the subsequent rapprochement of anthropology with the psychological disciplines have led to a plethora of studies which attempt to relate cultural factors to specific personality syndromes—to basic personality structure, modal personality, and national character. For an amplification of the many facets of the culture and personality field, the reader is referred to the many excellent volumes (Cohen, 1961; Haring, 1949; Hsu, 1961; Kaplan, 1961; Kluckhohn & Murray, 1948) and essays (Hallowell, 1953; Inkeles & Levinson, 1954; Kaplan, 1957; Margaret Mead, 1953) available.

Contributions of anthropologists to the understanding of personality and its relation to culture and social structure cannot be overestimated. It is from them that we became aware of cultural transmission via the socialization process and more recently of the interdependence that exists between personalities and social structure (Cohen,

1961). Another related aspect of significance to this chapter has been the range of studies dealing with child-rearing practices specifically and their relation to the development of personality and to social institutions in general (Kardiner, 1939; Kardiner, 1945; Whiting & Child, 1953). Whiting and Whiting (1960) ably delineate the methodological, conceptual, and substantive contributions anthropology has made to the study of child-rearing practices. Thus, we are able to note, and hopefully to utilize, the insights gained by anthropologists in their attempts to clarify the relation between socialization and personality.

Anthropologists probably have been the most influential in demonstrating the link between culture, socialization, and personality, but the seeds for many of their studies were planted by the theories of Freud (1949) and subsequent psychoanalysts. It was Freud who questioned the rationality of man and dramatized the importance of early experiences in the adult personality. It was he who gave the social sciences a new conception of man. Freud, however, was intent on relating personality variables to the biological structure of the individual, and it was left to his followers to broaden the base and demonstrate the utility of his ideas for the social organism. Some classic psychoanalysts still rely upon innate factors and instinct to explain personality. But among the neo-Freudians, Kardiner (1945) and others have shown the cultural relativity of human behavior, and Sullivan (1953) exemplifies those who see personality manifestations as the result of social interaction.

In addition, of course, psychoanalysis gives us the mechanisms of defense, the concepts of Oedipus, Electra, and other complexes, and most importantly the notion that neuroses and psychoses in adulthood are almost always related to experiences in early childhood. Some of these concepts have since been discarded and others modified, but the psychoanalyst's approach nevertheless stands as that which appears to have had the greatest influence in subsequent personality theories. It has practically dominated the field of child development and child-rearing.

Psychologists, in addition to their development of learning theory and the attendant perceptual and motivational processes of the individual, also have a fairly large investment in the general area of personality. This is especially true of the child psychologists and clinical psychologists. Unfortunately, of the many theories of personality that stem primarily from historical psychology, and of a substantial number of other theories extant today, few are oriented toward socialization and personality *development*. The development of personality is seen as somewhat tangential to other foci of interest, even among those few theories which involve development (R. R. Sears, 1959).

Among the latter, probably the most influential has been the behavioristic psychology of Watson, refined by such later associationists as Tolman, Hull, Guthrie, Miller, and Spence. The main concern of these theorists has been the learning process, and it was Hull who first inspired some of his students to apply learning theory to psychoanalytically discovered phenomena (R. R. Sears, 1959). Psychologists have become increasingly concerned about developmental factors in personality, and there is considerable evidence in the literature to indicate that they are applying the theoretical principles they have so painstakingly evolved to environmental factors—i.e., families, social class, group affiliation, and others—and the result is more than sheer behaviorism. It represents a dynamic interpretation, not just of personality, but also of personality *development*.

Sociologists have long studied the regularities and uniformities of groups and masses. The founders of sociology, such as Durkheim, Simmel, and Weber, recognized, however, that these were not mere "mass" movements but the result of interactions among individuals, ultimately combining to form groups of various sizes which had their own unique processes and their own structures. However, most sociologists traditionally have been concerned with the group per se and not with the individual—with organizations, mass movements, and *patterns* of behavior, not with the individuals in interaction which created those patterns.

Through the study of group processes, some sociologists, with influence from other disciplines, became vitally concerned with problems of socialization and attempted to answer the question of how individuals develop the capacity and the personality structure to participate in and to organize groups. Thus, the works of Cooley (1902), Thomas (Thomas & Znaniecki, 1918–1920), and Park (Park & Burgess, 1921) were instrumental in creating a distinct theoretical orientation toward personality development.

This is not to say that sociologists were uninfluenced by such men as George Herbert Mead, John Dewey, William James, and others from various disciplines, but sociologists have made a unique contribution to the study of personality, through such processes as interaction, i.e., taking into consideration the individual as well as the social patterns. Interaction became the key notion in the study of human behavior and, through the vehicle of cultural norms and the concepts of role and status (elaborated subsequently into role models), became the focus of the study of the individual in his social setting. Coupled with the study of attitudes and values, sociologists also began to see the individual as an actor in, as well as a reactor to, his social environment. [Cf. Ch. 4.]

Sociologists, too, were greatly influenced by psychoanalytic theories. The more recent push in this direction has come from the many writings of sociologists who, when dealing with socialization and personality formation, have very strong leanings toward the theories of Freud and his followers. The most comprehensive contribution along these lines has been made by Parsons (Parsons & Bales, 1955). Parsons, in this work and others, has made the herculean attempt to combine sociological and psychoanalytic theories into a fairly unified, fairly viable, schema. His work has stimulated many others to research, which has proven to be valuable to the understanding of the structural processes of society—especially the family and the dynamics of personality growth. Although this attempt is strongly sociological, the influence of psychoanalytic conceptions is clear.

Thus, it would seem that psychoanalytic theory has been the prime mover in practically all of the approaches to socialization and personality development. The major point to be made, however, is that at the juncture of the greatest cross-fertilization among disciplines is the greatest progress in our attempt at understanding human behavior. Furthermore, as one peruses the literature, it becomes increasingly clear that no one discipline of any significance is completely independent from the other disciplines. This is especially true in the study of socialization and personality development.

DEFINITIONS AND DELIMITATIONS

Socialization can be defined with relative ease, and with a consensus of opinion, as that process by which the infant learns the ways of a given social grouping and is "molded" into an effective participant of that group. The individual learns of the values, attitudes, norms, and other attributes of his culture; in time he becomes a social being. It is a long, tortuous, sometimes pleasurable, sometimes painful process, and the individual travels the route in his own unique way and acquires those minimal personality qualities deemed appropriate by the group. This is not to say that he becomes an exact replica of the expectations of his fellow members, because he doesn't. It is impossible to duplicate the experiences, perceptions, and interpretations of any given member of a group, even with twins. Therefore, each individual is unique at the same time that he has commonalities with his group.

We resist considering personality in either the extreme represented by Allport (1937;

1961), that the personality resides entirely "within the individual," or the other extreme initiated by Thrasher (1927), that personality is "the role which the individual plays in his group." Both of these conceptions are partially correct, since personality is in part a function of the roles one enacts and the norms one learns during the socialization process, and the individual in this process of internalizing expectations and other experiences does so intrapersonally. Personality therefore becomes a function of each of the above conceptions, and more— more, because personality evolves over the entire life span of the individual, and certain changes accrue to him from both group pressure and internal processes. Thus, to conceive of personality as being those traits and characteristics organized uniquely, but according to group expectations, fills the need for definition at a particular moment in time but ignores ongoing processes which facilitate change in the individual. However, both the persistent elements and the change must be taken into account.

Because the related fields of socialization and personality are so vast, involving a wealth of substantive material as well as a plethora of approaches, it is necessary to delimit this essay to a range of ideas which will be channeled by social structure (structural-functional approach) on the one hand and by the theory of symbolic interaction on the other. [See Chs 3 and 4 of this Handbook.] The literature brought to bear on the subject will be drawn mostly from the many contributors in the above-mentioned disciplines, but will use some data from other disciplines. Each has made substantive and methodological contributions without which adequate study of either socialization or personality development would be impossible.

Personality theory, if such exists, is a discipline most likely to be absorbed by and, in one way or another, deflected to other aspects of sociology, the psychologies, and anthropology. It is therefore becoming increasingly necessary to develop conceptualizations which deal, not with personality variables alone, but also with the social system within which the personality is involved. Thus, interaction, group process, culture, social structure, and other elements enter into and affect the inner dynamics of the individual.

To illustrate the necessity of interrelating the above: personality tests, though useful in other ways, seldom, if ever, shed any light on the interaction elements or the developmental processes in human behavior. As one example among many, Burchinal (1958) found no significant correlations between parental scale scores and the personality test scores of children and had, therefore, to conclude that parental attitudes toward children and children's personality and adjustment status were unrelated. If this actually exists in such an intimate relationship as that between the child and the parent, then we would have to conclude that social relations in general have little or no meaning. But the author would suggest this is not the case. The fault lies not in the researcher but in the diverse one-shot devices used in an attempt to measure personality and other complex variables. The need is not to conceptualize the variables as discrete entities and then have them compared to one another, but to conceive of them as interrelated units, parts of which have meaning and significance to a particular phenomenon or situation and parts of which do not.

Although socialization and personality development can be approached in many ways, it is our intention to limit this chapter to a consideration of two facets of the socialization process which have direct and indirect bearing upon the problem. (a) Initially, a synopsis of symbolic interaction theory will be presented to form the backdrop for the next two sections. (b) Then, an attempt will be made to demonstrate how social structure imparts to the agencies of socialization certain conditions to which the group tends to conform and, second, how these in turn affect the method and substance by which the child is transformed

from a piece of protoplasm into a human being. We shall proceed from the larger social system to the smaller—from some of the dominant value themes of United States culture to the many subcultural systems such as race, class, and ethnicity, each of which provides differential access to cultural values, ideologies, and material things. Finally, we shall turn to intimate small-group interactions from which the neophyte learns by imitation, learning, and other processes. The former is related to the latter and vice versa.

In the first instance, we see socialization and child-rearing practices as a dependent variable affected by the larger social structure, which in turn affects personality. In the second, socialization and child-rearing practices become the independent variable, studied so that we can refer directly to agencies of socialization, such as the family, as being responsible for a particular kind of personality. It appears that the point at which one begins his analysis determines whether he sees socialization as a dependent or independent variable. Here, we plan to approach our topic from both points, albeit at different times. Neither approach alone is sufficient to "explain" personality. Each becomes a necessary but not sufficient condition for elucidating personality variables; and both are here treated as reciprocal entities, one affecting the other. In this manner, we can avoid the circularity so clearly stated by Aberle (1961) where antecedent and consequent variables feed upon each other, one begetting a similar version of the other in a never ending circle providing no room for change.

SYMBOLIC INTERACTION THEORY OF SOCIALIZATION

Symbolic interaction is considered here as a middle range theory. [For a more detailed, though somewhat parallel, treatment of symbolic interactionism, see Ch. 4, especially pp. 127–143.] It does not pretend to cover the entire range of human behavior, as we shall see, but to focus upon the interaction element in human behavior and upon a limited range of the social structure. Given certain limiting conditions such as ethnicity, social class, or cultural system, one can deal with the individuals within such a subsystem and consider what influences certain individuals have on the development of other, less socialized individuals. Moreover, the study of interactional processes will permit us to determine the "how" and sometimes the "why" of cultural transmission, to understand the development of certain values and personality traits.

As with any theoretical scheme, certain preconditions exist which need to be spelled out. The basic assumptions and postulates follow.

The first assumption is that the individual is born *tabula rasa;* that is, he has nothing on his mind and no intra-uterine learning has taken place. This means that the new-born infant is neither social nor antisocial, but rather asocial (Stryker, 1959). Little evidence of merit exists about what exactly the fetus has learned in utero, although a fetus may be affected by diet or intake of toxic elements by the mother. The second assumption considers hereditary factors to be constant in any given population. We know this to be untrue in pure form, but the rationale for our making the assumption rests on three factors: (a) we are here dealing with social interactional processes and are not interested in biological factors per se; (b) in a statistically normal population, most individuals are constituted at birth with approximately like biological potentials, from which any deviation will probably random out; and (c) we are interested in studying the biologically normal individual, not the abnormal. Even such a factor as intelligence, once thought to be a biologically fixed entity, has been shown in recent years to vary with social class and time.

There are three postulates necessary for the delineation of this position, the first of which denies both the cultural determinists'

point of view and the classical behaviorism of Watson. It is that the individual is considered an actor as well as a reactor (Stryker, 1959). He is not merely a passive agent—a sponge, so to speak, soaking up and reacting to his environment—but an individual who, in the learning process, also acts on his environment and on others. The individual has the capacity for original thought and for combining existing knowledge in a way unique enough to induce change from previously accepted ways of behaving. Furthermore, the individual has the capacity to view himself objectively as well as subjectively, providing for man the special quality of rationality (G. H. Mead, 1934). Admittedly, the proportion of a given individual's behavior in the role of the "actor" is relatively small. We agree with learning theorists that perception always involves the past and that the interpretation one makes of his present perceptions permits him to predict the future, mostly on the basis of past experience. It follows then that one's initial experiences in infancy and childhood must have an effect on later personality organization. Nevertheless, the evidence available on personal as well as social change suggests that the individual has "actor" potential great enough in most cases to permit him the degree of control necessary to fashion his destiny within the limits of the prevailing culture.

The second postulate states that the basic unit for study is interaction (Stryker, 1959). It further states that both the individual and society stem from interactional processes—without interaction, individual existence, as we know it, would vanish and so, consequently, would society. As we shall see later, one's concept of self is dependent upon interaction.

The third and final postulate becomes the main focal point for the observation and measurement of behavior. This states that man attempts to put order into his world. As simple as this sounds, one cannot escape the conclusion that man's interaction with man is dependent upon the predictable ordering of his physical and social universe. Note the attempts of man at ordering the building of roads, dwellings, cities, etc., without which the physical world in which he lives would be chaotic.

Consider, then, what this means to the social scientist dealing with personality development. Among a host of other things, he must consider first of all language (or some other form of communication), because language provides the basis for structure in most social relationships. Language itself is ordered, and it in turn permits man to conceptualize and categorize his universe. The development of self is dependent upon language, for if we had no tools of communication, others would be unable to tell the neophyte who or what he was, and he in turn would have no way of categorizing himself. Furthermore, if the individual had no language with which to order his world, he would be devoid of memory, and without memory the past would vanish, culture would be unknown, and man would be unable to build a complex structure in his relations with other humans.

A corollary to the postulate of order, and in some ways dependent upon it, has to do with man's relative position to other men. His position always involves implicit or explicit evaluations of self made by others. Such evaluations are, in turn, interpreted by the individual, and he draws some conclusions as to what other people think of him (Cooley, 1902). Interpretations of this kind occur after the child has developed a concept of self, and result in a determination of his relative worth or status. A high degree of orderliness (predictability) will permit him to make distinct evaluations of his status, and integration of self is made easy. Should a drastic change in a pattern of behavior occur, or should the behavior patterns manifest ambiguity, a lack of integration exists, and one's status is in doubt; this may be interpreted as rejection, lack of acceptance, or some other disorganizing reaction. So, the corollary to the postulate of order is that man seeks to stabilize his

status. Such motivation occurs some time after the development of self.

Once the individual is able to distinguish self from others, however, other elements come into play: identification, generalized other, norms, roles, positions, reference groups, and additional factors, which will be considered in greater detail when socialization practices are treated as an independent variable. However, there is a "setting" in which these phenomena take place, so the next section will be concerned with the social structure as a backdrop, and with the impact this has upon child-rearing in particular and socialization in general.

SOCIAL STRUCTURE, SOCIALIZATION, AND PERSONALITY

In this section, socialization and child-rearing practices will be treated as variables dependent upon many facets of the larger social structure. However, they will be considered dependent only in the sense that they occur within a particular socio-cultural setting and that this setting functions as a necessary condition for the development of personality but does not include the *sufficient* condition for the ultimate determination of personality per se. For example, one can grant the notion of dominant cultural values to which the majority adhere, but one notes also that these values are internalized in varying degrees of intensity and in some segments of the culture not at all. Where these values are not inculcated, faulty socialization occurs; and faulty socialization usually takes place on the interactional, primary-group level.

Stability versus Change

Socio-cultural conditions have great influence, and it is to this aspect that we address ourselves here, with our aim being to demonstrate the interdependence of the larger social setting with socialization practices and to avoid attempting to explain personality outside the social system. At the same time, we wish to avoid the pure structural theories which do not explain the continuity of a social system primarily because they fail to deal with personalities.

Any social system, if it is to survive, must provide institutionalized means by which the young are positively oriented toward contemporary cultural values, thereby "building in" sufficient elements of social control to enable the system to perpetuate itself. Thus, socialization is not only basic to personality development, but also has manifest implications for and is requisite to social organization. The child learns by precept and by example those various age, sex, occupational, and other roles around which there is sufficient consensus to permit the stable expectations upon which socially organized behavior is based. At the same time, although there is nothing sacred about change, social or technological, the system must provide a latitude of expression to permit those changes necessary for the survival of that system. Thus, in American society today, under pressure of a cold war, innovation and creativity seem necessary for survival and are in great demand. But even under normal conditions, one of the primary values in our society is that of economic competition which demands the creation of new or different goods and ideas. The problem then becomes one of balance between stability and change—a strain toward consistency—in the operation of a social system which is not independent of but perpetuated by personalities which go to make up that system.

Systematic researches relating structural variables of a social system to socialization practices are comparatively few, and where data are available, they are often of the case study type. Moreover, the kinds of questions to which these studies are oriented do not meet our requirements directly, i.e., the treatment of socialization practices as dependent variables. Nevertheless, such studies will be of use, since we will be able to make inferences from the data presented.

"Culture and Personality" Studies

The general class of studies referred to are those concerned with culture and personality and which fall variously under such headings as basic personality structure, national character, modal personality, and the like. Distinctions can be made among these conceptualizations, but the utility for this exposition lies in the common notion that there are cultural patterns, dominant value themes, and institutions which permeate the total society, affecting ways of behaving which in turn affect personality. Otherwise put, there are conditions in the culture and social structure which are mediated by the agencies of socialization to the individual which produce similar personality syndromes. There is by no means a one to one ratio in this development, but however imperfect the relationship may be for individuals and subcultural groupings, there is enough evidence from presently available research to substantiate the existence of types of patterns in a given culture. Thus, members of any enduring group, large or small, will manifest some similar personality patterns. As Kluckhohn and Murray state,

By and large, the motivational structures and action patterns of Western Europeans seem similar when contrasted to the Near East or to Eastern Asiatics. Most white citizens of the United States, in spite of regional, ethnic and class differences, have features of personality which distinguish them from Englishmen, Australians or New Zealanders (1948, p. 39).

From this vantage point, one can note that central tendencies or common cultural patterns exist which pervade and transcend the individual. These are elements which are contingent upon the larger social structure. Florence Kluckhohn illuminates this by saying that our highly rationalized economic system produces " . . . achievement-minded, independent, and future oriented individuals who are largely free of ties that bind them in time and place" (1958, p. 70).

Some value of orientations of Americans can be put in historical perspective by relating them, at least partly, to the geography of the frontier and the demands of the physical environment. Such values as independence, initiative, freedom, and so on appear to have been prerequisites in that era, residues of which can be found today. Ecology, too, can act as the catalyst, as Erikson (1950) attempts to demonstrate by relating certain personality patterns of the Yurok to the fishing economy.

The area which has involved the greatest amount of research and reporting is the delineation of personality uniformities through the study of child-rearing practices. Although it is customary in studies of this kind to view child-rearing practice as a dependent variable, there is a circularity in them which implies that social institutions are reflections of personalities, which in turn are fed back into child-rearing practices, thereby resulting in national character, basic personality, modal personality, and so on. Kardiner (1945), for example, suggested that child-rearing practices result in certain psychological mechanisms which are reflected in art, religion, and magic, and he labeled this the "projective system."

Du Bois (1949), who was greatly influenced by Kardiner's conception, attempts to demonstrate that the children of Alor are socialized by adults who are unable to spend much time with them because of economic hardship. In this case, the mother must spend a great many hours gardening (economic pursuits). Consequently, children are fed twice daily and between times must shift for themselves. All this presumably leads to obsessive-compulsive behavior concerning food in adulthood.

Stephens (1962) attempts to demonstrate, à la Freud, and with the use of cross-cultural data, that young boys, under the optimal conditions of a long postpartum sex taboo, become sexually attracted to their mothers, which seemingly results in castration anxiety. It is reasoned that the mother-son sex attraction comes about in part by the fact that the mother's sexual frustration, resulting from the sex taboo, is redirected toward the child. The implications of this study are many, insofar as Stephens has related a significant quantity of the cross-cultural data of the Human Relations Area Files to one aspect of the classical Freudian Oedipus complex. From these data, he draws conclusions that the above-mentioned mother-son interaction has implications bearing upon later anxieties, menstrual taboos, initiation, totemism, and sorcery. We can extrapolate this to common personality characteristics for adults, which brings us full circle to child-rearing practices.

Similarly, Whiting and Child (1953) have related sorcery to patterns of illness in societies in which there was severe punishment for children in areas of sex and aggression; and McClelland and Friedman (1952), in a study of North American societies, report that achievement motivation was related to severe early training in independence. Gorer (1948), Fromm (1941), Riesman (Riesman, Glazer, & Denny, 1950), and others have found similar social characteristics of people in our own society, each from a somewhat different point of view, but their analyses point to personality similarities and common patterns.

Admittedly, most of these reports leave much to be desired. They are time bound, sometimes display a circularity which precludes change, often deal in inferences, and seldom if ever involve complete representation from the total society. But the purpose here is not to make a critical analysis, nor to review all the studies of this class. It is rather to point up the fact that any given culture, in a given time period, will display a consistency which results in certain values, ideologies, norms, and attitudes which in one way or another tend to affect the majority of the people in that culture and help to determine socialization practices. Linton has stated this nicely in a set of postulates:

1. That the individual's early experiences exert a lasting affect upon his personality, es-

pecially upon the development of his projective systems.

2. That similar experiences will tend to produce similar personality configurations in the individuals who are subjected to them.

3. That the techniques which the members of any society employ in the care and rearing of children are culturally patterned and will tend to be similar, although never identical, for various families within the society.

4. That the culturally patterned techniques for the care and rearing of children differ from one society to another.

If these postulates are correct, and they seem to be supported by a wealth of evidence, it follows:

1. That the members of any given society will have many elements of early experience in common.

2. That as a result of this they will have many elements of personality in common.

3. That since the early experience of individuals differs from one society to another, the personality norms for various societies will also differ (Kardiner, 1945, pp. vii–viii).

How Social Structure Affects Personality

Let us now turn to a class of studies which have come out in more recent years and in which socialization can be viewed more clearly and unambiguously as a dependent variable. Adapting from Fig. 1, we

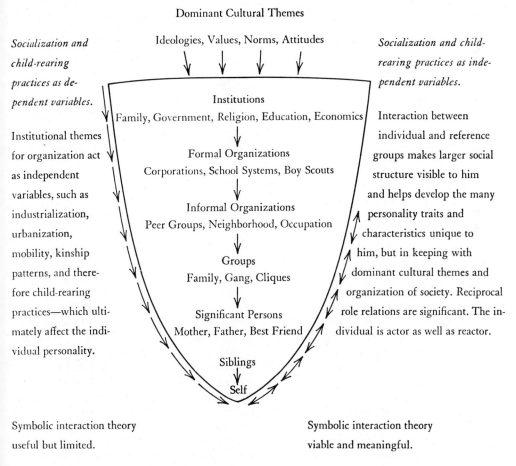

Socialization and child-rearing practices as dependent variables.

Institutional themes for organization act as independent variables, such as industrialization, urbanization, mobility, kinship patterns, and therefore child-rearing practices—which ultimately affect the individual personality.

Socialization and child-rearing practices as independent variables.

Interaction between individual and reference groups makes larger social structure visible to him and helps develop the many personality traits and characteristics unique to him, but in keeping with dominant cultural themes and organization of society. Reciprocal role relations are significant. The individual is actor as well as reactor.

Dominant Cultural Themes

Ideologies, Values, Norms, Attitudes

Institutions
Family, Government, Religion, Education, Economics

Formal Organizations
Corporations, School Systems, Boy Scouts

Informal Organizations
Peer Groups, Neighborhood, Occupation

Groups
Family, Gang, Cliques

Significant Persons
Mother, Father, Best Friend

Siblings

Self

Symbolic interaction theory useful but limited.

Symbolic interaction theory viable and meaningful.

Fig. 1.   Socialization-Personality Schema.

move from the larger social structure to the agencies of socialization, the former imparting certain conditions beyond the latter's control and to which the latter must adapt, thereby affecting the ways and means by which the young are socialized. This is depicted on the left side of Fig. 1; the arrows all point down, eventually reaching and affecting the individual. For example, family structure can affect socialization. Whiting (1961), using his own and other's data, was able to show that high infant indulgence was more likely to occur in polygynous or extended family households than in nuclear or mother-child households, with resultant differences in personality.

Economic factors play a dominant role in socialization also. Du Bois' study (1949) mentioned above illustrates that the means of livelihood of the Alor precludes great interaction between mother and child. Barry, Bacon, and Child (1957), in their cross-cultural study of socialization, found that boys are trained more for achievement, independence, and self-reliance in those cultures in which hunting, grain agriculture, or large animal herding was the means of livelihood. These traits appeared to be important for later role behavior and for societal functions. Girls, on the other hand, were trained for obedience, nurturance, and responsibility.

Such conditions as illustrated above are here taken as given, but they, too, have a history and are due to other factors. Moreover, it would seem that change would not occur if personalities feed back into the system the essence of the values and behaviors of the previous generation. Certainly some societies change far less rapidly than ours, so that change would appear imperceptible over several generations, but American society has changed measurably in less than a generation. It behooves us, therefore, to show the kind of interaction which produces personality change and, subsequently, change in role behavior and, ultimately, change in social organization.

A good example of how social structure affects personality is given by Miller and Swanson (1958) when they relate certain socialization practices to occupations. They proceed from explanations of economic needs which created conditions conducive to change from small business enterprises and small governmental agencies to large business and large government enterprises. This resulted in a shift from entrepreneurial to bureaucratic organizations, which provided conditions for new role requirements. They then compared entrepreneurial with bureaucratic child-rearing practices, and reported the entrepreneurial as being stricter and more achievement-oriented, whereas the bureaucratic were more "other" directed, more permissive, and oriented toward adjustment in child-rearing practices. Similarly, Aberle and Naegele (1952) view the parent (father) as socializing the child for the role he expects the child to hold as an adult, and the model for this role is the occupational orientation he himself holds.

Thus, the occupational structure appears to have an indirect but nevertheless meaningful impact on child-rearing practices and, although occupation itself is felt and transmitted most directly by the parent, so, too, are over-all value orientations which are part and parcel of the social class system and which also affect socialization.

A review of the literature comparing middle- and lower-class child-rearing practices by Bronfenbrenner (1958) and subsequent researches (Kohn, 1959a; Kohn, 1959b; Kohn & Carroll, 1960) reveal some generalized notions about differences between middle and lower classes. More middle-class mothers are permissive than are lower-class mothers. Middle-class parents are more concerned about the internalization of self-control by the child, and in this sense are future-oriented, while lower-class parents are more concerned about immediate consequences of child behavior and maintaining order and obedience. Furthermore, middle-class parents are more easily given to change in their child-rearing practices, primarily because they have access to or are more amenable to expert opinion, thereby creating change in practices over time. These differences in socialization practices between the lower and middle class undoubtedly have some impact on personality, and in this sense socialization practices become the dependent variable.

Few of the above examples are strictly one variety or another of the dependent-independent variable type but serve sufficiently well to illustrate the backdrop or setting from which personalities emerge. They illustrate those over-all generalized elements within a society which can have an effect on personality in an indirect or oblique way. These general patterns or general structures can have more or less impact on personality depending on other conditions and contingencies that may, by themselves or in combination, be most forceful.

Thus, the right side of Fig. 1 graphically portrays socialization practices as being the independent variable—that is, personality is dependent on agencies of socialization. The arrows go both ways to indicate interaction between the individual and those agencies with which he has direct contact. No matter how the social structure is made up, personalities can only develop and reflect what they perceive. What they perceive is part and parcel of the interaction process, and to the extent that the socializing agents have visibility of the component parts of the social structure, the individual will be able to incorporate them into his personality.

Although the social structure has an impact upon agencies of socialization, which in turn affect personality development, the internalization of those elements of the social structure necessary for its continuance are of a psychological nature and can be studied through the interaction process. Since interaction within the family is of primary importance, the family will be of major interest in this chapter. For an excellent treatment of the hypothesis that per-

sonality can serve as a mediator between the maintenance system (social structure) and the projective system (magic, art, religion) and for typologies drawn from this hypothesis, see Whiting (1961). For American society, we proffer the following paradigm, once again adapting from Fig. 1:

Economic factors: technology, industrialization, deruralization
lead to
physical and vertical mobility, urbanization, numerous job opportunities.
Subsequently,
extended family ties are weakened,
which leads to
development of isolated nuclear families,
which leads to
reliance upon external agencies of socialization,
which leads to
diluted identification.
Result:
Less continuity between generations.

Such a paradigm is purposely oversimplified to avoid, for the moment, the many possible tangents, such as effects of two world wars, greater freedom of women, greater specialization, population shifts, and the like. It is necessary to recognize that each social condition has a history, and that there is no single explanation for a given result.

With the assumption that the family is the single most important agency of socialization, and using the above as a frame, we can proceed to explain better the resultant emergence of change through the means by which infants are socialized. Yet, one cannot caution too strongly against the view that the nature of the social structure or culture is a sufficient explanation of the development of personality. One example of this fallacy is the conceptual framework sometimes used for the explanation of juvenile delinquency: juvenile delinquency becomes the result of differential association; young people are thought to become like those with whom they associate and use as reference groups. That this is a significant point of view, there can be no doubt. The discrepancies between the lower and middle classes do exist and undoubtedly provide the necessary conditions for delinquency to take place, but the theory does not embody all of the necessary conditions to explain delinquency, as we shall see. Such a notion may explain behavior patterns of some, or maybe most, children in a given category or locale, but not all. Why, for example, of a group of boys living side by side, do some become delinquent and others not? The answer lies, most likely, in the family, and in the pattern, intensity, frequency, and kind of interaction between individuals *within* that family. [For a related discussion of how child-rearing practices are affected by the culture, see Ch. 14, pp. 558–567 of this Handbook.]

SOCIALIZATION AS INDEPENDENT VARIABLE

One of the primary aims of adults in American culture is to produce an independent, autonomous human being skilled in those ways necessary to enact his roles in his future life. Concomitantly, he is to be embodied with those values and motivations deemed necessary for his participation in society. Exactly how is this done? It is not done on a direct line between the social structure and the individual or between an occupation and the individual but rather *between* individuals—the socializing agent and the neophyte.

It is on this level that the infant learns of his roles and other expected patterns of behavior, even though other elements, such as occupation, may affect the way the socializing agent approaches his subject. The child reacts, not to the occupation qua occupation, but to the individual, and it is this interpersonal relationship in which we are now interested. It is here that symbolic interaction theory is most viable and utilitarian. We now will begin at the other end of the spectrum, with the individual, and

work back toward social structure in general and to the above-mentioned paradigm.

Identification and Internalization

Beginning with the infant, then, in what ways is he able to internalize the values, norms, attitudes, etc., of his environment? Obviously, the infant is dependent and subject to forces external to him for his very survival and must rely on adults for the essentials of life, food, water, and shelter. If these were all that were provided for him, he would be little different from any other animal, as evidence from studies on isolated children (Davis, 1947) lead us to conclude. The development of social characteristics, however, separate from biological needs as they may seem, are related to the satisfaction of these needs, primarily because the socializing agent upon whom the infant is dependent cannot under normal conditions maintain a distinction between these two activities. Thus, as the child is being fed, he is also talked to, cuddled, etc., so that he learns behavior other than the mere satisfying of his biological needs. If we hark back to the postulate of predictability, we can note its applicability very early in his life. In this sense, the child is able to respond to his world in a meaningful way only after he is able to perceive a fairly orderly pattern. Such a pattern develops through learning processes after they have been repeated many times, and thus assume a consistency, so that he can perceive them as relatively orderly. From this point he can then identify them, and identify *with* the patterns and the person or persons creating those patterns. Since, initially, behavior by significant others is related to the satisfaction of his biological needs, it takes on added intensity of meaning, and he associates such behavior with his needs. The degree to which the child can perceive persistent and dependable behavioral patterns of the adult will affect the degree to which he will identify with that person.

A note on the concept of identification

seems necessary here. Identification has been treated variously by a number of writers in the field, and it is not our intention to give a comprehensive analysis of the term. For an excellent review of conceptions and a further attempt to delineate this concept, see Winch (1962). To be adultomorphic for a moment, the child, assuming the mother (socializing agent) is nurturant, does not necessarily want to be like his mother, but rather to be able to be near her, primarily because it is she who satisfies his needs. Thus, if the child can predict the mother's behavior, anxiety concerning needs is reduced. This is essentially a process of developing "norms" upon which the child can rely. It makes him feel secure. This process is purely egocentric. The results of such identification *later* develop into the imitation of, and the learning and internalization of, role behavior, values, etc., of the person with whom he identifies. Later, i.e., after the child is able to differentiate self from others, identification takes on different connotations; and at this later time, although the process of identification continues apace, *products* in the form of personality characteristics begin to emerge. We shall take these up later, but suffice it to say now that identification results in "the more or less lasting influence of one person on another" (Winch, 1962).

Then we can say that the greater the degree of predictability between the child and mother, assuming that the mother is predisposed to satisfy the child's needs, the greater the degree of identification. On the other hand, the more erratic or unpredictable the mother's behavior, the greater the anxiety and other psychological syndromes the child will experience, and the less likelihood that parents will be creating the kind of child personality that will enable them to "build in" positive orientations toward future roles (social control). If the degree of predictability or orderliness—i.e., patterned, consistent behavior—is not great enough to provide an atmosphere with which the child can identify, then the result is, without

other social elements entering the picture, a relatively disorganized personality.

An additional point deals with the learning of roles and behavior through identification, but where it is not consistent with roles and expectations of behavior outside and often inside the family setting. Thus, if parents are able to control rewards and punishments, but if at the same time they exhibit neurotic or psychotic traits and behavior, the child is very likely to learn and to internalize the same way of behaving, mainly because he doesn't know any other way. The child will thereby perpetuate in the next generation those learned responses considered to be neurotic or psychotic.

An attempt will be made to substantiate these hypothetical statements as soon as we complete the picture.

Under typical conditions in our society, the next step after identification with the mother is identification with the father. Optimum identification with the mother facilitates identification with the father, and this will occur, early or late, according to the frequency and quality of the interaction he has with the child. Identification occurs on the assumption that the father is predisposed to satisfy the child's needs. (The child, however, will tend to identify with the parent who wields power.) Thus, relatively stable norms develop between the child and two socializing agents who are representatives of the larger society and who provide for him initially the basic processes for interacting with other people. This ideal type might be graphically portrayed as in Fig. 2.

Dark lines indicate good identification. The heavier line between mother and self compared to father and self merely reflects the normative aspect of child-parent relations in American society. The mother usually spends more time with the child initially and exercises more frequent control over the child's activities. Those individuals and groups outside the circle— siblings, peers, teachers, etc.—are people he will normally interact with. He may iden-

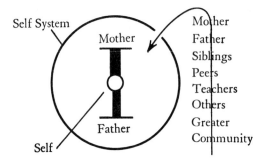

Fig. 2.

tify with a select number of these, or all of them, depending on the meaningfulness of his interactions with them.

If he does identify with one or many of them, they, too, would be drawn into the self system (graphically), and dark lines would appear between self and the meaningful agent. Thus, other people have the potential of modifying the initial identification processes laid down by the parents. For example, if identification with parents is such that the child is overly dependent upon them, and he subsequently develops meaningful relations with a peer or teacher who reflects this, it is probable that he would tend to modify his relations with his parents to attempt to become more independent.

Delineation of the self and self system and other concepts involves interpretation of many previous writers (Cooley, 1902; Lindesmith & Strauss, 1956; G. H. Mead, 1934; Sullivan, 1953).

The child is unable to differentiate self from other objects until he is able to use language. This is not to say that no learning takes place before this time, but only that he has no way to conceptualize who or what he is until he learns to view himself as an object, and he cannot do this until he has the tools (language) to categorize himself and other objects. This usually takes place approximately between the eighteenth and thirtieth months of life. After differentiation of self from not-self, the child then can begin to evaluate, in

Cooley's sense, reflections from other people, so that significant persons in his life in effect tell him who he is. If behaviors of significant others (i.e., others upon whom he is dependent) are consistent and repetitive to the point that they are reinforcing, thereby becoming normative, the child will be able to derive a fairly stabilized conception of self. When his world begins to broaden and take in other persons and groups, self will adapt to them to the degree that the parents and other early significant others accurately reflect to him behavioral patterns outside the family. This occurs both by precept and by example. The original conception of self can therefore be modified or changed within limits by subsequent persistent experiences. To elaborate, three basic notions need to be clarified.

Self Image, Self, and Self System

Self images are based initially on the interactional relationships the child has learned before the development of the self. But thereafter self image involves the child's perceiving, registering, and interpreting the repetitive reflections from distinctive and meaningful role relationships. He evaluates his behavior in terms of the response others make to him. From this process evolves his self image, and he will have a self image for each distinctive and meaningful role relationship experienced. This may involve a large number of psychological characteristics, often resulting in several qualities received from one person—especially if that one person is all things to the child, such as the mother. For example, a child could get the impression from his mother that he is "timid" and that he is "bright." The number of self images will be small initially but will broaden as the child enters more and more relationships.

The total number of self images he has accumulated at a given time become synthesized, and the resultant residues of each, some reinforced, others contradicted, become integrated into the self. Whether the ongoing experiences do or do not become integrated into the self is dependent, first, on how well the role relationships experience squares with his previous experiences or the degree of consistency and repetitiveness of the role he is enacting, and, second, whether the role relationship is in any way connected with his present or anticipated goals. In other words, these experiences become meaningful to him, and he evaluates them accordingly, i.e., he evaluates the reflections received from interpersonal relationships, and the resultant evaluations become residues of experience localized in the self. This is the *product*. The *process*, which involves modification or change of the self, occurs in the self system.

The self system is the continual process of ordering, integrating, and equilibrating the meaningful aspects of interaction. Unlike self images or the self, which are products, the self system is purely processual in that it is that aspect of the individual which is continuously attempting unity or balance among his perceived self images as they are related to the self. Order and congruence of his roles permit predictability that reduces anxiety and frustration and increases personality organization. Since all roles enacted by the individual are not always in keeping with the self, discordance can and often does exist among self images, and/or between the self and one or more of the self images.

Impaired Identification

When there is a lack of predictability and order, identification breaks down or never occurs, and the individual, especially in the very early years, judges his social environment to be so lacking in dependability that he does not trust the people around him. Also, if identification should take place initially, and conditions change to create a different order of things, anxiety and frustration result, and new adaptations need to be made. Moreover, if the identification process is chronically changed so that a

series of adaptations are followed by a series of changes, again in the early years when the child is unable to understand them except from an egocentric point of view (Piaget, 1928; Piaget, 1932), the result is a lack of orderliness and predictability and subsequent lack of ability to identify with *any* others. Since identification in the past did not occur to any great degree or was repeatedly broken, he relies only on self and becomes bereft of those emotions which permit him to identify with others (Fig. 3).

In Fig. 3, broken lines indicate a lack of integration of the self system and only a minimum of identification with parents. This is the basic pattern he tends to follow with other individuals and groups external to the family system. Should this pattern persist throughout the formative years of the child's life, he feels he can rely on no one but himself and therefore identifies with no one and no groups and becomes essentially psychopathic, i.e., he has little conscience, few feelings of remorse, only a minimum of guilt, and is highly exploitative of others.

Two ideal types of socialization have been shown: one in which there is a high degree of order and predictability, and therefore cohesiveness; and one in which there is little or none of these, or if there has been some, it has become broken.

Other types, however, can emerge under various conditions and at varying times. One is that in which the father is absent

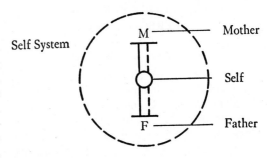

Fig. 3.

from the home and identification is only one way—with the mother. This could result, depending on other factors, in mother fixation, extreme dependency on the mother, or homosexuality. Another type in which the gang becomes the most predictable and satisfying unit for the individual could emerge at a later time; and if the family is relatively disorganized, strong identification with the gang becomes more probable. This type might lead to juvenile delinquency, crime, or other kinds of deviant behavior.

Fortunately, the family, although the most important single grouping in the socialization process, is not the only group with which the child will interact. It is possible, for example, for the child to develop meaningful relationships with other relatives—aunts, uncles, older siblings, etc., and with neighbors, schoolteachers, etc., to the point that he can modify the existent relationships within the family. As we shall see later, however, most relationships with individuals and groups outside the family are so evanescent that they often do not become meaningful enough to provide the identification necessary for the internalization of those values which can perpetuate the social system unchanged; hence change occurs. Change occurs even beyond that which one would expect from uncertainties in socialization, plasticity of roles, demographic imbalance, or population dynamics (Moore, 1960).

INDEPENDENT VARIABLES IN SOCIALIZATION AND PERSONALITY

Importance of the Family

Murdock (1949) has defined the family as a social group characterized by common residence, economic cooperation, and reproduction. It includes adults of both sexes, at least two of whom maintain a socially approved sexual relationship, and one or more children, own or adopted, of the sexually cohabiting adults. Whereas this definition is most applicable to the explanation of the near universality of the family, its applicability to the American family belongs to an earlier time. With greater opportunity for women to engage in remunerative work outside the home and to assume independent status, economic cooperation is not as functional as it once was. Not that the family has lost its economic function entirely; it hasn't. The family is still the major consuming unit of our economy, so it is functional for society but is becoming increasingly dysfunctional in an economic sense for individuals. Moreover, the fact that children are no longer economic assets but strictly economic liabilities removes the functional utility of having children. Finally, although sexual privileges continue to be legitimized through marriage, this function increasingly appears to be losing some of its former importance.

For these reasons, preference is given to the view of Parsons and Bales (1955, pp. 16–17) when they suggest that the "basic and irreducible functions" of the modern American family are (a) the socialization of children so they can become members of the society in which they are born and (b) the stabilization of the adult personalities of the population of the society.

The small group called the family, then, becomes functional to our society insofar as it inculcates values and attitudes in children which will give them a proper "fit" into society, i.e., inculcates those normative patterns necessary for the child, and later the young adult, to adapt himself into those extant or emerging roles which society provides. The degree to which any given family can do this successfully depends on the cohesiveness of the family group on the one hand and the institutional support the family receives from the society at large on the other.

In this section, we are viewing the family as an independent variable affecting the socialization process, while keeping in mind the fact that family interaction takes place on the interpersonal level but at the same time in a social setting including social class, dominant societal values, ethnicity, and the like. Too often the causal sequence is either circular or leaves a large gap between the independent variable, such as social class, and the dependent variable, personality (Hoffman & Lippitt, 1960).

The effects that internal processes of the family can have on children's personalities are many and varied. Here we shall consider such variables as parental personalities, interaction between parents, family composition, maternal employment, father's absence, mobility, and institutionalization of children.

Family Structure

Relationships within the family do not take place haphazardly—they are not merely chance relationships occurring in a setting no matter how organized, diffuse, or disorganized. They are structured; parents, implicitly or explicitly, have some notions about the way they want to rear their children. These may well vary between and within ethnic groups, social classes, and regions, but parents attempt to rear children according to their interpretation of their own socialization, the mass media, their reference groups, or some combination of these to achieve whatever ends they deem appropriate.

On this level, it would be far more proper to study the family as a small group and, in so doing, take cognizance of the same principles of behavior which have been found to apply to small groups generally. Elements such as structure, cohesion, consensus, power, and leadership are pertinent to understanding the impact the group has on the personality. This is not to say that the family as a group should be studied in isolation, but studied as a group within a socio-cultural setting; and if personality is

the phenomenon under consideration, one must descend in the level of abstraction from the large institutional setting to the interactional setting.

In this context, familial positions and roles are structured, and it is their structural aspects which permit the child to perceive and internalize the attitudinal and motivational sets of family members. Thus, if the father enacts the instrumental role and the mother the expressive role, and if these roles are distinct, unambiguous, and repetitive enough (i.e., structured), the child will be able to internalize them. Moreover, perception of sex roles will be clarified, and subsequent adaption of them is more likely to be appropriate. In reality, however, as Zelditch (1955) has indicated, in our culture family role differentiation is not an instrumental-expressive dichotomy, but rather one in which the father is high on instrumental and low on expressive activities and the mother is high on expressive and low on instrumental activities. There appears to be an increasing lack of exclusiveness between the sexes, and Brown (1958) asserts that there are definite signs of convergence of the two sex roles in our society. In addition, other studies demonstrate a general trend to greater democracy and equalitarian orientation on the part of both males and females (Blood & Hamblin, 1958). But, whichever way the family is structured, clearly delineated roles seem to be important to the child, and whether he is able to identify with and internalize his present and future roles depends on how clearly these emerge to him from his primary sources of information, namely, the family. The apparent trend toward convergence, then, would seem to befuddle the child with subsequent implications for personality organization.

Sex-role identification. The usual composition of the American family consists of father, mother, and children, with the father employed outside the home and the mother remaining at home with the children. The family is usually nuclear, not extended, and isolated from its kin group by virtue of neolocal residence and by social as well as geographic mobility. Under these conditions, it is the mother who spends the greatest amount of time with the children. It is she who rewards and punishes them most and with whom the children have the greatest amount of interaction. Even if the father is away from home for only eight hours a day (it is almost always more, especially in large metropolitan areas in which his absence frequently is upward of 10 hours), children still spend the bulk of their time with the mother. This usually means that it is the mother with whom the children are more likely to identify, especially during their more formative years.

Parsons (1954) has noted that this provides the girl with an appropriate role model, while, for the boy, an overwhelming dependence upon the mother seems inappropriate. In other words, the girl has good visibility of a position and series of roles which fit her sex in terms of present and future roles, whereas the boy does not. The boy, with the father and father's occupation outside the range of visibility, has relationships with adults, who are predominantly female: his mother and numerous teachers. Thus, his identification is with a cross-sex model, mainly his mother, which leads him to adopt cross-sex attitudes and behavior patterns until he is older. At a later age, peer group, male teachers, a realization that his father's sex role is more powerful than his mother's sex role (Emmerich, 1961), and the physiology of his sex urges combine to lead the boy to the realization of his sex and a subsequent attempt to refute most things feminine. Parsons (1954) has labeled this reaction "compulsive masculinity." Thus, we see the male child subject to a fairly radical change in the socialization of his sexual identity.

The female child, too, is subject to discontinuity due to misplaced identification and changing role patterns, but in reverse of that of the male. Her close identification with the mother would be more appropriate to an earlier time when there was greater institutional and kingroup support for women, particularly in helping her to become placed in marriage. Today, she is practically on her own in getting married or selecting an occupation or both. She is attaining independence increasingly, but as yet does not have the prerogative of "choosing" her spouse and only has limited access to the more prestigeful occupations. Thus, her identification with a mother role does not provide her with the means to compete in the outside world. In addition, although she initially sees the mother's sex role as containing the most power (Emmerich, 1959), as she increases in age she begins to perceive the father's sex role as being more powerful (Emmerich, 1961) and sees herself as having less power than a sibling brother (Emmerich, 1959). Such evidence gives credence to the notion that males enjoy a superior position (Parsons, 1954; Brown, 1958), with privileges not open to females. The girl, socialized predominantly for the wife-mother role, is left without proper guidelines when she discovers that this role is not within her power to achieve. In addition, her confusion is compounded by the absence of institutional support, and she is becoming increasingly ambivalent about the role of wife-mother. This does not mean she shuns this role; she doesn't. But it does mean her commitment to marriage will not be as great.

Such shifts that males and females have to make in their behavior patterns are disorganizing to the personality. Each sex becomes accustomed to repetitive and predictable patterns, only to find that these do not square with reality. Boys have to make a shift early and girls later in their respective roles, and on this basis one would expect greater personality disorganization among boys in the early years and among girls in later years of the socialization process. This is essentially what Lynn (1961), using demographic data from several sources, has found. The data he uses tend to confirm the notion that more boys than girls fail more or less completely in achieving same-sex identification, and, since this occurs early in socialization, it tends to have a more lasting effect. For those boys who do make a shift in early life, identification with the masculine role is facilitated by a societally stereotyped masculine role. Bennett and Cohen (1959), for example, found that both men and women share a common perception of the male role and that, as maturity approaches, both male and female begin to attach greater value to masculine traits.

Lynn's (1961) other main finding was that males, as they grow older, develop psychological disturbances at a more slowly accelerating rate than do females, as reflected by the frequency of referrals, admissions, and residence in mental health facilities. This finding tends to substantiate the existence of a masculine role supported and abetted by the larger social structure, whereas the female role becomes increasingly more ambiguous, leaving the female with the inculcations centering on the wife-mother role but without control or support for this role.

In addition, the incessant demands of the educational system subject her to standards of academic excellence, presumably geared to occupations other than wife-mother. The occupations available to her, however, are of low prestige value. Moreover, American society contains many elements denigrating the career woman. As a consequence, the female is left without structure and without support for either role. If she takes on both the mother-wife and career roles, the strain becomes great, and no matter how she manages it, something suffers: herself, her family, her career, or all three. In America, the female is thus probably experiencing her most perilous times since the later decades of the Roman Empire. Is it any wonder such inconsistencies prevent her from developing personal identity during adolescence (Douvan, 1960), or a commitment to a value system prior to marriage? Douvan's point is that a too clear or distinct self definition during adolescence might be maladaptive, in that a girl must remain malleable enough to "fit" the value system of her potential future spouse.

The important thing to note is that the female cannot commit herself without possible deleterious consequences for her life pattern. Thus, the pattern of early marriages would tend to insure the female (and male) an established place (status) in society. There still remains a fairly clear wife-mother role and, rather than face the ambiguities of the social system, many young girls jump at the chance to get married. Then later, after one, two, or three children, they decide to have still another child to continue to "justify their existence"—by insuring the wife-mother role for another few years.

Primary identification with the mother and the wife-mother role by the girl, then, appears to lead to complex personality problems for her throughout adolescence, and primary identification with the mother by the boy leads to earlier personality problems. For the boy and possibly for the girl as well, the relative occupational absence of the father and the resulting dominant interaction with the mother make such outcomes as personality problems seem unavoidable. Augmenting such conclusions are studies concerned with prolonged absence of the father.

Parental absence. When the father is absent, the mother tends to be a more functional parent to the children (Winch, 1962), that is, she is relied on more than in two-parent families. Winch's finding substantiates findings in Norway (Lynn & Sawrey, 1959; Tiller, 1958), which report mothers of father-absent children to be more overprotective and more concerned about their children than mothers in father-present families. The boys in the father-absent families tended to be infantile and dependent and to manifest conflict in their sex identification (compensatory masculinity) more than father-present boys. Along the same lines, Bach (1946), Sears, Pintler, and Sears

(1946), and Pauline S. Sears (1951) found boys of father-absent families to behave like girls, in overt as well as fantasy behavior, and to show less aggression in fantasy than boys whose fathers were present.

In a study of adolescent boys whose fathers were absent during early childhood (at least ages 3–5), compared to adolescent boys whose fathers were continuously present, Leichty (1960) found a greater Oedipal intensity among the father-separated boys and a closer identification with the father by father-present boys. Dager, in a similar unpublished study with a college sample, found that boys whose fathers were absent in early childhood, compared with boys whose fathers were not, were more feminine, viewed their mothers as more powerful, and tended to identify more with their mothers.

Girls, too, are affected by father absence, but perhaps not to the same degree. Lynn and Sawrey (1962) found girls to be more dependent in father-absent homes, and Winch (1962) reports that girls in father-absent homes tend to be more like their mothers than girls in father-present homes. However, in light of the tendency of children to identify with the same-sex parent, one would not expect father absence to be as important to girls as it appears to be to boys. Research with young children tends to corroborate this, but one could hypothesize that the absence of a male model for girls will at a later time, at least, have considerable effects on male-female relationships, say, in choosing a mate or in marriage. There is some evidence, for example, that girls with older brothers for a male model tend to be more "tomboyish" (Koch, 1956) than girls without older brothers. Also, Andrews and Christensen (1951) found tendencies toward earlier dating, earlier engagement, and more broken engagements among young people from homes with father absent as compared with those with father present. These differences were statistically significant for boys, though not for girls.

It should be recognized that the mere presence of the parents is not sufficient to create an integrative personality, as the parent-child section below will indicate. However, the presence of both parents or adequate substitute role models appears to be necessary for the learning of appropriate patterns of behavior of both sexes by the children. Adequate sex identification cannot take place where a parent is absent.

The implications that the father's absence has for personality development would seem to apply equally well, at least theoretically, to the absence of the mother when she is employed while the child is young and not in school, or the child is left with another person or agency with whom he has not built up any strong identification. The implications of training the child by others than members of the family are great. The rewards, punishments, and general interaction resulting from care by "others," whether it be diapering, disciplining, a form of training, or whatever, may well be inconsistent with the pattern the child had already developed with the mother. Moreover, although mother and child need not be together all of the time, the absence of the working mother means protracted blocks of time away from the child. There is also an absence of learning that could take place in that time with a dependable, significant, and meaningful person—the mother. In other words, identification with the parental role will not be as complete.

The research findings to date have been inconsistent and often contradictory in regard to the effects of maternal employment on children. Stolz (1960) and Hoffman (1963) have excellent summaries of these effects, and both have attempted to reconcile the inconsistent findings, but with little success. That there is an effect, there can be no doubt. That the effect is deleterious is still open to question, and more research is needed. At any rate, the working mother, for whatever reasons she is employed—necessity, career orientation, status, whether she likes her work or not, and so on—must be treated as an independent variable affecting the personalities of her children. Her absence and her concomitant reliance upon secondary agencies of socialization are bound to have some effect on her children's personalities.

The inconsistent findings cannot be reconciled here, but if we look at the processes of interaction leading to identification, and the subsequent adoption by the child of parental values and behavior patterns, perhaps we can develop some perspective on this problem. If we theorize that it is necessary for the child to have persistent and consistent interaction with meaningful persons for adequate development of self and personality traits in keeping with future roles, then we must propose the hypothesis that maternal employment, in the early years of the developing child, deprives the child of a consistent role model and teacher and therefore affects the personality. For example, Davis and Lawton (1960) demonstrate that the more ideal the mother-concept by young boys, the better the self concept. Wechsler and Funkenstein (1960) found that a perception of difference between the parents and self is related to a conflict of the individual's perception of himself, that is, he internalizes the conflicting role orientations of the parent. The experiencing of role conflict by the working mother would appear to be clearly visible to the child, thus affecting his concept of self.

Other studies relate personality variables to parental influence—especially the mother's. Winterbottom (1958) found children with high achievement motivation had mothers who made more demands upon them at early ages for independence, maturity, and achievement. Likewise, Crandall, Preston, and Rabson (1960) show that maternal rewards for achievement and approval-seeking are correlated with the child's degree of achievement.

Translated into behavioral patterns, one would expect some impact upon the activi-

ties of the children as a result of maternal employment. Whitehurst (1963) found that children of lower-class working mothers dropped out of school more frequently than those of nonworking mothers of the same class, despite the mothers' expressed value of education. Also Roy (1961) reports lower grades and lower educational aspirations among town boys and girls who have employed mothers. Moreover, withdrawal symptoms (Rouman, 1956) and a tendency toward maladjustment (Hand, 1957) were found among boys with working mothers. Admittedly, the ages of the children in some of the above researches are above the ages we are here concerned with, but if the results are this significant for older children, one would suspect, with the primary principle of learning operating, that the impact would be even greater at an earlier age.

When very young children are left in the care of others while the mother works, they experience some discomfiture, as Heinicke's (1956) study of day-nursery children points out (see institutionalization section below). Although the long-term effects of mothering by a series of others may not be directly observable, one would expect some cognitive discrepancy (Spiegal, 1957) in the child's ability to form any consistent notion of what is expected of him. Not only is the mother not around to be imitated, and to teach him in all the subtle and incidental as well as direct ways that mothers do, but the child is also subjected to the varying and sometimes contradictory modes of learning from "others." Thus, it would seem that cues would be misinterpreted and misunderstandings would arise (Spiegal, 1957), leading to frustrations and possibly other feelings, such as rejection or hostility. Such feelings may well become manifest at a more subtle level of personality than in the overt acting out of disorders. Thus, it is not too surprising that juvenile delinquency and personality (as we measure it) seem not to be clearly related to maternal employment.

Other variables such as the mother's attitudes, family integration, socio-economic status, and adequacy of supervision in the mother's absence must also be brought to bear on the subject. Certainly, a mother who hates children or is anxious to follow a career outside the home would be doing her children a favor by going to work, but this does not mean that her absence will better enable the children to inculcate values, norms, role prescriptions, and the like any better. On the contrary, her absence eliminates many hours of potential identification and learning time. Even with adequate supervision, secondary agencies of socialization may well prevent delinquency, but they lack the meaningfulness and the consistency that the mother can provide and which lead to identification and subsequent internalization of societal values. Such caretaking is even more inadequate than "multiple mothering," which would appear to hamper a consistent conception of self, create doubt about one's status, and subject the child to conflicting nuances of expectation and often diverse ways of behaving and learning. Researchers often refer to kibbutz children as examples of good adjustment, but have ignored Spiro's (1958) analyses of emotional adjustment (see below).

The fact that mothers work today is not new—mothers have always worked—within the home, to be sure, but also on the farm. Their "chores" were as demanding as were the men's, and practically as time consuming. The main difference today is *where* they work. On the farm, children were within earshort of their mother at least, and in fact learned many aspects of their future roles by so being, but today, when the mother works, there is a distinct separation from both parents.

Since the nuclear family is relatively isolated, the employment of the mother results in the children being subject to secondary persons and agencies of socialization, and the meaning of what is learned is not nearly so enduring or significant as when parent-child contact is sustained daily, especially during the formative years. Furthermore, this tends to increase conflict resulting from increased competition between parents and other authorities (Davis, 1940). Ultimately, such separation certainly has some effect on the nature of the child's personality, and the probable result is a considerable dilution of parental and societal values and a subsequent diminution in continuity from generation to generation.

Family composition. Although parents have by far the greatest influence on childrens' personalities, a child's siblings, if there should be any, intrude into the family situation a different structure and an entirely different set of interpersonal relationships. The family as a small group changes with the addition of each child, and as it does so, the changes in relationships and the degree of affect in relationships in turn bring about changes in personality. For example, the first child is usually the product of two young and inexperienced people who often view his arrival as a crisis (LeMasters, 1957). Such inexperience and the comparative lack of preparation for the parental role are intensified by the couple's relative isolation from their own families of orientation. They are essentially on their own and must rely on secondary sources of information on how to rear their children. As a consequence, young parents spend a great deal of time learning their roles, and the first child is therefore subject to an inordinate amount of attention.

The child becomes accustomed to this attention and orders his world accordingly. Upon the arrival of the second child, however, the firstborn's world is catapulted into chaos. The order he knew as an only child —the pattern of interaction that he could once depend upon—no longer obtains. This radical shift from formerly fairly predictable relationships to something considerably short of them leads to a great number of possible personality alterations. Most of the following consequences are inevitable in most families with more than one child and will occur in varying degrees, depending on other factors such as parents' personalities, ages of children, relatives present, and sex of children.

In the first place, the firstborn is likely to feel some rejection. Used to getting almost full attention, he now receives something considerably less, and he will undoubtedly feel the lack of it. Since the second child is normally born between the first child's eighteenth month and his third year, feelings of rejection occur at about the time the first child is developing a concept of self. Awareness of self, developing slowly with the accretion of symbols by which to recognize and differentiate self from others, does not necessarily coincide with the feelings of rejection at the birth of the second child. However, in the typical three- or four-child family, these two phenomena, awareness of self and feelings of rejection, are likely to overlap for some period of time. If these suppositions are correct, it would not be uncommon to find in firstborn children some general feelings of worthlessness and inferiority due to the resultant feelings of rejection. Such feelings would be greatest in first children but also occur in subsequent children, although with decreasing severity. This would partly explain findings among college students of which the writer has become aware from reading personality self-analyses for many years. Students almost invariably report that they have feelings of inferiority or, as they put it, an "inferiority complex."

Secondly, one would expect the first child also to generate feelings of hostility, primarily toward the second child. He associates the coming of the second child with the loss of parental attention and breakdown of the relational pattern he had learned to rely on. Third, the first child would learn something about being competitive. He now must learn to compete with his sibling(s) in order to gain attention or status from his parental figures. Finally, assuming parents will attempt to teach their children the art of getting along with their siblings, the child will also learn how to cooperate and accommodate his behavior to others.

The traits of hostility, competition, cooperation, and to some degree, feelings of rejection, so long as they are ordered and channeled along socially acceptable lines, are experiences the child must learn in order to interact adequately with others. The degree, intensity, and timing of this learning, however, are important.

If the second child is born at the time the first child is just beginning to differentiate self from others, and parents suddenly restrict and punish his hostility and competitiveness, the child may well develop increasingly inferior feelings and so withdraw completely. The sudden change in parental behavior confuses the child. Even though parents continue to love and nurture him, the child does not understand the difference in his parents' behavior and interprets it as being rejection.

The parents, with the addition of other children, cannot maintain the same qualitative or quantitative relationships with the child. Lasko (1954) has found in a longitudinal study that mothers are less consistent and more coercive and restrictive with a first than they are with a second child. This occurs after the birth of the second child, so it is perceived as change by the first child, with subsequent reactions of significance in personality. In a study of children with behavioral problems, Sewall (1930) found jealousy among older children and related this overwhelmingly to inconsistent homes.

The foregoing is merely illustrative of the way ordinal position qua position can affect personality. Other variables which affect the impact that birth order has on personality are many: size of family, socioeconomic status, spacing, sex, changing family atmosphere with each new child, learning about children by parents, weaning time, and many others. Some of the research findings follow. Because of the diversity of the studies, and the complexity of the phenomenon at hand, most of the findings are difficult to fit into a conceptual scheme of analysis.

In his attempt to regain the status he once had with his parents, the first child often meets with disappointment, and as his ever increasing efforts are met with frustration, he tends to become increasingly anxious. Anxiety ultimately results in withdrawal or aggression. Whether he withdraws or aggresses is partly determined by such factors as sex, spacing, and parental disciplinary measures. Sears, Maccoby, and Levin (1957) find first children to be slightly more aggressive. The causal link is unknown. Other studies, again with the causal link unknown, find first children more likely to be withdrawn and dependent (Karvin, 1934) and less aggressive (Sears, 1951). More recently, Schacter (1959) has found first children to be the most anxious and frightened when faced with standard anxiety-provoking situations. The firstborn child then, due to the accident of being born first, is subject to structural variables that are more likely to create personality problems. Available evidence indicates proportionately more firstborn are referred to clinics than children of other ordinal positions (Levy, 1931; Rosenow & Whyte, 1931). Although these data are dated, they square with the findings of Koch (1955) and Sears, Maccoby, and Levin (1957), who report stronger consciences for firstborn children. The assumption here is that the earliest child would be subject to greater and more stressful interaction with parents. Competition for status with a new sibling would make him more sensitive to his parents' expectations, with concomitant attempts to meet them, thus adapting adult-like characteristics earlier in his life than other siblings.

We know even less about children of other ordinal positions, but subsequent children do change the family structure and become part of a social system of considerably different proportions. If the second child remains the youngest, he receives treatment similar to the oldest child (Sears, Maccoby, & Levin, 1957), the main difference being that he is the younger of the two and not as subject to parental anxiety or to the feelings of rejection that the first child must cope with. If he, however, is followed by a third child, putting him in an intermediate position, then his world changes similarly to the first child's, although not to the same degree and with a somewhat different structure with which to contend.

Presuming a two- to three-year span between children, the middle child, theoretically at least, would be in a difficult position from the point of view of gaining status from his parents or from his sibs. As noted above, the oldest child would be hostile toward him and he in turn, having lost the infancy position of attention, would feel some hostility toward the youngest. In addition, the oldest, being five or six years of age, gains parental approval and status by his physical and mental prowess—the youngest also gains it, but because of infancy—but the middle child, having no one but his sibs to emulate to gain attention and approval, fails miserably because of his intermediate age. If he tries to compete with the oldest, he finds he lacks the physical and mental capacity. If he attempts to emulate the youngest, he is chastised for regressing. In this sense, he cannot win. Sears, Maccoby, and Levin (1957) indicate that the middle child was less likely to receive praise for good behavior and was most often required to do chores around the house. Moreover, except in large families, middle children received less of the mother's time for leisure activity.

The addition of more siblings would make an even larger family system, with an increasingly smaller number of intimate contacts between children and parents and a probable increase in the assumption of the parent-surrogate role by older children (Bossard, 1953). Whether personality adjustment is more favorable in large family systems as suggested by Bossard (1953), or more favorable in a small family system (Hawkes, Burchinal, & Gardner, 1958; Nye, 1952) is still in need of verification. There are obvious disadvantages to each type of family system. In the large family, economic factors plus a decrease in amount of parent-child interaction would seem to be deleterious. However, interaction with older siblings may substitute for the latter, with the additional experience of interacting with many sibs and whatever this implies in terms of learning. On the other hand, in the small family system, children are more likely to be open to overprotection, too much concern, and overindulgence. At the same time, they may be more prone to develop feelings of jealousy (Levy, 1931). However, children from small families are likely to have more economic advantages and, in this day of "enlightened" parenthood, to reap the benefits of greater intimate contacts with parents, possibly without the adverse effects of overprotection and indulgence mentioned above.

Another factor affecting the influence of ordinal position on personality is sex of child. Whether one has siblings of one sex or the other appears to make a difference in one's own sex-role learning. Koch (1956), for example, found that girls with older brothers tended to be more tomboyish than girls with older sisters. Brim (1958), in a further analysis of Koch's data, reports, among other things, the general finding that cross-sex siblings tend to assimilate traits of the opposite sex and that the assimilation is more pronounced in the younger siblings. Thus, boys with older sisters tended to be more feminine, and girls with older brothers tended to be more masculine. The very fact of having a sibling of the opposite sex, who would tend to have more power (Brim, 1958), would provide the younger sibling with another role model about which he could learn and from which he could predict behavior.

Once again, the accident of having an older sib of the opposite sex helps determine some traits of personality. However,

each sib, younger or older, same sex or opposite sex, will have an influence; and the permutations of age, sex, and position are so very great and research data so few that precise and complete pictures of the many patterns involved must await further research.

Parent-Child Relationships

Studies of parent-child relationships reported in the literature are not, in reality, of parent-child interactions but primarily of mother-child interactions (Peterson et al., 1961). Only a few studies deal with fathers' impacts upon the child, and most of these are concerned with father absence. Recognizing the possible influence of the father on both the mother and the child, one can, nevertheless, utilize the limited nature of these studies. Furthermore, because of the special relationship that mothers in our culture have with the children initially, the mother-child role relationships are of very great significance in patterning those experiences which will eventually become a part of the child's personality.

Although there is little doubt that interpersonal familial relationships have an impact upon the personality, there is little specific evidence which will permit us to conclude that a particular type of parent-child interaction will result in a particular personality. Certainly, the total atmosphere in the home and the totality of the personality configurations of mother, father, and siblings are of significance to the neophyte. In this sense, it is germane to heed the dictum of Martin (1957), who has suggested that dissimilar behavior patterns may actually reflect similar personality dynamics, and similar behavior patterns may reflect dissimilar personality dynamics. The intricate combination of a number of variables, therefore, precludes any hard and fast judgments in explaining or developing cause and effect relationships. Moreover, Frankiel (1959) and Child (1954) have noted in their reviews a lack of consensus among the studies dealing with parent-child interactions and, since only a few research findings are applicable to the type of analysis we wish to make, inferences from only some of the studies selected will be employed to substantiate our point of view. With this qualification in mind, let us look at some of the findings in research.

One of the most consistent findings regarding parent-child interaction which leads us to believe that home atmosphere is of significance in determining personality is that exemplified by Burgess and Cottrell (1939) and Terman (1938), which depicts happy marriages to be more frequent among children of happily married parents. Later studies tend to confirm this finding. In another vein, Strauss (1946) found a resemblance between the mate chosen and the chooser's parent of the opposite sex, if the child loved the parent. He also found that those who did not love their parent tended to select a mate opposite to that which the parent represented. Luckey (1960), too, found that men who did not identify with their fathers regarded their fathers as less loving and more dominant than themselves.

These data lend themselves to the interpretation that in order for children to identify with parents or a parent, there must first be a meaningful relationship established. This relationship must be one in which there is a nurturant, predictable, and status-giving set of interactions, such as can be inferred from a study by Mussen and Distler (1959), who found that kindergarten boys who strongly identified themselves with their fathers regarded their fathers not only as more rewarding and nurturant but also as more punitive and threatening. Payne and Mussen (1956) in another study found that when the father-son relationship is good and the son perceives his father as rewarding and affectionate, the son is more likely to identify with him. Hartup (1962) was able to establish a relationship between a

girl's femininity and a tendency on her part to imitate her mother; to which we add that she probably could not do so unless there were an established set of meaningful role relationships.

The studies cited in this section, as well as others too numerous to mention, deal with behaviors of the parent or parents leading to particular qualities or traits in the personality of the child. Such behavior patterns or personality sets of the parents as permissiveness, warmth, rejection, indulgence, overprotection, and so on, are presumed to have an effect on the child. Most of these studies are well conceived, with adequate controls and techniques for measurement, and permit us to draw some generalized, tentative conclusions:

Permissive (not extreme) and democratic parent-child interaction appears to be associated with children who demonstrate self-confidence, initiative, independence, creativity, and cooperation.

Restrictive or overprotective parent-child interaction is associated with children who are withdrawn, submissive, and dependent.

Rejection by parent(s) is associated with children who are aggressive.

Punishment by parent(s) is associated with children who are aggressive.

Warmth, however defined, also appears to be of some significance in parent-child interactions. Maccoby (1961) cites several studies in which "warmth emerged as a fairly clear factor" (p. 363) and goes on to point up its importance for identification.

The more specific effects from parent-child interactions are most difficult to contend with, since any given set of interactions at a given time may not be of direct, linear significance at a later time. Although clinical evidence would lead us to believe there is a relationship between specific infancy-childhood experiences and adult personality characteristics, there does not appear in the literature, nor can researchers demonstrate, a direct relationship, say, between punishing experiences in childhood to aggression in adulthood. Furthermore, some "traits" of personality may well be role-specific, that is, for example, a person can be aggressive in one role situation and submissive in another (Brim, 1960). All this really means is that personality is the result of a combination of experiences, does not become fixed at any given age, and is subject to change over time and with new experiences. However, since new experiences are interpreted through past experiences, we must take early experiences as being most meaningful and attempt to integrate the current and future findings into a more viable theory of socialization.

With this objective, let us look at these and other findings. It appears that either extreme permissiveness or extreme structure leads to deleterious effects on the personality of the child. Extreme permissiveness can be construed as rejection or indifference on the part of the parent, resulting in a lack of organization for the child. Development of self is most difficult under these conditions. The child's status is in doubt, and, since he is part of a relatively unstructured situation, he may well have difficulty in categorizing himself in relation to other members of the family.

Extreme structure in the form of overprotectiveness also impedes the development of self. The self in this case merely becomes an extension of an adult, leaving the child with little status and no independence. Is it any wonder he becomes dependent and withdrawing? Extreme structure in the form of punishment, on the other hand, does not impair the development of self but leads to a negative self concept. In this sense, the child can't do anything right, and a low or negative self concept develops, eventually culminating in excessive aggressive behavior in an attempt to achieve some semblance of status.

Baldwin, Kalhorn, and Breese's (1945) findings exemplify the nature of these conclusions in a study of parents' behavior in lower-class families. They found parents who attempted to divest themselves of the responsibility of child-rearing by maintaining minimum contact with them were punitive and rejecting when they did have contact. Psathas (1957) discovered the same type of "permissiveness" among lower-class families of adolescents. He feels, along with others (Sears, Maccoby, & Levin, 1957), that such permissiveness, although it leads to greater independence, is a reflection of a relaxation of controls, or rejection, rather than independence training.

Contrast this with the findings of Baldwin (1948) in a study of four-year-olds and additional findings by Psathas (1957) in studying adolescents, in which each found for middle-class homes a greater verbal contact between parent and child and a generally more democratic atmosphere. A higher middle-class parental regard for the sons' opinions was also found by Psathas, and we can safely infer the same from Baldwin's data. Thus, high verbal contact provides child and adolescent a more repetitive and predictable set of relations with parents, plus greater knowledge of norms and expectations on the one hand and a status with positive connotations on the other. It appears that lower-class children are less likely to receive this kind of treatment, which may well explain their higher rate of personality disorganization and their greater tendency to deviate. [Cf. pp. 563–567 of this Handbook.]

In this regard, Kohn and Clausen (1955) found that schizophrenic and manic-depressive patients recalled their mothers, compared to fathers, as being more dominating, more easily angered, more restrictive, and less satisfied with children's behavior. Fathers were recalled as being less strict, less certain of themselves, and more likely to give in in arguments. Of the various undesirable relationships recorded in another study (Schofield & Balian, 1959), overprotection and dominance were most prominent in schizophrenics. Both studies included adequate "normal" control groups to avoid spuriosity. Further evidence from Myers and Roberts (1959, p. 70) indicates, among other things, that schizophrenic patients from lower-class families were subject to parental control that was "physical, harsh and inconsistent, fathers were feared but uninvolved in family affairs, mothers had almost sole responsibility for family affairs, had little time for the patients and had difficulty maintaining order in the household, and patients had few rewarding relationships with their siblings."

Acting-out disorders have also been found to be associated with parent-child interaction. The well-known study of the Gluecks (1950) found an oversupply of delinquents in homes wherein there was overstrict or erratic discipline by the father, unsuitable supervision by the mother, indifference on the part of both parents, and a comparatively disorganized or noncohesive family organization. In another group of delinquents, Bandura and Walters (1958) found fathers who were hostile and rejecting of their sons, along with inconsistency in control handling by the mother. Andry (1960), in still another study, found that delinquents experience less adequate communication with their parents, especially their fathers.

The father's familial role seems to be taking on greater significance than was thought to have in the past, but a study by McCord and McCord (1958), in which they examine the criminal records of lower-class boys whose fathers were criminals, found that if paternal rejection and absence of maternal warmth or presence of maternal deviance is coupled with a criminal father model, the probability of criminality in the son is high. The important thing to note here is that consistent discipline and nurturance from one significant person, in this case the mother, despite the father's influence, tends to nullify the proneness toward delinquency. It takes paternal rejection *plus* an inadequate maternal relationship to have the necessary impact on the child for him to deviate.

These and other data reveal several distinct notions regarding parent-child rela-

tionships: (a) Faulty family relationships —such as inconsistencies, rejection or indifference, lack of warmth, and punitiveness—prevent the degree of identification that permits children to internalize those norms and values necessary for the development of normal self-control. Put another way, a lack of predictability prevents identification, which in turn prevents adequate development of self. Where predictability occurs and it takes the pattern of rejection, extreme punitiveness, or overprotection, the result is either a low and/or negative concept of self (low status) or lack of the development of self (no status). (b) Lower-class children are in the cultural and familial milieu in which the above is most likely to flourish. (c) Interaction with both parents seems necessary for the development of an integrated personality, but a predictable and status-giving relationship with only one significant other may be meaningful enough to help the child to avoid antisocial or extreme deviant behavior.

Institutional Care

Institutional care is in some ways similar to parental absence. Although parental absence includes both mother and father, when the mother is permanently absent, children often become wards of the state and are put in orphanages. These are the children to which we here refer, along with those children who are absent from parents for relatively long periods of time, in hospitals, in residence nursery schools, and the like.

As part of the learning process, the child must take as his cues those norms and expectations of behavior that his parents, or parent substitutes, set up for him through the wielding of reward and punishment. These, in time, become the orderly, dependable ways in which the child associates behavior with the satisfaction of his needs. The idea of predictability, of course, is not new. But stated in this form, it permits us to re-evaluate maternal deprivation studies

—as well as certain others that often have arrived at conclusions that seem to outreach their data for lack of an adequate theory— in a perspective that may give them greater meaning.

The Spitz-Ribble hypothesis of maternal deprivation is a case in point (Ribble, 1943; Spitz, 1945; Spitz & Wolfe, 1946). The hypothesis, simply put, states that maternal deprivation leads to serious deleterious effects on the personality of the young child. Research designed to test this hypothesis has been of some magnitude, and the overwhelming majority of the studies, comparing institutionalized with noninstitutionalized children, arrive at the conclusion that institutionalized children have personality disturbances that noninstitutionalized children do not have. Moreover, these disturbances are reported to be the result of mother-child separation or the absence of mother love. Bowlby (1951) brings together some 45 studies to support this hypothesis, and there are many others too numerous to mention here.

Pinneau (1950; 1955) and Orlansky (1949), among many, have, by pointing up methodological, sampling, and other weaknesses, attempted to demonstrate that such conclusions deriving from these researches are not necessarily valid. Casler (1961), too, has recently made an excellent critical review of the entire field and has brought other notions to bear upon the phenomenon of personality disorder. The past two decades have seen the arguments for and against maternal deprivation grow and grow with no adequate resolution of the dispute; critiques cannot demonstrate the Spitz-Ribble hypothesis to be invalid, and the maternal deprivation theory has not been scientifically substantiated. Baldwin (1956), in his review, states that after some 15 years of work on the effects of institutionalization on childrens' personalities, there is yet no clear indication of precisely what these effects are. That there are effects has been well substantiated, despite debunkings of this type of research, but pre-cisely to what they are due is still open to question. Maccoby (1958) has summarized the major findings of these studies relevant to us:

1. Some young children, when separated from their parents for a period of a week or more (owing to the necessity for hospitalization, for example), go into a depressed withdrawn apathetic state (designated "anaclitic depression" by Spitz) from which it is difficult to rouse them. When they are reunited with their parents they do not recover at once from their grief, but may become excessively "clingy" and may show deep disturbances that seem to reflect a fear that they will lose their parents again.
2. Children vary greatly in how vulnerable they are to separation trauma. Some seem to bear separation with little difficulty; others are deeply disturbed.
3. Very young infants show few such effects. Children between one and three years are most vulnerable. Later, children can begin to understand a little about the reasons for separation and can be comforted by a promise it will not last long.
4. While the most severe effects have been in long separations lasting for a week or longer, many young children show disturbance of lesser degree with very brief separations—e.g., when their parents go out for the evening and leave them with a sitter. Commonly, however, such disturbance disappears shortly after the parents are out of sight (pp. 164–165).

We can add to the third point above that Casler (1961), in his review of maternal deprivation, was able to establish fairly certainly that prior to the six-month period, few disturbances, if any, have been noted.

But to what can these disturbances and potential disorders of personality resulting from parental separation and institutionalization be attributed? Casler (1961) leans toward perceptual stimulation as an explanation and suggests that stimulation of this kind can be achieved in the institutionalized setting.

Leaving aside perceptual stimulation for the moment, but granting its necessity for development, the present writer would suggest that personality disorders deriving from this type of setting are due to the lack of order and subsequent felt rejection and not due to lack of mother love per se. As an example, cross-cultural studies point up the fact that many societies do not have the kind of mother-child relationship we think of as being "natural" but have relationships that involve the biological mother minimally very early. The difference here is that the child learns to relate to many people early and while he has had his mother to rely on. Consequently, when his mother is separated from him, there is little anxiety, because other predictable role relationships are available. He can trust his environment and enough of the people in it. If, as seems to be the case, these cultures perpetuate themselves, it means essentially that values are inculcated into the young and that there is a minimum of personality disorder. The difference for societies such as ours is that we do not have the institutionalized means to support and reinforce role relationships (orderliness in expectations) outside the family. Homogeneity is lacking, so that when the child is separated from his mother, either through hospitalization, foster parents, death, or whatever, the child usually must interact with strangers and within strange, unpredictable situations. This, we would argue, creates anxieties which may eventually lead to personality disorder. Whether the latter occurs depends to a great extent on the anticipatory learning before the change and on the degree of predictability or stability that ensues.

Bowlby (1960) reported a study made by his colleague Robertson, of children 15 to 30 months of age admitted to hospitals or residential institutions. The children are observed to go through

. . . a phase of protest, during which they cry, seem acutely distressed, look for their mothers everywhere and reject all substitute figures. This is followed by a phase of despair, in which they become withdrawn and inactive, and seem to be in a state of deep mourning. The final stage is one of detachment, in which they accept the care of nurses and the food and toys they bring, but are not interested in their mothers when they come to visit. If they lose several mother figures in turn, they may become permanently preoccupied with material things such as toys and food and not commit themselves further to personal relationships (p. 110).

The child cannot objectify or rationally appraise his situation and must rely on previously learned norms of behavior. He cannot predict what is going to happen in this strange social situation. Consequently, anxiety develops, and he takes recourse in defense mechanisms and perhaps eventually develops personality disorders. The symbol system which became common to the mother-child relationship over time (Parsons & Bales, 1955), and the means by which mother and child were able to predict each other's behavior, is not common to others at this point, which creates a situation that results in a breakdown in the system to which the child has been accustomed.

The children of the kibbutz have been studied, and there have been conflicting reports as to the nature of the socialization process that operates. However, the study by Spiro (1958) is probably the most comprehensive, and he reports that those children born and reared in the kibbutz (Sabras) were shy, reserved, tended to maintain psychological distance, and seldom formed emotional attachments. Moreover, there was a marked tendency for them to be withdrawn and hostile, which suggested to Spiro that these adolescents were insecure. Spiro's explanation of these personality characteristics is an admirable one, in which he discusses the discontinuity of nurses, the child's dethronement by a younger sib (the first child was overindulged by parents who now overindulge the youngest), and a seeming rejection by the entire kibbutz membership who also turn their love and attention to the younger ones.

Though kibbutz children have multiple mothering figures (nurses and parents), these are not consistent, which precludes strong identification. Without strong identification, due to a chronic shifting of nurses plus parental figures who often "go away" (every evening and sometimes for prolonged periods), the child cannot rely on anyone but himself. Perhaps this accounts for the psychological distance and the withdrawn nature of the Sabras. Furthermore, although, as Spiro points out, one will not find seriously disorganized personalities, one can't help wondering, along with some of the adult members of the kibbutz, whether the children have identified sufficiently strongly to inculcate this generation's values enough to perpetuate the system. The question is premature, and only the passing of another generation or two will provide the answer.

Separation of parent and child involves more than deprivation of affection and love. Again, parents in some societies do not necessarily involve themselves with children in this way, and there are enough data to indicate that children will inculcate and identify with those who hold a power position in relationship with them, and still be able to adapt to role prescriptions in the present and future.

Sharp breaks in group relationships leading to personality ramifications of one magnitude or another cause us to believe that the "gradualism" of Kirkpatrick (1963) is more in keeping with the needs of the child to adopt new practices or new roles while he still has a "home base" of mother or family; these provide security for him while he tests and anticipates how the new situation is structured. In this sense, Heinicke's (1956) study sheds very important light. He found that two-year-old day-nursery children, although they initially experienced some disturbance at being separated from their mothers during the day, became slowly adjusted to their situation over a three-week period, so that the separation did not substantially affect the mother-child relationship when the mothers picked them up after work. However, those children who were in residence in the nursery for a three-week period showed severe signs of hostility, cried excessively when parents visited, and sometimes failed to recognize them. Some affect was there for both sets of children, but it was more severe for those in residence for three weeks. Moreover, the day-care children were able to adapt, and there appeared to be a reduction of their symptoms, whereas the children in residence developed symptoms which tended to increase in severity as their stay progressed.

Horowitz (1940), too, presents evidence that a child is likely to be more independent if he can depend on and be assured of the affection of his parents. Presumably, a child is more likely to accept change, and perhaps even be freer to create or instigate change, when he can rely on a set of stabilized relationships.

SYNTHESIS

This chapter started out with a look at various approaches to personality analysis and at the broad setting in which socialization processes take place. This was followed by presentations of a theory of interaction, plus some of the interactional processes in which personality dynamics are formed within the setting of the family group. In terms of our interactional theory, socialization becomes the dependent variable in which the personality indirectly is subject to such broad indices as social class, economic factors, and over-all value themes. That is, there is seen to be a wide gap but nevertheless a connecting link between, for example, social class and personality development. In the second instance, socialization is seen as the independent variable, in which the personality is subject to interpersonal processes and is affected directly.

Neither the larger social structure nor the interpersonal relations are seen to be the *necessary* and *sufficient* conditions for understanding and explaining the development of personality; but each one must be considered within the framework of the other before any adequate explanation of personality development can take place.

An attempt will be made in this section to fuse social structure and socialization practices in order to explain those aspects of personality which seem to be emerging as dominant and those aspects of the sociopsychological environment which seem to be affecting the developmental process—which in turn affects personality.

Murphy (1956) has listed some of the most obvious aspects of United States culture which are affecting children:

1. The small family with its individualistic and competitive, but cooperative, values; its areas of spontaneity and rigidity; its mobility; its reliance on baby-sitters; its excitement about, but often sense of being burdened by, the babies;

2. Medical guidance, which dominates hygiene, feeding-elimination-sleep routines, inoculations, vitamins, separation of mother from the child immediately after birth and during hospitalization;

3. Property with its competitive values and its stimulus to interference with the freedom of the child; its comforts, play resources, creative stimulus;

4. The culturally heterogeneous and conflictful life of many communities—religiously, morally, sexually, aggressively, and structurally—in relationships between classes and shifts from one class to another;

5. Educational ambition which includes the requirement to meet standards of performance in every area, as well as to develop an understanding of oneself and the world one lives in;

6. Measurement .consciousness, with its stimulus to growth and also to standardization of the child by pressure to conform to norms which generally ignore or minimize the wide range of individual differences in normal samples;

7. Confusion regarding discipline, values, and demands made on the child;

8. Mobility: the frequency of moving which can increase confusion in values, make it hard for the child to sink in roots and develop a sense of stable harmony between his inner self and a familiar world outside; which at the same time may acquaint the child with a wider range of people and communities, and lead to broader awareness of ways of life;

9. Distorted or deprived parent-child relations growing out of the deprivations of the previous generation, in which the cumulative effects of two world wars are exacting an increasing toll; parents' compensatory efforts to create happy experiences;

10. The increasing dominance of irreality and secondhand experience as TV, added to movies and radio, becomes an easy pacifier for children from the age of 2 on, along with the increased information that TV brings to children (p. 216).

An evaluation of the above list leads one to agree with each of the 10 items, but the effect of such items of culture upon families and subsequently upon individual personalities remains to be clarified. In this sense, society, culture, and personality cannot be considered as separate variables (Parsons & Shils, 1951). Moreover, since the perpetuation of any given social system "requires organized relations, differentiated roles and patterns of social interaction . . ." (Hallowell, 1953, p. 601), and since this perpetuation is dependent upon the learning process which embodies identification and the development of order in individuals, it becomes obvious that "a human society is dependent upon psychological processes" (p. 602), insofar as the individual learns about those necessary elements which will permit him to function appropriately with the existing order of things.

If the social system is to persist, either in its present form or in some slightly modified form, the individual, as a recipient of the culture and also as a transmitter of it, must inculcate the values, norms, attitudes, and other aspects of the culture into his personality. Otherwise, continuity between generations would not exist, and the social system would be disrupted. Internalization of the culture occurs on a face-to-face, interpersonal basis, and identification is necessary to accomplish it.

In present-day America, although there is a semblance of continuity to the social system, the degree of social change is comparatively great and seems to be increasing, with a resulting increase in discrepancies and conflict between generations. It is our thesis that such conflict is primarily the result of the lack of adequate family relationships. Not that the family is the only agent by which the culture is transmitted, but it happens to be the most significant agent.

Basically, the family, as a socializer of children, is a conservative unit in almost all societies, including ours. To maintain its own unity and its own structure, it has to be. Ours is one of the few societies in which the family attempts to maintain its unity by training children to be obedient and loyal to the parents at the same time they are trained to be independent and autonomous. In the former sense, the family is conservative; in the latter, liberal. Thus, the change that occurs through the family comes about partly by design and partly by default. Couple this situation with the fact that there is little and decreasing institutional and community support for the family, and the potential for change becomes great.

Let us now turn to the mechanisms by which the above occurs. The reader will recall the paradigm given on page 751. We have stated that there has been a development of the isolated nuclear family due to several societal forces and, further, that the isolated nuclear family is the crucial social condition affecting identification, thereby creating personality problems and lack of continuity between generations. In light of recent studies to the effect that there still remains a *modified* extended family system, it remains for us to substantiate and justify our position of the isolated nuclear family. Axelrod (1956), Bell and Boat (1957), Litwak (1960a; 1960b), Scott (1956), Sussman (1953), and others have produced evidence indicating the existence of a modified extended family in contradistinction to the isolated nuclear family (Parsons, 1954; Wirth, 1938). The findings from these researches indicate in general that geographic and upward mobility need not necessarily isolate the nuclear family. The establishment of a new family in a neolocal residence or in a different occupation is sometimes aided and abetted by the parental family in the form of financial and other kinds of assistance, and the new family may continue to maintain ties with the parental family.

One cannot argue with these findings, as far as they go. However, one can question whether the "modified extended family" has any great effect on the development of personality. That is, do phone calls, sporadic visits, financial assistance, and prolonged physical presence only in dire circumstances provide the kind of atmosphere necessary for the facilitation of identification by the children of the new family?

Every new family is under stress. Marriage itself, since it is a rearrangement of the social structure, produces a temporary disequilibrium (Radcliffe-Brown, 1950), which in turn creates intrafamily tensions and stress as well as extended kinship stresses. Add to these occupational stresses, child-rearing stresses, community and other stresses common to the married pair, plus the loss of the continuous, day-to-day support (emotional as well as other) of extended family members, and the new family may become so caught up in problems that the atmosphere is not conducive to identification by the children. Rather, the atmosphere is disruptive for the identification process mainly because the married pair are so much "on their own" that they must turn to secondary agencies of socialization to help them rear their children. They cannot, on a daily basis, turn to extended family members. Extended family members are, in general, physically inaccessible in terms of geographic distance. This is especially true of the upwardly mobile.

Moving up the occupational ladder usually means moving away from one's family of orientation. This is not to imply that social or psychological unity necessary for the identification process occurs *ipso facto* because of physical proximity, but one cannot expect day-to-day interaction and emotional support from the extended family if the distance is too great. For the upwardly mobile, the psychological distance may be too great. Stuckert (1963), for example, has found that upward mobility among married women tends to produce social isolation, not only in regard to the extended family but also in the neighborhood.

The extended family may well continue to be an asset to the nuclear family in providing significant aid and friendship ties. But, in modern America, one will not usually find the type and intensity of extended family interaction which help in inculcating and reinforcing the values and attitudes of the nuclear family, let alone the support the new nuclear family needs to face the stresses and strains mentioned above.

The isolation of the nuclear family is due to several factors. First, the values of individualism, achievement, and neolocal residence all help to create conditions which lead to a relatively greater degree of isolation. Secondly, these values, combined with an economic structure based on industrialization, tend to force physical mobility. Mobility first came about with the centralization of industry and a rural to urban shift. Recently, however, there has been a decentralization of industry, and mobility now increasingly is not only rural-to-urban but across county, state, and regional lines.

Third, recent development of a far greater need for skilled and professional workers leads to higher educational achievement and therefore upward mobility. The social value of education has long been a part of the American scene, but only re-cently with deruralization and the needs of the economic system have people literally flocked to the schools in order to achieve and successfully compete. This would indicate that children are increasingly dependent on agencies other than the family for the functional means of fitting themselves for their future roles.

What implications for child-rearing and personality development do the above have? How have families accommodated themselves to these changing conditions? If we accept the notions of decentralization of industry and the accompanying articulation of the values of individualism (at least as it concerns personal autonomy in relation to the family of orientation), achievement, and education, then we must accept the fact that mobility, geographic and social, is a natural concomitant. Furthermore, it follows that there must be a breakdown in extended family relations, which in turn leads to the development of the isolated nuclear family.

Since the nuclear family is relatively isolated, the young married pair must perforce rely upon themselves for all kinds of support. With the advent of children, husband and wife are even more dependent upon each other. They ordinarily cannot shunt the children off to grandma, to an aunt or uncle. Their neighbors aren't readily accessible. Rossi (1955) has found that the neighborhood in the more mobile areas is likely to be perceived as unfriendly, and the residents there are less likely to form personal ties. So the pressures on the couple mount. Since domestic labor has all but vanished, the couple can expect no help from that quarter.

Moreover, the couple has received little or no training in child-rearing and is more than willing to turn to the mass media and the "experts" on how to rear their children. Unfortunately, it is difficult for parents to feel at ease with the experts' advice, since it often is ambiguous, sometimes contradictory, and, as Bronfenbrenner (1958) so ably pointed out, continuously changing.

With considerable uneasiness about the

way they are rearing their children, and the feedback they receive from children which often does not coincide with either their expectations or the experts' advice, parents begin to doubt their status and worth as parents. In addition, parents may not be able to help wondering about the reasons for having children. What function do they serve? They are strictly economic liabilities; they keep parents awake; they prevent parents from going anywhere of any significance for several years; they create continuous anxiety in parents lest they not grow up in accordance with "established" psychological principles, break a leg, fail a grade, get pregnant; *ad infinitum*. Is it any wonder parents become ambivalent about having and rearing children?

With such pressures, anxieties, and ambivalences, it is no surprise that parents create demands for kindergartens, prekindergartens, nursery schools, day nurseries, and other institutionalized vehicles to rid themselves of their children for a few hours every day. Such institutionalized baby-sitting seems necessary to parents of the isolated nuclear family—necessary in order for them to get relief. Thus, in relying on institutionalized baby-sitters, the nuclear family tends to subject children to many divergent personalities and many different patterns of behavior. In addition, of course, contacts with parents and other relatives are less frequent; this lessens the impact that the values, attitudes, and motivations of the parents will have on the children. Under these conditions, children begin to have fleeting doubts about the efficacy of parents' authority, since it is, on the one hand, less continuous and, on the other, in competition with other authorities (Davis, 1940).

The communication line between the child and his most significant others (parents) loosens, and ordinarily there are no extended family members to take up the slack. The evanescent character of his contacts with educational, religious, and other secondary persons is not intensive or enduring enough to permit the development of any meaningful identification, and so his personality suffers. Predictability of his social environment becomes relatively uncertain, his status is not clear enough to provide security, and the values to which he becomes exposed are not reinforced enough to permit him to identify with the community at large.

In a study of personality change, Dager (1956) found that a negative change occurred basically because of a series of inconsistencies in the child's environment. Testing the children twice, at the beginning and end of a nine-year interval, he found negative personality change occurring in those persons who had experienced broken homes, attendance at two or more schools, and a change in reference groups. A child under these circumstances would be unable to crystalize his position in his community. He would have to learn new roles in his family, his school, and his peer group. Given a certain amount of stability in one of his groups, say, the family, he would be better able to withstand or adapt to the inconsistencies reflected from other groups and agencies. The stable persons and those who experienced positive change were not, on the other hand, subject to this type of inconsistency.

Our position here is that a minimum amount of stability and integration are necessary for identification. Any group adequately providing these would be sufficient, but the group most likely to assume this responsibility today is the family. Whether the family is lower class or middle class, in a particular ethnic group, in an urban or rural area, or in any other social milieu should make no essential difference to the process of identification. For example, there are schizophrenics, neurotics, criminals, and juvenile delinquents from all social classes. The crucial element in each case is the family.

There are more juvenile delinquents from the lower classes, to be sure, but the fact of their low socio-economic status provides *only* the background conditions for juvenile delinquency. That is, low socio-economic status puts additional strains and pressures on the isolated nuclear family. The father has low status because he cannot remain employed, the mother has to work, aspirations go unfilled, the resultant frustrations lead to marital disharmony, and children are subjected to various child-rearing behaviors not conducive to identification. Lacking this, they pursue illegitimate means to satisfy their needs or resolve the resultant conflicts privately, by neuroses or psychoses. Social class may provide the necessary conditions, but only when coupled with family disorganization of one kind or another do we have the *necessary and sufficient* conditions for personality disorganization.

Essentially the same is true for personality disorders. Myers and Roberts (1959) state that schizophrenics in both lower-middle and lower classes were subject to intrafamilial stresses such as parental rejection, lack of warmth, and parental neglect. The fact that these were more extreme in the lower classes merely points up the added stresses experienced by low socio-economic groups.

It is our thesis that an integrated personality, that is, a personality imbued with the minimum values, attitudes, and motivations of the group to which he belongs, is necessary for an ordered society. Such a personality is dependent upon child-rearing and socialization processes consistent and predictable enough for the development of identification. The latter must perforce, because of its nature, occur in an integrated, enduring group. At the moment in American society, the most likely group for such a task happens to be the family.

The family, however functional it may be for the larger society, is becoming increasingly nonfunctional to individuals. Symbolic of this nonfunction is the increasing reliance by families upon many secondary agencies: social security, industrial retirement programs, care of the aged, a plethora of welfare agencies, care for the

young in the form of day nurseries, play schools, nursery schools, prekindergartens, and baby-sitting, fringe benefits, and so on. The passing of these activities from the family to other agencies is in no sense regrettable. It may be that this is as it should be for more efficient societal organization. However, such a shift in functions has occurred by default and not design. This indicates, at least in minor degree, a lack of identification with the family in particular and has implications for identification with the society at large.

In sum: with increasing mobility one can expect increasingly less contact with, and less support from, extended family members. From the point of view of personality development, a very great deal of the evidence, some of it presented in this chapter, indicates that enduring, nurturant contacts within a stable, integrated group structure are necessary before identification can take place. Support for the family by the society at large seems to be forthcoming only in the form of secondary agencies serving family members, and not for the family as an institution. Such secondary contacts, should they remain as evanescent as they are today, will create those conditions which lend themselves to less and less identification with parental or other figures. The attendant values, attitudes, and motivations which are concomitants of the identification process will become diluted and uneven, increasing the gap between generations and decreasing the degree of social control. In addition to an increase in personality disorganization (note the proliferation of mental health agencies), one also can expect the proportion of antisocial behavior to increase, thereby creating a less cohesive society.

Family organization has always been related to the fulfillment of the needs of the individual and to the fulfillment of the needs of the larger society. These needs are not separable. One is intimately related to the other. The history of man has demonstrated that a cohesive social group in which individuals are socialized (usually by the family) has accompanied a well-ordered society. In this era, we need not succumb to social nominalism on the one hand or revert to the extended patriarchal family on the other. We do need, however, to study the nuclear family and the socialization process within the social structure of which it is a part.

REFERENCES

Aberle, D. F. Culture and socialization. In F. L. K. Hsu (Ed.), *Psychological anthropology: approaches to culture and personality.* Homewood, Ill.: Dorsey Press, 1961. Pp. 381–399.

Aberle, D. F., & Naegele, K. D. Middle class father's occupational role and attitudes toward children. *Amer. J. Orthopsychiat.,* 1952, 22, 366–378.

Allport, G. W. *Personality: a psychological interpretation.* New York: Holt, 1937.

Allport, G. W. *Pattern and growth in personality.* New York: Holt, Rinehart & Winston, 1961.

Andrews, R. O., & Christensen, H. T. Relationship of absence of a parent to courtship status: a repeat study. *Amer. sociol. Rev.,* 1951, 16, 541–544.

Andry, R. G. *Delinquency and parental pathology.* Springfield, Ill.: Thomas, 1960.

Axelrod, L. Urban structure and social participation. *Amer. sociol. Rev.,* 1956, 21, 13–18.

Bach, G. R. Father-fantasies and father-typing in father-separated children. *Child Develpm.,* 1946, 17, 63–69.

Baldwin, A. L., Socialization and parent-child relationship. *Child Develpm.,* 1948, 19, 127–136.

Baldwin, A. L. Child psychology. In P. R. Farnsworth & Q. McNemar (Eds.), *Annual Review of Psychology.* Stanford, Calif.: Annual Reviews, 1956. Pp. 259–282.

Baldwin, A. L., Kalhorn, J., & Breese, F. H. Patterns of parent behavior. *Psychol. Monogr.,* 1945, 58, No. 3 (Whole No. 268).

Bandura, A., & Walters, R. H. Dependency conflicts in aggressive delinquents. *J. soc. Issues,* 1958, 14, 52–66.

Barry, H., Bacon, M. K., & Child, I. L. A cross cultural survey of some sex differences in socialization. *J. abnorm. soc. Psychol.,* 1957, 55, 327–332.

Bell, W., & Boat, M. D. Urban neighborhoods and informal social relations. *Amer. J. Sociol.,* 1957, 62, 391–398.

Benedict, Ruth F. Psychological types in the cultures of the Southwest. In *Proceedings of the 23rd Congress of Americanists.* Chicago: Univer. of Chicago Press, 1928. Pp. 572–581.

Bennett, E. M., & Cohen, L. R. Men and women: personality patterns and contrasts. *Genet. Psychol. Monogr.,* 1959, 59, 101–155.

Blood, R. O., & Hamblin, R. L. The effect of the wife's employment on the family power structure. *Soc. Forces,* 1958, 36, 347–352.

Bossard, J. H. S. *Parent and child.* Philadelphia: Univer. of Pennsylvania Press, 1953.

Bowlby, J. *Maternal care and mental health.* New York: World Health Organization, 1951.

Bowlby, J. Separation anxiety. *Int. J. Psychoanal.,* 1960, 41, 89–113.

Brim, O. G. Family structure and sex role learning by children: a further analysis of Helen Koch's data. *Sociometry,* 1958, 21, 1–16.

Brim, O. G. Personality development as role learning. In I. Iscoe & H. Stevenson (Eds.), *Personality development in children.* Austin: Univer. of Texas Press, 1960.

Bronfenbrenner, U. Socialization and social class through time and space. In Eleanor E. Maccoby, T. M. Newcomb, & E. H. Hartley (Eds.), *Readings in social psychology.* New York: Holt, 1958. Pp. 400–425.

Brown, D. G. Sex-role development in a changing culture. *Psychol. Bull.,* 1958, 55, 232–242.

Burchinal, L. G. Parents' attitudes and adjustment of children. *J. genet. Psychol.,* 1958, 92, 67–79.

Burgess, E. W., & Cottrell, L. S. *Predicting success and failure in marriage.* New York: Prentice-Hall, 1939.

Casler, L. Maternal deprivation: a critical review of the literature. *Monogr. soc. Res. child Develpm.,* 1961, 26, No. 2.

Child, I. L. Socialization. In G. Lindzey (Ed.), *Handbook of social psychology.* Vol.

2. Cambridge: Addison-Wesley, 1954. Pp. 655–692.

Cohen, Y. A. *Social structure and personality: a casebook.* New York: Holt, Rinehart & Winston, 1961.

Cooley, C. H. *Human nature and the social order.* New York: Scribner, 1902.

Crandall, V. J., Preston, A., & Rabson, A. Maternal reactions and the development of independence and achievement behavior in young children. *Child Develpm.,* 1960, 31, 243–251.

Dager, E. Z. Social factors in personality change. Unpublished doctoral dissertation, Ohio State Univer., 1956.

Davis, A., & Lawton, M. J., Self-concept, mother-concept and food aversions in emotionally disturbed and normal children. *Psychol. Repts,* 1960, 7, 143–149.

Davis, K. The sociology of parent-youth conflict. *Amer. sociol. Rev.,* 1940, 5, 523–524.

Davis, K. Final note on a case of extreme isolation. *Amer. J. Sociol.,* 1947, 52, 432–437.

Davis, K. *Human society.* New York: Macmillan, 1948.

Douvan, Elizabeth. Sex differences in adolescent character process. *Merrill-Palmer Quart.,* 1960, 6, 203–211.

Du Bois, Cora. Attitudes toward food and hunger in Alor. In D. A. Haring (Ed.), *Personal character and cultural milieu: a collection of readings.* (Rev. ed.) Syracuse, N.Y.: Syracuse Univer. Press, 1949.

Emmerich, W. Young children's discriminations of parent and child roles. *Child Develpm.,* 1959, 30, 403–419.

Emmerich, W. Family role concepts of children ages six to ten. *Child Develpm.,* 1961, 32, 609–624.

Erikson, E. H. *Childhood and society.* New York: Norton, 1950.

Frankiel, R. V. *A review of research on parent influences on child personality.* New York: Family Service Association of America, 1959.

Freud, S. *An outline of psychoanalysis.* Trans. J. Strachey. New York: Norton, 1949.

Fromm, E. *Escape from freedom.* New York: Rinehart, 1941.

Gerth, H., & Mills, C. W. *Character and social structure.* New York: Harcourt, Brace, 1953.

Glueck, S., & Glueck, Eleanor. *Unraveling juvenile delinquency.* Cambridge: Harvard Univer. Press, 1950.

Gorer, G. *The American people.* New York: Norton, 1948.

Hall, C. S., & Lindzey, G. *Theories of personality.* New York: Wiley, 1957.

Hallowell, A. I. Culture, personality, and society. In A. L. Kroeber (Ed.), *Anthropology today.* Chicago: Univer. of Chicago Press, 1953. Pp. 597–620.

Hand, H. Working mothers and maladjusted children. *J. educ. Sociol.,* 1957, 30, 245–246.

Haring, D. A. (Ed.) *Personal character and cultural milieu: a collection of readings.* (Rev. ed.) Syracuse, N.Y.: Syracuse Univer. Press, 1949.

Hartup, W. W. Some correlates of parental imitation in young children. *Child Develpm.,* 1962, 33, 85–96.

Hawkes, G. R., Burchinal, L., & Gardner, B. Size of family and adjustment of children. *Marr. & fam. Living,* 1958, 20, 65–68.

Heinicke, C. M. Some effects of separating two-year old children from their parents: a comparative study. *Hum. Relat.,* 1956, 9, 105–176.

Hoffman, Lois W. Effects on children: summary and discussion. In F. I. Nye & Lois W. Hoffman, *The employed mother in America.* Chicago: Rand McNally, 1963. Pp. 190–212.

Hoffman, Lois W., & Lippitt, R. The measurement of family life variables. In P. H. Mussen (Ed.), *Handbook of research methods in child development.* New York: Wiley, 1960. Pp. 945–1013.

Horowitz, E. L. Child-adult relationships in preschool years. *J. soc. Psychol.,* 1940, 11, 41–58.

Hsu, F. L. K. (Ed.) *Psychological anthropology: approaches to culture and personality.* Homewood, Ill.: Dorsey Press, 1961.

Inkeles, A., & Levinson, D. J. National character: the study of modal personality and sociocultural systems. In G. Lindzey (Ed.), *Handbook of social psychology.* Vol. 2. Cambridge: Addison-Wesley, 1954. Pp. 977–1020.

James, W. *The principles of psychology.* New York: Holt, 1890. 2 vols.

Kaplan, B. Personality and social structure. In J. B. Gittler (Ed.), *Review of sociology.* New York: Wiley, 1957.

Kaplan, B. (Ed.) *Studying personality cross*

culturally. Evanston, Ill.: Row, Peterson, 1961.

Kardiner, A. *The individual and his society.* New York: Columbia Univer. Press, 1939.

Kardiner, A., with Linton, R., Du Bois, Cora, & West. J. *The psychological frontiers of society.* New York: Columbia Univer. Press, 1945.

Karvin, E. *Children of preschool age; studies in socio-economic status, social adjustment and mental ability, with illustrative cases.* Chicago: Univer. of Chicago Press, 1934.

Kirkpatrick, C. *The family: as process and institution.* (2nd ed.) New York: Ronald Press, 1963.

Kluckhohn, C. The influence of psychiatry on anthropology in America during the past one hundred years. In J. K. Hall, G. Zilboorg, & H. A. Bunker (Eds.), *One hundred years of American psychiatry.* New York: Columbia Univer. Press, 1944. Pp. 589–617.

Kluckhohn, C., & Murray, H. A. (Eds.) *Personality in nature, society, and culture.* New York: Knopf, 1948.

Kluckhohn, Florence R. Family diagnosis: variations in the basic values of family systems. *Soc. Casewk,* 1958, 39, 63–72.

Koch, Helen L. Some personality correlates of sex, sibling position and sex of siblings among five and six year old children. *Genet. Psychol. Monogr.,* 1955, 52, 3–50.

Koch, Helen L. Sissiness and tomboyishness in relation to sibling characteristics. *J. genet. Psychol.,* 1956, 88, 231–244.

Kohn, M. L. Social class and parental authority. *Amer. sociol. Rev.,* 1959, 24, 352–366. (a)

Kohn, M. L. Social class and parental values. *Amer. J. Sociol.,* 1959, 64, 337–351. (b)

Kohn, M. L., & Carroll, E. E. Social class and the allocation of parental responsibilities. *Sociometry,* 1960, 23, 372–392.

Kohn, M. L., & Clausen, J. A. Social isolation and schizophrenia. *Amer. sociol. Rev.,* 1955, 20, 265–273.

Lasko, Joan K. Parent behavior toward first and second children. *Genet. Psychol. Monogr.,* 1954, 49, 97–137.

Leichty, M. M. The effect of father-absence during early childhood upon the oedipal situation as reflected in young adults. *Merrill-Palmer Quart.,* 1960, 6, 212–217.

LeMasters, E. E. Parenthood as crisis. *Marr. & fam. Living,* 1957, 19, 352–355.

Levy, J. A quantitative study of behavior problems in relation to family constellation. *Amer. J. Psychiatry,* 1931, 10, 637–654.

Lindesmith, A. R., & Strauss, A. L. *Social psychology.* (Rev. ed.) New York: Holt, 1956.

Litwak, E. Geographic mobility and extended family cohesion. *Amer. sociol. Rev.,* 1960, 25, 385–394. (a)

Litwak, E. Occupational mobility and extended family cohesion. *Amer. sociol. Rev.,* 1960, 25, 9–21. (b)

Luckey, Eleanore B. Marital satisfaction and parent concepts. *J. consult. Psychol.,* 1960, 24, 195–204.

Lynn, D. B. Sex differences in identification development. *Sociometry,* 1961, 24, 372–381.

Lynn, D. B., & Sawrey, W. L. The effects of father-absence on Norwegian boys and girls. *J. abnorm. soc. Psychol.* 1962, 64, 361–369.

McClelland, D. C., & Friedman, G. A. A cross-cultural study of the relationship between child-rearing practices and achievement motivation appearing in folk tales. In G. E. Swanson, T. M. Newcomb, & E. H. Hartley (Eds.), *Readings in social psychology.* (Rev. ed.) New York: Holt, 1952. Pp. 243–249.

Maccoby, Eleanor E. Effects upon children of their mother's outside employment. In National Manpower Council, *Work in the lives of married women.* New York: Columbia Univer. Press, 1958. Pp. 150–172.

Maccoby, Eleanor E. Choice of variables in the study of socialization. *Sociometry,* 1961, 24, 357–371.

McCord, J., & McCord, W. The effects of parental role model on criminality. *J. soc. Issues,* 1958, 14, 66–74.

Martin, W. E. Effects of early training on personality. *Marr. & fam. Living,* 1957, 19, 39–45.

Mead, G. H. *Mind, self, and society.* Ed. C. B. Morris. Chicago: Univer. of Chicago Press, 1934.

Mead, Margaret, *Coming of age in Samoa.* New York: Morrow, 1928.

Mead, Margaret. *Growing up in New Guinea.* New York: Morrow, 1930.

Mead, Margaret. National character. In A. L. Kroeber (Ed.), *Anthropology today.* Chicago: Univer. of Chicago Press, 1953. Pp. 642–667.

Miller, D. R., & Swanson, G. E. *The changing American parent.* New York: Wiley, 1958.

Moore, W. E. Theories of social change. *Amer. sociol. Rev.,* 1960, 25, 810–818.

Murdock, G. P. *Social structure.* New York: Macmillan, 1949.

Murphy, Lois B. Effects of childrearing patterns on mental health. *Children,* 1956, 3, 213–218.

Mussen, P., & Distler, L. Masculinity, identification and father-son relationships. *J. abnorm. soc. Psychol.,* 1959, 59, 350–356.

Myers, J. K., & Roberts, B. H. *Family and class dynamics in mental illness.* New York: Wiley, 1959.

Nye, F. I. Adolescent-parent adjustment: age, sex, sibling number, broken homes, and employed mothers as variables. *Marr. & fam. Living,* 1952, 14, 327–332.

Orlansky, H. Infant care and personality. *Psychol. Bull.,* 1949, 46, 1–48.

Park, R. E., & Burgess, E. W. *The introduction to the science of sociology.* Chicago: Univer. of Chicago Press, 1921.

Parsons, T. Certain primary sources and patterns of aggression in the social structure of the Western world. In *Essays in sociological theory.* (Rev. ed.) Glencoe, Ill.: Free Press, 1954. Pp. 298–322.

Parsons, T., & Bales, R. F., with Olds, J., Zelditch, M., Jr., & Slater, P. *Family, socialization and interaction process.* Glencoe, Ill.: Free Press, 1955.

Parsons, T., & Shils, E. A. (Eds.) *Toward a general theory of action.* Cambridge: Harvard Univer. Press, 1951.

Payne, D. E., & Mussen, P. H. Parent-child relations and father identification among adolescent boys. *J. abnorm. soc. Psychol.,* 1956, 52, 359–362.

Peterson, D. R., Becker, W. C., Shoemaker, D. J., Luria, Z., & Hellmer, L. A. Child behavior problems and parental attitudes. *Child Develpm.,* 1961, 32, 151–162.

Piaget, J. *Judgement and reasoning in the child.* New York: Harcourt, Brace, 1928.

Piaget, J. *The moral judgement of the child.* New York: Harcourt, Brace, 1932.

Pinneau, S. A critique on the articles by Margaret Ribble. *Child Develpm.,* 1950, 21, 203–228.

Pinneau, S. The infantile disorders of hospitalism and anaclitic depression. *Psychol. Bull.,* 1955, 52, 429–452.

Psathas, G. Ethnicity, social class, and adolescent independence from parental control. *Amer. sociol. Rev.,* 1957, 22, 415–423.

Radcliffe-Brown, A. R. Introduction. In A. R. Radcliffe-Brown & C. D. Forde (Eds.), *African systems of kinship and marriage.* London: Oxford Univer. Press, 1950.

Ribble, Margaret. *The rights of infants: early psychological needs and their satisfactions.* New York: Columbia Univer. Press, 1943.

Riesman, D., Glazer, N., & Denny, R. *The lonely crowd.* New Haven: Yale Univer. Press, 1950.

Rosenow, C., & Whyte, A. H. The ordinal position of problem children. *Amer. J. Orthopsychiat.,* 1931, 1, 430–434.

Rossi, P. *Why families move: a study in the social psychology of urban residential mobility.* Glencoe, Ill.: Free Press, 1955.

Rouman, J. School childrens' problems as related to parental factors. *J. educ. Res.,* 1956, 50, 105–112.

Roy, P. Maternal employment and adolescent roles: rural-urban differentials. *Marr. & fam. Living,* 1961, 23, 340–349.

Sapir, E. Cultural anthropology and psychiatry. *J. abnorm. soc. Psychol.,* 1932, 27, 229–242.

Schacter, S. *The psychology of affiliation: experimental studies of the sources of gregariousness.* Stanford, Calif.: Stanford Univer. Press, 1959.

Schofield, W., & Balian, L. A comparative study of the personal histories of schizophrenic and nonpsychiatric patients. *J. abnorm. soc. Psychol.,* 1959, 59, 216–245.

Scott, G. Urbanism reconsidered. *Amer. sociol. Rev.,* 1956, 21, 19–25.

Sears, Pauline S. Doll-play aggression in normal children: influence of sex, age, sibling status, father's absence. *Psychol. Monogr.,* 1951, 65, No. 6.

Sears, R. R. Personality theory: the next forty years. *Monogr. soc. Res. child Develpm.,* 1959, 24 (74), 37–50.

Sears, R. R., Maccoby, Eleanor E., & Levin, H. *Patterns of childrearing.* Evanston, Ill.: Row, Peterson, 1957.

Sears, R. R., Pintler, M. H., & Sears, Pauline S. Effects of father-separation on preschool children's doll-play aggression. *Child Develpm.,* 1946, 17, 219–243.

Sewall, M. Two studies in sibling rivalry: I— some causes of jealousy in young children. *Smith Coll. Stud. soc. Wk,* 1930, 1, 6–22.

Sorokin, P. A. *Society, culture and personality.* New York: Harper, 1947.

Spiegal, J. P. The resolution of role conflict within the family. *Psychiatry,* 1957, 20, 1–16.

Spiro, M. E. *Children of the kibbutz.* Cambridge: Harvard Univer. Press, 1958.

Spitz, R. A. Hospitalism: an inquiry into the genesis of psychiatric conditions in early childhood. Part I. *The psychoanalytic study of the child.* Vol. 1. New York: International Univer. Press, 1945. Pp. 53–74.

Spitz, R. A., & Wolf, K. M. Anaclitic depression: an inquiry into the genesis of psychiatric conditions in early childhood. Part II. *The psychoanalytic study of the child.* Vol. 2. New York: International Univer. Press, 1946. Pp. 313–346.

Stephens, W. N. *The oedipus complex.* New York: Free Press, 1962.

Stolz, Lois M. Effects of maternal employment on children: evidence from research. *Child Develpm.,* 1960, 31, 749–782.

Strauss, A. The influence of parent-images upon marital choice. *Amer. sociol. Rev.,* 1946, 11, 554–559.

Stryker, S. Symbolic interaction as an approach to family research. *Marr. & fam. Living,* 1959, 21, 111–119.

Stuckert, R. P. Occupational mobility and family relationships. *Soc. Forces,* 1963, 41, 301–307.

Sullivan, H. A. *The interpersonal theory of psychiatry.* Eds. H. S. Perry & M. L. Garvel. New York: Norton, 1953.

Sussman, M. B. The help pattern in the middle class family. *Amer. sociol. Rev.,* 1953, 18, 22–28.

Terman, L. M., with Buttenwieser, P., Ferguson, L. W., Johnson, W. B., & Wilson, D. P. *Psychological factors in marital happiness.* New York: McGraw-Hill, 1938.

Thomas, W. I., & Znaniecki, F. *The Polish peasant in Europe and America.* Boston: Badger, 1918–1920. 5 vols. (See especially vol. 3.)

Thrasher, F. M. *The gang.* Chicago: Univer. of Chicago Press, 1927.

Tiller, P. O. Father-absence and personality development of children in sailor families: a preliminary research report. In N. Anderson (Ed.), *Studies of the family.* Vol. 2. Göttingen: Vandenhoeck & Ruprecht, 1957. Pp. 115–133.

Wechsler, H., & Funkenstein, D. H. The family as a determinant of conflict in self-perceptions. *Psychol. Repts,* 1960, 7, 143–149.

Whitehurst, R. Employed mother's influences on working-class family structure. Unpublished doctoral dissertation, Purdue Univer., 1963.

Whiting, J. W. M. Socialization process and personality. In F. L. K. Hsu (Ed.), *Psychological anthropology: approaches to culture and personality.* Homewood, Ill.: Dorsey Press, 1961. Pp. 355–380.

Whiting, J. W. M., & Child, I. L. *Child training and personality.* New Haven: Yale Univer. Press, 1953.

Whiting, J. W. M., & Whiting, Beatrice B. Contributions of anthropology to the methods of studying childrearing. In P. H. Mussen (Ed.), *Handbook of research methods in child development.* New York: Wiley, 1960. Pp. 918–944.

Winch, R. F. *Identification and its familial determinants.* Indianapolis: Bobbs-Merrill, 1962.

Winterbottom, Marian. The relation of need for achievement to learning experiences in independence and mastery. In J. W. Atkinson (Ed.), *Motives in fantasy, action and society: a method of assessment and study.* Princeton: Van Nostrand, 1958. Pp. 453–478.

Wirth, L. Urbanism as a way of life. *Amer. J. Sociol.,* 1938, 44, 1–24.

Zelditch, M., Jr. Role differentiation in the nuclear family: a comparative study. In T. Parsons & R. F. Bales, with J. Olds, M. Zelditch, Jr., & P. Slater. *Family, socialization and interaction process.* Glencoe, Ill.: Free Press, 1955. Pp. 307–351.

CHAPTER 19 Families Under Stress

DONALD A. HANSEN
Purdue University

REUBEN HILL
University of Minnesota

Man suffering in a suffering family has been a favorite literary theme for centuries. In our day Wolfe, O'Neill, Agee, Lawrence, and Durrell have offered sensitive and often bitter insights into man and families under stress. Their images, at once profound and unusual, differ from those of earlier writers, but all are cast from the same life-stuff: the agonies which man suffers with and because of his loved ones.

Sensitive writers do not seek in family crises merely the surface facts of hardship and stress, but attempt also to capture the poignant drama that boils beneath. When a man meets stress, his family, willing or not, shares the anguish of his pains. He loses his job, and seeds of dissension are planted. Tensions course through the family as hardships increase; irritations chafe once smooth relationships and suppressed hostility crackles momentarily into view. The interplay within the family builds toward an emotional climax, and as the climax nears, bitter antagonisms creep from hiding and gnaw at the ties that bind the members. Often, unsuspected strengths appear to counteract antagonisms as the family stumbles toward its own tragedy or exaltation.

The writer of genius captures this drama as he feels his way through the stress-torn family, into the heart of intimate human life. The stress offers him a chance to watch rapid change; shifts in power and allegiance, which in a period of quiet take years, then develop suddenly, in a few weeks, days, or hours. Even more important, families under stress offer the writer a chance to view strengths and weaknesses that underlie the surface of family life, to discover dynamics and tensions which are normally hidden. And they allow him to show how seeds of dissension planted early in marriage can erupt later with vengeful destruction.

The intrigue of this drama holds dangers. Indeed, the creative artist—just as the family researcher—may fail to draw his eyes from it, to see more profound questions. Mere intrigue does not justify either the artistic or the research interests in the family under stress, nor does a simple desire to

782

help individual families from their sorrows. Intrigue can be satisfied with gossip, and a desire to help individuals is often too impatient to wait for sound investigation.

But the artist's and the researcher's interests are justified, perhaps even demanded, by the argument that understanding families under stress is crucial to understanding personality, family, and society. No one of these can be understood without understanding all, and their interrelationships cannot be fathomed without profound insight into the harshness of unusual stress and strain.

THE FOUR STREAMS OF RESEARCH

That social research is far from such *understanding* is obvious. For one thing, research is myopic; its focus is hazy, its scope narrow. When it attends to man, it often neglects family and society; when it attends to family or society, it neglects the other two.

Partly, the problem is in the tools and talents available. To conquer even simple problems, individual researchers, so limited in a complex world, must pool their efforts, must communicate and cooperate. Yet social research, like so many other developments in modern society, is splintered. Communications between men in related fields are often minimal. Study of families under stress is no exception. Today it develops in four parallel but unconnected bodies of research: disaster study, study of problem families, medical-psychiatric research, and study of sociological crises. Rarely does one group of researchers attend to the efforts and findings of the others; often they ignore the others' very existence.

These four bodies of research differ somewhat in specific focus (i.e., specific questions asked), in conceptual approach, in methods of research, and in assumptions and biases. A brief description of some of these differences and similarities will set the stage for a discussion of achievements and shortcomings of research into families under stress.

Disaster Study

It is almost a platitude in disaster research that family roles all but determine what a man does during and after disaster. Yet not one study has focussed specifically on *the family* in disaster, even though hundreds of catastrophes have been observed and carefully described since Prince's pioneering study in 1920. When the eye of the researcher is on individual victims and rescue operations, or on the recovery processes of the community, he does not seem to notice family activity. Nonetheless, as Hill and Hansen (1962) have shown, a number of propositions about the family can be uncovered from the mass of research reports available.

Disasters have been studied by psychologists, psychiatrists, social workers, and sociologists. The variety of skills and perspectives they bring to the study sets a good example for other researchers into families under stress, for it lures attention to the relationship of the family to both personality and community situations; a perspective rare in other streams of research.

On the negative side, disaster study tends to substitute sheer descriptions and weight of report for systematic and penetrating research. Increasingly, studies of real merit appear; but more often the reports not only fail to move beyond sheer description, they also fail to convince the reader that the description is entirely valid.

Nonetheless, a great body of undigested material is available for the student able to profit from case histories and reports of disaster experiences. And, occasionally, as will be seen in a later section, insights of real merit emerge.

Disasters pose special, demanding problems of research, for they happen suddenly and without warning. Data must be quickly gathered, and research teams must be able to form and move fast. Because disasters cannot be anticipated, only a lucky chance will allow the sort of study which brings comparison of families and communities before and after stress. Yet, because disaster problems are real and demanding, and because the respondents are so passionately immersed within the problem, there is less danger that this approach will slip into the reification of concepts which so strongly besets many sociological studies. (For reviews of this research, see Hill & Hansen, 1962; Nordlie & Popper, 1962.)

Study of the Problem Family

Social workers in America and England have long used the terms "problem," "hard core," and "multiproblem" to refer to families that are prone to crisis or to frequent conflicts with the community. Early social workers thought problem families were caused by poverty and saw a shoring up of economic resources as all important. Eventually, attention shifted to psychological factors, and problem families were seen, not as victims of the class structure, but as aggregates of neurotic or psychotic individuals. Only recently has attention begun to swing to more socially adequate analyses.

The term "problem family" was first consciously used in England during World War II in an effort to describe a group of families living in squalor and unwilling or unable to accept the help of social services. Such families have been characterized as "deviant," "antisocial," and "lower class." Studies of problem families, especially in England, have had a particularly biological bias, in addition to the middle-class bias so common to social workers in other countries.

Although problem families have been investigated in England, Holland, and the United States for some 20 years, the literature yields few systematic generalizations. Study of problem families suffers from the same difficulty as disaster study: lack of self-awareness, which allows sheer description and quasi-actuarial reports to substitute for systematic research. Surveys, the most popular method of research, have traditionally aimed, unsuccessfully, to determine the size and the cause of the problem, in order that effective measures could be taken to control it. In England, Blacker's study of problem families (1952) was so roundly criticized for its methodology, however, that the survey as a method has now fallen into some disrepute (Irvine, 1954; Philip & Timms, 1957).

Unlike disaster research, study of the problem family does not afford clear-cut views of the stresses families feel.

Research on the problem family faces special difficulties for it is hard to decide whether the "problem" is the family's or the community's. Researchers themselves apparently are unclear; often their attempts at simple description are hamstrung by logical circularity. Certain families are designated as problems, their characteristics are enumerated and described, and these characteristics are then taken as a criterion by which it is determined whether these and other families are problems.

Recently, however, certain students have consciously attempted to develop conceptual frameworks more adequate to an understanding of the problem family. Particularly noteworthy are the efforts of Parad and Caplan (1960), Baldamus and Timms (1955), and Geismar and his associates (1959, 1962). These researchers employ sociological frameworks, in contrast to the more common biological and psychiatric perspectives which threaded throughout the previous literature on problem families.

Geismar suggested in a personal communication that a major problem in research on multiproblem families is that studies compare stable and disorganized families and omit completely the dynamic aspect of the processes leading from one status to another. "For one thing we really do not know whether a family clearly diagnosed as multi-problem was not a stable one, a year or two earlier, or else had not passed through several stages of family disorganization; the converse could be true for stable families." For these reasons, Geismar is now engaged in longitudinal study of young families of low income. Whatever his results, his approach is a distinct step beyond the prescriptive stance so common in studies of problem families. His work suggests that, in spite of intrinsic difficulties they pose, such families offer excellent subjects for the study of the intricate and profound interworkings of personality, family, and society. (For reviews of this research, see Philip & Timms, 1957; Schlesinger, 1963.)

Medical-Psychiatric Research[1]

"Patients have families," Richardson announced in 1945, as if heralding a profound discovery. The title was humorously self-evident; yet the commonplace idea had been traditionally ignored in the medical profession. Today, however, medical research and practice are becoming profoundly aware of the implications of the idea, and many medical men would echo the words T. S. Eliot required of a central character in *The Cocktail Party:*

> . . . it is often the case that
> my patients
> are only pieces of a total situation
> which I have to explore. The single patient
> who is ill himself, is rather the exception
> (T. S. Eliot, 1950, p. 101).

Not surprisingly, medical research shows its greatest interest in families of patients with mental illness. *Folie à deux* is an older idea than psychiatry itself, and the analyst can hardly ignore the importance of his patient's social situation as he searches for causes and moves toward recovery. The great bulk of developing research reported in medical journals is couched in psychiatric terms, focussing on the individual's relationship to other individuals in small groups. The power of analysis of these approaches, particularly in relating personality to the family, holds great potential for studies of families under stress.

Not all reports in medical journals are psychiatric, however. With the rise of medical sociology, the functional and interactional frameworks, to be described below, appear more and more frequently. This development is encouraging, for it may lead to studies that are conceptually even more adequate to both personality and group; it may lead sociologists to concepts that permit simultaneous analysis of family and personality. The progress in this direction is depicted succinctly by Spiegel and Bell (1959) in their summary of a vast literature (over 200 publications) on "The Family of the Psychiatric Patient," much of which is relevant to crisis research. These authors reviewed the convergence between psychiatrists and sociologists in linking the concepts appropriate to personality, to family, and to culture. The most recent researches cited are those of Spiegel and his associates (Spiegel, 1957; Spiegel & Kluckhohn, 1954), which are based upon the transactional approach to personality and family study, the most encompassing of the medical-psychiatric frameworks to date. Essentially a field approach, the transactional point of view postulates that stressor events occur within a total complex of interdependent systems, any one of which—for example, the individual, the family, or the value system—may temporarily become a focus of observation. Each of these systems is seen as intimately and complexly interrelated, and no one has any greater "reality" than any other. As used by Spiegel and his associates in their studies of personality and family transactions in normal and pathogenic families, the transactional approach attempts to articulate the relation of the structure and process of stresses and strains within the individual to those in the family and in the value system shared by members of the family.

Thus, medical-psychiatric research on patients and families which began less than 20 years ago with simple questions, more often individual than family centered, has now developed promise of contributing theoretically cumulative findings on the interplay of family, personality, and culture

---

[1] The authors are indebted to R. J. R. King, University of Otago, New Zealand, for his collaboration in the mining of research literature in this area.

in the face of critical stresses (see Spiegel & Bell, 1959).

Sociological Studies of Family Crises

Study of family crises was one of the first areas to which pioneer sociologists gave attention. Reports on economic problems of low-income families appeared as early as the turn of the century but the early research was generally unsystematic and focussed only on isolated social and psychological bits of the family. Not until the great depression of the thirties did sociologists attain a degree of self-awareness necessary for theoretically relevant study. The depression arrived just as researchers were growing in sophistication and methodology and the general public was beginning to appreciate the potentials of social research. Doors opened just as the sociologist was discovering what questions to ask.

A distinct conceptual approach emerged in these studies and has developed over the years. Heralded in 1926 by E. W. Burgess' conception of the family as "a unity of interacting personalities," this framework tends to study the family as an intricate arrangement of roles:

The family is a unity of interacting persons, each occupying a position(s) within the family to which a number of roles are assigned, i.e., the individual perceives roles or norm expectations held individually or collectively by the other family members for his attributes and behavior. In a given situation, an individual defines these role expectations primarily in view of their source (reference group) and of his own self conception. Then he role plays. Most immediately the family is studied through analysis of overt interacts (interaction of role playing family members) cast in this structure (Hill & Hansen, 1960, pp. 302–303).

Interestingly, although the framework emphasizes "interacting personalities," and even though it rests on the works of George Herbert Mead and other social psychologists, it has never developed an adequate theory of personality. It tends to focus on pieces of persons in interaction with other pieces, or on various aspects of family structure. It has made little effort to study the relationship of personality to those sectors of society where the dynamics of families under stress take place.

Even more disappointingly, the framework fails to include the extrafamily relationships of family members and the relationship of the family unit to the community. It looks at family members when they are together, but not when they are with "outsiders."

Nonetheless, the approach has developed useful ideas and findings about families in stress, even though it has failed to come to grips with the wide sweep of community and interfamily relationships and personality. Indeed, the framework is quite well developed conceptually to analyze many aspects of *interpersonal* stress from dating conflicts to divorce.

Full understanding of families under stress, however, requires researchers to look beyond individual families, and even beyond individual persons in interaction. Both personality and community must be brought into theory and research if family stress is to be fully understood.

In the last 15 years, another frame of reference has developed in sociology. This framework, commonly called "structural-functional analysis," boasts the breadth of perspective necessary to full understanding of families under stress. It does, however, make assumptions about human nature which many interactionists resent (Hill & Hansen, 1960).

Two sets of concepts distinguish in practice this framework from the interactional: the concepts related to "function-dysfunction," and the concepts of "social system." Although the two sets are theoretically independent, in practice functional analysis so consistently combines the two that the framework is often labelled "system analysis."

Functionalists tend to see the family as

an open system of interdependent elements linked to the personality system of its members, to other small-group systems, and to the community system; what happens in any one system affects the others. Any of these systems may be made the focus of research attention. System analysis seems, on this count, well adapted to the requirements of crisis research. But it will be made clear in the next section that the concept "system" and its relatives must be used with utmost care, and only in analysis of certain problems.

THE CONCEPT "SYSTEM" IN STRESS RESEARCH

Words often hide their meanings. The concept "system" is a familiar follower of social and psychological camps, yet little effort has been made to specify exactly what it means. But it is crucial, in study of families under stress, to understand the concept, for one of the essential aspects of a system is its re-equilibration; when disturbed by external or internal stresses, the family is held, in system theory, to return to a quiet state.

This thesis leads to a number of questions: Does the family actually display the characteristics of a system, such as re-equilibration? Is system theory adequate to the full range of family dynamics? Can system theory offer an adequate theory of families under stress?

In a very general sense, the concept of family system merely holds that all parts of the family are in some way in mutual interaction. In this sense, the concept of system is familiar in research on families under stress. Burgess' description of the family as a unity of interacting personalities is very close to such a definition, and studies of families in depression, war reunion, and other stresses have emphasized the "readjustment" of families and the "equilibrating" of family troubles. Indeed, this focus on adjustment, to the exclusion of creative response or initiative, is the characteristic of

stress research most in need of revision. The bias toward static, reactive behavior under stress has allowed research to develop carefully and homogeneously, but also narrowly, in a way inadequate to capture the richness and anguish of human life. Useful as the static approach has been, it needs now to be enlivened.

Nonetheless, the static conception of "system" would pose few problems to social researchers. If, as Bell and Vogel (1961) have suggested, Webster's definition were accepted in family research, a mere broadening of focus would suffice. But the concept carries overtones of Bridgman's (1959) definition of system: "an isolated enclosure in which all measurements that can be made of what goes on in the system are in some ways correlated" (p. 188). Such a conception, hardly intended for social analysis, could lead to some very bizarre analyses of families under stress.

On the one hand, then, is the danger of distorting research and theory by too vigorously applying an inappropriate concept; but on the other hand, the concept may hold potentials as yet unappreciated in the study of families under stress.

It will be most useful to examine just what is meant, and what is not meant, by the popular and infectious concept. First, theorists generally conceive of the family system as "open" rather than closed. (A closed system would admit no matter or energy from the outside and thus settle into complete inactivity.) Psychologists and psychiatrists have been far more systematic than sociologists in discussions of "open systems"; from them, social researchers can gain crucial insights about theories of family and society. Allport, for one, offered a most penetrating statement on open systems:

If we comb definitions of open systems, we can piece together four criteria: there is intake and output of both matter and energy; there is the achievement and maintenance of steady (homeostatic) states, so that the intrusion of outer energy will not seriously disrupt internal form and order; there is generally an increase of order over time, owing to an increase in complexity and differentiation of parts; finally, at least on the human level, there is more than mere intake and output of matter and energy: there is extensive transactional commerce with the environment (Allport, 1960, p. 301).

These criteria offer useful tools in analyzing current conceptions of the family as an open system.

Criterion 1: Material and Energy Exchange

Material and energy exchange is crucial to study of families under stress, particularly under external stresses such as disaster, delinquency, and political persecution. In simplest form, the question posed by this criterion is: Does the family only *react* to stress or does it *actively and independently act* to meet and modify the stress?

In theory, both functional and interactional analyses attend carefully to the family dynamics that might modify members' perceptions of the stress. In practice and in conceptual development, however, interactionists are likely to give far closer attention to the effect of the individuals' "definitions of the situation" on their actions. Functionalists are likely to ignore the influences of ideas and definitions, as they focus intently on the relationship between stress and subsequent behavior (function or consequence) of the family, or its members.

Functionalists often make the working assumption that the individual is basically a reacting part of the social system, and a self-elicited (independent) action is rare and asocial. Interactionists emphasize, in theory at least, that the human is an independent actor, as well as a reactor to the situation (Hill & Hansen, 1960).

Psychiatric conceptions are far more sensitive than the sociological frameworks to problems of intake and output. But psychiatric theory and research is traditionally limited to energy exchange within the individual personality or between personality and personality. Rarely is the approach concerned with energy exchange of the family unit with the community. The coming decade may show psychiatry and sociology merging perspectives and concepts into frameworks increasingly sensitive to the effects of stress on personality and family dynamics.

Criterion 2: Homeostasis

Case after case demonstrates that re-equilibration is a common, apparently automatic process following disturbance of a family structure. Disaster research indicates that not only families but even entire communities (or the injured parts) tend to dynamic reaction following a tragedy, until the major shared problems have been overcome, and a new set of solutions has been found. Researchers often note the similarities, from family to family, in adjustment that follows death or addition of members.

Re-equilibration cannot be denied. But it is a large step from observation of readjustment in some, or even in almost all cases, to the assertion that homeostasis is an *essential* characteristic of even a group as closely organized as the family.

Allport, noting the popularity of the homeostasis concept in personality theory, suggested:

Some authors . . . regard this formula as logically fitting in with Cannon's account of homeostasis. Man's intricate adjustive behavior is simply an extension of the principles involved in temperature regulation, balance of blood volume, sugar content, and the like, in the face of environmental change. It is true that [some theorists] warn against extending the concept of homeostasis in personality theory. I myself doubt that Cannon would approve the extension, for to him the value of homeostasis lay in its capacity to free men from what he called the "priceless unessentials" of life. When biological equilibrium is obtained the priceless unessentials take over and constitute the major part of human activity (1960, pp. 303–304).

Seeking the priceless unessentials, the individual is likely to do things that do not contribute to the system, or are even destructive to it. If ever there was a time in the history of family associations to suspect that the tendency to homeostasis is not a necessary or universal characteristic of nuclear families, it is now. Today, with increased emphasis on companionship and personal happiness, the family develops a style of living which maximizes the priceless unessentials that bring new experience and change rather than routine and equilibrium of the homeostasis variety.

Consequences that are destructive to a designated system are recognized by functionalist theorists and are met principally by the concept of dysfunction and by the argument that much activity that *appears* destructive is actually constructive. Functionalists are yet rather hard pressed to account for behavior that is neither functional nor dysfunctional, although, presumably, such behavior is residual only to their research and not to their theory.

It is certainly most useful to analyze action for its part in maintaining or destroying a system. But overemphasis of such analysis seduces the researcher into an implicit claim that the movement to homeostasis is itself the motivating factor in stress behavior.

Emphasis on homeostasis leads the researcher into frustrating efforts to label all consequences as functional, dysfunctional, or eufunctional for a certain system, but not for others. Research thus becomes unduly complicated: the concepts originally intended only to sensitize and to be used as tools are extended beyond their useful limits and treated as real. The problems the researcher set out to study get lost, as he cleverly manipulates ideas to fit the concepts.

Most men do not like to live under stress. They seek solutions to their tensions, solutions that are often influenced as strongly by individual and community needs as by the needs of the family. The solution a man makes under stress may also be a solution for his family; but it may well add burdens to other members.

It is useful to be alert to the *possibility* that when a family is upset by stress, members may seek new solutions that readjust the entire family; such activity can be conveniently *described* as "equilibration." It is not useful, however, to be committed to the idea, for the behavior of many families and individuals belies it.

Criterion 3: Increase in Order Over Time

To this point we have (in spite of our critical remarks) endorsed using the concept "family system" as a sensitizing analogue in studies of families under stress. We have implied that both functional and interactional investigations in theory of families under stress do indeed use the analogue. Though they have different emphases, they both recognize the usefulness of analyzing energy exchange and re-equilibration. Thus, they emphasize, in differing degrees, orderly arrangement and stability rather than growth; adjustment, rather than creative activity.

If the analogue is to be used fully, however, family researchers must also take cues from the third criterion Allport offered. In theory and practice, students of families under stress minimize the possibility that the family might enhance its degree of order and become something more than it is at present. They fail to treat the family as anything more than a reacting system (or unity of personalities) which responds to the demands of the stress. It is entirely possible that time not only generates habits and an increasing differentiation of roles, but that it also stimulates and encourages an enhancement of personality and of the family as a unit.

The popularity of divorce, for instance, is often held to be due to frustration of the expectations for emotional satisfaction. It is possible that divorce is also a response to frustration of hopes for self-enhancement, self-actualization, and self-understanding.

The theoretical importance of the not-uncommon family which emerges from a crisis strengthened has been ignored. Is this just a happy confluence of stresses and re-actions, or is it possible that such a family found an opportunity to transcend its for-mer qualities? It is frequently recognized that a small crisis may be seized as a chance to readjust in areas where the family has fallen into nonsatisfying routines. Is it not also possible that members might seize on any small stress as an opportunity to de-velop or change the family, even though it was in a perfectly healthy state prior to the stress?

Sociologists commonly hold that the fam-ily has changed from the traditional to the companionship in *reaction* to demands of a more complex environment; wives, for in-stance, change after eye-opening experiences on entering the competitive labor market. Is it not also possible that the institution of the family has changed greatly because women, children, and even men have seized upon opportunities which *release* them, in-dividually and in their intimate relation-ship, to develop arrangements that are ordered more closely to their particular needs?

In short, is it not possible that families, individually and collectively (i.e., as the family system or institution), may *actively seek change* primarily because the society *allowed* the search and not because the society *requires* it? Such striving for en-hancement of order, a desire to find "greater fulfillment," is seen in the young couple's vow to make their marriage "more than other marriages," to realize in their union potentials not realized in families known to the couple.

Similarly, it is generally agreed that the family, collectively, is modifying in roles and functions within society to meet the demands of urbanization and industrializa-tion and other external pressures. This tra-ditional theme obscures the possibility that the family itself may be responsible for changes in society. Though families collec-tively are conservative, individual families are still the units which are most intimate and the most responsive to the individual. Might it not be that families, individually and collectively, are primary agents for transmitting to society, via family members, new solutions to problems shared within family circles; problems and solutions shared by individuals who face a world which calls for individual initiative and creativity in meeting its demands at the same time it increases its pressures for uniform solutions?

The family is seen as increasingly a unit of interpersonal relationships of members with one another, and less and less a unity of structural relationships. Power by coer-cion and punishment is dying, as cohesion and reward grow in motivating force. Might this suggest that the family is grow-ing in ability to respond to the efforts of members to find meaning in a complex and chaotic world; that the family is increas-ingly the meeting ground (as well as the battleground) on which individual mem-bers come together to find solutions to their individual and shared problems of identity and significance? Such possibilities empha-size the tendency of humans to strive for enhancement in the elaboration of internal order. Viewing the family as a system should sensitize researchers to these possi-bilities. But, in fact, the system approach has failed to do so: current conceptions of "system" limit attention to concepts of "re-action" and "adjustment." We have already suggested that the failure is shared through-out stress research: the concepts "stress" and "crisis" walk in constant companion-ship with the concept "readjustment." The relationship is fruitful in some respects, but in others it is only stifling.

A profound argument that modern man and his social groups do indeed strive for enhancement of internal order is found in the contemporary development of existentialism, existential analysis, and neo-Freudian theories which stress that a man strives for "understanding" and enhancement of the ego. Such theories, as well as the liberal theology led by Tillich, are among the most articulate voices contemporary man finds in his search for meaning in life. Significantly, these men make assumptions about man and about his relationship to society which are closely similar to those of actional sociologists, such as C. Wright Mills, Max Weber, and Don Martindale.

That such ideas are difficult to operationalize does not mean that they are unimportant or that they should be avoided. Perhaps, again, as psychiatric analysis blends with sociological, the possibility of "system enhancement" will gain the attention it deserves.

Criterion 4: Transactive Behavior

Understanding of the relationship between personality, family, and society is crucial to an understanding of families under stress. Sociologists in general disagree with psychologists on the relationship; even the sociologically sophisticated Gordon Allport (1960) holds that personality is in some way integumented, and resides "within the skin." Sociologists, by contrast, tend to think of personality in terms of social interaction, role relations, or situations. Some interactionists even claim that personality and society are two sides of the same coin: the mature adult is society and society is the mature adult. The claim is supported not only by their own research, but also by the discussions of anthropologists who note the closeness of the individual to both his physical environment and to his social group.

System theorists who follow the work of Talcott Parsons are closer to the psychologists; Parsons (1951) has posited that personality is indeed a system in itself, parallel to the system of social interaction and culture.

Strangely, through inconsistency of practice with theory, interactionists have traditionally studied families in stress as relatively "closed corporations." This focus is partially justified by the nature of the contemporary family, particularly in urban areas where the nuclear group of father, mother, and children is clearly differentiated from the surrounding community, and even from kin. Such focus, however, contradicts the interactionists' general theories of personality and society. The family is held to be not merely a number of socially isolated individuals interacting within the four walls of a house; each individual personality is also a member of a society and carries a complex and unique social world in his head. The deficiency could be at least partially corrected by the idea of "linked open systems" suggested by Caudill (1958). This idea is embraced by functionalists, who strongly emphasize the transactive behavior of families in stress with other systems in the community (Spiegel & Bell, 1959).

Similarly, psychiatric research is now emphasizing transactive behavior between personality and family systems. To date, little effort has been made to relate family to the community, and it may be unreasonable to expect psychiatrists to show great interest in this problem, even though they are now addressing the issue of the interrelationships of family and the value systems of the culture.

Summary

The general concept of "system" is not foreign to any of the three frameworks most commonly found in stress study. The frameworks—interactional, functional, and psychiatric—are quite different, however, in the precise definition of system and in the systematic aspects they choose to emphasize. Regardless of emphasis, a heavy price is paid when the concept "system" is reified into something more than an analogue (Hansen, 1964).

To answer the questions posed at the beginning of this section:

1. The family may in most cases be described with system concepts, but it does not necessarily display the characteristics of a system. Re-equilibration, in particular, is not essential in family life.

2. Current system theories are quite inadequate for even description of the full range of human life, for they emphasize orderly arrangement and stability, rather than growth or destruction; adjustment, rather than creative activity.

3. System theory is limited in developing an adequate theory of family functioning. It offers at most a methodological theory than can aid only in describing families. Current tendencies in using the system analogue (and the analogues of "function" and "dysfunction"), however, smack of three real dangers: (a) the danger of reifying the concepts so that families are seen as actually striving for homeostasis; (b) the danger of assuming that any such tendencies to homeostasis causally bring about action; (c) the neglect of the full range of individual and family life and activity in stress situations.

The analogue of social system can sensitize researchers to relationships otherwise ignored; it can also blind them and bind them to untenable assumptions. The idea of system does not offer a theory of families under stress. It is at best a useful descriptive tool.

SUBSTANTIVE THEORY AND FINDINGS

In studies of families under stress, it is hard to determine where methodological theory leaves off and substantive theory begins. This may be partly because social research is not yet quite aware of itself and has not yet developed even the basic tools it needs. It is also partly because the subjects of social research are man and society; constant change thus faces the researcher. No matter how abstract he may try to be, he cannot ignore that change is generated by individuals.

Man constructs an image of himself and of his society from symbols, and with symbols he just as truly constructs and changes social organization. No wonder, as Foote and Cottrell pointed out, social science does not really try to develop unchanging "laws" of human nature and society, but rather tends to specify the *methods whereby human nature and society develop and change*. Thus, they suggested, the methodological theories of social science are among its most valuable findings, and Poincaré's quip that natural sciences talk about their results while social sciences talk about their methods loses its sting (Foote & Cottrell, 1955)

Because of the confusion between methodological and substantive theory, it is important to remember that a statement in a developing discipline can be evaluated by two criteria. One is its utility, or how much it helps toward empirical or normative ends. The other is its cogency or truth. To say that the family is a system, or a unity of interacting personalities, or that family and society are reciprocal consequences of internalized meanings and values, may be acceptable as useful *tools* in studies of families in stress. Whether they are plausible explanations of families, personalities, and societies is quite another question.

Yet the utility of a concept or an idea may be influenced by its cogency; we can hardly claim it is useful to study the family as a unity of interacting druids. Such a study might be amusing and allow quick and sweeping causal analyses, but it simply isn't plausible. Utility must, at minimum, not violate substantive theory; utility is, rather, a compromise between the limitations of research ingenuity and the demands made by our conception and intuition of what is indeed most true or cogent.

In one sense, then, discussions in the following sections are methodological theories, but in another sense, they are substantive and the test of cogency must be applied. Though we may accept the *utility* of investigating the family as a social system, we cannot accept the idea that it is a cogent description of family life. Cogent description requires consideration of personality and family under the impact of a stressor, all taking place within the social context.

The Stressor

Stresses differ in their sources; some originate within, others outside the family. Some arise from the caprices of nature, some from the social community, others from the members themselves. Crises that result from stress such as economic depression or war, which are beyond individual families' control, present quite different problems from the crises arising out of the interpersonal relations within the family, such as infidelity, nonsupport, or alcoholism.

A number of efforts have been made in past years to categorize family stresses. Classified by source of trouble, stressor events divide into three types. (a) Extrafamily events which in the long run tend to solidify the family, such as war bombings, political persecutions, religious persecutions, floods, tornadoes, hurricanes, and other "acts of God." Though defined as stressful, these events are often solidifying, largely because they arise from sources external to the family. (b) Intrafamily events such as illegitimacy, nonsupport, mental breakdown, infidelity, suicide, and alcoholism. When these events are defined as stressful, they usually are disorganizing to the family, largely because they arise from troubles that members feel reflect poorly on the family's internal adequacy. (c) Some extrafamily events that are often not defined as critically stressful and are assimilable because other persons are in the same situation or worse, or events similar to others the family has previously undergone, such as some war separations, some war reunions, loss of home in a disaster, forced migration, sudden decrease in income during a depression, and premature births.

A second type of classification, first suggested by T. D. Eliot (1942) and expanded by Hill (1949), involves the combination of loss of family member (dismemberment) or addition of an unprepared-for member (accession) and loss of morale and family unity (demoralization), or all three.

TABLE 1

A CLASSIFICATION OF FAMILY CRISES OF DISMEMBERMENT-ACCESSION AND DEMORALIZATION

Dismemberment Only
* Death of child, spouse, or parent
* Hospitalization of spouse
* War separation

Accession Only
Unwanted pregnancy
Deserter returns
Stepfather, stepmother additions
* Some war reunions
* Some adoptions, aged grandparents,
    orphaned kin

Demoralization Only
* Nonsupport
Infidelity
* Alcoholism
Drug addiction
* Delinquency and events bringing disgrace

Demoralization Plus Dismemberment or Accession
* Illegitimacy
Runaways
* Desertion
* Divorce
Imprisonment
Suicide or homicide
* Institutionalization for mental illness or
    mental retardation

* Areas in which study has been reported.

Closely allied with this classification are stressor events that do not result in dismemberment in the sense of a change in the plurality pattern of the family, but do bring marked changes in the family configuration. Those family situations where roles are involuntarily vacated through illness, or are not fulfilled at all, as in families with mentally retarded children, are examples. Families experience significant strains when members become diabetics, rheumatic fever patients, or experience congestive heart failure and demand special considerations over prolonged periods. Such illnesses require a reallocation of the patient's roles to others within the family and a standardization of his role on a more or less indefinite basis (Parsons & Fox, 1952).

Most stresses of dismemberment, accession, and crippling illnesses sooner or later involve *demoralization,* since the family's role patterns are always sharply disturbed. Dismemberment creates a situation in which the departed one's roles must be reallocated, and a period of confusion and delay ensues while the members of the family cast learn their new lines. The addition of a new member resulting from the marriage of a divorced or widowed person strains the resources of a family that had previously "closed ranks" too well (Bernard, 1956; Goode, 1956).

Burgess (1947) has added two categories for further classifying family crises: (a) sudden change in family status, and (b) conflict among family members in the conception of their roles.

A sudden upturn in economic and social status may constitute a crisis quite as disruptive as that of economic loss or social disgrace. The price of upward mobility for some families may be family breakdown. We are only beginning to learn something of the conditions under which the family survives or goes to pieces when there is a swift change from poverty to riches or from obscurity to fame. More usually we think of stressor events bringing sudden changes

TABLE 2

Types of Stresses Involving Status Shifts

---

* Sudden impoverishment
* Prolonged unemployment
  Sudden wealth and fame
* Refugee migrations, political and religious
* Disasters, tornadoes, floods, explosions
* War bombings, deprivations
* Political declassing, denazification

---

* Areas in which study has been reported.

downward in status. The variety of crises of this type is well known, and the number of stars in Table 2 suggests that many of these crises have already been studied systematically by family sociologists.

Four themes run through these efforts to classify family stressors: (a) the effect of presence or absence of physical features of stress; (b) the tensions or hardships that precede impact of the stressor or evidence of strain; (c) the presence or absence of factors that allow members to blame one another for the stress; (d) the probable effect on the family of community response and resources. Two of these themes will be discussed in this section, two in the next.

Most stresses studied to date involve physical change or partial incapacity of at least one family member. The structure or status of a family is changed either abruptly or slowly, but it is physical change or condition that forces a family to make new definitions of its situation and to assign new roles. But in some stress, such as delinquency, there may be no observable physical or behavioral change; the stress or event arrives in the family only as an idea, and, though it is based on an established fact, it remains an idea. The act which touched off the idea is past; for one person it is a memory, for others it may be only a report. Such stress does not involve changed physical resources or physical burdens which might bring changes to families; it involves only an *idea* that brings change. Roughly, the influence of stress such as delinquency enters the family tree through the roots and seeps into its capillaries, while other stressors whack off a branch or two, thereby upsetting the organic balance of the tree's life. In delinquency, the idea is the *crucial* precipitate; in dismemberment and even stresses such as alcoholism and illegitimacy, the physical reality is crucial and greatly determines the resulting definitions.

The suddenness with which some stresses hit the family calls for behavior markedly different from that touched off by stresses which have a long history of development.

With increasing problems of alcoholism or loss of control of a child, the family is often forewarned and foreworried about a climax. The child who comes home a delinquent after months of rebellion at home doesn't so much surprise his parents as humiliate them. Quite different is the response of parents whose child "out of the blue" is suddenly involved in a gang fight or car theft.

Even more markedly, the family which loses its life possessions because of a fire or hurricane will often react quite differently from a family which suffers the same losses because of consistent economic reverses, over which it has no control. The first instance is unanticipated, the second foreseen.

One of the principal distinctions between disaster research and other stress research is the suddenness and intensity of impact; but even within disaster research, important insights will be lost if it is not recognized that some disasters, such as an annual flood, are anticipated and reactions are planned in advance. Other disasters, such as an explosion of a chemical factory, are completely unanticipated and catch family members and communities unprepared.

This point, and the third and fourth themes that run through the classification of stressors, require a discussion of the community contexts of families under stress.

Society and Families Under Stress

The tension between the individual and his society has been resolved in many ways over the history of mankind. To be a member of society, man must frustrate many of his desires, and he develops meanings and values that justify this sacrifice. The family has been a major buffer in easing this tension. It absorbs and protects the individual from many of the shocks he might receive from a harsh community, and tempers many of the wild rebellions of individuals against the social order. In another sense, the family is a battleground in the conflict. It transmits the demands of the community to the individual and insists that he meet these demands. At the same time, it modifies and transmits the individual's demands to the community.

Community contexts of stress. The importance of community contexts cannot be overstated. Stress can arise in the family not only because of interacting personalities, but also because of tensions and strains that follow changes in values held by the community. When a value changes, it threatens other values and tension results.

The modern family can be seen as in a state of constant stress. Rapid technological innovations and worldwide conflict impose real and undeniable stresses on families in modern times.[2]

In this sense, many of the most profound stresses on families through history have come not from disasters or individual pathologies, but from changes in social structure. These may require family members to change themselves too rapidly; or they may upset a family by requiring adjustments more quickly in some members than in others.

This chapter cannot attempt to examine the problems brought by such change; it must suffice to emphasize that the more dramatic stresses felt by individual families in a society cannot be fully comprehended unless the more pervasive stresses brought by the institutional change in meanings and values are also understood. Study of families under stress, as much as any study of the

[2] Indeed, Whyte's analysis of the organization man is, in this sense, one of the most incisive studies of families under stress. The stress Whyte saw is that felt by suburban families as a result of the new "Social Ethic," in which people not only conform, but feel a moral imperative to do so. They conform, Whyte suggested, in ignorance of the established fact that conflict between individual and society is an ever present element of human life:
"It is wretched, dispiriting advice to hold before him the dream that ideally there need be no conflict between him and society. There always is; there always must be. Ideology cannot wish it away; the peace of mind offered by organization remains a surrender, and no less so for being offered in benevolence. That is the problem" (Whyte, 1960, p. 372).

family, requires that the researcher understand both the history and structure of his society, in order to comprehend the behavior of families and of personalities under unusual stresses.

A community can even create some of these unusual stresses on families. The tensions and confusions felt within immigrant families because of indifference or even hostility of the community to which they have moved offer dramatic evidence.

Just as the community can create stress on the family, it can offer blueprints for behavior under stress. Many conventions are available to the individual numbed by the death of a loved one, and these conventions can help him cope with the difficulties involved. Just as truly, they can help other individuals in their efforts to aid and support the bereaved.

Disaster research yields the dramatic example of a mining town living under continued stress of the ever present danger of a cave-in. Within the community, ideas and expectations are developed that will help a family recover if the danger becomes reality (Beach & Lucas, 1962). This suggests that social institutions actually can *prepare* the family and its members for stress, by providing roles and norms for postimpact behavior even before the stress agent hits. It suggests that even some degree of continuing stress may be optimal in preparing the family or community for disaster stresses, for example, by predefining roles so that they will better fit emergencies, or by developing institutionalized ways of coping with chronic uncertainty (Hill & Hansen, 1962).

The effect of community norms, beliefs, and values has rarely been touched in disaster study, even though comparative studies illustrate their importance:

In an Indian background, catastrophic events are often ascribed to supernatural causes and are traced to the accumulation of sin . . . in this background it is legitimate to expect the catastrophe will not always be met vigorously by appropriate reactions on the part of the stricken people, but by an attitude of resignation which though consoling is quite inadequate to the situation (Sinha, 1954, p. 55).

The island of Yap is threatened periodically by typhoons which, though terrifying, are not highly dangerous if prepared for. Strangely, there is little "intelligent" preparation, and damage and death roar through unprotected villages. Schneider (1957) suggested that the reason is that the natives believe in supernatural powers that send the typhoons as "punishment" at the request of their tribal chief. Their only hope, they believe, is in ritual and magic. The importance of meanings and values—of community contexts—is underlined.

Such contexts have been ignored in all but a very few studies of families in stress. Even investigations of depressions and unemployment pay only passing attention to community contexts (Cavan, 1959). The potential of such a perspective is suggested in a few studies. Helmut Shelsky (1954), studying German families who had experienced severe bombing and the postwar deprivations of denazification and underemployment, found that the consequences were in general increased, rather than decreased, family solidarity. He looked for the explanation in the tendency for family members to find home and family a more secure haven from the uncertainties of the postwar world than the unstable social and community organizations which made up the family's community contexts. Ishwaran (1959) supported Shelsky's argument and carried it one step further. He found in Holland that the war, far from undermining family unity, strengthened it. Wartime stresses stimulated close cooperation between families and neighbors and the family even took over social functions normally performed by other agencies.

Somewhat similar findings were reported by Kent Geiger (1955), who studied refugee families from the USSR living in Europe and the United States. He found that families were far more frequently solidified than disorganized by the experience of political terrorism. The impact of economic deprivations on these same families, however, was seen to be detrimental to family solidarity. Reconciliation of these differences would require closer analysis of the community contexts of the stresses experienced by the families in these three studies to discover how the phenomenon of economic deprivation was distributed among families, that is, how universal was impoverishment among the families studied.

Disaster research, because it focusses on the community rather than on the family, yields a number of statements about community contexts of stress. Perhaps the most important concepts yet developed in study of disaster are those suggested by Fritz (1958; 1961) who posited that a "society of sufferers" arises in the wake of disaster impact. Survivors rescue the trapped and help the injured, support one another emotionally, and give shelter and comfort to neighbors and even strangers. A "therapeutic community" develops and helps heal the wounds of individuals, adds to the family's own resources, and ultimately contributes to the survival of the community itself.

This idea of the therapeutic community is furthered by scanty research which suggests that there would be differences in reactions of families in rural compared with urban areas, and in zones of transition compared with suburban areas. Hill and Hansen (1962) speculated on the impact of disaster on two ideal types of community ("individuated" and "kinship oriented"). They suggested that the individuated community may be more adaptive in short-term recovery from disaster impact and may give rise to a more marked therapeutic community. But in long-term adjustment, unless the hardships are very severe, kinship communities may be far better structured, because of the ready access they offer to extended families.

In any type of community, the extended family may offer more intense and lasting therapy to families under stress than does any other element of the society. In Hill's war separation study (1949), the families who adjusted least well or most slowly were often solitary families characterized by a history of mobility and transiency, whose relationship with relatives had become tenuous.

But, at least in disaster, kin become less and less helpful, especially when the impact is intense. Young (1954) reported that, during World War II, small communities in England were less resilient than large cities because when one family was hurt, chances were that all nearby relatives were also hurt. Young suggested, "What stands out is that the more scattered and extended the family, the less effective it is for the purposes of mutual aid in the process of recovery from a major disaster" (p. 389). On the other hand, if members of extended families are too closely grouped in a widespread disaster, all may suffer and none remain to aid.

When the doors and kitchens of neighbors are open to almost everyone, the long-term impact of stress may be resolved. This is suggested by the Perrys' (1959) comparison of two schoolhouse disasters in the Vicksburg tornado. Looking for children's emotional difficulties following the disaster, the researchers found far less severe trouble in communities which were predominantly Negro and similar to the "kinship-oriented" type employed by Hill and Hansen. This suggests that the community openness may be crucial in determining community and individual reaction to other stresses.

Although Tizard and Grad (1961) speculate that the solidarity of the social group may affect family response to mental deficiency in a child, medical research and problem family research yield virtually no research findings on community contexts. It is hardly surprising that medical researchers have neglected these contexts, for they have only recently broadened their scope from individual to family. More surprising, however, is that social work has so consistently neglected them.

Problem families cannot be understood apart from their social milieu, and yet in past research, neighborhood and community have not figured prominently in investigation. Geismar and his associates, however, have moved in recent years to an ever increasing awareness of the importance of social contexts. In the St. Paul project, analysis of the pattern of social functioning of 100 families showed that members who manifested trouble in bringing up children, taking care of the house, in social relationships and so forth, also tended to have problems in their relationships with neighbors, relatives, ministers, social workers and others (Geismar & Ayres, 1959).

In a more recent project on neighborhood improvement, Geismar (1961) emphasized that diagnosis and treatment of deviant behavior must take into account all those groups in which an individual plays the social role most characteristic of his personality system:

. . . almost every adult in Western society belongs to several social systems. He is, therefore, faced with the challenge of integrating a variety of roles in relation to self in such a way as to avoid inconsistencies, conflicts, and tensions. An individual's personality system reflects the manner in which these various roles are integrated. A disturbance in one or more of the roles within the personality system is likely to affect, adversely, other roles within the system (Geismar, 1961, p. 125).

A partial theory of community response to stress. No two communities are exactly alike in response, and even within one community, reactions differ among cases. Nonetheless, insight is gained by considering various *types* of community reaction. Three variables underlie the ideal types to be presented here; each will be considered simply as a dichotomy.

The first is *positional (or status) and personal relations.* When stress hits a family, aspects of community life such as legal, official, and professional bodies or position holders may respond or be affected. It is also important to recognize that within the community there are personal responses to family troubles. When a child goes delinquent, not only are courts and counselors alerted (positional responses), but also neighbors and friends act and react (personal responses).

The second variable is *community acceptance and rejection* of an individual family. Combining these two dichotomized variables yields four logical types, which may be labelled descriptively, "Therapeutic," "Social Welfare," "Repressive," and "Persecutive."

The therapeutic response is demonstrated in many disasters: family resources are greatly bolstered by both positional and personal relationships in the community. The Red Cross and less formal rescue and relief groups rush to aid victims (positional approval and help), and, among victims, a society of sufferers reaches great emotional heights (personal approval and help).

The social welfare response is demonstrated in the reactions to illegitimate births, middle-class delinquency, and drug addiction. Though positional help (which may involve repressed disapproval) is offered the unwed mother, the personal relationships are a powerful element of stress. The girl and her family are thus in a position of being shielded from censure and rejection by somewhat artificial means. Such a situation is highly disruptive for the family, for most primary supports are withdrawn and only the contractual (positional) support remains. In addition, individuals (other than the one shamed) are sometimes offered at least partial forgiveness or forgetfulness if they disassociate themselves from the shamed one. Thus there may be strong pressure from the community that makes adjustment more difficult and at the same time helps pull the family apart.

The repressive response is demonstrated in the arrest of income-tax dodgers or the reactions to so-called white-collar crimes. The family is forced to pretend it abides by one set of norms and values while it

TABLE 3

Types of Community Response to Unusual Individual and Family Behavior and Attributes[a]

Community Response Type	Community Positional Response		Community Personal Response
I. Therapeutic Response	e.g., to Disaster Victims	+	+
II. Social Welfare Response	e.g., to Illegitimacy	+	−
III. Repressive Response	e.g., to Opponents of a Police State	−	+
IV. Persecutive Response	e.g., to the American Communists	−	−

[a] Plus and minus signs indicate general acceptance or rejection of the individual or family.

really subscribes to another set, supported by its intergroup ties. A covert culture develops; repression from public view of actual ideas and actions is *expected* by the group. The group also often expects that certain other structural demands of the police agencies be circumvented; thus the actual values of the immediate group (personal relations) support the rebellious family, although the state (positional relations) persists in its prosecutions. Arrest under such conditions may win group sympathy and aid that can be quite therapeutic to the indicted one's family, and later to the prisoner when he is released.

The persecutive response is illustrated by political, racial, and religious persecutions which are supported by both state and people (for example, the California concentration camps for Nisei and Japanese in the early phases of World War II, and the persecution of American Communists today). Overt rejection by both positional and personal elements of the community can result in one of two general family reactions.

If the reason for persecution is fully endorsed and accepted by all members, the family will likely turn within, since it is denied all profitable intercourse with the community. Family integration and cohe-

sion will increase, as well as flexibility, as the family meets various threats. Family anomie will not be likely, for the family will generate its own value system and consensus. If the basis for persecution is not endorsed or accepted by all, however, the family may dissolve, or lose its objecting members if they can thereby escape persecution. If individual escape is not possible (as for Negroes under *apartheid* policies), even the low-consensus family will likely remain intact, festering within as it wards off blows from without. Thus, since physical characteristics are difficult to deny and at the same time are likely to be held in low value by the family members, family demoralization in crises is likely in families *persecuted for attributes,* but disintegration of the family is not likely. Families *persecuted for ideas and behaviors* would be more likely to dissolve, as dissenting or weak members leave the pressure area. But once the initial falling off in the latter type has occurred, the persecution may strengthen the family.

This distinction between persecution for attributes and for ideas or behavior is the third important variable in the basis for community attention to individual or family. Theoretically, a great difference can be expected in community attention which is

TABLE 4

Effect of Community Response (by Type) on Families Under Stress[a]

Community Response Type	Unusual Ideas or Behavior	Unusual Attributes or Change
I. Therapeutic	+ (*Demoralization Only*)[b] Depression Job Loss	+ (*Dismemberment-Accession*)[b] Disaster, War Bombings, Death of family member, War Separation Hospitalization
II. Social Welfare	— (*Demoralization Only*)[b] No studies yet done (e.g.: Middle-class Delinquency; Infidelity)	— (*Dismemberment-Accession with Demoralization*)[b] Illegitimacy, Divorce Desertion, Institutionalization for Mental Illness
		— (*Malfunctioning of Individual (s) with Demoralization*)[b] Alcoholism Mentally Retarded Child
III. Repressive	+ (*Demoralization Only*)[b] No studies yet done (e.g.: white-collar crime, Negro sit-ins)	+ No studies yet done (e.g.: State custody of baby born to blind parents)
IV. Persecutive	+ Persecution for political beliefs	— No studies yet done (e.g.: Persecution for racial characteristics)

[a] Plus sign indicates total response of community is helpful to the suffering family; minus signs indicate the total community response will increase the probability of family crisis.
[b] Hill's categorization of family crises of dismemberment-accession is indicated in the parenthetical titles.

precipitated by ideas or behavior, and attention which is precipitated by physical attributes or change. The general effect of adding this variable to the other two is shown in Table 4.

This discussion is necessarily speculative, for few data are available on which to rest solid theory. To date, research has only scratched the surface of the complex relationships between society and families in stress, and future studies must recognize that the community and social contexts can be the source of family troubles, and also that the community provides:

1. A dynamic structure of class status and power in which the position of any family may strongly affect either the range of behaviors actually possible or the range *thought* possible;

2. A reference framework—particularly of values and norms—in the definition the family will make of its own stress, and in the conception and evaluation of what the family is;

3. A source of verification or rejection of the family's definition of its situation or of its strategies to meet stress; and

4. A possible source of aid to be incorporated into, or to usurp, the family's stress-meeting services.

Researchers must not only view the community contexts as independent variables to which families react, but also seek for the dynamic exchanges between community and family during the course of family activity under stress.

Such a perspective has lead Foote and

Cottrell (1955) to propose a new direction for family research and theory which, they feel, is more closely attuned to present social realities. Their work emphasizes the importance of understanding social and historical perspectives of family and individual behavior. They also emphasize the issues of motivation and identity in personality and family development.

Personality Factors in Stress

One of the most costly shortcomings in the study of families under stress is neglect of personality. Though family researchers pay homage to personality factors in social behavior, no systematic theory of personality has developed, nor has any research stressed the full play of personality in families under stress.

The concepts "role" and "status" have served sociologists in their general descriptions of personality. These concepts, however, fall far short of full explanation and description of the dynamics and structure of individual personality. Inkeles (1959) suggested that both social structure and personality must be treated as important independent but interacting variables, which influence the flow of social process:

As this task is pursued, furthermore, sociologists will increasingly discover how impoverished and inadequate is their conceptual scheme in the very area in which they feel so secure. Although sociologists give a central place in their conceptual scheme to the role concept, it is surprising to discover how undeveloped this area of study is. There is, for example, no standard set of concepts or categories which could be used to describe *any* typical role or set of roles in a way that is sociologically meaningful, does some justice to its complexity, and permits systematic comparison with other roles (Inkeles, 1959, p. 267).

Devising such a set of categories which will do justice to personality variables, Inkeles suggested, is a necessary precondition for fruitful research in an area such as the family.

The family researcher is faced with the crucial task of attempting to investigate the reciprocal relationships of personality, family, and society. What effect does personality have on the processes and character of family life? Conversely, what effect does family structure and activity have on the development and nature of individual personality? How do both of these interact as social structure and processes?

To develop a theory of family reactions to stress also requires not only a knowledge of the general arrangement of statuses and roles in the family, but the distribution of personality characteristics in the population at large and among those who hold particular family roles (Inkeles, 1959). Without such knowledge we cannot predict or theorize about family reactions to a depression or to the introduction of a radical technology such as television or teaching machines.

Motivation. The question of motivation is perhaps the crux of the problem of personality theory for sociologists. Few researchers and theorists have concerned themselves with motivation, and when they do, their work is generally ignored. Foote (1951), an interactionist, and Parsons (1953), a functionalist, have suggested the concept "identification" as crucial in the theory of motivation. This concept is useful, but it does not cope with the full range of motivation apparent in human behavior. Even if identification or other concepts in role theory are interpreted in psychological terms (for instance, interpreting identification as a "redirection of drives"), it is still necessary to make decisions about the importance of the "unconscious" in motivation, about the relationship between the individual and society in determining motivation, and about the breadth or nature of goals or drives that may motivate an individual.

Without exception, personality theories, psychological as well as sociological, fail to account for the full range of human motivation. Allport (1960) suggested that we leave our cultural stockade and take a cue from the ancient Hindus, who said that most men have four central desires, which to some extent correspond to the developmental stages of life:

The first desire is for pleasure—a condition fully and extensively recognized in our Western theories of tension reduction, reinforcement, libido, and needs. The second desire is for success—likewise fully recognized and studied in our investigations of power, status, leadership, masculinity, and need-achievement. Now the third desire is to do one's duty and discharge one's responsibility. (It was Bismarck, not a Hindu, who said: "We are not in this world for pleasure, but to do our damned duty.") Here our Western work begins to fade out. Excepting for some pale investigations of parental punishment in relation to the development of childhood conscience, we have little to offer on the "duty motive." Conscience we tend to regard as a reactive response to internalized punishment thus confusing the past "must" of learning with the "ought" involved in programming our future. Finally, the Hindus tell us that in many people all these three motives pall, and they then seek intensely for a grade of understanding—for a philosophical or religious meaning—that will liberate them from pleasure, success and duty. (Need I point out that most Western personality theories treat the religious aspiration in reactive terms as an escape device to be classified along with suicide, alcoholism, and neurosis?) (Allport, 1960, pp. 304–305).

Most theories of personality emphasize the first two types of needs: the need to reduce tension and the need for success. Duty is perceived as merely a reaction to external pressures, particularly parental. Only rarely do theorists consider the idea that man "lives forward"; that he seeks to transcend what he is at the time and to move beyond and become something greater. These ideas are crucial in existential theories (notably of Victor Frankl and Rollo May); they enter the neo-Freudian theories of Fromm and Sullivan; they are seen in concepts of Erickson and Allport and in Foote and Cottrell's "interpersonal competence."

To date, most psychiatrists, medical researchers, and, even more markedly, sociologists fall far short of such conceptions of motivation; indeed, sociologists have tended to be content with a simple concept, "definition of the situation." This concept is almost alone in stimulating attention to the individual personality as a source of variation in family behavior under stress.

Definitions of the situation. In a real sense, interacting personalities are a family only because they *think* they are a family. They remain a family because each of them defines himself as a member and values this defined status more than the alternative statuses he thinks are available (divorcee, family deserter, runaway, parent neglecter, ingrate).

Family sociologists have traditionally ignored underlying organic or psychological influences on definitions of the situation. This concept is not incompatible with many psychological theories and can describe, in broad terms, even compulsive or instinctual behavior. Underlying motivation may be implicitly acknowledged by researchers, but they prefer to focus on the "middle man." In "definition of the situation" converge the underlying psychic influences and the overlying social influences.

In spite of theoretical statements, researchers infrequently give attention to private definitions of the situation. Indeed, crisis researchers even speak of family definitions as if the family presented a unified mind to all situations. That this is hardly the case need not be demonstrated; no two persons always think alike, and in a stress-worn family, it would be miraculous if adults and children defined confusing situations in the same ways.

A complex of individual definitions, however, would be extremely hard to investigate; it is difficult enough to conceive a unified strategy or definition of a crisis situation. Researchers, having voiced the idea that definitions are important in determining behavior, quickly turn their attention to the influences which modify a family's definition of the situation.

Hill (1949) suggested that the family defines a crisis on the basis of various influences, among which are: (a) the nature of the event or intrusive force; (b) the degree of hardship or kinds of problems the stress creates; (c) the resources or weaknesses available to the family, which may vary during the course of the crisis; and (d) the family's past experience with other crises, particularly with those of similar nature.

Hill's formulation has stood the test of 12 years. This is evidence not so much of its finished nature but rather of the minimal attention given by sociologists to definitions of the situation. Among other things, such a schema neglects the *ability of family members to perceive* various physical and psychological stresses on them (i.e., it neglects their phenomenological capacity). This ability to perceive is related, theoretically, to the presence or absence of neurosis or psychosis, as well as to the level of differentiation the individuals have gained in their perceptual fields.

This schema also neglects the possibility that even individuals who have the ability may still *fail to perceive a stress.* Even if perceived, it is not certain that the stress will be evaluated or interpreted in such a way that it is defined as a hardship or crisis. This evaluation is dependent upon such things as the values and beliefs of the individual, his needs, the perceived needs of significant others, and the expectations he thinks others hold for him.

In spite of limitations, the concept "definition of the situation" is important in stress research, for it insists that all social, psychological, cultural, and physical influences bearing on a family have a *personal* meaning. It is a concept that sensitizes researchers to the variable meaning of a stressor which differs for family members from situation to situation as well as from individual to individual.

The concept emphasizes that different social situations have different psychic meanings, and that these meanings can elicit behavior of a variable nature. Families, then, might be typed in terms of their cultural meanings and values, by economic class, by status or power, any of which may affect the definitions given to specific situations. The lower-class family, for instance, is theoretically no more likely to fall into crisis during a depression than is the middle-class family. Although the families of the working classes have fewer resources and may be less willing to use community resources (Myers & Roberts, 1959), the families of the middle classes display an Achilles heel in their greater proneness to definition of unemployment and sudden decrease of income as stressful. They are likely to overestimate the hardships which they define as threats to their social position and aspirations for their children.

As a first step toward integrating more personality data in their studies, crisis researchers might attend to the wide range of perceptions, evaluations, and definitions made by families under various stresses and various social conditions. Many methodological difficulties would arise, but it should be possible to make general statements about the probability that certain definitions will be made in various strata or statuses within the community.

Recognition of the interrelation of situations and definitions must, however, go hand in hand with understanding that the concepts represent different perspectives. The first perspective attempts to view the family and family members objectively, as through the eyes of an outside observer. The second attempts to view the family and its members phenomenally, through the eyes of the members themselves.

Most sociological research of families under stress views individual and family as objects rather than subjects. Even though the respondent is asked about his perceptions, opinions, and evaluations and plans, this information is treated objectively rather than phenomenally. That is, the researcher seeks to generate statements about the relation of behavior or adjustment in various family situations (e.g., level of integration, solidarity, or display of overt conflict), rather than about the relation of behavior to the member's perceptual reality.

Researchers confronted with the observation that similar families react to the same sorts of stress in various ways, however, have sought logical explanation in the concept, "definition of the situation." This search is most reasonable and promises insights not offered from an objective perspective.

Interactional research on families under stress has employed both perspectives, with an approach summarized by Hill (1949): *A* (the event) interacting with *B* (the family's crisis-meeting resources) interacting with *C* (the definition the family makes of the event) produces *X* (the crisis).[3]

Though this approach has the ring of truth to it, and though it has stood the test of recurrent examination for the past 15 years, it attempts to describe or explain a single phenomenon with two theories, one a partial restatement of the other, but couched in phenomenal rather than in objective concepts.

This is similar to saying that Adam ate the apple (we are here dipping far back into reported investigations of families under stress) both because Eve taunted him about it *and* because he decided he would. The concepts "family resources" and "family definitions" refer to two parts of the same family complex rather than to two different complexes.

It is not being argued that phenomenological and objective concepts cannot be used in a single description of family stress behavior. It is being argued, however, that they should not be used as complementary but as reciprocal statements about the same set of factors.

To avoid the confusion of concepts and findings, the approach might be more precisely represented as: *A* (the event) interacting with *B* (crisis-meeting resources) produces *X* (the crisis). Or: *A* interacting with *C* (the definition the family makes of

the event) produces *X*. Or: *A* interacting with *B* leads to *C* which leads to *X*.

A strong argument can be made for using the phenomenological approach for some research problems on families under stress. Indeed, this stance is often necessary to psychiatric understanding of the family life of mental patients and is usually employed by sensitive and effective social caseworkers. In the study of problem families, the phenomenological approach would force attention to the ideas, values, and standards of the individual families being studied, rather than to such objective conditions as poverty or scores on intelligence tests.

The phenomenological approach is limited, however, as studies of perception of social class give evidence. Even for problems to which it is appropriate, however, research may be impossible, for phenomenological concepts resist operational specification.

Davis (1956), in one of the few efforts to operationalize "definition of the situation," sought to discover how a hospital staff could help bring about a therapeutic definition. He focused on the definitions the individuals made of the time necessary for recovery from polio and of the definitions of "progress." If the patient saw "only walking" as progress, many steps might not be taken that would be necessary to the final goal of walking.

The meaning element of mental illness (Clausen & Yarrow, 1955; Freeman, 1961; Schwartz, 1957) and alcoholism (Jackson, 1956; Lemert, 1960) in the spouse of the afflicted individual has also been examined, particularly for its effect on processes of crisis and response. The importance of definitions is also suggested by the general finding that parents who define a child's mental illness as their fault are more adversely affected than parents who consider illness independent of them (Farber, 1959; Farber et al., 1961; Tizard & Grad, 1961).

Medical research contains many statements about the effect of various family attitudes or definitions and the importance

---

[3] Hill implicitly recognized the reciprocal relation of the *B* and *C* factors and combined them into a single concept of "family inadequacy," thereby refining his research project to a purely objective perspective.

of these in determining family behavior toward illness. The attitudes families adopt determine to a large extent the ways in which they attempt to cope with the problem of the ill member (Lewis & Zeichner, 1960). Mothers of younger children tend to be more accepting of retardation, and this acceptance is encouraged and supported by religious beliefs (Zuk, 1959). In some cases, definitions may be influenced by the particular diagnosis; parents may find it more acceptable to think their child a victim of cerebral damage rather than of mental retardation (Gordon & Ullman, 1956–1957).

Disaster research also suggests that the actual situation may be less important in determining behavior than the imagined situation. This was dramatically evident in the perception, evaluation, and definition that children made of the situation in wartime concentration camps (Vaughan, 1949).

The impact of such definitions cannot be overstressed. To the individual, these definitions constitute the real world. Indeed, if a man thinks he can fly, in a real sense he can; this idea may even lead to an attempt to soar from the top of the Empire State Building. Unfortunately, although such definitions greatly influence the action he takes, the consequences do not flow from his definitions, and he may experience the impact of unexpected stress.

From this quick overview of the insufficiencies of personality data in the research on families in crisis, we recognize major tasks to be undertaken, not the least of which involve bridging from community contexts to the family and from personality to the family.

The Family as Variable

Studies of families under stress have been more inventive conceptually and methodologically in their analysis of the family as variable than in their treatment of the personality contributions to behavior under stress. The family as variable may be viewed profitably from the many facets of value structure, internal role organization, and the course of activity following impact of the stressor event.

Compared with other associations in society, the average family is organizationally inferior. Its age composition is heavily weighted with dependents, and it cannot freely reject its weak members and recruit more competent teammates as do other associations. Its members receive an unearned acceptance, for there is no price for belonging. Because of its unusual age composition and its uncertain sex composition, it is intrinsically a puny work group and an awkward decision-making group. It is by no means ideally manned to withstand stress, yet the family is the bottleneck organization through which almost all troubles of modern society pass. No other institution so reflects the strains and stresses of life. The modern family experiences recurrent tension precisely because it is the great burden-carrier of the social order.

The family today is not only the focal point of frustration and tension, but also the source for resolving frustrations and releasing tensions. In our society, individuals hope that their family will show great capacity of sympathy, understanding, and unlimited support, and thus act as emotional therapy for personalities bruised in the course of competitive daily living.

The importance of meanings and values. It is largely because of these hopes that the family is so vulnerable to unexpected stress and crisis. The American family apparently operates at high levels of emotional intensity, with little margin for "shock absorption" (Parsons & Fox, 1952).

The importance of community norms and prescriptions for behavior is suggested in disaster research by Form and Nosow (1957) and in study of problem families by Baldamus and Timms (1955). Applying sociological concepts to the study of the problem family, the latter suggest that problem families characterized by Merton's "retreatism" show weak or poorly articulated goals, together with deviant standards of behavior. Such families, they suggest, should not be confused with families that appear to be deviant, yet which demonstrate strong goals and a nominal conformity to generally accepted standards. The distinction between nominal and real standards for conduct is most useful. Deviation may sometimes accompany apparent conformity (acceptance of nominal standards) or there may be outright rejection of standards (as demonstrated in deviant subcultures).

This discussion underlines the importance of looking not only at behavior, but also at the conflicts between competitive meanings and values, and standards and norms. Some people may be completely happy with a dishevelled home, with the daily excitement of volatile arguments and demonstrative love that picturesquely stereotype the immigrant Italian or Spanish family.

Goode has pointed out that

What is needed is a more precise disentangling of the standards by which people judge similar marital behavior and the responses they make to that behavior; their various patterns of behavior; and the words and phrases they use to describe the behavior (1961, p. 434).

Such precise descriptions await the development of concepts which can sensitively describe and analyze not only cognitive language but also a "language of the emotions" (Parsons, 1953). To date, in sociological theory and research on the family, as on personality, the question of meanings and values, norms and standards, converges in the concept "social role."

Family roles and mechanisms. Activity under stress that threatens the family depends in part upon the adequacy of the social roles played by members. What an individual does as a family member largely depends on the expectations that other members place upon him; the family succeeds only so long as its members agree on these expectations and try to meet them.

Stress causes change in these role patterns: expectations shift, and the family is forced to work out different patterns. In the process, the family is slowed up in its affectional and emotion-satisfying performances until new patterns are worked out and avenues for expressing affection are opened once more.

Sociological research on families under stress offers the most systematic investigation of the rearrangement of roles and other aspects of family organization that enable a family to cope with crises and to survive.

Sex activity, one of the most sensitive aspects of family life, changes sharply as families meet stress. Patterns of sexual relations alter, ceasing altogether for some couples (Komarovsky, 1940). In crisis involving interpersonal recriminations, where the crisis is regarded as the fault of any one member, the position of that member is greatly devalued (Koos & Fulcomer, 1948). Personality changes in members reflect the anxiety and feelings of insecurity engendered by the crisis, and in a sense each responsible member experiences personal shock, disorganization, recovery, and readjustment. This is particularly evident in bereavement.

Changes in parent-child relations are frequently reported in adjustment to crisis. In well-integrated families, Angell (1936) found few changes in relative position of parents and children as a result of the crisis of impoverishment, but did find changes in less well-integrated but more adaptable families. Some families withdraw from all activities until the shame is over and become more than ever closed in on themselves.

Farber and his associates (Farber, 1959; Farber, 1960; Farber, Jenne, & Romolo, 1960), have charted the impact of the severely mentally retarded child on the family as an instance of continuing stress over time. The emotional impact of discovering mental retardation is initially greater on the mother than on the father. Men are even less affected if the child is a girl. Lower-class families are less hesitant than middle-class to place the child in an institution, and both are less hesitant to institutionalize boys than girls. If not institutionalized, boys disrupt the family over the years more than do girls. The decision finally to institutionalize helps the family's integration and relieves especially the pressures on the retarded child's siblings.

Koos (1950) has noted other differences between middle- and lower-class families in their response to trouble. Difficulties that start small may build into crisis because of differences in role expectations held by family members. He found the adolescent-parent relationship to be a focal point in the crisis of the middle-class family. In upward-mobile families, the appropriate roles for wife and mother differ by socioeconomic groups, and the workaday housekeeper role of one's original class may have to be unlearned as the hostess role of the next class is learned.

Cavan (1959), attempting to generalize across class lines in a resumé of depression and unemployment studies, found that a husband's unemployment affects family roles in three ways: First, when the husband cannot find any work, his roles suffer in the eyes of other members of the family. Second, when some members of the family usurp the role of the father as chief wage earner, interpersonal relationships are strained. Third, when the family finally applies for relief and is accepted as a client, further rearrangement of roles is necessary.

Disaster research also emphasizes the importance of roles in study of stress, suggesting that few if any roles hold more powerful command over an individual than his roles in the family. A parent alone with children, for example, may react far more quickly and effectively to danger than if he were entirely alone. Sometimes his family roles may even lead him to act in ways an observer might think "crazy" or "panicky," though disaster reports reveal almost no cases of panic in intact families (Quaran-

telli, 1960). What appears "crazy" is often a rational effort to flee or find missing members.

In some situations, however, roles can hinder a family from meeting the threats of disaster. Hill and Hansen (1962) speculated that the democratization of family roles may help prepare individuals and small family units for atomic attack and recovery. The traditional, extended family with its intricate interlacings of loves and loyalties may well hold the individual or the intact family group in danger areas until escape is impossible.

In disaster threat, if the family is too rigidly organized, "low-status" dependent members may wait too long for the decision of the family head. When the high-status family member refuses to heed the warnings, or makes a poor estimate of the situation, the entire family may suffer. A similar status influence may have appeared in the schoolhouse disaster studied by Perry and Perry (1959), in which a white school inspector, present in the small Negro schoolhouse, purportedly failed to take charge until too late. The teacher and students, meanwhile, would not, or could not, act: they were waiting for his cue, and the delay set the scene for maladaptation to the disaster.

Most often, however, the more clear-cut the responsibilities, the more effectively a person meets a disaster. Marks and Fritz (1954) have shown that, compared to persons without dependents, men with homes and dependents both prepare better and act more rationally in all stages of disaster.

Roles which carry responsibility seem to affect a person's role conceptions: "Others need me," he seems to think. "What I do may save their lives." Such thoughts help him stay in "emotional check" during the first moments of stress and then to rise quickly to active aid. This thesis is supported by the observation that a woman depends on her husband to protect the family, but when he is absent, she quickly steps into the protective, leadership role.

The thesis is also supported by parents' reaction to the realization that in stress situations small children take their cues for behavior from adults (this cue-taking is also reported in medical research; see Caldwell & Guze, 1960). Vaughan (1949) wrote that in a concentration camp run by the Japanese, adults deliberately pretended to hold certain ideas and values in order to make the children's lives less wretched. The same strategy, though more spontaneous and less well developed, is illustrated time after time in interviews with parents after disasters.

In the study of problem families, roles have been recognized in efforts to categorize families by adequacy of role functioning. Geismar took an encouraging step beyond such a static conception. He raised the theoretical question of whether family malfunctioning is most pronounced in areas comprising "expressive" or "instrumental" roles. His exploratory research indicates that problem families are far more adequate in the instrumental than they are in the expressive areas; this suggests that disorganized families have greatest difficulty with interpersonal relationships, particularly those within the family, but that they show relative competence in the physical management of the family (Geismar et al., 1962).

Parad and Caplan (1960) suggested use of the central concept "family life style"—the reasonably stable patterning of family organization, subdivided into three dependent elements: value system, communication network, and role system. Use of this concept allows the researcher to study family life style in action; efforts of the family to cope with stress are analyzed as "intermediate problem-solving mechanisms."

Medical research also makes use of the role concept. Even psychiatrically oriented researchers depend on "role" to help them move from their focus on the individual to a focus on interpersonal relations. Spiegel has attempted to work out the processes involved in resolving role conflicts within a family. His analyses of strains in the family

system which may give rise to disequilibrium are stimulating for the general problem of families under stress (Spiegel, 1957). Da la Mata, Gingras, & Wittkower (1960) identified six possible mechanisms in reacting to illness of a father: (a) denial of the seriousness of the displacement, with the consequent minimizing of the emotional impact of the sick member; (b) overrating the effects and seriousness of the situation; (c) attempts to restore the balance in the power structure the family has set by the father's illness; (d) emotional support of the sick member to boost his morale; (e) emphasis on positive aspects of the member's illness, for example, gratitude that he still lives; (f) an unrealistic protection against depression and anxiety by affirmation of full recovery. Angry outbursts may develop from these unrecognized conflicts, for no one is sure what others expect.

Expectations not only encourage certain behaviors, but also deny others. Serious disturbance may result when, in spite of what parents encourage, certain activities are not discouraged. Incest may even be condoned and stimulated by parents. Incest thus may be not simply a matter of personalities, but also of family roles and rewards (Kaufman et al., 1954).

Not all stress results in equal strain on all members; one person may seek to take the brunt of the impact, or be forced or manipulated to absorb most of the stress. Recent psychiatric research offers insight into such mechanisms of family activity under stress. The concept of "double-bind" suggests that expectations can be such that no matter what he does, one individual cannot satisfy the expectations of another; the trouble is that contradictory expectations are held, and an individual may be frozen in confusion. Lichtenberg and Pao (1960) suggested that a double-bind, perhaps formed by a parent and continued through choice of marriage partner, may profoundly thwart recovery from mental illness. Ferreira (1960) refined this concept to suggest the "split double-bind," in which the expectations of one parent for a child conflict with the expectations of the other parent. The child who loves such parents equally is unable to satisfy one without frustrating the other; although the parents thereby maintain harmony between themselves, the child stumbles into trouble. Parents, Ferreira suggested, often express amazement at the child's behavior; they see the trouble as due to some peculiarity in him, rather than in their own relationship.

Vogel and Bell (1961) suggested a similar mechanism in using a child as the "family scapegoat." The child has an important function of maintaining equilibrium within the family; he indeed suffers beneath the weight of all the family's problems. If an individual in such a role—a most crucial one in his family—is treated, the family may break up and leave untouched important sources of family pathology (Rapoport, 1960). Or, possibly, the "suffering component" might be transferred to another member (Koskoff & Weniger, 1949).

A related concept, "emotional room," has found its way into disaster research. A family appears to be able to support only a certain amount of emotional disturbance among its members at any one time. Thus, following disaster, family members may have to take turns being emotionally disturbed; when one has finally improved, another may mysteriously "fall ill" (Hill & Hansen, 1962).

The expectations of family members can also be crucial in determining an individual's success in recovering from illness or readjusting to society (Evans et al., 1961). Parents who implicitly accuse a son on probation of further crimes or weakness of character may unwittingly push him toward the reformatory. Patients released from mental hospitals may be "protected" by their families to the point that they feel no need to improve; families who expect more of returned patients may prove quite therapeutic. Similarly, Freedman (1957) suggested that failure to set expectations appropriate to the limitations of a brain-damaged child may result in serious personality disturbance.

These and other psychiatric researches now developing underline the validity of the sociologists' earlier emphasis on roles in analyzing families under stress. But they also suggest that attention should not be frozen at the level of consciously perceived expectations, for many underlying mechanisms of interpersonal relations may be overlooked. The wedding of the sociological role concepts with the psychiatric conceptions of mechanisms and motivations promises to bear abundant fruit.

Stages of family activity under stress. Behavior over the period of stress varies from family to family. The common denominator of the various stages of reaction to stress situations may be charted, using the analogy of a truncated roller coaster. As a result of meeting stress, family members are collectively numbed by the blow. They meet friends at first, as if the blow had not fallen; then, as the facts are assimilated, organization slumps, roles are played with less enthusiasm, resentments are smothered or expressed, conflicts develop or are converted into tensions that strain relations. As the nadir of disorganization is reached, things begin to improve, new routines arrived at by trial and error or by thoughtful planning are put into effect, and some minimum agreements about the future are reached. The component parts of the roller-coaster profile of adjustment to crisis are:

stress → disorganization → recovery → reorganization (Fig. 1).

Refinements on this basic pattern have been worked out by Hill (1949) on adjustments to war separation and by Jackson (1956) on adjustments to alcoholism.

Jackson identified seven stages of adjustment: (a) attempts to deny the problem; (b) attempts to eliminate the problem; (c) disorganization; (d) attempts to reorganize in spite of the problem; (e) efforts to escape the problem: the decision to separate

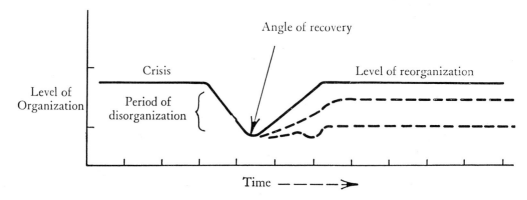

Fig. 1. Common Patterns of Family Adjustment to Crisis.

from the alcoholic spouse; (f) reorganization of the family without spouse; (g) reorganization of the entire family. Though Lemert's findings (1960) contradict Jackson's in a number of places, these stages are quite like the stages of adjustment and recovery to bereavement (T. D. Eliot, 1942; T. D. Eliot, 1960) and unemployment (Bakke, 1940). Several medical researchers also have attempted to identify stages or phases through which a family may pass in its efforts to cope with member illness (Archibald, 1950; Austin, 1955; Brodey, 1959; Schipper, 1959).

An interesting variation on the basic pattern of adjustment is seen in responses to disaster (Fig. 2). Following the initial disorganization, a "society of sufferers" and a "therapeutic community" appear to stimulate an almost euphoric rise in level of organization of individual families. The return to normal daily life in following days and weeks is accompanied by a return to adjustment patterns similar to those under other stresses (Hill & Hansen, 1962).

Some families appear almost invulnerable to stress; others slip easily into crisis under even the smallest of stresses. Since the depression studies of the 1930's, sociologists have attempted to explain this fact by pointing to variations in the resources a family has at its disposal.

Family resources. Robert C. Angell (1936) was the first among sociologists to suggest a set of resources that might help a family avoid the panic of a full-blown crisis in a stressful situation. He identified two primary concepts: "family integration" and "family adaptability."

Family integration refers to the "bonds of coherence and unity running through family life, of which common interests, affection, and a sense of economic interdependence are perhaps the most prominent" (p. 16). This concept is similar to Parad and Caplan's (1960) "need-response pattern," which describes the way in which the family as a group proceeds, respects, and satisfies the basic needs of its individual members.

Angell's concept of family adaptability refers to the family's capacity to meet obstacles and shift courses. It is a complex component, but Angell thought the families he studied evidenced three principal conditions of rigidity: (a) a materialistic philosophy of life among its members, (b) traditionalism in family mores, and (c) irresponsibility of one or both parents (Angell, 1936, p. 17).

Angell's greatest difficulty with the concept "integration" appears to be one of too great inclusion. Koos (1946) and Cavan and Ranck (1938) did specify some of the ele-

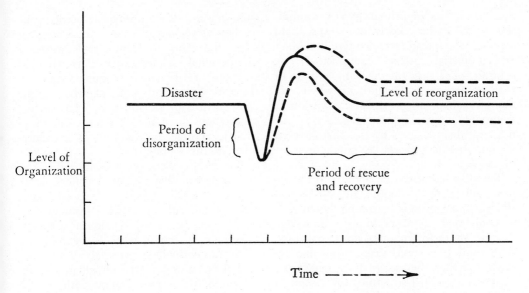

Fig. 2. Common Patterns of Family Adjustment to Community-Wide Disaster.

ments of "integration" as they focussed on family organization. Though the two studies differed in concepts, they agreed that a well-organized family would resist the formation of crisis. What is an organized family? It includes (a) agreement on role structure; (b) subordination of personal ambitions to family goals; (c) satisfaction with the family because it successfully meets the physical and emotional needs of its members; and (d) perceived and shared goals toward which the family is moving collectively. Lacking these, the family is inadequately organized and likely to succumb to stress.

Similar emphasis on the importance of a well-organized family is found in current medical research. In studies of families with brain-damaged children, the general impression is that where parents are integrated, realistic, and accepting, disturbance is minimal (Freedman, 1957). Families able to accept illness with sympathetic understanding, in comparison with those who could not, changed less in expectation and structure and were less likely to place the patient in complete dependency (Lewis & Zeichner, 1960). Medical research also parallels sociological research in suggesting that families in which roles are clearly defined function better than those where there is uncertainty of expectations.

Hill, building on the work of the depression unemployment studies, suggested the joining of concepts such as "family adequacy," "marital adjustment," "family integration," and "family adaptability" into one scale for "dynamic stability" (Hill, 1949). Hill's attempt provided a profile of several dimensions of interrelated measures rather than a new blend and did not lead to a solution of Angell's difficulty of defining, in operation and theory, the components of integration and adaptability. The problem remains unresolved today.

A theory of family strength and weakness. Societies, theorists have claimed, hold and attract individuals because of the rewards or punishments offered either through the primary (personal) relationship or through the contractual (positional) relationship. As the one relationship increases, the other decreases. Family researchers have used this idea, recognizing that family ties in primary-type communities tend to be closely knit and hold together widespread extended families. Modern, industrial societies (contractual), by contrast, offer a picture of family units of mother, father, and children, which, although perhaps not so isolated from kin as commonly supposed [see pp. 514–517], are held to other relatives by ties that may be all but invisible, except at holidays or in times of stress.

The idea has also been applied to the internal affairs of the family, suggesting that the modern family is becoming "atomized" as individual members splinter from one another in their daily activities, returning home only to eat and sleep, using one another (as they themselves have been used in the occupational structure) on a contractual basis.

But, although a single continuum (primary-contractual, or, in our terms, personal-positional) is appropriate for national analysis, in order to study families and

communities, two continua are needed: one to show development of structural relationships, the other to show development of interpersonal relationships. Personal and positional relations differ qualitatively, in the actor's goal and object of behavior, the consequences or functions of behavior, the expectations held for behavior, sources of behavioral force, and the stability and durability of the relationship.

These differences point toward the general statement that the family offers an individual certain status and power, and serves him with goods to consume, and, within this positional relationship, expects him to act in certain ways. But it may also offer him individual personalities to enjoy and to help, and these individuals also expect him to act in harmony with the expectations they hold for him. The two types of expectations may conflict, thus creating a stress on the individual and family. Even more important, one or the other type may be atrophied.

Theoretically, a family could exist without one or the other type of relationship, and in such a case every act of the individuals could be labelled either "positional" or "personal." But in real life families, pure relationships of either type seem highly improbable. Action is determined by a blend of interpersonal and structural expectations. The question is just "how much" force each relationship has on each member.

We might locate each dyad within a family within the quadrants formed by the intersection of the personal and positional continua. Though personal and positional relations are complex, in stress study we are primarily concerned with their behavioral influence (i.e., their strength in determining the actions of the family members). In logical types, a family can be: (a) strong in both personal and positional relations; (b) weak in positional but strong in personal (perhaps most rare in a family); (c) strong in positional but weak in personal; (d) weak in both.

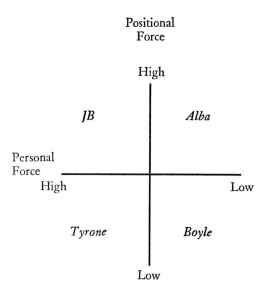

Fig. 3. Intersection of Positional and Personal Continua, Yielding Four Logical Types of Family.

Each type differs, theoretically, from the others in relationship and behavior.

Type A, the J.B.s[4]: high personal and high positional force, is represented by voluntary organizations such as a college fraternity, in which intimate contact is as important to most members as are the authority and status relationships among themselves and with the college community. A family of this type tends to stability of organization, probable durability, efficiency of operation, high degree of satisfaction felt by participants, marked conformity of members to group mores, sensitivity of individuals to the expectations of others, and marked ability to predict the behaviors of others.

Family members are highly cohesive, with mutual satisfaction in both personal and positional relations. This cohesion might be apparent to the observer or lie fallow, as a potential power ready when need arises. Families found in this quadrant are expected to be able to take heavy stresses without great deterioration. Enjoying both personal and positional force, they seem invulnerable to most stressor events.

Type B, the Tyrones[5]: high personal, low positional force, is rare in large-scale organizations. It is most easily seen in the relationship of man to mistress, in the relationship of some close siblings, or in dyads low in the ranks of highly structured organizations (such as privates in the army).

Families of this type—a subcategory of which might be the "pseudo-mutual" family (Wynn et al., 1958)—though probably rare, tend to be very unstable and of questionable durability. Although they may be mutually satisfying, they possess little power to withstand stress of many sorts, for such relationships are based directly on the mutual satisfaction of the members. If great

coercion is applied, the relationship may deteriorate under stress; either the family will drift apart or it will change to a type C or D relationship.

Type C, the Albas[6]: low personal, high positional force, is the most dramatic, for it contains those families which seem to resist completely certain amounts of stress and then suddenly splinter. This type is represented on an organization level by large business offices, by the army, and by such voluntary organizations as the PTA.

Families of this sort—a subcategory of which might be Goode's (1961) "empty shell" family—are typified by contractual behavior, in which services are exchanged on a profit-motive basis; by a tendency toward efficiency, in which behaviors are directed toward effective operation of the family; by stability, as long as there is no choice of escape by members; and by inflexibility. They tend to be coercive in relationships, in which one or more individuals (e.g., the patriarchal father) dominates all the activities of other members and forces them to behave as he wants them to behave. Internal conflict may build intensely as members fester in submissive roles. Such relationships are brittle, although the coercion may be so strong that only a dramatic, massive blow shatters the relationship. When a blow of sufficient strength comes, however, there is little flexibility to bend with the stress. Then the family breaks.

Type D, the Boyles[7]: low personal and low positional force, is illustrated by the couple considering divorce, the club about to die, or the ineffectual "service organization." It is also seen in the casual acquaintances made daily in an urban person's life, such as the cocktail party meetings of strangers. Families of this type can be hampered by instability, questionable durability, and little satisfaction for anyone. The person who tries to help is usually

---

[4] From Archibald Macleish's *J. B.* The names of these four types are taken from fictional descriptions of stress-worn families and are offered merely to help readers grasp the essence of the types.

[5] From Eugene O'Neill's *Long Day's Journey Into Night.*

[6] From Federico Garcia Lorca's *The House of Bernarda Alba.*

[7] From Sean O'Casey's *Juno and the Paycock.*

frustrated, and the person who needs help refuses it. Such families are highly vulnerable to stress; they evidence neither cohesion nor effective coercion. Indeed, all that holds them together may be inertia or the community sanctions against disorganization.

Crisis studies suggest that a family is more likely to weather stress if it is strong in involvement, integration, and adaptability, and that lacking one of these, the family under stress is likely to fall into crisis. The distinction between personal and positional relationships suggests that the statements are overly simple. The three variables contribute to family strength, but lack of any one need not leave the family vulnerable.

Families of type A can lack adaptability (for example, when positional force is entirely coercive) and yet still withstand a great deal of stress if there is a high degree of integration and involvement. The strengths will act as buffers against the impact, protecting the brittleness fostered by inflexibility.

A family can also be somewhat lacking in either integration or involvement (types B or C) and still withstand a certain amount of stress, if it can rely on strengths in the other variables. For example, inflexible families may even lack involvement (as in type C) and still withstand a certain amount of stress without changing much in functioning. Indeed, until the stress becomes intense enough, the family to all outward appearances will continue to function very efficiently and very effectively as a family. Such a family may stay together purely because of the coercive force of the structural relationship. When the stress becomes intense enough, however, the family may dramatically splinter, as the individual who has been coerced rebels, or in agony shouts, "I can't stand it any more!" and with that shout destroys the relationship.

To sum up; integration, involvement, and adaptability apparently are valid elements of family *strength,* but their relationship to family vulnerability is more complicated than is recognized in existing reports. Consensus buffers against stress; the family that agrees on values and goals and has cohesive agreements and expectations can ward off many intense blows. Involvement both buffers against stress and is therapeutic in recovery. Lack of adaptability leads to brittleness; this isolates the family from small stresses, but allows it to splinter under large stresses. Adaptability thus sometimes strengthens and sometimes weakens the family.[8]

To operationalize the concepts, personal and positional relationships, is not easy. It seems most profitable to seek information about behaviors (as distinct from *qualities*) that are likely to be loaded with behavioral influence (cohesions and coercions) of either personal or positional relationships.

Estimates of the behavioral force of personal and structural relations might be made by study of (a) the behaviors engaged in by the members of the family, and (b) the frequency of these behaviors. Highly promising are these areas of family life:

The range and frequency of topics of communication;

The range and frequency of topics of conflict;

The physical and emotional autonomy of dependents exhibited through the range and frequency of shared behavior and autonomous behavior;

The authority patterns and family roles adopted in solving family and individual prob-

---

[8] Another set of variables, cohesion and coercion, runs through this discussion. Coercion may either strengthen or weaken the family. If accompanied by cohesion, it can offer stability and definiteness to the relationship; indeed, without some coercion, a structural relationship might be almost as fickle as a purely personal relationship. Coercion without cohesion (or an overbalance of coercion) may result in added brittleness; it tempers the relationship as heat tempers steel, both hardening it and yet robbing it of its capacity to bend. Under great pressure it will only break.

lems (personal problems may be considered either family or individual, depending on their content);

The empathy between family members.

Each of these variables has interpersonal and structural components, and specific behaviors or patterns of behavior can be allied with either structural or personal force.

The above discussion should be taken as only suggestive of a direction for research into some problems of family strengths and weaknesses. The usefulness of the personal and positioned concepts, and of that of "behavioral force," has yet to be demonstrated in research. [Certain aspects of this discussion are also treated by Cavan in Ch. 14. See especially her section on downward mobility, pp. 573–575.]

CONCLUSION

Study of families under stress in each of the four areas considered in this chapter is beset with problems. Although accumulation of findings is promising, it is hardly as rich in firm theories as the abundance of studies would suggest.

Perhaps this is due partly to a limited focus and partly to a failure to understand the process of both research and theory development. No one conceptual framework so far evident in study of families under stress boasts the conceptual development necessary to meet the varied problems of personality, family as a unity or system, community, and society. Sociology in particular seems at a loss to cope with problems of human motivation, even though in its theory motivation is recognized as an essential of social life.

Current study also ignores cultural and physical factors related to families under stress. Although research, because of inadequate methods, must necessarily shortchange human life, theory need not. To study a family under stress, it must be broken into little conceptual pieces. It is

difficult to put the pieces back together again, but it is possible, and it is crucial. Unfortunately, traditional study either emphasizes analysis without synthesis, or attempts to synthesize without previous analysis. The first course leads to splintered and segmented pictures of the world, the second to disguised moralizing which seeks to convert rather than inform.

Crisis research has rarely risen above simple description, and when it does, it rises not toward general, or even middle-range theory, but rather toward isolated predictions of the response to stress by families which evidence various structural traits or qualities (such as family integration) or behavior (such as role conflict). In such studies, adjustment or maladjustment is usually taken as the criterion for evaluating behavior. Little attention is paid to what kind of adjustment it is, beyond a general, semiexplicit ideal of adjustment of family members to one another and to the changed situation.

Current efforts in research and theory might improve in a number of directions. For one thing, efforts might be made to develop, from existing data, generalizable though partial theories about families under stress; theories of family ability to withstand external and internal stresses, theories about the relationship of community structure and family placement in the community to the development and response to stresses, theories of the relationship of individual adjustment to family reaction. Such theories, it must be recognized, will be rather static and, regardless of the individual autonomy they claim to allow individuals, will treat the family as merely reactive elements to the situation. Nonetheless, such theories would be most useful both in the development of a more general theory of family and society and in aiding social-action researchers in making predictions necessary to effective action.

For another thing, stress research might recognize that individual families, and, derivatively, the family institution or system, lean toward the future. Individual families and institutions are constantly changing, and not all of the change is reactive to dynamic society. Families, as well as individual members, not only have a history and live in the present, they live in the future, and, indeed, behavior is often less closely determined by present situations than by what the individual anticipates and desires in future days, weeks, and even years. Likely, this forwardness is often as important in determining action as is the individual's history.

This forwardness is a significant factor not only when one looks at the individual family; its existence is easily seen in institutional patterns of middle-class families, who individually save and work so that they may retire independently or so that their children may attend a university.

Current stances in study of families under stress are ill equipped to treat such forwardness in contemporary life. This is partly because of the emphasis on "system," "equilibration," and "readjustment," an emphasis that is shared by interactionists and functionalists, as well as researchers of problem families and of families in disaster. The commitment to reactive change is most marked in current system analysis, in which behavior is analyzed for functional interrelationship; the analysis is laborious even for short, frozen periods of time. However useful such a perspective is for describing the relationship of personality and society, it is limited and static and can legitimately offer little explanation of causes.

In spite of the limitations of perspective and methodology, many incisive studies on families under stress have accumulated, and seeds of theory lie scattered over the fields of sociology, psychology, social work, and medical-psychiatric research. To gather these together is essential, but it is not enough: They must be imaginatively combined toward empirical theory, and the theory must be put to the test and refined. The process will be difficult; imagination will often have to substitute for knowledge, and researchers will have to be painfully aware of methodologies, as they keep a steady gaze on reality.

REFERENCES

Allport, G. W. The open system in personality theory. *J. abnorm. soc. Psychol.,* 1960, 3, 301–310.

Angell, R. C. *The family encounters the depression.* New York: Scribner, 1936.

Archibald, H. C. Disturbed child, disturbed family. *Arch. Pediatrics,* 1950, 67, 128–132.

Austin, E. Participation of the family and patient in a program of rehabilitation. *Amer. J. phys. Med.,* 1955, 34, 116–118.

Bakke, E. W. *The unemployed worker.* New Haven: Yale Univer. Press, 1940.

Baldamus, W., & Timms, N. The problem family—a sociological approach. *Brit. J. Sociol.,* 1955, 6, 318–327.

Beach, H. D., & Lucas, R. A. (Eds.) *Individual and group behavior in a coal mine disaster.* Washington, D.C.: National Academy of Sciences–National Research Council, Disaster Research Group, 1962.

Bell, N. W., & Vogel, E. F. (Eds.) *A modern introduction to the family.* New York: Free Press, 1961. Especially Parts III & IV.

Bernard, Jessie. *Remarriage.* New York: Dryden Press, 1956.

Blacker, C. P. *Problem families: five inquiries.* London: Eugenics Society, 1952.

Bridgman, P. W. *The way things are.* Cambridge: Harvard Univer. Press, 1959.

Brodey, W. Some family operations and schizophrenia. A study of five hospitalized families each with a schizophrenic member. *Arch. gen. Psychiatry,* 1959, 1, 379–402.

Burgess, E. W. The family as a unity of interacting personalities. *Family,* 1926, 7, 3–9.

Burgess, E. W. The family and sociological research. *Soc. Forces,* 1947, 26, 1–6.

Caldwell, B. M., & Guze, S. B. A study of the adjustment of parents and siblings of institutionalized and non-institutionalized retarded children. *Amer. J. ment. Defic.,* 1960, 64, 845–861.

Caudill, W. Effects of social and cultural systems in reactions to stress. *Soc. Sci. Res. Council Monogr.,* June 1958.

Cavan, Ruth S. Unemployment—crisis of the common man. *Marr. & fam. Living,* 1959, 21, 139–146. Reprinted in Ruth S. Cavan (Ed.), *Marriage and family in the modern world.* New York: Crowell, 1960. Pp. 425–437.

Cavan, Ruth S., & Ranck, Katherine H. *The family and the depression.* Chicago: Univer. of Chicago Press, 1938.

Clausen, J. A., & Yarrow, Marion R. (Eds.) The impact of mental illness on the family. *J. soc. Issues,* 1955, 11, 3–64.

Davis, F. Definitions of time and recovery in paralytic polio convalescence. *Amer. J. Sociol.,* 1956, 61, 582–587.

De la Mata, R. G., Gingras, G., & Wittkower, E. D. Impact of sudden severe disablement of the father on the family. *Canadian med. ass. J.,* 1960, 82, 1015–1020.

Eliot, T. D. Family crises and ways of meeting them. In H. Becker & R. Hill (Eds.), *Marriage and the family.* Boston: Heath, 1942. Pp. 489–536.

Eliot, T. D. Adjusting to the death of a loved one. In Ruth S. Cavan (Ed.), *Marriage and family in the modern world.* New York: Crowell, 1960. Pp. 438–444.

Eliot, T. S. *The cocktail party.* New York: Harcourt, Brace, 1950.

Evans, A. S., Bullard, D. M., & Solomon, M. H., Jr. The family as a potential resource in the rehabilitation of the chronic schizophrenic patient: a study of 60 patients and their families. *Amer. J. Psychiatry,* 1961, 117, 1075–1083.

Farber, B. Effects of a severely mentally retarded child on family integration. *Monogr. Soc. Res. Child Develpm.,* 1959, 24, No. 71.

Farber, B. Family organization and crisis. *Mongr. Soc. Res. Child Develpm.,* 1960, 25, No. 75.

Farber, B., Jenne, W. C., & Romolo, T. *Family crisis and the decision to institutionalize the retarded child.* Urbana, Ill.: Institute for Research on Exceptional Children, 1960.

Ferreira, A. J. The "double-bind" and delinquent behavior. *Arch. gen. Psychiatry,* 1960, 3, 359–367.

Foote, N., & Cottrell, L. *Identity and interpersonal competence.* Chicago: Univer. of Chicago Press, 1955.

Form, W. H., & Nosow, S., with Stone, S., & Westie, C. W. *Community and disaster.* New York: Harper, 1957.

Freedman, A. M., et al. Psychiatric aspects of familial dysautonomia. *Amer. J. Orthopsychiat.,* 1957, 27, 96–104.

Freeman, H. E. Attitudes toward mental illness among relatives of former patients. *Amer. sociol. Rev.,* 1961, 26, 59–66.

Fritz, C. E. The therapeutic features of disaster and their effects on family adjustment: some research orientations. Paper read at Groves Conference, Washington, D.C., 1958.

Fritz, C. E. Disaster. In R. K. Merton & R. Nisbet (Eds.), *Contemporary social problems.* New York: Harcourt, Brace & World, 1961. Pp. 651–694.

Geiger, K. Deprivation and solidarity in the Soviet urban family. *Amer. sociol. Rev.,* 1955, 20, 57–68.

Geismar, L. L. Three levels of treatment for the multiproblem family. *Soc. Casewk,* 1961, 42, 124–127.

Geismar, L. L., & Ayres, Beverly. *Patterns of change in problem families.* St. Paul: Family Centered Project, 1959.

Geismar, L. L., LaSorte, M. A., & Ayres, Beverly. Measuring family disorganization. *Marr. & fam. Living,* 1962, 24, 51–56.

Goode, W. *After divorce.* Glencoe, Ill.: Free Press, 1956.

Goode, W. Family disorganization. In R. K. Merton & R. Nisbet (Eds.), *Contemporary social problems.* New York: Harcourt, Brace & World, 1961. Pp. 390–458.

Gordon, E. W., & Ullman, M. Reactions of parents to the problems of mental retardation in children. *Amer. J. ment. Defic.,* 1956–1957, 61, 158–163.

Hansen, D. Nominal concepts, methodological theories and research bias. *J. Marr. & Fam.* (formerly *Marr. & fam. Living*), 1964, 26.

Hill, R. *Families under stress.* New York: Harper, 1949.

Hill, R. Generic features of families under stress. *Soc. Casewk,* 1958, 39, 139–150.

Hill, R., & Hansen, D. A. The identification of conceptual frameworks utilized in family study. *Marr. & fam. Living,* 1960, 22, 299–

311. Reprinted in M. Sussman (Ed.), *Sourcebook in marriage and the family*. (Rev. ed.) Boston: Houghton Mifflin, 1963. Pp. 494–503.

Hill, R., & Hansen, D. A. The family in disaster. In G. Baker & D. Chapman (Eds.), *Man and society in disaster*. New York: Basic Books, 1962.

Inkeles, A. Personality and social structure. In R. K. Merton et al. (Eds.), *Sociology today*. New York: Basic Books, 1959. Pp. 249–276.

Irvine, Elizabeth E. Research into problem families: theoretical questions arising from Dr. Blacker's investigations. *Brit. J. soc. Wk*, 1954, 9, 24–34.

Ishwaran, K. *Family life in the Netherlands*. The Hague: Uitjeverij Van Keulen, N. V., 1959.

Jackson, Joan K. The adjustment of the family to alcoholism. *Marr. & fam. Living*, 1956, 18, 361–369.

Kaufman, I., Peck, Alice, & Tagiuri, C. K. The family constellation and overt incestuous relations between father and daughter. *Amer. J. Orthopsychiat.*, 1954, 24, 266–277. Reprinted in Bell & Vogel (1961).

Komarovsky, Mirra. *The unemployed man and his family*. New York: Dryden Press, 1940.

Koos, E. L. *Families in trouble*. New York: King's Crown Press, 1946.

Koos, E. L., & Fulcomer, D. Families in crisis. In Evelyn M. Duvall & R. Hill (cochairmen), *Dynamics of family interaction*. New York: Woman's Foundation, 1948. Ch. 8. (Mimeographed.)

Koskoff, Y. D., & Weniger, F. L. Adverse effect on the family resulting from radical change of personality in one member after prefrontal lobotomy. *Prac. Ass. Res. nerv. ment Dis.*, 1949, 29, 148–154.

Lemert, E. M. The occurrence and sequence of events in the adjustment of families to alcoholism. *Quart. J. Stud. Alcohol*, 1960, 21, 679–697.

Lewis, V. S., & Zeichner, A. M. Impact of admission to a mental hospital on the patient's family. *Ment. Hyg., N.Y.*, 1960, 44, 503–509.

Lichtenberg, J. D., & Pao, P. N. The prognostic and therapeutic significance of the husband-wife relationship for hospitalized schizophrenic women. *Psychiatry*, 1960, 23, 209–217.

Marks, E. S., Fritz, C. E., et al. *Human reactions in disaster situations*. Chicago: National Opinion Research Center, 1954. (Unpublished rept.)

Myers, J. K., & Roberts, B. H. *Family and class dynamics in mental illness*. New York: Wiley, 1959. Especially Ch. 8.

Nordlie, P. G., & Popper, R. D. *Social phenomena in a post-nuclear attack situation*. Arlington, Va.: Human Sciences Research, 1962. Especially pp. 30–32.

Parad, H. J., & Caplan, G. A framework for studying families in crisis. *Soc. Wk*, 1960, 3–15.

Parsons, T. *The social system*. Glencoe, Ill.: Free Press, 1951.

Parsons, T. The superego and the theory of social systems. In T. Parsons, R. Bales, & E. Shils (Eds.), *Working papers in the theory of action*. Glencoe, Ill.: Free Press, 1953. Pp. 13–28. Reprinted in Bell & Vogel, 1961, pp. 636–648.

Parsons, T., & Fox, Renee C. Illness, therapy, and the modern American family. *J. soc. Issues*, 1952, 13, 31–44.

Perry, Helen S., & Perry, S. E. *The schoolhouse disasters: family and community as determinants of the child's response to disaster*. Washington, D.C.: National Academy of Sciences–National Research Council, Disaster Research Group, 1959.

Philip, A. F., & Timms, N. *The problem of "the problem family."* London: Family Service Units, 1957.

Quarantelli, E. L. A note on the protective function of the family in disaster. *Marr. & fam. Living*, 1960, 22, 263–265.

Rapoport, Rhona. The family and psychiatric treatment—a conceptual approach. *Psychiatry*, 1960, 23, 53–62.

Richardson, H. B. *Patients have families*. New York: Commonwealth Fund, 1945.

Schipper, M. T. The child with mongolism in the home. *Pediatrics*, 1959, 24, 132–144.

Schneider, D. M. Typhoons on tap. *Hum. organ.*, 1957, 16, 10–15.

Schwartz, C. G. Perspectives on deviance—wives' definitions of their husbands' mental illness. *Psychiatry*, 1957, 20, 275–291.

Schlesinger, B. *An annotated bibliography of the multi-problem family*. Toronto: Univer. of Toronto Press, 1963.

Shelsky, H. *Wandlungen in der Deutschen*

Familien in der Gegenwart. Stuttgart: Enk-Verlag, 1954.

Sinha, D. Psychological study of catastrophes. *Patna Univer. J.,* 1954, 6, 56–60.

Spiegel, J. P. The resolution of role conflict within the family. *Psychiatry,* 1957, 20, 1–16.

Spiegel, J. P., & Bell, N. W. The family of the psychiatric patient. In S. Arieti (Ed.), *Handbook of American psychiatry.* Vol. 1. New York: Norton, 1959. Pp. 114–149.

Spiegel, J. P., & Kluckhohn, Florence R. *Integration and conflict in family behavior.* Topeka, Kansas: Group for the Advancement of Psychiatry, 1954.

Tizard, J., & Grad, J. C. *The mentally handicapped and their families.* London: Oxford Univer. Press, 1961. Especially Ch. 10.

Vaughan, Elizabeth. *Communities under stress.* Princeton, N.J.: Princeton Univer. Press, 1949.

Vogel, E. F., & Bell, N. W. The emotionally disturbed child as the family scapegoat. In N. Bell & E. Vogel (Eds.), *A modern introduction to the family.* New York: Free Press, 1961. Pp. 382–397.

Whyte, W. H. *The organization man.* London: Penguin, 1960.

Wynn, L. C., Ryckoff, I. M., Day, J., & Hirsch, S. I. Pseudo-mutuality in the family relations of schizophrenics. *Psychiatry,* 1958, 21, 205–220.

Young, M. The role of the extended family in disaster. *Hum. Relat.,* 1954, 7, 383–391.

Zuk, G. H. The religious factor and the role of guilt in parental acceptance of the retarded child. *Amer. J. ment. Defic.,* 1959, 64, 139–147.

PART V Applied and Normative Interests

CHAPTER 20 Organizational Programs to Strengthen the Family

MURIEL W. BROWN

A "program" is here defined as a sustained activity which has a distinct purpose, procedures planned to accomplish that purpose, and a setting in which to operate. It is assumed that programs which strengthen family life are those designed to help families realize, as fully as possible, their own potentialities for creative living in the cultures to which they belong.

Family-related programs may be classified in many different ways. Some are governmental; some are conducted by voluntary organizations. Some of the latter are professional; some are formed by laymen. Some are single purposed; some are multipurposed. Some are tax-supported; some are financed by churches, industries, or foundations; some depend on contributions from individuals and groups interested in their aims. Some are local; some function at state or regional levels; some are national; a few are international. Some extend across all these lines of jurisdiction.

The organizations which sponsor these programs are as diversified as the activities themselves. They include: agencies that provide basic protection for all families through systems of national defense, law enforcement, and emergency aid; agencies that conserve and develop natural resources for the use of all families; agencies that keep track of conditions affecting families through surveys, studies, and the continuous collection of statistical data; agencies that interpret family needs and stimulate action to meet them; agencies that educate for parenthood, marriage, homemaking, and family living; agencies that give direct aid to individual families in the form of counseling, financial assistance, medical care, and other kinds of social service; agencies that provide recreational and cultural opportunities for the enrichment of family life; churches and other organizations that give spiritual comfort and guidance. Many agencies belong in more than one of these categories because they administer more than one type of program, have more than one source of support, or are federations with different kinds of organizations in their membership.

It would, of course, be impossible to review here all of the important work that has been done for and with families under these many different auspices. Included in this chapter, however, are many of the major programs that have been identified in recent years with the growth of movements to strengthen family life. To fully appreciate the significance of these, it is necessary to know why, where, when, and how they came into being. A little historical information has, therefore, been included in some of the descriptions. Programs in the United States are discussed in the first three sections; programs in other countries in the fourth section; and international programs in the final section. Both governmental and non-governmental activities are described in each section.

PROGRAMS IN THE UNITED STATES UNDER GOVERNMENT AUSPICES

The agencies of the United States government whose programs are most closely related to the concerns of American families are the Departments of Agriculture; Commerce; Defense; Health, Education, and Welfare; Interior; Justice; Labor; the Treasury; the Atomic Energy Commission; the Housing and Home Finance Agency; the Selective Service System; and the Veterans Administration. From time to time, the President is urged to create a federal Department of the Family, which would coordinate all government services to families. This is a complicated issue, however, and one not likely to be settled soon.

The federal government offers no direct service to families except in situations especially designated by the Congress. Examples of such exceptions are the direct service and financial aid given to families on Indian reservations and to needy repatriated Americans. Through carefully developed systems of cooperation with state governments, however, federal agencies perform a variety of backstopping functions that make it possible for families to set goals and work toward them with an ever increasing sense of security. Their programs protect the lives, the health, and the property of families. They provide insurance against loss of income through unemployment or old age, assistance for families in need, opportunities for family education, recreation, and cultural advancement, and good facilities for research to keep all of these activities in touch with the growing bodies of knowledge from which they derive their authenticity.

THE PROTECTIVE SERVICES

Only a person who has lived in places where there is no dependable law of the land can fully appreciate what it means to bring up a family in a country where contracts made in good faith are honored, where taxes are collected fairly, where court decisions are based on legal codes, where the right to own property is upheld by law, where sanitary regulations are enforced, where people have confidence in their systems of law enforcement and military defense.

In the United States, the Departments of Defense; Interior; Justice; Labor; and Health, Education, and Welfare all help to protect American families from many hazards no single family could cope with alone. The guardianship provided by the Army, the Navy, the Air Force, the Marine Corps, the Coast Guard, the National Guard, and state and local police departments is too often taken for granted, but if it were suddenly withdrawn, most of the energy families now spend meeting other needs would have to be used for survival. The welfare of families connected with these services is a major concern of our government, and many special arrangements are made for their benefit.

The chief responsibility for law enforcement rests with the Department of Justice and with state and local police forces. The Federal Bureau of Investigation plays a leading role in the never-ending war against crime. The Justice Department, as a whole, works closely with other agencies of government and with national voluntary organizations on such long-range problems as the prevention of juvenile delinquency and the protection of civil rights. The problem of narcotics is handled by the Narcotics Bureau of the Treasury Department.

When a member of a family goes to work today, he hopes to find working conditions that conform to existing regulations concerning hours, wages, safety precautions, and health conditions. The Department of Labor has been deeply involved for many years in the struggle to gain these protections for every citizen. The administration of labor laws is one of its important obligations, but not by any means its only function. The staff is in constant touch with both labor and management, and works endlessly with official and non-official groups to gain deeper insight into the problems of business and industry and to find new ways of solving these. Existing labor legislation is under continuous review so that necessary additions or revisions may be made. Issues in four major areas of special concern to families will probably confront this department for some time to come: automation, fair labor practices, child labor, and the employment of mothers outside of the home.

The agency of government with the most direct responsibility for family welfare is the Department of Health, Education, and Welfare. This was created in 1953 by the 83rd Congress to take over the powers and functions of its predecessor, the Federal Security Agency, established in 1939. It includes the Public Health Service, the Office of Education, the Vocational Rehabilitation Administration, the Food and Drug Administration, the Social Security Administration, and a newly created Welfare Administration. This last contains the Children's Bureau, the Bureau of Family Services (until recently the Bureau of Public Assistance), the Cuban Refugee Program, the Office of Aging, and the Office of Juvenile Delinquency and Youth Development.

The Food and Drug Administration monitors the nation's food and drug supply to prevent fraud and make sure that all products sold are truthfully labeled and safe if properly used. Its refusal to permit the drug thalidomide to be distributed in this country has given families throughout the United States a new understanding of the importance of its activities. This protective program is conducted along three main lines: law enforcement, education of the public, and appeals to business and industry for self-regulation.

Through a wide variety of technical and advisory services channeled through state departments of health, the Public Health Service makes important contributions to family and community health. For example, it helps communities to set up and maintain standards for environmental sanitation; for dealing with air and water pollution; for protecting food, including milk, from contamination; for the control of communicable diseases, including venereal infections; for community health practices; for public health nursing services; and for hospital and medical facilities. It administers congressional appropriations for grants-in-aid to the states for the improvement of health services, and takes initiative in the development of training programs to increase the number of qualified doctors, nurses, health educators, and other public health personnel.

The nine National Institutes of Health are the research arm of the Public Health Service. Seven of these are highly specialized, each studying a particular disease, group of diseases, or part of the body. All work closely with universities, medical schools, and voluntary health and welfare organizations, as well as with other government agencies. Intensive work is now being done under their auspices on some of the diseases most dreaded by parents: cerebral palsy, leukemia, asthma, epilepsy, arthritis, cystic fibrosis, and disorders of vision, speech, and hearing (USDHEW, 1963).

In October, 1962, two new institutes were established with non-categorical assignments: the National Institute of General Medical Sciences, and the National Institute of Child Health and Human Development.

The first was created to explore problems in the basic biomedical sciences; the second to make "an integrated approach to the health status, needs, and problems of people in the various stages of human development" (USDHEW, 1963b, p. 14).

A national program of poison control is maintained by the Public Health Service. This is, essentially, a system for communicating information about poisons and their antidotes. Any doctor can call the nearest of about 450 poison control centers, well scattered over the country, and find out in minutes what to do for a special poisoning case. Many of the new household cleaning preparations contain toxic substances which can be fatal to children, and it is sometimes hard to tell, from the symptoms, exactly what a baby has swallowed. The local centers all clear through the National Clearing House for Poison Control Centers, where the most expert diagnostic service in the world is available. Studies made by the Clearing House show that 90 per cent of the victims of accidental poisoning are youngsters under five years of age.

Modern conditions of living are constantly creating other new health hazards. One of these is the increasing amount of radiation, from many sources, to which people are exposed. The Public Health Service now has a radiological monitoring program that covers the entire country. Data for it are gathered by federal, state, and local health authorities. When the findings justify such action, the public is informed and steps are taken to reduce unnecessary exposure. The removal of X-ray machines from most of the stores selling shoes for children is a case in point.

When major disasters occur, practically every department of government steps in with some form of emergency aid. State and local public welfare agencies give extensive service and financial assistance to families in stricken areas. The Social Security Administration provides personnel and helps in other ways. The armed forces send men and supplies, as these are needed, to combat fire, flood, and earthquake damage, to preserve order and safeguard the lives and property of people.

On such occasions, the Public Health Service has an especially important part to play. In cooperation with the Army, the Red Cross, and many other state and national organizations, both public and private, it works constantly on measures to cope with health problems in disaster areas. It has in readiness plans for protecting and purifying water supplies in such emergencies, for helping to establish the necessary sanitary and hospital facilities, and for conducting large-scale immunization projects.

Another Public Health Service program not too well known is that of the National Center for Health Statistics. A subdivision of this is the National Vital Statistics Division (formerly the National Office of Vital Statistics), which has been working with the states since 1953 on a plan for the uniform and complete recording of marriages and divorces. This is an essential first step in a projected long-range study of family formation and dissolution in the United States. The findings of this research will be eagerly awaited by counselors, caseworkers, family life specialists, researchers, social welfare administrators, indeed by everyone who wants to help prevent family breakdown and strengthen marriage [cf. pp. 715–719].

The Veterans Administration administers the legislation which authorizes the payment of benefits to former members of the armed forces and to the dependents of servicemen who have died. It has two programs of special importance to families who are eligible: the Guardianship Service, which acts on behalf of beneficiaries under legal disability, including the children of deceased veterans, to make sure that the money paid to them by the government is wisely handled and that their welfare is otherwise protected; and the War Orphans Educational Assistance. The latter makes it possible for the sons and daughters of veterans who have died from service-connected illnesses or injuries to receive the education that would probably have been theirs if their parents had lived.

THE INSURANCE PROGRAMS

Most of the insurance programs now administered by the government date from the depression of the 1930's. When our economy suddenly collapsed in 1929, American families lost not only their savings but their incomes and, in many cases, their homes. To prevent the recurrence of such a disaster, the insurance principle was built into the long-range recovery plans. Bank deposits up to $5,000 (now $10,000) were insured by a new agency, the Federal Deposit Insurance Corporation. Later, under the Housing and Home Finance Agency, established in 1947, the Federal Housing Administration developed programs of federal mortgage insurance for the construction, purchase, and improvement of existing properties.

Among the chief features of FHA's mortgage insurance programs . . . are small down payments, reasonable financing charges, repayment of loan (including interest, principal, taxes, and insurance) in equal monthly installments, and long-term maturity. Millions of families are thus enabled to become home-owners who otherwise could not afford it (ICCY, 1961, pp. 82–83).

The Social Security Act was passed by the Congress in 1935, after months of careful study and preparation. Those sections of it which regulate insurance programs have been under almost constant review ever since to make sure that this legislation continues to serve the purposes for which it was intended: the protection of workers through retirement income, life insurance, unemployment insurance, and disability benefits. The program is financed by contributions from workers and their employers, under conditions set forth in the act (Larson, 1958). As it has matured, its basic concern with family welfare has become increasingly apparent.

The original plan made no provisions for family benefits. Insured workers who qualified were the only beneficiaries, except that amounts up to $250 were paid for funeral expenses when eligible workers died. In 1939, benefits were made payable not only to insured workers but also to their wives or widows when these women became 65, and to their minor children. A mother with a child beneficiary in her care became eligible for benefits regardless of her age.

In 1946, certain World War II veterans were taken into the program, which at that time was coordinated with the Railroad Retirement System. The year 1950 saw the extension of coverage to such groups as non-farm, self-employed persons and regularly employed farm and domestic workers. In that year, too, formulas for payments were adjusted to bring benefits more nearly into line with the changes in wage levels and cost of living that had taken place since 1935.

Between 1952 and 1954, benefits were again adjusted to bring their purchasing power back to the 1939 level, and coverage was again extended. The age of eligibility for women was lowered from 65 to 62 in 1956, and benefits became payable to widows at age 62, with no reduction in the amount. Also in 1956, the act was amended to permit a disabled worker who had reached the age of 50 to receive the same benefits he would have had if he had worked until he was 65 and then applied for retirement. At the time this change in the law was made, the benefits of dependents were extended to include handicapped children over 18 whose disabilities had originated earlier and would prevent their being gainfully employed. Provisions were also made for payments to mothers who had such children in their care.

Amendments to the Social Security Act in 1961 reflect a growing concern with the economic problems associated with health and medical care (USDHEW, 1962a, pp. 68–77). The age-50 requirement for disability benefits under the program, now called Old Age, Survivors, and Disability Insurance (OASDI), was dropped. The Congress was urged to include medical care under Social Security but authorized, instead, a new federal-state program of medical assistance for older people who could not afford to pay for this themselves. There is no disagreement about the need, but the question of how to provide medical care for the aged is still, in 1964, an unsolved problem.

Social Security is a decentralized program. Field offices were opened in 1936. When a community is too small to have a resident representative, staff from regional or state offices come to the local post office at regular intervals to advise people who have questions to ask about their social security payments or prospects. During these consultations, family problems often come up. These are referred to public welfare and other agencies and organizations likely to be able to help. The states are required to make public assistance available to all recipients of Old Age, Survivors, and Disability Insurance. Over one-third of those now receiving old age assistance have OASDI benefits also.

The need for this consultation and referral service is growing as more and more families feel the impact of social change. Since its program now covers nine out of every 10 workers in the United States, the Social Security Administration is in a strategic position to detect and interpret the changing needs and problems in American family life. Meanwhile, its own contribution to family stability is tremendous. It enables the breadwinner to spread his earnings over a lifetime and assures his family of at least a minimum income should he die or become disabled.

Helpful as it is, Old Age, Survivors, and Disability Insurance alone cannot relieve families of all financial anxiety. Unemployment is an ever present threat to the security of families dependent on current income for money to meet living expenses. The mine closes down, the company moves to another town, machines displace men, and with the job goes the pay check.

Through the unemployment security programs now carried on by the states in cooperation with the federal Department of Labor, a certain percentage of the wage loss due to temporary unemployment is covered, for a certain length of time, if the unemployed person is sincerely looking for work and is willing to take any suitable job that is offered to him.

There are actually two programs that go hand in hand in this package: unemployment insurance and a nationwide public employment service. At the federal level, both are located in the Bureau of Employment Security in the Labor Department. The administrative costs of this dual program are financed by taxes collected from employers. One state collects unemployment insurance taxes from employees also.

Some of the states take cognizance of the fact that a worker with a family needs more money for non-deferrable expenses than a single man. In these states, the amount paid as unemployment compensation is related to the number of dependents, as well as to past wages. Here again is evidence of the shift to the family focus in the development of policies for social action. One of the first measures taken by the Congress to counteract the effects of the 1960 business recession was the Temporary Extended Unemployment Compensation Act. This permitted payments for an additional 13 weeks to workers who had used up their regular unemployment benefits between specified dates in 1960 and 1961.

FAMILY SERVICES

The persons who wrote the Social Security Act knew that insurance alone could never solve the problem of social dependency. They therefore included in the bill provisions for a complementary program of public assistance to be administered by a Bureau of Public Assistance in the Social Security Administration. The Children's

Bureau was moved into SSA in 1946, from the Department of Labor, to share with the Bureau of Public Assistance responsibility for implementing those sections of the Social Security Act specifically concerned with child health and welfare.

For several reasons, a strong national welfare policy was slow to develop. The giving of relief has always been considered a local responsibility in the United States, and communities have differed greatly in the welfare policies and procedures they have adopted. Lack of money and lack of trained personnel have been perennial handicaps.

State departments of welfare did what they could to help the most needy between 1935 and 1960, and the federal government cooperated with these state agencies to the fullest extent possible under existing laws. Crises developed, however, in several states, and by 1960 the administration of public welfare had become a national issue.

Committees made up of lay and professional people with wide knowledge and experience studied the problems involved, with the help of the Department of Health, Education, and Welfare and several state welfare departments. Their recommendations led to the framing of new legislation which was presented to the Congress in the form of amendments to the public welfare sections of the basic Social Security Act. The passage of these amendments in 1962 established a national family-centered welfare policy for the United States which, at last, reflects our belief in the worth and dignity of the individual human being as a person in his own right and as a family member.

When he signed the new Public Welfare Amendments into law, President Kennedy said:

This measure embodies a new approach—stressing services in addition to support, rehabilitation instead of relief, and training for useful work instead of prolonged dependency. [It] will assist our states and local public welfare agencies to redirect the incentives and services they offer to needy families and children and to aged and disabled people. Our objective is to prevent or reduce dependency and to encourage self-care and self-support—to maintain family life where it is adequate and restore it where it is deficient (cited by Cohen, 1962, p. 1).

It is not possible to note here all of the important changes in social welfare policy in these 1962 amendments. A thorough analysis of these is contained in the *Annual Report* of the Department of Health, Education, and Welfare for 1961 (USDHEW, 1961, pp. 48–69). There are two new provisions, however, that should be mentioned because of their far-reaching implications: work relief and aid to families when the chief wage-earner is unemployed.

States may now, if they wish, arrange for recipients of public assistance to work out part or all of their relief on community projects that meet acceptable standards of dignity, health, and safety. Persons employed on such projects will have reasonable opportunities to look for more permanent work and will be helped to make full use of the counseling and job-finding facilities of the United States Employment Service. For many families, perhaps the most important feature of this new work relief program is the stipulation that some of the money earned by children may be saved for such future needs as their education. In the new plan are provisions for the training and retraining of unemployed men and women, to enable them to retain their occupational skills or learn new ones.

One of the services established under the original Social Security Act was known for many years as Aid to Dependent Children. The purpose of this program was, and is, to enable mothers to care for their children at home in the event of the death, disability, or prolonged absence of a father. Federal matching funds are available to help states defray the expenses of this service, which is state administered. In the past, some people in some states have thought that the granting of this aid should be largely dependent on the behavior of the mother. Whenever this question has become an issue, the Social Security Administration, through its Bureau of Public Assistance, has called hearings and refused federal matching funds if states were found to be using criteria for eligibility other than those specified in the Social Security Act.

The 1962 amendments re-emphasize the original purpose of the program: to make it possible for dependent children to be cared for in their own homes by their own mothers. To help these mothers maintain the best possible homes for their children, the new legislation authorizes counseling and other social services for the parents, as well as financial assistance. A fourth criterion of eligibility has been added to the original three: parental unemployment. The program has been renamed Aid to Families of Dependent Children (AFDC). That it meets a special and real need is evidenced by the fact that about two-thirds of the parents receiving temporary assistance through this channel are not eligible for any other form of relief.

The new provisions for social service to AFDC families highlight a problem that affects every social welfare program in the country: the lack of trained personnel in the social welfare field. The extent of this problem is indicated by the fact that there was only one trained welfare worker for each 23,000 people receiving public assistance in the United States in 1962 (USDHEW, 1962b, p. 16). The new legislation includes appropriations for research and for the demonstration of new approaches and techniques in program development, and also for the recruitment, preservice, and inservice training of men and women who will be able to give the wide variety of professional services on which the success of these programs depends.

The Welfare Administration of the Department of Health, Education, and Welfare is the agency of government that has major responsibility for implementing the social welfare sections of the Social Security Act, including the 1962 amendments. It carries out this responsibility through the Bureau of Family Services and the Children's Bureau.

The activities of the Children's Bureau in the fields of health and welfare are extensive. Under the Social Security Act of 1935, as amended, this agency makes available to the states technical and financial aid for three programs that reach hundreds of thousands of families each year: the Maternal and Child Health Program, the Crippled Children's Program, and Child Welfare Services. It also takes leadership in the search for solutions to such family-related problems as foster care, adoption, illegitimacy, juvenile delinquency, and day care for children of working mothers.

For some time, the bureau has been involved with other leading national health and welfare organizations in the development of a national Homemaker Service. This is a fairly new and much needed community resource for families. Under the supervision of a responsible local health or welfare agency, women are recruited and trained to go into homes, in response to requests for such help, to keep things going while mothers are ill or away. Public agencies in some states are providing this service on a demonstration basis. It is hoped that it will eventually be regularly included in public family welfare programs.

FAMILY LIFE EDUCATION

Every government agency considers the education of the public on matters pertaining to its work one of its most important functions. It is not surprising, therefore, that the two agencies that probably know most about American families and their problems should be conducting programs of education for parenthood, homemaking, and family living. These are the Department of Agriculture and the Department of Health, Education, and Welfare. A variety of methods and media are used, including printed materials, courses for youth and adults, conferences, and community organization for social action.

Programs of the Department of Agriculture

Most farm families and many city dwellers in the United States know the Cooperative Extension Service of the Department of Agriculture. It is a joint federal-state program established by the Congress in 1914 under the Smith-Lever Act to diffuse "among the people of the United States useful and practical information on subjects relating to agriculture and home economics, and to encourage application of the same" (Pope, 1958, p. 270). The work is based in the land-grant colleges and universities, and federal funds are available for it, when matched with state and local money. The federal allotments to states are based on the size of rural populations.

The structure of the service is simple. At each land-grant institution are experts in the specialized areas of agriculture and home economics. Some are research workers and do little traveling. Others spend most of their time in the towns and villages of their states, working with county agricultural and home demonstration agents, groups of farmers and homemakers, 4-H Clubs, and other youth organizations. A corresponding staff of specialists at the federal level assists the state leaders. Most state programs have usually culminated, each year, in a big meeting at the land-grant college called Farm and Home Week. As an outgrowth of these gatherings, there have developed, in many states, annual programs which provide opportunities for more intensive study of different aspects of agriculture and home economics. These take the form of short courses or institutes, last from three days to one week, are held at the land-grant colleges, and are variously known as homemakers' short courses, leadership training institutes, or homemakers' colleges.

The Cooperative Extension Service draws much of its vitality from its two-way communication with the "grass roots." To the rural homemaker it can bring the latest research findings in the fields of nutrition, clothing, home management, home furnishings, family financial planning, child development, family relationships, housing, family health, family safety, and family-community relationships. Through her, it can follow the flow of changing interests, concerns, and events in the life of the farm home. As the homemaker and her husband become active in the work of the Extension Service, they help to shape policies for and determine the content of the program.

Interest in the study of child development, human relations, and family life has grown so rapidly over the last 25 years that 33 states now employ 41 specialists in these subject matter areas. They are assisted in their work by the specialist in human development and human relations in the Washington office.

Another kind of change is illustrated by the fact that in 1935 only 11 per cent of American farms had electricity. Partly because of the facilities made available by the Rural Electrification Program, including loans for the extension and improvement of rural telephone services, and partly because the whole surrounding universe was moving into the electronic age, 97 per cent of American farm families had electricity in 1961. Rural consumers are doubling their power consumption about every seven years (ICCY, 1961, p. 14). Adult education has played an important part in this cultural transformation. Counselors representing the Rural Electrification Administration, home demonstration leaders, and county agricultural agents have helped rural families across the country to take advantage of the REA program, to reorganize their farming and homemaking methods for the most efficient use of electricity, to choose and care for the electrical equipment and appliances most appropriate in their situations.

The original charge to the federal Cooperative Extension Service was to develop an educational service for the rural areas.

The need for a similar service to urban families has since become apparent, and arrangements can now be made for cities to have cooperative extension programs. In 1959, home demonstration agents reached 8,452,636 families. Of these, 26 per cent were on farms; 22 per cent were rural non-farm; 52 per cent urban (ICCY, 1961, p. 11).

For many families who still live in the country and in small towns, life is becoming increasingly difficult. According to the 1960 census, 13 per cent of rural non-farm families and 36 per cent of farm families had less than $2,000 annual cash income. Other studies have shown that in some low-income areas up to 40 per cent of local families have less than $1,500 a year to live on. This means substandard housing, poor nutrition, inadequate clothing, little or no medical care—a generally miserable existence. About 800 counties, with a total population of 31 million, have been designated as areas where incomes are seriously low by the Area Redevelopment Administration of the Department of Commerce.

The Department of Agriculture has mobilized all of its resources and involved many other governmental and non-governmental agencies in a concerted effort to help people in these deprived areas improve the conditions under which they are living. This program is called Rural Area Development (RAD).

Information and counsel, loans, grants, and various kinds of technical aid are made available through the different agencies.

The planning is done by the rural people themselves—leaders from civic, farm, business, and other groups, in state and local committees —with assistance, as needed, from state, area, and county Technical Action Panels. These panels include representatives from USDA technical and credit agencies serving the territory, from the Cooperative Extension Service, the State Experiment Station, state and local governmental and other independent agencies. Responsibility for establishing the Technical Action Panel is assigned to the Farmers Home Administration. The Cooperative Extension Service helps committees get organized and provides educational leadership to the committees on planning and implementing programs. The broad planning aspect of RAD is indicated by the term applied to each plan for an area— Overall Economic Development Program (Wolgamot, 1963, p. 185).

This experiment should be a valuable learning experience not only for the families who benefit directly by it but for the country as a whole. The processes by which the national economy is nourished and stabilized in a free society are too little understood.

Programs Sponsored by the Office of Education

For many years, the federal Office of Education has worked with state departments of education, with other government agencies, and with national and international organizations to help parents and teachers understand better the developmental needs of children and make better provisions for meeting these needs in homes, schools, and communities. This service is chiefly rendered by specialists in the elementary education and home economics education branches of the office through consultations, publications, conferences, and assistance with preservice and in-service teacher education.

Among the projects sponsored by the Office of Education to further education for child and family development, few have been more rewarding than an experiment in community organization for family life education initiated in 1938 by the Home Economics Education Branch in four centers: Toledo, Ohio; Box Elder County, Utah; Wichita, Kansas; and Obion County, Tennessee.

This program was undertaken in the same creative spirit and with the same concern for human values that produced the Social Security Act and other new approaches to the solution of pressing social problems during the 1930's. Homemaking teachers had been especially close to the families of the children they taught during the bitter days of the depression. They sent home recipes that would help to conserve foods in short supply. They worked with nutrition specialists to get the school lunch program started. With the support of such organizations as the General Federation of Women's Clubs and the American Home Economics Association, and with the encouragement of school authorities, many of them became increasingly active in community affairs.

At this time, the community organization movement was only beginning. "Cooperative problem-solving," "leadership training," and "group dynamics" were hardly more than phrases heard on a few college campuses. When community groups wanted to do something themselves to solve local problems, they usually looked in vain for guidance. This lack of know-how was especially frustrating when it was evident that much could be done through local cooperative action to correct local conditions affecting families adversely.

After many consultations with organizations and individuals, the Home Economics Education Branch of the Office of Education decided to try to find communities willing to experiment with community organization for family life education, and to record their experiences. This venture was not the departure from the traditional concerns of home economics that it may have appeared to be. The Congress had recognized homemaking as a basic vocation for women by including home economics in the Smith-Hughes Vocational Education Act of 1917, legislation which authorized the payment of grants-in-aid to the states for vocational education. A Federal Board of Vocational Education, with a home economics education service, was created to administer the act. This was later merged with the United States Office of Education.

The states have always been free to make their own plans for the use of federal funds for vocational education, subject to stipulations in the Vocational Education Act as amended. The program is administered in accordance with policies cooperatively developed by federal and state personnel, in consultation with many individuals and groups. These policies are reviewed and, if necessary, revised from time to time.

It is now quite generally understood that state programs of home economics education receiving aid under the Vocational Education Act should have the following characteristics: They should be functional in the best sense of that word, geared to the interests and needs of the students served. They should provide for maximum teacher participation in the writing of state study guides. They should make maximum use of four practices known to be excellent means of creating mutual understanding between teachers, parents, and students: the home visit, the informal personal conference, the home project, and the small class. They should be comprehensive, including all phases of homemaking in programs for out-of-school youth and adults, as well as for high school students. They should be "school-centered" but "community minded," related in many ways to other community programs and services contributing to the improvement of family life. They should be dynamic, constantly gaining in breadth and depth by experimenting with new ideas along their growing edges (Brown, 1953, p. 4).

The proposed plan for experiments in community organization for family life education seemed to fit very well into this theoretical framework. To further test its feasibility, the Home Economics Education Service of the Office of Education gathered and made available to the states, in 1937, information about program developments along similar lines in several places (USDI, 1937). Such outstanding educators as George D. Stoddard and Ralph Tyler were called upon for advice by the then United States Commissioner of Education, John W.

Studebaker. In 1938, the project was formally approved and the four centers were chosen.

A joint planning conference with local, state, and federal people concerned was held in Washington in the fall of 1938. In preparation for this, members of the federal home economics education staff went to each of the centers to help the local superintendents of schools organize the steering committees that would take local responsibility for launching the programs.

The following paragraphs from the notebook of one of these consultants show how this was done:

Tuesday forenoon, the commissioner of education, the county superintendent of schools, the county director of instruction, and the chairman of the County Council of Parent-Teacher Associations discussed with us the general plans for the proposed program, and what such a program would entail as to personnel, financing, and other facilities. . . .

In the afternoon, we all met with all of the principals, all the agriculture and home economics teachers, two or three social science teachers, two or three elementary teachers, two representatives from the county department of public health, two representatives from the Extension Service, a representative from the Red Cross, two or three representatives from the County PTA, the chairman of the county board of education and a member of the county court. The proposed program was explained to these people and their hearty cooperation was promised. A planning committee of nine members was appointed to meet Wednesday morning to work out plans and procedures for getting a tentative plan for a county family life education program ready to send to Washington by the 15th of this month.

The state supervisor of home economics and I met with this committee Wednesday forenoon and plans and definite responsibilities for each member were decided upon. The data needed will be secured by the prospective committee members and the committee will meet again Saturday at one o'clock to compile data and formulate the plan. . . . The State Supervisor and the State Director of Vocational Education will return here for a meeting on Tues-

day and the plan will be edited by the group (Brown, 1953, p. 19).

These four programs are described in detail in the book just quoted, *With Focus on Family Living,* published by the Office of Education. They developed very differently, as the following brief accounts of major activities in each center clearly show.

The Toledo program. The files of the Toledo project are a rich source of original material on the dynamics of community organization for family life education. Long past the demonstration stage, the program continues to grow in depth and coverage after 25 years. This is the only one of the four that has been directed from the beginning by a professional staff: a coordinator, a parent education director, a nursery school specialist and, since 1961, a home economics specialist in adult education. Federal and state vocational education funds have been used for salaries, and the Toledo Board of Education has furnished maintenance.

The problem of basic structure has been a difficult one to solve, and one of the most significant contributions this center has made is the case history of its coordinating council. When a venture like this involves several disciplines and many autonomous groups, both lay and professional, the cooperative development of a flexible supporting structure, with plenty of channels within it for intercommunication, is a long and sometimes painful process.

The superintendent of schools sought community sanction for the experiment in 1938 by inviting representatives of 80 or more local agencies and organizations to a public meeting. Following this conference, two councils were formed: an Adult Council of 110 members from community groups wishing to participate, and a Youth Council of 62 persons representing high schools, colleges, church groups, out-of-school youth, and the youth-serving agencies. Neither of these two bodies functioned easily. The Adult Council soon turned over most of its responsibilities to an executive committee.

In 1946, it was converted into the Toledo Association for Family Living, with membership open to all interested persons and organizations. Forty agencies and 100 individuals were enrolled.

The list of officers elected at the 1946 annual meeting shows how far this school-based program had moved out into the community during its first eight years. It included the principal of an elementary school, the pastor of a church, a member of the American Association of University Women, a man from the American Federation of Labor, a Boy Scout executive, and a caseworker from the Lutheran Inner Mission.

The association made a good start but worked well for only a short time. In 1949–1950 it was reorganized again as the Citizens Committee for Family Life Education. This was in reality the Executive Committee of the association enlarged to 20: 10 citizens at large, chosen because of demonstrated interest in the program and 10 or more ex-officio members from the schools, the Council of Churches, the Council of Social Agencies, the Family Life Education Department of the University of Toledo, and other organizations to be agreed upon by the group as a whole. The Citizens Committee remained active for about 10 years, when it seemed to lose vitality. It was replaced in 1962 by an Advisory Committee to the staff composed of six to 12 members appointed by the superintendent of the Toledo public schools.

This freedom to experiment has been characteristic of the Toledo program from the beginning. Each of the projects developed under program auspices has been a new way of dealing with an existing need. Among the accomplishments are: a city-wide preschool council, an expanded parent education program, a consultation service for program planners, a premarriage education program, a demonstration nursery school, an inservice training course in child development for nurses, a course for expectant parents, a family life education library, and significant developments in family life education in the public schools and the University of Toledo.

An evaluation committee was set up in 1941 to be responsible for the ongoing analysis of program activities. On this committee were representatives of the Family Life Education Program, the Council of Social Agencies, the Child and Family Agency, and the Municipal League. Unable to find suitable readymade evaluative materials, this group reasoned out its own procedures for the appraisal of over-all gains and losses, and for the evaluation of individual projects. Occasionally, experts from research centers have been brought to Toledo for conferences, but the local plan has never seemed to need much changing. Insights gained from the study of past experiences are still applied at each new step in program development.

Box Elder County, Utah. The Box Elder County Program was active for 10 years, from 1938 to 1948. It functioned chiefly through standing committees which reported to a Central Sponsoring Committee. There were committees on studies and surveys, interpretation (public relations), local planning units, adult education, elementary school, library, curriculum revision, and youth. These were hardworking groups with almost no overlapping in membership. The county board of education provided a paid coordinator.

Two of the committees were especially active: Studies and Surveys, and the Youth Committee. The first did research for the program as a whole, and the second was primarily an action group. They both worked with the Utah State Agricultural College on a survey of the values, attitudes, and problems of about 1,000 older boys and girls in the area. This survey showed that the young people interviewed wanted more opportunities to take responsibility in home and community life, more experience with money and more instruction in the use of it, more community recreational facilities, and more vocational guidance.

The Youth Committee was given the task of interpreting to the public the findings of the survey. With help from many sources, including the Parent-Teacher County Councils, the Mutual Improvement Association of the Church of Jesus Christ of the Latter-day Saints, the Junior Chamber of Commerce, and state and county educational authorities, this group succeeded in arousing a great deal of interest in the problems revealed by the study. The local banks and credit companies entered the picture because they were concerned about the number of young married couples coming to them to borrow money, with ideas about earning and spending that seemed incredibly naive. New units of study were introduced into high school home economics and other courses, and a number of organizations developed programs and discussion materials relating to the needs highlighted by the study, with special emphasis on education for home responsibilities and money management.

One of the most memorable experiments in the program was a project of the Adult Committee. A woman who had been an unusually successful church worker was employed by the schools to try to find ways of helping families in low-income neighborhoods to raise their own standards of living. After several months of friendly visiting, the mothers began to respond. Two groups were organized to study topics suggested by the women: food for health, health habits, first aid, rug-making, family sewing. Fathers became interested, and families met in groups to talk about ways of getting sewers extended, roads gravelled, a small bridge built, street lights installed. The leader taught them how to get up petitions and how to approach the city council with their requests. She felt, when she ended the project, that the greatest service she had rendered to the families who worked with her was to teach them how to use the community resources that were available to them as citizens.

Although all county agencies and organizations were sincerely interested in the Box Elder County Family Life Education Program and gave a great deal of time to it, it was generally regarded as a public school project. Perhaps this was inevitable, since the schools provided the paid leadership and gradually took over most of the administrative responsibility for program activities.

The Wichita program. The Wichita Family Life Education Program will probably be remembered longest for its commitment to the principle of learning by doing. The city was at the beginning of a rapid industrial expansion during the late 1930's and early 1940's. It had not fully recovered, however, from the depression and the drought. The differences in conditions and standards of living between high- and low-income neighborhoods were very marked. There were needs and opportunities for services to families "across the board." Courses and classes for parents were already being given by lay leaders whose salaries were paid from state and local vocational education funds through the local board of education.

The Kansas State Board for Vocational Education sponsored the family life program and aided it financially. It was administered locally by the Vocational Education Division of the Wichita public schools. The leaders were anxious for it to be a community effort, cooperatively planned and actively promoted by all local family agencies and organizations, but this hope was never realized. Community groups and individual citizens responded generously when asked to help but considered the project a public school enterprise.

A local director was appointed and arrangements were made with the state board for the services of a specialist from its staff to act as coordinator. There were several changes in both of these positions during the eight years between 1938 when the program began and 1946 when it was consolidated with the home economics department of the Wichita public schools.

Among the many successful activities attributed to the Family Life Education Program were a community self-help center and a family fun project. The nucleus of the center was the Lend-A-Hand Club. This was a group of mothers who had banded together to help each other in the terrible winter of 1937–1938. Their families had come up from the dust bowls of Arkansas and Oklahoma and been stranded on the outskirts of Wichita. Most of the fathers had been out of work for months. The children were dressed in rags and going barefoot in all weathers because they had no shoes. Many of the families were living in patched-up chicken coops or tarpaper shacks.

The University Friends Church became interested through a member of the congregation who was also a parent education leader. It seemed to this Quaker teacher that the Lend-A-Hand Club was the place to start helping. She persuaded the women to let her have half the time at each meeting to talk with them about their problems. She felt sure, she said afterward, that guided discussions would give them more insight into some of their difficulties and would suggest new ways in which they might be able to help themselves.

The mothers asked for lessons in cooking and sewing, and a meeting place was found with the assistance of a real estate dealer and the Friends Church: half of an old store building, 21 feet wide, 10 feet high, and 40 feet long. The floor was cement, the roof leaked, and there was no heat. Classes started in January, 1939, with one old sewing machine, three pairs of scissors, and a pile of donated garments to be mended or made over.

This was the beginning of the center. Members "paid" their way by helping in the upkeep of the building, making rugs and quilts, or repairing clothing and furniture to be sold, or, in emergencies, given

away. The first 10 hours of this work earned a membership in the club, now the Southwest Wichita Community Center. Additional hours were credited to individual accounts at rates set by the members themselves, usually 20 or 25 cents an hour.

Among the classes held regularly was one on home living in which constant use was made of techniques for defining and solving problems. Often a meeting was held in the place where a difficulty had arisen, so that the situation could be studied at first hand. Word of these discussions spread, and people not in the class began bringing their troubles to it for analysis. In time the group came to be known as the Source Class and for a while took the place of the regular center business meetings. For several years, all proposals for new projects to be undertaken by the center were first referred to the Source Class for review and recommendations.

With the help of its friends, the center was able to do some remarkable things in a surprisingly short time. It acquired a director and a home of its own in 1940. In that same year, it took responsibility for planning, building, and selling a small house to study the transactions involved. In 1941, it organized a credit union. This made it possible for members to have group health insurance. By 1943, there was full employment again in the Wichita area, and the membership began to scatter. By this time, however, the families involved had practically completed their own rehabilitation.

The recreation program mentioned above met very different needs. Parents and teachers in a high-income neighborhood were concerned because the children who did not go to camp had so little to do during the long summer vacation. With the help of the coordinator of the Family Life Education Program and a parent education leader, they outlined a family fun program for six weeks in June and July. Children would meet in small groups to work at something they really enjoyed doing, with mothers and fathers as group leaders and teachers.

Somehow, the talents of parent leaders were matched with the choices of [the] children. School closed and the program got under way. School opened and youngsters [rushed to show their teachers] what they had made, or tell what they had done. Interest was so great that a public exhibit was arranged to display the results of the children's work. Even more significant than the impressive array of canned fruits and vegetables, plastic raincoats and hats, toys, knitted and crocheted garments, was the eagerness of the boys and girls to continue [the project] (Brown, 1953, pp. 182–183).

Several other schools had similar programs during that same summer. A total of 32 mothers and 12 fathers led groups without help, and 61 parents did so with assistance. The Boy Scouts, the YWCA, and the Red Cross contributed 37 additional lay leaders. At least one principal opened his school to parent leaders so that they might continue with their groups during the school year.

There were, of course, other outstanding achievements within the framework of the Wichita Family Life Education Program, during its lifetime. There were several "firsts" in adult education, including one of the first grandmothers' clubs in the country. The purpose of this one was to increase the members' understanding of themselves, their children, their in-laws, and their grandchildren. Several neighborhood councils were formed which succeeded in getting needed improvements in low-income residential areas. There were thought-provoking, if not always successful, excursions into the fields of housing, recreation, crime prevention, health, welfare, and counseling. The planting of thousands of redbud seedlings along the streets and in gardens was an early project. The springtime beauty of these trees today is one of the most enduring of the contributions made by the program to the city of Wichita.

Obion County, Tennessee. The program in Obion County, Tennessee, had a great deal of spontaneity and a minimum of formal organization. No one was employed to direct it, and it had no budget of its own. The county superintendent of schools and the senior public health nurse took charge and gave excellent leadership until the period of demonstration was over and the county had absorbed the program. Most of the projects were carried on by *ad hoc* committees.

A Library Committee formed a County Library Association, which obtained a charter for a county library. This was set up in the office of the county school superintendent and was heavily patronized from the day it opened. Books were obtained through purchase and gifts, and two branches were established in branch banks in two villages. Later, the library moved to larger quarters in the old Union City public health clinic. It will have a building of its own when the money being raised for it reaches the sum required for participation in the state library system—hopefully, in 1965.

A Nutrition Committee undertook to help parents in all parts of the county learn more about the nutritional needs of children and how to meet these in the home. The County Health Officer was in charge of this project. Teachers in every elementary school listed for him the names of the children who seemed to be undernourished. The doctor then visited each school, examined these youngsters, and conferred with their parents. The nurse worked out a food plan with the mother for each child whose diet needed correction, and the home economics teacher showed her how to make the new menus appetizing.

Hundreds of county residents were involved in these "clinics." PTA members were the hostesses. Young mothers visited local grocery stores to ask the proprietors to cooperate by stocking whole wheat bread and other nutritionally important items. About 80 new root cellars were dug and an unknown number of winter gardens were planted to assure a year-round supply of home-grown vegetables.

The work of the Health Education Committee reached its climax in 1950 with the opening of a new county hospital. Almost as important as the hospital itself were the techniques developed for convincing the public of the need for it. A leadership training course was organized to meet every two weeks on Saturday afternoons in the courthouse during the winter of 1943–1944, the sixth year of the Family Life Education Program. Each meeting highlighted a county health problem.

Each community in the county sent a delegation to this "class," consisting of two members from each parent-teacher association, the principal of each school, the home economics and agriculture teachers, two students from each high school, and two members from each Community Club. In addition to the delegations, there were representatives from each county organization and each service club. Each delegate was responsible for taking back to his community the facts presented and the conclusions reached at each session in the courthouse. The average attendance at these information sessions was 98, the lowest 43.

The meetings "back home" were often exciting. For example, more than 100 men and women, farmers and teachers, came to a village schoolhouse one evening after supper to hear the report on tuberculosis. The county nurse located all of the known active cases in this district on a large pin map. When it dawned on the group that these sick people were their neighbors and that 37 of them were at home without treatment, there was consternation. What about the danger of infection? "This is certainly a bad situation for everyone concerned," the nurse said. "But where can these patients go? There is absolutely no place in the county where they can be cared for, except at home."

After a long and heated discussion, the group appointed a committee to find out if a hospital could be built in the county with a wing for tubercular cases. At nine o'clock the next morning, one of the farmers was seen on the steps of the courthouse, stopping the magistrates as they went in to ask them to vote an appropriation for the hospital. That same day, a private citizen offered to give the building, under certain conditions, but the offer was refused. There seemed to be a general feeling that a county hospital was a public necessity which should be publicly supported, and this is the way this one was started.

The spirit of the original program is still very much alive in Obion County. The demonstration phase ended about 1950; when it became clear that the principles being demonstrated were already a "way of life" in the county. Cooperative action to strengthen family life has become a habit there.

From the standpoint of the Home Economics Education Service of the Office of Education, the results of these experimental programs were more than satisfactory. The insights gained have been reflected in the teaching of home economics in high schools, colleges, and teacher-training institutions in many of the states. Several successful community family life education programs have stemmed from the original four. Perhaps the most rewarding part of the whole experiment for those in the communities who involved themselves in it was the discovery that problems no one family can handle alone can often be solved by groups of families, especially when the agencies, the professions, and the people in a community pool their knowledge, experience, resources, and energies to help.

Programs in State Departments of Education

The states of California and New York both have parent education consultants in their state departments of education. In California this position is in the Bureau of

Adult Education, in New York in the Elementary Division. Both specialists give state-wide consultation service to state organizations and communities carrying on or wishing to institute programs of parent or family life education. They conduct leadership training conferences, workshops, and seminars, and prepare materials to help local discussion group leaders. The California *Handbook for Parent Education Leaders* is nationally known (Babitz, 1958).

In most of the states, the supervisor of home economics in the vocational division of the state department of education includes a consultation service in education for parenthood and family living in her program. Many of these women work closely with local groups on community family life education projects. They are all familiar with the experiments in the four centers described above, and extend the influence of these by watching for opportunities to stimulate similar activities. In New York and several other states, they help local supervisors and teachers of home economics to relate their high school and adult family life programs through a variety of cooperative projects with parents.

Parent Education in the Children's Bureau

The parent education program of the Children's Bureau began in 1913 with the publication of the first edition of the now world-famous pamphlet *Infant Care*. The bureau felt then, and still feels, an obligation to make available to American families the most reliable information about the growth, development, and guidance of children. This is done chiefly through a basic series of inexpensive booklets, prepared in the bureau and printed and sold, in enormous quantities, by the Government Printing Office. Titles in the series show the coverage: *Prenatal Care, Infant Care, Your Child from One to Six, Your Child from Six to Twelve,* and *The Adolescent in*

Your Family. These pamphlets are revised periodically to keep the series up to date.

A parent education specialist was first employed by the bureau in 1942 in the Child Study Division, later to become the Division of Research. Her chief responsibility, at first, was to work with the Reports Division on the basic pamphlets. Later, her program broadened to include a limited consultation service to state and national groups interested in parent education. At present, there are two parent education specialists in the Child Life Studies Branch of the Research Division, a man and a woman. Both have training and experience in social work, counseling, adult education, and research. They are in close touch with needs and trends in parent and family life education throughout the country and are especially interested in working with groups experimenting with new approaches in situations where the traditional methods of parent education have so far been ineffective.

The Health Services Division of the bureau is very much interested in helping to develop education for expectant parents through the public health nurses in maternal and child health programs. Since 1956, this division has been working with the Child Study Association of America on pilot training projects for nursing supervisors in state departments of health. Regional conferences, with a follow-up consultation service, have been successful in bringing to the participants important new concepts in group work and new insights into the emotional problems of pregnancy.

In the Social Services Division, there is interest in many aspects of parent education: how to help parents of predelinquent children; how to reach fathers and mothers in low-income families, in-migrant families, in once-rural families too quickly urbanized, in special ethnic and racial groups; how to make maximum use of child care centers for parent education. There is continuing interest, also, in a variety of procedures and techniques: educational guidance through casework and counseling; the organization of discussion groups; the teaching of homemaking skills, with guided conversations about the needs of children and families; cooperative projects in which families have opportunities to help themselves.

The Reports Division specializes in attractive, simple pamphlet materials for parents—small, illustrated leaflets that are widely distributed by public health nurses, doctors, social workers, and others in contact with young families. Examples are *So You're Going to Have a Baby* and *Your Baby's First Year*.

The several divisions exchange experiences and discuss their parent education problems in staff and committee meetings. When questions arise that require special consideration, the bureau frequently arranges small interdisciplinary conferences of experts, usually in cooperation with an interested institution. In 1958, the Research Division brought together, in this way, a group of research specialists in fields related to parent education to discuss the contributions of scientific research to the content of education for parenthood, and to identify areas in which more research is needed. The Institute of Child Development of the University of Minnesota co-sponsored this conference. The report of the proceedings was prepared at the university and published by the Children's Bureau in a booklet entitled *Parent Education and the Behavioral Sciences* (Grams, 1960). The Children's Bureau is issuing a directory of parent education specialists in the United States and Canada compiled by Armin Grams, in accordance with one of the conference recommendations.

RESEARCH UNDER GOVERNMENT AUSPICES

Programs that strengthen the family must themselves be constantly strengthened by knowledge gained through research. The two agencies of government primarily concerned with family-related research are the Agricultural Research Service of the Department of Agriculture, located at Beltsville, Maryland, and the National Institute of Mental Health of the Public Health Service, located in Bethesda, Maryland.

Some of the research carried on in these agencies is done by their own specialists, some by staff in cooperation with other research centers or qualified organizations, some through grants-in-aid to individuals and institutions. Recently, small grants-in-aid programs have been established in some of the operating units of the Department of Health, Education, and Welfare to encourage the study of problems relating specifically to family and child welfare.

The Agricultural Research Service

This service is organized administratively into two major program areas: Nutrition, Consumer and Industrial Use Research, and Farm Research. Nutrition, Consumer and Industrial Use Research includes four regional utilization research and development laboratories and three home economics divisions: Human Nutrition, Consumer and Food Economics, and Clothing and Housing. These three divisions carry out research formerly done under the name Institute of Home Economics.

Nutrition and consumer use research [in this program] covers investigations to define basic needs and wants of people for goods and services for daily living, to evaluate the contributions that various kinds of goods and services can make to satisfy these needs, to make periodic studies of levels of consumption by different economic and regional groups, to determine gaps between needs and consumption and suggest better ways in which these gaps may be filled, and to gain better understanding of human development and problems of living together in families, communities, and nations (personal communication from Kathryn Cronister, Assistant to Administrator, ARS, Oct. 15, 1963).

These studies involve the physical, biological, and social sciences. They are consumer-oriented, and seek "to provide the help that families need in selecting and using goods and services, in managing their money and time, and in developing and conserving their human resources. [They] also provide producers with important guides in bringing to market goods that are satisfying to consumers" (personal communication, Cronister). Among the many new products resulting from research in the four regional laboratories are such items as new types of baby foods, frozen concentrated orange juice, new types of wash-and-wear cottons, permanently creased woolens, better leather through new tanning processes, new plastics and paints. Self-help clothing for little children was developed by research in the home economics program.

The Cooperative State Extension Station Service of the Department of Agriculture administers grants to state experiment stations for researches, investigations, and experiments to develop and improve rural homes and rural life. Through county agricultural and home demonstration agents, the research specialists at these stations become very familiar with the patterns and problems of family living in their states, and give priority to studies that are likely to help parents, young people, children, and civic leaders with practical decision-making in matters pertaining to home and community life.

The National Institute of Mental Health

The National Institute of Mental Health was established in 1949 to give leadership and focus to an expanding program of government-sponsored research in the field of mental health. It was clear then, as it is now, that mental illness is an extremely serious public health problem about which far too little is known.

The program of the institute has four main objectives: to conduct and promote interdisciplinary studies of human development and behavior that will lead to a better understanding of the nature, treatment, and prevention of mental disturbance; to keep in touch with manpower needs in the mental health field and experiment with new ways of finding and training the people needed for research and services; to devise new methods and materials to meet a variety of clinical and educational needs in mental health work; and to provide consultation and demonstration services that will stimulate the development of mental health activities at state and local levels, and help states and communities to handle their mental health problems with increasing skill and understanding (USDHEW, 1963a).

Agencies and organizations working with families look upon this institute as an invaluable resource. Findings of studies made under its aegis are published in professional journals and discussed at the many interdisciplinary conferences in which the institute participates. Its excellent reading lists in mental health for teachers, parents, and others are widely used.

Although research on marriage and family living is not one of the primary responsibilities of the institute, much of its work has a bearing on family development. Staff and collaborators have made important contributions to the study of such questions as family interaction and mental illness, family structure and emotional disorders, the impact of cultural conflict on family relationships, factors that determine parental behavior, the effects of emotional disturbance during pregnancy on a mother's later relations with her child, the transmission of traits from parents to children, the improvement of communication between parents and adolescents, the value of the group discussion process as a method of influencing parental attitudes, parent-child relationships and children's behavior, the role structure of the urban, American, middle-class, three-generation family, and marriage counseling with special reference to the variables in divorce (Halpert, 1958).

Several projects supported in whole or in part by the National Institute of Mental Health have helped in the development of a strong and promising new clinical movement: family therapy. In this form of treatment, the unit of illness and health is the family group, not the family member who stands out in apparent isolation as The Problem. The setup for a major research project based on this hypothesis illustrates the cooperative character of much of the institute's work. This is the Study of Schizophrenic Communication which is financed by the National Institute of Mental Health, administered by the Palo Alto Medical Research Foundation as part of the Veterans Administration Hospital in Palo Alto, California, with the financial assistance of two private foundations.

Research in the Welfare and Social Security Administrations

The family-related projects of the Welfare and Social Security Administrations of the Department of Health, Education, and Welfare are essentially for the guidance and enrichment of the programs for which. these agencies are responsible. The first grants-in-aid for the study of the causes of dependency were announced by the Social Security Administration in March, 1961. They were authorized by the Congress "to add to existing knowledge or devise and evaluate new methods of applying knowledge with regard to such problems as the prevention and reduction of dependency, coordination and planning between private and public welfare agencies or improvement in the administration and effectiveness of programs carried on in relation to the Social Security Act" (USDHEW, 1961, pp. 21–22). These grants are awarded to nonprofit institutions with the advice of expert committees created to review applications.

When the Children's Bureau was created in 1912, it was given a mandate to investigate and report "upon all matters pertaining to the welfare of children and child life among all classes of our people" (USDHEW, 1961, p. 79). Research is, therefore, an essential part of its program. Its studies fall into three major categories: special investigations requested by the Congress, such as a study of children in migrant families; studies germane to its regular program of work, such as an analysis of independent adoptions in one state over a 10-year period; the routine compilation and publication of statistical data relating to the maternal and child health, crippled children's, and child welfare programs, day care, juvenile delinquency, and the like.

Since 1962, the bureau has administered a grant-in-aid program for the study of problems of child life. One such investigation, undertaken by a university, is a study of the gaps in the development of culturally deprived young children in a large metropolitan area. The bureau also offers technical consultant service to national and state private agencies contemplating research in its fields of interest. This is given by specialists permanently or temporarily on the bureau staff, usually through the Research Division. Group consultations with experts are frequently arranged.

OTHER GOVERNMENT PROGRAMS FOR FAMILIES

This review of family-oriented programs that are initiated and/or supported in whole or in part by government agencies is necessarily incomplete.

Much could be said about the contributions to family life made by the Housing and Home Finance Agency through its several operating units: the Urban Renewal Administration, the Federal Housing Administration, mentioned earlier, the Public Housing Administration, the Community Facilities Administration, and the Federal National Mortgage Association (ICCY, 1961, pp. 80–86).

The Tennessee Valley Authority has

several family-participation projects that belong on this list. Excellent facilities for camping and other forms of family recreation are maintained by the National Parks Service of the Department of the Interior. Each year, thousands of children and their parents come away from a visit to the Smithsonian Institution with a new appreciation of their American heritage. The Office of Education is providing leadership, under new legislation, for a program intended to help communities develop their resources for the enjoyment of art, music, and drama.

This is a splendid array of services. It is in no sense an integrated program, however. These many, varied activities are not formally coordinated. There is no over-all policy aimed at their standardization. Each has its own identity, its own life history, its own channels of communication with private and other public agencies. At the same time, these programs complement each other at community, state, and federal levels, so that the total impact on American family life is much greater than the sum of the parts.

From time to time, the government is urged to issue a policy statement specifying the values in family living to be respected in the drafting of all legislation and the planning of all official programs (Schorr, 1962). Discussion of this proposal has never yet led to a consensus of opinion about it. There are trends in the development of family service programs that have policy-making implications, however: increasing emphasis on the importance of helping families to help themselves; growing tendencies to begin work where families are, economically, socially, spiritually, and psychologically, to base action on facts about family living revealed by the families concerned, to involve families as much as possible in the planning, leadership, and evaluation of services designed for their benefit, to encourage families to recognize and build upon their own strengths and abilities, to adjust program goals and procedures to meet changing family needs and values.

Although there is no mandatory coordination of government programs serving families, the federal agencies with programs affecting children and youth have voluntarily established a mechanism for cooperative planning and the exchange of information about their work. This is the Interdepartmental Committee on Children and Youth. It was set up in 1948 to facilitate the participation of federal agencies in preparations for the Midcentury White House Conference on Children and Youth. Thirty-eight government agencies are now represented on it. The Children's Bureau furnishes the secretariat. This committee has recently formed a Subcommittee on Parent and Family Life Education.

PROGRAMS OF AMERICAN VOLUNTARY ORGANIZATIONS

Visitors from other countries are often astonished by the number and variety of privately supported voluntary groups active in the United States. Such organizations form naturally in a free society whenever people are drawn together by their desire to meet a felt need, try out a new idea, or work for a common cause. They play an important part in cultural evolution because they are free to move along the growing edges, exploring human needs, discovering new possibilities in human relationships, experimenting with new approaches to the solution of human problems.

Government agencies, operating under legislation which more or less prescribes their activities, have long since found that a working partnership with appropriate private organizations can have great value for both. The reader will have noticed that many of the government programs described in this chapter were developed in cooperation with private agencies.

Of the several hundred voluntary groups now active in the United States, over 200 have some form of family service as a major goal. Following are brief accounts of the work of a few of these, taken up alphabetically. Some of the programs described are included because they are outstanding examples of typical approaches; some because they are both outstanding and unique.

THE AMERICAN ASSOCIATION OF MARRIAGE COUNSELORS

Although marriage counseling is one of the activities of several clinical professions, the American Association of Marriage Counselors is the leading professional organization for those specializing in this field. For a description of this association and its work, see Chapter 22 of this Handbook.

THE AMERICAN COUNCIL OF PARENT COOPERATIVES

A parent cooperative is a nursery school founded, owned, and managed by parents, in compliance with the licensing requirements for preschool groups in force in their states. A trained nursery school teacher is usually employed as director, the mothers and fathers assisting her in a great many different ways. Professional supervision may be given through a sponsoring organization, such as a church, a social agency, a settlement house, or a board of public education.

The first parent cooperative on record was organized at the University of Chicago in 1916 by 12 faculty wives "who wanted to secure social education for their children, parent education for themselves, and a little free time for Red Cross work" (Taylor, 1954, p. 3). The university contributed space, professional guidance, and a trained teacher; it later took over the project entirely. According to the best available estimates, there are today about 1,000 parent cooperatives in the United States, and another 120 in Canada. The majority of the American groups are in the states of California, New York, Michigan, Washington, and Maryland. A few have been formed by parents of retarded, emotionally disturbed, and physically handicapped children.

Presently, the largest local program is probably the one in Seattle, Washington. This was started in 1940 by Katharine Whiteside Taylor, who has been the acknowledged leader of the parent cooperative movement for many years. In 1941–1942 there were only three child groups in the Seattle experiment and four classes for parents. Twenty years later, in 1961–1962, there were 120 preschool units and 94 parent groups with an enrollment of over 2,000. This work has been integrated into the expanding family life education program of the Seattle public schools, which employs a staff of five family life specialists, 24 instructors, and 26 special discussion leaders. It is supervised by an executive committee consisting of the director, the assistant in adult education, and the family life consultant of the department of home economics of the schools.

There has been for some time a growing tendency for parent cooperatives to work together in local associations or councils. Montgomery County, Maryland, is believed to have organized the first of these in 1944. The Seattle Council was formed in 1945, the East Bay Council in the San Francisco area in 1946. California organized the first state council in 1948; Michigan and New Jersey followed in 1950 and 1952. The American Council of Parent Cooperatives was formed at Teachers College, Columbia University, in 1960, in response to a demand from state and local groups for federation.

The purposes of the council are:

to promote interchange of information and help among cooperative nursery schools, kindergartens, and other preschool groups; to strengthen and extend the parent cooperative movement and community appreciation of parent education for adults, and preschool education for children; to promote desirable standards for the programs, practices and conditions in parent cooperatives, and encourage continuing education for their teachers and directors; to study legislation designed to further the health and well-being of children and families; to cooperate with family living adult education organizations in the interest of more effective service relationships with parents of young children (ACPC, 1962, p. 2).

The council is affiliated with the Association for Childhood Education International, and is establishing close working relationships with other national groups. It publishes a directory, service bulletins, and a newsletter, *The Parent Cooperative,* which is produced almost entirely by volunteers. The program is developed by the officers of the council, regional chairmen, and standing or special committees.

THE AMERICAN
HOME ECONOMICS ASSOCIATION

The story of the American Home Economics Association begins at the Chicago World's Fair of 1893. Among the attractions there was a household economics exhibit which featured a model working-class home. A man looking at this is said to have remarked, "This house may be run on $500 a year, but it would take a $5,000 wife to do it!" (Baldwin, 1949, p. 9).

Be that as it may, the exhibit aroused so much interest in home economics that a National Household Economics Association was formed to promote the idea of homemaking education for women. This organization worked primarily through women's groups, and often had a place on programs of the General and State Federations of Women's Clubs. After 10 years, it was disbanded because "the objects and aims of the association had become thoroughly incorporated in the work of the General and State Federations of Women's Clubs, and the Lake Placid Conference was now doing much better work along the same lines" (Baldwin, 1949, p. 10).

The Lake Placid Conferences were professional meetings for home economists held each year at Lake Placid, New York, beginning in 1899. These were, in fact, workshops at which intensive efforts were made to clarify and interpret the goals

and values of home economics. The general public and many home economists tended, at this time, to define education for homemaking as training in cooking, sewing, and household management—the basic housekeeping skills. Leading home economists, however, considered this position to be an abdication of professional responsibility. They saw home economics as the field of study primarily concerned with the development of the family as a whole.

This point of view was strongly advanced at Lake Placid in 1902 by Ellen H. Richards and other leaders. In her history of the association, Keturah Baldwin has written:

A larger vision unfolds in this conference— more subjects touching the intangible: the nature of the family and its significance in the development of the individual and of society, controlling ideals in the family of the future, current thought (including concepts as to the economic function of woman and theories of prosperity) as indicated by recent publications, use of new-found leisure, and social and industrial conditions (Baldwin, 1949, p. 15).

The American Home Economics Association was founded in Washington, D.C., January 1, 1909, during a meeting of the teaching section of the Lake Placid Conference, to provide administrative resources and centralized leadership for continuing growth of home economics as a profession. Its purpose as originally stated was "to improve the conditions of living in the home, the institutional household and the community." In 1930, this statement was revised to read: "The object of this Association shall be the development and promotion of standards of home living that will be satisfying and developing to the individual and profitable to society" (AHEA, 1931, p. 81). In 1958, the purpose was rephrased as follows:

The object of the American Home Economics Association shall be to provide opportunities for professional home economists and members from other fields to cooperate in the attainment of the well-being of individuals and of families, the improvement of homes, and the preservation of values significant in home life (AHEA Constitution, cited in AHEA, 1959, p. 6).

Each of these changes in wording represents an important advance in the development of program philosophy and policies.

The element missing in the early focus on skills was a core of basic values about human growth and development in the family setting that would give unity and direction to a total program of education for home and family living, however it might expand. To meet the need for this, the new association soon began to emphasize research and teaching in child development and family relationships. Its interest in these areas was so well established by 1926 that the Laura Spelman Rockefeller Memorial (see pp. 861–862) considered it eligible for substantial grants to strengthen this phase of its work.

With this financial assistance, the association was able to make a survey of experiments and new developments in home economics education relating to child care and parent education, and to prepare needed resource materials for teaching in these areas. A family life specialist was employed to give consultation service to home economists supervising home economics education programs in the states and to develop cooperative relationships with other organizations.

In 1927, the association was made custodian of Spelman funds for the Washington, D.C., Center for Child Study and Parent Education, a cooperative project involving the American Home Economics Association, the American Association of University Women, George Washington University, the University of Maryland, the National Research Council, the United States Office of Education, the Home Economics Education Service of the Federal Board for Vocational Education, and the United States

Public Health Service. The association terminated its formal connection with this project in 1932. The center is still in existence under the name of the National Child Research Center.

In 1941, the association decided that its special services in child development and family relations could be integrated with its regular publications and program of work. A Department of Child Development and Parental Education and a Division of the Family and Its Relationships had been created in 1931. In 1942, these became the Division of Family Relations and Child Development, now a section with the same name. This division initiated the idea of a national conference on the family in 1943 and helped to secure the cooperation from other organizations that made such a conference possible in 1948 (see pp. 175–176).

Under the leadership of the American Home Economics Association, the profession of home economics is contributing to the strengthening of family life here and abroad by "educating the individual for family living; improving the services and goods used by families; conducting research to discover the changing needs of individuals and families and the means of satisfying these needs, [and by] furthering community, national, and world conditions favorable to family living" (AHEA, 1959, p. 4).

THE AMERICAN SOCIAL HEALTH ASSOCIATION

Founded in 1912 as the American Social Hygiene Association, this organization seeks "to promote the conditions of living, environment and personal contact which best protect the family as a social institution" (cited in ASHA, n.d., p. 2). It conducts educational, research, and demonstration programs; makes surveys to define problems; disseminates information to the professions concerned and to the public. It works through its members, local affiliates, welfare councils, health councils, educational associations, and other voluntary groups, as well as with the armed forces and with federal, state, and local health, education, and welfare agencies. Its work is supported by individual contributions, foundation grants, community chests, and the cooperative financing of certain joint projects.

For many years, this association made a direct attack on venereal disease and prostitution. Long experience with deviant sex behavior, however, convinced staff and board that a better way of solving these problems would be to educate young people for wholesome personal and family living at an early age. In 1953, the association obtained funds from a foundation for an eight-year demonstration program in family life education. The object of this was to help education for family living find its place as an integral part of American education.

Projects were developed by committees representing school administrators, teachers, members of other professions, and state and community leaders in four different regions: the middle states (Colorado, Kansas, Missouri, Nebraska), New England (Connecticut, Maine, Massachusetts, New Hampshire, Rhode Island, Vermont), the central Atlantic states (Delaware, District of Columbia, Maryland, North Carolina, Virginia, West Virginia), and the Midwest (Iowa, North Dakota, South Dakota, Minnesota).

While these demonstrations were going on, family life education had high visibility in most of the states participating in the experiment. There were family life institutes, workshops, and conferences in schools, on college campuses, and in communities. Education for family living had a place on the program of nearly every large health, education, or welfare convention. Consultation services were requested by churches, social agencies, school systems, colleges and universities, teacher training institutions, and even a woman's reforma-

tory. A number of communities were surveyed to discover family needs and identify resources for family life education. Special committees were organized to work on family life emphases in school and community programs. Several excellent pieces of pamphlet material were produced and distributed widely with the help of the American Social Health Association. How many changes actually were made in the curricula of schools and colleges is not known.

In 1959, the association and the National Congress of Parents and Teachers together launched a different type of program, the Rocky Mountain Project. This involves Arizona, Nevada, New Mexico, and Utah. The over-all objectives are:

To increase the amount and improve the quality of family life education, to experiment with new approaches to family life education, to increase the number of trained leaders in this field, to improve public attitudes about family life education and family problems, to bring about better integration and coordination of community resources, to improve communication and understanding between and among family members, to disseminate and interpret pertinent information in this field (Cumings & Reed, 1961, p. 28).

Each state interprets those objectives in its own way. Arizona is experimenting with the use of radio and television, and has developed an excellent handbook for PTA leaders (Arizona Congress, 1961). Nevada is using one- and two-day institutes in selected communities to stimulate family life education and strengthen PTA's. It also has under way a pilot project in an elementary school where teachers, administrators, children, and their parents are looking for ways of improving the emotional climate in the school.

New Mexico is organizing discussion groups to deal with matters of local concern relating to family life. Leaders for these are being trained in institutes and workshops held at the state university and in communities. The Utah project has concentrated so far on the improvement of communication between young people and adults and between parents and children of all ages, using discussion groups as a means of bringing the generations together. These meetings have stimulated the development of several courses in family life education, and are being copied in other places in the state.

The Prescott, Arizona, program is a particularly good example of what can be accomplished through coordination. The following description is taken from an article appearing in the December, 1961, issue of the *PTA Magazine:*

The Prescott project is one of community organization for greater attention to local problems, but the school system has also been heavily involved from the outset. Following a kick-off meeting in August, 1960, attended by some nine hundred citizens, many activities have been inaugurated. These were climaxed last spring by a four-day community institute in family living, attended by a total of 1,139, including 520 young people from the schools. . . . Special sessions were held for ministers so that they could fulfill some of the community's counseling needs, and about thirty hours of personal counseling were given during the four days. To guarantee continuing activity in Prescott [a town of about 15,000 people, ed.] plans were made to follow up some of the results of the Institute.

Other activities . . . include the reestablishment of a chapter of Alcoholics Anonymous, the development of a library of family life education books and pamphlets, several evening courses in family living, and guidance to individual families needing help. . . (Cumings & Reed, 1961, p. 28).

On the national level, the American Social Health Association continues with its broad program. In 1958, it brought together the executives of national family-serving agencies to discuss problems and issues in family life education. The proceedings of this conference are a valuable summary of the points of view expressed on this occasion, and the recommendations made. In 1960, nearly a million booklists, pamphlets, and special reports were distributed free or at cost price to parents, teachers, nurses, members of the armed forces, health and welfare councils, social work agencies, and other professional groups.

Research into behavioral aspects of the problems it deals with is a permanent part of the general program of the association. Currently it is working intensively with federal and other agencies on the narcotics problem. Its activities are varied and responsive to emerging needs; all are in line with the policy of the association to work "for the development of school, college, and community programs designed to strengthen family life, and against individual and social circumstances which tend to weaken and undermine the family and its members" (Cumings, 1959, p. 1).

THE CHILD STUDY ASSOCIATION OF AMERICA

For more than 75 years, the Child Study Association of America has been so closely identified with parent education in the United States that the histories of the organization and of the movement are almost inseparable. It is the only national agency in the country devoted exclusively to parent education, and its leadership in this field is widely appreciated.

The founder of the Ethical Culture Society, Dr. Felix Adler, was also, indirectly, the founder of this association. In 1888, he advised a small group of mothers meeting in New York City to form a society for the study of child nature. The society became a federation when other groups organized and asked to affiliate. It was incorporated under its present name in 1925.

The founding mothers went eagerly to work to find out what was then known about children. They consulted authorities, read their books, and tried to apply their theories. As time went on, they and the theories became more sophisticated. They studied Pavlov and Freud, J. B. Watson and John Dewey, oriented themselves to the new social hygiene and mental hygiene movements, and to new developments in psychiatry. By 1920, the federation had a core group of experienced group leaders and members with special skill in sifting and interpreting professional materials for parents who were not prepared to go directly to the literature. One of these leaders was Sidonie Matsner Gruenberg, that remarkable woman who has been the heart and soul of parent education in the United States for over 50 years (Auerbach, Frank, & Wolf, 1956).

Major emphasis shifted in early years from the child as the subject of study to relationships within the family. To help clarify popular misunderstandings, the association began to publish basic articles on such topics as heredity, discipline, the importance of love and affection in family life, spiritual and moral values in character building. In 1923, the Laura Spelman Rockefeller Memorial provided the means for a monthly bulletin to keep groups in touch with current thinking and findings about child care and family life. At this time, Mrs. Gruenberg became the director of the association, an office she held for more than 25 years.

The money for the bulletin was the beginning of a close and fruitful relationship between the association and the Spelman Funds. Additional grants made it possible for the association to extend all phases of its program. Study groups were organized in new settings: settlement houses, churches, community centers, housing projects, some on the lower East Side of New York and in Harlem. Materials were written especially for parents, and earlier study group outlines were supplemented by readings and otherwise improved.

As the study groups multiplied, the need for leadership training became more and more apparent. A Spelman grant enabled Mrs. Gruenberg to give a course in parent education in 1924 at Teachers College. This was sponsored cooperatively by the college

and the Child Study Association. At the same time, the latter set up its own leader training program.

In 1925, again with the aid of the Spelman Memorial, the association convened two conferences, a Conference on Modern Parenthood for the general public, attended by 1,500 people from all over the United States, and a small conference of representatives of 13 national organizations conducting parent education programs. These have been repeated annually ever since. The meeting of agency representatives has become the Annual Institute for Workers in Parent Education, and is attended by 300 to 500 professional persons representing many different disciplines and agencies. The association's Annual Conference is open to the general public. It is usually attended by 1,000 to 1,500 persons, interested parents and professional workers, who are addressed by nationally and internationally prominent leaders on subjects of current concern.

The 1925 interagency consultation had a dramatic outcome. Participants recommended the organization of a national agency to coordinate, perhaps to integrate, activities in parent education carried on under many different auspices. The National Council of Parent Education was the result (see pp. 862-863). The Child Study Association worked closely with it until the council was dissolved in 1938.

A counseling service for parents was started in 1929. A psychiatrist was added to the staff, but the approach was educational rather than therapeutic. This was the first such service set up especially for parents. The counseling service is still functioning, and is staffed by trained psychiatric social workers, with psychiatric consultations. Short-term educational counseling interviews are offered to parents to help them deal more effectively with everyday difficulties related to their children's growth and development. This service is based on the concept that a change in parental attitudes may often prevent the development of serious problems in children.

Recently, a consultation service to nursery school and day care center staffs, focused on improving their contacts with the parents of children in their centers, has been inaugurated by the counseling service of the association.

The Child Study Association at one time shared with many other groups the belief that, with the right guidance, parent education would establish itself as a separate profession. As interest in education for parenthood increased, however, each of the helping professions found unique opportunities for parent education in its own work. Following this trend, the association adapted its leadership training program to the needs of other professional groups. The first request from another discipline for courses in the psychodynamics of human behavior and techniques of group leadership came from the New York City Board of Education for teachers. Similar courses have been held for social workers, public health nurses, clergymen and religious educators, and special persons from the field of education.

The study group program has changed, too, over the years. In 1949, a special series was offered for parents who were divorced, or were contemplating divorce. This was the first of many groups organized around special problems. There have been series for parents of brain-damaged children, for parents whose children were blind, deaf, or recovering from polio. Of late years, a good deal of emphasis has been placed on education for expectant parents.

The volunteer services are an important part of the program. Trained volunteers serve on the Book Review and Children's Book committees. With staff guidance, these committees evaluate books for children and parents, prepare basic booklists, review current materials, and the like.

And, finally, there is in the association a program of community services. This has been active since World War I, when it organized summer play schools for children whose parents were doing war work. These centers were under the auspices of different agencies, but they were planned and supervised by the Play Schools Committee of the Child Study Association. In 1939, this committee became an independent agency—the Play Schools Association. Today, this is a well-established organization with a large program in which parent education has an important place.

As members of the Child Study Association have worked, over the years, with parents and with persons in the professions serving families and children, they have had valuable opportunities to consider the problem of change in parental attitudes, from many different angles. On the basis of this experience, the association takes the position that parent education is not just an intellectual process, that emotional, social, and cultural factors are also involved in it; that it properly belongs, professionally, in the field of mental health; and that it is most effective when it is preventive. The role of the association, as its staff and board members now see it, is that of a national organization devoted to the task of developing programs of training, consultation, and research in mental health education for families (Buchmueller, 1961).

THE FAMILY SERVICE ASSOCIATION OF AMERICA

This organization is a federation, with a membership of more than 300 community-supported, family and community-serving agencies. It was founded in 1911 as the National Association of Societies for Organizing Charity. In 1919, it became the American Association for Organizing Family Social Work, took the name Family Welfare Association of America in 1930, and was renamed the Family Service Association of America in 1946. Each of these changes represents an important step in the evolution of the family service concept.

The scope of the work of the association is indicated by its official slogan: "Strength to Families Under Stress." Member agencies carry out its broad purposes in two ways: through marriage and family social work counseling on problems of marriage and child care, and through social planning and action undertaken to create community conditions as conducive as possible to wholesome family living. More than 400,000 families are served by these member agencies each year, an approximate total of 2 million individuals.

The program of the association is one of service to its member agencies and pre-member affiliates. The national office keeps in touch with local and regional problems and needs through field service, which includes field visits, institutes, regional meetings for board members, regional conferences, consultations, and correspondence. A consultation service is also available to citizen groups interested in setting up family service programs in their communities. "Direct services to help implement the programs of member agencies and pre-member affiliates provide a two-way flow of service, information materials and publications on administration, personnel, research, public relations, and professional training" (NSWA, 1961, p. 42).

The official channel of communication for FSAA membership is a magazine, *Family Service Highlights*. The association also publishes *Social Casework*, a fine professional journal which presents articles on developments in all fields of social work. A particularly timely and useful contribution to the entire field of family life education was the bulletin *A Review of Research on Parent Influences on Child Personality*, published by the association in 1959 (Frankiel, 1959).

The programs of member agencies vary greatly, but all offer family casework services and community leadership. An increasing number are experimenting with different forms of family life education in addition to their regular counseling services. In 1960–1961, Paget studied family life

education programs in the United States and Canada, defining family life education as "group education activities directed toward the improvement of family life" (Paget, 1961, p. 1). In his report, he briefly described family life activities in family service agencies in Boston, Memphis, New York, Philadelphia, St. Louis, San Bernardino, California, and Toronto, Canada. Only one of these organizations has a full-time family life director, although one has 14 staff members giving part time to family life education activities.

Each of these agencies provides professional leadership for single meetings and for discussion group series. Each also offers a counseling service to organizations interested in developing family life education activities—de-emphasizing the single meeting and urging the organization of small discussion groups when this is feasible.

Among the special projects reported were discussion groups in housing projects (Memphis and New York); community conferences (Memphis); a week-long program in a large department store to reach shoppers (St. Louis); long-term concentration on a single item—preparation for marriage (San Bernardino); a leadership training course for retired caseworkers (Toronto).

The Family Service of Memphis and the Jewish Family Service of New York both report success with groups in public housing projects, a type of program that is much needed but difficult to organize. The New York project was developed, at the request of housing authorities, for families about to be evicted for poor housekeeping. As a result of the discussions, housekeeping practices improved so much that eight of the 10 families were allowed to stay. Attitudes and behavior began to change when the tenants realized, apparently for the first time, that it takes a whole family to make a good home and keep a clean, tidy house—that no mother can do this alone. One of the important functions of the Family Service

Association of America is to help consolidate the gains when new ventures like this throw light on old problems.

THE GENERAL FEDERATION OF WOMEN'S CLUBS

From a very small beginning in 1890, the General Federation of Women's Clubs has been growing for almost 75 years in size and in its potentialities for service. Its basic program is designed for the thousands of American women's clubs which constitute its membership, all of these belonging through state federations. It welcomes appropriate groups from other countries, and participates extensively in projects intended to promote international understanding. Its purpose is "to bring into communication and to unite the women's clubs and like organizations throughout the world for the purpose of mutual benefit, and for the promotion of their common interest in educational, industrial, philanthropic, literary, artistic, and scientific culture as interpreted by established policy" (GFWC, n.d., p. 1).

The work of the federation is carried on through departments, divisions, and committees. This organizational pattern is defined by the GFWC bylaws and provides that, while the divisions and committees may be set up, discontinued, or changed from time to time, as new needs arise, the six departments (Conservation, Education, Fine Arts, Home Life, International Affairs, and Public Affairs) must be an integral part of every administration program.

It is through the Home Life Department that the federation makes its most direct contribution to family living. During the 1962–1964 administration of Mrs. Dexter Otis Arnold, the aim of this department is "to strengthen the Arm of Liberty by way of the American home, bringing fresh insight into the impact of a changing world on home and family" (GFWC, 1963, p. 1). Its program rests on four assumptions:

"[(a) that] the influence of the home is basic in building the character of the individual—his attitudes, values, and goals . . . [(b) that] the home should be the source of emotional and spiritual stability for all family members . . . [(c) that] the home should offer the first and best opportunity to learn the fundamentals of 'teamwork by agreement' and of individual responsibility . . . [(d) that] a woman should realize—and accept—her vital role as the central figure in the home" (p. 1).

There are, at present, four divisions in the Home Life Department: Family Economics and Home Management, Family Living and Child Development, House Improvement and Modern Food Trends, Religion and Spiritual Values. Each of these helps with the development of club programs in its area of interest: single meetings, study series, community action, workshops, seminars, or institutes. Special efforts are made to acquaint club members with sources of help in their communities. A strong appeal is made to junior clubs, and clubs with junior memberships, in order to reach young families.

Many of the projects undertaken by the federation have done much to raise standards of home living in the United States. The Household Economics Committee, through its Sub-committee on Pure Food, helped to secure the passage of the first national pure food bill, in 1906, and similar legislation in the states. Another of the early activities of this committee was a campaign to establish home economics courses in high schools.

Strong support was given to legislation for the education of rural women in home economics and, in 1922–1924, the federation worked hard for the appointment of county home demonstration agents. It made surveys of equipment in rural and urban homes in 1925 and 1927, obtaining such data as the number of houses with running water, gas, sewer connections, electricity, telephones, central heating, the kinds of

stoves used for cooking and heating, the
types of sanitary fixtures and labor-saving
appliances in use, the recreational facilities
available to families, and the number of
families having automobiles, radios, phono-
graphs, and pianos.

The results of these surveys were widely
publicized, and many Americans were
shocked to learn that there were thousands
of towns in the United States without public water or sewer systems, cities with no
trash or garbage collection, hundreds of
homes without modern conveniences of any
kind. A follow-up campaign to correct bad
conditions revealed by the surveys was carried out through state federations and local
clubs, in cooperation with state and local
agencies, both public and private. The General Federation prepared and published a
Home Equipment Primer that was in constant demand for several years. The information gathered in the course of these
activities was used to persuade the Census
Bureau to stop classifying women at home
as "non-productive" and count them as
"housewives." This change was made in
1930.

During the depression, the federation
helped farm women to organize cooperative markets for the sale of their produce,
and many of today's roadside markets are
descendants of these. In 1934, club women
in 63 cities made surveys of milk consumption among school children, and clubs
throughout the country supplied milk to
schools for youngsters who needed it
(Wells, 1953, pp. 182–192).

In 1946, the Home Life Department
published a pamphlet called *Family Living
Today,* now out of print. This included
articles by outstanding specialists on many
important phases of family life. It provided
inspiration and good basic content for a
wide variety of club programs on homemaking themes for a number of years. As
they have done so ably in the past, the
Home Life Department and the federation
as a whole still continue to ally themselves
with the forces in our society which work
for the enrichment of family life.

THE NATIONAL CATHOLIC
WELFARE CONFERENCE

In his encyclical on Christian marriage,
issued on December 31, 1930, Pope Pius XI
made an urgent appeal to people everywhere in the Christian world to "use every
fit means to restore the Christian family."
He called for positive social action and vigorous leadership to revitalize the Christian
family ideal.

The hierarchy of the Catholic Church in
the United States responded by setting up
the Family Life Bureau in the Social
Action Department of the National Catholic Welfare Conference, and the encyclical
became the charter of the new "secretariat."
Father Edgar Schmiedeler became the first
director and served in this capacity for 25
years. When Father Schmiedeler retired in
1956, Monsignor Irving DeBlanc was appointed director. In 1962, Monsignor De-
Blanc was succeeded by Monsignor John
C. Knott, the present bureau director.

The bureau does not try to supplant or
merge family life programs and movements
in the United States. Rather, its functions
are to service, encourage, and otherwise
strength these activities, to provide a means
of communication between them, and to
assist them to become more effective in
common action.

A National Advisory Board made up of
representatives from all major Catholic
family life movements and areas in the
country gives leadership in program development within the framework of Catholic
policy. Committees appointed by the board
are active in four general areas: (a) a committee on research and theory in the general family field; (b) a committee in which
the focus is on education and family life;
(c) a committee stressing action through
organization; and (d) a committee on family policy both domestically and internationally.

There are now family life directors in
nearly all American archdioceses. Most of
these are visited at least once a year by a
member of the staff of the bureau or a
member of one of its committees, and na-

tional and regional meetings are regularly held by the directors under the sponsorship of the NCWC Bureau.

The major objectives of the Family Life Bureau's program are: (a) fostering the growth and development of the Christian person; (b) preparing Christians for marriage; (c) educating husband and wife in Christian marriage; (d) educating parents and children in Christian family relationships; (e) servicing special persons and groups in family life; (f) relating the family to the life of the Church and community.

These objectives are implemented by the bureau through eight kinds of program services: (a) The bureau conducts its own research and fact-finding in the area of marriage and family life, and cooperates with institutions of higher learning and other agencies engaged in these activities, such as the Population Research Center at Georgetown University. (b) An exchange of information service is maintained through the publication of the bureau's newsletter, *The Catholic Family Leader,* and by participation in major national and international organizations related to its fields of interest. (c) The bureau sets standards and makes recommendations, as, for example, in its critically annotated bibliography of published Catholic materials in its field. (d) Numerous meetings are held throughout each year with priests and couples, and other bureau activities and materials are designed as leadership training instruments. (e) Technical assistance is rendered by the staff, advisory board members and other authorities enlisted by the bureau to assist Catholic and non-Catholic organizations and individuals with their needs in the bureau's area of competence. (f) Program aids are developed, whether through the bureau's Book Service Division, in the dissemination of discussion outlines, reprints, program suggestions, or preparation of and references to appropriate program aids, such as audio-visual materials. (g) The bureau measures performance by systematically reporting and evaluating its own operations and assisting others to do likewise in the light of the needs of the Church and her people. (h) The bureau recognizes achievement by paying public tribute, as in the Catholic Family of the Year Award, to those who exemplify the ideals of Christian marriage and family living.

The contributions the bureau makes to research in the family field are substantial

. . . [It] studies trends and tries to make professional studies available for students doing research. The research may be on housing problems, on family allowance laws, on standards of living as they are set by the families with no children, on the problems involved in "going steady," on the 19,000,000 women working outside the home, on family courts, on family laws, on mixed marriages, on the needs of family counselors, on the problems of urban, suburban, and rural life, on family vacations, on incessant moving as it affects family life, on maternity guilds, on the military life and the family (DeBlanc, 1957, p. 7).[1]

The Family Life Bureau welcomes new ideas and procedures in a complex, interdisciplinary, ever growing field of vital interest to Church and nation, as well as to the families themselves. Its basic assumption is that "many strong families working together under God's grace can restore family life as the chief stronghold of faith, and strength in our land" (Curtis, 1962, p. 4).

The National Congress of Parents and Teachers

For size, geographic distribution of members, and cultural penetration, the National Congress of Parents and Teachers is unique among lay organizations. In 60-odd years its memberships have increased from about 2,000 to more than 12 million. It was founded in 1897 as the National Congress of Mothers, became the National Congress of Mothers and Parent Teacher Associa-

[1] Reprinted with permission from *Grail Magazine,* St. Meinrad, Ind., Feb., 1957.

tions in 1908, and took its present name in
1924. The National Congress of Colored
Parents and Teachers is a similar organization functioning in southern states that still
have dual school systems. There is close
cooperation between the two groups.

The original congress was the outgrowth
of a mothers' club movement which spread
rapidly in the United States from the
1870's on. These clubs were study groups
formed more or less independently by
women who had heard of the new developments in child psychology resulting from
the work of such pioneers as G. Stanley
Hall, and who wanted to make use of these
insights in bringing up their own children.
As they came to understand better the
needs of their children and tried to meet
them, many of these mothers realized, for
the first time, how little they could do, as
individuals, to change conditions detrimental to child health and welfare. There
was, therefore, an immediate and warm
response when Mrs. Alice Birney, of Washington, D. C., proposed a national meeting
to which mothers would come from all
over America to translate their concerns as
mothers into social and legislative action.

The first official call to this convocation
was read at the biennial convention of the
General Federation of Women's Clubs at
Louisville, Kentucky, in May, 1895. The
next two years were spent preparing for
the meeting. Mrs. Birney and a team of
volunteers contacted as many women's organizations as possible, traveling by train
and carriage, on horseback or bicycle, sometimes on foot, to reach groups of mothers
in rural communities as well as in the
cities. Mrs. Phoebe Apperson Hearst gave
generous financial assistance.

When the Congress of Mothers was
founded, its purpose was stated as follows:
"The objects of this Association shall be
to promote conference on the part of parents concerning questions most vital to the
welfare of their children, the manifest interests of the home, and in general the

elevation of mankind" (cited in Overstreet
& Overstreet, 1949, p. 47). This is still the
general aim of the National Congress of
Parents and Teachers. The national organization consists of state branches (congresses) and their local associations
(PTA's). In some areas councils or districts
of parent-teacher associations are formed
by authorization of the state branch. *The
PTA Magazine,* first published in 1906, is
a strong integrating force.

From the beginning, parent education
has been one of the major concerns of the
congress. At first there was no standing
committee on parent education because
this had priority in the total program. In
1923, Professor Bird Baldwin of the University of Iowa took charge of parent education activities, under the supervision of
a standing committee on child development. Later, this became the Bureau of
Child Development, then, in 1928, the Bureau of Parent Education, which now is the
Standing Committee on Parent and Family
Life Education.

The first project to aid the study groups
was the preparation of loan packets of
papers written by experts, to be read at
meetings. Outlines to guide group discussion were first made available from the
national office in 1898–1899. These are now
carried in the magazine with lead articles
on major topics written by specialists. Publications and reading lists pertaining to
many phases of child and family development may be obtained free or at low cost
from National Congress headquarters. The
magazine itself is an excellent resource,
regularly containing authoritative articles
on family and child development, education, community organization, and national
and international issues affecting home and
family life.

In 1928, the National Congress of Parents
and Teachers employed a specialist to
strengthen its work in parent education.
This consultant traveled from state to state
for eight years, helping state congresses

and local parent-teacher associations to improve their study group programs by enriching the content, making better use of resources, securing more cooperation from educators, and promoting the coordination of all parent education activities at state and local levels. When the experiment ended in 1936, progress had been made in all these directions. Parent education conferences and institutes were being held regularly on college campuses and under a variety of other auspices. There were many more study groups in action, and nearly 3,000 persons were enrolled in National Congress correspondence courses.

An extensive leadership training project was carried on from 1949 to 1954 to meet the urgent demand of parents, in the postwar period, for more self-knowledge and knowledge of children's needs, for more cooperative study and discussion of parent-child relations under competent, well-informed leadership—in other words, more parent education "PTA style." Consultants were appointed to work with state congresses in each of the five regions into which the country had been divided. These specialists conducted demonstration workshops for state representatives, then helped them set up similar workshops for their local parent education chairmen and study group leaders. In most states, there were positive results. In Ohio, for example, all of the state universities combined in a plan to divide the entire state into six districts and hold training institutes in each one. Within a few months, more than 1,000 lay leaders had been trained in this way.

The Rocky Mountain Family Life Education Project, previously described (see pp. 848–849), broadens the scope of the study group approach in parent education and makes it part of a larger program of social action. This is consistent with long-established policy, since the National Congress of Parents and Teachers has always taken the position that the welfare of children, families, and communities cannot be separated. It joins other agencies in far-reaching cooperative efforts to deal with national and international problems affecting families. It has played an active part in such projects as the decennial White House Conferences on Children and Youth, using its resources to strengthen the follow-up of these in many ways. Its ultimate goal continues to be to help parents improve not only their methods of child rearing, but the home, school, and community environments in which children learn and test out their values (NCPT, 1944).

THE NATIONAL COUNCIL OF THE CHURCHES OF CHRIST IN THE U.S.A.

" 'My brother Juan was born in the potatoes,' the child said. 'Lupe died in the cotton' " (NCC, 1962, p. 8). Ramona, herself, is temporarily out of the lettuce, in a nursery at a community center in the migrant camp where her parents are working. At night there may be simple lessons in child care there for mothers who have the energy to attend. Perhaps some of the fathers will come to talk about their problems. There may be a club for teenagers. On Sundays, there will be religious services.

Such centers are a project of the National Council of the Churches of Christ in the U.S.A. Working through local committees in communities near labor camps, its Committee on Migrant Work is bringing both material and spiritual aid to families who follow the crops. This, of course, is only one of the ways in which the council helps to strengthen American family life (NCC, 1962).

This national coordinating body was formed in Cleveland in 1950 by the union of 12 national interdenominational agencies, including the Federal Council of Churches of Christ in Amercia. Its first purpose is "to make Christians more aware of the central unity of their faith [and to aid] Christians to direct their faith into channels of action" (NCC, n.d., p. 1).

There were representatives of 29 Protestant and Orthodox bodies at the founding meeting. The membership today includes 31 denominations, 960 local and state councils of churches, and more than 2,000 ministerial associations.

The four major divisions of the council are Christian Education, Christian Life and Work, Foreign Missions, and Home Missions. Within the divisions, there are departments, committees, and commissions to deal with different aspects of the total program, which has 70 different units. The Church World Service is a constituent part of the council.

The Department of Family Life is the successor to several units of the agencies which merged to form the National Council, particularly the Commission on Marriage and the Home of the Federal Council of Churches and the Department of Family Life Education of the International Council of Religious Education. It renders no direct service to families but acts as a consultation center and clearing house for the family life programs of all member communions. It assists councils of churches holding area conferences on family life, providing leadership, guidance, source materials, and help in the development of a basic family life philosophy.

This department also cooperates with seminaries and colleges on the organization of programs with special family life emphases: preparation for marriage, the church's leadership in family counseling, Christian family education in the community and on the campus. It develops patterns and needed resources for state and community institutes on Christian family life for area leaders, including manuals for leaders and audio-visual materials.

An important part of the work of the department has to do with research. It sponsors studies of family life and its Christian fulfillment around the world, in cooperation with the Rural Missions Cooperating Committee and the International Missionary Council; helps the Committee

on Migrant Work with its direct ministry to agricultural migrants; and rounds up information and resources for local councils of church women.

Members of the staff of the Family Life Department have written or helped to write a number of books and pamphlets on family and church-related subjects. One of the most recent is *Church Family Camps and Conferences, An Administrative and Program Manual* (Genné & Genné, 1962). This includes a chapter of suggestions for serving families with special needs: parents without partners, families with handicapped children, three-generation families, and so on.

An important project in which the department was recently involved was the North American Conference on Family Life, sponsored jointly by the National Council of the Churches of Christ in the U.S.A. and the Canadian Council of Churches. This was held at Green Lake, Wisconsin, in May, 1961. The purpose was to discover a new relationship between the social sciences and religion. There were 500 delegates and invited participants, including specialists from the psychological, sociological, medical, and allied professions.

An outstanding feature of this conference was the frankness with which it faced such problems as family, divorce, illegitimacy, and pregnant brides. Leaders called for an end to the platitudes in terms of which these subjects are too often discussed. Church men and women joined with behavioral scientists in the analysis of issues in sex education, mixed marriages, too-youthful marriages, and so on. There was a firm call for a valid sex code for Protestants, and praise for premarital counseling programs, although the group felt that the latter do not begin soon enough. Recommendations were drawn up for study by the churches.

Three important publications have resulted from this conference: *Sex Ways in Fact and Faith* (Duvall & Duvall, 1961), the collected working papers; *Christians and the Crisis in Sex Morality* (Genné & Genné, 1961), a summary; and *Foundations for Christian Family Policy* (Genné & Genné, 1962b), the verbatim compilation of proceedings and findings.

THE NATIONAL COUNCIL ON FAMILY RELATIONS

This is an interprofessional group which was organized in 1938 for the exchange of ideas and information among the several disciplines active in the family field. It accomplishes this purpose through annual conferences, through its *Journal of Marriage and the Family* (formerly *Marriage and Family Living*), through consultations with other agencies, and through the regional, state, and local councils on family relations affiliated with it.

Among the founders were Paul W. Sayre, professor of law at the University of Iowa, Ernest W. Burgess, professor of sociology at the University of Chicago, and Ernest R. Groves, professor of sociology at the University of North Carolina. Professor Sayre became the first president of the organization. The second president was the distinguished professor of psychiatry and neurology at The Johns Hopkins University, Adolph Meyer.

With the help of Professor Burgess, arrangements were made in 1938 for an office at the University of Chicago. The council maintained headquarters there until 1955, when it moved to Minneapolis.

Except for secretarial service, the work of this association was carried out almost entirely on a voluntary basis for several years. Evelyn Millis Duvall was made secretary-treasurer in 1941 and served for some time without salary, building up membership and program strength. She later became executive secretary, serving in this capacity until her resignation in 1951.

The council has now completed its twenty-fifth year, and is the leading interdisciplinary professional organization giving direct and specific attention to the process of family development. At present, its program has four major divisions: Research, Education, Counseling, and Special Emphases. This last includes all the areas of interest that do not seem to belong in any of the other three categories. It is here that new groups wishing a place in the council can make their contributions and test out their potentialities as future sections.

In recognition of Ernest W. Burgess' pioneering contributions to the study of family life, the council established a special research fund in his honor during the early 1950's. This fund was first drawn upon to finance a special issue of *Marriage and Family Living* in 1952. Awards for challenging research proposals and distinguished publications were made for several years. In 1962, the council decided to bestow the Ernest W. Burgess Award biennially upon a member whose work in family research has been, and promises to continue to be, of exceptional merit. Dr. Reuben Hill, Research Professor of Sociology and Director of the Family Study Center at the University of Minnesota, was the recipient in 1963.

The affairs of the council are administered by an executive committee and a 15-member elected board of directors who represent, as far as possible, the different regions of the United States and the different professional groups in the council. A standing International Liaison Committee maintains relationships abroad, especially with the International Union of Family Organizations. These two organizations cosponsored an International Conference on the Family held in New York City in 1960.

PLANNED PARENTHOOD—WORLD POPULATION (Formerly the Planned Parenthood Federation of America)

"Every human society," said Margaret Mead, "is faced with not one population problem but two: how to beget and rear enough children and how not to beget and rear too many" (in Rainwater, & Weinstein, 1960, p. 19). The Planned Parenthood Federation of America was founded in 1921 as the American Birth Control League to give leadership in the search for answers to both of these questions. It is now called Planned Parenthood—World Population. Its program includes research, education, and direct services to families. There is no reason to believe that it may now be nearing the end of a long struggle to see guidance in family planning universally recognized as an integral part of complete medical care (PPFA, 1962).

The name associated with the beginnings of the birth control movement throughout the world is that of Mrs. Margaret Sanger, once a visiting nurse on the lower East Side of New York. In 1912, Mrs. Sanger published her first pamphlet, *What Every Mother Should Know*. In 1916, she had rallied enough support to open the first public birth control clinic. In 1921, she organized the first American birth control conference, which resulted in the founding of the American Birth Control League. The first birth control clinical research bureau was established by her in 1923 and is still functioning in New York as the Margaret Sanger Research Bureau. In 1927, Mrs. Sanger organized the first world population conference, which led to the later formation of the International Union for the Scientific Investigation of Population Problems, headed by the famous geneticist Raymond Pearl.

There was, of course, a great deal of opposition to the movement in those early days. Leaders were arrested and sometimes imprisoned, clinics were closed, equipment and literature destroyed, meetings broken up. Even so, support for the program grew stronger, particularly among people in the medical, educational, and religious professions. In 1930, the New York Academy of Medicine passed resolutions favoring birth control. In 1937, the American Medical Association unanimously accepted birth con-

trol as an integral part of medical practice and education. Three years later the United States Public Health Service ruled that states which included child-spacing services in their state programs did not forfeit their right to federal assistance by doing so.

Meanwhile, the number of cooperating agencies increased and birth control centers multiplied. Soon it became clear that excess fertility was not the only problem, but that infertility could be very destructive to many families, and services to overcome it were frequently as unavailable as contraceptive services. Inevitably, the program grew to include both kinds of assistance in Planned Parenthood centers (PPFA, n.d.).

With increasing clinical experience came an increasing awareness of the need for more knowledge, for research that might give more insight into motivation and suggest better ways of helping people deal with their own sexual problems. The practice of birth control is a voluntary individual commitment, but the need for population control is urgent and world-wide. What the behavioral sciences can do to relate these two problems remains to be seen.

One practical next step is to complete the integration of family planning services into public health programs (PPFA, 1962). This is the present goal both of Planned Parenthood—World Population and of the International Planned Parenthood Federation. In a policy statement issued at its 1959 convention, the American Public Health Association placed on record its own commitment to the principle that family planning services should be an integral part of preventive medical practice. Indeed, in seven states this has been so for a number of years, and several other states included such services in maternal and child health programs in the year 1962–1963. Financing of state programs which include family planning services is on the same basis with relation to federal government support as any other state health program.

Planned Parenthood—World Population

has worked to minimize the religious issues involved by providing the rhythm method in its centers, and by engaging in cooperative activities with Roman Catholic leaders. There is hope that new and expanded research will help to resolve the major differences, which are on methods rather than on basic principles. Planned Parenthood stands for all medically approved methods of contraception, but does not propagandize for any of them. It recognizes and respects moral and cultural barriers when they exist, and believes that each individual couple must deal with the problem of family planning in the way that seems best to them. Planned Parenthood, in this program, means fertility control, the correction of sterility, and the promotion of responsible parenthood.

PARENT AND FAMILY LIFE EDUCATION IN PERSPECTIVE

A careful study of goals, practices, problems, and accomplishments in parent education was made in the early 1950's by Orville G. Brim, Jr., under the joint auspices of the Russell Sage Foundation and the Child Study Association of America. In *Education for Child Rearing* (1959), a report of this research, Brim pointed out two principal trends in parent education in the United States: the tendency to expand and diversify activities, and the drive to professionalize this originally lay movement.

Partly because the idea that one could learn how to be a better parent was exciting to many mothers, and partly because group experiences in themselves can be very satisfying, mothers' study groups multiplied, until by the early 1920's they far exceeded the number of people qualified to direct them. At this time, the flow of new scientific content for these programs was hardly more than a trickle. The social sciences were becoming more interested in the experimental study of human behavior, but facilities for research in child and family development were almost nonexistent.

FOUNDATION SUPPORT

Numerous interdisciplinary conferences, initially stimulated by Lawrence K. Frank, later vice president of the Josiah Macy, Jr., Foundation, resulted in the formulation of a plan for centralizing the parent education movement, tying it more closely to growing bodies of knowledge about children and family living, and providing more professional leadership through the recruitment and training of people for positions in parent education at federal, state, and local levels. A new foundation, the Laura Spelman Rockefeller Memorial, became interested in this program and supported it generously from 1923 to 1928, under the direction of Lawrence K. Frank. The Spelman Fund of the Rockefeller Foundation took it over when the memorial was dissolved in 1929, and carried it until 1938. These two funds and the General Education Board were the main support of parent education activities in the United States for almost two decades (Brim, 1959; Fosdick, 1962).

The work was carried on simultaneously along three lines: research, leadership training, and program development. Money was provided initially for a number of research centers, including St. George's Nursery School at the University of Toronto; the Institute for Child Research at Teachers College, Columbia University; the Institutes of Child Welfare at the Universities of Minnesota and California; an expanded Child Welfare Research Station at the University of Iowa; and the Child Study Center at Yale. Research programs were also established at the Medical School, in Denver, of the University of Colorado; at the Universities of Michigan and Chicago and Harvard University; at the Fels Fund Research Center in Yellow Springs, Ohio; at Antioch College; and at the Merrill-

Palmer School, now the Merrill-Palmer Institute of Human Development and Family Life. Most of these centers continued their work after the grants expired and are now internationally known for their achievements.

The training phase of the program was implemented through grants to colleges and universities for the professional training of parent educators. Many of these grants went to the schools where the research centers had been established or expanded. Numerous fellowships were offered, and among the first trainees were psychologists, teachers, nurses, social workers, and a number of home economists. A few of these Spelman Fellows went on to become supervisors of parent education in public school systems or in state departments of education. Most of them, however, returned after their training to work directly with parents through their own organizations, or took part-time positions as group leaders.

Courses in child development and parent education were introduced into college home economics curricula. By 1928, more than 20 colleges and universities were offering this training in nursery school settings. Today, a nursery school laboratory is standard equipment in practically every college home economics program, and nearly every high school provides some kind of supervised experience with preschool children in connection with courses in child care, child development, home management, personal and family relationships, or general home economics.

The principal recipients of grants to organizations for the expansion and improvement of their work in parent and family life education were the American Association of University Women, the American Home Economics Association, and the Child Study Association of America.

These were successful investments. The Child Study Association used its grants to lay a firm foundation for national leadership. Its work has reflected, through the

years, a deepening interest in psychiatric theory, and has shown the close interrelationship between parent, family, and mental health education. The American Association of University Women still gives consultant service to branches wanting help with projects in early childhood education. The grants to the American Home Economics Association turned out to be trend setting. Through the projects these made possible, the family orientation of home economics became firmly established. The outlines of a new professional field—family life education—began to appear, an interdisciplinary field in which home economics would have a significant place.

THE NATIONAL COUNCIL OF PARENT EDUCATION

The centralizing mechanism set up under Spelman auspices was the National Council of Parent Education. This consisted of a small staff and a board of directors which included such leaders in education, social work, and the social sciences as Lawrence K. Frank, Sidonie Matsner Gruenberg, Eduard Lindeman, George D. Stoddard, William Heard Kilpatrick, and Edna Noble White.

The council worked for more sound research in child growth and development and family life; better interpretation and wider dissemination of research findings; more interdisciplinary consultation in regard to policies, programs, and problems; and better communication among practitioners throughout the field. One of its most influential projects was the publication of the journal *Parent Education,* edited by Ruth Kotinsky. The five volumes that appeared "remain the primary repository of theoretical writings in the field of parent education, and the articles are as timely for the problems of today as for those of 20 years ago" (Brim, 1959, p. 334). Among the other council publications were a *Handbook for Parent Education Leaders,* one of the first of its kind, and two research monographs which have become classics: *The Field of Parent Education: A Survey from the Viewpoint of Research,* by Helen Leland Witmer (1934), and *Can Parents Educate One Another?* by Mary Shirley (1938), a study prompted by the still-debated question of lay versus professional group leadership.

In 1933, the council initiated an experiment of unusual interest in cooperation with the Works Progress Administration of the federal government. The WPA nursery school project had already been started, and qualified women were needed in preschool and other child care centers to help parents with problems of child rearing and homemaking. The National Council of Parent Education volunteered to arrange for their training, if WPA would recruit persons who could be prepared to meet this emergency. This seems to have been the first large-scale effort on behalf of parents in low-income or no-income families.

The program spread so rapidly that by 1934 more than 20 state departments of education had employed professionally trained workers to supervise WPA parent education activities. As the national economy straightened out, public support for these programs was gradually withdrawn, but many of the women who had found much-needed employment in them went on to distinguished careers in the various helping professions.

The National Council of Parent Education was well accepted by other agencies. It was fully used as a clearing house and consultation center, and the interprofessional conferences it organized performed a valuable integrative function. In 1938, however, the fund supporting it was dissolved and the council went out of existence. With it went the hope of establishing parent education as a separate field of professional specialization by means of strong central leadership. Intensive efforts were made to replace the council with a voluntary National Committee for Parent Education, but money enough to really activate this was never forthcoming. It merged in 1948 with the Parent Education Section of the National Conference (now the Council) on Family Relations, which is today included in a Section on Special Emphases.

Lack of money is, of course, not the only reason why parent education has become increasingly multiprofessional since 1938. The National Council of Parent Education itself encouraged this trend by stimulating an interest in education for parenthood in a wide variety of cooperating organizations, institutions, and disciplines. Each of these began to look more closely at the needs of parents, from the standpoint of its own professional orientation and practical experience, in order to define more precisely its unique contribution to American family living.

Partly because an increasing number of social agencies became interested in education as a supplemental approach to casework in family rehabilitation, and partly because parent educators themselves discovered that parents could not be abstracted from their family settings for educational purposes, parent education has tended to merge with the broader field of family life education.

ADVANCES IN THE BEHAVIORAL SCIENCES

There have been many significant developments in education for family living in the United States, and elsewhere, since 1940. Some of these are advances in the behavioral sciences; some are new experiments in cooperative programming; some are new educational projects.

Among the theories that have had a strong influence in recent years on practice and research in the family field are the concept of the family cycle as presented by Reuben Hill and Evelyn Millis Duvall at the National Conference on Family Life in 1948; Erik Erikson's theory of personality development, elaborated for the Fact-Finding Committee of the Midcentury White House Conference on Children and Youth

(Witmer & Kotinsky, 1952); Moreno's sociometry (1953); Rogers' non-directive counseling (1942); and the theories of group therapy developed by Slavson (1956), Ackerman (1958), and others. The National Training Laboratory in Group Development was opened at Bethel, Maine, in 1947, by Lippitt, Bradford, and their co-workers (Lippitt, 1950). This gave tremendous impetus to the further study of group dynamics, a field for research in which a great deal of interest had already been generated by Kurt Lewin's creative thinking about the nature of group processes.

NEW EXPERIMENTS IN COOPERATIVE PROGRAMMING

There are now a number of research and training centers specializing in family studies. In several universities, notably Teachers College at Columbia University and Florida State University, interdepartmental programs of family life education have been introduced. At Brigham Young University, a College of Family Living has recently been established. A pilot project, the Minnesota Family Study Center, was initiated at the University of Minnesota in 1957, with private funds, "to strengthen family life research and instruction" (Hill, 1962). This is under the direction of Reuben Hill, and is now "clearly established as an operational entity within the university structure" (Hill, 1962). Important studies of family problems are made by research specialists employed by trade unions, as a basis for programs of legislation and social action.

Outstanding among the independent centers for research and training in the family field are the Merrill-Palmer Institute of Detroit, opened in 1920 under private endowment, with Edna Noble White as director; the American Institute of Family Relations in Los Angeles, founded by Paul Popenoe in 1930; and the Family Institute set up in New York City in 1960 by Nathan Ackerman. This last is the heart of a comprehensive psychiatric program for the study of family stresses. Its purpose is to promote family health and prevent family illness by helping families to achieve healthier forms of family interaction.

An interesting group of new national organizations consists of associations formed by parents themselves to meet their own special needs. Among these are the American Council of Parent Cooperatives (see pp. 845–846), the National Association for Retarded Children, and Parents Without Partners, an organization which brings together in discussion groups parents who are rearing children without the help of a mate and who feel the need for consultation and exchange of experiences with other mothers and fathers in similar situations.

NEW VENTURES IN EDUCATION

In several states, there are strong state-wide programs of parent education. In Michigan, for example, the state department of mental health conducts a three-year training program for leaders of parent groups. The "graduates" have formed an organization known as Parent Education Associates and are taking major responsibility throughout the state for the recruitment of qualified volunteers for training and service.

In churches of every denomination, interest in education for parenthood and family living is expressed in a rich variety of activities. Today, there are few congregations without classes, group meetings, and/or special programs on family life themes for parents and adolescents. Materials and guidance for these are usually available from national church offices, such as the Board of Education of the Methodist Church, the Family Life Bureau of the National Catholic Welfare Conference (see pp. 854–855), and the National Council of Churches (see pp. 857–859).

A significant feature of this emphasis on family guidance is the increasing extent to which religion is asking for service from science in the form of research. Two examples of important current studies to strengthen programs of action are the long-range, cooperative Character Research Project of Union College, involving scores of participating families (Eward & Ligon, 1962), and the nationwide study of American Protestant family life conducted by the Board of Christian Education of the now United Presbyterian Church in the United States of America (Fairchild & Wynn, 1961).

Local projects throughout the United States give parent and family life education the community anchorage so essential to the vitality of any national movement. A census of these has never been taken but several of them are widely known. The Association for Family Living in Chicago, founded in 1925, is an educational social service agency, the purpose of which is to help parents rear emotionally healthy children. Its work includes study group leadership, individual counseling, the selection and distribution of educational materials, and extensive participation in community activities. It reaches parents in high and low, as well as middle-income, groups and does considerable work with families in housing projects.

The Clara Elizabeth Fund for Maternal Health is a community family life program established in Flint, Michigan, in 1937, with the support of a grant by William Knudsen, then president of General Motors. It works closely with other local agencies, helping to strengthen families in the city and county of Flint through the enrichment and coordination of educational and other services available to them. David Treat became the first director and continued to give leadership in that capacity for more than 26 years.

The program started with an emphasis on education for expectant parents. Knowing, however, that preparation for parenthood is a long growth process and that attitudes toward, and beliefs about marriage, child-bearing, child-rearing, and family living are forming during all of the years before marriage, Mr. Treat and his associates soon began to add to the classes in prenatal care courses in family life education for children, older youth, and young adults. In 1963, the program included such varied activities as parent cooperative nursery groups, parent-child reproduction classes, growth and development classes in junior high school, family living classes in ninth and twelfth grades, a family living course in the junior college, study groups for engaged couples, as well as classes for husbands and wives expecting babies.

The fund maintains a well-equipped center for teaching, counseling, and demonstration, where most of the work with out-of-school youth and adults is carried on. More than 5,500 parents and children attended the parent-child reproduction classes during the school year 1962–1963. In this same year, 3,338 students were enrolled in classes in the schools taught by specialists from the fund. All courses for school children are held in the schools, except for the class in reproduction. For this, the pupils come to the center. Through teaching, counseling, and personal service, the expectant parent program now reaches most of the families in Flint having babies in any given year. Although the Clara Elizabeth Fund for Maternal Health is a local organization, its work has influenced developments in family life education in many places.

Community family life education in St. Louis and St. Louis County, Missouri, has several unusual features (Gildea, 1959). It is not one but many programs, closely related to each other, and informally coordinated through consultation and joint planning by the agencies involved. Leadership is given by five strategic organizations: the St. Louis County Health Department, the Mental Health Association of St. Louis, the Family and Children's Service of Greater St. Louis, the Social Health Association of Greater St. Louis, and the Board of Education of the City of St. Louis.

The Mental Health Association, formed some time ago by the merger of the Mental Hygiene Society and the St. Louis Council of Parent Education, has four sectors in its present program: mental health education for parents of normal children of school age, school services, child guidance clinics, and residential treatment services. The Social Health Association works with teachers, school administrators, and parents to provide programs for parents of young children, materials and guidance for teen-age groups, workshops and conferences for professional personnel and, for the public, courses in family life education, discussion groups in churches, camps, and recreation centers. Its emphasis is on sex education for marriage, parenthood, home and family living.

Family and Children's Service provides the usual skilled social work counseling services for families with problems of unhappy marriage, difficult parent-child relationships, school problems, and poor work adjustment. In addition, it conducts an extensive preventive program of family education through mass meetings, conferences, institutes, and small discussion groups. A unique feature of its program is the generous cooperation it receives from certain businesses and industries.

The Divisions of School Mental Health and Research and Development of the St. Louis County Health Department play a leading role in the development of the program as a whole. They consult with other agencies in the various projects, and assist with the planning and implementation of research to meet program needs, especially the need for continuous evaluation (Glidewell, 1960). The Pupil Welfare and Adjustment Division of the St. Louis Board of Education is in touch with both home and school. Although most of its work is with youngsters, one of its major goals is to help parents and teachers gain a better understanding of children and of the ways in which they influence children's behavior. Research is one of the functions of the division, which recently made and published an interesting study of parental attitudes toward school attendance (BOE, St. Louis, 1962).

Public schools in many cities offer programs of parent education. Kansas City, Missouri, for example, has had one for a long time. In 1935, there were 18 of these directed by full-time specialists who were attached, in most cases, to the office of the superintendent. Today, the ways in which this work is related to the total school program are more varied. Sometimes parent education is assigned to adult education, sometimes to vocational home economics, sometimes to early childhood education. Group activities at the elementary level are usually carried on in cooperation with PTA's.

New Trends in Teaching Materials

A steady flow of materials has fed the stream of the parent and family life education movement since its very early days. The popular magazines have more or less regular contributions from such eminent authorities as Dr. Benjamin Spock, Margaret Mead, David Mace, and Evelyn and Sylvanus Duvall. There are few daily newspapers that do not carry syndicated columns of advice on child guidance and family relationships. Pamphlets on these subjects are so numerous that the Mental Health Materials Center of New York has set up a screening service. Small collections of selected items are sent to subscribers four or five times a year. This is called the Human Relations Aids Packet Service. The paperback libraries now include many excellent books, both fiction and non-fiction, dealing with family life.

Three sets of special-purpose materials have been widely used in recent years: (a) "Plays for Family Living" were originally produced by the American Theatre Wing but are now distributed by the Family Service Association of America. Most of them are written by Nora Stirling. Each one is built around a familiar problem in family relationships. Under certain conditions, these plays are available to study groups and for special meetings to stimulate and guide discussion.

(b) Loyd W. Rowland, Director of the Louisiana Mental Health Association, has prepared a series of letters to parents, originally intended for state distribution, which has now become internationally famous as the *Letters of Pierre the Pelican*. They are mailed at regular intervals to expectant parents and to parents of babies and young children. This material has been translated into several foreign languages and, since 1959, has been especially successful in West Berlin, Germany.

(c) The Parent Education Project of the University of Chicago was organized in 1953, supported as an experimental program by grants from the Fund for Adult Education until 1961, and carried since then by the American Foundation for Continuing Education. The materials developed by the project provide a course outline in child development and guidance, with basic readings and reference lists prepared by Ethel Kawin. They were tried out by approximately 1,500 study-discussion groups in the United States and Canada before being made generally available through publication in a four-volume series entitled *Parenthood in a Free Nation* (Kawin, 1963). These groups were sponsored by universities and colleges, public schools and their PTA's, mental health associations, agricultural extension services, family service agencies, adult education centers, churches, religious education organizations, and other community agencies.

This has been the long view of the stream of activities in education for parenthood and family living which bubbled up from countless small grass-roots sources into a national professional movement still highly dependent on lay cooperation. The tide of interest and effort has ebbed and flowed, but it has never run dry, and today is reaching new heights as the United States is being asked to distill and share its experiences in parent and family life education with countries around the world where families are feeling the impact of rapid social change (Stern, 1960).

SOME PROGRAMS IN OTHER COUNTRIES

The close connection between family, community, and national welfare has never been more evident than at the present time, when differences in standards of family living within and between countries are giving rise to acute national and international problems. Most of the governments concerned are taking drastic steps to reduce the tensions created by these discrepancies through reforms of various kinds: the redistribution of land, vast land reclamation and irrigation projects to increase the food supply, the building of new low-cost housing, rapid industrialization to spread employment, programs to combat major health hazards.

In many critical situations, remedial programs big enough to make a real impact require such vast expenditures of money and other resources that the countries involved cannot afford to undertake them alone. International cooperation in one of its many forms then becomes a necessity.

Governments not so gravely threatened are in a better position to utilize the slower processes of cultural evolution to safeguard their family values in their own culturally acceptable ways. In general, they use one or more of four approaches: (a) long-range government action by decree or social legislation, (b) education, (c) the encouragement of family initiative, and (d) emergency aid. The following programs fall, more or less, into one or more of these categories.

Programs for Families in Transition in Morocco

The Royal Kingdom of Morocco is a newly independent nation with an ancient civilization, which many different ethnic groups have helped to create. It is, however, a young country. More than half of its people are under 20 years of age. The streets of the cities teem with children, and the rate of population increase is one of the highest in the world.

The typical Moroccan family in the past has been the extended family. Now the old system is breaking down.

Young people . . . are leaving the villages in ever-increasing numbers to look for work in the cities or on the roads, dams, power plants, schools, harbor facilities, and airfields now under construction in many places. Their going weakens the solidarity of the tribal family. The gulf between the generations widens. There develops a loss of respect for parental authority, a lessening of parental supervision. Children and young boys and girls are having many new kinds of experiences and opportunities for education which their parents do not share. Parents, however, must not be allowed to abdicate, because [they are the child's first, most natural and most important teachers. As long as they are able to function to this role], the family remains the chief stabilizing influence in the process of cultural change (Brown, 1963, pp. 100–101).

To help families meet the requirements of the unfamiliar environments in which most of them are now living, the Moroccan government is developing a broad program of family assistance which includes new legislation, new opportunities for the education and advancement of women, and a strong emphasis on parent education. Services are keyed to the needs of young families because there are so many of them, and because they are probably the age group best able to make maximum use of the resources provided for them.

The permanent base of the Moroccan family is Moslem law, and recent legislative changes are in no sense a departure from this. The Statute of Personal Law enacted in 1958 is a thoughtful attempt to "adapt intelligently the riches of traditional law to the needs of modern life" (cited by Zeghari, 1962, p. 36). The first article of the new statute is concerned with the marriage contract. One of its major purposes is to strengthen the mother's position in the

family, and, consequently, the mother-child relationship. It requires mutual consent, limits the right of fathers to interfere, raises the age of marriage to 18 for men and 15 for girls, limits the husband's right to repudiate his wife, and considerably reduces polygamy.

There are also new laws to protect the family:

. . . the employment in industry of women and children is controlled, certain social welfare measures have been introduced to cover hardship in cases of disablement and the death of parents, family allowances are available to assist those in the lower income groups. Three-hundred-thousand laborers benefit from these measures which have only recently been put into effect and which can only be extended as the prosperity of the country increases (Zeghari, 1962, p. 37).

In recent years the Moroccan woman has taken an increasingly important place in national affairs and community life. There is, therefore, an urgent need to provide more and better opportunities for her education. This is being done through the development of programs of basic adult education, and through the organization of rural centers for women. The basic education program includes courses in the reading and writing of Arabic, and the teaching of domestic science (cooking, sewing, embroidery, infant and child care). The rural centers are, in reality, community workshops equipped with sewing machines, laundry and ironing facilities, sanitary equipment, and other necessary teaching aids and materials.

Leaders for these programs are being readied at a new national training center. Young women prepared there go out into the country to teach modern methods of hygiene and home management in rural communities. This part of the work is growing but is still handicapped by the extreme shortage of qualified leaders. Only a small proportion of Moroccan girls are yet in school.

The new parent education projects have

two major purposes: to help mothers and fathers with problems of child rearing that are strange to them, and to win parental understanding and support for changes in the educational system of the country. The government is expecting the schoolteachers to carry the main responsibility for parent education. Inservice and preservice courses are being developed to give them a new understanding of the dynamics of the parent-child relationship and of the possibilities in home-school cooperation. Courses are offered for parents at the People's Education Centers which deal with problems of daily family life, family finances, the parental role and how to prepare for it, parent-teacher teamwork in childhood education. The organization of parent-teacher associations is being encouraged.

Parent education is an important part of the work of the neighborhood youth centers of the High Commission for Youth and Sport. These centers provide wholesome recreational and vocational activities for unorganized youth. The leaders are responsible for bringing parents into the life of the centers, winning their confidence, and helping them to understand their children's needs. The guides furnished by the High Commission for the work with parents reflect a knowledge of group dynamics, and special training is provided for the teachers and youth leaders at the centers who work with parent groups.

The aim of the entire family adjustment program in Morocco is not to westernize Moroccan family life but to help young and old alike adapt themselves quickly to the modern, technical society which is growing up around them, while at the same time remaining faithful to the best traditions of the past (Zeghari, 1962).

THE GERMAN FAMILY "PACKAGE"

By 1962, 17 or more countries of western Europe had set up departments of government to coordinate their services to families. The program of family assistance developed by the Republic of West Germany since 1951 incorporates most of the benefits offered, to a greater or lesser degree, by other governments in that part of the world.

The damage done to the German family during the National Socialist regime was both physical and psychological. Millions of husbands and fathers were killed or imprisoned. Countless homes were destroyed or so badly shattered that families had to separate, finding shelter where they could. The economic system collapsed, wiping out incomes, savings, and insurance for all except the most privileged members of the National Socialist Party. More insidiously destructive, perhaps, were the results of the Nazi drive to alienate parents and children. Thousands of young people detached themselves from what was left of family and community life, leaving a stunned older generation to cope as it could with the wave of refugees from conquered German territories to the east—9 million people to be resettled in already devastated territory.

The upturn began with currency reform in 1948, but special family legislation had to wait until the framework for the new government was completed. The first formal step in the development of the family program was the establishment in October, 1953, of the Federal Ministry for Family Affairs. In 1957, the Office of Youth Affairs was transferred from the Ministry of the Interior to the Family Ministry, which then became and is now the Ministry for Family and Youth Affairs. It has major responsibility for promoting and coordinating government programs affecting families, but since six other ministries are also involved, there are still administrative problems to be solved.

The benefits now legally provided for German families, and paid for, for the most part, from public funds, include family allowances, tax relief, special rates for family transportation, special services for mothers traveling with children, subsidies for family vacations, rest homes for mothers, special arrangements for financing home building at low cost, and premiums for systematic saving, with special advantages for engaged and young married couples (Deutsche Bundesregierung, 1961).

Bills to further liberalize legislation providing payment of wages during illness, health insurance, and family allowances were before the German Parliament in 1963 and their passage seemed assured. With the enactment of these laws, "the free part of Germany will have completed the biggest stride forward in social welfare since the days of Bismarck" (Ger. Fed. Gov't, 1963, p. 4).

Funds for payment of these different benefits are made available to local authorities through cooperative arrangements between federal and state governments. Private social organizations receive government subsidies for performing many of the services provided through social legislation. The largest of these are Catholic and Protestant welfare associations. This means that many of the programs function in an ideological framework. The national nonsectarian agency conducting extensive programs of social welfare and family education is the Worker's Welfare Association (*Arbeiterwohlfahrt*). This was originally an arm of the Social Democratic Party but is now an independent organization.

Long before the war, there were schools for mothers (*Mütterschulen*) in Germany, centers where mothers who had or were expecting babies could receive instruction in their care. This program suffered during the war but is growing again. Many child guidance clinics were opened after 1945 with the help of the British and American military governments, and this movement is now strong. There is a new and growing interest in family research, and a small but promising young German Federation for Mental Health. Most public schools have parent-teacher councils, and parent education is increasingly included in adult education programs. Intensive efforts have been and are still being made to increase the number of social workers trained in the newer concepts of public welfare and family casework, and Germany is active again in international organizations concerned with family and child care.

PARENT EDUCATION IN FRANCE

One of the strongest centers for parent education in western Europe is the School for Parents and Teachers (L'École des Parents et des Éducateurs) in Paris, directed by M. André Isambert. It was founded in 1929 by a woman, Mme. Vérine, who believed that French parents should have an opportunity to prepare themselves for parenthood, especially for the task of guiding the sex development of their children. Since World War II, this school has become the model for similar organizations in a number of French-speaking European countries.

The present aims of the school are: "To re-establish a modern basis for the role and authority of parents; to choose the most useful knowledge to communicate to them; to develop, but without worrying or discouraging, a sense of responsibility" (L'École, 1960, p. 4).

In recent years, there has been in France, as in the United States, an increasing sensitivity to the subtleties of parent education: the hazards of giving advice, the danger of complicating personal problems by offering learning experiences that parents are not ready to use. To minimize such possibilities, the School for Parents has added to the dissemination of psychological information about child and family a personal service which brings parents and adolescents into direct relation with the parent educator. To foster this relationship, the school is stressing the use of educational methods, such as group discussion and the individual interview, which encourage the exchange of ideas and experiences between expert and parent (Isambert, 1960).

Courses are offered for young people on problems of emotional development and personal adjustment. Discussion groups for teenagers are organized in cooperation with schools, apprenticeship centers, recreation centers, homes for young workers, and social centers. However, direct aid to parents is still the school's most important activity. This assistance is given through consultations, small meetings, discussion groups, film showings, large meetings and conferences, reading materials, and special television, radio, and screen productions (L'École, 1960–1961).

The school maintains a large leadership training program, not to build up a corps of specialists but to increase the skill of people working with parents in all the helping professions. Each year it arranges a basic course of lectures at the Faculty of Medicine of the University of Paris for those who wish to keep in touch with advancing knowledge in the scientific fields that contribute to education for parenthood. Seminars are also conducted in the Faculty of Letters and Humanities of the Sorbonne. The publications of the school include a *Monthly Bulletin* (L'École des Parents) and *The Family Group* (Le Groupe Familial), a quarterly journal of research in the psychology and sociology of family life.

About 70 associations for parent education in France are more or less closely connected with the School for Parents and depend upon its leadership. Working relations are cultivated with all major private and public family-serving agencies and organizations, particularly the government Bureau of Family Allowances, which considers parent education an important part of its work. The school meets the larger part of its expenses through its own activities. It also receives subventions from the Ministry of Health and Population, the Ministry of National Education, the Youth Commission, the Bureau of Family Allowances, the Social Security Administration, and the city of Paris.

In 1956, the School for Parents brought together at Sèvres about 50 French organi-zations engaged in parent education to find a way of coordinating their activities. A group was formed for study and communication. The Schools for Parents of Belgium and Switzerland joined this group in 1958, and a Permanent Committee for the Coordination of Schools for Parents using the French language was established. In 1961, this association took on a more international character, receiving into membership groups from countries of western Europe, eastern Europe, Africa, and Latin America, including Italy, the Federal Republic of West Germany, the Netherlands, Poland, Yugoslavia, Turkey, Greece, Morocco, Tunisia, Senegal, Cameroon, Brazil, Argentina, Uruguay, and Venezuela. One can now foresee that this grouping could serve as a basis for an international union of schools for parents.

THE PECKHAM EXPERIMENT IN ENGLAND

Unless families have an inherent capacity for self-organization and self-development, the phrase "helping families to help themselves" has relatively little meaning. There have not been many serious attempts to test this hypothesis, but among them the London Pioneer Health Centre, more widely known as the Peckham Experiment, holds a place of special importance. Although this was a casualty of World War II and its aftermath in Great Britain, analysis of the records is still yielding valuable results (Pearse & Crocker, 1945).

The purpose of the project was to demonstrate that no man is, in fact, an island; that the family, not the individual, is the functional unit of society; that the mental and physical health of each family member ultimately depends on the well-being of the family as a whole; that given the right opportunities, families can generate health through the activities they undertake spontaneously to meet their own creative needs.

The experiment began modestly in the London borough of Peckham in 1927, when a small group of parents asked a staff of research-minded medical specialists to tell them what they could do to ensure the health of their children. The doctors offered to provide health guidance on a group basis if enough families could be found in the neighborhood to form a family club, with a small weekly membership fee. Within three years, 112 families, with a total of more than 400 members, had joined in the venture. A little house was rented to serve as a consultation center and clubhouse.

The only major requirement for membership in the plan was a periodic health examination at the center for everyone in every family belonging to the club. These examinations led to the early detection and treatment of many illnesses, but families continued to have about as much sickness as before. Apparently, health was a positive state of well-being to be sought as an end in itself.

The staff had not expected this finding. It showed the need for a wider range of activities for the cultivation of health than the pilot project afforded. The first small health center was, therefore, closed, and a group of parents and scientists, led by Dr. G. Scott Williamson and Dr. Innes H. Pearse, began a seven-year period of preparation for the new plan. "It was to be a health centre to cater for 2,000 families, in which were to be offered consultative services as before, and in which the member-families would find equipment for the exercise of capacities for which there was little or no possible outlet in the ordinary circumstances of their lives" (Pearse & Crocker, 1945, p. 13). Funds for the experiment were raised by private subscription.

The center was again located in Peckham, a section roughly representing a cross-section of the British nation, from the standpoint of both occupation and income. It was again presented to the neighborhood as a family club, and all families were invited to join who lived within a radius of about a mile, the distance a mother could comfortably push a baby carriage. There was a small family membership fee, and a moderate charge for each special activity in which members chose to participate.

When a family decided to join, appointments were made for an "enrollment talk" with one of the doctors, who explained the requirements: First, the "overhaul" to estimate the physical efficiency of the family and all its members for individual, family, and social life. Second, the family consultation, with all members of the family present, to discuss the findings of the "overhaul." Third, the unrestricted use of the center as a club by all family members.

The building itself facilitated this program in innumerable and ingenious ways. It consisted of three spacious floors supported by pillars, with a big swimming pool in the center. The outer walls and the few partitions inside were of glass so that everything going on in the building could be seen from almost anywhere. When the center opened, it contained only a few books, a billiard table, games for children, a record player, and one or two pianos. There was no receptionist, no social director, no program. Members were told that the club was theirs, to use and to enjoy.

In four and a half years, the place was transformed. Mothers, babies, school children, fathers, grandparents, adolescents, found there a setting in which, together or separately, they could be happily busy. The shyest of families might sit for a while in the cafeteria, watching a dance or a play in rehearsal, fun in the swimming pool, a basketball game, a father and son making a kitchen cabinet in one of the workshops. Sooner or later, most of them found themselves involved. Leaders emerged, as they were needed, and a pattern of organization evolved that was orderly, appropriate, and efficient. As groups set up projects, they raised the money for the equipment they needed.

The membership finally included about 1,600 families, 400 short of the hoped for 2,000, but enough to sustain an extremely varied program maintained almost wholly on the self-service principle by the members themselves. On a Saturday night there were often 700 to 1,000 people at the center, all busily carrying on their chosen activities. Although children were free to go off with their agemates, families came as families and enjoyed themselves as families. This was an attitude encouraged by the medical staff, who felt that children learned best when they worked and played side by side with parents who shared feelings and thoughts with them, and provided models of adult behavior.

When the war came, the center activities were suspended. The building was used as a factory and the swimming pool was filled with concrete. The area was heavily bombed, families moved away or were evacuated. At the close of the war, every possible effort was made to revive the project, at the insistence of the remaining member families. For a time, it seemed as if this effort might succeed but, in the end, the necessary supplemental funds could not be obtained from private sources, and the national plans for health and housing limited the scope of large, independent, cooperative family projects.

The French Family Movement

There are no groups in the United States exactly like the family associations of western Europe. These are organizations formed by heads of families who have banded together to gain and maintain social and economic security for their families. They are something like trade unions and something like lobbies. Their function is to represent families before their governments, and to work with other agencies toward the improvement of conditions affecting family life.

The French family movement dates from the end of the nineteenth century, when the first family associations were founded. These were associations of Protestant families. The character and purpose of such groups were defined in basic legislation enacted in 1901. Between 1910 and 1939, the movement gained momentum through the formation of several large federations of family-oriented organizations, among them the Catholic family associations, the Women's Civic and Social Union, the School for Parents and Teachers, and the People's Family Movement. The work of this period was climaxed by the proclamation, in Lille, in 1920, of a Declaration of Family Rights. In 1939, the government established a High Commission for Population, which issued an official Family Code.

All of this early, organized family action was motivated by a growing concern about the birth rate and the demographic problems connected with its decline. Between World Wars I and II, the emphasis shifted. Economic conditions were making it increasingly difficult for families to assume the responsibilities normally expected of them. There were no wage differentials in favor of men with many dependents, adequate housing was extremely hard to find, and employment was irregular. Urban and rural families were suffering alike from lack of food, clothing, and proper shelter. Before much could be done to meet any of these needs, World War II brought utter desolation to millions of homes.

Fully aware of the urgent need to protect and strengthen the nation's most precious asset, its family life, the French government decided to create a Ministry for Family Affairs. This was accomplished on June 5, 1940, just nine days before the fall of Paris. Soon afterward, associations within the family movement set up centers for the coordination of their work, one in each of the provinces (Departements), and two at the national level, one in the free and one in the occupied zone.

Under the German occupation, there continued to be official action on behalf of families, but the administrative arrangements for this were not in keeping with the French tradition of free association. The Family Ministry became a secretariat, then a commissariat, with regional deputies appointed to conserve family interests. In 1943, under a new law (le Loi Gounot of 1942), a huge national plan for organizing and controlling the French family movement was put into effect. Each canton or commune was allowed one association, which would speak for all of its families. These local groups were represented in departmental unions and linked, through these, with a national union at the summit. This machinery turned out to be cumbersome, and provided few opportunities for the free expression of family opinion or the exercise of family initiative.

In March, 1945, the Loi Gounot was rescinded, and an order proclaimed by General Charles de Gaulle restored to the French Family Movement much of its former autonomy. As soon as France was liberated, steps to revitalize this program were undertaken with enthusiasm. The National Centers for Coordination of Family Activities were replaced by the present National Union of Family Associations (Union Nationale des Associations Familiales). The most far-reaching changes, however, took place at the local level. Instead of the one-to-a-canton (or commune) plan, families were now free to organize as many, and as many different kinds of private local associations as they wished. There continued to be departmental unions of family associations, but affiliation with these was not obligatory. At departmental and national levels, the unions retained their semi-official status.

Family associations already established were urged to assist with the formation of new ones. Handbooks explaining the movement, the laws relating to it, and the procedures to be followed in setting up new groups were made available to local leaders. A great deal of emphasis was placed on the right of each organization to develop its own program within the ideological and legal framework of the movement as a whole. "In a country as diversified as France," wrote the author of one of these

manuals, "solutions are nowhere identical. There is little in common between the founding of a family association in a crowded quarter of a great city, and in one of our tiny villages" (Petitjean, 1946, p. 10).

This is, essentially, the pattern of organization of the family movement in France today (UNAF, 1963). Family affairs are handled for the government in the Ministry of Health and Population. The National Union of Family Associations, with its departmental, communal, and cantonal subdivisions, is the central body representing families. It advises the public authorities with respect to the wishes and needs of families; sees that delegates are appointed or proposed to the various commissions, assemblies, or bodies set up by the state, the departments, or the communes; makes sure that families are officially represented when the public authorities are considering matters of concern to them; provides needed services for families, whether these are requested by the government or not.

The services rendered are of a highly practical nature. For example, some family associations provide a homemaker service very similar to our own. Competent women are engaged to look after children and do the housework in emergencies, when the mother is ill or absent. It is estimated that, in one recent year, 5,000 of these aides assisted 100,000 mothers in families where there were 400,000 youngsters. Family associations also maintain day nurseries and baby-sitting services. Some of them arrange for the loan of such pieces of household equipment as vacuum cleaners, floor polishers, sewing and knitting machines. No avenues through which family life education can be carried on are neglected (UNAF, n.d.).

Family associations have few membership requirements, but these are specific. Families joining must be French. The husband and wife must be legally married and have, or have had, at least one legitimate or adopted child. They must live or own property in the commune or canton where the association is formed. The family must not have experienced a total breakdown of parental authority, and the father must be a citizen in good standing.

Financial support for family associations in France comes from public or private grants, donations, legacies, cash or reimbursement for services, income from properties owned by the group, and from authorized, organized festivals and exhibitions of activities. These organizations have an abiding sense of their dual responsibilities: to the families who belong and to the state. They work with their member families

to advise them; to group them; to awaken in them the consciousness of their vocation; . . . to prepare the young members for marriage; to create services of mutual help, schools for parents, and services of assistance to mothers. But when they have done all this, the task of the family associations is not finished. They then must turn to the state in order to remind it of the existence of the family group, to request its legislation to take account of the economic situation of the family, to prevent it from interfering with questions and problems which are outside of its competency, to turn to it on behalf of a certain cleanliness in the streets and in the shows, and also to make it hear the voice of the family heads (UNAF, 1947, p. 49).

There is behind all of this intensive effort to stabilize and enrich French family life a great seriousness of purpose. At the inspiring World Congress for Family and Population called in 1947 by the National Union of Family Associations, it was repeatedly pointed out that demographic problems are not the main reason for the measures now being so widely taken to strengthen family life. It is, in the minds of these leaders, a question of social justice, indeed, of necessity, "to serve effectively the cause of the family as an institution" because the fate of mankind is bound up with it (UNAF, 1947, p. 54).

Some Projects Here and There[2]

Many travelers in Pakistan have seen the refugee village built and maintained on the outskirts of Karachi by the All Pakistan Women's Association. Here, in pleasant surroundings, families made homeless in 1947 by the partition of Pakistan and India are earning a living by making the scarves, the woodcarvings, the jewelry, and other native products sold by APWA. In Dacca, there is a nursery school for 300 children established by a member of this organization—a distinguished woman chemist—which has become a center for parent education and the training of girls in child care and homemaking. The first village nursery schools in Egypt were established by a similar group of women.

In Uganda and several other African countries, women from the villages come, with their children, to residential centers for workshops in child care and homemaking. Experimentation with smokeless cook stoves, at table height, to bring food preparation up off the floor, has been an important part of the work in centers of this kind in many places. On another level, a recent seminar in Rangoon, Burma, brought together parents, professional workers, and government officials, to determine "what parents, men and women as individuals, voluntary organizations, local authorities, and government can do for the child to become a useful member of society" (Society for the Improvement of Youths, 1960, p. 1).

[2] The reader will have noticed that there is no reference in this chapter to organizational programs related to family life in the Soviet Union of Socialist Republics or the People's Socialist Republic of China. The materials which might have made it possible to include these programs are either lacking altogether or are too meager to be useful for this purpose. Interesting references in this connection are: Mace, D., & Mace, Vera. Marriage in Communist China, in *Marriage: East & West*. Garden City, N.Y.: Doubleday, 1960, pp. 303–326; Mace, D., & Mace, Vera. *The Soviet Family*. Garden City, N.Y.: Doubleday, 1963; Kharchev, A. G., Problems of the Family and Their Study in the USSR. *International Social Science Journal: Changes in the Family*, 1962, (14), 539–549.

The government of India is, at present, concentrating its efforts to raise standards of family living throughout the country on two fronts: family planning and community development. Less extensive family-related programs are numerous, however, in the different Indian states. In 1960, the Indian Institute of Social Welfare and Business Management in Calcutta opened a guidance clinic for emotionally disturbed children, with special advisory services for parents, the first, it is hoped, of a network of such clinics throughout the country (Indian Institute of Social Welfare, 1962).

The list of such "firsts" is almost inexhaustible. In Japan, for another illustration, the farm home demonstration worker on her green bicycle is joyously welcomed by rural housewives who have learned from her how to perform their tasks more easily and efficiently. The same thing is happening in places as far apart as the barrios of the Philippines and the villages of Turkey. The best of these efforts are indigenous. They heavily underscore the role of women in family conservation and development, and the need for giving high priority to women's education in all present and future schemes for national, social, economic, and political development.

INTERNATIONAL PROGRAMS

As groups in different parts of the world discover their common interests and concerns, they tend to join forces, to become members of existing international associations or to form new ones. It does not follow, however, that all organizations active in more than one country are "international" in the same way. Some are essentially national with foreign affiliates. Some are national voluntary agencies conducting cooperative programs in foreign countries. Some are intergovernmental structures, carefully set up to give equal representation to all member nations. Some are international federations of voluntary agencies with programs that are regional or worldwide in scope.

A fairly careful review of directories listing these many different kinds of programs organized for humanitarian purposes reveals only one international body devoted exclusively to family welfare. This is the International Union of Family Organizations (L'Union Internationale des Organismes Familiaux), which was founded at the World Congress for Family and Population convened in Paris, in 1947, by the French Union of Family Associations (L'Union Nationale des Associations Familiales). In 1948, the International Union was granted consultative status, under Category B, by the United Nations Economic and Social Council. It has since established consultative relations with UNESCO, UNICEF, the United Nations Food and Agriculture Organization (FAO), and with the Council of Europe. It has also been placed on the special register of cooperating non-governmental organizations by the International Labor Office (UIOF, 1959).

The headquarters and administrative offices of the union are in Paris. It has a membership of about 250 organizations, well distributed throughout the world. Among these are family associations and family movements, parent and parent-teacher organizations, women's groups and mothers' associations, child welfare, marriage counseling and marriage guidance groups, schools for parents, social work councils and associations, research centers, social security administrations, national health insurance offices, housing institutes, cultural and educational associations, family holiday organizations, population and family institutes, ministries and ministerial departments.

The work of this organization is carried on by a secretariat, and by permanent commissions and study groups. There are Commissions on Family Housing, Family Standards of Living, Parent-Teacher Relations, and Marriage and Marriage Guidance. Permanent study groups have been set up to deal with family movements, family action among the working classes, special problems of rural families, the family and social techniques, and European problems.

A basic purpose of the union is to establish a strong link between public and private organizations concerned with family welfare. The number of governmental bodies and public services dealing with social and family problems has greatly increased throughout the world, and these agencies are in a strategic position to help determine standards of family living by influencing legislative, social, and educational measures affecting family life. They strengthen the union by their activities, their technical knowledge, and the information they provide. In turn, they find in the union a valuable means of maintaining direct contact with families and with experts from voluntary groups working for family welfare.

Although it has only been in existence for a relatively short time, the International Union of Family Organizations has to its credit three particularly interesting and important achievements: (a) It has helped the leaders of the European Community to realize that family welfare is a primary consideration in the building of a strong economy. (b) It has established warm consultative relationships with several of the newly independent African countries facing serious problems of family readjustment. (c) It has formulated a statement of family policy which has universal application and has become the basic program of the union and its member associations. This is called the "Bill of Rights of the Family" and much of its content is an elaboration of those sections of the Universal Declaration of Human Rights of the United Nations which have a family reference.

Each country must interpret the meaning of a document like this in terms of its own cultural realities. In the absence of any other coordinating mechanism, such a statement can be a dynamic, unifying force in the far-reaching movement to strengthen family life which has been outlined in this chapter.

REFERENCES

Ackerman, N. W. *The psychodynamics of family life: diagnosis and treatment of family relationships.* New York: Basic Books, 1958.

American Council of Parent Cooperatives. *The Parent Cooperative.* A newsletter. Indianapolis, Box 40123: Author, 1962. Vol. 5 (3).

American Home Economics Association. *Home economics—new directions: a statement of philosophy and objectives.* Washington, D.C.: Author, 1959.

American Social Health Association. *Programs, services, activities.* New York: Author, n.d. (Brochure.)

Arizona Congress of Parents & Teachers. *Parents are the key.* New York: American Social Health Association, 1961.

Auerbach, Aline B., Frank, Josette, & Wolf, Anna W. M. Sidonie Matsner Gruenberg and the Child Study Association. *Child Stud.,* 1956, 33, 16–25.

Babitz, M. *Handbook on parent education.* (Rev. ed.) Bull. 27 (3). Sacramento, Calif.: State Department of Education, 1958.

Baldwin, Keturah E. *The AHEA saga.* Washington, D.C.: American Home Economics Association, 1949.

Board of Education of the City of St. Louis, Division of Pupil Welfare & Adjustment. *A study of attitudes of parents of children in public elementary schools of St. Louis toward school attendance.* St. Louis: Author, 1962.

Brim, O. G., Jr. *Education for child rearing.* New York: Russell Sage Foundation, 1959.

Brown, Muriel W. *With focus on family living.* Voc. Div. Bull. 249, Home Econ. Educ. Ser. 28, U.S. Office of Education. Washington, D.C.: U.S. Government Printing Office, 1953.

Brown, Muriel W. The "confrontation": a report on the 1962 conference of the International Union of Family Organizations. *Marr. & fam. Living,* 1963, 25, 100–102.

Buchmueller, A. D. The place of parent education in preventive mental health. Paper read at 6th Int. Cong. Ment. Hlth, Paris, 1961.

Cohen, W. J. The new public welfare legislation. Paper read at the conference with state administrators of public welfare, U.S. Dept Hlth, Educ., & Welf., Washington, D.C Sept. 24, 1962.

Cumings, E. C. *The family life program of the American Social Hygiene Association.* New York: American Social Hygiene Association, 1959. (Release.)

Cumings, E. C., & Reed, C. H. Accent on family living: the Rocky Mountain project. *PTA Magazine,* Dec. 1961, pp. 27–30.

Curtis, Bishop W. W. Goals of a family life program. *Catholic fam. Leader,* 1962, 11(1). (Abstr.)

DeBlanc, Msgr. I. A. Serving your family: a report on the work of the National Family Life Bureau. *Grail Magazine,* Feb. 1957, pp. 2–7.

Deutsche Bundesregierung, Bundesministerium fuer Familien und Jugendfragen. Fuer Familie und Jugend: Sonderdruck aus dem Taetigkeitsbericht der Bundesregierung. In *Deutsche Politik, 1961.* Bonn: Author, 1961, pp. 1–19.

Duvall, Evelyn M., & Duvall, S. M. (Eds.) *Sex ways in fact and faith: bases for Christian family policy.* New York: Association Press, 1961.

Eward, Frances, & Ligon, E. M. *Exploring Christian potential. Character research project.* Schenectady, N.Y.: Union College, 1962.

Fairchild, R. W., & Wynn, J. C. *Families in the church: a Protestant survey.* New York: Association Press, 1961.

Fosdick, R. B. *Adventures in giving.* New York: Harper & Row, 1962.

Frankiel, Rita V. *A review of research on parent influences on child personality.* New York: Family Service Association of America, 1959.

General Federation of Women's Clubs. *Facts about the General Federation of Women's Clubs and International Headquarters.* Washington, D.C.: Author, n.d.

General Federation of Women's Clubs, Home Life Department. *To strengthen the arm of liberty.* Washington, D.C.: Author, 1962.

Genné, Elizabeth, & Genné, W. (Eds.) *Christians and the crisis in sex morality.* New York: Association Press, 1961.

Genné, Elizabeth, & Genné, W. *Church family camps and conferences: an administrative and program manual.* Philadelphia: United Church Bookstore, 1962. (a)

Genné, Elizabeth, & Genné, W. (Eds.) *Foundations for Christian family policy.* New York: National Council of the Churches of Christ in the U.S.A., Department of Family Life, 1962. (b)

German Federal Government, Press and Information Office. Parliament gets broad, pioneering social-welfare plan. *The Bulletin: a weekly Survey of German Affairs,* 1963, vol. 11(5).

Gildea, Margaret C.-L. *Community mental health.* Springfield, Ill.: Thomas, 1959.

Glidewell, J. C. (Ed.) *Parental attitudes and child behavior.* Springfield, Ill.: Thomas, 1961.

Grams, A. *Parent education and the behavioral sciences.* Children's Bureau Publ. 379. Washington, D.C.: U.S. Government Printing Office, 1960.

Halpert, H. P. Activities of the National Institute of Mental Health which affect American families. *Marr. & fam. Living,* 1958, 20, 261–269.

Hill, R. *Minnesota Family Study Center: second biennial report, 1960–1961.* Minneapolis: Univer. of Minnesota, 1962.

Indian Institute of Social Welfare & Business Administration. *Child Guidance Centre: first report.* Calcutta: Author, 1962.

Interdepartmental Committee on Children and Youth. *Programs of the federal government affecting children and youth.* Washington, D.C.: U.S. Department of Health, Education, & Welfare, Social Security Administration, Children's Bureau, 1961.

Isambert, A. *L'éducation des parents.* Paris: Presses Universitaires de France, 1960.

Kawin, Ethel. *Parenthood in a free nation: basic readings.* New York: Macmillan, 1963. (a)

Kawin, Ethel. *Parenthood in a free nation: manual for group leaders and participants.* Chicago: Fund for Continuing Education, 1963. (b)

Larson, Neota. Family security under Old-Age and Survivors Insurance. *Marr. & fam. Living,* 1958, 20, 224–232.

L'École des Parents et des Éducateurs. *Qu'est-ce que L'École des Parents?* Paris: Author, 1960–1961.

Lewin, K., & Lewin, Gertrude W. (Eds.) *Resolving social conflicts.* New York: Harper, 1948.

Lippitt, R. *Training in community leadership.* New York: Harper, 1950.

Mead, Margaret. *Male and female.* New York:

Morrow, 1949. Cited by L. Rainwater & Karol K. Weinstein, *And the poor get children*. Chicago: Quadrangle Books, 1960. P. 19.

Moreno, J. *Who shall survive?: foundations of sociometry, psychotherapy, and sociodrama*. (Rev. ed.) New York: Beacon House, 1953.

National Congress of Parents and Teachers. *The parent-teacher organization: its origins and development*. Chicago: Author, 1944.

National Council of Churches. *The National Council of Churches: What it is. What it does*. New York: Author, n.d.

National Council of the Churches of Christ in the U.S.A. *The National Council of Churches: the churches working together for a Christian America*. New York: Author, 1962.

National Social Welfare Assembly. *Service directory of national organizations affiliated and associated with the National Social Welfare Assembly*. (6th ed.) New York: Author, 1961. Pp. 42–43.

National Union of Family Associations. *World congress for family and population*. Paris: Author, 1947. (English trans.)

Overstreet, H., & Overstreet, Bonaro. *Where children come first: a study of the PTA idea*. Chicago: National Congress of Parents & Teachers, 1949.

Paget, N. V. *Family life education—program profiles*. San Bernardino, Calif.: Kendal, 1961.

Pearse, I. H., & Crocker, Lucy H. *The Peckham experiment: a study in the living structure of society*. New Haven: Yale Univer. Press, 1945.

Petitjean, A. *Comment fonder une association de familles*. Paris: L'Édition Sociale Française, 1946.

Planned Parenthood Federation of America. *Birth control services in tax-supported institutions*. New York: Author, 1962.

Planned Parenthood Federation of America. *Birth control, U.S.A.: highlights of the program*. New York: Author, n.d.

Pope, E. V. Extension service programs affecting American families. *Marr. & fam. Living*, 1958, 20, 270–277.

Rogers, C. R. *Counseling and psychotherapy: newer concepts in practice*. Boston: Houghton Mifflin, 1942.

Schorr, A. L. Family policy in the United States. *Int. soc. sci. J.*, 1962, 14, 452–467.

Shirley, Mary. Can parents educate one another?: a study of lay leadership in New York State. *Parent Educ. Monogr. No. 111*. New York: National Council of Parent Education, 1938. (Out of print but available in some large libraries.)

Slavson, S. (Ed.) *The fields of group psychotherapy*. New York: International Univer. Press, 1956.

Society for the Improvement of Youths & the Rangoon Social Service Council. *Report of the seminar on child welfare*. Rangoon: Author, 1960.

Stern, H. H. Parent education: an international survey. *Stud. in Educ., Special Monogr.* Hull, Eng.: Univer. of Hull, & Hamburg, Germany: UNESCO Institute for Education, 1960.

Taylor, Katharine W. *Parent cooperative nursery schools*. New York: Teachers Coll., Columbia Univer., Bureau of Publications, 1954.

Union Internationale des Organismes Familiaux. *Brochure*. Paris: Author, 1959.

Union Nationale des Associations Familiales. *Congrès mondial de la famille et de la population*. Paris: Author, 1947.

Union Nationale des Associations Familiales. *Sommaire*. Paris: Author, 1963.

Union Nationale des Associations Familiales. *Problèmes familiaux—action familiale*. Paris: Author, n.d.

U.S. Department of Health, Education, & Welfare. *Annual report 1961*. Washington, D.C.: U.S. Government Printing Office, 1961.

U.S. Department of Health, Education, & Welfare. *Annual report 1962*. Washington, D.C.: U.S. Government Printing Office, 1962. (a)

U.S. Department of Health, Education, & Welfare. *Background information on the public welfare amendments of 1962*. Advance release. Washington, D.C.: Author, 1962. (b)

U.S. Department of Health, Education, & Welfare, Public Health Service. *Background material concerning the mission and organization of the Public Health Service*. Washington, D.C.: U.S. Government Printing Office, 1963. (a)

U.S. Department of Health, Education, & Welfare. *National Institutes of Health.* Public Health Service Publ. No. 81. Washington, D.C.: U.S. Government Printing Office, rev. 1963. (b)

U.S. Department of the Interior, Office of Education, Vocational Division. *Community programs of family life education from the viewpoint of home economics.* Misc. No. 1983. Washington, D.C.: Author, Nov. 1937. (Mimeographed.)

Wells, Mildred W. *Unity in diversity: the history of the General Federation of Women's Clubs.* Washington, D.C.: General Federation of Women's Clubs, 1953.

Witmer, Helen L. The field of parent education: a survey from the viewpoint of research. *Parent Educ. Monogr. No. 1.* New York: National Council of Parent Education, 1934. (Out of print but available in some libraries.)

Witmer, Helen L., & Kotinsky, Ruth (Eds.) *Personality in the making: the fact-finding report of the Midcentury White House Conference on Children and Youth.* New York: Harper, 1952.

Wolgamot, Irene H. RAD offers opportunities for home economics to contribute to better rural living. *J. home Econ.,* 1963, 55, 184–186.

Zeghari, M. The evolution of the family in newly developing countries. *National Educ.* Special issue regarding the International Conference of Family Associations. Rabat, Morocco: Ministry of Education, Management of Cultural Affairs, 1962. (English trans.)

CHAPTER 21 Family Life Education in America[1]

RICHARD K. KERCKHOFF
Washington School of Psychiatry

Many of the people who taught the first family life courses their schools ever had are teaching similar courses today. It is easy to forget that this is a very young field—a field which is living with its founders. How did the family life education movement begin? Where did it come from?

BEGINNINGS OF THE MOVEMENT

Long before the study of the family reached the sophisticated scientific level represented by much of the work reported in this Handbook, there was recognition of the importance of the family to human beings, and there was even curiosity about the dynamics of family life. There were also plans put forth from time to time to improve family life, usually to create a more ideal state or society.

With the social-cultural upheavals of the nineteenth and twentieth centuries, however, came an intensified recognition of specific inadequacies in American family

life. For example, some beliefs and skills which formerly had been learned in families were no longer being taught there. At the same time, shifts in other social institutions, such as the church and the neighborhood community, were being viewed as problems or problem-creating situations. The result of many of these institutional changes was a loss of social control: parents, religious institutions, and local communities seemed unable, for example, to obtain the same socialized behavior from children as had previously been possible (Brown, 1935).

Other radical changes in the roles of women, in occupational and economic behavior, and in the whole industrialization-urbanization movement let everyone know that the world was not what it had been a few years earlier. Imbued with what some sociologists refer to as a planning ideology, Americans appealed to their schools, legislatures, and other agencies of the state for a return to "old-fashioned sanity" or for the creation of a more ideal situation. Insofar as their unhappiness was directed toward family life, their appeal was creating the American family life education movement.

[1] This chapter focuses upon family life education within the schools of the United States. For treatment of family agencies outside the schools, and family life education in other countries, see Chapter 20 above.

The end of the nineteenth and the beginning of the twentieth centuries was a
period of change and ferment, which presented materials for building new social
structures. In the case of family life education, there were already movements afoot
which could be utilized in the founding of
this new field.

There was, for example, a new and growing body of knowledge about human behavior and about children. Psychiatry and
psychoanalysis, the beginnings of a mental
health movement, and an evolving child
development brand of home economics
presented data for fact-hungry parents.
Community child study courses tried to
help parents convert these ideas into answers to such practical questions as how to
make children behave correctly. Meanwhile, psychology and sociology, along with
economics and biology, had enough interesting facts and new ideas to make it
possible for a college course on family
relationships to look like an academically
respectable contribution.

Health education, character education,
citizenship education, home management
education, and other inventions of the
school world fit well enough with the new
effort to be seen as sometime allies of family education. The whole progressive education movement gave heart to those who
wanted the new family field to be functional, real, and useful education. Sex education, which had started as a rather limited movement, also began to show signs of
conversion into something more positive
for family living.

There were other professional advance-
ments which fed into the new field. In
medicine, not only the psychiatrist but the
pediatrician and obstetrician sometimes felt
a relationship to it. Domestic relations lawyers, or those who felt domestic relations
law was in a sad state, were ready for the
new educational effort. There would be,
soon, a breed of social scientists, the cultural anthropologists, who would travel to
all parts of the world studying the family

as one of their basic units of investigation
Also, many social workers were certain to
see family education as an ally in their
struggle with the problems experienced by
urban families.

The chronology of these historic events is
difficult to portray with complete accuracy,
but some of the highlight dates would be
the following:

By the 1880's, there was already some
movement toward the organization of parent groups with an interest in child management. Early in the twentieth century,
the importation of concepts and therapeutic
approaches from the field of psychoanalysis,
as well as the first interest in what was
later called child psychology and child development, added to this movement. It was
not until 1929, however, that the National
Council of Parent Education was organized, and parent education appeared to be
a firmly established field.

Home economics also had its beginnings
in the nineteenth century; it seems to have
been an outgrowth of urbanism. By 1908,
the movement had formed itself well
enough to support a national organization,
the American Home Economics Association, which from then on became of great
importance to the family life education
field. Because of the close tie between home
economics and the Extension Service of the
Department of Agriculture, this field often
had funds to promote training and research
designed to improve family life. Land-grant
colleges have become leading agents in the
training of family-oriented specialists of
various kinds.

The child was always an object of interest to home economists, but in the 1920's
child development started to become a recognized speciality within the field. The
Washington Child Research Center (now
called the National Child Research Center)
was established in 1928 by a Laura Spelman
Rockefeller Memorial grant, and the American Home Economics Association became
custodian of the funds. Along with a nursery school, courses in child behavior, and

research efforts, the center, located in Washington, D. C., published important pioneering works by leading home economists. From 1926 to 1935, three association representatives held conferences in every state, so that teachers might be encouraged to develop work in this field (Rockwood, 1948).

Sociologists became active in the family field about the same time. In addition to many major books on historical and institutional aspects of family life, sociology produced leaders in family education. Ernest R. Groves taught the first college course in the new area and wrote the first textbook, and Ernest W. Burgess was an early president of the National Council on Family Relations and first editor of its journal, *Marriage and Family Living* (now called the *Journal of Marriage and the Family*). Both of these men set a pattern in sociology classes by combining the learnings of many disciplines rather than hewing to a strict sociological line.

The sex education boom came at about the time of World War I. Perhaps the greatest contribution of this field to family life education has been made in more recent years, however, as the American Social Health Association added to its traditional concerns about the venereal diseases and prostitution a strong program of positive family life education. Through nine years of project efforts, this program has been instrumental in training teachers, principals, and supervisors to handle the family life education aspects of their work, and in assisting schools, colleges, and communities to advance family life education programs.

It was after World War I that the progressive education movement became an important force. Funds from the Progressive Education Association later helped develop high school programs for teaching child development and family relations.

Another sign of the times was the beginning of local, state, and even national conferences of people from various fields of specialization who met to discuss their common interest in family life. For example, in 1934 a Conference on Education for Marriage and Family Social Relations was held in New York City, cosponsored by the American Home Economics Association, the American Social Hygiene Association, and Teachers College of Columbia University. One outcome of this meeting was the organization in 1938 of the National Conference on Family Relations, which later was renamed the National Council on Family Relations, and became the most important organization in the field of family education.

As new as the field of family education is, there is a belief among many of its pioneers that some of its history, particularly its earliest history in the child development area, may be in danger of becoming lost. A library of early materials, the Historical Library in Child Development and Family Relations, has been established at the Merrill-Palmer Institute in Detroit, to help preserve the history of the movement.

THE NATURE OF THE FIELD

Focus and Boundaries

As now conceptualized, family life education includes facts, attitudes, and skills related to dating, marriage, and parenthood. Obviously, then, it includes—but is more than—homemaking education, or parent education, or family sociology, or sex education. Throughout the concept of family life education is woven the idea of relationships—parent-child, husband-wife, boy-girl, and so on.

H. T. Christensen (1958, p. 8) has pointed to the fact that family life education is "broad in field but narrow in focus." Many things affect family life; therefore, many things which are taught in school could be called family life education. However, only specific aspects of most school courses could actually qualify as family life education, since only they focus on the family.

Avery (1962) has proposed this working definition:

Family life education involves any and all school experiences deliberately and consciously used by teachers in helping to develop the personalities of students to their fullest capacities as present and future family members—those capacities which equip the individual to solve most constructively the problems unique to his family role (p. 28; cf. Avery & Lee, 1964).

He emphasized the words "deliberately and consciously" to distinguish purposive education for family living from the more incidental influences other school experiences may have on a student's family life.

Other definitions put emphasis on developing human relationships, bettering mental health, strengthening the family unit, and even on reforming society through improved family life.

Although it seems premature to expect agreement on a definition of the field, it is possible to note trends and emerging consensus. In particular, two trends run through the descriptions of family education programs presented below. First, there has been a move toward a more personal approach. Family life teachers are less interested in the family as a social institution and are more interested in actual preparation for personal participation in various stages of family living. A second trend historically has been toward increased educational activity in lower grades: more family life education in secondary and even in elementary schools.

The following review shows emerging recognizable differences in the focus of family education at different grade levels. College courses are often clearly labeled as preparation for marriage. In secondary schools, special courses in marriage preparation and family life exist, but so do family units incorporated into various home economics, social science, health, and other courses. In elementary schools, the emphasis is more apt to be on the improvement of family attitudes and understandings

indirectly through the incorporation of appropriate materials into various parts of the curriculum (Avery, 1962, pp. 28–36; H. T. Christensen, 1958, p. 593; Kirkendall, 1961, pp. 698–700).

College and University Programs

Sociologist Ernest Groves offered the first college courses in marriage preparation, first at Boston university in the early 1920's and then a few years later at the University of North Carolina. These usually are considered the beginning of formal family life education in the United States. However, family courses of a more academic nature had been found in American colleges prior to that time.

A 1926 study by Wells noted that 15 colleges gave instruction in the family field as early as 1920, and 22 courses were mentioned by 1923. There were even four courses which seem to have been started before 1910 (Drummond, 1942, p. 13). These early courses tended to be historical studies of the family as a social institution. However, Drummond said that between 1930 and 1940 there was a growing belief that education for marriage and family living could aid both individual happiness and social welfare. College students began asking for such courses, and in 1937 the American Youth Congress came out in support of marriage education. Drummond noted that by 1933–1935 more women's than men's colleges were offering courses on the family. About 80 per cent of these courses were taught in sociology departments. She contrasted the 50 colleges which offered courses in this field early in the 1930's with the more than 450 in 1940 (1942, p. 17).

The status of the field of family life education in colleges was documented in a 1948–1949 survey by Bowman (1949). He studied responses from 1,270 colleges and junior colleges (of 1,370 to which he had sent questionnaires) and found 632 had at least one marriage education course in their curriculum. The survey was designed to omit from its findings most purely historical courses on the family as well as courses on foods, clothing, child care, and the like. Of those who gave a date of origin, 37 per cent had initiated their courses within the five years prior to the study, and 55 per cent after 1939. Bowman thought that about two out of every 100 college students enrolled in such courses. He attempted to sketch a composite picture of a fairly "typical" situation:

There is only one course offered in the school and it is offered in the sociology department. It was started within the past 10 or so years. The course is elective but not open freely and without restriction to all students. It extends through one semester and carries three semester hours credit. Classes meet three times per week. They are coeducational.

The instructor has some background in sociology or psychology or both but has had no specific training in marriage education. He is married and living with his wife. The marriage course is only a small part of his load. . . . One of the instructor's problems is to keep enrollment down to the point where he can handle . . . one section effectively.

The instructor handles all topics within the course. . . . He assigns a textbook and collateral reading. He considers at least part of his course to classify as functional education for marriage. . . . He devotes considerable time to individual counseling upon student request . . . (Bowman, 1949, p. 415).

A 1956 study by Landis found:

. . . Eighty two percent of 768 responding colleges were offering one or more courses in marriage and the family. The 630 colleges offering courses were giving 1,027 courses and these courses had an enrollment of 77,000 students for the academic year 1955–1956. More than 1,000 professors were teaching the marriage and family courses during that year. This does not give an accurate picture of the total program in the colleges since less than half the colleges responded in the study. There were doubtless well over 100,000 students registered in marriage and family courses during the academic year 1955–1956. Percentagewise this would probably be less than 5 percent of the total student body registered in marriage and family courses in any one year. The survey gives some indication of the rapid growth of marriage education in colleges. More than half of the 1,027 courses reported had been added to the college curriculum in the ten-year period from 1945–1955. The most rapid growth had been in the functional courses in preparation for marriage, and almost two thirds of the students were registered in this type of course (Landis, 1958, p. 2).

Landis (1959) found that there were slightly more women than men students in the class enrollments. The instructors of the courses had been trained in sociology and psychology, typically, and were usually teaching in departments of sociology.

Those courses which were offered by junior colleges tended to be functional classes in preparation for marriage, that is, the emphasis was on practical preparation rather than on academic learnings about marriage. The junior college course was usually open to all students, with no prerequisites, and probably came into existence within the 10 years preceding Landis' study.

The typical teachers' college offering was a functional marriage course limited to upper division students, but often there was a second course which gave students a chance to study the institutional aspects of the family.

Catholic colleges, Landis found, usually had an institutional family course for upper division students. These courses often included a strong religious emphasis.

The average college or university in the Landis study offered a functional marriage course without prerequisites, an institutional family course limited to those who had upper division standing and prerequisite work in sociology, and additional advanced and specialized courses for upper division and graduate students.

Landis reported that many new specialized courses had come into the college curricula by the mid-1950's. These dealt with marriage counseling, child development, family research, adolescent development, aging family members, methods of teaching family life, teacher and community leadership training, and research training.

It must be kept in mind that many of the courses Landis studied would not have been included in the Bowman sample by definition, and, therefore, the two studies are not strictly comparable.

Bowman focused on the course which was designed at least partly to give functional preparation for marriage. He has suggested the following as main topics for a functional marriage course:

1. Differences between men and women.
2. The reasons for marriage.
3. The permanently unmarried.
4. Can a woman successfully combine wage earning and marriage, homemaking and child rearing?
5. When to marry.
6. Courtship.
7. Engagement.
8. Choosing a marriage partner.
9. Wedding and honeymoon.
10. Personality adjustment in marriage.
11. The importance and use of money in marriage.
12. The use of leisure time in marriage.
13. Reproduction.
14. Divorce (1952, pp. 361–363).

Landis' 1958 report noted that the functional marriage courses usually followed a sequence of family stages from dating to marriage to parenthood. Most of these courses included something on changing roles of men and women, dating and courtship, marriageability, mixed marriages, premarital sex standards, mate selection, engagement, legal aspects of marriage, religious differences in marriage, money, sex, and in-laws. Also, the biology of reproduction, fertility, and infertility was included, as was something on child-rearing practices. Sometimes the course dealt with aspects of aging.

Outlines such as these suggest that the courses are not within the sole domain of any one academic department or discipline.

Who, then, should offer them? American colleges and universities have provided a variety of answers to this question. Their family-centered work has also ranged from those institutions which have no formal course to those which offer a minor or major or even a master's or doctor's degree in the family.

In those universities where there is a curriculum focused on the family area, it is most typically either the sociology or the home economics department which provides this concentration, both at the undergraduate and the graduate levels. Sometimes, however, the family courses are not offered exclusively by these two departments. Several examples of how courses are being presented follow.

One pattern is the family center, epitomized by the Family Study Center of the University of Minnesota, directed by sociologist Reuben Hill. The center, which is not attached to any one university department, makes use of facilities among all of the departments and professional schools in offering training in family life education and research. It offers interdisciplinary courses for undergraduate credit but leaves the granting of degrees to other departments. By providing research and training opportunities for graduate students from various departments, and by maintaining a teaching and research staff, it pursues its goal of being truly a focus for family-centered activities on the campus and in the community.

Another system is seen in the interdivisional doctoral program in marriage and family living offered at Florida State University. This program is staffed by members of the Home and Family Life Department of the School of Home Economics, by faculty from the School of Social Welfare, and by staff from the Sociology Department.

A third illustration is Brigham Young University's Department of Human Development and Family Relationships, where graduate study is offered leading to the M.S. and Ph.D. degrees. This training is designed to prepare students for nursery school work, for university teaching in child development, marriage, and family relations, for marriage counseling, for child guidance work, for child welfare work, and for research positions. The department is in the College of Family Living. The undergraduate training in this department is designed to lead to certification for teaching in elementary and secondary schools, as well as to give general academic preparation and specific family living education.

At most colleges, the marriage preparation courses have tended to exclude many students on the campus because of prerequisites or because of such traditions as that barring men from taking home economics courses. For these and other reasons, the marriage course is sometimes cross-listed by several departments. More effective, probably, has been the practice followed earlier at The Ohio State University, of having the marriage course listed as a general studies course and conducted by a multi-departmental committee.

Elementary and Secondary School Programs

In recent decades there has been a pronounced acceleration of the family life education movement in American elementary and secondary schools. Although total national statistics are difficult to obtain, it is clear that thousands of high schools now have family living courses. Some states report more than 90 per cent of their high schools offering units in this new field. One estimate is that more than a million and a half high school students take homemaking subjects each year, most of them girls enrolled in home economics courses.

Observers of this growth have pointed to several explanations. As noted earlier in this chapter, the rapid changes in society, and particularly in family life itself, are often seen as contributing factors in the growth of family course work in the schools. The need for democratic alternatives to former authoritarian child-rearing patterns is also noted as a factor encouraging this growth. So, too, is the fact that other areas of life have responded well to direct education, leading to the assumption that family life may also be positively affected.

Landis found that of 286 high schools he studied in the state of California, 76 per cent were giving some family education either in units of study or as separate courses (1958). Typically, the social studies course in the twelfth grade included a unit of several weeks' length on the topic of courtship and marriage. This course was often required of all students. He found the functional courses in high schools to be very similar to those in colleges. However, he noted that high school marriage preparation courses put less emphasis on research findings and, because of possible administrative disapproval, gave little attention to the topic of sexual adjustment. Complete family life courses in California tended to be required and coeducational if they were offered in the social studies curriculum. If a home economics course was offered, it usually was an elective and was for girls only (Landis, 1956).

Landis (1958) has described the typical ninth-grade family course as less specifically designed as education for marriage and parenthood. Instead, it usually deals with personal adjustment, mental health, understanding oneself and others, and getting along within the family and with the opposite sex.

The better high school courses, Landis claimed (1958, p. 3), often give teenagers an opportunity to work with nursery school children; this is seen as increasing their understanding of children and helping them prepare for parenthood.

Family life education at the elementary school level is usually designed to help children improve their relationships with the other members of their own families. Some sex education, at least insofar as it deals with menstruation, reproduction, and other biologically oriented subjects, is seen as part of the elementary school offering. For several decades, the dominant philosophy among American family life educators concerning the elementary schools has been that family teachings should be diffused throughout the curriculum rather than being condensed into a separate course.

Throughout the decisions made concerning family life subject matter at various academic levels is the philosophy that family education should be geared to the child's developmental stage (Duvall, 1962). Brown (1941) put it this way:

Just as there are steps in learning to do arithmetic or in learning to read, there are steps in learning to be a mature adult. This is not the place to discuss this developmental sequence in detail, but even a quick look at the outline shows how well it serves as a basis for curriculum planning in family life education:

During the period of uterine development, there is, first of all, the need for experiences which facilitate the unfolding of fundamental growth patterns. . . .

During infancy, the baby needs to begin to learn how to sustain life in the outside world, how to coordinate his muscles, and how to cooperate with other people.

During the years of early childhood, he goes on with these earlier learnings and undertakes some new ones. On this level he needs, specifically, to learn how to accept the cultural pattern of his social group as this is transmitted to him by his parents. He also needs to begin to learn how to know and use his environment; to build a rich store of sensory impressions and ideas—raw materials for the progressive development of concepts.

During the years of middle childhood, he goes on with these earlier learnings and concentrates energy on some new ones. He needs to begin specifically to learn the attitudes and skills which will make him a good solver of life problems. He also needs to learn how to understand and accept the fact of his own sex.

During adolescence, he goes on learning in all of these general directions and brings some learning to a point of culmination. He needs to complete the adolescent cycle of physical growth. He needs to achieve emotional emancipation from his parents. He needs to learn to take final personal responsibility for his own behavior. He needs to learn how to make a vocational choice. He needs to learn how to make a good adult adjustment to members of the opposite sex. He needs to organize the values he has been developing during childhood into a fairly consistent philosophy of life.

During early adult life, he needs to learn how to adjust as a self-sustaining individual in home and community relationships, with or without marriage and parenthood.

During the years of middle life, he needs to learn how to enjoy the fruits of all previous learnings . . . to re-orient the self with respect to earlier plans and purposes; to find increasing opportunities for community service. . . .

During the last years, the years of old age, he needs to learn how to live a life of increasing spiritual significance as physical energy diminishes and he becomes more and more dependent, physically, on other people (p. 307).

Brown further stated that there are certain characteristics successful family life education in the schools must have. It must be coeducational, must be developed cooperatively among parents, students, teachers, and others, must really allow for individual differences, must be geared to the developmental needs of individuals, and must be a community program in the true sense of the expression (1941, p. 310).

In his statement of principles for family life courses in high schools, Kirkendall (1949) further suggested that the courses should include sex education (not just reproduction education), provide facilities for adequate counseling, and carefully be coordinated with other subjects in the curriculum.

Some of the courses and some of the state programs that exist at the elementary and secondary school levels are discussed in the remainder of this section.

It would be impossible to find a course at the high school level to match the claim of Ernest Groves's Boston and North Carolina courses to being first in the college field. *One* of the first known to current national leaders in family education, however, is the Personal Relationships course taught in the Tulsa, Oklahoma, public schools (Tulsa, 1949).

This course had its roots in a 1918 required class called Home Crafts for Girls, which included units in home nursing, infant care, house planning and furnishing, and household management. It became very popular, and the idea arose of having a similar offering for boys. Questionnaires were sent to the parents of the approximately 500 boys in the junior year at Tulsa Central High School, and parents were given the opportunity to discuss the idea of a home economics course for their sons. The response was so positive that a new, required course called Home Crafts for Boys was added in 1925. This had units on adequate diets, selection of clothes, personal allowances, house planning, building, furnishing, and management. There were also discussions of boy-girl relationships, and soon the boys were wanting to know the girls' views. For a while there was an exchange of students between the two Home Crafts classes, but finally the students asked that the classes be combined. The name of the course was changed to Home Living, and much later to Personal Relationships. By 1934, students in these courses were observing children in two of Tulsa's federal nursery schools. Later, well-equipped laboratory nursery schools were built into the new Tulsa high schools (Tulsa, 1949).

A later but better-known program was the one developed at Toms River, New Jersey. This elective course for eleventh- and twelfth-grade boys and girls was set up very carefully and has been closely observed and studied since it was first offered in 1941. A faculty committee worked for three years on the course before it was offered; excellent administrative support and the choice of an outstanding teacher, Elizabeth S. Force, seem to have helped the course

become accepted and highly respected in a brief period of time. The specific aims of the course, as noted in its study guide, have been:

I. To show through the various biological types of families, and by tracing the anthropological foundations, that family relationships are as old as civilization itself.

II. To show the influences of ancient civilizations on the family.

III. To show the importance of the family, particularly to the mother and children.

IV. To guide the individual in the selection of a proper mate. To teach individuals so to adjust themselves that neither one's personality is dwarfed. To help individuals find an agreeable method of courtship. To give them the knowledge necessary in the legal preparation for marriage.

V. To teach the necessary influences for happiness in marriage. To prepare the future parent to adjust himself if his family life becomes disorganized. To show what processes are involved in the reorganization of a family.

VI. To clarify the family's biological aspects. To stress the importance of a well-organized economic program. To aid in the working out of a satisfactory formula for getting along with the other members of the family.

VII. To extol the family and the home as the true sources of real, wholesome fun. To show the many ways in which the various members of the family can make use of their leisure time.

VIII. To encourage a better relationship between the family and the community (Force, 1962, p. 10).

In some large cities, well-coordinated family life programs have been developed in the schools. In Washington, D. C., a large program ranging from the kindergarten through the twelfth grade is in an experimental stage. More than in other cases, this program's central focus is health education.

Another example of an extensive program is found in Kansas City, Missouri. Some professional work in family life education has existed there since 1930 and since 1944 there has been a Department of Family Life Education. The department's head, Dr. Esther E. Prevey, has also provided national leadership in the family education movement. Her Kansas City program is largely built around two foci, an extensive parent education program and a senior-class course in marriage and family living. During each school year, thousands of parents enroll in the approximately 45 classes of preschool parents, 60 classes of elementary school parents, and eight classes of high school parents. The course for seniors runs for a full year, meeting daily in nine high schools, and is attended by about 900 students (personal correspondence with Dr. Prevey, 1963).

Many states offer guidance to the various family life classes within their borders through their state departments of education. In Michigan, for example, the Department of Public Instruction leaves curriculum-building up to the individual communities but stimulates thinking, planning, and action to improve programs of home and family living through a state curriculum committee.

The state committee comprises a cross section of individuals. Invited to serve on the committee are home economists, sociologists, guidance personnel, administrators and some from the elementary, high school and college and university programs. The Chief of Homemaking and Family Life Education serves as secretary of the committee (Withers, 1962, p. 2).

This committee and the state Chief of Homemaking, then, work with various departments in schools throughout the state—the home economics, biology, physical education, social studies, and guidance departments which handle courses in family education in Michigan. Part of the work of the Homemaking and Family Life Education Service of the Department of Public Instruction is to encourage more and better preparation of teachers of family life in the state, and to obtain in-service training for teachers trying to upgrade their offerings.

Michigan also was the home of one of the well-known and widely studied family life programs. In the city of Highland Park a required course for seniors emphasized a strong combination of academic learnings and free discussions built around their personal concerns. Early in the history of the course, all boys and girls were required to spend four days a semester in the laboratory nursery school. This program was somewhat curtailed during recent criticisms of American education for containing "frills," or courses other than basic skill and science subjects (see discussion below).

The New York State Education Department met the challenge of recent criticisms, not by abolishing family courses, but by revising them.

The 12th year course for boys and girls is currently being revised and strengthened to better challenge today's talented learners. Basic concepts include: 1) Families in our Society, with consideration for the contemporary family, families in a changing society, concerns of families today, the family life cycle and families in the community. 2) Families in Other Countries, giving attention to their similarities and differences, and inter-relationships among families of all cultures. 3) The Individual in the Family, considering the nature of the individual, roles of an individual in the family, family inter-action, management and achievement of goals. 4) Marriage as a Way of Life, concerned with partner selection and preparation for marriage, adjustments in marriage and children in the family (Lawson, 1962, pp. 5–6).

In contrast to states with active and well-developed programs, there are many states in which the incidence of family life education is low. In a recent study, Kenkel (1957) found that of the Iowa high schools from which he could obtain data, only 11 per cent offered a full course in family living, leading to the conclusion that very few high school students in Iowa are being reached (p. 381). He found that a common reason put forth in many schools for not offering a family course was that educators feared adverse community reaction, but he reported no actual adverse reaction in communities which did have such courses.

In a state-wide study involving high school principals in Indiana, Dager and Harper (1959) learned that some kind of family life education was offered in over 90 per cent of the 661 schools reporting. Only 61 principals claimed no work at all in this field. Most of these academic offerings, however, were units of study rather than complete courses. Two or more units of some courses were focused on family life in 256 schools; 236 schools offered one unit only. Fifty-three schools reported full family life courses *and* units on the family in other courses. Fifty-five schools had a complete family course but no additional family units in other courses. A total of 1,081 family offerings were reported in the 600 schools which had some work in the field; this number is made up of 108 complete courses and 973 units in other courses. Home economics curricula provided most of the family teaching in the Indiana schools.

Methods and Techniques

Recent studies such as G. A. Christensen's (1958) show that family life teachers as a group do not have a unique set of methods and techniques for teaching. However, it has been obvious from the literature that many individuals have attempted to make their teaching less "bookish" and more functional by applying methods not frequently used in other classes. Some critics of the field, in fact, believe family life teachers have been so taken up with certain methods of teaching that more emphasis has been put on the techniques than on the goals of the courses. Probably the matter would be a good deal clearer if there were more rigidly controlled experiments within the field to compare and evaluate various teaching methods.

Meanwhile, however, individual teachers report success with many techniques. Morgan found the following noted by elementary and secondary school teachers in the "Teacher's Exchange" section of *Marriage and Family Living* (now called the *Journal of Marriage and the Family*):

1. Autobiographies, profiles, or self-portraits written by students.
2. Check-lists used as "ice-breakers" for student-teacher conferences.
3. Debates.
4. Discussion technique, with the following variations:
   a. Buzz groups.
   b. Circle discussion (each person contributing, in turn).
   c. Open discussion.
5. Films.
6. Novels.
7. Opinion polls.
8. Problem-solving approaches.
9. Personal counseling.
10. Problem-detecting inventories to serve as guides in planning course content.
11. Participation in nursery school laboratories.
12. Panels.
13. Using photographs to stimulate discussion. (One teacher has sent such pictures home with students for family discussion.)
14. Studying needs of wider community in planning broad family life program.
15. Sociodrama skits, with variations.
16. Role playing, with variations.
17. Senior seminar idea.
18. Student panels going out to tell community groups about family life classes. Also sample classes for student body or community groups.
19. Team-teaching.
20. Tape recordings
    a. Of resource persons from the community.
    b. Of class discussions, then listening to them again.
    c. Of role playing sessions.
21. Watching TV programs, then following with discussion.
22. Working with P.T.A. or other commu-

nity groups in planning family life programs.

23. Using resource persons from wider community.

24. Individual or group research projects by
students (1962, pp. 11–12).

School-Related Programs

Although discussed more fully elsewhere
in this volume (see Ch. 20), mention should
be made here of the great variety of other
kinds of family education programs which
have an influence on school family life education.

For example, the work of some of the
family service agencies has direct relationships with school programs. An illustration
is the Family Service Agency of San
Bernardino, California, which has, as part
of its family education program, a premarriage counseling service in cooperation
with four local senior high schools. This
experimental program may point the way
for important agency-school cooperation to
provide students with both skilled teachers
and skilled counselors.

It has already been noted how nursery
schools, even when not part of the public
school system itself, have become a major
part of the family life education of some
schools. Other examples in the schools in
San Francisco, Berkeley, Oakland, Los
Angeles, Rochester, Schenectady, and elsewhere could be cited. Extensive use of
parent cooperative nursery schools has been
made in the Seattle and Baltimore public
schools under Dr. Katharine Whiteside
Taylor's leadership. The cooperative nursery
school movement has generally been seen
as a parent education venture as well as a
child education effort, and it has close
ties with kindergartens, where they exist,
as well as being used in some areas for
observational purposes by older students.

It is of interest to note that some of the
nation's very first institutional nursery
schools (not parent cooperatives), such as
those founded in the early 1920's at the
Harriet Johnson School in New York City

and the Merrill-Palmer Institute in Detroit,
had an experimental family life education
purpose along with a child-care and child-
rearing goal. Preschool facilities at the
Merrill-Palmer Institute have, from their
origin, been seen as laboratories for learning
and teaching about children and their
families.

The parent education movement is
viewed in this chapter as a part of the family life education movement which has
some school-related aspects (Brim, 1959;
Grams, 1960). Of great historical importance was the founding of the National
Council of Parent Education, a professional
organization financed by the Laura Spelman Rockefeller Memorial Fund, which
in the late 1920's trained parent educators,
prepared materials in the field, and in general gathered support for parent education.
Today, large and important organizations
such as the National Congress of Parents
and Teachers carry on extensive parent education programs which are tied in with
school programs.

The American Social Health Association
has had increasing interest in school-related
family life education programs, and recently, along with the National Congress of
Parents and Teachers, conducted a large
experimental program in four western
states. This Rocky Mountain Project involved various approaches to family life
education from elementary school classes to
television programs.

The purpose of the Rocky Mountain Project
is to make programs of family life education
in schools and communities stronger and better
coordinated and where such programs do not
exist, to create them. . . . [Its] objectives are:

1. To increase the amount and improve the
quality of family life education.
2. To experiment with new kinds of family
life education.
3. To increase the number of trained leaders in this field.
4. To improve public attitudes about family
life education and family problems.
5. To bring about better integration and coordination of community resources.
6. To improve communication and under-

standing between and among family members.

7. To disseminate and interpret pertinent information in this field (Amer. Soc. Hlth Ass., 1961, pp. 4–5).

Other examples of school-related programs are: the work of the Center for Research and Development on Family Life in Kansas City, Missouri, including the development of teaching-machine techniques for family life education in cooperation with the University of Kansas City; the community education program of the Civic Education Center of Washington University in St. Louis; and the preparation of teaching materials for high school students and for expectant parents by the Louisiana Mental Health Association (Paget, 1961).

In some cases, city-wide programs of family education in and out of the schools have been so well coordinated and formulated as to receive national attention. In Flint, Michigan, the Clara Elizabeth Fund for Maternal Health and the Mott Foundation have provided the school system with specialists and with funds for experimental family programs. In Toledo, Ohio, a community family life education committee of citizens was created to consult with the schools' family life education program, and four full-time staff members for family education both in and out of the schools were provided (Brown, 1953; Paget, 1961).

Oregon, one of the first states to provide leadership for large programs of family life education and particularly sex education, has been the home of the Oregon Development Center Project in Family Life Education, sponsored since 1951 by the E. C. Brown Trust. The first three goals of this experimental project were:

1. To provide an in-service education program for teachers which would orient them to basic concepts of family life education.
2. To acquire experience in the development of school and community family life education programs, and in the process to de-velop outlines and units, methods, techniques, and ideas in family life education which could be used by other teachers, school administrators, and community leaders in Oregon and elsewhere.
3. To discover ways of developing community understanding and support of the schools' efforts to provide family life education (Avery & Kirkendall, 1955, p. 1).

To these goals soon was added the necessary one of working out a usable definition or description of family life education itself (Avery, 1962; Avery & Kirkendall, 1955, pp. 7–11).

Perhaps this reaching out into the community of school-based family life programs, and reaching into the schools by community family programs, is to become the pattern for the future.

PROFESSIONALIZATION PATTERNS

The Making of a Family Life Teacher

Where do family life teachers come from? In the first place, it has been true historically, although less so today, that most family life teachers did not start out to be such. They were usually trained to be something else—home economists, sociologists, psychologists, physical education specialists, and so on. But, because of circumstances existing in their schools, they found themselves recruited into the field of family life education by their principal, superintendent, or department head. A new course in this field was to be taught, and the administrator picked a teacher to give it. Perhaps the teacher had had a little training in this or in some conceivably related field. Or often, the teacher was simply more or less available and seemed to be "good with children" and a fairly good model (perhaps having the reputation of successful marriage and parenthood). Or perhaps this teacher, more than others, recognized the need for family courses. Sometimes it was the students who requested the course and asked for a particular teacher.

G. A. Christensen (1958) found in his survey of family life teachers at all levels of education that the most common reason given for entering the field was "To help people." Next came "My interest in the family as a result of my happy family background." (A sizeable proportion of his sample—22 per cent—also noted that their own *stressful* family background led them into the field.) Other important motivations for entering the field were the need that a department or school had for such a teacher, and the influence of a professor or of a course they once took. Older respondents tended to report the former, and younger ones the latter.

Of course some teachers do train especially for this field of family education. High school teachers, for example, may at least prepare for the field within the limits of the major and minor system in their college of education and of the teacher certification system in their state. It may be that only a minor may be taken in the subject, and in many cases the teacher-in-training must accept certification in another subject, since certification in the field of family education is comparatively rare.

Longworth noted:

Failure to establish requirements for the certification of teachers of family living may eventually jeopardize the growth of the program. Most school administrators would hesitate to hire a coach without a thorough examination of his credentials and assurance that he was certified to teach in the area. Although it is recognized that teaching family living is a "touchy subject," in many instances a very haphazard system of selecting teachers is utilized (1952, p. 103).

He suggested a master's degree in education, which would include training in biology, economics, sociology, psychology, and, helpfully, law, religion, home economics, and recreation (p. 104). Longworth challenged the National Council on Family Relations to work on such a curriculum and to help achieve certification in various states. Meanwhile, some states train many

family life teachers who look for jobs in other states: Utah State University and Brigham Young University, for example, have trained more family teachers than have most other universities in past years, but since Utah has no specific family life certification for teachers in the public schools, many look to other states for employment.

In a number of teacher training institutions, persons who seek training in family life teaching find relatively few family courses. Also, they are offered very little actual practice teaching in family education. The courses they do take in their college work are mainly offered by home economics, sociology, and education departments.

For many, then, training comes at the graduate level. This is true not only of those college professors of family life who receive their advanced degrees in sociology, psychology, home economics, and so on, but also for secondary and elementary school teachers. Secondary school teachers, for example, increase their preparation for family life teaching by taking graduate courses in the traditional academic departments as well as by graduate work in the interdisciplinary programs of such institutions as Teachers College and Florida State University. This degree-oriented study may be supplemented by work at institutions such as the Merrill-Palmer Institute which provide intensive special training in family education without awarding degrees or certificates.

Formal training programs, however, do not produce a very large number of family life educators in any one year. School systems are still dependent to a large extent on finding various forms of in-service training for their family teachers.

In a study of Indiana public schools (Dager, Harper, & Whitehurst, 1962), 80 per cent of 547 teachers who were teaching family living reported having had some training in family life education, but only one-third of these had been trained before being hired as family teachers. When asked if they wanted more training in family life,

45 per cent responded in the negative. Similarly, in a Florida study (Bayer & Nye, 1963) only 5 per cent of the family teachers had as much as 15 hours of college work in the subject they were teaching, and about a third had none at all. The researchers concluded that the result was an "untrained" and "amateur" teaching force.

To help meet this situation, large city school systems often have a series of meetings for family teachers at which there are lectures and reports about teaching family classes. Some school systems make attendance at local and national professional family conferences attractive to their family life teachers, hoping to add to the professionalization process and provide more vital instruction.

It is generally believed in the family education field that the supply of teachers, whether from formal training sources or from conversion of teachers from other fields, lags far behind the demand. Year after year, family life educators have tried to deal more helpfully with the problem of recruitment and selection. While it has been true that the growth of family courses has created a demand for teachers greater than the supply, it has also been true that there has been an element of risk for any specific teacher who trained for a job in this field. There has always been a good chance that, because of the small size of the field when compared with more traditional ones such as English and history, there would be no job for the newly trained teacher.

There has also been much discussion about better selection methods for people wishing to teach family life subjects—selection procedures that would help weed out the more obvious neurotics, for example. However, not much has been done in this regard. In general, if a person can be accepted by a college of education or of home economics, he can be accepted in the family life education training program. This leads to a dilemma: How can the standards of selection be raised at the same time that attempts are being made to increase the number of recruits?

G. A. Christensen's study (1958) of school and college family life teachers showed that of 475 respondents, 340 agreed that family life educators should have exceptionally high moral standards, 107 were in doubt about this, and 28 disagreed with the statement. He reported that 183 said they would limit family life teaching roles to people who believe in God, 127 were doubtful, and 165 disagreed. Also, 204 thought the family teacher should be a fairly regular church attender, which, among other things, means that some thought church attendance was more important than belief in God. The largest proportion, 447, said that the family teacher should be a person who can respect the dignity and worth of the individual. It is highly desirable that these teachers should be married, 261 said. Only 23 said they would exclude divorcees, although another 140 had some doubt; 188 thought divorce might help a family teacher in his work. Almost all, 434, thought that only people who have a high level of emotional and social maturity should enter the field. Only 78 would limit this work to people who had had a successful marriage. The respondents thought sociology, psychology, home economics, child development, and counseling were most important as preparatory subjects for the would-be family teacher (parenthetically, 141 of these respondents had their own degrees in sociology). Adult education, philosophy, religion, and anthropology were not rated very high on this item.

G. A. Christensen listed 15 possible goals for family education and found that his respondents most frequently chose "To assist the student in developing an understanding of the relationships in modern marriage, and to help him understand himself in relation to the other members of his family." Self-understanding was the second most popular goal, and it should be noted that it is not specifically family-oriented. Scientific knowledge about the family was chosen third.

The major tasks of the family life field were seen by his sample of family educators to be to: (a) develop more and better research and theory, (b) improve teaching, (c) develop adequate evaluation procedures, (d) develop higher personal and academic requirements for family life educators, and (e) develop common principles for family life.

Organization and Organizations

Because family life teachers come from a variety of disciplines, there are many professional organizations which claim their allegiance, such as the American Sociological Association, American Home Economics Association, and so on. It becomes more and more obvious, however, that the National Council on Family Relations is the parent professional organization of this field. In their roles as family life educators, the teachers tend to relate to this organization.

The National Council on Family Relations was founded in 1938, "To bring together men and women in different fields of family living as a permanent association for the consideration of family relations." In addition to providing yearly national conferences and fostering 37 state, regional, and local family councils, the NCFR publishes the *Journal of Marriage and the Family* and provides teachers with kits of materials and an exchange of ideas dealing with problems of family life education. It provides leadership for workshops and is a clearinghouse for announcements concerning family education through its newsletter and other publications.

The organization had about 3,000 members in 1962. In 1959, an analysis of its then 2,661 members showed that among the largest categories 815 were teachers, 442 were students, 218 were ministers or Protestant religious educators, 180 were in social service agencies (with another 80 listed as social workers), 113 were medical doctors, 109 were marriage counselors, and 82 were parent and adult educators. Of the college teachers, the three largest categories were 195 sociologists, 131 home economists, and 101 family life and child development teachers. Among the largest classifications of high school teachers, 63 were in home economics and 38 in family living. These categories left over 600 members who belonged to a wide variety of occupations and professions, underlining the fact of a multiprofessional membership.

Family sections within other organizations such as the American Sociological Association provide professional material (research findings, and so on) for family life educators also. Of course, family educators, like teachers of all kinds, increase their professional status as educators through membership in such groups as the National Education Association, the American Association of University Professors, and their labor unions.

The only family life organization other than the NCFR to obtain wide interest among family teachers has been the Groves Conference on Marriage and the Family. Started by Ernest Groves in 1934, this is not actually a membership organization but an annual invitational conference. However, each year's invitation list is made up largely of people who have recently attended a conference, and a national organizational strength has tended to build up. This has been especially true in recent years, since the Groves Conference left its traditional home in Chapel Hill, North Carolina, and has moved around the country. Having larger meeting places, the conference has grown in membership size and now resembles the NCFR enough to arouse feelings of competition and to cause some family life leaders to wonder if the conference still has a unique role to play in the field. Unlike the NCFR, the Groves Conference does not have a between-conference program of activities, regional or state affiliates, or a journal.

The *Journal of Marriage and the Family* is the official journal of the National Council on Family Relations and has become the most consistent spokesman for the family education field. Over the years, its various editors have tended to include more research reports; this change has been seen both as a reflection of the higher professional standards of the field and as an internal effort to raise these standards. Other journals widely used by teachers of family life are the sociological, social work, and home economics publications, and a few other family life journals.

It should also be mentioned that there has been a recent movement of the American family education field to align itself more closely with international family organizations. The joint conference of the NCFR and the International Union of Family Organizations in New York City in 1960 was an indication of the trend. There also has been increased recognition of the family field by foundations and sponsoring organizations; money for research projects has become available on a modest scale, and in-service training programs for teachers have begun to receive support from outside the school systems.

Standards and Codes

In a 1950 issue of *Marriage and Family Living,* the editorial asked, "Are We Developing a Profession?" Many members of the family education group are still asking that question.

Writing about another field, Hayes has postulated a natural history of professions:

Professions appear to have a natural history. This may suggest the direction many professions are likely to take in the near future. . . . The postulated natural history of a given profession includes the following stages: (1) Social problem emerges when general recognition of difficulty or frustration spreads throughout a group. (2) Problem is first treated by unspecialized persons who respond to social need. (3) Persistence or extensive character of difficulty calls out persons with somewhat related or pertinent skills who address themselves to problem. (4) Conscious procedures grow out of trial and error. (5) Apprenticeships are set up and accumulated skills transmitted. (6) Theoretical foundations are formulated from experience and from the mobilization of seemingly pertinent bodies of knowledge and sciences. (7) Education becomes prolonged in order to learn theory and skills. (8) Group consciousness, organization, and organs of communication emerge. (9) When services become directly purchaseable, codes and standards are developed for defining and controlling relationships. (10) Sub-specializations to deal with more particularized phases of the original problem develop as refinements of theory, experience, and technique become possible and support becomes available. Corresponding standardization occurs. (11) Sub-specialization is carried to a point of completely solving the special phase of difficulty, or to a point of diminishing returns, or to a partial or complete loss of original functions. (12) There is a recognition of need for broader orientation of the original problem, and synthesis of what is known (Hayes, 1948, p. 293).

Using the standards noted in this hypothesized "natural history" as guidelines, it is possible to estimate the progress of family education along the pathway to professional status. However, individual judgments and measurements would still seem to differ. Looking at this formulation, Rockwood (1948) concluded that family life education is well along the road to professionalization. However, basing his views on his own findings from an extensive study of the family life educators themselves, G. A. Christensen (1958) noted:

Thus, though the family life movement has begun to assume some of the characteristics usually associated with an established discipline, it is obvious that it is as yet more divided than it is unified, that the loyalties of the family life educators themselves are expressed more strongly in the direction of their own parent disciplines than they are in the direction of the new and developing field of education for marriage and family living (p. 272).

Others who doubt that family life education has reached maturity as a profession often make reference to the scarcity of specific certification for teachers in this field, to the still inadequate selection and preparation of educators, and particularly to the comparative lack of professional codes and standards. There are many important value questions involved in the teaching of marriage and family relations, and many delicate issues which could strain the relationship between the family teacher and his students, their parents, and the community as a whole. Nevertheless, there have been very few serious attempts to work out a code of ethics or standards of professional behavior in this field. Insofar as family courses are taught by people who belong to fields which have their own codes bearing on the relationship between the professional person and his client, it might be said that codes are operative in family life courses. Psychologists teaching college family life classes would be an illustration. However, most of the sociologists, home economists, and other teachers of family courses at any academic level are not committed to any code other than that generally found in teaching.

If codes are to be developed in this field, they will probably come from the leadership of the NCFR. This organization, in fact, has upon occasion sponsored conference discussions of codes and has appointed committees to look into this and related matters. The difficult task of actually writing a code has not been accomplished, however, and it may be that this is partly an indication that some members of the field are not fully in favor of increased professionalization. As in other new fields, there are those who point out that professionalization brings with it its own set of rigidities, rivalries, and other difficulties.

ISSUES AND PROBLEMS IN NEED OF RESOLUTION

Family life education probably has no more problems or more pressing issues to be resolved than do most other fields of education. The analysis should not imply that it is in danger of dissolving into oblivion; the data seem to show that the field is growing and is meeting a conscious social need. However, there are problems in family life education today which will influence the direction the field will take and its ability to obtain a strong place in American education.

Questions of Values

Family education, as has been noted earlier, arose in response to a felt social need. It had many of the aspects of a reform movement; it was designed to correct a bad situation. Values, therefore, were part and parcel of the field from the beginning. Some persons thought there were better ways of doing things and that these ways should be taught. This is certainly not unique to family life education, nor is it unique that there is disagreement about which values the field should support.

This situation did not appear as a problem to many of the early family teachers. Assertions as to the rightness or wrongness of specific family behaviors abound in the literature and seem to have gone relatively unchallenged. There was a strong assumption that *of course* everyone—or at least everyone who counted—believed the same things about family life. The job was, evidently, to convince people to do these things, and the divorce rate would drop, children would be reared properly, and the institution of the family would be saved.

Such sentiments can still be heard at almost any conference of family teachers, but today they are almost always challenged. Probably most leaders in the field today agree that family life education should not consist of foisting one set of values, the teacher's, in place of another set, the pupil's. However, there is no agreement as to just what position the teacher *should* take when value conflicts arise.

Searching for principles involved in this issue of values, two family life teachers who are sociologists took opposite positions. One said:

. . . my thesis is two pronged but simple, namely, teaching ethical values through the marriage course is both desirable and unavoidable. . . .

Granting that in the last analysis the student must make his own judgments relative to ethical values, is he prepared to make intelligent judgments without guidance? If we assume that we are not to teach ethical values, are we, figuratively speaking, throwing the student into deep water without first giving him some instruction in swimming on the assumption that, if water and shore are both present, he will find a way to get from one to the other?

Certainly we can agree that the instructor should not attempt to make the student's judgments for him, should not moralize, condemn, or condone. Every student and every point of view is accepted. But if we assume marriage as it is now found in the United States, we cannot assume that there are no values operative in it, or that there is no difference among the practices associated with it.

There are relatively few who would reject the values inherent in such things as monogamy, legitimacy, healthy interpersonal relations, individual growth, emotional health and maturity, happy stable marriage, sexual exclusiveness in marriage, and the equality of the sexes. On the other hand, there are few who either advocate or condone adultery, family disunity, destructive interpersonal relations, extreme conflict, or the domination of one individual by another. If, then, we assume that the student will live in a given cultural framework, we must also assume the importance of teaching him the values by and through which his life may be made consistent with this framework (Bowman, 1957, pp. 325–327).

The other sociologist took this position:

. . . my main argument against the teaching of ethical values in the marriage course is the sociological one: Ethical systems are always related to groups of people; in fact, a dictionary definition of ethics is "the rules of conduct for a particular group." Now, in our multigroup kind of society, with its various religions, social classes, ethnic groups, individual family cultures, and all, which particular group is the teacher to use as his source of a specific set of rules of conduct?

Those who want the teacher to pass on a set of ethical values to the student, I suspect, have their own set of values in mind as the model of what is to be passed on. People would be far less free to demand that the teacher teach values if they suspected that the teacher's values were not the same as their own. And yet, except for the case of those few values which are universally accepted in our society ("accepted" but not universally implemented by behavior, it should be noted), it seems highly unlikely that the taxpayers, the school trustees, the administration, the teachers, the student, and the student's parents would all agree regarding what is right and wrong in many crucial areas of marriage.

What it amounts to is that there are only two sets of values which can safely be taught in our schools:

(1). Those upon which there is this rather unlikely unanimous agreement. (And it hardly seems necessary to me for the teacher to waste his time teaching the socially obvious. . . .)

(2). Those which represent the most powerful, or influential, and often the most conservative, and out-of-date groups in the society (Kerckhoff, 1957, pp. 332–333).

What position, for example, should the high school teacher take regarding divorce? If the family course is committed to contributing to family stability (not an uncommon goal in this field), should divorce be portrayed as an evil, a menace? Or should it be seen as an unfortunate occurrence in an otherwise healthy institution of marriage? Or should it be shown as a social invention which allows individuals to move toward their goal-values (and those who oppose divorce would then be seen as opposed to human beings solving their own problems)? Or should divorce simply not be studied in such a course because, as one teacher said, "This is a course in marriage, not in divorce"?

This problem was discussed by Leslie:

If any social predictions are warranted, it is probably safe to predict that divorce rates in the United States will be high indefinitely. . . . Many young couples will marry only to find out later that they are growing apart instead of together and that this is a matter of the occupational-social context in which they find themselves and not simply a function of their personal rigidities and inabilities to adjust. Increasingly this is a risk that must be faced by your students and mine, and by your children and mine. Should we as family life educators give support to divorce norms that will force these people to view a situation over which they certainly do not have complete control in terms of self blame? Or, should we, as qualified authorities who know that divorce is with us to stay, exert our influence to alter the present day conception of divorce? (1959, pp. 9–10).

If the solution to such a question seems easy, one can move to even more difficult ones regarding the teacher's position in relation to the topics of birth control and chastity. Again, the global goals of the course, such as the preservation and improvement of family life, will not guide the teacher much if the value questions arise. Should a high school teacher tell a class that premarital virginity is a matter of personal preference? Or should he condemn lack of chastity even though many members of his class are neither virginal nor committed to the value of virginity? He can tell them that premarital virginity is held to be a modal American value and is observed in practice by some but not by others, but he will not have told the students anything they did not already know. Or he can attempt to teach the "facts" about chastity without attempting to inculcate a value, but would he then have done his job? Or he can decide that discussions of chastity have no place in a class on fam-

ily life education, but he can't really believe this, and the students won't.

When he discusses marriage, he must in some way deal with the topic of birth control, being guided to some extent by his knowledge of laws regarding the teaching of this subject. But teachers are not generally being prosecuted for going beyond the law in the teaching of birth control. The law, it is suspected, is more often used by timid teachers as an excuse for not dealing with the topic honestly. In one major school system, for example, family life teachers had not been introduced to the current, more liberal law on the subject, but were operating on the assumption that older, more restrictive laws still existed. The teacher is well aware that Catholics do not hold the same views on the subject of birth control as do Protestants. He may only vaguely know of other differences, but he knows the topic is a "dangerous" one. Can he maintain his resolve to be as "functional" —that is, helpful, practical, sound, and not simply academic and theoretical—when he approaches the topic of birth control, as, for example, he was when he discussed the topic of family budgets?

Nor should it be assumed that all the difficult value problems deal with the topics of divorce and sexual or reproductive behavior, dramatic as these areas are. The value problems involved in the previously mentioned area of family budgeting can be as critical as those involved in the study of chastity, although they usually are not recognized as such. Only recently have critics of the family education field been pointing out that much of the current teaching about spending and saving money represents the values of an obsolete economic system and is inappropriate to today's economy.

Values related to the treatment of disagreements between marital partners are challenged in family life classes by values relating to the mental health of individuals. Values concerning permissive child-rearing, equalitarian sex-linked roles, working mothers, and the treatment of older members of the family must by their very nature conflict with other values related to these topics. Unlike the teacher of other courses, where value conflict is relatively unknown or at least unrecognized, the family life teacher deals daily with systems of right and wrong, good and bad.

Teachers react to this challenge in many ways, of course. To some it is no problem, or challenge, because they are convinced that they know the right way and the good values, and they are unaware of a dilemma. Others try to deal honestly with value clashes by presenting "all sides" and by clearly labeling values as their own, or as middle class, or as Catholic, or whatever. Other teachers make their aim the encouragement of students to build their own value systems, and they are relatively nonpersuasive where choices must be made. Still others search various value systems for areas of agreement and dwell on these. And some build supervalue systems—systems which are made up of values which seem *above* or superior to those linked to social class, religion, and so on; some teachers seem to regard mental health values in this manner.

For certain teachers, such problems are discouraging; and there are some who seek to return to the sociology theory class or the home economics food laboratory where they are not plagued by these kinds of decisions. The popularity of the field of family education, however, leads to the conclusion that concern with questions of value is a challenge and an attraction to many teachers; they know that they are teaching something of importance to their students' lives.

Along with questions of "Should we teach values?" and "Whose values?" the field comes up against questions of *"Can* we teach values?" or *"How* can we teach values?" Are values, in a phrase currently popular in the field, taught or caught?

Perhaps the whole issue is academic if it turns out that students are not changing their values in these classes anyhow.

For the future of the field, however, the issue of values is not academic. Individual teachers, whole school systems, and the field of family life education itself are being challenged to make vital decisions regarding value questions.

Individual teachers who seem to be violating cherished values of the community, or of powerful persons in the community, are in peril of losing their jobs. School boards have been split and school superintendents have been criticized because the supposed values of the family life classes fell into disfavor with segments of the public. The family education field itself has been accused by professionals of smuggling middle-class, conservative, and religious values into schools in the guise of scientific facts and secular education, while at the same time it has been accused by laymen of smuggling revolutionary and inappropriate sex education into the classrooms disguised as attempts to support family life. Again, this very problem makes the field more challenging to teachers who welcome a struggle or who like to feel that they are dealing with issues that are helpful and important.

Some observers think that one of the dangerous results of this unresolved value dilemma is the inability of the field of family education to support its teachers when they are caught in a value conflict. Lacking value consensus, family life educators find themselves unsure how far they can go. There are today almost no signs of effective support from the field, either from its leaders or its organizations, when a family teacher is threatened with the loss of his job because of what he taught or how he taught it. Although the problem has been the subject of discussion by the leading organization in the field, the National Council on Family Relations, this has not taken the form of systematic study, nor has this organization chosen to view itself in the role of a pressure group dealing with public policy; rather it so far has considered its role to be that of a forum for the expression of opinion. This position leaves its members relatively unprotected in matters of this kind, except through recourse to the courts and to such organizations outside the field as the American Association of University Professors.[2]

Questions of Acceptance and of Respectability

Part of the dilemma of contemporary family teachers is that they often are caught between criticisms by the lay public and by their academic peers from other disciplines. It seems confusing to say that a field which came into being because of public demand should have to fight for public acceptance, but such has been the case. Not everyone has been enthusiastic about adding or maintaining family life courses in the schools. And the opposition to such education has not simply been a reaction to the value dilemmas noted in the preceding section. [Some of these same issues pertaining to values and public acceptance of the field are discussed by Ehrmann as applying to sex research; see Ch. 15, pp. 616–620. Also consult Ch. 24, below.]

Is there room in the crowded curriculum for a new course? That is an age-old question in educational circles. If that course, along with being new, also seems to infringe upon courses already taught, opposition is aroused. The layman is also often quite suspicious of a course designed to teach about such a personal thing as marriage and the family. "Can these things be taught in school," he asks? If the teacher is very young and unmarried, or perhaps not

so young and divorced, old stereotypes come into play, and the suspicious layman becomes fairly well convinced that this is not really a legitimate class.

Also, if the instigator of the new course refuses to "sell" it as a cure for divorce, delinquency, and other great social issues, and further, refuses to promise that the layman's values will be taught in the class, even more opposition can be aroused.

Sometimes rivalry is engendered in other social institutions. Although family education in the schools has generally been able to find supporters among the clergy and social workers, for example, instances are not uncommon where individuals from these professions have seen the new courses as infringing on the role of the churches or of being inadequate attempts at "cheap" social work by untrained individuals.

In the face of recent criticisms of modern education as being unequal to the tasks of the space age, school boards have had to re-examine their belief in family education. At times they have withdrawn support and referred to family courses as "frills."

Some teachers have joined the criticism of the field and have made changes in their courses designed to show that they are "scientific" and sufficiently difficult to be respectable.

Landis called for a sterner defense of the field:

As teachers I believe that we have been too timid and too willing to run for cover on the occasions when certain kinds of attacks are made upon family life education programs. Those who have met such attacks constructively have found that minority opposition to the program diminishes when people become informed of the true facts concerning purposes, content and methods in family living classes today (1951, p. 1).

In some cases, family educators have taken steps to achieve and maintain public acceptance. With many teachers this means working with PTA's and other groups. It means sending material home with their

[2] For a report of AAUP action on a recent case involving the suspension of a professor subsequent to his expressing liberal views on sex, see "Academic Freedom and Tenure: The University of Illinois," *AAUP Bull.*, 1963, 49, 25–43. Also see pp. 616–618 of this Handbook.

students, visiting in homes, and consulting with parents regarding methods and materials used in the courses. Especially in cases where the community has had what it considers a bad experience with a family life class or family life teacher are such steps thought to be necessary. They are more frequent at the elementary and secondary school levels; almost never at the college level.

The relationship of the family life teacher to other teachers and to other disciplines also involves several unresolved issues. In a field as status conscious as education, the problem of acceptance of any discipline is of importance. Some observers as well as some family teachers would claim that family life education is low in the status hierarchy in American colleges and high schools. As a new field of education, family life education suffers the same status problem as any newcomer.

Family life education also may suffer from the self-imposed label of functionality. To be "functional," in this sense, means to be useful and practical. Since this is sometimes assumed to mean lack of respectability in educational circles, some college family educators play down their functional goals and emphasize the theoretical aspects of their courses. Theory in this field, however, must be related to psychological, sociological, economic, biological, and other theory. Few family life teachers are capable of building consistent and adequate master-theories which will silence their critics from other disciplines. The critics ask, "Why not have students take courses in these other fields and get the material first hand?"

In cases where the family life course is very popular with the students, representatives from other disciplines may feel threatened. Naturally, they claim, a course is popular if it is just a bull session about sex and if anyone can get a good grade in it. Many family life teachers claim that one of the most useful skills they have had to learn is the ability to handle the not-too-humorous jibes directed at them by other teachers who thought the marriage course was becoming too popular with students.

The uneasy relationship of family life education to research deserves a special note. To some extent, even in the most functional and most student-centered class, there would be an expectation that classroom material would be based on research more strongly than on personal opinion. Most family life teachers today have a serious problem with this assumption, a problem which is not unique to this particular field, of course. Actually, there are two problems: (a) Is the available research useful to the teacher? (b) Is the teacher capable of using the research?

The contributions and shortcomings of family research are discussed in early chapters of this Handbook. Teachers themselves, particularly those in high schools, are the first to admit they do not have the time to be fully aware of all the existing research and are not sufficiently trained to make adequate interpretations of it. To remedy this situation, attempts are being made to provide teachers with summaries and interpretations of current research. There are also in-service training institutes and workshops where teachers are taught more about what is found in current research and how to read research reports.

Questions of Common Goals and Methods

At conferences of family life educators, relatively few discussions have dealt with questions of the values held or taught by teachers. In the corridors, discussion might turn to problems of rivalry with other disciplines, but, on the floor, this has seldom been a popular topic. There is another set of problems, dealing with the goals and methods of the field, which traditionally has been featured in official conference deliberations.

For example, a frequently asked question is, "Do family courses have a specific content?" This question often springs from the dispute between those teachers who are subject-oriented and those who are student-oriented, if such a distinction is legitimate. Some family teachers feel a responsibility for presenting specific categories of information. Others think courses should be based on the needs and interests of their current students.

These two philosophies result in different approaches to the family course. Take the matter of grading students as an example: Those teachers who go into class with specific material to be presented usually find examinations and grading fairly easy. The examination measures and the grade reports the nearness of the student to mastery of the specific subject matter. But student-centered teachers experience much greater trouble with examining and grading. Some, consistent with their basic philosophy, involve students in these processes also. But many say that it is difficult if not impossible to grade individual students according to their progress in such a class. Often teachers claim that the memorizing of specific facts is not what they are encouraging; it has little to do with helping marriage and family life, they think. It is difficult to discover just what they do want to encourage. Sometimes it is attitude change, and teachers experiment with before-and-after attitude scales or opinion tests. Others are interested in teaching certain skills in human relationships, and these skills are difficult to measure.

Other similar problems are involved. For example, there is the question of immediate versus long-term gains. That is, who should receive the A, the student who knows all of the "right" answers when the course is over, or the student who can apply certain principles to his marriage later in life? Also, should students be graded on the progress they made in the course or simply on the level they are at when they finished the course? That is, who gets the A, the student who learned a lot, or the student who knew a lot when the course began as well as when it ended?

We have already become aware that these

problems of subject matter, examining, and grading are related to the field's struggle with the question of how academic it should be. For some teachers, the perfect solution is to remove most of the academic trappings from the family life course. Some would make it strictly elective. Others would make it non-credit bearing. And many favor not giving examinations or grades for such courses.

There are arguments against these "solutions," however. If family life education is strictly elective, will it reach those students "who really need it"? If such courses do not bear credit, will they appeal to credit-conscious students and add to the status of the field? And if examinations and grades are abolished, won't there be further problems of student motivation for taking the courses and student aspiration while in the classes?

In some areas controversy still exists concerning whether or not elementary and high school family classes should be composed of boys and girls or should be segregated by sex. Those who believe in mixed classes claim that there is educational value in bringing together the points of view of the two sexes. Also, they point to the negative results of treating this subject as though it were something boys and girls should not discuss together. Proponents of segregated classes usually point to the age level involved and claim that junior high students, at least, are more comfortable discussing matters of sex and personal relationships separately.

Sounding out family life educators themselves on some of these questions, G. A. Christensen (1958) found that most thought the courses should be elective, but encouragement should be given students to elect them. Also, most thought that boys and girls should take the courses together.

Another problem involves the ages at which American boys and girls are getting married and having children of their own. Since the "early marriage problem" has become of such concern to Americans, family educators have more and more wondered about the value of courses which are at the college and late high school levels. Perhaps these courses are coming later in the lives of many boys and girls than they should to be of maximum value.

Other questions deal with the role teachers should play vis à vis students, and with whether family courses should be taught by one person or by a team.

Since the early days of family life education there have been courses taught by one person and courses taught by teams. Those taught by one person sometimes involved bringing other resource persons— such as physicians and clergymen—into class for special lectures, with the teacher acting as coordinator as well as instructor. The argument in favor of team teaching is that the topics covered in a family class are usually far beyond the competency of any one teacher. In favor of the one-teacher method, however, is the kind of relationship students can form with one person but not so easily with a team.

One of the teacher-role problems which has been of interest to the field of family life education is the question of whether the teacher can and should be a counselor to his students. From the beginning, it was found that dealing with family life subjects in a personal manner encouraged students to see teachers after class for personal counseling and guidance. Some teachers saw this as an opportunity to further their teaching goals; for others, it was just another demand on time, energy, and talents. For the perceptive teacher who tried to be both instructor and counselor, some new problems appeared. Questions concerning how, if at all, to use information derived from counseling in class or in grading were bound to arise. Switching from an instructive role to a listening, non-judgmental, and guiding role, and then switching back again, was difficult for some teachers. Many began to ask for training in counseling along with training as teachers. Since the marriage counseling profession itself was

struggling for status and professionalization, there was a notable reluctance on the part of marriage and family counseling centers to provide short-term training for teachers. Those that did offer such training usually found many to take advantage of it.

Bowman pointed to certain practical aspects of the situation:

Recognition of the importance of premarital counseling in a program of education for marriage is widespread. But a question is sometimes raised as to who can and should do this counseling. Should a person trained primarily for classroom teaching also serve as counselor on premarital problems? For some time to come there will not be enough trained counselors to meet the need. Therefore, counseling on premarital problems must be done in considerable measure by teachers. The immediate problem is to assist teachers to improve their counseling. Furthermore, counseling and teaching may be helpful allies. Teaching affords contacts with students, opportunities to establish rapport, core information, and the stimulation of questions. Counseling suggests problem areas to be included in teaching, aids in making teaching more functional, and helps prevent the teacher from allowing his course to crystallize (1947, p. 1).

It may well be that teaching and counseling are mutually supportive endeavors and that good family life education should include both. About 80 per cent of American family life teachers claim that they do some counseling, as well as teach. It may also be that the attitudes and approaches demanded by these two processes are contradictory, and hence difficult for one person to use effectively. At any rate, if school systems are to expect teachers to counsel as well as to teach, there will have to be much greater provisions made for training and functioning than are now available. For example, counseling demands both time and privacy, which a great majority of public school teachers today do not have in sufficient abundance.

The questions involved in working out the teacher-counselor role have led many

family educators to ponder the problem of
what is education and what is therapy. Can
counseling be limited to educational goals,
or should it be? Can teaching be therapeutic as well as educational, and should
it be?

One formulation popular among some
family educators is:

Education and therapy are complementary
phases of a single process—the *learning* process
as directed to the achievement of effective maturity. The extent of their identity has been
obscured by their more salient differences in
emphasis; the one upon mastery in the handling of *judgments,* the other in the handling
of *feelings.* By an oversimplified aphorism, we
could say education teaches the individual how
to examine *what he thinks* about what he
feels important; therapy, to examine *how he
feels* about what he thinks important (Powell,
Stone, & Frank, 1952, pp. 33–34).

A final question of goals and methods
deserves attention. Stated simply it is this:
Should family life education in the schools
be a course, a unit in a course, or an emphasis throughout the curriculum? In elementary schools, family life education is
often an emphasis and is diffused throughout the curriculum, with a coordinator
rather than a specific teacher. Some educators believe this is a healthy method and
recommend it for higher education also.
Others feel that when family education is
everybody's business it becomes nobody's
business.

CONCLUSIONS, EVALUATIONS, AND PREDICTIONS

Gigantic social forces have united with
extant social values and produced what has
aptly been described as the folk movement
of family life education. There were other
responses to these forces and values, but
family life education has moved ahead of
them in public acceptance and could be-

come an almost universal American mechanism for dealing with family life. It has
student support; it was student demand
which brought about functional marriage
courses in university after university. It has
community support—mostly. At least there
is more acceptance than there is resistance;
and there is more fear of resistance than
actual resistance.

What can stop this field? If it represents
a socially approved American response to
felt social needs, why do so many school
systems not have family living courses
(Bayer & Nye, 1963)? If college students
in Wisconsin, California, and Indiana demand courses, why don't all colleges everywhere have them? Even today, many students are not being reached by such courses,
and successful family life, it has been noted,
is still seen more as a by-product than a
major objective of our educational system.

Each observer of the field will reach his
own conclusions about what is holding it
back—and some probably will not think it
accurate to claim that the field is being
held back. Noted here are just three factors
which seem to be retarding an otherwise
growing social movement: (a) confusion
regarding the definition of the field and the
division of labor within it, (b) overcaution
in teaching about sex, and (c) inadequate
evaluation of the results of family life education.

There is a deceptive clarity in written
definitions of the field. To realize this, one
has only to compare the definitions with
the actual courses being taught. Or one
may reach the same conclusion by studying
the research of the field; different researchers report different results partly because
they define, or their respondents define,
family life education differently. G. A.
Christensen (1958) asked his respondents
about the chief objectives of family life
education and found such diverse answers
as: to achieve interpersonal competence, to
reduce divorce, to give self-understanding,
to master factual material, to aid in self-
insight, to provide emotional maturity, and

to facilitate adjustments to cultural change. Can family life education be all of these?

Agreement on a definition for the field, and a statement of its objectives, might clarify the question of who should teach it. At present, the field is dominated at the secondary school level by home economists and at the college level by sociologists and home economists.

At a recent family life education conference, a nationally known home economist asked, "What, if anything, is the difference between family life education and home economics?" Many home economists would claim that there is no difference—that the Department of Home Economics should be called the Department of Family Life (and some colleges already have made this change). Family life teachers who are not home economists, however, do not see this convergence. Coon (1962) even found that secondary school home economists themselves reported only a small portion of their time spent in teaching family life, and they evidently did not usually consider their foods and clothing classes to be family life education.

One problem for home economics is that it has not been able to overcome the reluctance of boys to take the course. This is obviously of more importance to family life education at the secondary school level, where boys are especially sensitive to being identified with a "girlish field." It is also of importance in teacher training for work at the elementary and secondary levels. Many family life teachers are trained in home economics colleges rather than in colleges of education or of social science, and, again, fewer young men than young women find there way into the field because of the label it carries.

However, if the Department of Home Economics is an imperfect place for family courses to be based, so are other departments. Critics of the family education offered by sociologists, for example, claim that the sociological interest has not always been in practical, student-requested, func-

tional kinds of family courses. G. A. Christensen (1958) found, for example, that in his sample the sociology teachers of family life courses were less functional in their approach than were the home economists.

Another of his findings was that most secondary school and college family life educators thought that family life teachers should be members of a Family Life Department rather than a sociology or home economics department. Perhaps they were pointing to one way out of the present confusion regarding division of labor. There are those who believe that the family life field would prosper if it were less tied to traditional academic departments.

Some of the value dilemmas this field is experiencing have already been noted. Many of these revolve around the teaching of matters related to sex, and it is understandable that, in a society where sex is a confusing matter, education about it might be confused. However, family life education cannot gain the support of adolescents unless it recognizes the role of sex in the family. Today, many students doubt the ability of their family life teachers to deal with sexual topics in a mature and helpful manner. That their suspicions are sometimes well-founded is seen in the curious omission of sexual topics from many family courses (Bayer & Nye, 1963) and textbooks (Hudson, 1956). Bayer and Nye found the avoidance of sexual topics prevalent in Florida high schools. Hudson found only three high school texts giving treatment to sexual matters among the 10 books he examined, and these but briefly. "Most authors treat sex by implication, as if young people were unaware of the sexual aspects of life. When these aspects emerge in discussions of kissing, necking, and petting, the emphasis is on control and sublimation" (1956, p. 91). Some authors may have wanted to treat sex differently in their texts, of course, but may have met objections from publishers.

Historically, the literature of the family life field has reflected very little interest in the search for sexual values other than very conservative ones. Some recent exchanges of ideas such as those of the Harpers (1957; 1959), Kirkendall (1960), and Stokes (1962), however, indicate some change in this matter. Certainly, if the field is to deal realistically with family life in America today, it must take some position other than shocked disapproval regarding such facts of life as the divorce rate, the degree to which sexual relations are not confined to marriage, and the radical changes taking place in sex-linked roles of husbands and wives. If not, the "folk movement" will not be moving with the folk. [Cf. Ehrmann's discussion, pp. 616–620.]

Evaluation

Student demand and enthusiasm have carried the new field of family life education along, but so has the faith of family life educators. As with most action programs, faith, rather than proof of results, seems to keep the machinery running. However, tools for measuring the results of this kind of education are becoming available, and as family life teachers meet their critics today, they find themselves wishing that they had used the tools and documented the results of their brand of education.

At present, it seems impossible to say that there is proof that family life education improves family life. And if it does not, or if there is a suspicion that it does not, then critics may ask, "What is it for?"

Attempts at evaluation have not been lacking, however; they have simply been inadequate. Some are rather impressionistic statements by people who have been engaged in the work of family education. Numerous testimonials to the value individual teachers, students, or administrators place on this kind of education abound in the literature. For example:

When we turn our glance to the future and contemplate the magnitude of the problems that lie ahead, we can still rest assured that

[the] beachhead has been established once and for all; that marriage education will never move back to the zero point . . . that the scratch [it has made], though neither long nor deep, will never be removed. Marriage education has become a permanent part of the American educational process. . . . There has been set in motion a new movement in American education. . . . It will involve a reevaluation of education in general (Bowman, 1953, p. 308).

There also have been research-based evaluations of courses and programs within the field, but probably not more than two dozen have ever been reported in the literature, and these have almost all been studies of college programs. Hill has summarized:

This discussion of evaluation of the consequences of family life education suggests the need to make our objectives, I think, much clearer. They have been so lofty it has been almost impossible to evaluate our progress or lack of progress with respect to them. There is justification for the belief that specific techniques and factual knowledges can be successfully taught and carried over into marriage. It remains to be seen, of course, whether these are important to the over-all success or failure of marriage.

The evidence from the attitude changes achieved in the marriage course leads us to the conclusion that persons who have had marriage education are somewhat more realistic in their anticipation of problems and in their general marriage expectations. Marriage education also seems to result in an ability to verbalize somewhat more freely about marriage, its problems, solutions, and nature. Marriage becomes objectified, a vocabulary is learned along with some concepts and principles. Our better students, especially, develop an ability to discuss marriage with an emotional detachment and an apparent understanding which many of us believe to be good because it permits freer marital communication. We have, as yet, to prove that this is conducive to marital success (1960, p. 38).

Hill (1960) sees at least four major methodological problems in this kind of research: How can we isolate one factor, the marriage course, from all other factors which prepare us in one way or another for marriage? What can we use as a definition of marital success? When should the evaluations take place, at the end of the course, after the wedding, or when the marriage is five years old? And who should make the evaluative judgment, teacher, student, or a third party?

Kerckhoff (1960) invited consideration of the philosophical and ethical considerations which evaluators must face. Evaluation, according to some critics, is too apt to be a measurement by some "outer" source of something that is best known only by "self." Ethically, it borders on exploitation, it has been charged, because it can be used as a tool of administration to control a teacher by comparing him with other teachers or with some standard.

However, most present-day researchers are willing to use what research methods they have available, and they have not been very discouraged by philosophical and ethical arguments against evaluation. Researchers, in fact, seem to be encouraging family life teachers to request and support evaluation studies. If the field does *not* obtain such studies, it will be increasingly vulnerable to growth-frustrating attack.

Some Hunches and Forecasts

From time to time, family life educators play prophet and make predictions about the future of their field. Let us add a few hunches of our own concerning the direction of family education.

Many students of the field reach the conclusion that there will be an important change in the theoretical structure of the family life educator's body of knowledge in future years. This guess is based on the condition of this body of knowledge today—it invites systemization. It is also based on the impact being made on the field by theoretically oriented academicians, often to the discomfort of the more action-oriented practitioners among the family life educators.

A similar and related prediction is that scientific thinking and scientific research will have more influence in family education in the future. Textbooks in the field have shown more deference to research in recent years, and teachers who are able to understand research findings may be expected to rely more and more on this kind of data, as contrasted with more value-laden and impressionistic materials.

Leslie's guesses seem similar:

Critical analysis of what is currently done in family life education suggests that there are many aspects of hidden valuation in our work. . . . I have indicated that I believe that over the next twenty years family life education must become more firmly based in a more adequate comparative scientific framework, that family life educators must concern themselves not simply with adjusting people to the kind of society in which they live but must also assume responsibility for making it a better society in which to live, and finally, that, before they can be of much help to others, family life educators must resolve some of their own attitudes, particularly in the area of sex behavior . . . (1959, p. 12).

In general, we would see family life education, if it is to prosper, becoming more sensitive to two opposite influences on the family: (a) the strivings of the individual personalities within the family, and (b) the needs of human beings in the world outside the family.

This will mean that the field must recognize that the family is not an end in itself. The demands of the world community today are so vital, so much a matter of human existence itself, that that family life education which teaches children to hold marriage and family life as the highest goal might be regarded as education for suicide.

It will also mean the recognition by the field that human institutions are made for human beings, not human beings for human institutions. There is no point in making the preservation of the family institution the exclusive goal of family life education. If the family is to be preserved, it must be because it helps human beings achieve their highest values; and if it does that it will not need to be bolstered by schoolroom indoctrination.

REFERENCES

American Social Health Association & National Congress of Parents and Teachers. *Rocky Mountain project in family life education.* New York: ASHA, 1961.

Avery, C. E. Inside family life education. *Fam. life Coordinator,* 1962, 11, 27–38.

Avery, C. E., & Kirkendall, L. A. *The Oregon Developmental Center project in family life education.* 220 S. W. Alder St., Portland, Ore.: E. C. Brown Trust, March, 1955.

Avery, C. E., & Lee, Margie R. Family life education: its philosophy and purpose. *Fam. life Coordinator,* 1964, 13, 27–37.

Bayer, A. E., & Nye, F. I. Family life education in Florida public high schools. Paper read at Nat. Counc. on Fam. Relat., Denver, Aug., 1963.

Bowman, H. A. The teacher as counselor in marriage education. *Marr. & fam. Living,* 1947, 9, 1–8.

Bowman, H. A. Marriage education in the colleges. *J. soc. Hyg.,* 1949, 35, 407–417.

Bowman, H. A. The content of a functional marriage course. *Coll. & Univer.,* 1952, 27, 355–364.

Bowman, H. A. A critical evaluation of marriage and family education. *Marr. & fam. Living,* 1953, 15, 304–308.

Bowman, H. A. Teaching ethical values through the marriage course: a debate (pro). *Marr. & fam. Living,* 1957, 19, 325–330.

Brim, O. *Education for child rearing.* New York: Russell Sage Foundation, 1959.

Brown, Muriel W. Trends in parent education. *Annals Amer. Acad. pol. & soc. Sci.,* 1935, 182, 73–81.

Brown, Muriel W. Education for family adjustment today. *J. home Econ.,* 1941, 33, 225–228, 305–311.

Brown, Muriel W. *With focus on family living.* Washington: U. S. Department of Health, Education, & Welfare, Office of Education, 1953.

Christensen, G. A. An analysis of selected issues in family life education, 1958. Unpublished doctoral dissertation, Michigan State Univer., 1958.

Christensen, H. T. *Marriage analysis: foundations for successful family life.* (2nd ed.) New York: Ronald Press, 1958.

Coon, Beulah I. *Home economics in the public secondary schools: a report of a national study.* Washington: U. S. Department of Health, Education, and Welfare, Office of Education, 1962.

Dager, E. Z., & Harper, G. A. Family life education in Indiana public high schools: a preliminary report. *Marr. & fam. Living,* 1959, 21, 385–388.

Dager, E. Z., Harper, G. A., & Whitehurst, R. N. Family life education in public high schools: a survey report on Indiana. *Marr. & fam. Living,* 1962, 24, 365–370.

Drummond, Laura W. *Youth and instruction in marriage and family living.* New York: Teachers Coll., Columbia Univer., Bureau of Publications, 1942.

Duvall, Evelyn M. *Family development.* (2nd ed.). Philadelphia: Lippincott, 1962.

Force, Elizabeth S. *Teaching family life education: the Toms River Program.* New York: Teachers Coll., Columbia Univer., Bureau of Publications, 1962.

Grams, A. *Parent education and the behavioral sciences.* Washington: U. S. Department of Health, Education, & Welfare, Social Security Administration, Children's Bureau, 1960.

Harper, R. A. The responsibilities of parenthood: a marriage counselor's view. *Eugenics Quart.,* 1959, 6, 8–13.

Harper, R. A., & Harper, Frances R. Are educators afraid of sex? *Marr. & fam. Living,* 1957, 19, 240–246.

Hayes, W. J. The place of sociology in professional education. *Soc. Forces,* 1948, 26, 292–298.

Hill, R. Education for marriage and parenthood in the United States. Paper read at Soc. Scientists' Advisory Meeting sponsored by Soc. Security Admin., June 20–21, 1960. (Mimeographed.)

Hudson, J. W. A content analysis of selected family life education textbooks used at the secondary level. Unpublished doctoral dissertation, The Ohio State Univer., 1956.

Kenkel, W. F. A survey of family life education in Iowa high schools. *Marr. & fam. Living,* 1957, 19, 379–381.

Kerckhoff, R. K. Teaching ethical values through the marriage course: a debate (con). *Marr. & fam. Living,* 1957, 19, 330–334.

Kerckhoff, R. K. Evaluating family life education. *Merrill-Palmer Quart.,* 1960, 6, 187–191.

Kirkendall, L. A. Principles basic to education for marriage and family life in the high school. *Marr. & fam. Living,* 1949, 11, 131–133.

Kirkendall, L. A. Values and premarital intercourse—implications for parent education. *Marr. & fam. Living,* 1960, 22, 317–324.

Kirkendall, L. A. Education for marriage and family living. In A. Ellis & A. Abarbanel (Eds.), *The encyclopedia of sexual behavior.* New York: Hawthorn Books, 1961. Pp. 696–704.

Landis, J. T. Utilizing community support for family life education. *Marr. & fam. Living,* 1951, 13, 1, 34.

Landis, J. T. Attitudes and policies concerning marriages among high school students. *Marr. & fam. Living,* 1956, 18, 128–136.

Landis, J. T. Education for marriage in the United States. Paper read before Stud. Group V, World Fam. Cong., Paris, June 16–21, 1958. (Mimeographed.)

Landis, J. T. The teaching of marriage and family courses in colleges. *Marr. & fam. Living,* 1959, 21, 36–40.

Lawson, Dorothy S. Education for home and family living in New York State. Paper read at Conf. on Teaching Fam. Life, Merrill-Palmer Inst., Detroit, May 7, 1962. (Mimeographed.)

Leslie, G. R. Personal values, professional ideologies, and family specialists. *Marr. & fam. Living,* 1959, 21, 3–12.

Longworth, D. S. Certification of teachers of family living: a proposal. *Marr. & fam. Living,* 1952, 14, 103–104.

Morgan, O. W. New approaches in family life education. Paper read at Nat. Counc. on Fam. Relat., Storrs, Conn., Aug. 24, 1962.

Paget, N. W. *Family life education program profiles.* San Bernardino, Calif.: Kendal, 1961.

Powell, J. W., Stone, A. R., & Frank, J. D. Group reading and group therapy: a concurrent test. *Psychiatry,* 1952, 15, 33–51.

Rockwood, Lemo D. Highlights of a study of the sources and history of family life education. Ithaca: Cornell Univer., New York State Coll. of Home Economics, 1948. (Mimeographed.)

Stokes, W. R. Our changing sex ethics. *Marr. & fam. Living,* 1962, 24, 269–272.

Tulsa Public Schools. *Personal relationships: eleventh grade: a revision of the course in home living.* Tulsa, Okla.: Author, 1949.

Withers, Rex T. Home and family life education in Michigan. Paper read at Conf. on Teaching Fam. Life, Merrill-Palmer Inst., Detroit, May 7, 1962. (Mimeographed.)

GERALD R. LESLIE
Oklahoma State University

As a professional emphasis of adequately trained family specialists, marriage counseling is so new that its character is not yet fully determined (Harper, 1953; Mace, 1954). Analyses of it are apt to vary, depending somewhat upon whether the writer is oriented to social science, psychotherapy, medicine, social work, the ministry, or the law; for few of the persons practicing marriage counseling today were trained primarily as marriage counselors. Rather, they were trained in one or more of the conventional academic disciplines and have moved into marriage counseling in response to demands from students, clients, patients, or parishioners, and in response to their own professional and personal needs to develop a new form of theory and practice. Yet the outlines of a new clinical profession are emerging, and a solid core of definitions, principles, goals, and techniques may be described.

MARRIAGE COUNSELING DELIMITED

Marriage counseling is a specialized field of counseling focussing upon the marital

relationship. Thus it both overlaps and is distinct from other fields of counseling and psychotherapy. In a not wholly facetious sense, marriage counseling also may be described as "what marriage counselors do." In a rapidly developing field, where theory and practice are not yet fixed, one may learn more about the parameters of the field and about its structure by observing the evolving practices of a representative group of trained counselors than through a synoptic definition. For an indirect exposure to this range of conceptualization and technique the reader is referred to standard textbooks in the field (Cavanagh, 1957; Cuber, 1948; Johnson, 1961; Mace, 1948; Mudd, 1951; Skidmore, Garrett, & Skidmore, 1956; Vincent, 1957) and to the Casebook of the American Association of Marriage Counselors (1958). In the absence of complete familiarity with the field, the following distinctive features of marriage counseling are presented.

Focus on Marital and Premarital Relationships

Marriage counseling is more specialized than other comprehensive fields of family counseling and social casework. Although

[1] The author is indebted to Edward Z. Dager and David R. Mace for helpful suggestions on an earlier draft of this chapter.

marriage counselors attempt to include the total family group in their diagnostic formulations and treatment plans, they seldom deal directly with more than two or three family members. As marriage counselors, they do not specialize in work with preadolescent children and are prone to refer such children who may be involved to other specialists. Similarly the work of the marriage counselor is likely to be restricted to the conduct of clinical interviews in his office. The home visit and the extension of material aid to families go beyond marriage counseling as such.

The problems treated by marriage counselors fall broadly into three groups: (a) those encountered in premarital relationships as a couple move toward marriage, (b) marital problems, and (c) problems encountered by divorced and widowed persons that stem from prior marriages or are directly relevant to possible future marriages. The general age range of marriage counseling clients is from mid-adolescence to about 55 or 60. Although marriage counselors occasionally work with older or younger persons and occasionally deal with problems that are not directly related to marriage, these are the exception rather than the rule.

Clients who seek marriage counseling also are likely to come with problems which they conceive to be related to marriage. They are likely to say, however embellished, "Something is wrong between my spouse and me," or "Something is wrong with my marriage." Ordinarily, they do not come seeking help with specifically personal problems or with vague, unspecified complaints. Thus, from the beginning of counseling, the problem focusses sharply upon marriage and, if anything, that focus becomes even sharper as counseling proceeds.

The Case Unit is the Relationship

Since marriage counselors treat relationship problems, rather than personal problems as such, diagnosis and treatment planning ideally involve two or more clients. At this level, marriage counseling is more complex than traditional psychotherapy, where persons often are treated outside the context of immediate relationships with others.

Whereas in many forms of therapy the counselor eschews all contact with other family members of his client, marriage counseling ideally involves the same counselor working concurrently, and sometimes jointly, with two or more parties to the relationship. This radical departure from traditional practice has both advantages and disadvantages and inevitably increases the complexity of counselor-client interaction.

Obviously, marriage counselors believe that the advantages in working concurrently with both partners to a relationship outweigh the disadvantages. The marriage counselor can more quickly evaluate and employ therapeutically whatever distortions exist in the productions of each partner, something that is ordinarily denied to the psychotherapist. Moreover, he is in a position to coordinate the counseling of the partners so that whatever gains they achieve are mutually reinforcing. He thus seeks to avoid the familiar pattern of one partner becoming more disabled as a function of the other's improvement. Distortions in the counseling process itself, commonly labeled transference (Wolstein, 1954) or referent reactions (Johnson, 1961), are held somewhat in check by the lack of exclusiveness in the counselor-client relationship. The major disadvantage probably lies in the conscious and unconscious efforts of the partners to seek the counselor as an ally in their struggles against one another (Johnson, 1961).

In some proportion of cases, the ideal of working with both partners is not met. Either because of the physical unavailability of one partner or because of his or her inability or unwillingness to be involved, the counselor may be forced to work with one partner only. In this situation, some of the advantages cited above are lost, but the diagnostic and treatment problem remains the same. The counseling goals include not only improved mental health for the client, but improvement of the client's total relationship with the unavailable partner.

Interprofessional Character

The interdisciplinary character of marriage counseling is apparent on at least two levels. First, marriage counselors have been trained in different academic disciplines and give allegiance to different professions. Their theoretical orientations may be based in the concepts and findings of modern sociology and psychology, in psychiatry and social work, in psychoanalysis, or even in religion. It probably is true that most counselors strive for some degree of electicism and that, not having any truly eclectic theory, they use multiple, overlapping frames of reference. The marriage-counseling practice of a person trained in psychoanalysis may be quite different from that of a sociologist, and still different from that of a man trained in educational guidance. Yet, these practitioners probably each use concepts and techniques employed by the others and seek consistent, if not common, treatment goals.

Whatever the original discipline in which a marriage counselor is trained, his training in that specialty almost certainly is not broad enough for the competent practice of marriage counseling. The range of relationship problems brought to marriage counselors requires, in addition to training in personality theory and the theory and technique of counseling, training in at least the sociology of the family, genetics, anatomy, physiology, sexology, elements of psychiatry, religion, and domestic-relations law. Thus, long after his professional degree is secured, the aspiring marriage counselor must steep himself in other fields of knowledge. Eventually, as a marriage counselor, he is more than a sociologist, psychiatrist, or social worker. He practices in an interprofessional area.

From Education to Deep Therapy

Disputes over whether marriage counseling is a form of psychotherapy have occasionally occupied the field (Harper, 1953; Karpf, 1951a). Those who argue that it is psychotherapy usually stress unconscious motivation and the role of personal pathology in marital problems. Those who insist that it is not psychotherapy are prone to emphasize the relative normality of marriage-counseling clients and their ability to cope with their relationship problems consciously. Most practitioners probably recognize the partial validity of each position.

There are many definitions of psychotherapy, but for our purposes the broadest of them is most appropriate. If psychotherapy includes the exercise of any determinant interference in the course of a client's life, then it is quite clear that marriage counselors practice psychotherapy. The important question is, "What kind of psychotherapy do they practice?"

Marriage-counseling practice differs from other forms of psychotherapy in that marriage counselors are less prone to assign priority to the clients' personal problems or to factors operating early in the clients' lives. Marriage counselors focus on present relationships as much as possible and work backward through the clients' development only as far as necessary to resolve the present relationship problems. Thus, rather than stressing the analytic notion of regression to the stage of greatest pre-oedipal weakness, marriage counselors assume that most clients need not work through all early developmental problems in order to be helped to cope with current interactional difficulties.

Clients who seek marriage counseling cover a very wide range of health and illness. Some of the more extreme levels of personal pathology are ruled out by the fact that clients generally must be ambulatory and sufficiently well organized to seek help on their own initiative. That there are profound neurotics and psychotics among them, however, is quite certain. Yet most clients are neither psychotic nor extraordinarily neurotic. Most of them cope reasonably well with most life situations most of the time. Even more important, most clients do not come because of illness per se. How much effort will have to be directed toward the cure of personal pathology must be determined anew in every marriage-counseling case. And how much effort *can* be directed toward curing individual pathology varies with the training, experience, and skill of the counselor. Some marriage counselors are well equipped to do depth therapy and some are not. Some clients who require it may get intensive psychotherapy as part of a program of marriage counseling, and some have to be referred to other specialists for it.

It follows, then, that marriage counseling cannot be distinguished by whether the counselor works at conscious, preconscious, or unconscious levels. Many counselors work in varying degree at all three levels. Most prefer to work as much as possible at relatively conscious levels and some, because of limited training, work exclusively at these levels. More thoroughly trained counselors often work at preconscious levels, and the most skilled among them work at levels as deep as other psychotherapists.

The Value Position on Marriage

A common misconception among laymen and some professional persons is that marriage counseling has the promotion and preservation of marriages as its primary goal. Such persons view marriage counseling as directed toward buttressing traditional, conservative standards of family life and being generally opposed to solutions involving unconventional personal behavior, separation, and divorce. The value position assumed by most professional marriage counselors is, in fact, quite different.

Marriage and family life are not unfailingly productive of healthy personalities, or of happiness and satisfaction. Although the potential in healthy families is great, although many, even most, persons can attain maximum personality fulfillment only in harmonious family relationships, the potential for maladjustment, frustration, and unhappiness also is great. Some persons at some time in their lives are not at all well prepared for marriage. To help or encourage them to marry would be utmost folly. Some premarital relationships are so neurotically based as virtually to ensure marital conflict. And some marriages that produce pervasive undesirable effects in parents or children might better be discontinued. In a society where family living is virtually synonymous with adult living, and where the basic satisfactions of childhood are experienced in a family setting, most people will find maximum fulfillment in the development of healthy families of their own. Thus marriage counseling more often than not exerts its influence toward the development, maintenance, and restoration of marriages. But in some instances, marriage counselors aid clients to dissolve unsatisfactory marriages and either to live without partners or to develop new and healthier relationships.

Professional marriage counselors are "analysts of" rather than merely "propagandists for" marriage. Being of varied religious persuasions as well as of different primary training, they do, however, vary in their acceptance of divorce as a solution to relationship problems and in their intellectual commitment to the positive benefits that marriage brings. Each counselor must judge anew with each client how the goals of personal satisfaction and relationship stability can best be attained. The marriage counselor's evaluation of the continuance of a marriage also is influenced by the probable selectivity operating in bringing clients to a marriage counselor rather than to some other form of counseling. It is reasonable to expect—and the evidence generally supports the view—that marriage counseling clients disproportionately include those who need to work out their difficulties within the context of marriage.

An Art Grounded in Science

There is both an art and a science to marriage counseling. The science includes the basic principles of human interaction, personality development, interviewing, and other knowledge in which counselors must be competent. These principles stem from sociology, psychology, psychiatry, and so on, and may be taught in the classroom. Presumably, any intelligent human being of proper academic background can master them.

The phrase "art of counseling" refers to the relationship aspects of the counseling process itself. Not all who are capable of mastering the relevant theory and factual information can become qualified counselors. In addition, counselors must be able to form enabling, permissive relationships with a wide variety of clients and at the same time remain objective and nonjudgmental. A very crucial variable is the counselor's ability to use his own personality effectively in the service of his clients (Johnson, 1953).

This art of counseling cannot really be taught in the classroom. Indeed, there are persons who by reason of their own previous experience cannot learn it well under any circumstances. Others, by virtue of broad empathic capacity and the possession of adequate security and satisfaction in their own lives, can become increasingly skilled (Fromm-Reichmann, 1950). Ordinarily, this skill is acquired in actual counseling practice under the direct supervision of experienced counselors. Counselor training programs provide for a lengthy period of internship in which the emphasis is upon the increasingly effective use of the counselor's own personality. Even after the period of formal training is completed, the need for supervision or systematic consul-

tation with one's colleagues remains. The need for continuing personal development of the counselor and for increased skill in interpersonal relationships is never ending.

THE DEVELOPMENT OF MARRIAGE COUNSELING

Although the history of modern marriage counseling is very short, its roots extend back through most of human existence.

Premodern Agencies and Emphases

Marriage counseling, like all counseling, probably stems originally from folk recognition of the value of catharsis to people in trouble. The sense of emotional relief derived from merely talking problems through with a sympathetic listener often has great therapeutic value and has been recognized through the ages. Probably every era has included the role of the wise man whose wisdom lay more in simply serving as a sounding board against which people could work out their troubles than in the possession of technical competence. If such wise men had been truly wise, and if their numbers had been adequate, most modern forms of counseling might never have been necessary. Unfortunately, then as now, the therapeutic listening often was accompanied by naive admonitions to "do what is right," and the problem would be solved. Many popularizers of the present operate in much the same fashion, imploring people whose problems lie in the inability to conform to established ways to solve their problems by conforming.

One of the first agencies to offer aid with family problems undoubtedly was the church. As part of its inherent charge, the church long has been interested in stabilization of the marriage relationship and has employed the personal relationship between minister and parishioner in an effort to do so. The Roman Catholic Church, through the confessional, combined in a way that is still sound today the value of catharsis with a close, supportive, disciplined relationship with a father figure. The efforts of the church in this area, however, were oriented toward the conservation of traditional values to the point where those who could not easily conform to its teachings often were driven away.

The medical profession began early to take on counseling functions as an adjunct to physical healing. Many taboos about bodily and sexual functions were lowered in the physician-patient relationship, providing physicians with ready access to emotional and relationship problems centering in this part of married life. Over the decades, physicians have numbered disproportionately among the acknowledged specialists in family problems. Unfortunately, the impression grew up among physicians and laymen alike that physicians by virtue of their medical training acquired competence to work with relationship problems. It requires no special brilliance today to see that ordinary medical training does not provide the knowledge, attitudes, and skill required for effective counseling. The occasional wise man among physicians who was able to combine ready access to patients' problems with intuitive skill in human relationships became a symbol or stereotype of the profession. Physicians today often have neither the necessary skill nor the inclination to devote the time to deal with relationship problems.

Modern Agencies and Emphases

Over the past several decades, developments in several professions, disciplines, and agencies have contributed directly and indirectly to the emergence of modern marriage counseling.

Developments in psychiatry. Psychiatrists, of course, were among the first to treat problems of personal and interpersonal adjustment. Several factors in the nature of psychiatry, however, forestalled developments which might have led to the incorporation of marriage counseling into medicine.

First among these was the orientation of psychiatry to biology and the associated concept of illness. Great emphasis was placed upon organically based disorders, and even when emotional disorders were incorporated into the field, the emphasis was upon the decidedly abnormal and bizarre, with the concept of "cure" being extended to these also. Thus, while psychiatry gradually broadened to include the so-called functional disorders, it still dealt with these in terms of the original bio-medical model.

The development of psychoanalysis provided for the first time a comprehensive theory of personality and system of therapy which departed significantly from this model. Although Freud based his original theories in biological mechanisms, subsequent experience proved him simply to have been a good ethnographer, and the neo-Freudians have gradually substituted ideas of social causation for those of biological causation. Psychoanalysis today provides the foundation for virtually all psychotherapy, whether practiced by medical or nonmedical personnel.

The concern with psychodynamics and individual psychotherapy, however, has prevented psychiatrists generally from moving very far in work with interpersonal relationships. Fairly typically, psychiatrists treat patients apart from their significant relationships with other people. Psychiatrists often will not treat a husband and wife concurrently—let alone jointly—and may refuse even to see or to interview other family members. Although this emphasis upon individual psychotherapy has tended to keep developments in marriage counseling and psychiatry quite distinct, the recent emphasis in psychiatry upon family therapy (Ackerman, 1958) may signal imminent rapprochement of the two fields.

Clinical psychology. Until about the time of Wundt and James, psychology also had its roots in physiology. And, although clinical psychology developed later, it, too, has been much influenced by the bio-medical model. It has followed psychiatry in its concern with abnormal behavior, while departing from psychiatry in its greater emphasis upon learning in the development of that behavior.

Although hampered somewhat by the vested interest of psychiatry, clinical psychologists have long practised psychotherapy and indeed have probably worked with a broader range of deviant behavior. Particularly in academic settings, clinical psychologists encounter the whole spectrum of personal and relationship problems, thus being drawn inadvertently into the treatment of marital problems. Whatever preparation the psychologist has for working with marital problems ordinarily is incidental to his training in individual behavior disorders. He is apt to lack both a theoretical framework for the analysis of marital problems and the necessary familiarity with sexology, domestic-relations law, sociology of the family, and religion.

Social work. During the early 1900's, social work began to give up its charity orientation and catering to the physical wants of people to move toward a casework emphasis on the total adjustment of individuals and families. In so doing, it became less attached to the social sciences and adapted the psychoanalytic model to casework practice. For about 30 years, there was a hiatus between the social-work ideology of fostering total family adjustment and its theoretical and clinical grounding in individual psychotherapy. Even during this period, casework was more broadly based than either psychiatry or clinical psychology. Caseworkers frequently worked concurrently with two or more family members and, through devices such as the home visit, were concerned with the total family. In the early years and under the influence of psychoanalysis, the two family members frequently in treatment were mother and child. In recent decades, however, caseworkers have gravitated more and more into marriage counseling. As this occurred,

social work again began to look to social science for its theoretical formulations and today is contributing significantly to the development of marriage-counseling theory (Gomberg, 1956; Pollak, 1956; Weiss & Monroe, 1959a; Weiss & Monroe, 1959b).

Direct Antecedents

Each of the fields just discussed has contributed to the development of professional marriage counseling, but marriage counseling did not grow directly from them. Instead, certain developments in education and social science led straight to it.

Social hygiene and sex education. World War I and the publicity it gave to problems of prostitution and venereal disease gave impetus to the social-hygiene movement in the United States. The American Social Hygiene Association (now the American Social Health Association), as the major organization in the field, soon began to stress the control of prostitution, premarital blood tests, prenatal examinations, and the treatment of infants' eyes. Starting as a narrow sex-education movement, it soon broadened to a concern with the whole family-adjustment problem. Some counseling services were provided through regional officials of ASHA, and gradually an emphasis upon the development of family-life education programs emerged.

It was during the 1920's, and as part of this general movement, that the now ubiquitous sex manuals began to appear. These books stressed the promotion of sex adjustment, and indirectly marital adjustment, through the provision of sound information and the encouragement of healthy attitudes. People were encouraged to take their sex- and marital-adjustment problems to professional people, and the demand for marriage counseling began to grow.

Home economics and child development. Counseling in the field of child development generally has been secondary to course work and research. However, as child-development departments in colleges of home economics have been drawn into providing functional family-life education, some counseling has appeared. Such functional course work may have started at the Merrill-Palmer Institute in Detroit about 1920. The early courses, wherever taught, were largely courses in infant and child care and training. Gradually, the emphasis shifted to more significant problems of child development, and then, as it became apparent that the social and emotional development of children is significantly influenced by family relationships, to child development and family life.

The marriage-education movement. Functional preparation for marriage in American colleges and universities began with the work of Ernest R. Groves, first at Boston University and later at the University of North Carolina. Groves taught a course in preparation for marriage at Boston in 1924. From this beginning, courses developed relatively independently at several universities, and the movement was under way.

Early courses tended to be a series of lectures given by different persons who were experts in separate fields such as sociology of the family, psychiatry, gynecology, religion, and household economics. Instructors seldom felt competent to cover the whole range of material necessary to preparation for marriage and dealt with these feelings of inadequacy by refusing to accept the whole responsibility. The resulting product often was abstract, unintegrated, and of very uneven coverage. There was a heavy emphasis upon factual material and neglect of the development of attitudes and values. Such early courses hardly were designed to stimulate students to take their personal marital problems to their instructors for help, but many of them did so anyway.

From the beginning, some instructors recognized that academic preparation for marriage implied the learning of relationship skills and the development of healthy attitudes as well as the mastery of factual information. Since attitudes and values could hardly be handled in the typical large lecture sections, a trend appeared toward small classes, with one instructor handling the entire semester's work. This trend occurred simultaneously with repudiation of the naive idea that "being happily married qualifies one to teach the course," and the development of the area as a professional specialty of well-trained people.

With the passage of time, courses emphasized more and more the personality, social, and cultural factors involved in successful marriage, and correspondingly less emphasis was placed on such topics as budgeting and household management. They became mental-hygiene courses, often bordering upon group therapy. Naturally, the line between classroom instruction and counseling blurred, and instructors, often without formal training, found themselves expected to do counseling on a substantial scale. Many universities granted released time from teaching duties for this purpose.

The first generation of instructor–marriage counselors was largely self-taught. Moving into counseling after their formal training was completed, there was no alternative. Undoubtedly, the quality of the counseling was very uneven and reflected heavily the personalities and social values of the counselors. As these men trained graduate students, however, they sought to provide their successors with what they themselves lacked, and the formal training of social scientists in marriage counseling was under way.

College and university programs in marriage education and marriage counseling have become large and widespread. A recent survey (Landis, 1959) has shown over 1,000 courses on the family, and counseling training programs have developed at a number of institutions. These will be discussed more fully below.

Conferences and Organizations

As marriage education grew, and as it merged with the interest in marriage counseling developing in other professions, several conferences and organizations focussing on teaching, research, and counseling appeared.

The Groves Conference on Marriage and the Family. In 1934, Ernest R. Groves invited to a conference at Chapel Hill, North Carolina, a group of professional persons interested in the improvement of educational techniques. The conference became an annual affair and gradually broadened its scope to include teaching, research, and counseling. As an invitational conference, it was able to set extremely high standards, and through a series of lectures, seminars, and research groups to stimulate the professional development of the area. The emphasis has been and remains today upon the sharing of concepts, ideas, and experiences among the leaders in the profession rather than upon the dissemination of materials to a broad public.

The National Council on Family Relations. An interprofessional and lay group to promote successful family living was formed in 1938. Organized originally by a sociologist and an attorney, the National Council has grown to a membership of nearly 3,000, organized into local, state, and regional groups. The Council publishes the *Journal of Marriage and the Family* (formerly *Marriage and Family Living*), a quarterly devoted to family-life education, counseling, and research, and holds annual conferences attended by several hundred members. The Council is divided into sections, one of which is on marriage counseling. This counseling section is led by many of the same people who participate in the Groves Conference and also has overlapping membership with the American Association of Marriage Counselors. Through its journal and conferences, the Council serves as a major publication outlet and educational medium for people interested in marriage counseling.

The American Association of Marriage Counselors. Founded in 1942, the American Association of Marriage Counselors is the major professional organization of marriage counselors in the United States. From the beginning, it has assumed the role of developing and maintaining high professional standards in the field. Consequently, its membership is small, numbering approximately 450 in 1962. The academic backgrounds of members are difficult to state precisely, because many of them have had formal training in more than one discipline. According to their current professional identifications, the largest groups of members are psychologists and psychotherapists and educators. There are somewhat smaller numbers of social workers, sociologists, physicians, and ministers, and a scattering of attorneys. Only about one out of three applicants is accepted for membership.

The AAMC has established standards for marriage-counseling centers, for postdoctoral training centers, and, more recently, for university doctoral programs emphasizing training for marriage counseling. It has published a casebook (1958) and contemplates publishing a journal. Recently, it adopted a formal code of ethics governing marriage-counseling practice. The AAMC, as an organization, provides no counseling services, but both the national office and some regional affiliates maintain formal or informal referral services. The Association carries on a continuing program of education through clinical meetings arranged both on regional and national bases and held several times each year.

Counseling Agencies

Agencies and organizations offering marriage-counseling services directly appeared first in Europe. The first counseling center for problems of sex was established by Magnus Hirschfeld in Germany in 1919. Another opened in Austria in 1922. By 1930 there were perhaps 100 of them. Most of these centers closed after the coming of the Hitler regime. Since 1945, there has been some revival.

Outside of the United States today, marriage counseling is more highly organized in England than anywhere else (Mace, 1958). The National Marriage Guidance Council has established approximately 100 local councils which offer counseling services on a community basis. The Catholic Marriage-Advisory Council, maintaining its own set of locals, was formed so that Catholics could work with counselors of their own faith, particularly in the areas of family planning and divorce. The entire movement is partly supported by the British goverment, although it maintains its private, voluntary nature.

The philosophy of counseling and counselor training is very different from that which characterizes professional marriage counseling in the United States. The British argue, with merit, that other countries simply cannot afford such highly professional services and have developed a system of selecting and training counselors who work on a part-time, unpaid, volunteer basis. There is relatively more emphasis on the personal suitability of persons for doing counseling, less emphasis on formal training, and more emphasis upon the relationship and supportive elements in counseling. Proponents of the English and American systems each believe their system to be superior in its own context. No definitive comparison of the two systems has yet been possible.

The first center in the United States was opened by two German immigrants, Abraham and Hannah Stone, at the Community Church in New York City in 1929. Abraham Stone later became Director of Counseling at the Margaret Sanger Research Bureau.

The American Institute of Family Relations opened in Los Angeles in 1930. Over the years, this organization has developed a large staff and offered a variety of services, ranging from education for parenthood to publishing family-life education literature and conducting workshops and courses for counselor training. Its professional reputation has suffered somewhat

from too much popularization, although recently there have been signs of attempts to return it to full professional status.

The Marriage Council of Philadelphia, which has a casework emphasis, opened in 1932. In addition to its service function, the Marriage Council has become a major postdoctoral training center. It is affiliated with the University of Pennsylvania schools of medicine and social work and has conducted considerable research into the techniques and results of counseling (Mitchell, Preston, & Mudd, 1953; Mudd & Froscher, 1950; Preston, Mudd, & Froscher, 1953).

The Merrill-Palmer Institute, a non-degree-granting institution, has developed an integrated counseling service emphasizing clinical and counseling psychology, family sociology, and group work. It has an elaborate internship program and, with the Marriage Council of Philadelphia, is approved by the American Association of Marriage Counselors as a postdoctoral training center.

In 1950, the Menninger Foundation established, and operated for several years, a postdoctoral marriage-counseling training program which gradually became confined to ministers. Recently, the program has been altered to become a program in pastoral care and training. At this writing, it is uncertain how much emphasis there will be on marriage-counseling training.

A large volume of work with marital problems is done by the approximately 300 member agencies of the Family Service Association of America. These are private social-work agencies whose approach to marriage counseling is through the broader framework of social casework. As more and more of the problems brought to social agencies are relationship problems, the initial resistance of some social workers to using the phrase "marriage counseling" is breaking down.

Considerable marriage counseling also is done through about 250 local branches of the Planned Parenthood Federation of

America. Perhaps best known for their contraceptive service, various Planned Parenthood centers provide informal and formal counseling services, either through staff physicians or through nonmedical counselors who also conduct educational programs. Both counseling and education, under these auspices, range from a fairly narrow concern with sex problems to highly professional marriage counseling.

A unique approach to marriage counseling, and a rapidly developing one, is to be found in various family-court centers over the nation (Bridgman, 1959; Elkin, 1962). Although they are organized in various ways, their essential feature is the use of the influence of the court to urge participation in marriage counseling upon couples in conflict or seeking divorce. Some of these programs have operated for at least two decades and have dispelled the notion that forced participation in counseling is doomed to failure. The apparent success enjoyed by family-court centers in areas like Toledo, Ohio, and Los Angeles has led several states to consider or enact legislation providing for mandatory state-wide predivorce counseling. So far, however, the legal and staffing problems created by these efforts generally have rendered them unworkable. It is entirely possible that over the next generation, most of these problems will be solved. [Cf. p. 956.]

The most direct participation of social scientists in the development of marriage-counseling agencies has been through the establishment of counseling and counseling-training services at colleges and universities. Over the past two decades, at least a dozen major universities have been involved and, currently, Teachers College, Columbia University, Florida State University, the University of Minnesota, Purdue University, and the University of Southern California have active counselor-training programs which maintain regular contact with the American Association of Marriage Counselors.

University marriage-counseling centers have varying emphases upon service, training, and research, but typically emphasize counselor training as part of the program of study leading to the doctoral degree. The staffs generally include two or more of the disciplines—sociology, psychology, and social work—and usually provide for some psychiatric participation.

The long-range significance of these centers lies in the provision of a regular mode of recruitment into marriage counseling as a profession. Most present-day marriage counselors had to get their training in addition to, and after, their formal academic training. Now, with university graduate programs developing to feed students into the approved postdoctoral training centers, the characteristics of a true profession are beginning to emerge.

MARRIAGE-COUNSELING THEORY

Alleged Eclecticism

Marriage-counseling theory customarily is described as eclectic. In fact, it is seldom so. An eclectic theory is one which successfully integrates into a new theory elements from two or more existing ones. The temptation to describe marriage-counseling theory as eclectic derives from the fact that practitioners come from various academic disciplines and typically have had some training in two or more of these disciplines. In practice, they find that the concepts and theories of any one discipline are inadequate. They may use, at various times and in various ways, concepts from sociology, psychology, psychoanalysis, and social casework, together with applied knowledge from medicine, genetics, religion, and domestic-relations law. The specific integration of these diverse elements into practice is seldom explicit and is not likely to be constant even for the same counselor, let alone from one counselor to another. Such usage is more nearly omnium gatherum than eclectic.

It appears that marriage counselors' insistence upon their "eclecticism" may be partly a matter of conviction and partly defensive. To the extent that they believe that marriage counseling is truly an interdisciplinary art, it is a matter of conviction. But there may also be, lurking near awareness, some doubt over whether there really is *a* theory of marriage counseling and whether practice does not suffer from the lack of clearly articulated theory. Doubtless, different marriage counselors would take different positions on this matter, and it is not the purpose of this chapter to resolve the issue. Once it is recognized that these elements may be operating, energy which might have been expended in futile debate over an abstract ideal of eclecticism may be turned to the task of theory-building itself.

Personal and Relationship Problems

A starting point is the simple fact that the problems typically presented to marriage counselors may have two somewhat distinct but overlapping components, personality impairment in one or both of the partners, and conflict between the partners. Or, to put it differently, the problem may lie in the people involved, in the relationship between them, or, perhaps more often, personal and relationship difficulties combine to create an ever worsening, ever more complicated problem.

The situation often is not so simple as to resolve itself into determining whether either personality impairment or relationship difficulties are present or absent. There are occasional cases where "the problem" is to be found in one profoundly neurotic or even psychotic partner. Or both partners may be emotionally ill, and there are cases where "the problem" lies in extreme cultural differences between the spouses; where they are of different national, racial, religious, educational, or economic backgrounds. But, more often, the pervasiveness and the acuteness of both personality and relationship problems must be considered.

Personal problems may be pronounced in many different areas of living, for example, in a wife who not only is unable to manage the routines of everyday living such as housecleaning and meal preparation, but who can give no affection, controls and rejects her children, is afraid of social contacts, detests sex, and has headaches, stomach trouble, and arthritis. Or her emotional difficulties may be confined virtually to a single area—a distaste for sex born out of early rigid training. Similarly, role conflict may exist only in the in-law area, or it may extend through earning a living, housekeeping, sex relationships, parent-child relations, and social life. Hence, the marriage counselor must determine not only whether emotional illness or role conflict is the major problem but, also, how pervasive or segmental the personal and relationship difficulties are.

In some instances, persons who have functioned relatively well for three decades or more suddenly confront adjustments that they are unable to make. Or there may be a history of maladjustment which began in early childhood and characterized each subsequent period of life. Marriages differ in the same way. Some of them go along very smoothly for a while, only to confront a crisis that cannot be resolved. Others are embroiled in conflict from the premarital period through 20 years or more of living together. Acute personal and relationship difficulties present very different counseling problems from longstanding, chronic ones.

When a marriage counselor sees his clients for the first time, he must seek answers to these questions: What kind of problems does this couple have? Are they primarily emotional problems within each of the partners? Are they role conflicts between two relatively normal people? Are there elements of both? How pervasive or confined are these difficulties? Are they confined to just one or two areas or are they involved in almost everything these people do? How long has this been going on? Is it something they brought with them into the marriage, or is it something that developed last year or last month? The number of combinations of answers to these questions is quite large; the problems brought to marriage counselors are quite varied. An adequate theory of marriage counseling must be capable of embracing all of the possible combinations.

For the elements upon which to build marriage-counseling theory, one may look to the concepts of psychology, including psychoanalysis, or to those of sociology and anthropology. Some individual marriage counselors look predominantly to one or another. It is the thesis of this chapter, however, that neither of these disciplines alone offers a conceptual system adequate to embrace the range of marriage-counseling problems outlined immediately above. Each makes certain assumptions about human behavior that are essential to accurate understanding of marital problems, and each ignores certain ranges of causation that also are essential to the understanding of marital problems. In a synthesis of concepts from the two disciplines can be found the most comprehensive and useful approach to a theory for marriage counseling available today.

Social-System Theory

The case unit in marriage counseling is the relationship, typically between husband and wife. That relationship can be conceptualized in different ways. It is regarded here as comprising a social system, a social system being constituted by the interaction of any number of persons (Parsons, 1951).

A social system is made up, not of people, but of behavior. Viewed from the standpoint of the individual, every person participates in many different, and often overlapping, social systems. Husband and wife in interaction constitute one system, mother and child a second, father and child a third, and so on. There is also the social system which embraces the whole family. Each family member participates, in addition, in a variety of systems involving nonfamily members. Some of the more significant of these revolve around the occupational role of the husband, the family's religious affiliation, and the members' social and community affiliations. Society may be viewed as a complex network of interdependent, interlocking social systems.

Until the appearance of social-system theory, sociological analyses of marriage-counseling problems were handicapped by the practice of making the individual the basic unit of analysis. The individual was typically set over against the society, society being composed of a plurality of individuals. The individual-society dichotomy, however, failed to provide adequate conceptual tools for the analysis of the relatively small social units within which most "societal" interactions actually are carried out. Thus, there were no satisfactory concepts for handling the interactions of work groups, play groups, families, and so on (Lantz, 1959).

When marital relationships and all other relationships are characterized as social systems, however, the individual no longer is the basic unit of analysis. Instead, the units become the roles which individuals play in the multiple social systems in which they participate (Parsons, 1951). The marital relationship, then, is viewed not simply as two people who must be dealt with, but as a system of interactions possessing certain properties which make for either satisfaction or dissatisfaction. These properties are more than the simple products of the personalities of husband and wife. They derive from the ways in which the personalities of the partners impinge upon one another in a particular social context. Once in existence, the system of interaction becomes a dynamic force in its own right, influencing the way in which "personality" is manifested.

Once this is accepted, the dangers of sociological reductionism must be avoided. Parsons has pointed out that discussions of behavior by sociologists and psychologists frequently bog down in sociological reductionism if the writer is a sociologist, or psychological reductionism if the writer is a psychologist (Parsons, 1954). Each tends to reify the particular units of analysis with which he deals and to attempt to derive the other's concepts therefrom. It is Parsons' contention, and the writer's also, that neither sociological nor psychological concepts have any inherent primacy in the explanation of human behavior. Instead, they constitute equally valid explanations of different ranges of behavior. They complement one another, being, at one and the same time, dependent upon one another but not reducible to one another.

What has been briefly described above as social-system theory is, in effect, the common-sense interpretation of the sociologist. The psychologist also works with concepts which can be viewed in terms of systems, but the systems with which he deals lead him to a different "common-sense" interpretation of behavior.

Just as sociology focusses on interaction, psychology focusses on certain elementary processes of behavior like perception and learning and with the organization of these into the personality of the individual as a system. The common sense of the psychologist indicates that interaction *between* individuals should be explained by knowledge of their behavior *as* individuals. This is the typical approach of psychologically grounded psychotherapists to problems of marital interaction.

It requires no great prescience to see that social systems and personality systems are overlapping. Social systems involve segments of behavior and thus segments of the personalities of individuals. These segments are the roles which comprise the interactions. Conversely, personality involves a system of roles, role being the basic unit of social systems. So far, there would seem to be no reason why each of these systems of concepts should not be reducible to the other—why personality could not be completely explained as a system of social roles, and why interaction could not be com-

pletely extrapolated from knowledge of personality. In fact, neither is possible, for both personalities and relationships have unique properties of their own.

Each personality is unique in at least two respects. One type of uniqueness is based in the biological organism. Though biological characteristics assume meaning only through experience, each physical organism presents a unique set of reward objects. From such gross characteristics as size, regularity of features, and coloration, to more socially determined ones such as intelligence and aggressiveness, the individual always responds as an organism, with the organism being an important determinant of the enactment of any particular role. Thus, a tall, light-skinned, well-proportioned, intelligent man brings to the role of husband (or any other role) a very different set of potentials than does a small, misshapen one. Any interpretation of personality which neglects this element cannot approach reality.

Personalities are unique also in the particular combination of social systems in which they participate. Although most men eventually play the roles of husband and father, no two men have an identical number and combination of roles in their total experience. The ways in which they enact the roles of husband and father are influenced by the sequence and the pattern of roles from earliest childhood on through adolescence and adulthood. The final combination of a specific physical organism encountering an idiosyncratic pattern of roles produces a uniqueness in personality which is not adequately portrayed simply by description of the combination of roles enacted at a particular moment in time.

Nor is it sufficient to envision relationships merely as the social expression of particular personalities. Each relationship has unique properties of its own above and beyond the elements which compose it. Therapists who stress the neuroses of individual marriage partners are particularly prone to fail to see this. Consider, for example, a wife whose striving behavior accentuates her husband's existing doubts about his ability to advance occupationally. Each spouse may be said to be neurotic and to suffer from anxiety related to perceived failures in earlier experience. Take each of these persons, however, and place him in a different relationship, and his or her "neurosis" may manifest itself quite differently. This woman married to a driving, highly successful man may feel even more inadequate than if she were married to a less successful husband. Her anxiety may now focus on her own feared inability to keep up with him, and she may resort to any number of ways of coping with this situation. She may, for instance, sabotage her husband's ambitions, or she may resort to hypochondria in order to divert attention from her personal failures. It may even be that, married to this successful man, her feelings of inadequacy become much less conspicuous and problem-causing. By identification with his success, she may for all practical purposes become much less neurotic. The husband in the original example, married to a different kind of woman, may also reveal his neurosis in a very different pattern of behavior. Married to a hypochondriacal woman, his strength may seem relatively much greater, and his feelings of inadequacy may be virtually lost in his care of his sick wife.

The forms in which particular personality components may express themselves are many and varied. While some of these forms may cause problems, others may be quite benign. Whether problems result is significantly a function of the particular relationships in which the individual finds himself, and counseling efforts may be quite successfully directed toward altering the relationship while leaving other aspects of the personality system relatively untouched. In theoretical terms, relationships cannot be extrapolated from the personality systems which enter them any more than personality can be reduced completely to a set of roles.

The Element of Culture

The conceptual system is not complete even with the inclusion of both social systems and personality systems. The element of culture is yet to be added. A typical failure among counselors and therapists is to conceive of culture as essentially something external to personality. This leads to the reification of culture and statements to the effect that "the culture does . . . ," or "the culture causes . . . ." In fact, culture neither does anything nor causes anything. Culture is internalized into the personality system, just as institutionalization occurs in social systems. Men and women hold particular attitudes and behave in certain ways because they have learned these patterns in their own social milieu. Culture may only be inferred from systematic observation of the behavior of large numbers of persons, and it has no existence outside the commonalities in that behavior. Thus, at one and the same time, the influence of culture may be both overestimated and underestimated. When it is conceived of as a thing apart from personality, it is endowed with a force it does not possess, and its true significance for behavior is missed.

Most counselors, in marriage counseling and other fields, probably are inadequately aware of the cultural dimension. This shows up in many ways. For example, it appears frequently in Freudian interpretations of masculinity and femininity, when men are regarded as universally aggressive and dominating and women are supposed to achieve many goals by indirection. These notions may work well in middle-class European and American groups but be almost inapplicable to the situations of many lower-class people. Ambition on the job may bring only despair to lower-class males, who will be laid off at the first downswing of the business cycle. Their wives often must work if the family is to survive even in prosperous times, and in periods of recession the wives' incomes may be more steady than their husbands'. To diagnose the partial role reversal found among such couples as being of psycho-sexual origin is not only faulty, but may lead to a treatment program that will increase, rather than ameliorate, their problems.

Countless other examples could be given. Weeping on the part of males, a predisposition to physical violence, and exploitative attitudes toward the opposite sex are phenomena completely acceptable and constituting functional adjustments in different social groups. Without thorough familiarity with the cultural influences in his clients' lives, the counselor may be unable to assess properly the ways in which personality and relationship elements impinge upon one another. With adequate knowledge of personality influences and role relationships operating within a given cultural context, the counselor is in the best position to develop a treatment plan that not only will reduce the currently recognized problems but will avoid inadvertently causing new ones.

The Counseling Relationship as a Social System

Even while stressing the husband-wife relationship as a social system, it is easy to overlook the fact that the relationship between counselor and clients also is a social system with properties that have much to do with the outcome of counseling (Spiegel, 1954). As in all social systems, there are roles laid down for counselor and clients which specify both the range and type of interaction that should occur.

Traditionally, the role of counselor or therapist in this society is that of "healer." The usual analogy here is to medical practice, where the patient comes to the physician to be "cured of his illness" (Parsons & Fox, 1952). The marriage counselor, like the physician, stands in an interstitial position between his clients and the larger society. Clients who come for counseling ordinarily are engaging in deviant behavior

(not following accepted norms governing husband-wife interaction). They talk with the counselor about unconventional attitudes and behavior which in other social systems would result in sanctions being imposed upon them. In their roles as clients, however, they are temporarily exempted from normal social obligations. The counselor, as counselor, is permitted and even obligated to be accepting of behavior which in other circumstances he might regard as reprehensible. This temporary suspension of normal social obligations to both clients and counselor carries with it, however, corresponding obligations. The clients have their deviant behavior accepted, but only on the condition that they cooperate with the counselor to work toward removal of that deviancy. Similarly, the counselor is permitted temporary entrance into the clients' deviancy, but only for the purpose of bringing them back to acceptable behavior.

Parsons has elaborated the client-counselor system in terms of the stages in the Freudian paradigm of psycho-sexual development and the succession of stages in the counseling process. Viewed thus, the stages appear in Table 1. The remarkable parallel between stages seems to apply to virtually all forms of counseling and therapy. Whatever the range of problems upon which the counseling focusses, and whatever the theory from which the counselors operate, the counselor-client system is much the same. This may help explain the often noted fact that counselors of very different theoretical persuasions seem to have comparable success in dealing with the same kinds of problems. The common elements in the counselor-client social system may have as much or more to do with counseling outcome than does the theory upon which the counseling presumably is based.

Marital Conflict as a Form of Deviancy

Counseling and psychotherapy have been influenced greatly by earlier developments in medicine and psychoanalysis. These

TABLE 1

STAGES IN THE COUNSELING PROCESS IN TERMS OF THE
FREUDIAN PARADIGM OF PSYCHO-SEXUAL DEVELOPMENT (AFTER PARSONS, 1954)

Stage	Freudian Paradigm	Counseling Process
First	Maternal care focussed on gratification of organic needs. Mother completely permissive.	Counselor permissive to relieve clients' fears.
Second	Establishment of active love relationship between child and mother.	Transference stage in which support encourages attachment to counselor.
Third	Disciplines become more prominent. Child denied reciprocity for aggressive and dependent impulses, and his achievements rewarded.	Counselor begins to manipulate rewards, making them contingent upon clients' responses to counseling.
Fourth	Child becomes emancipated from family. Seeks rewards in new family.	Clients weaned from counselor.

specialties have contributed much to modern marriage counseling but have left, also, a legacy of concepts that makes it more difficult to conceptualize marital conflict adequately.

One of the concepts that causes difficulty is that of "illness." Medical people and, more recently, nonmedical psychotherapists have posed the problems with which they deal in terms of sickness and health. The model here is a biological one. Illness is conceived as a disturbance in the organism which can be explained in biological terms. Such a model is most appropriate in traditional medical practice. It begins to become less applicable in the practice of psychiatry where functional, as contrasted with organic, disorders are recognized. By definition, these are behavioral rather than biological disorders. Instead of developing a new and more appropriate model, however, medicine by and large has forced its analyses of nonbiological problems into the original biological model.

In the broader field of psychotherapy dominated by academic psychology, a somewhat similar situation is found. Here, the concept of emotional illness is even further removed from the biological concept of illness, but a mode of analysis stemming from roots in physiology and medicine remains. The client is conceived somehow to have become possessed of an entity (illness) which must be removed. Although biological causation may now be explicitly denied, many therapists continue to operate with concepts of illness and cure, and considerable research focusses upon establishing interrelations among biological and behavioral elements in the etiology and amelioration of emotional problems.

The final move from consideration of emotional problems within the individual to that of conflict between persons renders the biological model grossly inappropriate. To conceive of marital conflict as stemming from illness in one or both partners overlooks the facts that: (a) there is no evidence that marital conflict occurs more often between neurotic partners than between relatively nonneurotic ones; (b) neurotic needs may be complementary and strengthen a relationship; and (c) the incidence of severe marital conflict undoubtedly is far greater than the incidence of severe mental illness. The attribution of marital conflict to emotional illness reminds one of the now discredited interpretations of masturbation as a cause of mental illness and religious participation as a cause of mental health. Just as masturbation is a near-universal male practice outside of mental hospitals as well as inside them, and religion can be an outlet for emotional illness as well as a contributor to mental health, so is the correlation between neurosis and marital conflict partly spurious.

It is an acknowledged fact that the "cure" of mental illness in one partner to a relationship often serves to disrupt rather than to better the relationship. To say, as some therapists do, that this is because the other partner is neurotic, although it has some plausibility in terms of the notion of neurotic equilibrium, smacks strongly of circular reasoning. The second partner's alleged neurosis may be established from the fact of a worsening relationship following the cure of the first partner rather than from any other objective evidence of prior emotional impairment. The fact that worsening of the relationship may occur is evidence, however, that the relationship itself possesses dynamic force that must be taken into account at both the level of diagnosis and the level of treatment. A concept of the relationship as a social system provides a far more appropriate model than does a biologically based model of illness.

That marriage partners in conflict may manifest signs of widespread behavior disorder is indisputable. To find an explanation for these, one may look either into the remote personal history of the individuals and, by seeking to lessen the impact of early frustrations, enable them to cope more adequately with present problems. Or one can begin with the present relationship and work backward *in the relationship* to the point where the partners began to violate one another's expectations. At some point in time, the roles that they played in relation to one another were more satisfying than at the point where they seek counseling. Somewhere, the partners began to deviate from expected behavior. The original deviation may have involved the withholding of affection or approval, attacks upon one another, flight into the escapes of alcohol, sex, work, or what have you. What-

ever the original deviation, it encouraged compensating deviation in the other partner, which in turn stimulated further deviation. Interaction, whether it be satisfying or frustrating, tends to become cumulative and circular (Kirkpatrick, 1955), and soon the partners find themselves unable to reverse their mutually defeating behavior.

Contributions of Freudian Psychology to Analysis of the Family as a System

The personality theory most consistent with social-system theory is the psychoanalytic. Freud, more adequately than most of his successors in academic psychology, developed an essentially structural view of personality and saw the significance of the role of interpersonal relationships in determining the organization of personality. It is true that Freud based his theory in biology, but subsequent experience has shown that he was simply a good ethnographer (Malinowski, 1927). His concept of instincts was quite vague and not at all important to his theory of personality. At the same time, his concept of the unconscious tended to "layer" personality and to force a structural view.

One of Freud's most significant contributions lay in his analyses of several aspects of the relationship between the child and his parents. Earlier than anyone else, he saw the terrific importance of early emotional learning in the family for personality development. Unfortunately, he did not adequately visualize the entire social-system network of either child or parent and overgeneralized the development of personality from a restricted range of relationships. Failing to see the whole family as a system, or the relationship between that system and other subsystems such as the occupational, he placed undue stress on the child-father relation and was prevented from seeing that personality can and does continue to change after the childhood years.

In the concept of the superego, Freud also saw that culture is internalized into personality, and that this occurs originally and primarily in the family. He thus corroborated the earlier analyses of Durkheim. Even so, he had an overly narrow conception of pathology and was not able to allow for significant variation among kinship systems.

Marital Diagnosis and Treatment

It should be clear by now that in dealing with deviancy in social relationships, traditional diagnostic and therapeutic tools are inadequate. A broader framework is needed within which family dynamics may be understood. This requires both analysis of the personality systems of the partners and of the role relationships between them.

At the personality level, the level of continuing impairment in each partner must be determined. Following Rutledge's modification of the Freudian model (1960), four somewhat distinct levels of functioning and impairment may be postulated as in Table 2. This personality diagnosis must be made separately for each partner and may involve any combination of the four possibilities. It is one thing to plan treatment for a couple both of whom are functioning as healthy personalities, another thing to plan it where one partner suffers impairment at the level of early identity and role confusion, and still another where both partners suffer from earliest emotional deprivation.

This model may help to explain some of the variability in definitions of and approaches to marriage counseling. Some counselors may refer clients who show many signs of emotional impairment and work only at the "healthy personalities in marital conflict" level. Such counselors stress the differences between counseling and psychotherapy and consider counseling as a conscious-level process. Other counselors may select for themselves clients who manifest considerable pathology, and these counselors may operate in the tradition of conventional psychotherapy. To be able to work at either level consistently, however, considerable selection of clients must take place. Married couples do not automatically come separated into healthy and impaired categories. Most counselors operate at many different levels, both from case to case and even within individual cases.

TABLE 2

LEVELS OF FUNCTIONING IMPAIRMENT AND INDICATED LEVELS OF TREATMENT (AFTER RUTLEDGE, 1960)

Level	Indicated Level of Treatment
1. Healthy personalities in marital conflict	Relatively brief, conscious-level counseling is possible even though bizarre symptoms may be presented.
2. Later identity and role confusion (age 7–13)	Combination of support and conscious-level counseling, with some insight development.
3. Early identity and role confusion (age 2–7)	Requires intensive therapy. Emphasize development of healthy aspects of personality rather than concentrate upon exorcising of pathology.
4. Earliest emotional deprivation	Not generally amenable to therapy. Recognize early crippling. Guide to as much meaning in life as possible.

Personality-level diagnosis must be completed at least concurrently with social-role diagnosis but, by itself, does not constitute an adequate basis for treatment planning. The counselor also must do an equally complex analysis of the history and present structure of the relationship between the couple. What can be done with the personalities of the partners is a function not only of their childhood histories but also of current and past marital dynamics.

Models for analyzing marital dynamics generally are not so compact as those which have been developed for personality analysis. Whether this indicates greater complexity or less adequate conceptualization is uncertain. It is true that those who emphasize the necessity for role analysis are more aware of the need for proper personality diagnosis than most psychotherapy-oriented counselors are aware of the need for social diagnosis. Therefore, outlines for the analysis of marital dynamics customarily include the analysis of personality characteristics. The outline reproduced below is a modification of one developed by Weiss and Monroe (1959a).

Outline for Marital and Family Dynamics

I. Identifying data
   A. list of persons by family role and age
      1. significant relatives out of home
      2. significant nonrelatives
   B. significant family dates (marriages, divorces, births, deaths)
   C. social and economic facts (race, religion, occupation and income, education, housing and neighborhood, group affiliations, ethnic background)
II. Current social and psychological situation
   A. pertinent elaboration of identifying data; physical descriptions of couple, home and neighborhood; cultural patterns
   B. family functioning, including:
      1. housekeeping and living arrangements
      2. eating and food preparation
      3. money handling
      4. discipline
      5. recreation

      6. family routines and rituals
      7. family values
   C. description of each client in terms of:
      1. problem as client sees it; verbalized feelings about it
      2. client's current life adjustment including work, family, health, and recreation
      3. nature of important relationships in client's life, including feelings about these persons
      4. physical and emotional symptoms
      5. evaluation of client by other partner
      6. client-counselor relationship
   D. if information is available and pertinent, similar descriptions of other family members
III. Social history
   A. history of each client
   B. marital history
IV. Present interaction
   A. degree and kinds of environmental stresses upon couple and their effects upon family integration; the precipitating stress
   B. nature and degree of cultural and subcultural conflicts, if any, in terms of:
      1. value differences within family
      2. members' acceptance of family values
   C. characteristic handling of social roles
      1. roles accepted, rejected, and so on
      2. complementarity of roles, or refusal to accept complementarity, giving reasons
      3. disparity between explicit (conscious) roles and implicit (unconscious) roles
      4. evaluation of failures to accept social roles
         a. internal stress (inner conflict)
         b. external stress (not permitted to play role)
      5. culturally inappropriate roles
      6. evaluation of client's role playing by other partner
      7. deviations from characteristic handling of roles
      8. attempts at re-establishing equilibrium
   D. dominance pattern
      1. stability or fluctuation
      2. rebellion against hierarchy of dominance

E. family goals
    1. common goals, if any
    2. appropriateness of goals
    3. success in achievement
    4. willingness of clients to sacrifice personal satisfaction to joint goals
F. degree and kinds of satisfactions interaction provides to each client
V. Historical perspective on marital interaction
VI. Psychodynamics of each partner
  A. characterological descriptions
    1. main and subsidiary traits and/or outstanding symptoms
    2. areas of inhibition and substitutes for inhibited areas
  B. basic conflicts
  C. developmental dynamics
  D. diagnosis
VII. Marital treatment
  A. counseling goals for couple as a unit
    1. what each client wants counselor to provide
    2. prediction of optimal marital adjustment to be expected through counseling
      a. modifications of individual behavior necessary to attain goal
      b. effect of behavioral modifications upon marital interaction
      c. problems modification might create in family equilibrium
  B. counseling techniques needed to achieve modifications
    1. how many clients, how many counselors
    2. specific techniques to be employed and degree of their use
    3. timing of various techniques

Section I of the outline, in addition to providing for the gathering of conventional background data, serves to identify the relevant social systems in which the clients participate. Preliminary information on the spousal relationship is supplemented by data on previous marriages, larger family relationships, and relationships with nonrelatives who may be directly involved. In addition, the couple is placed in a fairly specific, detailed, social and cultural context.

From this general background, the counselor moves, in Section II, into detailed evaluation of the spouses' current problems. He determines how efficiently the couple is functioning in the various areas of living; whether the conflict has become pervasive and disruptive, or whether it is confined to one or a few areas. He finds whether fairly typical marital roles are followed, or whether there is widespread unconventionality. The material on family values is likely to be especially important. Some couples are greatly involved with their racial, nationality, religious, and family backgrounds, while others make few such identifications. Some emphasize striving and achievement, while others eschew competition. Some seek material possessions, some seek professional accomplishment, and some are without explicit goals. Some emphasize sexuality, and some deny it almost completely. Beyond further placing the couple, this information reveals the areas where there is cohesiveness and where there is strife. These evaluations are secured from both partners so that the relationship, as an entity, emerges alongside the definitions held by each individual.

Through Sections IV, V, and VI, the descriptive material is formulated into a specific marital diagnosis. The roles expected, played, and rejected by each partner for himself and the spouse, at both conscious and preconscious levels, are determined to be either fixed or potentially modifiable. The diagnosis is not just of the two clients, but of the relationship between them and of the larger system of relationships within which they function.

Then, and only then, is the counselor in a position to plan a program of treatment that will yield the expected benefits for each of the partners and for the relationship. Only thus can therapeutic gains in one area be used to reinforce those in another, and the disheartening spectacle of gains in one area being cancelled by deterioration in another be avoided. The counselor may conclude that both partners can change considerably, that only one of them can, or that for neither is change possible. His goals may be broad or very limited. He may recognize that certain changes in one partner, while possible, may have to be foregone because ultimately they would bring that client to grief. He is in a position to know whether he can work concurrently with both partners, whether treatment for one should be delayed, or whether aspects of the client-counselor relationship will require that two counselors be used. Herein lies the crucial difference between conventional psychotherapy and marriage counseling. Marital diagnosis and treatment require a framework that is broad, inclusive, and focussed upon current interactional problems.

DISTINGUISHING FEATURES OF PRACTICE

Marriage-counseling practice shares many features with other forms of counseling and therapy. There are some features of marital diagnosis and treatment, however, that are distinct enough to merit systematic discussion. These include: (a) the practice of having two or more parties to a relationship work concurrently with the same counselor, and (b) the use of conjoint therapy.

One Counselor, Two or More Clients

Most marriage counselors prefer to work with all of the significant parties to a relationship rather than to accept only one client and refer the others to different specialists. In conventional psychotherapy, of course, the position is taken that the person's relationships are part of his difficulty, and he must be aided to solve his problems without regard for those relationships. It is often stated, further, that the therapist must avoid contact with the other parties in order not to become entangled in their conflicts and in order to work through transference phenomena with his client properly. To the writer's knowledge, no

very convincing evidence of the validity of these assumptions ever has been presented. Moreover, treatment so oriented often has the effect of seriously disrupting relationships whose continuance and improvement is extremely important to the client. It is not uncommon for therapeutically guided resolution of neurotic difficulties to result in divorce, and for the divorce then to produce emotional difficulties as severe as those which led the individual into treatment originally. Some clients give evidence early in therapy of wanting and needing to terminate certain of their relationships, while others demonstrate equally convincingly that they want and need to work out their difficulties in a fashion that will sustain and enhance important relationships. Whatever selection process operates in bringing certain types of clients to certain specialists probably works to bring large numbers of this latter type to marriage counselors. It may even be assumed, until there is adequate proof to the contrary, that clients who seek out marriage counselors have the preservation of their marriages as an important source of motivation.

Hence, marriage counselors prefer to work concurrently with both husband and wife. This does not necessarily mean that both will enter treatment immediately or that they will be paced at the same rate. This depends on the marital diagnosis and whether similarly paced treatment will be of maximum advantage both to the parties and to the relationship. Ordinarily, marriage counselors prefer at least to interview both partners at the beginning of counseling in order to make a more rapid, accurate, and complete diagnosis, and then to work toward a pattern of treatment that will actively involve them both. In many instances, and in the preferred situation, both partners enter treatment early and proceed at roughly the same rate.

The distinct orientation of the marriage counselor in this respect is not intended merely to identify marriage counseling. Nor does it represent a defensive posture.

Instead, it has important advantages in the handling of relationship problems.

One of the difficult problems in therapy lies in identifying and working through the distortions in the client's productions. Inevitably, the client presents an inaccurate picture of his situation. There may be considerable distortion of which he is fully aware. He has thought and done things of which he himself does not approve and of which he does not expect others to approve. Both to avoid arousing anxiety in himself and to avoid the possibility of being rejected by the therapist, he conceals important information. At another level he presents a one-sided account. No matter how carefully he avoids concealment or how hard he tries to present a fair, balanced picture of his relationship problems, he simply is unable to see them in proper perspective. He is deeply emotionally involved, and he has been hurt. It is not unusual to listen to separate but honest descriptions of the marriage by husband and wife and to have difficulty realizing that they are talking about the same relationship. At still a third level, there often are distortions that arise out of repression. Too-painful memories simply have been excluded from consciousness. The three kinds of distortions combined present a formidable diagnostic and therapeutic problem.

In long, intensive therapy, the therapy may continue for months without either the therapist or the client being able to break through the barriers which are thus presented. The marriage counselor, through interviewing both partners, has several advantages. First, there is less likelihood of conscious concealment. Each spouse knows that the counselor is hearing of embarrassing incidents from the other partner. Therefore, he is both relieved of the necessity to conceal and motivated to give as complete an account as possible. Second, the unwitting distortions introduced by the clients are immediately identified as areas of distortion, at least, by the lack of congruence between the partner's descriptions. And,

third, the identification even of areas of repression is aided by seeing each client, not only through the screen of his own production, but also through that of the partner.

A second significant area in therapy that is altered by working with both partners involves transference and countertransference phenomena. These terms are used broadly here to refer to all emotional responses of one participant in the counseling relationship to another that are inappropriate to the reality situation between them. That transference reactions tend to develop in most marriage-counseling relationships is assumed. But how elaborate and involved the transference needs to be and should be is another matter.

In classical analysis, of course, the development and resolution of the transference neurosis is the very heart of therapy. Marriage-counseling problems, however, do not inevitably or even customarily derive directly from unresolved pre-oedipal situations. The conscious problem-solving abilities of clients are much more adequate, and the development of full-fledged transference phenomena often delays and makes more difficult the resolution of the marital problems. Some marriage-counseling clients do have the kinds of emotional impairment that require extreme dependence on the counselor for resolution. But, even then, working with both partners is not usually contraindicated.

In more typical marriage-counseling situations, incipient transference reactions early in counseling tend to be held in check because the participation of the other partner discourages development of a private world between counselor and client. Each partner's tendencies to maneuver the counselor into the role of father, mother, lover, what-have-you, immediately come into conflict with the other partner's contrary view and with the fact of the relationship of the other partner with the counselor. Thus, regression is discouraged, and both clients are forced to cope with their problems at more current, conscious levels. This has the effect both of shortening the period of counseling and of encouraging solutions more in harmony with the clients' existing relationships.

In those instances where transference reactions become pronounced, most counselors appear not to have significantly more difficulty working the distortions through than are encountered in more traditional psychotherapy. The added task of having to control the development of distortions in both partners simultaneously is offset by the lesser likelihood of the counselor being unwittingly caught up in either pattern of distortion. Working with both partners not only helps limit the development of transference but of countertransference also.

Conjoint Therapy

A logical extension of the practice of having the same counselor work with both parties is to have the counselor work with them not only concurrently but jointly. To work with them jointly is to conduct interviews with both partners present rather than to see them alternately. Joint interviews have long been a distinguishing feature of marriage counseling. Until fairly recently, however, the literature has stressed the limited uses to which they could be put (Karpf, 1951b; Skidmore & Garrett, 1955).

Traditionally, joint interviews have been used at the beginning and again toward the end of counseling. During intake, husband and wife often are seen together so that the counselor may observe their interaction in the counseling session. Nonverbal gestures and attitudes thus displayed, along with the verbal interaction, are an important aid in arriving at an early and accurate marital diagnosis. Couples in conflict, however, are likely soon to begin to quarrel and to seek to draw the counselor into their struggles. At this point, counselors ordinarily begin to see the clients in individual sessions until their major hostility toward one another has been worked through and each has made

substantial progress in understanding his own role in the development of the conflict. As this happens, joint interviews may be reintroduced on a trial basis to determine whether the couple now are capable of reinforcing one another's motivation to make the marriage work. If this proves to be the case, then a combination of individual and joint interviews may be used to speed the counseling toward termination.

In spite of the obvious advantages in having the couple work together where improvement in the relationship is a major goal, counselors' attitudes toward joint interviews long were reluctant and cautious. Probably there were several reasons for this. For one thing, most professional marriage counselors were trained in a tradition of therapy that stressed the exclusiveness of the counselor-client relationship and the dangers of becoming embroiled in the clients' conflicts. Persons so trained and oriented seldom had much skill in the conduct of joint interviews, and whatever efforts they made along these lines often were discouraging. It was easier to acknowledge the unworkability of joint interviews than to develop the skills necessary to use them effectively.

Moreover, the simultaneous interviewing of two clients requires the counselor to attend to a far broader range of stimuli than does the interviewing of a lone client. Not only must the counselor simultaneously hear, accept, and reflect the emotional communications of both partners, but he must protect each one against undue attack by the other and, most important, he must constantly support the relationship as an entity distinct from the perceptions of either client. This is both intellectually and emotionally very demanding work. Most counselors are simply not up to the alert conduct of joint interviews over the same time period that they can successfully conduct individual interviews.

A final factor may lie in the effect of marital conflict upon the counselor as a person. The traditional stress upon preventing the couple from fighting in the counseling sessions has been justified upon the grounds that as the counselor loses control of the interviews, he loses his ability to help the clients. Within limits, of course, this is true. One might suspect, however, that this is an inadequate explanation.

Marriage-counseling clients do not stop fighting when they enter counseling. Indeed, entrance into counseling may have the effect of intensifying the conflict for a while. A counseling structure which does not permit the expression of the accompanying feelings to the counselor, at least, makes the client-counselor relationship somewhat artificial. Each partner is likely to be somewhat aware of not revealing himself fully, or of being able to reveal himself fully, to the counselor. To have the couple fight before the counselor may be more honest for them and, indeed, may have no more negative effect upon them than does the fighting which occurs outside the counselor's presence. Their fighting in the counseling interview may make the counselor exceedingly uncomfortable, however.

What masquerades as the counselor's concern for what is happening to the relationship between his clients may be in good measure his own anxiety at being so intimately involved in their conflict. Actually, there is no reason to assume that the counselor has lost control of the interview simply because the clients are fighting. He permits and encourages the expression of other kinds of feelings without worrying about loss of control. Why is this different? It may be different only because the counselor fears an inability to control himself when so much hostility is being expressed. He may be afraid of his own impulses to behave hostilely or to withdraw from the clients. If these or other feelings emerge actively, he does indeed lose control of the interview. If he is secure enough to remain uninvolved in the conflict, however, there is nothing inconsistent between permitting his clients to fight and remaining firmly in control of the counseling process.

Therapists in a variety of areas are evolving a new pattern of conjoint therapy (Ackerman, 1958). Instead of making hesitant, limited use of joint interviews, they are making of them a major therapeutic tool. In some instances, clients seen together for the initial interview may be continued in joint interviews throughout the counseling process. In other cases, a combination of joint and individual interviews may be used. And in still other settings, the pattern of joint interviews may be begun after the separate clients have made considerable progress through individual therapy.

Where conjoint therapy is used as a major therapeutic procedure, there are several distinguishing features. In the main, these are extensions of the processes which come into existence when the same counselor sees both partners in individual interviews.

Conjoint therapy has tremendous impact upon the appearance of distortions in the clients' productions. Distortions are less numerous, less bizarre, and are more quickly revealed, to the clients as well as to the counselor, as distortions. When both partners are present, fantasy is held in check. Neither partner can escape the reality of immediate scrutiny of his statements by another who has detailed knowledge of the relationships under discussion. The common situation where the counselor is left to fathom and eventually to reveal the distortions is thereby avoided. What otherwise might require weeks and months is often accomplished in a session or two. Moreover, the counselor is able to retain his position in support of the relationship without having eventually to reject some of what each client has told him.

A second distinguishing feature of conjoint therapy is its greater emphasis upon *current* relationships. Clients seen together do not face great encouragement to concentrate upon and to relive their early family experiences. The emphasis is upon what hurts them right now. Moreover, even the current situation is faced, not in terms of what pains the clients as individuals, but in terms of what is wrong between them. They will, of course, search for the basis of their conflicts both in what has transpired between them and in what each partner brought into the relationship in the first place. The development of insight into the effects of earlier experience occurs. Indeed, it may be very prominent. The emphasis, however, is upon the contribution of early experience to the relationship conflict and not upon early frustration or personality impairment as such.

In frequent joint sessions, the counselor also can aid the couple to alter their interaction directly. This is in contrast with the conventional therapy situation, where there may be marked disparity between the behavior of each client in the counseling sessions and their behavior in relation to one another at home—a process that may continue for quite a long time. In conjoint therapy, the partners typically fall into habitual modes of interaction, admitting the counselor directly into their conflicts and learning, in turn, that the counselor can empathize with them both and not be drawn into taking sides. As the counselor helps protect each partner against the onslaughts of the other, the clients can afford to be somewhat more objective, both about the other's attacks and about their own contributions to forcing the attacks. Each partner can make tentative overtures toward a less hurtful pattern of interaction, and the counselor is there to help the other partner respond in kind. Once begun, this process becomes cumulative and circular, leading the couple out of conflict according to dynamics analogous to those which led them into it in the first place.

This process does not proceed smoothly, of course. In early joint sessions, there may be bitter outbursts that virtually ignore the counselor's presence. After the hostility has run its course, however, the counselor helps the clients to analyze the basis for their hurts and how the hurts led them into attack and counterattack. Initial tentative insights and slightly modified interactions then often are followed by lapses back into destructive conflict. For a while, new areas of conflict may even be opened up, as the clients give vent to long-suppressed antagonisms and as they test the counselor's and one another's ability to accept these feelings and to deal with them constructively. Gradually, the hostile outbursts become less frequent, less intense, and less prolonged. Gradually, the clients become more adept at and more confident in the newer, more constructive, interaction. The whole process may be telescoped into a very few sessions, or it may require a good many. But its potential for foreshortening the counseling and increasing its effectiveness is great.

The most significant advantage of this use of the counseling hours lies in its effects upon the clients' behavior between the sessions. The interaction in the counseling office sets a pattern for interaction outside it. As soon as the partners show any ability to modify their earlier pattern, each becomes a kind of subtherapist working throughout the day and week. This happens following conventional counseling procedure, too, but in conjoint therapy, the clients are apt to become involved earlier and more actively. More of the responsibility for improvement in their relationship is shifted to the clients, where it belongs. Less dependence upon the counselor is built up, and eventually less weaning away from the counselor is required.

That this process actually occurs has been demonstrated time and again in practice. Undoubtedly, however, there are instances where conjoint therapy cannot be used or can be used only with considerable modification. It is not apt to be useful, for example, in cases where there is not adequate motivation to continue the relationship. Clients who are committed to separation or divorce may only be handicapped by joint sessions. Even when this is suspected, however, a joint session may reveal whether there is unrecognized potential for reconciliation. Where one or both partners are excessively paranoid, joint sessions may only help to consolidate the delusional system. And, finally, this procedure requires some strength on the part of both partners. A nearly defenseless client may not be able to participate adequately, even with the counselor's help, and may face further destruction. The context indicates that such clients are exceptions—that the majority of marriage-counseling clients do have considerable motivation to work at their relationships, they are not excessively paranoid, and they are not without substantial personal resources. The exact limitations on the use of conjoint therapy in marriage counseling are not yet known. There simply has not been enough experience with it. Significant exceptions, in addition to those listed above, undoubtedly will be found. That conjoint therapy will be more and more widely used in the future, however, is virtually certain.

TRAINING FOR MARRIAGE COUNSELING

The whole problem of training marriage counselors hinges upon the conception of what marriage counseling is and what it should become.

During the short 20 years of its existence, the American Association of Marriage Counselors has been influenced heavily by the generation of essentially self-taught specialists who moved into marriage counseling after they had completed their training in other professions, such as sociology, psychology, medicine, and social work. It is only natural that they should have stressed the interdisciplinary character of the field and the necessity for extensive postdoctoral training. The problems in providing such training were great. There were relatively few self-taught marriage counselors available, training centers were very few, and no standards existed to indicate whether existing centers were at all adequate. The only test of whether an individual's training was sufficient came when and if he applied for

membership in the Association. Membership committees struggled mightily to admit qualified persons and yet to keep standards of training and personal qualifications high enough to assure the truly professional development of the field.

The membership standards laid down by AAMC have varied but slightly over the years, so that the most recent standards can be taken as representing accurately those that have prevailed throughout the organization's existence. The general qualifications for clinical membership stress academic training, professional experience and qualifications, and personal qualifications.

Under academic training, the qualifications include a graduate or professional degree (Ph.D., M.S.W., M.D., etc.), plus the acquisition of basic knowledge in the fields of psychology of personality development and interpersonal relations; elements of psychiatry; human biology, including the fundamentals of sex anatomy, physiology, and genetics; sociology of marriage and the family; legal aspects of marriage and the family; and counseling techniques. Since few, if any, formal training programs provide work in all of these areas, considerable work beyond the doctorate or other professional degree is implied.

The necessity for such additional training is made explicit in the requirements for professional experience. These state that a candidate for clinical membership in AAMC should have at least three years of professional experience in some recognized field subsequent to obtaining his degree. In addition, he should have had actual experience as a clinical assistant under approved supervision. The experience thus gained should be reflected in: (a) diagnostic skill in differentiating between the superficial and the deeper levels of maladjustment, and the ability to recognize when the latter requires referral to other specialists; and (b) a scientific attitude toward individual variation and deviation, especially in the field of human sex behavior, and the ability to discuss sexual problems objectively.

Finally, the personal qualifications stress professional integrity, conformity to accepted ethical standards, and a high degree of emotional maturity. Although these personal qualifications are more difficult to assess accurately than either academic training or professional experience, they are deemed to be of utmost importance.

These standards were laid down originally, in 1948, by a joint subcommittee of AAMC and the National Council on Family Relations. They have undergone minor revision since that time, but have guided the selection of AAMC members through the development of standards both for postdoctoral training centers and for graduate education in marriage counseling.

Postdoctoral Training Standards

The AAMC wrestled with the problem of establishing standards for postdoctoral training centers for approximately 10 years. The standards that gradually emerged emphasized the setting in which the training is offered, the qualifications required of trainees, and the training program itself.

Only training centers having established administrations, clearly defined financial policies, and high professional standards are considered. At least one member of the staff must be a member of AAMC and, in addition, two or more of the clinical professions must be represented on the staff. At least one staff member must have skill and experience in supervision. If not included on the staff, consultants from the fields of psychiatry, psychology, and social casework are required. Further specified standards concerning record keeping, confidentiality, fees, the number and variety of cases carried, and evaluation of trainees' work must be met.

Trainees must bring to the center the usual professional degree in their fields (Ph.D., M.S.W., M.D., B.D., etc.), and must have had two years of experience working with people in that field. Unless distance prevents it, the trainee's personal qualifications must be examined in a face-to-face interview before admission to the program, and he is required to submit a reasonably realistic plan for the professional use of his marriage-counseling training.

At the training center, full-time residence for 12 months is recommended, and a minimum of half-time residence for an academic year is required. The trainee spends from 6 to 15 hours weekly actually doing marriage counseling, has from $1\frac{1}{2}$ to 5 hours of individual supervision weekly, has ample time to dictate and record interviews, and has from 6 to 15 hours of seminars and case conferences.

Any training center which believes it meets these standards can apply to AAMC for investigation and approval. If approved, the center is required to provide factual information justifying its continued approval every two years and must undergo complete re-evaluation every four years. Over the years, three centers in the United States have received approval under these standards, and, at this writing, there are two approved centers. Five additional centers are awaiting evaluation and show good evidence of being able to meet requirements. Even by the time this appears in print the total number should be at least seven.

A very large part of marriage-counseling training to date has been offered at the postdoctoral level and has been carried out under these standards. This sole mode of recruitment into the field presented problems, however. From the point of view of professional marriage counseling, there was no steady supply of candidates with a common background of training and experience. From the viewpoint of the trainees, the necessity for embarking upon a new pattern after many years already spent in professional training often was quite burdensome. Consequently, the centers were unable to use their full potential for advanced training, and many persons desiring adequate training were unable to avail themselves of it. Part of the solution was to extend the marriage-counseling training process downward into the graduate schools. Several major graduate schools now offer marriage-counseling training as part of the preparation for the doctoral degree.

Graduate Training Standards

Standards for graduate-school training in marriage counseling have been modelled upon the postdoctoral training standards. Two types of doctoral programs have been approved: a four-year program, and a three-year program. In both instances, there is emphasis upon the provision of formal academic training in the several areas of competence required for membership in AAMC. In addition, practicum experience is required. If the undergraduate major was in the social sciences, practicum work may be begun during the first year of graduate study. In any event, approximately 10 hours per week of practicum are recommended for the second year, and approximately 20 during the third year. The three-year program then terminates with the awarding of the doctoral degree. In the four year program, an additional year of full-time internship in a training center meeting AAMC standards for postdoctoral training is urged.

The significance of the establishment of graduate training standards in marriage counseling probably cannot be overestimated. It represents a very long step toward the development of a profession of marriage counseling. For the first time, students may begin pointing toward a career in marriage counseling from their undergraduate days. Even prior to the approval of doctoral training, AAMC had a membership category of Associate-in-Training to involve interns in the affairs of the Association. Now, as university programs are approved and their students become affiliated with AAMC, one of the last requirements of a distinct profession—the establishment of a regular mode of recruitment—will be met. Most persons in the field welcome this development. It has, however, major implications for the academic disciplines involved and for relationships between scholars and practitioners.

Sociology of the Family, Family-Life Education, and Marriage Counseling

Sociologists are but one of the academic groups involved in doing marriage counseling and in training marriage counselors. The professional identity problems that they face, however, are quite similar to those faced by other academicians.

Some concern with social action has been present in family sociology from the beginning. Prior to about 1920, that concern was likely to be registered chiefly in the emphasis, in course work and writing, given to various ills associated with families—divorce, illegitimacy, poverty, desertion, and so on. Few sociologists, as such, were recruited for positions in social agencies or were practitioners in any direct sense. As explicitly functional family courses emerged during the 1920's and 1930's, however, a growing body of sociologists acknowledged a major interest in family-life education.

Most such persons carved dual identities for themselves. Working in academic settings, they stressed their identities as general sociologists, interested in theory-building and research apart from their applied interests. Their identification with family-life education tended to be expressed concurrently, but through somewhat distinct publication outlets and professional organizations. Thus, one reference group was the sociological profession as represented by the American Sociological Association. Another was interdisciplinary and represented in many instances by the National Council on Family Relations. There is oversimplification in this, of course. Some of the interest in family-life education was expressed through distinctly sociological channels, and both essays and research on functional topics were published in the traditional sociological journals. Nonetheless, some real division occurred also. Family sociologists as individuals became known as having only academic interests or as having both academic and applied interests. And those who had both faced a growing problem of professional identity.

As the role of marriage counselor was added to those of family sociologist and family-life educator, the problem became even more acute. Just as the interests of family-life educators had gone beyond those of purely academic sociology, so those of marriage counselors went beyond and were more specialized than those of family-life educators. The three professional functions very often were combined in the same person. Those persons, however, now found themselves facing in as many as three different directions. As sociologists, they addressed themselves to their sociological colleagues; as family-life educators, they addressed themselves to a broad interdisciplinary audience; and as professional marriage counselors, they cultivated a small, almost superdisciplinary audience of other professional marriage counselors. In the process, professional identities became increasingly confused.

The present confusion is not shared equally by all family specialists. Those persons whose interests lie solely in the family as an institution give undivided allegiance to the sociological profession. Although some of their courses include functional material, they acknowledge no need for special competence in the handling of such material and face no resulting identity problems. Similarly, some specialists have identified so completely with family-life education or with marriage counseling that they have ceased to have other significant professional reference groups. For an increasingly large number, however, continuing commitment to two or more of these specialties poses difficulties.

As a profession, sociology has been slow to take cognizance of this situation. The emphasis upon research in professional journals and at annual meetings has worked against the existence of an adequate forum for the developing applied interests. Family-life educators and counselors have contributed to this situation by their own ambivalence concerning their action interests. Being trained academicians, they share the high value placed by academic people upon theory development and pure research. The combination of lack of organizational encouragement and defensive withdrawal gradually widened the gap between various groups of family specialists and confounded the identity problems of those with multiple interests.

There are forces operating at the present time that may alter this situation. Perhaps significantly, much of the impetus for these changes has come from outside professional sociology. The concerted efforts of psychologists to secure certification legislation has been one influence. In promoting certification, psychologists have directly threatened the legal right of sociologists to do many kinds of applied work outside of academic settings (Goode, 1960). Although the American Sociological Association's new section on social psychology probably would have developed without this influence, the need for an accrediting body within the profession undoubtedly was one factor. Sociologists are now asserting their right to practice in the very broad field of social psychology. It appears that in support of this claim and in defense against the actions of psychologists, sociologists will have to develop specific accreditation procedures to define which sociologists are competent to engage in social psychological practice. As this happens, applied interests such as marriage counseling may become incorporated more directly into the profession.

The American Association of Marriage Counselors was wrestling with the whole problem of accreditation before the certification of psychologists became a major issue (Ellis, 1951; Stokes, 1951). The organization decided against the direct accreditation of marriage counselors, at least for the time being, and has emphasized high membership standards and the development of training centers instead. The extraordinary prestige attaching to AAMC membership has resulted, however, in an almost *de facto* accreditation. Marriage counselors of all persuasions, including sociologists, have looked to AAMC both for recognition and for professional interaction. That this identification of sociologist-marriage counselors with AAMC will continue seems certain. Both the number of sociologists involved and the degree of their commitment to professional marriage counseling seem destined to increase. What is less certain is whether this interest, which usually is only one of the interests of sociologist-marriage counselors, will also find direct expression within professional sociology. This problem of professional identification is not a simple one, but it is likely to be resolved in our time.

REFERENCES

Ackerman, N. *The psychodynamics of family life.* New York: Basic Books, 1958.

American Association of Marriage Counselors, Inc. *Marriage counseling: a casebook.* New York: Association Press, 1958.

Bridgman, R. Counseling matrimonial clients in family court. *Nat. Probation & Parole Ass. J.,* 1959, 5, 187–199.

Cavanagh, J. *Fundamental marriage counseling: a Catholic viewpoint.* Milwaukee: Bruce, 1957.

Cuber, J. *Marriage counseling practice.* New York: Appleton-Century-Crofts, 1948.

Elkin, M. Short-contact counseling in a conciliation court. *Soc. Casewk,* 1962, 43, 184–190.

Ellis, A. Legal status of the marriage counselor: a psychologist's view. *Marr. & fam. Living,* 1951, 13, 116–120.

Fromm-Reichmann, Frieda. *Principles of intensive psychotherapy.* Chicago: Univer. of Chicago Press, 1950.

Gomberg, R. Family-oriented treatment of marital problems. *Soc. Casewk,* 1956, 37, 3–10.

Goode, W. Encroachment, charlatanism, and the emerging profession: psychology, sociology, and medicine. *Amer. sociol. Rev.,* 1960, 25, 902–914.

Harper, R. Should marriage counseling become a full-fledged specialty? *Marr. & fam. Living,* 1953, 15, 338–340.

Johnson, D. Understanding and use of the self in counseling. *Bull. Menninger Clinic,* 1953, 17, 29–35.

Johnson, D. *Marriage counseling: theory and practice.* Englewood Cliffs, N.J.: Prentice-Hall, 1961.

Karpf, M. Marriage counseling and psychotherapy. *Marr. & fam. Living,* 1951, 13 169–178. (a)

Karpf, M. Some guiding principles in marriage counseling. *Marr. & fam. Living,* 1951, 13, 49–51, 55. (b)

Kirkpatrick, C. *The family: as process and institution.* New York: Ronald Press, 1955.

Landis, J. The teaching of marriage and family courses in colleges. *Marr. & fam. Living,* 1959, 21, 36–40.

Lantz, H. Sociological theory and marriage counseling. *Merrill-Palmer Quart.,* 1959, 5, 176–179.

Mace, D. *Marriage counseling.* London: Churchill, 1948.

Mace, D. What is a marriage counselor? *Marr. & fam. Living,* 1954, 16, 135–138.

Mace, D. Marriage counseling in Britain today. *Marr. & fam. Living,* 1958, 20, 379–383.

Malinowski, B. *Sex and repression in savage society.* New York: Harcourt, Brace, 1927.

Mitchell, H., Preston, M., & Mudd, Emily H. Anticipated development of case from content of first interview record. *Marr. & fam. Living,* 1953, 15, 226–331.

Mudd, Emily H. *The practice of marriage counseling.* New York: Association Press, 1951.

Mudd, Emily H., & Froscher, Hazel B. Effects on casework of obtaining research material. *Soc. Casewk,* 1950, 31, 11–17.

Parsons, T. *The social system.* Glencoe, Ill.: Free Press, 1951.

Parsons, T. Psychology and sociology. In J. P. Gillin (Ed.), *For a science of social man.* New York: Macmillan, 1954. Pp. 67–101.

Parsons, T., & Fox, Renee. Illness, therapy, and the modern urban American family. *J. soc. issues,* 1952, 8, 31–44.

Preston, M., Mudd, Emily H., & Froscher, Hazel B. Factors affecting movement in casework. *Soc. Casewk,* 1953, 34, 103–111.

Pollak, O. *Integrating sociological and psychoanalytic concepts.* New York: Russell Sage Foundation, 1956.

Rutledge, A. A further look at marital diagnosis. Detroit: Merrill-Palmer Institute, 1960. (Mimeographed.)

Skidmore, R., & Garrett, Hulda. The joint interview in marriage counseling. *Marr. & fam. Living,* 1955, 17, 349–354.

Skidmore, R., Garrett, Hulda & Skidmore, C. *Marriage consulting.* New York: Harper, 1956.

Spiegel, J. The social roles of doctor and patient in psychoanalysis and psychotherapy. *Psychiatry,* 1954, 17, 369–376.

Stokes, W. Legal status of the marriage counselor. *Marr. & fam. Living,* 1951, 13, 113–115.

Vincent, C. (Ed.) *Readings in marriage counseling.* New York: Crowell, 1957.

Weiss, Viola, & Monroe, R. A framework for understanding family dynamics: part I. *Soc. Casewk,* 1959, 40, 3–9. (a)

Weiss, Viola, & Monroe, R. A framework for understanding family dynamics: part II. *Soc. Casewk,* 1959, 40, 80–87. (b)

Wolstein, B. *Transference: its meaning and function in psychoanalytic therapy.* New York: Grune & Stratton, 1954.

CHAPTER 23 Legal and Procedural Aspects of Marriage and Divorce

WILLIAM M. KEPHART
University of Pennsylvania

Marriage has not always been under the control of the state; indeed, even at the present time, some primitive groups provide for neither legal nor religious control of the marriage bonds. Over the millennia, however, civilized societies have found it necessary to impose strict legal controls over both marriage and divorce. As is so often the case with statutory controls, the provisions themselves tend to become more numerous, more diverse, more complex—and more controversial. The Law now spells out minimal ages for marriage, consanguineous proscriptions, health standards, grounds for divorce and annulment, and a variety of other legal enactments. In parallel fashion, it has become necessary to make statutory provision for the various licensing, recording, and reporting aspects of marriage and divorce.

What has been the sociologist's concern with this welter of marriage and divorce laws and registration procedures? Traditionally, sociological interest has centered on the reform aspects of marriage and divorce legislation. The sociologist has been bothered by the fact that most divorces are collusive in nature, that Gretna Greens continue to exist, that more than one-third of the states still permit common-law marriage, that Nevada can with impunity make a joke of existing divorce law, and so on. The sociologist has been bothered by these things, and he would change the Law, or change the System, so as to correct what he feels are abuses.

In some instances, however, sociological zeal has tended to reach beyond the implications of substantive research. The present account tries to bridge the gap, i.e., to point up the areas of research as they relate to the law. Another aim is to describe the statistical procedures involved in the derivation of official marriage and divorce data, since it is from this material that much analytical research has developed. To put the matter succinctly, a case is made for the proposition that reform, research, and reporting are interlocking functions of the socio-legal approach to marriage and divorce, and that the role of the interlocker is a rightful one for the sociologist.

MARRIAGE LAWS IN THE UNITED STATES: RANGE AND MEANING

The Constitution of the United States delegates authority over marriage and divorce to the individual states. There is no federal marriage and divorce law in the United States, there never has been, and, in spite of longstanding complaints on the part of many social scientists, it is doubtful whether there ever will be. Some abortive attempts have been made to nationalize our marriage and divorce laws, but no real political backing for the move has been forthcoming, and today the issue has all but died in our federal legislature. For better or worse, the fact must be faced that the United States has 50 different sets of marriage and divorce laws. This section examines, in sociological perspective, some of the implications involved.

Age at Marriage

Americans are generally surprised to learn that in some states it is legal for 12-, 13-, and 14-year-old children to marry, but such is indeed the case. It should be remembered that in the Judaeo-Christian heritage, marriages frequently took place when children reached puberty, which was arbitrarily set at 12 for the female and 13 or 14 for the male. This provision still applies in most South American countries and is quite common in Asiatic nations. In our own society, it is legal for a girl to marry at age 14 in Alabama, Georgia, Iowa, New York, South Carolina, Texas, and Utah, provided she obtains parental approval. In the state of Washington, a girl can legally marry at 12, if her parents consent. Similarly, the minimal age at which boys can marry, in some states, is 14. At the other extreme, in Connecticut, Florida, Kentucky, Louisiana, Nebraska, Ohio, Pennsylvania, Rhode Island, Virginia, West Virginia, and Wyoming, both parties must be 21 years of age before they can legally marry without their parents' consent. In a very real sense, therefore, the legal range of age for marriage in our culture is from 12 to 21. For more detailed information, see Mackay (1959) and *Information Please Almanac* (1962).

It is a common assumption that youth who marry below the legal age can have their marriage annulled, but this is more false than true. If the age without consent is 21, and a given couple, by falsifying their dates of birth, marry at 19, it is extremely doubtful whether the court would grant an annulment. Annulments for under-age marriages usually are granted in cases where the couple were under the *minimal age,* i.e., the age with consent.

Insofar as the state laws are concerned, the most common minimal age is 18 for the male and 16 for the female; the most common maximal age (without consent) is 21 for the male and 18 for the female. Note, however, that in no less than 11 states (listed above) the age without consent is 21 for the female. The remarkable thing about this latter figure is that, in practice, the average (median) age at first marriage for females in the United States is now 20 (USDHEW, 1959, p. 19). (The corresponding age for males is 22.5.) Stated differently, 11 states have age-at-marriage requirements for the female which are higher than the average (median) age at which United States females are marrying.

What is the role of the sociologist as regards the legal age at marriage? One task would be to ascertain whether a relationship exists between age at marriage and subsequent marital adjustment. This relationship has been explored in a number of studies, and the findings are consistent: very early marriages are associated with marital maladjustment (Burchinal, 1959; Burgess & Cottrell, 1939; Goode, 1956; Groves & Ogburn, 1928; Locke, 1951; Monahan, 1953; Moss & Gingles, 1959; Terman, 1938). The next logical step would be to determine whether it is the *fact* of early marriage which leads to the marital discord, or whether the people who marry at a very early age are those who tend to have marital conflicts. This kind of study has not yet been attempted, although with the type of computer research now being done, such an effort should certainly be possible. Until it is, however, the sociologist is on thin ground when he advocates that the minimum age at marriage in a given jurisdiction be raised.

The socio-legal factor is complicated by the fact that a couple who are too young to marry in their home state can go to a nearby state with lower age requirements and marry. The marriage is usually binding, the general stipulation being that a marriage which is valid in the state where it is performed is valid in all states. In any event, it seems clear in this instance that the role of the sociologist is to pin down the *causative* relation, if any, between age at marriage and marital adjustment rather than to mount a premature crusade against specific marriage-age laws. It may be that when the relation between age at marriage and marital adjustment is fully understood, formulation of statutory policy will take care of itself.

Consanguinity

The term "consanguinity" refers to blood relationship, and in the legal sense has been employed to denote the degrees within which individuals may not marry. In all 50 states, marriages are prohibited between mother and son, father and daughter, sister and brother, grandfather and granddaughter, grandmother and grandson, uncle and niece, aunt and nephew. The majority of states also forbid the marriage of first cousins, a prohibition which in some jurisdictions is extended to second cousins as well (Mackay, 1959).

Most states prohibit marriage to a half-brother or half-sister, a prohibition which, again, is extended in some jurisdictions to include half-cousins, half-nephews, and half-nieces. Moreover, about half of the states have statutory restrictions pertaining to *affinity*, a term which has nothing to do with blood ties but denotes a *marital* relationship. Kentucky, for example, prohibits marriage to a "half sister, first cousin, grandniece, first cousin once removed, stepmother, stepdaughter, grandfather's wife, grandson's wife, mother-in-law, wife's

grandmother, and daughter-in-law" (Mackay, 1959, p. 22).

What is the purpose of such an extended list of affinal prohibitions? Kirkpatrick has given a succinct but convincing explanation.

It is startling to find concern about *affinal* relationships in the laws of the various states. Yet if one presumes to attribute to an abstraction, the State, the desire to prevent familial jealousy, one can understand why a score of states . . . prohibit marriage to father's wife and son's wife. Twenty-three jurisdictions prohibit marriage between stepparents and stepchildren. The older male is thus warned that the fresher charms of the stepdaughter can never legally replace those of the wife in the marriage bed. It would certainly surprise the purveyor of mother-in-law jokes to learn that it seemed necessary in a dozen states to prohibit marriage with the wife's mother (Kirkpatrick, 1963, pp. 422–423).[1]

It would be an interesting sociological endeavor to ascertain (a) the percentage of couples who, by the fact of their marriage, are breaking the laws pertaining to consanguinity or affinity, and (b) the proportion of marrying couples who actually know what these laws are. The methodology involved in a study of this kind might prove to be difficult, inasmuch as a random sample would perhaps have to be combined with unsigned questionnaires, thus making it hard to employ follow-up procedures. Nevertheless, if the details could be worked out, the results might lead to an equalization of the various state laws. At present, the range of consanguinity and affinity statutes is tremendous. Some of them seem downright purposeless. If it could be shown that the statutes are being circumvented, or that people are ignorant of the laws of their own state, it might be that more realistic legislation would be forthcoming. At the present time, it is doubtful whether the average marriage-license clerk ever inquires into the consanguinity or affinity of the

[1] Clifford Kirkpatrick, *The Family: As Process and Institution.* (2nd Ed.) Copyright © 1963 The Ronald Press Company.

applicants. This is not to suggest that state legislators are eagerly awaiting the results of empirical research so that they can alter the marriage and divorce laws in conformance with sociological expectations. Still, it is a thesis of the present chapter that in the absence of valid research findings, needed reform in the areas of marriage and divorce legislation will be a long time coming.

Miscegenation

The *American Collegiate Dictionary* defines miscegenation as "mixture of races by sexual union," or "interbreeding between different races." As used by sociologists, however, the term is more likely to denote interracial marriage. In the legal sense, no less than 30 of the states have miscegenation statutes, or laws which prohibit the marriage of whites to members of such groups as Negroes, Mongolians, Hindus, Malayans, Chinese, Japanese, and American Indians.

As might be imagined, the bulk of the miscegenation statutes are concentrated in the southern states, all of which have laws banning interracial marriage; in fact, some of them have maximum penalties of a 10-year jail term for violators. A number of southern states not only outlaw interracial marriage but any sexual activity between the races. Some states, like Florida, make it illegal for Negroes and whites of opposite sex even to occupy the same room (maximum penalty: a year in jail and/or a $500 fine). Also, Sherwin noted, "In Arkansas if a mulatto child is born to any woman, this in itself is evidence that she has committed the crime of miscegenation and it is possible for her to be convicted without any further evidence" (1949, p. 53).

While all the southern states take pains to prevent interracial mixing, a number of jurisdictions outside the South also have miscegenation statutes, including California, Colorado, Idaho, Indiana, Montana, Nebraska, Nevada, North Dakota, Oregon, South Dakota, Utah, and Wyoming. In some of these states, the intent of the law was apparently to discourage unions between whites and orientals, or between whites and American Indians. It should be noted that in some states the miscegenation laws have been challenged as unconstitutional. In most instances, however, constitutionality has been upheld on the ground that these laws discriminate against neither race, it being as illegal for Negroes to marry whites as for whites to marry Negroes.

In practice, there is nothing to prevent a white and a Negro who are residents of an anti-miscegenation state from marrying, despite what the law says, provided they marry in a state which has no such law. If the couple in question are residents of a southern state, it would nevertheless be inadvisable for them to return home, for southern states generally will not recognize the validity of an interracial marriage, regardless of where it occurred.

From the sociological view, of course, it is questionable how much effect a state law has on interracial marriage. For those whites and Negroes who have strong feelings against miscegenation, the laws are quite unnecessary. And for those of both groups who have contrary feelings, it is likely that they will intermarry regardless of state law, simply by moving to a more permissive jurisdiction.

It can be effectively argued that some restrictive statutes are on the books for purposes other than deterrence. In the southern states, for instance, it may well be that the anti-miscegenation statutes serve as an expression of public will as much as anything else. And the fact that the northeastern states have no laws prohibiting interracial marriage might be taken as an indication that public opinion is more kindly disposed toward such unions. The defect in this reasoning is that in those same northeastern states, interracial dating and interracial marriages seem to be almost negligible, with no indication that an increase is in the making.

Appearances may be deceptive, though, and the role of the sociologist would seem to be that of determining the actual rate of interracial dating and marriage. Based on vital-statistics data, there has been only one estimate of the interracial marriage rate in the United States, that made by Jacobson. The latter reported, "Marriages between white persons and Negroes or members of other nonwhite races are relatively infrequent in the United States. In 1939, the only year for which data are available, such interracial marriages accounted for only 8 out of 10,000 marriages in the country" (Jacobson, 1959, p. 62). Whether the rate has increased or decreased since then, or whether the over-all picture varies by regions, is not known. There is even less information about interracial dating, inasmuch as this material would have to be drawn from segmental studies rather than from vital statistics. [Cf. Ch. 16, pp. 646–648, 655–656.]

At any rate, by ascertaining geographical and temporal patterns in interracial dating and marriage, and by comparing the results with the variations in state miscegenation statutes, it might be possible to make some definitive statements regarding these laws. It should be remembered that they have generally been held to be constitutional, and that the whole concept of interracial marriage is a sensitive one in many sections of the United States, on the part of both Negroes and whites. It would seem, therefore, in this instance, that the family sociologist could best serve social interests by assuming the role of fact-gatherer.

PROCEDURAL LEGALITIES RELATING TO MARRIAGE

Although no two states have precisely the same procedural requirements for marriage, certain legalities are rather general throughout the United States, e.g., such things as the marriage license, waiting period, physical examination, and the marriage ceremony itself. The licensing, reporting, and recording aspects of marriage are extremely important to the sociologist, for it is this sequence which provides the vital-statistics component. The recording and reporting aspects, however, together with the research opportunities involved, are examined in the concluding section of this chapter. The purpose of the present section is to describe the more important procedural aspects of marriage.

The Marriage License

Although there are some similarities between a marriage contract and a private contract, there is one essential difference: once made, the marriage contract cannot be changed or rescinded simply by the voluntary actions of the two parties involved. Since the marriage contract is more than a private contract, it is incumbent upon the state to set up a procedural mechanism which insures that the statutory provisions are being fulfilled. This mechanism, in essence, is the marriage-licensing procedure. The marriage license attests to the fact that the necessary legal requirements have been fulfilled. The converted license, or marriage certificate, serves as proof of marriage in the eyes of the law, proof which is often invaluable with respect to inheritance rights, social security, insurance, and so on.

Marriage licenses are issued by the individual states and must be used within the state of issuance. Nonresidents may procure a license provided they fulfill the stated legal requirements. The license itself, however, cannot be taken as proof of marriage; it is merely *legal permission* to marry. Details vary from state to state, but in general the license must be *converted* to a marriage certificate by a legally recognized officiant. It is the latter's signature on the marriage record form which attests to the fact of marriage.

Serological Examination

Unknown a generation ago, blood tests are now a legal requirement for marriage in all states except Maryland, Minnesota,

Nevada, South Carolina, and Washington, D.C. The serological certification is generally to the effect that neither party has syphilis, or that the disease is not in the communicable stage. Oddly enough, some states require a blood test to be taken, but if the test discloses syphilis the marriage license will still be issued! All that is required is that both parties be informed of the affliction. Another anomaly occurs in the state of Washington, where only the male is required to take a serological examination. In those states where the examination procedure follows a more logical course, however, it is still possible for a couple to marry without a blood test by the simple expedient of leaving the home state and getting married in one of the six jurisdictions which have no such requirement.

The 1950's saw some question raised regarding the advisability of requiring a blood test, some officials being of the opinion that with advanced techniques available in the control of syphilis, the premarital blood tests were serving little purpose (Hedrich & Silverman, 1958). In recent years, however, the problem of syphilis has again increased, and hence it is unlikely that the serological requirement will be removed in those states which now have such a law. On the contrary, it may be that the handful of states which either have no law, or have an ineffective one, will adopt the standard type of serological test procedures.

Waiting Period

The purpose of the waiting period, obviously, is to put a legal brake on "quickie" marriages. It may come as a surprise to learn, therefore, that in some 20 states there is no legally prescribed waiting period. In most of these states, however, the blood test serves as a built-in waiting period, as it takes time before the results of the serological examination can be determined. Also, some states require a certain amount of time to transpire between the date the license is issued and the date the ceremony

can take place. In a class by itself is Nevada, which has neither a waiting period nor a blood-test requirement.

For those states which do require waiting periods, the time varies from one to five days, the average being three days. A few states, in order to discourage nonresidents from entering for the sole purpose of marrying, impose a longer waiting period on nonresidents than residents. In general, though, the very purpose of the waiting period is partially negated by the fact that residents of states requiring such a period can always rush their marriage by going to a state where no waiting period is necessary.

Solemnization

Forty-seven out of the 50 states permit either a clergyman or a civil official to preside over the marriage ceremony. Three states—Delaware (although an exception here is that the Mayor of Wilmington can serve as marriage officiant), Maryland, and West Virginia—require that the ceremony be performed by a clergyman, a procedure which originated in the Colonial South, where marriage was held to be religious rather than civil in nature. In the 47 states which permit a civil official to preside, marriage ceremonies may be performed by governors, mayors, judges, magistrates, recorders, justices of the peace, and other persons authorized by the court.

Despite the fact that nearly all the states permit civil ceremonies, most American couples prefer their marriage to be under religious auspices. According to the Jacobson survey of regional vital-statistics reports, about four-fifths of all first marriages are presided over by a clergyman. Among widowed and divorced persons, however, civil ceremonies are almost as common as marriages held under religious auspices (Jacobson, 1959).

Although most states require witnesses to be present, the actual form of the ceremony is largely unregulated. As Clarke pointed out, "The statutes do not attempt to impose detailed rules as to the form of the religious marriage ceremony, for such requirements would probably run counter to the constitutional guarantee of religious freedom. Over half the jurisdictions have not attempted to legislate on the subject at all" (Clarke, 1957, p. 91). About the only statutory provision involved is the requirement, in some states, that the two parties swear in front of an officiant that they take each other as husband and wife.

COMMON-LAW MARRIAGE

To understand common-law marriage, it is necessary to turn to the historical antecedents of present-day matrimony. We are accustomed to thinking of marriage as being under joint church-state auspices; that is, the license must be procured from the state, but the ceremony and the signing of the marriage certificate can be either civil or religious. Historically, marriage was neither civil nor religious but private in nature, a relationship solely between the two parties, or two families, involved. During the Middle Ages, when the Church gradually assumed control over marriage, there was some resentment on the part of certain groups, many of whom refused to accept ecclesiastical authority. As a result, private marriages, or *self-gifta,* continued to be undertaken long after the Church had refused to recognize them as valid.

It was inevitable that the United States would have to face the issue of common-law marriage sooner or later. In a frontier nation, it was simply a fact of life that the facilities for obtaining a marriage license and an officiant were sometimes cumbersome. In the cities, licensing procedures might present no difficulties, but for the pioneers who pushed westward, amorous activities did not always lend themselves to the red tape involved in securing the marriage license. At any rate, during the nineteenth century, one state court after another took the position that common-law marriages were valid *in the absence of express statutory prohibitions to the contrary.* In 1877, the United States Supreme Court reaffirmed this general position in a decision which remains the law of the land: common-law marriages are valid unless the state in question has a specific law which declares them to be illegal.

At the present time, prohibitory statutes are lacking in 19 states (Mackay, 1959, p. 6), while the other states recognize common-law marriages if they were legal in the state where contracted. Exactly what constitutes a common-law marriage is difficult to say, inasmuch as the interpretation seems to vary from state to state, and sometimes from court to court. In general, all that is necessary is for a man and woman who are legally marriageable to affirm in the present tense that they take each other as man and wife. It is not necessary for the agreement to be in writing.

The recognition of common-law marriage throughout much of the United States is indeed an anomaly. As the writer has stated elsewhere,

It is almost as if the right hand of the state were in opposition to what the left hand was doing. That is to say, through its statutory provisions the state says: "You must be of such and such an age. You must take a physical examination. You must procure a marriage license and abide by the recording procedures." But the same state also says: "You really need not comply with any of these provisions. So long as you take one another, in the present tense, as man and wife, we will consider you to be validly married" (Kephart, 1961, p. 416).

The recognition of common-law marriage has worked innumerable hardships, not only on the individuals involved, but on their families as well. What happens to a common-law wife and her children when the husband dies? Unless she can prove that a common-law marriage existed— seldom an easy task—neither she nor her children are entitled to the property rights or inheritance that normally are theirs.

Contrariwise, when a wealthy, unmarried man dies, it is not unusual for one or more "common-law wives" to step forth and claim the bulk of the estate. In both instances, legitimate and illegitimate claims, much bitter and costly litigation could have been prevented by the presence or absence of a single record form: the marriage certificate.

Society at large also suffers from the use, or misuse, of common-law marriage. One of the purposes behind the licensing and recording procedures is to provide a comprehensive program for the collection and publication of marriage and divorce statistics, statistics which tell how many marriages are occurring every year, the age at which people marry, what the rate of divorce is, what the temporal and geographical variations in marriage and divorce are, and so on. The authorization of common-law marriage simply throws another wrench into statistical machinery which by its very nature is sometimes difficult to keep in running order.

The role of the family sociologist as regards common-law marriage seems to be a clear one: it is to press for statutory revision. The wisdom of many of the laws dealing with marriage, divorce, social welfare, and the like, can be debated pro and con. And as has been pointed out, a number of these laws are in need of some underlying sociological research before their true significance can be assessed. But such is not the case with common-law marriage. There are no pros and cons to debate, and no needed research which would bear on the advisability of statutory support. Common-law marriage may at one time have served a legitimate purpose, but that day has long since passed. What is needed now is not research or debate, but reform.

SOCIO-LEGAL ASPECTS OF DIVORCE

The problem of divorce is nearly as old as man himself. In virtually all times and all places, man has had to wrestle with the fact of unhappy marriage and the procedures which officially sever the bonds of matrimony. In few other societies, however, has the problem of divorce given rise to the legal spectacle that now exists in the United States. The reasons for this plight are not hard to find. When the colonists began to formulate divorce law they were guided by traditional Christian principles and by marriage as it was then practiced.

With regard to the first, divorce had traditionally been frowned upon by Christians almost irrespective of sect or denomination; indeed, the only real difference of opinion was over whether divorce should be allowed for *any reason*. Even the most liberal of the Christian denominations believed that divorce should be permitted only for serious causes. With regard to marriage, Colonial legislators, in looking at the marriage structure then current, could certainly be excused if they saw no reason for alarm. Quite obviously, America was an agrarian society, and the husband-wife-children unit formed a functional team: they raised their own food, made their clothes, served as their own school and hospital, and so forth. Functional marriage was a necessity, and divorce was all but unknown. Among other things, how could a farmer run his farm without a wife and children? And in the Colonial era, exactly what was a divorced woman supposed to do? Woman's place was in the home, and a homeless female was headed for trouble.

So, when the Colonial laws were formulated, the legislators conceived of divorce as a very exceptional act, something a man or a woman would turn to as a last resort. The permissible grounds gave evidence of the philosophy that divorce would be allowed only for the most serious of reasons, e.g., cruelty endangering life, desertion, adultery, conviction of a crime. Divorce was not only a rare phenomenon in Colonial America, but some of the colonies actually made no provision by which a divorce could be obtained. Those colonies which did often made the legal grounds, such as adultery or cruelty, punishable as criminal offenses. In general, however,

Colonial divorce was so infrequent as to be handled by the governor or by the state legislature rather than by the courts.

With the coming of the nineteenth and twentieth centuries, vast changes took place on the American scene. The women's rights movement took hold, and, for better or worse, the old idea about woman's place being in the home was tossed into limbo. Women were able to achieve a measure of economic independence and no longer had to spend their lives under patriarchal authority. The Industrial Revolution and the rise of the factory system made serious inroads into the *functional* aspects of family life. And, finally, urbanization and the growth of metropolitan areas changed the traditional agrarian family almost beyond recognition. In brief, the forces which had held the family together for hundreds of years were disappearing at a rapid rate.

Although it was to be expected that the divorce rate would rise, no one could have predicted the veritable flood of cases which inundated the courts: from less than 10,000 in 1867 to some 400,000 in 1961! It became obvious that something had to give; that is, with almost one out of every four marriages ending in divorce, it was evident that one of two things would happen: (a) the divorce laws would be made more liberal, or (b) the enforcement of the laws—the divorce procedure itself—would become more lenient. As it turned out, it was the latter practice which came to the fore, hence the development of the American divorce paradox: relatively stiff laws on the one hand versus lax enforcement on the other.

Although the laws and procedures may vary from one state to the next, the *essence* of the American divorce process is pretty much the same in all jurisdictions. One spouse, generally the wife, brings suit under a convenient legal ground as defined by the state. The other spouse perfunctorily denies the charges. During the hearing, the "guilt and innocence" concept of divorce is developed, with one spouse assuming the role of the good and innocent party, and the other depicted as the villain in the case. As Rheinstein put it:

The plaintiff must be absolutely lily-white. He or she has to allege, usually under oath, that he or she has always and at all times conducted himself or herself as a true and faithful husband or wife; and, if he or she should have been guilty also of one of these kinds of marital misconduct, then under the so-called doctrine of recrimination there can be no divorce. In other words, if the marriage has been shattered by one party's misconduct, you can get a divorce. If the marriage has gone on the rocks so completely that both parties have been guilty of marital misconduct—no divorce. That is the official law (Rheinstein, 1952, pp. 40–41).

In view of this system, it is easy to understand why most divorce proceedings are cut-and-dried affairs. Questioning of the plaintiff by the court is generally of a routine nature, with no real probing of veracity attempted; as a matter of fact, in many cases witnesses are not even called. Another important feature of American divorce proceedings is the fact that the defendant generally does not appear in court to defend himself. And if he does not appear for the purpose of refuting the charges made against him, the court will assume that the allegations are true. The divorce will thereupon be granted.

Grounds for Divorce

As is well known, the only recognized ground for divorce in New York State is adultery. On the other hand, some states list over a dozen different grounds. All told, there are some 40 different grounds for divorce in the United States, with none common to all the states. Adultery is but a partial exception to this statement, since Texas recognizes only the wife's infidelity as a statutory ground. Contrary to popular opinion, however, adultery is a seldom-used ground for divorce today, comprising 2 or

3 per cent of all divorce actions. Only in New York State is it significant (Jacobson, 1959, p. 124). The fact is that a large majority of all divorce suits are based on two grounds, cruelty and desertion, even though their names and descriptions are far from uniform throughout the states. There are dozens of other grounds—drunkenness, conviction of a crime, impotence, vagrancy, drug addiction, incest, epilepsy, venereal disease, and so on—but for reasons which are not entirely clear, divorce in the United States has come to signify the legal grounds of cruelty or desertion.

Cruelty is variously defined as "inhuman treatment," "intolerable cruelty," "cruel or barbarous treatment," and so forth. Some states go so far as to construe the term to mean "mental suffering." Still other jurisdictions have added a closely allied ground called "indignities," by which is meant a continuing action or sequence of events rather than a single action. Interestingly, two states (New Mexico and Oklahoma) have added a ground which is simply entitled "incompatibility." However, as defined by statute, cruelty often has a catchall connotation and is a more or less convenient legal repository for domestic strife which cannot readily be tabbed by any other name. The fact that it is so variously and loosely defined helps to explain why cruelty is easily the most popular ground for divorce in the United States. The precise figure is difficult to determine, in view of the varying definitions of the term, but it is probably safe to say that nearly two-thirds of the divorce suits in this country use cruelty as the legal ground.

Desertion is used as a legal ground in about 30 per cent of all American divorce actions. It is variously referred to as "desertion," "abandonment," or "willful absence," and is recognized in nearly all the states as a basis for divorce, the only real exception being North Carolina. Even New York courts are empowered to dissolve a marriage where one spouse has been "absent without tidings for a period of five years," if a diligent search fails to turn up the missing party. (The legal severance is known as an Enoch Arden decree.)

With regard to the required length of absence, there is much variation among the various state laws, with Hawaii specifying six months, Rhode Island five years. All states, however, require the absence to be continuous for the prescribed period of time. It should be noted that the mere *fact* of a continuous absence is not sufficient grounds for divorce. It must be shown that the deserting spouse had no just cause for his or her leaving. If, for example, the wife refuses to perform the necessary household duties such as cooking and cleaning, the husband would have just cause for leaving, and the wife would be unable to procure a divorce on the ground of desertion. Interestingly enough, some courts have consistently ruled that sexual refusal on the part of the wife constitutes desertion *on her part*. It should be kept in mind, however, that the questioning by the court on matters pertaining to just cause is of a routine and perfunctory nature. Typical divorce testimony might read as follows:

Court: And you say your husband has been gone for 26 months?

Wife: Yes.

Court: Have you heard from him during this period?

Wife: No, not a word.

Court: Have you seen him at all?

Wife: Not since the day he left.

Court: Why did your husband leave you?

Wife: I've no idea. He just packed and left.

Court: You have no idea why he left?

Wife: None.

Court: Did you take care of the house properly?

Wife: Yes, even the neighbors knew I was an immaculate housewife.

Court: Did you cook his meals properly?

Wife: I had hot meals ready for him every day, whether he came home or not.

Court: Did you fulfill your wifely duties
properly; that is, did you satisfy
your husband's sexual needs?

Wife: Certainly, unless I was sick.

Court: Will you tell the court of the events
leading up to his departure. . . .

Since in all likelihood the husband will
not be in court to defend himself, even
though he has been notified of the date and
place of the hearing, the judge normally
takes the word of the plaintiff and grants
the divorce. The letter of the law has been
fulfilled: the wife has been shown to be a
good and loving spouse, while her husband
is portrayed as the culpable and guilty
party. The reader can but conjecture the
real reasons which prompted the husband
to leave his home. It is reasonable to suppose, in most such cases, that there are two
sides to the story, but under current procedures the court has no real desire to get involved with the complexities of the situation. Among other things, it would take a
tremendous amount of time to adjudicate
a case so as to hear both sides of the conflict,
together with evidence, witnesses, testimony, and so on, and in view of the present
high rate of divorce the machinery of the
courts would surely clog. It may be that the
system should be changed in order to provide ample hearing of marital disputes. Before exploring this possibility, the next
sections consider the legal alternatives to
divorce, annulment and legal separation.

Annulments

In distinguishing between divorce and
annulment, popular impression has it that
whereas the former legally dissolves the
marriage as of the date specified on the
decree, an annulment is a legal declaration
that the marriage never existed. Theoretically, this distinction is a true one, but in
actuality it may be misleading. For example, it is quite usual for a court, upon granting an annulment, to order the father to
support minor children, should there be
any. Moreover, the court may order the

husband to make regular alimony payments
to the wife. All well and good for the court
to make a legal declaration that this marriage "never existed," but in point of fact
the husband knows better—and he can
prove it!

A more realistic difference between annulment and divorce relates to the time factor. In general, annulments are based on
causes or conditions which predated the
marriage and involve grounds such as the
existence of a prior marriage, fraud, consanguinity, or the couple's being under age.
Divorce, on the other hand, generally involves an action which occurred after the
date of marriage—adultery, cruelty, desertion, and the like.

In practice, annulments have often been
obtained on rather questionable grounds.
For instance, "In New York a court
granted a husband an annulment where he
said that his wife had falsely told him that
she had $6,000 in the bank which she
would give him to set himself up in business after they were married" (Pilpel &
Zavin, 1952, p. 263). It will be remembered
that in New York State the only ground
for divorce is adultery. Rather than go
through with the rigmarole of "hotel
adultery," many couples in New York turn
to annulment, and apparently the courts
are lenient in their handling of these cases.

Legal Separation

Viewed objectively, the concept of legal
separation is a strange one. In a sense, it is
neither one thing nor another. The couple
remain legally married, yet they may not
live together. They are not permitted,
legally at least, to have sex relations with
each other, yet if either party were to have
sexual intercourse with someone else, he or
she would be guilty of adultery. The husband is still liable for the support of his
wife and children, yet a legal separation
does not permit either party to remarry. In
the event of a trial, neither husband nor
wife can testify against the other.

Referred to by a variety of terms—limited

divorce, legal separation, partial divorce, semidivorce, *divortium a mensa et thoro* (divorce from bed and board)—the concept of legal separation has its roots in canon law rather than statutory law. Although they refused to acknowledge the validity of absolute divorce (*divortium a vinculo matrimonii*), the early ecclesiastical courts recognized that there were individual cases where the husband and wife could no longer live together. This was particularly apparent in those marriages where the wife faced the problem of living with a drunken or cruel husband. In such instances the Church permitted the couple to live apart.

Today, even though it is a legal rather than a religious concept, limited divorce serves much the same purpose; namely, to permit (or more accurately, to require) a man and wife to live apart in those instances where the marriage has become intolerable. Most generally, it is the wife who brings suit; in fact, in some states, like Pennsylvania, only wives are permitted by law to bring suit. A legal separation thus serves the purpose of "freeing" the wife from an intolerable situation and at the same time assuring her and her children of financial support.

The statutory grounds for a legal separation are quite similar to those for absolute divorce: cruelty, desertion, conviction of a crime, drunkenness, adultery, impotency, etc. In practice, cruelty is the ground employed in the large majority of cases. It should be noted that bringing suit for a legal separation does not prevent the plaintiff from suing for divorce later, either on the same or on different grounds; in fact, one state (Louisiana) provides that an absolute divorce must be preceded by a one-year legal separation.

As might be imagined, legal separations are numerically insignificant in the United States. Except in rather unusual cases, they serve a limited purpose, and over one-third of the states make no statutory provision for legal separations. On the other hand, many European countries utilize legal separation extensively. A common practice there, for example, is for a couple contemplating a divorce to apply to the court for a legal separation. After a stipulated period of, say, three years, the parties may, upon application to the court, have the separation converted to a divorce. During the period of separation the court usually will attempt to bring about a reconciliation of the two parties. It was this reconciliation process in Europe which served as the forerunner of the family-court movement in America.

The Integrated Family Court

It is evident to both social scientists and the legal profession that the handling of divorce and other types of marital disruption leaves much to be desired. The sad fact is that the legal muddle of divorce is much the same today as it was a generation ago. The only reasonably bright spot to have appeared is the family-court movement, and even there the outcome is by no means certain.

The family court bears certain conceptual and operational similarities to the juvenile court, although the latter has had a much wider and more enthusiastic acceptance in this country. The first juvenile court was founded in Chicago, in 1899, and today these courts have become an integral feature of our antidelinquency program. The first family court was founded in Cincinnati, Ohio, in 1914, and at the present time many if not most of our large cities have such a court in operation.

Family courts vary widely both in name and in function. Some courts which are actually called "family courts" or "courts of domestic relations" are not integrated family courts at all, but courts which handle a specific type of family problem, such as desertion. The true family court, as that term is used by sociologists, is a court empowered by law to handle *all family problems* of a *justiciable* nature, e.g., divorce, annulment, legal separation, desertion and nonsupport, alimony, custody, adoption, delinquency, bastardy, neglect, and intrafamily conduct problems. Conceptually, the family court is to the family what the juvenile court is to the child. With a staff which may include social workers, nurses, psychiatrists, marriage counselors, and probation officers, the court attempts to ameliorate family difficulties, aid in interpersonal marital conflicts, offer professional guidance, and otherwise strengthen family ties. In an integrated family court, such as the widely cited courts in Ohio, a couple applying for a divorce has the benefit of professional marriage counseling. [Cf. p. 922.]

The integrated family court also has a marked administrative advantage over the courts which, operating separately, handle problems of divorce, desertion, adoption, and so forth. All family cases are heard under one roof, and all records can therefore be centralized. In the absence of a centralized court, there is bound to be a great deal of jurisdictional and administrative inefficiency. For example, in New York City, there are actually six different courts which handle family matters: the Supreme Court (divorce, annulment, custody); Special Sessions (illegitimate children); Family Court (support claims); Children's Court (delinquency and neglect); Surrogate's Court (adoptions); and Home Term (disorderly conduct within the family). Most of the larger cities have three or more separate courts for the handling of various types of domestic-relations cases.

The difficulty with the family-court movement has been twofold. In the first place, because of the extensive staffing involved, such courts are expensive to operate, and in most jurisdictions the budget has been inadequate for the size of the task. In the second place, the family courts now operative have, for the most part, failed to provide statistics which would indicate something of the effectiveness of their program. With regard to marriage counseling, for instance, there are no figures which would tell what percentage of the litigants in divorce actions are reconciled (or of those reconciled, what proportion remain reconciled) as compared to parallel figures

in a regular divorce court which has no counseling service.

What the final outcome of the family-court movement will be is open to some question. Certainly, there is no public clamor in favor of the integrated court. On the other hand, many family courts have already won the support of both family sociologists and the community, in spite of severely restricted budgetary appropriations. It is to be hoped that the problem of budgetary limitations can be overcome, for in the last analysis the family court is a socio-legal *experiment,* and as such is deserving of a fair trial, particularly in view of the fact that no better method of handling family problems has even been suggested.

Research Opportunities in the Socio-Legal Area

Over and above the strictly legal aspects of divorce, annulment, and separation, the important question remains as to the kinds of research that can be done in the socio-legal area. One of the first questions that comes up is the relationship between the underlying factors involved in the marital dispute and the party who actually sues for the divorce. It is well known, for example, that it is generally the wife who becomes the plaintiff in divorce suits. It is more or less assumed that this is mainly for the sake of appearance, that it looks a little more chivalrous for the wife to be permitted to become the plaintiff. Yet anyone who has had any connection with divorce suits knows that by the time a marriage has reached the stage of litigation, the husband is likely to feel anything but chivalrous. Nor would chivalry explain why a substantial minority of husbands actually do become plaintiffs.

When the divorce figures for "party to whom granted" are examined in more detail, some curious variations are found to occur. In the first place, there is a variation over time. In the 1860's, when the United States divorce statistics were first collected,

Census Bureau tabulations showed that the husband was plaintiff in about one-third of the cases. By the 1960's, the figure had declined to less than 25 per cent. In the second place, there are variations from state to state, 56 per cent being wife-plaintiff cases in Georgia, as compared to a figure of 82 per cent in Wisconsin (USDHEW, 1959, pp. 2–28).

In the writer's survey of Philadelphia divorce records, it was possible to make tabular breakdowns of a more detailed nature than those provided by the national vital statistics figures. Again, a number of interesting variations were evident, as shown in Table 1.[2]

TABLE 1

PERCENTAGE DISTRIBUTION OF DIVORCES BY
PARTY TO WHOM GRANTED
PHILADELPHIA SAMPLE, 1950

| | No. of Divorces | Percentage Granted to: | |
		Husband	Wife
First marriage total	1,256	30.6	69.4
Native white	939	29.3	70.7
Negro	142	44.4	55.6
Foreign born	175	26.8	73.2
Remarriage total	178	37.1	62.9
Native white	119	34.4	66.6
Negro	19	47.4	52.6
Foreign born	40	40.0	60.0
Total, all cases	1,434	31.4	68.6

As can be seen, there are divergences among the subgroupings. Among Negroes, for example, the husband is much more likely to sue for divorce than is the case among whites. The same is true for the remarried group as compared to those married once only.

Why should these differences exist? Why, as time goes on, should relatively more and more wives assume the role of plaintiff? Why are there such marked differences

[2] Philadelphia data shown in the present chapter have not been published heretofore. For methodological references, as well as a bibliography of works stemming from the Philadelphia study, see Kephart (1955).

among the states? What accounts for nativity and marital-status differentials? And why should the Negro male be so much more likely than the white male to become plaintiff in a divorce action? This fact hardly squares with the stereotype of the Negro family, in which the wife is often looked upon as the more stable partner.

The important thing, of course, is not so much the observed variation in *legal* procedure, but the possibility that these variations stem from *actual* differences in marital behavior on the part of the various subgroupings. Although space precludes an attempt to answer all of the questions raised above, an examination of the Negro-white differential can serve as illustration. Hypothesize that the reason for the Negro husband's relative propensity to become plaintiff stems from behavioral factors which may be inherent in the low socioeconomic status accorded most Negro families. If this hypothesis is valid, then it follows that among white divorces, the lower socioeconomic group would show a higher husband-plaintiff proportion than would the upper socioeconomic level. To test this hypothesis, the Philadelphia data were retabulated to include occupational groupings among native-white first marriages, with the results shown in Table 2.

TABLE 2

PERCENTAGE DISTRIBUTION OF DIVORCES BY
PARTY TO WHOM GRANTED AND
OCCUPATIONAL LEVEL
PHILADELPHIA SAMPLE, 1950

| | No. of Divorces | Percentage Granted to: | |
		Husband	Wife
Professional-proprietory	87	29.1	70.9
Clerical	192	28.0	72.0
Skilled	188	37.2	62.8
Semiskilled	362	29.5	70.5
Labor-service	110	19.5	80.5
Total	939[a]	29.3	70.7

[a] Native white first marriages.

TABLE 3

PERCENTAGE DISTRIBUTION OF DIVORCES BY
LEGAL GROUND, RACE, AND NATIVITY
PHILADELPHIA SAMPLE, 1950
(N: 1,256 FIRST MARRIAGES)

	No. of Divorces	Percentage of Divorces Involving:		
		Desertion	Cruelty[a]	Other Grounds
Native white	939	46.8	49.6	3.6
Foreign born	175	50.3	45.7	4.0
Negroes	142	61.3	35.2	3.5

[a] Including indignities.

Contrary to expectations—that is, contrary to the Negro pattern—the lowest occupational grouping among whites (the labor-service category) shows the highest percentage of divorce suits being granted to the *wife*. The original hypothesis, therefore, must be rejected. Whatever the answer, it does not appear to lie in the realm of broad socioeconomic classification.

Start on a different tack. Perhaps an examination of the legal grounds for divorce might shed some light on the question. These data are presented in Table 3.

Again, racial and nativity differentials manifest themselves. Negroes tend to use the ground of desertion, while among whites the principal legal ground is cruelty. This tendency does not appear to be a class difference among whites, as can be seen

from the occupational figures in Table 4.

Thus far, tabular data have been presented which show the distribution of divorce by party to whom granted and legal grounds. There remains the question whether any association exists between these two factors, whether, for example, one spouse is more often the plaintiff in desertion cases. This breakdown is shown in Table 5.

The figures show a marked tendency in all the subgroups for the husbands to use desertion as a legal ground and the wives to use cruelty. Among Negroes, in fact, cases involving desertion are *more likely* to show the husband rather than the wife as plaintiff. To answer the original question, the reason why the husband is so much more likely to be the plaintiff in Negro divorce

TABLE 4

PERCENTAGE DISTRIBUTION OF DIVORCES BY
LEGAL GROUND AND OCCUPATIONAL LEVEL
PHILADELPHIA SAMPLE, 1950
(N: 939 NATIVE WHITE FIRST MARRIAGES)

	No. of Divorces	Percentage of Divorces Involving:		
		Desertion	Cruelty[a]	Other Grounds
Professional-proprietory	87	40.5	53.2	6.3
Clerical	192	51.1	45.6	3.3
Skilled	188	51.1	47.8	1.1
Semiskilled	362	46.0	50.0	4.0
Labor-service	110	48.1	48.0	3.9

[a] Including indignities.

TABLE 5

PERCENTAGE OF DIVORCES BY
MAJOR LEGAL GROUND AND PARTY TO WHOM GRANTED
PHILADELPHIA SAMPLE, 1950
(N: 1,434)

| | All Cases Granted To: | | | Desertion Granted To: | | | Cruelty[a] Granted To: | | |
	No.	Husband	Wife	No.	Husband	Wife	No.	Husband	Wife
First marriages	1,256	30.6	69.4	614	42.0	58.0	596	19.5	80.5
Native white	939	29.3	70.7	439	40.9	59.1	466	18.2	81.8
Negro	142	44.4	55.6	87	50.6	49.4	50	34.0	66.0
Foreign born	175	26.8	73.2	88	37.5	62.5	80	17.5	82.5
Remarriages[b]	178	37.1	62.9	81	55.5	44.5	91	22.0	78.0
Native white	119	34.4	66.6	48	52.1	47.9	66	22.7	77.3

[a] Including indignities.
[b] Negro and foreign born remarriages not included because of smallness of numbers.

suits, as compared to white cases, apparently lies in the fact that the legal ground of desertion is the principal ground used in Negro divorce suits.

The final question to be answered is why the Negro group tends to overuse the legal ground of desertion, a tendency which does not seem to be explainable in terms of socioeconomic factors. Although it is perhaps possible that inherent racial differences between the two groups provide the answer, the sociological explanation is more plausible. It must be remembered that the American Negro family had its origin in slavery, and from a financial point of view it paid the plantation owner to discourage strong marital and familial ties on the part of the slaves. To the owner, slavery was a business, and it was felt that marital ties between male and female slaves would complicate the buying, selling, and breeding which were integral parts of a slave economy. In consequence, liaisons between male and female slaves were likely to be informal and temporary, without backing either by church or state. After emancipation, this looseness of family organization tended to perpetuate itself because of the economic plight of the Negro male. As a result, the Negro family tended to become matriarchal

in nature, a pattern well known to sociologists.

Family traditions are neither made nor broken overnight, and vestiges of the loose, matriarchal type of family can still be seen among lower-class Negroes. Family courts which handle such cases have long known of the high desertion and nonsupport rates of Negro males. The Philadelphia divorce data reported above, however, suggest that the Negro wife may be leaving her husband more often than has been realized. The point is that when the Negro husband leaves his family the chances are good that the wife will report him to the authorities on charges of nonsupport. But when the Negro wife leaves her husband, the latter will not report her for the simple reason that the wife is not liable for his support. The only realistic legal action for the husband is to sue for divorce on the ground of desertion. That this may actually be the case is suggested by the above data, which indicate that the Negro husband is much more likely than the white husband to become plaintiff in divorce actions.

It may well be, because of historical factors as well as present-day cultural differentials, that *patterns of conflict* in Negro families are different from those in white

families. The former may be characterized
by desertion, nonsupport, and a general
syndrome involving frequent absence from
the home by one spouse or the other. Marital conflict among whites, on the other
hand, may involve bickering, disagreements, affectional discord, and other manifestations of personality conflict. Verification or rejection of this hypothesis, of
course, must come from methods of investigation other than the analysis of legal divorce data.

It can be argued that the legal causes of
divorce have nothing to do with the real
causes, and that therefore an analysis of
statutory grounds is meaningless. It was
the writer's impression, however, based on
the examination of thousands of pages of
testimony as well as discussions with lawyers and court clerks, that incidents depicted in a divorce hearing do not arise out
of thin air. They may be exaggerated, even
distorted, but they often appear to have
enough basis in fact to afford the investigator some insights regarding differential
conflict among *broad classes* of the population.

Thus far, some illustrative research implications of divorce legalities, such as the
statutory grounds and the party to whom
granted, have been discussed. Marriage and
divorce record forms contain a much wider
array of data, however, and the following
section is devoted to this larger recording
and reporting area.

THE RECORDING AND REPORTING
OF MARRIAGES AND DIVORCES[3]

Stated in simplest terms, family sociologists gather information in one of two
ways: they conduct their own studies, or
they analyze available records of some sort,
an example of which was given in the previous section. There is not an equal balance
between the two types of inquiry, however.
For every study involving official records,

[3] The reader may find it helpful to compare this section
with Ch. 9, and especially pp. 329–330, of this Handbook.

there are dozens in which data are procured by questionnaires, interviews, tests,
case histories, or some other method
wherein the investigator, in a sense, *creates*
the data. As a matter of fact, it is doubtful
whether many family sociologists have ever
seen a standard record of marriage (or
divorce) other than their own.

This is not to belittle the efforts of the
data-makers; after all, most of our substantive information relative to the family has
come from them. It is undoubtedly true,
though, that much more could be done in
the analysis of marriage and divorce records, particularly at the local and state
levels. At present, only a handful of family
researchers are working in this area. And
although there are probably many reasons
for this dearth of record analysts, the main
one seems to be that the recording and reporting of marriages and divorces is a
rather complicated process, and the records
themselves are replete with difficulties.
Take, for instance, the actual processing of
a marriage record. Procedures vary somewhat from state to state, but the following
flow is fairly typical:

1. Couple applies to appropriate local official for a marriage license.
2. Local official determines whether couple
   meets the qualifications as to marriageability, blood test, waiting period, etc.
3. If all requirements are met, the local official issues a marriage license.
4. Couple takes the marriage license to person authorized to perform the ceremony.
5. Officiant performs the ceremony and
   signs the marriage certificate.
6. Officiant sends a copy of the marriage
   certificate back to the local official.
7. Local official then registers the marriage.
8. Local official sends record-of-marriage to
   the State Board of Health's Vital Statistics Division.
9. State Vital Statistics Division records,
   indexes, and files the record-of-marriage.
10. At year-end, State Vital Statistics Divi-
    sion tabulates all recorded marriage
    records and forwards tabulations to the
    National Vital Statistics Division.

11. The National Vital Statistics Division periodically issues bulletins containing statistical information derived from above tabulations (adapted from USDHEW, 1956).

It can be seen that the analysis of marriage and divorce records (divorce reporting follows a similar process) can be made at either local, state, or national levels. There are advantages and disadvantages at all three levels, and it might be well to consider some of them. For richness and completeness of data, local marriage and divorce records (city or county) are clearly superior. As transcripts or extracts are forwarded to state and national vital-statistics centers, individual items contained in the original records are often eliminated. This attrition is particularly significant in the case of divorce. Unlike marriage, divorce involves litigation, in the course of which a great deal of sociological information is often elicited, such as race, religion, nationality, family background, occupation, education, and income, as well as phenomena relating to the so-called cause of the divorce. Much of this material, however, is available only at the local level.

The difficulty in attempting to work with local marriage and divorce records is that in a number of jurisdictions officials are reluctant to open their files, even to qualified research workers. In some instances, the records are actually impounded. Even where the researcher is given access to marriage and divorce records, it is often difficult to transcribe the desired information. In the Philadelphia study, for example, it was necessary to read through voluminous testimony. Another drawback in working with local records is that when all is said and done, the findings are still local. They may or may not be representative of the nation at large. Nevertheless, in spite of the difficulties involved, sociologists who are willing to spend the requisite time and effort will find the results rewarding, as evidenced by the works of Christensen, Hemperley, Kephart, Monahan, Schroeder, and Sullenger.[4]

At the state level, also, it is often difficult to gain access to the necessary records, and, of course, the question of geographical representativeness still remains. On the other hand, the number of cases is relatively large, and the problem of transcribing the data may be easier than at the local level. Some of the finest sociological studies, e.g., by Jacobson (1959), Monahan (1952), and Lewit (1961), are those in which state records have been utilized.

As might be imagined, it is from the national level that the major marriage and divorce statistical reports have emanated. The first national report on marriages and divorce covered the years 1867–1886 and contained, in addition to numerical totals, some detailed statistics pertaining to legal causes, duration of marriage, regional variations, and the like. Statistical reports were also published for the period 1887–1906, for the year 1916, and for the successive years 1922–1932. Unfortunately for all concerned, from 1932 until the end of World War II the federal program lagged. It was not until 1946, when the Vital Statistics Division was moved from the Census Bureau to the Public Health Service, that regular publication was resumed. Even then, the statistical data involved were "slim pickings" indeed, and it has only been in recent years that the national program has begun to supply reasonably detailed marriage and divorce statistics.[5]

The difficulty with the federal system has been that the Constitution provides for state control of marriages and divorces, and the laws and procedures relating to marriage and divorce in one state may be very different from those in another. For example, the National Vital Statistics Division

---

[4] References to these and other studies using record data can be found in Kephart (1957).

[5] For a more detailed account of the development and need for nationwide marriage and divorce statistics, see ASA Committee on Marriage and Divorce Statistics (1958).

has recommended a Standard Record of Marriage (Fig. 1) and a Standard Record of Divorce or Annulment (Fig. 2), yet a number of states continue to use forms which lack the required items of information. There are still some states which do not have centralized reporting, that is, a system whereby county marriages and divorces are reported to the state capital. Family researchers who are interested in working at the state level would do well to consult Figs. 3 and 4, which show those states that do and do not maintain centralized marriage and divorce files.

In an effort to prod the "slow" states and to maintain a consistent and comprehensive level of marriage and divorce reporting, the National Vital Statistics Division has re-

cently established a Marriage Registration Area (in 1957) and a Divorce Registration Area (in 1958). In the words of Dr. Hugh Carter, Chief of the Marriage and Divorce Statistics Branch of the National Vital Statistics Division:

In order to stimulate State improvement in registration and statistics, we have established statistical reporting areas from which uniform and comparable data are obtained. The Divorce Registration Area (DRA) now includes 21 States. The Marriage Registration Area (MRA) now includes 35 states. We hope all other States will soon participate. Then we will have statistics on a par with most of the countries of the Western World (Carter, 1961, pp. 8–9).

As can be seen from Figs. 5 and 6, a

Fig. 1.

_____ DEPARTMENT OF PUBLIC HEALTH
(State)
_____ OF VITAL STATISTICS
(Division)

FORM APPROVED
BUDGET BUREAU NO. 68-R547

STATE FILE NO.

COUNTY

STANDARD RECORD OF
☐ DIVORCE OR ☐ ANNULMENT

LOCAL FILE NO.

HUSBAND

1. NAME a. (First) b. (Middle) c. (Last)   2. DATE OF BIRTH (Month) (Day) (Year)

3. USUAL RESIDENCE a. (City) b. (County) c. (State)   4. PLACE OF BIRTH (State or foreign country)

5. NUMBER OF THIS MARRIAGE   6. RACE OR COLOR WHITE NEGRO OTHER ☐ ☐ ☐ (specify) _____   7a. USUAL OCCUPATION   7b. KIND OF BUSINESS OR INDUSTRY

WIFE

8. MAIDEN NAME a. (First) b. (Middle) c. (Last)   9. DATE OF BIRTH (Month) (Day) (Year)

10. USUAL RESIDENCE a. (City) b. (County) c. (State)   11. PLACE OF BIRTH (State or foreign country)

12. NUMBER OF THIS MARRIAGE   13. COLOR OR RACE WHITE NEGRO OTHER ☐ ☐ ☐ (specify) _____   14a. USUAL OCCUPATION   14b. KIND OF BUSINESS OR INDUSTRY

15. PLACE OF THIS MARRIAGE a. (County) b. (State or foreign country)   16. DATE OF MARRIAGE (Month) (Day) (Year)

17. NUMBER OF CHILDREN UNDER 18   18. PLAINTIFF HUSBAND WIFE ☐ ☐   19. DECREE GRANTED TO HUSBAND WIFE ☐ ☐   20. LEGAL GROUNDS FOR DECREE

I hereby certify that the above persons were divorced on: (Month) (Day) (Year)   DATE OF RECORDING (Month) (Day) (Year)

SIGNATURE OF COURT OFFICIAL   TITLE OF COURT OFFICIAL

DEPARTMENT OF HEALTH, EDUCATION, AND WELFARE · · PUBLIC HEALTH SERVICE   PHS-2040 6-54

Fig. 2.

number of the states not yet participating in the MRA and DRA are located in the South and Southwest, and it is hoped that these states can be induced to join. The criteria for admission to the MRA and DRA are certainly moderate enough: (a) maintenance of centralized marriage and divorce records; (b) adoption of satisfactory report forms, such as the standard records shown in Figs. 1 and 2; (c) regular reporting by all local areas to the state vital-statistics division; and (d) agreement between state and national vital-statistics divisions relative to joint testing of reporting for completeness and accuracy. All things considered, it is a reasonable expectation that within the foreseeable future the goal of complete national marriage and divorce registration can be achieved in much the same manner that national birth and death registration was attained.

Research Implications

Although no particular mention has been made of it in the sociological literature, establishment of the MRA and DRA is of tremendous importance to family sociologists, particularly those who are interested in demographic analysis. Thus far, there has been relatively little demographic analysis of national marriage and divorce data by family sociologists, one reason being that up to now there has been a limited amount of tabular and other official data to analyze. With the inauguration of the Marriage and Divorce Registration areas, however, plus the recently adopted sampling program (Carter, 1961), the picture has begun to brighten. Tabular information already available from reports issued by the National Vital Statisics Division includes:

All marriages, first marriages, and remarriages, by resident status of bride and groom in state where married

First marriages and remarriages, by age and color of bride and groom

First marriages of both bride and groom, by age of bride, by age of groom

Marriages by age and previous marital status of bride and groom

Marriage and divorce rates per 1,000 female population in specified age groups

Percentage distribution of marriages, by month

Median age of bride and of groom at first marriage and remarriage

Marriages and marriage rates: United States, each division, and state

Percentage distribution of divorces and annulments, by color of husband and wife

Percentage distribution of divorces and annulments, by legal grounds

Percentage distribution of divorces and annulments, by number of children reported

Percentage distribution of divorces and annulments, by duration of marriage

Divorces and divorce rates: United States, each division, and state

Fig. 3.

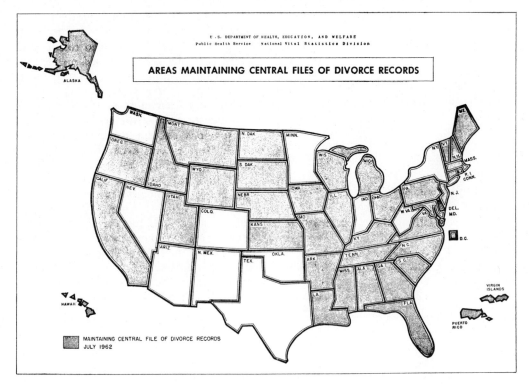

Fig. 4.

Annulments reported: United States, each division, and state

Divorces and annulments, by month

Divorces and annulments, by age and color of husband and wife

Divorces and annulments, by party to whom granted

Divorces and annulments, by age of husband and of wife and duration of first marriage or remarriage in years

Divorces and annulments, by age of husband and of wife and number of times married.

The above list, representing only a portion of the marriage and divorce data now published by the National Vital Statistics Division, has been included to show some of the opportunities available for family students interested in demographic analysis.

Nor does the information published by the National Vital Statistics Division exhaust the research opportunities for family

demographers. To repeat, a great deal of rich statistical information pertaining to marriage and divorce is available at the county and state levels for sociologists willing to dig it out. At these levels, in fact, certain demographic information is available which goes far beyond present compilations of the National Vital Statistics Division. Examples of these surveys, done in the postwar period, are as follows (Jacobson, 1959; Kephart, 1957; Monahan, 1952; Lewit, 1961):

Age at first marriage, by occupational level
100-year trend in median age at first marriage
Relative age differences between husband and wife, by occupational level
Ecological distributions of marriages and divorces
Duration of marriage, by separation and divorce dates

Importance of residential propinquity in marriage

Relation between premarital propinquity and divorce

Divorce rates, by occupational level

Distribution of first marriages and remarriages, by educational level

Ratio of observed to expected number of marriages, by previous marital status

Stability of remarriages

Percentage distribution of divorces, by religious affiliation

Success or failure of Gretna Green marriages

Rate of interracial marriage

Rate at which divorced couples remarry each other

Stability of interreligious marriages

Comparative divorce frequency of whites and Negroes

Premarital pregnancy as a factor in divorce

It should be kept in mind that the present chapter has dealt with *vital-statistics data only*. The Census Bureau also collects and publishes family statistics based on the regular decennial enumerations as well as on special sample surveys (see Ch. 9).

There has been more family research of all kinds in the postwar period than in all the previous decades combined. Prospects for the future look even brighter. In this concluding section, the attempt has been made to point up some opportunities for the family sociologist interested in the analysis of national marriage and divorce statistics as well as for the researcher concerned with local and state data. For those interested in the former, data provided from MRA and DRA and from the improved sampling procedures will open up new horizons. For family sociologists interested in

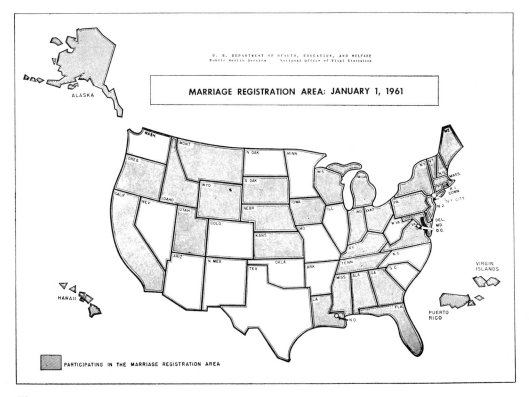

Fig. 5.

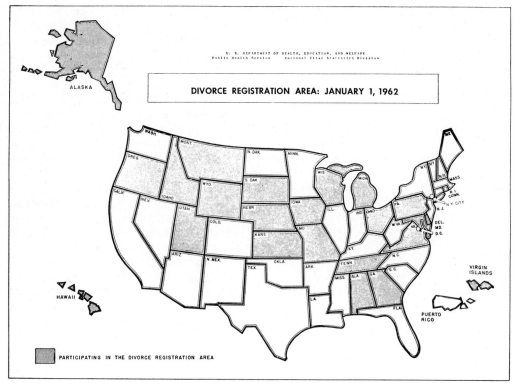

U. S. DEPARTMENT OF HEALTH, EDUCATION, AND WELFARE
Public Health Service   National Vital Statistics Division

DIVORCE REGISTRATION AREA: JANUARY 1, 1962

PARTICIPATING IN THE DIVORCE REGISTRATION AREA

Fig. 6.

the actual transcription of marriage and divorce data, the materials available at the local and state level look most inviting. In any event, it seems reasonable to assume that demographic research in the family field has reached the point best described as the end of the beginning.

REFERENCES

American Sociological Association Committee on Marriage and Divorce Statistics. The need for nationwide marriage and divorce statistics. *Amer. sociol. Rev.*, 1958, 23, 306–312.

Burchinal, L. Adolescent role deprivation and high school age marriage. *Marr. & fam. Living*, 1959, 21, 378–384.

Burgess, E. W., & Cottrell, L. *Predicting success or failure in marriage.* Englewood Cliffs, N.J.: Prentice-Hall, 1939.

Carter, H. The program for improved registration and statistics. Paper read at Amer. Bar Ass. Section on Fam. Law, St. Louis, Aug. 8, 1961.

Clarke, Helen I. *Social legislation.* New York: Appleton-Century-Crofts, 1957.

Goode, W. J. *After divorce.* Glencoe, Ill.: Free Press, 1956.

Groves, E. R., & Ogburn, W. F. *American marriage and family relationships.* New York: Holt, 1928.

Hedrich, A. W., & Silverman, Charlotte. Should the premarital blood test be compulsory? *Amer. J. publ. Hlth,* 1958, 254, 125–132.

Information please almanac. New York: Simon & Schuster, 1962.

Jacobson, P. *American marriage and divorce.* New York: Rinehart, 1959.

Kephart, W. M. Occupational level and marital disruption. *Amer. sociol. Rev.,* 1955, 20, 456–465.

Kephart, W. M. Some knowns and unknowns in family research: a sociological critique. *Marr. & fam. Living,* 1957, 19, 8–15.

Kephart, W. M. *The family, society, and the individual.* Boston: Houghton Mifflin, 1961.

Kirkpatrick, C. *The family: as process and institution.* (2nd ed.) New York: Ronald Press, 1963.

Lewit, Sarah. Selected characteristics of marriages: Georgia. U. S. Department of Health, Education, and Welfare, National Vital Statistics Division. *Selected stud.,* 1961, 47, 289–325.

Locke, H. *Predicting adjustment in marriage.* New York: Holt, 1951.

Mackay, R. V. Law of marriage and divorce. New York: Oceana Publications, 1959.

Monahan, T. P. How stable are remarriages? *Amer. J. Sociol.,* 1952, 52, 280–288.

Monahan, T. P. Does age at marriage matter in divorce? *Soc. Forces,* 1953, 32, 84–85.

Moss, J. J., & Gingles, Ruby. The relationship of personality to the incidence of early marriage. *Marr. & fam. Living,* 1959, 21, 373–377.

Pilpel, Harriet, & Zavin, T. *Your marriage and the law.* New York: Rinehart, 1952.

Rheinstein, M. Our dual law of divorce: the law in action versus the law of the books. Univer. of Chicago Law School, Conference Series No. 9, *Divorce,* 1952.

Sherwin, R. V. *Sex and the statutory law.* New York: Oceana Publications, 1949.

Terman, L., with Buttenwieser, P., Ferguson, L. W., Johnson, W. B., & Wilson, D. P. *Psychological factors in marital happiness.* New York: McGraw-Hill, 1938.

U. S. Department of Health, Education, and Welfare. *Manual for the registration of marriages.* Document No. 390—Rev., May 28, 1956. Reproduced by National Office of Vital Statistics, Public Health Service, Washington, D. C.

U. S. Department of Health, Education, and Welfare. *Vital statistics of the United States, 1959.* Section 2. Marriage and divorce statistics. Washington, D. C.: Author, May 28, 1959.

CHAPTER 24 The Intrusion of Values

HAROLD T. CHRISTENSEN
Purdue University

At several points throughout this volume, attention has been focused upon the problem of values. In Chapter 1, for example, it was argued that science must be value-free in its method, although it can and does deal with values as data (pp. 11, 27–28). Following this, there have been discussions of the reputed preoccupation ·of family scholars with normative and ethical issues (pp. 8, 387–391, 618–620); of value factors explaining the rise of the nuclear family (pp. 91–94); of the responsiveness of sexual behavior to differing and changing sex codes (pp. 588–597); of the so-called definition of the situation as a factor in behavior and adjustment (pp. 129–131, 802–805); of the importance and place of motives, values, and expectations in the decisions and patterns of marriage (pp. 702–711, 723–727); of the disorganization that comes from failure to meet expectations (pp. 573–575, 805–809); of methodological problems involved in "response errors," the "social desirability effect," and other kinds of value-caused distortion (pp. 234–236, 258–268, 292–295, 383–388); and of public relations problems due to value conflict between the family specialist and both his subjects and

the consumers of his data (pp. 268–272, 616–618, 898–903, 940–942). Since the present chapter attempts to pull together these and other aspects of "the value problem," without repeating the detailed arguments, the thoughtful reader may find it profitable to review the pages indicated above and also to check the index for additional page references.

Values are the mental and emotional sets which aid persons in judging the relative worth or importance of things, ideas, or events. They are more action-oriented than are beliefs. According to Williams, "a belief is a conviction that something is real, whereas a value is a standard of preference" (1961, p. 406). In decision-making theory, values, simply stated, are *the criteria one uses for choosing among alternatives*. Thus, in family living, one might value such things as premarital chastity, fidelity to the spouse, husband-wife equality, small number of children, and the avoidance of divorce. But others may hold different values on these and other points, depending mainly upon their upbringing and upon the dominant norms of their respective cultures. And the decisions and adjustments of family members will to a large extent depend upon the particular values which they cherish, whatever these are.

If data could be examined independently of the value systems of the examiners there would be no "value problem." It is only when values intrude themselves within the scientific process, to upset the objectivity of this process, that the difficulty arises. This difficulty is an everpresent potential for the social sciences.

In this concluding chapter, attention is focused upon four separate but interlocking aspects of the value problem: the interrelatedness of science, values, and social action; the question of assessing research and action programs in the family area; the legitimacy of values used as data in family research; and image problems in family sociology. The first of these is treated from the standpoint of science and sociology in general; the last three with special reference to *family sociology* in particular.

VALUES, SCIENCE, AND SOCIAL ACTION

The story is told of an aspiring biologist who had spent many years studying and classifying all of the bugs found within a given geographic area, and who now had his work completed and his dissertation ready to hand in. But just at this point he discovered a new specimen which had previously escaped him. "Do you know what he did?" (long pause) "He stepped on it." This facetious account illustrates the temptation faced by the less-than-objective scholar to distort facts for personal or group advantage. But "stepping on" the evidence is not in accordance with the spirit of science.

Within the physical sciences, where the data are inanimate, for the researcher or engineer to keep his generalizations and decisions free from personal preference comes relatively easily; within the biological sciences, because the data are alive and hence to a greater extent "human," this ceases to be quite so easy; but within the social sciences, where the data are apt to

involve the same kinds of feelings and behaviors that the researcher himself experiences, the task becomes most difficult of the three. Furthermore, certain of the social science subfields are especially close to the emotions and to personal interests, making objectivity among them even more difficult to obtain. Marriage and the family is one of these.

Writing of family research in the period immediately following World War II, Komarovsky and Waller had this to say:

The worker in this field is shackled by taboos and ancestral superstitions, which he has the more trouble in combating because they are in his mind as well as in his environment. We are able to observe only what the mores permit us to see. At any given period sociological writing on the family reflects the moral problems of the time, and that is as true today as it ever was; but nevertheless we have made progress toward the scientific understanding of family relations (1945, p. 443).

It should be added that the most striking progress in family study has been made during the two decades since these authors expressed themselves (see Ch. 1), but the fundamental difficulty remains. Furthermore, although this value problem is particularly bothersome in the field of study that is of present concern, it exists in essentially the same form in other branches of science as well; the difference is one of degree rather than of kind.

The Requirements of Science

It is in the nature of science that generalizations spring directly and solely from the data examined, rather than from either the desires of the scientist or the pressures of society. Science seeks to discover *what is* rather than what ought to be; it looks for *truth,* not proof; it cuts new trails, letting the chips fall where they may, rather than defending old ones or catering to vested interests.

The point of view which espouses this value-free search for reality has been called the "scientific attitude" or "scientific" frame of reference." Assumptions behind such an attitude are that the world of phenomena is an orderly one, capable of being understood and controlled; that to know is better than not to know, hence the pursuit of knowledge is good; and that phenomena are causally related, or at least are so related that A can be observed to follow B under the conditions specified (cf. Martinson, 1961, p. 281).

Science aims at the accretion of facts and theories toward the goal of prediction and potential control. A *fact* is simply "an empirically verifiable observation," whereas "*theory* refers to the relationship between facts, or to the ordering of them in some meaningful way" (Goode & Hatt, 1952, p. 8). With facts one can *describe*. With theory one can *generalize* concerning cause and effect relationships, and hence *predict* outcomes under specified conditions. Predictive power is the ultimate aim of science. In the hands of the engineer it makes *control* possible, for with causal sequences understood, one merely has to manipulate the independent variable(s) to obtain the desired result in the dependent variable(s). But note that actual control is for the engineer, not the pure scientist. Applications of scientific knowledge (applied science) involve value judgments and are outside the province of science proper—although some persons wear two hats, so to speak, and attempt to be both scientist and engineer.

Furthermore, science as such must be distinguished from both the value-free attitude upon which it is based and the predictive theory in which it results. Essentially, it is a *method* for investigating phenomena. In this it differs from both the intuitive-inspirational method of the religionist and the speculative-deductive method of the pure philosopher. Science confines itself to *empirical data,* or in other words to phenomena which man is capable of experiencing. It *observes* these data through one or more of the five senses, then *tests* for relationships, and finally *generalizes* on the basis of these testings. Since it

moves from particular facts to general principles or laws, its process is essentially *inductive*. Science may or may not start with *hypotheses,* but where successful it will always end with the discovery of dependable facts and/or relationships—which are its generalizations and which add up to *theory*. Since the discoveries of science must be dependable, that is, must be capable of replication by others using comparable data and techniques, one of the most important ingredients of the method is *verification*.

Thus, science is rather precise and focused; it should not be permitted to be "all things to all men." Since it strives for *objectivity,* it its no respecter of "sacred" domains or vested interests; hence, it almost inevitably runs into conflict with persons and groups who seek to promote some chosen value or point of view. Typically, the promoters of values—and to a certain extent this includes everyone—either become *anti-science* or *pro-science* in approach; and if the latter, they either use the prestige of science to try to support their value positions, by selecting just those facts that "fit" (a particularly common tendency in this age when the prestige of science is high), or they honestly attempt to adjust the differences, to build a system of values based upon—or at least compatible with—science.

Alternative Positions of the Social Scientist

Values, as has been said, present the social sciences with a particularly knotty problem. There have been numerous attempts to deal with this problem and to develop a theory of values that is manageable (e.g., Catton, 1959; Goode & Hatt, 1952; Lundberg, Schrag, & Larsen, 1958; Morris, 1956; Williams, 1961). Yet, social scientists today are far from agreement about the relation of their efforts to values; in a sense, they take different value positions on the value problem.

Two issues have been especially troublesome in past decades, and each has generated considerable controversy. The first asks, simply, how research can be made "objective," or free from value-bias (the relation of empirical theory to normative theory). The second asks when the sociologist's responsibility for his research ends (the relation of empirical theory to action).

The lines of the first issue are sharply drawn in the contrast of Lundberg's work with that of Myrdal and Popper.

Lundberg (1939) built a strong case for developing the social sciences by modeling them on the value-free methods of the physical sciences. He argued for a "positivistic" social science, in which methodology is so carefully developed, and the units of study so carefully chosen and controlled, that values have little or no chance of distorting research. Ideally, according to this line of argument, methods can be so carefully constructed and employed that the problem of value-bias is no greater for the social scientist than for the physical scientist.

Myrdal's (1944) classic analysis of evaluation in the social sciences boldly contradicts such a position:

Scientific terms become value-loaded because society is made up of human beings following purposes. A "disinterested social science" is, from this viewpoint, pure nonsense. It never existed, and it never will exist. We can make our thinking strictly rational in spite of this, but only by facing the valuations, not by evading them (p. 1064).

Today, the position represented by Myrdal is, for most social scientists, nearly "popular knowledge"; the controversy continues, but it is sporadic and pallid compared to 25 or even 15 years ago.

But Myrdal's position (which essentially suggests that values can be controlled if they are identified and thereby rendered "objective") is not entirely satisfactory to all sociologists, who question whether any individual can effectively identify all his values; for, even though he may perceive that in some values he differs from most persons, it is extremely difficult to recognize the values implicit in his culture, which are almost second nature to him.

Popper (1952) argued that this difficulty in gaining objectivity can be approached only through the collective and critical efforts of a community of scientists. But even such communities may fail to identify some basic prejudices, for bias can be shared by generations of thinkers, as was evidenced in Hitler's Germany and as is currently seen in the contrast of Soviet and United States social theorists. The only workable path toward objectivity in research, Popper claimed, is "to tackle the practical problems of our time with the help of the theoretical methods . . . of trial and error, of inventing hypotheses which can be practically tested, and of submitting them to practical tests" (p. 222).

Problems of controlling bias in research are far from resolved today, but, perhaps because solutions are more elusive than was once thought, the emotion-packed arguments of 20 years ago have subsided into more gentlemanly and leisurely discussion.

But active debate continues over the second issue, which asks when the sociologist's responsibility for his data ends, or, more plainly, should the social scientist work for the application of his findings? The positions in this debate can be categorized into three major clusters: value rejection, value espousal, and value separation.

Value rejection. This position represents the most extreme dissociation of the scientist from the value world in which he lives. Its defenders argue for disinterested research and unconcern for ethical problems and the applications of research findings. Not only has it been argued that science is non-ethical by definition and that it is the scientist's duty to make sure that his own values are excluded from the investigative process, but also it has been claimed that the scientist should remain scientist throughout, staying "pure" and uncontaminated by association with value judgments, and hence with social action. Lundberg, one of the most forceful advocates of this position, argued:

It is not the business of a chemist who invents a high explosive to be influenced in his task by considerations as to whether his product will be used to blow up cathedrals or to build tunnels through mountains. Nor is it the business of the social scientist in arriving at laws of group behavior to permit himself to be influenced by considerations of how his conclusions will coincide with existing notions, or what the effect of his findings on the social order will be (1929, pp. 404–405).

This position—which would present the social scientist as a technician, who is not to reason why—is not very popular today; significantly, Lundberg (1947; Lundberg, Schrag, & Larsen, 1958a; Lundberg, Schrag, & Larsen, 1958b) has more recently declared himself for the less extreme position of value separation.

Value espousal. The other extreme of the debate argues that the social scientist not only has values, but that it is impossible for him to compartmentalize his life clearly and completely into separate areas of "science" and "action." Hence, he must make his own value position explicit so as to forewarn his public and aid them in interpreting his generalizations; and further, since he is better informed on public matters than the layman, he has an obligation to assume active leadership in helping society decide what to do and what not to do (see Lynd, 1939). In other words, holders of this position argue that the scientist is necessarily involved with the world, and cannot avoid influencing it.

Mills argued:

Whether he wants it or not, or whether he is aware of it or not, anyone who spends his life studying society and publishing the results *is* acting morally and usually politically as well. The question is whether he faces this condition and makes up his own mind, or whether he conceals it from himself and from others and drifts morally (1959, p. 79).

After approving Popper's argument for social engineering (see above), Hansen (1963) claimed that he did not go far enough; whereas Popper would have the scientist enter the field of social action in order to test knowledge and pursue objectivity, Hansen believes that he also has a responsibility to help shape action for the benefit of society:

The responsibility of the sociologist is certainly met in part by his search for objective facts and empirical theory. Indeed, to confine himself solely to research aimed at social action would endanger his search, his science, and eventually, his society. Development of factual theory requires many projects with little immediate relevance; without facts and understanding, action is at best ineffectual and at worst destructive.

But in insulating himself from practical problems, in insisting on his detachment, in pursuing a false image of objectivity, the sociologist is in danger of allowing the power he creates to be delivered into the hands of men who not only hold different values, but who are often less able than he to evaluate his findings (p. 324).

Advocates of value espousal argue that it is not enough for the social scientist to investigate social phenomena without regard for the application of his findings (as in value separation). He must, while still wearing the robes of the expert, urge that the most promising course be adopted; he must speak ex cathedra; he must identify himself as a sociologist, and allow this identification to lend weight to his proposals. In short, although in most political and social issues he should not identify himself as different from any other citizen, in matters in which he is an expert, he must speak as an expert, act as an expert, and influence others as he can only as an expert.

Value separation. This position is more moderate than the other two, and is held by most sociologists today, including the present writer (see the sections below on legitimate and illegitimate value intrusions).

Value separation frankly recognizes the legitimacy of values in the scientist but stresses the need for keeping his citizen-self and his scientist-self entirely separate—even on issues on which he is "expert." Those taking this position feel that it is all right, perhaps even desirable, for the scientist to assume value-laden roles in society, just so he does not either use the prestige of science to promote his other values or permit his values to enter into the scientific process. The important thing is not that the scientist be *exclusively* scientist, but rather that he keep his roles of scientist and citizen separate, so that neither is spoiled by the other and so that the public will always know from which position he speaks (cf. Bain, 1939; Becker, 1941).

But there are real difficulties in maintaining such a separation. These difficulties may not be so great in the physical and biological sciences as in the social sciences. Certain atomic physicists, for example, have spoken out against nuclear testing, and certain biologists have declared themselves on one side or the other of the euthanasia controversy; yet it is doubtful that these public commitments have made them either less objective in their work or less respected by society. With the social scientist the problem is different, in degree if not in kind, for he may personally hold or reject the very values that he must study objectively, and to avoid mixing the two is, some critics say impossible.

Legitimate Value Intrusions

Since there is lack of consensus on the value issue among social scientists, it can be expected that each scientist's position will in some part depend upon his personal value system; in other words, choosing a value position is in and of itself making a value judgment. It is the writer's judgment—rational, it is to be hoped, but undoubtedly also evaluative—that the following are legitimate intrusions of values into the scientific realm:

1. *Accepting the scientific method as a valid approach to truth.* Science itself is a value (cf. Bain, 1939; Becker, 1941; Goode & Hatt, 1952, p. 24)—not its method, but its basic premise that "to know is better than not to know." Science values the pursuit of knowledge, and in accepting this the scientist makes his first and most basic value choice—the choice which starts him as a scientist.

2. *Selecting research problems that have potential utility.* Although there is a place for the "pure" scientist who is interested only in "knowledge for knowledge's sake," there also is room and need for scientists with applied or practical interests. Since there is no dearth of problems to be researched, perhaps preference should be given to those with close-range utility *plus* long-range theoretical importance. Letting values enter in at the point of problem selection need not in any way affect the research process or the results obtained.

3. *Supplying interpretive judgments to link with the outside.* Strictly speaking, interpretations are not a part of the scientific process. They are speculative and often involve value judgments. Nevertheless, they are important, both from the standpoint of future research and from the standpoint of application possibilities. No one is in a better position to bridge these gaps than is the researcher himself, with his fresh and intimate knowledge of the data. Interpretations coming at the end of the research report can be the source of new hypothesis generation as well as of engineering programs. But they must be clearly labeled as such and not made to appear to be a part of the generalizations proper.

4. *Determining the best means to a chosen end.* Science cannot decide upon the goal to be sought after, but once this is known, it can determine the alternative means for achieving this goal as well as the relative efficiency of each alternative. In other words, it can use some goal or desired end (value) as the criterion against which to measure its phenomena—but of course without making

any judgment as to whether the end itself is good or bad. Thus, in analyzing marriage and family phenomena, Christensen (1958a, pp. 17–19) adopted the "happiness criterion of success," Kirkpatrick (1963, pp. 178–180, 655–659) the "happiness-adjustment criterion of ultimate goodness," and Martinson (1960, pp. 14–17) "the American ideal—belief in the dignity, freedom, and equality of man—as the core value complex against which to judge the efficacy of choices." Each of these authors pointed to other value-framework possibilities. The important point here is that the framework is *adopted* by the scholar, *not proved,* although generally with a concern that it fit the value structure of the group being studied.

5. *Using values as data in the research.* Although the scientist is denied value judgments of his own while engaging in research, he certainly can and (if social scientist) must deal with the value judgments his subjects make. Values, as is demonstrated in more detail in a later section of this chapter, are extremely important data for the understanding of human behavior.

In summary, it may be considered legitimate for the scientist to make a value choice in becoming a scientist, to let values enter in at both the beginning (problem selection) and the end (interpretation) of his research, to adopt value criteria as standards against which he measures his phenomena, and to study the values which people hold in order to understand their behavior.

The position taken here is that it is impossible for the social scientist to free himself *entirely* from values (since he is human), and also impossible for him to be scientist while at the same time shaping his data to the defense or promotion of desired ends (involving a contradiction of terms). In other words, the position is the one that in the previous section was labeled *value separation:* it avoids both the unrealistic position of complete value rejection and the nonscientific position of out-and-out value espousal.

Exponents of the value-separation position have argued for both the feasibility and the desirability of combining *scientist role* and *citizen role* within the same person,— although with adequate precautions to keep the two roles separate. Bain, for example, after pointing out that the scientist, as scientist, cannot *advocate* anything (although he may serve as factual expert to policy-making agencies), had this to say: "If we are too holy to descend into the market place to counsel with our fellow citizens, the market place may rise and destroy science and many of our cherished values as well" (1939, p. 364). Becker expressed it as follows: "Insofar as our work is professionally scientific, it must be judged by scientific standards, not by patriotic, humanitarian, or religious standards. Insofar as we have time, energy, and inclination to be patriots, humanitarianists, or religionists, we have the right to play these roles up to the hilt" (1941, p. 171).

Illegitimate Value Intrusions

It may be said that values are legitimate to science if and when they are kept out of the research process itself, but that they intrude illegitimately whenever they enter into this process and thus distort the results. Science is only science insofar as its generalizations are based solely upon objective measurements of empirical data, so that replication will result in verification. This, of course, becomes impossible whenever either the values of the subjects get in the way of the measuring instruments and obscure the objective reality these instruments were trying to get at, or the value systems of the investigators blind these investigators to the nature of their problem and/or tempt them into deserting their science. Thus, value distortion may come from either the side of the subjects being studied or from the side of the researcher himself.

Distortions emanating from the value positions of the research subjects often become accentuated because of imperfections in the measuring instruments—or at least because of the relative inability of these instruments to bypass the distortions already there. Problems of this order have been treated earlier at several points, and so the discussion is not continued here (see the page references given at the beginning of this chapter).

Distortions of the other variety, that is, those stemming from the value positions of the researcher, are particularly difficult to eliminate. Although, as has been argued above, the value-separation point of view seems most tenable for the scientist, achieving it is not easy. In the first place, one's values tend to intrude into the scientific side of his nature in subtle ways, and just recognizing their presence may be difficult. Secondly, even when recognized, there may be the temptation to leave them there—the temptation, in other words, to put personal desires above scientific integrity, to value other things more than science itself. Thus, sometimes the researcher will let values into his work unknowingly, at other times deliberately; but in either case the intrusion is illegitimate.

The particular vulnerability of the social scientist to value intrusion has been pretty well demonstrated. Mills (1943), for example, after examining a representative number of textbooks in the social disorganization area, concluded that workers in this field tended to be reform-oriented and to sanction tacitly and promote unconsciously the norms of rural, middle-class, Protestant America. He showed how the basic ideology of social pathologists is built around value-loaded concepts such as "normal," "healthy," "stable," "conforming," and "adjusting"; and that these concepts reflect the backgrounds of the pathologists and hence the structure of American society.

In a similar kind of analysis, Davis (1938) showed how the mental hygiene movement has unconsciously incorporated into itself the Protestant ethic, characterized by such traits as equal opportunity, achieved rather than ascribed status, the legitimacy of wealth properly earned, self-reliance, personal ambition, sobriety, thrift and hard work, sensory and rational alignment with nature, and the pursuit of practical ends. He argued that mental hygienists, by allegiance to this typically American open-class ethic, have become blinded to the *social* determinants of mental health, which prevents them from properly taking their own value systems into account and thus inclines the movement to self-defeat. "Normal," he pointed out, tends to be used in a normative sense, that is, as a nonstatistical concept and with an absence of established criteria. The dilemma which workers in this field find themselves in was described as follows:

In so far as the mental hygienist retains his ethical system, he misses a complete scientific analysis of his subject and hence fails to use the best technological means to his applied-science goal. But if he forswears his ethical beliefs, he is alienated from the movement and suffers strictures of an outraged society (p. 65).

C. C. Bowman (1946) alluded to "hidden valuations" which exist throughout sociological interpretation. He claimed that with the maturing of the discipline and the recent recognition of its many complexities, there is developing a new humility and a declining self-righteousness over sociology's alleged objectivity. The correction for errors introduced by concealed values, he believed, is to lay bare or make explicit the value premises which so often underlie the generalizations. This he tried to do, using the area of sexual and family relationships to illustrate. He then described how the family sociologist's typical interpretations regarding such things as sexual behavior, birth control, and the treatment of women and children are influenced by values from the general culture —individualism, democratic ideals, a welfare philosophy, and the like. "The main conclusion to be drawn from all of this is that objectivity would be greatly enhanced if there were explicit formulation of ideological attachments instead of implicit valuations covered over by a deceptive terminology" (p. 544).

Donald Hansen, in a paper to appear in

a future issue of *Journal of Marriage and the Family,* has pointed out an increasing danger to which family sociologists are exposed due to the growing sophistication of their methodology: the danger of error due to the nominal content of the methodological theories they use. Whereas early family theories were tested primarily on frameworks of "real concepts," which refer to substantive reality (e.g., "family," "activity"), today's vastly more complicated theories make heavy use of frameworks built from "nominal concepts," which can be defined only by reference to other concepts (e.g., "role," "system," or simply "x"). Unlike substantive theories, which are accepted only if true, methodological theories are accepted largely for their utility in gaining research ends. Yet, as Hansen shows, the researcher frequently unconsciously lets his value commitments affect the nominal definitions within his theory, leading him into unwarranted assumptions and propositions about reality. Hence, problems of value control are today substantially different from the past, and require more than stepped-up effort along traditional lines (i.e., suspending normative judgments). He suggests four promising efforts: (a) to develop conceptual frameworks and methodological theories that are appropriate to the tasks at hand and that clearly define and interrelate the nominal concepts involved; (b) to differentiate adequately between assumptions which are substantive and those which are accepted as methodologically expedient; (c) to recognize the limitations of the developed frameworks and avoid the reification that may come from holding to any single methodological framework; and (d) to work toward the construction of methodological theories that can be applied universally and not just within a particular value system.

As has been said previously, there is no place for personal biases or vested interests within the scientific process: facts must be allowed to speak for themselves. The scientist has personal values of his own, and is entitled to them. But he must be on constant guard to avoid being either deceived or seduced by these values and thus prostitute his science.

For a somewhat contrary view, that values and science—in this case, sociology—cannot be separated and that to try to do so is to work toward the detriment of each, see Gouldner (1962); also compare the writings of Mills, Davis, C. C. Bowman, and Hansen just cited. However, the difference between their positions and the present one may be more apparent than real. On both sides there is recognition that values have certain legitimate roles *outside of the research process,* that within the research process they should be controlled *insofar as possible,* but that complete elimination is not now and *may never be possible within such a discipline as family sociology.* Furthermore, all seemingly agree that some control over values is established simply by making them explicit. Certainly, as things now stand, personal bias and vested interest very frequently (and perhaps to some extent inevitably) play a part. But it is the writer's position, at least, that insofar as these value slantings can be discovered and controlled within the research process and are not, their intrusions are illegitimate.

ASSESSING FAMILY RESEARCH AND ITS APPLICATIONS

Science, as science, is value-free. Yet, as has been seen it is premised upon initial value assumptions of its own, it may expediently use existing value norms as "standards" against which its data may be ordered, and it may deal with values as data relevant to human behavior. Furthermore, the scientist may legitimately use his values in choosing the problem to be investigated, in interpreting the research results, and in his private or citizenship roles—providing what he does in these respects is clearly labeled and is not allowed to influence his scientific generalizations. It is when the investigator's values enter into the research process itself, shaping the results, that the endeavor ceases to be scientific.

Applications lie outside of the research

process and inside of the field of values. This is the realm of the engineer, not the scientist, although it is possible for the same person to wear two hats, each at a different time and in a different context. Furthermore, the age-old contention between pure and applied science seems largely pointless, since the possibility of an absolutely "pure" science is problematic; since even the applied scientist, to remain a scientist, must be as value-free (pure) as possible within the research process; and since applied research can contribute to "pure" research, and vice versa (cf. Goode & Hatt, 1952, pp. 29–40).

With regard to the marriage and family field, research applications may be seen within the realms of mass communication, education, counseling, legislation, and various other programs of social action. In a sense, this entire volume has dealt with the assessment of family research and its applications, and Part V has especially focused upon the latter, the assessment of applications. All that remains is a filling in of certain gaps and a pulling together of loose ends into a kind of summary.

The Media of Mass Communication

An important feature of contemporary Western culture is the very extensive development of its communication systems. This applies to both private and public communication, although it is the latter that is of special concern here. Whether it be via newspapers, magazines, books, motion pictures, radio, or television, modern man is being almost constantly bombarded with facts, ideas, persuasions, and emotional stimulations of one sort or another. Some of these are for entertainment, others for sales promotion, others for propagandistic purposes, and still others for educational or cultural development. But whatever the medium or the purpose, the exposure of man to this bombardment is extensive, continuous, and the results frequently bewildering. Furthermore, it is

relatively new in the history of civilization.

Since the profit motive is central to the operation of all of these media, and since sex, love, marriage, and parenthood are intrinsically interesting (they are focal points for most of the human emotions and many of the personal difficulties universally experienced), it is understandable that a large proportion of the mass-communication barrage is directed toward the family. Almost every publication one reads or program one hears or sees carries *something* on a family-related theme (see the opening paragraphs of this Handbook, p. 1). The question becomes: What are the qualities of the materials presented and their effects upon the persons and families so exposed?

For one thing, these marriage and family products of the mass media are spotty, that is, they are not of uniformly high or low quality, but range all the way from responsible discussions by eminent authorities (cf. Brown's treatment, pp. 866–867) to sensationalized trash (cf. Ehrmann's treatment, p. 597). At their best, these outpourings both inform and motivate the consuming public toward accepted goals in family living; at their worst, they only distort and destroy. Of course, the great bulk of what is offered lies somewhere between these two extremes. Short of out-and-out censorship, the only practical solution seems to be the kind of family life education that teaches one to be discriminating.

Censorship remains a highly controversial issue in our society. Those who favor it point to both the offensiveness and the seductiveness of a forced exposure to filth, while those who oppose it argue that the dignity of man requires that he be free to make his own decisions. The trend in recent years has been away from control and toward the liberal view. This movement has been reinforced by several United States Supreme Court decisions (e.g., the Roth and Alberts cases in 1957) which have reduced obscenity tests to two: (a) Is the work without any social importance? (b) Does it, taken as a whole, appeal to the prurient interests of the average person, applying contemporary community standards? Since people cannot always agree on what is or is not important (e.g., Does it have literary merit?), and since community standards are known to vary greatly in time and place, these tests must be recognized as being both loose and liberal.[1] Perhaps most contemporary Americans would recognize the need for some control (censorship) over the mass media—enough, at least, to protect the public against forced exposure to things it regards as offensive and to protect the young against types of seduction (e.g., hard-core pornography) that they are too immature to resist. Yet, the lid is off, and certain irresponsible commercial interests are pushing their advantage to the limit. Radio and television have resisted the trend more than have the other mass media, although certainly not completely and who knows for how long?

But pornography—whether it be mild, borderline, or hard-core—is not the only objectionable feature found in the mass dissemination of family-related materials (Christensen, 1958a, pp. 590–592). There is a tendency to treat complex personal problems much too briefly, even flippantly, and with distorted emphases, for the sake of the "fast buck." This, for example, may be seen in many of the current syndicated newspaper columns emitting "advice to the lovelorn." They usually draw upon folklore and "common sense" more than research findings; and, even when they use the latter, it would seem that the temptation to overgeneralize and plagiarize is frequently irresistible. Of course, the information is not always incorrect, nor is the advice always misleading; but they *may* be and frequently

[1] It also may be noted that both of these tests use existing values—personal judgment in the first test and community norms in the second—as the criteria against which obscenity is measured. Certainly this is a legitimate position; it conforms with the notion of value relativism discussed below. Nevertheless, it is so relative that it leaves the situation greatly confused and changing.

are, because the reporter is untrained in the substantive field and/or is guided chiefly by profit or success motives. Superficial answers and distorted information may only increase the anxiety and personal problems of the receiver, and thus in turn increase the family disorganization in which he is involved. Research in this area may prove most fruitful.

It is recognized, of course, that the conscientious editor or reporter frequently is caught in an almost impossible situation. The structural demands of his job often leave him with little choice: he must interest his public or he will lose his job. Whereas the teacher and research worker normally have tenure positions and captive audiences, the publisher is less sheltered. Hence the temptation to oversimplify, to sensationalize, even to misquote. Kirkendall (1964) has taken the position that the professional worker must be willing to "compromise" to a degree in order to get his materials before those who need them most.

The tendency for popular writers to steer clear of research reports has been demonstrated by Brieland (1957). In a careful study of a sample of book, pamphlet, magazine, and newspaper feature material written for parents, he found that an extremely small proportion of the authors even mentioned research; instead, they presented anecdotal material, used successful parents as models (rather than the experts), and often expressed extreme viewpoints. This last was thought to be the result of "having to attract attention for their views among a tremendous number of parent education articles and books" (p. 65). Five possible reasons for this apparent distrust of experts were suggested: (a) Parents don't like their children to be used as research "guinea pigs"; (b) they aren't interested in many of the highly technical problems that are being researched; (c) studies often are contradictory and hence fail to give final or dependable answers; (d) statistical terms present a barrier in making the reports understandable and interesting; and (e) the researcher often writes just for other researchers and so doesn't make his materials meaningful for parents.

Hillman (1954), in an analysis of over 6,000 letters received by an advice columnist of a popular magazine, concluded that these letters gave graphic evidence of unmet needs in the population, and that the most urgent of these needs was for "sound, practical education for personal and family living" (p. 54).

England (1960), in a study of family-magazine fiction spanning most of the first half of the twentieth century, concluded: "While the direction of fictional changes in images of love and courtship is consistent with actual trends in American courtship patterns, the magnitude is not. Fictional love is changing more rapidly than love in real life" (p. 165). This would suggest that family fiction not only reflects the times, but also influences the future.

Irresponsible journalism (or the irresponsible use of any of the media of mass communication) probably needs two positive types of correction, which if made would largely preclude the need for negative censorship. The first is for more public concern and more self-policing on the part of the popular disseminators. The second is for a greater willingness on the part of the social scientist to enter the marketplace, in other words, to go at least part way in interpreting his data for lay consumption, either personally or by cooperating with the would-be "science writers" (cf. Kirkpatrick, 1963, pp. v–vi).

But there are at least two dilemmas involved in this latter suggestion: (a) how to present one's material to the public in an interesting and understandable way without watering it down or distorting its meaning; and (b) how to become a part-time popularizer without losing status with one's professional colleagues. If the first could be solved, the second would probably be resolved in the process, for the thing that most makes scientists lose respect for other scientists is the feeling that the others are

prostituting their training and professional commitment. It may be that the problem is too formidable ever to be completely resolved. It could be alleviated, nevertheless, both by eliminating unnecessary and confusing jargon in the communications of science, and by raising the levels of public tolerance and comprehension of scientific matters.

The More Formal Agencies or Dissemination

Family research materials are utilized, not only by the mass communications media, but more systematically and formally by agencies such as the school, the church, the government, and the various helping professions. Here, too, there are value dilemmas.

Detailed treatments of the major agencies and some of their dilemmas have been presented in the four chapters immediately preceding this one (for the value problems involved, see especially pp. 844, 898–903, 915–916, 940–942, 944). All that is attempted in the present section is a brief and largely supplementary summary of the value problem in the family life education area, regarding this area as representative of the whole.

According to Charters:

. . . the significant aspect of the teaching-learning process in the classroom is the transmission of value orientations from teacher to pupil. It proceeds not so much through didactic teachings as through the reward and punishment system and other subtleties of the flow of interaction. . . . Which values will be transmitted depends upon the teacher's own value orientation, which, in turn, is determined by his practice in the groups and subcultures of the social structure. Problems arise in those cases where classroom participants (teachers and pupils) are located at different points in the larger social structure and enter the classroom with conflicting value orientations (1963, p. 726).

Charters then proceeded to review a rather

large number of investigations which have dealt with social-class selectivity in teaching, and concluded that, although there does seem to be a middle-class bias, as many have contended, the research has been methodologically weak and the evidence as it stands is inconclusive.

Family life educators are in disagreement about which of several value positions is most appropriate for their role. Some argue that values have no business in the classroom and others that the teacher would be remiss in his duty if he did not guide students to value positions that are culturally acceptable (cf. Bowman et al., 1957). Still others see their role as being somewhere in between these two positions. Harper, for example, has reminded us that the time has come "for we marriage counselors and family life educators to lift ourselves from our conventional moralistic thinking about marriage and family life" (1959, p. 13). He argued that "rational evaluation" should supplant moral judgment, yet some of his own stated positions on divorce, children, and sex are so extreme as to be regarded by the more conventional end of the continuum as themselves irrational (see Letters to the editor, 1959). Leslie also invited a re-examination of the value premises which underlie the field, and concluded that "family life educators must concern themselves not simply with adjusting people to the kind of society in which they live but must also assume responsibility for making it a better society in which to live . . ." (1959, p 12). Marsh and Humphrey (1953) argued against the existing dominance of middle-class conventions in marriage education and counseling, and proposed instead a kind of cultural relativism, whereby the success of a given marriage would be measured against the norms of the subculture which applied. But with rather different positions are such writers as Mason (1959), who felt that family life teachers should promote the generally accepted values of self-realization and satisfying relationships, and should use their own values

affirmatively, although at the same time encouraging students to make their individual choices. Luckey argued similarly:

Every person who thinks of himself as a parent educator needs to work through, or be busily working through, a set of values which he recognizes as his, not only because he can avoid unintentionally imposing these on others when the occasion is inappropriate but because he can better seize every possible opportunity to indoctrinate in a legitimate setting! It is sneaky to infiltrate, but it's satisfying to lead a group that is aiming at the same objectives you are (1961, p. 264).

Of the sensitive areas which invite controversy, premarital sexual behavior seems especially receptive. In an attempt to get away from abstract moral judgments, Kirkendall (1960) has developed the position that premarital coitus should be judged almost solely on the basis of what it does to the interpersonal relationships of those involved; but Poffenberger (Poffenberger et al., 1962) has attacked this thesis, arguing that such a standard is so relative that it is ineffective as a control, and that teachers need to inculcate group sex norms for the sake of social survival. Reiss (1963) has taken some of his professional colleagues to task for what he believes to be their moralizing approach to sex ethics, saying in effect that science can't determine morals and that what we need to do is stop the debates and get on with the research. Rubin (1963) has answered the attack by arguing that family life educators have a moral responsibility to society, that debate is needed for the clarification of issues, and that these functions can be carried out without detracting from the function of science. And so rages the controversy.

As Kerckhoff has pointed out in Chapter 21 of this Handbook (p. 901), family life educators distribute themselves on the values question about as follows: those who "know what is right" and hence see no problem; those who honestly try to present all sides and to label everything properly, including their own values; those whose emphasis is to encourage students to think through and develop their own positions; those who search for common areas of agreement and then stress these; and those who adopt some general or superior value that few could quarrel with, such as mental health or interpersonal competence. To these might be added a sixth: those who rebel against convention or tradition as such, seeking their guideposts in reason and science. Of the six named, the first listed—claiming to know what is right and dogmatically teaching it—is the most out of line with the spirit of this scientific age and, thus, has been losing ground.

An intriguing possibility for helping resolve the value dilemma in teaching is suggested in research reported by Muuss. He found that the causal nature of human behavior can be taught in the schools, even to very young children, and that where this method supersedes the traditional judgmental approach, the child is "less punitive, less anxious, more tolerant, more democratic, more responsible, more secure, has fewer conflicts, and shows better school adjustment" (1960, p. 155). Muuss thought that this argues for a *causal orientation* to family life education. If he is right, perhaps science itself should be taken as the central or guiding value. But a word of caution is in order, since the dissemination of scientific facts may not always produce the results desired. C. C. Bowman, for example, claimed that "objective discussions about sexual experimentation may lead to—sexual experimentation" (1946, p. 544).[2] The problem needs further research.

Legislation and the Question of Family Policy

In contrast to many European countries and some in other parts of the world, the United States has never developed a national family policy. There is no federal department or bureau of families, for example, and no system of family allowances or "mother's wages." Instead, this country has maintained a diversity in family values and a hands-off policy by the government. Still, the difference is a relative one, and there is evidence that we may be in the early stages of developing such a policy (Schorr, 1962).

Schorr has attributed the relative lack of a national family policy in this country to three strong traditions within the culture: individualism, diverse interest and pressure groups, and opposition to governmental intervention. He has seen a weakening of these traditions, however, especially of the last. This, he argued, along with certain other trends—increasing affluence, which makes easier financial supports to families; closer international relationships, which make us more accepting of foreign influence; and greater stress upon the person-serving functions of family life, which increases the importance with which it is regarded—is clearing the way for the development of a national family policy. Furthermore, "The need for such a policy has been urged with increasing frequency of late, at the White House Conference on Children and Youth, at the Advisory Meeting to the Commissioner of Social Security by the National Association of Social Workers, and in professional literature" (p. 463).

Although we cannot be said to have had a national family policy as such, there are numerous ways in which the federal government has intervened on behalf of fam-

---

[2] An interesting example of this point, illustrating the entire controversy, is described in a recent issue of *Time*, March 6, 1964, p. 35. In sexually permissive Sweden, some 140 eminent physicians have decried the sexual laxity which is resulting in new increases in venereal disease and extramarital pregnancies and which, they believe, is a "menace to the vitality and health of the nation." They further believe that the blame lies with the country's liberal approach to sex education in the schools, "pointing out that young minds—unless taught differently—can confuse in-

struction with encouragement." This group of doctors has petitioned the government to take swift steps to remedy the situation, but their petition has resulted in a sharp reaction from liberal advocates of sex freedom.

ilies. Examples are slum clearance and public housing; the social security act, including provisions for unemployment insurance, old age assistance and insurance, and aid to dependent children; dependent deductions in filing the graduated income tax; special services to families of veterans; school lunch programs; and many others. An entire issue of *Marriage and Family Living* was devoted to describing these government services affecting American families (National Council on Family Relations, 1958). Many of them have roots reaching far back, but the trend has been toward elaboration and expansion.

Nevertheless, the development has not been deliberate or uniformly planned: it has, so to speak, grown up like Topsy. Furthermore, help to families has frequently been incidental to programs set up to serve other interests (Schorr, 1962, pp. 456–463).

Brown, in Chapter 20 of this Handbook, points out that, although governmental family programs are diverse and lack integration, there are trends toward convergence in point of view and toward voluntary coordination among agencies (p. 844). Mogey, in Chapter 13, discusses some of the practical considerations and problems involved in sociological intervention to promote the values that a community or national policy might take; he deals with what are called "the melting-pot approach," "the community approach," and "the caretaker approach" (pp. 522–523). Kerckhoff, in Chapter 21, stresses the need for seeing family values in perspective with community, national, and world values; and argues that in a world as torn with strife and with issues as large as they are today, "education which teaches children to hold marriage and the family as the highest goal might be regarded as education for suicide" (p. 909).

It would seem that the trend toward consensus in family policy will continue, which in effect will produce a more truly national policy than we have today. To be compatible with long-range American ideals, such a policy will need both to coordinate family values with nonfamily values, and to allow for the legitimate existence of a diversity of family values. The policy, in other words, will need to be multifocused. It will recognize what later in this chapter is described as the *principle of value relevance*. In this, it will be adopting a position comparable to that taken by the United States Supreme Court in its recent obscenity rulings—that is, gearing its standards to current community norms (see above). It will be a policy of *value pluralism* (cf. the position taken on theory pluralism, pp. 23–24, 171–172).

Evaluation Research as a Means of Self-Correction

Ordinarily, research is focused upon some substantive problem of the family, such as factors associated with child socialization, or the relationship between family size and marital adjustment, or the effects of cultural norms upon behavior and behavior consequences. It is possible, however, to turn the searchlight of science inward, that is, to focus it upon the research process itself or upon one or more of the application areas, such as teaching, counseling, or legislation. This procedure is comparable to introspection in personality dynamics, and it is known as *evaluation research*. However, testings of this kind are not to be confused with subjective judgments or simple armchair assessments.

Science may only analyze means to an end, not the "goodness" or "badness" of the end itself. True evaluation research involves the measurement of the phenomenon being considered against some criterion that has been adopted. Decisions involved in the choice of criteria are, of course, nonscientific. But once such decisions have been made, by others or by the investigator who for the moment has stepped outside of his scientific role, the researcher can proceed to determine where his data are with reference to the adopted criterion. Thus, where evaluation research can be built into any program, that program may become self-correcting with regard to desired ends.

Efforts to evaluate family research itself have included the various bibliographical listings, abstracts, and inventories; the formulations of tentative frames of reference; the reachings toward criteria for judging excellence; and certain additional critiques, all of which were outlined in Chapter 1 (see especially pp. 13–15, 18–19). There is no need to repeat.

Illustrative of attempts to evaluate family life education are studies by Behlmer (1961), Dorothy Dyer (1959), Gillies and Lastrucci (1954), H. A. Bowman (1953), Landis (1948), Moses (1956), and Schilling (1961). These differ greatly in conceptualization and level of research sophistication. In general, it can be said that, although family life teachers increasingly are recognizing the need for program evaluation, few of them go further than subjective impressions of what is being accomplished; and of those who try research, very few do it in such a way that the outcomes can with certainty be related to the course experiences (cf. Luckey & Neubeck, 1956, pp. 352–353). Of the studies mentioned, for example, only Dyer made use of a control group.

Cuber (1949) and Longworth (1953), in urging family life educators to take a close look at their own work, pointed to a number of methodological problems which need to be overcome. Chief among these are: (a) settling upon standard criteria of marriage and family success; (b) deciding when, during the learning experience, to take the measurements; (c) eliminating, insofar as possible, all normative elements from the evaluation; and (d) isolating the effects of the marriage course from all other forces which may have caused the changes that were measured. It is the last two named that generally present the greatest difficulties.

Going from the least to the most sophisticated (and hence most valid and reliable) evaluation designs for family living courses would produce something like the following:

1. *Good feelings.* This, of course, is not research at all, nor does it involve any design. Mere self-satisfaction with what one does in the classroom is largely subjective and is likely to be quite unreliable.

2. *Goals without measurement.* Here there is a step in the direction of objective evaluation, but no real measurement. Course objectives are formally set up, but the degree to which they are realized remains at the level of impression and inference.

3. *Ex post facto evidence.* This is obtained by either observing or measuring what are thought to be changes in the students. It may be impressions of changed behavior or be based on testimonials, assigned papers, questionnaires, or projective tests. At any rate, such evidence comes only after the fact, and there is no way of being sure that the presumed change is real.

4. *Test-retest procedures.* When these are used, one or more tests are given near the beginning of the course and then repeated at the end, to determine if there has been movement. Or the retesting may come some time after the students have left school, to determine how the course experience may have affected their lives. These procedures, if carefully followed, can measure change, but since this change may have occurred anyway, there is no way of proving that it was a function of the course.

5. *Longitudinal experiments.* In this type of procedure, an experimental group (those exposed to the family life education experience) *and* a control group (those not given this experience) are set up, and *both* are studied over time (test-retest procedure). Furthermore, the two groups are *matched* on other factors which it is presumed might influence the change, in order to hold these factors constant. When this is done, any difference in change between the experimental and control groups is attributable to the experimental variable, in this case, family life education. Longitudinal design of the control-group va-

riety is the only one that can establish cause and effect relationships. It also is the most difficult to apply.

It must be remembered, of course, that even with the most sophisticated design, all that can be said is that the experimental program has caused a specified change in a specified direction. This is important knowledge. Nevertheless, before there is ' evaluation, the change must be described as either detracting from or contributing to accepted goals. [Cf. Kerckhoff's discussion of evaluation problems in family life education, pp. 908–909.]

Similar evaluational problems and patterns exist in other areas of family research application. Three examples only will be mentioned: Mudd and her co-workers (1950; cf. Hollis, 1950) attempted to evaluate the effectiveness of marriage counseling by measuring client "movement" toward desired goals as the counseling progressed over time. Schorr (1960) attempted to assess the effectiveness of public social security programs (especially those pertaining to old age assistance and insurance) by relating them to filial responsibility in the American family. Brim (1957) summarized attempts that have been made to evaluate parent education, pointing to deficiences in these attempts and new directions which the research needs to take.

VALUES AS DATA IN FAMILY RESEARCH

Up to this point, concern has been with value intrusions into the over-all methodology and life activity of the researcher; values have been seen as having both legitimate and illegitimate functions in regard to science and the scientist. In the present section, special attention is given to an entirely legitimate function of values: their rightful place within the *substantive content of the social sciences*. Neither the physical nor the biological sciences deal with values as data,

simply because the entities they study are nonevaluating in nature. But, since the social sciences are concerned with man, and since man is an evaluating organism, the values of man might be viewed as intruding themselves into the subject-matter areas of the scientific disciplines involved.

Shakespeare wrote, "There is nothing either good or bad, but thinking makes it so." Sometimes men's thoughts have objective validity, and sometimes they are no more than subjective fantasy; nevertheless, whatever they are, if they are believed they will be acted upon. To the family sociologist, whose job it is to understand behavior within the family context, the beliefs and values of people become important data to enter into the research equations. If "thinking makes it so," then it is necessary to get at the thought in order to understand the behavior, regardless of the ultimate validity or lack of validity of the thought itself (this latter being a question more for the philosopher than the social scientist).

Ways of Viewing the Value Variable

Values considered as data may be viewed in three different ways: as a dependent variable, wherein the family causes values to be formed in the personalities of its members; as an independent variable, wherein the values held by family members cause them to behave according to predictable patterns; and as an intervening variable, wherein values intrude themselves into the interactions of other variables in ways which affect the outcomes.

As a dependent variable. It has been emphasized repeatedly in this Handbook (Chs 3, 4, and 18 especially) that the family is society's chief socializing agent: by internalizing group norms within the personalities of the young, it provides a necessary amount of value continuity from generation to generation. The family is society's most important conveyor of values.

Hobart (1963) has challenged the assertions of certain writers that the family, as we know it, has outlived its usefulness and will eventually be eliminated from society. Instead, he argued that the family is perhaps more than ever needed in contemporary United States, due to the alienation of modern man resulting from the highly mobile and materialistic nature of his culture. He then called for a far-reaching "value revolution" in which the family would play a key role—a revolution that would displace "the now pre-eminent success, efficiency, productivity, prosperity values by the more human oriented being, knowing, caring, loving values" (p. 409). This he saw as the necessary prerequisite to the preservation of human society. Note the following:

One linkage between values and the family lies in the fact that the original unit of human community and the universal humanizing unit of all societies is the family. It is in the family that many of the most important values, bases for choice, are learned. The family not only transmits values; it is predicated on, and in fact symbolizes some of the distinctively "human" values: tenderness, love, concern, loyalty. . . .

But the priority of these love and concern values is directly challenged by success and achievement values which may imply that status symbols are more important than babies; that what a child *achieves* is more important than what he *is;* that what we *own* is more important than what we *are.* Thus the stage is set for conflict between a success oriented husband and a child-people welfare oriented wife, or for a rather inhuman family which values things over people, and which may raise children who have difficulty living down this experience of worthlessness (p. 407).

. . . Increasingly, the family is the only security base available to man today. Where a commitment-based family security is dependably available to man, he will have a basis for relating fearlessly to the greater varieties of people available to him in a society organized in terms of achieved statuses, deepening and enriching himself and others in the process (p. 412).

Toby has demonstrated that "the better integrated the family, the more successful it is as a bulwark against the anti-social influences emanating from the neighborhood or the peer group" (1957, p. 512). This conclusion is in general agreement with a considerable literature which relates juvenile delinquency to disorganized family life.

It seems reasonable to conclude that the family will transmit to its children either socially acceptable or socially unacceptable sets of values, depending upon both the nature of values started with and the degree of value conflict between parents; and that the child's, and later the next generation adult's, behavior will be greatly influenced by the kinds of values so acquired.

As an independent variable. The latter part of the preceding sentence refers to values as the independent variable, as *acting upon* the persons who hold them and *inducing behavior.* The idea is almost a truism and hardly needs to be labored; as a matter of fact, this aspect of the relationship between values and behavior becomes clear from the very definition of values given earlier: "the criteria one uses for choosing among alternatives."

"The mores can make anything right." This now classic statement by William Graham Sumner explains the fact that ethical standards differ greatly in both time and space, and that people's behaviors, which also differ, must be judged in the light of the particular standards or values which apply, rather than seen exclusively in terms of any notion of "the ultimate" or "the absolute" or "the eternal." The theory which has been built up around this idea is known as *cultural relativism.*

Since cultural norms (values) are internalized within the individual personalities of the society, it follows that behavior will differ from culture to culture and from subculture to subculture. It is because of the variety of these internalized norms that family behavior—dating and mate-selection practices, extramarital sexual activity, number and spacing of children, authority patterns within the home, or whatever—has been found to vary in predictable or patterned ways. Thus, as has been demonstrated throughout this volume, family behavior varies according to: (a) the time or historical dimension; (b) the space or cross-cultural dimension; and (c) certain bio-social factors or categories within the general culture, such as age, sex, religion, ethnic origin, and social class.

Aside from this acknowledgement of the influencing role of values by historical, cross-cultural, and category research, it has become well recognized in social psychology that certain of each person's values are unique to him, and that these individual aspects help explain his own particular behavior. Although many of one's values are shared with the larger society, being culturally induced, others have come from either individual or small-group experience and are more or less unique to the person holding them. Yet they also affect behavior. Seen as an independent variable, values need to be studied across time, across space or cultures, across bio-social categories within each culture, and across personality structures within each category or subgroup.

As an intervening variable. Not only do values affect behavior directly, but they are known to *affect the effects of behavior,* that is, to help determine the *outcomes* or the *consequences* of a line of action. When this is so, their effects are indirect and they may be viewed properly as intervening variables. And the notion of cultural relativism applies here as well as above, for, to some extent at least, *both behavior and the consequences of behavior are relative to the normative systems within which they occur.*

Here again one finds use for the concept known as *definition of the situation* (for expanded treatments, see above, pp. 129–131, 802–805). In coining this phrase nearly a half-century ago, W. I. Thomas made a most valuable distinction between objective situations and one's perception of these situations, and emphasized the previously under-recognized importance of the latter. He demonstrated that reality factors (objective) get their meaning in and through interpretive factors (subjective), which today would in large part be labeled "values." "If men define situations as real, they are real in their consequences" (Thomas & Thomas, 1928, p. 572).

Ellis, in discussing some of the dynamics of marriage counseling, presented what he called "the A-B-C Theory of personality:"

There are at least three factors in emotional disturbance: A—what happens to the individual from the outside or from within his own physical body; B—what he thinks or tells himself about what happens; and C—his final reaction or disturbance. C often seems to stem directly from A, since human beings can think or make interpretations of A in a split-second. Actually, however, there is always B, our own beliefs and prejudices, which causes C (1960, p. 17. Cf., in Ch. 19 above, Hansen & Hill's more sophisticated discussion of the interaction of four factors: A, the event, B, the family's crisis-meeting resources; C, the definition the family makes of the event; and X, the crisis.).

A further illustration of what is meant here may be taken from the closely related field of demography and the concept "population pressure." Christensen (1942) distinguished among *potential* population pressure, which refers simply to the surplus of births over deaths; *nominal* population pressure, which refers to the pressure of population upon an average or optimum man-land ratio according to accepted criteria; and *real* population pressure, which is defined as the pressure of population upon the feelings and behavior of people. This latter was looked upon as "real" (in contrast to both of the former) in a true sociological sense, in that it is recognized and responded to in the lives of those it reaches, and hence is a genuine social force.

Real population pressure is the imbalance of three variables: population, income, and subjective standards. When people feel it, they either discontentedly endure, or they adjust; and if the latter, they adjust either psychologically by substituting non-economic values for economic deficiencies or they adjust overtly by seeking supplementary income, migrating into other areas or other occupations, or cutting down their birth rates. Sometimes the adjustment is in one of these ways, sometimes in another, and sometimes in several; but always real population pressure is accompanied by discontent and/or adjustment (pp. 160–161).

So, to the sociologist, values represent an intervening variable which must be taken into account if behavior and its consequences are to be explained. In the family, as in other segments of life, one cannot expect the same in one historical period as another, in one culture as another, in one subcultural category or group as another, or even in one person compared with another, simply because there are varying definitions of the situation, varying values or norms, which affect the behavior and its outcome. In short, family phenomena are relative to the values held by its members.

Types of Value Conflict Affecting the Family

Values create a problem for family members only when they diverge or are in·conflict. Several types of value conflict may be recognized: (a) among norms within the general culture, (b) between family and societal norms, (c) between expectations and realizations, and (d) among values held by members of the particular family.

Disorganization of values within the culture. Sorokin (1941) has developed a cyclical theory of social change which sees the major segments of the culture responding to shifts in the dominant value systems—"culture mentality types"—of the over-all society. He named these systems the "ideational," in which the core values are essentially other-worldly; the "sensate," in which the core values are opposite to this, that is, are centered upon temporal pleasures and materialism; and the "idealistic," in which there is something of a harmonious blending between these two. Society was described over the centuries as alternating between the two extremes, with periods of idealistic balance intervening; and the contemporary scene was pictured as an "over-ripe sensate age." A particular characteristic of present-day sensate mentality is value conflict, resulting in social disorganization. And the family, like the other sociocultural systems considered, is in serious crisis today because of this disorganization.

Similarly, Zimmerman (1947) has recognized a basic interrelationship between family stability and social stability. In tracing the history of the Western family from early times to the present, he has seen three periods of family crisis correlated with similar crises in the civilizations then extant: the first was in Greece around 300 B.C.; the second in Rome about A.D. 300; and the third is in the Western world at the present time. Indices of family crisis were found to be approximately the same in each of these periods: low fertility, a revolt of youth, accent on individualism, open sensualism in public life, high rates of marital breakup, and the like. In the first two crisis periods, civilization fell, and it was argued that unless ways can be found to strengthen the contemporary family, it can be expected that Western civilization also will go under. The family was seen both as responding to norms of the general culture and as contributing to its strengths or weaknesses (cf. Hobart's thesis given above).

Martinson (1960, Chs 1, 3, & 4) has stressed the confusion existing among marriage educators in modern America due to the heterogeneity of value systems within the culture, the *lack of specific norms.* He described three marriage models competing within the present culture: the *Judiac-Christian model,* which is the longer tradition and which stresses that marriage is a sacrament ordained of God, with the idea of permanence, based upon sexual exclusiveness, and for the purpose of companionship and the procreation and rearing of children; the *romantic model,* which arose in the twelfth century around extramarital love relationships, but which later spread to influence modern dating and individualistic mate-selection practices; and the *rationalistic model,* which came in most recently as a challenge to both the dogmatism of the Judaic-Christian model and the irresponsibility of the romantic model, and which attempts to incorporate the values of both our scientific age and our democratic society. The first of these three coexisting models stresses *faith,* the second *feeling,* and the third *reason.* Some family specialists hold to one or another of these models exclusively—the "pure" family sociologist, for example, relies upon the third—but others combine them in some fashion. Nevertheless, there is value confusion, which leaves the teacher with only about three alternatives: (a) to present the facts without any interpretation; (b) to discover the factors which relate to happiness in marriage and then stress these as guides; and (c) to use the American ideal of dignity, freedom, and equality as the "core value complex" against which the decisions and adjustments of family living can be measured. Martinson favored this last, and he developed his treatise to illustrate and support it.

To illustrate the nature of value conflict and of the decisions facing contemporary American families, Kirkpatrick (1963) pointed to the existence of *ten major dilemmas:*

Freedom in family experience versus order and efficiency
Work achievement versus the love-reproduction function
Personal self-expression versus devoted child-rearing
Flexible general training versus rigid specific training
High aspiration level for children versus realistic expectations

Family loyalty versus community loyalty
Extensive, casual association versus restricted, intensive association
Love experience versus love safety
Free sex expression versus sex restraint
Early marriage versus mature, discriminating mate selection

"Some dilemmas," he said, "are peculiar to our culture; others are interwoven with the life of human beings at all times, in all places, and in all cultures" (p. 95). Furthermore, perfect solutions to these dilemmas are not attainable: whichever "horn" one climbs on, or if he straddles the middle, there is always a price.

These and other writers have made abundantly clear that the problems of the modern family are to a large extent related to the conflicting nature of contemporary culture—complex, heterogeneous, transitional, and rapidly moving—which makes for confusion and anomie. Bain (1935), to give still another example, has written of our "schizoid culture" and described how the various cultural contradictions, including some within the family area, put people under tension and cause breakdowns in the personality and in relationships.

Nonalignment with the cultural norms. The kind of tension just examined is that which originates in the general culture; value conflicts outside of the individual become internalized within his personality system and affect his behavior. Another type of tension arises when the personality system is out of line with the social system within which it operates. This can happen even when the social system is itself well integrated, although it is likely to be greater in a society that is disorganized. It may come about either through (a) inadequate socialization of the individual by his society, (b) movement into a society which possesses different norms than those to which one is accustomed, or (c) an exposure to and acceptance of alien norms by means of the mass media or cross-cultural contacts. There is the strong probability that the heterogeneity, the high mobility, and the elaborate communication existing in most contemporary societies cause them to experience more of this type of personality tension than formerly—as well as of the previously mentioned type.

Kluckhohn (1958) has analyzed the process of acculturation for Italian and Irish immigrant groups, whose basic family values are quite different from those of the middle-class American system to which they become exposed. Numerous personal and family strains were found to result from the value conflicts engendered, and the necessary shifts in value position if assimilation was to take place were not the same for the two groups, which had different positions to start with. She said:

It has long been my contention that the assimilation process for peoples coming into this country will vary in accord with the degree of goodness of fit between the value orientations they brought with them and the dominant values of the society. When people have markedly different value preferences on all the orientations, the process will be slower and more fraught with difficulties than if there were agreement on some one or two. And the most difficult change of all is the radical shift to value positions that formerly had been the least favored of all (p. 70).

In Chapter 19 it was demonstrated that problem families cannot be understood apart from their social milieu, that family stress needs to be viewed within its community context. For example, studies were cited to show that families who have relationship problems with their neighbors, relatives, and others are the ones most likely to experience internal trouble of various sorts, and that problem families generally show poorly articulated goals and deviant standards of behavior (see especially pp. 795–801, 805–806).

One of the important findings of the pioneer researches of Terman (1938) and of Burgess and Cottrell (1939) was that marital success comes easier for *conventional*

husbands and wives. It is those who have conservative and conforming attitudes, who get along well with parents and others, who attend church and participate in community affairs that are most successful; whereas those who rebel against convention and do things their own way are the ones most likely to have their marriages fail.

The kinds of strains brought upon intrafamily relationships by deviating members is illustrated in Jackson's study (1956) of alcoholism on the part of the husband-father. Typically, such a family goes through several stages, beginning with a sense of shame or guilt and an attempt to conceal the problem from others; continuing through successive phases of disorganization and partial recovery involving, among other things, the reassignment of roles; and ending with either a cure, a separation, or a realistic acceptance of the situation along with some permanent adjustment to it. Furthermore, alcoholism frequently results in such additional problems as nonsupport and sexual infidelity.

Mizruchi and Perrucci (1962), while recognizing that strains within social systems may come about through divergence between norms and behavior, tried to discover if and how certain *qualitative* aspects of the social norms are related to personal pathology. They concluded that, when deviation occurs, *prescriptive* norms are less likely to lead to extreme pathological reactions than are *proscriptive* norms. Although their analysis was confined to drinking norms and behavior, there was the strong suggestion that it could be fruitfully applied to other normative systems as well, and the sexual area was specially mentioned as offering promise. This point is discussed again a little later under the heading "Toward a Theory of Value Relevance."

The gap between expectation and realization. Whereas the two types of conflict just described involve the clash of norms—either among norms within the society, or between the norms of the society and those of the individual, but, in either case, internalized within the individual and affecting his behavior—attention is now being turned to problems of discrepancy between norms and actual situations. Through the socialization process, individuals build up sometimes vague and in other instances precise expectations for the marriage and family experience: the qualities expected in a mate, the nature of the roles each will play, the kinds of satisfaction that will come out of living together and rearing a family. It would seem indisputable that some of the problems of family life result directly from the gap between what its members have come to expect and what they are able to realize.

Quite probably, all married couples experience this gap to *some* extent, although with many it is narrow or they have the personal resources to adjust to it with a minimum of discomfort or disorganization.

In a study of nearly 1,000 university students, Christensen (1958a) found for both date selection and mate selection a tendency to either compromise one's "ideal" by settling for someone with qualities short of those desired, or to become disillusioned after the choice had been made, or some of both. Thus, dating practices did not entirely measure up to dating preferences (pp. 244–245), and the person actually chosen for marriage did not measure up to the respondents' ideal of a mate (pp. 263–264). Strauss (1946) earlier found a similar discrepancy in the mate-selection process.

A rather common explanation given for divorce is the heavy romantic emphasis of our dating culture, which blinds young people to the facts concerning marriage and the person they marry and hence invites disillusionment following the wedding (cf. Hobart, 1958; Hobart, 1960). Perhaps this helps explain why most divorces occur relatively early in the marriage, soon after the romantic bubble has burst.

Pineo (1961) studied this disillusionment —which he called disenchantment—in both the early and later years of marriage and described it as "reality shock." From his data, both sexes were found to experience a gradual decline in marital satisfaction or euphoria from early to middle marriage, but the husbands suffered most disenchantment in the earliest years and the wives most later on. Furthermore, divorce percentages showed up highest for those husbands and wives whose adjustment scores (enchantment) showed the greatest drops

In separate studies, LeMasters (1957) and E. D. Dyer (1963) demonstrated the prevalence of a similar crisis following initial parenthood. The majority of each set of couples studied experienced extensive or severe crisis after the birth of their first child. This forced these couples to reorganize family roles from an adult-centered pair to a child-centered triad. Most of them recovered from the initial shock and made satisfactory adjustments, but the transition was generally difficult. The authors felt that their findings should suggest to family life educators a more realistic approach to preparation for parenthood.

W. G. Dyer (1956) has analyzed families from the standpoint of the satisfaction or dissatisfaction of family members with the father's job. He found that the less satisfied—whether it be father, mother, or children—were also low on satisfaction in other areas, both familial and nonfamilial, and experienced more family disagreements over the father's work. This demonstrates how dissatisfaction in nonfamilial areas can carry over into the family arena.

In Chapter 14 of this *Handbook* it was shown how economic depression puts the family in crisis and in many instances results in its disorganization (see especially pp. 573–574). Depression upsets roles and causes a reorganization of expectations—or at least a suspension in their fulfillment. The great depression of the 1930's affected upper-class families least and middle-class families most, probably because the latter were upward climbing (high expectations) and were without adequate resources to fall back on. Upper-class families usually had reserves that they could call upon, and lower-class families had lower expectations to start with; but middle-class families had neither, and so were left with the largest gap between expectation and realization.

Disagreements among family members. Role conflict within the family itself is the fourth and final type of value disjunction that requires attention. This sometimes is the result of one or more of the other types, for if the individual is confused or disenchanted or put under tension by the value clashes earlier described, he or she is more likely to behave neurotically and hence to foul up his relationships. Furthermore, even if the individual is non-neurotic, there is a chance that these other conflicts will have engendered *different* values within him than he held previously or than are held by other family members. Conflict among family members has perhaps been the subject of more study than has any of the other three types, and reference has been made to the phenomenon at numerous places throughout this volume. For present purposes, all that will be needed is a few examples and a pointing up of the general nature of the problem.

Buerkle, Anderson, and Badgley have argued for viewing the family as a social system, with husbands, wives, and children occupying specific statuses and each playing or acting out the role appropriate to his status in each separate situation. They explain as follows:

. . . husbands and wives approach a given situation from different role perspectives, i.e., their roles represent a sexual division of labor. Ideally, these sex roles are interlocking to the point where interaction process within marriage and the family can operate smoothly. However, due to several cultural factors, conflicts of interest can easily replace role reciprocity. For example, marital conflict in a culture like our own may result from, among other things, social change, where the transition from ascribed to achieved roles makes sex prerogatives in various situations less clear. Accompanying this, subcultural differences between males and females may produce incompatible value orientations between the spouses. Also, it must be remembered that husbands and wives are the representatives of two separate kinship organizations whose background and orientation may not always coincide (1961, p. 25).

Success in marriage seems to be dependent upon how well husband and wife agree on basic values. In a study of university married couples, Ort (1950) reported a negative correlation of −.83 between the expressed happiness of the spouses and the number of value conflicts they experienced. His research led him to conclude that there is no general formula for happiness in marriage, but rather, happiness depends upon the degree to which the mates play the roles expected of them. Somewhat similarly, Keeley studied a sample of married couples to determine if husband-wife value convergence is related to marital success. He found that it was, and then went on to say:

When a couple is married, two value systems are brought together in interaction with each other. Depending upon the quality of interaction, its duration, and other factors, these two initially divergent value systems may experience a degree of value convergence, divergence, or rigidity. Other things being equal, the degree of convergence will be highest in cases where the interaction is of a cooperative, shared sort; where the marriage is longest; where the more basic values are involved; where the values are mutually functional to the behavior of both husband and wife; where the couple has similar socioeconomic backgrounds; where the role-taking ability of the couple is high; where the social distance between husband and wife is low; and where the marriage is the most successful (1955, p. 345).

Any number of studies deal with problems of convergence versus divergence in the role perceptions of family members. Dunn (1960), for example, has pointed to a trend in the culture away from a clearly defined division of labor between the sexes, and has shown that boys and girls tend to differ from each other in expectations regarding some important areas of family interaction. Christensen (1958a, pp. 406–407) has cited several pieces of research to show that young men and young women tend to perceive the future wife's role differently; more of the former expect or desire the wife to be in homemaking and not in employment, whereas more of the latter define the situation as the reverse of this. Connor, Greene, and Walters (1958) have shown that family members often have divergent conceptions of what constitutes "good father," "good mother," and "good child" roles, with disagreement being greatest between fathers and their children. Luckey (1960) has reported positive associations between marital satisfaction and several kinds of perception congruence: between self-perception and perception of self by spouse, between self-perception and perception of parent of the same sex, between perception of spouse and perception of parent of the opposite sex, and between perception of spouse and perception of an ideal self. Farber and McHale (1959) have demonstrated that consistent child-rearing —which is known to favor mental health in children—is most likely when husband and wife are integrated with regard to basic values and roles.

Nevertheless, Turk (1963) has shown that system maintenance does not depend on value consensus alone, that sometimes disparate values can be integrative. Although his analysis was in the area of formal organization, it was suggested that the theory would apply also to other areas— especially when different sex roles are involved. In this connection, the reader may want to review this Handbook's earlier treatment of the somewhat controversial "theory of complementary needs" (see especially pp. 665–670).

Processes involved in the resolution of family disagreements have been treated in a number of places throughout this volume (see especially Ch. 17).

Toward a Theory of Value Relevance

It has been shown that values may be even more important in explaining behavior than are the external reality factors, and that it is how people perceive or define a situation that often determines their action and even the effects of this action. Thus, for the social scientist, values are relevant data. It has further been shown that values may be treated either as dependent, independent, or intervening variables; and that the value conflicts which affect the family may come either from disorganization within the norms of society, nonalignment of individual with social norms, gaps between expectation and realization, or disagreements among family members.

A paradigm of harmony and dissonance. Each married pair may be placed at some point on a continuum of harmony or disharmony with the outside world, and at another point on another continuum of harmony or disharmony with respect to each other. The couple's position on the first will depend upon how well the personal values of each line up with the norms of the cultural system in which they are located and/or with the realities of the situations within which they operate: it will depend, in other words, on the extent to which there is nonalignment with the general culture or there are gaps between expectation and realization. The couple's position on the second of these continua will depend upon both the adequacy of personality matching in the mate-selection process and the distance that the pair has moved toward love and adjustment in the interactional process. Internalized norms or norm conflicts from the general culture may serve indirectly to either narrow or widen the gaps in either instance, and hence may influence the couple's location on either of the continua.

It may be helpful to view this relationship in the form of a paradigm, as shown in Fig. 1. Here the two continua have been reduced to dichotomies for the sake of

Intramarital interaction between husband and wife	Interaction between married pair and external systems	
	Value consensus	Value conflict
Value consensus	**A** Maximum harmony	**B** Pair agreement, strained by external conflict
Value conflict	**C** Pair disagreement, mollified by external support	**D** Maximum dissonance

Fig. 1. Relationship of the Consensus-Conflict Dichotomy to Intramarital versus Extramarital Systems.

simplicity. On the vertical axis is pictured consensus-conflict categories with respect to intrapair interaction, and on the horizontal axis these same categories with respect to the couple's interaction with systems external to itself. Four types or patterns emerge (although it must be remembered that the presentation is schematic and does not explicitly portray the many variations from type that occur in real life; nevertheless, these variations are differences only in degree of fit, not in type): Type A combines value consensus from both inside and outside of marriage and thus provides the conditions for maximum harmony. Type B links pair consensus with stress brought in from the outside; it very likely comes second in harmony, for love and understanding at the close interpersonal level of marriage are known to provide reinforcement against pressures which otherwise could be devastating. Type C links pair conflict with support for the marriage from the outside; it (so one could hypothesize) would be third in harmony potential. Type D is characteristic by value conflict from both inside and outside the marriage and so provides the conditions for minimum harmony or maximum dissonance.

Although this schema needs the substantiation, alteration, or refutation that only additional systematic empirical research could bring, it possibly now can serve to help organize one's thinking regarding the interrelationship of the different levels of value harmony and conflict, and to suggest leads for future study. For example, by selecting groups of families that fit types B and C and comparing them, it should be possible to isolate the relative importance to marital success of intrafamilial as compared with nonfamilial harmony-disharmony. This is a problem in value intervention.

Further examples of value intervention. There have been a few family studies which deal with values as intervening variables affecting the outcomes of the behavior being considered. Some of these have been alluded to above (pp. 987–988); others are considered here.

This approach has been applied rather fruitfully to the problem of the working wife or mother. Gianopulos and Mitchell (1957) reported poorer marital adjustment when the wife worked and the husband disapproved than when she worked with his approval. Nye confirmed this finding and added the further generalization that "dissatisfaction with the wife's occupational role by *either* the wife or the husband is related to poorer marital adjustment" (1963, p. 280, italics added). Yarrow, Scott, and de Leeuw (1962) reported that the mother's work status *as such* is not related to child-rearing practices, but that there is a relationship when the mother's motivations and education are taken into account; most serious child-rearing problems are experienced by mothers who prefer to work but do not because of a sense of "duty." Hoffman reported that the feelings mothers have about their outside employment are apt to have more effect upon the child than just the fact of working or not working. She concluded:

The over-all pattern of findings suggests that the working mother who likes working is relatively high on positive affect toward the child, uses mild discipline, and tends to avoid inconveniencing the child with household tasks; the child is relatively nonassertive and ineffective. The working mother who dislikes working, on the other hand, seems less involved with the child altogether and obtains the child's help with tasks; the child is assertive and hostile (1963, p. 102).

In examining the question of family size as a factor in marital adjustment, Christensen and Philbrick (1952) found that success in controlling births to the number desired is a more crucial factor than is the number itself. It was the coming of unplanned children, which violated the couple's values, that was found to be responsible for most of the difficulty. Nevertheless, Farber and Blackman (1956) failed to find support for this position.

Although a great deal more research is needed, it can be hypothesized that this same pattern of value intrusion will apply in most areas of family behavior. For example, one might expect that the impact of economic deprivation upon family stability will vary according to how well the couple's *level* of living comes up to its

standard of living; that the most functional marital power structure will be that which most closely aligns with the respective values of husband and wife, even permitting successful "role reversal" arrangements for certain couples; and that the negative-versus-positive effects of premarital sexual intimacy will depend more than anything else upon the violation or nonviolation of the value positions of the cultures and the persons involved.[3]

An illustration from the author's research. It was this last named hypothesis that prompted the writer to undertake the cross-cultural investigation about to be described. Cultural norms rather than personal values were the units of comparison, although it was believed that the two would produce similar results, and that work with the latter should eventually follow in order to complete the theory. Premarital sexual attitudes and behavior were chosen as the substantive area to be studied, mainly for convenience, since it was believed that cross-cultural differences would be greater in this area than in most others, and hence the analysis would be sharpened; interest was primarily in value theory and only secondarily in subject-matter content. The following brief summary draws from several previous publications (Christensen, 1958b; Christensen, 1960; Christensen, 1962; Christensen, 1963a; Christensen, 1963b; Christensen & Carpenter, 1962a; Christensen & Carpenter, 1962b).

The design attempted to sharpen the analysis not only by selecting sex as the substantive area to be investigated, but also by

[3] Cf. Reiss (1960, pp. 191–194 and passim), who recognized four standards of premarital sexual behavior as existing within the American culture: the traditional double standard, a restrictive single standard, permissive single standard without affection, and permissive single standard with affection. He saw the consequences of sex acts as depending to a considerable extent upon conformity to existing standards; hence, in America, "permissive with affection is the permissive standard most closely integrated with the positive value consequences, such as psychic satisfaction, and most weakly integrated with the negative-value consequences, such as guilt feelings" (p. 192).

selecting cultures with greatly divergent sex norms as the populations to be compared. These turned out to be Denmark, which is known to have a rather liberal or permissive normative system in regard to sex, similar to all of Scandanavia; midwestern United States, which is thought to be somewhat typical in this regard of the country of which it is a part, and hence more restrictive than Denmark; and, finally, Mormon society in the intermountain region of western United States, which is known to have very conservative or restrictive sex norms and which, therefore, could form the other end of a cross-cultural continuum.

Samples were drawn from each of these three cultures and studied by means of two separate though complementary research methods. In the first instance, the marriage, birth, and divorce records from a defined area within each culture were matched to yield measures of the phenomenon of premarital pregnancy (where the interval between marriage and birth of the first child was "too short," premarital conception was assumed). In the second instance, carefully constructed questionnaires were administered to selected classes in a university from each culture, in a manner that would keep the respondents anonymous and make the responses comparable to yield measures of both attitudes and behavior in the area of sex.[4]

To avoid possible embarrassment from too close identification, the three samples are referred to simply as Danish, Midwestern, and Intermountain. Findings are summarized below in terms of value patterns, behavior patterns, and value-behavior discrepancies.

1. Value patterns were obtained by means of the questionnaire. On virtually every measure, Danish respondents appeared most permissive and Intermountain respondents most restrictive; Midwestern respondents were in between, though closer to the lat-

ter than to the former.[5] Thus, for example, significantly more Danish respondents approved both premarital and extramarital coitus, approved every form of intimacy starting earlier in the courtship process,[6] and thought of premarital intimacy as progressing more rapidly from necking, through petting, to coitus. In contrast, the smallest percentages of respondents held these values in the Intermountain sample.

2. Behavior patterns presented a similar cross-cultural picture. The Danish subjects were by far the highest and Intermountain subjects lowest in percentages who had experienced premarital coitus (questionnaire data) and in rates of premarital pregnancy (record-linkage data). Since very few of the questionnaire respondents were married, no measure of the *extra*marital relations actually occurring could be made.

An exception to the usual cross-cultural picture was found in the case of petting experience. Percentages who engaged in petting as a terminal activity, that is, who petted and stopped there, were highest in the Intermountain and lowest in the Danish—a reversal—suggesting that, as the severity of the sanction against premarital coitus increases, the greater is the tendency

---

[4] George R. Carpenter collaborated in the student survey phase of the research.

[5] It will be noted that this cross-cultural pattern substantiates or validates the beginning assumption of a continuum extending from permissive Denmark to restrictive Intermountain, and so does the cross-cultural pattern on *behavior* to be reported in the next paragraph. Furthermore, with both value measures and behavior measures, the Midwestern sample almost always came closer to the Intermountain than to the Danish; the largest gap was between the Danish and the two American samples.

Sex of respondent was controlled in every cross-cultural comparison. In most instances, for each culture, females showed up as more conservative than males.

[6] Cross-cultural differences in approval were least for necking, next for petting, and greatest of all for coitus. Since this means that cross-cultural differences are accentuated by each increase in degree of intimacy, it gives plausible though presumptive support to the original assumption that the sex area (which is more intimate and more emotionally involved than others) has the methodological advantage of sharpening up the comparisons.

to use petting as an alternative activity. Percentages who had *either* petted or experienced coitus premaritally were highest in the Danish and lowest in the Intermountain, although differences here were not as great as when coitus alone was considered.

3. Value-behavior discrepancies were of special interest, since, by considering values as an intervening variable, they can help get at the problem of behavioral consequences. Several important discoveries were made. It was found that more Danish students approved premarital coitus than had actually experienced it, whereas the reverse was true in the two American samples and especially so in the Intermountain. This suggests that as cultural norms become more restrictive, there is an increasing tendency for persons to overstep the limits, for behavior to violate the standards. In view of this discrepancy pattern, a logical expectation would be lowest guilt in the Danish sample and highest in the Intermountain sample. In tapping feelings following first premarital coitus, this is exactly what was found; furthermore, the opposite of guilt, as measured by first premarital coital experience being "voluntary because of desire" and being accompanied by "pleasant feelings," was in reverse order—Danish highest and Intermountain lowest.

Two measures of effect were derived from the record-linkage data. The first had to do with the timing of the wedding following premarital pregnancy. It was found that Danish couples, feeling little stigma, typically marry about five months after the conception; Midwestern couples typically marry about two months after, or as soon as they can, in order to conceal the fact; and Intermountain couples, it may be presumed, marry soon after premarital coitus starts—feeling guilty as it is, without waiting for a pregnancy to force them. The second measure had to do with divorce rate as affected by timing of first pregnancy. In considering this from the standpoint of premarital conception, it was found that, although in all three cultures divorce rates were higher in the premarital as compared with the postmarital pregnancy categories, the *differential* in divorce rate between premarital and normal postmarital pregnancy cases was lowest in Denmark and highest in Intermountain. In considering postmarital conception only, it was found that early conception generally was associated with higher divorce rate than later conception, and, more important, that the *differential* in divorce rate between early and late conceivers was lowest in the Intermountain sample (the Midwestern was highest in this respect and the Danish in between, an exception to the usual pattern).

Thus, the *effects or consequences* of the behavior studied seem related, not just to behavior considered alone, but to value-behavior discrepancy. The Danish culture, which sexually is the most permissive of the three, showed the lowest amounts of terminal petting as a substitute for coitus, of premarital coitus by couples who held values against it, of guilt feelings accompanying premarital coitus, of hurried weddings forced by a pregnancy, and of divorce-rate differential between premarital and postmarital conceivers. In contrast, the Intermountain culture, which sexually is the most restrictive of the three, showed the highest rates in each of these areas. Furthermore, the Intermountain culture, whose normative pattern includes early postmarital conception, showed the lowest divorce rate differential between early and late postmarital conceivers—presumably because early postmarital conception is in line with the value system there.

Summary and theory. In two earlier publications (Christensen, 1958a, pp. 22–25; Christensen, 1958b, pp. 41–43) the writer has briefly described what he calls "the principle of value relevance." A recapitulation, with some recent additions, will serve to summarize this section.

In simplest terms, *the principle of value relevance means that the values people hold are relevant to their behavior and to the outcomes or effects of this behavior:* in other words, it means that the family sociologist not only may but *must* deal with values as part of his data. What people believe, or perceive, or desire, or expect determines how they act and react in reference to the situations they face—even more so, very often, than the reality factors outside their mental-emotional systems.

Values may be dealt with as *dependent variables,* shaped by forces outside the individual, such as family interaction; as *independent variables* which influence one's behavior and relationships, including that which takes place within the family; and as *intervening variables,* which are so because they intrude themselves into a process to affect both its direction and its outcome. Since the meanings attached to things and events depend upon the values people hold, it is this last named—values as intervening variables—which carries the most promise for the family researchers of the future.

Married-pair unity and family harmony are dependent upon at least a reasonable amount of value consensus. Family members may conflict either among themselves or with systems or conditions on the outside; where it is neither, harmony is maximized; where it is both, dissonance is maximized. *External family conflict* comes when its members either hold values vastly different from the general culture, or different from the reality situations in which they find themselves. *Internal family conflict* comes when its members hold values essentially different from each other. *Value conflict within the general culture* is also external to the family, at least to start with, but the trouble is that it usually cannot be kept that way; after being internalized within the family, it seems likely to add to the strains of conflicts already there.

Although a great deal more research is needed before the value phenomenon can be well understood, certain answers already have been provided, at least tentatively. It is pretty well known, for example,

that the relationship of level of living to standard of living is more important in the effects of economic deprivation than is level of living considered alone; that the attitudes family members hold about a mother being employed outside the home are apparently more important in knowing its consequences than is the sheer fact of her working; that the ability of a married couple to control family size in line with its desires is more important to its adjustments than is number of children in and of itself; and that certain measurable effects of premarital sexual intimacy are greater in cultures where the practices are most strongly condemned. In other words, it is value-behavior discrepancy, rather than behavior alone, that determines the consequences. At the societal level, this has been labeled *cultural relativism.* At the personal level, it could be referred to as *value relativism.* At either level, and both, it is *the principle of value relevance.*

IMAGE PROBLEMS IN FAMILY SOCIOLOGY

Although the marriage and family field has attracted a disproportionate amount of attention, both with the lay public and among professional sociologists (see pp. 3, 13–14), there are a number of image problems which need to be reckoned with. Recently, these problems have been coming to the fore, primarily because the field is maturing and, with this, its workers are growing more status conscious. It seems appropriate to end this volume by an introspective look at the field and how its workers and others regard it.

"Natural" Advantages and Disadvantages

To start with, it may be noted that the field is characterized by some more or less intrinsic advantages and disadvantages. Its advantages lie chiefly in its almost universal appeal: family phenomena are naturally interesting to most people. Its disadvantages rest mainly in its relatively low status among academicians, in its tendency to incite public opposition in sensitive areas, and in its vulnerability to value seduction.

It may appear contradictory to say that a field which enjoys a great deal of public and professional interest also must fight for acceptance, yet this is the situation. Earlier chapters have shown how the family field—most especially the sex area—has met with opposition regarding both research and teaching; furthermore, this resistance has come from both the lay public and the academic community (see especially pp. 269-272, 616-620, 898-903). Although the amount of opposition has varied from place to place and has fluctuated over time, the long-range trend undoubtedly has been toward its diminution and an increasing respectability of the field (cf. Ch. 1, especially pp. 12-13). Nevertheless, this "progress" should not blind one to the fact that the problem has only been lessened, not eliminated.

It is a sociological fact that the various intellectual disciplines are not equal in prestige, nor are the subfields within a given discipline. There is an almost universal struggle for status, and this is not just interpersonal but also among the groups and institutions to which one belongs. In the United States today, scientific disciplines have an edge over nonscientific ones, and the so-called natural sciences (the physical and biological) have higher prestige than the social or behavioral sciences. Within this last category, it seems probable that economics and political science rate higher than the others, primarily because they deal more directly with elements of social power. Finally, within sociology, it seems probable that such subfields as industrial sociology and political sociology enjoy more prestige in the academic world than does family sociology, for the reason just given. Power (potential or actual) carries with it prestige. Since family sociology deals with some of the "softer" things of life—those that have little to do directly (although con-

siderably indirectly) with the broad issues of social control—it tends to be downgraded. This fact puts it at a "natural" disadvantage.

In addition to this disadvantage coming from the lower power potential of its subject matter, sociology in general, and family sociology in particular, may have relatively lower prestige because they are in earlier stages of development than are certain other of the social sciences.

It could be, too, that the field's advantage in attracting interest (both public and professional) puts it ultimately at a disadvantage because of the professional jealousy that may be engendered. Although this cannot be substantiated with data right now, it represents a plausible hypothesis capable of being tested. The assumption of professional jealousy directed toward the family worker seems most plausible in situations where family courses are of the "functional" variety (which colleagues may reject as being neither scientific nor sociological) and where they pull, as they often do, disproportionately large enrollments (which colleagues are likely to view as unfair competition).

It is also at the point of functional family life education and marriage counseling that the various value problems previously discussed come most strongly into play. Leslie (1959; Ch. 22 of this Handbook, pp. 940-942) has described the confusion of professional identity that has characterized family workers who have tried to combine applied and academic interests. He believes, however, that this combining is possible, and that the problem of professional identification, though difficult, "is likely to be resolved in our time" (see above, p. 942; cf. Ehrmann's discussion of "doctrinal quarrels," pp. 618-620).

Perspective Distortions

As pointed out earlier, the only commitment allowed the scientist, as scientist, is a commitment to the premises of science itself—that knowledge is better than ignorance and that the value-free investigation of empirical evidence is the best way to knowledge. Two distortions of this perspective, somewhat opposite in nature, are found among marriage and family specialists: (a) preoccupation with normative interests and (b) preoccupation with professional status.

The first of these has been alluded to a number of times up to this point in the discussion. It may be made up of a humanitarian bias, a stability bias, or both. Straus (pp. 388–391 of this Handbook) distinguished between "evaluative" and "descriptive" measures in family research and found the latter to be more useful and to be gaining ground. Kolb (1948; 1950) criticized the family field for promoting the values of adjustment and stability, arguing that this works against individualism and progress and toward the preservation of the *status quo*. A mature scientific perspective, it is believed, will require an essentially nonnormative approach.

The second distortion in perspective has come about largely as a reaction against the first. Family workers with a scientific bent have tended to rebel against the traditional moralistic-humanitarian, preservation-of-values approach, as have certain of the less scientific who follow along because of the prestige which the scientific stance brings them. But in either case, the reaction has sometimes become an over-reaction, a swinging from one extreme to the other. In writing of this tendency as applied to sociology generally, C. C. Bowman said:

Whatever the socio-psychological genesis of this frame of mind, its development at the professional level is partly explicable in terms of the dialectical process. Noting that the mores contain irrationalities, gross generalizations and many other illogical elements, one may easily fall prey to the unwarranted conclusion that diametrically opposed beliefs will be rational, logical, scientific. If the mores are looked upon as the thesis, then this type of naive sociology becomes the antithesis (1946, p. 543).

Who today wants to be a moralist? Some persons, of course, but not nearly so many as earlier when morality was more the fashion. "In a day when religious virtues were valued, men wished to appear godly. Similarly, in an age of science, many hold opinions which they fondly consider to be 'objective'"—and, Bowman later added, "progressive" (p. 543). But this clamor for objectivity and liberality is sometimes little more than following a fashion, acquiring status or rationalizing behavior by climbing on the bandwagon of science. Today there is pressure to "play it cool" and to appear objective whether one is or not; those in the social science world who are morally or religiously inclined tend either to keep quiet, to pretend to be different than they are, or to bear ridicule from the scientifically and materialistically oriented.

Thus, the family field today may be said to have both a radical right and a radical left—with, of course, what is probably the majority falling in between these two extremes. The radical right gives uncritical support to the *status quo* and gets tangled up in its own value positions. The radical left over-reacts to the approach of the right by prematurely or irresponsibly attacking norms which may be socially useful without replacing them with something more useful. The first puts a damper on science by opposing innovation; the second does so by making a virtue of innovation as such, without reference to consequences. The one is as lacking in objectivity as is the other (cf. Carpenter, 1962).

Terminological Difficulties

Another problem reflecting upon the image of the family specialist lies in the difficulty of the language he is apt to employ. Part of this problem is the same as that faced by sociology generally, and perhaps to some extent by every scientific discipline, for, with specialization, comes a tendency to develop a terminology unique to the particular focus. This practice interferes with effective communication, both among scientists from the varying disciplines, and between scientists and the lay public (discussed earlier in this chapter).

Sociology in particular has been singled out for criticism concerning the awkwardness of its jargon (e.g., Mills, 1959, pp. 217–226). Insofar as the sociologist needlessly uses complicated diction or coins new words to appear scholarly, the criticism would appear justified. It must be remembered, however, that the communications of science require precision, and that criticisms of sociology on this score can be at least partly explained by the reluctance of others to give up their traditional, rather loose, "common-sense" modes of thinking on matters which concern the sociologist. (For an answer to the jargon criticism and other criticisms which have concerned the "anti-sociologist," see Merton, 1961, pp. 14 ff.). And the problem of the *family* sociologist is no different from that of his professional colleagues in this respect. The answer to it requires that the specialist resist any temptation to be difficult in communication just to impress; in fact, it asks that he strive toward language that is as simple and clear as possible in view of the precision necessary.

An additional terminological difficulty of the family specialist lies in the value-loaded nature of some of the terms he employs: "happiness," for example, and "adjustment," and "chastity." When he uses value-loaded words such as these, he seemingly employs value judgments to the effect that something is "better" or "worse" than something else, and this corrupts his image in the eyes of purists regarding the separation of science and values. Yet, as was pointed out earlier, values may be recognized as existing in the group studied, and then used as criteria against which data are measured, without judging as part of the scientific process the intrinsic goodness or badness of the values themselves.

An example of the trend in sociology away from value-loaded terminology is the recent abandonment by some of the word "primitive," which tends to connote inferiority, and the substitution of the word "preliterate," which is purely descriptive. Gouldner has argued that the area of sociology dealing with sexual relations has tended more than other areas to cling to value-loaded terms. He used "exploitation" as an example, and said: "Doubtless 'exploitation' is by now so heavily charged with misleading ideological resonance that the term itself can scarcely be salvaged for purely scientific purposes and will, quite properly, be resisted by most American sociologists" (1960, p. 167). Gouldner suggested "reciprocity imbalance" as a possible non-evaluative substitute. But the proposed substitute is more awkward and difficult than the original, and so presents a communications problem.

This illustrates where family sociology is at its present stage of development. There is self-examination and, with it, progress in resolving the pressing issues; nevertheless, the theoretical problems still facing it—and particularly the value problems—represent basic conflicts of interest. These problems are not easy and much remains to be accomplished.

CONCLUSIONS

At its twenty-fifth anniversary conference in 1963, the National Council on Family Relations took a close and careful look at developments and needs in the marriage and family field. The three major papers dealt explicitly with past developments, prognostications for the future, and the tasks and challenges that lie ahead (Bernard, 1964; Duvall, 1964; Hill, 1964). There was general consensus that the family will not completely disintegrate to be replaced by some other institutional arrangement, that there are measurable evidences of accomplishment in the study and treatment of families, and that numerous discontinuities and unresolved issues make continued professional development highly important.

This Handbook, too, and in a much more comprehensive fashion, has reviewed the many scholarly and applied approaches to family study and betterment. The attempt has been to pull together and integrate into meaningful theory the great mass of empirical materials presently existing, and to evaluate the field in terms of where we have been, where we now are, where we will be going, and what we need to get there. Five different but interrelated aspects of the over-all phenomena have been focused upon, separately or in combination: theoretical orientations, methodological tools, substantive generalizations, workable applications, and value premises.

In this final chapter, ways in which values intrude themselves into the work of the family sociologist have been examined. (a) The first major section dealt broadly with relationships among science, values, and social action. It was recognized that, although values can legitimately intrude in certain well-defined ways, they must, insofar as possible, be kept out of the research process itself, so that the generalizations come only from the data and hence are verifiable. Virtually all social scientists today hold this point of view, but differ on the question of the scientist's role in social action. Regarding this latter, the position here adopted was that the scientist role and the citizen-role—both valid—should be kept separate. (b) The second section turned to the problem of assessing family research, education, and the various action programs. Pointed out were the needs for responsible journalism; for a resolution of the value issue in teaching and counseling; for the further development of a family policy, even though it be multifocused; and for more sophisticated evaluation research in order to make the programs self-correcting. (c) The third section focused upon the legitimacy and utility of considering values as data in family research. Values were viewed as dependent variable, as independent variable, and as intervening variable, with special attention to the latter and to various kinds of value conflict. A theory or principle of value relevance was constructed. (d) The fourth section pointed to an emerging status consciousness among professional family workers and to the so-called image

problems involved. The image ascribed to the field was seen as coming from both the self-image of its workers and an imposed image from the outside, and as deriving from the way family specialists are meeting the conceptual, methodological, and value problems which challenge them. There has been developing an increasing respectability —as seen internally, from the consuming public, and from the academic community.

An additional encouraging sign in this coming of age of the field is the recent movement toward self-policing by the adoption of codes of ethics. The American Association of Marriage Counselors now has such a code, and the American Psychological Association has had one for some years. The American Sociological Association in 1960 appointed a Committee on Professional Ethics, which now has made an extensive report as a step toward setting up a code to guide its members in a wide range of matters pertaining to research, teaching, consulting, professional practice, writing and publishing, and relationships with the public. At least preliminary consideration has been given to the formulation of a code for family life education (cf. pp. 897–898 of this Handbook).

As a final word, let it be said that workers in marriage and the family need not feel apologetic or defensive—need not, at least, so long as they understand and carry out their professional responsibilities. But they must take care not to let image concerns seduce them from the methodological rigors required of all science. Insofar as family specialists are able to do their jobs, image and status problems will take care of themselves.

REFERENCES

Bain, R. Our schizoid culture. *Sociol. & soc. Res.*, 1935, 19, 266–276.

Bain, R. Science, values, and sociology. *Amer. sociol. Rev.*, 1939, 4, 560–565.

Becker, H. Supreme values and the sociologist. *Amer. sociol. Rev.*, 1941, 6, 155–172.

Behlmer, R. H. Family life education survey. *Marr. & fam. Living,* 1961, 23, 299–301.

Bernard, Jessie. Developmental tasks of the NCFR—1963–1988. *J. Marr. & Fam.* (formerly *Marr. & fam. Living*), 1964, 26, 29–38.

Blake, Judith, & Davis, K. Norms, values, and sanctions. In R. E. L. Faris (Ed.), *Handbook of modern sociology.* Chicago: Rand McNally, 1964. Pp. 456–484.

Bowman, C. C. Hidden valuations in the interpretation of sexual and family relationships. *Amer. sociol. Rev.,* 1946, 11, 536–544.

Bowman, H. A. A critical evaluation of marriage and family education. *Marr. & fam. Living,* 1953, 15, 304–308.

Bowman, H. A. Kerckhoff, R. K., Davis, F. K., & Sussman, M. B. Teaching ethical values through the marriage course: a debate. *Marr. & fam. Living,* 1957, 19, 325–339.

Brieland, D. Uses of research in recent popular parent education literature. *Marr. & fam. Living,* 1957, 19, 60–65.

Brim, O. G. Evaluating the effects of parent education. *Marr. & fam. Living,* 1957, 19, 54–60.

Buerkle, J. V., Anderson, T. R., & Badgley, R. F. Altruism, role conflict, and marital adjustment. *Marr. & fam. Living,* 1961, 23, 20–30.

Burgess, E. W., & Cottrell, L. S. *Predicting success or failure in marriage.* Englewood Cliffs, N. J.: Prentice-Hall, 1939.

Carpenter, G. R. An analytical paradigm of the problem of subjectivity in family life education. *Marr. & fam. Living,* 1962, 24, 186.

Catton, W. R., Jr. A theory of value. *Amer. sociol. Rev.,* 1959, 24, 310–317.

Charters, W. W. The social backgrounds of teachers. In N. L. Gage (Ed.), *Handbook of research on teaching.* Chicago: Rand McNally, 1963. Pp. 715–813.

Christensen, H. T. Population pressure among Wisconsin farmers. In E. B. Fred (Ed.), *Summaries of doctoral dissertations, University of Wisconsin.* Vol. 7. Madison: Univer. of Wisconsin Press, 1942. Pp. 160–162. (Complete original dissertation filed in the University library.)

Christensen, H. T. *Marriage analysis: foundations for successful family life.* (2nd ed.) New York: Ronald Press, 1958. (a)

Christensen, H. T. Value variables in preg-

nancy timing: some intercultural comparisons. In N. Anderson (Ed.), *Studies of the family.* Vol. 3. Göttingen: Vandenhoeck & Ruprecht, 1958. Pp. 29–45. (b)

Christensen, H. T. Cultural relativism and premarital sex norms. *Amer. sociol. Rev.,* 1960, 25, 31–39.

Christensen, H. T. A cross-cultural comparison of attitudes toward marital infidelity. *Int. J. comp. Sociol.,* 1962, 3, 124–137.

Christensen, H. T. Child spacing analysis via record linkage: new data plus a summing up from earlier reports. *Marr. & fam. Living,* 1963, 25, 272–280. (a)

Christensen, H. T. Timing of first pregnancy as a factor in divorce: a cross-cultural analysis. *Eugenics Quart.,* 1963, 10, 119–130. (b)

Christensen, H. T., & Carpenter, G. W. Timing patterns in the development of sexual intimacy. *Marr. & fam. Living,* 1962, 24, 30–35. (a)

Christensen, H. T., & Carpenter, G. W. Value-behavior discrepancies regarding premarital coitus in three Western cultures. *Amer. sociol. Rev.,* 1962, 27, 66–74. (b)

Christensen, H. T., & Philbrick, R. E. Family size as a factor in the marital adjustments of college couples. *Amer. sociol. Rev.,* 1952, 17, 306–312.

Connor, Ruth, Greene, Helen F., & Walters, J. Agreement of family member conceptions of "good" parent and child roles. *Soc. Forces,* 1958, 36, 353–358.

Cuber, J. F. Can we evaluate marriage education? *Marr. & fam. Living,* 1949, 11, 93–95.

Davis, K. Mental hygiene and the class structure. *Psychiatry,* 1938, 1, 55–65.

Dunn, Marie S. Marriage role expectations of adolescents. *Marr. & fam. Living,* 1960, 22, 99–111.

Duvall, Evelyn M. American families and NCFR—since 1938. *J. Marr. & Fam.* (formerly *Marr. & fam. Living*), 1964, 26, 10–19.

Dyer, Dorothy. A comparative study relating marital happiness to university courses helpful in marital adjustment. *Marr. & fam. Living,* 1959, 21, 230–232.

Dyer, E. D. Parenthood as crisis: a restudy. *Marr. & fam. Living,* 1963, 25, 196–201.

Dyer, W. G. A comparison of families of high and low job satisfaction. *Marr. & fam. Living,* 1956, 18, 58–60.

Ellis, A. Marriage counseling with demasculizing wives and demasculinized husbands. *Marr. & fam. Living*, 1960, 22, 13–17.

England, R. W., Jr. Images of love and courtship in family-magazine fiction. *Marr. & fam. Living*, 1960, 22, 162–165.

Farber, B., & Blackman, L. S. Marital role tensions and number and sex of children. *Amer. sociol. Rev.*, 1956, 21, 596–601.

Farber, B., & McHale, Julia L. Marital integration and parents' agreement on satisfaction with their child's behavior. *Marr. & fam. Living*, 1959, 21, 65–69.

Gianopulos, A., & Mitchell, H. E. Marital disagreement in working wife marriages as a function of husband's attitude toward wife's employment. *Marr. & fam. Living*, 1957, 19, 373–378.

Gillies, D. V., & Lastrucci, C. L. Validation of the effectiveness of a college marriage course. *Marr. & fam. Living*, 1954, 16, 55–58.

Goode, W. J., & Hatt, P. K. *Methods in social research*. New York: McGraw-Hill, 1952. Pp. 18–40.

Gouldner, A. W. The norm of reciprocity: a preliminary statement. *Amer. sociol. Rev.*, 1960, 25, 161–178.

Gouldner, A. W. Anti-minotaur: the myth of a value-free sociology. *Soc. Probl.*, 1962, 9, 199–213.

Hansen, D. A. The responsibility of the sociologist to education. *Harvard educ. Rev.*, 1963, 33, 312–325.

Hansen, D. A. Nominal concepts, methodological theories and research bias. *J. Marr. & Fam.* (formerly *Marr. & fam. Living*), 1964, 26.

Harper, R. A. Marriage counseling and the mores: a critique. *Marr. & fam. Living*, 1959, 21, 13–19.

Hill, R. The American family of the future. *J. Marr. & Fam.* (formerly *Marr. & fam. Living*), 1964, 26, 20–28.

Hillman, Christine H. An advice column's challenge for family-life education. *Marr. & fam. Living*, 1954, 16, 51–54.

Hobart, C. W. Disillusionment in marriage, and romanticism. *Marr. & fam. Living*, 1958, 20, 156–162.

Hobart, C. W. Attitude changes during courtship and marriage. *Marr. & fam. Living*, 1960, 22, 352–359.

Hobart, C. W. Commitment, value conflict and the future of the American family. *Marr. & fam. Living*, 1963, 25, 405–414.

Hoffman, Lois W. Mother's enjoyment of work and its effects on the child. In F. I. Nye & Lois W. Hoffman, *The employed mother in America*. Chicago: Rand McNally, 1963. Pp. 95–105.

Hollis, Florence. Evaluating marriage counseling. *Marr. & fam. Living*, 1950, 12, 37–38.

Jackson, Joan K. The adjustment of the family to alcoholism. *Marr. & fam. Living*, 1956, 18, 361–369.

Keeley, B. J. Value convergence and marital relations. *Marr. & fam. Living*, 1955, 17, 342–345.

Kirkendall, L. A. Values and premarital intercourse. *Marr. & fam. Living*, 1960, 22, 317–322.

Kirkendall, L. A. Shelter in academia vs competition in the magazine world (a letter to the editor). *J. Marr. & Fam.* (formerly *Marr. & fam. Living*), 1964, 26, 108.

Kirkpatrick, C. *The family: as process and institution*. (2nd ed.) New York: Ronald Press, 1963.

Kluckhohn, Florence R. Family diagnosis: variations in the basic values of family systems. *Soc. Casewk*, 1958, 39, 63–72.

Kolb, W. L. Sociologically established family norms and democratic values. *Soc. Forces*, 1948, 26, 451–456.

Kolb, W. L. Family, sociology, marriage education, and the romantic complex. *Soc. Forces*, 1950, 29, 65–72.

Komarovsky, Mirra, & Waller, W. Studies of the family. *Amer. J. Sociol.*, 1945, 50, 443–451.

Landis, J. T. An evaluation of marriage education. *Marr. & fam. Living*, 1948, 10, 81–84.

LeMasters, E. E. Parenthood as crisis. *Marr. & fam. Living*, 1957, 19, 352–355.

Leslie, G. R. Personal values, professional ideologies, and family specialists. *Marr. & fam. Living*, 1959, 21, 3–12.

Letters to the editor. *Marr. & fam. Living*, 1959, 21, 185–188.

Longworth, D. S. Critique of attempts to evaluate marriage teaching. *Marr. & fam. Living*, 1953, 15, 308–312.

Luckey, Eleanore B. Marital satisfaction and its association with congruence of perception. *Marr. & fam. Living*, 1960, 22, 49–54.

Luckey, Eleanore B. Value as the content of parent education programs. *Marr. & fam. Living*, 1961, 23, 263–266.

Luckey, Eleanore B., & Neubeck, G. What are

we doing in marriage education? *Marr. & fam. Living,* 1956, 18, 349–354.

Lundberg, G. A. The logic of sociology and social research. In G. A. Lundberg, R. Bain, & N. Anderson (Eds.), *Trends in American sociology.* New York: Harper, 1929. Pp. 389–425.

Lundberg, G. A. *Foundations of sociology.* New York: Macmillan, 1939.

Lundberg, G. A. *Can science save us?* New York: Longmans, Green, 1947.

Lundberg, G. A., Schrag, C. E., & Larsen, O. N. The functions and influence of scientists. In *Sociology.* (Rev. ed.) New York: Harper, 1958. Pp. 736–742. (a)

Lundberg, G. A., Schrag, C. E., & Larsen, O. N. The scientist's and the citizen's role in sociology. In *Sociology.* (Rev. ed.) New York: Harper, 1958. Pp. 15–17. (b)

Lynd, R. *Knowledge for what?* Princeton: Princeton Univer. Press, 1939.

Marsh, C. M., & Humphrey, N. D. Value congeries and marital counseling (with discussions by H. T. Christensen & J. W. Hudson, and a rejoinder by the authors). *Marr. & fam. Living,* 1953, 15, 28–34.

Martinson, F. M. *Marriage and the American ideal.* New York: Dodd, Mead, 1960.

Martinson, F. M. Value assumptions in family research with reference to population. *Sociol. Quart.,* 1961, 2, 281–292.

Mason, Madeleine. The teacher's value system in relation to family life education. *Marr. & fam. Living,* 1959, 21, 75–77.

Merton, R. K. Now the case for sociology. *N. Y. Times Magazine,* July 16, 1961, pp. 14 ff.

Mills, C. W. The professional ideology of social pathologists. *Amer. J. Sociol.,* 1943, 49, 165–180.

Mills, C. W. *The sociological imagination.* New York: Oxford Univer. Press, 1959.

Mizruchi, E. H., & Perrucci, R. Norm qualities and differential effects of deviant behavior: an exploratory analysis. *Amer. sociol. Rev.,* 1962, 27, 391–399.

Morris, R. T. A typology of norms. *Amer. sociol. Rev.,* 1956, 21, 610–613.

Moses, Virginia M. A study of learning derived from a functional course in marriage and family relationships. *Marr. & fam. Living,* 1956, 18, 204–208.

Mudd, Emily H., Preston, M. G., Froscher,

Hazel B., & Peltz, W. L. Survey of a research project in marriage counseling. *Marr. & fam. Living,* 1950, 12, 59–62.

Muuss, R. E. Mental health implications of a preventive psychiatry program in the light of research findings. *Marr. & fam. Living,* 1960, 22, 150–156.

Myrdal, G. A methodological note on valuations and beliefs, and a methodological note on facts and valuations in social science. In *An American dilemma.* New York: Harper, 1944. Pp. 1027–1064.

National Council on Family Relations. Government services affecting American families. Special issue of *Marr. & fam. Living,* 1958, 20, 211–321.

Nye, F. I. Marital interaction. In F. I. Nye & Lois W. Hoffman, *The employed mother in America.* Chicago: Rand McNally, 1963. Pp. 263–281.

Ort, R. S. A study of role-conflicts as related to happiness in marriage. *J. abnorm. soc. Psychol.,* 1950, 45, 691–699.

Pineo, P. C. Disenchantment in the later years of marriage. *Marr. & fam. Living,* 1961, 23, 3–11.

Poffenberger, T., Klemer, R. H., Reiss, I. L., Stokes, W. R., Kirkendall, L. A., & Porter, B. M. Premarital sexual behavior: a symposium. *Marr. & fam. Living,* 1962, 24, 254–278.

Popper, K. R. *The open society and its enemies.* (Rev. ed.) Vol. 2. London: Paul, 1952.

Reiss, I. L. *Premarital sexual standards in America.* Glencoe, Ill.: Free Press, 1960.

Reiss, I. L. Letter to the editor. *Marr. & fam. Living,* 1963, 25, 113–114.

Rubin, I. Letter to the editor. *Marr. & fam. Living,* 1963, 25, 229–230.

Schilling, Margaret. Evaluation of a family life education program. *Marr. & fam. Living,* 1961, 23, 297–299.

Schorr, A. L. *Filial responsibility in the modern American family.* Washington, D. C.: U. S. Department of Health, Education, & Welfare, 1960.

Schorr, A. L. Family policy in the United States. *Int. soc. sci. J.,* 1962, 14, 452–467.

Sorokin, P. A. *Social and cultural dynamics.* New York: American Book, 1941. 4 vols.

Strauss, A. The ideal and the chosen mate. *Amer. J. Sociol.,* 1946, 50, 204–208.

Terman, L. M., with Buttenwieser, P., Ferguson, L. W., Johnson, W. B., & Wilson, D. P.

Psychological factors in marital happiness.
New York: McGraw-Hill, 1938.

Thomas, W. I. *The unadjusted girl.* Boston:
Little, Brown, 1923.

Thomas, W. I., & Thomas, Dorothy S. *The
child in America.* New York: Knopf, 1928.

Toby, J. The differential impact of family disorganization. *Amer. sociol. Rev.,* 1957, 22,
505–512.

Turk, H. Social cohesion through variant
values: evidence from medical role relations.
Amer. sociol. Rev., 1963, 28, 28–37.

Von Mering, O. *A grammar of human values.*
Pittsburgh: Univer. of Pittsburgh Press,
1961.

Williams, R. W. *American society: a sociological interpretation.* (2nd ed.) New York:
Knopf, 1961. Pp. 372–470.

Winch, R. F., McGinnis, R., & Barringer, H.
R. Scientific method and the study of the
family. In R. F. Winch, R. McGinnis, and
H. R. Barringer (Eds.), *Selected studies in
the family.* New York: Holt, Rinehart &
Winston, 1962. Pp. 1–17.

Yarrow, Marian R., Scott, Phyllis, & de
Leeuw, Christine. Childrearing in families
of working and nonworking mothers. *Sociometry,* 1962, 25, 122–140.

Zimmerman, C. C. *The family and civilization.*
New York: Harper, 1947.

Name Index

Subject Index